Essentials of Victimology

Essentials of Victimology

Crime Victims, Theories, Controversies, and Victims' Rights

Jan Yager, Ph.D.
John Jay College of Criminal Justice
The City University of New York

ASPEN PUBLISHING

Cover image: iStock.com/LightFieldStudios

To contact Customer Service, e-mail customer.service@aspenpublishing.com,
call 1-800-950-5259, or mail correspondence to:

Aspen Publishing
Attn: Order Department
PO Box 990
Frederick, MD 21705

Printed in the United States of America.

2 3 4 5 6 7 8 9 0

ISBN 978-1-5438-2933-4

Library of Congress Cataloging-in-Publication Data application is in process.

SUSTAINABLE FORESTRY INITIATIVE
Certified Chain of Custody
Promoting Sustainable Forestry
www.sfiprogram.org

ABOUT ASPEN PUBLISHING

Aspen Publishing is a leading provider of educational content and digital learning solutions to law schools in the U.S. and around the world. Aspen provides best-in-class solutions for legal education through authoritative textbooks, written by renowned authors, and breakthrough products such as Connected eBooks, Connected Quizzing, and PracticePerfect.

The Aspen Casebook Series (famously known among law faculty and students as the "red and black" casebooks) encompasses hundreds of highly regarded textbooks in more than eighty disciplines, from large enrollment courses, such as Torts and Contracts to emerging electives such as Sustainability and the Law of Policing. Study aids such as the *Examples & Explanations* and the *Emanuel Law Outlines* series, both highly popular collections, help law students master complex subject matter.

Major products, programs, and initiatives include:

- **Connected eBooks** are enhanced digital textbooks and study aids that come with a suite of online content and learning tools designed to maximize student success. Designed in collaboration with hundreds of faculty and students, the Connected eBook is a significant leap forward in the legal education learning tools available to students.
- **Connected Quizzing** is an easy-to-use formative assessment tool that tests law students' understanding and provides timely feedback to improve learning outcomes. Delivered through CasebookConnect.com, the learning platform already used by students to access their Aspen casebooks, Connected Quizzing is simple to implement and integrates seamlessly with law school course curricula.
- **PracticePerfect** is a visually engaging, interactive study aid to explain commonly encountered legal doctrines through easy-to-understand animated videos, illustrative examples, and numerous practice questions. Developed by a team of experts, PracticePerfect is the ideal study companion for today's law students.
- The **Aspen Learning Library** enables law schools to provide their students with access to the most popular study aids on the market across all of their courses. Available through an annual subscription, the online library consists of study aids in e-book, audio, and video formats with full text search, note-taking, and highlighting capabilities.
- Aspen's **Digital Bookshelf** is an institutional-level online education bookshelf, consolidating everything students and professors need to ensure success. This program ensures that every student has access to affordable course materials from day one.
- **Leading Edge** is a community centered on thinking differently about legal education and putting those thoughts into actionable strategies. At the core of the program is the Leading Edge Conference, an annual gathering of legal education thought leaders looking to pool ideas and identify promising directions of exploration.

For the co-founders of victimology, such visionaries whose efforts we all enjoy today, as well as for all the past, current, and future victims, their dedicated service providers, the academics who conduct research and teach in the growing field of Victimology, and for my former, current, and future students.

For my older brother, Seth Alan Barkas (1945-1969), and my great nephew, Billy "Webb" Yager (1991-2017). Gone but never forgotten.

For my terrific husband Fred, our wonderful family, and friends. Thanks for your continual love and support.

—Jan Yager, Ph.D.

Brief CONTENTS

Detailed CONTENTS

CHAPTER **TEN**

CHILD VICTIMS: ABUSE, NEGLECT, AND OTHER VICTIMIZATIONS 371

CHAPTER **ELEVEN**

TEEN AND COLLEGE VICTIMS 415

PREFACE

Jennifer Ann Crecente at age 16 on a trip in 2004 to Hawaii for an APA (American Psychological Association) conference. Photo credit: Dr. Elizabeth L. Richeson, Jen's grandmother

- On February 15, 2006, 18-year-old Jennifer Ann Crecente, a senior in high school, accompanied her ex-boyfriend to check out a car he wanted to buy. Unfortunately, he had made up that story to get Jen into the woods where he had hidden the shotgun that he would use to shoot her in the back of the head. Her body was found two days later. (See Chapter 7, "Primary and Secondary Victims of Homicide," for more details about Jen's murder based on interviews with her father, Drew.) (Crecente, 2020)

- From 2004 to 2018, Rachel W. was sexually harassed by a member of her congregation. Victimized over a period of 14 years when she was in her 50s and 60s, Rachel wants those studying victimology to know that sexual harassment can happen at any age and that it can be prolonged and not just a one-time occurrence. (Interview with the author, 2020)

- Six-year-old Danny vanished on December 1, 1992. A year later, Jeffrey Rinek, an FBI agent specializing in missing children, was assigned to Danny's cold case (defined as an unsolved crime that occurred at least a year before). It took until 1998 for Rinek to find Danny's remains. For various technical reasons, no one could be charged in the case but finding Danny's remains enabled his sister (Danny's mother had already passed away) to have a memorial service for her brother which was attended by Rinek, his wife, and their sons, among others. (Rinek and Strong, 2018; Rinek Interviews with the author, 2021.)

These three real-life examples are just a few of the types of cases and victims that are included in this new textbook on victimology, *Essentials of Victimology*. What is victimology? It will be defined again in the first chapter, but for those who are reading this Preface, it is the scientific study of victims, especially victims of crime, including the victim-offender relationship and the aftermath of the victims' experiences such as how crime impacts the victim physically, emotionally, legally, and financially. Victimology also addresses the interactions of crime victims with the criminal justice system, if they decide to report the crime.

Victimology has become a popular undergraduate course for anyone pursuing a career in criminology, criminal justice, forensic psychology, victimology, and such related professions as law enforcement, law, corrections, rehabilitation counseling, social work, and victim advocacy. It is also being taught at the graduate level in master's programs in criminal justice, criminology, victim services, and forensic psychology; as part of police academy training; and in some law schools. Crime victim advocacy training at rape crisis centers, domestic violence shelters, and counseling centers offering help to a wider range of victims also look to victimology for a greater understanding of those who are victimized as well as those who respond to victims including police, medical personnel, crime victim advocates, lawyers, and prosecutors.

Essentials of Victimology is a new textbook for anyone seeking to gain a fundamental understanding of victimology.

The victimology courses I teach are almost always closed out because the course is so popular. What might account for that popularity? A frequent comment from my students is, "All my other courses focus on the criminal. I wanted to learn more about the victim."

Essentials of Victimology will provide you with an awareness of the evolution of the discipline of victimology, as well as an understanding of the early and current victimology theories, and a discussion of such key concepts as *victim blame, victim precipitation, repeat victimization*, the *just world hypothesis*, and *system blaming*, among others. (All these terms are defined in Chapter 3, "The Discipline of Victimology: Founders, Theories, and Controversies.")

The question, "Who are the victims?" is a pervasive theme in the study of victimology and all its related issues. By reading this textbook, you will acquire a deeper insight as to *who the victims are* of all the major violent, property, and economic crimes such as murder, rape and sexual abuse, robbery, burglary, larceny/theft, child abuse, dating violence, school violence, workplace violence, hate crimes, terrorism, stalking, domestic violence, elder abuse, cybercrime, white-collar crime, and even some rarely addressed victim issues such as animal cruelty and natural disasters.

Essentials of Victimology is based on the research, teaching, writing, and victim advocacy that this author has been participating in for more than four decades and, since August 2014, at John Jay College of Criminal Justice, a senior college in The City University of New York. Every semester since Fall 2015, including most winter and summer breaks over the last few years, this author has taught "Victimology" at John Jay College of Criminal Justice and, in Spring 2021, at Iona College as well.

WHAT *ESSENTIALS OF VICTIMOLOGY* COVERS

The first six chapters of *Essentials of Victimology* cover the basics that a student of victimology needs to know, including definitions of major crimes experienced by the victims discussed in this textbook (Chapter 1), an anthropological and historical view of how the rights of crime victims have evolved over time (Chapter 2), the founders, theories, and controversies behind victimology, such as *victim blame* and *victim precipitation* (Chapter 3), and why and how we measure crime and victimization (Chapter 4).

In Chapter 5, there is a discussion of victims and their interactions with the criminal justice system, namely the police, the courts, and corrections, including prisons. You will also read about related issues, such as the need for the criminal justice system to avoid inflicting on victims what has been referred to as the "second injury," a concept popularized by former police officer and psychiatrist Dr. Martin Symonds, who specialized in crime victims. (Symonds, 1980).

In Chapter 6, the discussion focuses on medical, psychological, and financial help for victims, including ER examinations, crisis intervention, trauma therapy, PTSD, and Eye Movement Desensitization and Reprocessing Therapy (EMDR). Also discussed in Chapter 6 is the option of civil suits that victims could consider pursuing since technically that is outside of the criminal justice system.

From Chapter 7 through Chapter 15, major violent, property, and white-collar or economic crimes are explored in separate chapters beginning with the primary (direct) and secondary (family members and friends) victims of homicide (Chapter 7); followed by property crime victims including robbery, burglary, larceny/theft, motor vehicle theft, graffiti, vandalism, and arson (Chapter 8); and cybercrime, white-collar crime, and economic crime victims (Chapter 9).

The next two chapters focus on child and teen victims, addressing issues such as abuse, neglect, and family violence affecting children and teen under age 12 (Chapter 10) and teen and college victims (Chapter 11) including dating violence and school violence.

Chapter 12 covers victims of sexual violence including rape, sexual abuse, assault, and harassment and Chapter 13 deals with assault, domestic violence, stalking, and elder abuse.

Victims of the criminal justice system including inmates who have been hurt or even extorted during imprisonment, those who have been falsely arrested, and challenges faced by the families of the incarcerated, are explored in Chapter 14.

Chapter 15 looks at various special victim populations including victims of workplace crime, terrorism, and human trafficking; people with intellectual, physical, and mental disabilities and disorders; and substance abuse victims. Also discussed in this chapter are victims of hate crimes related to race, ethnicity, religion, or sexual orientation, including victims because they are members of the LGBTQ (lesbian, gay, bisexual, transgender, and questioning) community. The chapter concludes with a discussion of animal cruelty and wildlife crime victims, natural disaster victims, and cruise ship victims. In addressing those situations, the focus is on the victim of a crime rather than a more general examination of those issues.

Finally, Chapter 16 provides information about more than 60 careers that are directly or indirectly related to victimology, victims, and the media, as well as considerations about the future of the field.

TYPICAL QUESTIONS THAT *ESSENTIALS OF VICTIMOLOGY* WILL ANSWER

Some of the myriad of questions this textbook will answer (in addition to "Who are the victims?") include:

- What are the rights of a crime victim?
- Is it possible to be concerned about the rights of victims without diminishing the rights of the offender?
- What are the earliest theories of victimization that relied on victim typologies?
- What are the next victimization theories, the so-called "opportunity" theories?
- What about alternatives to incarceration, like restorative justice? Does the victim have to agree to participate in it?

- Who is the typical victim of each type of major violent or property crime? In terms of age, gender, race, ethnicity, location (rural, suburban, urban), and socioeconomic factors, who is most likely to be a victim of each particular crime?
- What is white-collar crime and who are its most common victims?
- What are the reasons behind reporting or non-reporting to the police for different types of crime victimization?
- What is *victim blame* and why is it so harmful to victims?
- What is a clearance rate and why do clearance rates matter?
- What is the likelihood, even if a victim reports the crime, that the case will go to trial rather than be resolved through plea bargaining?
- What is the distinction between crime prevention and crime victimization reduction? How can we accomplish either or both?
- In addition to becoming a victimologist or crime victim advocate, what other careers will benefit from the study of victimology?

INTRODUCING YOU TO THIS TEXTBOOK

Publishing a new textbook on victimology does not take away from the many excellent victimology textbooks already available (Karmen, 2020; Doerner and Lab, 2021; Daigle, 2018; Burgess, 2019; Daigle and Muftic, 2020; Fisher, Reyns, and Sloan III, 2016; Wallace and Roberson, 2018; Turvey, 2014; and Clevenger, et al., 2018). So why another one? Some of the reasons are delineated below. For starters, *Essentials of Victimology* takes a more multi-disciplined approach than most other textbooks. In addition to sociology, criminology, and victimology, this textbook looks to anthropology, history, law, psychology, psychiatry, social work, medicine, nursing, and communication studies for insights and answers. For example, in Chapter 2, you will discover a discussion about the way victims and their families and communities have dealt with violent or property crimes in two cultures: the Comanches of North America and the Inuit (previously known as the Eskimos) of the Artic.

In Chapter 6, when addressing the medical and psychological aftermath of victimization, this author studied the research or interviewed practitioners from psychology, psychiatry, forensic psychology, medicine, and social work, as well as sociology and criminology. You will learn about psychological research into how to conduct a better or cognitive victim interview. (Fisher and Geiselman, 2010)

Certain topics receive more extensive treatment in this textbook than in others. For example, in Chapter 10 on child victims, there is a more in-depth discussion about sibling sexual abuse, a type of child and teenage sexual abuse that is rarely or minimally addressed in other textbooks even though researchers, such as David Finkelhor, estimate that sibling sexual abuse is *five times* more common than father-daughter (parent-child) incest. (Finkelhor, 1980).

In this textbook, child victims have their own chapter (Chapters 10), as do teens and college victims (Chapter 11).

Chapter 14, on victims *of* the criminal justice system, is a unique chapter in a victimology textbook that includes a discussion of victims of police brutality, prisoners who are victims, those who have been falsely accused, as well as the too often overlooked plight of the families of the incarcerated.

In Chapter 15, special situations, like hate crimes, and animal cruelty, wildlife crime, and natural disaster victims, are highlighted.

According to peer reviewers, one of the many strengths of *Essentials of Victimology* is the inclusion of numerous first-person interviews with crime victims or experts. Rather than just paraphrasing what victims, or those working with victims, have to say, you will read verbatim quotes from those interviews. Although verbatim quotes may sometimes only be just a line or two, other times, quotes are shared in a more extensive way, especially in the Profiles included in a majority of chapters.

More than 125 respondents were interviewed by this author in researching this textbook. Interviewees were found by posting multiple queries between April 2020 and April 2021 requesting respondents through HARO (Help a Reporter Out), a free three-times-a-day publicity newsletter that is distributed to an estimated database of 800,000 potential readers, according to Cision, the company that owns and administers it. The decision whether an interviewee would be used anonymously or, with permission, for attribution was made on a case-by-case basis. (You will know if an interviewee is named or anonymous by the name associated with that interview. Complete names indicate attribution. Pseudonyms are indicated by a first name and last initial, such as Christine R.)

Additional interviewees were found through the social media site Linkedin.com, as well as by following up on press releases sent by publicists whose clients had just published a book, released a study, or announced a new website or program related to crime or victimization. I also followed up on my own internet and print publication research, e-mailing victims or, in the case of homicide, their family members. On May 10, 2020, through Survey Monkey Audience, this author purchased a survey panel that enabled contact with 225 male and female respondents from throughout the United States to complete a 10-question survey developed about crime victimization. Key questions included whether respondents had been the victim of a crime and if they had, if that crime had been reported to the police.

Whether named or anonymous, all the quotes from interviews included as examples in this textbook are true even if some of the identifying details had to be changed to conceal and protect the identity of those who wished to remain anonymous.

Consider that beginning on January 1, 2021, the National Incident-Based Reporting System (NIBRS) replaced the Uniform Crime Reports (UCR) which was how crime data had been collected and published by the FBI since 1930, for almost 100 years. The NIBRS and the other major U.S. source of crime data, the National Crime Victim Survey (NCVS), are explored in Chapter 4, "Measuring Victimization: Why and How."

In this textbook, you will also read quotes from memoirs, TED Talks, or original interviews with victims who might surprise you because these victims have not been anyone's focus before. For example, Kerri Rawson shared in our phone interview and in the guest interview via Zoom that she did with three of my classes at John Jay College of Criminal Justice (Victimology, Criminology, and Penology) about her life ever since she learned that her father was a serial killer. Author of *A Serial Killer's Daughter,* Kerri revealed how she sees herself, her brother, and her mother as crime victims. Kerri says she was unaware that her father was leading the double life of a husband, devoted father, and worker when, 16 years ago, in 2005, when Kerri was 26 years old, an FBI agent knocked on her door. Once inside, he told her that her father had just been arrested for killing eight people. (The death toll was increased to ten, partly based on information that Kerri was able to provide related to one of their neighbors who was murdered.) (Rawson, phone and Zoom interviews, 2020; Rawson, 2019)

THE CHALLENGE OF OVERLAPPING CRIMES

Some information discussed in one chapter may also be an issue addressed or mentioned in other chapters. Take cybercrime, for example. Although it is primarily an economic crime, including identity theft and credit card fraud it is discussed in Chapter 9 on white-collar and economic crimes, not conventional property crimes. But cyberstalking, a form of cybercrime, is mentioned in reference to stalking in Chapter 13 ("Victims of Assault, Domestic Violence, Stalking, and Elder Abuse"). Because cybercrime also includes cyberbullying, it is mentioned in Chapter 10, "Child Victims." Just be aware as you read *Essentials of Victimology* that you might find information about a particular crime and its victims in more than one chapter. These seeming repetitions are unavoidable, and intentional.

CHAPTER STRUCTURE

Here is what you can expect in each of the chapters that follow.

1. Learning Objectives

   These learning objectives list what you can expect to have learned after you have read the chapter.

2. Core of the Chapter

   You will read facts, examples, excerpts from verbatim interviews, statistics, tables, and charts related to that chapter's content.

3. Profile

   This is a section in many chapters; it is one or more extensive interviews that is related to the topics explored in the chapter.

4. Summary

   At the end of each chapter, there is a summary of what you have just read, highlighting key information covered in that chapter. The summary will reinforce what you are learning and better prepare you for any quizzes or tests.

5. Key Terms

   This is a list of the key terms that were presented and defined, in the chapter. The style is to bold face a key term the first time it is defined or where it is significant, not incidental, in a chapter. (Key terms are also defined again, in alphabetical order, in the master Glossary for the entire textbook at the end of the textbook.)

6. Review Questions

   Every chapter has a list of questions to help you to review the chapter's essential information that you have learned. By asking, and answering, these questions you can keep yourself on track throughout the semester.

7. Critical Thinking Questions

   You will find critical thinking questions intended to help you apply what you have learned. These questions are constructed in a way that will hopefully challenge you to think creatively and critically about what you have learned.

8. Activities and Exercises

   At least one or more activities or exercises related to the chapter's subject matter are provided. You could carry out these activities on your own or as class work if your professor organizes one or all of these activities together. Group activities can be organized in person or online via the Breakout Room function if the videoconferencing program your professor is using offers that feature.

9. Resources

   This section includes related associations, agencies, or organizations of note, annotated listings, with their websites.

10. Cited Works and Additional References

    Any works that were cited in the previous chapter will be listed in alphabetical order, beginning with the last name of the author. Additional references are also included.

11. Videos, Films, Documentaries, or Podcasts

    This last section includes any videos, films, documentaries, or podcasts related to the chapter.

MY BACKGROUND

Although a fine arts major in college, I was fascinated by sociology and took undergraduate courses in that field. Then, in my senior year, something happened that would lead to my personal motivation to study crime victims. My older brother, Seth Barkas, who was 23, an NYU graduate, married, the father of a five-year-old, with another son on the way, was stabbed by a teenage gang during a robbery as he was walking to his car to return home to his apartment in Forest Hills, Queens. A freelance writer, he had been attending an off-off Broadway play in Manhattan that he was assigned to write about for a major national theater newspaper. He died several days later from his injuries.

Seth Alan Barkas (1945-1969)
Contributed photo.

At this funeral, I had my first experience with what I now know is referred to as *victim blame*. Even though my brother was a freelance theater critic, doing his job, reviewing a play in Manhattan on assignment, several people at the funeral asked me in an accusatory tone why he was out at night as if he was to blame for what happened to him. Although I did not act on the way that question made me feel right away, it did stay with me. It would, indeed, within a few years, shape my future career path.

My brother's murder was traumatic and a complete shock, but I did not initially do anything related to crime or crime victims. Instead, after I graduated college, I spent a year studying art therapy at Hahnemann Medical College in Philadelphia. My two semester-long internships included working with those diagnosed with a psychotic disorder at Philadelphia General Hospital and then interning at a city-run home in South Philadelphia where children who had been removed from an abusive household had been temporarily placed.

At the end of that year, I decided against becoming an art therapist and began working as an editorial assistant at Macmillan Publishing Company in the school division. Three years later, after working for a year at Grove Press, Inc., Scribner's published my first nonfiction book on the history of vegetarianism, *The Vegetable Passion*.

While that book was in production, I found myself drawn to trying to understand the criminal justice system and what happened to my brother five years before. I enrolled in the master's in criminal justice program at Goddard College Graduate Program. My mentor and advisor was Dr. Arthur Niederhoffer, a former police officer who was a Professor in the Department of Sociology at John Jay College of Criminal Justice and author of *Behind the Shield*. My master's thesis was on "Victims of Crime and Social Change."

The year after I graduated with my masters, Scribner's published my book on crime victims, *Victims,* that I had been researching and writing for four years. A year later, it was published in the United Kingdom by Peel Press.

Even before I completed my master's degree, I began teaching college level courses. The first course, "The Roots of Violence," I taught at The New School. To conduct research for that course, I visited the morgue, went on several ride-a-longs with the New York City Police Department (NYPD), and immersed myself in the criminal justice system by interviewing crime victims, offenders, police officers, ADAs (assistant district attorneys), victim advocates, criminologists, judges, and defense attorneys as well as attending criminal proceedings, visiting prisons such as Attica Correctional Facility in New York State, and even interviewing the head of Scotland Yard in London. I also visited police departments in Paris and Amsterdam and throughout the U.S. including Boston, and shelters for domestic violence victims in London and Texas. I taught courses in criminal justice and juvenile delinquency at Temple University.

I followed up by spending the next four years obtaining my Ph.D. in sociology from The City University of New York Graduate Center. One of my three areas of expertise was deviance and crime, which I studied under deviance expert and criminologist Edward Sagarin. After graduation, I taught criminology and sociology courses fulltime for two years at the New York Institute of Technology.

I took time off from college teaching to raise my two sons but once they were older, I returned to teaching, first at the University of Connecticut, at the Stamford campus (1999-2006), and then, since 2014, in the Department of Sociology at John Jay College of Criminal Justice. At John Jay, where I am an Adjunct Associate Professor, I have taught Victimology along with courses in Penology, Criminology, International Criminology, and, alternatively, other courses including Race and Ethnic Relations, Introduction to Sociology, among others. I have also taught undergraduate courses in victimology, criminology, penology, sociology, forensic health (graduate), qualitative research (graduate), and public speaking at other colleges and universities in the Tri-State area including William Paterson University, Kean University, New York Film Academy, and Iona College.

Over the years, my practical experience has included working at a crime victim hotline, taking the 40-hour training to become a volunteer at a local rape crisis center, participating in a reentry volunteer program for women at Bedford Hills Correctional Facility, developing and running a part-time crime prevention resource center in New York City for two years, that was housed at Marymount Manhattan College, and, for 1-1/2 years, being a participant observer in a support group for adult survivors of childhood and teenage sexual abuse.

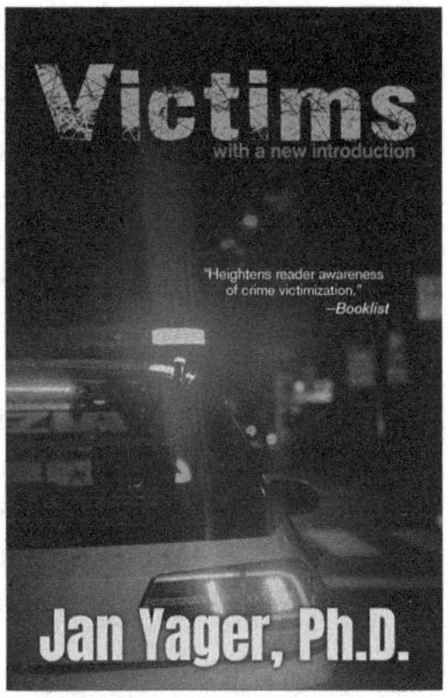

2021 version of *Victims* with a new introduction, originally published by Scribner's.

I have continued conducting original research by interviewing crime victims, and those who help them, including adding excerpts from some of those interviews in the newer introductions, along with the updated bibliography, resource section, and statistics, to my book *Victims*, most recently updated and published by Hannacroix Creek Books, Inc. Additional victim and service provider interviews have been conducted by phone and via Zoom as recently as August 2021.

A SPECIAL NOTE TO STUDENTS WHO ARE READING THIS TEXTBOOK

I have written this new victimology textbook as if you are a student in my Victimology class. I have discovered from years of teaching victimology, as well as criminology, penology, and the sociology of deviance, that what students find most interesting are the original interviews with crime victims and other experts who graciously consented to be guest speakers in my courses. Some of those guest presentations, as well as additional interviews that I conducted in-person, by phone, or via Zoom, are excerpted throughout this textbook.

But students also need to learn the statistics about who are the most typical victims of a particular crime and if there are any notable trends to consider. For example, in 2019, of the 267,988 reported robberies in the United States, 509 resulted in the death of the victim or what is known as a robbery-homicide. The phrase, "Your money or your life," may be a cliché, but it is often said by the robbers and, as that 509 number indicates, for 509 victims, for them the robbery was fatal. (FBI, *2019 Crime in the United States*, "Expanded Homicide Data Table 10") Students also need to be aware of the classic and contemporary peer-reviewed articles related to crime victims that are pivotal to the study of victimology.

This textbook is structured for a traditional twice a week, or once a week, 16-week course over 4 months, assigning and covering a chapter a week. If your college or university follows a 14-week semester schedule, your professor can double up chapters over several weeks. Because of my experiences with in-person as well as distance or online learning, I know this textbook will work in either in-person or remote learning formats; it should also work in a hybrid one.

At the product page for this book at the publisher's website, www.AspenPublishing.com, there are materials available in two sections: the Instructor's portion, which is password protected, and the Student section, which is not. Instructors will be advised how to make any password protected materials available to their students, such as the chapter-by-chapter Power Points unique to *Essentials of Victimology*, if they choose to do so.

Students may freely download any of the materials posted at the product page for this book archived in the Student portion of the product page. Materials will include Appendices such as The Crime Victims' Rights Act (CVRA) (2004) or Tips on Responding to Survivors of Homicide Victims. Students will also find additional Resources, References, and listings for Videos, Podcasts, Films, or Documentaries, organized chapter by chapter.

Please note that all these materials, unless it is a government publication and/or in the public domain, are copyright protected meaning the materials are for individual educational use only. Please do not repost, copy, publish or share these materials without written permission from the publisher.

A SUGGESTION TO THOSE OFFERING TRAINING AT CRISIS CENTERS OR IN OTHER PROGRAMS

Essentials of Victimology was written with the idea that every chapter is pivotal to the field of victimology. However, if this textbook is being used for training at a crisis center, depending upon the type of crime victim that the center focuses on, some chapters could be optional or skipped. If this textbook is being used as part of police academy training, although police officers would benefit from reading the entire book, if there is only time to cover a couple of chapters, these chapters would be recommended: Chapter 5, "Victims and the Criminal Justice System," Chapter 6, "Helping the Victim," and as many of the chapters on specific crime victims as possible, from Chapter 7, "Primary and Secondary Victims of Homicide," through Chapter 15. For a training for crime victim advocates specializing in sexual violence victims, these chapters might be most pertinent: Preface, Chapters 1, 2, 3, 5, 6, and especially Chapters 10, 11, and 12, "Sexual Violence."

Please visit my website, https://www.drjanyager.com, where you will find blogs on a range of topics and a resource section that you might want to explore.

Although personal replies cannot be guaranteed, you are welcome to write to me with suggestions, comments, or additional materials related to *Essentials of Victimology*.

Jan Yager, Ph.D.
(the former J.L. Barkas)
John Jay College of Criminal Justice
The City University of New York (CUNY)
Sociology Department
Adjunct Associate Professor
https://www.drjanyager.com
e-mail: drjanyager123@gmail.com

Jan Yager, Ph.D.
Photo credit: Fred Yager

CITED WORKS AND ADDITIONAL REFERENCES

Barkas, J.L. *Victims.* 1978. New York: Scribner's.

__________. "Victims of Crime and Social Change." May 1975. Master's Thesis for completion of an M.A. in Criminal Justice, under the supervision of Arthur Niederhoffer, Ph.D. Goddard College, Plainfield, Vermont.

Burgess, Ann Wolbert. 2019. *Victimology: Theories and Applications.* Third edition. Burlington, MA: Jones & Bartlett Learning.

Clevenger, Shelly, Jordana N. Navarro, Catherine D. Marcum, and George E. Higgins. 2018. *Understanding Victimology: An Active-Learning Approach.* New York: Routledge.

Crecente, Drew, J.D. Wednesday, December 9, 2020. Guest presentation via Zoom, "Victimology," John Jay College of Criminal Justice.

__________. Tuesday, February 23, 2021. Guest presentation via Zoom. "Social Deviance." Kean University.

__________. Monday, December 28, 2020. Phone interview with author.

Daigle, Leah E. 2018. *Victimology: A Text/Reader.* Second edition. Los Angeles, CA: SAGE.

Daigle, Leah E. and Lisa R. Muftic. 2020. *Victimology: A Comprehensive Approach.* Second edition. Los Angeles, CA: SAGE.

Doerner, William G. and Steven P. Lab. 2021. *Victimology.* 9th edition. New York: Routledge.

Dussich, John P. J. 2005. "Victimology: Past, Present and Future." 131st International Senior Seminar. Visiting Experts' Papers.

Fisher, Bonnie S., Bradford W. Reyns, and John J. Sloan III. 2016. *Introduction to Victimology: Contemporary Theory, Research, and Practice.* New York: Oxford University Press.

FBI (Federal Bureau of Investigation). 2019. *2019 Crime in the United States.* U.S. Department of Justice, Criminal Justice Information Services Division, posted online.

__________. 2018. *2018 Crime in the United States.* "Expanded Homicide Data 2018." "Murder Circumstances by Relationship, 2018."

Finkelhor, David. 1980. "Sex Among Siblings: A Survey on Prevalence, Variety, and Effects." *Archives of Sexual Behavior.* 9: 171-194.

Karmen, Andrew. 2020. *Crime Victims: An Introduction to Victimology.* 10th edition. Boston, MA: Cengage.

Quinn, Elizabeth and Sara Brightman. 2015. *Crime Victimization: A Comprehensive Overview.* Durham, NC: Carolina Academic. Press.

Quinney, Richard. 1979. *Criminology.* Second edition. Boston, MA: Little, Brown and Company.

__________. 1972. "Who Is the Victim?" *Criminology.* 10: 314-323.

Rawson, Kerri. April 29, 2020. Guest presentation via Zoom, John Jay College of Criminal Justice.

__________. April 17, 2020 and April 29, 2020. Phone interviews with the author.

__________. 2019. *A Serial Killer's Daughter.* Nashville, TN: Nelson.

Rinek, Jeffrey L. Thursday, February 25, 2021. Phone interview with the author.

Rinek, Jeffrey L and Marilee Strong. 2018. *In the Name of the Children: An FBI Agent's Relentless Pursuit of the Nation's Worst Predators.* Dallas, TX: BenBella Books.

Symonds Martin. 1980. "The "Second Injury" to Victims of Violent Acts. *American Journal of Psychoanalysis.* 70: 34-41.

Tischler, Henry L. 2019. *Introduction to Sociology.* 12th edition. New York: Wessex. Press, Inc.

Turvey, Brent E. 2014. *Forensic Victimology: Examining Violent Crimes in Investigative and Legal Contexts.* Second edition. Waltham, MA: Academic Press.

__________. May 22, 2020. Phone interview with author.

Von Hentig, Hans. 1948. *The Criminal and His Victim: Studies in the Sociobiology of Crime.* New Haven, CT: Yale University Press., 1948. (Reprint edition, 1979, with a Preface by Marvin E. Wolfgang. Schocken. Books)

Wallace, Harvey and Cliff Roberson. 2018. *Victimology: Legal, Psychological, and Social Perspectives.* Fifth Edition. New York: Pearson.

Yager, Jan. 2021. *Help Yourself Now: A Practical Guide to Finding the Information and Assistance You Need.* New York: Allworth, Press, an imprint of Skyhorse Publishing, Inc.

__________. (a/k/a/ J.L. Barkas) 2021, 2015 *Victims.* (Scribner's, 1978.) Stamford, CT: Hannacroix Creek. Books, Inc. (with new introduction)

Essentials of Victimology

Chapter **ONE**

Victimology

An Overview

Learning Objectives

After you finish reading this chapter, you should be able to

1. Define *victimology.*
2. Know when the term *victimology* was first coined and by whom.
3. Explain the differences among primary, secondary, tertiary, and quaternary victims.
4. Identify and define eight major violent and property crimes previously known as the Part I offenses of the Uniform Crime Reporting (UCR) Program, which is now tracked by the National Incident-Based Reporting System (NIBRS).
5. Define *bystander* and *witness.*
6. Be able to compare the varied approach to a research topic by victimologists versus criminologists.
7. Offer at least three reasons for studying victimology.

DEFINING VICTIMOLOGY

This textbook is a comprehensive study of **victimology**. Just what is victimology?

It is the scientific study of the **victim**. Just what does the word *victim* mean? It is derived from the Latin word *victima* which was originally tied to the idea of a religious sacrifice. (Burgess, 2019: 11) Other definitions of victim include "a person who suffers from a destructive or injurious action or agency." Add on *ology* which means "any science or branch of knowledge" and you arrive at *victimology*, the scientific study of victims. (Dictionary.com)

You will learn in this textbook, and some of you may already know, that for many, the term *survivor* has become the preferred term since many have negative associations with the term *victim* and its implication that someone has lost to the criminal. But *survivorology*, as some have proposed, does not work as a replacement for the discipline of victimology. (Karmen, 2020) When *victim* is used throughout this textbook, it could be interchanged with *survivor*. No negative connotation is implied by the word *victim*. (Harding, 2020)

Victimology, the focus of this textbook, is the scientific study of **victims** of crime as well as the treatment of crime victims by the criminal justice system including the services provided for victims. It is considered one of the **social sciences**. What is a social science? *Social science* is defined as "all those disciplines that apply scientific methods to the study of human behavior." (Tischler, 2019) Psychology, cultural anthropology, social work, political science, and economics, are considered social sciences. (Tischler, 2019)

There is also a narrower definition of victimology that focuses on victims of crime as part of what is known as the "**penal couple**," the offender and the victim, a term first attributed to Romanian lawyer Beniamin Mendelsohn (he spelled his first name with an "i" rather than a "j"). (Schafer, 1968)

Victimology is a relatively new branch of the social sciences. Its origins can be traced back to 1924, when renowned criminologist Edwin Sutherland included a chapter on the crime victim in his popular criminology textbook. (Sutherland, 1924)

Next, the concept of this new approach of considering the relationship between the victim and the criminal is attributed to Mendelsohn who wrote an article entitled "Method to be Used by Counsel for the Defense in the Researches Made into the Personality of the Criminal." It was published in a French journal, *Revue de Droit Penal et de Criminologie* in 1937. (Mendelsohn, 1963; Siegel, 2018; Schafer, 1968; Dussich, 2005).

Mendelsohn based his article on the results of the 300-question survey that he distributed to his clients that probed the relationship between the offender and the victim. His focus was on victims of rape and, according to criminologist Schafer, "on the extent of their resistance." (Schafer, 1968: 41) Schafer continues, "In his basic study of criminal-victim relationships he [Mendelsohn] proposes the term 'victimology' in order to develop an independent field of study and perhaps a new discipline." (Schafer, 1968: 41)

Mendelsohn's initial publications were followed, in 1940, by the publication by criminologist Hans von Hentig of his ground-breaking journal article entitled, "Remarks on the Interaction of Perpetrator and Victim," which appeared in *Journal of Criminal Law and Criminology* (von Hentig, 1940;). Von Hentig's article was followed by his book, *The Criminal and His Victim*, published by Yale University Press in 1948. (von Hentig, 1948; Schafer, 1968; Mendelsohn, 1963, 1974)

Victimology evolved out of a multidisciplined approach that draws on sociology and criminology as well as social sciences, noted above, and science fields such as psychiatry, biology, social work, nursing, medicine, and even statistics. It seeks to answer the question, "Who are the victims?" and to discover a unique and broader perspective as to their interactions with the offenders and the responses of the criminal justice system to the victims of crime. (Mendelsohn, 1974)

WHO ARE THE VICTIMS?

Who are some of the victims that victimologists study? Here are thumbnail sketches of real-life victimizations:

Diana Rodriguez-Martin. Contributed photo.

- Diana Rodriguez-Martin was a beautiful, trusting 43-year-old woman who was separated from her husband. But in February 2017, she agreed to meet with him again and that is when tragedy struck. Only two people were present at that last meeting and one of them ended up dead and dismembered, with her body parts put into dumpsters, never to be found again. Exactly what happened that fateful day may never be completely known, but Diana's estranged husband confessed to the killing, claiming it was in self-defense, even though Diana was unarmed. He received a ten-year sentence in a **plea bargain** deal for first-degree manslaughter "since her body was never recovered" according to reporter Jennifer Bain. (Bain, 2018; Frangipane, 2017; interviews by the author with Diana's first cousin, Valerie Reyes-Jimenez, 2017, 2018.)
- Alvin and Bernadette Fazande were married 58 years when Hurricane Katrina devastated New Orleans and surrounding communities including Jefferson Parish where they lived. Taking a bottle of water along as well as a plastic bag that contained their will and other documents, the two 79-year-olds retreated to the attic of their one-story home as the water quickly rose. Unfortunately, they did not survive the storm. A week later, when their son was finally able to visit his parents' home, he could still see the red "Send Help" sign that they had placed in their window. The failure of the levee system to stop the waters the way it was supposed to, the slow government response time afterwards, and the reluctance of residents like the Fazandes to evacuate when they had a chance, are three reasons that have been given for a death toll ranging from a low estimate of 986 to a high estimate of 1,440, including Alvin and Bernadette. (Associated Press, 10/25/2005; Lindsey Cook and Ethan Rosenberg, *U.S. News & World Report*, 8/28/2015)
- When Jack F. was eight years old, he was sexually molested by his 16-year-old cousin. (He called him his cousin but he was actually a boy with a troubled childhood who had been adopted by Jack's grandparents when he was 12.) "It happened on my grandparents' farm in a small little ranch house," says Jack, who is now 35. "I blocked it out for 10 years. It all came to a head when I was 18. I was back there at my grandparents' house and I remember it vividly. I was writing a story and it all flooded through and just came out." Jack did not report it, nor has he ever confronted his "cousin" about it, although he hopes to someday. "I don't have any evidence to take to the police. The **statute of limitations** has passed. We were both minors when it happened. It would be his word against mine. My grandmother knows everyone in [her state]. It would break up that family or put them under undue stress and it would drag our family's name through the mud. It's something I don't wish to do." (Interview with the author, 2021)
- In North London, a 28-year-old man was robbed at night by two assailants who took his wallet and his expensive watch. He suffered a broken jaw and a brain bleed. The Metropolitan Police appealed to any witnesses of the robbery to contact them by e-mail, tweet, or calling their Crimestoppers number. (O'Reilly, November 2020)

- Between the ages of 4 and 11, Christina R. was the victim of **sexual molestation** by her older first cousin. When she was 11, she told her best friend what was going on and her friend encouraged her to tell her middle school advisor, which Christina did. The police immediately got involved and they all soon learned that her cousin had previously been molesting Christina's older sister, starting when he was 11. When he began his victimization of Christina, her cousin was 17. By the time Christina confided about the **incest,** he was a man of 24. He took a plea deal of 10 years for each victim, for a total of 20 years, with the sentences to be served consecutively. The 2018 National Crime Victimization Survey (NCVS), the second major source of crime data in the U.S. (which you will learn more about in Chapter 4) reported that only 24.9% of rapes were reported to the police. (Morgan and Oudekerk, 2019) Even fewer of those rape and sexual assault victims who report the crime see an arrest made or a sentence imposed. RAINN (Rape, Abuse & Incest National Network) estimates that out of 1,000 sexual assaults, of the 310 that are reported to the police, only 50 reports will lead to an arrest, only 28 of those cases will lead to a felony conviction and of those convictions, only 25 perpetrators will get prison time. (RAINN.org). Considering those realities, Christina's case is an exceptional one. (Interviews with the author, 2019, 2020.)
- Jeffrey Bright, a 16-year-old transgender boy, and his sister, Jasmine Cannady, 22, were allegedly shot and killed by their mother, who confessed at the scene to the police. (Farberov, 2021)

Dorri Olds as a teenager. Contributed photo.

- Dorri Olds shares about being gang-raped by classmates when she was only 13 years old. She kept her secret until age 26 after waking up in a Florida Drug rehab. Olds had no memory of leaving New York City after a three-day bender on cocaine and alcohol. The first time Olds spoke about her ordeal was with her counselor at that facility. In 2009, soon after her father's death, Olds turned to a therapist for help. Years later, she felt blindsided by a particular Facebook "friend" suggestion. Before going public with her story, Olds finally confided in her mother and two older sisters. Her related essay, "Defriending My Rapist," was published in the Sunday Styles section of *The New York Times* on January 13, 2012. (Olds, 2012; Olds, 2020; Olds, 2021)
- Lillian C., who was unemployed and desperate for work, became the victim of a mystery shopper cybercrime which led to her losing $2,400. She also suffered feelings of humiliation that she fell for the scam. Because she had voluntarily deposited the phony check into her account, her bank explained to her that she had to cover the losses and pay the overdraft fees after the check bounced. (Interview by ES with victim, 2019)
- Lynn Julian Crisci developed numerous physical problems including internal injuries such as blast force trauma when she was hurt by the bombs that went off during the April 2013 Boston Marathon terrorist bombing. (Read more about her ordeal in the section on "Terrorism" in Chapter 15.) (Interview with the author, 2020)

These are just twelve victims—of murder, first-degree manslaughter, incest, cybercrime/identity theft, natural disaster, robbery, aggravated assault, domestic terrorism, and rape. In 2019, according to the FBI Uniform Crime Report, there were 16,425 murder and nonnegligent manslaughter victims in the United States. (FBI, *2019 Crime in the United States*) Although the United States leads the world in the number of homicides for what is referred to as a Westernized nation, homicide is certainly not just an American phenomenon or problem. In the study of homicide throughout the world, the United Nations Office on Drugs and Crime (UNODC) released a study in 2019 stating that in 2017, when their data was gathered, there were an estimated 464,000 murders around the world, "surpassing by far the 89,000 killed in armed conflicts in the same period." (UNODC, 2019)

Although few would disagree that homicide is the most serious of all crimes, there are many more crimes that are cause for concern that injure, psychologically traumatize, or financially damage their victims. In just the United States in 2019, as noted in Table 1.1, there were hundreds of thousands (and in some categories, millions) who were victims of aggravated assaults, robberies, rapes, motor vehicle thefts, and burglaries, not to mention those who were victims of natural disasters or even of being falsely accused and imprisoned. It seems that victimization is a fact of life.

Remember that these statistics, based on the FBI annual report, are only *reported* crimes. As will be discussed further in Chapter 4, "Measuring Victimization: Why and How," according to the Bureau of Justice Statistics, which compiles the second major source of information on crime in the United States, the National Crime Victimization Survey (NCVS), less than half, or only 41 percent, of violent crime victimizations were reported to the police in 2019. (Morgan and Truman, Bureau of Justice Statistics, 2020)

TABLE 1.1. Number of Reported Victims of Eight Major Violent and Property Crimes in the United States, 2019

Offense	Number of Reported Crimes
Reported murders	16,425
Reported rapes	139,815
Reported robberies	267,988
Reported aggravated assaults	821,182
Reported burglaries	1,117,696
Reported larceny/thefts	5,086,096
Reported motor vehicle thefts	721,885
Reported arsons	33,395
Total reported major crimes in the U.S. (adding up all the above crimes)	**8,204,482**

Source: Federal Bureau of Investigation (FBI), *2019 Crime in the United States*

We will explore these statistics and the victims of major violent, property, and economic crimes in greater detail in the chapters that follow. For now, you at least have an overview about reported crime victims in the United States for 2019, as well as an awareness that official FBI statistics of reported crimes do not represent the totality of crime because so many crimes are not reported.

PUTTING VICTIMOLOGY IN A HISTORICAL CONTEXT

Regardless of whether you date victimology back to Sutherland's crime victim chapter in his 1924 textbook, Mendelsohn's 1937 article, von Hentig's 1940 journal article, Mendelsohn coining the term *victimology* in 1947, or von Hentig's 1948 book, victimology is still a relatively new area of study, not even 100 years old. (Sutherland, 1924; Mendelsohn, 1974; von Hentig, 1940; von Hentig, 1948; Schafer, 1968: 39-42, 157). Compare that timeline of victimology to its parallel discipline, the scientific study of the criminal or *criminology*, an academic discipline and social science that dates back to the 1870s, and is usually attributed to Cesare Lombroso, or to his student Raffaele Garofalo for coining the term *criminology* in 1885, (Adler, Mueller, Laufer, 2007:10). Some, like criminologist Richard Quinney, date *criminology* back even further, to the 1830s "when crime was first studied as a social, not an individual phenomenon." (Quinney, 1979).

That would put criminology's origins around the same time as *sociology*, defined as the scientific study of groups and society, a discipline that most deem the parent social science to both criminology and victimology. The coining of the term *sociology* is usually attributed to August Comte, who first used *sociology* in his major work, the six-volume *Cours de Philosophie Positive* (*The Course on Positive Philosophy*), written between 1830 and 1842. (Tischler, 2019) Harriet Martineau (1802-1876) translated Comte's treatise into English (1853), condensing it into a more manageable two-volume version. She is credited with bringing the new social science of sociology to England. (Tischler, 2019)

It is often said that the development of sociology and criminology as a field of study grew out of the transformation during the early eighteenth century through the late nineteenth century from a way of life organized primarily around agricultural means of production to an urban society employing an industrial means of production. (American Sociological Association, 2008)

Chapter 2, "An Anthropological and Historical View of Crime Victims and Victims' Rights" and Chapter 3, "The Discipline of Victimology: Founders, Theories, and Controversies" provide more detailed discussions about how the victims' rights movement of the 1970s was an outgrowth of other movements, such as the Civil Rights Movement of the 1960s and the women's movement of the 1970s and 1980s. What this author is referring to here is why even the concept of victimology started when it did. Why, in the 1930s and 1940s, did a lawyer, like Mendelsohn, and a criminologist, like von Hentig, shift their focus from solely on the criminal to exploring how and why some people become victims of various crimes ranging from theft to terrorism?

Could it be that victimology unfolded at a time of great unrest in Europe from the 1930s through to 1945 with the rise of Nazism and the outbreak of World War II, which resulted in millions of victims? This is something to be considered since so many of the early victimologists—Mendelsohn, von Hentig, Schafer, and Wolfgang, among others—were looking to understand the role of the victims in any of the crimes that they endured. In the course of his studies, Mendelsohn, for example, created typologies that categorized victims on a scale from "completely innocent" to "most guilty." (Mendelsohn, 1963). Is it possible that the development of victimology was facilitated by a concern over why some became victims whereas others had managed to avoid it? (Huebel, 2018; Kalczewiak, 2019; Shirer, 1960)

It has been said that one of the motivations behind psychologist Stanley Milgram's infamous experiment in obedience to authority was to understand whether just anyone could be forced to become a Nazi and kill those whose only "crime" was being Jewish, disabled, homosexual, or a gypsy. (Milgram, 1974; Gibson, et.et al., 2017). It is probably not a coincidence that Milgram's experiments began at Yale University in July 1961, three months after the start of one of the most famous post-war trials of a high-ranking Nazi war criminal who was tied to sending countless Jews to their deaths in the concentration camps. Adolf Eichmann had been captured in Argentina on May 11, 1960 and taken to Israel for trial.

The trial began in Israel beginning on April 11, 1961, and Eichmann, who had proclaimed that he was just doing what he was ordered to do, was sentenced to death by hanging on December 12, 1961. (United States Holocaust Memorial Museum, 2021; Harvard University, Department of Psychology, website biography, n.d.; Arendt, 1963; Berenbaum, 2021)

There are actually two distinct categorizations of victimology. The first classifies victimology as a branch of criminology and focuses on crime and the victims of crime. (Dussich, n.d.; Drapkin and Viano, 1974.)

The second is a much broader view that reflects the approach advocated by lawyer Mendelsohn who, due to his early work in this field as discussed above, is considered the "father of victimology." As Mendelsohn wrote, "Victimology should be a separate and autonomous science, have its own institutions and be allowed to develop for the well-being and progress of humanity." (Mendelsohn, *Excerpta Criminologica*, 1963)

Yes, Mendelsohn envisioned victimology "apart from criminology, since criminologists can be only criminologists and nothing else, as a physician cannot be also an engineer or a chemist or a physicist. . . . There should be a separate institute for the research of all victims of all factors in which society is interested . . ." (Mendelsohn, personal correspondence with the author, November 24, 1978.)

The Show of Violence by Dr. Fredric Wertham

Agreeing with Mendelsohn's broader definition, criminologist Dr. Brent E. Turvey defines victimology in his own textbook, *Forensic Victimology*, in this way: "The study of victims in the broadest sense, including those that have been harmed by accidents, natural disasters, war, and so on." (Turvey, 2014)

One of the first popular books to use the term *victimology* and to draw attention beyond *The Criminal and His Victim*, the scholarly book by Professor Hans von Hentig that had been published the previous year, was *The Show of Violence* by psychiatrist Dr. Fredric Wertham.

Best known for his later 1954 controversial crusade against comics, *Seduction of the Innocent*, (Wertham, 1954), Wertham wrote: "The murder victim is the forgotten man. When we have sensational discussions on the abnormal psychology of the murderer, we have failed to emphasize the unprotectedness of the victim and the complacency of the authorities. One cannot understand the psychology of the murderer if one does not understand the sociology of the victim. What we need is a science of victimology." (Wertham, 1949)

In the following sections, we will take a closer look at victims and victimology.

PRIMARY, SECONDARY, TERTIARY, AND QUATERNARY VICTIMS

There are two basic overall categories of victims that you will be studying in your Victimology class: **primary (direct) victims**, those who directly experience a crime or traumatic event, and **secondary (indirect) victims** or **co-victims**, those who are the family, friends, or even the co-workers of the victims. They suffer too, but in quite a different way. Diana Rodriguez-Martin, the primary victim of homicide featured as an example at the beginning of this chapter, was the first cousin of Valerie Reyes-Jimenez, who is a secondary victim of homicide. Because Diana's estranged husband said he dismembered her and disposed of her body parts in garbage bags in dumpsters, Valerie has shared that she thinks of her cousin whenever she passes by those receptacles. Valerie has said in guest presentations in Victimology class, as well as in newspaper interviews, "I can't even cut up a whole chicken without thinking of Diana and hearing the bones crunch." (Carrega, 2018; Reyes-Jimenez, 2017; 2018). Valerie is also a primary victim because she revealed that she was the victim of domestic abuse but, fortunately, her marriage ended before it had a fatal tragic outcome like her cousin's.

There are **tertiary victims** as well, especially in circumstances related to homicide, sexual violence including rape or sexual assault, and child abuse. What is a tertiary victim? A tertiary victim refers to those who work with crime victims on a daily or regular basis including police officers, crime victim advocates, healthcare providers, and therapists. Researchers, social workers, and help providers have applied other terms derived from the symptoms exhibited by the same group including **vicarious traumatic stress** (McCann and Pearlman, 1990), secondary traumatic stress (Figley, 1999; Bride, 2007) and even **compassion fatigue** (Mottaghi et al., 2020). This author prefers the term *tertiary victims* since that is consistent with the terms *primary victims* and *secondary victims*.

For those who deal with victims on a continual basis, hearing about their victimizations can have psychological consequences. Those who provide services to victims of trauma have to be careful that their own mental health needs are addressed since they are spending more time than the average person investigating crime especially violent criminality or working with victims. Those who deal with victims of child abuse and homicide are especially vulnerable to being a tertiary victim. Anyone who has to make a death notification has to be concerned about being a tertiary victim as well. A Nevada police officer, a veteran of 22 years on the force, shared in an interview that doing a death notification was for him the hardest thing he ever had to do on the job. (Interview with the author, January 12, 2021)

This author also realized that there is a fourth level of victimization, although it may not be as severe and certainly it is not as well-known a form of victimization as the first three. To be consistent with the three other general categories of victims, those are the individuals this author refers to as **quaternary victims**. That is because quaternary is what goes in the sequence following primary, secondary, and tertiary. So who are the quaternary victims? These are the family members, friends, and even classmates or co-workers who may hear about what the tertiary victims are experiencing. In trying to avoid keeping all those images and real-life stories to themselves, some tertiary victim may share with their loved ones, being mindful of confidentiality and anonymity issues, of course, unwittingly creating quaternary victims.

Former FBI agent Jeffrey L. Rinek, who specialized in searching for missing children for 30 years, writes about this in his book, *In the Name of the Children*, co-authored with Marilee Strong. Rinek also shared about this phenomenon in a phone interview with the author (Rinek and Strong, 2018; Rinek, 2021) as have others that the author has interviewed. A reader of this chapter shared the following insight about quaternary victims: "Great point. In a way we may all be quaternary victims just from what the news media covers and what is shown relentlessly on the evening news (e.g., "the following is hard to watch . . .") (Communication with the author, May 6, 2021)

It is also important to keep an open mind about who is the victim when examining the facts in each crime as well as how each victim is treated. For example, Boston Marathon bombing victim Lynn Julian Crisci shared that she has felt that those who had visible injuries, such as the loss of a limb, were treated differently by the medical work force as well as by the media compared to those who had 'invisible injuries." (Crisci, 2021) Lynn refers to her injuries as invisible because they are internal. So, no one is able to see the brain injuries and other harms related to the blast force trauma that she suffered because of the Boston Marathon bombing including her **post-traumatic stress disorder (PTSD)**, hearing loss, or the chronic back pain that she still endures. (Crisci, 2020)

In a 14-minute video, "This is My Story," posted by Algonquin College in Ottawa, Canada, Jen shares about the way her life changed forever when she was told that her sister had been murdered. This author usually has students watch this video on the first or second day of Victimology class. In the words of Jen, a secondary victim of her sister's homicide, the video, posted at YouTube (the link is in the Resources at the end of this chapter), dramatically shows how she and her family were impacted by her sister's murder. It even affected her sister's funeral since the police told the family they had to videotape it because a suspect had not yet been arrested. They were told to look for any questionable or unfamiliar attendees at the funeral. It turned out that her sister's killer was someone known to her. Jen continues, sharing how the family finally dealt with her sister's death when, ten years later, when her killer was up for parole, they had to bring everything up again if they wanted to make a victim impact statement at the parole hearing. The video concludes with Jen recounting about how much the victim advocate she worked with helped her and her family to deal with her sister's murder. That was why Jen decided to study victimology and why she wanted to help other victims. (Jen, Algonquin College, Victimology Interview, 2016)

CATEGORIES OF CRIMES AND VICTIMS

Chapter 4, "Measuring Victimization: Why and How," goes into the topic of crime and crime victim categories in greater detail. For now, let us just define the eight major crimes that used to be the Part I offenses in the old **Uniform Crime Reporting (UCR) Program,** which was used by local law enforcement for tracking crime and providing those totals to the FBI since 1930. A new reporting system, known as the **National Incident-Based Reporting System (NIBRS)**, with a much-expanded list of 49 crimes to be tracked, was phased in over the last decade or two. Beginning January 1, 2021, it officially replaced the UCR. (FBI, "A Guide to Understanding NIBRS," 2019)

Violent and Property Crimes

The most common crimes to consider are the so-called **conventional crimes**—violent and property crimes. Over the years, these crimes have also been referred to as **street crimes**, because so many of these crimes, like robbery and, to a lesser degree, murder, take place in the street. It has been suggested that the term *street crime* be retired since so many of these so-called conventional crimes actually occur at home or in offices, not in the street.

Violent and property crimes make up the eight major crimes that, as mentioned above, the UCR had always grouped into the category of Part 1 offenses also referred to as the **Crime Index**. You will find a more detailed discussion of the NIBRS, including all the offenses it covers and the official definition for each one, in Chapter 4, "Measuring Victimization: Why and How." Here are the eight major crimes that were part of the old Part I offenses section of the UCR (and that are part of the 49 crimes now tracked by the newer NIBRS):

1. Murder and nonnegligent manslaughter;
2. Rape;
3. Aggravated assault (Assault offenses);
4. Robbery;
5. Burglary (Breaking and Entering);
6. Larceny/theft offenses;
7. Motor vehicle theft; and
8. Arson

Definitions of these eight major conventional violent and property crimes are included in Box 1.1. These definitions are the ones provided by the NIBRS.

White-Collar Crimes (Economic or Financial Crimes as well as Cybercrime)

Another category of crime victim involves those of the so-called **white-collar crimes**, such as **fraud**, **bribery**, **money laundering**, **embezzlement**, **blackmail**, and **forgery**. Criminologist Edwin H. Sutherland coined the phrase *white-collar criminality* back in 1939 in a speech he delivered at an association meeting, followed by the 1940 article he wrote on the topic entitled, "White-Collar Criminality," published in the *American Sociological Review*. These crimes are included in the Group A Offenses of the NIBRS list of offenses and discussed in

Box 1.1. Definitions of Eight Major Violent and Property Crimes (Previously Known as the Part I UCR Offenses)

Crimes Against Person

1. Murder and Nonnegligent Manslaughter—"The willful (nonnegligent) killing of one human being by another."

Homicide—"The killing of one human being by another."

2. Rape

Sex Offenses, Forcible—"Any sexual act directed against another person, without the consent of the victim including instances where the victim is incapable of giving consent."

Forcible Rape—(Except Statutory Rape) "The carnal knowledge of a person, forcibly and/or against that person's will or not forcibly or against the person's will in instances where the victim is incapable of giving consent because of his/her temporary or permanent mental or physical incapacity."

3. Assault Offenses—"An unlawful attack by one person upon another."

Aggravated Assault—"An unlawful attack by one person upon another wherein the offender uses a weapon or displays it in a threatening manner, or the victim suffers obvious severe or aggravated bodily injury involving apparent broken bones, loss of teeth, possible internal injury, severe laceration, or loss of consciousness. This also includes assault with disease (as in cases when the offender is aware that he/she is infected with a deadly disease and deliberately attempts to inflict the disease by biting, spitting, etc.)."

Simple Assault—"An unlawful physical attack by one person upon another where neither the offender displays a weapon, nor the victim suffers obvious severe or aggravated bodily injury involving apparent broken bones, loss of teeth, possible internal injury, severe laceration, or loss of consciousness."

Crimes Against Property

4. *Robbery—"The taking, or attempting to take, anything of value under confrontational circumstances from the control, custody, or care of another person by force or threat of force or violence and/or by putting the victim in fear of immediate harm."

5. Burglary/Breaking and Entering—"The unlawful entry into a building or other structure with the intent to commit a felony or a theft."

6. Larceny/Theft Offenses—"The unlawful taking, carrying, leading, or riding away of property from the possession, or constructive possession, of another person."

7. Motor Vehicle Theft—"The theft of a motor vehicle."

8. Arson—"To unlawfully and intentionally damage, or attempt to damage, any real or personal property by fire or incendiary device."

Source: NIBRS (National Incident-Based Reporting System) Offense Definitions, 2012

*This author considers categorizing Robbery, since it involves face to face confrontation with a robber, as one of the Crimes against Property instead of Crimes Against Person as a controversial labeling by the NIBRS.

more detail in Chapter 4, "Measuring Victimization: Why and How," as well as Chapter 9, "Cybercrime, White-Collar Crime, and Economic Crime Victims."

As you probably know, the United States could be said to have 51 sets of laws—the laws that each state sets for its citizens and the laws set by the federal government. In most cases, white-collar crimes fall under the jurisdiction of the federal government. For example, in 2019, the charges behind what came to be known as the College Admission Scandal included bribery, money laundering, and document fabrication. Bribery and money laundering are listed as crimes against property in the NIBRS Group A offenses. More than 50 offenders were charged in that college admission scandal including such high-profile individuals as actresses Felicity Huffman and Lori Loughlin. (Taylor, 2019) Both served time in jail in their plea-bargained sentences for their role in the crimes.

Although the crimes of bribery and money laundering are listed in the NIBRS, which is tracked by local law enforcement, both Lori Loughlin and Felicity Huffman were sentenced according to federal guidelines. (Taylor, December 28, 2020) They both served their jail time at FCI Dublin, a low-security federal prison with the capacity for 761 female inmates. (Federal Bureau of Prisons, n.d.)*

Other white-collar crimes include theft of intellectual property, corporate financial fraud, and healthcare fraud. **Cybercrimes** include identity theft, credit card fraud, ransomware, phishing, hacking, and internet employment scams. You will learn more about these crime victims in Chapter 9, "Cybercrime, White-Collar Crime, and Economic Crime Victims."

Victimless Crimes

There is a third category of crime victims; the so-called **victimless crimes**, as sociologist and lawyer Edwin M. Schur put it in his classic book on this topic, *Crimes Without Victims*. (Schur, 1965). Some of the victimless crimes, like prostitution, will be mentioned at the appropriate point in this textbook, such as in the discussion of human trafficking in Chapter 15, "Additional Victim Situations or Populations," as well as in Chapter 7, "Primary and Secondary Victims of Homicide." The Netflix movie *Lost Girls* drew attention to the murder of Shannan Gilbert and as many as nine other victims, many of whom were believed to be **sex workers** (the newer, preferred term for **prostitution**). Those unsolved murders dating back to 2010, with bodies discovered in 2011, came to be known as the victims of the Long Island Serial Killer, also known as the Gilgo Beach Killer. (Vincenty, 2020)

Considering prostitution a crime is controversial, particularly when applied to underage **runaways**, usually teenagers, who have run away from home often because of some kind of abuse they were experiencing at home, either physical, sexual, or both. Complicating the labeling of some acts, like prostitution, as a victimless crime are state-by-state or even in-state differences in how the crime is treated. For example, whether or not arrests are made for prostitution in the state of Nevada, where it is legalized in several rural counties but not in Las Vegas, Reno, or Lake Tahoe. (Macionis, 2020) There are also some countries, including Germany, Switzerland, Greece, and Australia, where prostitution is legal and regulated. (Business Insider, 2019)

* n.d. means "no date" was available for a source.

It should be noted that there are some who do not believe there is such a thing as a victimless crime. Intellectual property theft, also known as piracy, is an example of that. Although some mistakenly refer to it as a victimless crime, there are victims. The creator of the product is a victim because he/she is cut out of any profits for the product that is illegally being pirated. The company that developed and is marketing the project is a victim because all the money they put into creating the product is not being recouped through sales especially if a competing company has stolen their intellectual property and produced a duplicate product probably at a lower cost. The NIBRS may be trying to reinforce the concept that there are crimes that may not have a direct victim but are still crimes in the creation of a third crime category namely Crimes Against Society. (As you may recall, the other two categories are Crimes Against Person and Crimes Against Property.) That category includes many of the crimes that previously were consisted victimless, like prostitution.

Bystanders

Another category of individuals related to crime victimization that you need to be aware of is the **bystander**. A bystander is someone who sees or hears a crime as it is taking place. There are bystanders at all kinds of crimes, from murder to aggravated assault, from rape and sexual assault cases, to sexual harassment. Some bystanders choose to intervene; others do not.

Should a bystander intervene or not? Is it legal or required to intervene? Researchers have discovered that someone is more likely to intervene if alone. The more people that are bystanders, the less likely someone is to get involved because of the phenomenon known as the **bystander effect**, whereby people who witness a crime assume that someone else will step up so they do not. (Dwyer Gunn, "Won't They Help?", 2014; Gidycz, et al., 2011; Levine, et al., 2001; Darley and Latane, 1968; Katz, 2018)

A contradiction to that notion is what happened in the case of Chanel Miller. Back in January 2015, Chanel, who was 22 at the time, attended a party in Palo Alto, California. Upon leaving the party, she was sexually assaulted by 19-year-old Brock Turner, a student athlete at the university. Two bystanders intervened and stopped him, holding him down until police arrived. Turner was found guilty and sentenced to six months in prison plus three years' probation. Originally referred to as "Emily Doe," to protect her identity, Chanel decided to follow up on the powerful Victim Impact Statement she read in court that went viral on the internet with her bestselling memoir, *Know My Name*. (Miller, 2020)

Cover of audiobook version of *Know My Name*, Chanel Miller's memoir.

Even if the bystander was not the actual crime victim, being present or within earshot of a crime as it is unfolding can be traumatizing. But is it illegal to fail to intervene? In the United States and most other countries, it is not. Most Americans are familiar with the widely publicized case of Kitty Genovese whose murder was allegedly ignored in 1964 as 38 neighbors were supposedly bystanders to the crime from their Queens, New York apartments but failed to intervene. Over the years, there have been disagreements over whether or not bystanders failed to intervene. The 2016 documentary, directed by James Solomon, by Bill Genovese, Kitty Genovese's younger brother who was 16 when she was murdered, explores what really happened. (Genovese, 2016)

The two men who intervened and saved Chanel Miller would probably be considered witnesses rather than bystanders. Bystanders are those who just happen to be present when a crime occurs but they may not hear or see anything.

"Bystander training" is an emerging movement on college campuses. With estimates that 20 to 25 percent of female college students are affected by interpersonal violence, which includes sexual assault, stalking, dating violence, and intimate partner violence, bystander intervention training programs for college students, such as One Act, developed in 2010, have shown positive outcomes in terms of date rape attitudes and behaviors, bystander's confidence, and willingness to help to those who have participated in a two-year study. (Alegria-Flores, et al., 2017) Writing in the *New York Times*, Claire Cain Miller discusses some of the key approaches that bystanders could take if they observe behavior that could be labeled sexual harassment. (Miller, 2017)

Witnesses

By contrast, a **witness** is someone who has actually seen some or all of the crime occurring. The witness may also be someone who just happened to be there, similar to a bystander. But a witness has seen enough to be able to give testimony or even to possibly identify the suspects.

The witness may also be the actual crime victim. One or more witnesses may play a key role in any crime victimization, especially if there is a suspect. When there are many witnesses, the police or attorneys may look for consistencies or inconsistencies in their accounts. Just how vital the testimony of a witness can be to a case is emphasized by the following example from a rape case shared with this author by the victim who was also the only witness. As Beverly N. explained, "I was sexually assaulted eight years ago. It was someone that I knew that I had previously dated. He kept on calling and texting and I finally agreed to meet him. It was at that point that he assaulted me."

Beverly called her friend after the rape happened and her friend called the police. She went to the hospital, had an examination, and a rape kit was done.

It turned out that her rapist had not disconnected his call to her, so the entire rape was recorded on Beverly's phone. You could hear her yelling "Stop" and "What are you doing?"

Initially, Beverly cooperated with the assistant district attorney but then she decided to withdraw her complaint. Without her testimony, the case did not go forward. Soon afterwards, Beverly changed her phone number, moved, and never saw her rapist again. There was so much evidence in her case she had been told that a plea-bargained guilty plea or even winning at trial was pretty much a sure thing if she had not withdrawn her support of the case.

Why did she change her mind about pursuing a case against her rapist?

"I'm Latino," Beverly shared. "My brother and my father have both been in prison for various reasons. So, I did not want to be responsible for taking away someone's freedom where they end up going to prison. I felt so bad about being that person who had some of that control. I decided I didn't want to do that." (Yager, 2020; Yager, 2021)

WHAT VICTIMOLOGISTS MIGHT STUDY

Before we move on to why studying victimology is important, let us look at some hypotheticals of what victimologists might study:

- Remember Beverly, described above, who decided to withdraw her testimony which stopped her rape case from going forward? A victimologist might study. What are the consequences of their actions to the victim, to the perpetrator, or to the community?
- A study of the siblings of primary crime victims what are their immediate and long-term reactions to their sibling's victimization?
- Why do some people evacuate when there is a natural disaster and others refuse to leave, with near fatal or deadly consequences?
- For family members who have lost a loved one to homicide, who seeks out crime victim compensation and who does not? What are their reasons?
- Victims who fight back. Is fighting back linked to a higher or lower chance of injury or death in crimes of rape, robbery, or homicide?
- What is the percentage of incarcerated women, and men, who were victims of incest? What crime are they incarcerated for?
- Who reports being victimized to the police and why?
- What percentage of crime victims were intoxicated or high on drugs at the time of their aggravated assault? What percentage of their perpetrators?
- Is victim-precipitated homicide a valid concept to apply to homicide or is it a version of victim blame?
- What are the hot spots for increased crime in a community or city?

TABLE 1.2. A Comparison of What Victimologists and Criminologists Might Study

Victimologists	Criminologists
Who are the victims of crime?	Who are the criminals?
Theories of victimization: What causes someone to become a crime victim?	Theories of criminality: What causes someone to become a criminal?
Treatment of victims who report crime by the crime justice system: police, courts, and penal system.	Treatment of those suspected of a crime who are arrested and found innocent and freed or found guilty and punished.
The short-term effects of victimization.	The short-term effects of being arrested and found guilty.
How the media depicts and treats the victim.	How the media depicts the criminal.
Victimization trends—locally and internationally.	Criminal trends—locally and internationally.
The reasons behind repeat or recurring victimization.	What causes **recidivism** (when an offender is rearrested and/or sent back to jail or prison)?

TABLE 1.2. Continued

Victimologists	Criminologists
Who becomes a victim on the basis of gender, race, ethnicity, age, educational level, immigration status, occupation, marital status, and socioeconomic status?	Who becomes a criminal on the basis of gender, race, ethnicity, age, educational level, occupation, parents' occupation, marital status, and socioeconomic status?
How effective are victim services in helping victims?	How successful is probation in preventing future criminality?
What type of therapy is best for victims of violent or property crime?	How and why is cognitive behavior therapy the most effective current treatment to change criminal behavior?
How and when should victims be involved in the punishment of the perpetrator?	When and why should parole be granted?
Who are the victims of homicide?	What motivates someone to kill someone?
How can someone avoid becoming a victim of cybercrime and, if they are victimized, what should they do about it?	What drives someone to hack a computer?
Who are the secondary victims of crime?	How does being accused or found guilty of a crime impact on the criminal's family and close friends?
What are the short- and long-term effects of terrorism on the primary, secondary, and tertiary victims?	Who are domestic or international terrorists?
How do victims whose family member has been killed feel about capital punishment?	What is the relationship between capital punishment and crime rates?
Has broader focus than just crime against humans addressing animal cruelty as well as broader victimizations such as natural disasters and war.	Focused mainly on conventional violent, property, or white-collar crimes.

TEN REASONS TO STUDY VICTIMOLOGY

1. In gathering valuable information about crime victims, the criminal justice system is better equipped to deal with crime and punish its perpetrator.
2. Studying victimology offers the opportunity to focus on the other key element in every crime, the victim.
3. Victimology helps those who will be dealing with crime victims including police officers, lawyers, social workers, psychologists, and anyone else associated with the criminal justice system or counseling, to do their jobs.
4. Studying victimology helps anyone who is going to be working with crime victims, or even offenders, to look beyond the stereotype of the "good" victim or the "bad" offender." Instead, victimology advocates probe what really happened in every criminal situation.
5. Without blaming the victim, victimology can teach us about who is more likely to become a victim or what behaviors are more apt to help a victim survive in any criminal situation.
6. Since much of the criminal justice system is focused on criminals their rights, and punishment, victimology addresses how victims are treated by the criminal justice system.

7. Because of victimology and the efforts of its researchers and teachers, categories of victims that cannot even be handled by laws have been addressed. For example, some victims of domestic violence suffer emotional abuse, not physical or sexual abuse, but there is no crime that those abusers have technically violated. Those victims next help extricating themselves from the abusive situation, before it does become violent and a crime.
8. Victimologists look at how the intellectually and mentally disabled are at greater risk of being victims than the general population as well as the lack of training by most law enforcement programs and agencies into how to better handle taking the mentally ill into custody. (Cochran, 2000; Steadman and Morrissette, 2016; Kennedy, 2010)
9. Victimologists may do their own data collection and analysis, and in that way they contribute their findings to our overall knowledge about crime, its victims, its offenders, its reduction, and its prevention.
10. Because victimology grew out of a multidisciplined approach, drawing on diverse social sciences and medical fields it offers an exceptional understanding of crime and the criminal justice system from the victims' point of view.

SOME QUESTIONS TO CONSIDER

When you finish reading and studying *Essentials of Victimology*, you should be able to answer these questions about each of the major types of victimization:

- In terms of such demographic factors as age, gender, race, ethnicity, location (rural, suburban, urban), and socioeconomic factors, who are the most likely victims of each major violent or property crime?
- What percentage of each crime is estimated to be reported to the police?
- What is the clearance rate for that crime?
- What is the likelihood, even if a victim reports the crime, that the case will go to trial rather than being resolved through plea bargaining?
- Is there a stigma to being a crime victim?
- Should victims be called survivors instead of victims?

Profile ▪ **Bill W., Survivor of Child Sexual Abuse**

Here are excerpts from the self-report shared by 31-year-old Bill W. You will find the complete self-report posted at the publisher's website, www.AspenPublishing.com, in the student portion of the site.

In 2000, when I was 10 years old, I fell victim to sexual abuse. I remember it like it was yesterday, and I think about it often. As a kid I went camping with my aunt and uncle all the time. . . . The one thing I remember most about this day was that when everything ended, my parents were getting ready to head back home to . . . , and I was asked if I wanted to stay . . . I opted to stay, but given what happened, I wish more than anything I hadn't.

My parents left . . . That night while I was sleeping, I woke up to my uncle touching my private parts. I didn't cry, make any noise, or move at all. It's like I was frozen. I was so afraid to move or tell him to stop, that I just pretended I was still sleeping, and waited for it to end. . . .

For the next few days I would go into my room alone and cried thinking about what had just happened to me. I knew it was wrong, and I struggled to come to terms with it. I was devastated. It felt like someone ripped away my sanity for a while, as the thought of it consumed me every single day for months. I didn't know what to do. I went back and forth in my mind if I should tell my brothers. . . . my parents. Should I call the cops and report what had happened? I decided not to do any of those things. Instead, I kept it to myself. I figured I would just try to bury it in the back of my mind and never tell anyone about it. . . .

Experiencing something like this at just 10 years old has impacted my life tremendously. . . . As the years passed, I turned my sadness into anger. Growing up I fought a lot in school and took my anger out on people who never deserved it. In middle school I was banned from riding the bus for fighting . . .

When I was a senior in high school, I actually mustered up the courage to confront my uncle about what happened as a 19 year old, nine years later . . . We both cried a lot, and he apologized to me. And he told me that he was sexually assaulted by one of his older brothers when he was a kid. We talked a little while longer, and I told him I forgave him.

Confronting him, and having that talk with him . . . felt like a weight had been lifted off of my shoulders, and for the first time since I was ten, I felt a sense of relief. . . . [But} I still struggle with some anger issues. . . .

One of the best decisions I have ever made in my life was to talk to a mental health professional. Although I have not told my provider about what happened, we do talk about my anxiety and anger and PTSD (post-traumatic stress disorder), which has helped tremendously. Although I have not yet told my provider about this [the sexual abuse], I will in time when I am ready.

SUMMARY

In this first chapter, we have explored a definition of victimology, when this new discipline is said to have been started, and even why it emerged at that time, why it is important to study victimology, and who are the main categories of victims that victimologists study.

Victimology is the interdisciplinary scientific study of victims. It is an outgrowth of both sociology and criminology with contributions from anthropology, economics, social work, police science, psychology, psychiatry, and statistics. There is a discussion of the two different approaches to victimology: one sees it as a subdiscipline within criminology and the other sees it as a completely separate discipline, studying all victims, not just criminal ones, and parallel to criminology.

You learned that Beniamin Mendelsohn, the Romanian lawyer mentioned above, is considered the "father of victimology" because he first published about the victim-offender relationship in a 1937 journal article and then he coined the term in 1947; he also wrote extensively about crime victims beginning with his initial study of rape victims based on his 300 questionnaire survey to his clients. Other pioneers include Hans von Hentig, whom some considered a co-founder of the discipline, whose 1940 scholarly article, "Remarks on the Interaction of Perpetrators and Victims," and his related follow-up book, *The Criminal and His Victim*, published by Yale University Press in 1948, reinforced the path that Mendelsohn had initiated.

This chapter covered the four categories of victims: primary, those who are the actual crime victim; secondary, those who are related to the crime victim, or close friends or concerned employers or community members, especially important in the crime of murder; tertiary victims, those who are helping crime victims who may suffer from stress related to that role such as police officers, emergency room personnel like nurses and physicians, crime victim advocates, lawyers, or prosecutors; and, finally, quaternary victims, those who live with, are close to, or even work with the tertiary victims who find hearing about the victimizations that their loved ones or colleagues are dealing with can cause stress.

In discussing who are the victims of crime that victimologists study, you learned about the major official crime statistic reporting system that the local police offices use, sharing that information with the FBI (Federal Bureau of Investigation). The FBI uses that data to issue its annual report of crime in the United States.

On January 1, 2021, the National Incident-Based Reporting System (NIBRS), which had been gradually introduced over more than a decade, replaced the Uniform Crime Reporting (UCR) system, a paper system that was established almost 100 years before (in 1930). For the purposes of this introductory chapter, the original Part I eight major violent and property crime offenses from the old UCR were listed and defined, including: murder or nonnegligent manslaughter; rape; aggravated assault; robbery; burglary; larceny/theft; motor vehicle theft; and arson. Each of those crimes was briefly defined using the NIBRS official definition.

That discussion was followed by an overview about white-collar crimes, including its original definition by criminologist Edwin Sutherland back in 1940, as well as a discussion of victimless crimes, especially prostitution, or the newer preferred term, sex workers, and, finally, a definition and brief discussion of bystanders and witnesses.

There was a comparison in Table 1.2 of what victimologists might study compared to criminologists. It was followed by a listing of 10 reasons to study victimology.

The chapter ends with a brief Profile, excerpted from Bill, a 31-year-old man's self-report about his sexual assault by his uncle when Bill was ten.

KEY TERMS

aggravated assault
arson
assault
breaking and entering
burglary
bystander
bystander effect
compassion fatigue
conventional crimes
co-victims
Crime Index
cybercrimes
direct victims
embezzlement
forcible rape
forgery
fraud
homicide
incest
indirect victims
larceny/theft
money laundering
motor vehicle theft
murder
NIBRS (National Incident-Based Reporting System)
nonnegligent homicide
penal couple
plea bargain
primary victims
prostitution
PTSD (post-traumatic stress disorder)
quaternary victims
rape
recidivism
robbery
runaways
secondary traumatic stress
secondary victims
sexual molestation
social sciences
street crimes
sex worker
tertiary victims
UCR (Uniform Crime Reporting)
vicarious traumatic stress
victim
victimless crimes
victimology
white-collar crimes
witness

REVIEW QUESTIONS

1. How do you define *victimology*?
2. When was victimology founded and by whom?
3. In 2019, how many victims of murder were reported and tabulated by the FBI in the United States?
4. What is a primary victim?
5. What is a secondary victim?
6. Who are some of the service providers who might be considered tertiary victims?
7. Who might be put in the category of a quaternary victim and why?
8. What is a brief definition of homicide according to the NIBRS?
9. What is the meaning of murder and nonnegligent manslaughter according to the NIBRS?
10. What is a description of forcible rape according to the NIBRS?
11. What is the NIBRS definition of aggravated assault?
12. What is the NIBRS classification of robbery?
13. What is the NIBRS definition of burglary, also called "breaking and entertaining?"
14. How does the NIBRS define motor vehicle theft?
15. What year was the term "white-collar criminality" coined and by whom?

CRITICAL THINKING QUESTIONS

1. Do you think victimology should be its own discipline or part of criminology? Support your point of view.

2. After considering the ten reasons for studying victimology noted in this chapter, what is *your* number reason for studying victimology? If your reason is missing from that list, please add it and explore your reasoning.

3. Of all the types of crime victims that could be examined, or the issues that crime victims face, which ones do you think deserve the most attention today, and why? Is it more important to consider how much crime there is in the United States, or other countries, in general, across all populations withing that country, or to break it down by gender, race, ethnicity, age, or other factors such as location, and whether or not someone has a disability?

4. The author suggests that the reason victimology began as a separate discipline at the end of the 1930s and throughout the 1940s might be related to what was happening in the world at that time, especially the rise of Nazism in Germany and World War II. Do you agree with that point of view? Why? Why not? If you disagree, what is your alternative explanation for why victimology arose at that time, compared to the reasons that are usually given for why sociology and criminology arose in the 1800s?

ACTIVITIES

1. What do you want to learn about crime victims and victimology? Write down your goals for this course so you can check back when you finish reading *Essentials of Victimology* to confirm that you have learned what you set out to explore. Look over the goals that you wrote down. Order or reorder those goals by importance.

2. Take one of the true-life cases that you learned about in this chapter and do a search on the internet through Google or another search engine. If you find an article or two about the case, read it and see what additional information you learn about the victim, the offender, and any secondary victims of the case. What have you learned about the case that sheds even more light on what happened to the victim and the aftermath of the crime, if anything? For example, did you discover that a Facebook page has been set up in the victim's memory or that there is now a scholarship in that victim's name through his or her alma mater? Has the offender been released from jail or prison? Are there any follow-up articles about the victim or about the victim's family?

3. In groups of four, do a Google search to find a crime that is not included in this chapter and discuss some of the issues you might want to consider about the victims of that crime. For example, if the crime is a burglary of a residence, what are some questions you would ask the apartment dwellers or homeowners about whether or not the crime was reported? If it was a homicide, do you want to find out whether the case was ever solved and, if it was, what punishment the perpetrator received? Do you want to read interviews with the family and friends of the victim if none are readily available? Is there any information in the article and case you are reading about as to how the victim was dealt with by the criminal justice system? If so, was it reported as a positive or negative experience? (This exercise can be done in-person or via online videoconferencing if the program that is being used has a breakout room function whereby the class can be divided electronically automatically into groups.)

   The recommended amount of time for this group exercise, whether done online only or in person, is 10-15 minutes. That permits enough time to search for a new article and case and to discuss it as a group. Each group should pick someone to take notes for your team (room) and someone to be the spokesperson, although the same person could perform both functions. You might also want all four to contribute feedback when the exercise is over. All teams (rooms) should come back together to discuss the results of the exercise.

4. Consider what happened to Alvin and Bernadette Fazande, who are two of the estimated 1,000+ victims who died during Hurricane Katrina in New Orleans in 2005. Do research into Hurricane Katrina and see what factors might have exacerbated this natural disaster, including the local, state, and federal responses to it, that might justify victimologists studying this event and its victims. (Associated Press, 10/25/2005; Lindsey Cook and Ethan Rosenberg, *U.S. News & World Report*, 8/28/2015)

RESOURCES

Academy of Criminal Justice Sciences (ACJS)
acjs.org
Founded in 1963, there is a victimology section to this international professional membership organization that is dedicated to education and scholarly research related to the criminal justice system.

American Society of Criminology (ASC)
Division of Victimology
asc41.com/divisions/dov/
Dating back to the 1940s, this international professional membership organization of criminologists and practitioners in the criminal justice field are dedicated to research, networking, and sharing knowledge. There is a division focused on victimology. As of 2021, the official journal of the DOV is *Victims and Offenders*.

Federal Bureau of Investigation (FBI)
fbi.gov
Founded in 1908, the FBI is the principal law enforcement agency of the United States. From the usa.gov website: "The Federal Bureau of Investigation (FBI) enforces federal law, and investigates a variety of criminal activity including terrorism, cybercrime, white collar crimes, public corruption, civil rights violations, and other major crimes."

National Center for Victims of Crime
https://victimsofcrime.org
A nonprofit educational, information, and advocacy organization founded in 1985 by Ala Isham and Alexander Auersberg, motivated by victimization of their mother, Sunny von Bulow. Activities include the Center for Victim and Survivor Services (CVSS), National Crime Victim Bar Association, the National Training Institute, Center for Victim Service Professionals (CVSP), and other efforts.

National Organization of Victim Assistance (NOVA)
trynova.org
A nonprofit membership educational organization founded in 1976 that is has various trainings available for those who work with crime victims including Crisis Response Team (CRT) Training™. Holds an annual training event and conference in the summertime.

National Sexual Violence Resource Center (NSVRC)
nsvrc.org
Started in 2000, NSVRC is a leading nonprofit information source on materials related to sexual violence as well as bystander intervention. For bystander intervention material, check out the "Bystander Intervention Resources" at their site. It includes extensive annotated listings of websites as well as fact sheets, web pages, and webinars.

Susan Schechter Domestic and Sexual Violence Social Justice Laboratory (Schechter Lab) Prevention Innovations Research Center (PIRC)
unh.edu/research/prevention-innovations-research-center/about-us/susan-schechter-laboratory
This is a training institution for students, faculty, researchers, and those who work with crime victims to focus on prevention of domestic and sexual violence. The laboratory, based in Durham, New Hampshire, is named in honor of Susan Schechter, co-author of a groundbreaking study of alternative ways to intervene in domestic violence and maltreatment cases. (See listing below)

World Society of Victimology (WSV)
worldsocietyofvictimology.org
This international membership organization had its roots in the First International Symposium on Victimology that was organized by Israel Drapkin in Israel in 1973. Every three years, there is an

international conference in a different global location. Over the years, international conferences have been held in Tokyo, Montreal, Amsterdam, and Orlando, among other locations.

CITED WORKS AND ADDITIONAL REFERENCES

Adler, Freda, Gerhard O. W. Mueller, and William S. Laufer. 2007. *Criminology and the Criminal Justice System*. Sixth edition. New York: McGraw Hill.

Alegria-Flores, Kei, Kelli Raker, Robert K. Pleasants, Mark A. Weaver, and Morris Weinberger. 2017. "Preventing Interpersonal Violence on College Campuses: The Effect of One Act Training on Bystander Intervention." *Journal of Interpersonal Violence*. 32: 1103-1126.

American Sociological Association (ASA). 2008. "The Field of Sociology." Published online by the American Sociological Association. www.asanet.org

Arvay, Marla J. 2001. "Secondary Traumatic Stress Among Trauma Counsellors: What Does the Research Say?" *International Journal for the Advancement of Counseling*. 23: 283-293.

Associated Press. Updated October 25, 2005. "Portrait of Many of Katrina's Victims Emerges." Posted at nbcnews.com

Bain, Jessica. February 7, 2018. "Man Gets Prison for Beating Wife to Death, Chopping Up Her Body." *New York Post*. Posted at nypost.com

Barkas, J.L. (a/k/a Jan Yager). September 10, 1978. "Let's Give Crime Victims Their Due." *Newsday*.

____________. March 1977. "Victims of Crime and Social Change." Master's Thesis, Goddard College Graduate Program, Plainfield, VT.

Barkas, Janet (a/k/a Jan Yager). July 1972. "Frau Wagner." *Opera News*. 37: 20-21.

BBC News. September 24, 2020. "Male Domestic Abuse Victims 'Sleeping in Cars and Tents.'" Posted at BBC.com.

Berenbaum, Michael. May 27, 2021. "Adolf Eichmann." Posted at Britannica.com.

Blume, Harvey. December 19, 2001. "The Other NYPD Murder." *The American Prospect*.

Briche-Saddler, Michael. May 22, 2020. "Man Who Filmed Ahmaud Arbery's Death Arrested for Murder Charges, Georgia Authorities Say." Posted at the Washingtonpost.com site.

Bride, Brian E. 2007. "Prevalence of Secondary Traumatic Stress Among Social Workers." *Social Work*. 52: 63-70.

Bureau of Justice Statistics, National Crime Victimization Survey, 2019. See Morgan, Rachel E.

Burgess, Anne W. 2019. *Victimology*. Third edition. Burlington, MA: Jones & Bartlett Learning.

Business Insider. March 13, 2019. "Prostitution Is Legal in Countries Across Europe, But It's Nothing Like What You Think." Posted at www.businessinsider.com

Carrega, Christina. December 20, 2017. "Family of Brooklyn Woman Killed, Dismembered by Husband Not Satisfied with Guilty Plea." *New York Daily News*, posted at nydailynews.com

Cochran, Sam. October 2000. "Improving Police Response to Mentally Ill People." *Psychiatric Services*. 51: 1315.

Cook, Lindsey and Ethan Rosenberg. August 28, 2015. "No One Knows How Many People Died in Katrina." *U.S. News & World Report*. Posted at USNews.come.

Crecente, Drew, J.D. Wednesday, December 9, 2020. Guest presentation via Zoom, "Victimology," John Jay College of Criminal Justice.

____________. Tuesday, February 23, 2021. Guest presentation via Zoom. "Social Deviance." Kean University.

____________. Monday, December 28, 2020. Phone interview with author.

Crisci, Lynn. February 28, 2021. E-mail to author.

____________. June 14, 2020. Phone interview with author.

Darley, John M. and Bibb Latane. 1968. "Bystander Intervention in Emergencies: Diffusion of Responsibility." *Journal of Personality and Social Psychology*. 8: 377-383.

Dictionary.com. "Victim." Posted at Dictionary.com.

Ellenberger, Henri. 1955. "Relations Psychologiques Entre Le Criminel et la Victime." *Revue International de Criminologie et de Police Technique*. 8: 757-790.

Farberov, Snejana. February 23, 2021. "Pennsylvania Mother is Found Caked in Dried Blood After 'Fatally Shooting her Daughter, 22, and Trans son, 16, in the Head and Face' as Teen Begged Her 'Please Don't Shoot.'" DailyMail.com (UK) Posted online.

Federal Bureau of Investigation (FBI). *2019 Crime in the United States.* Washington, D.C.: U.S. Department of Justice.

________________. 2012. NIBRS Offense Definitions. Posted at nibrs-offense-definitions (fbi.gov)

______________. July 2019. "A Guide to Understanding NIBRS." Six-page fact sheet. Posted at the FBI.gov website.

Figley, C.R. 1999. "Compassion Fatigue: Toward a New Understanding of the Costs of Caring." In B.H. Stamm (ed.), *Secondary Traumatic Stress: Self-Care Issues for Clinicians, Researchers & Educators.* (2d ed.). Lutherville, MD: Sidran Press, 3-28.

Finkelhor, David. 1980. "Sex Among Siblings: A Survey on Prevalence, Variety, and Effects." *Archives of Sexual Behavior.* 9: 171-194.

Fisher, Ronald P. and R. Edward Geiselman. 2010. "The Cognitive Interview Method of Conducting Police Interviews: Eliciting Extensive Information and Promotion Therapeutic Jurisprudence." *International Journal of Law and Psychiatry.* 33: 321-328.

Frangiapane, Paul. July 10, 2017. "Lawyer for Man Who Allegedly Dismembered Wife Says Death was 'Totally Accidental.'" *Brooklyn Daily Eagle.* Posted at brooklyneagle.com

____________. February 7, 2019. "Man Who Chopped Up Wife and Threw Her in Garbage Gets 10 Years for Manslaughter." *Brooklyn Daily Eagle.* Posted at brooklyneagle.com

Gibson, Stephen, Grace Blenkinsopp, Elizabeth Johnstone, and Aimee Marshall. 2017. "Just Following Orders? The Rhetorical Invocation of 'Obedience' in Stanley Milgram's Post-experiment Interviews." *European Journal of Social Psychology.* 48: 585-599.

Gidycz, Christina A., Lindsay M. Orchowski, and Alan D. Berkowitz. 2011. "Preventing Sexual Aggression Among College Men: An Evaluation of a Social Norms and Bystander Intervention Program." *Violence Against Women.* 17: 720-742.

Goldsmith, Maurice. 1973. "The Thalidomide Affair." *Science and Public Affairs, the Bulletin of the Atomic Scientists,* 40-41.

Goodman, J. David. April 29, 2015. "A Decades-Old Quarrel Is Said to Be at the Center of a Fatal Brooklyn Shooting." *New York Times.* A19.

Gunn, Dwyer. July 24, 2014. "Won't They Help?" Psyche magazine, part of Aeon.com.

Harding, Kate. February 27, 2020. "I've Been Told I'm a survivor, Not a Victim. But What's Wrong With Being a Victim?" *Time.* Posted at time.com.

Huebel, Sebastian. Winter 2018. "Disguise and Defiance: German Jewish Men and Their Underground Experiences in Nazi Germany, 1941-1945." *Shofar: An Interdisciplinary Journal of Jewish Studies.* 36: 110-141.

Jones, Stephen. 2017. *Criminology.* 6th edition. Oxford, UK: Oxford University Press.

_____________. Personal correspondence with author, May 17, 2020.

_____________. Personal correspondence with author, May 23, 2020.

Kalczewiak, Mariusz. January 2019. "We Hope to Find a Way Out from Our Unpleasant Situation: Police-Jewish Refugees and the Escape from Nazi Europe to Latin America." *American Jewish History.* 103: 25-49.

Karmen, Andrew. 2020. *Crime Victims: An Introduction to Victimology.* Tenth edition. New York: Cengage.

Katz, Jackson. 2018. "Bystander Training as Leadership Training: Notes on the Origins, Philosophy, and Pedagogy of the Mentors in Violence Prevention Model." *Violence Against Women.* 24: 1755-1776.

Kennedy, Brendan. September 1, 2010. "Dead Man's Family Called for Help; Pickering Man Killed by Police Was Paranoid, Mentally Ill, Family Says." *The Toronto Star.* Posted online.

Knight, Carolyn. 2004. "Working with Survivors of Childhood Trauma: Implications for Clinical Supervision." *The Clinical Supervisor.* 23: 81-105.

Kolker, Robert. 2013. *Lost Girls.* New York: Harper.

Levine, Robert V., Ara Norenzayan, and Karen Phlbrick. September 2001. *Journal of Cross-Cultural Psychology.* 32: 543-560.

Macionis, John J. 2020. *Social Problems.* Eighth edition. New York: Pearson.

Manning, Rachel. September 2007. "The Kitty Genovese Murder and the Social Psychology of Helping." *American Psychologist.* 555-562.

Martin, Erika. February 5, 2021. "LAPD: 4 Sought in Caught-on-Video Robbery of Man Shot, Pistol-Whipped While Shopping with Toddler in DTLA." Posted at KTLA.com.

McCann, I. Lisa and Laurie Anne Pearlman. 1990. "Vicarious Traumatization: A Framework for Understanding the Psychological Effects of Working with Victims." *Journal of Traumatic Stress*: 3, 131-149.

McInnes, Mitchell. August 31, 2015. "Opinion: Should the Law Require Bystanders to Help?" published online by the EdmontonJournal.com

Mendelsohn, Beniamin. August-October 1937. "Methods to Be Used by Counsel for the Defense in the Researches Made into the Personality of the Criminal." *Revue de Droit Penal et de Criminologie*. France.

___________. "The Origin of the Doctrine of Victimology." Chapter 1: 3-11, in Israel Drapkin and Emilio Viano (eds.). 1974. *Victimology*. Lexington, MA: Lexington Books.

___________. Personal correspondence with the author, November 24, 1978.

___________. Personal correspondence with the author, January 19, 1978.

___________. Personal correspondence with the author, March 26, 1981.

Merriam-Webster dictionary. Definition of *victim*. Online version. Posted at https://www.merriam -webster.com/dictionary/victim

___________. Definition of *victimology*. Online version. Posted at https://www.merriam-webster.com/ dictionary/victimology#h1

Milgram, Stanley. 1974. *Obedience to Authority*. New York: Harper & Row.

Miller, Chanel. 2020. *Know My Name: A Memoir*. New York: Penguin Books.

Miller, Claire Cain. December 12, 2017. "The #MeToo Moment: How to Be a (Good) Bystander." *The New York Times*. Posted online at nytimes.com.

Morgan, Rachel E. and Barbara A. Oudekerk. September 2019. *Crime Victimization 2018*. U.S. Department of Justice, Bureau of Justice Statistics. Washington, D.C.

Morgan, Rachel E. and Jennifer L. Truman. September 2020. *Crime Victimization 2019*. U.S. Department of Justice, Bureau of Justice Statistics. Washington, D.C.

Mottaghi, Shekoofeh, Hanieh Poursheikhali, and Leila Shameli. 2020. "Empathy, Compassion, Fatigue, Guilt and Secondary Traumatic Stress in Nurses." *Nursing Ethics*. 27: 494-504.

Morse, Dan. 2013. *The Yoga Store Murder: The Shocking True Account of the Lululemon Athletica Killing*. New York: Berkeley True Crime.

Mizne, David. November 13, 2018. "How to Create a Culture of Safety With Bystander Intervention Training." Article originally appeared on The Next Web. Reprinted at the www.15five.com site as a blog.

Muftic, Lisa R. and Donald E. Hunt. 2012. "Victim Precipitation: Further Understanding the Linkage Between Victimization and Offending in Homicide." *Homicide Studies*. 17: 239-254.

Murray, Jayna Troxel (1980-2011). 2011. Obituary with 41 pages of comments posted at www.legacy.com

Newman, Andy. August 31, 1999. "Disturbed Man Wielding a Hammer Killed by Police in Brooklyn." *New York Times* posted at nytimes.com.

Olds, Dorri. March 2, 2021. E-mail to author.

___________. January 13, 2012. "Defriending My Rapist." *The New York Times*. The Opinion Pages.

___________. April 15, 2020. Guest presentation. John Jay College of Criminal Justice, Victimology course.

O'Reilly, Luke. November 11, 2020. "Man, 28, Left With Broken Jaw and Bleed on Brain During Rolex Robbery in North London." *Evening Standard* (UK). Posted online.

Quinney, Richard. November 1972. "Who Is the Victim?" *Criminology* 10: 314-323.

RAINN (Rape, Abuse, & Incest National Network). "Statistics." Posted at rainn.org

Rawson, Kerri. April 29, 2020. Guest presentation via Zoom., John Jay College of Criminal Justice., April 29, 2020.

___________. April 17, 2020 and April 29, 2020. Phone interviews with the author.

___________. 2019. *A Serial Killer's Daughter*. Nashville, TN: Thomas Nelson.

Rinek, Jeffrey L. Thursday, February 25, 2021. Phone interview with the author.

Rinek, Jeffrey L and Marilee Strong. 2018. *In the Name of the Children: An FBI Agent's Relentless Pursuit of the Nation's Worst Predators*. Dallas, TX: BenBella Books.

Ryan, William. 1971. *Blaming the Victim*. New York: Pantheon Books.

Samenow, Stanton E. January 22, 1981. Personal correspondence with author.

Schafer, Stephen. 1968. *The Victim and His Criminal: A Study in Functional Responsibility*. New York: Random House.

Schecter, S. and J.L. Edelson. 1999. *Effective Intervention in Domestic Violence and Maltreatment Cases: Guidelines for Police and Practice.* Reno, NV: National Council of Juvenile and Family Court Judges.

Schwartzbach, Micah. 2021. "Can I Settle a Criminal Case with Money?" Posted at Nolo.com.

Schur, Edwin M. 1965. *Crimes Without Victims: Deviant Behavior and Public Policy: Abortion, Homosexuality, Drug Addiction.* Englewood Cliffs, NJ: Prentice-Hall, Inc.

Seattle Times. March 22, 2011. "Once a Star Athlete, Decatur Grad Now Accused of Murder." *The Seattle Times.* (By wire reports and *The News Tribune Tacoma*)

Shapland, Joanna and Matthew Hall. 2007. "What Do We Know about the Effects of Crime on Victims?" *International Review of Victimology.* 14: 175-217.

Shirer, William. 1960. *The Rise and Fall of the third Reich: A History of Nazi Germany.* New York: Simon & Schuster, Inc.

Siegel, Larry J. 2018. *Criminology.* Thirteenth edition. Boston: Cengage Learning.

Stashower, Daniel. November 29, 2013. "'The Yoga Store Murder: The Shocking True Account of the Lululemon Athletica Killing" by Dan Mors. *The Washington Post.* Opinions. Posted online.

Steadman, Henry J. and David Morrissette. August 15, 2016. "Police Responses to Persons With Mental Illness: Going Beyond CIT Training." *Psychiatry Services.* 67:10: 1054-1056..

Sutherland, Edwin H. 1924. *Criminology.* Philadelphia, PA: J. B. Lippincott Company.

_______________. "White-Collar Criminality." February 1940. *American Sociological Review.* 3: 1-12.

Taylor, Kate. December 28, 2020. "Lori Loughlin Released from Federal Prison." *New York Times.* Posted online at nytimes.com.

_______________. Updated October 22, 2019. "Parents Paid to Open College Doors. Now They're Spending to Limit Prison Time." *New York Times* Posted online.

Tischler, Henry L. 2019. *Introduction to Sociology.* Twelfth Edition. New York: Wessex Press, Inc.

Treatment Advocacy Center. n.d. "Law Enforcement and People with Severe Mental Illnesses." Briefing Paper. Arlington, VA.

Turvey, Brent E. 2014, 2009. *Forensic Victimology.* Second edition. Waltham, MA: Academic Press, an imprint of Elsevier.

UNODC (United National Office of Drugs and Crime). 2019. *UNODC Global Study on Homicide, 2019.* Vienna, Austria. Posyted at UNODC,org.

Vincenty, Samantha. March 13, 2020. "Neflix's Lost Girls Is Based on the Terrifying Gilgo Beach Murders." *OPRAH* Magazine. Posted online.

Von Hentig, Hans. September-October 1940. "Remarks on the Interaction of Perpetrators and Victims." *Journal of Criminal Law and Criminology.* 31: 303-309.

_______________. 1948. *The Criminal and His Victim.* New Haven, CT: Yale University Press.

Walklate, Sandra (ed.).2018, 2007. *Handbook of Victims and Victimology.* Second edition. New York: Routledge.

Werber, Sarah. "Mental Health Professionals, Trauma Exposure, and Role Conflict: A Qualitative Study." Master's Thesis. Long Island University, CW Post, n.d.

Wertham, Fredric, M.D. 1954. *Seduction of the Innocent.* New York: Rinehart & Company.

_______________. 1949. *The Show of Violence.* Garden City, New York: Doubleday

Wolfgang, Marvin. 1967. *Studies in Homicide.* New York: Harper and Row.

_______________. January 10, 1985. Personal correspondence with author.

_______________. May-June 1957. "Victim-Precipitated Homicide." *Journal of Criminal Law and Criminology.* 48: 1-11.

Yager, Jan. *Victims.* 1978 (Scribner's) 2021, 2015 (Hannacroix Creek Books). With new introduction, bibliography, and resources.

Young, Marlene and John Stein. December 2004. "The History of the Crime Victims' Movement in the Unites States." A Component of the Office for Victims of Crime Oral History Project. Posted online at https://www.ncjrs.gov

Videos, Documentaries, and Films

The Definition of Insanity: One-hour documentary on the Miami Dade's Jail Diversion Program for those who are arrested who are mentally ill. Premiered April 14, 2020 on PBS.

Clip related to the PBS documentary, *The Definition of insanity* (described previously).

Jen. "This is My Story." May 31, 2016. Victimology interview. 14:31 minutes. Algonquin College. Posted at youtube.com https://www.youtube.com/watch?v=EaxKT5onf-o

Lost Girls. 2020. Based on the book of the same title. Directed by Liz Garbus. Produced by NetFlix. Starring Amy Ryan, Oona Laurence, Thomasin McKenzie, and Gabriel Byrnes.

The Witness. 2015. Written by Bill Genovese, James D. Solomon, Russell Greene, and Gabriel Rhodes. Directed by James D. Solomon. Documentary.

Just Mercy. 2019. Directed by Destin Daniel Cretton. Starring Michael B. Jordan, Jamie Foxx, Brie Larson. Released by Warner Bros. Pictures.

Richard Jewell. 2019. Directed and produced by Clint Eastwood. Written by Billy Ray. Starring Kathy Bates, Paul Walter Hauser, Olivia Wilde, John Hamm, Sam Rockwell.

Chapter **TWO**

An Anthropological and Historical View of Crime Victims and Victims' Rights

Learning Objectives

After you finish reading this chapter, you should be able to:

1. Explain the legal system of individual retribution by victims or the victims' families characteristic of two simpler societies: the Inuit (previously known as the Eskimos) and the Comanches.
2. Gain an understanding of how the victim was treated when there was a "victim justice system," before written laws evolved into the "criminal justice system."
3. Understand the victim-related issues addressed in such major written codes or laws as the Code of Ur-Nammu, the Code of Hammurabi, the Mosaic Code, the Draco Code, the Laws of Solon, the Twelve Tables of Rome, the Laws of Manu, the *Corpus Juris Civilis* of Emperor Justinian, the *Leges Henrici* of Henry I, and the *Magna Carta*.
4. Understand the shift from victims or victims' kin handling the offender directly to crime becoming a "public" wrong.
5. Examine what it was like to be a crime victim in Colonial America and how that changed after the Declaration of Independence and the break from England.
6. Be able to discuss vigilantism in the Old West.
7. Explain the development of the victims' rights movement in the 1970s and 1980s.
8. Name at least two of the landmark U.S. Supreme Court cases related to granting victims certain rights.
9. Identify at least three key federal victims' rights legislation.
10. Define Marsy's Law, when it was first introduced, and by whom, and the advances it has made for victims' rights on a state level in the states that have passed it.

HOW A VICTIM'S JUSTICE SYSTEM EVOLVED INTO TODAY'S CRIMINAL JUSTICE SYSTEM

If you sit in a courtroom anywhere in the United States where a murder, rape, or robbery case is about to be tried, and the crime is under the jurisdiction of a state, the court clerk will preface the proceedings by declaring: "The People of the State of ________________ v. ________ __________ (the defendant)."

If it is a federal crime, it would be the federal government versus the defendant.

What is being stated at the beginning of any trial is that it is *the state*, or *the federal government*, and not the *victim* that is charging the defendant of the crime of murder or any other major violent, property, or economic crime, even though that crime was against a person or persons.

However, this is not the way it always used to be. Crimes, even such major violent crimes like murder, forcible rape, and aggravated assault with the intent to kill, were once treated as crimes *against the victim*. It was the victim or, if the victim was deceased, the victim's family or **kin** who could deal directly with the offender. As criminologists Daigle and Muftic explain it: "The justice system operated under the principle of **lex talionis**, an eye for an eye.... Punishment based on these notions is consistent with retribution. During this time period [before and throughout the Middle Ages (about the 5th through the 16th century)] a crime was considered a harm against the victim, not the state. Criminals were expected to pay back the victim through restitution. During this time period, a criminal who stole a person's cow likely would have to compensate the owner (the victim) by returning the stolen cow and also giving him or her another one." (Daigle and Muftic, 2016: 1-2) Other ways of handling criminal behavior included exile and banishment and the death penalty. (Abbott and Lotha, 2007; Brouwers, 2018)

How did the right of the victim to directly seek punishment or restitution from the criminal shift to the state or federal government? How did we go from what this author calls a **victim justice system** to what everyone today refers to as a **criminal justice system**?

There is no simple or easy answer, nor is the disappearance of the victim's right to retaliation readily explained. It is, however, a fascinating history that is worth understanding in a textbook on victimology since it places the current way victims are treated within a historical and even a cross-cultural context.

Anthropologists and legal historians have noted that law may be divided into two major types: **private law** and **public law**. *Private law* is a term applied to the unwritten systems that are based on community mores, sanctions, or taboos. In private law, the right to deal with the offender by collecting compensation or imposing punishment such as exile (banishment) or execution is given to the wronged person (the victim) or the victim's kinship group (in the case of homicide). *Public law* is when that right is instead exercised by the government because wrongs are considered crimes against the society as a whole and not just against the individual victim.

One way to explore how the victim of a major violent or property crime was treated before law became codified is to look at earlier cultures and their systems of law.

This chapter begins with a look at two different primitive cultures characterized by private law systems: the Inuit of the Arctic (previously referred to as Eskimos) and the Comanches, a tribe of Native Americans. What is a **primitive culture**? Anthropologist

Elman R. Service defines it in this way: ". . . any of numerous societies characterized by features that may include lack of a written language, relative isolation, small population, relatively simple social institutions and technology, and a generally slow rate of sociocultural change. In some of these cultures history and beliefs are passed on through an oral tradition and may be the province of a person or group especially rained for the purpose." (Service, 2018)

Next, the chapter presents a historical review of the evolution of victims' rights from ancient times to the present including the period after the Middle Ages when the "state" replaced the victim as the recipient of any blood or money **restitution** that was once directly due the victim or the victim's kin.

This chapter then traces how the rights of the tribal victim of violence and property crime differ from the rights of victims in contemporary culture. By looking at a selection of early legal codes, starting with the **Code of Hammurabi**, the **Mosaic Code**, the **Code of Draco** of ancient Athens, the ***Corpus Juris Civilis*** of ancient Rome, and the **Laws of Manu** of India, an idea begins to emerge about disparities in the violent and property crime victim's rights for redress that have occurred across time and cultures.

The chapter ends with an overview of **The New Age for the Victim**, an outgrowth of the Civil Rights Movement and the attention on child abuse victims in the 1960s, followed by the women's movement of the 1960s and 1970s, which led to an increased awareness of the rights of rape and domestic abuse victims. The 1970s were also the beginning of a genereal victims' movement which spilled over into the 1980s when key victims' rights legislation was passed by the federal government. A notable act is the **Victims of Crimes Act** (42 U.S. Code Chapter 112), also known as VOCA, enacted in 1984. That act authorized crime victim compensation and other assistance to crime victims through the Crime Victim Fund which was to be financed from funds from convicted federal offenders and, in an amendment passed in 2002, through additional sources including private donations. (Office for Victims of Crime [OVC] 1999; OVC, 2020) (You will also find a list of key federal victims' rights legislation in Table 2.6 at the conclusion of this chapter.)

You may find it useful to consult or review the key concepts related to the law, as defined in Box 2.1, as you continue reading this chapter.

Box 2.1. Definitions for Key Concepts and Terms in Criminal Law

Deviance: An act that goes against the norms of a society but is not a crime because it has not broken a law. Examples include someone continually talking in a loud voice during a movie or live theatrical performance or drinking too much in the privacy of one's own home.

Crime: An action or behavior that breaches a criminal law and is open to punishment.

Box 2.1. Definitions for Key Concepts and Terms in Criminal Law (continued)

Criminal law: Violating criminal law is necessary to be convicted of a crime.

State and federal constitutions: Two of the three sources of criminal law. The third are court decisions. The state or federal government brings action against the criminal because the crime is considered to do harm against the entire society as well as the victim.

Civil law: Under civil law, the victim may initiate legal action against the accused or a third party deemed negligent such as a hotel, a company, or a school. The punishment may be the payment of a fine and other legal actions, such as being required to stop doing certain acts. However, taking away someone's freedom—sentencing someone to jail or prison time—an option if someone has been found guilty of breaking a criminal law, cannot be imposed. (This is discussed further in Chapter 6, "Helping the Victim: Medical, Psychological, Financial Aid, and Civil Suits.")

Misdemeanor: A less serious crime; if incarceration is imposed, it is for a shorter period of time in jail, less than a year. A fine, probation, or another alternative to incarceration, such as restorative justice, whereby an agreement is reached among the injured parties, may be imposed.

Felony: This is a more serious crime which can result in a prison sentence of one year or much longer, or even the **death penalty** in the 27 states where **capital punishment** is still allowed or by the federal government, which technically can impose the death penalty in selected situations including murder, espionage, or terrorism. (Death Penalty Information Center, 2021)

***Mala in se*:** Crimes for which there is a general consensus that the acts involved, such as murder, robbery, rape, arson, burglary, and larceny/theft, are inherently immoral.

***mala prohibita*:** Crimes that are only crimes because the acts involved, such as getting drunk in public or interrupting funeral services, are forbidden.

Sources: Legal Dictionary, 2017; Reid, 2018; Ruane, 2017; Adler, Mueller, and Laufer, 2007; Wormser, 1949, 1962; Banning, 2004.

A CROSS-CULTURAL VIEW OF CRIME VICTIMS

The in-depth monographs based on **ethnography**, field trips undertaken by such anthropologists as R.F. Barton (1883-1947) and Bronislaw Malinowski (1884-1942), helped to dispel the myth that primitive cultures were completely unstructured, lacking any recognizable and cohesive system of dealing with crime and related legal problems. Let us look at the rights of the victim to deal with the criminal in two primitive cultures: the Inuit of the Arctic and the Comanches of North America. Please note that some of these observations are based on the reports of anthropologists from decades ago or even from early in the previous century rather than contemporary accounts. The two cultures highlighted below had victim-focused justice systems that, although varied in some ways, had elements similar to those of other non-westernized cultures, such as the Ifugao people of the Northern Philippines. (Barton, 1919)

Inuit of the Arctic

The Inuit (the preferred term in Canada, Greenland, and even among Alaska Natives instead of "Eskimos") are well-known for their carnivorous diet, their adaptability, and their hunting, fishing, and caribou economy. At the time of the first European contact around 1740, an estimated 40,000 Inuit were living in Alaska alone. Present-day Inuit live in areas other than just Alaska, thinly spread in Arctic isolation along the northern fringe of North America, and western and eastern Greenland—a distance of some 6,000 miles from the handful of Siberian Inuit to the settlements of East Greenland.

Picture of the Inuit from 1999. Image provided by Ansgar Walk/CC BY 2.5.

There is no "Eskimo tribe" or centralized Inuit population, but instead there are bands of Inuit, usually numbering fewer than one hundred persons, with a total population estimated in 2012 at around 59,000 throughout the world, if we include the Greenland population who refer to themselves as the *Inuit*. (Chavez, n.d.)

Explorer and anthropologist Peter Freuchen lived among the Polar Inuit from 1910 to 1921, trading with them and marrying an Inuit girl. In his monograph about the Inuit, he vividly described the Polar Inuit since he was one of the last to observe them untouched by extensive Western influence. (Freuchen, 1961: 13-14)

The Inuit were once characterized by "legalized" **infanticide** (killing of a newborn), **senilicide** (killing the elderly and senile), and **invalidicide** (killing an invalid) before the rules of Western cultures intervened. If a family did not feel that they could take care of a new baby, infanticide was permitted and not punished nor were the parents scorned. A fierce, almost brutal struggle against severe cold necessitated a sanctioning of the elimination of the "weaker" from the group. Suicide was also permitted; hanging was typical. Usually the suicide was done with outside assistance since outright suicide provoked too much mental anguish for the victim. All these acts were socially approved homicides so that they would not provoke blood vengeance (also known as a **blood feud**) by the victim's kin. But repeated or recidivist homicide, perceived sorcery or witchcraft, and chronic lying did lead to a publicly demanded execution.

Anthropologist Franz Boas, in his 1888 monograph, *The Central Eskimo*, indicated that blood revenge—killing the murderer by the nearest relative of the victim—was not uncommon. Boas also noted that in certain quarrels, where the murderer himself could not be apprehended, the family of the murdered man would retaliate by killing one of the nearest relations of the murderer. (Boas, 1964: 174)

But a system found among the Inuit that was unique regarding retribution for murder was the requirement that the murderer care for the victim's widow and children. In *Man's Rise to Civilization as Shown by the Indians of North America from Primeval Times to the Coming of the Industrial State*, Peter Farber notes a related situation that might develop in these circumstances, such as when a murdered man's son, reared as a stepson, might, on reaching manhood, kill his stepfather in revenge for his biological father's earlier killing. (Farber, 1968: 44-45) (See Table 2.1 for a summary of how the Inuit dealt with crime and punishment.)

In the case of a recidivist murderer, the offender would be declared a public nuisance. Some community-minded man would then take on the task of interviewing all the adult males in the community to ask their opinion as to whether an execution should follow. A unanimous decision for the death penalty would then be carried out by an executioner, thereby averting the risk that a blood feud might follow. (Hoebel, 1972)

The desire to steal a certain woman was the most frequent cause for attempted or successful murder, as noted by later explorers such as Geert van den Steenhoven and Knut Rasmussen. Canadian anthropologist Asen Balikci, in analyzing the seven murders reported by Steenhoven, summarizes the deliberate nature of the acts as well as the trend of surprising the victim, usually by coming up from behind, to avoid a struggle. (Balikci, 1970: 178-179)

Comanches of North America

The Comanches were known in the sign language of the Great Plains as "the snake people" and are also known as "Lords of the Southern Plains." (Gelo, 2018) Estimates of the Comanche population are that there were approximately 20,000 Comanches in the early 1800s with that number diminishing to just 1,500 in 1900 because of disease and conflict. (Gelo, 2018) According to comanchenation.com, the current enrolled tribal members of the

TABLE 2.1. Crimes and Punishment Among the Inuit

Single murder	Private wrong ". . . results quite regularly in the murderer taking over the widow and children of the victim" Blood revenge—"immediate or long postponed"
Homicidal recidivist	Public crime Legal execution
Witchcraft (sorcery)	Execution
Chronic lying	In theory, execution, but anthropologist Hoebel could not find any actual examples
Adultery	With husband's consent, considered permissible wife-lending
Assisted suicide	Acceptable
Infanticide	Legally acceptable
Senilicide	Legally acceptable
Invalidicide	Legally acceptable
Cannibalism caused by starvation	Legally acceptable
All disputes except homicide	Settled by boxing and butting (hitting/pushing)

Source: Hoebel, "Law-Ways of the Primitive Eskimos" (Spring 1941)

Comanche Nation is approximately 17,000 with an estimated 7,000 residing near Lawton, Ft Sill, Oklahoma, and nearby counties. (Comanchenation.com, n.d.) These nomadic warrior people were known for their courage and for measuring their wealth in horses, which they introduced to the Plains after originally acquiring some from early Spanish traders and settlers.

What type of law operated with the nomadic Comanches? There was no state, clan, or tribe; kin or family had to carry out any form of retribution. There was one right or wrong and the pressure of custom, not a written law or code, forced adherence. Certain crimes, such as rape and theft, were rare. Rape, except upon captives, was infrequent. Generosity was so highly valued that just by asking someone for an object, it would be given.

Killing a murderer did not lead to a blood feud; it was the permissible act of the victim's family and accepted by the family of the murderer. There was no counter-killing, as in the Inuit culture. However, the killing of a wife by a husband or the killing by a brother of his sister passed without judgment by the larger community since this was the personal responsibility of the family unit, not open to inter-family laws.

There were two types of chiefs: the war chief and the peace chief. The war chief's functions were to determine the objectives of a raid, designate scouts, decide where to camp and when to take periods of rest, appoint cooks and water carriers, formulate attack strategies, order the expedition to turn back, make a truce with the enemy, and divide the winnings. But the peace chief, or "headman," had a function like a mediator. The headman's advice was followed more than anyone else's and the authority was completely arbitrary, remaining only if he kept the respect of his fellow Comanches. Civil (police chief) and military (war chief) affairs were separate. (Wallace and Hoebel, 1952: 12)

There were nine common legal offenses against the individual recognized by the Comanches:

- adultery
- wife absconding
- violation of **levirate** (when a man marries his brother's widow) privileges
- homicide
- killing someone's favorite horse
- causing another person to commit suicide
- excessive sorcery
- failure to fulfill a contract
- theft (Hoebel, 512)

(See Table 2.2 for a summary of how the Comanches handled crime and punishment, according to anthropologist E. Adamson Hoebel.)

T.R. Fehrenbach, author of *Comanches,* provides these insights about Comanche law:

> Since no state, clan, or tribe existed, the only form of retribution had to be carried out by kin or family. What was somewhat peculiar to the Comanche form of feud was that, almost always, retributive killing was only carried out in response to a murder that was recognized as murder within the general band mores, and the justice was accepted—that is, the family acted as official judge and jury and executioner, and the "feud" stopped there. So, really, these were not blood-feuds, as carried on by Inuit, (very bloody, despite some anthropologists' denials) or Scots intra-tribal warfare, which carried act and reprisal over a broad spectrum of blood relationship, and usually involved the slaying of totally "innocent" parties—guilty only of being kin to the offending party. The Comanches carried on this kind of feud, in fact, with Texas, but never within [their] own circles.
>
> Within the Comanche society and culture, certainly this form of feud was more direct and "just" (in that the justice was accepted by all) than anything in so-called civilized societies. After all, in social terms, perfect justice occurs when a felon is hanged, he, his kin, the offended, the judge, society at large, and the hangman all agree that the hanging is deserved, whether they actually like it or not. . . . But then, we don't even agree on what is "criminal." Tribal cultures have no such problems. (T.R. Fehrenbach, 1975, personal communication)

Anthropologist E. Adamson Hoebel (1906-1993), who spent much of his lifetime studying the Comanches as well as primitive law in general, suggested these postulates and corollaries to be basic to the Comanche way of life:

Postulate V. Engaging in sexual relations with kin (incest) constitutes subhuman behavior.
Postulate VII. The great spirits (Sun and Earth) have powers of legal judgment.
Postulate VIII. Each Comanche is to cooperate with others and help them in their life's activities.
Corollary 1. Altruism and sharing of goods are socially desirable.
Corollary 2. The killing of a fellow tribesman is not permissible. (Hoebel, page 131)

TABLE 2.2. Victim Rights in Comanche Culture According to Anthropologist Hoebel

Crime	Victim Remedy
Land dispute	Peace Chief to settle with awarding of damages especially prized horses as well as blankets, saddles, clothing, robes
Adultery	Ridicule; ask a war chief to intervene on plaintiff's behalf; kill accused's horses; unfaithful wife can request damages from her lover; may have to compensate with 1 to 10 horses or favorite horse
Wife-stealing or absconding	Demand return of the wife; husband can gash the soles of her feet, whip her, or cut off her nose; may have to compensate with 1 to 10 horses or favorite horse
Murder	Kin of victim can take the life of the murderer
Murder within the family	Rare but acceptable; considered private matter; if husband kills wife, will not be revenged by wife's kin
Slaying of favorite horse	Death
Accidental homicide	Settled by proper payment to the family of the deceased
Sorcery	Concern of the affected family; may ask for execution

Source: W. Adamson Hoebel, *The Political Organization and Law-Ways of the Comanche Indians* (1940).

RECAP: THE VICTIM IN PRIMITIVE CULTURES

In examining the unwritten but highly specific legal systems of the Inuit and Comanche, we find that the victim, and not the criminal, was the supreme consideration. It was a victim justice system. Justice was specific and definite. If a deliberate murder was committed—one that was not sanctioned by the community (e.g., infanticide was sanctioned previously in Intuit society), the murderer was put to death (a death for a death). Less heinous offenses, such as theft or violating certain taboos, had specific fines and penalties as well. Sorcery was deemed a capital crime in most primitive cultures and treated accordingly.

Those judged guilty of recidivist or repeat homicide or pathological lying were dealt with severely.

In contrast to today's criminal justice system of law and justice, primitive cultures focused on the victim seem to be almost callous in their denial of the rights of the criminal once guilt is proven. Primitive cultures sought to prevent blood feuds and further acts of violence, or sorcery, preferring to keep the peace of the society. Fairness meant a fair sense of retribution for the injured party —the victim—not the injuring one.

Primitive cultures had a legal system exemplified by:

1. individual retribution
2. collective responsibility or liability
3. private law with the privilege of applying force vested in the wronged individual or kinship groups
4. the conditional curse, ordeal, or oath as methods of determining guilt or innocence

5. blood feuds that, although they do not occur as often as previously believed, usually end with the payment of blood money (compensation); although killing the murderer does sometimes happen, it stops there
6. **mediators** or **go-betweens**, which exist in all primitive cultures for settling disputes

There is little chance of complex contemporary societies replacing public law with the private law of primitive cultures. Nor would modern societies want to completely adopt a private law system. That is because coupled with the right of the victim to get payment or compensation from the criminal or the criminal's kin are things most would view as excessively harsh or even barbaric, such as the right of the husband to kill his wife or the justifiable homicide of someone found guilty of adultery or sorcery. Yes, so-called **honor killings** still occur in some parts of the world, whereby someone is killed, usually a woman and often by her male family member, such as a brother, husband, uncle, or father, for allegedly shaming the family, for example it might be for showing a face in public where it is forbidden, do still happen in some parts of the world. (Brown, 2016) There is a push to get tougher on those who commit so-called honor killings; the Associated Press reported that "'more than 1,000 women were killed last year in so-called honor killings in Pakistan.'" (Kennedy, 2016)

A better alternative might be the adaptation of specific principles from private law that might improve the current public law system. Fortunately, that has been occurring in many communities. For example, the practice of having a go-between or mediator, which we have seen is universal in private law, is becoming more common in contemporary public law as more and more communities are offering arbitration or mediation as a way to divert certain types of cases away from criminal court. Applying the principle of **collective responsibility** from primitive cultures to the detection, treatment, and even prevention of juvenile delinquency might be a welcome development in seeing that problem as a societal challenge instead of a problem afflicting just that one juvenile and his or her solitary family. (In Table 2.3 you will find a summary of how the Inuit and Comanches demonstrate the principles of "individual retribution" and "collective responsibility.")

TABLE 2.3. Two Representative Primitive Cultures Evidencing the Principles of "Individual Retribution" and "Collective Responsibility"

People	Mediator	Location	Economy	Punishment for Murder
INUIT	Self-appointed community-minded man	Arctic and subarctic regions of North America	Hunting, fishing, caribou	Killing on single occasion leads to feud. Recidivist homicide necessitates male adult community decision to retaliate or not. If unanimous, execute without revenge; permissible forms of homicide include assisted suicide, infanticide, senilicide, invalidicide
COMANCHES	Peace chief or "headman"	Great Plains (Oklahoma)	Nomadic hunters	Husband may kill wife. Brother may kill sister. Outside family called for counter-killing by victim's family. No feud results.

Sources: R.F. Barton; Franz Boas; Peter Freuchen; Knud Rasmussen; E. Adamson Hoebel; T.R. Fehrenbach; M. Fortes; Ernest Wallace (See Cited Works and Additional References at the end of the chapter for complete citations).

A HISTORICAL VIEW OF CRIME VICTIM TREATMENT IN PUBLIC LAW

Primitive law seems wise and pro-victim in some instances, but very harsh in others. What about the earliest written legal codes and the first examples of public law? Was it more lenient to the offender or the victim? Whose rights—the accused or criminal or the victim—seemed to be the dominant concern, or did it depend? Although the Code of Hammurabi, which dates from the eighteenth century B.C.E. (around 1754 **B.C.E.—Before Common Era**) was thought to be the first major legal document, it was discovered that there was an earlier one: the **Code of Ur-Nammu**.

Code of Ur-Nammu

According to Josh Mark, writing in the *Ancient History Encyclopedia*, The Code of Ur-Nammu was written by King Ur-Nammu, who ruled from 2047-2030 B.C.E., as the founder of the Third Dynasty of Ur in Sumer. As Mark notes, however, there might be an even earlier text. But since the actual earlier text has not been found, Ur-Nammu is considered the first example of written law. Mark writes: "An earlier law code (known as the Code of Urukagina from the twenty-fourth century B.C.E.) is only known through partial references to it and so, since the actual text itself has not been found, Ur-Nammu's code is considered the oldest extant."

Mark continues: "The Code of Ur-Nammu assumed a universal understanding on the part of the people that law descended from the gods and the king was simply the administrator of those laws. Harsh penalties were considered unnecessary for most crimes since people were assumed to know how they should behave toward each other; a monetary fine as a reminder of how to behave was sufficient."

Here are samples from the written laws that are said to have consisted of 40 paragraphs:

> *If a man committed a kidnapping, he is to be imprisoned and pay fifteen shekels of silver.*
>
> *If a man proceeded by force, and deflowered the virgin slave-woman of another man, that man must pay five shekels of silver.*
>
> *If a man appeared as a witness, and was shown to be a perjurer, he must pay fifteen shekels of silver.*
>
> *If a man knocked out the eye of another man, he shall weigh out half a mina of silver.*
>
> *If a man knocked out a tooth of another man, he shall pay two shekels of silver.*
>
> *If a man, in the course of a scuffle, smashed the limb of another man with a club, he shall pay one mina of silver.*

In these examples from the Code of Ur-Nammu, the universal application of financial restitution to the victim for all crimes is quite significant since it even covers knocking out another man's eye or tooth. This is definitely a far cry from the much more famous "an eye for an eye" in the renowned Code of Hammurabi, described below. In the Code of Ur-Nammu, even rape, what is referred to as "deflowering the virgin slave-woman of another man," will result in the victim getting financial compensation.

Code of Hammurabi

Now we turn to the much more famous of the early examples of written law, the Code of Hammurabi, written by Hammurabi, the sixth king of the first known dynasty of Babylonia (an area that today makes up Iraq and Syria), who reigned from about 1728 to 1686 B.C.E. His code is inscribed on a block of black diorite and was first discovered in modern times in 1901 on the acropolis of Susa by an expedition sent out by the French government under H. de Morgan.

About one fifth of the code has been erased; the remaining 44 columns contain 248 separate provisions, relating almost exclusively to civil and criminal law. The sections of top concern to this chapter are sections 6-14, the penalties for theft, and sections 194-233, criminal law. (Pritchard, 1973)

Picture of the Code of Hammurabi. Image provided by Mbzt/CC BY 3.0.

The most progressive aspect of the Code is the concept of restitution. In most cases, repaying a theft or loss was insufficient, and an additional penalty was paid as well. Thus, the theft of foods in transportation was punished by a five-fold restitution; the embezzlement of a merchant's money by his agent called for three-fold restitution.

Another unique feature, and one of vital significance to developing a historical view of how the crime victim was considered and treated by its rulers, was provision 23. In that provision, the city or government in whose territory or district a robbery was committed would be accountable for replacing the stolen property if the thief had not been caught and if the victim had itemized his losses "in the presence of god . . ." This is an especially interesting provision since, as you will see in Chapter 6, "Helping the Victim," in the section of the chapter that discusses what is available today from the state or federal government in terms of crime victim compensation. Rarely or never are property or economic losses because of crimes, such as robbery or burglary, or **cybercrimes** such as identity theft, compensated or replaced by the government. There is, however, a growing trend to change that, as you will see in later chapters, especially Chapters 8 and 9, "Property Crime Victims" and "Cybercrime, White-Collar Crime, and Economic Crime Victims," respectively. (Chouhy, 2018)

According to the Code of Hammurabi, the ruler would pay out if no arrest was made; in contemporary society, whether or not an arrest is made, it is from the offenders, court fees or the federal VOCA (Victims of Crime Act) from 1984 that the state crime compensation funds are derived. As the National Association of Crime Victim Compensation Board explains: "... most of this money comes from offenders rather than tax dollars, since a large majority of states fund their programs entirely through fees and fines charged against those convicted of crime. Federal grants to compensation programs, providing about 35 percent of the money for payments to victims, also come solely from offender fines and assessments." The funds are paid out through the state compensation boards, not directly between offender and victim. Not only do offender and victim rarely have any contact; in fact, it is usually expressly forbidden. But there may not be a known assailant just a reported crime. (NACVB website)

In Box 2.2 you will find examples of restitution and punishments from the Code of Hammurabi. Note the victim emphasis in many of these examples. The numbers preceding the stipulations refer to its corresponding number in the entire code:

Box 2.2. The Code of Hammurabi

6. If any one steal the property of a temple or of the court, he shall be put to death, and also the one who receives the stolen thing from him shall be put to death.

14. If any one steal the minor son of another, he shall be put to death.

15. If any one take a male or female slave of the court, or a male or female slave of a freed man, outside the city gates, he shall be put to death.

21. If any one break a hole into a house (break in to steal), he shall be put to death before that hole and be buried.

22. If any one is committing a robbery and is caught, then he shall be put to death.

23. If the robber is not caught, then shall he who was robbed claim under oath the amount of his loss; then shall the community, and ... on whose ground and territory and in whose domain it was compensate him for the goods stolen.

154. If a man be guilty of incest with his daughter, he shall be driven from the place (exiled).

155. If a man betroth a girl to his son, and his son have intercourse with her, but he (the father) afterward defile her, and be surprised, then he shall be bound and cast into the water (drowned).

195. If a son strike his father, his hands shall be hewn off.

196. If a man put out the eye of another man, his eye shall be put out. [An eye for an eye]

197. If he broke another man's bone, his bone shall be broken.

198. If he put out the eye of a freed man, or break the bone of a freed man, he shall pay one gold mina.

199. If he put out the eye of a man's slave, or break the bone of a man's slave, he shall pay one-half of its value.

200. If a man knocks out the teeth of his equal, his teeth shall be knocked out. [A tooth for a tooth]

Box 2.2. The Code of Hammurabi (continued)

202. If any one strike the body of a man higher in rank than he, he shall receive sixty blows with an ox-whip in public.

204. If a freed man strikes the body of another freed man, he shall pay ten shekels in money.

205. If the slave of a freed man strikes the body of a freed man, his ear shall be cut off.

206. If during a quarrel one man strike another and wound him, then he shall swear, "I did not injure him wittingly," and pay the physicians.

207. If the man die of his wound, he shall swear similarly, and if he (the deceased) was a free-born man, he shall pay half a mina in money.

208. If he was a freed man, he shall pay one-third of a mina.

209. If a man strike a free-born woman so that she lose her unborn child, he shall pay ten shekels for her loss.

210. If the woman die, his daughter shall be put to death.

229 If a builder build a house for some one, and does not construct it properly, and the house which he built fall in and kill its owner, then that builder shall be put to death.

230. If it kill the son of the owner the son of that builder shall be put to death.

231. If it kill a slave of the owner, then he shall pay slave for slave to the owner of the house.

232. If it ruin goods, he shall make compensation for all that has been ruined, and inasmuch as he did not construct properly this house which he built and it fell, he shall re-erect the house from his own means.

Source: Translated by L.W. King, the Avalon Project, Yale Law School Lillian Goldman Law Library, posted at https://avalon.law.yale.edu/ancient/hamframe.asp

Criminologist Stephen Schafer indicated that the cruelty that characterized so many of the Hammurabi codes were not done in the interest of the victim but for its deterrent effect on the criminal and the society. He also noted that the criminal "paid as an object of the victim's vengeance, not in compensation for the victim's injury." (Schafer, 1960: 4)

Mosaic Code

Harvey Wallace and Cliff Roberson point out the origins of the Mosaic Code or Ten Commandments as well as its historical and legal significance: "According to legend, Moses returned from a mountaintop carrying the Ten Commandments, which were inscribed on two stone tablets. These commandments subsequently became the foundation of Judeo-Christian morality. The Mosaic Code also became the basis for many of the laws in our modern society: The prohibition against murder, perjury, and theft was present in the Mosaic Code thousands of years before the founding of the United States." (Wallace and Roberson, 2019: 4-5)

One of the earliest stories in the Bible, in Genesis, is the slaying of Abel by his brother, Cain. In primitive cultures, the slaying of Abel by Cain would be a deed that was outside the province of the social legal system since it happened within the family. But it evoked this punishment: Cain was to be a fugitive and a wanderer over the earth and to wear a mark. If anyone killed Cain, a sevenfold vengeance was to be taken for him.

Thus the punishment for Cain is not a step backwards—because the life of the murderer was not demanded in exchange for the life of the victim—but as a step forward since there was punishment meted out despite the fact that he killed his brother. Thus, the Bible documents that murder was becoming unacceptable whether close kin or not. It is important to see the punishment for Cain in a light that reflects the ancient culture the priests and scholars who wrote the Bible were trying to explain, rather than wondering what might have happened if Cain had been slain for killing Abel.

It is in Exodus that The Decalogue or Ten Commandments first appears. The Decalogue in the original way it is given to Moses resembles the story of Hammurabi being give the Code by the sun god himself in that Moses was given the tablets by God. The indirect relationship between the Code of Hammurabi and the Bible was probably through the Canaanites, upon whom Babylonian culture exercised an influence for some centuries. Included below is an abridged version of the Mosaic Code, starting with the Sixth Commandment:

The Decalogue*

6. Thou shall not kill.
7. Thou shall not commit adultery.
8. Thou shall not steal.
9. Thou shall not bear false witness against your neighbor.
10. Thou shall not covet your neighbor's house, wife, or his servant, man or woman, or his ox, donkey, or anything that is his.

Source: *Abridgment from Exodus 20:1-21

The Book of the Covenant clearly states punishments for major offenses: death for anyone causing the death of another. If it be an accident, there will be a place where the murderer can seek refuge, but if it be through "treacherous intent," then the murderer must die. Abducting another? Death. Cursing a father or a mother? Death. Intercourse with an animal? Death. Death to the sorcerer.

But for certain thefts, restitution is offered: "If a man steals an ox or a sheep and then slaughters or sells it, he must pay five oxen for the ox, four sheep for the sheep." There is blood vengeance if a thief is killed while breaking and entering, but if after the act, there shall be vengeance. The thief must make full restitution; if he does not have the means, he must be sold to pay for what he has stolen. If a stolen animal is found alive in his possession, ox, donkey, or sheep, he must pay double.

In the Book of Moses, the selling of the criminal might be necessary because tangible retribution could not be made. There is no discussion about right or wrong, punishment or rehabilitation. The issue is that theft had to be discouraged by imposing harsh repayment burden on the offender—returning goods at four or five times the value of the stolen property. (*The Old Testament of the Jerusalem Bible*)

Ancient Greece

As early as Homer, who flourished in the eighth or ninth century B.C.E., we find references to retribution in *The Iliad* where, if the relations of the murdered person were willing, a fine might be paid to prevent the more customary exile of a murderer. Thus, by that time, the death penalty for murder was rarely invoked. As Danielle Allen points out in her article about Athenian law, exile allowed the convicted murderer to relocate to another town or city and to even start a new life. As Allen puts it, "In departing the community, the wrongdoer freed the victim and the prosecutor of the anger, and also put an end to the social disruption plaguing the city. . ." (Allen, 2003)

The Greek city-state experienced four governmental phases: a limited monarchy, an oligarchy, a despotic rule, and a democracy. The government, once in the hands of the hereditary monarchy, passed to the control of the nobles, or "cupatrids," and the Age of Nobles was initiated by the middle of the eighth century B.C.E., a time when the power of jurisdiction previously given to the king passed to the supreme Council of State, which met on the Areopagus Hill.

Economic and political discontent in the seventh century B.C.E. provided the climate for the dictatorship of Cylon to be set up in 630 B.C.E. Although by the next year Cylon's supporters had been starved out and slaughtered, the nobles paid heed to the warning and agreed to the first written code. Thus, the famous code of Draco or **Draco's Code** was codified in 621 B.C.E.

Draco collected the laws, rather than writing them, although his name has become an adjective—Draconian—which still is used to describe harsh or cruel laws. Written down, the obvious harshness of the laws cannot be denied. For example, the penalty for most offenses was death. There was no distinction in terms of punishment among someone who stole a piece of fruit, someone who robbed a temple, or someone who killed a man. But Draco's Code signified an important change, namely that the state, and not the vendetta, now resolved murder violations.

Solon, a Chief Magistrate, was appointed in 594 B.C.E. to revise the Code of Draco. His new local code and law courts survived over the next three centuries in Athens. When the Romans were compiling their own legal code, the Twelve Tables, described below, they sent a commission to Athens in 454 B.C.E. to examine the laws of Solon. (Freeman, 1963: 9-39)

Known as Mediator, Solon restored mortgaged land and abolished all debts. He instituted the policy that the qualification for all offices of states would be annual income, rather than birth, and therefore opened the way to all citizens. Eventually the old Court of the Areopagus became a purely democratic body. It met in the open air and tried cases of intentional homicide, intentional wounding, or arson.

The trying of cases of involuntary homicide met in the court building called Palladion. The Delphinion was used if a case of justifiable homicide was to be tried. If someone already exiled for a verdict of guilty of manslaughter committed another murder, the court met at Phraetto. It is said the accused pleaded from a boat rather than being allowed to stand on native soil. A special trial was held in the City Hall or Prytaneion if an animal or inanimate object was said to have caused the death of a man.

Most trials came before the popular jury courts if they were non-homicidal. The Heliaea was the first jury court created by Solon. It became the supreme judicial power in the state. All cases except homicide and arson came before it, and the jury was chosen by lot from the citizen body. An Athenian jury could number from 500 to 2,000 members, depending on the case it was to hear.

The state only considered crimes against itself, not crimes against the community; cheating the public treasury or treason were deemed crimes against the state. One change brought about by Solon was that any citizen, not only the person injured or the next of kin, could bring an indictment against another except in the case of murder, where the right of prosecution was still left in the hands of the relatives of the deceased. There was no public prosecutor. The penalty imposed was executed by the state. There were prisons supervised by the annually chosen officers known as The Eleven. Foreigners could not address the Athenian courts, nor could women or slaves. Only free male citizens of full Athenian parentage could address the courts.

Ancient Rome

Around 509 B.C.E., the traditional beginning of the Roman Republic, all criminal justification was a matter for officers of the state, the consults and the praetors, and the Assembly of the Roman People. Initially, each sentence had to be pronounced by an officer of the state. If the defendant was a Roman citizen, if a capital sentence or if a fine above a certain limit was imposed, it would not be carried out until confirmed by the Assembly on appeal. (Cicero, *Murder Trials*, 1975: 12)

Like in Greece, there was nothing such as a public prosecutor or attorney general in ancient Rome. Each citizen had the right to charge another citizen. Greed often motivated prosecutions since there were large rewards promised to those who were victorious; even a share of confiscated property was granted if there was a conviction on a capital charge.

Punishment for murder had a long history in Rome, dating back to the **Twelve Tables**, a series of laws composed on tablets during the mid-fifth century B.C.E (circa 451 B.C.E.) The laws that are written down on the Twelve Tables had been known for centuries but, as Wallace and Roberson point out, "applied only to the ruling patrician class of citizens." (Wallace and Roberson, 2019: 5) The plebian class protested and the result was the creation of the Twelve Tables which was put on display for all residents of Rome.

Here are several examples cited by Dr. Schafer in *The Victim and His Criminal* from Twelve Tables regarding the position of the victim or restitution to the victim:

> *A thief who was not caught in the act of committing the theft was obliged to pay double the value of the stolen object.*
>
> *In cases where the stolen object was found in a search of his house, he was to pay three times the value.*
>
> *He was to pay four times the value if he resisted the execution of the house search.*
>
> *He was to pay four times the value of the object if he had stolen it by force or the threat of force. (Schafer,* The Victim and His Criminal, *1968: 13)*

Mark Cartwright points out additional civil laws, crimes, and penalties in his article, "Twelve Tables." Here are other civil actions and penalties covered in the Twelve Tables: arson could be punished by death by burning; using magic on crops was punishable by death by crucifixion; banishment from Rome, loss of citizenship, confiscation of property for being the accessory to a crime; paying compensation to the victim as a way of avoiding court. (Cartwright, "Twelve Tables" 2018)

Roman citizens who murdered received a show of leniency that might be regarded as excessive today. Killing one's parents was a charge that probably meant exemption from the death penalty and even the chance of avoiding detention. Executions were rare. The reason for this was that the accused person would remain free until the verdict and penalty was announced. Hence, they almost always left Rome for non-Roman territory to escape from imprisonment or a death sentence. After the first century B.C.E., it was customary to allow someone to depart before even pronouncing the verdict. It was the threat of death if the guilty party were to return that kept the convicted away. (Cicero, *Murder Trials*, 1975: 18-19)

Dolus (evil intent), *culpa* (negligence) and *casus* (accident) are three standards of liability that Roman law is particularly admired for since it contributed to the development of Western legal thought. The roots are in civil law, concerned with compensation, the awarding of money for **misdemeanors**, rather than in criminal law, which is more concerned with punishment or retribution for major **felonies**.

The Greek influence in this area is apparent. In an intriguing article by F.J. Lawson, "Roman Law," he expands on the above thesis: "In fact it is difficult to define the historic importance of Roman law, more difficult to see what is peculiarly Roman in it and still more difficult to explain either its importance of its Roman character." (Lawson, "Roman Law," 1973: 113)

Lawson points out that direct evidence of Roman law really begins with Cicero. He also makes the point that the Republican constitution did not give the citizen the right to assert power against the sovereign people, although it did protect the citizen against the abuse of power by the magistrates. As was the case in Athenian law, the blood feud, or anything like it, had been suppressed even before written history began. Lawson writes:

> But although murder and treason were already crimes against the State, most of what would not be treated as criminal offenses were redressed by way of civil action brought by the victim against the wrongdoer. Moreover, a person seeking justice against another person got no help from the State in bringing him before the courts. Nor was private law for the most part the product of legislation, though the Roman people could in its assemblies modify private law if it chose. (Lawson, 1973: 114)

Corpus Juris Civilis

A century after the Twelve Tables, to update Roman laws, the *Corpus Juris Civilis,* also known as The Justinian Code because it was created by Emperor Justinian I, were set down in 528-529 C.E. There were four main parts to the Justinian Code: According to Frederick W. Dingledy, the project took three years and one of the four parts of the Code was organized into 50 books including one book devoted to Criminal Law. (Dingledy, 2016)

The Laws of Manu

The Laws of Manu come at the end of a tradition that started with the *Dharma Sutras*, or "Instructions in the Sacred Law," the earliest sources of Hindu law, that were probably composed between the sixth and second centuries B.C. (600-200 B.C.E.) and are attributed to Gautama, Baudhayana, Vasistha, and Apastamba. (Basham, 1954: 112-113)

The early *sutras* (instructions or principles), had fines for punishment of murder that were dependent on the **caste** [class] that the victim belonged to: 1,000 cows for killing a member of the warrior-caste (*kastriya*); 100 for a *vaisya* and 10 for a *sudra* or a woman of any class. However, the murder of a Brahman, the highest caste, could not be appeased with a fine. Nor would a Brahman be subjected to the death penalty in ancient India.

Although fine and caste were closely tied in criminal cases, in matters of moral conduct, the high Brahmans were fined more stringently than the lower castes since Brahmans were believed to have higher standard of behavior. Thus a theft by a Brahman would be seen and dealt with as a more heinous offense than if the lower castes committed it.

By about 200 B.C.E. to 200 C.E., the probable time of Manu, compensation to the victim was regarded as a form of penance. Therefore, the compensation might be given to the priests instead of to the injured party. That change in who received the compensation money is a significant one for the victim. It is a similar change that would later occur in Germanic England beginning in the eighth century C.E.

Some of the Laws of Manu and provisions for compensation or retribution are illustrative of how the Indian development compared to what was happening at that time in Rome. Here are some of the Laws of Manu:

Assault

- With whatever limb a man of a low caste does hurt to a man of the highest castes, even that limb shall be cut off.
- He who raises his hand or a stick, shall have his hand cut off; he who in anger kicks with his foot, shall have his foot cut off.
- If a blow is struck against man or animals in order to give them pain, the judge shall inflict a fine in proportion to the amount of pain caused.
- If a limb is injured, a wound is caused, or blood flows, the assailant shall be made to pay to the sufferer the expenses of the cure. (*The Laws of Manu*, 1969: 303-304)

Theft

- With whatever limb a thief in any way commits an offense against men, even of that the king shall deprive him in order to prevent a repetition of the crime.
- On him who steals more than ten kumbhas of grain corporal punishment shall be inflicted; in other cases he shall be fined eleven times as much, and shall pay to the owner the value of his property.

Violent Crime

- He who commits violence must be considered as the worst offender, more wicked than a defamer, than a thief, and then he who injuries another with a staff.
- But the king who pardons the perpetrator of violence quickly perishes and incurs hatred.
- Neither for friendship's sake, nor for the sake of great lucre, must a king let go perpetrators of violence, who cause terror to all creatures. (*Laws of Manu*, 1969: 308, 310, 312, 314)

In Table 2.4 you will find a summary of the major codes and laws covering from Ancient Times through the Laws of Manu.

TABLE 2.4. Major Codes and Laws from Ancient Times (2047 B.C.E.) through Laws of Manu (200 B.C.E.-200 C.E.)

Code	Originator	Place	Dates	Why Significant
Ur-Nammu	King Ur-Nammu	Sumer	2047-2030 B.C.E.	First written code; restitution to the victim
Code of Hammurabi	King Hammurabi	Babylonia	1728 B.C.E.-1686 B.C.E.	Levels of restitution from financial to execution; sums based on class
Mosaic Code	Moses	Ancient Israel	1393-1273 B.C.E.	Extolled a conduct code of exemplary behavior
Draco Code	Draco	Athens	621 B.C.E.	Harsh; death penalty for almost every crime
Laws of Solon	Solon	Athens	594 B.C.E.	Prescribed new fines for rape; legislated against slander; abolished all Draco laws except murder-related
Twelve Tables	The Demviri (Ten Men appointed by the Senate)	Rome	451 B.C.E.	Important transition from blood feuds to settle crime to restitution to the victim
Laws of Manu	Manu	India	200 B.C.E.-200 C.E.	Restitution to victim seen as a penance and may be given to a priest; spells out punishments for violent and property crimes with higher caste getting steeper fines because supposed to be a role model

WHEN CRIME BECAME A PUBLIC WRONG

Gradually the development of public law versus private law changed the function of the courts, as well as the redress open to the victim. The courts no longer were the peacemakers between feuding families, like the headman of the Comanches, but were to maintain public order, to protect the rights of innocent citizens, and to try those accused of a crime.

The shift began during the Middle Ages, and it was characterized by the lord or king taking a portion of the victim's share of compensation for a criminal wrong. The term for this was from ancient Germanic law, ***wergild* or *wergeld*,** which meant "payment." Wergild (also known as *Busse+, emenda, lendis*) was the payment or compensation to the victim when a crime was committed or to the victim's family or kin in the case of homicide. Some have also referred to the wergild as **blood money**.

The size of the wergild indicated what value was placed on the slain person's life. The portion that the king got was known as the ***Friedensgeld*** or *gewedde*. In Saxon England, notes Dr. Schafer in *The Victim and His Criminal*, the payment to the victim for homicide was known as ***Wer*** and the compensation for injury was known as ***Bot***; the king or overlord payment was known as the ***Wite***. (Schafer, 1968: 18)

In time, the pattern of the king taking just a portion of the victim's share of the *wergild* continued and developed into one where the king, or head of state, was taking everything that should have gone to the victim. In effect the victim was cut out of any restitution or compensation for losses related to being a crime victim.

According to Dr. Schafer, this occurred after the **Treaty of Verdun** in August 843 A.D. when the Frankish Empire was divided into three kingdoms. (Schafer, 1968) The victim gained nothing from the change in focus from the victim's rights being primary to an emphasis on the rights of the criminal.

The victim was powerless to prevent the erosion of his standing or to reactivate his claims to compensation. But as the victim lost his right to exact blood revenge, so too the criminal was unable to make peace with the victim or his kin. Crime became a public affair. In criminal matters, a crime was seen as an act against society as a whole as well as against the victim. But the victim was a distinct second in the process. The victim could neither kill the criminal nor could the criminal completely absolve his guilt through monetary compensation.

The crime victim was left with nothing. The king got it all. The criminal was punished as he would have been anyway, but perhaps even more severely because disputes among the victim, the victim's kin, and the criminal could no longer be settled through compensation or exile. That was no longer an option.

Leges Henrici

Between 1114 and 1118, a legal treatise that is known as ***Leges Henrici*** was written down by an unknown Norman under the reign of King Henry I of England. The *Leges Henrici* contain Anglo-Saxon and Norman laws formalizing that offenses were now crimes against the king or government. This was a distinct shift from allowing the victim, or the victim's family in the case of murder, to deal directly with the offender. These crimes, now considered a breach of the "king's peace," would result in a fine being paid to the king, an execution, or maiming. At first, the king, or the feudal barons, got only part of the compensation that would have gone to the victim or the victim's kin. But, as mentioned above, in time the rulers got all the money and the victim was left out in the cold up until the modern rebirth of the victim's rights, beginning in the 1960s.

Common law developed that made it impossible for the victim to receive restitution unless he had first done everything to make sure that the criminal was brought to justice. The crime of ***theftbote*** was even created making it a misdemeanor for the victim to retrieve his stolen goods or to make a deal with the criminal that would avoid the criminal's prosecution. (Laster, 1970: 71-98)

Furthermore, the previous adjustment of punishment to mirror the severity and type of injury to the victim was gradually replaced with a consideration of the personality of the criminal and the offender's chances to be rehabilitated. This approach further diminished any semblance of psychological recompense to the victim in the form of public vengeance for his wrong. What was left, by the twentieth century, was only the slim chance that the victim could bring a civil, or tort, action against the defendant, a rather inadequate and inefficient method of compensation because most criminals were ***judgment proof***, meaning that most criminals, whether or not they were incarcerated, lacked the funds to pay the victim if they were found guilty in a civil suit. Further reducing the likelihood of a civil suit as a successful recourse for crime victims was the large financial investment it might take for the victim to bring a lawsuit. In addition to legal fees, victims considering a civil suit had to consider the time lost from work and the possibility of losing one's job for that reason because of the numerous court appearances that a civil suit might require.

THE HISTORY OF CRIME VICTIMS IN THE UNITED STATES

Today's laws in the United States, on both the state and federal levels, are derived from **English common law**. Federal laws apply to everyone in all 50 states, while state laws apply just to that state. In essence, there are 51 legal systems in the United States: the federal laws and the fifty state laws, each state having its own laws. Occasionally there is agreement among all the states, such as in the passage of the National Minimum Drinking Law in 1984 when states raised the minimum drinking age to 21. Before that, the minimum drinking age varied from 18 to 21.

Law in the United States is based on English Law, Mosaic Law, Continental Law, and American Law. (Wormser, 1962)

Treatment of Criminals and Victims in Colonial Massachusetts

One of the earliest documents addressing acceptable behavior in Colonial America was the Massachusetts ***Body of Liberties*** developed in December 1641. The emphasis in the 98 sections is on curbing the power of elected representatives. It is important to remember that the early colonialists left England because they wanted to get out from under the absolute rule of the monarchy in England. Yet it is ironic that the early colonists, who had left England because they felt they were not being treated fairly by the government of England, seemed to create their own set of harsh rules in the New World. For example, Anne Hutchinson was tried and ordered banished for expressing her religious beliefs that were different from what the recognized ministers were preaching. Or consider how Roger Williams (1604-1684) had to flee Massachusetts because of his belief that church and state should be separated. He also made it known that he felt the lands had been unfairly taken from the Indians, another unpopular point of view. He was found guilty and received a sentence of banishment but instead left on his own, founding the colony of Rhode Island. (Wormser, 1962)

The 13 American colonies were based on English common law and on religious beliefs. Since there were initially no formal police departments it was not until 1838 in Boston that one was formally established—one in which victims had a primary role in righting any wrongs done to them. From 1640 to 1680, according to Elizabeth Pleck, the Puritans in colonial Massachusetts "enacted the first laws anywhere in the world against wife beating and 'unnatural severity' to children. A second reform epoch lasted from 1874 to about 1890, when societies for the prevention to cruelty to children (SPCCs) were founded, and smaller efforts on behalf of battered women and victims of incest were initiated." (Pleck, 1989: 19-20)

Maintaining social order was important in colonial America. One of the first buildings to be constructed in a new town in colonial America was "a house of detention" even when there were just 40 houses to the city. (Lynch, 2011) Debtors were the only ones held in confinement although it was soon realized that putting someone in prison for failure to pay a debt was counterproductive since they would be unable to work and earn the money to repay the victim. The building was mostly used not as a prison for someone convicted of a crime but for someone awaiting trial. (Cullen and Johnson, 2017)

By studying court records, Pleck discovered that imposing a fine was the way that the few recorded domestic assaults were punished. Between 1603 and 1802, according to the court records for Plymouth Colony, there were just 19 cases of wife or husband beating, incest, or a child assaulting a parent. It is interesting to note that Pleck discovered that victim blame, a concept whereby blame is put on the victim for directly or indirectly provoking the offender and that will be mentioned quite often in this textbook, came into play in cases of wife beating; "judges tended to inquire whether a wife provoked her husband into beating her." (Pleck, 1989: 26)

But the Puritans were certainly a group of dramatic contrasts. Pleck, as noted above, points out how they were innovators in enacting laws against wife beating and child abuse. But they are probably much better known for the infamous Salem witch hunts which resulted in hundreds of arrests and trials of alleged witches which led to at least 19 of those convicted getting hanged and one being "pressed to death." (Wormser, 1962)

According to Pleck, an important change occurred in the eighteenth century in colonial America that would impact what, if anything, was considered a crime that the community should address. In *Commentaries on the Laws of England*, initially published between 1765 and 1769, William Blackstone noted that private vices should not be controlled by the law. As Pleck states, "The family became a private institution, separated from public life" and the Puritans no longer concerned themselves with family violence. (Pleck, 1989: 28)

According to Lynch, offenses were dealt with in four main ways: fines, public shaming, physical chastisement, or the death penalty. In England, the number of capital crimes had risen from 50 in the late 1680s to more than 200 by 1776. Known now as the Bloody Codes in England these laws meant that something as relatively minor as stealing a handkerchief could lead to an execution, after the American Revolution, the number of offenses that could lead to the death penalty was severely reduced. Within a few years, murder was the only reason for capital punishment. (Lynch, 2011)

Exemplary Democratic Documents

The United States has been hailed as a model of democracy for the rest of the world, and many credit the ***Magna Carta*** (signed in 1215) as its model. It is said to have inspired such pivotal legal documents as the Declaration of Independence (1776), the Bill of Rights (1789), and the Constitution of the United States (1787) as well as the Declaration of the Rights of Man and the Citizen in France (1789). (Besa Arifi, 2015)

There are definitely concerns for the rights of the accused in those epic documents. The Fourth Amendment to the Constitution of the United States prohibits "unreasonable searches and seizures." Due process of law is covered by the Fifth and Fourteenth Amendments. The Fifth Amendment also grants the accused the right to avoid self-incrimination or to be tried twice for the same crime (double jeopardy). The right to a trial by jury in civil cases is protected by the Seventh Amendment. The right to a speedy trial and to a trial by an impartial jury are covered in the Sixth Amendment, as well as the right "to be confronted with the witnesses against him." Prohibiting the courts from imposing excessive bails or fines, or punishments that are "cruel and unusual" is prohibited, according to the Eighth Amendment.

However, there are no amendments directly applicable to the crime victim. That was left to the states to determine and enact. A crime victims' rights bill was enacted in 2004, known as the Crime Victims' Rights Act or Justice for All Act, but it only applies to federal criminal cases. (See Appendix II where that act is reprinted which is available at the publisher's website for this textbook, www.AspenPublishing.com.)

A Return to a Victim Justice System in Some Parts of the Wild West

The earliest settlers had to fend for themselves. Formal police departments did not emerge until the mid-1800s. In the Wild West, there was a return to the earliest types of victim justice systems but unfortunately it was too often done in a reckless way that in too many instances led to the deaths of innocent people who were victims rather than offenders. Two terms from those times are associated with lawlessness: **vigilantism** (the enforcement of laws by self-appointed people without any official legal authority) and **lynchings** (or hangings by a mob for alleged offenses).

The reason that bands of men (women were rarely part of these groups) in so-called **vigilante committees** took shape and were deemed necessary included the potential for stealing and murder caused by the discovery of gold including the California Gold Rush of 1849. An interesting essay by Gabriel Furshong, "Montana's Vigilante Obsession Obscures the Truth," published online in High County News, discusses his conflicted feelings about the glorification of vigilantism that he grew up with. They even had a Vigilante Day Parade in the 1980s and 1990s.

According to criminologist Andrew Karmen, lynchings grew out of public whippings in Virginia in the late 1700s. The escalation of these whippings to vigilance committees is attributed to a Colonel Lynch as the term became associated with the violent punishments that mobs carried out, usually by hanging. (Karmen, 2020).

Reflecting on the vigilantism of Montana from the vantage point of an enlightened adult, Furshong describes how, according to historian Frederick Allen, writing in his history, *A Descent, Orderly Lunching: The Montana Vigilantes,* over a six-year period, 50 men were killed. One of those men was Ah Chow, a Chinese immigrant who had killed someone although he said that his victim, John R. Bitzer, was the aggressor. (What you may already know, or what you will learn, criminologist Marvin Wolfgang would call "victim precipitated homicide" in his seminar work in 1957.)

Before Chow could prove his innocence at a trial, he was lynched. (Furshong, 2019)

Although we usually associate vigilantism with bygone days of the Wild West, in Iowa in the 1920s and 1930s, when an epidemic of bank robberies occurred, the Iowa Bankers Association (IBA) formed Vigilante Committees. According to Darcy Maulsby's research into this unique group, they "frequently engaged in gunfights with criminals. At one time, there were 4,303 vigilantes covering 881 banking towns in 84 Iowa counties." (Darcy Maulsby, 2020.)

This caption is provided by Darcy Maulsby, who reprinted this photo in her book, *Calhoun County*. "According to notes on the back of this photo, these are Calhoun County vigilantes. . . . They are standing near the Calhoun County, Iowa, courthouse. The photo appears to have been taken in the late 1920s or early 1930s. (Courtesy of Calhoun County Museum)"

Other than these dramatic and too often negative examples of victims or potential victims taking the law into their own hands, the pendulum had swung toward the criminal justice system and the rights of the criminal as protected by the various amendments to the Constitution. But beginning in the 1940s, and especially in the 1960s until the present day, that pendulum was going to swing again, back, at least partially, to the victim and victim's rights.

How Victims Became a Key Issue in the Twentieth Century

From the late 1880s into the early 1900s, the plight of the victim was mentioned at various interactional prison congresses including the Sixth International Penitentiary Congress held in Brussels in 1900. At that meeting, restitution to victims was discussed. However, nothing was successfully decided that would improve returning to the victim the right to compensation or direct involvement in the fate of the criminal, a right that had been taken away centuries before.

The Rise of the Victim's Rights Movement

America would be at the forefront of drawing attention to the mistreatment of children beginning in the late 1800s with the founding of the Society for the Prevention of Cruelty to Children. As discussed in greater detail in Chapter 3, "The Discipline of Victimology," it was in the late 1930s and in the 1940s that two key figures in the history of victimology would emerge to shine a spotlight on the victim. As noted in Chapter 1, "Victimology: An Overview," first it was lawyer Beniamin Mendelsohn, beginning in 1937, and then again in 1947, when he coined the term *victimology,* and, almost simultaneously, criminologist Hans von Hentig, whose article on the role of the victim in the crime, published in 1940 and followed by his seminal book, *The Criminal & His Victim*, published in 1948. By then, the shift back to the victim had started. We can date "The New Age for the Victim" from 1937 or 1940, but unfortunately, at least initially, as you will see in greater detail in Chapter 3, "The Discipline of Victimology," when the founders of victimology are discussed in detail, the shift was to the culpability of the victim in the commission of a crime.

There were other factors besides Nazism and World War II that led to the development of victimology and over the next several decades that led to "The New Age for the Victim." As discussed in Chapter 10, "Child Victims," beginning in the 1960s, America drew worldwide attention to child neglect and abuse. This was a crime that was previously figuratively shoved under the rug and considered a private, family matter.

Elizabeth Pleck in "Criminal Approaches to Family Violence, 1640-1980," published in *Crime and Justice*, points out that Stephen Pfohl attributes the awareness of the child abuse problem to the discovery of radiology in the 1950s. Radiology provided a way of seeing that a child had multiple injuries and might be a victim of abuse, which was brought to light by the medical journal article in 1962 on the battered child syndrome, co-authored by several pediatricians, most notably C. Henry Kempe. (Pleck, 1989. Pfohl, 1977)

The rights of children to be free of physical, sexual, or verbal abuse, or neglect, in the 1960s was joined by the Civil Rights Movement of the decade leading to an greater awareness about racial discrimination. The Civil Rights Act of 1964 was a turning point.

In terms of restoring financial compensation to crime victims, long ignored, was another issue that is part of the rediscovery of the crime victim. The impetus to crime victim compensation in modern times is credited to British prison reformer Margery Fry and her 1951 article, "Justice for Victims." Another reason that the 1960s are hailed as the beginning of the victims' rights movement is that concrete help for victims begins. For example, in the United States, California became the first state to offer a compensation program in 1964. Within a decade, 18 states had programs and soon every single state complied. During the 1960s, victim assistance programs were also established beginning with California and Missouri. (Boateng and Abess, 2017; Kyl, Twist, and Higgins, 2005.)

In addition to the dramatic and important step forward in the 1960s whereby those who were victimized could be granted compensation from the government if they applied for those funds, Dr. Stephen Schafer, discussed in detail in the next chapter, published his landmark book, *The Victim and His Criminal: A Study in Functional Responsibility.* This was the first major work in the field since von Hentig's book 20 years before.

The Victims' Movement Gains Momentum in the 1970s

It is probably not a coincidence that in the 1970s the victims' movement, also characterized by the strides of the women's movement, gained its momentum. Although Betty Friedan's bestseller, *The Feminine Mystique*, which became the bible of the women's movement, was published in 1963, and helped to get the movement going, it was in the 1970s that the women's movement really took off. Related to the advancement of a woman's right to work outside the home (Friedan, 1963; Kaufman, 1968) was the development of places outside the home or family that women could turn to if they were victims of domestic violence or rape. (Pizzey, 1974)

Picture of the Chiswick Women's Aid in England, the first shelter for victims of domestic violence, and their children

Erin Pizzey is credited with the founding of the first women's shelter, known as Chiswick Women's Aid, in 1971 in London, England. It was renamed the Refuge and still operates today, offering help to domestic violence victims and their families.

The organization Women's Advocates of St. Paul, Minnesota, dates its domestic violence shelter to 1972. Domestic violence shelters became a safe haven for those seeking help or protection from victimization even by their spouses.

That is the same year that rape crisis centers were started in such major cities as Washington, D.C., Boston, Philadelphia, and Berkeley, California, and Chicago. These centers offered free individual and group counseling.

In 1974, the National District Attorneys Association received a grant from the Office of Justice Programs (OJP). Those grants were provided to several major cities to create what became known as the Victim Witness Assistance Programs (VWAPs). The cities to initiate these much-needed programs to provide information and especially to help crime victims who might be witnesses in a case included New York City and Milwaukee, Wisconsin. Over the next few years, adding a VWAP program became standard in most district attorney offices.

A major step forward for rape victims occurred in 1976, when Nebraska became the first state in the United States to enact a law that made rape by a spouse a crime.

In 1978, Charlotte and Robert Hullinger co-founded Parents of Murdered Children (POMC) three months after the murder of their daughter Lisa by an ex-boyfriend. That same year, this author's book on victims of major violent and property crimes, *Victims*, was published by Scribner's to much attention. Beginning with an appearance on *The Today Show*, and interviewed by veteran journalist Edwin Newman, *Victims* seemed to rally the public and media to finally pay attention to the crime victim. That was a major shift from focusing on, and even often glorifying, the criminal. Most Americans knew the names of Bonnie and Clyde, who robbed banks in the 1930s and became the subject of a hit movie in 1967, or gangster Al Capone, or even Richard Speck, who had killed 13 nurses on July 14, 1966. But could they name even one of their victims? What about the victim? That was becoming a question that more and more people were asking even if they had not personally been the victim of a major crime. (Barkas, a/k/a Yager, 1978; Charlotte Hullinger, 2020; Robert Hullinger, 2020)

The following year, 1979, psychologist Morton Bard, a former police officer and CUNY professor, published his book, *The Crime Victim's Book*, co-authored with Dawn Sangrey. (Bard and Sangrey, 1979) Dr. Bard articulated the difference between crime victimization and other tragedies when he said, "The impact of a crime is far more devastating than a natural disaster like a tornado because it is a person doing this to you . . . In an instant, the crime creates a social world for you in which people are threatening, and you are no longer safe." (Pace, 1997)

The 1970s also saw the 1976 establishment of the National Organization of Victim Assistance (NOVA), which is still active today. John Dussich was a founding member and a co-founder in 1979 of the World Society of Victimology. (Dussich, n.d.)

Full Speed Ahead for the Victims' Movement from the 1980s Through Today

The 1980s began with Mothers Against Drunk Driving (MADD) starting up in 1980. It was initiated by the mother of 13-year-old Cari Lightner who was killed by a three-time repeat drunk driver. Cari's mother, Candace Lightner, through her nonprofit organization, MADD, has helped to raise consciousness about the dangers of driving under the influence, lobbied for stiffer penalties for those found guilty of driving drunk. MADD is credited with reducing the number of annual injuries and fatalities tied to drunk driving. (MADD, 2021; Reinarman, 1988)

In 1981, President Reagan brought attention to crime victims by declaring a week in April as National Crime Victims' Rights Week, a tradition that still continues today. The following year, President Reagan issued an Executive Order that asked for a Task Force on Victims of Crime.

Throughout the 1980s, all the way through today, victimology has continued to grow as a field, a topic explored in greater detail in the next chapter. For example, the victims' movement grew with the establishment in 1985 of another major research, educational, and advocacy association, the National Center for Victims of Crime. It was co-founded by Ala Isham and Alexander Auersperg, the children of Sunny von Bulow. As the website states, "Motivated by their mother's victimization and their family's traumatic experience with the criminal justice system." (Victimsofcrime.org)

Beginning in the 1990s, a new approach to victim-offender interaction known as **restorative justice** started to develop as an alternative to incarceration, in addition to confinement, as well as a way to help victims to heal. (Restorative justice is discussed in Chapter 5, "Victims and the Criminal Justice System.)

It was in 1994 that a federal law was passed that has come to be known as Megan's Law requiring that convicted sex offenders register in their state, even after release. As discussed in Chapter 10, "Child Victims," as well as in Chapter 12, "Sexual Violence: Rape, Sexual Abuse, Assault, and Harassment Victims," Megan's Law was motivated by the rape and murder of 7-year-old Megan Kanka in suburban New Jersey. It was suggested that Megan's death might have been prevented if her parents knew a convicted sex offender was living near Megan.

Parents of Murdered Children (POMC) founded in the 1970s, MADD founded in the 1980s as well as the National Resource Center and Clearinghouse on Missing & Exploited Children, started in 1984 through the efforts of Reve and John Walsh, whose son, Adam, had been abducted and killed, among others (missingkids.org), and Megan's Law, passed in 1994 with the rape and murder of Megan Kanka as the catalyst, are three of the many examples of the way that the victim movement has been shaped by families wanting to make changes or get help, because of the victimization they suffered, and addressed by the government.

VICTIMS' RIGHTS

In 1982, Congress passed the Victim and Witness Protection Act, following the steps that states had taken to provide witness protection, restitution, and fair treatment of victims of crimes being prosecuted by the state. However, this act would apply to federal victims and witnesses of violent crimes. Two years later, a most important legislative event occurred with the passage of VOCA, which stands for Victims of Crime Act. With the establishment of a Crime Victims Fund, it would now be possible to fund local victim assistance programs as well as state victim compensation programs with the money coming from federal criminal penalties, bond forfeitures, and criminal fines.

The National Crime Victim Law Institute points out that in the Supreme Court's 1991 decision *Payne v. Tennessee*, allowing victim impact statements at sentencing, the victims' rights movement gained enormous momentum. (Payne had been found guilty of two counts of first-degree murder and two counts of attempted murder in the stabbing deaths of his neighbor and her two-year-old daughter.) In addition to the right of a victim give a victim impact statement during the sentencing phase of a trial, victims were now seen as having these additional rights:

- The right to be present and heard at criminal justice proceedings
- The right to protection
- The right to financial recompense for losses suffered because of a crime
- The right to information (National Crime Victim Law Institute, "History of Victims' Rights")

In the 30 years since *Payne v. Tennessee*, the pendulum has definitely been swinging more in favor of victims and their rights at any time since the Middle Ages when the king first claimed the victim's share of the compensation from the offender and did not offer anything in return.

In Table 2.5, you will find a list of some of the U.S. Supreme Court decisions that had a positive impact on the protection or expansion of the rights of the crime victim. Each decision is noted as an expansion or protection of victims' rights or the opposite.

TABLE 2.5. Supreme Court Decisions Impacting the Rights of the Crime Victim

Year	Case	Decision	Impact on Victims
1987	*Booth v. Maryland*	Not okay to use victim impact statements in capital cases	Not positive for victims
1990	*Pennsylvania Dept. of Public Welfare v. Davenport*	Offenders could get out of paying restitution to victims	Did not advance victim rights
1990	*Maryland v. Craig*	Child abuse victims could testify via closed circuit TV	Positive for victim rights
1991	*Payne v. Tennessee*	(Basically overturned *Booth v. Maryland*) Victim Impact Statements could be allowed at sentencing	Positive for victim rights
1991	*Simon & Schuster v. New York Crime Victims Board*	Struck down the so-called "Son of Sam"* Law, thereby making it difficult for victims to claim earnings from criminals because of their crimes	Did not advance victim rights
2001	*TRW v. Andrews*	Victims of identity theft could not get extra time to sue credit bureaus	Did not advance victim rights
2000	*United States v. Morrison*	Victims of rape and domestic violence could not sue their attackers in federal court	Did not advance victim rights
2005	*Gonzales v. Castle Rock Police*	Case was brought by Gonzalez, whose 3 daughters were murdered by her husband. Victims could not sue police department for failing to enforce an order of protection	Did not advance victim rights
2006	*Davis v. Washington*	The hearsay statements in a 911 emergency call could be used as evidence if the caller is unable to testify at trial	Positive for victim rights
2008	*District of Columbia et al. v. Heller*	The Second Amendment protects an individual's right to have a gun in their home	Positive for victim rights
2011	*Michigan v. Bryant*	A jury can hear a victim's dying words	Positive for victim rights
2013	*Maryland v. King*	Police can collect DNA from those who are arrested and use DNA to solve crimes	Positive for victim rights

*Son of Sam was a notorious serial killer who in the 1970s terrorized New York City. The original Son of Sam law was to prevent the criminal from profiting from any books or movies that he or she wrote or allowed to have written based on their crimes.

You will also find a list of no fewer than 33 key federal victims' rights legislation beginning in 1974 with the Child Abuse Prevention and Treatment Act up through the 2016 Native American Children's Safety Act. The three acts that are considered most monumental in advancing the rights of victims are the 1984 Victims of Crime Act, also known as VOCA, the 1994 Violence Against Women Act, also known as VAWA, and the 2004 Justice for All Act. It has indeed become the golden age for victims as victimology has advanced and so have the rights of victims. But there is more work to be done. What once was a victim justice system, that became a criminal justice system, now needs to become a justice system for all. Table 2.6 summarizes the key federal victims' rights legislation by year and title of the act.

TABLE 2.6. Key Federal Victims' Rights Legislation

Year	Title of the Act
1974	Child Abuse Prevention and Treatment Act
1980	Parental Kidnapping Prevention Act
1982	Victim and Witness Protection Act
1982	Missing Children's Act
1984	Victims of Crime Act
1984	Justice Assistance Act
1984	Missing Children's Assistance Act
1984	Family Violence Prevention and Services Act
1985	Children's Justice Act
1988	Drunk Driving Prevention Act
1990	Hate Crime Statistics Act
1990	Victims of Child Abuse Act
1990	Victims' Rights and Restitution Act
1990	National Child Search Assistance Act
1992	Battered Women's Testimony Act
1993	Child Sexual Abuse Registry Act
1994	Violent Crime Control and Law Enforcement Act
1994	Violence Against Women Act
1996	Community Notification Act (Megan's Law)
1996	Mandatory Victims' Restitution Act
1997	Victims' Rights Clarification Act
1998	Identity Theft and Deterrence Act
2000	Trafficking Victims Protection Act
2001	Air Transportation Safety and System Stabilization Act (established after September 11 Victim Compensation Fund)
2003	PROTECT Act (Amber Alert Law)
2003	Prison Rape Elimination Act
2003	Fair and Accurate Credit Transactions Act
2004	Justice for All Act (including Title I: The Scott Campbell, Stephanie Roper, Wendy Preston, Louarna Gillis, and Nila Lynn Crime Victims' Rights Act)

TABLE 2.6. Continued

Year	Title of the Act
2006	Adam Walsh Child Protection and Safety Act
2010	Tribal Law and Order Act
2015	Justice for Victims of Trafficking Act
2016	Native American Children's Safety Act

Source: 2020 NCVRW (National Crime Victims Rights Week) Research Guide.

In reviewing the 1976 article by William F. McDonald, sociologist and Research Director of the Institute of Criminal Law and Procedure at Georgetown University, "Towards a Bicentennial Revolution in Criminal Justice: The Return of the Victim," it is clear just how far the victims' movement has evolved since that article was published. McDonald notes that his research led him to conclude that it was the rise of the office of public prosecutor that led to the diminishing of the victims' role. According to McDonald, the first public prosecutor office was established by **statute** in Connecticut in 1704. (McDonald, 1976) Declaring it difficult to trace the history of the victim's role in criminal case prosecutions from 1810 to 1976, he chose to focus on the current state of victims' rights in criminal cases in 1976. Of course this is now a historical description but it is definitely worth reprinting because it emphasizes how far we have come in these past four decades:

> Today [1976], in the opinion of many commentators, both victims and witnesses of crimes receive from public prosecutors what has been called the "administrative runaround." Both are required to make numerous trips to the courthouse to tell and retell their stories to a series of prosecutors responsible for different stages of the case, and often to sit for prolonged periods of time in dirty waiting rooms or corridors, frequently with the defendant nearby. Witness fees are generally inadequate to cover actual expenses, much less to compensate for the emotional stress. In many jurisdictions they are not paid at all. (McDonald, 1976)

Just how far the victims' rights movement has gone at the federal and state level is highlighted by the passage in many states of what is known as "Marsy's Law." Marsy's Law was named after Marsalee (Marsy) Nicholas. In 1983, she was stalked and killed by her ex-boyfriend. Marsy was a student at University of California, Santa Barbara at the time of her tragic death.

According to the website for Marsy's Law for North Carolina, a week after Marsy's murder, Marsy's mother, Mrs. Marcella Leach, after visiting her daughter's grave, walked into a grocery store where she found herself face to face with her daughter's accused killer. Marsy's mother had not been informed that he had been released on bail. That experience led to the drafting of what became known as Marsy's Law. It was passed on November 4, 2008, in the state of California. Since that time, it has been passed in Illinois, North Dakota, South Dakota, Ohio, Florida, Nevada, Georgia, North Carolina, Oklahoma, Kentucky, Wisconsin, and Pennsylvania.

Here is a list of the rights that Florida's Marsy's Law, passed in November 2018, guarantees for victims:

A. The Right to Notice of Case Proceedings
B. The Right to Attend Court Hearings
C. The Right to Be Heard at Relevant Proceedings
D. The Right to Proceedings Free from Unreasonable Delay
E. The Right to Reasonable Protection and Other Safety-Related Provisions
F. The Right to Protection of Privacy and Dignity
G. The Right to Restitution
H. The "Victim" Definition Problem
I. Implementation and Enforcement Provisions (Cassell and Gravin, 2020)

Especially important is Florida's definition of *victim*, which is "H" in the guarantees for victims. If not for this definition in the state's constitution, courts or the legislature could decide just who is a victim. Here is what the Amendment says in that regard: "[a] used in this section, a 'victim' is a person who suffers direct or threatened physical, psychological, or financial harm as a result of the commission or attempted commission of a crime or delinquent act or against whom the crime or delinquent act is committed." (Cassell and Gravin, 2020) The co-authors point out that "the Amendment makes clear that '[t]he term 'victim' does not include the accused.'" (Casell and Gravin, 2020)

The last provision, "Implementation and Enforcement Provisions" guarantees that the new rights are in "automatic legal effect without the need for any subsequent action by the Florida Legislature." It also guarantees that victims will receive information about their rights. (Cassell and Gravin, 2020)

Hopefully the rest of the states in the United States will follow the lead of Florida and the other 12 states and enact their own Marsy's Law. There has long been a discussion about adding such an Amendment to the U.S. Constitution. That would be a huge achievement but at least there is the VOCA act and the Crime Victims' Rights Act (CVRA) establishing crime victim rights in federal cases, and the subsequent federal acts advancing victims' rights as well as the trend toward guaranteeing more victim rights at the state level.

SUMMARY

There was a time when victims could solve their disputes directly with the criminal, including getting compensation. That was more common before written law. Two primitive cultures—the Inuit and the Comanches—are described as a way of looking at the contrasting treatment of the victim in those societies. What distinguishes those cultures is the ability of the victim to work things out directly with the offender, or through a mediator, with compensation or exile as an alternative to the death penalty or injury.

In this chapter, there is also a discussion about how the victim was compensated during Ancient Greece and Rome, and in the Laws of Manu, for violent or property crimes. The term *wergild*, also known as blood money, refers to the compensation that the offender gave to the victim for violent or property crimes or, in the case of homicide, to the victim's family. Then, beginning in the Middle Ages, and the transfer of power to the king, some of the compensation that went to the victim was now given to the king instead.

Eventually, the king got all the money that would have gone to the victim. The term *theftbote* describes how it even became a misdemeanor to try to retrieve your stolen goods and work out a private compensation settlement with the criminal so he could avoid prosecution.

This chapter also discusses how the rights of the victim were treated in Colonial America. Citing the extensive research of Elizabeth Pleck, you learned that the Puritans, strict in some ways, were actually quite innovative in that they were the first to make wife beating a crime as well as child abuse. How widely any males or parents were punished for violating those laws is questionable, but they were ahead of their time in calling attention to those social issues.

In the mid to late 1800s, around the time that there began a movement to found an association for the prevention of cruelty to animals, a similar association was founded to deal with children who were being abused at home.

But it was not until the 1960s, alongside the Civil Rights Movement and the women's movement of the 1960s and 1970s that the rights of crime victims begin to be addressed after an almost 1,000-year hiatus. President Ronald Reagan declared the first National Crime Victims' Week in 1981.

The chapter also discussed the groundbreaking federal legislation and U.S. Supreme Court decisions highlighting the rights of a victim. One of the many notable rights granted was *Payne V. Maryland* (1991) which granted the right of a victim to provide a Victim Impact Statement at sentencing. (In Appendices, posted at the publisher's website www.AspenPublishing.com, see the blank Victim Impact Statement provided by the U.S. Department of Justice of the U.S. government related to financial crime victimization.)

Although many rights of the accused are protected in Amendments to the U.S. Constitution, an Amendment protecting victims' rights has not yet been passed. But the Crime Victims' Rights Act (CVRA) is a key federal legislation granting crime victim rights in federal criminal cases. Progress has also been made in having states pass legislation covering nine basic victim rights including the right to get notified about case proceedings. This effort is known as Marsy's Law and it came about after Marsalee (Marsy) Nicholas, a student at the University of California, Santa Barbara, was stalked and murdered by her ex-boyfriend in 1983. Her brother and her mother started an advocacy group known as Marsy's Law for Us All. California was the first to enact Marsy's Law in 2008. As of November 2018, 11 additional states had enacted it. The list of rights that Marsy's Law guarantees to the victim, passed as a statute in Florida, were noted earlier in this chapter and include the right to be told about court proceedings and the right to receive restitution, among others.

KEY TERMS

B.C.E. (Before Common Era)
blood feud
blood money
Body of Liberties
Bot
caste
Code of Daco
Code of Hammurabi
Code of Ur-Nammu
collective responsibility
Colonel Lynch
Comanches

Corpus Juris Civilis
crime
criminal justice system
criminal law
cybercrime
death penalty
deviance
ethnography
felony
Friedensgeld
gewedde
go-between
honor killings
infanticide
Inuit
invalidicide
judgment proof
kin
Laws of Manu
Leges Henrici
levirate
lex talionis
lynching
Magna Carta
mala in se
mala prohibita
mediator
misdemeanor
Mosaic Code
New Age for the Victim
primitive culture
private law
public law
restorative justice
restitution
senilicide
state and federal constitutions
statute
theftbote
Treaty of Verdun
Twelve Tables
victim justice system
Victims of Crimes Act (VOCA)
vigilante committees
vigilantism
wer
wergild or *wergeld*
Wite

REVIEW QUESTIONS

1. What do the Inuit and the Comanches have in common when it comes to how they view and treat the victim of a crime?
2. What is the famous phrase associated with the rights of the victim and the Code of Hammurabi?
3. What is the *wergild*?
4. Who started taking some and eventually all the monies due the victim for the wergild?
5. What were some of the innovative pro-victim laws that were passed by the Pilgrims of Massachusetts in the seventeenth century?
6. Who attributed the unique position of the prosecutor as the reason that the victims' rights were so eroded from colonial times until the victims' movement of the 1960s and 1970s?
7. How does the vigilantism of the Wild West in the United States differ from the rights of victims or a victim's family to work things out with the accused?
8. What are some of the movements that contributed to "The New Age for the Victim"?
9. Name one U.S. Supreme Court ruling that advanced victim's rights between 1987 and 2013.
10. Name one U.S. Supreme Court ruling that was not positive for victim's rights.

CRITICAL THINKING QUESTIONS

1. Do you think exile or banishment would work as a contemporary option for convicted offenders instead of prison? If yes, what kinds of crimes would you apply it to? How would you enforce it?
2. Today some sentences, particularly for property or economic crime offenses, do include restitution to the victim as a mandated part of the sentence or punishment. Should that be an option instead of prison even for violent crimes including murder? Why? Why not?
3. The phrase "The New Age for the Victim" is used to describe what happened beginning in 1937 and in the 1940s with the founding of victimology. Do you agree that the rights of victims to be directly involved in the outcome of their criminal case as well as to be compensated had been ignored for centuries? Why? Why not?

ACTIVITIES

1. In this chapter you learned about severael different associations or movements that led to a change in the laws that were started because the founders experienced a tragedy related to crime including MADD, Parents of Murdered Children, Megan's Law, and Marsy's Law. Do research on the internet by using a search engine like Google, Google Scholar, or Bing, and explore at least one other association or law related to victims whose founded organization was motivated by a crime-related tragedy. What year was it founded? What was the crime that inspired the founder's activism? What are the advantages and challenges of founding an association, or drawing up new legislation, when the impetus was a personal one?
2. Pick one topic from this chapter and find a scholarly article or a book published by an academic or well-recognized popular book publisher. Read the article, or at least several chapters in the book, and summarize how it furthers your understanding of that particular topic in this chapter.

RESOURCES

MADD (Mothers Against Drunk Driving)
madd.org
A role model of how one mother, whose daughter was tragically killed by a drunk driver, turned her grief into a campaign to draw attention to the drunk driving problem that has helped to save countless lives. Cari Lightner was just 13 when she was hit and killed. Her mother, Candace Lightner, founded MADD. (She now has her own website (www.candacelightner.com) and does speaking and consulting on activism.) The mission of MADD, which continues, is still to increase awareness about the hazards of driving impaired.

Marsy's Law for All
marsyslaw.us
Like the founder of MAAD, it was tragedy that was the catalyst to the development of Marsy's Law, a plan to get states to adopt a bill of rights for crime victims. Marsy's brother, Dr. Henry T. Nicholas III, co-founded Marsy's Law for All with Marsy's mother.

National Association of Crime Victims Compensation Boards (NACVCB)
nacvcb.org
This membership association has a directory that links to the state crime victim compensation boards. Those who work for state crime victim compensation boards are its members.

National Crime Victim Law Institute (NCVLI)
law.lclark.edu/centers/national_crime_victim_law_institute
This nonprofit legal education and advocacy organization is housed at Lewis & Clark Law School in Portland, Oregon.

National Organization of Victim Assistance (NOVA)
trynova.org
Founded in 1976, NOVA offers educational programs including credentialing and victim advocacy. There is an annual conference usually held in August.

CITED WORKS AND ADDITIONAL REFERENCES

Abbott, Geoffrey and Gloria Lotha and editors of *Encyclopedia Britannica.* August 9, 2007. "Exile and punishment." Posted at Britannica.com.

Adler, Freda, Gerhard O.W. Mueller, and William S. Laufer. 2007. *Criminology and the Criminal Justice System.* Sixth Edition. New York: McGraw-Hill.

Allen, Danielle S. March 23, 2003 "Punishment in Ancient Athens" in Adrienne Lanni (ed.). "Athenian Law in Its Democratic Context." Posted at stoa.org.

Allitt, Patrick N. December 1, 2017. "Vigilante Justice in the American Wild West." *The Great Courses Daily.* Posted at thegreatcoursesdaily.com

Arifi, Besa. 2015. "Relevance of Magna Carta to Rights of Victims of Abuse of Power." *SEEU (South East European University) Review.* Vol. 11, Issue 1.

Baker, David V. December 2007. "American Indian Executions in Historical Context." *Criminal Justice Studies.* 20: 315-373.

Balikci, Asen. 1970. *The Netsilik Eskimo.* Garden City, NY: Natural History Press.

Bard, Morton and Dawn Sangrey. 1979. *The Crime Victim's Book.* New York: Basic Books.

Barkas, J.L. *See also* Jan Yager.

Barkas, J.L (a/k/a Jan Yager). 1978. *Victims.* New York: Scribner. 2021. Stamford, CT: Hannacroix Creek Books, Inc.; updated bibliography and resources, new introduction and cover.

____________. "What About the Victims" 1979. *Journal of Current Social Issues.* 27-33.

Barksdale, Nate. June 15, 2014, updated July 1, 2019. "6 Things You May Not Know About Magna Carta." History.com.

Barton, R.F. February 13, 1919. "Ifugao Law." *American Archaeology and Ethnology.*Vol.15, No. 1.

Basham, A.L. 1954. *The Wonder That Was India.* New York: Grove.

Boas, Franz. 1988, 1964. *The Central Eskimo.* Lincoln, Nebraska: University of Nebraska Press.

Boateng, Francis D. and Gassan Abess. 2017. "Victims' Role in the Criminal Justice System: A Statutory analysis of Victims' Rights in U.S." *International Journal of Police Science & Management* 19: 221-228.

Brown, Robert A. 2019. "Policing in American History." *DuBois Review.* 16: 189-195.

Brown, Ryan P. August 11, 2016. "How to Understand Honor Killings." *Psychology Today.* Posted at psychologytoday.com.

Carrington, Frank. 1975. *The Victims.* New Rochelle, NY: Arlington House.

Cartwright, Mark. April 24, 2018. "Corpus Juris Civilis." *Ancient History Encyclopedia.* Posted online.

____________. "Twelve Tables." April 11, 2016. *Ancient History Encyclopedia.* Posted online at https://www.ancient.eu/Twelve_Tables/.

Cassell, Paul G. and Margaret Garvin. Spring 2020. "Protecting Crime Victims in State Constitutions: The Example of The New Marsy's Law for Florida." *Journal of Criminal Law and Criminology.* 110: 99-139.

Cassell, Paul G., Nathanael J. Mitchell, and Bradley J. Edwards. Winter 2014 "Crime Victims' Rights During Criminal Investigations? Applying the Crime Victims' Rights Act Before Criminal Charges are Filed." *Journal of Criminal Law and Criminology.* 104: 59-104.

Chavez, Holly. n.d. "Not Eskimos: Ten Enlightening Facts About the Inuit." Blog. Posted at oceanwide-expeditations.com

Chouhy, Cecilia. August 2018. "Moving Beyond Punitive Interventions: Public Support for Government-Funded Victim Compensation for White-Collar Crime Victims." *Criminology & Public Policy.* 17: 547-551.

Cicero. 1975. *Murder Trials.* Translated by Michael Grant. Harmondsworth, Middlesex, England: Penguin

Comanchenatin.com. n.d. "About Us." Posted at comanchenation.com

Cullen, Francis J. and Cheryl Jonson. 2017. *Correctional Theory.* Second edition. Thousand Oaks, CA: SAGE.

Cuomo, Mario M. Fall 1992. "The Crime Victim in a System of Criminal Justice." *Journal of Civil Rights and Economic Development* 8: 1-20.

Daigle, Leah E. and Lisa R. Muftic. 2016. *Victimology.* Los Angeles: SAGE.

Dingledy, Frederick W. 2016. *The Corpus Juris Civilis: A Guide to Its History and Use. College of William & Mary Law School*, Library Staff Publications.

Farber, Peter. 1968. *Man's Rise to Civilization as Shown by the Indians of North America from Primeval Times to the Coming of the Industrial State.* New York: Dutton

Fehrenbach, T.R. 1974. *Comanches.* New York: Random House.

__________. November 7, 1975. Personal communication.

FindLaw. January 23, 2019. "Burglary Sentencing and Penalties.". Posted at criminal.findlaw.com

__________. March 14, 2019. "Robbery Sentencing and Penalties." Posted at Criminal.findlaw.com

Fortes, M. and E.E. Evans-Pritchard (eds.). 1940. *African Political Systems.* London: Oxford University Press.

Freeman, Kathleen. 1963. *The Murder of Herodes: And Other Trials from the Athenian Law Courts.* New York: Norton.

Freuchen, Peter. 1961. *Book of the Eskimos.* New York: Fawcett.

Friedan, Betty. 1963. *The Feminine Mystique.* New York: Norton.

Furshong, Gabriel. May 29, 2019. "Montana's Vigilante Obsession Obscures the Truth." *High Country News.* Posted at hcn.org.

Gagarin, Michael. March 27, 2003. "Athenian Homicide Law: Case Studies. Posted at stoa.org

Gelo, Daniel J. May 23, 2018. "Comanche." Posted online at Encyclopedia.com

Greensite, Gillian. November 1, 2009. "History of the Rape Crisis Movement." Posted at CALCASA (California Coalition Against Sexual Assault).

Hammurabi, King. Hammurabi Code. Translated by L.W. King. The Avalon Project, Yale Law School Lillian Goldman Law Library. Posted online at avalon.law.yale.edu

Harrington, L.H. (Chair). 1982. *President's Task Force on Victims of Crime: Final Report.* Washington, D.C.: U.S. Government Printing Office.

Hazeltine, H.D. January 1917. "The Influence of Magna Carta on American Constitutional Development." *Columbia Law Review*, Vol. 17, No. 1: 1-33.

Hodge, Frederick Webb (ed.). 1971. *Handbook of American Indians North of Mexico.* Part One. New York: Rowman and Littlefield.

Hoebel, E. Adamson. 1954. *The Law of Primitive Man: A Study in Comparative Legal Dynamics.* Cambridge, MA: Harvard University Press.

__________. March-April 1941. "Law-Ways of the Primitive Eskimos." *Journal of Criminal Law and Criminology.* 31: 663-683.

__________.1940. *The Political Organization and Law-Ways of The Comanche Indians.* Menasha, WI: American Anthropological Association.

Hullinger, Charlotte. December 30, 2020. Personal communication.

__________. January 7, 2021. Phone interview with the author.

Hullinger, Robert. January 7, 2021. Phone interview with the author.

Jarrell, Melissa L. and Joshua Ozymy. 2012. "Real Crime, Real Victims: Environmental Crime Victims and the Crime Victims' Rights Act (CVRA)." *Crime Law and Social Change.* 58: 373-389.

Jenkins, Owen B. May-June 1905. "The Code of Hammurabi and American Law." *The American Law Review.* Vol. XXXIX.

Johnson, Kirk. May 30, 1987. "Goetz Case Jury Takes Short Trip On the Subway." *New York Times.*

Jones, Alexander (ed.).1973. *The Old Testament of the Jerusalem Bible.* Reader's Edition. Vol. 1. Genese-Ruth. Garden City, NY: Doubleday and Company.

Kajubi, W. Senteza, L.J. Lewis, and C.O. Taiwo (eds.). 1974. *African Encyclopedia.* London: Oxford University Press.

Kaufman, Sue. 1968. *Diary of a Mad Housewife.* New York: Bantam Books.

Kennedy, Merrit. October 6, 2016. "Pakistan Toughens Penalties for 'Honor' Killings." National Public Radio. Posted at npr.org.

Laster, Richard E. 1970. "Criminal Restitution: A Survey of Its Past History and an Analysis of Its Present Usefulness." *University of Richmond Law Review.* Vol. 5.

The Laws of Manu. 1969. Translated by George Buhler. New York: Dover Publications.

Lawson, F.H. 1973. "Roman Law" in *Western Civilization: Recent Interpretations.* Charles D. Hamilton (ed.). New York: Crowell.

Loukacheva. Natalia. February 2012. "Indigenous Inuit Law, 'Western' Law and Northern Issues." *Arctic Review on Law and Politics.* 3: 200–217.

Lynch, Jack. Summer 2011. "Cruel and Unusual: Prisons and Prison Reform." *CW (Colonial Williamsburg) Journal.* Posted online.

MacLeod, William Christie. July-August 1937. "Police and Punishment Among Native Americans of the Plains." *Journal of Criminal Law and Criminology.* 28: 181-201.

Maine, Sir Henry. 1883. *Dissertations on Early Law and Custom.* New York: Henry Holt.

Mark, Joshua. June 16, 2014. "Ur-Nammu." *Ancient™ History Encyclopedia.* Posted at www.ancient.eu

Marsy's Story. 2021. FAQ. Posted at www.marsyslawfornc.com

Maulsby, Darcy. Dougherty. 2015. *Calhoun County.* Charleston, SC: Arcadia Publishing.

__________ June 4, 2020. "Iowa's Vigilante Crime Fighters of the 1920s and 1930s." Blog post at darcymaulsby .com

McDonald, William F. 1976. "Towards a Bicentennial Revolution in Criminal Justice: The Return of the Victim." *The American Criminal Law Review.* 13: 649-673.

Meany, Paul. August 31, 2018. "Cicero's Natural Law and Political Philosophy." Posted at libertarianism .org

Miller, Wilbur R. 2012. *The Social History of Crime and Punishment in America: An Encyclopedia.* "Victim Rights and Restitution." Thousand Oaks, CA: SAGE.

Mince-Didier, Ave. "Incest Laws and Criminal Charges." Criminal Defense Lawyer. Posted at criminaldefenselawyer.com.

Mowat, Farley. March 1, 1952. "They Sometimes Murder But Never Steal." *Maclean's.*

Naegele, Charles J. "History and Influence of Law Code of Manu." Theses and Dissertations, Golden Gate University School of Law, GGU Law Digital Commons, 2008.

National Association of Crime Victim Compensation Boards, "Crime Victim Compensation: An Overview." Posted at nacvcb.org/

National Center for Missing & Exploited Children. n.d. "Our Beginnings." Posted at www.missingkids.org.

Office for Victims of Crime. July 1999. U.S. Department of Justice. "OVC Fact Sheet."

Pace, Eric. December 14, 1997. "Morton Bard, 73, Authority on Crime Victims." *New York Times.* posted at nytimes.com

Pfohl, Stephen. 1977. "The Discovery of Child Abuse." *Social Problems.* 24: 310-321.

Pizzey, Erin. 1979. *Scream Quietly or the Neighbors Will Hear.* New York: Penguin.

Pleck, Elizabeth. 1989. "Criminal Approaches to Family Violence, 1640-1980." *Crime and Justice.* 11:19-57.

Pritchard, James B. (ed.). 1973, 1958. *The Ancient Near East Vol. 1: An Anthology of Texts and Pictures.* Princeton, New Jersey: Princeton University Press.

Refuge. Homepage. "History." refuge.org.uk

Reid, Sue Titus. 2018. *Crime and Criminology.* Fifteenth Edition. New York: Wolters Kluwer.

Reinarman, Craig. January 1988. "The Social Construction of an Alcohol Problem: The Case of Mothers against Drunk Drivers and Social Control in the 1980s." *Theory and Society.* 17: 91-120.

Ruane, Janet M. December 2017. "Re (searching) the Truth About Our Criminal Justice System: Some Challenges." *Sociological Forum.* 31: 1127-1139.

Schafer, Stephen. 1960. *Restitution to Victims of Crime.* London: Stevens and Sons.

Schafer, Stephen. 1968. *The Victim and His Criminal.* New York: Random House.

Stefansson, V. 1913. *My Life with the Eskimos.* New York: Macmillan Company.

Turvey, Brent E. 2014. *Forensic Victimology: Examining Violent Crimes in Investigative and Legal Contexts.* Second edition. Waltham, MA: Academic Press, an imprint of Elsevier.

U.S. Constitution. Posted at senate.gov

U.S. Department of Justice, Office of Victims of Crime. 2020. *2020 NCVRW (National Crime Victims Rights Week) Research Guide.*

Wallace, Ernest and E. Adamson Hoebel. 1952, 1987. *The Comanches.* Berkeley, CA: University of California Press, reprint.

Wallace, Harvey and Cliff Roberson. 2019. *Victimology.* 5th edition. New York: Pearson.

Weiden, David Heska Wanbli. July 19, 2020. "This 19th-Century Law Helps Shape Criminal Justice in Indian Country." Opinion. *The New York Times.* Posted at www.nytimes.com

Wormser, Rene A. 1962. *The Story of the Law and the Men Who Made It—From the Earliest Times to the Present.* Revised. New York. Simon and Schuster.

Yager, Jan. 2021. *Help Yourself Now.* New York: Allworth Press, an imprint of Skyhorse Publishing.

__________. *Victims.* 2021. With a new introduction and updated statistics, bibliography, and resources. Stamford, CT: Hannacroix Creek Books, Inc. (First edition published in 1978 by Scribner's under the name J.L. Barkas)

_____________. (a/k/a J.L. Barkas). 1977. "Victims of Crime and Social Change." Master's Thesis. Goddard College Graduate Program in Criminal Justice. Thesis advisor: Dr. Arthur Niederhoffer, Sociology Professor, John Jay College of Criminal Justice.

Young, Marlene, and John Stein. December 2004. "The History of the Crime Victims' Movement in the United States." A Component of the Office for Victims of Crime Oral History Project. Sponsored by the Office for Victims of Crime, Office of Justice Programs, U.S. Department of Justice. Posted at ncjrs.gov

Videos, Films, Documentaries, and Podcasts

Office of Victims of Crime. March 20, 2016. "What is the Crime Victims Fund?" 2:33 minutes. Short video developed by the OVC to explain the Crime Victim Fund. https://www.youtube.com/watch?v=0sWgbUigNIE

Denver District Attorneys Office. February 22, 2010 "A Brief History of the Victims' Rights Movement." Part 1. Written and produced by Joshua Thurmond.5:47 minutes Posted at https://www.youtube.com/watch?v=o5zsnL1cWgc

Chapter **THREE**

The Discipline of Victimology

Founders, Theories, and Controversies

Learning Objectives

After you finish reading this chapter, you should be able to:

1. Identity the early founders of victimology, including Mendelsohn and von Hentig, and discuss their victim typologies.
2. Identify and explain the research of criminologist Marvin Wolfgang and how it led to his controversial victim-precipitation theory of homicide.
3. Identify and explain Routine Activity Theory (RAT).
4. Describe Lifestyle Theory.
5. Explain Deviant Place Theory and how it applies to victimology.
6. Discuss the application of Edwin Sutherland's learned theory of criminal behavior to victim behavior and how this might relate to repeat victimization.
7. Examine the need for a multidisciplined approach to theories of crime victimization.
8. Define and describe some of the key controversies around the concepts of *victim blame, victim facilitation, victim precipitation, repeat victimization, system blaming,* and the *just world hypothesis.*

EARLIEST ROOTS OF VICTIMOLOGY

In Chapter 1, "Victimology: An Overview," we addressed a definition of **victimology** and mentioned its "father" Beniamin Mendelsohn, who is discussed in greater detail below. The discipline actually has much older roots. Italian jurist and philosopher Cesare Beccaria (1738-1794), whose treatise *On Crimes and Punishments*, initially published anonymously in 1764, focused on crimes and their punishment. However, it does include a few paragraphs related to the victim even though the emphasis in the treatise is on the offender. In section XX, "The Certainty of Punishment, Mercy," for example, Beccaria reinforces that the victim lost the right to intervene in criminal matters. Beccaria writes: "The right to inflict punishment is a right not of an individual, but of all citizens, or of their sovereign. . . ." (Beccaria, 1764, 1963 reprint: 58). (The evolution of a victim justice system to a criminal justice one, with the state being seen as the wronged party, was discussed in Chapter 2, "An Anthropological and Historical View of Crime Victims and Victims' Rights.")

Becarria's treatise was a *tour de force* for the rights of the criminal, including his denouncement of torture, capital punishment, and, most famous of all, the concept that the punishment should fit the crime. In advocating for better and more humane treatment of the offender he was, in fact, trying to reverse the extreme mistreatment of offenders all too common in those days, inhumane behavior that too often blurred the line between offender and victim.

Addressing victims as a separate issue, however, the rare times that Beccaria does mention the victim of a crime, it is to emphasize that he is truly the odd man out in the crime and punishment scenario. Note that the title of Beccaria's treatise even reinforced that: *On Crimes and Punishments*, not "On Crimes, Victims, and Punishments." (Beccaria, 1764, 1963)

Expanding on the above quote from Beccaria he wrote, "Sometimes a man is freed from punishment for a lesser crime when the offended party chooses to forgive—an act in accord with beneficence and humanity, but contrary to the public good—as if a private citizen, by an act of remission, could eliminate the need for an example, in the same way that he can waive compensation for the injury. The right to inflict punishment is a right not of an individual, but of all citizens, or of their sovereign." (Beccaria, 1764, 1963: 58) Beccaria seemed to be saying that if a victim does allow a criminal to escape punishment, that is a bad thing. Only all citizens or their sovereign ruler should have the power to do that. (Beccaria, 1764, 1963: 58)

Criminologist Dr. Stephen Schafer, in his influential 1968 book, *The Victim and His Criminal*, points out that the "holy three of criminology"—Lombroso (1835-1909), Garofalo (1851-1934), and Ferri (1856-1929)—mentioned the victim. As Schafer writes:

> Cesare Lombroso, in admitting to factors other than atavistic biological degeneration, considered that there were passionate criminals who acted under the pressure of victim-provoked emotions. Raffaele Garofalo called attention to victim behaviors that could be regarded as provoking the offender to criminal action. Enrico Ferri, in a somewhat indirect reference, mentioned those 'pseudo-criminals' who violate the law because of the 'inevitable necessity' of self-defense. (Schafer, 1968:3)

As mentioned in Chapter 1, "Victimology: An Overview," criminologist/sociologist Edwin Sutherland included a chapter on victims, chapter 3, "The Victims of Crime," in his 1924 criminology textbook, *Criminology*. (Sutherland, 1924) The inclusion of a chapter on crime victims in a criminology textbook is often cited as the turning point for the new field, which would emerge in an even bigger way two decades later. (Ironically, the 9th edition of Sutherland's *Criminology*, co-authored with Donald R. Cressey, and published in 1974, no longer had the chapter on victims. That edition had no fewer than five chapters related to prisons.) (Sutherland and Cressey, 1974: ix)

It should be pointed out, however, that a year earlier than Sutherland's chapter on victims in his 1924 textbook, in 1923, the Lebanese-American poet and artist Kahlil Gibran wrote about the crime victim. Gibran's views were expressed in his classic book of prose poems and essays, *The Prophet*, illustrated with his own drawings, a perspective that would actually be at the root of one of the biggest controversies in the study of the victim, namely, what is the victim's role in any crime? In the section on Crime and Punishment, Gibran writes:

> *And this also, though the word lie heavy upon your hearts:*
>
> *The murdered is not unaccountable for his own murder.*
>
> *And the robbed is not blameless in being robbed.*
>
> *The righteous is not innocent of the deeds of the wicked,*
>
> *And the white-handed is not clean in the doings of the felon.*
>
> *Yea, the guilty is oftentimes the victim of the injured.*
>
> *And still more often the condemned is the burden bearer for the guiltless and unblamed.*
>
> *You cannot separate the just from the unjust and the good from the wicked;*
>
> *For they stand together before the face of the sun even as the black threated and the white are woven together.*
>
> *And when the black thread breaks, the weaver shall look into the whole cloth, and he shall examine the loom also.*
>
> (Gibran, 1926, reprinted 1969: 50-51; Schafer, 1968: 51).

Could the criminologist be considered the "weaver," the "whole cloth" be considered the crime and the criminal, and the victim, together with the emerging future field of victimology, be deemed "the loom"?

However, the more traditional credit for helping to launch the study of the crime victim is not given to Kahlil Gibran but shared between a a Romanian lawyer, Beniamin Mendelsohn and a German criminologist Hans von Hentig (discussed after Mendelsohn in this chapter). In 1937, Mendelsohn published an article, "Method to be Used by Counsel for the Defense in the Researches Made into the Personality of the Criminal," published in the French journal, *Revue de Droit Penal et de Criminologie.* That article discussed the results of the offender-victim 300-question survey that Mendelsohn had conducted with his clients, focusing on rape victims, which is usually credited with planting the seeds for the new discipline. (Schafer, 1968: 3)

VICTIMOLOGY FOUNDERS AND THEIR THEORIES: TYPOLOGIES

Please consider referring back to the discussion, "Putting Victimology in a Historical Context," in Chapter 1, "Victimology: An Overview" to review a possible explanation, tied to the Nazi oppression that was happening in Europe at that time, as a possible reason why, in the late 1930s through the 1940s, the new discipline of victimology emerged. In this section, you will find out more information about the founders of that new discipline. You might also want to refer to Chapter 2, "An Anthropological and Historical View of Crime Victims and Victims' Rights," where you will find an exploration of how a focus on the victim, the core of victimology, grew in the 1970s, 1980s, and beyond.

Beniamin Mendelsohn (1900-1998)

If there is a "father" of victimology, it would be Beniamin Mendelsohn, a Romanian attorney who eventually moved to Jerusalem, Israel. (Schafer, 1968; Dussich, 2005; Doerner, 2021). As early as 1937, as noted above, Mendelsohn researched and published an article about the relationship between the victim and the criminal in the rape cases he was representing. He discovered these connections by asking his clients to fill out an extensive 300-question survey that explored those details. The results of his research appeared in French in the August-October 1937 issue of *Revue de Droit Penal et de Criminologie.* (Schafer, 1968: 41, 157)

Mendelsohn's even bigger contribution would come a decade later, in 1947, when he proposed the term *victimology* for this brand-new field. According to Mendelsohn, in his article, "The Origin of the Doctrine of Victimology" (originally published in 1963 in *Excerpta Criminologica* and reprinted in the anthology *Victimology*, published in 1974), it was in a speech delivered at the invitation of the Romanian Society of Psychiatry, in March 1947, in which he set forth the foundation for a discipline to be known as *victimology.* (Mendelsohn, in Drapkin and Viano, 1974: 6)

Beniamin Mendelsohn, considered by many to be the "father" of victimology.

But would it be a branch of criminology or a separate discipline? Mendelsohn advocated for the latter. As he wrote in that 1963 article, "The Origin of the Doctrine of Victimology," "The majority—almost the unanimous opinion—is in favour of Victimology, but solely within the bounds of Criminology. The minority—which is becoming less of a minority—supports my view that Victimology should be a separate and autonomous science, should have its own institutions and should be allowed to develop for the well-being and progress of humanity." (Mendelsohn, in Drapkin and Viano, 1974: 11)

Among others, criminologist Stephen Schafer concurred. In his 1968 book, *The Victim and His Criminal*, Schafer states that Mendelsohn did not see victimology as a branch of criminology but, instead, as "'a science parallel to it' or, better, 'the reverse of criminology.'" (Schafer, 1968: 42) Schafer noted that Mendelsohn also suggested new terminology for the study of victims. He created parallel words to those for the criminal, "victimal" as a juxtaposition to "criminal," "victimity" in contrast to "criminality" (Schafer, 1968: 41)

A true pioneer in the field of victimology, Mendelsohn might have held an even bigger place in its history if he had published a book that synthesized all his theories, typologies, and insights in one place. Unfortunately, it is up to scholars, criminologists, victimologists, sociologists, and others to piece together his ideas from his various journal articles, often published in French although some are also translated into English, and even from personal correspondence. It is said that Mendelsohn was the first one to refer to the offender-victim relationship as the "**penal couple**" (as Mendelsohn called the criminal and his victim). But Schafer notes that Mendelsohn objected to the " 'co-existence of two parallel ways' and asked that they be separated." (Schafer, 1968: 41)

Most references to Mendelsohn, after it is noted that he first used the term *victimology* in 1947, focus on the typology of victims that he created. That typology of victim categories that he developed is shown in Table 3.1.

TABLE 3.1. Mendelsohn's Six Categories of Crime Victims

Typology	Description
1. Completely innocent victim	children
2. Victim with minor guilt	victims due to ignorance
3. Victim who is as guilty as the offender	voluntary victims
4. Victim who is guiltier than the offender	precursor to Wolfgang's victim precipitation
5. Most guilty victims	victims who are guilty alone
6. Imaginary victims	simulating victims what police currently refer to as "un-founding" of a victim's account of the crime

Source: Schafer, 1968: 42-43 (based on Mendelsohn's 1956 article, "The Victimology.")

Here are Dr. Schafer's comments on Mendelsohn's typology:

1. "completely innocent victim"—"ideal" (children and those who are unconscious)
2. "victim with minor guilt" and "victim due to his ignorance" ("example is the woman who 'provokes' a miscarriage and as a result pays with her life")
3. "victim as guilty as the offender" and "voluntary victim"
   Suicide; euthanasia; suicide committed by a couple
4. "the victim more guilty than the offender"
   Someone who provokes someone to crime ("provoker victim")
   Someone who induces someone to commit a crime ("imprudent victim")

5. "more guilty victim" and "victim who is guilty alone"
   "example, the attacker who is killed by another in self-defense"
6. "simulating victim" and "imaginary victim"—"mislead the administration of justice in order to obtain a sentence of punishment against an accused person . . . paranoids, hysterical persons, senile persons, and children" (Schafer, 1968: 42-43)

Hans von Hentig (1887-1974)

On a par with Mendelsohn in importance to the origins of victimology is criminologist Hans von Hentig. Von Hentig, a German criminologist, was born in Berlin. According to the University of Colorado at Boulder, which houses von Hentig's papers, his father was Secretary of State during the German Empire period. Von Hentig attended the universities of Paris, Berlin, and Munich and served in the German Army during World War I as the "commandant of a machine gun detachment in France (Verdun), the Balkans, and in Arabia, 1914-1918." (University of Colorado, n.d.) According to the biography at the university with his archived papers, "He was full professor of criminal law and criminology at the University of Bonn, 1934-1935. Discharged November 1, 1935 for not making the mandatory Hitler salute and identified as politically unreliable to the Nazi government, he escaped to the United States in September 1936." (University of Colorado, n.d.)

Dr. von Hentig was a visiting lecturer at the University of Colorado from 1938-1939 and 1942-1943. He left to start a program at the University of Iowa which ended in 1944. (University of Colorado, n.d.) He held other teaching positions but is most remembered for the 1948 publication of his book, *The Criminal and His Victim,* by Yale University Press.

Although most point to the more extensive 13 typologies in von Hentig's influential, seminal book, there were already 4 typologies that he described in his earlier 1940 article, "Remarks on the Interaction of Perpetrator and Victim," published in the *Journal of Criminal Law and Criminology.* As von Hentig wrote in "Remarks on the Interaction of Perpetrator and Victim," "If there are born criminals, it is evident that there are born victims, self-harming and self-destroying through the medium of a pliable outsider." (von Hentig, 1940: 303)

The first page of von Hentig's 1940 article reads as a precursor to the victim-precipitation orientation of Marvin Wolfgang almost 20 years later. (Wolfgang, 1957) The four types of victims that von Hentig includes in this article are: the depressive type; the greedy of gain type; the wanton type; and the tormentor type. (von Hentig, 1940: 304-307)

Eight years later, in his book, *The Criminal and His Victim,* von Hentig expanded on those four victim types as he looked at the psychological and biological characteristics of crime victims, generalizing from murder to crime in general. (von Hentig, 1948, reprinted 1979: 383-450)

As von Hentig wrote in *The Criminal and His Victim,* emphasizing the victim's role in crime: "Crime, for the most part, is injury inflicted on another person . . . . there are always two partners: the perpetrator and the victim." (von Hentig, 1948, reprinted 1979: 383)

What makes von Hentig's 1948 book so important to the development of victimology? Probably it is Part IV, "The Victim." In this extensive section (67 pages in the reprinted edition), von Hentig, taking the spotlight off the criminal for a change, shares statistics about the victim in various crimes. The variables that he is addressing are remarkably contemporary and the statistical breakdowns are surprisingly consistent with those of today, as you will see in the chapters on each of these victims that follow later in this textbook. For example, von Hentig addresses murder victims in Memphis, Tennessee, by the race and gender of the victim and the race and gender of the murderer, during the years 1920-1925. (von Hentig, 1948/1979: 394)

He also looks at the reported motives for murders and manslaughters in New York City during a five year period (1936-1940). Von Hentig discovers that the reasons for those murders and manslaughters included altercations of various causes having the largest percentage (34.3%), followed by passion or marital conflict (25%). When he looked at the age of the victims, he discovered that the largest percentage (33.8%) were in the 20-29 year-old age group for both males and females. For the crime of rape, for the victims of rape by age over a four-year period, 63% were in the 14-18 year-old age group. In terms of arrests for assault in New York City from 1937-1941 by gender, males were assaulted 95.5 percent of the time by males and only 4.5 percent by females versus 14.3 percent of females were assaulted by females with the majority of the assaults still by males, 85.7 percent. (von Hentig, 1948, in reprint edition, 394-396; 402; 404)

The rest of that chapter focuses on von Hentig's annotated discussions of his 11-victim typology. In Box 3.1, you will find further comments about each of these types, based on von Hentig's original writings.

Box 3.1. A Detailed Look at von Hentig's Victim Typologies

General Classes of Victims According to Hans von Hentig

1. The Young—Von Hentig makes the strong statement, "Youth is the most dangerous period of life," which, as you will see when you read Chapter 10, "Child Victims," is still true today. (von Hentig, 1948/1979: 404) Yes, homicide is a real issue in the United States and globally for children, who may be beaten or suffocated by a parent or caregiver with an untold number of additional deaths that are not listed that way. Von Hentig notes that for some parents, there are no maternal instincts. For others, there may be more sinister motives for murder such as money, if the child was insured, or getting rid of the child, if he or she was an obstacle to a romantic relationship. (von Hentig, 1948/1979: 405)

2. The Female—According to von Hentig, "Female sex is another form of weakness recognized by law—numerous rules of our criminal code embody the legal fiction of an ordinarily weaker and a stronger sex. The groups of crimes against chastity and against family and children are meant to be a protective device against the superior physical force or the neglect of the male." (von Hentig, 1948/1979: 406-407) But he continues, ". . . but women do not easily become victims of this inequality except as special circumstances supervene" such as older women being murdered because of their wealth. (von Hentig, 1948/1979: 407)

3. The Old—Many today would disagree with von Hentig's depiction of the elderly as "ideal victims of predatory attacks" (von Hentig, 1948/1979: 410) since there have been advances since 1948 that make it possible for the elderly to still be strong. Today, those who are that old and weak will be indoors with caregivers or in nursing homes, less available to criminals although, as noted in Chapter 13, "Victims of Assault, Domestic Violence, Stalking, and Elder Abuse," which addresses the topic of elder abuse, some of the elderly unfortunately

Box 3.1. A Detailed Look at von Hentig's Victim Typologies (continued)

are more likely to be victims. Wrote von Hentig, "In the combination of wealth and weakness lies the danger." (von Hentig, 1948/1979: 410)

4. The Mentally Defective and Other Mentally Deranged—Von Hentig includes in this category the feeble-minded, insane, drug addicts, and alcoholics. (von Hentig, 1948/1979: 411)

5. Immigrants, Minorities, Dull Normals—Von Hentig groups these more likely victims into one type. He writes, "The inexperienced, poor, sometimes dull immigrant is an easy prey to all kinds of swindlers." (von Hentig, 1948/1979: 415)

Psychological Types of Victim

6. The Depressed—It is in this type that von Hentig foretells the victim precipitation theory that Wolfgang set forth a decade later. Von Hentig lists four distinct ways that the depressed might bring about a crime including "the detrimental result would not have followed without the actual instigation or provocation of the victim." (von Hentig, 1979: 419)

7. The Acquisitive—According to von Hentig, "The greedy can be hooked by all sorts of devices which hold out a bait to their cupidity." He uses the term "sucker" in regard to the acquisitive as a more likely victim. (von Hentig, 1979: 422)

8. The Wanton—This type is quite outdated since more contemporary laws do make it possible for a male to be the victim of rape although back in 1948, by definition, "Legally speaking, rape can only be committed by the male" and, he continues, "'any man, who, by means of temptation, deceptions, arts, flattery or a promise of marriage, seduces any unmarried female' is guilty of seduction." (von Hentig, 1979: 426)

9. The Lonesome and the Heartbroken—Von Hentig points out how the lonely and broken hearted, including those who are grieving, set them up as more likely victims. He points out that "uprooted" boys as well as prostitutes may be more likely victims of mass murderers because their isolated and lonely situations make them more vulnerable. Von Hentig, 1979: 427-431)

10. The Tormentor—This section is an expansion of von Hentig's 1940 article, "Remarks on the Interaction of Perpetrator and Victim," where he describes the boy who witnessed his mother's abuse by his father throughout his childhood. That child grows up to commit parricide, killing his father, the tormentor. (von Hentig, 1979: 431-432)

11. Blocked, Exempted, and Fighting Victims*—In this last category, von Hentig includes what he describes as a blocked victim meaning ". . . an individual who has been so enmeshed in a losing situation that defensive moves have become impossible or more injurious than the injury at criminal hands. Such is the case of the defaulting banker, swindled in the hope of saving himself. It is a self-imposed helplessness and an ideal condition from the point of view of the criminal." (von Hentig, 1979: 433)

*Note that Dr. Schafer listed these three types of victims separately so that he attributes 13 typologies to von Hentig in his book whereas von Hentig combined these three types into one category so there are only 11 typologies in von Hentig's book. (Schafer, 1968: 44)

Henri Ellenberger (1905-1993)

Ellenberger is being included here as one of the early originators of victimology. He is often mentioned as an early advocate of the new field of victimology because of his 1955 article, published in French, "Relations psychologiques entre le criminel et la victim," in the journal, *Revue International de Criminologie et de Police Technique*. The translation of the title of that article is "Psychological Relationships Between the Criminal and the Victim."

Ellenberger was a Canadian psychiatrist whose most famous work is *The Discovery of the Unconscious*, published in 1970. He originally studied medicine and psychiatry but beginning in the 1950s, he switched to criminology. He was an associate professor at McGill University in Canada and then became a Professor of Criminology at the University of Montreal. There he conducted his research and wrote about the relationship of the criminal and the victim, including the publication of his frequently-cited article listed above. (Delille, 2016)

* * *

But it was Dr. Wolfgang's 1957 journal article "Victim-Precipitated Homicide" and his related follow-up book *Patterns of Homicide*, published a year later, that did for the study of crime victims what Durkheim's empirical study *Suicide*, published at the end of the nineteenth century, did for the study of suicide. In Durkheim's study, one of the first to use statistics to look at sociological trends, Durkheim was able to show that what had previously been seen as an individual act, suicide, was actually an act influenced by social factors, such as marital status, having children, age, and gender, with single, childless, males having higher suicide rates than married women with children. (Durkheim, 1897/1963) Basically, victimology, and the way victims were viewed by the criminal justice system, and even by the public, would never be the same.

Criminologist Marvin E. Wolfgang.

EMPIRICAL VICTIM STUDIES

Marvin E. Wolfgang (1924-1998)

Criminologist Dr. Marvin Wolfgang is credited with the very influential Victim-Precipitation Theory. Dr. Wolfgang received his M.A. and Ph.D. from the University of Pennsylvania and for several decades he was a professor there. He authored many leading books including *Patterns of Homicide* (1958), which followed up on his controversial article, "Victim Precipitated Criminal

Homicide," published the year before and *The Subculture of Violence* (1967), among others That article summarized his in-depth analysis of 588 homicide victims that occurred in the city of Philadelphia between January 1, 1948 and December 31, 1952. He was able to get access to the data of the Homicide Squad of the Philadelphia Police Department. What Dr. Wolfgang discovered would become a major empirical study of crime victims and their relationship to offenders in terms of causation. Instead of telling academics and the public not to blame the victim, Wolfgang looked at each case and came up with his theory that in 26 percent of the cases that he studied, the victim could be said to have precipitated the crime. In those cases, the victim could be seen as blameworthy for the crime.

However, Wolfgang was very specific about what he meant by **victim-precipitated homicide.** He was not referring to an angry word or an offensive gesture. He was clear that it referred to those homicides where the victim was the first one to precipitate the crime. Or, in Wolfgang's words, "those criminal homicides in which the victim is a direct, positive precipitator in the crime. The role of the victim is characterized by his having been the first in the homicide drama to use physical force directed against his subsequent slayer. The victim precipitated cases are those in which the victim was the first to show and use a deadly weapon, to strike a blow in an altercation—in short, the first to commence the interplay or resort to physical violence."

Here are some examples of victim-precipitated homicides from Wolfgang's study that he shares in his journal article:

- In an argument over a business transaction, the victim first fired several shots at his adversary, who in turn, fatally returned the fire.
- The victim was the aggressor in a fight, having struck his enemy several times. Friend tried to interfere, but the victim persisted. Finally, the offender retaliated with blows, causing the victim to fall and hit his head on the sidewalk, as a result of which he died.
- A drunken victim with knife in hand approached his slayer during a quarrel. The slayer showed a gun, and the victim dared him to shoot. He did.
- During an argument in which a male called a female many vile names, she tried to telephone the police. But he grabbed the phone from her hands, knocked her down, kicked her, and hit her with a tire gauge. She ran to the kitchen, grabbed a butcher knife, and stabbed him in the stomach. (Wolfgang, 1957: 3)

Here are some of Dr. Wolfgang's additional findings about what was distinctive about victim-precipitated (VP) crimes:

- In VP cases, victims are more likely to have a previous arrest or police record (62% of VP victims versus 54% of offenders)
- Alcohol was present in the homicide situation in 74 percent of VP cases compared to 60 percent in non-VP cases.
- There is a *significant* association between the sex of the victim and VP homicide in that males comprise 94 percent of VP homicides but only 72 percent of non-VP homicides.
- Of the 588 criminal homicides that Wolfgang studied, 150 or 26 percent were designated as VP cases.

Dr. Wolfgang deemed 150 or 26 percent of the homicides he studied to be victim-precipitated. There are a couple of key issues to keep in mind when considering Dr. Wolfgang's empirical study since his term, victim-precipitated, and his findings have had such far a reaching impact on the way the crime victim is viewed and on victimology.

1. Although he deemed 26 percent of the murders were victim-precipitated, that still left 74 percent that were *not* victim-precipitated.
2. His definition was that someone struck the first blow or was the first to show a weapon. It was not a term used in a more general way.
3. Some of the examples that he shared as examples of his definition of victim precipitation are questionable. Consider this example: *"A drunken victim with knife in hand approached his slayer during a quarrel. The slayer showed a gun, and the victim dared him to shoot. He did."* (Wolfgang, 1957) Does daring someone to do something justify doing it?

It is interesting that a decade later, two sociologists, Harwin L. Voss and John R. Hepburn, took it upon themselves to attempt to replicate Dr. Wolfgang's study to see if his influential findings would hold up. They studied Chicago homicides during 1965 (in all, 395 cases committed by 429 offenders). As the co-authors wrote in the overview to their study: "All cases in which a charge of criminal homicide was filed in Chicago in 1965 were examined in a replication of Wolfgang's *Patterns in Criminal Homicide.* Nonwhite males between 15 and 39 years of age were the victims or offenders more frequently than any other age-race-sex category. It was found that 37.9 per cent of the cases were victim-precipitated and nonwhite males were most likely to precipitate their own deaths." Although far less as well-known as Dr. Wolfgang's study, certainly the Voss and Hepburn study deserves noting especially since it found victim precipitation of homicide in their sample to be even higher—37.9 percent versus the 26 percent that Wolfgang suggested. (Voss and Hepburn, 1969)

It is an understatement that Dr. Wolfgang's victim-precipitation theory, even after all these years, is still considered controversial. But as criminologist Wayne Petherick points out in his article, "Victim precipitation: Why We Need to expand Upon the Theory," "Victim precipitation is not victim blaming." (Petherick, 2017: 263) The author points out that some studies, such as Amir's study of rape, discussed below, complicated matters since his use of the term *victim precipitation*, when applied to rape victims and their behavior, could be seen as victim blaming. (Amir, 1967)

THE VICTIM FINALLY TAKES CENTER STAGE

Stephen Schafer (1911-1976)

Originally from Budapest, Hungary, Stephen Schaefer received his doctorate from the University of Budapest. He taught criminology there until 1951 when he moved to England, followed by a move to the United States in 1961. After teaching at several universities in the United States, Dr. Schafer landed at Northeastern University in Boston, where he was a professor of sociology and criminology. (Schafer, 1968: back cover)

Schafer's 1968 book, *The Victim and His Criminal: A Study in Functional Responsibility*, is a *tour de force* in the field of victimology. His contribution to the field of victimology ranks him with Mendelsohn, von Hentig, and Wolfgang (discussed previously) as one of the early pioneers who helped to advance the fledgling field of victimology to the important place it holds in criminology and sociology today. Dr. Schafer's first accomplishment was to put the victim front and center when he titled his book, *The Victim and His Criminal.* Compare that title to Dr. von Hentig's: *The Criminal & His Victim.* The former title shows a major shift in emphasis.

Schafer's book is well-written, thorough, and detailed. In Part 1 he begins with a discussion about the Golden Age of the Victim, followed by the victim's decline in prominence, and, to complete that first chapter, the revival of the victim's importance. It is possible that the revival of interest in the crime victim is tied to movements in the 1960s and 1970s that addressed the status of women and African Americans—two major groups that, like the victim, were considered underdogs. (Schafer, 1968: 7-38) (One of the first rape crisis center was established in the United States in 1972 in Washington, D.C.; the first battered women's shelter was opened in 1971 in London, England and the first one in the United States was launched in 1974 in St. Paul, Minnesota.) (DCRCC, dcrcc.org; Pizzey, 1979; awomansplace.org)

In Part 2 he covers the "Criminal-Victim Relationship as a Crime Factor" starting with "The Beginnings of 'Victimology.'" It is intriguing that Schafer chose to put the discipline's name within quote marks. (Schafer, 1968: 39-103)

Part 3 covers compensation and restitution to crime victims with the last part devoted to Schafer's concept of "The Functional Responsibility" of the crime victim. Schafer's very first paragraph in this key part of his groundbreaking book highlights not just the complexity of the establishment of culpability in the offender-victim relationship in every crime but Schafer's somewhat "**victim blame**" or "shared responsibility" perspective: "In the matter of criminal-victim relationships, alarm and indignation had been directed for a long time exclusively against the offender; this was coupled with indifference toward the victim's role. Now the importance of the victim's role is gaining in acceptance, but only slowly." (Schafer, 1968: 137)

Schafer's contribution includes the excellent way he summed up the development of victimology in *The Victim and His Criminal* as well as his own views on the functional responsibility of the victim. Echoing the perspective of Mendelsohn, von Hentig, and especially Wolfgang, Schafer concludes his book: ""Crime is not only an individual act but also a social phenomenon. . . . There is hardly any doubt that the crime-caused injury, harm, or other disadvantage of the victim was generated by the criminal and that the latter was thereby instrumental in curtaining the victim's performance of his role in society. . . . Also, it is far from true that all crimes 'happen' to be committed; often the victim's negligence, precipitative action, or provocation contributes to the genesis or performance of a crime. The norm-delineated functional role of the victim is to do nothing to provoke others from attempting to injure his ability to play his role. At the same time, it expects him actively to prevent such attempts. . . ." (Schafer, 1968: 152)

Menachem Amir (born 1930)

Menachem Amir is included in this history of victimology because he applied Dr. Wolfgang's victim-precipitation theory to rape victims. A former graduate student of Dr. Wolfgang, Dr. Amir summarized his findings in his controversial book, *Patterns in Forcible Rape.* His findings were based on his analysis of 646 rapes that were reported to the Philadelphia Police

Department from 1958 to 1960. Based on his analysis and criteria, Dr. Amir found that 19 percent of the rape cases could be deemed victim-precipitated. Dr. Amir also found that there were four characteristics that were more likely to be associated with victim-precipitated (VP) rapes, namely:

1. Victim was between the ages of 15 and 19
2. Alcohol was used by the victim or both the victim and the offender
3. Victim and offender knew each other
4. Victims were more likely to have a "bad" reputation (Fisher, et al., 2016: 9-21)

"Bad reputation" was an important concept in Amir's study since he used the term no fewer than eight times in his article: "bad repute" once and "bad reputation" seven times. (Amir, 1967: 495, 497, 502.). However, "bad reputation" of the victim is a contentious characteristic of VP cases and characteristic number 4 from the above list is probably one of the two causes for controversy about Dr. Amir's research findings. (Amir, 1967: 502)

Referring back to the section of Amir's research article, "Victim Reputation and Previous Arrest Record," Amir writes, ". . . if the victim has a 'bad reputation' that fact would be known to the offender, and would contribute more strongly to the offender's imputation that she is sexually available. Hence, it is necessary to determine whether an association exists between VP rape and victim ("bad") reputation. Such association was, indeed, found to be statistically *significant*. Thus, in VP cases the victim is more likely to have a 'bad' reputation (33%) than in non-VP events (17%)." (Amir, 1967: 497)

The second reason that Dr. Amir's article was so controversial and probably never achieved the level of importance that his mentor Dr. Wolfgang, did, with his work related to homicide, is that he was unsuccessful in drawing a precise analogy between "asking for rape" and "precipitating murder." That is probably because rape, a violent crime, does not have the rape victim "throwing the first punch," one of the precipitating actions that Dr. Wolfgang used to categorize a victim-precipitated homicide.

If Dr. Wolfgang's study, "Victim-Precipitated Homicide," added an important concept to the victimology research—even if it was controversial when first advanced in 1957 and even if it is still debated to this day—his former student's study was a step backwards. Amir's questionable concept of a "bad" reputation and questionable definition of victim-precipitated rape (as when the victim "agreed to sexual relations but retracted before the actual act or did not react strongly enough when the suggestion was made by the offender (s)") made it unpopular to explore victim precipitation for decades. (Amir, 1967; Muftic and Hunt, 2012)

Characterizing some of the rape victims that he studied as having a "bad reputation" unfortunately could easily slip into the victim blame mindset. Victim blame is explored in greater detail in the Controversies section of this chapter that follows. But it is certainly a concept which has unfortunately been applied to rape victims far too often when it was completely unjustified. Labeling a rape victim as someone with a "bad reputation" could infer that she was "asking for it."

As noted above, Dr. Wolfgang suggested a much more concrete and clear definition of victim-precipitated homicide, namely, "the victim is a direct, positive precipitator in the crime." He continues, "the victim was the first to show and use a deadly weapon, to strike a blow in an altercation—in short, the first to commence the interplay or resort to physical violence." (Wolfgang, 1957:2)

THE NEXT GENERATION OF THEORIES: AN OPPORTUNITY APPROACH

As we can see, the earliest victimologists and criminologists created victim typologies as well as advancing the idea of victim precipitation. Discussed below are the main theories, in chronological order. The typologies and the victim precipitation orientation lean toward a subtle and a not-so-subtle victim blame approach. In the 1970s, a different theoretical view of what causes someone to become a crime victim emerged, one that seemed to place more blame on opportunities or circumstances rather than on the individual victim.

Lifestyle Exposure Theory

Criminologists Michael Hindelang, Michael Gottfredson, and James Garofalo are associated with the opportunity victimization theory approach, which is related to their book, *Victims of Personal Crime: An Empirical Foundation for a Theory of Personal Victimization*, published in 1978. **Lifestyle exposure theory**, also known as **lifestyle theory**, is based on the premise that differences in victimization rates can be explained by the differences in the exposure to crime based on such demographics as age, gender, even occupation. Hence, you could use lifestyle theory to explain why there was initially a drop in violent crime when the lock-downs were required because of the 2020 pandemic in such cities. (Marley Coyne, *Forbes*, 2020.) Fewer people on the street, more people at home, less crime. In non-pandemic times, bar fights and the assaults or even homicides that occur in those locations require going to the bar in the first place for those crimes to occur. Some seniors may be more likely victims of fraud because too many are gullible, but they are less likely to be victimized at night out in the street because they are much more likely to be home. Unlike seniors, the group with the highest homicide rate in any age group, young adults aged 18 to 24, are more likely to be out and about, even on work or school nights and especially throughout the weekend.

Lifestyle also refers to job choice as a risk factor. Those working night shifts without security nearby where cash is available, those who drive a taxi or shared car services, police officers, and journalists, are some of the occupations that put someone at greater risk of becoming a crime victim.

Other lifestyle choices, such as who you associate with, can put you at greater or reduced risk for being a crime victim. Historically we know that marital status is a lifestyle factor as well; marrieds are less likely to be victims than those who are single. Consider some of the traditions associated with the college lifestyle that may put some students at greater risk of becoming crime victims; for example: excessive drinking; functioning on too little sleep (which can lower alertness and make someone more vulnerable); or drug use (which could put someone in harm's way if where they go to buy the drugs is in a questionable neighborhood). The concept of lifestyle choices leads into the next theory, **Routine Activity Theory**.

Routine Activity Theory (RAT)

This victimization theory is associated with the seminal article, "Social Change and Crime Rate Trends: A Routine Activities Approach," by Lawrence Cohen and Marcus Felson, published in the *American Sociological Review* in 1979. According to Cohen and Felson, there are three factors that need to coincide for a crime and victimization to occur. Those factors are: "(1) motivated offenders, (2) suitable targets, and (3) the absence of capable guardians against a violation." (Cohen and Felson, 1979: 589)

Although in their original article Cohen and Felson do not spell out just who are these "motivated offenders," over the years it has been suggested that those who are unemployed, teenagers with time on their hands, or addicts desperate to get money to feed their habit might fall into that category.

What targets that will most likely be factors in victimization? Cohen and Felson listed "expensive and movable durables, such as vehicles and electronic appliances, have the highest risk of illegal removal." (Cohen & Felson, 1979: 595)

Based on more contemporary reports by crime victims, smartphones and similar pricey electronic devices could be substituted for electronic appliances. (It should be noted that "suitable targets" can be a store, and not just a person.)

This means that security systems are broken, nonexistent, or easily immobilized; police officers are not around; and homeowners are absent, increasing the likelihood of a burglary. Insufficient guardianship applies to the conditions encouraging crime, such as the lack of supervision of teenage boys, some of whom might be deemed "motivated offenders."

The capable guardian that can be a deterrent to victimization, according to Routine Activity Theory (RAT), might include everything from the police to what is known as closed circuit television (CCTV) or video surveillance in stores, apartment complexes and, increasingly, outside of homes in the United States, United Kingdom, Australia, and elsewhere. Cohen and Felson proposed that when all three of these scenarios are present—motivated offenders, suitable targets, and the absence of capable guardians—it is the perfect storm for a crime to occur. They write, "the lack of any one of these elements is sufficient to prevent the successful completion of a direct-contact predatory crime. . . ." (Cohen & Felson, 1979: 589)

One of the basic premises of RAT is that the shift in activities away from the home that occurred after World War II, including the growth of women having outside jobs resulting in homes being unattended during the day, were factors in the "significant increases in the movement of valuable goods through its ports and terminals" (Cohen & Felson, 1979: 592-593)

Notice how dramatically different this approach to explaining victimization is from the victim typologies in the earliest generation of victimization theories where the emphasis was on the victim's traits, such as "young," "female," "old," or "acquisitive" (greedy.)

Cohen and Felson wrote that "household and family activities entail lower risk of criminal victimization than nonhousehold-nonfamily activities . . . ." (Cohen and Felson, 1979: 594) Pratt and Turanovic, however, disagree. In their 2016 article, "Lifestyle and Routine Activity Theories Revisited: The Importance of 'Risk' to the Study of Victimization," published in *Victims & Offenders*, they propose that Cohen and Felson did not go far enough with their theory. They also object to Cohen and Felson's suggestion that as long as you stay home, you are less likely to become a victim, pointing out that intimate partner violence and child abuse are most likely to occur in the home. (Pratt and Turanovic, 2016: 339). SAMHSA Substance Abuse and Mental Health Services Administration (SAMHSA) and other government and private agencies and companies were concerned about the rise of these types of victimizations during the pandemic of 2020 because of the stay at home orders. (SAMHSA, n.d.; Abramson, 2020)

However, there was a positive unintended consequence of the stay-at-home orders that started in the United States in March 2020 because of the pandemic. It was announced that March 2020 was the first March in nearly two decades, since 2002, when there was not one school shooting. (Lewis, 2020)

Deviant Place Theory

Somewhat in tandem with lifestyle theory is **deviant place theory**. Consider the cliché that you hear from realtors when you are figuring out where to move, or what your property is worth if you are trying to sell, namely, "location, location, location." Rodney Stark points out 30 propositions in his article, "Deviant Places: A Theory of the Ecology of Crime," published in the 1987 issue of *Criminology*, that form the foundation of what he calls "a theory of deviant places." Here are several of Stark's propositions:

- "Proposition 5: *Where homes are more crowded, there will be lower levels of supervision of children."*
- "Proposition 6: *Reduced levels of child supervision will result in poor school achievement, with a consequent reduction in stakes in conformity and an increase in deviant behavior."*
- "Proposition 22: *Stigmatized neighborhoods will tend to be overpopulated by the most demoralized kinds of people."*
- "Proposition 23: *the larger the relative number of demoralized residents, the greater the number of available 'victims.'"*
- "Proposition 30: *The higher the visibility of crime and deviance, the more it will appear to others that these activities are safe and rewarding."* (Stark, 1987: 897-904)

Stated more simplistically, by being in a deviant place, you increase the chance that you will become a victim of crime or violence. Hence, living, working, or visiting a high crime area raises the possibility that you will become a crime victim. Victimology and sociology both consider how the rates of victimization are impacted by poverty and population density, and how the prevalence of other risk factors, like gang activity, can make a place more or less deviant. Walking alone at night down a street, or in a deserted parking garage, known to have a lot of crime, is in line with Deviant Place Theory. The cost of housing may even depend on the risk of victimization as a factor in pricing: having a lower risk of becoming a crime victim because there is less crime in an area may be one of the considerations accounting for the higher housing costs.

Situational Victimization

Situational victimization, also known as **environmental criminology**, means that by applying certain strategies to an environment, someone may be more or less likely to become a victim. The situation or environment decreases or increases the opportunity for a crime, and victimization, to occur. The rationale behind **situational victimization** is that increasing or decreasing the likelihood of becoming a crime victim is put on the environment, rather than the characteristics of the individual. Also known by the acronym **CPTED—crime prevention through environmental design** or, alternatively, **SCPT—situational crime prevention theory**—the concept is that there is something that can be done to decrease opportunities for victimization. Co-authors Huisman and van Erp distinguish SCPT to be an "offence-based perspective on crime as opposed to offender-based approaches . . . ." (Huisman and van Erp, 2013: 1178)

For instance, consider the ATM where you may still do your banking. You might want to avoid going to an ATM alone to withdraw cash at 2 a.m. because doing so could put you at greater risk of being victimized than if you went during the day (or used a credit card or paid a bill electronically). Obviously equally risky is frequenting an ATM that is hidden behind bushes and trees or located in a secluded place where no one could intervene if a criminal were to try robbing you.

Categorizing SCPT as "opportunity-based" approach, Huisman and van Erp write: "Opportunity-based analyses have led to the design of many simple street-crime prevention strategies such as improved street lightning, ink merchandise tags, and ignition immobilizers in cars, to prevent burglary, shoplifting and car theft (Clarke 1997)." (Huisman and van Erp, 2013);

In instances of potential street crime, like robbery, motor vehicle theft, or shoplifting, it is clear how environmental criminology might reduce the likelihood of becoming a victim or having property stolen. Those in the security business, including police officers, employees in security, and the military might refer to this idea as **target hardening**, namely that by increasing the security to a building or an area where vulnerable potential victims might congregate, victimization including theft might be reduced or eliminated.

Example of target hardening in front of a government building in London

As Wim Huisman and Judith van Erp explain in "Opportunities for Environmental Crime: A Test of Situation Crime Prevention Theory," the focus is "on the specific characteristics of a situation, and study [ing] the process through which an offence is committed, rather than focusing on the offender, root causes or the broader political, socio-economic and regulatory context of crime" (Huisman and van Erp, 2013).

ADDITIONAL VICTIMOLOGY THEORIES

Radical Victimology

There have been some additional theoretical developments in victimology to note. In 1983, sociologist/criminologist David O. Friedrichs published an article in *Crime & Delinquency*, "Victimology: A Consideration of the Radical Critique." In this article, a follow-up to a paper Friedrichs presented at the First World Congress of Victimology held in Washington, D.C. from August 20-24, 1980, the author suggests the need for a more **radical victimology** perspective. Friedrichs quotes from the 1972 article by radical criminologist Richard Quinney in his "Who Is the Victim?" where Quinney suggested an expanded view of crime victims from the prevailing focus on street crimes to also include "'victims of police force, the victims of war, the victims of the 'correctional' system, the victims of state violence, the victims of oppression of any sort.'" (Quinney, quoted in Friedrichs: 287). Friedrichs recommends the development of a radical victimology with that expanded focus just as Quinney and others had advocated a radical criminology that expanded classic criminology with its historical focus.

Environmental Victimology

Flint, Michigan and Bhopal, India are just two environmental tragedies that environmental victimologists study. As you may know, in Flint, Michigan, beginning in April 2014, water contaminated with undetected lead flowed into homes and was being consumed, leading to high levels of lead in the population, especially children. In Bhopal, India, in December 1984, a pesticide leaked toxic gases causing an estimated 4,000 fatalities. Environmental victimology is concerned with more than just chemical disasters. It includes physical disasters such as earthquakes and tornadoes. Christopher Williams, writing in his article, "An Environmental Victimology," sees environmental victimology fitting within a framework of radical victimology "which is broadly concerned with human rights, abuses of power, and human suffering irrespective of whether the circumstances are within the ambit of law." (Williams: 1996: 18)

Williams points to what he dubs a "victim syndrome" that environmental victimology needs to address. In addition to the issue of avoidance of liability that is tied to avoiding or dealing with victimization, Williams notes there is a need to look at the psychosocial outcomes of environmental victimization. He notes that in Bhopal, India, since so many women became infertile because of the toxic gas leak, it became difficult for them to marry because any young woman was suspected of being unable to bear children whether it was true or not. (Williams: 28) Research into the aftermath of the dropping of the nuclear bomb on Nagasaki and Hiroshima documented that survivors had to deal with work discrimination, being consider poor marriage prospects, and panic that any minor illness might cause hereditary health problems. (Williams: 29)

Forensic Victimology

Forensic victimology is another notable approach to victimology. Practitioners go into the field, studying specific crime scenes and presenting their findings in court. In his 2014 textbook, *Forensic Victimology*, Dr. Brent E. Turvey defines forensic victimology in this way: "a subdivision of interactionist victimology, in which victims are defined by having suffered harm or loss due to a breach of law. It involves the thorough, critical, and objective outlining of victim lifestyles and circumstances, the events leading up to their injury, and the precise nature of any harm or loss suffered." (Turvey, 2014: 21).

Turvey continues to explain that forensic victimology, in contrast to traditional victimology, is an "applied discipline as opposed to a theoretical one." (Turvey, 2014: 21) Here are some of the activities in which forensic victimology would be engaged:

1. Assist in understanding elements of the crime.
2. Assist in developing a timeline.
3. Define the suspect pool.
4. Provide investigative suggestions.
5. Assist with crime reconstruction.
6. Assist with contextualizing allegations of victimization.
7. Assist with the development of offender modus operandi.
8. Assist with the development of offender motive.
9. Assist with case linkage.
10. Assist with public safety response.
11. Educate the court. (Turvey, 2014: 21-24)

Psychologist Lenore E. Walker, Ed.D., author of the classic study, *The Battered Woman*, published in 1979 by Harper & Row. Contributed photo.

A typical case for a forensic victimologist could be studying a crime scene and all the forensic evidence related to it to figure out if a suicide or the crime of homicide occurred.

Theories Related to Specific Crime Victimizations

Please note that the theoretical contributions of Victimology pioneers Dr. Ann Wolbert Burgess and Dr. Lynda Lytle Holmstrom, with their groundbreaking empirical research into rape victims in the 1970s and beyond, is discussed in Chapter 12, "Sexual Violence." The insights of psychologist Dr. Lenore E. Walker, an early contributor to a better understanding of victims of domestic violence with her research and publications including *The Battered Woman*, published in 1979, and the 1984 follow-up, *The Battered Woman Syndrome*, are explored in Chapter 13, "Aggravated Assault, Domestic Violence, Stalking, and Elder Abuse."

THREE BASIC PERSPECTIVES IN VICTIMOLOGY

John Hegger, who has worked in the probation field, served as a law enforcement officer, and taught as an adjunct professor, nicely sums up the three basic victimology perspectives: Conservative, Liberal, and Radical-Critical. The conservative approach, more often applied to the so-called street crimes—major violent and property crimes—"maintains that every individual is somewhat responsible for their own victimization." (Hegger, 2015)

By contrast, the liberal approach is more closely association with such crimes as white-collar crimes and "acts that may involve complex involvement between criminals and victims." (Hegger, 2015) An example Hegger provides is that of a bank patron blaming the bank if they are the victims of identity theft because the bank did not offer adequate protection.

Finally, the radical approach, described earlier as radical victimology, "focuses on the overall bigger picture regarding victimization." (Hegger, 2015) Hegger sees the radical approach falling between the liberal and the conservative. It even goes to bigger crimes than either street crimes or identity theft. Proponents of radical victimology would see the government as the party at fault, for not having tougher laws that might have prevented a crime like insider stock trading. Hegger sees this approach as a way to get those in charge to take a greater responsibility for victimization. But the negative side of that view is when individuals fail to see themselves as culpable for doing their own due diligence to avoid becoming a victim in the first place.

The best approach, according to Hegger, is to combine all three approaches into one blended approach.

APPLYING SUTHERLAND'S LEARNING THEORY OF DEVIANCE TO CRIME VICTIMS

Sutherland's Learned Theory of Deviance (Differential Association Theory)

Edwin Sutherland left his home state of Nebraska, in 1906 to attend the University of Chicago. From then on, he devoted the rest of his life trying to understand the social basis of criminal behavior. Sutherland received his Ph.D. in 1913 and taught at the University of Illinois and the University of Minnesota. He then taught at the University of Chicago for five years before leaving for the sociology department of Indiana University, where he taught until his death in 1950. His approach to criminal behavior and its causation would always be tied to that of the Chicago School of scholars and researchers, especially the writings of Clifford Shaw and Henry D. McKay, who had developed a theory of juvenile delinquency, and to Frederick Thrasher, who had studied 1,313 gangs in Chicago. (Shaw and McKay, 1942; Thrasher, 1927)

Criminologist Edwin Sutherland.

Sutherland rejected Lombroso's theory that criminals had a distinctive physical trait—that criminals were born not made—for his belief in social organization as the cause of crime—that the group in which an individual is raised and nurtured will determine whether that individual will become a criminal. Sutherland does, however, give himself an "out" to that theory in his 9th postulate which acknowledges that not all criminality can be explained by associations.

Here are the nine principles that sociologist and criminologist Edwin Sutherland set forth in 1939 that reinforces his perspective that criminal behavior is learned. This version is excerpted from the 9th edition of the textbook *Criminology*, originally by Sutherland, who died in 1950, with Donald R. Cressey co-authoring this 1974 edition:

1. Criminal behavior is learned.
2. Criminal behavior is learned in interaction with other persons in a process of communication.
3. The principal part of the learning of criminal behavior occurs within intimate personal groups.
4. When criminal behavior is learned, the learning includes (a) techniques of committing the crime, which sometimes are very complicated, sometimes very simple; and (b) the specific direction of motives, drives, rationalizations, and attitudes.
5. The specific direction of motives and drives is learned from definitions of legal codes as favorable and unfavorable.
6. A person becomes delinquent because of an excess of definitions favorable to violation of law over definitions unfavorable to violation of law. This is the principle of differential association.
7. Differential associations may vary in frequency, duration, priority, and intensity.
8. The process of learning criminal behavior by association with criminal and anticriminal patterns involves all the mechanisms that are involved in any other learning.
9. While criminal behavior is an expression of general needs and values, it is not explained by those general needs and values, since noncriminal behavior is an expression of the same needs and values. (Sutherland and Cressey, 1974: 75-77)

An Application of Sutherland's Learned Theory of Victimization

So now just substitute "victim" for "criminal" and you see how easily there could be a learned theory of victimization. If criminal behavior is learned, why not victim behavior? When does the learning of victim behavior begin? In the earliest years. We know that those who are neglected or treated badly during pregnancy, infancy, and the early formative years are more likely to become delinquents. But they are also more likely to become victims. Here are those principles of what could be called the learned theory of victimization:

1. Just as criminal behavior is learned, so is victim behavior. It is learned from the first experience of victimization which can occur as early as the socialization during infancy and childhood.
2. Because victim behavior is learned by the experience of being a victim, every effort must be made to avoid victimization in the first place.
3. If victimization occurs, however, it is important to avoid a second or repeated occurrence. In the realm of certain types of crime, such as sexual assault, especially of minors, the pull to stop the victimization or, if it occurs once, to reveal it has to be stronger than the push to maintain the secrecy, the secret, and to allow the victimization to occur.
4. Victim behavior is learned by observing someone else being victimized as well as being a victim yourself.
5. What starts off as a crime victimization can generalize to other areas of the victim's life including relationships, school or work, and in other areas.

6. When someone becomes a victim of a crime, a line has been crossed. Society must do everything it can to help the victim to never cross that line again and to feel safe and whole again.
7. There may be a pull by a victim to victimize others. A victim may need outside or therapeutic help to understand and resist this tendency.
8. Being a victim can be passed down from generation to generation just like other family traditions. This tendency, however, with help and insights, can be reversed.
9. Everyone's reaction to being a victim is as unique as they are.

Here is just one example of the way that victim behavior is learned. It is from Bonnie T., a woman who was horribly abused by her first husband. She put up with the abuse for years but one night, after he had brought his mistress to live with them in their apartment, along with their two children, he accused his wife of cheating on him. She protested that it was not true, but he beat her so badly anyway that she was finally forced to call the police, partly because her children were watching this beating and partly because he was really hurting her.

Bonnie's husband did spend a few nights in jail, and soon afterwards they divorced. For many years, she was single, raising her children alone. But then she met someone, fell in love again, and got married. Her second husband treated her well. But much to her shock and surprise she would ask him to beat her. In sharing with her daughter about the abuse she suffered with her father, Bonnie said about her second marriage: "But at the beginning of the marriage, it's like I would yell at him to hit me and I am not sure why. When we would have our fights and I would yell that out to him, he would just walk away and leave until I was calm. But I never understood why I asked or challenged him [to hit me]. I [guess] still had anger towards your father. [But] now we don't fight. We get along fine."

Being a victim sets someone up to be a victim again and, as the research into child abusers has shown, can even increase the likelihood that someone will become a perpetrator. (For a more extensive discussion of *repeat victimization*, see the Controversies section below.)

A MULTIDISCIPLINED APPROACH TO CRIME VICTIMIZATION

The typology approach to who becomes a victim, and why, espoused by the earliest victimologists depends on such sociological variables as age, gender, race, and ethnicity, as well as such psychological and mental concerns as being depressed, lonesome, or even mentally defective.

That gender is a factor in victimization was reinforced during the interview with Kerri Rawson, the daughter of the BTK serial killer, Dennis Rader. When asked why 8 out of 10 of the murder victims of her father were women, she answered that he knew that he could overpower them, that they were weaker. (Rawson, 2020)

We have addressed sociological variables, psychological ones, and even economics, but there are other disciplines that all have to be factored into why someone becomes a victim and someone else does not. Or why someone becomes a victim more than once. **Repeat victimization** is a real thing as we saw in the example that was shared about Bonnie and, later, when you read about lawyer Nance Schick in the chapter on robbery. Just as going to prison is the number one reason for recidivism—you cannot become a statistic for recidivism, or getting rearrested and returned to prison, unless you went to one in the first place—similarly, becoming a victim once increases the likelihood you will become a victim again. A line has unfortunately been crossed and it is easier to cross that line a second, third, or even a seventh time than to cross it for the first time.

So prior victimization, and the way that you are consciously or unconsciously set up to become a victim again, is a variable from the world of psychology or psychoanalysis that needs to be considered as to whether someone becomes a victim once or repeatedly.

From the field of communications, we can add body language. Robbers and purse snatchers share that they watch body language to decide who might be a good target. For example, if you take money, especially a large sum, out of an ATM, avoid clutching your handbag too tightly or patting down a wallet in your back pocket because to a criminal those are telltale signs there is money that you are concerned about. Criminals have reported that having an especially nice hairstyle indicates that you are more likely to have nice jewelry or money on you just as burglars may look for homes with nicely manicured lawns indicating enough money to pay for a landscaping service as a signal that there might be more valuable goods inside.

There's Safety in Numbers

What about group dynamics as a factor in who is more likely to become a victim? Offenders generally do not want to get caught. One way of increasing the likelihood of overpowering a victim and getting away with a crime is to kill the only witness. Another is having more criminals against single victims. However, the downside of having two or more criminals working together, whether it is during a violent or a property crime, is that one could turn on the other if caught. But if they stay a devoted pair, threesome, or group, they do stand a better chance of overpowering the lone individual, whether that means stealing their property or committing a gang rape. The adage, "safety in numbers," applies to criminals and to potential victims. If you go out to a bar at 11 at night with a group of friends, and they all want to go home, avoid staying behind by yourself. Go home with them! Unfortunately staying behind is what a young woman did years ago only to be killed by the bar's bouncer. It is unlikely that bouncer would have succeeded if she was still part of her original group of friends. The statistical proof of this truism about how to avoid being a victim of a major violent crime or even of personal larceny with contact is irrefutable. For instance, the statistics compiled by Cohen and Felson in their 1979 seminal article on routine activity theory indicate that out of 182 rapes that were committed, 179 happened to single (alone) victims; 3 to 2 victims; none to three or four or more victims. Out of 713 victims of robbery, 647 were alone, 47 were in pairs, only 13 were 3 people, and 6 were 4 or more. The numbers supporting the increased likelihood of being an aggravated assault victim if you are alone are equally dramatic: 2,116 aggravated assault victims were alone versus 257 with 1 more person, 53 with 3, and 43 with 4 or more. Finally, only 25 out of 1,062 larceny with contact were not alone.

TABLE 3.2. Number of Victims Present During Their Victimization for Selected Major Crimes

Number of Victims	Rape	Robbery	Aggravated Assault	Personal Larceny with Contact
1	179	647	2,116	1,062
2	3	47	257	19
3	0	13	53	3
4 plus	0	6	43	1

Source: Cohen and Felson, 1979: 595.

ASSOCIATIONS AND JOURNALS FOR VICTIMOLOGISTS

Although victimologists publish in such peer-reviewed criminology journals as *Criminology, Crime & Delinquency,* and sociology journals such as the *American Sociological Review*, victimology has its own peer-reviewed journals: *The International Review of Victimology*, published by SAGE and the *Journal of Victimology and Victim Justice*, also published by SAGE.

Victimologists are members of criminology and sociological organizations with divisions related to that specialization including the Division of Victimology within the American Society of Criminology (ASC) and the Victimology Section within the Academy of Criminal Justice Sciences (ACJS). In 2021, *Victims and Offenders* became the official journal of the DOV. There is also an international association dedicated to victimology research and its researchers namely the World Society of Victimology, established in 1979 in Germany. Its beginning in 1973 followed the First International Symposium on Victimology in Israel which had been organized by Israel Drapkin. World symposiums continue to be held on a biannual basis bringing researchers and practitioners involved in the field of victimology from around the world to network and to share their latest research findings and concerns.

CONTROVERSIES

Victim Blame

One of the biggest steps forward in the field of victimology has been a move away from the blaming the victim mindset. As noted in the beginning of this chapter, victimology unfortunately started out with the typologies of Mendelsohn and von Hentig. Those typologies, although not directly blaming the victim, might, by indicating that some individuals could be more likely to become victims, in an indirect way be seen as factors in why someone was victimized.

I have discovered there are four types of victim blame:

1. Victim self-blame by the victim about himself/herself;
2. Victim blame by others known to the victim;
3. Victim blame by officials including police, lawyers, prosecutors, and medical personnel; and
4. Victim blame by the media or society in general.

Here are some examples of each of these situations:

Victim Self-Blame

Victims this author has interviewed, as well as experts who work with victims, confirm that, unfortunately, too often it is the victims who blame themselves. "If only" is a phrase you may hear victims say when they are expressing their victim self-blame. Another common phrase is, "I should have known better."

As noted in Chapter 1, "Victimology: An Overview," Dorri Olds wrote about her gang rape when she was 13 by five boys ages 14 to 15. She wrote about her experience in the *New York Times* in 2012. At that point, Dorri was in her 40s. Except for a therapist she confided in when she was in her mid-20s and in rehab, she kept the rape a secret for decades because she thought she was to blame for it. "I thought it was my fault because I wore a sexy shirt and flirted," Dorri said when speaking to a Victimology class. (Olds, 2012; Olds, 2020)

In a follow-up e-mail, when asked to explain what happened in rehab with her counselor in more detail, Dorri wrote: "The counselor asked me if anything had happened to me that fueled my drinking and drugging. I burst into tears and told her about that horrible night. I felt it was my fault because I had wanted a boy to ask me out on a date. But I thought my sexy shirt must've given the wrong message. I was confused and ashamed. My rehab counselor Mary (a social worker) said, "Girls aren't attacked because of their clothes. What happened to you was rape. Those boys raped you. And, the only cause of rape is rapists. It's not your fault. It was never your fault." Then she opened her arms to me and I leaned my head against her pretty sweater and wept. She held me for a long time. That was a life-changing moment for me." (Olds, 2021)

Jill C. was raped by a platonic friend when she was in high school. She had cut school and was smoking marijuana with some friends when she was held down and raped. Jill suffers from victim self-blame over what happened. "I shouldn't' have cut school," she says. "Every act has consequences. I shouldn't have gotten high." (Anonymous interview shared with author.)

Maya Angelou, acclaimed poet and college professor, wrote about victim self-blame in one of the most powerful ways in her first autobiography, *I Know Why the Caged Bird Sings*. Angelou shares how at the age of eight, the man her mother brought into the house, Mr. Freeman, raped her. He warned her not to tell because if she did, he would kill her beloved brother, Bailey. So, Angelou initially kept quiet. But eventually Angelou's told her brother Bailey because "I had to tell who did that to me, or the man would hurt another little girl." (Angelou, 1969)

So Angelou told, Mr. Freeman was arrested, There was a trial. He was found guilty and sentenced to "one year and one day, but he never got a chance to do his time." (Angelou, 1969) His lawyer got him released, and he was soon kicked to death.

Angelou's reaction to this news and, as she tells it in her autobiography, "I had to stop talking." Her victim self-blame was not tied to why the rape happened but to her self-disclosure that somehow in her child mind that led to Mr. Freeman's death.

She did not speak for five years. Elizabeth Street, writing at LearningLiftOff.com, says that it was a teacher who inspired Angelou to speak again. Bertha Flowers, a teacher, who knew that Angelou loved poetry told her, "'You do not love poetry, not until you speak it.'" (Street, May 8, 2017)

Victim Blame by Others

- A 16-year-old is raped by her best friend's 26-year-old brother. The only person she confides in about what happened is her grandmother. The victim is shocked that her grandmother's response was, "She asked what I was wearing for him to push himself on me like that."
- Jill C., mentioned above under victim self-blame, shared with her interviewer, "I told my boyfriend at the time. He blamed me and said I was a whore." However, fortunately for Jill, and her relationship with her boyfriend, he apologized for his initial hurtful declaration. Jill continues, "But then we talked about what exactly happened in that bedroom and he told me, 'You realize that is rape.'"

The above examples are of victim blame of those close to the victim, a trusted extended family member and authority figure (Valerie's grandmother) and a romantic partner (Jill's boyfriend). There is another fundamental person in a discussion of this type of victim blame and that is the offender. In their classic article, "Techniques of Neutralization: A Theory of Delinquency," published in 1957, the same year as Wolfgang's "Victim-Precipitated Homicide" article, Gresham M. Sykes and David Matza put forth their theory that there are five major techniques that delinquents learn that enable them to become deviant and commit victimization. Those techniques are listed below; for the study of victimology, note the all-important third technique:

1. The denial of responsibility;
2. The denial of injury;
3. The denial of the victim;
4. The condemnation of the condemners; and
5. The appeal to higher loyalties. (Sykes and Matza, 1957: 667-670)

The excerpts that follow, from the section of Sykes and Matza's classic article entitled, "The Denial of the Victim," reinforce why this author sees the theory of neutralization as akin to victim blame:

> the moral indignation of self and others may be neutralized by an insistence that the injury is not wrong in light of the circumstances. The injury, it may be claimed, is not really an injury; rather, it is a form of rightful retaliation or punishment. By a subtle alchemy the delinquent moves himself into the position of an avenger and the victim is transformed into a wrong-doer . . . To deny the existence of the victim, then, by transforming him into a person deserving injury is an extreme form of a phenomenon we have

> mentioned before, namely, the delinquent's recognition of appropriate and inappropriate targets for his delinquent acts. (Sykes & Matza, 1957: 668)

Criminologist Sykes and Matza's important journal article highlights the worst believers of victim blame, namely, the offender. It is their blame of the victim, a form of denial of the victim, that allows them to neutralize the victim. They considered that denial of the victim one of the five techniques that they saw as a means of justifying criminal behavior. Just as Sutherland saw his nine postulates of differential association as a way of explaining how criminal behavior is learned, the theory of neutralization, especially its denial of the victim by seeing the victim as deserving of whatever fate befalls him or her, squarely places the blame on the victim. (Sutherland and Cressey, 1974; Sykes & Matza, 1957)

Victim Blame by Officials, including Police, Lawyers, Prosecutors, Medical Personnel, and Employers

Those who work in law enforcement as well as those who interview victims for rehab, crime victim assistance programs, rape or domestic violence crisis centers, and other criminal justice-related situations need to be mindful of victim blame, and the necessity of avoiding it. Here are examples:

- Jill, mentioned above, actually suffered three types of victim blame. Her third type was the victim blame by officials. Jill explained in her interview that she reported her rape to the police "but they wouldn't investigate because they said I [was] lying and that I wanted it."
- Banu P., whose attack by a rickshaw driver in Egypt that you will read about in greater detail in Chapter 13, "Victims of Assault, Domestic Violence, Stalking, and Elder Abuse," shared that a senior teacher at the college where she was working commented, "She is a foreigner and she took a rickshaw!" (Personal communication with author, 2021)

Victim Blame by the Media and Society

When you read an article in the newspaper or a story on the internet, and the inference is that the victim "was asking for it," that is a type of victim blame that is hurtful to the victim or, in the case of homicide, to the victim's family. That is media victim blame. This author requested an interview with the parents of a murder victim back in the 1970s when she was doing the research for her book *Victims*. The case was a famous one, leading to a big Hollywood movie and no fewer than two books on the case, a novel and a nonfiction true crime. Those parents were the only victims who turned down the interview explaining that the media had painted their daughter in a very unflattering light. Instead of the dedicated hard-working teacher that she was, who was single and who went home with a man she met at a bar, like so many single women in their 20s used to do—and some still may do so—she was depicted as promiscuous.

Unfortunately, this type of media blaming of the victim happens far too often. Training the media in how to deal with survivors of crime as well as the families of homicide victims would be a welcome step in helping to reduce this type of unnecessary victim blame by the media.

Victim Precipitation

The three concepts of victim precipitation, victim facilitation, and victim provocation need to be clarified since these concepts are pivotal to victimology. **Victim precipitation** is easiest since Dr. Marvin Wolfgang, discussed earlier in this chapter, was quite clear on his definition: "The role of the victim is characterized by his having been the first in the homicide drama to use physical force directed against his subsequent slayer." (Wolfgang, 1957)

However, criminologists Leah E. Daigle and Lisa R. Muftic define victim precipitation in a much more general way: "the extent to which a victim is responsible for his or her own victimization." (Daigle and Muftic, 2020: 4)

This controversial concept has permeated victimology almost from its beginning. (von Hentig, 1940; Mendelsohn, 1963; Wolfgang, 1957; Amir, 1967; Gobert, 1977; Schafer, 1968). In 1985, Terance D. Miethe published an article in the Sociological Focus, "The Myth or Reality of Victim Involvement in Crime: A Review and Comment on Victim-Precipitation Research," which included an analysis of the flaws in victim-precipitation research to date. Those included: methodological issues (the studies had relied on police files) and conceptual/definitional problems: whose definition do we use? A legal one that would deem someone's actions self-defense? Should it be restricted to only certain crimes? (Miethe, 1985: 211-214)

Victim Facilitation

The victim has a much more passive role in the crime that occurs when it is deemed victim facilitation. An example would be if someone has not locked his or her car door (or the door to an apartment or house). For example, in a Connecticut town, the police reported that of the 42 cars that were stolen or broken into during the month of December 2020, only one was locked. (Laguarda, 2021)

If someone goes to the cafeteria and puts his or her cell phone on the table, rushing to get some condiments for lunch, only to return a few seconds later to find the cell phone is missing, that would be considered victim facilitation. Some criminologists consider victim facilitation a term that is applied to property crimes rather than violent personal crimes. A controversy could be fueled, however, when it is noted that victim facilitation should not be confused with, or seen as a justification for, victim blame. These are quite distinct concepts.

Victim Provocation

In *Crime Victimization*, Elizabeth Quinn and Sara Brightman define **victim provocation** in this way: "the individual who starts a fight with someone in a bar and ends up getting stabbed. The person may be seen as both an offender and a victim at the same time as he may have initiated the event, but also experienced harm as a result of it (and perhaps greater harm than the other victim)." (Quinn and Brightman, 2015: 19)

Daigle and Muftic define victim provocation to be a concept that takes the idea of the victim as offender even further than Wolfgang's concept of victim precipitation with the victim the first to show violence. Here is their definition of victim provocation: "when a person does something that incites another person to commit an illegal act. Provocation suggests that without the victim's behavior, the crime would not have occurred. Provocation, then, most certainly connotes blame. In fact, the offender is not at all responsible." (Daigle and Muftic, 2020: 4)

The Just World Hypothesis

A textbook on victimology and a discussion of controversies, including the all-important victim blame phenomenon, would be incomplete if this author left out psychologist Melvin J. Lerner's groundbreaking work on what has become known as the just world hypothesis. This author first learned about the just world hypothesis during the 1970s, while researching victims and studying for a master's in criminal justice. (Barkas a/k/a Yager, *Victims,* 1978) In his co-authored article, "Just World Research and the Attribution Process: Looking Back and Ahead," published in 1978, Lerner and Miller even begin by addressing victim blame. The very first sentence of their article reads: "Various sources have noted the tendency of people to blame the victims of misfortunes for their own fates." (Lerner and Miller, 1978: 1030)

Based on various studies conducted in the 1960s by Dr. Lerner and others, such as Walster, Lerner developed the **just world hypothesis**. As Lerner and Miller write: "The just world hypothesis is easily stated: Individuals have a need to believe that they live in a world where people generally get what they deserve. The belief that the world is just enables the individual to confront his physical and social environment as though they were stable and orderly. Without such a belief it would be difficult for the individual to commit himself to the pursuit of long-range goals or even to the socially regulated behavior of day-to-day life." (Lerner and Miller, 1978: 1030; Lerner, 1965; Walster, 1966; Miller, 1977).

Now that you know the definition of the just world hypothesis, you can probably see how it is easy to make a quick leap from that hypothesis to victim blame. If you blame the victim for what happened, then the world is still just. If the victim is not to blame, that means that what happened to that victim could happen to anyone. That is a frightening, terrifying, and numbing thought.

Since victim blame is a misleading term, we also know that the concept of a just world, however comforting that might be, is also a misleading concept and term.

False Victimization

You may have heard of false accusation, whereby someone is falsely accused of a crime, false confession, when someone confesses to a crime he or she did not commit, or false imprisonment, when someone is falsely convicted of a crime but is really innocent. A phenomenon that is less widely known but that still needs to be addressed because it does occur is something known as false victimization. In Chapter 5, "Victims and the Criminal Justice System: Police, Courts, and Correction," you will learn that the police call **defounding** when an investigation into the facts of a reported crime lead to the conclusion that the victim's version of events are not born out by the forensics, witness accounts, or other evidence. In Chapter 10, "Child Victims," you will learn about the SAID syndrome, an acronym for Sexual Allegations in Divorce. This occurs when a parent coaxes a child or teen to make false accusations against the other parent to gain an upper hand in divorce proceedings relating to custody issues or the financial settlement. (Karmen, 2020: 300)

If someone claims to have been the victim of a burglary, putting in an insurance claim for the theft of an expensive antique vase, but no burglary occurred and no vase was stolen, that is an example of a false victimization related to a property crime. That alleged victim would be guilty of insurance fraud and making a false police report, among other possible criminal charges. Probably the most infamous examples of false victimization are when someone cries rape and none occurred. (See Chapter 12, "Sexual Violence Rape, Sexual Abuse, Assault, and Harassment Victims," for a summary of famous cases in this category which eventually led to the alleged rapist's acquittal and charges against the person who turned out to be a pseudo-victim.)

False victimization is a concern that is often brought up in the case of rape, especially after sexual assault laws were modified so that victims did not have to show resistance and even injury to "prove" that they had been raped. However, false claims of rape are in reality fairly infrequent. In their article, "Rape and Child Sexual Abuse: What Beliefs Persist About Motives, Perpetrators, and Survivors?" by Hannah McGee, Madeleine O'Higgins, Rebecca Garavan, and Ronan Conroy, it was noted that the rates of false rape allegations is between 2 percent and 9 percent. That was based on a study by Kelly and Lovett of rape cases in 11 European countries. (McGee, et al., 2011: 3582; Kelly & Lovett, 2009; Rumney, 2006; Piggott and Soothill, 1999; Heaney, 2018; Lind, 2015).

Repeat Victimization or Polyvictimization

Why does someone become a victim more than once? Laura K., a 55-year-old single marketing entrepreneur, has been the victim of seven different crimes: childhood sexual abuse, molestation, rape, aggravated assault, rape, hate crime, and motor vehicle theft. Nance Schick has been the victim of multiple crimes as well including, most recently, aggravated assault in a robbery attempt. (You will read Nance Schick's story in Chapter 8, "Property Crime Victims.")

Those are anecdotal examples, as is the previous example of Bonnie and repeat victimizations that were shared earlier in this chapter. Criminologists Jillian J. Turanovic and Travis C. Pratt co-authored a quantitative study on repeat victimization, "Can't Stop, Won't Stop": Self-Control, Risky Lifestyles, and Repeat Victimization," published in the *Journal of Quantitative Criminology*. Turanovic and Pratt conclude that "repeat victimization is a complex phenomenon." (Turanovic and Pratt, 2014) But it is certainly a situation that is worth studying; if the first victimization could not be prevented, hopefully there is a way to prevent a second, third, or even more victimizations.

Researchers are discovering that just as there are repeat offenders, there are those who suffer victimization repeatedly. It is not feasible to generalize from Turanovic and Pratt's sample of teenagers involved in risky lifestyles and how it was possible to reduce repeat victimization. However, their suggestion about how their findings relate to repeat victimization should be heeded: "Helping victims to limit their use of drugs and alcohol, to avoid participating in violence or in unstructured and unmonitored social activities, and to minimize friendships with violent peers may substantially decrease the likelihood that they are repeatedly victimized." (Turanovic and Pratt, 2021: 46)

System Blaming

Another controversial concept we will discuss in this chapter is **system blaming**, whereby victimization is not considered the fault of the criminal, nor is blame shifted to the victim. Instead, it is the system that is to blame. System blaming was particularly popular by the so-called Chicago School of Sociology in the 1930s. A book that was the quintessential example of that was Clifford Shaw's *The Jack-Roller: A Delinquent Boy's Own Story* (Shaw, 1930, 2013 reprint). Based on extensive interviews with "Stanley," "whose career in delinquency began at the age of six and a half years . . ." (Shaw, 1930/2013: 24) By eight years old, he was arrested because he was truant from school and placed in the Detention Home. (Shaw, 1930/ 2013: 47) After many times in prison, 22-year-old Stanley finally seemed to get his life on track, finding a job. The blame for Stanley's brush with the law is placed on the neighborhood he grew up in. The emphasis is on the social issues that Stanley had to deal with during his formative years, rather than on Stanley's choices.

A more contemporary system blaming example is whether the change in the bail system in New York City— eliminating cash bail when someone is arrested except in the most serious offenses—and any other criminal justice reforms were the cause of the dramatic increase in gun violence, violent crime, and even homicide in 2021 compared to previous years. Is system blaming the reason is reflected in the title of the PBS News Hour interview, "Is Criminal Justice Reform to Blame for the Rise in Crime in NYC?" (PBS News Hour, 2021)

Identification with the aggressor

The last controversy we will address in this chapter is a psychological concept, the phenomenon of identification with the aggressor, first described by Sigmund Freud's youngest of six children, his daughter Anna, an influential psychoanalyst in her own right, in 1936, when the German edition of her book, *The Ego and the Mechanisms of Defense*, was published. (Freud, 1936, English translation, 1937, 1992 reprint). You might associate the concept of identification with the aggressor with the Stockholm Syndrome, a related idea based on an actual bank robbery in Stockholm on August 23, 1973. It was said that after the two-day ordeal, "the hostages still saw compassion in their abductors." (Klein, 2019) The term Stockholm Syndrome became even more popular after newspaper heiress Patty Hearst was kidnapped in 1974; nineteen months later, she was captured by the FBI and eventually tried for her alleged participation in illegal activities with her captors. Others thought she was the victim of the Stockholm Syndrome. (Latson, 2015)

In victimology studies, identification with the aggressor applies more often to the syndrome that you will read more about in several chapters dealing with specific victimizations such as in Chapter 10, "Child Victims." Yes, research has been validating that being exposed to violence in the home, whether it is observing parents fighting violently or siblings abusing their brothers or sisters, without intervention, increases the likelihood that those primary and secondary victims may become perpetrators. Of course the concept of identification with the aggressor does not excuse criminal behavior. But it might help us to better understand the consequences of victimization, such as witnessing violence or being bullied, on shaping those who might go on to become aggressors themselves.

Too often mass murderers will point to alleged bullying during their formative years as the reason they became a killer. A study by the U.S. Secret Service National Threat Assessment Center, studying 41 school attacks in the U.S. from 2008 through 2017, concluded, according to the Associated Press report by Colleen Long: "Most students who committed deadly school attacks over the past decade were badly bullied, had a history of disciplinary trouble and their behavior concerned others but was never reported . . ." (Long, 2019)

SUMMARY

The earliest "victimology" theories were typologies developed by Beniamin Mendelsohn, who is said to have coined the term *victimology* in 1947 and to have first written about the victim-criminal relationship in 1937, followed by Hans von Hentig, whose 1940 and 1947 typologies were important to the development of the discipline. Empirical research on victimization trends was pioneered by University of Pennsylvania criminologist Marvin Wolfgang as reported in his influential 1957 article, "Victim-Precipitated Criminal Homicide." His finding that 26 percent of the 588 homicides that he studied had what he called victim-precipitation, meaning the victim was the first to render the initial blow or show a weapon became one of the leading theories in victimology even though victim precipitation factored in only 26 percent of the cases. Opportunity-based theories were advanced in the 1970s, including Lifestyle Theory proposed by Michael Hindelang, Michael Gottfredson, and James Garofalo; Cohen and Felson's Routine Activity Theory; and, almost a decade later, Rodney Stark's Deviant Place Theory. (Cohen and Felson, 1979; Hindelang, Gottfredson, and Garofalo, 1978; Stark, 1987).

Other theoretical approaches include radical victimology, environmental victimology, and forensic victimology. In this chapter, this author showed how Edwin Sutherland's classic 1939 learned theory of criminal behavior, based on the truism that criminal behavior is, by and large, learned, could be reapplied to victim behavior. This chapter includes the suggestion that a multidisciplined theory of victimization that reflects the various social sciences and communication arts will further our understanding about who is more likely to become a crime victim, and why.

Key controversies in victimology are highlighted, including victim blame, victim precipitation, victim facilitation, victim provocation, repeat victimization, defounding, and system blaming. The related concept, Lerner's just world hypothesis, is also discussed. A concept first introduced by psychoanalyst Anna Freud, identification with the aggressor, is also mentioned including its related to the so-called Stockholm Syndrome and the correlation between being bullied and some of the shoot shooters in the U.S. between 2008 and 2017. These are just some of the controversial concepts related to victimology that will appear throughout *Essentials of Victimology* as specific crimes and victimizations are explored in greater depth.

KEY TERMS

CPTED (crime prevention through environmental design)
defounding
deviant place theory
environmental victimology
forensic victimology
just world hypothesis
lifestyle exposure theory
lifestyle theory
penal couple
radical victimology
repeat victimization
(RAT) routine activity theory)
SCPT (situational crime prevention theory)
situational victimization
target hardening
victim blame
victim facilitation
victimology
victim precipitation
victim-precipitated homicide
victim self-blame

REVIEW QUESTIONS

1. Who is considered the "father of victimology"?
2. What is Hans von Hentig's contribution to victimology theory?
3. How did criminologist Stephen Schafer's contribute to the growth of victimology?
4. What percentage of homicides in Philadelphia did Dr. Wolfgang find to be victim-precipitated and why is this concept, first proposed in 1957, so important to the discipline of victimology?
5. Why did Dr. Amir's follow-up study, trying to compare victim-precipitated rapes to victim-precipitated homicides, fail to get the same positive attention accorded Dr. Wolfgang's study?
6. What do Cohen and Felson say are the three elements that, when present, increase the likelihood of victimization, or what they called the routine activity theory?
7. What is Sutherland's learned theory of criminal behavior and how could it apply to crime victims?
8. What is victim blame?
9. Who advanced the just world hypothesis and how does it tie into the concept of victim blame?
10. What is the concept of repeat victimization and why is being aware of it important to the study of victimology?

CRITICAL THINKING QUESTIONS

1. Do you agree that the fact that the co-founders of victimology, Mendelsohn and von Hentig, were in Europe during the rise of Nazism and World War II, both leaving for other countries, Mendelsohn to Israel and von Hentig to the United States, could have been a factor in the development of this new approach to crime, namely, the study of the

victim (victimology)? Support your view. (If you like, refer back to this related discussion in Chapter 1.)

2. Of all the early and more contemporary theories of victimization that you learned about in this chapter, which one seems to be the most likely explanation for the greatest number of victimizations in all types of crime including violent personal crimes, conventional property crimes, and white-collar crimes? Explain your answer.

3. If you studied criminology, you know there are half a dozen criminological theories about what causes criminal behavior including rational choice theory, trait theories, psychological, biosocial, and psychoanalytic theories, social structure theories, socialization theories, and developmental theories. (Siegel, 2018) Can you pick one of those criminological theories and apply it to an explanation for why someone is more likely to become a victim without falling into the victim blame mindset?

4. Do you agree or disagree that victim behavior, like criminal behavior, is learned? Share one or more examples from your readings or observations that support your answer.

5. Pick one of the controversies you learned about in this chapter and discuss your views of it: victim blame, victim precipitation, victim facilitation, system blaming, the just world hypothesis, and system blaming. Do you think the concept is valid? Outdated? Useful? Misunderstood? Support your views.

ACTIVITIES

1. Do a "ripped from the headlines" activity. Search the internet for information about whatever crime you and your "team" want to discuss. It could be rape, robbery, murder, aggravated assault, burglary, motor vehicle theft, larceny/theft, cybercrime, or another crime that is not listed here. Your professor can put you into groups of four. Assign one of your group to be the notetaker. Write down the main details about the crime. Who was the victim? Age? Gender? Occupation? Marital status (if known)? Time of day that the crime occurred? Who was the perpetrator (if known)? What was their relationship (if known?)? Then take 10 minutes to discuss among yourselves which of the following theories your group thinks applies best to this "ripped form the headlines" victimization:

    1. Routine activity theory;
    2. Lifestyle theory;
    3. Deviant place theory;
    4. Wolfgang's Victim-precipitation theory;
    5. Situational victimization theory;
    6. Yager's victim behavior as learned behavior theory (an adaptation of Sutherland's original differential association theory); or
    7. Sykes and Matza's theory of neutralization.

    When the 10 minutes is up, be prepared to present your case for one of these theories to the rest of the class. (This group activity can be done in in-person, hybrid, or online only teaching settings using the breakout room function if one is available in the videoconferencing program.)

2. Access the website for the online library collection for your college, university, or law school. Pick the one article related to victimology theories and typologies that you are

most interested in reading in its original format. Put into the search engine the title of the journal article and any other key details to help you locate that original article such as author's name, place and year of publication. Write a detailed summary about everything you learn by reading the original article. Especially if the article goes back decades or even almost a century ago, what examples are still relevant? Which ones are dated? What more contemporary examples could you substitute? Is there anything about the theory that is dated? What is still relevant, and why?

3. Pick one of the early founders of victimology—Mendelsohn, von Hentig, or Schafer—and do additional research on your chosen figure. Consider what was happening in the world, in the United States, and even in their own lives, that might explain why they developed, and expanded, the new discipline of victimology at that particular time in history.

RESOURCES

Academy of Criminal Justice Sciences (ACJS)
Victimology Section
acjs.org
There is a victimology section to this international professional membership organization dedicated to education and information gathering related to the criminal justice system.

American Society of Criminology (ASC)
Division of Victimology
asc41.com
Founded in 1941, this international membership association for criminologists, victimologists, sociologists, and penologists hosts an annual meeting. There are number divisions within the association including a Division on Victimology (DOV). It was created in 2012 by Dr. Bonnie S. Fisher and Dr. Robert Jerin. There is an international conference every year, usually in November, in a different U.S. city unless it is held virtually.

NOVA (National Organization of Victim Assistance)
trynova.org
Nonprofit membership educational organization founded in 1976 that is especially focused on training those who work with crime victims. Holds an annual conference in the summertime. They also offer NOVA Crisis Response Team Training.™

World Society of Victimology
worldsocietyofvictimology.org
This international membership organization had its roots in the First International Symposium on Victimology that was organized by Israel Drapkin in Israel in 1976. Every three years there is an international conference held in a different global location.

CITED WORKS AND ADDITIONAL REFERENCES

Alexander, Cheryl S. March 1980. "The Responsible Victim: Nurses' Perceptions of Victims of Rape." *Journal of Health and Social Behavior*. 21: 22-33.

Amir, Menachem. *Patterns in Forcible Rape*. 1971. Chicago, IL: University of Chicago Press.

______________. December 1967. "Victim Precipitated Forcible Rape." *The Journal of Criminal Law, Criminology and Police Science*. 58: 493-502.

Angelou, Maya. 1969. *I Know Why the Caged Bird Sings*. New York: Random House, Inc.

Beccaria, Cesare. 1764, 1963. *On Crimes and Punishments.* Translated by H. Paolucci. Indianapolis, IN: Bobbs-Merrill.

Brownmiller, Susan. 1975. *Against Our Will: Men, Women and Rape.* New York: Simon & Schuster.

Burgess, Ann Wolbert. 2019. *Victimology.* Third edition. Burlington, MA: Jones & Bartlett.

Burgess, Ann Wolbert and Lynda Lytle Holmstrom. 1974. "Rape Trauma Syndrome." *American Journal of Psychiatry.* 131: 981-986.

_______________. 1973. "The Rape Victim in the Emergency Ward." *American Journal of Nursing.* 73: 1741-1743.

Clarke, R.V. 1997. *Situational Crime Prevention: Successful Case Studies.* Second edition. Australia: Harrow & Heston.

Claster, D.S. and David, D.S. 1977. "The Resisting Victim: Extending the Concept of Victim Responsibility." *Victimology.* 2: 109-117.

Cohen, Lawrence and Marcus Felson. 1979. "Social Change and Crime Rate Trends: A Routine Activities Approach." *American Sociological Review.* 44: 588-608.

Coyne, Marley. April 11, 2020. "Crime Rates Across U.S. Drop Amid the Coronavirus Pandemic." *Forbes.* Posted online at Forbes.com

Cunningham, Katherine C. and Lisa DeMarni Cromer. 2016. "Attitudes About Human Trafficking: Individual Differences Related to Belief and Victim Blame." *Journal of Interpersonal Violence.* 31: 228-244.

Curtis, Lynn A. April 1974. "Victim Precipitation and Violent Crime." *Social Problems.* 21: 594-605.

Delille, Emmanuel. 2016. "Teaching the History of Psychiatry in the 1950s: Henri Ellenberger's Lectures at the Menninger Foundation." *Zinbun.* 47: 109-128.

Doerner, William G. and Steven P. Lab. 2021. *Victimology.* Ninth edition (Eighth edition published 2017). New York and London: Routledge.

Durkheim, Emile. *Suicide: A Study in Sociology.* 1897, 1963 reprint. Translated by John A. Spaulding and George Simpson. London: Routledge & Kegan Paul.

Dussich, John P.J. January 9-10, 2003. "History, Overview & Analysis of American Victimology and Victim Services Education." Proceedings of the First American Symposium on Victimology: Exploration of Higher Education and Professional Practice. Kansas City Community College, Kansas. 4-17.

_______________. January 9-10, 2003. Introduction. "Proceedings of the First American Symposium on Victimology: Exploration of Higher Education and Professional Practice." Kansas City Community College, Kansas. 2-3.

_______________ "Victimology: Past, Present and Future." n.d.131st International Senior Seminar Visiting Experts Papers.

Ellenberger, H. 1954. "Psychological Relationships Between the Criminal and His Victim." *Revue Internationale de Criminologie et se Police Techniquer.* 2: 103-121.

Fattah, Ezzat A. 2000. "Victimology: Past, Present and Future." *Criminologie.* 33: 17-46.

Finkelhor, David and Richard Ormrod. October 2001. "Homicides of Children and Youth." *Juvenile Justice Bulletin.* U.S. Department of Justice. Posted at https://www.ncjrs.gov/pdffiles1/ojjdp/187239.pdf

Fisher, Bonnie S. and Steven P. Lab. 2010. *Encyclopedia of Victimology and Crime Prevention.* Thousand Oaks, CA: SAGE.

Fisher, Bonnie S., Bradford W. Reyns, and John J. Sloan III. 2016. *Introduction to Victimology: Contemporary Theory, Research, and Practice.* New York: Oxford University Press.

Freud, Anna. *The Ego and the Mechanisms of Defense.* 1937 reprinted, 1992. New York: Routledge.

Friedrichs, David O. April 1983. "Victimology: A Consideration of the Radical Critique." *Crime & Delinquency.* 283-294.

Gangloff, Bernard and Crisanta-Alina Mazilescu. 2015. "Is It Desirable or Useful to Believe in a Just World?" *Revista de Cercetare Si Interventie Sociala.* 51: 150-161 (published in English by Expert Projects Publishing House).

Garofalo, Baron Raffaele. 1914. *Criminology.* Boston: Little, Brown and Company.

Gibran, Kahlil. 1923, reprinted 1969. *The Prophet.* London: Heinemann.

Gobert, James J. May 1977. "Victim Precipitation." *Columbia Law Review.* 77: 511-553.

Goffman, Erving. 1963. *Stigma: Notes on the Management of a Spoiled Identity.* Englewood Cliffs, NJ: Prentice-Hall.

Gottfredson, Michael R. Summer. 1981. "On the Etiology of Criminal Victimization" *The Journal of Criminal Law and Criminology.* 72: 714-726.

Gottfredson, Michael R. and Travis Hirschi. 1990. *A General Theory of Crime.* Stanford, CA: Stanford University Press.

Gramazio, Sarah, Mara Cadinu, Stefano Pagliaro, and Maria Giuseppina Pacilli. 2018. "Sexualization of Sexual Harassment Victims Reduces Bystanders' Help: The Mediating Role of Attribution of Immorality and Blame." *Journal of Interpersonal Violence*. 1-25.

Griffin, Brenda Sue. 1977. "Rape: Risk, Confrontation and Normalization." Ph.D. Dissertation. University of Illinois at Urbana-Champaign, Department of Sociology: Urbana, IL.

Griffin, Susan. September 1971. "Rape: The All-American Crime." *Ramparts*. 26-35.

Gromet, Dena M. 2012. "Restoring the Victim: Emotional Reactions, Justice Beliefs, and Support for Reparation and Punishment." *Critical Criminology*. 20: 9-23.

Heaney, Katie. October 5, 2018. "Almost No One Is Falsely Accused of Rape." Posted at thecut.com.

Hersey, Jon. 1946. *Hiroshima*. New York: Knopf.

Hindelang, Michael J., Michael Gottfredson, and James Garofalo. 1978. *Victims of Personal Crime: An Empirical Foundation for a Theory of Personal Victimization*. Cambridge, MA: Ballinger.

Holstein, James A, and Gale Miller. 1990. "Rethinking Victimization: An Interactional Approach to Victimology." *Symbolic Interaction*. 13: 103-122.

Huisman, Wim and Judith van Erp. 2013. "Opportunities for Environmental Crime: A Test of Situational Crime Prevention Theory." *British Journal of Criminology*. 53: 1178-1200.

Klein, Christopher. April 9, 2019. "Stockholm Syndrome: The True Story of Hostages Loyal to their Captor." Posted at history.com

Korellis, Patrick. March 2, 2021. Zoom interview with author and Social Deviance class. Kean University.

Kubrin, Charis E. 2010. "Clifford R. Shaw and Henry D. McKay: Social Disorganization Theory." *The Encyclopedia of Criminological Theory*. Edited by Francis T. Cullen & Pamela Wilcox. Thousand Oaks, CA: SAGE. Published online

Laguarda, Ignacio. February 1, 2021, updated February 5, 2021. "42 Cars Stolen or Broken Into in December; All but 1 Were Unlocked, Stamford Police Say." *Stamford Advocate*. Posted online.

Latson, Jennifer. September 18, 2015. "How an American Heiress Became the Poster Child for Stockholm Syndrome." *Time* magazine. Posted at time.com

Lerner, Melvin J. 2003. "The Justice Motive: Where Social Psychologists Found It, How They Lost It, and Why They May Not Find It Again." *Personality and Social Psychology Review*. 7(4): 388-399.

___________. 1971. "Observer's Evaluation of a Victim: Justice, Guilt. and Veridical Perception." *Journal of Personality and Social Psychology*. 20: 17-35.

___________. 1997. "What Does the Belief in a Just World Protect Us From: The Dread of Death or the Fear of Undeserved Suffering?" *Psychological Inquiry*. 8:29-32.

Lerner, Melvin J. and Dale T. Miller. 1978. "Just World Research and the Attribution Process: Looking Back and Ahead." *Psychological Bulletin*. 85: 1030-1051.

Lifton, Robert Jay. 1967. *Death in Life: The Survivors of Hiroshima*. London: Weidenfeld and Nicolson.

Linda, Dara. June 1, 2015. "What We Know About False Rape Allegations." Vox.com.

Luckinbill, D. F. 1977. "Criminal Homicide as a Situated Transaction." *Social Problems*. 25: 176-186.

Long, Colleen. November 7, 2019. "Secret Service Study: Chool Shooters Were Badly Bullied, Showed Warning Signs." Associated Press. Published by the *Colorado Sun* newspaper and posted online at coloradosun.com.

Mawby, R. and S. Walklate. 1994. *Critical Victimology: International Perspectives*. Thousand Oaks, CA: SAGE.

McGee, Hannah, Madeline O'Higgins, Rebecca Garavan, and Ronan Conroy. 2011. "Rape and Child Sexual Abuse: What Beliefs Persist About Motives, Perpetrators, and Survivors?" *Journal of Interpersonal Violence*. 26: 3580-3593.

McShane, Marilyn D. and Frank P. Williams III. April 1992. "Radical Victimology: A Critique of the Concept of Victim in Traditional Victimology." *Crime and Delinquençy*. 38(2): 258-271.

Meier, Robert F. and Terance D. Miethe. 1993. "Understanding Theories of Criminal Victimization." *Crime and Justice*. 17: 459-499.

Mendelsohn, B. May-June 1963. "The Origin of the Doctrine of Victimology." *Excerpta Criminologica*. 3(3). Reprinted in Israel Drapkin and Emilio Viano (eds.). 1974. *Victimology*. Lexington, MA: Lexington Books. 3-11.

Mendelsohn, Beniamin. "Methods to be used by Counsel for the Defense in the Researches made into the Personality of the Criminal." *Revue de Droit Penal et de Criminologie*. France. August-October 1937.

_______________. 1963. "The Origin of the Doctrine of Victimology." Reprinted in Chapter 1: 3-11, in Israel Drapkin and Emilio Viano (eds.). 1974. *Victimology*. Lexington, MA: Lexington Books.

_______________. November 24, 1978. Personal correspondence.

________________. January 19, 1978. Personal correspondence.

________________. September 1973. "Victimology and the Needs of Contemporary Society." *The Israel Annals of Psychiatry and Related Disciplines.* 11: 1-9.

Miethe, Terance D. August 1985. "The Myth or Reality of Victim Involving in Crime: A Review and Comment on Victim-Precipitation Research." *Sociological Focus.* 18: 209-220.

Ministry of Children, Community and Social Services. n.d. "Review of the Roots of Youth Violence: Literature Reviews." Volume 5, Chapter 3, "Rational Choice and Routine Activities Theory." (Section prepared with the assistance of Nicole Myers).

Moody-Ramirez, Mia and Hazel Cole. 2018. "Victim Blaming in Twitter Users' Framing of Eric Garner and Michael Brown." *Journal of Black Studies.* 49: 383-407.

Muftic, Lisa R. and Ronald E. Hunt. 2012. "Victim Precipitation: Further Understanding the Linkage Between Victimization and Offending in Homicide." *Homicide Studies* 17: 239-254.

Niemi, Laura and Liane Young. June 24, 2016. "Who Blames the Victim?" *The New York Times.* Posted at nytimes.com

Olds, Dorri. 2012. "Defriending My Rapist." *The New York Times.*

__________. April 15, 2020. Guest speaker, "Victimology." John Jay College of Criminal Justice, Department of Sociology.

_________. November 27, 2017. Guest speaker, "Victimology." John Jay college of Criminal Justice, Department of Sociology.

__________. March 3, 2021. Personal e-mail communication.

Oxford Reference. 2021. "Identification with the aggressor." Posted online at oxfordreference.com

Pane, Lisa Marie. December 29, 2020. "In a Year of Pain, One Silver Lining: Fewer Mass Shootings." Associated Press. Posted at apnews.com

Park, Robert E., Ernest W. Burgess, and Roderick McKenzie. 1925. *The City.* Chicago, IL: University of Chicago Press.

PBS News Hour. May 29, 2021. "Is Criminal Justice Reform to Blame for Rise in Crime in NYC?" Transcript of interview with Christopher Booker, Hari Sreenivasan, NY Governor Andrew Cuomo, and Julian Harris-Calvin,

Petherick, Wayne. 2017. "Victim Precipitation: Why We Need to Expand Upon the theory." *Forensic Research & Criminology International Journal.* 5: 262-264.

Piggott, Linda and Keith Soothill. April 1999. "False Accusation of Rape in the News." *The Police Journal.* 72: 151.

Pratt, Travis C., Kristy Holtfreter, and Michael D. Reisig. 2010. "Routine Online Activity and Internet Fraud Targeting: Extending the Generality of Routine Activity Theory." *Journal of Crime and Delinquency.* 47: 267-296.

Quinney, Richard. June 24, 2020. Personal communication.

_______________. 1970. *The Social Reality of Crime.* Boston: Little, Brown.

_______________. November 1972. "Who Is the Victim?" *Criminology.* 314-323.

Roberts, Julian V. 2009. "Listening to the Crime Victim: Evaluating Victim Input at Sentencing and Parole." *Crime and Justice.* 38: 347-412.

Roberts, Kayleigh. October 6, 2016. "The Psychology of Victim-Blaming." *The Atlantic* magazine. Posted online at theatlantic.com.

Rosoff, Stephen, Henry Pontell, and Robert Tillman. 2019. *Profit Without Honor.* Seventh edition. New York: Pearson.

Rumney, Philip N.S. March 2006. "False Allegations of Rape." *Cambridge Law Journal.* 128-158

Samenow, Stanton E. 2014, 1984. *Inside the Criminal Mind.* Revised and Updated edition. New York: Broadway Books, Random House, Inc.

Schafer, Stephen. 1968 *The Victim and His Criminal: A Study in Functional Responsibility.* New York: Random House, Inc.

Schur, Edwin M. 1965. *Crimes Without Victims: Deviant Behavior and Public Policy.* (Abortion, Homosexuality, Drug Addiction). Englewood Cliffs, NJ: Prentice-Hall, Inc.

Shaw, Clifford R. 1930, reprinted 2013. *The Jack-Roller.* Chicago, IL: University of Chicago Press.

Shaw, Clifford R. and Henry D. McKay. 1942. *Juvenile Delinquency and Urban Areas.* Chicago, IL: University of Chicago Press.

Shimon, Marilyn. 2020. *First One In, Last One Out: Auschwitz Survivor 31321.* Mirror Books.

Siegel, Larry J. 2018. *Criminology.* Thirteenth edition. Boston, MA: Cengage.

Stark, Rodney. November 1987. "Deviant Places: A Theory of the Ecology of Crime." *Criminology.* 893-910.

Street, Elizabeth. May 8, 2017. "The Moving Story of How a Teacher Inspired Maya Angelou to Speak." Posted at LearningLiftOff.com.

Sutherland, Edwin H. 1924. *Criminology*. Philadelphia, PA: J.B. Lippincott Company.

______________. 1947. *Principles of Criminology*. Fourth edition. Philadelphia, PA: Lippincott.

______________. February 1940. "White-Collar Criminality." *American Sociological Review*. 5: 1-12.

Sutherland, Edwin H. and Donald R. Cressey. 1974. *Criminology*. Ninth edition. Philadelphia, PA: Lippincott.

Sykes, Graham M. and David Matza. December 1957. "Techniques of Neutralization." *American Sociological Review*. 22: 664-670.

Thrasher, Frederic. 1927, 2013. *The Gang*. Chicago, IL: University of Chicago Press.

Trevino, A. Javier and Richard Quinney. 2019. *Clinard and Quinney's Criminal Behavior Systems*. Fourth edition. New York: Routledge.

Turvey, Brent E., et al. 2014. *Forensic Victimology: Examining Violent Crime Victims in Investigative and Legal Contexts*. Second edition. Boston, MA: Academic Press, an imprint of Elsevier.

Tyler, Kimberly A. and Morgan R. Beal. 2010. "The High-Risk Environment of Homeless Young Adults: Consequences for Physical and Sexual Victimization." *Violence and Victims*. 25: 101-115.

University of Colorado, Boulder. Universities Libraries. n.d. Hans von Hentig Papers. Collection. Identifier: COU: 1646. Summary of contents of papers posted online.

Van den Bos, Kees and Marjolein Maas. December 2009. "On the Psychology of the Belief in a Just World: Exploring Experiential and Rationalistic Paths to Victim Blaming." 35: 1567-1578.

Von Hentig, Hans. 1948. *The Criminal and His Victim: Studies in the Sociobiology of Crime*. New Haven, CT: Yale University Press. (Reprint edition 1979 with a Preface by Marvin E. Wolfgang: Schocken Books).

______________. September-October 1940. "Remarks on the Interaction of Perpetrator and Victim." *Journal of Criminal Law and Criminology*. 31(3): 303-309.

Voss, Harwin L. and John R. Hepburn. 1969. "Patterns in Criminal Homicide in Chicago." *Journal of Criminal Law, Criminology, and Police Science*. 59:499-508.

Walker, Lenore E.A. 1979. *The Battered Woman*. New York: Harper & Row.

______________. 1984. *The Battered Woman Syndrome*. New York: Springer.

______________. Wednesday, August 4, 2021. Correspondence with the author.

Walster, E. 1966. "Assignment of Responsibility for an Accident." *Journal of Personality and Social Psychology*. 36: 73-79.

Wertham, Frederic. 1949. *The Show of Violence*. New York: Doubleday.

Williams, Caroline. November 18, 2014. "How Pickpockets Trick Your Mind." Posted at BBC.com.

Williams, Christopher. 1996. "An Environmental Victimology." *Social Justice*. 23: 16-40.

Wolfgang, Marvin. 1958. *Patterns of Criminal Homicide*. Philadelphia, PA: University of Pennsylvania Press.

______________. May-June 1957. "Victim-Precipitated Homicide." *The Journal of Criminal Law, Criminology, and Police Science*. 48: 1-11.

Yager, Jan. *Help Yourself Now*. 2021. New York: Allworth Press, an imprint of Skyhorse Publishing.

___________. *Victims*. 2021, 2015. With a new introduction. Stamford, CT: Hannacroix Creek Books, Inc. (First edition published in 1978 by Scribner's under the name J.L. Barkas)

Yar, Majid. 2005. "The Novelty of 'Cybercrime': An Assessment in Light of Routine Activity Theory." *European Journal of Criminology*. 2: 407-427.

Zaykowski, Heather and Lena Campagna. 2014. "Teaching Theories of Victimology." *Journal of Criminal Justice Education*. 25: 452-467.

Videos and Radio Programs

MTV, "Decoded." "How to Stop Victim Blaming" hosted by Franchesca Ramsey. 4:35 minutes. Excellent, short perspective on victim-blaming including reference to Dr.Melvin Lerner's experiments and his concept of the just world hypothesis. Posted at https://www.youtube.com/watch?v=pij_4PNuAaA

Psych2Go. "What is Stockholm Syndrome? Psych 101 ep1" Mar 26, 2019 4:16 minutes Posted at https://www.youtube.com/watch?v=F-6VkeBv3G0

Gross, Terry, interviewer. May 28, 2014. National Public Radio (NPR) "'Fresh Air' Remembers Poet and Memoirist Maya Angelou" 15 minutes. Posted at https://www.npr.org/2014/05/28/316707321/fresh-air-remembers-poet-and-memoirist-maya-angelou

Chapter **FOUR**

Measuring Victimization

Why and How

Learning Objectives

After you finish reading this chapter, you should be able to:

1. Identify when and by whom the earliest crime statistics were gathered.
2. Provide at least three reasons why measuring crime at the local, state, national, and global level is a worthwhile effort.
3. Explain the three different ways that crime data is expressed through several rates: victimization, incident, or prevalence.
4. Define a clearance rate and why those rates are important.
5. Be aware of the history of the UCR (Uniform Crime Report), dating back to 1929, how the data is reported, and what federal agency analyzes and published it, and its replacement by the National Incident-Based Report System (NIBRS) beginning on January 1, 2021.
6. Recall at least a dozen of the 49 Group A Offenses in the NIBRS.
7. Be aware of the definitions for the crimes that the NIBRS tracks as well as the offender and victim data that is being recorded.
8. Know about the secondary major source of crime statistics about the United States, the National Crime Victimization Survey (NCVS), including when it was initiated as well as who and what it surveys.
9. Name at least two additional sources of crime victimization data in the United States.
10. Examine specific crime statistics in the United States and globally.
11. Recognize and understand research techniques for measuring crime used by victimologists.
12. Identify at least one of the four global crime studies described in this chapter.
13. Highlight the research methods used by criminologists for some of the key studies that have shaped victimology.

WHY STATISTICS ABOUT CRIME AND CRIME VICTIMIZATION MATTER

- A family is house hunting. Will the crime rate in a particular community be one of their considerations?
- A police precinct must make budget cuts and the first to go may be their community policing efforts. Are there any statistics that could support the effectiveness of community policing in lowering the community's crime rate?
- Several new laws have been passed, such as decriminalizing possession of a small quantity of marijuana or, in some states, making recreational marijuana legal. Is there a way to track if these new laws are having a positive or negative impact on a city or state's crime rates?
- Lydia wants to visit her partner when she finishes work. She will be walking alone from where she parks her car to her partner's apartment a block or two away. What do the statistics say about the safety of that neighborhood?
- Brian is a 20-year-old single male living and working in a major city. Does he have a greater, lesser, or similar chance of becoming a victim of one of the major personal violent crimes—murder, robbery, aggravated assault, or rape—than a 59-year-old married woman working from home in a suburb?

Crime data is a way of knowing where a community or even a country compares to others on certain types of crime, from robbery, burglary, homicide, and kidnapping to **cybercrime** and **white-collar crime**. Using the statistics shared in the United Nations Office of Drugs and Crime (UNODC) *2019 Global Study on Homicide*, if you are traveling to Venezuela, where the murder rate is 56.8 per 100,000 persons per year—one of the highest murder rates in the world—you may want to be super cautious compared to if you are visiting the Netherlands, where the murder rate is 0.6 per 100,000 persons in one year. (UNODC, 2019: 21)

Researchers, and even the average layperson, will want to know whether being robbed by a stranger is more likely than by someone they know, as well as any trends in crime victimization that might help them to take specific steps that might make them a less likely victim. For example, as you will see in Chapter 10, "Child Victims: Abuse, Neglect, and Other Victimizations," a family member, trusted adult known to the child, and even a same age peer acquaintance is the more likely perpetrator. So why do most parents send out the inaccurate message to their children that they should only be afraid of strangers without also teaching them how to recognize threats from the more likely perpetrators who are known to them?

Police departments have found that **crime mapping**, whereby crime data is used to see when, and where, crime is occurring, has been found to reduce crime. (Crime mapping is referred to in the quote that follows as "spatial predictions of crime.") For example, Fitterer, Nelson, and Nathoo report that the Los Angeles Police Department has used spatial predictions of crime to preemptively allocate patrol units and has estimated that geographical criminal intelligence has decreased violent crimes by 5.4 percent and homicides by 22.6 percent. (Fitterer, et al., 2015, referencing Uchida et al., 2012.)

Crime mapping also helps to identify what are known as **hot spots**, high-crime-density areas in a community or city. (Eck et al., 2005) Police department researchers and analysts have found that crime mapping of hot spots "significantly improved the ability of crime analysts and researchers to understand crime patterns and victimization." (Eck et al., National Institute of Justice, 2005)

A BRIEF HISTORY OF THE GATHERING OF CRIME STATISTICS

Many sociology textbooks date the empirical study of behavior by sociologists to the study of the statistical pattern of suicides that Emile Durkheim described and discussed in *Suicide*, published in 1897. As Durkheim notes in the Preface to *Suicide*, the source of the documents in his book that form the basis of his theories about suicide, and sociology, were from the Ministry of Justice. (Durkheim, 1897, reprinted 1970).

However, gathering crime statistics actually dates back to 1827 in France when Andre-Michel Guerry, a French lawyer, and Adolphe Quetelet, a Belgian mathematician and astronomer, both explored the completely new field of crime statistics. Their conclusions were similar: there was a pattern to crime. For example, Guerry discovered that in the richest parts of France, property crime was more common. (Fisher, Reyns, and Sloan, 2016)

Adolphe Quetelet, statistician

Michael Friendly, a York University Professor of Psychology and statistics expert, has studied Guerry extensively. He writes that Guerry (1802-1866), is one of the co-founders of the field of crime statistics, which had an immense influence on the development of criminology and sociology. In 1827, he was designated to work with the crime data that the Ministry of Justice had collected. He published his first major work on statistics, *Statistique Comparee de L'etat de L'Instruction*," 68 years before Durkheim's much more celebrated empirical study of *Suicide*. (Friendly, 2006; Friendly, 2007; Durkheim, 1897)

Then, in 1830, Guerry was appointed Director of Criminal Statistics at the Ministry of Justice. He published two more major works on statistics, in 1883 and 1864. (Friendly, 2006; Friendly, 2007)

One of Guerry's "'social fact'" discoveries was that crimes against persons were unrelated to literacy, but crimes against property increased with literacy. (Friendly, 2006)

Adolphe Quetelet (1796-1874), a Belgian astronomer, mathematician, and statistician, traveled to Paris in 1823 at the age of 27 where he studied at an astronomical observatory. He shares with Guerry the distinction of being one of the forerunners of modern crime measurements. He is said to have organized the first International Statistical Congress in 1853. (Tikkanen, 2021)

Upon his return to Belgium the following year, Quetelet was involved in various pursuits including publishing studies in mathematics, astronomy, and physics. But what is most central to our discussion of the growth of crime statistics was his proposal for a Belgian national census and the collection of crime statistics and the research and writings he conducted about patterns in crime victimization. (Beirne, 1987: 1150)

One of Quetelet's contributions, based on his analysis of crime statistics, was his theory that those lacking wealth who see wealth might be motivated to commit crime because of that disparity. Piers Beirne, better known for his animal abuse studies and green (environmental) criminology studies, quotes Quetelet's 1831 writings: "'These are the rough alternations from one state to another that give birth to crime, especially if those who suffer from them are surrounded by subjects of temptation and find themselves irritated by the continual view of luxury and of an inequality of fortune which disheartens them.'" (Quetelet, 1831, quoted by Beirne, 1987: 1155).

AN OVERVIEW OF CRIME VICTIMIZATION OFFICIAL DATA IN THE UNITED STATES

Let us jump ahead to the 1920s in America. **The International Association of Chiefs of Police (IACP)**, a nonprofit organization founded in 1893 and still in operation today, established a Committee on Uniform Crime Records to create a structure of uniform police statistics. (North Carolina State Bureau of Investigation, n.d.; IACP website)

Initially, seven offenses were chosen to be part of the data collection program. Those offenses were to be known as the **Crime Index**: murder and nonnegligent manslaughter, forcible rape, robbery, aggravated assault, burglary, larceny-theft, and motor vehicle theft. (In 1979, a Congressional mandate added arson to the list.)

In January 1930, according to the "UCR History" from the North Carolina State Bureau of Investigation, 400 cities representing 20 million people in 43 states were participating in the **UCR (Uniform Crime Report)** program. At that time, Title 28, Section 534 of the United States Code was enacted, which empowered the Attorney General to also gather crime data. The Attorney General chose the FBI (Federal Bureau of Investigation) to gather, analyze, and disseminate the annual data, a responsibility that it handles to this day. In addition to the cooperation of local police precincts through the IACP is the participation by the sheriffs throughout the United States via the National Sheriff's Association (NSA).

Keep in mind that the crime statistics sent by the local police departments and sheriffs to the FBI only includes reported crimes. There used to be a controversial **hierarchy rule** under the UCR. That stated that if someone was the victim of multiple crimes, such as rape, robbery, and aggravated assault, only the most serious offense would be recorded. The 2019 FBI Uniform Crime Report states that 15,261 police departments and county, city, and state law enforcement agencies sent data to the FBI for tabulating. Bear in mind, however, that this data only covers reported crimes since that is the only information that law enforcement can collect. (FBI, 2020)

NIBRS (National Incident Based Reporting System

The new NIBRS eliminated the hierarchy rule. Now one crime incident can be counted under up to 10 different offenses for any of the 52 offenses they now track. But you should know about the hierarchy rule because you may be using UCR data from recent or even many years ago for comparisons with today or for a historical review of crime rates and trends in the United States. So, the UCR data and the NIBRS data is technically not identical. But since the NIBRS became the standard on January 1, 2021, in time any discrepancies and disparities will be worked out. (FBI, 2013) The NIBRS is administered through what the FBI still refers to as the **Uniform Crime Reporting (UCR) Program**. (FBI, 2020)

The NIBRS will be discussed in greater detail below.

In Table 4.1 you will find one of the last UCR reports under the old system with the total number of crime victims indicated for the eight crimes of the Crime Index noted.

TABLE 4.1. Reported Crime in 2019 in the United States*

Type of Crime	Number of Reported Crimes
All reported violent crimes	**1,135,093**
Murder and nonnegligent manslaughter	15,020
Rape	126,958
Robbery	248,681
Aggravated assault	744,434
All reported crimes including property crimes	**9,626,836**
Burglary	998,474
Larceny-theft	4,659,007
Motor vehicle theft	667,300
Arson	33,395

*Population covered: 307,140,768. Number of police agencies reporting: 15,261

Source: 2019 FBI UCR (Uniform Crime Reporting) (Table 12, "Crime Trends")

Crime Statistics That Victimologists, Criminologists, and the Criminal Justice System Want to Know

In addition to the frequency of a crime, victimologists want to know about the relationship between the criminal and the victim. This is one of the key pieces of data that a victimologist would find especially useful in developing a better understanding of who becomes a victim, and why. Was this victim chosen randomly, like the 58 men and women attending an outdoor concert, shot to death by a lone Las Vegas mass shooter on October 1st, 2017? (Belson, Medina, and Perez-Pena, 2017) Or was there a family, friendship, acquaintance, or work relationship between the criminal and the victim, such as in the case of Ana Charle, the head of a shelter who, back in April 2015, was stalked, raped, and gunned down and killed by a former resident? (Baker, 2015)

Victimologists might also want to know the age, race, ethnicity, and occupation of the criminal and his or her victim, as well as where the crime occurred, whether there was a weapon present, and whether the victim put up a fight or complied. If a weapon was present during the crime, what kind of weapon was it and was it used? Was the crime reported to the police is another key question that helps to understand a crucial part of the criminal justice system. If it was not reported, why not? Was this the victim's first victimization? If not, how many other times has he or she been victimized? What were those crimes? Other statistics that victimologists might find useful to know are how often a particular crime occurs in an area, city, state, or country, during what days, or at what time, and whether the number of incidents is higher or lower than the year before or even during the previous decade.

DEFINING VICTIMIZATION, INCIDENT, PREVALENCE, AND CLEARANCE RATES

The amount of crime can be reported in terms of **raw number** or according to **victimization rate**, **incident rate**, or **prevalence rate**. Another important rate to know about is the **clearance rate**. All these terms are described below.

The *raw number* refers to the actual number of victims. Using Table 12 of the 2019 FBI Uniform Crime Report, there were 15,020 reported murders and nonnegligent manslaughters in the United States during that year. (FBI, *2019 Crime in the United States*, Table 12)

Official law enforcement crime statistics usually count crimes by the number of incidents instead of by the number of victims. For example, if three people are robbed, that would be calculated as one incident even though it was actually three victimizations. Because of that, victimization rates tend to be higher than incident rates. Incident rates permit us to examine crime rates across different cities. An *incident rate* refers to the number of new victims per 1,000 or per 100,000 individuals annually.

Prevalence rates are based on the number of persons or households in the population who experienced at least one victimization during a specific time period. Prevalence rates estimate the number of individuals per 1,000 or per 100,000 who have ever suffered a specific crime As Lauritsen and Rezey note in, "Measuring the Prevalence of Crime with the National Crime Victimization Survey," "Prevalence rates do not take into account the number of victimizations each victim experiences. These rates tell about the risk of experiencing at least one crime in a given period." (Lauritsen and Rezey, 2013)

The equation used to get the crime rate is on the basis of 100,000 people and is as follows:

$$\frac{\text{Number of Reported Crimes} = \text{that number} \times 100{,}000}{\text{Total U.S. Population}} = \text{Rate per 100,000 population}$$

To clarify, let us use actual numbers. Take the number of a specific crime in a state or a country, such as 15,020 reported murders in the U.S. in 2019. Divide that by the U.S. population in 2019 of 328,200,000. That answer is 0.00004576. Now multiply that number by 100,000 and you get the murder crime rate in the U.S. for 2019 based on reported murders of per 4.57 per 100,000 population.

Yes, rates can sometimes be confusing. Take the homicide rate for the United States. As will be mentioned in several chapters in this textbook, including in Chapter 7, "Primary and Secondary Homicide Victims," the United States has one of the highest homicide rates for a Westernized country, of approximately 5 murders per 100,000 individuals. Compare that to the much lower rate of such countries as Germany, with a 0.9 rate. But if we look more closely at just one American city, Baltimore, Maryland, in 2019 it had 348 homicides. With an estimated population of 593,490, that is a homicide rate of 57 per 100,000 persons, a far cry from the average of 5 murders per 100,000 for the country as a whole. (Prudente, 2020; Knezevich, 2020)

Another crime statistic that is useful to know about in understanding crime in America, or in any country for that matter, is the **clearance rate** for each offense. Simply put, clearance rate refers to the percentage of the reported offenses for a specific crime that is cleared by an arrest of a suspect. According to the FBI, the crime with the highest clearance rate in 2019 was, as you may have guessed, murder and nonnegligent manslaughter. That clearance rate was 61.4 percent. The crime with the lowest clearance rate was motor vehicle theft, at 13.8 percent, followed by burglary (14.1%) and then larceny-theft (18.4%). Stated another way, 85.9 percent of all reported burglaries and 81.6 percent of all larceny-thefts did not lead to the arrest of a suspect. (FBI, 2019)

Aggravated assault, considered a violent crime, had the second highest clearance rate, behind murder, at 52.3 percent. The clearance rate for reported rapes was only 32.9 percent, just a little higher than for robberies, at 30.5 percent. (FBI, 2019)

For all violent crimes in 2019 that were reported, the number of crimes that were cleared by an arrest was 45.5 percent (FBI, 2019)

Figure 4.1 shows this information in a clearer way.

FIGURE 4.1 **Percent of Crimes Cleared by Arrest or Exceptional Means,* 2019**

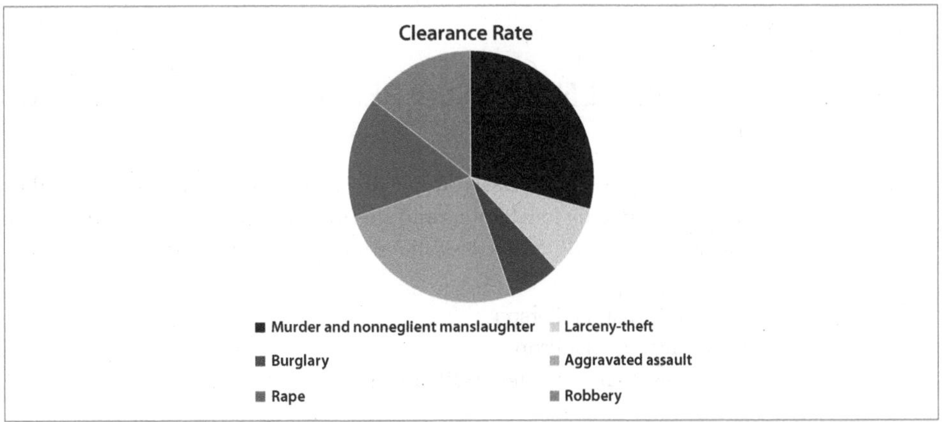

FIGURE 4.1 | Continued

Clearance rate for ALL violent crimes	**45.5%**
Murder & nonnegligent manslaughter	61.4%
Rape	32.9%
Robbery	30.5%
Aggravated assault	52.3%
Clearance rate for ALL property crimes	**17.2%**
Burglary	14.1%
Larceny-theft	18.4%
Motor vehicle theft	13.8%
Arson	23.8%

Source: FBI (Federal Bureau of Investigation), *2019 Crime in the United States*. Criminal Justice Information Services Division, Table 25. "Percent of Offenses Cleared by Arrest or Exceptional Means."

*This is what the FBI explains about the concept of "cleared by exceptional means."

Cleared by exceptional means

In certain situations, elements beyond law enforcement's control prevent the agency from arresting and formally charging the offender. When this occurs, the agency can clear the offense exceptionally. Law enforcement agencies must meet the following four conditions in order to clear an offense by exceptional means. The agency must have:

- *Identified the offender.*
- *Gathered enough evidence to support an arrest, make a charge, and turn over the offender to the court for prosecution.*
- *Identified the offender's exact location so that the suspect could be taken into custody immediately.*
- *Encountered a circumstance outside the control of law enforcement that prohibits the agency from arresting, charging, and prosecuting the offender.*

Examples of exceptional clearances include, but are not limited to, the death of the offender (e.g., suicide or justifiably killed by police or citizen); the victim's refusal to cooperate with the prosecution after the offender has been identified; or the denial of extradition because the offender committed a crime in another jurisdiction and is being prosecuted for that offense. In the UCR Program, the recovery of property alone does not clear an offense.

(Source: FBI, 2010)

THE NATIONAL INCIDENT-BASED REPORTING SYSTEM (NIBRS)

The **National Incident-Based Reporting System (NIBRS)** is the official crime data based on crimes reported by local police and sheriffs with the data sent to the FBI to compile, analyze, and share. The NIBRS divides crimes into three categories:

1. Crimes Against Person
2. Crimes Against Property
3. Crimes Against Society (FBI, 2013)

Tables 4.2 and 4.3 list the offenses that the NIBRS tracks, along with what type of crime it is considered. In Table 4.2, you will find a list of the offenses as well as which of the three categories that crime falls into: against person, against property, and against society. Note that the NIBRS lists robbery as a crime against property.

Definitions of all the crimes that NIBRS covers are included in Box 4.1. As stated in "Effects on Crime Statistics," the classification of these offenses is "based solely on police investigation as opposed to the determination of a court, medical examiner, coroner, jury, or other judicial body; these are law enforcement statistics." (FBI, "Effects of NIBRS on Crime Statistics," 12.) You may also access the NIBRS Offense Definitions provided by the FBI, U.S. Department of Justice, at this URL: https://ucr.fbi.gov/nibrs/2012/resources/nibrs-offense-definitions

TABLE 4.2. Group A Offense NIBRS Listings

There are 28 Group A offense categories made up of 71 Group A offenses. The offense categories are listed below in alphabetical order.

Offense	Crimes Against
Animal Cruelty	Society
Arson	Property
Assault Offenses	
Aggravated Assault	Person
Simple Assault	Person
Intimidation	Person
Bribery	Property
Burglary/Breaking & Entering	Property
Commerce Violations	
Import Violations*	Society
Export Violations*	Society
Federal Liquor Offenses*	Society
Federal Tobacco Offenses*	Society
Wildlife Trafficking*	Society
Counterfeiting/Forgery	Property
Destruction/Damage/Vandalism of Property	Property
Drug/Narcotic Offenses	
Drug/ Narcotic Violations	Society

(continued)

TABLE 4.2. Group A Offense NIBRS Listings (continued)

Offense	Crimes Against
Drug Equipment Violations	Society
Embezzlement	Property
Espionage*	Society
Extortion/Blackmail	Property
Fraud Offenses	
False Pretenses/Swindle/Confidence Game	Property
Credit Card/Automated Teller Machine Fraud	Property
Impersonation	Property
Welfare Fraud	Property
Wire Fraud	Property
Identity Theft	Property
Hacking/Computer Invasion	Property
Money Laundering	Property
Fugitive Offenses	
Harboring Escapee/Concealing from Arrest*	Society
Flight to Avoid Prosecution*	Society
Flight to Avoid Deportation*	Society
Gambling Offenses	
Betting/Wagering	Society
Operating/Promoting/Assisting Gambling	Society
Gambling Equipment Violations	Society
Sports Tampering	Society
Homicide Offenses	
Murder and Nonnegligent Manslaughter	Person
Negligent Manslaughter	Person
Justifiable Homicide	Not a Crime
Human Trafficking	
Commercial Sex Acts	Person
Involuntary Servitude	Person

TABLE 4.2. Group A Offense NIBRS Listings (continued)

Offense	Crimes Against
Immigration Violations	
Illegal Entry into the United States*	Society
False Citizenship*	Society
Smuggling Aliens*	Society
Re-entry after Deportation*	Society
Kidnapping/Abduction	Person
Larceny Theft Offenses	
Pocket-picking	Property
Purse-snatching	Property
Shoplifting	Property
Theft from Building	Property
Theft from Coin-Operated Machine or Device	Property
Theft from Motor Vehicle	Property
Theft of Motor Vehicle Parts or Accessories	Property
All Other Larceny	Property
Motor Vehicle Theft	Property
Pornography/Obscene Material	Society
Prostitution Offenses	
Prostitution	Society
Assisting or Promoting Prostitution	Society
Purchasing Prostitution	Society
Robbery	Property
Sex Offenses	
Rape	Person
Sodomy	Person
Sexual Assault with an Object	Person
Fondling	Person
Incest	Person
Statutory Rape	Person

(continued)

TABLE 4.2. Group A Offense NIBRS Listings (continued)

Offense	**Crimes Against**
Failure to Register as a Sex Offender*	Society
Stolen Property Offenses	Property
Treason*	Society
Weapon Law Violations	
Weapon Law Violations	Society
Violation of National Firearm Act of 1934*	Society
Weapons of Mass Destruction*	Society
Explosives*	Society

Source: NIBRS. This is an edited version of the Group A Offense Listing, posted at Mississippi NIBRS (ms.gov).

*Denotes offenses for federal and tribal LEA reporting only.

TABLE 4.3. Group B NIBRS Offenses Listed in Alphabetical Order

Bad Checks
Bond Default/Failure to Appear*
Curfew/Loitering/Vagrancy Violations
Disorderly Conduct
Driving Under the Influence
Drunkenness
Family Offenses, Nonviolent
Federal Resource Violation*
Liquor Law Violations
Peeping Tom
Perjury*
Trespass of Real Property
All Other Offenses

Source: NIBRS. This is an edited version of the Group B Offense Listing, posted at Mississippi NIBRS (ms.gov)

*Denotes offenses for federal and tribal LEA reporting only.

Box 4.1. NIBRS Offense Definitions (National Incident-Based Reporting System)

Source: Reprinted from "NIBRS Offense Definitions," Uniform Crime Reporting (UCR) Program, National Incident-Based Reporting System (NIBRS), U.S. Department of Justice, Federal Bureau of Investigation, NIBRS 2012.

NIBRS Offense Definitions

"The definitions that were developed for the NIBRS are not meant to be used for charging persons with crimes. To the contrary, they are simply a way of categorizing or organizing the crimes committed throughout the United States. State statutes must be very specific in defining crimes so that persons facing prosecution will know the exact charges being placed against them. On the other hand, the definitions used in the NIBRS must be generic in order not to exclude varying state statutes relating to the same type of crime.

Accordingly, the offense definitions in the NIBRS are based on common-law definitions found in *Black's Law Dictionary*, as well as those used in the *UCR Handbook* and the NCIC Uniform Offense Classifications. Since most state statutes are also based on common-law definitions, even though they may vary as to the specifics, most should fit into the corresponding NIBRS offense classifications.

If a state statute for an offense includes additional offenses not fitting the NIBRS offense definition, the non-conforming offenses are reported according to their NIBRS offense classifications. For example, some states have larceny statutes that are so broadly worded as to include the crime of embezzlement. If an embezzlement is perpetrated within such a state, it is reported to NIBRS as Embezzlement, not Larceny."

Group A Offenses

Arson—To unlawfully and intentionally damage, or attempt to damage, any real or personal property by fire or incendiary device.

Assault Offenses—An unlawful attack by one person upon another.

Aggravated Assault—An unlawful attack by one person upon another wherein the offender uses a weapon or displays it in a threatening manner, or the victim suffers obvious severe or aggravated bodily injury involving apparent broken bones, loss of teeth, possible internal injury, severe laceration, or loss of consciousness. This also includes assault with disease (as in cases when the offender is aware that he/she is infected with a deadly disease and deliberately attempts to inflict the disease by biting, spitting, etc.).

Simple Assault—An unlawful physical attack by one person upon another where neither the offender displays a weapon, nor the victim suffers obvious severe or aggravated bodily injury involving apparent broken bones, loss of teeth, possible internal injury, severe laceration, or loss of consciousness.

Intimidation—To unlawfully place another person in reasonable fear of bodily harm through the use of threatening words and/ or other conduct, but without displaying a

Box 4.1. NIBRS Offense Definitions (National Incident-Based Reporting System) (continued)

weapon or subjecting the victim to actual physical attack.

Bribery— (Except Sports Bribery) The offering, giving, receiving, or soliciting of anything of value (i.e., a bribe, gratuity, or kickback) to sway the judgment or action of a person in a position of trust or influence.

Burglary/Breaking and Entering—The unlawful entry into a building or other structure with the intent to commit a felony or a theft.

Counterfeiting/Forgery—The altering, copying, or imitation of something, without authority or right, with the intent to deceive or defraud by passing the copy or thing altered or imitated as that which is original or genuine; or the selling, buying, or possession of an altered, copied, or imitated thing with the intent to deceive or defraud.

Destruction/Damage/Vandalism of Property—(Except Arson) To willfully or maliciously destroy, damage, deface, or otherwise injure real or personal property without the consent of the owner or the person having custody or control of it.

Drug/Narcotic Offenses—(Except Driving Under the Influence) The violation of laws prohibiting the production, distribution, and/or use of certain controlled substances and the equipment or devices utilized in their preparation and/or use.

Drug/Narcotic Violations—The unlawful cultivation, manufacture, distribution, sale, purchase, use, possession, transportation, or importation of any controlled drug or narcotic substance.

Drug Equipment Violations—The unlawful manufacture, sale, purchase, possession, or transportation of equipment or devices utilized in preparing and/or using drugs or narcotics.

Embezzlement—The unlawful misappropriation by an offender to his/her own use or purpose of money, property, or some other thing of value entrusted to his/her care, custody, or control.

Extortion/Blackmail—To unlawfully obtain money, property, or any other thing of value, either tangible or intangible, through the use or threat of force, misuse of authority, threat of criminal prosecution, threat of destruction of reputation or social standing, or through other coercive means.

Fraud Offenses—(Except Counterfeiting/Forgery and Bad Checks) The intentional perversion of the truth for the purpose of inducing another person, or other entity, in reliance upon it to part with something of value or to surrender a legal right.

False Pretenses/Swindle/Confidence Game—The intentional misrepresentation of existing fact or condition, or the use of some other deceptive scheme or device, to obtain money, goods, or other things of value.

Credit Card/Automated Teller Machine Fraud—The unlawful use of a credit (or debit) card or automated teller machine for fraudulent purposes.

Box 4.1. NIBRS Offense Definitions (National Incident-Based Reporting System) (continued)

Impersonation—Falsely representing one's identity or position and acting in the character or position thus unlawfully assumed, to deceive others and thereby gain a profit or advantage, enjoy some right or privilege, or subject another person or entity to an expense, charge, or liability which would not have otherwise been incurred.

Welfare Fraud—The use of deceitful statements, practices, or devices to unlawfully obtain welfare benefits.

Wire Fraud—The use of an electric or electronic communications facility to intentionally transmit a false and/or deceptive message in furtherance of a fraudulent activity.

Gambling Offenses—To unlawfully bet or wager money or something else of value; assist, promote, or operate a game of chance for money or some other stake; possess or transmit wagering information; manufacture, sell, purchase, possess, or transport gambling equipment, devices or goods; or tamper with the outcome of a sporting event or contest to gain a gambling advantage.

Betting/Wagering—To unlawfully stake money or something else of value on the happening of an uncertain event or on the ascertainment of a fact in dispute.

Operating/Promoting/Assisting Gambling—To unlawfully operate, promote, or assist in the operation of a game of chance, lottery, or other gambling activity.

Gambling Equipment Violations—To unlawfully manufacture, sell, buy, possess, or transport equipment, devices, and/or goods used for gambling purposes.

Sports Tampering—To unlawfully alter, meddle in, or otherwise interfere with a sporting contest or event for the purpose of gaining a gambling advantage.

Homicide Offenses—The killing of one human being by another.

Murder and Nonnegligent Manslaughter—The willful (nonnegligent) killing of one human being by another.

Negligent Manslaughter—The killing of another person through negligence.

Justifiable Homicide—The killing of a perpetrator of a serious criminal offense by a peace officer in the line of duty, or the killing, during the commission of a serious criminal offense, of the perpetrator by a private individual.

Kidnapping/Abduction—The unlawful seizure, transportation, and/or detention of a person against his/her will, or of a minor without the consent of his/her custodial parent(s) or legal guardian.

Larceny/Theft Offenses—The unlawful taking, carrying, leading, or riding away of property from the possession, or constructive possession, of another person.

Pocket-picking—The theft of articles from another person's physical possession by stealth where the victim usually does not become immediately aware of the theft.

Box 4.1. NIBRS Offense Definitions (National Incident-Based Reporting System) (continued)

Purse-snatching—The grabbing or snatching of a purse, handbag, etc., from the physical possession of another person.

Shoplifting—The theft, by someone other than an employee of the victim, of goods or merchandise exposed for sale.

Theft From Building—A theft from within a building which is either open to the general public or where the offender has legal access.

Theft From Coin-Operated Machine or Device—A theft from a machine or device which is operated or activated by the use of coins.

Theft From Motor Vehicle—(Except Theft of Motor Vehicle Parts or Accessories) The theft of articles from a motor vehicle, whether locked or unlocked.

Theft of Motor Vehicle Parts or Accessories—The theft of any part or accessory affixed to the interior or exterior of a motor vehicle in a manner which would make the item an attachment of the vehicle, or necessary for its operation.

All Other Larceny—All thefts which do not fit any of the definitions of the specific subcategories of Larceny/Theft listed above.

Motor Vehicle Theft—The theft of a motor vehicle.

Pornography/Obscene Material—The violation of laws or ordinances prohibiting the manufacture, publishing, sale, purchase, or possession of sexually explicit material, e.g., literature, photographs, etc.

Prostitution Offenses—To unlawfully engage in or promote sexual activities for anything of value.

Prostitution—To engage in commercial sex acts for anything of value.

Assisting or Promoting Prostitution—To solicit customers or transport persons for prostitution purposes; to own, manage, or operate a dwelling or other establishment for the purpose of providing a place where prostitution is performed; or to otherwise assist or promote prostitution.

Robbery—The taking, or attempting to take, anything of value under confrontational circumstances from the control, custody, or care of another person by force or threat of force or violence and/or by putting the victim in fear of immediate harm.

Sex Offenses, Forcible—Any sexual act directed against another person, without the consent of the victim including instances where the victim is incapable of giving consent.

Forcible Rape—(Except Statutory Rape) The carnal knowledge of a person, forcibly and/or against that person's will or not forcibly or against the person's will in instances where the victim is incapable of giving consent because of his/her temporary or permanent mental or physical incapacity.

Forcible Sodomy—Oral or anal sexual intercourse with another person, forcibly

Box 4.1. NIBRS Offense Definitions (National Incident-Based Reporting System) (continued)

and/or against that person's will or not forcibly or against the person's will in instances where the victim is incapable of giving consent because of his/her youth or because of his/her temporary or permanent mental or physical incapacity.

Sexual Assault With An Object—To use an object or instrument to unlawfully penetrate, however slightly, the genital or anal opening of the body of another person, forcibly and/or against that person's will or not forcibly or against the person's will in instances where the victim is incapable of giving consent because of his/her youth or because of his/her temporary or permanent mental or physical incapacity.

Forcible Fondling—The touching of the private body parts of another person for the purpose of sexual gratification, forcibly and/or against that person's will or not forcibly or against the person's will in instances where the victim is incapable of giving consent because of his/her youth or because of his/her temporary or permanent mental or physical incapacity.

Sex Offenses, Nonforcible—(Except Prostitution Offenses) Unlawful, nonforcible sexual intercourse.

Incest—Nonforcible sexual intercourse between persons who are related to each other within the degrees wherein marriage is prohibited by law.

Statutory Rape—Nonforcible sexual intercourse with a person who is under the statutory age of consent.

Stolen Property Offenses—Receiving, buying, selling, possessing, concealing, or transporting any property with the knowledge that it has been unlawfully taken, as by Burglary, Embezzlement, Fraud, Larceny, Robbery, etc.

Weapon Law Violations—The violation of laws or ordinances prohibiting the manufacture, sale, purchase, transportation, possession, concealment, or use of firearms, cutting instruments, explosives, incendiary devices, or other deadly weapons.

Group B NIBRS Offenses with Definitions

Bad Checks—Knowingly and intentionally writing and/or negotiating checks drawn against insufficient or nonexistent funds.

Curfew/Loitering/Vagrancy Violations—The violation of a court order, regulation, ordinance, or law requiring the withdrawal of persons from the streets or other specified areas; prohibiting persons from remaining in an area or place in an idle or aimless manner; or prohibiting persons from going from place to place without visible means of support.

Disorderly Conduct—Any behavior that tends to disturb the public or decorum, scandalize the community, or shock the public sense of morality.

Driving Under The Influence—Driving or operating a motor vehicle or common carrier while mentally or physically impaired as the result of consuming an alcoholic beverage or using a drug or narcotic.

Drunkenness—(Except Driving Under The Influence) To drink alcoholic beverages to the

Box 4.1. NIBRS Offense Definitions (National Incident-Based Reporting System) (continued)

extent that one's mental faculties and physical coordination are substantially impaired.

Family Offenses, Nonviolent—Unlawful, nonviolent acts by a family member (or legal guardian) that threaten the physical, mental, or economic well-being or morals of another family member and that are not classifiable as other offenses, such as Assault, Incest, Statutory Rape, etc.

Liquor Law Violations—(Except Driving Under The Influence and Drunkenness) The violation of laws or ordinances prohibiting the manufacture, sale, purchase, transportation, possession, or use of alcoholic beverages.

Peeping Tom—To secretly look through a window, doorway, keyhole, or other aperture for the purpose of voyeurism.

Runaway—A person under 18 years of age who has left home without permission of his/her parent(s) or legal guardian.

Trespass of Real Property—To unlawfully enter land, a dwelling, or other real property.

All Other Offenses—All crimes that are not Group A offenses and not included in one of the specifically-named Group B offense categories listed previously.

Source: FBI (NIBRS (National Incident-Based Reporting System), 2012.

Keep in mind that the definitions that are shared in this chapter, as set forth in the NIBRS, are just general guidelines. The definition of an offense, as well as the punishment for those found guilty of a particular offense, may vary from state to state, and as to whether or not it is a federal crime. These explanations are just a broad way of describing each of these offenses.

Here, in a nutshell, is what the NIBRS provides for each offense:

1. The offense (type of offense, location, type of weapon involved)
2. Property (description, value, quantity)
3. Victim(s) (age, relationship to offender, injury)
4. Offender(s) (age, sex, race)
5. Arrestee(s) (race, ethnicity, resident status)

Box 4.2 provides a more detailed listing of the 53 pieces of information that the NIBRS can provide for each Group A offense.

Box 4.2. Information That the NIBRS Records on Each Crime Incident

Administrative segment:
1. ORI number
2. Incident number
3. Incident date/hour
4. Exceptional clearance indicator
5. Exceptional clearance date

Offense segment:

6. UCR offense code
7. Attempted/completed code
8. Alcohol/drug use by offender
9. Type of location
10. Number of premises entered
11. Method of entry
12. Type of criminal activity
13. Type of weapon/force used
14. Bias crime code

Property segment:

15. Type of property loss
16. Property description
17. Property value
18. Recovery date
19. Number of stolen motor vehicles
20. Number of recovered motor vehicles
21. Suspected drug type
22. Estimate drug quantity
23. Drug measurement unit

Victim segment:

24. Victim number
25. Victim UCR offense code
26. Type of victim
27. Age of victim
28. Sex of victim
29. Race of victim
30. Ethnicity of victim
31. Resident status of victim
32. Homicide/assault circumstances
33. Justifiable homicide circumstances
34. Type of injury
35. Related offender number
36. Relationship of victim to offender

Offender segment:

37. Offender number
38. Age of offender
39. Sex of offender
40. Race of offender

Arrestee segment:

41. Arrestee number
42. Transaction number
43. Arrest date
44. Type of arrest
45. Multiple clearance indicator
46. UCR arrest offense code
47. Arrestee armed indicator
48. Age of arrestee
49. Sex of arrestee
50. Race of arrestee
51. Ethnicity of arrestee
52. Resident status of arrestee
53. Disposition of arrestee under 18

* *Source:* Ramona R. Rantala with Thomas J. Edwards. Bureau of Justice Statistics, Office of Justice Programs, U.S. Department of Justice, "Effects of NIBRS on Crime Statistics," Special Report, July 2000.

With the switch over from the traditional UCR, which was based on something called the **Summary Reporting System (SRS)**, to the new NIBRS, only one UCR SRS will remain. That is the **Law Enforcement Officers Killed and Assaulted Information (LEOKAI)** that is reported to the FBI from law enforcement agencies participating in the program. Otherwise, as noted before, NIBRS replaced the UCR as of January 1, 2021.

The Resource section at the end of this chapter provides the web address you can copy and paste into your browse to access a video developed by the FBI that highlights the NIBRS system and the key benefits of the NIBRS new reporting system. As noted before, one such advantage is the elimination of the controversial hierarchy rule. As stated in the "30 Questions and Answers About NIBRS Transition," published in October 2018 by the Federal Bureau of Investigation, Uniform Crime Reporting Program, National Incident-Based Reporting System, "SRS has a Hierarchy Rule that says only the one most serious crime in a criminal incident will be counted as part of the statistics collection. For example, a murder and a robbery happen in the same incident, then only the murder will be counted." (FBI, October 2018; 8)

Summary for NIBRS, 2019

Before we move on to the second major source of crime data in the United States, the National Crime Victimization Survey (NCVS), let us just get an overview of what you can expect from the FBI's annual NIBRS crime data. (Please note that since the NIBRS only became a mandatory replacement of the UCR on January 1, 2021, the 2019 data represents only 8,497 law enforcement agencies reporting, just 51.3 percent of the 16,551 law enforcement agencies that submitted data to the UCR Program in 2019. The data for 2021 and beyond should include 100 percent of the law enforcement agencies.)

Usually in the Fall, the FBI releases its crime data for the previous year. In addition to the detailed reports that are posted online, the FBI National Press Office issues a press release summarizing the crime data's findings including trends from the previous year. (There is also a Summary posted online by the FBI entitled "Summary for NIBRS, 2019." (NIBRS, 2019) The press release regarding the 2019 data, for example, notes that of the 5,547,758 reported crime victims in the United States, 23.6 percent were between 21 and 30 year of age, 51 percent were female and 48.2 percent were male with 0.8 percent of unknown gender, and where the race was known, 68 percent of victims were white, 23.3 percent Black or African American, 1.9 percent Asian, 0.7 percent American Indian or Alaska Native, and 0.5 percent native Hawaiian or other Pacific Islander.

In terms of victim-offender relationship, the FBI press release summarizes the information for 2019 with these facts: 25.1 percent of the victims were strangers; 24.4 percent were related to their offender, and just over half (50.4%) of the victims knew their offender but were not related. (FBI, 2020)

At the actual statements posted at fbi.gov, there are tables and charts covering the violent (rape, murder and nonnegligent homicide, aggravated assault, robbery) and property (burglary, arson, motor vehicle theft, larceny-theft) offenses. For some crimes, there may be as many as 25 or more additional tables. These tables cover the number of offenses as well as such expanded information as rates by location such as city, state, or larger areas, by type of weapon used, and other key facts on reported crimes for that year.

As a victimology student, it will help you in your studies, as well as with any reports you might have to research, if you get comfortable accessing the FBI data in its original format. Table 4.4 provides a sample of data from the newer NIBRS reporting system. It shows victims in the United States for 2019 by offense category and in age groups from 10 and under to 66 and over, and unknown age. As you will see in Table 4.4, there were 5,547,758 reported victims in the United States in 2019, according to the NIBRS, in all offense categories. In *Crimes Against Person*, the biggest number of victims were of assault (1,892,509), followed by sex offenses (121,331), followed by kidnapping/abduction (25,445), followed by homicide (7,495), and followed finally by human trafficking offenses (1,246). In those offense categories, those in the 11-15 year-old age group had the least number of victims (120) followed by those aged 61-65 (255 victims), compared to the highest number by age group (26-30, 1,083; 21-25, 1,061; 16-20, 915). Although those in the 66 and over age group seem to have a higher number of homicide victims than expected (423), this covers such a wider age group than any of the other categories (from 66 through the 70s, 80s, and even 90s) comparisons of the frequency of homicide by age are less reliable for that particular age group. Remember that this is based only on 51.3 percent of the law enforcement agencies.

For sex offenses, the age group with the highest number of victims was ages 11-15 (33,098) with ages 10 and under having the second highest number of victims (24,914). Once again, the age range for 10 and under, basically birth-10, limits making comparisons of that number with the higher number in the 11-15 age group, just a 4 year span. The different age group categories also make it challenging to see how the NIBRS data for sex offenses by age for 2019 fits in with the findings by Putnam, as reported by Gewirtz-Meydan and Finkelhor, that the highest age for first onset of child sexual abuse was 12 years and older (36.9%) followed by ages 4 to 7 (28.4%), followed by ages 8 to 11 (25.5%). (Gewirtz-Meydan and Finkelhor, 2020; Putnam, 2003; Finkelhor, 2009)

REVIEWING A SAMPLE OF THE TRADITIONAL UCR REPORTS

Especially when the new data is released for the previous year, there is a flurry of popular newspaper and online publication articles about the results as well as more in-depth analysis by various criminal justice and general research center sites, or think tanks. Learning to go to the original data yourself, and getting familiar with it as well as comfortable reviewing the actual data, will serve you well. As you go forward in your career, whether it is in law enforcement, corrections, law, forensic psychology, social work, or any number of additional occupations, being able to read and understand the annual FBI crime data should prove to be a useful skill. Look over the information in Box 4.3 from the 2019 UCR report for the offense of Robbery by Location.

TABLE 4.4. Incidents, Offenses, Victims, and Known Offenders by Offense Category, 2019

Victims Age by Offense Category, 2019														
		Age												
Offense Category	Total Victims[1]	10 and Under	11-15	16-20	21-25	26-30	31-35	36-40	41-45	46-50	51-55	56-60	61-65	66 and Over	Unknown Age
Total	**5,547,758**	**99,951**	**173,716**	**407,984**	**627,685**	**681,316**	**617,042**	**552,725**	**445,588**	**427,082**	**374,910**	**345,202**	**264,475**	**453,632**	**76,450**
Crimes Against Persons	**1,892,509**	**88,752**	**144,181**	**205,659**	**243,739**	**254,702**	**219,033**	**185,412**	**137,360**	**120,158**	**95,535**	**75,793**	**45,725**	**52,343**	**24,117**
Assault Offenses	**1,736,992**	60,686	108,978	179,038	228,047	241,991	209,286	177,336	132,068	115,990	92,671	73,605	44,427	50,223	22,646
Homicide Offenses	**7,495**	346	120	915	1,061	1,083	820	730	560	430	356	335	255	423	61
Human Trafficking Offenses	**1,246**	48	283	323	125	103	58	59	22	29	10	11	2	12	161
Kidnapping/ Abduction	**25,445**	2,758	1,702	3,209	3,855	3,755	2,881	2,508	1,548	1,140	729	513	301	337	209
Sex Offenses	**121,331**	24,914	33,098	22,174	10,651	7,770	5,988	4,779	3,162	2,569	1,769	1,329	740	1,348	1,040
Crimes Against Property	**3,655,249**	**11,199**	**29,535**	**202,325**	**383,946**	**426,614**	**398,009**	**367,313**	**308,228**	**306,924**	**279,375**	**269,409**	**218,750**	**401,289**	**52,333**
Arson	**13,217**	324	164	451	817	1,141	1,290	1,372	1,138	1,252	1,108	1,051	818	1,420	871
Bribery	**376**	4	11	43	48	69	47	34	31	19	14	19	1	11	25

Burglary/Breaking & Entering	**448,257**	2,014	2,623	18,342	41,046	48,606	47,385	44,517	37,537	38,567	36,087	36,485	30,391	58,414	6,243
Counterfeiting/ Forgery	**50,844**	126	140	1,991	2,969	3,535	3,969	4,064	3,804	4,036	4,081	4,685	4,205	10,925	2,314
Destruction/ Damage/ Vandalism	**690,888**	1,493	2,409	37,315	74,694	81,998	75,481	71,685	61,045	60,733	55,098	52,077	41,297	67,101	8,462
Embezzlement	**5,887**	8	12	130	272	423	545	555	515	602	571	537	438	1,075	204
Extortion/ Blackmail	**5,733**	22	282	1,072	972	608	456	418	314	336	286	289	244	390	44
Fraud Offenses	**407,393**	773	995	19,810	34,603	39,689	39,161	36,993	32,082	33,159	31,412	32,164	30,074	69,320	7,158
Larceny/Theft Offenses	**1,585,165**	4,999	18,473	94,989	176,664	193,630	178,509	160,974	133,071	130,229	117,236	111,384	88,896	158,850	17,261
Motor Vehicle Theft	**287,149**	254	165	10,548	30,000	36,711	34,308	31,888	27,105	26,631	23,644	21,628	16,153	24,990	3,124
Robbery	**107,237**	764	3,975	15,562	17,262	14,670	11,622	9,825	7,421	6,826	6,031	5,212	3,494	3,850	723
Stolen Property Offenses	**53,103**	418	286	2,072	4,599	5,534	5,236	4,988	4,165	4,534	3,807	3,878	2,739	4,943	5,904

[1]This table includes only data for the victim types of individual and law enforcement officer. It does not include business, financial institution, government, religious organization, or other victim types. Victims are counted once for each offense type to which they are connected.

Source: FBI, NIBRS 2019, "Victims" Table, Age by offense Category.

Box 4.3. Screen Shot Showing a Sample Page from the 2019 FBI Crime in the United States Report: Robbery by Location

U.S. DEPARTMENT OF JUSTICE • FEDERAL BUREAU OF INVESTIGATION • CRIMINAL JUSTICE INFORMATION SERVICES DIVISION

2019 CRIME in the UNITED STATES

Criminal Justice Information Services Division

Feedback | Contact Us | Data Quality Guidelines | UCR Home

Home | Offenses Known to Law Enforcement | Violent Crime | Property Crime | Clearances | Persons Arrested | Police Employee Data

Robbery Table 1

Robbery, Location
Percent Distribution within Region, 2019

Download Excel

Region	Total[1]	Street/ highway	Commercial house	Gas or service station	Convenience store	Residence	Bank	Miscellaneous
Total	100.0	34.3	16.7	3.0	6.6	15.8	1.4	22.2
Northeast	100.0	39.3	10.8	2.0	4.1	14.2	1.6	27.9
Midwest	100.0	36.9	12.9	4.4	5.4	19.1	1.8	19.4
South	100.0	31.8	16.1	3.4	7.2	20.7	1.3	19.5
West	100.0	34.4	20.8	2.5	7.3	9.7	1.3	24.2

- [1] Because of rounding, the percentages may not add to 100.0.

NATIONAL CRIME VICTIMIZATION SURVEY (NCVS)

The second major source of crime data in the United States, besides the data provided by local law enforcement to the FBI annually through the NIBRS, is the **National Crime Victimization Survey**, also known by the acronym **NCVS.** It started in 1972 and at that time, it was known as the National Crime Survey (NCS). The concept was to collect information about reported and even unreported crimes directly from Americans participating in the survey through interviews to be conducted in a **self-report** manner. Initially, there was a sample of 72,000 households in the NCVS sample. According to the National Academy of Sciences history of the NCVS, 15,000 businesses were also included in the survey plus samples from 26 major cities (12,000 households and 2,000 businesses). (National Academy of Sciences, 2014)

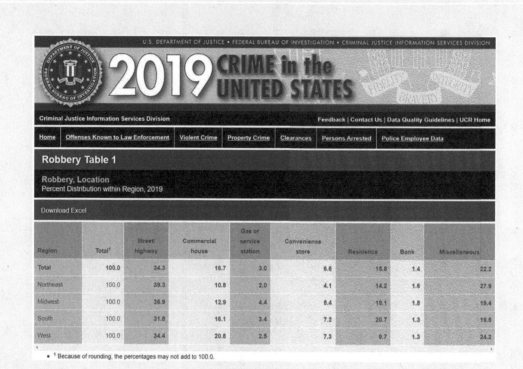

In 1992, after a redesign of the survey, the name was changed to the National Crime Victimization Survey (NCVS). The survey is usually conducted in person, or it might be administered by phone, by a member of the U.S. Census Bureau (under the U.S. Department of Commerce) on behalf of the Bureau of Justice Statistics (BJS), under the U.S. Department of Justice.

This secondary major source of crime data in the United States evolved because of the realization that almost half of all crimes are not reported to the police. If the UCR (and now the NIBRS) was to remain the only source of official crime data, the actual crime victimizations in the United States would be underreported and additional details about those crimes would be unknown, information that might be gained by talking to the victims. The NCVS was an outgrowth of the crime data collection work previously accomplished by the National Opinion Research Center and the President's Commission on Law Enforcement and Administration of Justice in response to the soaring crime rates in the 1960s.

Twice a year, a national representative sample of approximately 49,000 households (or more, depending on the year and the funding for the program), that include approximately 100,000 persons, are interviewed. (ICPSR—Institute for Social Research, 2021)

Homicide is not included but these violent and property crimes are part of the NCVS interview and data:

Violent crimes:

1. Rape and sexual assault
2. Robbery
3. Aggravated assault
4. Simple assault

Property crimes:

1. Household burglary
2. Motor vehicle theft
3. Theft

Till now, the NCVS provided the most comprehensive information about crime victims, reported and unreported, because it also finds out the following information about the crime victim for each victimization:

- victim's age
- gender
- race
- sexual orientation
- gender identity
- veteran status
- citizenship
- disability
- type of crime

- where and when it occurred
- victim-offender relationship
- offender characteristics (requested, if known)
- type of property that was stolen
- whether or not the crime was reported to the police
- whether drugs or alcohol was involved
- extend of the victim's injury
- weapon involvement
- relationship to the offender
- whether the victim has sought help
- information about other criminal justice system actions such as the police making an arrest or a judge or prosecutor getting in touch with the victim

(Source: "National Crime Victimization Survey," Bureau of Justice Statistics, November 2017, information sheet; ICPSR, 2021).

NCVS does provide another source of ongoing data that gives a more complete view of crime patterns and rates since unreported as well as reported crimes are included. But there are some shortcomings to the NCVS, including that:

1. It is based on self-reports. Memories can be faulty. Time frames about when a crime occurred can be blurred.
2. The survey is 20 pages long, causing some to skip questions, answer in a very sketchy manner, or opt out of the survey altogether.
3. It looks at losses at home and not in workplaces (e.g., bank robberies or office burglaries).
4. It asks about only two kinds of theft: personal larceny with contact such as purse-snatching or without any direct contact, like pickpocketing.
5. Because respondents in the NCVS must be over 12 years of age, there is no information on crimes such as child abuse or larceny-theft that have occurred to those under the age of 12.
6. Although the NCVS is hailed as providing a nationally representative sample, in a country with more than 300 million residents, interviewing approximately 100,000 persons over the age of 12 twice a year about their crime victimization actually covers just a relatively small number of individuals.

Here are two additional challenges with the NCVS. The first is what is known as **memory decay**. That is when the **respondent** (interviewee) fails to share a victimization with the interviewer because he or she forgets about it. The second issue is known as **forward telescoping**. That is when the respondent includes victimizations that actually happened much earlier than the screening period that is being considered, such as within the last 6 or 12 months prior to the interview.

In Table 4.5, you will find a comparison between the two major ways crime is reported in the United States: the NIBRS and the NCVS.

TABLE 4.5. Comparing the two main official sources of crime data in the United States: NIBRS and the NCVS

Consideration	NIBRS	NCVS
Date started	1988 but officially replaced the UCR (which had been used since 1930) on January 1, 2021	1972 but first survey was collected in 1973
Collection method	Reported crimes submitted by the local precincts and sheriffs to the FBI for analysis (8,497 precincts in 2019 but should go up to 96% which was the reporting area of the UCR, 16,551 precincts)	Covers 49,000 households or approximately 100,000 persons being interviewed but this number can vary if changes in budgets reduce or expand the sample size
Compiler of data	Police and sheriff departments with data compiled and released by the FBI	U.S. Census Bureau Representative on behalf of the Bureau of Justice Statistics (BJS), part of the U.S. Department of Justice
Data collectors	Police officers and sheriffs	U.S. Census Bureau representative
Method/Mode of collection	Police officer files a report based on information provided over the phone, in writing, or in person by a victim, witness, third party, or police officer's own investigation	An interview usually is conducted in person with a Census Bureau representative, but it could also be conducted by phone
Age of those reporting	Any and all ages and in all locations	Does not record any crimes for those 12 or under or those living in nursing homes, prisons, or military barracks
Type of crimes included	Only crimes reported to the police	Reported *and* unreported crimes
Commitment from those reporting crime	Can be a one-time report	Households included in study must agree to be surveyed once every 6 months and remain in the survey sample for 3 years
Types of crimes reported/recorded	Usually only recent occurrences which are compiled and submitted to the FBI on an annual basis	Because of telescoping, memory lapses, or embellishments, respondents may include crimes outside the 6-month window that the survey supposedly covered
Response rate	The estimate is that as many as 96% of the police and sheriff departments throughout the United States share their crime data annually with the FBI for its comprehensive reports	Response rate for participation in the survey has been going down from as high as 96% between 1993 to 1998 to 73% in 2018
Type of crime or victims not covered	Only those who do not report it; the NIBRS covers 49 Group A offenses and 10 Group B offenses	Any crimes happening to those under 12 as well as crimes outside of the 11 that it covers (see answer below to "Offenses covered")
Recording of murder	Data covers 3 categories—murder, nonnegligent manslaughter, and a 3d category, justifiable homicide (counted separately from the other two)	Excluded

(continued)

TABLE 4.5. Comparing the two main official sources of crime data in the United States: NIBRS and the NCVS (Continued)

Consideration	NIBRS	NCVS
How many victim and offender variables are studied	58 data elements about the victim, offender, property, arrestee including age, sex, race, ethnicity, victim-offender relationship	Age, injury, location of incident, presence of weapon, race, ethnicity, reporting to police, sex (gender), type of crime, victim-offender relationship, year, whether victim services were provided
Excluded victims	None	Businesses, those under 12
Offenses covered	See Table 4.2 for a complete list of offenses covered in 23 major crime categories covering 49 specific crimes in the Group A category (rape, robbery, murder, nonnegligent manslaughter, arson, aggravated assault, simple assault, motor vehicle theft, larceny/theft, etc.) and 10 additional crimes in Group B offenses	Covers 11 offenses including completed, attempted and threatened rape; sexual assault; aggravated assault; simple assault; completed and threatened robbery; burglary; motor vehicle theft; property theft; purse-snatching; vandalism; and pick-pocketing. (Does not record arson, embezzlement, kidnapping, or murder, among other crimes)

Sources: Compiled by author based on multiple sources including Bureau of Justice Statistics, "NCVS Personal Victimization Variable Descriptions"; Addington, 2008; Sheriff Wickersham and Edwin Roessler, n.d.; Gramlich, 2020; FBI, NIBRS (fbi.gov); BJS, NCVS (bjs.gov; FBI, 2013).

Similar to the NIBRS (and the previous UCR), a year after the compiling of the data, a report will be issued by the statisticians at the Bureau of Justice Statistics. The 2019 report, for example, was released in September 2020. (BJS, 2020) Similar to the way the new data from the FBI is handled, the Bureau of Justice Statistics will summarize its findings for each new report. A one-page summary, "Criminal Victimization, 2019," was released in September 2020 by the U.S. Department of Justice, Office of Justice Programs (OJP), summarizing in a few paragraphs the NCVS (National Crime Victimization Survey) report by Rachel E. Morgan and Jennifer L. Truman. One of their key findings was that 41 percent of the violent victimizations were reported to police, according to those in the NCVS sample related to crimes experienced from July 1, 2019 and November 30, 2019. (PJP, 2020) The U.S. Department of Justice also releases occasional reports, such as the technical report entitled, "Measuring the Prevalence of Crime with the National Crime Victimization Survey." This report, released in September 2013, highlighted trends in crime in the United States from 1993 to 2010, based on the NCVS annual reports that had been compiled over those years. Co-authors Janet L. Lauritzen and Maribeth L. Rezey summarize some of their key findings on the first page in a section entitled, "Highlights." Here is just one of their eight highlights: "Victims of violent partner violence (21%) were more likely to experience repeat victimization with the year than were victims of stranger violence (9%)." (Lauritsen and Rezey, 2013)

However, unlike the extensive charts and tables for the FBI's NIBRS for the previous year, the NCVS report will be two main documents: a summary report (for 2019 it was 53 pages), highlighting certain crimes and trends, and a longer, even more detailed and extensive version of the report with additional charts and tables. (OJP, 2020) The Bureau of Justice Statistics, like the FBI, posts all of its reports online so you may access each report online or download and print it out.

OTHER SOURCES OF DATA

National Violent Death Reporting System (NVDRS)

In 2003, the **National Violent Death Reporting System (NVDRS)** started collecting crime data from 6 states. By 2016, it was collecting data from 32 states. By 2018, NVDRS had expanded to include data from all 50 states, the District of Columbia, and Puerto Rico. (CDC, n.d.)

Unlike the previous two major official crime data collection efforts, the NVDRS collects data rather than conducts research. It links data on violent deaths—homicide and suicide—from law enforcement, social service, and health agencies. The data collection efforts are organized through the National Center for Injury Prevention and Control, which is part of the Centers for Disease Control and Prevention.

Here is the description of this initiative from information provided by the CDC (Centers for Disease Control and Prevention):

> In the United States, more than seven people per hour die a violent death. More than 18,000 people were victims of homicide and over 48,000 people died by suicide in 2018 alone.
>
> To help find ways to prevent violent deaths, we need to know the facts. The National Violent Death Reporting System (NVDRS) links information about the 'who, when, where, and how' from data on violent deaths and provides insights about 'why' they occurred.
>
> NVDRS is the only state-based surveillance (reporting) system that pools more than 600 unique data elements from multiple sources into a usable, anonymous database. NVDRS covers all types of violent deaths—including homicides and suicides—in all settings for all age groups.

The data compiled by the NVDRS is available to approved researchers as well as law enforcement, medical examiners, and data providers through their NVDRS Resources webpage.

Mercy, Barker, and Frazier of the CDC in their article, "The Secrets of the National Violent Death Reporting System," share an example of just how this data could help to better understand, and even prevent, violent deaths: "For example, as part of their death investigation, medical examiners and coroners typically gather information on the presence of alcohol and drugs in the blood and tissues of homicide victims. On the other hand, law enforcement agencies, as part of their criminal investigation, gather details of the circumstances under which the homicide occurred, such as whether the homicide was precipitated by an argument or a gang fight or a robbery. By linking these types of information together, we can now determine the circumstances under which homicide victims are most likely to be intoxicated. Combined with information on the location of homicides, this may shed greater light on the relevance of, for example, alcohol serving policies and guidelines at bars where violence may erupt. . . ." (Mercy, Barker, and Frazier, 2006)

Qualitative Data

The emphasis in this chapter so far has been on the collection of **quantitative data**. That information is important of course. We need those crime statistics that are gathered and distributed through the NIBRS and the NCVS. But qualitative data, based on interviews and even participant observation, can help contribute to our understanding about crime and other victimizations. One case study, or even one victim story, or what some refer to as **narrative victimology**, has a place in victimology research. (Walklate, et al., 2019) Qualitative research can contribute to our understanding about crime and victimization in different ways than the insights that we gain from quantitative or big data research and studies.

For some inexplicable reason, we do not yet have in victimology research the timeless qualitative studies like Sutherland's *Professional Thief*, or sociologist Clifford R. Shaw's *The Jack-Roller: A Delinquent Boy's Own Story*. (Sutherland,1937; Shaw, 1930).

There is no shortage of books about individual crime victims, but those works tend to be popular books in the true-crime genre rather than qualitative studies by criminologists, victimologists, or sociologists. Just a few of the popular books in that category that immediately come to mind are Robert Kolker's *Lost Girls*, which became a Netflix original movie in 2020, and memoirs by victims, including Chanel Miller's *Know My Name* or Debra Puglisi Sharp's *Shattered*. (Miller, 2019; Sharp, 2004). Former FBI agents also write memoirs, such as Jeffrey Rinek's *In the Name of the Children*. (Rinek and Strong, 2018)

Hopefully there will be more qualitative case studies written by victimologists about one or more victims that will contribute to our understanding of victims in much the same way that Mitch Albom's *Tuesdays With Morrie*, a best-seller written on the basis of interviews with terminally ill sociology professor Morrie Schwartz, helped millions to better understand aging and dealing with a terminal illness and an impending death.

Victimologists, criminologists, and sociologists also compile their own research. There are countless groundbreaking studies, mostly published in peer-reviewed journals, some becoming books based on that initial research as well, that contributes crime victim data beyond the major official statistics. Because of the time and cost involved in compiling crime victim data, government grants or funds from foundations or universities are often necessary to fund such undertakings, regardless of whether it is qualitative or quantitative victimization research or a combination of the two that is being undertaken. Government sources for potential funding include the U.S. Department of Justice's Office of Justice Programs (OJP), Office for Victims of Crime, National Institute of Justice (NIJ), and other agencies and foundations such as the Charles Koch Foundation. (Lee, 2019; Charles Koch Foundation website, n.d.)

MEASURING CRIME GLOBALLY

The International Criminal Police Organization (INTERPOL)

It is challenging to track crime internationally because of differences in definitions for the types of crime and inconsistencies in reporting procedures. The International Criminal Police Organization (**INTERPOL**), established in 1914, is a coordinated effort among the 194 member countries to deal with crime on an international level including tracking major criminals across borders. But because INTERPOL no longer publishes crime statistics, it unfortunately is not a source of crime data for researchers or the public.

INTERPOL stopped releasing its data because it was becoming a political issue when the tourism of cities or countries was impacted on the basis of perceived crime levels.

The argument advanced for stopping the release of the data was that the way crimes were classified was different in various countries. For example, in England and Australia, attempted murders are included as "other homicides" but in the United States it is counted as "aggravated assault." (Smith, et al., 2011) What INTERPOL, which is headquartered in Lyons, France with a branch office and research center in Singapore, does offer is an international arm to policing. See Chapter 5, "Victims and the Criminal Justice System: Police, Courts, and Corrections," for further discussion of INTERPOL, including the use of the "Red Notice" which flags someone as being sought by the police and their travel being limited.

The United Nations Office on Drugs and Crime (UNODC)

The **United Nations Office on Drugs and Crime (UNODC)** is leading the global effort to gather and standardize crime statistics. As noted at their website: "Better data and improved national capacity to collect data are needed to support and enhance the international community's response to the challenges of crime." In 2010, UNODC published a book entitled *Manual on Victimization Surveys*. This 200+ page book is available for free at the UNODC as a downloadable PDF. It does not recommend any one survey but instead looks at trends in the 52 surveys submitted to the UNODC for review. These were the most popular concerns being measured by those surveys:

1. victimization
2. fear of crime
3. unreported crimes
4. attitudes towards the police and the criminal justice system
5. crime prevention measures
6. security systems and strategies

The International Crime Victim Survey (ICVS)

In 1987, several European criminologists initiated the International Crime Victim Survey (ICVS). Since that time, there have been five rounds of surveys in 1992, 1996, 2000, and 2004/2005. It is estimated that by the end of 2005, more than 140 surveys had been conducted in more than 78 countries. The basic survey of the ICVS was developed from the national crime victim surveys of Switzerland, the Netherlands, and England and Wales. (ICVS, 2021; Van Dijk, Mayhew, and Killias, 1990). It is estimated that there are more than 300,000 unique respondents in the ICVS database. (ICVS, 2021)

Any respondents who note that they have been victimized within the last five years are then asked additional questions, such as whether the police were notified, how they then treat the victim; and what sentence might be recommended for the offender. (ICVS, 2021)

The Crime Survey for England and Wales

The British Crime Survey (BCS), as of April 2012, changed its name to the Crime Survey for England and Wales. Since the late 1980s, the British Crime Survey no longer included

Scotland. A new unique survey, the Scottish Crime and Justice Survey, was initiated for Scotland. (Office for National Statistics, ons.gov.uk)

Face-to-face interviews are the method of data collection for the Crime Survey for England and Wales. In 2010/11, approximately 1,000 interviews were conducted in each police force area. The survey got a 76 percent responses rate. A total of 51,000 people were interviewed including approximately 47,000 adults from the ages of 16 and up and 4,000 children, ages 10 to 15.

Here are some sample questions:

- The next few questions are about things that may have happened to you PERSONALLY [not the other people in your household] over the last 12 months, that is since the first of [DATE], in which you may have been the victim of a crime or offence. Again, I only want to know about things that have happened in the period marked on the calendar, so we can build a picture of crime in the last 12 months. Please include anything that happened to you during that time – at home, in the street, at work, in a shop, in a park, on a train or anywhere else.
- Since the first of [DATE], [apart from anything you may have already mentioned], was anything you were carrying stolen out of your hands or from your pockets or from a bag or case?
- During the last 12 months, have you been sexually interfered with, assaulted or attacked, either by someone you know or by a stranger? (Office for National Statistics, 2018)

Crime Victimisation (Australia)

Each year, a Crime Victimisation Survey (CVS) is a topic on the Multipurpose Household Survey (MPHS) that is conducted throughout Australia by the Australian Bureau of Statistics (ABS). It is a supplement to the monthly Labour Force Survey (LFS). (Australian Bureau of Statistics, 2021)

For the June 2019 to June 2020 survey, the sample size was 29,793 with a response rate of 76.4 percent. The latest release that discusses the most recent survey's findings points out that domestic violence cannot be measured by that particular survey since it may be an ongoing situation. (Australian Bureau of Statistics, 2021)

For the purposes of comparison, and to give you an indication of the kind of crime victimization data you will find in this survey, here are some of the results: 24 percent reported a break-in; 23 percent reported a physical assault; and .03 percent reported experiencing a robbery. (ABS, 2021)

CRIME STATISTICS AND STUDIES THAT HAVE SHAPED VICTIMOLOGY

Locally, nationally, and internationally, measuring crime victimization is more than an academic effort. It can influence attitudes toward victims, and by gaining a more realistic understanding about when and where crime is occurring, and to whom, it may help in the reduction or even the elimination of some types of victimization. Such preventable child neglect crimes like the hot car deaths that have claimed the lives of more than 851 infants and children since 1998 immediately comes to mind. Measuring when those deaths occur, and by whom, may help in eliminating those situations as a type of child victimization. (https://www.noheatstroke.org/)

Until now, this chapter has focused on how crime and victimization is measured by government statistics collected by the FBI from local law enforcement agencies or the sampling of thousands of Americans through the NCVS (National Crime Victim Survey); other international surveys were described. In this section, we will look at the research approach of individual victimologists, beginning with the typologies of the earliest founders in the field (Mendelsohn and von Hentig), the empirical studies of Wolfgang and Amir, and more recent empirical studies and research techniques including the **qualitative methods**, most notably in-depth interviewing or observation or participation observation. Constructing a **typology**, defined as "organization systems of types" is a "well-established analytic tool in the social sciences," as Collier, LaPorte, and Seawright wrote in their journal article about typologies. However, it is quite possible that because Mendelsohn and von Hentig started the new discipline on the basis of typologies, rather than empirical data, the acceptance of victimology as a new social science discipline might have been slowed. Empirical data, like the statistics that Durkheim relied on for his classic study of suicide back in 1897, tend to get far more attention in academic circles as well as by the public than the more generalized approach of a typology. (Durkheim, 1897)

It is probably not a coincidence that it took the empirical study of Dr. Marvin Wolfgang, "Victim-Precipitated Homicide," published in 1957, to catch academic and public attention for the new discipline. Although both Mendelsohn and von Hentig had, within their writings, attested to the controversial idea that some victims do, indeed, precipitate their own victimization, it was the 26 percent statistic out of the 588 homicides perpetrated by 621 offenders that Dr. Wolfgang studied, courtesy of the Philadelphia Police Department, that shook up academia and made its way into the general public's view of some incidents of crime as being potentially victim precipitated.

Wolfgang studied every homicide committed in the city of Philadelphia over a four-year period from January 1, 1948 to December 31, 1952. His definition of "victim precipitation," as noted in Chapter 3, "The Discipline of Victimology," and Chapter 7, "Homicide: Primary and Secondary Victims of Homicide," was quite specific. **Victim precipitation** was when the victim was the first one to strike the first blow. That finding gave rise to an entire approach and perspective in the new field of victimology known as **victim-precipitated homicide**. The concept of victim-precipitated homicide and the related wider concept of victim precipitation could not have developed without the statistics that Dr. Wolfgang meticulously documented in his journal article and books related to his findings.

The concept of victim precipitation, particularly victim-precipitated homicide, is well-known today especially among victimologists and criminologists. But it was groundbreaking when Dr. Wolfgang first proposed it and it is still probably one of the most controversial concepts in victimology even today. (The second related controversial concept in victimology is probably **victim blame** or the notion that the victim was "asking for it.")

Another empirical study that had impact because of the use of statistics to support its thesis was the study of rape victims by Menachem Amir, who had studied under Dr. Wolfgang at the University of Pennsylvania. Amir's study was published in 1967, a decade after Dr. Wolfgang's study. Based on an examination of 646 rape cases committed by 1,292 offenders that occurred in Philadelphia between January 1, 1958 and December 31, 1958 and between January 1, 1960 and December 31, 1960. (You may recall that Dr. Wolfgang studied the homicides that occurred during a continuous four-year period.) Amir's examination of those cases applied one of these definitions of victim precipitation: "The term 'victim precipitation' describes those rape situations in which the victim actually, or so it was deemed, agreed to sexual relations but retracted before the actual act or did not react strongly enough when the suggestion was made by the offender(s). The term applies also to cases in risky or vulnerable situations, marred with sexuality, especially when the victim uses what could be interpreted as indecency in language and gestures or constitute what could be taken as an invitation to sexual relations." (Amir, page 495)

Dr. Amir's results were that 122 or 19 percent of the cases that were studied could be labeled "victim-precipitated." As noted in the previous chapter, however, the responses to Dr. Amir's study, and results, was decidedly more negative than Dr. Wolfgang's. It has been suggested that is because Dr. Amir referred to women who had a "bad reputation" as a precipitating factor in their rape and the notion that the criteria for a victim-precipitated rape is not at all comparable to someone striking the first blow in a homicide deemed victim-precipitated. (Amir, 1967)

Amir's results may not have been as revolutionary a concept as Dr. Wolfgang's initial study on victimology, but rightly or wrongly, it certainly reinforced the notion of victim precipitation. The way that both Drs. Wolfgang and Amir used statistics and crime data to substantiate their theories and hypothesis is instructive to anyone studying victimology and why statistics and crime data matter.

We have seen that Mendelsohn and von Hentig used the social science research technique of creating typologies. Wolfgang and Amir used an empirical approach, but they did not gather the original data themselves. They instead used a quantitative research technique that is now known as nonreactive, meaning they did a secondary analysis of pre-existing data. This is obviously faster, easier, less expensive, and more efficient than gathering the data from scratch. But it also introduces the possibility that those who original collected the data, in their cases, the various police department and law enforcement officers inputting the data, did not categorize it properly.

Probably one of the most important statistical studies of crime victims done to date is the work of Michael J. Hindelang, Michael R. Gottfreson, and James Garofalo, based on a secondary analysis of data provided by their own *Crime Victimization in Eight American Cities*, published in 1976, based on the newer crime data provided by the LEAA (Law Enforcement Assistance Administration)-Census surveys, and highlighted in their 1979 book, *Victims of Personal Crime: An Empirical Foundation For a Theory of Personal Victimization*. Most well-known for their contribution, based on their crime victimization data analysis, of the lifestyle-exposure theory of victimization, in their pioneering book, the co-authors state, "Of the estimated 208,719 victims of personal crime in the eight cities, 25 percent reported that they had suffered some form of injury." (Hindelang, et al, page 38) Based on their extensive analysis of voluminous data, the co-authors found that their lifestyle-exposure theory depended on four propositions:

1. Being outside, especially at night, increases the likelihood of being a crime victim.
2. Lifestyle will dictate if someone is more likely to be out especially at night.
3. Those who share a similar lifestyle are more likely to interact, which will make them more or less likely to be crime victims.
4. The more the crime victim shares demographic characteristics with the offender the greater the likelihood of victimization.

5. The amount of time spent in activities with nonfamily members is a "function of lifestyle."
6. The more nonfamily time a victim spends, the greater the likelihood of becoming a victim, especially of personal theft.
7. Lifestyle will dictate how easily someone can isolate themselves from offenders, reducing or increasing their chances of victimization.
8. Victims become more desirable to an offender if they are geographically more convenient, being within a short distance of the offender's residence.

The well-documented decreases in crime rates in various cities throughout the United States and internationally during the dramatic shutdowns initially when the COVID-19 pandemic was at its peak seem to reaffirm the crime victimization findings of Hindelang, et al. from 1979, and their lifestyle exposure theory, namely, that being off the streets at night will lower the chances of becoming a violent crime victim.

See Box 4.4 for a review of the various research methods that are available to all social scientists, including victimologists.

Box 4.4. Research Methods for Gathering Victimization Data Used By, or Available to, Victimologists

Typologies	grouping together similar types to substantiate the formulated concepts
Survey	conducting an original inquiry through written questionnaires and/or interviews
Experiment	manipulating real-life individuals and events to see before-and-after or side-by-side comparisons
Nonreactive research measures (also known as **materials-based methods**):	using pre-existing data collected by others to do a secondary data analysis of the results applied to different considerations or measures; other types of nonreactive research are content analysis (of text), analysis of existing statistics, or reviewing previously gathered physical evidence
Ethnography	finding out about a group by becoming a complete participant, **participant observer, observer**, or covert observer
Qualitative research	relies on **in-depth interviewing**; may be based on as few as one or as many as 25, 50, or more
Evaluation research	looks at whether an intervention or activity has led to the desired outcome. For example, do community-based crime prevention programs lead to lower rates of victimization compared to comparable communities without a similar program?
Quantitative research	relies on data gathered from large samples using surveys

Sources: Deborah Carr, et al., *The Art and Science of Social Research*; Neuman, *Understanding Research*

Four researchers into family violence have shaped what we know about victims partly because their studies relied so heavily on crime data and partly because their concerns, children and family violence, had become key issues in the 1970s when they began their dedicated research efforts. Drs. David Finkelhor, Murray Straus, Richard J. Gelles, and Susan Steinmetz did studies over the last forty years that have helped victimologists and those working in the child welfare fields, as well as physicians and nurses, to see how widespread child abuse and family violence really were in America. In 1994, for example, David Finkelhor pointed out in his article "Current Information on the Scope and Nature of Child Sexual Abuse," based on adult retrospective interviews that 70-to-90 percent of the child abuse experiences were with someone known to the child, not a stranger. Dr. Straus's analysis of statistics helped to support his claim that spanking and corporal punishment could have negative effects on a child. He discovered research supported by data that children who were spanked had an IQ 5 points lower than a comparable group of children who were not spanked. (Cloud, *Time*, September 26, 2009)

* * *

Gathering official and unofficial crime statistics to be used for research purposes as well as to inform the public about whether crime is going up or down, who is being victimized, and how that data could be used to lower crime rates, is one of the justifications for the continued time, energy, and expense that goes into collecting and disseminating, crime and victimization data. Victimologists are involved in that data collection as well as criminologists, sociologists, ethnographers, statisticians, and other social scientists. Victimologists need to continue to collect original data about crime and other victims and victimizations, as well as to do a secondary analysis of existing data, so the discipline can continue to advance.

SUMMARY

Crime data started back in the early 1830s when Frenchman Adolphe Quetelet and Belgian Andre-Michel Guerry pioneered the use of statistics to study the distribution of crime and victimization.

Crime data is useful for assessing how a community, state, country, or even a continent is doing as it deals with violent and property crimes. Comparing victimization data year by year, as well as the various factors associated with each type of crime, can help victimologists to see any patterns that can help to better understand who becomes a victim with the goal of reducing or eliminating further victimizations.

No measurement system is perfect, but the United States does spend a great deal of time and resources collecting data about who commits crime and who are its victims. That information is shared with the public as well as law enforcement, politicians, researchers, and decision makers to get a picture of the frequency of each major crime and who its victims are. In 1929, the International Association of Chiefs of Police initiated what became the UCR, the Uniform Crime Report. On January 1, 2021, the NIBRS—National Incident-Based Reporting System—replaced the UCR with its mandate to gather data on 52 offenses including the 8 that the UCR considered the Crime Index (murder and nonnegligent manslaughter, forcible rape, aggravated assault, robbery, burglary, larceny-theft, motor vehicle theft, and arson), as well as with the inputting of 53 potential pieces of information including more than a dozen about the victim such as the victim-offender relationship, if known. The FBI compiles, analyzes, and disseminates the annual NIBRS.

This chapter includes the official definitions for all 52 offenses that the NIBRS tracks. The definition, as well as the punishment for those found guilty of a particular offense, may vary from state to state and as to whether or not it is a federal crime. These definitions are just a general way of describing each of these offenses.

The secondary main source of information on crime in the United States is the NCVS, National Criminal Victimization Survey, initiated in 1972. It is administered annually to approximately 90,000 households. Only those over the age of 12 can participate but it does cover unreported as well as reported crimes. The Bureau of Justice Statistics administers, analyzes, and publishes the reports on the NCVS.

This chapter also noted that qualitative data is a possible source of information about crime victims although there have been more notable scholarly case studies about offenders, such as Sutherland's classic *The Professional Thief*, published in 1937, than about crime victims. The in-depth studies of crime victims tend to be written by popular writers in the true crime genres or by the victims themselves in their powerful memoirs (self-reports).

It is challenging to track crime internationally because of the difference in definitions for the types of crime and inconsistencies in reporting procedures. INTERPOL, established in 1914, is a coordinated effort among more than 100 member nations to deal with crime on an international level including tracking major criminals across borders. But they do not publish crime statistics. Other international sources of crime data are the ICVS (International Crime Victim Survey), the Australian Bureau of Statistics annual Crime Victimisation Survey (CVS), and the Crime Survey for England and Wales.

KEY TERMS

clearance rate
Crime Index
crime mapping
cybercrime
ethnography
evaluation research
forward telescoping
hierarchy rule
hot spots
IACP (International Association of Chiefs of Police)
incident rate
in-depth interviewing
INTERPOL
(LEOKAI) Law Enforcement Officers Killed and Assaulted Information
materials-based methods
memory decay
narrative victimology
NCVS (National Crime Victimization Surveys)
NIBRS (National Incident-Based Reporting System)
NVDRS (National Violent Death Reporting System)
Nonreactive research
observer
participant observer
prevalence rate
qualitative methods
quantitative data
raw number
respondent
self-report
SRS (Summary Reporting System)
survey
typology

UCR (Uniform Crime Report)
Uniform Crime Reporting (UCR) Program
UNODC (United Nations Office on Drugs and Crime)
victim blame
victim-precipitated homicide
victim-precipitated rape
victim precipitation
victimization rate
white-collar crime

REVIEW QUESTIONS

1. Who are the European crime statistics pioneers?
2. When did the first effort to gather reported crime statistics from local, city, and state law enforcement agencies start in the United States and who gathers the statistics annually?
3. What newer initiative that was started in 1989 replaced the older, paper system on January 1, 2021?
4. Name at least 10 of the major crimes that the NIBRS track.
5. What are at least three aspects of the victim that the NIBRS records?
6. Name three ways that gathering crime statistics can help victimologists to do their job.
7. What is the secondary source of crime data collection, started in the United States in 1972?
8. Identify at least two of the pioneering studies in victimology that relied on collecting data. What type of research method was used?

CRITICAL THINKING QUESTIONS

1. Do you agree that it is useful to spend time, money, and resources collecting crime data? Why? Why not?

2. Look over the categories of crimes and the victim information that the NIBRS is collecting. Do you see any categories that should be changed? Edited? Deleted? Added?

3. What is the No. 1 piece of crime data that is most important to you and why?

4. As you know, the NIBRS categorizes robbery as a crime against property (rather than a crime against a person). Do you agree or disagree with this distinction? Explain your answer.

5. How might the additional data that is being collected by police for the NIBRS compared to the UCR benefit victims, the criminal justice system, and even police officers? Critically discuss the differences between the UCR, which was used since 1930, and the newer NIBRS, which became mandatory as of January 1, 2021. Why is this change useful or do you disagree with this transition and permanent change? Why?

6. INTERPOL stopped releasing the crime data that it collects from its member countries to any government agencies or tourist or other companies, or the public, outside of law enforcement. Is their reasoning for no longer sharing that information valid or would the benefits of having that information known outweigh any potential abuses?

7. Consider the reluctance of INTERPOL to share their crime data information with the way that the FBI's annual UCR report, now the NIBRS report, is presented to the media. Do you see any similarities? Differences? How could the media be retrained to present the annual FBI crime data differently rather than just labeling a city or state more or less violent than others?

ACTIVITIES

1. Do an electronic search across a variety of social media platforms, newspapers, or magazines, and see whether you find one or more examples of the misuse of crime statistics or statistics that have been gathered in a questionable or sloppy way. Why is that a cause of concern? What can be done to avoid these types of situations from happening so often?
2. Some states have their own crime statistics available for review. Do a search on Google or another search engine or go to the law enforcement department for your state and access those statistics for the most recent year available. Pick a crime, such as "murder" or "burglary," or a category of crimes, such as "violent crimes" or "property crimes" and compare your state's crime levels to the ones posted by the FBI for the entire country. How does your state compare on that particular crime or category of crime? Were you pleasantly surprised or disappointed by what you just learned about your state?
3. Go to the website for the latest version of the FBI NIBRS (National Incident Reporting System). Pick one of the crimes that you are most interested in learning more about such as murder, rape, robbery, burglary, larceny-theft, motor vehicle theft, or aggravated assault, among others. Find that crime in the report. Pick at least three different specific pieces of data that you want to learn more about, such as what weapon was used most often in murders, what were the relationships between the victim and the offender in reported murders, or what age group was most often the victim of a rape. Now pick a previous year and compare that exact crime and line of inquiry to that previous year. What are the similarities or differences in the crime data between the two years?
4. You have been asked to develop a victim survey. What are some of the questions you would ask?

RESOURCES

Bureau of Justice Statistics
Office of Justice Programs, Washington, D.C.
bjs.gov
Responsible for administering the NCVS (National Criminal Victimization Survey) since 1973 and compiling and releasing the data. The NCVS is done through a collaboration with the U.S. Census Bureau.

Federal Bureau of Information (FBI)
U.S. Department of Justice, Washington, D.C.
fbi.gov
For almost 100 years, the FBI has compiled and released its annual **Uniform Crime Report (UCR)** based on the data provided by all the local, state, federal, and any other police departments. Beginning

January 1, 2021, the NIBRS (National Incident-Based Reporting System) replaced the UCR. However, the FBI will continue compiling, analyzing, and releasing the annual reports on how much crime occurs in the United States.

National Violent Death Reporting System (NVDRS)
cdc.gov/violenceprevention/datasources/nvdrs/
What started out in 2002 as an effort to collect data on violent deaths from just six states expanded to include all 50 states in 2018. Administered by the CDC (Centers for Disease Control and Prevention), the NVDRS covers all violent deaths including homicides, suicides, and unintentional firearm death.

Pew Research Corporation
pewresearch.org
A think tank with more than 180 experts representing a range of disciplines including social scientist researchers.

United Nations Office on Drugs and Crime (UNODC)
Vienna, Austria
unodc.org
Established in 1997. Crime prevention is one of its core considerations. UNODC conducts research and has educational forums.

CITED WORKS AND ADDITIONAL REFERENCES

Addington, Lynn A. February 12, 2008. "Current Issues in Victimization Research and the NCVS's Ability to Study Them." Bureau of Justice Statistics, Washington, D.C.

Amir, Menachem. December 1967. "Victim Precipitated Forcible Rape" *The Journal of Criminal Law, Criminology, and Police Science.* 584: 493-502.

Aniyar, Daniel Casto. 2019. "'Paintings for a Crime': Composed Cognitive Maps for Measuring Crime and Situation." *Journal of Victimology and Victim Justice.* 2: 141-163.

Australian Bureau of Statistics. 2021. "Crime Victimisation, Australia." Posted online at abs.gov.

Beirne, Piers. March 1987. "Adophe Quetelet and the Origins of Positivist Criminology." *American Journal of Sociology.* 92: 1140-1169.

Biderman, Albert. Summer, 1981. "Sources of Data for Victimology." *The Journal of Criminal Law and Criminology.* 722: 789-817.

Breo, Dennis L. and William J. Martin. 2016. *The Crime of the Century: Richard Speck and the Murders That Shocked a Nation.* New York: Skyhorse Publishing.

Bureau of Justice Statistics, Office of Justice Programs. "National Crime Victim Survey (NCVS)." Posted at bjs.gov

____________. Personal victimization variable descriptions. n.d. Posted at bjs.gov

Carr, Deborah, Elizabeth Heger Boyle, Benjamin Cornwell, Shelley Correll, Robert Crosnoe, Jeremy Freese, and Mary C. Waters. 2007. *The Art and Science of Social Research.* New York: Norton.

Cave, Damien, Livia Albeck-Ripa, and Iliana Magra. June 6, 2020, updated June 7, 2020. "Huge Crowds Around the Globe March in Solidarity Against Police Brutality." *New York Times.* Published online.

Cloud, John. September 26, 2009. "Kids Who Get Spanked May Have Lower IQs." *Time.*

Cohen, Shawn, Reuven Fenton, Frank Rosario, and Daniel Prendergast. April 28, 2015. "Shelter Worker Gunned Down by Ex-Resident After Escaping Rape." *New York Post.*

Collier, David, Jody LaPorte, and Jason Seawright. 2012. "Putting Typologies to Work: Concept Formation, Measurement, and Analytic Rigor." *Political Research Quarterly.* Vol. 65.

Daigle, Leah E. and Lisa R. Muftic. 2016. *Victimology.* Thousand Oaks, CA: SAGE.

Doerner, William G. and Steven P. Lab. 2017. *Victimology.* Eighth Edition. New York: Routledge.

Dupont-Morales, M.A. 1998. "Constructing the Case Study in Victimology." *Journal of Criminal Justice Education.* 9: 293-302.

Durkheim, Emile. 1897, 1951 *Suicide.* Translated by John A. Spaulding and George Simpson. Glencoe, IL: Free Press.

Eads, David. August 10, 2018. "Too Many Politicians Misuse and Abuse Crime Data." *New York Times.*

Eck, John E., Spencer Chainey, James G. Cameron, Michael Leitner, and Ronald E. Wilson. August 2005. "Mapping Crime: Understanding Hot Spots." National Institute of Justice (NIJ)

Federal Bureau of Investigation (FBI). 2019. "Law Enforcement Officers Killed and Assaulted." Posted at ucr.fbi.gov/leoka/2019

___________. 2019. *2019 Crime in the United States.* "Robbery."

___________. 2019. *2018 Crime in the United States.* Clarksburg, WV: Criminal Justice Information Services Division.

___________. UCR (Uniform Crime Reporting). Posted at fbi.gov

___________. 2013. "A Guide to Understanding NIBRS." U.S. Department of Justice, NIBRS Posted online.

___________. October 2018. "30 Questions and Answers about the NIBRS Transition." 15 pages Posted online at fbi.gov.

___________. *2018 Crime in the United States.* Table 12. U.S. Department of Justice.

___________. *2018 Crime in the United States.* Table 16. U.S. Department of Justice.

___________. 2019. "Hate Crime Statistics." NIBRS/U.S. Department of Justice.

___________. 2013. "The Advantage of NIBRS Data." Fact sheet. Posted online.

___________. Released Fall 2020. "Summary for NIBRS, 2019. U.S. Department of Justice, Federal Bureau of Investigation.

___________. 2019. National Incident-Based Reporting System. Overview. "UCR Focuses on NIBRS and Other Tools to Make More Relevant Data Available to Users."

___________. Released Fall 2020. "Victims" One-page summary. Posted by the NIBRS, 2019, UCR Program/NIBRS.

Finkelhor, David. Summer-Autumn, 1994. "Current Information on the Scope and Nature of Child Sexual Abuse." *The Future of Children.* 4: 31-53.

___________. Fall 2009. "The Prevention of Childhood Sexual Abuse." *The Future of Children.* 19: 169-194.

Fisher, Bonnie S., Bradford W. Reyns, and John J. Sloan III. 2016. *Introduction to Victimology: Contemporary Theory, Research, and Practice.* New York: Oxford University Press.

Fitterer, J., T.A. Nelson, and F. Nathoo. 2015. "Predictive Crime Mapping." *Police Practice and Research.* 16: 121-135.

Friendly, Michael. May 2006. "Andre-Michel Guerry and the Rise of Moral Statistics." Presentation at the Joint Statistical Meetings.

___________. March 4, 2021. Personal communication.

Gewirtz-Meydan, Ateret and David Finkelhor. 2020. "Sexual Abuse and Assault in a Large National Sample of Children and Adolescents." *Child Maltreatment.* 25: 203-214.

Glaser, Daniel. 1974. "Victim Survey Research: Theoretical Implications." *Victimology,* Ch. 4. Israel Drapkin and Emilio Viano (eds.). Lexington, MA: Lexington Books.

Gramlich, John. November 20, 2020. "What Data Says (and doesn't say) about Crime in the United States." Facttank, Pew Research.

"Heat Stroke Deaths of Children in Vehicles." Updated June 1, 2020. Posted at.noheatstroke.org/

Hindelang, Michael J., Michael R. Gottfredson, and James Garofalo. 1978. *Victims of Personal Crime: An Empirical Foundation for a Theory of Personal Victimization.* Cambridge, MA:

ICPSR (Institute for Social Research, University of Michigan). 2021. "Resource Guide: National Crime Victimization Survey."

Karmen, Andrew. 2010. *Crime Victims: An Introduction to Victimology.* Tenth Edition. Boston, MA: Cengage.

Lau, Tim. June 12, 2019. "Crime Rates in Largest U.S. Cities Continue to Drop." Brennan Center. Posted online at brennancenter.org

Lauritsen, Janet L. and Maribeth L. Rezey. September 2013. "Measuring the Prevalence of Crime with the National Crime Victimization Survey." Technical Report. Bureau of Justice Statistics, U.S. Department of Justice.

Lee, Stacy. June 9, 2019. "Crime Victim Awareness and Assistance Through the Decades." National Institute of Justice (NIJ) Posted online at nij.ojp.gov

MacFarquhar, Neil and Serge F. Kovaleski. May 28, 2020. "A Pandemic Bright Spot: In Many Place, Less Crime." *New York Times.*

Meier, Barry. February 18, 1993. "Reality and Anxiety: Crime and the Fear of It." *The New York Times,* A14.

Morgan, Rachel E., Ph.D. and Barbara A. Oudekerk, Ph.D. September 10, 2019. "Criminal Victimization, 2018." Bureau of Justice Statistics. Office of Justice Programs. Washington, D.C.

National Academy of Sciences. 2014. Panel on Measuring Rape and Sexual Assault in Bureau of Justice Statistics Household Surveys; Committee on National Statistics; Division on Behavioral and Social Sciences and Education; National Research Council; Kruttschnitt C, Kalsbeek WD, House CC, editors. Estimating the Incidence of Rape and Sexual Assault. Washington, D.C. National Academies Press. Posted online at ncbi.nih.gov

National Incident-based Reporting System. Federal Bureau of Investigation. Posted at fbi.gov

Neuman, W. Lawrence. 2017. *Understanding Research*. Second edition. New York: Pearson.

Office for National Statistics. 2015 [errata]. "2017-18 Crime Survey for England and Wales Questionnaire (from April 2017). Kantar Public.

Pemberton, Antony, Eva Mulder, and Pauline G.M. Aarten. 2018. "Stories of Injustice: Towards a Narrative Victimology." *European Journal of Criminology*. 16: 391-412.

Posten, Ben, Joel Rubin, and Anthony Pesce. October 15, 2015. "LAPD Underreported Serious Assaults, Skewing Crime Stats for 8 Years." *Los Angeles Times*. Posted at latimes.com

Putnam, F. W. 2003. "Ten-year Research Update Review: Child Sexual Abuse." *Journal of the American Academy of Child and Adolescent Psychiatry*. 42: 269-278.

Rinek, Jeffrey L. and Marilee Strong. 2018. *In the Name of the Children*. London: Quercus.

Schafer, Stephen. 1968. *The Victim and His Criminal: A Study in Functional Responsibility*. New York: Random House.

Sharp, Debra Puglisi. 2015. Personal interviews.

___________. 2004. *Shattered*. New York: Atria, Simon & Schuster.

Shelley, Louise. 2010. *Human Trafficking: A Global Perspective*. New York: Cambridge University Press.

Southall, Ashley and Neil MacFarguhar. June 23, 2020. "Gum Violence Spikes in N.Y.C., Intensifying Debate Over Policing." *New York Times*.

Sullivan, Christopher J. and Jean Marie McGloin. 2014. "Looking Back to Move Forward: Some Thoughts on Measuring Crime and Delinquency over the Past 50 Years." *Journal of Resaerch in Crime and Delinquency*. 5: 445-466.

Sutherland, Edwin (ed.). 1937. *The Professional Thief*. Written by a Professional Thief. Chicago, IL: University of Chicago Press.

United Nations. July 9, 2019. "Global Study on Homicide-2019." UN Information Service. Posted online.

___________. Office on Drugs and Crime. "Compiling and comparing International Crime Statistics" Posted online

https://www.unodc.org/unodc/en/data-and-analysis/Compiling-and-comparing-International-Crime-Statistics.html

___________. 2010. *A Manual on Victimization Surveys*. Geneva, Switzerland: UNODC.

Van Dijk, J.J.M., P. Mayhew, and M. Killias. 1990. *Experiences of Crime Across the World: Key Findings from the 1989 International Crime Survey*. Deventer, Netherlands: Kluwer Law and Taxation Publishers.

von Hentig, Hans. 1948. *The Criminal and His Victim: Studies in the Sociobiology of Crime. New Haven*. CT: Yale University Press. (Reprint edition with a Preface by Marvin E. Wolfgang. 1979. Schocken.)

Walklate, Sandra, JaneMaree Maher, Jude McCulloch, Kate Fitz-Gibbon, and Kara Beavis. 2018. "Victim Stories and Victim Policy: Is there a Case for a Narrative Victimology?" *Crime Media Culture*. 15: 199-215.

Wickersham, Sheriff Anthony and Edwin Roessler. Getting ready for the NIBRS transition. National Police Foundation. Posted at policefoundation.org

Wolfgang, Marvin E. 1958. *Patterns of Criminal Homicide*. Philadelphia, PA: University of Pennsylvania Press.

___________. Editor. 1967. *Studies in Homicide*. New York: Harper & Row.

___________. May-June 1957. "Victim Precipitated Homicide." *Journal of Criminal law, Criminology, and Police Science*.48(1), 1-11.

Videos

Anne Milgram, "Why smart statistics are the key to fighting crime" TED. Jan 28, 2014 12:41 minutes Posted at https://www.youtube.com/watch?v=ZJNESMhIxQ0

Federal Bureau of Investigation (FBI). "NIBRS 101" 7:12 minutes. Posted at https://www.fbi.gov/video-repository/nibrs-101.mp4/view.

CHAPTER **FIVE**

Victims and the Criminal Justice System

Police, Courts, and Corrections

Learning Objectives

After you finish reading this chapter, you should be able to:

1. Understand the complexities about why victims do or do not report crime victimization to the police.
2. Analyze the pros and cons of reporting a crime to the police from the victim's point of view.
3. Examine the pluses and minuses of reporting a crime to the police from the perspective of the police and the criminal justice system.
4. Understand "defounding" and "unfounding" and how that impacts what police officers see when they respond to a crime scene.
5. Understand the realistic range of police response times for noncritical and high-priority calls.
6. Create a list of do's and don'ts for police officers who interview victims at the scene of a crime.
7. Describe the processing of a criminal case from the point of a crime taking place.
8. Explain what a photo array is and why it is so important if there is a suspect arrested in a case.
9. Describe the processing of a criminal case from the point of the crime taking place.
10. Define what a plea bargain is and its prevalence in the American criminal justice system.
11. Understand what it means to be a witness in a trial.
12. Describe the services offered by a victim witness assistance unit in the office of the district attorney.
13. Have a basic knowledge of the scope of the penal system in the United States today including the number of local, state, and federal prisons.
14. Define the evidence-based correctional theories, especially restorative justice, and how those theoretical approaches to punishment apply to victims.
15. Know what rights a victim has if an incarcerated offender is up for parole.

OVERVIEW

This chapter covers many key issues that crime victims face related to the criminal justice system beginning with the decision about whether or not to report the crime to the police. If the police are called, you will learn about what victims might expect from that point on. But calling 911 is not as simple or easy a matter as it might seem. (As former 9-1-1 Operator Holmes points out in her Profile in Chapter 6, calling 911 does not necessarily mean that someone wants the police. Two other options are emergency medical services or the fire department.)

As you will learn in this chapter, victims, witnesses, or bystanders have a range of reasons they may prefer not to report a crime to the police. Therefore, in addition to assessing how often victims report, and why, we will also explore the reasons victims avoid reporting.

Following the discussion of victims and the police, this chapter will provide you with an overview of the criminal justice system since anyone who works for, or with, victims, as well as victims, should understand that process. In this chapter, you will also find an overview of the punishment options that a convicted offender faces. **Restorative justice,** whereby the victim, the offender, a restorative justice representative or mediator, or a community representative work out a punishment that usually does not include jail or prison time. That punishment option, which is discussed below in the section on the penal system, is increasing in popularity. It is also the punishment alternative that most directly involves the victim of the crime. (Restorative justice is mentioned again in Chapter 6 in the section on financial compensation possibilities for victims.)

The next goal of this chapter is to review the rights that victims have won over the last several decades related to the criminal justice system. You will learn as well about the victim's role in the criminal justice system. (Please note: The right of a victim to sue in civil court is covered in Chapter 6, "Helping the Victim," in the section on financial assistance.)

CALLING 911 AND REPORTING TO THE POLICE

When a victim or a bystander calls 911, it is because a crime is either in the process of being committed or has just occurred. What kind of crime just happened may vary widely, from any of the six major violent crimes—murder, rape, robbery, aggravated assault, child abuse, or domestic violence—to the myriad of property crimes including burglary, larceny/theft, motor vehicle theft, arson, embezzlement, fraud, money laundering, cybercrime, and more. As mentioned above, calling 911 might mean that the caller wants the 911 operator to contact either the police, emergency medical help, the fire department, or all three.

The Decision to Report a Crime

Many people will view the decision to report a crime to the police as a no brainer: Get victimized, call the police. Unfortunately, for victims, it may not be that clear-cut a choice.

For example, if the victim is undocumented and fears deportation, if the victim has had prior dealings with the police and, as a result, is fearful of interacting with them again, if the victim feels that the police will not do anything so why bother, if a victim may fear being scrutinized by the police about what happened and, directly or indirectly, be blamed for the incident, or if the victim fears retaliation from the assailant for going to the police, then the victim may be reluctant to call the police. These are just some of the reasons a victim may not report a crime right after it occurs or soon afterwards. A pivotal issue in understanding criminal victimization, patterns of reporting and nonreporting were discussed in Chapter 4, "Measuring Victimization." It has been the object of study by academics and government agencies for decades. (Skogan, 1976; Harrell and Davis, Bureau of Justice Statistics, 2020; Payne, 2008;Tolsma,Blaauw, and te Grotenhuis, 2012; Singer, 1988).

As mentioned in earlier chapters, the estimated percentage of victims who report a crime to the police varies by type of crime. The Bureau of Justice Statistics, based on the National Crime Victimization Survey results, estimated that 52 percent of all violent crime victimizations were not reported to the police between 2006 and 2010. (Langston and Berzofsky, Bureau of Justice Statistics, 2012) The 2019 National Crime Victimization Survey discovered that the reporting to police rate had fallen even lower: just 41 percent of violent victimizations were reported to the police. (Morgan and Truman, 2020) As pointed out in a previous chapter, only 24% of rapes were reported to the police according to the 2018 National Crime Victimization Survey (NCVS). (Morgan and Oudekerk, 2019)

In their article, "Victim Willingness to Report Crime to Police: Does Procedural Justice or Outcome Matter Most?" published in *Victims and Offenders*, Kristina Murphy and Julie Barkworth, identify the following as typical reasons that victims do not report the crime to the police:

1. Offense was not serious enough
2. Victim considered the crime a private matter
3. Police distrust
4. Did not think the police would help
5. Victim had a previous negative experience with police or "legal authorities"
6. Victims felt the criminal justice system further victimized them including feeling **victim blame** (Murphy and Barkworth, 2014)

This author did a survey on May 10, 2020, with 225 men and women who were part of the Survey Monkey Audience. They participated in a 10-question anonymous survey administered through the online research software, Survey Monkey. Question 5 asked the respondents to consider their most recent victimization and whether or not they reported it to the police. Of the 174 who answered that question, 44.83 percent did not report it and 41.95 percent did.

Question 6 asked those who did not report it to indicate their reason. The reason was shared by 115 respondents and included the following rationales, listed in descending order of popularity. The results are summarized in Box 5.1. (Yager, 2021)

Box 5.1. Reasons for Not Reporting the Most Recent Crime in Yager Survey

I didn't think they would be able to do anything about it.	37.39%
I didn't have enough information to help them make an arrest so why bother reporting it.	16.52%
I considered it a private, family matter.	9.57%
I was too upset to want to talk about it with anyone.	7.83%
I was worried about retaliation or repercussions of reporting it.	6.96%
I wanted to put the crime behind me and not discuss it with anyone.	6.09%
I didn't want to take the time to report it to the police.	5.22%
I was worried about what might happen if I reported it.	5.22%
I heard that reporting might lead to me spending a lot of time in court appearances.	1.74%
My insurance company didn't require reporting to put in a claim.	1.74%
I didn't want to tell anyone about what happened, not even police.	1.74%

(*Source:* Yager, *Victims*, 2021)

The criminal justice system's involvement with a crime begins with the victim, witness, or bystander reporting the crime to the police during or immediately after the crime has occurred. Yes, a victim may be on the cell phone, calling the police on speakerphone, while domestic abuse is occurring. If someone is burglarizing the house and the criminal does not know there is a homeowner still present, the victim may be hiding in a locked bathroom, calling the police. But in most cases, as in a robbery or a fight, the victim will call the police *after* the criminal leaves or the criminal act is over. If the victim is incapacitated, and if there are bystanders or witnesses, they might call for the victim. In domestic violence cases, for example, a neighbor or even a child or teen might call the police during the assault.

Reporting to the police usually is the first step for victims to take to get police involvement in their victimization. Police are the first part of, or initial step in, the criminal justice system. The other parts, also discussed in this chapter, are the courts, including the defense attorney and the district attorney's office, especially the prosecutor assigned

Example of the police helping a victim.

to the case, and, if a defendant is found guilty, the corrections or punishment part of the system.

If a victim, or someone witnessing or having knowledge about a crime, calls 911, that is just the first step. Locating, or arresting, a perpetrator, let alone guaranteeing that the perpetrator is brought to justice, is something police cannot promise. No one can assure victims, or the family of a murder victim, of the outcome of their case. Unless the police have personally observed a crime happening, unless a victim—or a witness, bystander, Good Samaritan, or neighbor—alerts the police that a crime is in progress, or that a crime has taken place, the situation may remain a private matter.

Here are two real-life examples of victims who chose to report their victimizations to law enforcement:

- Dawn Burnett was the victim of a somewhat unusual burglary situation. Her house was for sale and while she was away on a trip, it was broken into and squatters were living in it. "I reported it to the police," Dawn shared in this author's survey. "It became local news as it was a ring of house break ins, squatters, and fraudulent rentals."
- Six years ago, Adriana H. was the victim of domestic violence with her boyfriend. "I called 911 and then hung up," she writes in this author's survey. "They called back and I reported it." That led to the police arriving and she went to a magistrate (judge) That led to her boyfriend being removed from the home that they shared so she could remain. Adriana was also granted a permanent protective order against him.

Here are a few examples of victims who *did not report* their victimization to the police:

- Lisa W. was drugged and raped on a date when she was 17 years old. "I woke up the next morning on a dirty mattress in the center of a garage, naked," Lisa shared with this author. She continues, "I did not speak of the event for twenty-eight years as I was too fearful of what others especially my father, would think in particular, that I must have done something to provoke it, and that it was my fault." (Interview with the author, 2020)
- In Chapter 1, in the section entitled, "Who are the Victims?" you may recall that Jack F., who was sexually molested at the age of 8 by his 16-year-old so-called "cousin," did not report the abuse to the police. He explained to this author in our phone interview why he decided not to report it: "We were both minors when it happened. It would be his word against mine. My grandmother knows everyone in [her state]. It would break up that family or put them under undue stress and it would drag our family's name through the mud. It's something I don't wish to do." (Interview with the author, 2021)

In the next chapter, Chapter 6, "Helping the Victim," we will explore the medical, emotional, and financial help from the government in the form of crime victim compensation that is available for victims. That is what is still possible for victims who do not report the crime even if they have chosen to opt out of the criminal justice system. However, when you read the section on government-sponsored financial reimbursements, you will see that to be eligible, reporting the crime, within a certain time period, is usually a requirement. An exception is the cost of a rape kit, which could cost thousands of dollars. The federal Violence Against Women Act (VAWA), first passed more than 25 years ago, in 1994, stated that if a state wanted to be eligible for certain federal grants, they had to certify that the cost of the rape kit would be covered. Updates to the law added that reporting the crime to the police was not a requirement to get those out-of-pocket expenses covered. (Andrews, 2019) Some states, like New York, reimburse directly to the medical providers for the forensic rape examinations. (Office of Victim Services, New York States, 2021; Office of Victim Services, State of Connecticut, n.d.)

In this chapter, we discuss what happens after a victim (or a bystander or neighbor) calls 911 and the police respond to the call. Sometimes the case goes no further. Sometimes there are further involvements with the criminal justice system.

Why Should a Crime Be Reported to the Police?

Calling the police has enormous implications. On the plus side, it can set in motion a police response that can stop a crime in progress, if the police are called while the crime is being committed, especially in situations of domestic violence or robbery in progress. Even if the crime has already occurred, it can enable police and investigators to get descriptions of the assailants and collect evidence that could be useful in arresting a suspect and, if it goes further, leading to a conviction.

As will be noted in Chapter 6, "Helping the Victim," most state compensation programs require reporting a crime to the police. Some states have a 72-hour time period for a victim to report the crime to the police if he or she plans to apply for crime victim compensation, as discussed in Chapter 6. Although some states, like Ohio, have waived the time element for reporting the crime, reporting to the police is still required. For those victims, a delay needs an explanation. Most insurance companies for homeowner claims or motor vehicle theft reports also require formally reporting the crime to the police. (As noted above, there are exceptions to the requirement to report to the police to apply for government compensation, such as receiving a sexual assault forensic examination without first reporting to the police.)

But some victims may take longer to call 911 than the time allowed by some government reimbursement programs if they are in shock or denial or just need time to gain enough composure to make the call. As you read in Chapter 2 on an anthropological and historical view of crime victims and their rights, in most cases, victims can no longer deal directly with offenders the way they could in primitive cultures or before that right was transferred to the king or state.

Today, involving the criminal justice system is usually the best way to get the justice or even the compensation that victims deserve. However, the criminal justice system is just one of two options. A second option, which may not involve the police if a firearm or knife was not used in the commission of the crime, which would have required mandatory reporting of the injured party to authorities in a majority of cases, is the civil justice system option. As discussed in the next chapter, the civil justice option is not as well-known as a possibility. It involves a **civil suit**, under which the victim could sue and seek financial redress from the offender or a responsible third party. (See Chapter 6, "Helping the Victim: Medical, Psychological, Financial Aid and Civil Suits, for a discussion of civil suits.)

Nonreporting of crimes is a challenge in the United States and globally. You know from Chapter 4, "Measuring Victimization: Why and How," that the **NIBRS (National Incident-Based Reporting System)** is the newer and more detailed reporting system that reflects information provided by the local police precincts and any other participating law enforcement agencies to the FBI, solely on the basis of reported crimes. But how much crime is reported? The National Crime Victimization Survey (NCVS), the secondary source of national crime data in the United States, based on interviewing with a representative sample, covers reported and nonreported crimes that occurred within the last 12 months for anyone in the household above the age of 12.

In Table 5.1 you will find a list of crimes and the percent reported to the police during 2017 and 2018 as well as the victimization rate reported per 1,000 population. This is based on the probability samples that comprise the National Crime Victimization Survey (NCVS). Note that the only major violent crime that is missing from this table is murder. The property crime of arson is also missing. (The NCVS excludes asking the respondents about certain crimes.) The Table, based on the *Criminal Victimization, 2018* report developed by Bureau of Justice Statistics statisticians Rachel E. Morgan, Ph.D. and Barbara A. Oudekerk, Ph.D., also breaks down reporting of crime to the police in the subcategories of violent crime, namely domestic violence, stranger violence, violent crime involving injury, and violent crime involving a weapon.

TABLE 5.1. Percent and Rate of Victimizations Reported to Police, by Type of Crime, 2017 and 2018

	Percent Reported		Victimization Rate Reported per 1,000	
Type of Crime	**2017**	**2018**	**2017**	**2018**
All violent crimes	44.9%	42.6%	9.2	9.9
Rape/sexual assault	40.5	24.9	0.6	0.7
Robbery	49.0	62.6	1.1	1.3
Assault	44.7	43.0	7.6	7.9
Aggravated assault	57.2	60.5	2.1	2.3
Simple assault	41.3	38.4	5.5	5.6
Violent crime excluding simple assault	51.4%	49.9%	3.8	4.3
Domestic violence	47.2%	47.0%	2.1	2.3
Intimate partner violence	47.5	45.0	1.2	1.4
Stranger violence	46.9	44.5	3.5	4.0
Violent crime involving injury	52.2	54.3	2.4	2.9
Violent crime involving a weapon	52.5	60.3	2.4	2.9
All property crimes	35.7%	34.1%	38.7	36.9
Burglary/trespassing	49.1	46.6	10.1	9.9
Burglary	51.1	47.9	6.6	6.6
Trespassing	45.7	44.2	3.6	3.2
Motor-vehicle theft	79.0	78.6	3.3	3.4
Other theft	30.2	28.6	25.3	23.7

Source: *Criminal Victimization, 2018*, Bureau of Justice Statistics, based on the National Crime Victimization Survey, page 8.

The first notable change is the evident drop in rape/sexual assault crimes reported to the police between 2017 and 2018. In 2017, 40.4 percent of rapes/sexual assaults were reported but that percentage dropped dramatically to just 24.9 percent in 2018.

Why is that drop so alarming? Because 2018 is the year that there was more attention on sexual assault than in most years because of several high profile developments related to rape and sexual assault. Going chronologically, the first was the conviction on April 26, 2018 of megastar TV actor and comedian Bill Cosby on three counts of aggravated indecent assault. He was sentenced on September 25, 2018 to serve 3 to 10 years in a state prison, fined $25,000 and required to repay the $43,611 prosecution costs. (Bowley and Coscarelli, 2018)

The next major sexual assault event was the indictment of movie mogul Harvey Weinstein on May 30, 2018. And the third event was the testimony on September 27, 2018, from Dr. Blasey Ford and her allegations against Supreme Court nominee Judge Kavanaugh. Televisions throughout the country were tuned to the hearings. (Stolberg and Fandos, 2018) The follow-up was that on October 6, 2018, by a Senate vote of 50 to 48, Judge Kavanaugh was confirmed as a Justice on the Supreme Court. (Stolberg, 2018)

Was there a cause-and-effect among these high-profile sexual assault-related cases and the dramatic drop in victims reporting rape/sexual assault victimizations to police in 2018? It is only conjecture but it does highlight how potentially complicated the issue of reporting and nonreporting can be in all types of crimes especially rape/sexual assault. It will be interesting to see if there is an upswing in the reporting of rape cases tied to the publication in September 2019 of the memoir by Chantel Miller, *Know My Name*. You may recall from previous chapters that Miller was originally only referred to as Emily Doe when, several years before, she was raped by a college athlete who was found guilty at trial, receiving a six-month prison sentence, which led to a huge outcry with the public consensus that was much too light a sentence for such a serious crime. The victim statement she read in court went viral, but the victim was anonymous until her memoir was published. Would coming forward publicly inspire more rape victims to come forward and report their victimizations? (Miller, 2019)

Another notable statistic as revealed in Table 5.1 about reporting by percentages and rates is that the property crime with the highest reporting rate to the police, by far, is motor vehicle theft. That rate is 78.6 percent. Compare that to the relatively lower rate of 47.9 percent for burglaries and the even lower rate of 28.6 percent for 2018 for other thefts.

What these statistics show is that there can be higher percentages of reporting when there is a reason, such as a financial incentive, to report. Although as noted in Chapter 8, "Property Crime Victims," it's rare that the owner of a stolen car gets reimbursed at the rate the victim paid for the car, most insurance companies will reimburse at the current market value, which could be many thousands of dollars and enough to buy another car. However, the first step that insurance companies require is that a report is made to the police about the stolen car.

Ditto for burglaries and robberies. Although crime victim compensation does not reimburse for property, private insurance companies do, such as homeowners' insurance. They require a police report as well.

If more apartment dwellers had renters' insurance, we might see an increase in burglary reports to police since there would be an economic incentive for apartment dwellers to do so.

Another finding about reporting to the police becomes evident by studying Table 5.1. Violent crime involving a weapon had the highest reporting rate for 2018 (60.3%) followed by violent crime involving injury (54.3%). If the offender is a stranger, victims are more likely to report the incident than if they are when the offender is someone they know like a family member or friend.

What Happens After a Crime Is Reported?

Victims need to understand that reporting to the police about the crime that just happened, making a **statement** about the crime, even if the victim did not see the offender's face so a visual identification is unlikely, may still be helpful to the authorities. It could establish the ***modus operandi***, or pattern, of victimization, that could help the police in solving this and even other similar offenses committed by the same perpetrator. There could also be **forensic evidence,** such as DNA analysis, fingerprints, or ballistics that could help to solve this and other cases.

In the next chapter, Chapter 6, "Helping the Victim," there is a discussion about the medical help that victims of crime may receive after suffering injuries related to their victimization. These physical injuries may be "invisible" because the injuries are internal, such as those shared by the victim of the Boston Marathon bombing who, because of blast force trauma, has been left with memory issues, cognitive impairment, and hearing loss. These kinds of injuries are not something that can easily be seen, like cuts requiring stitches, or the loss of a limb.

If someone is severely injured or unconscious and incapacitated, an ambulance may have been called to take the victim to the hospital. For those victims, whether treated at a hospital or by a private physician, if the injuries were caused by a firearm or knife, and that state has mandatory reporting to police in such cases, involving the criminal justice system may be automatic. At their website, in the report entitled, "Mandatory Reporting of Non-Accidental Injuries: A State-by-State Guide," The Victim Rights Law Center, with offices in Massachusetts and Oregon, there is a list of states requiring mandatory non-accidental injury reporting, as of 2014. Some states, such as Alabama, do not require mandatory reporting of non-accidental injuries but others, like Alaska, Colorado, and Delaware, do require it. Some states, like Arkansas, require mandatory reporting if the bullet or knife wound was intentionally inflicted. So, victims who have suffered those types of injuries requiring medical attention may have their victimization reported to the police whether they want to or not. (Victim Rights Law Center, 2014)

When a victim seeks out medical help may be a factor in voluntary reporting to the police. For example, in 2010, when Joseph F. was an 18-year-old college freshman, he met a man he connected with on social media to sell his $400 designer sports sneakers, as described in Chapter 8, "Property Crime Victims." As Joseph explains, "When he pretends like he's going into my backpack to get the money, all of a sudden he pulls out a gun and tells me, 'Motherfucker, give me everything you got." I froze for a minute and told him, 'No.' That's when he pistol whips me in the face and I started bleeding." It was the Emergency Room nurses that told Joseph to call the police. Says Joseph, "When I was at the hospital, the nurses had asked me what happened, and I told them the whole story. They recommended I tell the cops and make a report, so I did." (Anonymous interview shared with the author.)

It is important to help victims understand that calling police and filing a report when a crime has occurred is usually the right thing to do. But it is also good to be realistic about what, if anything, the police may be able to do about any case. As noted before, the police have staffing issues that require them to prioritize what cases they are able to investigate and which ones they unfortunately cannot pursue. Money alone may not be the criteria, although back in the mid-1970s a police officer shared with this author that they were required to investigate any burglary where the theft was valued at $10,000 or higher.

The amount that is stolen, however, may not be the only factor. Cases where there were multiple offenders and a weapon was present, especially if the weapon was used and victim or victims were injured, usually get a higher priority level by the police.

Reporting the crime, if it is safe to do so, is a step to consider. Victims do have their reasons for being reluctant report a crime, as summarized in Box 5.1. But, as stated above, victims also have to be realistic about what, if anything, the police may do related to a specific crime. If an investigation does not ensue, if offenders are not arrested, if there is not even the courtesy follow-up that some would like, that should not be used to judge *all* police and all situations. That judgment, unfortunately, is too often the case.

Whenever a crime is reported, victims should avoid considering that one situation is a reflection on the entire police force. But since it is human nature to generalize from one experience, anyone who plans to become a first responder needs to realize that your behavior as a police officer in response to a victim's experience may be the way you and maybe even the entire police force is judged. (Miller, et. al., 2004)

Another reason to report a crime is based on what researchers have discovered: that calling 911 actually helps to reduce **repeat victimization** defined as the tendency to become a victim of the same or additional crimes, more than once or multiple times. As Dr. Kay Lang writes in her dissertation, "911: Help or Hindrance in Reducing repeat Victimization," "My results suggest that those people who call police experience less repeat victimization than those who do not call the police. This pattern remains the same for both violent victimization and residential burglary. In addition, those people who call the police experience repeat victimization later than people who do not call the police, and, again this holds true for violent attacks and residential burglary." (Kay Lang, pages vii-viii)

Let us consider why reporting a crime to the police might make a victim *less* likely to suffer repeat victimization. Take a burglary. When the police are called about a burglary, they will show up at the victim's apartment or home. They will take a statement from the victim. They will usually ask the victim for any details about what happened. They will ask whether anyone having access to their home might have done the burglary. Some police might even check the apartment or home for security measures, advising the victim about what better measures could be taken to avoid a second burglary. Asking the apartment dweller or home owner for an inventory of stolen property could help the victim to become more organized about what is valuable and where it is stored. The police may advise the victim about crime prevention tips to reduce their likelihood as a repeat target.

Statute of Limitations

For some crimes, especially for rape and sexual offenses, there may be a **statute of limitations (SOL)** for a victim to file a report against an alleged offender. This varies by state and by crime. That means that a report must be filed by the victim within a certain time limit for the case to be pursued. Some states have different statute of limitations for criminal or civil suits. The SOL may range to as short a time frame as within one year of the victimization or the victim becoming aware of the victimization, due to delayed processing of the events because of the crime's emotional toll, to as long as 10, 20, or 30 years from commission of the crime, to no SOL for Wyoming, West Virginia, Virginia, Utah, or South Carolina, to name just a few states. Some states, like New Mexico, have a DNA exception; in that case, SOL only begins when DNA evidence is obtainable. Some of the most serious acts, like murder, have no SOL.

Failure to Report

There are situations where the victim considers it unsafe to report. Those situations, with examples, are discussed in Table 5.2.

TABLE 5.2. Reasons for Not Reporting to the Police, Including Fears, Provided by Victims

Fear of retaliation.	"I just didn't want to do anything that could make things worse even if it was the right thing." (He recognized the perpetrators.) "I feel that they would be out on the street the next day and would come looking for me."
Fear of getting arrested.	1. Victim was robbed while he was illegally dealing unlawful prescription drugs. 2. Victim was undocumented immigrant afraid of deportation.
Victim was too traumatized.	"I was too scared from what happened."
Victim didn't think police could do anything.	"I know the place [where he was robbed] well enough to know there are no cameras, so there was no lead."
Victim did not know he could report it.	"Being so new to the country [only here 6 months] I didn't know where to turn to. I didn't know I could go the station and make a report." (Robbed of his mother's cell phone when he was 13)
Victim minimized the crime.	"No real amount of money was taken from me." (Same victim as in previous reason.)

Source: Direct quotes are excerpted and compiled by this author from victim interviews and surveys.

If during the commission of the crime there is no firearm or knife wounds requiring medical attention with mandatory reporting, or if the victim chooses to avoid making a report with the police, there may be no victim involvement with the criminal justice system. The NCVS (National Crime Victimization Survey) conducted annually by the U.S. Census Bureau for the Bureau of Justice Statistics for the U.S. Department of Justice indicates that as many as fifty nine percent (59%) of violent crimes went unreported in 2019. (Morgan and Truman, 2020) So, we know that for many victimizations, there is no involvement with the criminal justice system.

What crime victim advocates and others who may help victims who seek medical or counseling services related to their victimization need to know is that, in most states, as noted in the next chapter, Chapter 6, "Helping the Victim," failing to report the crime to the police means that they will not be eligible to apply for crime victim compensation. Also, if they plan to report the crime to the police at a later time point, the longer they wait to make their statement, if there is **evidence** at the crime scene that might be helpful in solving the crime, the harder it might be for such evidence to be **admissible** in court or even preserved.

For the sake of argument, unless crime victims seek to pursue a civil suit, for victims who decide not to report their victimization to the police, their victimizations will become negative experiences that they will have to deal with privately or, if they choose to seek out professional help, with a therapist or a crime victim advocate. As noted before, reporting a crime, especially a violent one, means that the police may receive information that might help them to see a pattern of victimization which could lead to a subsequent arrest. That arrest, if it is a repeat offender, could help to solve older cases or even prevent further victimizations. The consequences of a reported rape being disallowed by the police is retold dramatically in the real-life story of *Unbelievable,* a Netflix 2019 series. The series was based on the Pulitzer-Prize winning 2015 ProPublica and The Marshall Project article by Marie Adler, who was 18 when she was raped. (Mcafee, 2020)

It should be noted that some types of crime, such as cybercrime, identity theft, and fraud, may be reported to the FBI, the bank, a credit card company, and other agencies. Even if the local police are not be able to investigate those types of economic crimes, filing a formal report provides value; for example, the criminal might be involved in more conventional property crimes as well.

Trends and current events may also influence whether victims report or not. The Academy Award-winning 2015 movie *Spotlight* chronicled the investigative reporting of the *Boston Globe* that followed up in 2001 on reports of priests sexually abusing children that first came to light in 1976 and again in the 1990s but were never pursued. *The Globe*'s new editor, Marty Baron, assigned the investigation to the paper's Spotlight team of investigative reporters. *Spotlight* dramatized how the controversial truth of priests engaging in sexual abuse emerged after all those years as reporters found and interviewed victims willing to share their story.

Police Response Time

One of the biggest issues that victims have with police is how long it takes them to arrive once 911 is called. If a crime is in progress, victims may be on their own or deal with the aftermath before even the fastest police department can arrive. Someone could bleed out in just five minutes if there is a fatal gunshot or knife wound. Removing oneself from a dangerous situation when possible (for example, if there is a burglar coming in the front door, can you and your family run out the back) may be the prudent thing to do since even the fastest police department may take 5 to 10 minutes to arrive.

Remember that all police departments have two response times: highest priority calls and average response time. So, keep that in mind when you are considering the rates below. Here are police response rates provided by Security Sales & Integration for November 2018:

Los Angeles—5.7 minutes
Seattle—7 minutes
Dallas—under 8 minutes
Miami—just over 8 minutes
New York City—average response rate of 9.1 (high priority calls: 4.6 minutes; noncritical situations: 13.3 minutes).
Atlanta—9 minutes 35 seconds
Houston—10 minutes
Detroit—12 minutes (down from over 50 minutes in 2013)
Denver—13 minutes (down from 15 minutes between 2013 and 2016)

Source: Steve Karantzoulidis, "The Best and Worst Police Response Times of 10 Major U.S. Cities"

One of the biggest debates about police response times is the question of whether or not shorter response time actually makes a difference in the **clearance rate**, which basically means an arrest was made. It is commonly believed that only an unrealistically fast response time of one minute will make a difference in clearance rates. (Vidal and Kirchmaier, 2018). Jordi Blanes I. Vidal of the London School of Economics and Tom Kirchmaier, also of the

London School of Economics, set out to do research that might prove or disprove just how much quicker police response time could make in clearance rates.

The co-authors begin their journal article, "The Effect of Police Response Time on Crime Clearance Rates," published in the *Review of Economic Studies*, with two rather harsh views negating the belief that improved response time can make a difference in catching a criminal. The first quote from L.W. Sherman from *Crime and Justice* is that there: "'is no direct evidence that rapid response can make any difference in detection or crime rates and some indirect evidence that it cannot. It is very rare that rapid response can catch an offender.'" (Sherman, 2013, quoted in Vidal and Kirchmaier, 2018: 856) The second quote affirms that point of view. Quoting Bayley, Vidal and Kirchmaier state: "'If police can arrive within one minute of the commission of an offense, they are more likely to catch the suspect. Any later and the chances of capture are very small, probably less than one in ten.'" (Bayley, 1996, quoted in Vidal and Kirchmaier, 2018: 856)

One of the goals of the Vidal and Kirchmaier research was to dispel the belief, held for more than four decades, according to the co-authors, that response time is irrelevant. They attribute that overarching theory to the prominent 1976 Kansas City Response Time Analysis Study. They point out one of the flaws in that study was that it only related to "on-scene arrests . . . ignoring arrests later in time." (Vidal and Kirchmaier, 2018: 858)

Vidal and Kirchmaier studied the internal records of the Greater Manchester Police force between 2008 and 2014. One of the pieces of information in those records is the response time to a crime scene. That police force is the second largest in Great Britain, supervising a population of 2.6 million. Their findings were that faster response time *does* matter in clearance rates. They conclude: "a 10% increase in response time leads to a 4.7 percentage points decrease in the clearance rate." They also discovered a related benefit of a better response time: "conditional on clearing a crime, the police take less time to do so if the initial response time was faster." (Vidal and Kirchmaier, 2018: 858)

There are many reasons that an improved response time logically should make a positive difference in the outcome of a victimization including the practicality of having witnesses still present who could provide descriptions of the assailant, and that the physical evidence at the crime scene might still be intact. But whether it takes just a few minutes, or longer, victims and witnesses should be prepared for the next steps once the police arrive.

What to Expect When Law Enforcement Arrives

When a victim is reporting a crime, regardless of whether it is a sexual assault or the theft of a bicycle, the victim should feel validated and respected. Since the police are often the first on the scene of the crime unless, if there are injuries, the EMTs or ambulance arrives first, they will examine the crime scene for evidence and assess the situation to determine what transpired. To give an example, a domestic violence victim, had to be arrested along with her abusive partner because police could not figure out who the real perpetrator was. The boyfriend was accusing the girlfriend and the girlfriend was accusing her partner. They both had injuries. At the stationhouse, it got sorted out, based on various interviews, that the girlfriend was indeed the victim. In that case, the boyfriend's account of things was considered **unfounded**. If the case was exaggerated or not at all in actuality the way the victim depicted it, that might be seen as an instance of **defounding.**

Some municipalities, like in Maryland, have ruled that unless there are injuries, a mandatory arrest is no longer required in domestic violence cases. The reason for this is to encourage reporting because under the mandatory arrest rule, too many victims were not reporting for fear their partner would automatically be arrested and jailed. (Melissa Hoppmeyer, 2021)

The National Sheriffs Association manual, *Training and Technical Assistance to Law Enforcement on Responses to and Investigation of Domestic Violence, Dating Violence, and Stalking,* provides the following guidelines of what to expect when the police arrive:

> When responding to a crime scene, the officer must first locate and secure the scene and ask his/herself the following questions:
>
> - Are there any weapons?
> - Is anyone injured?
> - Who is involved? (victim, offender, witnesses)
> - If the offender is not on the scene:
>   - Where is the suspect?
>   - Are they in continuing danger?
>   - Is the suspect in possession of a weapon?
>
> *Source:* National Sheriffs Association, n.d.)

Because police officers may be the first on the scene. they may have to initiate life-saving medical emergency strategies. The NYPD, in recognition of this, has specialized training through their Police Academy as well as additional instruction. The training entitled "Medical Emergency Response and Critical Intervention Training Unit," is provided to uniformed police officers as well as civilian members of the police service on a recurring periodic basis. (NYPD, "Specialized Training Section.")

In addition to just being common sense responsive policing, **Briana's Law** was passed in New York State on August 27, 2017, by New York Governor Andrew Cuomo. The law requires that all police officers receive CPR training and get recertified every two years. Briana's Law was seven years in the making. The efforts to get the law passed were initiated in 2010 after the untimely death of 10-year-old Briana Amaryllis Ojeda from an asthma attack. Briana's mother had been pulled over by a police officer because of a driving error when rushing her daughter to the hospital following a severe asthma attack. Unfortunately the police officer did not know CPR and Briana died. Although the NYPD did train its officers in CPR, the responding officer claimed that his training was inadequate and out of a textbook. Because of that, he did not feel confident to perform CPR. Briana's law will hopefully save more lives by police officers who may be the first responders to a life-threatening scene because of a health or crime-related emergency requiring CPR. (New York State Assembly, 2014.)

Death notification is a crucial part of a police department's interactions with victims. An officer will be communicating with the secondary victims of crime, the immediate family of the deceased. If those family members are present at the time of the murder or homicide, the police officer will be taking statements, offering comfort, and providing referrals. If the murder or homicide occurred in another location, they will have to make the death notification. This is a pivotal duty for police officers. Further discussion of death notifications by police is provided in Chapter 7, "Primary and Secondary Victims of Homicide" with additional information in the Appendices posted at the publisher's website, www.AspenPublishing.com.

The Office for Victims of Crime (OVC) of the U.S. Department of Justice suggests that police officers consider the three basic needs of victims when they respond to a 911 call:

1. The need to feel safe
2. The need to express their emotions
3. The need to know "What Comes Next" after their victimization (OVC, "Basic Guidelines on Approaching Victims of Crime")

The OVC recommends that any medical needs are attended to first. Law enforcement should introduce themselves to victims by name and explain what their role is. To help victims feel safe they could even say, directly, "You're safe now" or "I'm here now."

"I don't believe this happened to me" is the most common response to victimization, according to the OVC. They also point out the feelings of self-blame, anger, shame, sadness, or denial that victims initially experience. Responding police officers need to avoid compounding those feelings in how they initially respond. The OVC suggests countering self-blame by saying something like, "You didn't do anything wrong. This was not your fault."

Letting victims know what may happen next in the process should help them deal with the "what comes next" part of the post-victimization process. Police officers who are first to respond can describe, briefly, what law enforcement tasks need to be completed such as filing a report, investigating the crime, and the arrest and arraignment of a suspect. If there will be any medical forensic examinations that need to be carried out, police officers should explain why these examinations are required. They may speak with victims about normal reactions to what they have experienced such as depression, physical problems, concentration and memory loss, and other emotions. Providing referrals to available resources including crisis intervention centers, victim-witness assistance programs at the prosecutor's office, the state crime victim compensation program, national services, and hotline numbers would be helpful.

Improving the Police Reporting and Interaction Experience

How police talk to victims at the scene or, if they come down to the station, in the police precinct will color the way they view the police for this case and possibly for years to come. For example, Susan shared about her police reporting experience regarding her grandfather's previous molestation of her from the ages of 6 to 12: Susan has no regrets about going to the police. But "I wish the police made me more comfortable while asking me questions," she confides. She was only interviewed by a male officer and wonders if a female officer might have helped with her tough situation. (Anonymous interview shared with author.)

Here are some tips that law enforcement can keep in mind to improve the reporting to police experience:

1. Determine whether someone is a victim or actually the offender is of course part of the job of the police officer but it has to be done in a way that a victim does not feel discounted or distrusted.
2. Listen empathetically and carefully.
3. If it is a sex crime, when possible have two officers doing the interviewing including one of the same sex as the victim.
4. Take detailed notes.

5. If it is a murder, follow death notification guidelines.(See Chapter 7)
6. If it is a domestic violence situation, follow local and state guidelines. Most communities now have requirements for mandatory arrest and possibly even obtaining a restraining order. Know the laws in your area regarding domestic violence calls. Remember also that these can be the most dangerous of all calls to respond to since one or both parties might have weapons; also, the 911 call may have been placed by concerned neighbors or family members and one or both parties in the situation might turn against the officer.
7. Offer victims help from a variety of sources: medical, financial, or psychological. Have booklets from free counseling services as well as information on the state crime compensation board and its application procedures.
8. If your department says it's okay to do this, have a business card that you provide victims to allow for convenient follow-up directly with you. If you know you are hard to reach, let the victim know about alternative individuals at the precinct who can provide information about the case.
9. Have a brochure about the criminal justice system part of the process in case an arrest is made and the case goes further.
10. Avoid making promises you cannot realistically keep such as "We're going to find whoever it was that did this to you," if it was a stranger assault, or "Maybe you'll be able to locate some or all of your stolen items."
11. You may reassure victims that what happened was not their fault, negating the victim blame mentality.
12. Make sure someone that the victim trusts arrives so the victim is not alone after the interview. It could be a crime victim advocate from a local victims' center, someone attached to the victim-witness unit at the district attorney's office, or even the crime victim advocate at the local precinct who is usually on call in these situation. Alternatively, a victim's family member, friend, or a trusted neighbor can stop by to offer comfort while the victim deals with all the issues related to their particular violent or property victimization.
13. Police officers should learn about the cycle of violence that is common in domestic violence situations. This will help them to be better prepared to deal with these very complex and sometimes quite volatile situations. (See a discussion of domestic violence and the cycle of violence in Chapter 13, "Victims of Assault, Domestic Violence, Stalking, and Elder Abuse."

Dr. Martin Symonds' Four Phases of Victims Reactions to Violent Crime

It is rare that we have the insights from a psychiatrist who specializes in crime victims who also worked as a police officer for seven years before attending medical school and becoming a psychiatrist specializing in the treatment of crime victims and the training of police. That was the case with Martin Symonds, M.D., who also taught courses on crime victims and criminal behavior at John Jay College of Criminal Justice. In his classic article, "The 'Second Injury' to Victims of Violent Acts," published in 1980 in *The American Journal of Psychoanalysis*, Dr. Symonds shares his findings about the four phases that victims to violent crime go through in their reaction to the trauma. Dr. Symonds based these phases on an analysis of the psychological responses of nearly 600 victims of violent crimes. On the basis of that analysis, he came to the conclusion that victims of violent

TABLE 5.3. Dr. Martin Symonds' Four Phases of Reactions to Violent Crime

Phase	Reaction
First phase	"shock, disbelief, and denial." temporary paralysis and denial of sensory impressions.
Second phase	Victim can no longer deny the experience. Develops "Frozen Fright" or "Traumatic Psychological Infantilism" "Terror-induced pseudo calm, detached behavior." Victim behaves in way that seems to be ingratiating, appeasing, complying, even cooperative and voluntary acts.
Third phase	"There are generally alternating cycles of apathy, anger, depression, resentment, phobic reactions, and constipated rage."
Fourth phase	". . . the victim "hopefully integrates their unfortunate experience into their life style. . . ."

Source: Symonds, 1980, reprinted 2010.

crime display the same psychological responses that he often noticed in physically injured police officers and Vietnam veterans. According to Dr. Symonds, these reactions are the same whether the victim did not have contact with a criminal, such as in a burglary, or there was extended contact, such as in a rape or robbery. These phases and reactions are summarized in Table 5.3.

To avoid victims feeling like they are experiencing a "second injury" usually directed at law enforcement or hospital personnel, Dr. Symonds offers suggestions about how police officers should deal with crime victims. He even developed a training program for police and emergency personnel that was entitled, "Psychological First Aid for Victims of Crime." Dr. Symonds' emphasizes that police need to understand that victims have "silent expectations" for "nurturing and non-blaming." If those unspoken needs are not met by first responders, unfortunately they will bemoan their treatment by them. Fortunately, according to Dr. Symonds, that can be avoided by understanding what victims are going through in the third phase of victimization. Dr. Symonds suggests that the victim interview will be less stressful if it is more like a "therapeutic interview:"

> I encouraged the interviewer to identify himself to the victims' satisfaction such as presenting his ID card without being asked. To express his recognition of the victims distress by saying, "I'm sorry it happened. I am glad you are all right." And by demeanor and statements indicate that the victim did nothing wrong. Restoration of power to the victim can be accomplished by the interviewer asking permission to conduct the interview. "Is this a good time to talk to you? Do you mind if I ask you the following questions? Do you mind if I write your answers down?" The entire spirit of the interview has to be a non-challenging, non-contradictory, and supportive interview. (Symonds, 2010: 39-40.)

Avoiding the "Just Another Day at the Office" Syndrome

A major challenge for police officers and how they handle victims is avoiding the "just another day at the office" syndrome. This might happen to officers after they are on the job, and responding to victims, after a certain period of time. It may differ for each officer, from a few months or years, to decades. The Catch-22 is that police officers have to develop a "thick skin" when it comes to the violence, crime, murder, and mayhem they may see on a daily basis so they avoid burning out or feeling excessive stress related to their job. But if they stop feeling the empathy, compassion, sympathy, and concern that victims expect and need from them, they may be seen as callous and uncaring.

In interviews, police officers share that it is a challenge to treat victims they encounter in a demanding situation as if they are the only case they are working on. This is not just true for police officers. This phenomenon is something everyone dealing with the public in a personal and major way, such as medical doctors, nurses, psychologists, or psychiatrists, need to do. Patients, or victims, do not want to feel as though they are a faceless "number." Everyone wants to be treated as if their case is the first and only case that the police officer (or doctor or therapist) is dealing with.

But preserving that sense of unique interest is a challenge. As this officer explains, ". . . after a while you deal with a lot of sad and shocking cases that you begin to become immune to it. It's like, what's going to happen next? You know something crazy is going to happen, and you just have to prepare yourself to handle it. I do feel compassion for these victims because the acts that are done against them are really traumatizing. But on my end, it is just another day in the office and I have to handle it right."

Dr. Martin Symonds referred to this "just another day at the office" syndrome as part of the "second injury" that victims of violent crime may experience. The "second injury" is basically when those who are dealing with, or treating, victims of crime, including police officers, emergency medical personnel, agencies, family and friends, and even society in general, make them feel dismissed or ignored. As Dr. Symonds notes:

> Though the victim may be in a state of passive submission following victimization, he is unusually sensitive and often misperceives the ordinary professionalism of the police and hospital personnel as unfeeling, uncaring, indifferent and sometimes hostile. This misperception is often heightened by the victim coming in contact with the emotional insulation that all professionals develop in order to function without distress in crisis work. Early in my career, I worked in an emergency ward of a large general hospital, which was also the receiving ward for all the very serious cases of other hospitals in the city. Though the ward only had 30 beds, half of those patients would die within 24 hours. In order to survive and function, workers on that ward developed an emotional insulation that to an outsider would be seen as cruel and heartless. It was only years later that I thought of what the relatives of the sick patients much have felt when we would take time off from work and eat lunch on the ward. (Symonds, 2010: 37)

All jobs have some amount of stress but few would disagree that being a police officer or state trooper, or working for the government's law enforcement agencies including FBI, CIA, DEA, ICE, or Homeland Security, has even higher levels of stress. As Solomon and McGill point out in their book, *The Price They Pay*, almost 50 percent of all police officers may get assaulted "in any given year," adding to the stress they feel. (Solomon and McGill, 2015) As Luke Barr reports, police officer suicides in the United States reached a record high in 2019. That year, 228 current or former police officer died by suicide according to Blue H.E.L.P., a nonprofit organization that tracks this information. It is also concerned with eliminating the stigma of mental illness in police departments so that more at risk officers will get help before it is too late. (Barr, 2020)

AFTER THE POLICE REPORT IS FILED

The first step in the criminal justice system response to a crime is reporting it, but in the majority of cases, the case may go no further. There are numerous reasons for that but the most common one is that there is just not enough evidence to find a suspect and make an arrest. As mentioned before, there also tends to be a hierarchy on what cases the police can pursue just based on the sheer volume of reported crimes and the number of officers available to pursue those cases. This can be frustrating to victims. But reporting the crime is still the first step since there might be DNA evidence that clearly links a repeat offender to the crime scene, such as a burglar who had no other possible link to being present at the apartment dweller or homeowner's residence. For burglaries or motor vehicle thefts, even though the clearance rate (the number of reported crimes cleared by the arrest of an offender) may be quite low at just 13.9 percent for burglary and 13.8 percent for motor vehicle thefts, filing a police report with the police is the prudent thing to do because private homeowners' or renters' insurance companies and car insurance companies usually require a report.

Depending on the type of crime that was committed, the circumstances of the case, the seriousness of the crime, and other factors, after the report is filed, an investigation may follow. That investigation may lead to the arrest of an alleged offender. If that occurs, the next phase of the criminal justice system and the victim's involvement with it commences. This is where the victim is also a witness for the prosecution if the prosecution decides to pursue the case.

Note: A different version of this key information was shared in Box 2-1 in Chapter 2, "An Anthropological and Historical View of Crime Victims, and Victims' Rights." Since some students may be reading the chapters out of order, and since this material is so fundamental, it is included here as well. You may skip this box if you like,or read it over as a review.

Box 5.2. A Quick Review of Some Criminal Justice Basics including Misdemeanor versus Felony and State versus Federal

Deviance: An act that goes against the norms of a society but is not a crime because it has not broken a law. Examples include someone continually talking in a loud voice during a movie or live theatrical performance or drinking too much in the privacy of one's own home.

Crime: An action or behavior that breaches a criminal law and is open to punishment.

Criminal law: Violating criminal law is necessary to be convicted of a crime.

State and federal constitutions: Two of the three sources of criminal law. The third are court decisions. The state or federal government brings action against the criminal because the crime is considered to do harm against the entire society as well as the victim.

Civil law: Under civil law, the victim may initiate legal action against the accused or a third party deemed negligent such as a hotel, a company, or a school. The punishment may be the payment of a fine and other legal

Box 5.2. A Quick Review of Some Criminal Justice Basics including Misdemeanor versus Felony and State versus Federal (continued)

actions, such as being required to stop doing certain acts. However, taking away someone's freedom—sentencing someone to jail or prison time—an option if someone has been found guilty of breaking a criminal law, cannot be imposed. (This is discussed further in Chapter 6, "Helping the Victim: Medical, Psychological, Financial Aid, and Civil Suits.")

Misdemeanor: A less serious crime; if incarceration is imposed, it is for a shorter period of time in jail, less than a year. A fine, probation, or another alternative to incarceration, such as restorative justice, whereby an agreement is reached among the injured parties, may be imposed.

Felony: This is a more serious crime which can result in a prison sentence of one year or much longer, or even the **death penalty** in the 27 states where **capital punishment** is still allowed or by the federal government, which technically can impose the death penalty in selected situations including murder, espionage, or terrorism. (Death Penalty Information Center, 2021)

male in se: Crimes for which there is a general consensus that the acts involved, such as murder, robbery, rape, arson, burglary, and larceny/theft, are inherently immoral.

Male prohibita: Crimes that are only crimes because the acts involved, such as getting drunk in public or interrupting funeral services, are forbidden.

Sources: Legal Dictionary, 2017; Reid, 2018; Ruane, 2017; Adler, Mueller, and Laufer, 2007; Wormser, 1949, 1962; Banning, 2004.

If you are taking this Victimology course as a follow-up to a Criminology or Criminal Justice course, you will know the information in this quick review. Furthermore, this information is discussed at various points throughout this textbook. But since it is useful background to have in a discussion of the criminal justice and civil justice systems that follow, let us do a quick review.

A **misdemeanor** is a less serious crime that can result in a fine, probation, jail time of less than a year or other alternatives to incarceration such as successful completion of a rehab program or restorative justice.

A **felony** is a more serious crime that can result in a fine, probation, and prison time of one year or more. In those 27 states that still have the **death penalty**, it can even lead to a sentence of **capital punishment** or death. (deathpenaltyinfo.org)

In the United States, there are specific laws in every state that are unique to that state and the punishments for breaking those laws can range widely. For example, conviction for a third degree felony in Texas can lead to a sentence of no less than 2 years or more than 10 years. By contrast, in New York, a conviction for burglary in the third degree is punishable by up to 7 years in prison. If convicted of a crime in a state, and sentenced to prison, there are 1,719 state prisons with minimum, medium, and maximum security-designated facilities as well as what is known as a "camp" institution that has security restrictions even more lenient than the minimum security facilities. (Sawyer and Wagner, "Mass Incarceration")

There are crimes that are also considered federal crimes, pursued by federal law enforcement officers and, if convicted, and sentenced to prison that result in serving time in one of the 109 federal penitentiaries, not in a state prison. (Sawyer and Wagner) Federal crimes include kidnapping across state lines, tax fraud, treason, counterfeiting, mail fraud, drug trafficking, piracy, and white collar crimes. Bank robbery is both a state and federal crime.

MAKING AN ARREST

Since this is a textbook on victimology, this topic will not get the attention it would get in a criminology textbook. This has also become one of the most controversial issues in policing since the tragic death of George Floyd on May 25, 2020, as he was being arrested as well as the many other contentious arrests where the suspect died during the arresting process. What should be noted here is that every arrest should be done "by the book" meaning it is a fair and just arrest according to all the laws that insure the rights of the accused. In Chapter 7, "Primary and Secondary Victims of Homicide," we address police uses of force ending in death that are unjustified.

Another topic related to making an arrest is the use of reasonable force. What is especially tragic is when fatal mistakes are made that cannot be sorted out because the situation led to an outcome that is irreversible. Several cases come to mind including the Australian yoga instructor who called in to 911 that she thought someone was being sexually assaulted in the alley behind her home. Justine Ruszczyk was shot and killed by the responding police officer, who was later convicted of third-degree murder and manslaughter; he alleged that he thought she had a weapon when Ms. Ruszczyk approached his police cruiser. (Romo, 2019) Or the tragic mistaken killing of Breonna Taylor, a 26-year-old African American emergency room technician. She had been shot because the police were trying to serve what is known as a **no-knock warrant** which, according to the *New York Times* report by Oppel and Taylor on Taylor's death, "allowed the police to enter without warning or without identifying themselves as law enforcement." According to Oppel and Taylor, "After a brief exchange, Mr. Walker fired his gun. The police also fired several shots, striking Ms. Taylor." (This case is still pending so we will have to see what facts are presented at trial if there is one.) (Oppel and Taylor, 2020)

AFTER AN ARREST IS MADE

What follows is a general overview of what happens after an arrest is made. Remember that in the United States, we have 50 different state legal systems as well as a federal one so there may be some variation in the overall steps after the arrest that are described below. It is pivotal to know what the procedure in the state is where you will be working with victims, either as a victim advocate, lawyer, assistant district attorney, police officer, or even as a researcher and victimologist.

In the complaint room, or in the Witness Aid Services United, a formal complaint is written. The victim/witness signs an affidavit as to the facts of the crime.

Based on that complaint, the police will arrest the accused unless he or she voluntarily turns himself in.

You might think that if the victim can identify who the perpetrator was, he or she is going to share that information with the police, and, if there is enough evidence to substantiate the victim's claim, an arrest will be made. Unfortunately, that is not always that simple or obvious. For example, 15 years ago, Marvin J., a 28-year-old, was playing dice with his friend. They got into an argument and his friend shot his friend. Unfortunately, the bullet caused the victim to become paralyzed from the neck down. "For the first three years, I wanted to commit suicide," the victim explained to the interviewer. Marvin lives in a hospital setting and finds he is most comfortable when he is around others who share his situation and are also in wheelchairs. He never revealed to the police who the perpetrator was, and he does not plan to. Whether it is out of fear of retaliation, or a loyalty to his friend because of a friendship bond that few others would understand, his friend has never been arrested for what happened to his friend all those years ago. (Anonymous interview shared with author.)

At this point in the process, the victim has moved into the category of being a **witness** to the crime. The witness may not have been the actual victim of the crime—he or she was just right there or nearby when it happened—but the victim is always a witness (unless he or she was unconscious or nonresponsive at the time of the crime).

If the victim or witness provides enough information that a suspect could be arrested, there is evidence that points to a possible offender, without even an eyewitness testimony from the victim, the offender confesses, or there is DNA or other evidence that points to a possible offender, an arrest will be made. Even in the case of a murder, if the victim is deceased, there may be bystanders or other attempted murder victims who survived who can provide eyewitness testimony. Or there may be enough DNA evidence to make an arrest.

Unless a suspect walks into a police precinct and turns himself or herself in, a **warrant, arrest warrant,** or **bench warrant** will be issued that grants the police the authority to make an arrest.

The victim or witness should be notified that an arrest was made. Depending upon the details of the case, the victim may be asked to pick out the alleged perpetrator from a **photo lineup**, also known as a **photo display**, or a **photo array**, with as many as six or more photos, or a **police lineup** or an **in-person lineup** of actual people. Whether it is a photo lineup or a police lineup using real people, the principle is the same. The accused suspect may or may not be included in the in-person lineup. Usually the lineup is conducted behind a one-way mirror.

Let us assume that things have moved far enough along that an arrest has been made.

In a courtroom, with a judge, the defendant is arraigned in criminal court. The defendant, represented by private or court-appointed counsel, is informed of the official charges as stated in the victim/witness' affidavit.

Bail, or the terms under which a defendant may be released with the assurance that they will return for their next court appearance, is determined. There now is a growing tendency away from automatic cash bail. If there is no cash bail, the defendant is told to report back to court on a certain date. Depending on the municipality or state, there may be an incentive to report back or the threat that a bench warrant will be issued for arrest if the defendant fails to report back. Adureh Onyekwere, writing at The Brennan Center, shares this innovative alternative to cash bail program that was tried in New York City in 2016: "New York City instituted an alternative-to-bail project in 2016, called the Supervised Release Program. It gives judges the discretion to release defendants unable to afford bail, under the condition that they periodically meet with social workers and complete regular phone check-ins.

By March 2019, the program had delivered an 88 percent court appearance outcome, comparable to results of a defendant being released on their own recognizance or bail." (Onyekwere, 2019, updated 2021)

If cash bail is set and the offender is able to make bail, the case is adjourned for a preliminary hearing which should take place within 72 hours. If bail is denied, the accused will be remaindered to jail.

HOW THE CRIMINAL JUSTICE SYSTEM WORKS

Even before a crime occurs, it is useful for potential victims to have an understanding of how the criminal justice system works. That will enable them to feel less helpless and befuddled by quite a complex system. It is possible if more victims understood the criminal justice system, they might be more likely to report crimes, to be more active participants in the process that could help their case, or, if they decide not to pursue the case, to at least make that decision based on knowledge and not fear or unfamiliarity. They should also know that there is the option to sue in civil court the accused or a third party without having to get involved with the criminal courts, or in addition to participating in the criminal case, if that is their choice

The information about the criminal justice system could be provided to victims by the police, by the victim-witness assistance program at the local distinct attorney's office, by the crime victim compensation board, by the local crime victim crisis center, and the crime victim advocate that is assigned to victims who agree to that service, and even by the ER at the hospital where victims may be treated for their injuries. Today, because of search engines like Google, information about the criminal justice system is also readily available for anyone with a smartphone or a computer or access to one such as at the local library.

Victims of crimes and even potential crime victims need to know that they have to be aware of the laws, and the rights of victims, in their particular state or, if it is a federal offense, federal crimes and victim rights.

After a Crime Has Occurred

As you know, not all crime is reported. But if it is, letting the criminal justice system know that a crime has occurred is an important first step in the criminal justice system process. If the victims, a bystander, or someone who knows the offender and decides to turn him in, does report the crime to the police, or to the prosecutor's office, that will start the process of involving the criminal justice system. If police are called while a crime is in progress, an arrest might be made at the crime scene.

Investigation and Arrest

Reporting a crime leads to writing up an **incident report** about what happened. As discussed previously in this chapter, the police must collect enough evidence that there is **probable**

cause to believe the accused individual committed the crime or was a participant. At the time the incident report is written, police will ask the victim to fill out a **Victim Notification Form**. This will facilitate communication between the police and the victim about the progress in their case.

Depending upon the type of crime that was committed, the circumstances of the case, the seriousness of the crime, and other factors, after the report is filed, an investigation may follow.

Investigations can take just a few hours, a few days, weeks, months, or years. Victims can get frustrated by what seems to be lack of progress in their case, especially if it is a major crime, like robbery with severe injuries, or homicide. Everyone is familiar with the hit TV show *CSI* which enjoyed more than a decade on TV where cases are often solved by the **DNA evidence**. Then you have similar crime-theme programs such as *Law and Order* or *Criminal Minds* where the crimes are solved by police work—following the evidence, interviewing victims and witnesses, tracking down suspects until there is enough evidence to justify an arrest or they confess. The subspecialty of victimology, **forensic victimology**, is based on examining and reexamining crime scenes. Confessions that lead to arrests might not be from the suspect. It could be someone who does a deal with the prosecution for their testimony in exchange for immunity in their own case. All the collected evidence will be presented to the court. The reality is that neither extreme is what really happens. Victim and witness statements count. Good old-fashioned police work matters. DNA evidence can help crack a case. Perpetrators sometimes confess, to the police or to family members or friends who tip off the police, whether they are named or anonymous.

The Complaint

A **complaint** is also an important step. This is the official court document that has to be signed. In that complaint, either a police officer or a victim will accuse someone of committing a crime. The person signing the complaint is the **complainant**.

The court signs a warrant complaint when the crime is an **indictable offense**. Here is a list of indictable offenses:

Murder	Kidnapping
Aggravated manslaughter	Manslaughter
Robbery	Aggravated sexual assault
Sexual assault	Aggravated criminal sexual contact
Aggravated assault	Aggravated arson
Arson	Burglary

For other offenses, a summons complaint is issued. These are non-indictable offenses that are heard in municipal or family courts, rather than superior criminal court. Those types of offenses include:

Simple assault
Criminal mischief
Theft under $200

Unfortunately, in the majority of cases, the case may go no further. There are numerous reasons for that but the most common one is that there is just not enough evidence to find a suspect and make an arrest. There also tends to be a hierarchy on what cases the police can pursue based on the sheer volume of reported crimes and the number of officers available to pursue those cases. This can be frustrating to victims.

Reporting the crime is definitely the first step since there might be DNA evidence that clearly links a repeat offender to the crime scene, as noted before, such as a burglar who had no other possible link to being present at the apartment or home. In the case of burglary or motor vehicle theft, even though the clearance rate—the number of reported crimes cleared by the arrest of an offender—may be quite low, in 2019, just 13.9 percent for burglary and 13.8 percent for motor vehicle thefts—since private homeowners or renters insurance companies or car insurance companies require a report on the theft, filing a report with the police is the prudent thing to do. (FBI, 2019)

Clearance rates for major crimes besides burglary and larceny in 2019 in the United States are: Larceny-theft 18.4 percent, Robbery 30.5 percent, Rape 32.9 percent, aggravated assault 52.3 percent, and murder and nonnegligent manslaughter 62.3 percent (FBI, *2019 Crime in the United States*, Clearance Figure.) That means that except for homicide, with a 61.4 percent clearance rate, the highest for all major crimes, there is a strong likelihood that there will not be an arrest following a major crime. But since there were more than 10 million arrests in the United States in 2019 (10,085,207 to be exact, according to the FBI), although the proportion of arrests per major crime might be a low percentage, there are certainly a lot of arrests that occur. (FBI, 2019 Crime in the United States, "Persons Arrested.")

If an investigation leads to the arrest of an alleged offender, the next phase of the criminal justice system and the victim's involvement commences. This is where the victim goes from crime victim to witness for the prosecution if the prosecution decides to pursue the case.

Police do not need a warrant to make an arrest if there is probable cause. That means that there is reason to believe the suspect was involved in an indictable offense or in a domestic violence incident.

In all other cases, as discussed previously, unless the police observe someone committing a crime, or a suspect walks into a police precinct and turns himself or herself in, a **warrant, arrest warrant,** or **bench warrant** is issued. This grants the police the authority to make an arrest. In the complaint room, a formal complaint is written. The victim/witness signs an affidavit as to the facts of the crime.

Based on that complaint, the police will arrest the accused unless he or she voluntarily turns himself in.

Presentation to the Grand Jury

The prosecutor presents their evidence to the **grand jury**, a group of citizens who have been selected to decide if there is enough evidence to indict someone for a major crime. There are grand juries at the federal level. At the state level, all but two states and the District of Columbia do not use a grand jury. The grand jury dates back to the Fifth Amendment The Fifth Amendment to the U.S. Constitution states: "No person shall be held to answer for a capital, or otherwise infamous crime, unless on a presentment or indictment of a Grand Jury."

If the grand jury decides it is likely the accused defendant committed the crime, the formal charge, known as an indictment, will be issued. It grants the defendant the right to a jury trial.

A Suspect Is Arrested and Booked

The person who was arrested is now considered a **formal defendant**. Previously, someone was considered a suspect or the "target of an investigation." But upon arrest, the status changes to defendant.

When someone is taken into custody, he or she has to be read their **Miranda rights** (*Miranda v. Arizona*). The Miranda rights advise the accused that:

- You have the right to remain silent.
- If you do say anything, it can be used against you in a court of law.
- You have the right to have a lawyer present during any questioning.
- If you cannot afford a lawyer, one will be appointed for you if you so desire.

Upon arrest, defendants are searched and processed by the police or *booked*. The defendants' key information will be taken along with a photograph (a "**mug shot**") and fingerprints.

First Court Appearance

This first court appearance is supposed to happen within 48 to 72 hours of the arrest, depending on the particular jurisdiction. At the preliminary hearing, judge will be told about the charges, the defendant will be advised of his or her rights, and the defendant will be asked if he or she is guilty or not guilty. The judge has to decide if the defendant could be released before the trial, with or without bail. The judge needs to decide if the defendant can be released on his or her own recognizance (**released on personal recognizance** or **ROR**).

If the judge feels the defendant needs a financial incentive to return to court on the assigned date, the defendant is given the option of buying a **bail bond**. If the defendant is unable to make bail, he or she will be held in jail until the next court date. If there is no cash bail, the defendant, as noted before, is free to go, but must return on the next court date. If there was a bail bond and the defendant fails to appear in court, the bail bond is forfeited and a bench warrant will be issued for the defendant's immediate arrest, as we said earlier. The same applies if there was no cash bail required: a bench warrant will be issued.

When the defendant returns to court on the assigned date, the judge has the ability to refund the bail money. As part of the bail agreement, the judge can order the defendant to avoid any contact with the victim. If the defendant attempts to contact or intimidate the victim (who is now a witness in the case), bail can be revoked,

Case Review

Now the prosecutor's office will review the case and decide if the case will be prosecuted. Assistant district attorneys (ADAs), also called assistant prosecutors, and investigators will read the police reports on the crime as well as interview witnesses.

Victims may get upset with this phase of things because prosecutors have a lot of power about what happens with a case. They may do any of the following:

1. Prosecute the defendant while keeping the charges intact.
2. Upgrade the charges to a more significant crime.
3. Downgrade the charges to a less serious crime.
4. Dismiss the charges completely and close the case.

Remember that the rule in a criminal case is that guilt must be proven "beyond a reasonable doubt," which means that a high evidentiary standard needs to be met.

Arraignment

This is similar to the first court appearance. If the defendant was arrested before, bail is reviewed. The judge will make a date for a **plea disposition conference** or **a pre-trial conference**.

"Cop a Plea" and the Reality of Plea Bargaining

On television, especially in such long-running shows as *Law and Order: SVU (Special Victims Unit)*, the majority of cases that led to the arrest of a suspect go to trial. Not only do the cases go to trial, the cases go to trial quickly! After all, the case has to be solved within a one- hour time slot! The reality is far from that Hollywood fantasy. Writing at the website for the American Bar Association, Suja A. Thomas shares these shocking realities in her article, "What Has Happened to the American Jury?": "The jury has gone missing from the American legal system. Juries today decide only 1 percent to 4 percent of criminal cases and less than 1 percent of civil cases. Some civil cases do not even make it to the court system and instead are decided by other bodies such as agencies or arbitrators." (Thomas, 2017)

At the federal level, retired attorney Robert Katzberg, who began his career in the 1970s, shares in his book, *The Vanishing Trial* how it used to be: "As a young federal prosecutor in the 1970s, I was in the courtroom on a regular and repeated basis, trying bank robberies, tax frauds, narcotis cases, and other crimes enumerated in the Untied State Code." (Katzberg, 2020: 28)

Alas, Katzberg also shares how it was to change over the next several decades. He points out that by 1990, only nine percent of federal cases went to trial (instead of being plea bargained) and by 2018, the number had shrunk to just 2 percent. (Katzberg, 2020: 2)

What this means for the victim, who may also be the witness, is that having his or her "day in court" has become a myth. Victims, who are also the witness in the case, who once feared the cross examination when he or she took the stand, ironically do not have to fear that situation any more since, in the majority of cases, there will be no trial.

For some victims, this may be a relief. That means they do not have to deal with the time and emotional angst of going back and forth to court any number of times or with the emotional angst of reliving what happened.

Although the potential trauma is associated with seeing the accused again face to face in court is averted, also absent is the catharsis associated with telling his or her side of the case in court, especially before a jury of the accused's peers, with justice hopefully being served.

Including the Victim in the Plea-Bargaining Process

There is some attempt going on to at least bring the victim into the plea-bargaining process. According to the Office for Victims of Crime's Legal Series Bulletin, "Victim Input Into Plea Agreements," in 22 states, "the victim's right to confer with the prosecutor requires a prosecutor to obtain the victim's views concerning the proposed plea."

The victim's right to be consulted regarding a proposed plea deal is open to a wide range of interpretation from state to state. As noted in the "Victim Input Into Plea Agreement" Legal Series Bulletin #7, issued by the Office for Victims of Crime, "In no state is the right to confer interpreted as the right to direct the prosecution of the case or to veto decisions of the prosecutor. As the applicable law in Wisconsin specifically states, 'The duty to confer . . . does not limit the obligation of the district attorney to exercise his or her discretion concerning the handling of any criminal charge against the defendant.' " (Wisc. Stat. 971.095 (2000) as quoted in Legal Series Bulletin #7)

Yes, the victim's right related to plea bargaining varies from state to state. For example, in Maine, the state prosecutor must advise the court of its attempt to share the plea agreement details with the victim and the victim's reaction to the deal including any objections.

The chief misconception about this victim right is that if a victim objects to a recommended plea deal, he or she can decline it, which will stop the prosecutor from making that offer, or at least modifying it. In reality, a victim's opinion may be heard but he or she does not have veto power. A few states allow a victim to write a written **victim impact statement (VIS)** that the court could consider when offering the plea agreement. The state of Arizona has one of the stricter efforts at enforcing the right of the victim to provide input into the plea deal with three mandates, namely (1) that the prosecuting attorney advised the court that it made "reasonable efforts" to confer with the victim before requesting the negotiated plea; (2) that reasonable efforts were made to give the victim notice of the plea proceeding, letting the victim know that he or she has to the right to be present at the hearing and if, present, to speak; and (3) that the prosecutor has informed the court of the victim's position, if known, regarding the negotiated plea. ("Victim Input Into Plea Agreements, Ariz. Rev. Stat 13-4423)

Pre-Trial Conference

If the ADA and defendant cannot agree on a plea, they will go before the judge at the pretrial conference or the plea disposition conference. At that conference, the judge will be advised that they could not reach a plea agreement. At that point, the judge will set a date for the trial.

The Trial

Why does it take so long for a case to get to trial? Some of the reasons include the volume of cases, that has led to a backlog, the expense of putting a jury trial together, the challenge of coordinating the schedules of all those who are part of the trial including the prosecutor, lawyers, and witnesses, and even the time necessary to gather the evidence and for the defendant's attorney to be able to do discovery.

Before the trial, many hearings may be held to suppress evidence or to demand certain information for the defense. If the ADA or the defendant's lawyer needs more time, they may ask for a **continuance**, which is an extension of time.

At the trial, a jury will be selected (the Sixth Amendment of the Constitution guarantees the right to a jury trial). Criminal cases with serious felonies have 12 jurors. The selection of a jury is a process known as the ***voir dire***, which is French for "to speak the truth." During voir dire, potential jurors are asked a series of questions; the defense attorney and the assistant district attorney can accept or refuse a particular juror until the required number are agreed upon.

When the Victim/Witness Is Called to Testify

After the trial begins, the victim/witness may be called to testify. However, it may at this stage be inconclusive as to who the victim/witness might be because there may be several cases and victim/witnesses against the same defendant. The prosecution may decide to have a different victim/witness testifying for a variety of reasons; e.g., the prosecutor may feel that the jury will be more sympathetic to a certain victim/witness or that the victim/witness testimony will help build a stronger case. The prosecutor's goal is to win the case so he or she will pick the "best" testimony and victim/witness to testify. For example, in the case of Nicole Anderson, whose sexual assault from the ages of 10 to 14 by a church elder is discussed in greater detail in Chapter 12, "Sexual Violence: Rape, Sexual Abuse, Assault, and Harassment Victims," her brother's case was the one the prosecutor decided to pursue. In our interview, Nicole explained that she was told that her brother, who was abused from the ages of 8 to 16 by the same man, was the case to pursue. It turned out the offender took a plea deal so there was no trial anyway. But Nicole felt that she missed out on having her own day in court.

If a victim/witness is chosen to testify, he/she may not be allowed to be part of the proceedings of the trial. This is because the lawyer for the accused does not want the victim/witness knowing what others have said since that could impact on the testimony that is offered. There are some states that are trying to get victims the right to sit through the entire court proceedings.

When a victim/witness is only allowed in court to testify it can be very upsetting to some victims. For example, Roberta Roper, whose 22-year-old daughter Stephanie was raped and murdered on April 13, 1982, was so upset that she and her husband were not allowed to be present throughout the trial of the two men charged with the crime that she founded the Stephanie Roper Committee and Foundation in Upper Marlboro, Maryland. In the Associated Press (AP) article, "Victims' Rights Amendments Pass in 5 States," Roper was quoted as saying, " 'By being a presence at the trial, we as a family could bear witness to the fact that Stephanie lived, and she mattered,' Mrs. Roper recalled. "We were denied that.'" The men were convicted and sentenced to two concurrent life sentences." (AP, *New York Times*, 11/8/1992)

One of the advances in victim/witness rights in the last few decades has been the establishment of separate victim/witness rooms where those individuals can await their day in court. Previously they might have been in the same room with those giving testimony in defense of the accused.

At the end of the trial, the defense and the prosecutor will make their final statements. The judge will advise the jury and they will withdraw to deliberate.

When they return to the courtroom, the verdict will be read. The court will be advised that they are to maintain decorum upon hearing the verdict.

If the defendant is found innocent, he or she will be free to go.

If he or she is found guilty, the defendant will be escorted to jail to serve time, if it is a misdemeanor conviction, or to await processing about what state prison he or she will be sent to, if it is a felony conviction.

How Victims Can Become Better Witnesses

In most criminal cases today, the victim serves as a witness and the state brings the charges against the defendant. In 1974, the first Victim Witness Assistant Projects (VWAP) were federally funded through the Law Enforcement Assistance Administration (LEAA) in the Brooklyn and Milwaukee District Attorney Offices, as well as seven additional programs through the National District Attorneys Association. The goal was to help victims to become better witnesses so they could facilitate a better outcome for the prosecution.

As you recall, it is the State (or the federal government) vs. the Defendant, not the individual victim. In order to help victims become better witnesses, many brochures and pamphlets have been printed and distributed, with titles such as "25 Suggestions to a Witness," "Information for Witnesses;" "The Witness Guide to Court Proceedings," or a three-page flyer, by District Attorney Robert M. Morgenthau, entitled "Rights of Witnesses in a Criminal Proceeding." In addition to sharing what services are available to the victims and witnesses, including crime victims compensation, referral to the social services department, emergency relocation and housing assistance, a witness fee, if qualified including partial reimbursement for travel and lunch, the main point to the victim/witness is that "You should realize that the Assistant District Attorney presents the People's case in court" and "you are a witness for the People."

The 25 suggestions to the witness from the Distinct Attorney of Jefferson County is much more detailed, including guidelines on how to speak to the jury, dress, and tips such as avoiding chewing gum, speaking spontaneously, not memorizing; avoiding laughter in the courtroom; thinking before speaking; answering directly and simply ONLY the question asked, then stopping. Other suggestions include "do not volunteer information not actually asked for;" avoid losing your temper; say "I don't know" rather than making something up; avoid mannerisms or acting nervous, which might make someone think you are not telling the truth; avoid nodding your head "yes" or "no" since the court reporter has to hear your answer; avoid arguing with the defense attorney; "when you leave the witness stand after testifying, wear a confident expression no matter how you may feel about your testimony" and more.

In Box 5.3 you will find a summary of the previous discussion of how the criminal justice system works.

Box 5.3. Steps in a Criminal Case Following a Crime and a Subsequent Arrest

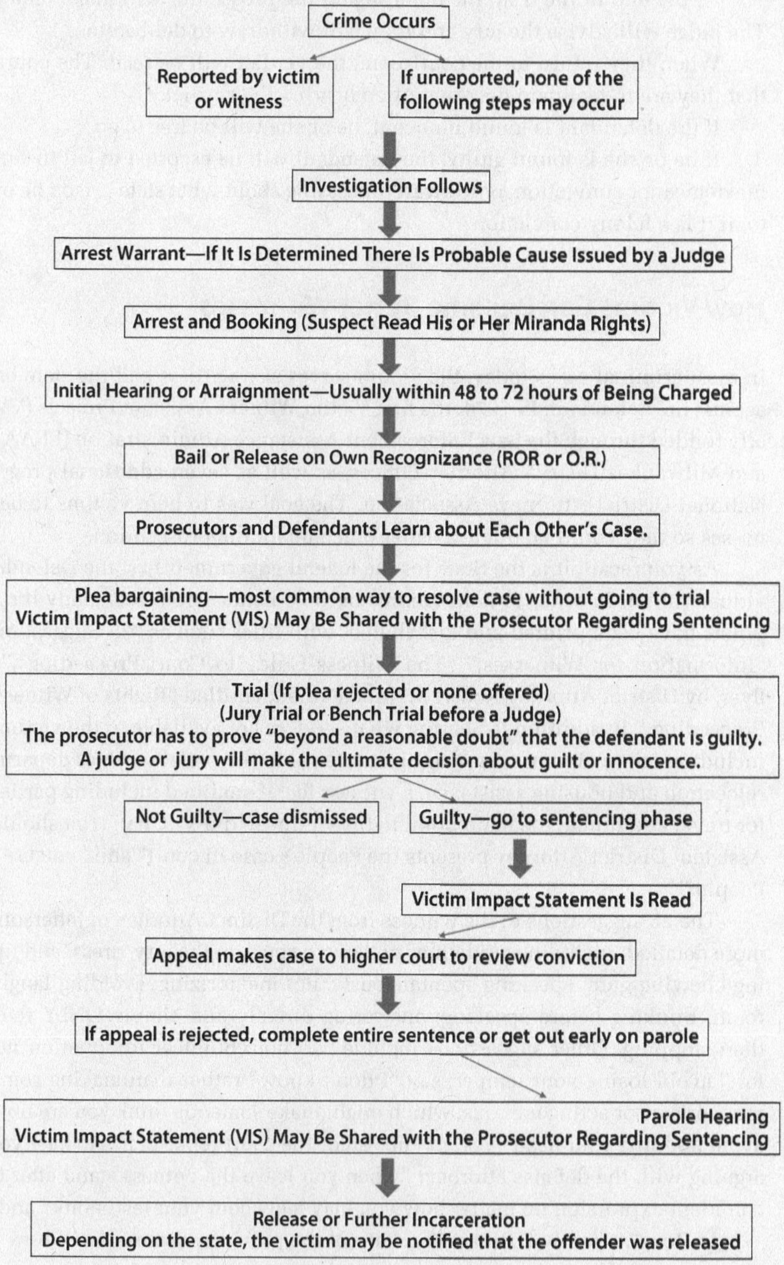

A REVIEW OF VICTIM RIGHTS

As noted in Chapter 2, "An Anthropological and Historical View of Crime Victims and Victims' Rights," and at many other points in this textbook, the pendulum has been swinging back in the direction of granting more rights to crime victims. Although victims do not get paid in livestock or other goods as they were centuries ago, there are now more rights for victims other than being "just" a witness to a crime. Some of those rights include the right to privacy, the right to know if a defendant has been released on bail, the right to comment on a defendant's sentencing, the right to be notified if an offender was sentenced to a correctional facility about work release, furlough, parole, or release from a community treatment center, the right to know whether a defendant is committed to a mental health facility and, if he or she is, notification of any discharge, transfer, or escape from the facility, and more. See Box 5.4 for a summary of victims' rights.

Box 5.4. Summary of Victims' Rights

- the right to information;
- the right to be present at criminal justice proceedings;
- the right to due process, i.e., the right to notice of and opportunity to be heard at important criminal justice proceedings;
- the right to financial recompense for losses suffered as a result of a crime, such as restitution and/or compensation/reparations;
- the right to protection; and
- the right to privacy.

Source: Reprinted from "History of Victims' Rights," National Crime Victim Law Institute (NCVLI)

Marsy's Law for All LLC was founded to encourage states to adopt a constitutional amendment guaranteeing rights to crime victims on the state level. It was an initiative started by Dr. Henry Nicholas in 2009 in honor of his sister, Marsy, whose ex-boyfriend murdered her in 1983. By April 2020, 14 states—California, Illinois, North Dakota, Ohio, Florida, Georgia, North Carolina, Nevada, Oklahoma, South Dakota, and Wisconsin—had passed Marsy's Law, which states that victims have the constitutional protections mentioned above that pertained to federal crimes but at the state level. (Please refer back to the more extensive discussion of Marsy's Law in Chapter 2.)

Many states have a Crime Victim Bill of Rights covering the rights stated above and many more. Based on New Jersey's "A Crime Victim's Guide to the Criminal Justice System," here are the key rights concerning crime victims are the rights:

- To be free from intimidation
- To be informed about social services

- To financial remedies, and available compensation for losses
- To have stolen property or anything in evidence returned as promptly as possible
- To make a victim impact statement prior to sentencing
- To be able to wait in a secure area at court before testifying
- To be advised of the progress of a case and its final disposition
- To be notified if and when an appearance in court is required
- To be able to submit a written statement to the prosecutor prior to the prosecutor's final decision about whether formal criminal charges will be filed.

Victims should also be notified in writing about the various key events related to their case beginning with an initial introductory letter followed by communications regarding the grand jury, an indictment, a negotiated plea, conditions of bail release, sentencing date, the sentence imposed by the court, the defendant's filing of an appeal, if there is a mistrial/retrial or mistrial/retail, and post-conviction release.

Box 5.5. Laws Granting Rights to Victims

1965 First crime victim compensation program is launched in California.

1984 Federal Bureau of Prisons establishes a victim/witness notification system.
Victim/witness coordination positions are created in the U.S. Attorney's Offices within the U.S. Department of Justice.
Wisconsin is the first state to approve a Bill of Rights for child victims.

1986 Rhode Island passes a victims' rights constitutional amendment granting victims the right to restitution, the right to submit a victim impact statement, and the right to be treated with dignity and respect.

1988 *State v. Ciskie* is the first case to allow the use of expert testimony to explain the behavior and mental state of an adult rape victim.

1989 Washington and Texas pass victims' rights constitutional amendments.

1991 U.S. Supreme Court in a 7-2 decision in *Payne v. Tennessee* rules that a victim impact statement in death penalty cases does not violate the defendant's constitutional rights.

1992 Congress re-authorizes the Higher Education Bill which contained the Campus Sexual Assault Victims' Bill of Rights.

1994 Kentucky becomes the first state to institute automated telephone voice notification to crime victims of their offender's status, location, and release date.

1999 The National Crime Victim Bar Association is founded by the National Center for Victims of Crime to encourage civil justice for crime victims.

2002 By this year, all 50 states plus the District of Columbia, U.S. Virgin Island, Guam, and Puerto Rico have crime compensation programs.

2003 Congress passes the PROTECT Act of 2003, also known as the AMBER ALERT law, creating a national network known as AMBER (America's Missing Broadcast Emergency Response)

Box 5.5. Laws Granting Rights to Victims (continued)

to help law enforcement and the public to be able to respond more quickly in child abductions.

2003 Congress passes the Rape Elimination Act to address the problem of rape in prisons.

2004 Congress passed the Crime Victim's Rights Act (CVRA) (Also known as the Justice for All Act).

2006 *Davis v Washington*—Victims' 911 Call Can Be Used as Evidence If They Can't Testify

2011 *Michigan v Bryant*—Victims' Dying Word Can Be Reported to a Jury

2013 *Maryland v King*—Police Can Collect DNA from Arrestees to Solve Other Crimes

THE VICTIM'S ROLE IN SENTENCING

The verdict is in and the offender is found guilty. Or the defendant may have decided to forego trial and enter into a plea arrangement with the prosecution. At the local, state, and federal levels, victim impact statements have become an important part of the sentencing process including at parole hearings. These statements can be made in writing or can be made orally or through electronic or audio means.

Being sentenced to jail or prison are the punishments that have the most popular exposure in TV series, like *Orange is the New Black*, or movies, like the classic *The Shawshank Redemption*. It would be hard to imagine much interest in a drama entitled, "Ankle Monitor House Arrest." There are options that judges can follow, unless there is a mandatory minimum sentence that must be imposed and it must be a state or federal penitentiary, such as probation, with supervision, including community service and possibly even payment of a fine or restitution, house arrest, or even restorative justice, as discussed in Chapter 6, "Helping the Victim."

The Victim Impact Statement

Canada adopted Victim Impact Statement admissibility at sentencing in 1988 (Wemmers and Cyr, page 260), followed by the United States, in 1991. It was then that the U.S. Supreme Court in *Payne v. Tennessee* declared that allowing a victim impact statement at sentencing in death penalty cases did not violate the Constitution. By 1997, 44 states were allowing the presentation of victim impact statements at sentencing as well as at later parole hearings.

A victim impact statement does not have to be a lengthy statement. Victims or, in the case of a crime against a minor, the victims' parents, or in the case of homicide, the victims' survivors, can share briefly to the judge and in the court about the impact of the crime. If the victim and their support network remain in the courtroom when the sentence is imposed, it can be an emotionally charged experience. The convicted offenders' and their loved ones may cry out in disbelief if the sentence seems too harsh and the victims may react strongly if they feel the sentence is too lenient. Everyone in the courtroom will be admonished for any outbursts since calm and decorum are required at all times. (A sample Victim Impact Statement for federal crimes involving financial matters is included in the Appendix, which is posted in the Student section of the publisher's website for this text book. No password is needed.)

In Box 5.6 you will read what the state of Ohio writes about the victim impact statement in their comprehensive booklet for victims entitled, "Ohio Crime Victims' Rights."

Box 5.6. Making a Victim Impact Statement

In all felony cases, the court shall order the preparation of a victim impact statement. You may provide a written or verbal statement, which should include:

- An explanation of any physical, psychological or emotional harm suffered as a result of the offense.
- An explanation of any property damage or other economic loss suffered as a result of the offense.
- An opinion regarding how much compensation is needed for harm the offender caused because of the offense.
- Information about any previous compensation the victim has applied for or received.
- A recommendation for an appropriate penalty for the offender's illegal behavior.

In all criminal or juvenile cases, the court may order the preparation of an investigation report prior to sentencing or disposition. If the court orders such a report, you may make a written or oral statement regarding the impact of the crime.

Before sentencing or disposition, the court must permit the victim to make the statement orally.

Any written statement that you provide is confidential and is not a public record, although it can be shared with the offender and the defense attorney. The court must consider the statement, along with other required factors, in imposing the sentence or determining the disposition. (ORC 2947.051, 2951.03; 2930.12; 2930.13; 2930,14)

Source: Reprinted from "Ohio Crime Victims' Rights" Pages 24-25.

Victims have the right to write, or speak, a Victim Impact Statement before the judge and with the prosecutors. A victim may write a written statement but also ask that it be read aloud. There is of course no guarantee as to how much impact, if any, the victim's statement will have on the judge or the prosecutor or the sentencing part of the criminal justice procedures.

Victim Impact Evidence in Death Penalty Cases

As noted above, *Payne v. Tennessee* in 1991 declared it constitutional for victims to make impact statements in death penalty cases. This was expanded to all cases. However the Death Penalty Information Center points out in its "Victim Impact Evidence" statement at its website that it is still "unconstitutional for the prosecution to present evidence or argument that the victim's family members want the defendant to be sentenced to death." (Death Penalty Information Center)

In their article, "Victims' Family Says They Were Retraumatized by Government's Conduct During Federal Executions," posted on July 27, 2020, 10 days after Daniel Lewis Lee was given the death penalty for the murder 20 years before of Nancy Mueller and her 8-year-old daughter, the Death Penalty Information Center issued a reminder. It wrote that the murder victims' family "long opposes his execution." Commenting on the first federal execution in nearly two decades, the article continues, "The Department of Justice did not consult them [the victims' family] in announcing the execution, ignored their pleas for clemency, and derided as 'frivolous; their request that the execution be delayed until after the COVID-19 pandemic, so they could attend without risking their lives. The way the government behaved throughout the course of killing Daniel Lee in their names, they say, has retraumatized them and prevented them from attaining peace." (Death Penalty Information Center, 2020)

In a powerful essay, "A Tiger by the Tail: The Mother of a Murder Victim Grapples with the Death Penalty," included in a unique book, *Wounds That Do Not Bind: Victim-Based Perspectives on the Death Penalty*, Linda L. White explains why she is opposed to the death penalty. White's pregnant daughter, Cathy, who also had a 5-year-old daughter, was raped and killed by two 15 year olds. Because of their age, they were ineligible for the death penalty, and White was glad about that so she did not have to deal with it being applied in her daughter's case. But in a general way, White thought the death penalty put too much emphasis on that one event in the healing that all murder victims' families have to do. White sees the healing as something that has to come from within. An external event, like the death penalty imposed on their loved one's killer, will not give closure. White describes how she had heard about, or read about, families who made statements after the death penalty was carried out like this one: "We can finally go on with our lives!"

White condemns putting off living until after the death penalty is carried out as the way victims will heal. As White writes, "I cannot imagine having lived for many years awaiting what I perceived to be justice for her [her daughter]." (Aker and Karp, 2006: 65)

Instead, White shares about an uplifting experience for her when she met with one of the two teens who had killed her daughter. He told White that her daughter's last words, before she was shot to death, were, "'I forgive you, and God will forgive you too.'"

A study by the Capital Jury Project (CJP) of 353 cases from 14 different states where the decision would be made about whether the sentence of capital punishment would be imposed has some interesting findings. As reported on by Karp and Warshaw in *Wounds That Do Not Bind*, after the *Payne v. Tennessee* decision, VIE (Victim Impact Evidence) was presented in a majority (52%) of the cases. There was only a 5 percent increase in sympathy for the victims' family (what they refer to as co-victims but others refer to homicide survivors or the secondary victims of homicide). Jurors who did not hear a VIE were 85 percent likely to be sympathetic toward the victims' family versus 90 percent if they did hear a VIE. (Not a huge difference.)

The extensive study concluded: "the influence of families on sentencing, if there is any at all, is very small. The conclusion that we draw from this is that co-victim testimony does not have a notable influence on sentencing outcomes." (Acker & Karp, 2006: 290)

THE CORRECTIONS SYSTEM AND THEORIES: WHAT YOU SHOULD KNOW

The third part of the criminal justice system is corrections. The first two parts are police and the courts. First let us review the scope of the corrections systems in the United States today. In the United States today there are 110 federal prisons, 1,833 state prisons, 1,772 juvenile correctional facilities, 3,134 local jails, 218 immigration detention facilities, and 80 Indian Country Jails. In addition to the 2.3 million men, women, and juveniles incarcerated in those facilities there are 3.6 million on **probation**, in lieu of jail or prison, and 840,000 on **parole**, also known as supervised release meaning getting out of prison early and serving the remaining of the sentence for a set number of months or years and by meeting certain conditions. (Wendy Sawyer and Peter Wagner, Prison Policy Initiative, March 24, 2020)

Incarcerated person in a prison cell.

Many victims may be unaware that traditional prisons are just one option for sentencing. There are other possibilities related to correctional theories.

Victims need to consider these correctional theories since they may even be asked by the assistant district attorney, if there is an arrest and if a plea is offered, whether they agree to a plea. If probation is offered in lieu of jail or prison time, it is important to know that probation is not a "piece of cake" as there are restrictive rules that the defendant must follow and violating those rules can result in being sent to jail or prison. Understanding these factors might make more victims open to probation as an alternative to incarceration since the evidence points to jail or prison, in most cases, as not working. The decision depends on the offense. Restorative justice, which has become much more popular in the last decade, is mostly applied to non-violent property crimes although there are a few programs, such as the Drug Court in the Brooklyn Criminal Court in New York City, that is successfully doing restorative justice with violent offenders with drug problems who agree to go into rehab, make restitution payments to their victims, and to apologize to their victims, as well as stay out of trouble going forward. The Mental Health Court in Dade County, Miami, Florida is another program that is offering an alternative to incarceration for those whose crimes even if violent ones involved mental health and drug issues. (Judge Steve Leifman, 2020)

Having a better understanding about what works and what does not work, if the victim is asked for his/her opinion about a fair punishment for the perpetrator of the crime they or their family member endured, is more than a theoretical issue. It can mean a dramatic shift in the way that justice is served in the United States. That shift would not only free up billions of dollars that are currently spent incarcerating criminals, especially nonviolent ones, since running a prison is an expensive proposition. It is a 24/7 operation that also requires feeding, housing, and hopefully educating and offering programs to the inmates not only to keep them occupied but also to help with the rehabilitative aspects of their confinement.

Very few victims want to meet with, or even think about, the perpetrators of their crime while that offender is incarcerated. There are exceptions. Debra Puglisi Sharp wanted to meet with the man who raped her, held her hostage and killed her husband.. The convicted murderer, who was sentenced to several life sentences, turned her down. (Sharp, 2015)

In their book, *Law & Disorder: Inside the Dark Heart of the Murderer*, authors John Douglas and Mark Olshaker write: "Crime victims and their survivors tend to be leery of the term 'vengeance' because of its implications of vindictiveness and retaliation. . . . The term many of them prefer is 'retribution,' meaning something justly deserved, a punishment or repayment based on action or performance. Either way, the point is that the justice system in the limited way in which it is able, attempts to balance the scales between the victim and the offender." (Douglas and Olshaker, 2013)

Criminologists and penologists highlight six correctional theories as well as one additional concern, **early intervention**, which is not a theory per se but definitely worth mentioning. Here are the seven main correctional theories:

1. **Just deserts** or **retribution:** Obtaining justice through punishment. Whether the criminal will commit another crime upon release, or whether crime in society will go down, is not the concern. Punishment for the sake of punishment.
2. **Deterrence:** Punishment that makes the individual offender less likely to commit another crime, known as *specific deterrence*, or making an example of the offender so others will be less likely to commit that crime, known as *general deterrence.*
3. **Incapacitation:** The correctional philosophy behind incapacitation is that there may be a benefit to putting convicted offenders in prison, especially violent ones, because at least if they are locked up, they will not be victimizing the general public. However, other inmates, correctional officers, and staff are of course potentially at risk.
4. **Restorative justice:** As an alternative to incarceration, the offender, the victim, a mediator, and possibly one or more members of the community, or criminal court, if it is a court-based program, get together and agree on a plan to restore the victim and punish the criminal without jail or prison time.

5. **Rehabilitation:** Whether the offender is housed in a jail or prison, or gets probation including community service, the goal of rehabilitation is to deal with the criminogenic cause of the offender's actions in the first place so the criminal is less likely to victimize others or commit violent personal or property crimes again. The current preferred method of treatment for offenders is Cognitive Behavior Therapy, rather than psychoanalytic therapy. In Cognitive Behavior Therapy (CBT), the offender works with a trained counselor to correct his or her faulty thinking that is behind the criminal behavior.
6. **Reentry:** This evidence-based theory is that it is necessary to help the offender to prepare for a return to society since the majority of inmates, excluding those who are serving life without parole, will go back into society at some point. Finding a place to live, a job that is legal, reconnecting with family and finding new friends rather than the ones who may have led the criminal astray, can help the offender to have a better chance at staying out of trouble with the law.
7. **Early intervention:** This can start as early as in utero, when the fetus is developing, by encouraging pregnant women to avoid drinking or doing drugs, as well as during the formative years when nurturing behavior is more likely to have a better outcome than being physically or emotionally abusive or neglectful to a child or teen. (Cullen and Jonson, 2017)

UP FOR PAROLE: CONSIDERING THE VICTIM'S RIGHTS

Being able to share a Victim Impact Statement for the parole board is a victim right that has been hard won. But you have to check with your state to see the conditions of that right in your particular state. For example, in Florida, victims have the right to attend the parole hearing along with other members of the public, attorneys, members of the media, the inmate's family, and other members of the public. The hearings are public hearings, open to the public. The offender will not be in attendance. Offenders will have been interviewed at their institution. Florida states that "Written comments may be submitted for consideration prior to a **conditional release** hearing." Conditional release may be used synonymously for parole.

There is a very powerful video posted at YouTube entitled, "Victimology Interview." Mentioned previously, the secondary victim of homicide that is the subject of the interview, Jen, shares the story of her sister's murder. She details how her family finally moved on after ten years but then they were notified that the convicted killer was up for parole. They had to go through everything all again. But you can see that Jen and her family were still grateful that they were notified and had a chance to plead their case about why they did not want their family member's killer to get parole.

Having the chance to share a victim impact statement (VIS) at sentencing and again before the parole board are major victories for victim rights. Do judges and prosecutors take the VIS into account? They are supposed to. In addition to considerations about whether the victim impact statement has an effect on the offender's sentence or parole release, there is the value to the victim. Is it a catharsis? Does it help in their healing from the crime? A Dutch study of 142 victims, "Delivering a Victim Impact Statement: Emotionally Effective or Counter-Productive?" published in the *European Journal of Criminology*, determined that those who delivered an oral victim impact statement had a stronger sense of "procedural justice" and their feelings of anger and anxiety were reduced by the process. (Lens, et al., 2015: 30)

SUMMARY

The criminal justice system includes the police, the courts, and corrections. Unless a victim, a bystander, or another party calls the police, a crime may never be known to the authorities.

If the crime is reported, and an arrest is made, the victim may become a witness in the government's case against the defendant. What the criminal justice process is like is discussed including what a trial is like with a reminder that approximately 95 percent of most criminal cases are settled through plea bargaining, not going to trial.

The first step of the criminal justice system is for the victim, witness, or a third party to report a crime to the police or another representative of law enforcement. It is by notifying the police that victims begin their journey to get justice for the wrong done to them. We know, however, that underreporting is a fact of life with the National Crime Victimization Survey estimating that just 41 percent of all violent crimes were reported to police. (Morgan and Truman, 2020)

There are many reasons victims may not want to report a crime including everything from fear of being embarrassed to being engaged in criminal activity at the time the crime occurred to telling the wrong person about the crime and getting discouraged from reporting it.

In this chapter we also covered some of the ways that police can be more positive in their interactions with victims so there is a greater likelihood that victims will feel an effort is being made to help them, whether or not an offender is caught or property is returned. At a certain point after the arrest is made, the next part of the criminal justice system takes over—the defense attorney, the district attorney, the courts, the judge, and the potential punishment or corrections if the arrestee is found guilty. At that point, the victim has become a witness in the crime in a criminal case brought by the state or federal government against the defendant.

In this chapter, you learned an overview of the correctional theories associated with the third part of the criminal justice system, corrections. Of the correctional theories—rehabilitation, incapacitation, deterrence, just deserts, early intervention, reentry, and restorative justice—it is the restorative justice option, discussed at greater length in Chapter 6, "Helping the Victim," that the victim might get involved once a defendant is found guilty and sentenced. (Or as an alternative to incarceration.)

Victim rights, also discussed in Chapter 2, "An Anthropological and Historical View of Crime Victims and Victims' Rights," are highlighted in this chapter. Some of those rights, related to the criminal justice system, include, in most states, and in federal cases, that victims have the right to provide a victim impact statement at an offender's post-conviction sentencing or parole hearing.

KEY TERMS

admissible
arrest warrant
bail
bail bond
bench warrant
Briana's Law
capital punishment
civil suit
clearance rate
complainant
complaint
conditional release
continuance
death notification
death penalty
defounding
deterrence
DNA evidence
early intervention
evidence
felony
forensic evidence
forensic victimology
formal defendan
grand jury
incapacitation
incident report
indictable offense
in-person lineup
just deserts
Marsy's law
Miranda Rights
misdemeanor
modus operandi
mug shot
NCVS (National Crime Victimization Survey)
NIBRS (National Incident-Based Reporting System)
no-knock warrant
photo array
photo display
photo lineup
plea disposition conference
police lineup
pre-trial conference
probable cause
rehabilitation
retribution
reentry
restorative justice
statement
SOL (statute of limitations)
third party victim rights litigation
victim blame
victim impact statement)
voir dire
warrant
witness

REVIEW QUESTIONS

1. What is the first step in involving the criminal justice system in a crime that has occurred?
2. What are two reasons a victim might not report a crime to the police?
3. Why is a faster response time important in trying to achieve a better clearance rate for a crime?
4. What is one promise that police officers should avoid making to victims and why?
5. What percentage of criminal cases resulting in an arrest go to trial?
6. If a criminal case does not go to trial, what is the term for how the case is handled?
7. If an offender is found guilty, name at least four of the seven correctional theories related to punishment of the offender.
8. What are some of the rights of a crime victim in the criminal justice process?

CRITICAL THINKING QUESTIONS

1. Why do you think someone would be reluctant to report a burglary to the police if it would increase the likelihood that they would be able to put in an insurance claim and possibly even get back some or all of their stolen items?
2. Do you think police have an unfair negative reputation in the United States? Why? Why not?
3. Why do you think the rate for reporting crimes to the police in 2019 in the United States for violent crimes was only 41 percent? What are some of the reasons for so many being reluctant to report violent crimes? How could that trend be reversed?
4. Is it fair to allow victims to read their victim impact statements at parole hearings? What if the offender has been rehabilitated in prison? Should that count more toward whether an offender gets parole or not?

ACTIVITIES

1. Divide into pairs. One will be the police officer interviewing someone about a crime that has just occurred. The other will be the victim. After seven minutes, switch places. See what questions you ask each other and how you feel about the interview process. Is there anything that the police officer should have asked about what happened that was left out? Is there anything as a victim you noticed in the way it felt being interviewed by a police officer? (If this is an online only course, this activity could still be done through the "Breakout room" or "Collaborate" function that the leading popular videoconferencing programs provide to educators/students.)
2. Go to the main website for the U.S. Justice Department: https://www.justice.gov/ In the search engine at the site, put in a topic that you learned about in this chapter. The emphasis at this site is on federal crimes, but there is still useful information that applies to all victims. This activity will help you to get familiar with the wealth of information that is available for free from the U.S. government on crime related matters. (Every country has a government website for its justice department.)

RESOURCES

Blue Help
bluehelp.org

Blue Lives Matter NYC
bluelivesmatternyc.org
Advocacy organization increasing public awareness about the job of police officers.

International Association of Chiefs of Police
theiacp.org
Membership organization for police officers offering education and networking opportunities.

Maryland Crime Victims' Resource Center, Inc. (MCVRC)
mdcrimevictims.org
In 2002, the Stephanie Roper Committee and Foundation, Inc., merged into the MCVRC.

National Police Accountability Project
nlg-npap.org
Project of the National Lawyers Guild

The National Crime Victim Bar Association
victimbar.org

National Police Association
nationalpolice.org

National Sheriffs' Association
sheriffs.org
Membership organization for those working in sheriff departments.

Office of Victims of Crime, U.S. Department of Justice
ovc.ojp.gov/help-for-victims/victim-notification
Right to Notification

CITED WORKS AND ADDITIONAL REFERENCES

Abraham, Henry J. 1975. *The Judicial Process.* Third edition. New York: Oxford University Press.

Acker, James R. and David R. Karp (eds.). 2006. *Wounds That Do Not Bind: Victim-Based Perspectives on the Death Penalty.* Durham, NC: Carolina Academic Press.

Adler, Freda, Gerhard O.W. Mueller, and William S. Laufer. 2007. *Criminology and the Criminal Justice System.* Sixth Edition. New York: McGraw-Hill.

Andrews, Michelle. July 10, 2019. "Years After Sexual Assault, Survivors Hounded to Pay Bills for the Rape Kit Exam." NPR (National Public Radio) Posted at npr.org

Associated Press. October 1, 2020. Court Oks $800M settlement for Las Vegas shooting victims. *Los Angeles Times.* Posted at latimes.com

_________. November 8, 1992. "Victims' Rights Amendments Pass in 5 States." *New York Times.* 29.

Avakame, E.F., J.J. Fyfe, and C. Mccoy. 1999. "Did you call the police? What did they do? An empirical assessment of Black's theory of mobilization of law." *Justice Quarterly.* 16: 765-792.

Bayley, D.H. 1996. *Police for the Future.* New York: Oxford University Press.

Barkas, J.L. (Janet Lee) *See also* Jan Yager.

Barkas, J.L. January 6, 1976. "Citizen Observer Precinct Tour." Unpublished report. Goddard College Graduate Program.

_________. January 25, 1976. "Second Radio Patrol Car Precinct Tour with the 9th Precinct." Unpublished report. Goddard College Graduate Program.

_________. September 10, 1978. "Let's Give Crime's Victims their Due." *Newsday.* 1, 10.

_________. December 12, 1980. "Reflections on Murder, Criminals, Handguns. . . ." *Newsday.*

_________. 1979. *Understanding the Criminal Justice System.* Public Affairs Pamphlet No. 574. New York, NY. 28 pages.

_________. Summer 1979. "What About the Victims." *Journal of Current Social Issues.* 27-33.

Barr, Luke. January 2, 2020. "Record Number of US Police Officers Died by Suicide in 2019, Advocacy Group Says." ABCNews.com. Posted at https://abcnews.go.com/Politics/record-number-us-police-officers-died-suicide-2019/story?id=68031484

Bennett, Thomas L., Iowa Organization for Victim Assistance (IOVA), MADD/Polk County Chapter, Polk County Victim Service, Crime Victim Assistance Division, Iowa Department of Justice, and Bonnie J. Campbell. September 1992. "In Person, In Time"—Recommended Procedures for Death Notification." Des Moines, Iowa: Crime Victim Assistance Division.

Bennett-Sandler, Georgette and Earl Ubell. "Time Bombs in Blue." March 21, 1977. *New York*. 47-61.

Blum, Howard. September 9, 1977 "Witness Paying a Price for Federal Protection." *New York Times*. B1, B22.

Bok, Sissela. 1978. *Lying: Moral Choice in Public and Private Life*. New York: Pantheon.

Bowley, Graham and Joe Coscarelli. September 25, 2018. "Bill Cosby, Once a Model of Fatherhood, Is Sentenced to Prison." *The New York Times*. Posted online at nytimes.com

Carmody, Deirdre. January 13, 1976. "Civilian Patrol Lens a Hand." *New York Times*. 37.

Carrington, Frank. 1975. *The Victims*. New Rochelle, NY: Arlington House.

Caunitz, William J. 1984. *One Police Plaza*. New York: Bantam.

Center for Victim Research. July 2019. *Losing a Loved One to Homicide: What We Know about Homicide Co-Victims from Research and Practice Evidence*. 33 pages. Posted at https://ncvc.dspacedirect.org/bitstream/item/1440/CVR%20Research%20Syntheses_Homicide%20Covictims_Report.pdf?sequence=1

Chapman, Ben. December 8, 2019. "New York City Jail Costs Reach Record Level" *Wall Street Journal*. Posted online at https://www.wsj.com/articles/new-york-city-jail-costs-reach-record-level-11575833362

Civiletti, Denise. May 1, 2019. "New State Law Eliminating Cash Bail for Misdemeanors, Nonviolent Felonies Will have Public Safety and Budget Impacts, Officials Say." Posted online at riverheadlocal.com

Cox, Clinton. January 18, 1976. "A Community Divided." *New York Sunday News Magazine*, 8+.

Cullen, Francis T. and Cheryl Lero Jonson. 2017. *Correctional Theory: Context and Consequences*. Second edition. Thousand Oaks, CA: SAGE.

Daley, Robert. March 28, 1977. "The Cop Who Knew Too Much." *New York*. 36-41.

Dawsey, Josh and Pervaiz Shallwani. July 17, 2013. *Wall Street Journal*, Eastern edition. A17.

DeathPenaltyInfo.org. "States With and Without the Death Penalty—2020." Posted at https://deathpenaltyinfo.org/state-and-federal-info/state-by-state

__________. July 27, 2020. "Victims' Family Says They Were Retraumatized by Government's Conduct During Federal Executions." Posted at https://deathpenaltyinfo.org/news/victims-family-says-they-were-retraumatized-by-governments-conduct-during-federal-executions

Dembroff, Randa. "The Ninth Precinct: A Tale of Frustration in the Urban Jungle." Unpublished Master's Thesis for Columbia University, Graduate School of Journalism, Class of 1976.

diGrazia, Robert J. November 19, 1975. Police Commissioner, Boston Police. Personal correspondence.

Doerner, William J. and Steven P. Lab. 2017. *Victimology*. 8th edition. New York: Routledge, Taylor & Francis Group.

Douglas, John and Olshaker, Mark. 2014. *Law & Disorder: Inside the Dark Heart of Murder*. New York: Pinnacle.

Druzin, Bryan H. and Jessica Li. Spring. 2011. "The Criminalization of Lying: Under What Circumstances, If Any, Should Lies Be Made Criminal?" *Journal of Criminal Law and Criminology*. 101(2): 529-573.

Durk, David. October 20, 1975. Guest presentation, The New School. "The Roots of Violence," Janet Barkas, Instructor.

Elwell, Laurie. March 1993. "Results of Survivor Survey." Parents of Murdered Children newsletter. 1-2.

Federal Bureau of Investigation (FBI). *2017 Crime in the United States*. Uniform Crime Reports. Table 29. Estimated Number of Arrests.

__________. *2018 Crime in the United States*. "Clearance Figure" Posted at https://ucr.fbi.gov/crime-in-the-u.s/2018/crime-in-the-u.s.-2018/topic-pages/clearances#:~:text=In%20the%20nation%20in%202018,by%20arrest%20or%20exceptional%20means.

Felson, R.B., S.F. Messner, A.W. Hoskin, and G. Deane. 2002. "Reasons for Reporting and Not Reporting Domestic Violence to the Police." *Criminology*. 40: 617-648.

Fisher, Bonnie S., Bradford W. Reyns, and John J. Sloan III. 2016. *Introduction to Victimology: Contemporary Theory, Research, and Practice*. New York: Oxford University Press.

Fisher, Franklin. April 29, 1979. "Shot Cops." *Sunday News Magazine*. 9, 18, 44-45, 50-51.

Fisher, Ronald P., R. Edward Geiselman, and Michael Amador. 1989. "Field Test of the Cognitive Interview: Enhancing the Recollection of Actual Victims and Witnesses of Crime." *Journal of Applied Psychology*. 74(5): 722-727.

Forer, Lois G. 1980. *Criminals and Victims: A Trial Judge Reflects on Crime and Punishment*. New York: Norton.

Franklin, H. Bruce. 1998. With a Foreword by Tom Wicker. *Prison Writing in 20th Century America*. New York: Penguin.

Franks, Lucinda. September 3, 1975, "Slain Auxiliary Is Given a Police Funeral." *New York Times*. 40.
Galvin, Miranda A. and Aaron Safer Lichtenstein. July 20, 2017. "Same Question, Different Answers: Theorizing Victim and Third Party Decisions to Report Crime to the Police." *Justice Quarterly* (35): 1073-1104.
Graham, Fred. September 9, 1977. "Complaints from the Invisibles." *New York Times*.
Gramlich, John. March 1, 2017. "Most violent and property crimes in the U.S. go unsolved." Pew Research Fact Tank. Posted at https://www.pewresearch.org/fact-tank/2017/03/01/most-violent-and-property-crimes-in-the-u-s-go-unsolved/
Gorman, Judge Walter T. April 5, 1976. Interview. State Supreme Court Judge, Court of Claims. New York, NY.
Greenburg, Dan. January 21, 1979. "The Ninth Precinct Blues." *New York Times Magazine*. 31+.
Greenstone, James L. and Sharon C. Leviton. 1982. *Crisis Intervention: A Handbook for Interveners*. Dubuque, IA: Kendall/Hunt.
Hamilton, Jesse. August 28, 2017. "Briana's Law: A Victory for the State of New York." Posted at https://www.nysenate.gov/newsroom/articles/jesse-hamilton/brianas-law-victory-state-new-york
Harrell, Erika and Elizabeth Davis. December 2020. Contacts between police and the public, 2019-statistical tables. Bureau of Justice Statistics, U.S. Department of Justice, Office of Justice Programs.
Hickman, Blair. April 3, 2015. "Inmate, Prisoner, Other, Discussed." Commentary. The Marhsall Project. Posted at www.themarshallproject.org
Hickman, Matthew J., Nicole L. Piquero, and Alex R. Piguero. 2004. "The Validity of Niederhoffer's Cynicism Scale." *Journal of Criminal Justice*. 1-13.
Hoppmeyer, Melissa. January 8, 2021. Interview with the author.
Jarvis, John P. 2017. "Police Responses to Violent Crime: Reconsidering the Mobilization of Law." *Criminal Justice Review*. 42: 5-25.
Johnson, Richard J. November 10, 1977. "Beat." *New York Times*. A23.
Karantzoulidis, Steve. November 20, 2018. "The Best and Worst Police Response Times of 10 Major U.S. Cities." Security Sales & Integration. Posted at https://www.securitysales.com/news/best-worst-police-response-times/
Katzberg, Robert. 2020. *The Vanishing Trial: The Era of Courtroom Performers and the Perils of Its Passing*. Herndon, VA: Mascot Books.
__________. September 23, 2020. Zoom interview with the author, "Penology" course, John Jay College of Criminal Justice.
Kerik, Bernard B. 2015. *From Jailer to Jailed*. New York: Simon & Schuster.
Koster, Nathaltie-Sharon Nandita. February 1, 2018. *Crime Victims and the Police: Crime Victims' Evaluation of Police Behaviour, Legitimacy, and Cooperation: A Multi-Method Study*. Leiden University (Netherlands).
Lang, Kay. 2015. "911: Help or Hindrance in Reducing Repeat Victimization." A Dissertation submitted to the University at Albany, State University of New York, School of Criminal Justice.
Langton, Lynn and Marcus Berzofsky. August 2012. Victimization not reported to the police, 2006-2010. Special Report, National Crime Victimization Survey, Bureau of Justice Statistics, U.S. Department of Justice.
Leifman, Judge Steven. November 19, 2020. 11th Judicial Circuit Florida. Guest speaker via Zoom, "Forensic Health Issues, The Law, and the Criminal Justice System," graduate course, Iona College.
Lens, Kim ME, Antony Pemberton, Karen Brans, Johan Braeken, Stefan Bogaerts, and Esmah Lahlah. 2015. "Delivering a Victim Impact Statement: Emotionally Effective or Counter-Productive?" *European Journal of Criminology*. 12: 17-34.
Lynch, Karen. 2014. *Good Cop, Bad Daughter: Memoirs of an Unlikely Police Officer*. San Francisco, CA: Nothing But the Truth LLC.
Maas, Peter. March 16, 1976. "The Roots of Violence." Guest presentation, The New School. Janet Barkas, Instructor.
__________. 1973. *Serpico*. New York: Viking.
Malcolm, Andrew H. October 3, 1974. "The Modern Sheriff: A New Breed." *New York Times*. 45.
Maslach, Christina and Susan E. Jackson. May 1979. "Burned-Out Cops and Their Families." *Psychology Today*. 12(12): 59-62.
Mcafee, Tierney. January 5, 2020. "The Harrowing True Story Behind Netflix's 'Unbelievable.'" *Country Living*. Posted at counryliving.com

McCart, Michael R., Daniel W. Smith, and Genelle K. Sawyer. April 2010. "Help Seeking Among Victims of Crime: A Review of the Empirical Literature." *Journal of Trauma Stress.* 198-206.

McKinley, James C. May 30, 2018. "Harvey Weinstein Indicated on Rape and Criminal Sexual Act Charges." *New York Times.* Posted at https://www.nytimes.com/2018/05/30/nyregion/weinstein-indicted-rape.html#:~:text=A%20grand%20jury%20voted%20on,Weinstein.

Meislen, Richard J. August 21, 1977. "Fugitives from Bench Warrants Linked to 'Thousands of Crimes.'" *New York Times.* 1, 31.

Miller, Chanel. 2019. *Know My Name.* New York: Viking Press.

Miller, Joel, Robert C. Davis, Nicole J. Henderson, John Markovic, and Christopher W. Ortiz. May 2004. "Public Opinions of the Police: The Influence of Friends, Family, and News Media." Reported published by the U.S. Department of Justice.

Morgan, Rachel E. and Barbara A. Oudekerk. September 2019. *Criminal Victimization, 2018.* Bureau of Justice Statistics, U.S. Department of Justice, Office of Justice Programs.

Mueller, Benjamin. October 27, 2016. "Police to Install Advocates for Crime Victims in Every Precinct." *New York Times.* A25.

Murphy, Kristina and Julie Barkworth. 2014. "Victim Willingness to Report Crime to Police: Does Procedural Justice or Outcome Matter Most?" *Victims and Offenders.* 9:178-204.

The National Crime Victim Bar Association. "Civil Justice for Crime Victims." 2-page brochure. Posted at the association's website, victimbar.org

National Crime Victim Law Institute. "History of Victims' Rights." 2011. Posted at https://law.lclark.edu/centers/national_crime_victim_law_institute/about_ncvli/history_of_victims_rights/

National Sheriffs Association. July 2010. *First Response to Victims of Crime: A Guidebook for Law Enforcement Officers.* Office for Victims of Crime, U.S. Department of Justice.

__________, n.d. *Training and Technical Assistance to Law Enforcement on Responses to and Investigation Of Domestic Violence, Dating Violence, and Stalking,* (153 page manual)

New Jersey Department of Law and Public Safety. Office of Victim-Witness Advocacy. Division of Criminal Justice. September 1997. "A Crime Victim's Gide to the Criminal Justice System." Second edition. Posted at https://www.passaiccountynj.org/Prosecutor/Crime%20Victims%20Guide.pdf

New York State Assembly. February 11, 2014. "Assembly Passes Legislation establishing 'Briana's Law.'" Press release. Posted at nyassembly.gov

NYPD. n.d. "Specialized Training Section." Fact sheets. Posted at 1.nyc.gov/site

O'Connell, Michael and Sarah Fletcher. 2018. "Giving a Victim a Voice in Parole Hearings: South Australia's Experience." *Journal of Victimology and Victim Justice.* 42-62.

Office for Victims of Crime (OVC) and NCJRS.gov. "Basic Guidelines on Approaching Victims of Crime." n.d. Posted at https://www.ncjrs.gov/ovc_archives/reports/firstrep/bgavoc.html

__________. November 2002. "Status of the Law: Right to Confer with Prosecutor." Posted at ncjrs.gov/ovc

__________. November 2002. "Victim Input into Plea Agreements." Legal Series Bulletin #7. "Status of the Law." Posted at https://www.ncjrs.gov/ovc_archives/bulletins/legalseries/bulletin7/2.html

Office of Victim Services, State of Connecticut Judicial Branch. n.d. "Sexual Assault Forensic Examiners Program" Posted at https://www.jud.ct.gov/crimevictim/safe.htm

Office of Victim Services, State of New York. June 7, 2021. "Services: Forensic Rape Examination (FRE) Direct Reimbursement Program. Fact sheet. Posted at ovs.ny.gov

Officer.com. March 1, 2008. "Death Notification: Breaking the Bad News."

__________. *Training and Technical Assistance to Law Enforcement on Response to and Investigation of Domestic Violence, Dating Violence, and Stalking.* n.d. Posted at https://www.sheriffs.org/sites/default/files/CurriculumFinalRedux.pdf

Onyekwere, Adureh. February 24, 2021 (originally published December 10, 2019). "How Cash Bail Works." The Brennan Center. Posted online at brennancenter.org

Oppel, Richard A., Jr. and Derrick Bryson Taylor. July 18, 2020. "Here's What You Need to Know about Breonna Taylor's Death." *New York Times.* Posted at https://www.nytimes.com/article/breonna-taylor-police.html

P., Kim. "Study: Average Police Time." n.d. Posted at Creditdonkey.com

Pate, T. Ferrara, A. Bowers, R.A., et al. 1976. "Police Response Time: To Determinants and Effects." Washington, D.C: Police Foundation.

Payne, Brian K. 2008. "Elder Physical Abuse and Failure to Report Cases: Similarities and Differences in Case Type and the Justice System's Response." *Crime & Delinquency.* 59: 697-717.

Potter, Dr. Gary. Published July 16, 2013. "The History of Policing in the United States, Part 1." EKU (Eastern Kentucky University) School of Justice Studies.

Pristin, Terry. July 16, 1978, "Choke Holds: Killers or Life-Savers?" *Los Angeles Herald Examiner*. A-8.

Raab, Selwyn. September 19, 1976. "New System Will Free Policemen from Appearing at Arraignments." *New York Times*. 1, 25.

Reid, Sue Titus. 2018. *Crime and Criminology*. Fifteenth Edition. New York: Wolters Kluwer.

Rheingold, Alyssa A. and Jonah L. Williams. 2015, "Survivors of Homicide: Mental Health Outcomes, Social Support, and Service Use Among a Community-Based Sample." *Violence and Victims*. 870-883.

Romo, Vanessa. June 7, 2019, "Ex-Minneapolis Officer Sentenced to 12½ Years in Death of Unarmed 911 Caller" NPR.org

Sawyer, Wendy and Peter Wagner. March 24, 2020. "Mass Incarceration: The Whole Pie." Prison Policy Initiative. Posted at https://www.prisonpolicy.org/reports/pie2020.html

Schwartz, Emma. December 13, 2007. "Giving Crime Victims More of Their Say." *U.S. News & World Report*. Posted at
http://www.usnews.com/news/national/articles/2007/12/13/giving-crime-victims-more-of-their-say

Shapland, Joanna and Matthew Hall. 2007. "What Do We Know About the Effects of Crime on Victims?" *International Review of Victimology*. 14: 175-217.

Sharp, Debra Puglisi. 2015. Interview with the author.

__________. 2010. *Shattered: Reclaiming a Life Torn Apart by Violence*. New York: Atria.

Sherman, L.W. 2013. "The Rise of Evidence-Based Policing: Targeting, Testing, and Tracking." *Crime and Justice*. 42: 377-451.

Singer, Simon I. September 1988. "The Fear of Reprisal and the Failure of Victims to Report a Personal Crime." *Journal of Quantitative Criminology*. 4: 289-302.

Skogan, Wesley G. February 1976. "Citizen Reporting of Crime: Some National Panel Data." *Criminology*. 13: 535-549.

Slaikeu, Karl A. 1984. *Crisis Intervention: A Handbook for Practice and Research*. Boston: Allyn and Bacon.

Smith, Mitch. April 30, 2019. "Minneapolis Police Officer Convicted of Murder in Shooting of Australian Woman." *New York Times*. Posted at https://www.nytimes.com/2019/04/30/us/minneapolis-police-noor-verdict.html

Snider, Brett. June 4, 2014. "What Happens in a Police Lineup?" Posted at Findlaw.com.

Solomon, Karen and Jeffrey M. McGill. 2015. *The Price They Pay*. Worster, MA.; Bluehelp.org.

Stolberg, Sheryl Gay. October 6, 2018. "Kavanaugh Is Sworn In After Close Confirmation Vote in Senate." *The New York Times*. Posted at nytimes.com

Stolberg, Sheryl Gay and Nicholas Fandos. September 27, 2018. "Brett Kavanaugh and Christine Blasey Ford Duel With Tears and Fury." *The New York Times*, posted at nytimes.com

Symonds, Martin. 1980, reprinted 2010. "The 'Second Injury' to Victims of Violent Acts." *The American Journal of Psychoanalysis*. 70: 34-41.

__________. 1975. "Victims of Violence: Psychological Effects and Aftereffects." *American Journal of Psychoanalysis*. 35: 19-26.

State of Alaska. February 5, 2020. "Victim Impact Statements." U.S. Department of Justice. Posted at https://www.justice.gov/usao-ak/victim-impact-statements

Thomas, Suja A. 2019; Spring 2017. "What Has Happened to the American Jury?" American Bar Association. (Abridged and edited version of article that appeared initially in *Litigation* on page 25) Posted at https://www.americanbar.org/groups/gpsolo/publications/gp_solo/2019/january-february/what-happened-american-jury/

Tolsma, Jocehm, Joris Blaauw, and Mafred te Grotenhuis. 2012. "When Do People Report Crime to the Police? Results from a Factorial Survey Design in the Netherlands, 2010." *Journal of Experimental Criminology*. 8:117-134.

United States Parole Commission. "Participation of Victims and Witnesses in Parole Commission Proceedings." October 178, 2002. Posted at https://www.justice.gov/uspc/usdoj-uspc-participation-victims-and-witnesses-parole-commission-proceedings

Vicens, A.J. and Jordan Michael Smith. 2014, 2020. "Map: How Long Does Your State Give Rape Survivors to Pursue Justice?" *Mother Jones*. Posted at https://www.motherjones.com/politics/2014/11/rape-statutes-of-limitation-maps-table/

Victim Rights Law Center. May 2014. "Mandatory Reporting of Non-Accidental Injuries: A State-by-State Guide." Manual. Boston, MA: Victim Rights Law Center. Posted online.

Vidal, Jordi Blanes I. and Tom Kirchmaier. 2018. "The Effect of Police Response Time on Crime Clearance Rates." *Review of Economic Studies.* 85: 855-891.

Walklate, Professor Sandra. "Who Is the Victim of Crime? Paying Homage to the Work of Richard Quinney." 22-page paper.

Walklate, Sandra; Gabe Mythen; and Ross McGarry. "Trauma, Visual Victimology, and the Poetics of Justice." Unpublished manuscript. To be published in M. Haviid-Jacobsen (ed.). 2014. *The Poetics of Crime.* Surrey, UK.

__________. 2011. "Witnessing Wootton Bassett: An Exploration in Cultural Victimology." *Crime Media Culture.*7: 149-165.

Wambaugh, Joseph. 1973. *The Onion Field.* New York: Dell.

Weinstein, Judge Jack. Fall 1974. Guest presentation at the author's course, "The Roots of Violence," The New School.

Welling, Sarah N. January 1987. "Victim Participation in Plea Bargains." *Washington University Law Review.* 65: 302-338+

Wemmers, Joanne and Katie Cyr. 2004. "Victims' Perspectives on Restorative Justice: How Much Involvement Are Victims Looking For?" *International Review of Victimology.* 11: 259-274.

West, Brian West and Matthew Varacallo. May 27, 2019. "Good Samaritan Laws" Posted at https://www.ncbi.nlm.nih.gov/books/NBK542176/ (National Center for Biotechnology Information, U.S. National Library of Medicine).

West's Encyclopedia of American Law. 2008. "Photo Lineup." The Gale Group.

Whelton, Clark. September 19, 1976. "In Guards We Trust." *New York Times Magazine.* 20+.

Williams, L.S. 1984. "The classic rape: when do victims report?" *Social Problems.* 31: 459-467.

Williams, Lena. September 4, 1977. "Off-Duty Officer Kills Youth Who Allegedly Cut Him." *New York Times.* 30.

Yager, Jan. May 20, 2020. "Crime Victim Survey of 225 Men and Women Throughout the United States Ages 18 and up." Through Survey Audience, Surveymonkey.com. 10 question survey.

__________. "How to Avoid Ponzi Schemes" Posted 7/11/2010 at http://www.consumeraffairs.com/boomerific/2010/018_avoiding_ponzi_schemes.html

__________. 2021, 2015. *Victims.* Originally published 1978 by Scribner's. Reprint edition published with a new introduction and updated bibliography and resources by Hannacroix Creek Books, Inc. Stamford, CT.

Videos

National Victim Assistance Academy. Office for Victims of Crime. "Listen to My Story Communicating with Victims of Crime Video" 13:34 minutes. November 7, 2007.
https://www.youtube.com/watch?v=vOU_wLC34_k

Department of Justice Canada. November 27, 2017. "Transforming the Criminal Justice System: Victim's Experience." 4:56 minutes. This is the story of Nicole, who was raped. It took 5-1/2 years from the rape till the acquittal of her rapist. Posted at: https://www.youtube.com/watch?v=BOrwmgd_l5g

Southeast Texas Criminal Justice Studies. October 19, 2015. "Criminal Justice System." 3:13 minutes. This short video provides a summary of the American criminal justice system. Posted at https://www.youtube.com/watch?v=C45agsIsvWs

Chapter **SIX**

Helping the Victim

Medical, Psychological, Financial Aid, and Civil Suits

Learning Objectives

After you finish reading this chapter, you should be able to:

1. Understand how important response time is when a crime victim has major injuries and needs medical attention.
2. Evaluate the dual role that an EMT (Emergency Medical Technician) may have to play when responding to a victims' need for medical help.
3. Describe the procedures a rape victim goes through at the hospital.
4. Explain the difference between informal and formal victim emotional help.
5. Identify positive ways family and friends can help a victim to heal.
6. Explain some of the reasons people might not want to share about their victimization.
7. Understand the ways that victims cope with traumatic events with and without the help of counseling and other service providers.
8. Discuss why some people get PTSD following victimization and others do not.
9. Pinpoint the first state to offer crime victim compensation for violent crime victims.
10. Identify the basic eligibility requirements for receiving state crime victim compensation.
11. Discuss if restorative justice is a practical way that crime victims can get compensation and emotional healing from their victimization.
12. Understand the right of a crime victim to sue in civil court.
13. Define the two types of damages that a judge and jury can award to a victim in a civil suit.

WHAT VICTIMS NEED: AN OVERVIEW

Being the primary or secondary victim of a crime is usually horrific and traumatizing enough, but that situation can be either compounded or helped by the speed and quality of medical care that is received, if there are injuries, or by the psychological help that is provided, if needed. Getting help to deal as effectively as possible with the aftermath of the crime including getting financial compensation are all ways to try to facilitate victims and, in the case of homicide, their immediate family, in dealing with and eventually recovering from the crime

Here are the basic needs of most crime victims:

1. Medical (if there were any injuries);
2. Psychological (to help deal with the immediate and potentially long-term emotional trauma related to the victimization);
3. Financial (to cover medical or counseling costs or other costs related to the victimization, such as crime scene cleanup; relocation, if necessary; installation of new locks; loss of earnings; or in the event of a homicide, funeral costs); and
4. Dealing with the criminal justice system (if victims choose to do so).

The fourth concern, legal issues including reporting to the police, were explored in the previous chapter, Chapter 5, "Victims and the Criminal Justice System: Police, Courts, and Corrections." This chapter deals with the other three victim concerns.

As someone who is reading this textbook to learn about victimology, it is important for you to understand what help might be available to victims, how the availability of that aid evolved historically, and any controversies surrounding that assistance. The words that anyone interviewing a crime victim does not want to hear, regardless of whether the crime occurred today, last week, last year, ten years, or even decades ago, are, "I did not know that was available to me," or words to that effect.

The experience of being victimized is traumatizing enough in most cases that victims should at least be made aware of available help. Whether victims will choose to pursue or decline that help is a different issue. If a victim goes without assistance, the reason should not be that help was never offered in the first place. This is especially true with such time-sensitive services such as medical assistance or state-funded crime victim compensation, discussed below.

GETTING MEDICAL HELP

In Chapter 13, "Victims of Assault, Domestic Violence, Stalking, and Elder Abuse," you will learn that the speed with which an ambulance arrives or medical help, such as **CPR** or stopping a bleed, is offered may make the difference between an aggravated assault or attempted murder and a homicide or murder. There is an expression that goes like this: "Don't add insult to injury." That is exactly what happens when, for example, a completely innocent citizen, just trying to get home at night, is accosted by a gang and stabbed, and then a family member is told, years later, that inadequate medical treatment at the hospital after the mugging might have been equally or even more responsible for the victim's death than the muggers.

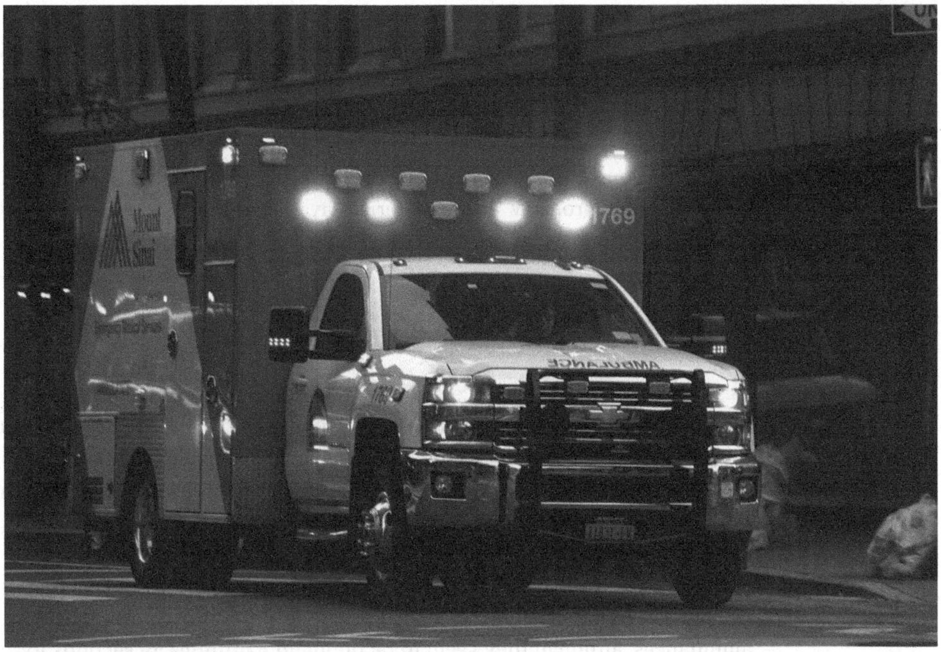

Emergency medical help has arrived.

Preventing the victimization in the first place is an issue that we will explore in Chapter 16, the concluding chapter. This chapter, Chapter 6, deals with the medical attention that every victim has the right to receive immediately or soon after the crime occurs or, in some cases, even while the crime is in progress if it can mean the difference between life and death. Whether that victim has the best insurance in the world, or no insurance, the speed and quality of the medical attention a crime victim receives may literally be a life or death situation. If there is an offender, that offender may be charged with the more serious crime even if the reason that aggravated assault became a homicide or murder was a medical issue which, in most cases, is hard to prove.

There is a very important point that Jonathan Shepherd, a Senior Lecturer in Oral and Maxillofacial Surgery at the Bristol Royal Infirmary in Bristol, Great Britain, makes in his short one-page article, "Supporting Victims of Violent Crime," published in the *British Medical Journal*. It seems the reporting rate of victims in the United Kingdom is even worse than in the United States. Fewer than 25 percent of the victims of crime in the United Kingdom report their crimes to the police. That means "more than three quarters of victims of violent crimes who attend accident and emergency departments are not recorded in the crime statistics kept by the police," writes Shepherd. (Shepherd, 1988)

Shepherd quotes these astonishing statistics from the U.K. version of the NCVS, a survey of one person over the age of 16 in 11,000 randomly selected households in England and Wales and 5,000 in Scotland recorded crimes during the previous 12 months. The reporting rates to police were as follows: only 11 percent of robberies, 26 percent of sexual offenses, and 23 percent of "woundings." (Shepherd, 1988)

The reason those statistics are important, and what that has to do with seeking medical help, is that for the vast majority of victims, around 50 percent in the United States and as high as 75 percent in the U.K., medical help may be the only way they can learn about services available to crime victims with the exception of family and friends, if they do tell them about what happened. (Skogan, 1976; Payne, 2008; Tolsma and Blaauw, 2012; Harrell and Davis, 2020)

Shepherd recommends that hospitals, ERs, and doctors interact more with local crime victim centers and sources of help. These medical services should be able to refer victims to information or direct help with legal issues, crime prevention officers, how to repair or recover stolen property after robberies, available funds from crime victim compensation boards, and other social services. (Shepherd, 1988)

Calling or Going for Medical Help

Response time is a real concern when it comes to crime-related injuries. Response time is a measure of how long it takes for an ambulance to arrive. It could also refer to how long it takes for the police to respond since most police have basic CPR and first aid training.

Here is a startling fact from the **Stop the Bleed®** program of the American College of Surgeons: the average time to bleed out as 5 minutes. Five minutes! As noted in the previous chapter, although the preferred response time for police to arrive is five minutes or under, longer wait times do happen. Writing in the *Journal of Emergency Medical Services (JEMS).* Jay Fitch, Ph.D. notes that there is no universally accepted ideal response time for ambulances, although they seem to recommend 8 minutes 59 seconds for urban areas. (Fitch, "Response Times," 2005) That's almost double the length of time that it would take for someone to "bleed out."

In his article, "Be Prepared for Ambulance Wait Times," Andrew M. Seaman notes that a study of data collected in 2015 from 486 U.S. agencies analyzing their emergency media service data found that the average wait time was 8 minutes. In rural areas, the wait time was as high as 14 minutes. (Seaman, 2017)

The study's lead author, Dr. Howard Mell, is quoted as saying, "It's long enough that if CPR isn't done before the ambulance gets there, it's not going to turn out well for the patient."

What these ambulance response times mean to those concerned with saving the life of a crime victim is that bystanders as well as even victims themselves need to learn basic first aid to keep themselves alive until help arrives. The U.S. government has a program entitled, "You Are the Help Until Help Arrives." It includes these five steps:

1. Call 9-1-1.
2. Stay safe.
3. Stop the bleeding.
4. Position the injured.
5. Provide comfort.

Or should you just drive to the hospital instead of waiting for medical help? Here's when to call an ambulance, according to guidelines from the American College of Emergency Physicians:

- The person's condition appears life-threatening.
- The person's condition could worsen and become life-threatening on the way to the hospital.
- Moving the person could cause further harm or injury.
- The person needs the skills or equipment used by paramedics or emergency medical technicians (EMT).
- Driving would cause significant delay in getting to the hospital.

(*Source:* https://www.mainlinehealth.org/)

Now that you understand that someone could "bleed out" in just 5 minutes and that there might not be enough time to drive to a hospital, it might be prudent to take a Stop the Bleed® course so that, if you someday find yourself in a situation where time, not the perpetrators, may be the life and death factor, you will be able to render timely assistance. The organization Stop the Bleed® listed in the Resources section at the end of this chapter, has classes throughout the United States as well as in the U.K., Australia, and even online.

Crime Scene Responsibilities of EMS (Emergency Medical Services) Responders

Timothy G. Price and Rory M. O'Neill, in "EMS, Crime Scene Responsibility," point out the unique situation that **EMS (emergency medical services)** responding to a 911 call might have to deal with if the situation is a crime scene and not just a medical call because of a possible heart attack. The first step is for EMS personnel to know that a situation they are responding to may be a crime scene. What is a *crime scene*? According to Price and O'Neill, "A crime scene is considered any location where a criminal act occurred or where evidence from a criminal act may be found. This includes but is not limited to violent acts, drug manufacturing, and fires. EMS providers should be careful to consider as crime scenes the location of runs that appear to be obvious or reported suicides or accidents. Reported self-inflicted or accidental injuries must be investigated by law enforcement to confirm these reports. These scenes should be treated like any other potential crime scene in terms of evidence preservation and documentation." (Price and O'Neill, "EMS, Crime Scene Responsibility," 2019)

EMS may arrive on the scene before the police so they need to be careful to handle the medical emergencies while preserving the crime scene as much as possible. If police arrive before EMS, or at the same time, they can take over the evidence collection and documentation part of the crime scene tasks. Price and O'Neill recommend that "If the nature of the run is dispatched as a potential crime scene, EMS should always wait for police officers to arrive on the scene and declare it safe for medical responders."

This can create an extremely challenging situation for EMS who will be eager to treat the victim upon arrival.

If EMS arrives before police, Price and O'Neill suggest that they record their impressions of the crime scene since this could be valuable to the investigation of the crime. Observe any signs of forced entry, how the body is positioned, lighting, if any doors are open. EMS personnel are cautioned to avoid stepping in any blood or bloody footprints.

Possibly most important of all is for EMS personnel to take notes verbatim of anything the victim or any witnesses say. It has to be verbatim to be valid. Indicate it is an exact quote by putting the words in quotation marks. This can be especially useful related to domestic violence cases since the victims may share initially about what happened but later on, out of fear of retaliation or a reluctance to say anything that might lead to their partner getting jail or prison time, some victims may stop talking about what happened.

Profile ▪ 911 Operator Karima Holmes

Here are excerpts from the phone interview this author conducted with Karima Holmes, a 20-year veteran of emergency communications and the former 911 director for Washington, D.C. Karima began working as a 911 operator when she was just 19 years old. She is now 41.

Karima Holmes at her console at the 9-1-1 Call Center.

When a victim calls 911, the person on the other end of the line, a 911 professional, has been trained to gather pertinent information about the situation and to get field responders on the way as quickly as possible. Understandably 911 callers are usually in a heightened emotional state and may even be rendered speechless. A 911 call taker never knows what the next call will bring and is prepared to use special techniques to get as much information from the caller as possible to send them the most appropriate help.

This is a hefty responsibility that requires one to be passionate about helping others. Successful 911 call takers also possess executive functioning skills such as the ability to make quick decisions and act reasonably, and the ability to multitask to continue to actively listen while entering critical details into the dispatching system. There is no margin for error.

Fortunately, 911 call takers follow a set of protocols that provide if/then guidelines that make the most efficient dispatching of police, fire and EMS possible even given the variability of circumstances. Essentially, protocols are a series of probing questions that assist call takers in identifying the risks the emergency presents, the type of resources to send, where to send them, and how quickly help is needed.

For example, if a victim calls 911 to report that they were just involved in a hit and run car accident and sustained no injuries, just the police will be dispatched. If during the call, the victim shares that smoke is billowing out from under the hood of the car, a fire engine would be dispatched too. Then, of course, if the victim mentions that they just realized when they exited the damaged vehicle that they cannot bear any weight on their left foot, an ambulance would be sent to the accident scene as well.

For crimes that just occurred, like hit and run accidents and robberies, victims usually call 911 right away. During this time, their emotions may be extreme. When the 911 call taker is the first person the victim interacts with following a crime, call takers must be able to use techniques to help them calm down and deescalate so that the right help can be sent to them as quickly as possible.

Often, 911 call takers are the first to hear crime reports, in many cases just seconds or minutes after they occur. Victims of crime at the hands of strangers are more likely to quickly report crimes by calling 911. Domestic abuse survivors are sometimes hesitant to report those intimately known to them. However, when they do, they often turn to

911 as a way to quickly get professional and practical advice on what steps they should take immediately to regain their safety.

Very often, 911 call takers are the first "helpers." In addition, 911 call takers can play a significant role in helping victims rebuild their lives by dispatching first responders to apprehend criminals and thereby ensuring that justice is served, for example.

With the more serious crimes, such as rape or especially domestic, one of the things I know happens is that when an individual calls 911, they are usually unsure if they want to report [to the police]. I always found that amazing.

With rape victims, someone usually calls for them. Sometimes people call themselves, but most of the time, she tells her best friend, "I was raped," and her best friend says, "We're calling 911."

Of all the calls I took in my career, the most memorable is one that I handled about 15 years ago. I was in my late twenties and in a supervisory position but still helping to answer 911 calls when the call volume was high, or when we were short staffed.

This particular call came in in the middle of the day, around noon. We had already gotten several calls from people who had driven past an 18- or 19-year-old woman who was walking down a major highway with two young children. The woman was violently hitting and abusing the children along the way. As the 911 calls were coming in, we were trying to pinpoint exactly where the woman and children were so we could dispatch the police to the right location. Eventually, we got enough information to know that the woman and children had made it to a gas station and the woman had locked herself and the children inside the gas station's bathroom. The next call we got is from the gas station clerk. I took that call.

The clerk says, "There's a girl in the bathroom. A girl just walked in with these two kids. She's locked herself in the bathroom with the kids and they're screaming at the top of their lungs. She's probably beating them."

I can hear the kids screaming in the background, and then there is complete silence. I was in the middle of typing in the information the clerk gave me and I realize he is quiet too now. So, I stop, and I say, "Is she still in there?"

He says, "Yes. But the kids are not crying anymore."

I say, "What do you mean they're not crying?"

I know immediately that something tragic has happened. Then, the clerk tells me that "there is so much blood". I immediately stand up and I start yelling across the room to my colleagues to make sure that the police and emergency medical services are on their way to that gas station.

When the first responders did get to there, they found that the woman had basically beheaded the younger child and had stabbed the older one to death in the bathroom.

When I took that call, I had just come back from maternity leave after having my son. I remember those moments like they happened yesterday. I remember saying out loud to no one in particular, "She stabbed her kids!" I think that incident was so personally traumatic for me because I had just had my son. I was in disbelief.

After that, you could hear a pin drop in that 911 center. It felt like we were in suspended reality. Each one of the 911 call takers had taken one or more calls from concerned motorists and I took the last one. It was horrific.

We later learned that the woman suffered from bipolar disorder and had not been taking her medicine. Just before she walked down the highway to the gas station, she had offered her children to her significant other and to one or two of her relatives. She had told them, "I don't want them anymore." Apparently, nobody would take the kids. They told her, "They are your responsibility."

Later when the young woman was in a more lucid state and was told what she had done, she was devastated and did not recall the incident at all. I followed that case for a long time and the last information I had was that the woman was still in jail.

I would not be human if I did not admit that there are some calls that I will never forget. But what comforts me is that, in being a victim's first contact, I always did what I could in those moments to get them the help that they needed. When I started my career, I knew it would not be easy to take call after call from people experiencing the worst circumstances of their lives, but I found deep purpose in helping in any small way that I could.

That said, the idea of secondary trauma, or indirect exposure to duty related distress for 911 call takers, is very real. In fact, recent studies have shown that some experience symptoms of PTSD. There is a lot of work being done in the 911 industry to address this growing concern.

One specific outlet that I relied on to help me cope with stress and anxiety from taking 911 calls was the practice of yoga. For me, learning to regulate my breathing helped me control my energy and focus it inwards, leading to a feeling of deep stillness. My practice of yoga served to decrease my stress response and increased my relaxation response, which I found to be invaluable in becoming the best 911 call taker I could be.

At the Hospital

Family members, or a close friend if family members are unavailable or very far away, should be called to the hospital so a victim is not alone while any medical procedures are administered. If a victim is incapacitated, a family member, or next of kin, may be required for consent for surgical procedures. The unique requirements for victims of sexual assault are discussed below. If the police were called, they may have a **crime victim advocate** that they will alert to the situation who will offer their services to the victim. Meeting the victim at the hospital, if the victim agrees to it, can be a source of information and comfort to a crime victim. If they do not have a crime victim advocacy program at their local precinct, the police may be partnered with a crime victim center to offer their help to a victim. If victims are up to it, they may even call a crime victim center themselves asking for someone to meet them at the hospital. Remember that most of these services offer assistance 24 hours a day, 7 days a week. A volunteer or staff member will provide help to injured victims if they request it.

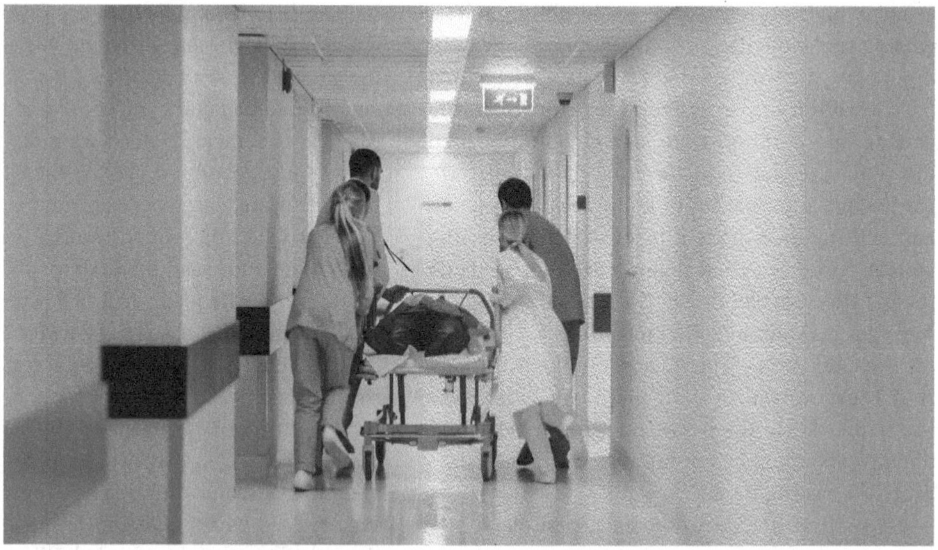

Hospital, by Gorodenkoff/Shutterstock.

One of the requirements to be a volunteer with one of these centers is usually that volunteers are able to get to a hospital that is affiliated with the center within a certain amount of time, which could be as long as 45 minutes or as brief as 20. If an advocate is assigned to a victim, the advocate will meet the victim at the hospital. The advocate is not there to interfere with any interactions between the victim and her or his family, friends, or medical staff, but to help deal with the issues specifically-related to being a victim of a crime. That is his or her area of expertise. Crime victim advocates may stay through the entire medical proceedings. They may also help the victim through any other related experiences such as dealing with the police or the courts.

Referring to the medical victim-related experiences, the victim knows that a cut because someone knifed him in a robbery attempt is very different than the stitches that are necessary because someone dropped a plate in the kitchen and stepped on it by mistake. Both injuries may require stitches but the emotional angst related to these wounds and the administrative issues involved, especially if there was an arrest made at the scene, or a police report filed, will highlight the unique challenges of hospital care related to victimization.

In addition to hospital visits, there are visits to private physicians. As will be noted in Chapter 10, "Child Victims," and Chapter 11, "Teen and College Victims," the Federal Child Abuse Prevention and Treatment Act (CAPTA) requires each state to have provisions for certain individuals to report suspected child neglect or abuse. Most pertinent to this chapter are those in the medical field that are mandatory reporters namely, nurses, physicians, and other health care workers. It will be noted below, in the section on emotional help for victims, that these are additional mandatory reporters in those related fields: therapists, counselors, and other mental health workers.

Most states also require the reporting of suspected abuse of the elderly. See the Elder Abuse section in Chapter 13, "Victims of Assault, Domestic Violence, Stalking, and Elder Abuse, for more details on that mandatory reporting requirement.

Finally, a majority of states also have provisions for the mandatory reporting of non-accidental gun shot or knife wounds to the police. This is a state-by-state requirement, however. Alabama, for example, in 2014 did not have mandatory reporting by healthcare professionals; Alaska did have mandatory reporting by health care professionals of non-accidental gunshot, knife, and burn injuries.

So except for suspected child abuse cases, or, depending on the state, mandatory reporting of non-accidental gunshot, knife, or other wounds, crime victims receiving medical care at the hospital, including in the ER (Emergency Room), or from a private physician, should be treated the same way as anyone else. All medical personnel at the hospital have to be savvy enough to avoid in any way making victims feel **victim blame**. Victims are going through enough physical trauma after the crime that they need everyone that they encounter after the victimization to treat them with respect, empathy, and understanding. There may be additional procedures that assault victims need at the hospital such as photographs or x-rays that must be taken to document injuries for legal reasons or the rape kits that rape victims need (described below).

Forensic Evidence Collection at the Hospital or by the Doctor

When a patient arrives at the ER, it may still be debatable whether the injury is related to a crime or accident or is self-inflicted. Although the medical staff may prefer to only focus on the patient's physical injuries, ignoring the forensic data related to the situation can seriously jeopardize the chances of pursuing the case if it turns out to be a crime.

Collecting evidence in the case of rapes is discussed below but there are other crimes that may need evidence collection at the hospital or by the physician if a crime has occurred. *Forensic medicine* has emerged as a subdiscipline within the medical field. Other terms for it are *forensic pathology* and *legal medicine*. It has related associations with the International Forensic Medicine Association. Within nursing, the subspecialty of **forensic nursing** has emerged. It has its own association, the Association of Forensic Nurses.

What needs to be emphasized is that medical personnel at the hospital, and in a doctor's office, need to be aware that the injuries they are treating have to be handled on more than one level. The first level is the medical one. That is first and foremost. But the second level, since that can make a difference if a case has evidence that is admissible in court, or even evidence at all, is the criminal investigation and documentation part of things. That is where the forensic medicine or forensic nursing expertise comes in.

Here is a list of the responsibilities of forensic medicine specialists who are dealing with a patient whose presence in their hospital or office is because of crime-related injuries according to B.R. Sharma's article in the *Journal of Clinical Forensic Medicine*:

1. Role of ambulance and rescue workers—if they are trained in some or all of the issues that follow, especially the importance of identifying and preserving evidence. The forensic aspect of any case should be improved.
2. Investigation of trauma—it is suggested that a hospital liaison is designated to work with the police and the medical team coordinating the necessary forensics in the case. That liaison has to understand forensic concepts, legal obligations, and victim issues.
3. Preservation of evidence—an acceptable method of preserving evidence needs to be developed at the point of admission.
4. Physical evidence or **trace evidence**—evidence such as gunshot residue, hair, or fibers that are transferred between individuals during the commission of a crime need to be collected in an acceptable manner.
5. When to collect evidence—ER staff needs to know that collecting evidence in a "legally acceptable manner" is essential.
6. Processing of clothing—forensic medical specialists could handle this key concern but if someone with those credentials is unavailable, nurses need to be trained in how to handle a victim's clothing in the preferred way including how to seal and clearly mark each item.
7. Investigation of wound characteristics—there are no fewer than nine different injury types that those treating the patient should know about. Being educated in these matters can increase the medicolegal outcomes of an investigation.
8. Certifying death—"Manner of death is the fashion or circumstance in which the cause of death arose that may be natural, accident, homicide, suicide, or undetermined," notes Sharma.
9. Standards and liability issues—Sharma notes that since 1992, the joint Commission on Accreditation of Health Care Organizations (JCAHO) USA has published standards that are aimed at making sure all hospital staff are trained in the identification of crime victims and procedures required in abuse survivor work.
10. Role of photography in clinical forensic medicine—photography is no longer only done at the crime scene. It is being used in ERs. (Sharma, 2003)

THE SEXUAL ASSAULT FORENSIC EXAM AND RAPE KIT

A rape victim may be asked to agree to a **Sexual Assault Forensic Exam**, also known as **SAFE.** The purpose of being able to provide it as evidence that will become part of what is known as the Rape Kit. Once processed, the information in that kit might help the prosecutor to make its case against any accused rapist. The DNA evidence could also be put through the FBI's extensive database of thousands of profiles. The database is referred to by the acronym **CODIS**, which stands for the **Combined DNA Index System**.

Box 6.1 describes what is in a typical rape kit. Students can download a more detailed 15 step version, based on the New York Health Department collection kit guidelines, summarized at the product page that accompanies the text at www.AspenPublishing.com.

Preparing for the Exam

To help with a possible conviction, if possible, DNA evidence should be collected within 72 hours. RAINN (Rape, Abuse & Incest National Network), the leading provider of direct help through its hotline and information, suggests a victim avoid doing any of the following before providing samples for the rape kit, described in Box 6.1, namely, do not bathe, shower, comb hair, change clothes, use the bathroom, or clean up the area where the rape occurred.

Rape Kits Processing and Delays

DNA evidence usually helps to convict an accused rapist; it might also help to get charges dropped. So, testing rape kits seem to be a way to see that justice is served in rape cases.

Box 6.1. What Is a Rape Kit?

You may have heard the term "rape kit" to refer to a sexual assault forensic exam. A **rape kit** is a container that includes a checklist, materials, and instructions, along with envelopes and containers to package any specimens collected during the exam. A rape kit may also be referred to as a Sexual Assault Evidence Kit (SAEK). The contents of the kit vary by state and jurisdiction and may include:

- Bags and paper sheets for evidence collection
- Comb
- Documentation forms
- Envelopes
- Instructions
- Materials for blood samples
- Swabs

Source: RAINN

Having a notorious backlog of hundreds, even thousands, or more, rape kits hurts everyone. Victims and medical professionals should not hold back on doing a SAFE or putting together a rape kit because they fear it will just sit around for months or even years. Now that the rape kit backlog has become public and there is pressure to get kits tested, hopefully the situation will continue to improve.

In December 2019, President Trump signed into law legislation to cover the cost of testing an estimated 100,000 backlogged rape kits. (Lantry, ABCNews.com),

Actress Mariska Hargitay, star of the two decades old TV crime drama *Law and Order: SVU*, has a program called End the Backlog. It is part of the Joyful Heart Foundation, a national nonprofit that she founded whose goal is to make a difference in the way sexual assault, domestic violence, and child abuse victims are responded to by society. End the Backlog is committed to drawing attention to the rape kit backlog problem in America.

Mariska Hargitay, actress and founder of the END THE BACKLOG initiative of her nonprofit organization, Joyful Heart Foundation, on the left, together with Kym Worthy, Wayne County prosecutor, at the National Press Club.

In some instances, there might even be emergency medical care funding available for victims of sexual assault. See Box 6.2 for information about what compensation the state of Texas offers to sexual assault victims related to their SAFE.

THE PSYCHOLOGICAL IMPACT OF BEING A VICTIM

We know two things about help-seeking behavior of victims:

1. Less than half of all crimes are reported to the police. (Morgan and Truman, 2020)
2. The majority of victims are reluctant to seek formal counseling related to their victimization. (McCart, Smith, and Sawyer, 2010)

Box 6.2. Sample from the Attorney General of the State of Texas

Emergency Medical Care Compensation—Sexual Assault Exam

Eligibility Requirements

You may apply for compensation for **only the emergency medical care** you received during a sexual assault exam at a hospital after August 31, 2015. Learn more about Emergency Medical Care—Sexual Assault Exam.

You will not be considered for compensation for any other crime-related costs, such as follow-up medical care, mental health care, or lost wages. You have three years from the date of the crime to request compensation for other crime-related costs.

To receive reimbursement **for only the emergency medical care** costs, you do not need to meet all CVC eligibility requirements.

You must meet the following eligibility requirements:

1. The crime must occur in Texas to a U.S. resident; or the victim is a Texas resident and the crime occurred in a country that does not offer crime victims' compensation.
2. You must apply within three (3) years from the date of the crime unless good cause is shown e.g., age of the victim, mental or physical capacity of the victim, etc.
3. You are:
   - A victim who received emergency medical care during a sexual assault exam at a hospital after August 31, 2015.
   - A person who legally takes on the responsibilities or pays the cost of the eligible emergency medical care.
   - Someone authorized to act on behalf of the victim listed above, such as a parent or guardian.
4. You did not give false information to the program.
5. You were not incarcerated at the time of the crime.

Source: Posted on the internet by Ken Paxton, Attorney General of Texas.

Why do these two facts matter? Most people look at the reporting of a crime to the police as the beginning of the victim's involvement in the criminal justice system. The necessary paperwork of filing a report and, if there are any suspects, of viewing them in a possible photo or in-person lineup and, if there is a formal charge, of becoming a witness to the charges whether that means there is a plea bargain or a trial. All this was discussed in greater detail in Chapter 5, "Victims and the Criminal Justice System: Police, Courts, and Corrections".

What is rarely mentioned is that if victims opt out of reporting the crime to the police, they eliminate police providing them with information about what services are available to crime victims. Police should know that counseling services are available to crime victims. If they report the crime, those services are usually free. If they do not report it, they may have to pay out of pocket, or through their insurance plan. However, there may also be community-based crime victim services that offer free counseling to victims whether or not they report the crime.

In their journal article, "Help Seeking Among Victims of Crime: A Review of the Empirical Literature," Michael R. McCart et al. point out that there are two types of sources of help: the formal, such as police, mental health workers, and physicians as well as the informal, family and friends. (McCart, et al., 199.) The percentage of those seeking formal help is much lower than informal. For example, according to a study by Prospero and Vohra-Gupta, as summarized by McCart et al., reportedly only 16 percent sought help from a mental health professional among the college students who reported being intimate partner violence victims. (McCart, 2010:199)

We will start our discussion with the more common type of help that all crime victims seek, namely, the informal support from family and friends.

Informal Help from Family and Friends

Prospero and Vohra-Gupta pointed out that in that same sample of college students, a whopping 42 percent sought support from family and friends after their intimate partner violence victimization, compared to the 16 percent mentioned earlier who sought formal mental health aid. (McCart, 2010: 199) As noted before, around half of all victims will not report their crime to the police, so they may not even know that there is free counseling available, or victims may prefer to avoid formal counseling for personal reasons that have nothing to do with cost.

For all victims, the first line of defense in their post-victimization recovery is therefore the victim's own support system of family and friends. A victim's grandmother blamed her granddaughter for the rape because of how she was dressed and she even told her it was not a real rape because her granddaughter knew the man—it was the 20-year old brother of the victim's best friend and the grandmother said it had to be a stranger to be a "real rape". That example is a reminder that those working with victims need to be reminded that family and friend responses can facilitate or delay a victim's recovery. Since so many victims may not know about, or wish to pay for or even involve themselves, with formal counseling services, family and friends have to understand some of the basic issues that crime victims will be dealing with so they help, and do not further victimize the victim.

Most crime victims, if they have opened up with loved ones about the crime, want to be listened to with empathy, not pity. Being heard without judgment or **victim blame** can go a long way in helping in the healing process. Avoiding such comments as, "Why did you have to go out by yourself, anyway?" or "Do you think what you were wearing had anything to do with it?" or "I told you not to bring that up when she was upset" smack of victim blame.

Even if the victim blames himself or herself (**victim self-blame**), it is key to reassure the victim that she or he is not to blame. That does not mean that what happened cannot serve as some kind of a learning experience to prevent future victimization. So the family and friends who are supporting and helping the victim have to walk a very thin and careful line between victim blame and helping the victim to feel like greater understanding will give him or her a stronger feeling of control over the future. If all crime is totally random, then this could happen again? That can be a frightening thought as blaming a victim can lead to a self-incriminating mindset.

Jennifer Storm, the former Victim Advocate for the Commonwealth of Pennsylvania, shares in her powerful memoir, *Blackout Girl*, how tough it was for her when she did not receive support from her family or friends following her rape at the age of 12 by a 28-year old whom she had met through friends. When she came back from the hospital where she had been examined, having under her finger nails scraped and her clothes removed and placed into a brown paper bag—this was in 1988—it was not the reaction from her family or her friend that would help her on her long road to recovery. Quite the opposite. As she writes in *Blackout Girl:*

> After that day we never spoke about what had happened. No one ever told me it wasn't my fault. No one held me and said, "It's okay to cry, baby, it will all be okay." No one ever told me that the noises at night were just our house creaking and not that man coming to get me. No one ever said, "Jennifer, that is *not* what sex is; *this* is what it is." No one ever said anything. Meanwhile, I interpreted their silence as meaning they thought the rape was my fault. The strange new way people looked at me meant I was dirty, and we don't speak of these things. I was bad and not worthy of consoling.
>
> I told my best friend what had happened, and she thought I was dirty, too. The next day she passed a note to everyone in the cafeteria saying that I was a slut and that I deserved it.
>
> I must have been bad. (Storm, 26-27)

With reactions like this from family and friends—her family's silence was an action even if it was an act of omission—may explain why victims are reluctant to share about what they have gone through. Those who do share, however, need encouragement, understanding, and support. As mentioned in previous chapters, emotional consequences of victimization include post-traumatic stress disorder (PTSD), depression, and substance abuse issues, to name just a few of the many consequences. If a victim does not seek out formal help from a therapist or even a support group, informal help from family and friends may at least help to deal with these emotional reactions to the victimization until formal help is sought or even if it is never an option.

In the chapter on rape we will look at how the rape victim recovers, going from the acute reaction when the rape first happens and the integration of the experience, in time, by the victim. In Chapter 7, we will also look at the pattern of recovery in the secondary victims of homicide, using a modification of Dr. Kubler Ross' stages of grief, from the shock of hearing the news through the 6th stage of grief, contributed by Dr. Ross' former associate, David Kessler, namely the "finding meaning" stage. That information would be helpful to make known to the family and friends of the victim so he or she can be as supportive of their victimized loved one as soon as possible. (Kubler-Ross, 1969; Kessler, 2020)

There may be a temptation to say to yourself, "What would I want from my family or friends if something like this happened to me?" but that is a temptation you might want to resist. No two people are alike and your job, as someone who is helping crime victims, professionally, or even just as the family or friend of a crime victim, is to discover what he or she wants. You may want to talk nonstop about what happened. Your friend may prefer to tell you about it once and never mention it again. You may want to go into "If only" scenarios, because it makes you feel better, even if you know it was not your fault. Your family member may prefer to avoid such hypotheticals.

Family and friends need to listen without judgment. You can ask for details about what happened if it is done in a way that does not seem like you are interrogating your family member or friend but instead are showing interest. The best way is if your family member or friend volunteers whatever he or she wants to share. Since victims often need to repeat what happened again and again until they no longer have a need to do so—it is a way of gaining mastery over the situation—if possible, resist saying, "You told me that already," even if you have heard something one or a dozen times. Saying "You told me that already" can be very off-putting and insensitive to this tendency to need to repeat what happened.

Why Some Do Not Confide About the Crime

In terms of failing to share about the crime, there are two groups of victims that fall into this situation: those who are not emotionally able to share, but they hope their family members will guess that they are hiding something and will ask them to confide because they really want to share and, the second group, those who adamantly want to hide what happened.

If you think a friend or family member falls into the first group of victims who are withholding about the victimization, you can try to open your loved one up by saying something like, "You seem different lately. Sadder. Even depressed. Has something happened recently that you want to talk about?" Your family member or friend may say no. If she or he does, that will be the end of it since you do not want to push or prod. Pushing someone to share if he or she is not ready can backfire. But this type of questioning could be the "in" to the situation that you need to get your loved one to open up so you can offer the support that he or she needs.

In the second situation, unfortunately you have to patiently wait until your friend or family member will open up. If he or she is determined to keep what happened from you, you will probably not even see any telltale signs that something has happened. Also, there may be someone that the victim is able to disclose to, such as a counselor.

Since you cannot force someone to share about a situation that is especially traumatic, you can at least create an atmosphere that would encourage such opening up. For instance, be careful not to express victim blame attitudes about popular culture situations that might lead a family member or friend to think that there would be judgment of her or him if he or she opened up. Without being too obvious, if someone shares about their victimization in the media, or in a publication, you might point out how brave you think he or she was and reaffirm your positive attitude toward those who share.

It is almost universal that any victim, whatever the crime, feels like he or she has lost control over his or her life. Deciding when, and to whom, the victim shares about the victimization is part of that process of regaining control over his or her life. You do not want to take that renewed control away from him or her by forcing him or her to share before he or she is ready.

If the reason a victim will not open up and seek support from family or friends is a fear of reprisal by revealing about the crime, that may be an imaginary or a real fear. You have to trust the victim's judgment about what of those two realities it might be. Or, as sociologist William Thomas said, along with his wife Dorothy, when they formulated the **Thomas Theorem**, in 1928, if you define a situation as real, it is real in its consequences. If you discover fear of reprisal may be stopping your friend or family member from sharing about the crime he or she has endured, you might consider pursuing any actions that would minimize that fear including a step as radical as moving to a new neighborhood or even a new state or, if necessary, a new country. You might even talk about the general benefits of getting support from family and friends, not pertaining to crime at all. That might inspire your loved one to consider sharing about what he or she has gone through recently or even long ago, whenever the victimization occurred.

Formal Counseling

Formal help for victims in the aftermath of a crime is available in many forms, ranging from calling a hotline for a one-time chance to share what the victim is experiencing to scheduling private consultations with psychiatrists, psychologists, social workers, mental health counselors, or other types of psychotherapists. These specialists usually have undergone academic or post-graduate training in helping victims of crime with short or long-term therapy. Other sources of help include talking with coaches, clergy, rabbis, and substance abuse counselors, or joining a peer support group, which can be either run by peers only or facilitated by a trained therapist.

Psychologist having session with her patient in office, by wavebreakmedia/Shutterstock

Why does formal help matter? Because researchers, victims, and even prosecutors point out that victims who seek help seem to do better than those who do not.

There are national hotlines for specific crime victims, such as hotlines for domestic violence, rape and sexual assault, victims of terrorism and mass violence, child abuse, human trafficking, disaster distress, teen dating abuse, identify theft, missing and exploited children, elder abuse, scams and frauds, and other crimes. See listings in the Resources section at the end of this chapter.

Most local crime victim centers or specialized crime victim crisis centers, such as for rape or domestic violence victims, have hotlines staffed by trained volunteers. Hot lines provide information as well as counseling. Sometimes the victim calls asking for information, such as how to apply for crime victim compensation, but he or she is really also trying to start a dialogue that might lead to more emotional support. The best way to give emotional support to those who seek out help, even if it looks as if they only want information about available services, is to ask questions. Deal with the reason for the call first. "You can find out what you need to qualify for crime victim compensation by going to this website or I can answer any specific questions you have right now." After you direct the caller to the website that will have extensive and detailed information, you can add, "So-and-so, I know this-and-that happened. It's been (fill in the time frame). How are you doing?" After you hear the answer, if there is something said that gives you a chance to ask more questions, and to get into a dialogue with the victim, take that opportunity to build rapport.

WORKING WITH A COUNSELOR

Post-traumatic stress disorder (PTSD) is a condition that was initially diagnosed in veterans who were having flashbacks and adjustment problems upon returning home after combat. In their scholarly article, "Mental Health Needs of Crime Victims: Epidemiology and Outcomes," by Dean G. Kilpatrick at the National Crime Victims Research and Treatment Center, Medical University of South Carolina and Ron Acierno, the co-authors reanalyzed the results of various victim studies in regard to PTSD levels. Those levels were compared to reported PTSD levels in "noncrime victims." Here is what they found for all crime victims: a lifetime PTSD rate of 25.8 percent and a current rate of 9.7 percent compared to a lifetime and current PTSD rate for nonvictims of only 9.4 percent and 3.4 percent respectively. (Kilpatrick and Acierno, 2003)

In Box 6.3 you will find a list of popular ways of treating primary or secondary victims of crime with a short definition of those treatment methods.

Box 6.3. Popular Ways of Treating Primary and Secondary Victims of Crime
(in alphabetical order)

Eye Movement Desensitization and Reprocessing (EMDR): A unique way of treating trauma that was developed by Francine Shapiro in 1988.

Cognitive Interview: Developed by psychologists Ronald Fisher and Edward Geiselman in 1984-85 as a method to improve memory and recall.

Cognitive Therapy or Cognitive Behavior Therapy (CBT): Started by Dr. Aaron T. Beck in the 1960s.

Grief Counseling (also known as ***bereavement counseling***)**:** Some base it on the five stages of grief that Dr. Kubler Ross described in 1969, namely: denial, anger, bargaining, depression, and acceptance.

Group Therapy: When several people get together to share about their similar experience such as being a victim or a crime or having a family member who was murdered. Groups may be completely peer groups or there could be a trained counselor leading it.

Individual Therapy: One-on-one therapy with a range of therapists or counselors who can help the victim or the victim's family to work through the trauma.

Box 6.3. Popular Ways of Treating Primary and Second Victims of Crime (continued)

PTSD Therapy: May rely on other therapies, such as cognitive behavior therapy (CBT), exposure therapy, or EMDR, to help victims to minimize or eliminate some or all of the symptoms of PTSD, namely: sleep disturbances, re-experiencing the trauma when something connected to it is experienced, anger, feeling anxious, having trouble concentrating.

Substance Abuse Therapy: Focusing on addictions that may be longstanding or could have been exacerbated by the primary or secondary victimization. There are various ways to treat the addiction including inpatient rehab or outpatient counseling. In either case, treatment may include medication which is usually only prescribed by a physician.

Trauma Therapy: Talking therapy that helps someone to work through the trauma of a particular event such as a crime. Some therapists have victims walk through the trauma. Others instead deal with the behavioral and emotional consequences to it and helping the trauma to have less of a grip on the victim.

Mary Joye is a Florida-based licensed mental health counselor who has been treating clients including crime victims as well as veterans for the last 12 years. She is a trauma certified therapist. How does Mary Joye work with a crime victim who is experiencing PTSD related to their victimization? "I try to move a crime victim forward," says Joye. "A lot of regular therapy digs into the past. But they've done that in the police station and they do that with the detective. By the time they get to me, they have become a victim. They identify with being a victim. That defines them. I help them to move forward. Something bad happened to them, but that is not their identity. They acknowledge its presence, but they learn not to allow it to take over. It happened. Rape happened *to* me instead of saying 'I am a rape victim,' 'Murder happened in my family, but I am not defined by my family member's murder. Something horrible happened. It's a part of my life but it's not all consuming my life."

Sarah Fogel is a social worker who is also a trauma therapist. She has worked with sexual assault victims and she describes trauma therapy this way, "There are a few different schools of thought in trauma therapy. One is you don't bring up the trauma. The other is that you deal with it in every single detail—the sights, the sounds, the feelings. I am in the middle. If someone doesn't want to talk about it, we can talk about all the things going on around them." Fogel feels it is important to "meet a person where they're at." For example, she had a client that "in our first conversation, she went into all of the sexual abuse by her father, and figuring out why her relationship patterns are the way they are."

This author asked psychotherapist Carrie Mead if her clients want to confront the source of their trauma. She recalled she only had one who had done that. It was an eight-year old girl whose mother had physically abused her. She was not in her mother's custody.

Carrie explains, "She said, 'Ms. Carrie. I want to call her and tell her what she did was wrong.'

"We didn't have a protective order. She hadn't talked to her mother in months."

Carrie put through the call to the little girl's mother.

'"Mom, I know what you did was wrong."'

Her Mom was crying. 'I didn't mean it.'

"She hung up the phone [on her]."

Carrie points out how that little girl was fortunate since she knew who the perpetrator was and could confront her. She has other patients who know they were victims, but they do not know who the perpetrator was. "They are enraged. They would like to have it out with them but they don't know who the person is. They tell me they would [confront them] if they knew who it was."

Although we usually think of victims seeking out counseling right after victimization, it may still be helpful to a victim a decade or even longer after the crime occurred. You may recall the brief Profile with Bill W. at the end of Chapter 1 in which he shared in his self-report that when he was 10, he was sexually assaulted by his uncle. Now 31, he never reported the crime to the police and does not intend to. But Bill did recently go into therapy:

Bill explains:

> . . . I was always mad at myself as a kid for that happening to me, i don't know why. But today as an adult, I find that I'm very edgy and defensive. I absolutely do not like to be touched by anyone for obvious reasons, which kept me from going out to crowded bars and concerts in my 20's. When I turned 23, I decided I wanted to just get away, and start my life so I decided to join the—[military]. I have been in the—[military] for eight years now, and I wouldn't change a thing. The military has been a great outlet for me. . . . [I] recently just re-enlisted . . .
>
> [But] These experiences did not influence what I wanted to do with my life. I have always wanted to do something with law enforcement or military well before any of this ever happened to me. My oldest brother was in the Marines and ended up taking his own life as a result from severe PTSD. It's a huge reason why I have decided to dedicate my life to the service. I am also a huge mental health advocate, especially when it comes to veteran suicide and PTSD awareness.
>
> One of the best decisions I have ever made in my life was to talk to a mental health professional. Although I have not told my provider about what happened, we do talk about my anxiety and anger and PTSD (post-traumatic stress disorder), which has helped tremendously. Although I have not yet told my provider about this [the sexual abuse], I will in time when I am ready.
>
> One piece of advice I would give is that if anyone out there is struggling with a traumatic experience, or is suffering with mental health, it is never too late to seek professional help. You would be surprised at what talking to a professional could do for you. You don't have to face your demons alone!

In the United States, depending on where you live, there may be free or sliding scale counseling individual or group sessions available for crime victims. Some services, even if direct programs are local, such as Safe Horizons in New York City, founded in 1978, offer support for all victims of violence and abuse through a toll-free hotline. (See the listing in the Resources section.)

Ashleigh Diserio is a behavioral consultant who has 13 years of experience working with the U.S. government and private sector clients consulting on felony-level crimes that includes mass shootings, child abuse, homicide, and sexual assault. Diserio, who has a master's in forensic psychology, shares her key insights about helping victims, reprinted with permission from Victims (2021):

1. Until you have been the actual victim of that particular crime, or something similar, do not think you can fully understand what victims are feeling and going through.
2. A commonly-known resource that victims can seek support form is therapists. A more obscure resource used to help victims grow, heal, and prosper is life coaches. Life coaches work with clients to examine where their client is at in the present moment and where they want to be in the future. The client and life coach work together to help identify the client's goals and to develop an actionable plan to achieve them. Seeking assistance from one or both resources is a positive step to dealing with the challenges that victims might be facing.
3. Law enforcement agencies who implement evidence-based best practices when conducting interviews seem to gather more information and build better rapport with interviewees. I teach law enforcement the **cognitive interviewing** approach* which was developed by Dr. Ronald Fisher at Florida International University. My agency interviews victims, subjects, and witnesses using the same interview style, and we conduct all interviews in the same room. Some law enforcement would not think of conducting interviews of subjects in "soft rooms," which are typically used for victim interviews. "Soft rooms" have couches, chairs, comfy pillows, and calming artwork. It took years to get some law enforcement on board with conducting interviews using evidence-based best practices, but we have seen great results in the amount of information obtained with these techniques.
4. Help domestic violence victims to become more proactive in pressing charges before it is too late. Law enforcement often does not understand why victims become hesitant to press charges. We must be understanding about the reasons behind why these victims go back to abusive situations. Throw as many resources at them and keep showing up every time these victims seek help. Domestic violence victims typically try to leave abusive situations eight times before they leave for the final time. (Yager, 2021)

Crime Victim Assistance Centers

Most towns and cities have at least one or maybe more publicly-funded or non-profit organizations offering free help to victims of crime. Some of these centers focus on only one type of victim, such as victims of rape and sexual assault, or victims of domestic violence. Others are available for all victims of all crimes. Some of these centers offer information and referrals, others offer counseling by volunteers who are trained through an intensive program, usually lasting around 40 hours spread out over several days or weeks, or even social workers or psychologists might staff the centers.

What is important to know about these sources of help is that victims may call about one concern but they are actually calling about much more including other issues. For example, 37-year-old Alice W. called a crime victim hotline that this author worked at because she said she wanted information about her eligibility for financial compensation from the state crime victim compensation program. She explained that a neighbor heard about the program and told Alice she should look into it. Alice shared with the counselor that she had three

* Cognitive interviewing is a form of interviewing that suggests using all five senses for victims or witnesses to describe a crime scene, and it even recommends looking at the crime scene from various perspectives, including the criminal.

children, ages 14, 15, and 16, and that three weeks before, her husband, a truck driver, had trouble with his vehicle so he pulled over to the shoulder on the highway to check it out. As he got out of the car, a tractor trailer hit him from behind and fled the scene. Mrs. W. found out from the police that her husband lived an hour and a half before he died. He was able to give them a description of the truck but since his glasses were knocked off by the impact, he was unable to offer a description of the driver.

She shared that a witness came forward and said that she saw a man get out of the truck, look at the injured man, and get back into the truck. Based on that witness' testimony, the charge was upgraded to murder.

Her husband did not have any insurance and the reason for her call initially was to discuss the possibility of getting crime victim compensation. But it was also clear that Mrs. W. wanted to talk about what happened to her husband and that counseling on an ongoing basis, individual or in a group, might be beneficial to her. Helping her to apply for financial compensation, however, was definitely an important part of that call.

THE FINANCIAL IMPACT OF VICTIMIZATION

Many are shy about looking at the financial toll of victimization, except when it comes to burglary, robbery, or motor vehicle theft, because with violent crimes the attitude might be, "At least I am alive." All but the 508 robbery-homicide victims in 2019 in the United States—the 266,988 who were robbed but lived—they may be thinking, "It's only money." (FBI, *2019 Crime in the United States*)

It *is* only money, but when it comes to homicide, it is not just the funeral costs for buying or cremating the victim that are a direct financial consequence of the crime but the victim's lost wages over a lifetime. If that victim is a college or graduate school graduate, there is the cost of that education that never got recouped, depending on the age of the victim.

The economic toll of homicide was made quite clear when the September 11th terrorist attacks led the government to appoint someone who would decide on the economic value of each of the 2,977 victims based on a number of factors such as age, estimated earning capabilities if they had lived. If someone has a private life insurance policy, there will be money paid out to the victim's family when someone is killed. (Gordils, 2019)

But many citizens do not have life insurance. According to the Insurance Information Institute, Inc., in 2018, approximately 60 percent of Americans had life insurance. (III, 2019)

In addition to the lost earnings of homicide victims, there are the lost earnings of hospitalized victims whose salary is cut because their time off is not covered by sick days, or the lost earnings of victims who are freelancers or contract workers who only get paid if they work. There are also medical bills related to the victimization that need to be paid, as well as other costs related to the victimization such as replacing locks on doors, even installing new doors, if the burglar broke it down, or relocating to a new place because of a domestic violence threat.

As you know from Chapter 2, "An Anthropological and Historical View of Crime Victims and Victims' Rights," victims lost the right to directly get revenge or compensation from their offenders by the Middle Ages. For centuries, the victim was merely the witness for the prosecution if a case went forward. That started to change in the 1940s with the development of victimology and then again, in the 1960s, when the victim began to reemerge as a wronged party in the criminal-victim or "penal couple" dyad deserving of financial compensation for being wronged. Later in this chapter, we will address the civil right to compensation that became an option beginning in the 1970s. We will also focus on crime victim compensation programs and restitution programs that are court ordered.

Government Crime Victim Compensation Programs

Margery Fry, a British penal reformer, is credited with starting the modern crime victim compensation movement with the publication of her article, "Arms and the Law," in 1951, with her article about offenders paying victims of their crimes. But several years later, in a widely-circulated article in 1957 in *The Observer*, she called for a government compensation program for crime victims.

In 1963, New Zealand was the first country to start a government-funded **crime victim compensation program.** In 1965, California became the first state to have a state compensation program. In 1984, when the federal government passed VOCA, The Victims of Crime Act, funding for state crime compensation programs would now come from the fines and forfeitures from federal criminals. By 2002, all 50 states, Guam, Puerto Rico, District of Columbia, and the U.S. Virgin Islands had crime victim compensation programs.

Although there is some variety from state to state in terms of the maximum award, eligibility requirements and what is covered is quite similar. The similarities include the necessity of reporting the crime to the police. Some states require the report to be filed within 72 hours. Other states, like Ohio, eliminated the timing restriction but still require that a report is filed, and that reimbursements are paid based on submitted receipts; a decision is usually made within 60 days. In the meantime, the victim must pay the bills on his or her own.

Except for Florida, which does consider covering losses up to a certain amount related to property crimes, the criteria is that to be eligible for state crime victim compensation, it had to have been a violent crime with medical expenses, funeral costs, crime scene cleanup, counseling, loss of wages, in the case of homicide, with the requirement that all other insurance first be exhausted. Each state is able to set its own crime victim compensation rules, regulations, and even how much reimbursement is available.

Unfortunately, it can be confusing and complicated to get reimbursed if there is any other funding available such as insurance. Here is the wording from the California compensation program regarding that policy: According to California law, "CalVCB can only reimburse victims for crime-related expenses if there are no other sources of reimbursement. If CalVCB reimburses a victim for losses, but another source of funds becomes available because of the same criminal incident, CalVCB is entitled to be reimbursed."

There are other stipulations. The person requesting compensation cannot be the perpetrator of the crime. But most programs also will not compensate anyone who is on parole, in jail or prison, or on felony probation.

There is a cap on how much can be paid for the various eligible expenses including funerals for homicide victims (usually around $7,500 to $10,000), death claims ($25,000 to $70,000), injury claims (ranges, in West Virginia the maximum is $35,000). The claim must be filed within a certain time period, anywhere from two to seven years after the crime occurred.

Every state has certain unique features, and maximums, to its plan so check with your state's crime compensation board, that is the state where the crime occurred. Tennessee has a maximum of combined expenses through their Criminal Injuries Compensation Fund of $32,000. You can find that state's compensation board information online through Google or go to the website for the National Association of Crime Victim Compensation Boards (http://www.nacvcb.org/) which allows you to search by state.

Box 6.4. Sample of Crime Victim Compensation Eligibility from Texas

Crime Victims' Compensation

Eligibility Requirements

You may apply for compensation for all eligible crime-related costs, including payment of medical costs from a sexual assault exam. To receive compensation for these costs, you must meet the following eligibility requirements:

1. The crime must occur in Texas to a United States resident; or the victim is a Texas resident and the crime occurred in a country that does not offer crime victims' compensation.
2. The crime must be reported to an appropriate law enforcement agency.
3. The victim or claimant must cooperate with the law enforcement investigation.
4. You must apply within three (3) years from the date of the crime unless good cause is shown e.g., age of the victim, mental or physical capacity of the victim, etc.
5. You are either a victim or a claimant.
6. You did not:
   - Participate in the crime.
   - Commit illegal activity at the time of the crime. Does not apply to a person who seeks compensation if the illegal activity the person engaged in was the result of human trafficking.
   - Share responsibility for the crime due to your behavior.
   - Give false information to the program.
7. You were not incarcerated at the time of the crime.

Covered Crimes

Crimes or attempted crimes that caused physical or mental injury or death.

Assault	Family Violence	Kidnapping
Child Abuse	Hit and Run	Robbery
Child Sexual Assault	Homicide	Sexual Assault
DWI	Human Trafficking	Stalking
Elder Abuse		

Identity theft and property crimes are not covered.

Source: Posted by Ken Paxton, Attorney General of Texas

When Deserving Victims Slip Through the Bureaucratic Cracks

As Alysia Santo points out in her article published in The Marshall Project, seven state crime victim compensation programs will not provide compensation to victims who have a criminal record. Whereas all the programs will not allow the perpetrator of the crime to get compensation, or someone on felony parole or probation to get compensation, denying crime victim compensation to legitimate crime victims because of past convictions is a policy that needs to be reconsidered in light of the spirit and mission of the funds. The example that Santo begins her article with is powerful and telling. Anthony "Amp" Campbell's father was murdered in Sarasota, Florida. Campbell was a football coach at Alabama State University. Even after using his savings, he did not have enough money for his father's funeral. The Sarasota police told him that he should apply to Florida's compensation board for the funds. Unfortunately, his request was denied because his father had been convicted in 1983 of burglary. Despite his father turning his life around and becoming a model citizen by the time of his murder in 2015, the eligibility requirements were clear: convictions of certain kinds of previous felonies ruled out entitlement to the crime victim compensation fund. (Santo, 2018)

What other options are available to victims who have had expenses or losses due to a crime? Restitution and the related option of restorative justice programs are discussed below. The chapter also explores private funding as well as the option of filing a civil suit to collect damages from the criminal offender or from a third party.

Box 6.5. Victim Compensation Application

State of Colorado—Page 1 of a 5-page application

The Victim Compensation program operates pursuant to C.R.S. 24-4.1-101 et seq.

Eligibility Requirements:

1. The crime must be one in which the victim sustains mental or bodily injury, dies, or suffers property damage to locks, windows or doors to residential property as a result of a compensable crime.
2. The victim must cooperate with law enforcement officials (e.g. district attorney, police, sheriff)
3. The law enforcement agency was notified within 72 hours after the crime occurred.
4. The injury or death of the victim was not the result of the victim's own wrongdoing or substantial provocation.
5. The victimization occurred on or after July 1, 1982.
6. The application for compensation must be submitted within one year from the date of the crime; six months for residential property damage claims.

General Information:

1. There does not have to be an arrest made for a victim to be eligible for compensation.
2. Compensation may be made for medical expenses, mental health counseling, dentures, eyeglasses, hearing aids, or other prosthetic or medical devices, loss of earnings, outpatient care, homemaker or home health services, funeral expenses, and loss of support to dependents.
3. Compensation for property damage may be awarded for the cost of replacement or repair to exterior doors, locks or windows that are damaged during the commission of the crime.
4. By law, you must apply for all other available sources of financial assistance or reimbursement, including private insurance, Medicaid and Medicare.

Box 6.5. Victim Compensation Application (continued)

5. Please attach all bills and receipts. You may apply even if you have not received any bills as of this date.
6. Your claim will be investigated and presented to the Victim Compensation Board. This process may take up to 60 days.
7. Total recovery may not exceed the statutory limit of $30,000. Compensation for some categories is limited by Board policy. Some jurisdictions do not pay up to the statutory limit of $30,000.
8. Should your claim be denied, you have a right to request reconsideration of the Board's decision and have the right to submit new or additional information related to the reason(s) for the Board's denial or reduction of your claim. You may arrange for reconsideration by contacting the Victim Compensation program within 30 days from the date on which you receive notice of the denial or reduction of your claim. If you request reconsideration of the Board's decision, further information concerning the reconsideration process will be mailed to you. In the event the denial is upheld by the Board, you have a right to have the Board's decision reviewed in accordance with the Colorado Rules of Civil Procedure within 30 days.

Source: Page 1 of the Victim Compensation Application of the State of Colorado posted online at https://cdpsdocs.state.co.us/ovp/Vic_Comp/VC_English_Application_2_18_16.pdf

Restitution

The prosecution can order restitution, or payment, also known as **reparations**, to the victim by the offender as part of their punishment. Although some defendants are what is known as **judgment proof**, meaning they do not have any funds, especially if the defendant is on probation, rather than doing jail or prison time where he or she might only earn 10 cents to 90 cents an hour, it might be possible to put a lien on the perpetrator's salary, if employed, or on the defendant's property, to make sure the payment is settled.

In some cases, the defendant could be offered restitution in lieu of another type of punishment, such as prison time. If the defendant goes to prison, and the judge has ordered **restitution** as part of the prison sentence, the account set up for the defendant at the time of incarceration, which will include payments for commissary items, or from wages for work done within prison, can have as much as 50 percent passed along to the victim, as stipulated. Although work-release programs are rare in the United States, one program, which unfortunately was moved to another facility after decades on the upper West Side, Lincoln Correctional Facility, had inmates working at jobs during the day that brought in thousands of dollars by the time they were ready to finish their sentence. The inmates had up to 80 percent of their earnings held in escrow for them until their release. The rest was paid to the state to help defray the cost of their room and board. A situation like that would be an excellent option for restitution to the victim since there were enough earnings to be able to make such a payment.

On April 24, 1996, the Mandatory Victims Restitution Act of 1996 became a federal law by Congress that restitution had to be made by defendants in many federal crimes. The crimes included violent crimes, a property crime including offenses committed by fraud or deceit. These four crimes that were included for mandatory restitution under the *Violence Against Women Act* were still to have restitution, namely: domestic violence; sexual abuse; sexual exploitation; and telemarketing fraud. Of course if the defendant has no available funds, it is a requirement that will not be met. (Office for Victims of Crime, 1997-98)

Restorative Justice Programs

Most **restorative justice** programs are tied to nonviolent property offenses. This is an alternative to incarceration that is growing in popularity. Since almost no state crime victim compensation programs offer financial compensation to victims for their losses related to such property crimes as robbery, larceny-theft, burglary, and white collar crimes including fraud, embezzlement, and identity theft, a restorative justice program with a financial compensation element to the victim could be a win-win for the victim, the state, and the offender. Most restorative justice programs require that the offender get into a drug rehab program, if the offense was drug related, or the offender has a drug addiction, and that the offender apologize to the victim for their crime, and that they get a job that is legitimate. Since most restorative justice programs are an alternative to prison, the offender will be making at least minimum wage if not more so there is a great likelihood that the court-ordered restitution to the victim will be paid.

Restorative justice usually involves getting the victim, the offender, a mediator or facilitator, and a member of the community together to discuss a plan to make the victim whole again and to rehabilitate the offender so that he or she will not commit another crime. That is a simplistic explanation of it but it is based on a different model for criminal justice, a far different one than the one based on punishment.

In many ways, the idea of restorative justice is similar to the social justice practices of some primitive cultures that we studied in Chapter 2, whereby the victim and the offender, or the victim's family, if the victim was killed, could work out a way of dealing with the crime that satisfies all parties. Making the victim whole again was the emphasis more than just punishing the offender. Is it a coincidence that we associate the idea of restorative justice with the **Maori** indigenous Polynesian people of New Zealand? Restorative justice is the idea of dealing with conflict and dispute resolution, including crime, within the criminal justice system, through approaches like the Navajo peacemaking or the Maori restorative justice practices. (Cullen and Jonson, 2017)

Private Funding

For those victims who do not qualify for state crime compensation, do not want to deal with the required paperwork, or do not want to wait 60 days for a decision to be made regarding possible reimbursement, there are other options for help from private sources that those who work with victims should be aware of and recommend where practicable. As a basic source of help, friends and family might assist with funeral expenses if a death has occurred, temporarily take in victims after a fire that renders a home or apartment out of commission, or with financial assistance or gifts when high insurance policy deductibles mean that stolen items such as laptops or TVs are not entirely covered by the payout.

For those who have it, private life insurance can help surviving family members by replacing lost wages of a victim in the case of homicide. However, as noted before, only 60 percent of Americans have life insurance. What has in the last decade become a very popular mechanism for raising funds is organizing **crowdfunding** campaigns using sites like GoFundMe or Kickstarter. There is generally a nominal service fee or platform fee for using such a site but once an appeal is up and running, funds from donors can be received quite quickly in anywhere from 30 to 90 days depending on how long the campaign lasts. Some sites, such as Kickstarter, require organizers to offer donors "perks" (e.g., mugs or t-shirts) to motivate them; other sites, such as GoFundMe, instead suggest that donors include optional "tips" to help fund administrative costs. Kickstarter requires that you meet or exceed your financial target or you cannot get the funds but GoFundMe will allow you to keep the funds even if you miss the target, although the commission may be slightly higher in that case.

THE CIVIL COURT SYSTEM OPTION

Some victims choose to seek justice through the civil court system. You have seen some of the reasons that it is challenging for victims to actually get money from government crime victim compensation programs or enough money to fit their needs. For example, the typical cap on monies to those whose family member died from homicide ranges from $10,000 to $25,000, although some states have higher amounts. The reality is that if a family has lost its main breadwinner, and there is no life insurance policy, that money is not going to go very far.

Another option, as mentioned earlier, is the possibility of filing a civil suit against the offender or a civil suit against a third party.

A **civil suit** is brought by an injured party for compensation for harm due to wrongful actions (or sometimes the inaction) of a defendant. For example, a wrongful death civil suit might be filed in a murder case. The settlement in a civil suit in the case of murder if won, can run in the hundreds of thousands or millions of dollars in damages.

A **third-party civil suit** is a suit brought against another party for compensation due to injuries suffered by the plaintiff. One of the more famous third-party suits is the settlement reached in 2016 of a sports reporter, Erin Andrews, who was awarded $55 million ($27 million to be paid by two hotel chains named in the suit and the remainder by the convicted perpetrator). The case involved a stalker who found out the hotel room number where the victim was staying, booked the adjacent room, and secretly took a compromising video of the victim that was posted on the internet. The civil suit awards were decided six years after the convicted stalker was sentenced to 30 months in prison for his illegal actions. (Bieler, 2016)

More recently, in October 2019, 4,440 plaintiffs agreed to a proposed settlement by the hotel chain of approximately $800 million related to the mass shooting that occurred on October 1, 2017, in Las Vegas when Stephen Paddock killed 58 people and injured hundreds more. (Associated Press, 2020)

Those are just two famous cases involving large settlements. There are civil suits being settled related to crime victimization that are for much smaller amounts and not well known. The pioneer in this field was the late Frank Carrington, a federal law enforcement officer and attorney who in the 1970s founded the Victim Rights Center as part of Americans for Effective Law Enforcement, Inc. Currently, the National Crime Victim Law Institute is a leading source of information with this organization providing information and advocacy for victims' rights.

To win a criminal court case, the burden to prove guilt is "beyond a reasonable doubt." In a civil suit, winning is based only on the "mere preponderance of the evidence" considered a somewhat easier standard of guilty to prove.

Civil suits are usually taken on by lawyers on a *contingency basis*. What that means is that victims generally do not pay unless they win their case. If they win, the lawyer's contingency fee may be up to 33 percent. Since lawyers on contingency cases only get paid if they win the case, it may be hard for victims with questionable cases to find lawyers to represent them in a civil suit or to find a lawyer if the potential damages to be awarded are not likely to be a big enough amount or there is only a small likelihood that the accused will actually pay. In those situations, it might be possible for victims to pay a lawyer on an hourly basis for the civil suit or to contact firms that handle a certain number of pro bono cases a year. They might find a victims' case appealing enough that they will take it on for free.

In "Memorandum of Law on Third Party Victims Rights Litigation," prepared by the Victims Rights Center of the Americans for Effective Law Enforcement, Inc., pioneer Frank Carrington and his team, including Richard J. Vittenson and Vicki A. Marani, outline six situations when third-party victim lawsuits are brought. All six are relevant for crime victimization:

1. Against government entities for failure to protect the plaintiff from criminal harm.
2. Against private parties for failure to protect the plaintiff from criminal harm.
3. Against landlords for failure to maintain secure premises.
4. Against innkeepers for failure to maintain secure premises.
5. Against those who fail to exercise proper care of mental patients.
6. Against those who fail to exercise proper care of prisoners.

In their brochure, "Civil Justice for Crime Victims," the National Crime Victim Bar Association explains the difference between civil justice and criminal justice: "A significant difference between the criminal and civil court systems is that in a civil case, the victim controls the essential decisions that shape the case. It is the victim who decides whether to sue, accept a settlement offer, or go to trial. The civil justice system does not attempt to determine the innocence or guilt of an offender. Offenders are also not put in prison. Rather, civil courts attempt to determine whether an offender or a third party is liable for the injuries sustained as a result of the crime. Rather than holding defendants accountable for their crimes against the state, the civil justice system holds defendants who are found liable directly accountable to their victims." (NCVBA, "Civil Justice for Crime Victims")

This is a stark contrast to the victim's part in the criminal justice system. As previously noted, in the criminal justice system, the victim has been relegated to the role of witness for the prosecution. Unlike what is at stake in the civil justice system, if a defendant is found guilty, they can be fined but they can also be put in jail or prison, or on probation or parole. The offender's freedom is at stake.

Here is an example of a successful civil suit that a victim brought. It applies to the second category of liability, "liability of private persons for criminal attacks by another." In this case it was the "duty to maintain a safe place to work." The Memorandum of Law noted previously cites the U.S. Supreme Court ruling, *Lillie v. Thompson*, "which held that a young female employee who was required to work at night in an isolated, unguarded building had a right to sue her employer as a result of a criminal attack by a third party. The injury was held to be reasonably foreseeable."

The Memorandum continues, pointing out an Arizona case whereby a "store clerk who was shot by a robber and lost an eye while working alone after midnight was enabled to cover damages either on the basis of the corporation's negligence in failing to provide a reasonable safe place for him to work or for its breach of a promise that he would not be required to work alone at night." (Memorandum of Law on third Party Victims Rights Litigation," page 5.)

Filing a Civil Lawsuit

The victim files a **complaint** which details the case and the legal claims being made. (Here is where having a lawyer who is an expert in this sub-specialty should be advantageous.) The defendant will respond to the complaint with the **answer.**

If the plaintiff wins, the judge and jury are able to award **compensatory damages** for losses that the injured party suffered and **punitive damages**, which are intended to have a deterrent effect.

Winning the civil suit against an offender is just the first step. Getting the money that the court has awarded paid to the victim is the next big step. The National Crime Victim Bar Association (NCVC) points out that victim's privacy in filing the suit may be protected if the suit is filed under a Jane or John Doe pseudonym. Confidentiality agreements may prevent the offender or third-party defendant from sharing information about the case. ("Civil Justice for Crime Victims.") Oftentimes victims who do win their civil suits, as part of the agreement, are prohibited from publicly disclosing the size of the financial settlement that they received.

Types of Civil Lawsuits

NCVC notes that in civil suits, the wrongful act or crime is referred to as a **tort.** Here is a list of civil torts that have corresponding criminal offenses:

- Assault ("putting the victim in fear of immediate injury while the perpetrator has the ability to inflict such injury")
- Battery (rape, sexual battery, molestation, fondling, forcible sodomy, malicious wounding, and attempted murder)
- Wrongful death (this includes vehicular homicide, murder, or manslaughter)
- False imprisonment (often occurs in rape and kidnappings)
- Intentional or reckless infliction of emotional distress (stalking)
- Fraud (white-collar or economic crimes including criminal fraud, racketeering, telemarketing schemes)
- Negligence
- Conversion (larceny, concealment, embezzlement) (*Source:* "Civil Justice for Crime Victims" NCVCA)

Free referrals to attorneys for a consultation about various issues that need to be considered if a victim is thinking of filing a civil suit are available through the National Crime Victim Bas Association (victimbar.org).

Small Claims Court

Suing the accused, such as an abuser, in Small Claims Court may be another option. There is usually a cap on how much can be awarded. It could be as low as $5,000. Some states have a higher limit. Texas, for example, allows justice suits that can go as high as $10,000. Also, there may be a statute of limitations form when the crime occurred to when the small claims suit can be filed. Usually individuals represent themselves in small claims court rather than having an attorney since the amounts involved are not that huge.

SUMMARY

When someone is a victim of a crime, he or she has certain needs that should be met. Those needs can be medical, if injured; psychological, to deal with the trauma of being victimized; financial, because of losses related to the crime, and legal, including reporting the crime to the police and dealing with the criminal justice system. The later of these concerns were addressed in Chapter 5 "Victims and the Criminal Justice System." This chapter summarizes what victims can expect when they call an ambulance if they are injured and go to a hospital and provides information about rape kits in cases of sexual assault, especially rape. Also addressed are sources of formal and informal support and counseling that are available for victims. An excerpt from Jennifer Storm's memoir about the response by her family and her friend to her rape at the age of 12 highlights how pivotal the reactions of family and friends can be. Those sources are the main ways that victims get emotional support after a crime and they need to be positive and supportive at all times; avoiding victim blame is a key need.

The benefits and limitations of the state compensation programs, now available in all 50 states plus the U.S. Virgin Islands, Guam, Puerto Rico, and the District of Columbia, are summarized. Some of the regulations that victims must comply with in order to qualify for state crime victim compensation, such as making a police report and filing within a certain time period after the crime, are discussed. Each state has its own guidelines so it is important to look into what the state where the crime occurred requires if an application is to be started.

Restitution and restorative justice are described and applied to the victim experience. Restorative justice is a newer approach in the United States although it has its roots in the Maori people of New Zealand.

Although restitution through the courts is a possibility, as noted in this chapter, many defendants are unable to make any payments, especially if they are going to jail or prison for a long time. Another option discusserd in this chapter is for a victim is a civil suit which may be against the offender or a third party that is being held responsible for a civil tort. A majority of criminal offenses have a corresponding civil tort that could be the basis for receiving damages if the case is won such as assault, battery, false imprisonment, and wrongful death. There are lawyers who specialize in civil suits brought by crime victims. The National Crime Victim Bar Association will make a free referral to an attorney for a consultation about this option.

KEY TERMS

civil suit
CODIS (combined DNA index system)
cognitive interviewing
CPR
compensatory damages
complaint and answer
crime victim advocate
crime victim compensation program
crowdfunding
EMS (emergency management services)
forensic nursing
judgment proof
Maori
PTSD (post-traumatic stress disorder)
punitive damages
rape kit
reparations
response time
restitution
restorative justice
SAFE (Sexual Assault Forensic Exam)
Stop the Bleed®
third-party civil suit
Thomas Theorem
tort
trace evidence
victim blame
victim self-blame

REVIEW QUESTIONS

1. What type of crime victims require mandatory reporting of the crime to the police by medical personnel?
2. What type of DNA evidence is collected at the hospital after a rape and why?
3. Which counseling option is most popular with victims?
4. Were the PTSD (post-traumatic stress disorder) rates higher or lower in crime victims compared to those who had not experienced victimization?
5. When was the first crime victim compensation program made available in the United States and in what state?
6. What is restorative justice?

CRITICAL THINKING QUESTIONS

1. When someone is hospitalized because of a crime-related injury, does it matter to the victim or his/her family why he/she was injured or are all injuries the same regardless of what caused it? Explain your answer.

2. Why do you think there is such a backlog of rape kits? Is it a money question or is there some other cause?

3. Is the maximum amount available through state crime victim compensation programs for injuries or loss of wages for crime victims in the United States a realistic amount? What should it be? If the amount is raised, how would it be funded?

4. What kind of crimes is restorative justice best suited for in place of jail or prison time? Explain your answer.

ACTIVITIES

1. Choose a state and access the website for its compensation program. Look over its eligibility requirements and what it offers to victims. Consider the rules and regulations. Now redesign the program taking into account some of its limitations. How much additional funding will be necessary for your new plan if it expands the types of crimes that are covered or the monetary awards for each item? How will you fund this new plan?
2. Pretend you are a 911 dispatcher. You get a call that someone has been shot but the victim is still alive. At this point, you are unsure whether the location is a crime scene or the site of a suicide attempt. What are some of the crime scene protocols and concerns that the EMS personnel who respond to the call need to keep in mind? Make a list of do's and don'ts. What are some of the ways that EMS personnel can help or hinder future prosecution of the case if it is indeed a crime scene?
3. Make a list of three crimes you have studied in this textbook so far and line it up with the civil tort that a victim might pursue in a civil suit.

RESOURCES

International Association of Forensic Nurses
forensicnurses.org
Membership professional organization.

National Coalition Against Domestic Violence (NCADV)
ncadv.org
A membership organization concerned with domestic violence.

National Association of Crime Victim Compensation Boards
nacvcb.org
Membership organization of crime victim compensation boards.

National Center for PTSD
ptsd.va.gov
A research and education center related to PTSD and traumatic stress.

National Center for Victims of Crime
victimsofcrime.org
Membership and educational association with extensive information at its website.

The National Domestic Violence Hotline
1-800-799-7233 (SAFE)
www.ndvh.org
The website offers information. The hotline provides peer support and information about how to handle the situation and what options are available.

National Organization of Victim Assistance (NOVA)
trynova.org
Founded in 1976, this membership organization offers training for crime victim advocates and other service providers.

National Resource Center on Domestic Violence
nrcdv.org
Training and education center dedicated to ending domestic violence.

National Suicide Prevention Lifeline
suicidepreventionlifeline.org
800-273-8255
A 24/7 hotline throughout the United States. This network of 100+ local suicide prevention centers offers peer counseling and information. If the threat is immediate, call 911.

Joyful Heart Foundation
joyfulheartfoundation.org
This is a national educational and advocacy organization founded in 2004 by actress Mariska Hargitay, who plays Olivia Benson on the long-running hit TV series, *Law and Order: SVU (Special Victims Unit).* From their website: "The vision of the Joyful Heart Foundation is a world free of sexual assault, domestic violence, and child abuse."

Office on Violence Against Women
U.S. Department of Justice
justice.gov/ovw

Safe Horizons
Safehorizon.org
New York-based resource for domestic violence including referrals to shelters and counseling services. They cover a wide range of victim issues from sexual assault, domestic violence, and child abuse to human trafficking, stalking, and youth homelessness.

Stop the Bleed®
stopthebleed.org
A program of the American College of Surgeons to train civilians to be able to stop a bleed until medical or emergency service providers arrive.

Violence Policy Center
vpc.org
An educational organization especially concerned with gun violence.

Office for Victims of Crime (OVC)
"Help for Victims"
ovc.ojp.gov/help-for-victims/overview
At this page at this government agency, you will find links to toll-free hotlines for crime victims including a page for victims for terrorism and mass violence and links to elder fraud help.

CITED WORKS AND ADDITIONAL REFERENCES

Allen, Roy B. 1986, "Measuring the Severity of Physical Injury Among Assault and Homicide Victims." *Journal of Quantitative Criminology.* 2(2): 139-156.

Americans for Effective Law Enforcement, Inc., Victim Rights Center. "Memorandum of Law on Third Party Victims Rights Litigation." Frank Carrington, President. n.d. 25-page paper.

Andrews, Bernice, Chris R. Brewin, Suzanna Rose, and Marilyn Kirk. 2000. "Predicting PTSD Symptoms in Victims of Violent Crime: The Role of Shame, Anger, and Childhood Abuse." *Journal of Abnormal Psychology.* 109: 69-73.

Barkas, J.L. (a/k/a Jan Yager). September 10, 1978. "Let's Give Crimes' Victims Their Due." *Newsday.*

__________. Summer 1979. "What About the Victims." *Journal of Current Social Issues.* 2733.

Bell, Randall. 2021. *Post-Traumatic Thriving: The Art, Science, & Stories of Resilience.* Core IQ Press.

Bieler, Des. March 7, 2016. "Erin Andrews awarded $55 million in peephole lawsuit" *The Washington Post.*

Bowen, Alison. November 14, 2018. "She's Been Waiting 15 Months for Her Rape Kit to Be Processed. A New Proposal to Track Evidence Aims to Change That." *Chicago Tribune.* Posted online.

Brewin, Chris R., Bernice Andrews, and Suzanna Rose. April 2003. "Diagnostic Overlap Between Acute Stress Disorder and PTSD in Victims of Violent Crime." Brief report. *American Journal of Psychiatry.* 160: 783-785.

Burgess, Ann Wolbert. April 1975. "Family Reaction to Homicide." *American Journal of Orthopsychiatry.* 45: 391-398.

Calhoun, Lawrence G. and Richard G. Tedeschi. 2004. "The Foundation of Posttraumatic Growth: New Considerations." *Psychological Inquiry.* 15: 93-102.

Carrington, Frank. 1975. *The Victims.* New Rochelle, NY: Arlington House.

Cullen, Francis T. and Cheryl Lero Jonson. 2017. *Correctional Theory.* Second edition. Los Angeles: SAGE.

Danis, Fran S. April 2003. "The Criminalization of Domestic Violence: What Social Workers Need to Know." *Social Work.* 48(2): 237-246.

FEMA. U.S. Department of Homeland Security. "You Are The Help Until Help Arrives." Posted at https://community.fema.gov/until-help-arrives

Fenney, Alethia Z. 2012. "Navajo Peacemaking and Maori Restorative Justice: a Comparison of Process and Procedure." Thesis. Regis University.

Fisher, Ronald P., R. Edward Geiselman, and Michael Amador. 1989. "Field Test of the Cognitive Interview: Enhancing the Recollection of Actual Victims and Witnesses of Crime." *Journal of Applied Psychology.* 74(5): 722-727.

Fitch, Jay. August 31, 2005. "Response Times: Myths, Measurement and Management." *JEMS (Journal of Emergency Medical Services).* Posted online.

Fogel, Sarah. January 11, 2021. Phone interview with author.

Frankl, Viktor. 2006 (originally published in 1946). *Man's Search for Meaning.* Boston, MA: Beacon.

Gobert, James. May 1977. "Victim Precipitation." *Columbia Law Review.* 77(4): 511-553

Gordiles, Chloe. Winter 2019. "Victim Compensation Fundamentals: Kenneth Feinberg and Guidelines for Future Compensation Fund Czars." *The Review of Litigation.* University of Texas at Austin School of Law. 164-190.

Greenstone, James L. and Sharon C. Leviton. 1982. *Crisis Intervention: A Handbook for Interveners.* Dubuque, IA: Kendall/Hunt.

Gross, Karen. January 13, 2021. Zoom interview with author.

Hagerty, Barbara Bradley. July 22, 2019. "An Epidemic of Disbelief." *The Atlantic.* August 2019. Posted online.

Hanson, Rochelle F., Genelle K. Sawyer, Angela M. Begle, and Grace S. Hubel. April 2010. "The Impact of Crime Victimization on Quality of Life." *Journal of Traumatic Stress.* 23: 189-197.

Harrell, Erika and Elizabeth Davis. December 2020. Contacts between police and the public, 2019—statistical tables. Bureau of Justice Statistics, U.S. Department of Justice, Office of Justice Programs.

Joyce, Mary. January 13, 2021. Phone interview with author.

Kanin, Eugene J. February 1994. "False Rape Allegations." *Archives of Sexual Behavior.* 23: 81–92.

Karmen, Andrew. 2020. *Crime Victims: An Introduction to Victimology.* 10th edition. Boston, MA: Cengage.

Kessler, David. 2020. *Finding Meaning: The Sixth Stage of Grief.* New York: Scribner.

Kilpatrick, Dean G. and Ron Acierno. 2003. "Mental Health Needs of Crime Victims: Epidemiology and Outcomes." *Journal of Traumatic Stress.* 16: 119-132.

Kushner, Harold S. 2004 (originally published in 1981). *When Bad Things Happen to Good People.* New York: Anchor Press.

Lantry, Lauren. December 31, 2019. "Trump signs bill to help eliminate backlog in rape kit testing." Posted at https://abcnews.go.com/US/trump-signs-bill-eliminate-backlog-rape-kit-testing/story?id=67997113

Insurance Institute. 2019. "Facts + Statistics: Life Insurance."

Luber, Marilyn and Francine Shapiro. 2009. Interview with Francine Shapiro: Historical overview, present issues, and future directions of EMDR. *Journal of EMDR Practice and Research.* 3: 217-231.

Maercker, Andreas and Astrid Mehr. 2006. "What if Victims Read a Newspaper Report about Their Victimization? A Study on the Relationship to PTSD Symptoms in Crime Victims. *European Psychologist.* 11: 137-142.

McCart, Michael R., Daniel W. Smith, and Genelle K. Sawyer. April 2010. "Help Seeking Among Victims of Crime: A Review of the Empirical Literature." *Journal of Traumatic Stress.* 23:198-206.

Mead, Carrie. January 15, 2021. Phone interview with author.

Mendelssohn, B. 1937. "Method to be Used by Counsel for the Defence in the Researches Made into the Personality of the Criminal." *Revue de Droit Penal et de Criminologie.* Bruxelles.

Miller, Susan L. 2005. *Women as Offenders: The Paradox of Women's Violence in Relationships.*

Missouri Hospital Association. September 11, 2018. "Treatment of Crime Victims." Posted at https://web.mhanet.com/treatment-of-crimc-victims.aspx.

Morgan, Rachel E. and Jennifer L. Truman. September 2020. *Criminal Victimization, 2019.* Bureau of Justice Statistics, Office of Justice Programs, U.S. Department of Justice, Washington,D.C.

Mowell, Barry D. 2012. "Victim Rights and Restitution." In *The Social History of Crime and Punishment in America: An Encyclopedia.* Wilbur R. Miller (ed.). Thousand Oaks, CA: SAGE.

The National Crime Victim Bar Association. "Civil Justice for Crime Victims." 2-page brochure. Posted at the association's website, victimbar.org

National Institute of Mental Health. January 2020. "Coping with Traumatic Events." Posted at https://www.nimh.nih.gov/health/topics/coping-with-traumatic-events/index.shtml

__________. "Post-Traumatic Stress Disorder." n.d. Posted at https://www.nimh.nih.gov/health/topics/post-traumatic-stress-disorder-ptsd/index.shtml

Office for Victims of Crime (OVC), Initiatives for improving the mental health of traumatized crime victims. n.d. Archived at the ncjrs.gov website.

__________, "Mental Health Issues." April 2005. Posted at ncjrs.gov website.

__________. "Restitution." 1997-1998 Academy Text Supplement. Ch. 21-10.

P, Kim. Updated April 14, 2020. "Study: Average Police Response Time." Creditdonkey.com. Posted online.

Payne, Brian K. 2008. "Elder Physical Abuse and Failure to Report Cases: Similarities and Differences in Case Type and the Justice System's Response. *Crime & Delinquency.* 59: 697-717.

Price, Timothy G. and Rory M. O'Neill. February 25, 2019. "EMS, Crime Scene Responsibility." NCBL Bookshelf, a service of the National Library of Medicine, National Institutes of Health. Posted at https://www.ncbi.nlm.nih.gov/books/NBK499999/

RAINN. "What Is the Sexual Assault Forensic Exam?" Posted at https://www.rainn.org/articles/rape-kit

Roman, Carmen, Ph.D. January 15, 2021. Phone interview with author.

Rosenfeld, Richard. April 18, 2008. "Understanding Homicide and Aggravated Assault." For presentation at the conference on The Causes and Responses to Violence, Arizona State University. Uploaded on January 10, 2014 and posted to researchgate.com

Santo, Alysia. Data analysis by Michael Corey and graphics by Yolanda Martinez. Septembe 13, 2018. "Seven States Ban Victim Aid to People with Criminal Records." The Marshall Project. Posted at themarshallproject.org.

Schur, Edwin M. 1974. *Victimless Crimes: Two Sides of a Controversy.* NJ: Prentice Hall.

Seaman, Andrew M. July 19, 2017. "Be Prepared for Ambulance Wait Times." Reuters. Posted at https://www.reuters.com/article/us-health-emergency-response-times/be-prepared-for-ambulance-wait-times-idUSKBN1A42KQ#:~:text=On%20average%20in%20the%20U.S.,30%20minutes)%2C%20researchers%20found.

Shapland, Joanna and Matthew Hall. 2007. "What Do We Know About the Effects of Crime on Victims?" *International Review of Victimology.* 14: 175-217.

Sharma, B.R. December 2003. "Clinical Forensic Medicine—Management of Crime Victims from Trauma to Trial." *Journal of Clinical Forensic Medicine.* 10(4): 267-273.

Shaw, Clifford and H. McKay. 1942. *Juvenile Delinquency and Urban Areas.* Chicago, IL: University of Chicago Press.

Shepherd, Jonathan. November 26, 1988. "Supporting Victims of Violent Crime." *BMJ: British Medical Journal.* 297: 1353.

Skogan, Wesley G. February 1976. "Citizen Reporting of Crime: Some National Panel Data." *Criminology.* 13: 535-549.

Slaikeu, Karl A. 1984. *Crisis Intervention: A Handbook for Practice and Research.* Boston: Allyn and Bacon.

State of Colorado. "Victim Compensation Application." Posted at https://cdpsdocs.state.co.us/ovp/Vic_Comp/VC_English_Application_2_18_16.pdf

Storm, Jennifer. 2020, updated edition. *Blackout Girl.* Center City, MN: Hazelden Publishing.

Tedeschi, Richard G. and Lawrence G. Calhoun. 1996. "The Posttraumatic Growth Inventory: Measuring the Positive Legacy of Trauma." *Journal of Traumatic Stress.* 9: 455-471.

Tolsma, Jochem and Joris Blaauw. 2012. "When Do People Report Crime to the Police?" Results from a factorial survey design in the Netherlands, 2010. *Journal of Experimental Criminology*. 8: 117-134.

Turvey, Brent E. 2014. *Forensic Victimology*. Second edition. Waltham, MA: Academic Press, Elsevier.

Victim Rights Law Center. March 30, 2019. *Mandatory Reporting of Non-Accidental Injuries: A State-by-State Guide*. Updated May 2014. 51 pages. Posted online. https://www.victimrights.org/

Vincent, Lynn. "False Accusations of Rape, Ruined Lives." *World Magazine*. Posted online at https://world.wng.org/2019/03/false_convictions_ruined_lives

Von Hentig, Hans. 1948. *The Criminal and His Victim*. New Haven, CT: Yale University Press.

Wemmers, Jo-Anne. May 19, 2008 (published online). "Victim Participation and Therapeutic Jurisprudence." *Victims and Offenders*. 3(2-3): 165-191.

Wemmers, Jo-Anne and Katie Cyr. "Victims' Perspectives on Restorative Justice: How Much Involvement Are Victims Looking For?" *International Review of Victimology*. 11(2-3): 259–274.

Wilkinson, Richard G., Ichiro Kawachi, and Bruce P. Kennedy. 1998. "Mortality, the Social Environment, Crime and Violence." *Sociology of Health & Illness*. 20(5): 578-597.

Wolfgang, Martin F. May-June 1957. "Victim Precipitated Criminal Homicide." *Journal of Criminal Law and Criminology & Police Science*. 48: 1-11.

Workman, Kim. Excerpt from *Journey Towards Justice*. Posted at https://e-tangata.co.nz/reflections/restorative-justice-in-a-maori-community/

Workman, Kim. November 18, 2018. Restorative justice in a Maori community. E-Tangata. Posted at e-tangata.co.nz

Yager, Jan. 2021. *Help Yourself Now*. New York: Allworth Press, an imprint of Skyhorse Publishing.

Zehr, Howard. 2015. *The Little Book of Restorative Justice*. Revised and updated. New York: Good Books, an imprint of Skyhorse.

Videos and TED Talks

Office of Victims of Crime, U.S. Department of Justice. "If You're a Victim of Crime, Help is Available." 2:29 minutes. Posted at https://ovc.ojp.gov/help-for-victims/overview

__________. March 30, 2016. "What is the Crime Victims Fund?" 2:33 minutes Short video explaining the federal legislation known as VOCA which created a fund based on federal crime-related to fund state and nonprofit crime victim help initiatives. Posted at https://www.youtube.com/watch?v=0sWgbUigNIE

Raymond, Michelle. "The Invisible Victims of Crime." TEDx Royal Tunbridge Wells talk. April 8, 2019. 8:38 minutes. Posted at https://www.youtube.com/watch?v=HEFezmxePAk

Michelle discusses how she was impacted when her husband was accused of a crime.

CHAPTER **SEVEN**

Primary and Secondary Victims of Homicide

Learning Objectives

After you finish reading this chapter, you should be able to:

1. Define a primary or direct and a secondary or co-victim of homicide.
2. Understand what a clearance rate is and how it pertains to trends in homicide over the last few decades.
3. Identify and define the various types of homicide and degrees of murder, and compare them to manslaughter.
4. Summarize what we know about the average homicide victim today including the most typical relationship between the victim and the offender.
5. Compare and contrast homicide rates in major cities and countries throughout the United States and around the world.
6. Describe the dynamics to such homicide situations as murder-suicide, mass murder, serial murder, intimate partner homicide, robbery-homicide, rape-homicide, burglar surprise killings, child killings, and capital punishment.
7. Review the controversy over the theory of victim-precipitated homicide.
8. Explain and describe the various needs of secondary victims of homicide.
9. Describe the six stages of grief and how it applies to secondary victims of homicide.
10. Define Prolonged Grief Disorder (PGD) and why it is especially dangerous if untreated.
11. Discuss the challenges faced by an overlooked secondary victim of homicide, namely, the family of the murderer.

PRIMARY HOMICIDE VICTIMS

Homicide victims are the first victims explored in the chapters in *Essentials of Victimology* discussing victimizations (Chapters 7-15). It is one of the worst and most violent crimes. Yet statistically, it is the least frequently committed type of violent crime. Compare the number of reported homicides in 2019 in the United States—16,425—to the number of reported rapes—131,959—and the relative scale becomes apparent. There are even more reported victims of robbery—261,241—and far more reported aggravated assaults—821,182. (FBI, *2019 Crime in the United States*) However, most will agree that homicide is the ultimate crime because it results in the death of the victim.

Still, to start understanding the scope and magnitude of this crime, we need to set aside the statistics and recognize homicide victims as individuals with hopes and dreams: children, teenagers, and adult men and women whose lives were cut short and whose family and friends were left bereft.

Every killing represents a life that has ended prematurely and violently. It is untimely death, not death due to "natural causes," fatal disease, pandemic, or unavoidable accident, but death because someone or several people killed somebody.

Contributed photo of firefighter Stephen Siller, killed in the World Trade Center Terrorist attacks in Manhattan, September 11, 2001.

Mary Siller-Scullin, older sister of Stephen Siller, the firefighter whose courage in going back to the World Trade Center buildings at the time of the 9/11 (September 11, 2001) tragedy is commemorated every year with the Tunnel2Towers run, commented on this. Pointing out why dealing with murder or intentional death because of criminal actions including terrorism is such a major grief, Mary said in a phone interview with this author: "The sudden impact of a sudden traumatic event makes the grief to me very pronounced. You really have no time to prepare for the loss, and then you have to slowly take in what has happened, and learn how to integrate that into your being." (Siller-Scullin, 2021)

Other horrific crimes involving personal violence such as rape or robbery at gunpoint are traumatic but the victims survive. Although dealing with the trauma may take a lifetime for some and for others it means coping with **Post-Traumatic Stress Disorder (PTSD)**, for most it is a surmountable trauma. Homicide victims, unfortunately, are denied that opportunity. Their life is over, snuffed out by someone else. Their families and friends are left behind to pick up the pieces from this greatest of violent crime victimizations. Homicide victims are usually in their prime or younger, according to the statistics related to homicide. As Mary Siller-Scullin, mentioned above, explains, "It's the age of the person. It's not their time, so to speak. They leave parents and older siblings left behind."

This first part of this chapter explores what we currently know about homicide and murder victims. Who are typical homicide or murder victims? Although the focus will be on homicide and murder victims in the United States, the chapter will also consider homicide and murder victims internationally, including trends that transcend borders. What are the controversies surrounding homicide and murder victims, especially the concept of victim-precipitation that still persists, that victimologists address?

The second part of this chapter will discuss those who are known as **co-victims** or **secondary victims of homicide:** the family and friends of the deceased and even their co-workers and neighbors. These secondary victims are also sometimes referred to as **homicide survivors**.

Here are sketches about real-life murder victims:

- Terrell Henry, a 22-year-old student at John Jay College of Criminal Justice, was fatally shot, allegedly by a gang member who mistook him for a rival gang member. Terrell, who was completely innocent and had no gang affiliations, was in his last year at John Jay and planned to join law enforcement as an FBI agent. Terrell had just left a party with his twin brother and a childhood friend and was coming out of a deli in the Brownsville section of Brooklyn, New York, when the attack took place. (Various reports including Paul Frangipane, August 22, 2017; NY1 News, August 13, 2016; CBSNew York, August 12, 2016)
- In Los Angeles, a man in his 20s was shot in the chest outside a popular taco stand. He died at the hospital. The suspect fled the scene. So far there was no known motive. (CBS Los Angeles, with the victims's other 2020)
- A 15-year-old boy used a golf club to hit an 18-year-old female bicyclist and then stole her bicycle. When the boy's mother asked him where he got the bicycle, he lied and said that he had bought it for $45. The victim died several days later from her injuries. The remorseful teen was arrested, found guilty, and sentenced to 6 to 18 months in jail, with weekends at home. (Interview by the author with the victim's mother, 1976; Barkas, 1978)
- Eight years ago, a 33-year-old African-American husband and father went to a bar to relax and hang out with a friend. A disagreement ensued, but observers thought the two seemed to resolve matters. However, upon leaving the bar, the father was shot and killed by a second individual. It turned out that the victim's friend had called the shooter and told him to take care of things when the victim left the bar. The friend and his accomplice both got prison time. The victim left behind a 12-year-old son and a widow. (Phone interview with the author, with the victim's mother 2020)
- In Detroit, a 29-year-old mother was violently assaulted and allegedly killed by her boyfriend, who was arrested four days later. (Fox 2 Detroit. 2020)
- Seventeen-year-old Linda (not her real name) was killed by her 24-year-old boyfriend, the father of their young child. They had an abusive relationship and right before the stabbing murder, she had informed her boyfriend that she was ending their relationship. (Phone interview with Melissa Hoppmeyer, Chief Prosecutor of the Family Violence Unit, Prince George's County, Maryland, 2021)
- A 33-year-old San Diego woman was found guilty of second-degree murder, gross vehicular manslaughter while intoxicated, hit-and-run causing death, and driving under the influence. She had run over and killed her 25-year-old friend and co-worker who had tried to get her to stop driving drunk by holding on to the driver's car door. Still holding on to the car, her friend fell onto the street; he was then run over as the driver did not stop driving. (City News Service, *San Diego Union-Tribune*, 2020)

HOMICIDE: AN OVERVIEW

The above true-life thumbnail sketches of murder victims, based on interviews or newspaper, TV, and online reports, are just a few of the sizable number of victims of homicide and murder in any given year. In just the United States in 2019 that number was 16,425, according to the FBI (FBI, *2019 Crime in the United States*, "Murder"). That number was up 0.3 percent from 2018 and 34 percent from 2015.

The definition of murder and nonnegligent manslaughter by the FBI's **Uniform Crime Report (UCR)** Program is "the willful (nonnegligent) killing of one human being by another." (FBI, *2019 Crime in the United States*, Released Fall 2020)

However, homicide is not just an American concern. The United Nations Office on Drugs and Crime (UNODC) Global Study on Homicide 2019 shared its finding that in 2017, around the world, there were an estimated 464,000 victims of homicide. (UNODC, 2019) As you will see in this chapter, which cities and countries have fewer or greater numbers of murder victims varies widely. Unfortunately, the United States has the dubious distinction of having the highest homicide rate compared with similar westernized countries like Australia, the United Kingdom, Norway, or France, to name just a few.

In the United States, which unfortunately has become the homicide capital of the so-called Westernized world, we have become far too accepting of these astronomical homicide statistics. That we have reduced the number of homicides in the United States from a higher 21,606 in 1995 to a comparatively lower 16,425 in 2019 is certainly an improvement. But that drop in the rate is not a reason to become complacent about murder in America. (FBI, *Crime in the United States, 1996*; FBI *2019 Crime in the United States*, 2020). Indeed, the New York Police Department (NYPD) announced in April 2021 that there had been a year to date increase in homicides in New York City of 17.9% (132 murders in April 2021 compared to 112 in April 2020 or, comparing April 2021 to the previous year, 44 versus 38 murders, respectively. (NYPD, 2021) Whether the murder rate is going up or down, however, there are still simply too many homicides in a country revered for achievements in technology, cinema, science, medicine, and other fields. People seek to emigrate here because it is supposedly safer than from some of the more violent countries they are fleeing from as a place to raise their families and make their living.

Why do so many people accept that the America that is so innovative that it gave us the iPhone and the internet could be the same country that puts up with a homicide rate of 5.3 per 100,000? That rate is disproportionately high when it is compared with the dramatically lower homicide rate of 1.2 in the United Kingdom, 1 per 100,000 in Germany, or .06 in Japan. ("Murder Rate by Country," World Atlas, 2020, based on the UNODC figures and (FBI, *2019 Crime in the United States*.) Of course the U.S. rate is still a lot lower than these countries with dramatically higher murder rates: El Salvador (61.8 per 100,000), Jamaica (57 per 100,000) and Honduras (41.7 per 100,000). (World Atlas, 2020; Kuang Keng Kuek Ser, 2016)

It is useful to note that the homicide rate of 5 per 100,000 in the United States is only an average. The FBI Uniform Crime Reporting System cautions against using their annual data to rank particular towns or cities since how the information is collected can vary among the more than 18,000 police precincts reporting their data. (FBI, *2019 Crime in the United States*) But if we just look at one city with a high crime rate, Baltimore, Maryland, in 2019 it had 348 homicides. With an estimated population of 593,490, that is a homicide rate of 57 per 100,000 persons, a far cry from the average 5 per 100,000 for the country as a whole. (Prudente, 2020; Knezevich, 2020)

Consider that Chicago hit the dubious milestone of 700 homicides in just one year by late November 2020. (NBC Chicago, 2020) In "Homicide Mortality by State," the CDC (Centers for Disease Control) through the NCHS (National Center for Health Statistics) ranks all the states by their murder rate per 100,000. This information was last reviewed on February 16, 2021 and here are the two states with the least number of murders —Maine, with a rate of 1.8 per 100,000 and Idaho, with a rate of 1.7 per 100,000, although Vermont would have a very low rate as well since there were 11 murders but no rate was indicated. Compare those low rates to the states with the highest murder rates per 100,000: Alabama (12.8), Louisiana (14.7), Missouri (10.8), Mississippi (15.4), New Mexico (11.8), and South Carolina (11). (CDC/NCHS, 2021)

Table 7.1 highlights the homicide rates in selected countries around the world based on the UNODC (United Nations Office on Drugs and Crime) in 2014, in Europe and Asia as well as Latin and South America. As initially mentioned above, note the dramatic differences in homicide rates, by country. You will find the rate, number of murder victims (in parentheses), and the country's population so you can better interpret what that number of victims means.

TABLE 7.1. Homicide Rates by Selected Countries, 2014

Country	Rate per 100,00/Number	Population
United States	4.5 (14,249)	318.9 million
China	1 (13,410)	1.26 billion
France	1.2 (792)	66.03 million
United Kingdom	.9 (602)	64.1 million
Belize	34.4 (120)	331,900
El Salvador	62.2 (3,921)	6.34 million
Germany	.9 (716(	80.62 million
Honduras	84.6 (5,936)	8.098 million
Jamaica	44.9 (1,193)	2.7 million
Japan	.3 (395)	127.3 million
Norway	.6 (29)	5.084 million
The Netherlands	.7 (125)	16.8 million
South Korea	.7 (392)	50.22 million
United States/Virgin Islands	52.6 (56)	104.737
Venezuela	62 (19, 030)	30.41 million

Sources: United Nations Office on Drugs and Crime. 2014; OSAC (United States Department of State, Bureau of Diplomatic Security); Jamaica 2016 Crime & Safety Report; infoplease.com (world populations).

To help put the Table 7.1 homicide victim numbers by country in a clearer perspective, consider that the United States has over 300 million people and Japan has 127 million. If you multiply the number of homicide victims in Japan—395—by three, which would give you roughly the same population density as the United States, the outcome would be about 1,185 murder victims, controlling for population. Compare that number to the more than 14,000 homicide victims in the United States that year and you can see how disproportionate the American homicide rate is compared to Japan's.

Rates help measure homicide victimization but are much less tangible than looking at what the actual numbers represent. Yes, the United States was doing better in 2015 with 15,696 homicide victims compared to 24,700 in 1991, but can and should do much better still.

TABLE 7.2. Murder Victims in the United States, 1991-2020

Year	Murder Victims	Year	Murder Victims
1991	24,703	2006	17,309
1992	24,506	2007	17,128
1993	24,536	2008	16,465
1994	23,326	2009	15,399
1995	21,606	2010	14,772
1996	19.645	2011	14,661
1997	18.208	2012	14,858
1998	16,974	2013	14,319
1999	15,522	2014	14.164
2000	15,586	2015	15,883
2001	16,037	2016	17,413
2002	16,229	2017	17,294
2003	16,528	2018	14,123
2004	16,148	2019	16,425
2005	16,740	2020	20,000*
	(continued next column)	Total:	474,542

*This is an estimate based on the preliminary report that murder increased by 25% over 2020. Final statistics are being released in September 2021. (Asher, 2021)

Sources: Federal Bureau of Investigation (FBI), *Crime in the United States* (Murder from 1991 through 2010) Posted at https://ucr.fbi.gov/crime-in-the-u.s/2010/crime-in-the-u.s.-2010/tables/10tbl01.xls FBI, *2018 Crime in the United States*, posted at https://ucr.fbi.gov/crime-in-the-u.s/2018/crime-in-the-u.s.-2018/topic-pages/tables/table-1; FBI *2019 Crime in the United States;* Asher, 2021).

DEFINITIONS AND TYPES OF HOMICIDE AND MURDER

Homicide refers to the taking of someone's life. Those killings can be felonious (**criminal homicide**) or non-felonious. Non-felonious homicides are **excusable homicide** and **justifiable homicide**, as defined below.

Within the category of criminal homicide, there are four types of crimes: **first-degree murder, second-degree murder, felony murder**, and **manslaughter**. You will find a brief description of each of those crimes below.

Excusable Homicide

An example of an excusable homicide would be if someone driving within the speed limit hits a child that has suddenly run out in front of the car. If the driver hits and kills that child because he or she is unable to stop, that death would be an excusable homicide.

Here is another example: "Two children were being taught to swim by a swim instructor. One of the children had an asthma attack and needed his inhaler. The instructor told the other child to stay out of the pool even though she was a good swimmer. While the instructor was retrieving the inhaler, the girl got back in the pool and drowned." (Daigle and Muftic, 2016: 108-109).

Justifiable Homicide

Justifiable homicide cases can be quite controversial because what one person considers justifiable homicide another might consider murder. One case that comes to mind is the 2012 shooting of Treyvon Martin by George Zimmerman. Treyvon Martin, at the time of the shooting, was a teenager living in Florida on his way to visit his father who lived in a gated community. Zimmerman justified his shooting of Treyvon because he believed he was posing a risk to the neighborhood. The stand your ground law in Florida allegedly gave Zimmerman the right to defend himself (and his neighborhood) against Martin. In a controversial decision, Zimmerman was acquitted of the charge of second-degree murder, although some still considered him guilty in the court of public opinion. It should also be mentioned that charges in cases such as this can vary by state. Florida, where Martin's death occurred, has a stand your ground law; Colorado, by contrast, has a duty to retreat requirement. (Florida abolished the duty to retreat in 2005.) (Bell, 2015) Depending on the state, justifiable homicide could also refer to self-defense. (Bell, 2015) "The most fundamental component required for using deadly force in self-defense is proportionality," writes Florida attorney Pamela Cole Bell. (Bell, 2015:391) She continues, "A person must be confronted with deadly force before using deadly force."

Was the action justified? In the UCR (Uniform Crime Report) Program, there are just two situations that are considered justifiable homicide. Those situations are

- The killing of a felon by a peace officer in the line of duty.
- The killing of a felon, during the commission of a felony, by a private citizen.

(FBI, *Crime in the United States, 2013*)

Criminal Homicide

If a homicide is neither justified nor excused, it is considered a **criminal homicide**. The legal definition of criminal homicide is to intentionally, knowingly, recklessly or with criminal negligence cause someone else's death. Within the category of criminal homicide are four types of crimes: first-degree murder, second-degree murder, felony-murder, and manslaughter.

First-Degree Murder

In most states, in order for a criminal homicide to be considered first-degree murder, there has to be premeditation. In Colorado, it is after deliberation.

First-degree murder is the only type of murder for which a sentence of **capital punishment** or the **death penalty** may be imposed in those 27 states that still have the death penalty. An example of a first-degree murder conviction was the decision in the case of a 47-year-old white man who in 2012 shot a 17-year-old Black teenager, Jordan Davis, in a dispute over loud music outside a store, by firing into the car Jordan was in with three friends. Since prosecutors did not seek the death penalty, the perpetrator's mandatory sentence was life without parole. He appealed his sentence, claiming he thought Jordan had a gun, so his actions were self-defense. That appeal was denied in November 2016. (Saunders, News Service of Florida, 2016)

Second-Degree Murder

If there is no premeditation or deliberation, but there is malice, then it is considered **second-degree murder**. In Raleigh, North Carolina, in February 2014, a woman named Amanda was found guilty of second-degree murder in the killing, aided by her husband, in July 2011 of 27-year-old Laura Ackerson. The murder was the result of a custody dispute over Amanda's husband's two oldest children. Her husband was convicted the previously year in the murder and was serving a life sentence. Amanda received a sentence of 13 to 16-and-a-half years in prison. (ABC11.com, 2014)

Felony Murder

When someone is unintentionally killed during the commission of another felony that is considered **felony murder**.

There are two types of felony murder. The first is holding someone responsible for felony murder if he/she kills someone when he/she is committing another crime, such as rape, robbery, or burglary.

The second type of felony murder is especially controversial. This type of felony murder holds an accomplice accountable for murder if a murder occurred during a rape, robbery, or burglary even though the accomplice had nothing to do with the actual murder. Parliament ended it in the United Kingdom in 1957 even though the doctrine has been tracked to the felony murder rule in English common law. (Prabhu, 2019: 444) Canada and India, as well as the states of Hawaii and Kentucky, have also ended it. (VanSickle, 2018)

There are distinct benefits to the criminal justice system of the felony murder doctrine. Since someone who drove the car in a hold-up where someone was killed can be charged with felony murder, which could carry a very stiff prison sentence, offering the accomplice a plea deal or even immunity from prosecution provides the prosecution with a powerful bargaining chip to get the eyewitness testimony that could help convict the actual killer.

But it can also lead to controversial and questionable situations like the one highlighted in the *New York Times* article, "Serving Life for Providing Car to Killers" by Adam Liptak. The article describes how in 2004, 20-year-old Ryan Holle lent his car to a friend. His friend, along with three of his friends, then used the car to drive to the Pensacola, Florida home of a marijuana dealer. The burglary became violent when one of the burglars killed the dealer's 18-year-old daughter by beating her over the head with a shotgun.

When it came to trying the case, it was considered irrelevant that Ryan was a mile and a half away when the burglary and the murder were committed. He was offered a plea of 10 years but chose to go to trial instead. The outcome of going to trial was a lot worse for Ryan than accepting the plea would have been because he admitted to knowing that his car would be used in a burglary. Even though he was not present when the crime occurred, he was found guilty of felony murder and sentenced to life without parole.

In Liptak's article, Terry Snyder, the father of the victim, is quoted as saying that he finds nothing wrong with Ryan's felony murder conviction. "It never would have happened unless Ryan Holle had lent the car,'" Snyder is quoted as saying. "It was as good as if he was there." (Liptak, 2007.)

Here is an update on Ryan's felony murder case: Governor Rick Scott commuted Ryan's sentence from life without parole to 25 years. At this time, he is incarcerated at a minimum-security facility in Florida convicted of first-degree murder, armed burglary, and armed robbery. His release date is tentatively scheduled for June 2024. (Offender search, Florida Department of Corrections)

In Abbie VanSickle's article, "If He Didn't Kill Anyone, Why Is It Murder?" another of many controversial examples of felony murder is cited. In 2012 in Indiana, four young men broke into a home to burglarize it. The homeowner, who was asleep upstairs, awoke and fatally shot and killed one of the four burglars. Under the felony murder rule, the remaining three defendants were convicted of first-degree murder. Although three of the four convictions were later overturned by the State Supreme Court, the felony murder rule was not eliminated. (VanSickle, 2018)

Manslaughter

Compared to murder, there is less responsibility for killing someone when it is considered manslaughter, but it is still a crime. In manslaughter, someone dies but there was no intent to kill that person. A true-life example of manslaughter is the conviction of a 27-year-old Florida woman who was sentenced to 14 years in prison for the death of a 32-year-old man. She had supplied that man with the drugs that led to his fatal overdose. At the joint press conference hosted by Sheriff Tommy Forst and State Attorney Larry Basford, Sheriff Ford was quoted as saying, "This is a warning to those who are selling drugs in Bay County. If you provide drugs to an individual who passes away, then both the Bay County Sheriff's Office [and] our local police departments are going to come after you and try to put a case together for manslaughter.'" The maximum sentence the woman who supplied the methamphetamine to the victim ("'as he was in an overdose state' from taking heroin and fentanyl") could have received was 15 years. An additional detail related to this case that the *New Herald* reporter Nathan Cobb adds is that "she also prevented the man's brother from calling 911, which potentially cost Peters [the victim] his life." (Cobb, 2021)

Involuntary or Vehicular Manslaughter

Within the category of manslaughter is **vehicular manslaughter**, or **vehicular homicide**, which is the charge if a driver drives drunk, on drugs, or recklessly, resulting in someone's death. According to the Legal Information Institute, posted by Cornell Law School, vehicular homicide is defined as: "A crime in which the defendant's unlawful or negligent operation of a motor vehicle results in the death of another person. Also called automobile homicide and vehicular manslaughter. Such laws vary by jurisdiction, but vehicular homicide is generally easier to prove than manslaughter because it requires an even less culpable ***mens rea***." The term *mens rea* refers to criminal intent with its literal meaning "guilty mind."

In some states, within the category of criminal homicide, it is possible to be convicted of vehicular homicide, which includes causing the death of another while driving a car in a grossly negligent or reckless manner. For example, in the state of Tennessee, vehicular homicide is considered a Class B felony which can result in a sentence of not less than 8 years or more than 30 and a fine of not more than $25,000. (MADD, Mothers Against Drunk Driving)

Aaron was an 18-year-old in Massachusetts when he made history in 2012 by becoming the first to be convicted of motor vehicle homicide by texting. After pleading not-guilty, he was convicted and received a sentence of 2 years in prison and revocation of his driver's license for 15 years. The circumstances leading to this outcome occurred during the previous year when Aaron had been in a head on collision with Donald Bowley, a 55-year-old father of three. Although Aaron denied texting while driving, according to the police, his phone showed that he had sent a text at 2:34 PM, got a response at 2:35 PM, and the accident occurred at 2:36 PM. (Linsey Davis, June 6, 2012))

Here are just a few additional examples of involuntary or vehicular manslaughter.

- On December 20, 2016, a 32-year-old Baltimore man was found guilty of involuntary manslaughter for leaving his 2-1/2-year-old daughter in a hot car for 16 hours during the previous summer, resulting in her death. He was acquitted of the more serious charges of second-degree depraved-heart murder and first-degree child abuse resulting in several physical injuries with death. The incident occurred on June 21, 2015 after the toddler's father returned home from celebrating Father's Day and drinking with a relative. He parked the car, went into the house, and slept until 4 P.M that day before his daughter's body was discovered. The temperature had reached 89 degrees that day. (Fenton, 2016)
- A Kansas City sixteen-year-old was charged with second-degree involuntary manslaughter, third degree assault, and texting while driving. She was allegedly texting on her smartphone when she lost control of her car and hit and killed Loretta J. Larimer, who was 72 at the time of the crash in September of 2011. If found guilty of the charges, the driver faced four years in state prison on the manslaughter charge, a year in jail on the assault charge, and a $200 fine on the texting while driving charge.

Russell L. Weaver and Steven I. Friedland cite four dramatic examples of the outcome of texting while driving in their article "Driving While 'Intexticated': Texting, Driving, and Punishment," published in the *Texas Tech Law Review* in 2014. The first mentions that a man in "Colorado who was engaged in text messaging died in a crash mid-sentence." The authors plead in their article that serious sanctions or punishments for texting and driving need to be imposed to act as a deterrent in much the same way that the sanctions associated with drinking and driving have helped to reduce drunk driving injuries and deaths. (Weaver and Friedland, 2014:110)

Going back to the previous Kansas city example, although she was only sixteen, Rachel was to be tried as an adult. (KCTV, "Teen charged with manslaughter in texting while driving case.") Personal injury lawyer Ray Hodge updated about the case: Rachel got a plea deal that sentenced her to 48 hours in jail and 72 hours on house arrest as well as probation for five years, serving 300 hours of public service or employment, and losing her license until she graduated from high school. Rachel was indeed fortunate that the children of the victim of that fatal crash agreed to the plea deal. (Ray Hodge, "City Teen Served Time for Texting While Driving;" Gaug, 2012)

Photo of the victims of the vehicle manslaughter case that claimed 27 lives.

Included above are images of the 27 victims of the deadliest drunk driving vehicle manslaughter case in U.S. history that took place on May 14, 1988. The victims were on their way to their homes in Kentucky from a church-sponsored trip to an amusement part in Mason, Ohio, just three hours away. The wrong way driver was a repeat drunk driver offender. He was convicted and served 10 years and 11 months in prison. (Keneally, 2018) Karolyn Nunnallee lost her daughter Patty in that bus crash. A former MADD National President, she has been working to put an end to the crime that caused her young daughter's life; it is an enduring quest for her. (Witty, 2020)

THE MAGNITUDE OF THE HOMICIDE PROBLEM

In the United States, some cities, like Chicago, New Orleans, or Detroit, have developed the dubious reputation of having much higher homicide rates than the rest of the country. By December 2020, 753 children, teens, and adults had been killed in Chicago during that year.

Police at crime scene. Image provided by LightField Studios/Shutterstock.

By late November 2020, the Los Angeles Police Department reported 300 murders, the highest number of homicides in a decade. (Selva and Silverman, November 23, 2020).

Homicide rates vary from city to city, from state to state, and even from country to country. As you saw from Table 7.1, there are dramatic differences among cities and countries around the world in the homicide rate per 100,000 and in the numbers who are killed.

Compared with other Westernized countries, a disproportionate number of Americans die from violence each year. Covering one year until March 2019 (although the *exact* dates do not match up for the two countries), just over 671 individuals were killed in the United Kingdom (England, Scotland, Wales, and Northern Ireland)—with a population of 64.1 million—compared to the 16,425 killed in the United States—with a population of 328.2 million in 2019. Since the United States has a population that is approximately five times larger than the United Kingdom, in order to arrive at a comparative statistic, multiplying the 671 U.K. murder victims by five would mean approximately 3,355 homicide victims, allowing for the population difference, which is still significantly fewer than the 16,425 murders that the United States actually had that year. (Office for National Statistics, 2020; FBI, *2019 Crime in the United States*, 2020)

THE RELATIONSHIP BETWEEN THE VICTIM AND THE MURDERER

The relationship between the victim and the offender is one of the areas of investigation that victimologists are especially interested in. That information can hopefully help us to understand the reason behind each murder where the circumstances behind the crime are known. Comprehending why a particular homicide occurred not only has potential legal implications in determining how the killer will be charged or if the crime might even be considered an excusable or a justifiable homicide, situations previously define in this chapter. Gaining a greater understanding into each homicide, however, might also be beneficial with one of the goals of those in law enforcement, criminology, and victimology, namely the reduction of homicide to the lowest possible levels. For starters, we must find a way to dramatically reduce the number of homicide victims in the United States, so we can forego the dubious distinction of having the highest homicide rate of all Westernized countries.

As we said earlier, murder has one of the highest reporting rates of all crimes, besides motor vehicle thefts. Table 7.3, "Relationship of Victim to Murderer in 2019," identifies the **victim-offender relationships** of the 13,927 reported murders in 2019. (Note that this number of murders is somewhat different from the totals in other parts of the FBI UCR. Unfortunately there is no explanation for those differences. It is being pointed out, however, so you do not assume there is a mistake in this total number.)

Please note the largest number of relationships unfortunately falls into the "unknown" (meaning unknown relationship) category (6,808). The 1,372 that are attributed to strangers may look exceedingly high since other relationships, such as friend (345) or employee (9), seem quite low. But look at the number of victims and offenders who were acquaintances—2,778, almost twice the number who were strangers. If you add up the number of victim and offenders who knew each other, the numbers tell a different story: family members, friends, boyfriend or girlfriend, acquaintances including neighbors, employee, or employer (totaling 5,747), strangers (1,372) and unknown relationship (6,808).

It is tempting to suggest that being killed by a stranger is much less likely than being killed by someone known to the victim (5,747 known to the victim versus 1,372 who are strangers). But you have to factor in that it is more than likely that a preponderance of those victim-offender murders with an unknown relationship (6,808) were actually strangers because those are the harder murders to solve. Those are also, obviously, the murders with the least amount of information known including even the relationship between the victim and the murderer.

TABLE 7.3. Relationship of Victim to Murderer in 2019
Total number of murder victims in the United States—13,927

Husband	Wife	Mother	Father	Son	Daughter	Brother	Sister	Other Family	Acquaintance
85	482	166	178	259	171	115	27	327	2,778
Friend	**Boyfriend**	**Girlfriend**	**Neighbor**	**Employee**	**Employer**	**Stranger**	**Unknown**		
345	187	505	100	9	13	1,372	6,808		

Source: FBI, *2019 Crime in the United States*, Expanded Homicide Data, Table 10, "Murder Circumstances by Relationship, 2019."

Certain questions need to be asked and answered when the police, detective, or the forensic investigators arrive at a scene since homicide and murder is sometimes not that easy a crime to figure out. Who was responsible for the blows that started the fight that led to the fatal punch? The victim or the killer? Was it self-defense, an accident, an intentional or an unintentional killing? Was the crime caused in the heat of the moment or premeditated? Were the victim and perpetrator strangers, acquaintances, family members, friends, former friends, or is their relationship unknown?

ADDITIONAL FACTS ABOUT MURDER VICTIMS

In the United States, as the statistics in Tables 7.3 and 7.4 demonstrate for the years 2018 and 2019, out of the 14,123 reported murders you were more likely to get killed if you were male than if you were female (10.914 males versus 3,180 females). You were also more likely to be killed by an acquaintance (2,692) or a family member (1,869) with the third category by a stranger (1,392). There is a category that could throw all those statements aside if the actual victim-offender relationship behind the 6,808 murders noted in Table 7.3 that are classified as having an "unknown" victim-offender relationship get solved. Also, if you add friends to the acquaintance category, as some crime data does, the number of acquaintances and friends that were murder victims in 2018 increases to 3,067. If you add the neighbors who killed their neighbor (104), that number gets even high (3,171). Based on these Supplementary Homicide Reports of the UCR, workplace violence is underrepresented in victim-offender relationships with nine employers and 18 employees listed in the victim-offender relationship table.

More Blacks or African Americans were murdered in 2018 (7,407) compared to whites (6,088) and if you consider that Blacks in 2018 made up only 12.1 percent of the population in the United States, you can recognize that Blacks were disproportionately killed. The FBI puts ethnicity into a separate category. More non-Hispanics or non-Latinos (9,066) were killed in 2018 compared to Hispanics or Latinos (2,173) although the ethnicity of 1,840 was unknown. The estimated percentage of Hispanics or Latinos in the United States in 2018 was 18.1 percent.

TABLE 7.4. Murder Victim Information by Age, Sex, and Ethnicity for 2018
Total number of murder victims: 14,123

Sex:	
Male:	10,914
Female:	3,180
Unknown:	29
Race:	
White:	6,088
Black/African American:	7,407
Other:	395

TABLE 7.4. Murder Victim Information by Age, Sex, and Ethnicity for 2018 (continued)

Unknown: 233
Ethnicity:
Hispanic or Latino: 2,173
Not Hispanic or Latino: 9,066
Unknown: 1,840
Age:
Under 18: 2,819
18 and over: 12,855
Unknown: 142

Source: FBI, 2018 Uniform Crime Reports, Tables 1-13.

TABLE 7.5. Type of Weapon Used in Murders in 2018 in the United States

Weapon	Percentage
Firearms	72.7%
Knives or cutting instruments	10.7%
Unknown weapons	11.8%
Personal weapons (hands, fists, feet)	4.8%

Source: FBI, *2018 Crime in the United States*, Table 7

Table 7.6 provides more details on the weapons used.

TABLE 7.6. Details on Weapons Used in Murders in the United States 2018
Total number of victims: 14,123

Weapons Used	Number of Weapons
Firearms	10,263
Knives, etc.	1,515
Blunt objects	443
Personal (Feet/Fist/Hands)	672
Poison	5
Explosives	4

TABLE 7.6. (continued)

Weapons Used	Number of Weapons
Fire	72
Drugs	78
Strangulation	70
Asphyxiation	90
Other Weapons or Not Stated	909

Source: FBI, *2018 Crime in the United States.*

Where Do Most Murders Occur?

Intimate partner homicide tends to occur at home, but in rarer instances it can also occur elsewhere, such as when a victim who was trying to get away is tracked down to his or her job by the perpetrator. Intimate partner homicide is not just an American problem. The World Health Organization estimates that one out of seven murders around the world is caused by domestic violence. Females are six times as likely to be the victim of intimate partner homicide as males. When the female is the killer, the homicide is often related to the intimate partner's inflicting prior abuse. But the abused spouse's actions are subject to scrutiny according to strict guidelines in order for the killing to be ruled as self-defense and justified rather than as a crime.

Based on what we know about the crime victim-offender relationship for solved murders, being killed by a stranger is less likely than being slain by someone known to the victim. During 2013, for example, a whopping 45 percent of all solved murders were committed by someone that the victim was acquainted with or by a former friend. Families and educators must get the word out about this because we are teaching children, teens, and even adults the wrong thing by emphasizing that they should only be afraid of strangers. If acquaintances, former friends, and even family members are more likely to be killers, it is important to teach everyone about the warning signs that someone is going to hurt them. They also need to be educated about how to avoid putting themselves in harm's way, such as going to someone's apartment alone especially someone they just met.

In 2010, the Census of Fatal Occupational Injuries (CFOI) recorded 518 workplace homicides, or 11 percent of all fatal work injuries that occurred that year. Of those workplace homicides, 405 were the result of a shooting. You can see that these statistics are dramatically higher than the statistics compiled by the FBI based on crimes reported to the local police precincts with data shared with the government. (For 2014, only 27 work-related murders were recorded. It is possible the relationship for the other workplace murders were put into different categories such as acquaintance, friend, unknown, or, if it was a family-owned business, categorized by the family relationship.)

What occupations puts someone at greater risk of being killed than others? According to the article by Danielle Kurtzleben, "America's Most Violent Jobs, in 5 Charts," in 2013 of the 400 homicides at work that year, the 7 jobs with the highest murder numbers from

2011-2013, based on the Bureau of Labor Statistics, were, in descending order of number of murders:

- Police officers
- Retail sales workers
- Security guards
- Taxi drivers and chauffeurs
- Cashiers
- Restaurant employees (bartenders, waitresses, cooks)
- Food service managers.

Males were more likely to be killed at work than females: 81.9 percent males versus 19.1 percent females.

As will be discussed at greater length in Chapter 10, "Child Victims," young children, especially infants and those under the age of 5, are at risk for child homicide or **infanticide**. As you will see from Table 7.7, not all areas of the United States are equal when it comes to murder, with the South having a much higher percentage of murders in 2018 (46.2%) compared to the other regions with the Midwest (22%), followed by the West (19.9%) with the Northeast having the lowest rate (11.9%).

TABLE 7.7. Murder by Region in the United States in 2018

Region	Percent
South	46.2
Midwest	22.0
West	19.9
Northeast	11.9

Source: Table 3, By Region, FBI *2018 Crime in the United States.*

HOMICIDE SITUATIONS

Although all of the crimes listed below resulted in the victim's death, as well as the three additional special cases listed later on in this chapter, namely, murder-suicide, mass murder, or serial murder, each of these killings has a unique legal definition. How the killer, and possibly even the victim, is viewed may differ based on the type of homicide or murder it is deemed.

Single Victim/Single Offender Homicides

Single victim/single offender murders were the most common type of murder in 2018, according to the FBI statistics. Almost 50 percent (49.2%) or 6,951 murders were of a single victim by a single offender. (FBI 2018 Crime Reports, Table 4). The least common victim/offender situation was multiple victims and multiple offenders (294 murder victims or 2.1%). An example of this type of typical murder victim is Alfred K. who was killed in September 2010. According to the student interview with Alfred's mother, Gloria K., the police figured out that the shooter had an argument with his girlfriend because he wasn't allowed into a party. Alfred tried to break up the argument, which he did, but as Alfred was walking away, the shooter started spraying gun shots in random directions and one of the bullets hit Alfred and killed him. A month later, the shooter turned himself into the police.

Gloria said, "I got to speak with the shooter and asked him why and the shooter replied that it was a mistake and that he felt terrible for what he'd done, but that he doesn't ask for forgiveness. And I told him I forgive you anyway because this is how my new beginning without my only son begins."

Another example of a single victim/single offender homicide that is "ripped from the headlines." is the stabbing death of 58-year-old Raquel Spohn Wehber, a driver for a rideshare company, who was from Tijuana, Mexico. On July 6, 2021, Raquel was driving in San Diego's National City when a teenage passenger allegedly stabbed her to death. (NBC7 Staff, July 7, 2021)

Intimate Partner Homicide

In 16 percent of murder cases where the victim-offender relationship is known, intimate partner violence (IPV), what used to be called "wife beating," or partner conflict, is estimated to be the cause of the murder. Although largely a male offender/female victim situation, males are also the victim of this type of murder. As noted in the previous FBI chart, Table 7.3, in 2019, there were 482 female victims of murder by a spouse and 85 male victims. Also killed were 505 girlfriends and 187 boyfriends.

In 2013, according to research conducted by the Violence Policy Center, 1,600 women were murdered by men in just one year; a gun was the most common weapon. Nationwide, 94 percent were killed by someone they knew; 62 percent were wives or had another intimate connection to the killer. (Violence Policy Center, September 15, 2015)

In their influential article, "Homicide: A Leading Cause of Injury Deaths Among Pregnant and Postpartum Women in the United States, 1991-1999," researchers Jeani Change, Cynthia J. Berg, Linda E. Saltzman, and Joy Herndon discovered that "homicide is a leading cause of pregnancy associated injury deaths." (Chang, et al., 2005: 471)

Out of the 7,342 deaths that were reported to the PMSS (Pregnancy Mortality Surveillance System), all but 1,993 were not related to pregnancy-related causes. Of those 1,993, the second leading cause of pregnancy-related injury deaths was homicide (31%) or 617 of those women died from homicide during pregnancy. (The second leading cause of pregnancy-related injury deaths was car accidents (44.1%). (Chang, et al., 2005:472) Black women had a pregnancy-associated homicide ratio that was seven times higher than the ratio for white women, with the racial disparity the highest among women aged 25 to 29 years of age. (Chang, et al., 2005: 472).

Robbery-Homicide

- Sixty-nine-year-old store owner Mark Vuono was shot and killed during a robbery at his jewelry store in Stamford, Connecticut over the weekend in late March 2020. A customer arrived at the store and discovered the crime scene. (NBCConnecticut.com, March 30, 2020). On April 9th, it was announced that arrests were made of three alleged robbers in their fifties who were caught trying to rob another jewelry store in nearby Greenwich, Connecticut. The federal government took over the case. (Nickerson, April 9, 2020).
- Crestview, Florida police arrested a 20-year-old woman and three of her friends for robbing her boyfriend, a 19-year-old, who was killed. A 25-year-old suspect, whom the victim had shot when he entered his room to commit the robbery, also died. Those arrested were charged with murder and robbery with a firearm and murder, robbery with a firearm, and accessory after the fact while in commission of a capital felony. (Mypanhandle.com, May 20, 2020)

These are just 2 of the 548 robbery-homicide victims out of the 14,123 total murder victims who died in 2018 in the United States. That number is down from the 2,488 who were killed in robbery-homicides in the year 1980 when there were 23,040 murders, at a rate of 0.21 percent (FBI Uniform Crime Report, 1980) The robbery-homicide rate for 2018 was similar to the rate for 2015 when out of 13,455 murder victims, 595 were murdered during the robbery at a rate of 0.10 percent. (FBI Uniform Crime Reports, 2015)

Although since 1980 the murder rate as well as the overall number of robbery-murder victims has gone down, as noted above, there were 548 robbery-homicides in 2018, which is still 548 too many. We might ask, robbers can't just take whatever property they're after and not kill the victim? Without blaming the victim, since victims have a right to defend themselves, and since the victim has been killed, it is challenging to recreate what happened from all points of view. Factors that need to be considered, however, are whether the robber or robbers had a gun and whether the victim also had a gun, and if he or she resisted or complied.

Rape-Homicide

It is hard to find statistics about how many murders were proceeded by rape because of the previous hierarchy rule in reporting data to the Uniform Crime Reports—only the most heinous or the more serious of the crimes were sent to the FBI for the annual national report. But one study estimates it to be two percent of all female murder victims. Since the FBI reported 15,980 murders in 2015, based on the police reports they received, that would mean around 319 women were raped before they were killed. The estimated number of reported rapes that year was 90,491. Keep in mind that it is a commonly held belief that less than half of all rapes are reported. However, murders are most likely to be reported, except for those incorrectly considered as a suicide, an accident, or a death from natural causes.

Burglar-Surprise Killings

A support group for survivors of homicide which this author attended as a participant observer was held in the kitchen of a family on Long Island whose son had been killed during a burglar-surprise. The burglar probably assumed the house would be empty that day, but the son was not feeling well, so he had stayed home from high school. The confrontation with the burglar proved deadly. Most burglaries are considered property crimes and not violent crimes because most burglars enter the residence during the day or the office at night, expressly to avoid the possibility of a confrontation with a victim or victims. But there are cases of what is called the "burglar-surprise," which turns the burglary into a robbery, and sometimes a robbery-homicide.

According to the Bureau of Justice Statistics review of the 2.1 million household burglaries that occurred in the United States between 2003 and 2007, 430 resulted in a burglary-related homicide, which accounted for less than 1 percent of all homicides during that period or 0.004 percent of all burglaries during those years. As with robbery-homicide victimizations, for those whose loved ones were one of those 430 burglary-homicide victims, that is 430 victims too many.

The victim in burglar-surprise situations may not always be the homeowner or apartment dweller or the burglar. For example, in Vancouver, Canada in February 2020, an intruder was shot and killed by the homeowner. (Fox 12 News, February 14, 2020) In Las Vegas, Nevada in December 2019, a woman who was home alone heard a knock on the door at around 11 in the morning. According to the police statement about the burglar-surprise, she ignored the knock. At that point, a 30-year-old man broke into the woman's house through her sliding door. She went to her bedroom, got her handgun, and when the burglar confronted her, shot him once. He then ran off, driving away in a car, but was found nearby by police and taken to the hospital where he died. The case was considered self-defense. (DeSilva, Fox5Vegas.com, December 28, 2019.)

Child Killings

Tragic homicide victims are the defenseless children. Here are two terms related to homicide of children: **filicide**—if a parent or caregiver kills a child; and **infanticide**, a subcategory of filicide, which refers to the killing of an infant under the age of one.

From the infants who die because a parent or caregiver shakes them to stop them from crying, thereby causing their death from shaken baby syndrome, to the 800+ children who died from 1998-2019 because they got heatstroke after being left in a hot car, to the toddlers or children who accidentally shoot themselves (or a friend or loved one) because they happen upon a gun, to the brutal abduction and murder by strangers or someone known to the victim, infants and children are the most vulnerable. (Rice, 2019)

How big a problem is this in the United States? Just looking at infants, according to the CDC (Centers for Disease Control and Prevention), homicide kills 10 times as many infants annually as the flu. In 2019, 154 infants under the age of one were killed in the United States. In Table 7.8 you will find out the reasons why. Remember that this is only reported killings.

TABLE 7.8. Killings of Infants under One Year in the United States in 2019

Method of Killing of Infants under One Year of Age	Number (Out of 154)
Firearms	8
Knives and other instruments	5
Blunt objects	10
Personal weapons (hands, feet, fists)	74
Poison	0
Explosives	0
Fire	1
Narcotics	6
Strangulation	1
Asphyxiation	8
Other undetermined/unspecified means	41

Source: FBI *2019 Crime in the United States*, Table 9, Expanded Homicide Data, Murder Victims by Age by Weapon

Sixty-three percent of children killed under the age of five between 1980 and 2008 were killed by a parent. (Alexia Cooper and Erica L. Smith, 2011: 6) Please read Chapter 10, "Child Victims" and Chapter 11, "Teen and College Victims," for a more detailed discussion about the various types of child abuse although child killings are the ultimate form of child abuse.

Additional Homicides That Are Generally Family-Related

Killing of one's parents is known as **parricide.** If the victim is the perpetrator's mother, it is known as **matricide. Eldercide** refers to the killing of a senior in the 60 and older age category.

Murder-Suicide

- Karthik, a 45-year-old father of three, husband, and business owner, distressed by the recent economic crisis, allegedly shot his wife, three sons, and mother-in-law before turning the gun on himself.
- In June 2007, wrestler Chris Benoit killed his wife and son before killing himself.
- In 1998, comedian Phil Hartman, who skyrocketed to fame as a regular on *Saturday Night Live* (SNL), was shot and killed, allegedly by his wife, who later killed herself.
- Back in 1980, Dorothy Stratten, *Playboy*'s 1980 Playmate of the Year, was shot and killed by her estranged husband, who then killed himself.

These are all real-life examples of victims of a unique type of homicide: murder followed by the suicide of the killer, known as **murder-suicide**, homicide-suicide, or "double headers."

These types of cases receive wide coverage in the media even though they are relatively rare. According to Marvin W. Wolfgang, University of Pennsylvania criminologist, who studied 588 criminal homicides in Philadelphia that occurred over a year period (from 1948–1952), only 3 percent of those killings were murder-suicides. In an interview three decades later he said, "That is a general percentage that still holds in the United States nationally." (Wolfgang, 1980)

Local or national statistics of "double headers" are not kept. Let us take the 2019 statistic for the United States, using the FBI statistic of 16,425 murder victims. Using Professor Wolfgang's 3 percent estimate, this means there were an estimated 492 victims of criminal homicide followed by the killer's suicide.

By contrast, in England, where the total number of homicide victims is small compared to the United States, there are an estimated 33 percent that are murder-suicides. Criminologist D.J. West studied 78 British "double headers" and in his classic study *Murder Followed by Suicide*, described them as predominantly family affairs, marked by severe depression, extreme jealousy, and aggressive psychopathology.

Unlike killings by strangers, crimes attracting an equal amount of attention, murder-suicides provoke more shock than fear.

The numbers and percentages of murder/suicides here may be different than in England, but the profiles that can be recreated from the scanty evidence suggest a similar pattern.

In the United States, the classic situation is of the spurned lover killing the erstwhile partner and then, in continuation of the emotional storm, or in remorse, immediately killing him- or herself.

Psychiatrist Dr. T.L. Dorpat has suggested that such murder/suicide cases are "an acting out of fantasies of reunion." Psychoanalyst David Abrahamsen, author of *The Murdering Mind*, has emphasized the frustration behind the typical murder/suicide: "Frustration is the wet nurse to violence and murder. "

A second pattern that these killings may fall into is that of the parent killing the child; fearing an inability to bring it up properly, or being unable to give it what the parent perceives the child needs, as well as custody battles that lead the murderer to fear he or she will never see the children again.

"Another situation," said Dr. Elliot Gross, former chief medical examiner of the City of New York, "is where a person who has killed someone has been surrounded by the police. With capture imminent, those circumstances may lead to the person committing suicide." It has become so common that there is even a term for it: suicide by cop.

Sometimes, the suicide does not immediately follow the killing such as the Connecticut man accused of killing his ex-wife and their maid who committed suicide some eight months after the murders. Other alleged killers, while being detained awaiting trial, commit suicide in their cells. A more recent example of an alleged killer who committed suicide before he could be tried and sentenced is the suicide of Fotis Dulos. That Connecticut man was accused of killing his estranged wife, Jennifer Dulos, a mother of five, who disappeared the year before and whose body was never found. Dulos suffered carbon monoxide positioning at his home in an attempted suicide; he died two days later. (Gold, 2020)

There are also euthanasia killings followed by suicide. Those cases, however, differ from the typical murder-suicide that stem from jealousy, rage about separation, or custody issues.

"In euthanasia killings," Professor Wolfgang said, "there is a love relationship and a strong affection, a bond."

Although far less common, some murders followed by suicide involve strangers. In 1976 in Jackson, Georgia, for example, an ex-convict shot and killed three persons before killing himself. "There's a real distinction between that kind of killing," said William B. McDonald of the Institute of Criminal Law and Procedure in Washington, D.C., "and those that result from interpersonal situations."

McDonald thinks it would be interesting to look at the differences between the type of murderers who kill themselves and those who do not.

"There are some methodological problems," he notes, it being manifestly impossible to interview the murderers in murder-suicide cases.

"I wouldn't want to put any brakes on media reporting," said criminologist Wolfgang, ""but there is some evidence that the wide dissemination of information about dramatic events, particularly suicide, can have a ripple effect."

He cited Marilyn Monroe's suicide as a timeless case study. Wolfgang continued: "I believe there were something like eleven suicides of that sort during the two days following her suicide by similar women of similar ages and situations."

More recently, Mary V. Seeman writes about this phenomenon in "The Marilyn Monroe Group and the Werther Effect." Seeman explains that the **Werther Effect**, a term coined in 1974 to describe imitative suicide, is actually traced back to 1774 when German writer Goethe, who was then 25, published *The Sorrows of Young Werther*. Goethe was himself suicidal following an unhappy romantic relationship. In the book, the disappointed lover commits suicide with a pistol. According to Seeman, the book led to "Masses of young men dressed in yellow pants and blue jackets (like Werther) and, carrying a copy of Goethe's novel, shot themselves." (Seeman, 2017)

Bernie Auchter summarized the key findings of several top researchers into murder-suicide in his article, "Men Who Murder Their Families," based on a panel discussion hosted by the National Institute of Justice in 2010. The three panelists were Jacquelyn C. Campbell of Johns Hopkins University, author David Adams, and family violence researcher Richard Gelles of the University of Pennsylvania.

Professor Campbell's summary of the findings of the 12-city study conducted by the Centers for Disease Control and Prevention's National Violent Death Reporting System looked at 408 cases of murder-suicide. In these cases, men were the perpetrator in 91 percent of the cases; they used a gun 88 percent of the time. (Auchter, June 2010) Another finding that Professor Campbell shared was that intimate partner violence occurred in 70 percent of those murder-suicides although only 25 percent of the perpetrators had domestic violence arrest records. Unemployment was considered a risk factor "but only when combined with a history of domestic violence." (Auchter, 2010)

Profile ■ An Interview with Tereson

Tereson and her son Eden. Contributed Photo.

Terrence "Terry" and his son Eden. Contributed Photo.

On Easter Sunday, April 12, 2020, Tereson got the phone call that no mother ever wants to receive. "My brother-in-law told me they were both dead." Her 21-year-old son, Eden, was dead and so was her ex-husband, Terry. Her husband was 50 years old. Tereson had three children including Eden's older sister, 25 and younger brother, 18. Eden was her middle child. He had gone to live with his father in a small Southern town two years before. At the time, Tereson thought it might be a good change for Eden. He had autism spectrum disorder and although he was never diagnosed, she suspected her husband had it too. She thought they would get along really well since they both found relationships challenging. Eden's father, Terence "Terry," was a Grammy-nominated audio engineer and producer with a B.A. in Broadcast Journalism and two master's degrees, one in mass communication with a concentration in public relations and another in teaching.

As noted in the section of this chapter on murder-suicides, in the majority of murder-suicide cases, it is a parent (husband) who shoots and kills his spouse and then himself. A rarer form of murder-suicide is *familicide* whereby the husband kills the entire family including children. But in Eden's case, he was actually the shooter. Tereson shares what she pieced together about what may have happened to cause her son to snap:

> I was told guns were involved. I just knew, there was no question in my mind, I knew my son did it. I know them so well. I know exactly what happened. I've been around them for so long and know both of their tempers and their impulsiveness.

It seems about a month before the tragedy, Eden's father got upset with Eden because he had not cleaned up his room. To make the point that he was upset, he shot up Eden's computer. What Tereson explained to this author is that Eden's computer was the one thing in the world that he truly enjoyed and felt comfortable doing. He enjoyed playing his videogames.

Tereson shares about the challenges of dealing with such a loss.

> I was suicidal for six months. I had PTSD so bad. My thoughts. My grief. I cried. That's what I did. I went to Vermont and I cried in this country settling.
>
> Guns were a huge factor. . . . My son should never have been able to buy a gun.

Tereson does not know where her son bought the AR-Style 15 rifle that he used to kill his father and then himself. "He might have bought it online." she says.

What is the one thing Tereson wants those who will be working with crime victims, or trying to prevent crime, to know?

If there's one thing that I'd like to see changed [is that] when there's a red flag, check it out. Police were notified several times. He was causing all kinds of waves in the city [where he lived.] [I think] He [my ex-husband Terry] was having a psychotic break. Terry was unhinged and causing problems in town by accusing government of a cover up. Be attuned to mental health. My son might have done the shooting, but [it is wrong] for anyone to believe that it was premeditated. Eden was a casualty of lacking to protect and serve. If you would have seen Eden walking down the street. He was sporting a trench coat, a black knit cap, and carrying a gun on his hip.

It was a completely impulsive thing. Neither of them [my husband or my son] had impulse control.

Police Related Deaths

It is a reality that people are killed by the police in either justified or unjustified killings. In this section, we will briefly look at civilians who are killed by police in the process of being arrested in situations that are determined to be unjustified killings. The most notable example of an unjustified killing during an arrest is the killing of George Floyd on May 25, 2020 by a police officer. The reason for detaining Floyd was that he was suspected of allegedly trying to pass a counterfeit $20 bill. Former Minneapolis police officer Derek Chauvin was found guilty on April 20, 2021 of two counts of murder in the death of George Flloyd. Three other officers, who were nearby and who allegedly did not intervene during the 8 minutes and 46 seconds that Chauvin had his knee on Floyd's neck, leading to his death, were also charged. The outrage that was sparked by the video showing the police officer's almost 9 minutes of keeping his knee on Floyd's neck even after he said, "I can't breathe," led to riots, lootings, and even the disbanding of the Minneapolis police department where Floyd's death occurred (Altman, 2020; Levenson and Cooper, 2021)

Police killings have become one of the most controversial issues in criminal justice, victimology, and criminology. Here are issues that have become paramount concerns:

- When, if ever, is the killing of a suspect by the police justified?
- How often do these justified police killings occur in the United States?
- What are the circumstances behind each unjustified police killing?
- Is racial bias a factor, meaning is it more likely that Blacks will get killed by police versus whites?
- What about Hispanics? Are they disproportionately killed by police during arrest or while in police custody?
- Are police killings related to racism or poor police training?
- How does the number of police killings in the United States compare to the number that occur in other countries?
- Does technology have any advances that can help in detaining those under arrest with less of a threat of fatality?
- What part do guns play in police killings?

These are just some of the many questions related to police killings that need to be answered through the acquisition and analysis of detailed crime data from every police agency.

According to the Prison Policy Initiative, U.S. police kill civilians at a higher rate than other countries. According to data compiled by the Prison Policy Initiative for 2017 and 2019 among various westernized countries, the U.S. rate is 33.5 per 10 million population. The country with the next highest rate is Canada at 9.8 per 10 million followed by Australia at 8.5 per 10 million. The next country listed, the Netherlands, has an even lower rate, at 2.3 per 10 million, followed by 2.0 for New Zealand. England and Wales, the part of Great Britain that the United States is most often compared to, has a rate of 0.5 per 10 million population. (Alexi Jones and Wendy Sawyer, 2020)

Police Killed in the Line of Duty

- In April 2020, in Baton Rouge, Louisiana, a man allegedly ambushed two police officers who had been sent to interview him about a killing several hours before. It was reported that after he shot and killed one of the officers, he stood over that police officer's body and continued to shoot. The second officer survived but was in critical condition. (McConnaughey and Lauer)

TABLE 7.9. Line of Duty Deaths

Total	**130**
9-11 Related Illness	8
Accidental	2
Aircraft accident	1
Assault	3
Automobile accident	27
Bomb	6
Drowned	1
Duty related illness	2
Fall	1
Gunfire	39
Gunfire (Accidental)	2
Heart attack	17
Motorcycle accident	3
Struck by vehicle	4
Vehicle pursuit	5
Vehicular assault	8
Weather/Natural disaster	1

Source: "Officer Down Memorial Page." https://www.odmp.org/search/year/2016.

- In July 2016, two snipers shot at 12 police officers in Dallas, Texas, killing five. At the time of the shooting, there were an estimated 800 people demonstrating. (F. Brinley Bruton, et al., 2016)

The Officer Down Memorial Page at odmp.org honors officer deaths in the line of duty. Table 7.9 includes the data for the most recent year listed at their site, 2015, by category.

The most dangerous category is officers killed because of gunfire. Being a police officer has definitely become more dangerous in the last year largely because of the anti-police sentiment fueled by the media focus on the controversial police force examples in the Minneapolis; Ferguson, Missouri; Baltimore, Maryland; Staten Island, New York; and other controversial cases.

CNN published an article announcing that 64 police officers were shot dead in the line of duty in 2016. You could compare that number to 39 in 2015, a dramatic increase. (Jason Hanna, et al., "Fallen officers: 64 shot dead in the line of duty in 2016")

Prisoner Killings

Between 2001 and 2012, approximately 670 inmates were killed while incarcerated in state prisons; approximately 100 were killed in federal institutions. The perpetrators in these killings tended to be other inmates, not correctional officers. A well-known case is that of Jack Henry Abbott. He was incarcerated beginning at an early age for minor offenses but as an adult, he killed a fellow inmate. Years later, he was released after Norman Mailer and others came to his defense on the strength of his bestseller, *In the Belly of the Beast.* But within a few weeks of his release, Abbott got into an altercation with a waiter and aspiring actor, whom he stabbed to death. He was returned to prison and given a lengthy sentence. The next time Abbott experienced violence in prison, however, was at his own hand. Upon being denied parole, Abbott committed suicide.

Those incarcerated in local jails also stand the risk of being killed; between 2000 and 2012, an estimated 270 males and 5 females were stabbed or beaten to death. As Karmen points out, almost 75 percent or 200 of those murder victims had not yet been found guilty of a crime. They were in jail "technically innocent and were being detained awaiting their trial." (Karmen, *Crime Victims*, 400)

On July 13, 2021, 39-year-old Tyrone Billups, who was serving a 45-year sentence for first degree burglary, bribing a witness, first degree possession of marijuana, and possession of controlled substances, died from the injuries he sustained from another inmate assaulting him. Billups' death, which occurred in a correctional facility in Alabama, is under investigation. (Chandler, 2021)

For more on inmate killings in jails and prisons, as well as because of suicide while incarcerated, go to Chapter 14, "Victims of the Criminal Justice System."

Mass Murders

In a **mass murder**, multiple victims are killed at one point in time. Some of examples of mass murders are the June 12, 2016 tragedy in Orlando, Florida, where 49 men and women were killed in a night club and, just a few months later, on December 20th, 2016, a hijacked oversized truck was driven into a crowded Christmas market in Berlin, Germany, killing 12 shoppers. The alleged murderer in the Berlin incident was killed in a gun battle several days later in Milan, Italy. A few years before, on July 20th, 2012, in Aurora, Colorado, 11 men and women and 6-year-old Veronica Moser-Sullivan were killed in a movie theater.

Whether it's the mass murder of nearly 3,000 by terrorists during the 9-11 tragedy in New York City, Pennsylvania, and Washington, D.C., or the Columbine High School mass shootings, the public remembers the circumstances of mass murders. The numbers are astonishing, and the magnitude of these murders are highlighted by the way that so many share such a somber fate all at the same time, like the 14 having a holiday party in San Bernardino, California, only to be gunned down by a terrorist co-worker and his wife. Sealed in everyone's memory are the tragic deaths of 9 worshippers at a church in Charleston, shot to death in a hate crime by a young man pretending to be part of their Bible study class.

Terrorist attack on the Twin Towers, September 11, 2001, Manhattan, downtown New York City.

These mass murders are indeed horrific and the loss to families of the murdered are as tragic as the killing of a young person on a deserted city street at night by a teenage gang or an abused wife killed by her enraged husband because she announced her intention of leaving him.

The victims of separate instances of murder or homicide can reach out to other homicide victim families through Parents of Murdered Children, the National Organization of Victim Assistance (NOVA), MADD (Mothers Against Drunk Drivers), and other victim organizations that offer self-help support groups or individual counseling for those who are dealing with the aftermath of murder. Secondary victims of isolated murders or homicides will be able to connect to other survivors because of their shared experience but those whose loved ones died in a mass murder have the unique situation of also sharing the circumstances of the murder.

See Chapter 15, "Additional Victim Situations and Populations," for a further discussion of the victims of terrorism.

Serial Murder

If there are three or more victims by the same killer, in separate incidents, the perpetrator is considered a **serial killer**. One of the most infamous serial killers in recent memory is Dennis Rader, also known as the BTK Strangler or BTK Killer. The letters BTK stand for "Bind" "Torture" and "Kill." Rader, a college graduate who had served in the Air Force and was married with two children, committed ten murders between 1974 and 1991. He was known for sending detailed letters about his crimes to the media and the police, but he was not caught until he sent out letters again in 2004, leading to his arrest and subsequent guilty plea in 2005.

Rader's entry in Wikipedia is almost 5,000 words long. No fewer than four films and five songs exist about this killer, and novelists Stephen King and Thomas Harris are each said to have based a novella or a novel on Rader. However, a film and a book focus on the survivors: the documentary *I Survived BTK* by Charlie Otero, who, as a teenager, discovered the bodies of four of his family members who had been killed by Rader, and *The Shadow of Evil* by Jeffrey M. Davis, the son of the final BTK victim Dolores Davis.

Spree Murders

A spree murder is when someone kills two or more individuals in several places over a relatively short time period. Spree murders are what happened in areas near Atlanta, Georgia on March 16, 2021 at three massage parlors where eight people were killed in separate locations. Four people were killed at the first massage parlor, near Acworth, a northwest suburb of Atlanta; less than an hour later, there was another shooting at a massage parlor in the northeast area of Atlanta. Three women died there. The police then received a report of a third shooting, which took place across the street. Another female victim was found in that third location. Relatively soon afterwards, the alleged shooter was arrested after his parents recognized him from the surveillance video and notified police. Six victims were Asian; two Caucasian. Hate crime charges have not yet been ruled out. One of the survivors was Hispanic. (Fausset and Vigdor, 2021)

CONTROVERSIES IN HOMICIDE THAT VICTIMOLOGY ADDRESSES

Victim Precipitation

Building on the groundbreaking work of Hans von Hentig about the possible role of the victim in a crime (von Hentig, 1940; von Hentig, 1948), University of Pennsylvania criminology professor Dr. Marvin Wolfgang analyzed the homicides reported by the Philadelphia police between 1948 and 1952. Based on Wolfgang's analysis of 150 cases, he determined that in 26 percent of the cases, it was the victim who started the physical altercation or showed a weapon, which in turn led to the escalation of violence that resulted in death.

Wolfgang identified three key factors associated with victim precipitation:

1. Drinking alcohol preceding the confrontation.
2. Minor disagreements that escalated into an explosion of anger that led to the slaying.
3. The existence of a prior relationship between the victim and the killer, such as being a family member, spouse, or close friend or acquaintance.

Is it possible to objectively look at a murder to determine if there was victim precipitation without automatically falling into the trap of blaming the victim?

Consider a situation in which a 17-year-old girl confesses to her mother, who shares the news with her husband, that his mother's new husband molested their daughter nine years earlier, when she was eight and spent the night at her grandmother's. Her father immediately drives to his mother's house to confront her husband. He brings a shotgun with him. He claims the gun goes off accidentally, killing the stepfather. The jury convicts him of voluntary manslaughter with the belief that he killed the victim intentionally during passion. He serves two years in prison. At that point, the South Carolina Court of Appeals rules that there was insufficient evidence and the guilty verdict was overturned and he is immediately freed.

Since the victim was a child molester, did his illegal behavior precipitate the father's violent confrontation and subsequent accidental shooting of the molester?

So-called "crimes of passion" might bring up the question of victim precipitation. Could a victim's behavior, such as being caught having an affair with the killer's spouse, or flirting with someone else's date at a bar, be construed as precipitating the murder? What about when victim of a bully is so traumatized that he or she feels the only recourse is to become homicidal? What if the objects of the homicidal acts are not even the original bullies? How does victim precipitation factor into those killings, if at all?

As you are learning in *Essentials of Victimology*, the field of victimology and other social scientists are moving away from a victim precipitation approach to homicide. For example, psychologists Lilia M. Cortina, Veronica Caridad Rabelo, and Kathryn J. Holland, in their article, "Beyond Blaming the Victim," published in the *Industrial and Organizational Psychology*, suggest what they refer to as perpetrator predation "as a way to understand workplace abuse without blaming the abused." (Cortina, Rabelo, and Holland, 2018: 81) They state, even more emphatically, "Victim precipitation, we conclude, is an archaic ideology. Criminologists have long since abandoned it, and so should we." (Cortina, et. al., 2018,: 81)

In the section of their article entitled, "Shifting the Paradigm," the co-authors continue, "Cortina (2017) has proposed *perpetrator predation* as a useful framework for understanding these dynamics. According to *Merriam-Webster*, a 'predator' is a person who 'lives by predation,' or 'looks for other people in order to use, control, or harm them in some way.' With a perpetrator predation lens, one can still 'fall prey' to victimization more often than others, which might be partly attributable to one's own characteristics (e.g., social skill deficits, personality quirks, intellectual disabilities); this framework, however, draws our attention to the individual who targets those characteristics. It also brings power into the picture, with power disparities often separating predator from prey. . ." (Cortina et. al., 2018: 91-92)

Clearance Rate

Clearing a crime by an arrest, the most common way clearance rates are measured, is discussed in other chapters. It is mentioned here, as a controversial issue in regard to homicide and murder, because of the dramatic decline in clearance rates for these violent crimes in the U.S., from a high of 93% in 1953 down to 76% in 1983, to an even lower 59% in 2016. (Karmen, 2020: 220) In 2019, according to the FBI annual report, the clearance rate for murder and nonnegligent manslaughter was 61.4%. (*FBI, 2019 Crime in the United States*) As low as that clearance rate is, however, it is the highest for any violent crime in the U.S. Those clearance rates for 2019 were 32.9% for rape; 30.5% for robbery; and 52.3% for aggravated assault. (FBI, *2019 Crime in the United States*) Why should victimologists care about a low clearance rate for murder?

FROM ATTEMPTED MURDER TO MURDER

Sometimes what was considered an attempted criminal homicide or murder turns into a case of homicide or murder when the victim dies. On March 30, 2020, three months after he was stabbed by an intruder at a Hanukkah party in Monsey, New York, Rabbi Josef Neumann died from his injuries. Originally charged with attempted murder and federal hate crimes, the assailant, who wounded four others, now faced a murder charge. In *the New York Times* article about the rabbi's death, reporter Azi Paybarah noted that Governor Andrew M. Cuomo considered the attack on the rabbi as both a hate crime and an example of domestic terrorism. (Paybarah, 2020)

Another example of this type of situation occurred when James Brady, who had survived a bullet to his head in the assassination attempt on President Ronald Reagan in 1981, died in 2014 from a series of health problems. Was Brady's death related to his attempted murder 30 years before? If so, woould the shooter now be charged with homicide? According to the *Washington Post* article by Peter Hermann and Michael E. Ruane, Brady's death was now ruled a homicide by the medical examiner. But they also noted, "There was no immediate word on whether the shooter, John W. Hinckley Jr., who has been treated at St. Elizabeths psychiatric hospital since his trial, could face new criminal charges." (Hermann and Ruane, 2014)

PREVENTING HOMICIDE VICTIMIZATION

Finally, without placing victim-blame, how can we use what victimologists have learned about homicide and murder to help you or your loved one to be less likely homicide victims? Here are some suggestions:

1. Help children, teens, and adults to be more careful about their behavior so they do not unwittingly contribute to their own victimization. Without perpetrating the "victim blame" mindset, get the word out that learning to be self-protective is essential around all individuals, not just strangers.
2. Provide guidelines about how to calmly deal with escalating situations, such as altercations at bars or road rage confrontations, to avoid a fatal outcome.
3. Address the very real situation in the United States today that 73 percent of homicides are committed with a firearm and, where the type of firearm is noted, 88 percent were handguns.
4. Spread the word about how to more likely survive a "burglar surprise," robbery, rape, or domestic violence. (Refer back to the information that was shared throughout this chapter as well as in the chapters about those crimes in the rest of this textbook.)
5. If you are planning on traveling, whether it is to another city or another country, check out what the government, for example, the U.S. Department of State, says about that destination. Is your destination on a travel advisory or a watch list because of a greater likelihood of visitors becoming victims of violent crimes, especially kidnapping and murder? Can you access articles about a city to check its safety rating and learn which areas to avoid because they pose risks that visitors need to be aware of?
6. Be careful what information you or your loved ones post on social media. You might unwittingly be setting yourself up as a victim because you mention your valuable possessions or broadcast the dates on which you will be traveling or the places at which you will be staying.
7. Sometimes the difference between attempted murder and murder is how quickly someone could get medical attention. Keep your smartphone charged and available to you.

8. Since most homicides are usually one offender and one victim, there is safety in numbers. Especially at night, have someone with you so you are a less likely target for rape, robbery, or murder.
9. Women especially must extricate themselves from escalating situations in intimate relationships that might lead to murder. If necessary, seek out help from a domestic violence shelter finding out the best course of action so you and your family are least likely to be harmed.

Just to reinforce how effective taking steps to reduce risks can be, look at how much was accomplished in understanding and controlling the causes behind AIDS and reducing the spread of HIV and AIDS, which was killing millions globally. Consider how many deaths from lung disease have been minimized or eliminated after aggressive reduction in smoking became a priority for so many individuals and societies.

What will it take to succeed at dramatically reducing the number of murder victims from 16,214, the number of murder victims in 2018, to as few as possible within the next decade?

Profile of a Homicide Victim ▪ **Jennifer Ann Crecente**

Jennifer Ann Crecente, an 18-year-old high school senior and honors student, highlighted in a previous chapter, was close with both her parents even after her parents divorced.

Over the years, Jennifer's friendship with a neighbor, who was also a classmate, grew into a romance. But because the relationship did not work out, Jennifer ended it.

A few weeks after their romance ended, her ex-boyfriend asked Jennifer if she could join him in looking over a car he wanted to buy. Being a kind and thoughtful person, Jennifer thought nothing of accompanying him to see the car.

They drove to the woods and Jennifer got out of the car, figuring she would be soon be looking over her friend's potential purchase. Instead, he quickly removed a rifle that someone else had bought for him and shot Jennifer in the back of the head (during an interview with this author, Jennifer's father shared that he had learned that the killer had Jennifer get on her hands and knees).

Jennifer's father, Drew, was unaware that his daughter had been missing for two days before her body was found. Since he had left his cell phone in another room and did not hear it ringing, his ex-wife, through Drew's mother, tracked down a friend and an ex-girlfriend of his to go to his house at 4 in the morning to share the news. His only daughter, Jennifer Ann, had been killed on February 15, 2006, the day after Valentine's Day.

CO-VICTIMS OR SECONDARY VICTIMS OF HOMICIDE

Secondary victims of homicide are those loved ones who have lost someone to homicide or murder. They are also known as **survivors of homicide**, homicide survivors, **indirect**, or **co-victims.** The primary victims might be a spouse, a significant other, a parent, a daughter, a son, a brother, a sibling, a cousin, an uncle, an aunt, a friend, or even a well-liked co-worker. Their murder will immediately impact secondary victims and forever change them.

Issues Facing Secondary Victims of Homicide

Other than being present and having to witness it, suddenly finding out about the murder of a loved one is a tremendous immediate shock. But there are additional concerns, many of which co-victims of homicide must contend with, including:

1. Death notification (how the news is received)
2. Stages of grief
3. Autopsy issues and/or funeral arrangements
4. Dealing with children and other family members and friends
5. Financial issues
6. Insurance
7. Media
8. Criminal Justice System and/or Juvenile Justice including dealing with the police
9. Physical manifestations related to being a homicide co-victim
10. Social relationships may be affected
11. Employment
12. Post-traumatic stress disorder, depression, and substance abuse disorders
13. Getting past the homicide or murder and remembering the victim.

Death Notification

How someone is notified that his or her loved one has been killed in a homicide is a crucial consideration on what is probably the worst day or one of the worst days in the life of any parent, spouse, sibling, extended family, or friend. How, and how well, a death notification is handled can make a big difference in how a secondary victim begins the long healing process that lies ahead. Often, this difficult notification is made by law enforcement first responders.

Fortunately, the National Sheriffs Foundation developed a booklet for law enforcement dealing with how to handle first response to all victims of crime. The section entitled, "Tips on Responding to Survivors of Homicide Victims" is reprinted in the Appendices for this textbook which you will be able to find online at the publisher's website, AspenPublishing.com.

In their article, "Tense Relationships between Homicide Co-Victims and Detectives in the Wake of Murder," published in *Deviant Behavior*, Mark D. Reed et. al. summarize best practices for death notifications. Although some jurisdictions may have the police chaplain or social workers give the death notification, these best practices are geared to the detective assigned to the case. Referring to the book *Homicide: The Hidden Victims* by Deborah Sprungen (Sage Publications, 1998), Reed et al. share these death notification best practices:

- Do not make the notifications over the phone
- Have at least two officers present at the notification
- Provide family members with thorough and precise details but avoid sharing unnecessary ones
- Be open to answering any questions that the family asks. (Reed, et. al., 2020)

How to Talk to a Secondary Victim of Homicide

Death notification is just the first time that anyone dealing with a secondary victim of homicide or murder must show a concern about what is said to these victims. If you are dealing with secondary victims in your job, as a police officer, lawyer, prosecutor, doctor, crime victim advocate, or even as a friend or family member, it is best to avoid uttering clichés that may be more harmful than helpful such as "Everything happens for the best" "I know what you're going through" or "At least he didn't suffer."

Listen to secondary victims whether you are a first responder or just a family member or friend whose loved one has been killed. Keep listening. You may feel like you have heard the story about how their loved one died many times before, but remember that some victims need to retell the story of their loved one's murder until they have mastered it and it is no longer too much for them to bear. Others may not want to talk about it at all, and you need to respect that reaction too. Some co-victims may even use how they feel when they retell what happened as a way of gauging how they are dealing with the trauma. Can they tell what happened without breaking down and crying? Are they able to share without getting PTSD, becoming enraged, or having an anxiety attack?

Remember that there is no consistent timetable about when someone will "get over" a loved one's murder. Some may never get over it. Others just learn to accept it, and go on.

Provide useful information, if asked. Many secondary victims are unaware that every state has a crime victim compensation program that has funds provided by the federal government to the states to give compensation to the primary or secondary victims of crime including murder. There are eligibility requirements, varying from state to state,but covering funeral costs up to a certain amount, usually between $6,000 and $10,000, is a common benefit. Someone will have to check if there is money available for counseling services for secondary victims. If the crime occurred in someone's apartment or your home, most state crime victim compensation programs will pay for the cost of crime scene clean up. There may also be private nonprofit organizations or associations offering services or even financial compensation to secondary victims of murder.

LOSS FROM HOMICIDE IS DIFFERENT THAN OTHER DEATHS

The secondary victims of homicide most directly affected by the crime are the spouse, their children, the deceased's parents and siblings, and extended family, such as cousins, especially if they were close with the victim.

Filipa Alves-Costa, Catherine Hamilton-Giachritsis, and Sarah Halligan have conducted one of the few qualitative studies of bereavement by secondary survivors of homicide. (Alves-Costa, Hamilton-Giachritsis, and Halligan, 2021: NP2953; Currier, Holland, Neimeye, 2006; Parkes, 1993; Shear, 2021) Alves-Costa wanted to explore if their sample's grief was unique because of the violent way their loved one died. (Alves-Costa, Hamilton- Giachritsis, and Halligan, 2021.) These three psychologists and academics were permitted to interview 21 individuals who had lost a loved one through homicide and who were attending a 4-day residential group program for secondary victims organized by Escaping Victimhood (EV), a charity located in the United Kingdom. These 21 participants included 18 females and 3 males ranging in age from 29 to 66 with a mean age of 47.81. The sample that they studied included 12 parents, 5 siblings, 1 partner, 1 daughter, 1 friend, and 1 grandmother of the homicide victim. Time since the homicide ranged from 12 months to 18 years with a mean of 2.48 years. (Alves-Costs, Hamilton-Giachritsis, and Halligan, 2021: NP2954.)

The co-author psychologists found three main themes to their interviews, which lasted from 20 minutes to 2 hours:

1. the uniqueness of the experience
2. the changed self and world
3. missed experiences of support. (Alves-Costa, et al., 2021: 2954)

Focusing on the first of their central findings, an astounding 19 out of 21 participants mentioned "the first subtheme (sudden, unexpected, and violent nature of the event)." (Alves-Costa et al., 2021: NP2960)

It was the deliberateness of homicide that the interviewees found most disturbeing. Participant 6 said: "We have had many other deaths in the family but, you cannot compare, they were nature, this is just another level, someone intended to kill her.'" (Alves-Costa et al., 2021: NP2960).

The second theme of these interviews shared by *all* 21 interviewees was that they had a *changed self* after their loved one's homicide. Participant 19 said: "'The shock, the trauma, the trauma, you just see everything happening again and again in your head, no matter if you are asleep or not.'" (Alves-Costa et al., 2021: NP2963)

In line with the changed self and altered view of the world response, the researchers found that 19 out of 21 reported having an "overall lack of energy and feeling of exhaustion" and 9 shared about physical issues including eating and sleep disturbances. (Alves-Costa et al., 2021: NP2960).

Finally, 15 out of 21 interviewees reported having different world views related to "overall safety and trust issues." Participant 20 said: "I think before I didn't think about crimes and things like that, because you do not have to, you see things on the news and you read things in the newspapers, but it is always very distant from you.'" (Alves-Costs et al., 2021: NP2964.)

Fred Guttenberg's daughter Jaime was one of the 17 victims who died in the shooting attack of the 19-year-old mass killer at Marjory Stoneman Douglas High School in Parkland, Florida on February 14th, 2018. Twelve were killed inside the school, three more were killed outside the school, and two died later at the hospital from their injuries for a total of 17 fatalities. Seventeen more were injured but survived. (Burch and Mazzei, 2018)

Fred Guttenberg and his 14-year-old daughter Jaime. Contributed photo.

In his book, *Find the Helpers*, Guttenberg writes about how his life changed that fateful day. He writes, "When you experience the death of your child, the world stops." Guttenberg continues, "Everything you know and feel breaks into pieces. In the days following Jaime's murder, that's what I kept saying: 'I feel broken.' But I had a deep desire to know what had happened to my child. I am Jaime's dad. I will always be Jaime's dad. Though I couldn't function for myself, I had to do certain things for her, including listening to the description of her school being turned into a battlefield of terror and violence by one crazed coward with an AR-15 semiautomatic rifle. I had to hear how my daughter was hunted down and shot with one bullet in the side, severing her spinal cord. Our lives were forever turned upside down by this six-minute murder spree of innocent teenagers and adults. Almost immediately, we had to meet with law enforcement and make plans. Time stood still, yet at the same time, it marched forward with the reality that my wife and I needed to make funeral arrangements for Jaime. We needed security for our house and for the funeral, and Scott and other friends in law enforcement assisted with this. His family rode through the horror with us." (Guttenberg, 2020: 57-58; Guttenberg, 2021)

DEALING WITH GRIEF

Secondary homicide victims agree that the murder of a loved one changes everything. Many turn to the work of psychiatrist Dr. Kubler-Ross, based on her experiences working with hospice patients, who know they will be dying within weeks or, at the most, months, for an understanding about dealing with catastrophic situations. Here are those five stages of grief that secondary victims of crime go through:

TABLE 7.10. Dr. Elisabeth Kubler-Ross' Five Stages of Grief

1. Denial	"No, it can't be true." "You've got the wrong person."
2. Anger	Anger can be directed at many different people or just one—the police, the perpetrator, the doctor, the ER nurse.
3. Bargaining	This stage might fit more if a violent crime may or may not lead to death. "Please don't let my loved one die. I'll promise to. . . ."
4. Depression	Starts once the finality of murder sinks in, and the loss feels even bigger after the initial attention from others is gone.
5. Acceptance	Some may accept what has happened relatively soon, within weeks or months, for others it may take years. For others, there may never be an acceptance.

Source: Elisabeth Kubler-Ross, M. D. *On Death and Dying* (1969), excerpted and adapted by this author.

Secondary victims may share that they simply do not believe it when someone tells them that their loved one has been murdered. There must be some mistake. You got my loved one mixed up with someone else. Then, once there is an awareness that it is true, there is anger. Strong anger. It could be directed at the killer. It could be directed at "the system" that let this happen. It could be directed at the loved one for "allowing" themselves to be killed. Next is bargaining. This stage works better in the hospice situation since the loved one in that life-and-death situation is still alive. The bargaining is that if someone does something then death will not be inevitable. The next stage, depression, applies to secondary victims. Some stay in this stage a long time, finding it hard to get past the horrific loss. Victims may find unique ways to assuage their depression such as the way a mother in Poland dealt with the murder of her 25-year-old son, knifed in the throat back in 1972 by a customer at a bar he was frequenting,. She vowed never to dance again after her son's murder. She kept that vow even refusing to dance at her grandson's wedding decades later.

The last stage is acceptance of the death and murder. When, or if, that happens is different for every secondary victim. There is no timeline that can be applied to this fifth stage of grief following murder. It may even be possible to get to what is now being known as the sixth stage of grief, described below, as a way of dealing with stage five.

The Sixth Stage of Grief

Grief expert David Kessler, who worked for many years alongside Dr. Kubler-Ross, contributed something valuable to the field when his book, *Finding Meaning*, was published in 2019. Kessler refers to this as the "sixth stage of grief." Secondary victims who reach this sixth stage of grief may do much better than those who get stuck at any of the earlier phases. We see that practically every organization and even many major laws that have helped crime victims in the last fifty years were brought about by secondary victims. Six-year-old Adam Walsh was abducted and subsequently killed. That tragedy was the catalyst to the victim rights activism of John Walsh and his wife. John Walsh, who has been the host of *America's Most Wanted,* along with his wife, helped to update and improve the way that missing and kidnapping children were handled. Their efforts led to the passage in 1984 of the Missing Children's Assistance Act as well as the established of the National Center for Missing & Exploited Children. MADD—Mothers Against Drunk Drivers—was started by the mother of a 13-year-old victim of a drunk driver.

In 1978, Robert and Charlotte Hullinger, whose 19-year-old daughter Lisa was murdered by her former boyfriend, founded Parents of Murdered Children (POMC). The organization has chapters throughout the United States offering support groups for victims whose loved ones have been murdered as well as training for those who work with victims. There are many additional organizations that survivors of murder have set up as they have unwittingly applied Kessler's sixth stage of grief, finding meaning.

The Hullingers actively ran their organization, which quickly grew from just a few members and chapters to dozens of chapters throughout the United States, for eight years. Then it was time to refocus their energies on their jobs and two surviving children while others continued on with POMC, an organization that is helping parents of murdered children to this day.

Back in the mid-1970s, the late Edith Surgan founded the New Mexico Crime Victims Assistance Organization. She was motivated by the killing of her 19-year-old daughter, a nursing student, who was stabbed to death as she walked across campus at her college in Staten Island, New York. In an article published in *Impact: Albuquerque Journal Magazine* in 1980, Surgan shared about what secondary victims of homicide deal with: "My husband and I were crushed by the loss of our daughter. We were in deep shock, unable to relate to the events around us. Neither of us could do anything for almost nine months. Just trying to get through half hour by half hour was very difficult. . . . You suddenly find yourself very lonely, and even your friends and family don't know how to relate to you. They don't want to hear about it. It's unpleasant. Yet your compulsion to talk about it is very strong. They just stay away from you."

Prolonged Grief Disorder (PGD)

According to the Center for Victim Research, homicide co-victims may suffer from **prolonged grief disorder**, a period of prolonged or complicated grief that is at a rate two to three times higher than the general population. What is complicated or prolonged grief? In their booklet, "What We Know About Homicide Co-Victims from Research and Practice Evidence" the Center for Victim Research defines it as "a form of grief characterized by preoccupation with and longing for the deceased." (Center for Victim Research, 9) Among bereaved individuals in general, rates of prolonged grief are between 7-10 percent. By contrast, according to a community-based study of homicide co-victims by Rheingold and Williams, two years after the homicide, 23 percent were experiencing prolonged grief. In their sample of 47 survivors of homicide, 34 percent were also suffering from **post-traumatic stress disorder (PTSD)** and nearly half of the sample (48.9%) met the criteria for a depressive disorder. One of the important findings from Rheingold and Williams is the importance of social support to secondary homicide victims. As they note in their article, "Survivors of Homicide: Mental Health Outcomes, Social Support, and Service Use Among a Community-Based Sample," "survivors who met criteria for PTSD reported less perceived social support than individuals who did not meet criteria for PTSD."

The Center for Victim Research emphasizes that dealing with prolonged grief disorder may be a life-threatening issue. That is because the condition is associated with a higher risk of suicidal ideation and suicidality. (Center for Victim Research, 2019: 8)

Getting Professional Help

For some secondary victims of homicide, self-help support groups, or just talking to friends and family, however supportive, may not be enough to help get over the life-changing experience of losing a loved one to homicide. Although all 50 states now have a crime victim compensation program that covers funeral costs and loss of support, up to a certain dollar amount, for those who have lost loved ones to homicide, secondary victims of homicide need to check with their state's plan if counseling for co-victims is a covered expense. If the state compensation plan does not cover counseling for secondary victims of homicide, co-victims can check with crime victim treatment centers in their local community. They may offer free or low-cost counseling to secondary victims of homicide. If free or low-cost counseling is not available through victim-related services, if a secondary victim is experiencing PTSD, depression, and prolonged grief disorder, a regular insurance policy through a place of employment, a private policy, or any other type of health insurance may cover some or all of the cost of counseling. When a co-victim is looking for an appropriate therapist, a professional who has worked with crime victims previously, and possibly even taken courses in victimology, criminology, and even gotten an advanced degree related to those fields, in addition to psychological training, may bring to the sessions an understanding of the unique trauma that co-victims face. For example, they will be receptive to admissions of **survivor guilt,** whereby the surviving family member or friend feels guilty that he or she was not the one to die, or **victim blame**, whereby the blame is placed on the victim and not the offender for the victimization. Therapists who are savvy about the unique issues that secondary victims of homicide must deal with may be helpful in coping with one of the most traumatic losses anyone should ever have to endure.

DEALING WITH THE MYRIAD OF ISSUES FACING HOMICIDE CO-VICTIMS

When you consider the issues that homicide co-victims face (listed earlier in this chapter), you see how much help may be needed. Depending upon the relationship of the co-victim to the murder victim, these issues may be dramatic, if it is a spouse or an adult child who was contributing to his parents or even acting as a caregiver, or if it is a friend or a more distant relative. If the co-victim was present when the murder occurred, there will be additional issues to deal with the criminal justice system as a witness. Secondary victims of homicide should be aware that there are victim advocates available to them, through the local police department, and especially if they are also a witness, through the victim-witness assistance program at the district attorney's office in their borough, town, or city.

There are also specialized associations and organizations that can offer assistance to homicide co-victims who especially fit their focus, such as the nationwide Parents of Murders Children (POMC), mentioned previously, which was co-founded by the parents of a homicide victim. Even though the focus in their organization and support groups is on parents who have lost a child, they also offer help to surviving siblings. Another organization, based in Arizona but offering information to all survivors of homicide, is Homicide Survivors, Inc. It was started in 1982, a year after Gail Leland's 14-year-old son, Richard, was murdered. Reaching out to these and other organizations for those who have lost a loved one, including Compassionate Friends, may help homicide co-victims to deal with the emotional aftermath of loss. Some homicide co-victims, however, may find they need to be in support groups with others who have lost a loved one from homicide rather than illness or accidents. Other issues, like employment, financial matters, dealing with the media, helping children to deal with such a unique type of loss of a sibling, parent, or grandparent, are all issues that homicide co-victims may need help with during the weeks and months after the murder.

TERTIARY VICTIMS

We have discussed primary and secondary victims of homicide. As noted in Chapter 6, "Helping the Victim," there is a third potential victim, those who are helping victims. Especially when it comes to dealing with homicide, everything from notifying the next of kin, to going to the morgue, to dealing with the family and friends of the victim as the criminal justice system unfolds, the potential for burning out or feeling what is also known as compassion fatigue is very real. Refer back to Chapter 6 for suggestions about how to deal with being a tertiary victim.

GETTING PAST THE HOMICIDE OR MURDER AND REMEMBERING THE VICTIM

For those who have been killed, the term *survivor* obviously does not apply to those victims. But at least who that person was should survive. That is why this author, in interviews with secondary victims of homicide, asks questions like, "Tell me about Jennifer?" or "Tell me about your son Eden or your ex-husband Terry."

Darcy Maulsby, an Iowa historian, author, and storyteller from Lake City, Iowa, shared with this author: "I'm amazed at how many people I encounter who've lost a family member or friend to murder. When I lived in the Des Moines metro in the early 2000s near a small town called Granger, Iowa, my next-door neighbor told me one day that her sister had been murdered a number of years ago. This sister, Lisa Peak, was an Iowa college student and journalism major. I've always thought that one of the many tragedies of a murder is that the crime not only ends the person's life, but often steals the victim's humanity. It seems like people are much less interested in knowing how the person lived but want every detail about how that person died. I always try to remind people that interest in true crime should focus on a desire to honor the deceased, tell their story and hopefully find justice. Here's Lisa Peak's: https://iowacoldcases.org/case-summaries/lisa-peak/" (Maulsby, 2021)

Profile: ▪ Charisse Coleman, Secondary Victim of the Homicide of Her Brother Russell Coleman

Russell Coleman and his younger sister Charisse, 1987.

In 1995, Russell Coleman was a 42-year-old artist who was working as a clerk in a liquor store in Shreveport, Louisiana, when three men entered the store to rob it. Russell was shot three times in the back by one of them during the commission of the robbery, and he died instantly at the scene. Within a few days, based on a tip that police received, the three robbers were identified. Two years later, the defendant identified as the shooter was found guilty of first-degree murder by a jury and sentenced to death.

I interviewed Russell Coleman's younger sister, Charisse, via Zoom. I had contacted Charisse after reading, "Matters of Life or Death," the chapter she contributed to the book entitled, Wounds That Do Not Bind: Victim-Based Perspectives on the Death Penalty, edited by James R. Acker and David R, Karp.

At the time my brother Russell was killed in 1995, I was pursuing auditions and acting work in New York City. I had gotten a BFA in Acting at NYU and had lived in Cleveland, Seattle, and Berkley.

One of the things the murderer took away was the future development of a relationship that I was hoping to transform with Russell. [At the time of his death] we had a very difficult relationship and I was [actually] trying to figure out what kind of relationship I could have with my older brother. There was never any doubt that he loved me. How all that got communicated and the interactions and [is what I was in the midst of sorting out when he was killed.] [Coincidentally] right before he was killed, he called up my Mom and was able to thank her. It was an enormous gift to her. She referenced it [that phone call] even after she got dementia. We would reminisce about Russell and one of the things is that in that same phone call, he told her that she was his best friend. It's both heartbreaking and heartwarming.

Charisse joined a sibling support group that met in Brooklyn, New York. She attended for four years.

That's one of the things I got very leery telling people in the early couple of years after Russell died. I would say he was in a store and there was an armed robbery and he was shot and killed.

They would want to know what kind of store it was.

I was really hesitant to say "liquor store."

I could see it in their eyes. The relief sometimes the rather scornful judgment about it which was really painful. I didn't talk to people that I didn't know.

They didn't mean to be cruel. They didn't mean to be unsympathetic. They really were concerned and felt bad but at the same time they were looking for a glimpse of what in this story that will never happen to me or somebody I care about. Because Russell wasn't a Black kid in the projects. Russell wasn't the guy on the corner doing the drug deal. Somebody who looks like them, who lived like them, with the same basic socioeconomic racial stratum could this happen to them? I want to use the clinical term, it scared the shit out of them. They wanted something that was the clue of information that would tell them well nobody I know is a clerk in a liquor store, so they're safe.

It doesn't bother me now as much. At the time, I was furious.

I asked what Russell was like.

Russell was a charmer. He was good looking and witty and funny. That's one of the things Mike [his boss] told me.That I didn't know. How if anyone was in a down mood, as soon as Russell came through the door, the customers lightened up, lighted up.

Profile of a Survivor ▪ **Drew Crecente, Jennifer Ann's Father**

Drew Crecente with his daughter Jennifer Ann.

It sounds like a cliché—that no parent should have to bury his child—but that is all too true for parents who have lost a child, teenager, or grown child to violent crime. That is what happened to Drew Crecente. There was a brief profile of Drew's 18-year-old daughter, Jennifer Ann, at the end of the primary victims of homicide section of this chapter. As you may recall, Jennifer Ann was killed by her ex-boyfriend. As any parent who has lost a child to homicide knows, Drew's life would be changed forever. Almost immediately, Drew founded Jennifer Ann's Group (www.jenniferann.org), a nonprofit organization dedicated to teaching teens, their parents, educators, and the media about the dangers of teenage dating violence. Two years later, to gain a better understanding of what he and his family were going through because of Jennifer Ann's murder, Drew went to law school, graduating with his JD three years later. This computer programmer turned lawyer and victim advocate is the fulltime executive director of Jennifer Ann's Group. In the follow-up phone interview to Drew's guest presentation via Zoom in my victimology class, he described how he learned about Jennifer Ann's death and what his life has been like coping with the murder of his only child on February 15, 2006. For more on Drew Crecente, see the discussion of Jennifer Ann's Group, the educational nonprofit he set up in his daughter's memory, in Chapter 11 in the section on dating violence.

CONTROVERSIAL HOMICIDE CO-VICTIMS: THE FAMILIES OF CONVICTED MURDERERS

Another category of secondary victims of murder are the family members of the convicted murderers. We are not referring to the accused murderers who are innocent. Those miscarriages of justice will be discussed in Chapter 14. We are instead referring to the family members whose loved ones have killed and are either serving time for those murders or have been killed themselves, either in a murder-suicide situation or in a fatal encounter with police, bystanders, or civilians who intervened to stop the killing. Two women who have written books about their situations and gone public with their unique plight are Sue Klebold, mother of Dylan Klebold, one of the two Columbine High School mass murderers, and Kerri Rawson, whose father is the BTK serial killer. Sue Klebold's son and his friend murdered a dozen classmates and a teacher at Columbine High School in April 1999. The killers committed suicide at the end of their rampage. Seventeen years after the tragedy, Sue Klebold published a memoir. In her 2016 TED Talk, "My Son was the Columbine Killer," as well as in a BBC interview that is also posted on YouTube, Klebold shares about what she has gone through, how her son's crimes continue to impact her, and the emotional complexities she faces everyday of losing a child that way. (Klebold, 2016) As Klebold writes in the Prologue to her memoir, "I will give my life to reverse what happened that day. In fact, I would gladly give my own in exchange for just one of the lives that was lost. Yet I know that such a trade is impossible. Nothing I will ever be able to do or say can possibly atone for the massacre." (Klebold, 2016)

Kerri Rawson, the daughter of the BTK Killer, Dennis Rader, considers herself a victim of her father's horrific acts. She only learned of his 30 years of murder when she was 26, back in 2005, when an FBI agent knocked on her door and let her know that her father had just been arrested for being the BTK Killer. In 2019, Rawson published her memoir, *A Serial Killer's Daughter*. Her situation is different than Sue Klebold's, not just because she is the daughter of a killer rather than the killer's mother, but because her father is in prison for life without the possibility of parole. Because he is still alive, he must deal with her mixed feelings about him. At this time, she has made the decision not to write to him or to visit him. She has cut off all contact.

***

The experiences of victims dealing with the criminal justice system, including law enforcement and corrections, was explored in Chapter 5, "Victims and the Criminal Justice System." Rather than repeat that information here, please refer back to Chapter 5 related to how the criminal justice system treats primary and secondary victims of crime especially homicide.

SUMMARY

This chapter looked at the primary and secondary victims of homicide or murder. It is pointed out that the United States has the highest homicide rate of any Westernized country: 4.5 victims per 100,000 population which, in 2019, equaled 16,425 individuals. That is a stark contrast to other countries like the United Kingdom, with a homicide rate of .9 per 100,000, which equaled 602 victims in 2014, or France, with a 1.2 rate per 100,000 and 792 victims. According to the FBI *Crime in the United States 2018* report, that year in the United States, there were 14,123 murder victims in the United States.

The various types of homicide and murder are defined: excusable homicide; justifiable homicide; criminal homicide; first-degree murder; second-degree murder; felony murder; and manslaughter. Key factors that we know about the victims of homicide are: Most homicide victims are male, except for the crime of domestic violence or spousal homicide, in which the victims are disproportionately female. Victims are typically males between the ages of 18 and 25. More Blacks and Hispanics are victims of homicide than whites. (Since the National Incident-Based Reporting System (NIBRS) replaced the UCR in 2021, we will have even more detailed information about all crimes including murder.)

Drinking or drugs are factors in homicide with one study finding that one third of victims and one fourth of suspects had been drinking at the time of the murder. In homicides where the victim-offender relationship is known, only 10 percent are committed by strangers. The rest are committed by someone known to the victim: 29-50 percent by friends or acquaintances; 12-17 percent by a family member. The rest are unsolved homicides.

Although most murders are one offender and one victim, there are other unique types of murders of homicides including murder-suicides; mass murders; and serial murders.

Victim precipitation means that the victim was the first one to act in a manner that caused the fatal outcome, such as the victim striking the first blow in an altercation. Criminologist Marvin Wolfgang in his study of homicides in Philadelphia found that 26 percent of the cases that he studied he deemed examples of victim precipitation.

Secondary victims must deal with the aftermath of homicide and murder. Whether it is a spouse, child, parent, sibling, or friend, there are stages of grief that have to be dealt with as well as practical issues, like getting the body autopsied, arranging for the funeral, looking into any compensation that is due, as well as going through the stages of grief that would be experienced whenever a family member dies. But there are added issues, such as guilt, rage, self-blame, as well as short- and long-term aftermaths of the homicide or murder. In this chapter, the five stages of grief that Dr. Kubler Ross outlined are discussed as well as the sixth stage identified by David Kessler, finding meaning. That sixth stage is especially applicable to homicide co-victims because starting an organization, like Parents of Murdered Children, or getting involved in advocacy for victims, like what the late Edith Surgan did after her daughter's murder, can help in their healing from such a horrific event.

Getting support so PTSD and what is known as prolonged grief disorder (PGD) are dealt with is important because PGD can lead to physical problems as well as an elevated risk of suicidal ideation and suicidality (suicide plans or attempts). Although support groups may be helpful, especially if it is made up of survivors of homicide who are going through the same experiences, but professional counseling may be necessary and recommended.

KEY TERMS

capital punishment
co-victims of homicide
criminal homicide
death penalty
eldercide
excusable homicide
felony murder
filicide
first-degree murder
justifiable homicide
homicide survivors
honor killings
indirect victim
infanticide
intimate partner homicide
intimate partner violence (IPV)
MADD (Mothers Against Drunk Driving)
manslaughter
mass murder
matricide
mens rea
murder-suicide
parricide
post-traumatic stress disorder (PTSD)
prolonged grief disorder
rape-homicide
robbery-homicide
second-degree murder
secondary victims of homicide
serial killer
sexual homicide
survivor guilt
UCR (Uniform Crime Report)
vehicular homicide
vehicular manslaughter
victim blame
victim-offender relationship
victim precipitation
Werther Effect

REVIEW QUESTIONS

1. What section of the United States had a higher number of murders in 2018?
2. In the United States in 2018, what gender are more likely to be murdered?
3. What is the most common relationship between the victim and the offender in murder?
4. What is the most common weapon used in murder?
5. What are the five stages of grief that survivors of homicide may go through?
6. What is the sixth stage of grief?
7. What is the #1 most important consideration for law enforcement in doing a homicide notification?
8. Why is it especially important to address prolonged grief disorder (PGD)?

CRITICAL THINKING QUESTIONS

1. If you were a judge and someone killed another person while driving and texting, what sentence would you give him or her? What crimes would you charge him/her with? Explain your answer.
2. What's the #1 most interesting or shocking fact about homicide or murder victims that you learned in this chapter? Why was it surprising?

3. Do you think it's appropriate to include the parents or children of murderers as secondary victims of homicide? Why? Why not?

4. Should the media be allowed to interview the family and friends of homicide victims right after the crime? Why? Why not? Explain your answer.

ACTIVITIES

1. Next weekend, from Friday night until Sunday night, pick one city, possibly the one where you are living and/or going to school, and monitor what murders happen in your area. Who is the alleged perpetrator? the victim? Is there an arrest? What was the relationship between the perpetrator and the victim, if any?

2. Divide up into pairs or groups of four and make a list of statements you should avoid saying if you are dealing with someone who has lost a loved one to homicide, whether it is in a professional capacity, like a police officer or a crime victim advocate, or just the family member or friend of someone you know.

RESOURCES

Compassionate Friends
compassionatefriends.org
Offers help to families who have lost a child including a child through homicide or murder. There are local chapters throughout the United States offering self-help groups.

Escaping Victimhood (EV)
Birmingham, United Kingdom
escapingvictimhood.com
A charitable organization sponsoring 3-4 day retreats for 10-12 individuals directly or indirectly impacted by serious violent crime including secondary victims of homicide. Trained facilitators run the workshops.

Homicide Research Working Group (HRWG)
hrwg1991.org
This research professional association was started more than 30 years ago. Through its efforts, the peer-reviewed academic journal, *Homicide Studies*, premiered in February 1997 and is published quarterly by SAGE Publications.

Homicide Survivors, Inc.
homicidesurvivorsinc.org
Arizona-based organization for homicide co-victims.

MADD (Mothers Against Drunk Driving)
madd.org
Started in 1980 by Candy Lightener after the death of her 13-year-old daughter, Cindi, by a drunk driver. Has raised awareness about the tragic consequences of driving impaired by drinking or drugs.

National Center for Victims of Crime
victimsofcrime.org
Started in 1985 by Ala Isham and Alexander Auersperg, the National Center for Victims of Crime, originally called the Sunny Von Bulow National Victim Advocacy Center, was set up after their mother's victimization which put her in a coma for 28 years, until her death at age 76.

National Organization for Victim Assistance (NOVA)
trynova.org
Advocacy and training organization that helps those who provide services for crime victims as well as for the victims themselves.

Parents of Murdered Children (POMC)
pomc.org
Started by the Hullingers in Cincinnati, Ohio, following the murder of their 19-year-old daughter by her ex-boyfriend, whom she had met in Germany when they were both in a college exchange program. Offers self-help groups for the secondary victims of homicide through their local chapters throughout the United States; they also have an annual conference.

Survivors of Homicide
survivorsofhomicide.com
Connecticut-based organization offering free help to secondary victims of homicide.

Tunnel to Towers Foundation
tunnel2towers.org
Nonprofit that was set up after Stephen Siller died working as a firefighter during the 9-11 terrorist attack on the World Trade Center. The foundation pays off the mortgage for widows or widowers of first responders including firefighters, police, and military who died in the line of duty.

CITED WORKS AND ADDITIONAL REFERENCES

Abrahamsen, David. 1973. *The Murdering Mind*. New York: Harper & Row.

______________. August 20, 1980. Phone interview with author for murder-suicide research.

Acker, James R. and David R. Karp, editors. Assistant editor, Jarrett B Warshaw. 2006. *Wounds That Do Not Bind: Victim-Based Perspectives on the Death Penalty*. Durham, NC: Carolina Academic Press.

Addington, L.A. 2007. "Hot vs. Cold Cases: Examining Time to Clearance for Homicides Using NIBRS Data." *Justice Research and Policy*. 9: 87-112.

Adinkrah, M. 2005. "Vigilante Homicides in Contemporary Ghana." *Journal of Criminal Justice*. 33: 413-427.

Altman, Alex. June 4, 2020. "Why The Killing of George Floyd Sparking an American Uprising." *Time* magazine. Posted at time.com. (Published in the June 15, 2020 issue of *Time*)

American Psychiatric Association (APA). 2013. *Diagnostic and Statistical Manual for Mental Disorders*. 5th edition. Washington, D.C.: APA.

Amick-McMullan, A.; D. Kilpatrick and H. Resnick. 1991. "Homicide as a Risk Factor for PTSD among Surviving Family Members. *Behavior Modification*. 15: 545-559.

Amnesty International. 2011. "Death Penalty Statistics, Country by Country." Reprinted in *The Guardian* online. Ghttps://www.theguardian.com/news/datablog/2011/mar/29/death-penalty-countries-world

Alves-Costa, Filipa, Catherine Hamilton-Giachritsis, and Sarah Halligan. 2021. "'Everything Changes': Listening to Homicidally Bereaved Individuals' Practice and Intervention Needs." *Journal of Interpersonal Violence*. 36: NP2954-NP 2974.

Arango, Tim, Shailia Dawan, John Eligon, and Nicholas Bogei-Burroughs. April 20, 2021. "Derek Chauvin is Found Guilty of Murdering George Floyd." *The New York Times*. Posted online at nytimes.com

Armour, M. 2006. "Meaning Making for Survivors of Violent Death." In *Violent Death*. Edward Rynearson (ed.) New York: Routledge.

_________. 2007. "Violent Death." *Journal of Human Behavior in the Social Environment.* 14: 53-60.

Asher, Jeff. March 16, 2021. "Murder rate Remains Elevated as new crime Reporting system Begins." *The New York Times.*

Auerhahn, K. 2007. "Just Another Crime? Examining Disparity in Homicide Sentencing." *The Sociological Quarterly.* 48: 277-313.

Auchter, Bernie. June 2010. "Men Who Murder Their Families: What Research Tells Us." *NIJ (National Institute of Justice) Journal.* 266: 10-12.

Avoyellestoday.com. April 20, 2020. "Eden James Dupuy, 21." Obituaries. Available online at avoyellestoday .com

_____________. April 20, 2020. "Terence 'Terry' Alfred Dupuy, 50." Obituaries. Available online at avoyellestoday.com.

Baldus, D.C., et al. 1990. *Equal Justice and the Death Penalty: A Legal and Empirical Analysis.* Boston, MA: Northeastern University Press.

Barkas, J.L. (aka Jan Yager). Syndicated August 26, 1980. "Double Headers: Murder Followed by Suicide: Who Commits Them—and Why." INA (Independent News Alliance), part of United Media.

Baumer, E.P., Messner, S.F., and Felson, R.B. 2000. "The Role of Victim Characteristics in the Disposition of Murder Cases." *Justice Quarterly.* 17: 281-307.

Burch, Audra D. and Patricia Mazzei. February 14, 2018. "Death Toll Is at 17 and Could Rise in Florida School Shooting." *New York Times.* Posted at nytimes.com

Bell, Pamela Cole. 2015. "Stand Your Ground Laws: Mischaracterized, Misconstrued, and Misunderstood." *University of Memphis Law Review.* 46(2): 383-436.

Black, Donald. 1976. *The Behavior of Law.* New York: Academic Press.

_____________. 1980. *The Manners and Customs of the Police.* New York: Academic Press.

Blough, Richard H. and Kimberly D. McCorkle. 2020. *American Homicide.* 2d edition. Los Angeles, CA: SAGE.

Boelen, P.A., J. Van den Bout, J.D. Keijser, and H. Hoijtink. 2003. "Reliability and Validity of the Dutch Version of the Inventory of Traumatic Grief (ITG)." *Death Studies.* 27: 227-247.

Boelen, P.A. and H.G. Prigerson. 2012. "Commentary on the Inclusion of Persistent Complex Bereavement-Related Disorder in DSM-V." *Death Studies.* 36: 771-794.

Borg, M.J. and K. F. Parker. 2001. "Mobilizing Law in Urban Areas: The Social Structure of Homicide Clearance Rates." *Law and Society Review.* 35: 435-466.

Bruton, F. Brinley, Alexander Smith, Elizabeth Chuck and Phil Helsel. July 7, 2016. "Dallas Police 'Ambush': 12 Officers Shot, 5 Killed During Protest." Posted at https://www.nbcnews.com/

Bucholz, J.A. 2002. *Homicide Survivors: Misunderstood Grievers.* Amityville, NY: Baywood.

Burgess, Ann Wolbert, Cheryl Regehr, and Albert R. Roberts. 2013. *Victimology: Theories and Applications,* 2d edition. Burlington, MA: Jones & Bartlett Learning.

Burstow, Bonnie. 2003. "Toward a Radical Understanding of Trauma and Trauma Work." *Violence Against Women* . 9: 1293-1317.

Carter, D.L. and Carter, J.L. 2016. "Effective Police Homicide Investigations: Evidence from Seven Cities with High Clearance rates." *Homicide Studies.* 20: 150-176.

Catalano, Shanna, BJS Statistician. September 2010 (covering 2003 to 2007). "Victimization During Household Burglary." U.S. Department of Justice, Office of Justice Programs, Special Report. Posted at https://www.bjs.gov/content/pub/ascii/vdhb.txt

CBS Los Angeles, KCAL9. May 21, 2020. "Man Killed, Boy Wounded in Shooting at Glendale Taco Stand." Posted at https://losangeles.cbslocal.com/2020/05/21/man-killed-boy-wounded-glendale -taco-stand-shooting/

Center for Victim Research. July 2019. *Losing a Loved One to Homicide: What We Know about Homicide Co-Victims from Research and Practice Evidence.* 33 pages. Posted at https://ncvc.dspacedirect .org/bitstream/item/1440/CVR%20Research%20Syntheses_Homicide%20Covictims_Report .pdf?sequence=1

Chandler, Kim. July 14, 2021. "Inmate Killed in Assault at Fountain Prison." Associated Press (AP). Posted at apnews.com.

Chang, Jeani, Cynthia J. Berg, Linda E. Saltzman, and Joy Herndon. March 2005. "Homicide: A Leading Cause of Injury Deaths Among Pregnant and Postpartum Women in the United States, 1991-1999." *American Journal of Public Health.* 95: 471-477.

City News Service. February 14, 2020. "Driver Guilty of DUI, Murder, for Dragging Co-Worker Alongside Car." *San Diego Union-Tribune.* Posted at https://www.sandiegouniontribune.com/news/courts/ story/2020-02-14/latisha-ingram-verdict

Clark, John R. 2017. "Vehicular Manslaughter." *Air Medical Journal.* 36: 229-230.

Coleman, Charisse. Friday, January 8, 2021. Zoom interview with the author.

Committee to Protect Journalists (CPJ). "51 Journalists Killed in 2016." https://cpj.org/killed/2016/

Cooper, A. & Smith, E.L. 2011. "Homicide Trends in the United States, 1980-2008." *Bureau of Justice Statistics, Department of Justice.* Accessed at https://www.bjs.gov/content/pub/pdf/htus8008.pdf

Cortina, Lilia M. 2017. "From Victim Precipitation to Perpetrator Predation: Toward a New Paradigm for Understanding Workplace Aggression." In N. Bowling and M.S. Hershcovis, editors, *Research and Theory on Workplace Aggression*, pages 121-135. New York: Cambridge University Press.

Cortina, Lilia M, Veronica Caridad Rabelo, and Kathryn J. Holland. March 2018. "Beyond Blaming the Victim: Toward More Progressive Understanding of Workplace Mistreatment." *Industrial and Organizational Psychology.* 11: 81-100.

Crepeau, Megan. February 7, 2020. "Reputed Gang Member Beat Rival to Death Just Half-Hour after Being Placed in Same Cell in Cook County Jail, Prosecutors Say." *Chicago Tribune.*

Criminal Justice Information Services Division. 2010. Crime in the United States, 2010. Murder by Offender/Victim Situations, Posted at https://ucr.fbi.gov/crime-in-the-u.s/2010/crime-in-the-u.s.-2010/tables/10shrtbl04.xls

Currier, J.L., J.M. Holland, and R.A. Neimeyer. 2006. "Sense-Making, Grief, and the Experience of Violent Loss: Toward a Medicated Model." *Death Studies.* 30: 403-428.

Davis, Linsey. June 6, 2012. "Massachusetts Teen Aaron Deveau Found Guilty in Landmark Texting While Driving Case." ABCNews.com.

Decker, Michele R., Sandra L. Martin, and Kathryn E. Moracco. May 2004. "Homicide Risk Factors Among Pregnant Women Abused by Their Partners." *Violence Against Women.* 10: 498-513.

DeSilva, Kristen. December 28, 2019. "Woman Fatally Shoots Burglar in Southeast Las Vegas Valley, Police Say" Fox5Vegas.com.

DNAinfo. "Chicago Murders." "2016 Death Toll: 730." Posted at https://www.dnainfo.com/chicago/2016-chicago-murders

Dogbite.org. May 2018. "U.S. Dog Bite Fatalities: Breeds of Dogs Involved, Age Groups and Other Factors Over a 13-Year Period (2005 to 2017)." Posted at https://www.dogsbite.org/dog-bite-statistics-multi-year-fatality-report-2005-2017.php?gclid=EAIaIQobChMIwMvHhYn36QIVcuW1Ch3JegHiEAAYASAAEgJikPD_BwE

Dominus, Susan. February 28, 2016. "Review of *A Mother's Reckoning* by Sue Klebold." *New York Times* (Book Review).

Dupuy, Tereson. Thursday, January 14, 2021. Zoom interview with the author.

Durkheim, Emile. 1897, reprinted 1955. . *Suicide.* New York: Free Press.

Edwards, Breanna. "Texas Woman Stabbed to Death by Stepson After 'Gloating' About Dallas Cowboys Win." http://www.theroot.com. Posted December 22, 2016.

Ewing, Jody. September 7, 1976. Iowacoldcases.org. "Marie 'Lisa' Peak.'" Iowa Cold Cases. Posted at https://iowacoldcases.org/case-summaries/lisa-peak/

Federal Bureau of Investigation (FBI). 2020. *2019 Crime in the United States.* Posted at https://ucr.fbi.gov/crime-in-the-u.s/2019/crime-in-the-u.s.-2019/topic-pages/expanded-homicide

______________. 2019. *2018 Crime in the United States.* Expanded Homicide Data Tables, 1 through 20. posted at https://ucr.fbi.gov/crime-in-the-u.s/2018/crime-in-the-u.s.-2018/home

______________. 2018. *2017 Crime in the United States.* Washington, D.C.: U.S. Department of Justice.

______________. *Crime in the United States* (Murder from 1991 through 2010). Posted at https://ucr.fbi.gov/crime-in-the-u.s/2010/crime-in-the-u.s.-2010/tables/10tbl01.xls

____________. 2015. *2014 Uniform Crime Report—Crime in the United States.* Washington, D.C.: Department of Justice.

______________. Table 25. *2017 Crime in the United States.* "Percent of Offenses Cleared by Arrest or Exceptional Means." https://ucr.fbi.gov/crime-in-the-u.s/2017/crime-in-the-u.s.-2017/topic-pages/tables/table-25

Fausset, Richard and Neil Vigdor. March 16, 2021. Updated March 19, 2021. "8 People Killed in Atlanta-Area Massage Parlor Shootings." *New York Times.* Posted at the nytimes.com site.

Felson, Marcus. 1997. "Routine Activities and Involvement in Violence as Actor, Witness, or Target." *Violence and Victims.* 12(5): 209-220.

Fenton, Justin. December 20, 2016. "Father Convicted of Manslaughter in Daughter's Hot Car Death." *The Baltimore Sun.* Posted at baltimoresun.com.

Flewelling, R.L., and K.R. Williams. . 1999. "Categorizing Homicides: The Use of Disaggregated Data in Homicide Research. In M.D. Smith and M.A. Zahn (eds.). *Homicide: A Sourcebook of Social Research.*

Flynn, Sandra, Linda Gask, Louis Appleby, and Jenny Shaw. 2016. "Homicide-Suicide and the Role of Mental Disorder: A National Consecutive Case Series." *Social Psychiatry and Psychiatric Epidemiology.* 51: 877-884.

Fox 2 Detroit. March 30, 2020. "Police Investigate Suspected Domestic Murder Cases in Hazel Park and Southfield." Posted at https://www.fox2detroit.com/news/police-investigate-suspected-domestic-murder-cases-in-hazel-park-and-southfield

Fox 12 News. February 14, 2020. "Police: Intruder Shot, Killed by Homeowner in Vancouver" Posted at https://www.kptv.com/news/police-intruder-shot-killed-by-homeowner-in-vancouver/article_6c2b818c-4f24-11ea-ac80-e3a88ed2e294.html

Freeman, L.N., D. Shaffer, and N. Smith. 1996. "Neglected Victims of Homicide: The Needs of Young Siblings of Murder Victims.' *American Journal of Orthopsychiatry.* 66: 337-345.

Gaug, Andrew. May 31, 2012. "Texting Death Nets Kansas City Girl Jail Time, House Arrest." St. Joseph News-Press, posted at newspressnow.com

Georges, Leah C., Richard L. Wiener, and Stacie R. Keller. 2013. "The Angry Juror: Sentencing Decisions in First-Degree Murder." *Applied Cognitive Psychology.* 27: 156-166.

Goethe, J.W. 2010 (originally published in 1774). *The Sorrows of Young Werther.* Oxford, UK: Oxford University Press.

Gold, Michael. January 30, 2020. "Fotis Dulos, Connecticut Man Accused of Killing Jennifer Dulos, Is Dead." *The New York Times.* Posted online at nytimes.com

Goleman, Daniel. March 18, 1987. "Patterns of Death: Copycat Suicides among Youths." *New York Times.* Available at nytimes.com

Goodman, J. David. April 28, 2015. "Fatal Shooting Outside Brooklyn Church Was Set Off by Longtime Dispute, Police Say." *New York Times.* Posted at https://www.nytimes.com/2015/04/29/nyregion/brooklyn-church-shooting.html

Goodwin, John. 1979. *Murder USA.* Ballantine.

______________. August 20, 1980. Phone interview with author for murder-suicide research.

Grant, Isabel. March-April 1997. "Sentencing for Murder in Canada." *Federal Sentencing Reporter.* 9: 266-272.

Gross, Elliott, M.D. August 20, 1980. Phone interview with author for murder-suicide research.

The Guardian. "Death penalty statistics, country by country" https://www.theguardian.com/news/datablog/2011/mar/29/death-penalty-countries-world (Includes reprinted chart from Amnesty International, "10 countries with the most executions.")

Guttenberg, Fred. 2020. *Find the Helpers.* Coral Gables, FL: Mango.

Hanlon, Robert E. with Thomas V. Odle. 2013. *Survived by One: The Life and Mind of a Family Mass Murderer.* Elmer H Johnson & Carol Holmes Johnson Series in Criminology. Carbondale, IL: Southern Illinois University Press.

Hannah, Jason; Ralph, Ellis; Steve Visser. December 13, 2016. "Fallen Officers: 64 Shot in the Line of Duty in 2016." http://www.cnn.com/2016/08/14/us/police-officers-fatal-shooting-line-duty-nationwide/)

Hermann, Peter and Michael E. Ruane. August 9, 2014. "Medical Examiner Rules James Brady's Death a Homicide." *The Washington Post.* Posted online.

Hodge, Ryan. July 18, 2012. "City Teen Served Time for Texting While Driving." Posted at http://www.kansaslaw.com/news/kansas-city-teen-served-time-for-texting-while-driving-20120718/

__________. July 4, 2012. "Convicted of Texting While Driving: Could This Happen in Kansas?" Posted at http://www.kansaslaw.com/news/teen-convicted-of-texting-while-driving-could-this-happen-in-kansas-20120704/

Hough, Richard and Kimberly McCorkle., 2019. *American Homicide.* 2d edition. Thousand Oaks, CA: SAGE.

Houghton, Howard. July 15, 1980. "Crime Victims: Demanding Justice from an 'Unbalanced' System." *Impact: Albuquerque Journal Magazine.*6-7, 12-13.

Hullinger, Charlotte. Thursday, January 7, 2021. Zoom interview with the author.

Hullinger, Robert. Thursday, January 7, 2021. Zoom interview with the author.

Imperatrice, Joseph. September 10, 2020. Founder, Blue Lives Matter, NYPD.NYC. Guest presentation via Zoom, Forensic Health Issue, The Law, and the Criminal Justice System. Graduate course, Iona College.

Jeffrey, Terence P. November 2, 2012. "CDC: Homicide Kills 10 Times as Many American Infants as the Flu." Posted at http://www.cnsnews.com/news/article/cdc-homicide-kills-10-times-many-american-infants-flu

Jiao, A. Y. 2007. Explaining homicide clearance: An analysis of Chicago homicide data 1965-1995. *Criminal Justice Studies.* 20: 3-14.

Jones, Alexi and Wendy Sawyer. June 7, 2020. "Not Just "a Few Bad Apples": U.S. Police Kill Civilians at Much Higher Rates Than Other Countries." Prison Policy Initiative. Posted at their website.

Kaltman, S. and G. Bonanno. 2003. "Trauma and Bereavement: Examining the Impact of Sudden and Violent Deaths." *Journal of Anxiety Disorders.* 17: 131-147.

Karmen, Andrew. 2020, 1990. *Crime Victims.* 10th edition. Boston, MA: Cengage.

KCTV. "Teen Charged with Manslaughter in Texting While Driving Case." Posted April 19, 2012. Accessed at: http://www.kctv5.com/story/17587020/teen-charged-with-manslaughter-in-texting-while-driving-case

Kelleher, Kevin. August 25, 1995. "Wave of Violent Robberies Puts Armored Cars under the Gun." *San Francisco Business Times.* Retired from Gale Business Insights: Global.

Keneally, Meghan. May 13, 2018. "30 Years After 27 Died in Worst Drunk-Driving Crash, Survivors Ask if Enough Has Changed." Published at abcnews.go.com

Klebold, Sue. 2016. *A Mother's Reckoning.* New York: Crown.

Knezevich, Alison. March 26, 2020. "Baltimore Population Drops below 600,000, the Lowest Total in a Century, Census Estimates Show." *Baltimore Sun.* Posted at baltimoresun.com

Kramer, Margaret and Jennifer Harlan. February 13, 2019. "Parkland Shooting: Where Gun Control and School Safety Stand Today." *New York Times.* Posted at nytimes.com

Kubler-Ross, Elisabeth. 1969. *On Death and Dying.* New York: Macmillan.

Kurtzleben, Danielle. December 2, 2014. "America's Most Violent Jobs, in 5 Charts." Vox. Posted at https://www.vox.com/2014/12/2/7313827/workplace-homicide-murder-violent

Latus, Janine. November 4, 2020. Guest presentation via Zoom, Victimology class, John Jay College of Criminal Justice.

__________. 2007. *If I am Missing or Dead: Sister's Story of Love, Murder, and Liberation.* New York: Simon & Schuster.

Lee, Catherine. December 2005. "The Value of Life in Death: Multiple Regression and Event History Analyses of Homicide Clearance in Los Angeles County." *Journal of Criminal Justice.* 33: 527-534.

Levenson, Eric and Aaron Cooper. April 21, 2021. "Derek Chauvin Found Guilty of all Three Charges for Killing George Floyd." CNN. Posted at cnn.com

Leverick, Fiona.2006. *Killing in Self-Defense.* New York: Oxford University Press.

Lichtenhal, W.G., D.G. Cruess, and H.G. Prigerson. 2004. "A Case for Establishing Complicated Grief as a Distinct Mental Disorder in DSM-V." *Clinical Psychology Review.* 24: 637-662.

Liem, Marieke and Manuel Eisner. 2020. "From Homicide to Imprisonment: Mapping and Understanding the Flow of Homicide Cases." *Homicide Studies.* 24: 207-219.

Liem, Marieke and F. Koenraadt. 2018. *Domestic Homicide: Patterns and Dynamics.* London: Routledge.

Lion, Patrick. December 20, 2016. "Berlin Timeline of Terror: The Hijacking and How Tragedy Unfolded at German Christmas Market." Posted at http://www.mirror.co.uk/news/world-news/berlin-timeline-terror-hijacking-how-9490123

Liptak, Adam. December 4, 2007. "Serving Life for Providing Car to Killers." *New York Times.* Posted at nytimes.com

Litwin, K.J. 2004. "A Multilevel Multivariate Analysis of Factors Affecting Homicide Clearances. *Journal of Research in Crime and Delinquency.* 41: 327-351.

Lockwood, R. and G.R. Hodge. Summer 1986. "The Tangled Web of Animal Abuse: The Links between Cruelty to Animals and Human Violence." *The Humane Society.* 1-6.

Losey, Butch. 2011. *Bullying, Suicide, and Homicide: Understanding, Assessing, and Preventing Threats to Self and Others for Victims of Bullying.* London, UK: Routledge.

Luckenbill, David F. December 197. "Criminal Homicide as a Situated Transaction." *Social Problems.* 25: 176-186.

MacIntosh, Thomas. December 31, 2018. "London Violence: How a Bloody Night Became a Deadly Year." BBC News. Posted at https://www.bbc.com/news/uk-england-london-46530919

MADD (Mothers Against Drunk Driving). http://www.madd.org/laws/law-overview/Vehicular_Homicide_Overview.pdf)

Madhani, Aamer. January 2, 2018. "Chicago Murders Down, but Death Toll Still High." *USA Today.*

Maulsby, Darcy. Wednesday, July 14, 2021. Written e-mail communication with the author.

Mazzei, Patricia. February 13, 2019. "Parkland: A Year After the School Shooting That Was Supposed to Change Everything." *New York Times.* Posted at nytimes.com

McDonald, William. August 1980. Phone interview with author for murder-suicide research.

Merz-Perez, L., K.M. Heide, and I.J. Silverman. 2001. "Childhood Cruelty to Animals and Subsequent Violence against Humans." *International Journal of Offender Therapy and Comparative Criminology.* 45: 556-573.

Morrall, Peter. 2011. "Homicide and Its Effect on Secondary Victims: Peter Morrall and Colleagues Discuss the Impact of Violent Crime on the Families, Friends and Associates of Its Victims, and the Potential Forensic Role of Mental Health Nurses. *Mental Health Practice* (cover story). 15.

Muftik, L.R. & Hunt, D.E. 2013. "Victim Precipitation: Further Understanding the Linkage between Victimization and Offending in Homicide." *Homicide Studies.* 17: 239-254.

Null, Jan. October 31, 2016. Department of Meteorology & Climate Science, San Jose State University. "Heatstroke Deaths of Children in Vehicles." Posted at http://noheatstroke.org/

Mypanhandle.com. May 20, 2020. "Two Dead & Three Arrested in Robbery-Homicide Incident." Posted at https://www.mypanhandle.com/news/two-dead-three-arrested-in-robbery-homicideincident/

Nadeau, J.W. 1998. *Families Making Sense of Death.* Thousand Oaks, Ca: SAGE.

National Sheriffs' Association. July 2010. *First Response to Victims of Crime: A Guidebook for Law Enforcement Officers.* Office for Victims of Crime, U.S. Department of Justice.

NBCChicago.com. November 19, 2020. "Chicago Nears 700 Homicides in 2020, a Milestone Reached Just One Other Time Since 1998." NBC Chicago.

NBCConnecticut.com. March 30, 2020. "Owner of Stamford Jewelry Store Killed During Robbery; Police." Posted at https://www.nbcconnecticut.com/news/local/owner-of-stamford-jewelry-store-killed-during-robbery-police/2247177/

NBC7 Staff. July 7. 2021, updated on July 9, 2021. "Police ID Driver Stabbed to Death by Teenage Passenger in National City." Posted at nbcsandiego.com.

New York Daily News. December 21, 2016. "Baltimore Man Convicted of Involuntary Manslaughter in Hot Car Death of Young Daughter." Posted online.

Nickerson, John. Thursday, April 9, 2020. "Feds Identify Suspects in Robbery-Homicide of Stamford Jewelry Store Owner." *Stamford Advocate* newspaper. Posted at https://www.stamfordadvocate.com/policereports/article/Feds-identify-suspects-in-robbery-homicide-of-15190733.php

Office of National Statistics. "Homicide in England and Wales: year ending March 2018." Updated February 7, 2019. Posted at https://www.ons.gov.uk/peoplepopulationandcommunity/crimeandjustice/articles/homicideinenglandandwales/yearendingmarch2018

O'Flaherty, Brendan and Rajiv Sethi. 2010. "Homicide in Black and White." *Journal of Urban Economics.* 68: 215-230.

Oliveira, Nelson. Saturday, December 24, 2016. "Smothered to Death." *The Advocate.* Stamford, CT.: A1, A4.

Ordway, Denise-Marie. John Wihbey, and Leighton Walter Kille. June 7, 2020. "Deaths in Police Custody in the United States: Research review." Posted at https://journalistsresource.org/studies/government/criminal-justice/deaths-police-custody-united-states/

Parkes, C.M. 1993. "Psychiatric Problems Following Bereavement By Murder or Manslaughter." *Bereavement Care.* 12: 2-6.

Paybarah, Azi. March 30, 2020. "Rabbi Dies Three Months After Hanukkah Night Attack." *The New York Times.* Posted online at nytimes.com

Prabhu, Dolly. 2019. "A Lifetime for Someone Else's Crime: The Cruelty of Pennsylvania Felony Murder Doctrine." *University of Pittsburgh Law Review.* 81: 439+.

Prudente, Tim. January 1, 2020. "2019 Closes with 348 Homicides in Baltimore, Second-Deadliest Year on Record." *Baltimore Sun.* Posted at baltimoresun.com

Puckett, J.L. and R.J. Landman. 2003. "Factors Affecting Homicide Clearances: A Multivariate Analysis of a More Complete Conceptual Framework. *Journal of Research in Crime & Delinquency.* 40: 171-193.

Parkes, C.M. 1993. "Psychiatric Problems Following Bereavement by Murder or Manslaughter." *British Journal of Psychiatry.* 162: 49-54.

Rawson, Kerri. April 29, 2020. Guest interview via Zoom. John Jay College of Criminal Justice.

____________. April 17, 2020. Phone interview with author.

____________. 2019. *A Serial Killer's Daughter.* Nashville, TN: Thomas Nelson.

Redondo, Diego, Ph.D. June 16, 2020 and October 14, 2020. "Active Shooter Training." Via Zoom. Penology course, John Jay College of Criminal Justice.

Reed, Mark D., Dean A. Dabney, Susannah Naomi Tapp & Glen A. Ishoy 2020. "Tense Relationships between Homicide Co-Victims and Detectives in the Wake of Murder." *Deviant Behavior.* 41: 543-561.

Regoeczi, W.C. and M. Riedel. 2003. "The Application of Missing Data Estimation Models to the Problem of Unknown Victim/Offender Relationships in Homicide Cases." *Journal of Quantitative Criminology.* 19: 155-183.

Rctadmin. March 30, 2020. "Monsey Machete Attack Victim Dies—Rockland County Legislators Ask Public Not to Attend Funeral Due to COVID Pandemic." Posted at https://www.rocklandtimes.com/2020/03/30/monsey-machete-attack-victim-dies-rockland-county-legislators-ask-public-not-to-attend-funeral-due-to-covid-pandemic/

Reuters Staff. June 8, 2007. "Tennessee Preacher's Wife Gets 2 Months in Killing." Reuters.com.

Rheingold, Alyssa A. and Joah L. Williams. 2015. "Survivors of Homicide: Mental Health Outcomes, Social Support, and Service Use Among a Community-Based Sample." *Violence and Victims*. 870-883.

Rice, Doyle. May 6, 2019, updated May 7, 2019. "In the Past 20 Years, 800 Children Died While Trapped Inside Over-Life Cars." *USA Today*. Posted at usatoday.com.

Riches, G. and P. Dawson. 1998. "Spoiled Memories: Problems of Grief Resolution in Families Bereaved through Murder." *Mortality*. 3: 143-159.

Riedel, M. 1998. "Counting Stranger Homicides: A Case Study of Statistical Prestidigitation. *Homicide Studies*. 2: 206-219.

_________. and T.A. Rinehart. 1996. "Murder Clearances and Missing Data." *Journal of Crime and Justice*. 19: 83-102.

Rogers, Katie. 2016. "At Least 27 Shot, 7 Fatally, in Chicago over Christmas Weekend." Posted at http://www.nytimes.com/2016/12/25/us/chicago-shootings-gun-violence.html?_r=0

Rydberg, J and J.M. Pizarro. 2014. "Victim Lifestyle as a Correlate of Homicide Clearance." *Homicide Studies*. 18: 342-363.

Rynearson, E.K. 1995. "Bereavement after Homicide: A Comparison of Treatment Seekers and Refusers." *The British Journal of Psychiatry*. 166: 507-510.

Rynearson, T. 1994. "Psychotherapy of Bereavement after Homicide." *Journal of Psychotherapy, Practice & Research*. 3: 341-347.

Samuels, Alex. March 1971. "Excusable Loss of Self-Control in Homicide." *The Modern Law Review*. 34: 163-171.

Santa Cruz, Nicole. October 25, 2017. "Three Men Plead Not Guilty to Murder in Compton Slaying of 1-year-Old Autumn Johnson." *Los Angeles Times*. Posted at https://homicide.latimes.com/post/autumn-johnson-charges/

Saul, Josh. December 15, 2016. "Why 2016 Has Been Chicago's Bloodiest Year in Almost Two Decades." *Newsweek*. Posted at http://www.newsweek.com/2016/12/23/chicago-gangs-violence-murder-rate-532034.html

Saunders, Jim. November 17, 2016. "Appeals Court Upholds Michael Dunn Conviction in Jordan Davis Murder." News Service of Florida. Posted at https://news.wjct.org/post/appeals-court-upholds-michael-dunn-conviction-jordan-davis-murder

Seeman, Mary V. 2017. "The Marilyn Monroe Group and the Werther Effect." *Case Reports Journal*. 1.

Shallwani, Pervaiz. April 2015. "Former Resident Charged in Fatal Shooting of Homeless Shelter Director" *Wall Street Journal*. Posted at https://blogs.wsj.com/metropolis/2015/04/28/former-resident-charged-in-fatal-shooting-of-homeless-shelter-director/

Shear, M. K. 2015. "Complicated Grief." *New England Journal of Medicine*. 37: 153-160.

Siller-Scullin, Mary. Thursday, January 14, 2021. Phone interview with the author.

Simon, D. 1991. *Homicide: A Year on the Killing Streets*. Boston, MA: Houghton Mifflin.

State of Florida. Offender Search for Ryan Holle. http://www.dc.state.fl.us

Steele, David. "August 29, 2014. "People with Mental Illness Are More Likely to Be Victims of Homicide than Perpetrators of Homicide." Posted at http://www.nationalelfservice.net/populations-and-settings/crime/people-with-mental-illness-are-more-likely-to-be-victims-of-homicide-than-perpetrators-of-homicide/)

Sturup, J., Kralberg, D., and M. Kristiansson. 2015. "Unsolved Homicides in Sweden: A Population-Based Study of 264 Homicides." *Forensic Science International*. 257: 106-113.

Surgan, Edith. July 16, 1979. Personal correspondence.

___________. June 7, 1980. Personal correspondence.

Stretesky, P.B., T.O. Shelley, M. Hogan, and N. Unnithan. 2010. "Sense-Making and Secondary Victimization among Unsolved Homicide Victims." *Journal of Criminal Justice*. 38: 880-888.

Thompson, M.P., F.H. Norris, and R.B. Ruback. 1998. "Comparative Distress Levels of Inner-City Family Members of Homicide Victims." *Journal of Traumatic Stress*. 111: 223-242.

Turvey, Brent. 2014, 2009. *Forensic Victimology*. Boston: Academic Press, Elsevier.

__________. May 22, 2020. Interview with the author.

U.S. Department of Labor. January 2013. "Workplace Homicides from Shootings." Retrieved from https://www.bls.gov/iif/oshwc/cfoi/osar0016.htm

U.S. Department of Justice, BJS. Released November 2011. "Homicide Trends in the United States, 1980-2008. https://www.bjs.gov/content/pub/pdf/htus8008.pdf

United Nations Office on Drugs and Crime (UNODC). 2019. *Global Study on Homicide 2019*.

____________. 2014. Research and Trend Analysis Branch (RAB), Division of Policy Analysis and Public Affairs (DPA). *Global Study on Homicide 2013.* Vienna, Austria: UNODC. 166 pages. Accessed at https://www.unodc.org/documents/gsh/pdfs/2014_GLOBAL_HOMICIDE_BOOK_web.pdf

____________. July 8, 2019. "Homicide Kills far more People than Armed Conflict, New UN Study Shows" Posted at https://news.un.org/en/story/2019/07/1041981

Van Denderen, M., J. deKeokser. M. Kleen, and P. Boelen. 2013. "Psychopathology Among Homicidally Bereaved Individuals: A Systematic Review." *Trauma, Violence & Abuse.* 16: 70-80.

VanSickle, Abbie. June 27, 2018. "If He Didn't Kill Anyone, Why Is It Murder?" *New York Times.* Posted online.

Varandani, Suman. April 13, 2020. "Louisiana Murder-Suicide: Son Shoots Father with AR-15 Style Rifle before Killing Self. Posted at ibtimes.com

Violence Policy Center. September 15, 2015. "More than 1,600 Women Murdered by Men in One Year, New Study Finds." Posted at http://www.vpc.org/press/more-than-1600-women-murdered-by-men-in-one-year-new-study-finds/

Von Hentig, Hans. 1948. *The Criminal and His Victim: Studies in the sociology of crime.* New Haven, CT: Yale University Press.

____________. September-October 1940. "Remarks on the Interaction of Perpetrator and Victim." *Journal of Criminal Law and Criminology.* 31: 303-309.

Voss, Harwin and John R. Hepburn. 1969. "Victim Precipitated Homicide in Chicago." *Journal of Criminal Law and Criminology.* 4(3): 499-508.

Weaver, Russell L. and Steven I. Friedland. October 1, 2014. "Driving While 'Intexticated': Texting, Driving, and Punishment." *Texas Tech Law Review.* 101-111.

Wertham, Frederic. 1949. *The Show of Violence.* New York: Doubleday.

West, D.J. 1965. *Murder Followed by Suicide.* London: Heinemann.

WFAA Staff. February 11, 2020. "Verbal Argument Leads to Fatal Shooting, Dallas Police Say." Posted at https://www.wfaa.com/article/news/crime/verbal-argument-leads-to-fatal-shooting-dallas-police-say/287-15f8e6e5-5f12-4a7b-bb95-2ae1ebc7bc77

Witty, Helen. May 28, 2020. "32 Years after the Deadliest Drunk Driving Crash in U.S. History, We Must Continue to Fight." Posted at MADD.org.

Wolfgang, Marvin E. 1958. *Patterns of Criminal Homicide.* Philadelphia: University of Pennsylvania Press.

____________. August 20, 1980. Phone interview with the author.

____________. 1957. "Victim Precipitated Criminal Homicide." *Journal of Criminal Law, Criminology and Police Science.* 48(1): 1-11.

Wong, Grace; Elvia Malagon; Rosemary Regina Sobel, and Katherine Rosenberg-Douglas. November 19, 2016. "Police: Two Held, Murder Charges Expected in Shooting of Grandson of U.S. Rep. Davis." *Chicago Tribune.* Posted at http://www.chicagotribune.com/news/local/breaking/ct-danny-davis-grandson-dead-20161118-story.html

Wright, Jeremy and Christopher Hensley. 2003. "From Animal Cruelty to Serial Murder: applying the graduation hypothesis. *International Journal of Offender Therapy and Comparative Criminology.* 47: 71-88.

Yager, Jan. 2020 (originally published in 1978 by Scribner's). *Victims.* With a new introduction and updated bibliography and resources. Stamford, CT: Hannacroix Creek Books, I.

Yardley, Elizabeth, David Wilson, and Morag Kennedy. 2017. "'To Me Its [Sic] Real Life': Secondary Victims of Homicide in Newer Media." *Women & Offenders.* 12: 467-496.

Zinzow, H.M., Rheingold, A.A., M. Ryczkiewicz, B.E. Saunders, and D.G. Kilpatrick. 2011. "Examining Posttraumatic Stress Symptoms in a National Sample of Homicide Survivors: Prevalence and Comparison to Other Violence Victims." *Journal of Traumatic Stress.* 24: 743-746.

Videos, Films, or TED Talks

Finding Jenn's Voice. Produced and directed by Tracy Schott. Documentary about Jennifer Snyder who was murdered in 2011. https://voies4change.net

Kleibold, Sue. 2016. "My Son Was a Columbine Shooter." TED Talk. https://www.ted.com/talks/sue_klebold_my_son_was_a_columbine_shooter_this_is_my_story?language=en

Jackie. 2016.. Starring Natalie Portman as Jackie Kennedy. Distributed by Fox Searchlight Films.

Newtown. 2016. Documentary about the Sandy Hook Elementary School mass murder told from the point of view of several of the families who lost a child. Directed by Kim A. Snyder.

Tower. 2016.. Documentary about the University of Texas mass murder told from the point of view of the victims and survivors. Produced by Meredith Vieira.

Nebraska Educational Broadcasting Company. 2012. *Until He Is Dead: A History of Nebraska's Death Penalty*. 2012. Produced by the NET News (Nebraska's Educational Broadcasting Company). Copyright 2012. Length: 56 minutes. http://video.netnebraska.org/video/2336565831/

Witness. 2016. Documentary about the famous Kitty Genovese murder in Queens, New York on March 13, 1964. Created by her brother, Bill Genovese.

CHAPTER **EIGHT**

Property Crime Victims

Robbery, Burglary, Larceny/Theft, Motor Vehicle Theft, Graffiti, Vandalism, and Arson

Learning Objectives

After you finish reading this chapter, you should be able to:

1. Know the estimated number of property crimes in the United States according to the two main sources of official crime data.
2. Define a fence and how the stolen goods market operates.
3. Identify and describe the key factors related to robbery victims, namely age, where the crimes take place, time of day, presence or type of weapon, victim-offender relationship, and clearance rate.
4. Explore the reactions that robbery victims may experience.
5. Highlight steps potential victims can take to reduce the chance of being a robbery victim especially in work-related situations.
6. Define a burglary, its prevalence, what time of day most burglaries occur, and the clearance rate.
7. Define a home invasion.
8. Identify at least three types of larceny-theft, the prevalence of larceny-theft in the United States, and its clearance rate.
9. Understand who are the victims of shoplifting.
10. Know the prevalence of motor vehicle theft and its victims.
11. Describe the typical victims of graffiti and vandalism.
12. Define arson and explore its victims.

OVERVIEW

Property crimes include robbery, burglary, larceny-theft, motor vehicle theft, graffiti, vandalism, and arson. Except for robbery, vandalism, and arson, most of these crimes involve taking money or goods from victims without the threat or use of force or causing damage to property or injury to individuals. Although the number of injuries or deaths due to property crime is much lower than in cases of violent personal crimes, to victims and their families, any injury or death because of a robbery-homicide, a burglary that turns into a deadly home invasion, or an arson-homicide, is altogether too real to the victims and their families.

Robbery is actually a crime of violence *and* property, but it is categorized by the National Incident-Based Reporting System (NIBRS) as a crime against property. (The Uniformed Crime Reports (UCR) previously categorized robbery as one of four violent crimes in the Crime Index reported on annually to the FBI.).

This chapter defines and explains each of the major property crimes. These property crimes fit into the category of so-called conventional property crimes, what were previously referred to as street crimes. In the next chapter, Chapter 9, "Cybercrime, White-Collar Crime, and Economic Crime Victims," you will learn about other types of property crime victims such as identity theft, financial and so-called white-collar crime, and even piracy of intellectual property that victimizes companies and individuals by stealing their earnings. (Cyberstalking victims are also discussed in Chapter 13, "Victims of Assault, Domestic Violence, Stalking, and Elder Abuse," within the section of that chapter that explores stalking victims.)

In *Criminal Victimization, 2018*, based on the self-reports of a sample of American households, the National Crime Victimization Survey (NCVS), Bureau of Justice Statistics statisticians Rachel E. Morgan, Ph.D. and Barbara A. Oudekerk, Ph.D. report that there were more than 13 million (13,502,840) property crime victims including burglaries (2,639,620), trespassing (1,724,720), motor-vehicle theft (534,010), and other thefts (10,329,210). The "other thefts" refer to the unlawful taking or attempted unlawful taking of property or cash without personal contact with the victim. (Morgan and Oudekerk, 2019)

The official FBI statistics, based only on crimes reported to the police, recorded 6,925,677 property crimes in the United States in 2019. It tracked burglary, larceny-theft, motor vehicle theft, and arson. (FBI, *2019 Crime in the United States*) In 2019, robbery was still included in the category of violent crime by the UCR. In 2019, there were an estimated 267,988 of reported robberies. (FBI, 2019)

CLEARANCE RATES FOR PROPERTY CRIMES

For the United States in 2019, here are the clearance rates, reported property crime offenses that were cleared by an arrest: motor vehicle thefts (13.8%); burglary (14.1%); larceny-theft (18.4%); arson (23.8%); and robbery (30.5%). (FBI, *2019 Crime in the United States*, "Clearances")

VICTIMS OF PROPERTY CRIMES

Here are real-life examples of property crime victims:

- Mail was stolen from mailboxes in a North Carolina neighborhood. A homeowner witnessed the mailbox thief in the act just after 7 P.M. on a Thursday night and was able to take a picture of the thief. It was not an elderly woman committing the crimes, as the neighborhood had assumed, but a man with a criminal record in Georgia. (Marusak, 2021)
- A National Guard firefighter in West Virginia was killed when responding to a fire at 2 A.M. on a Sunday morning. By that evening, it was determined that the cause of the fire was arson. (Kesslen, 2020)
- When Louisa T. went to visit her family in Puerto Rico, she left her pocketbook and wallet in her car. Her wallet was stolen, along with her credit cards. She called the police and canceled her cards. She suspected her relative's son but she did not say anything to the police since he was a family member. (Anonymous interview shared with the author.)
- Years ago, this author was standing on a crowded city bus when she was jostled by another passenger, who kept apologizing. Not once, but two or three times, the other bus passenger kept pushing, with the quick follow-up, "I'm sorry." The response was, something like, "Don't worry about it." Soon, the bus stopped and the passenger got off the bus, along with another passenger. It was soon discovered that the two-person team had managed to steal a wallet. That technique is actually a common one that pickpockets use. As James Brown, a United Kingdom hypnotist and "stage pickpocket" explains, ". . . it's actually about directing the mind towards something." (Williams, 2014)
- An 84-year-old woman who was shopping for Christmas presents had her purse snatched as the assailant ran out of the store. Captured on security video cameras, a 17-year-old was arrested and charged with robbery by snatching, grand theft, possession of crack cocaine, and violation of probation. (Florida newspaper report, 2019, specific details withheld pending the outcome of the case.)

THE STOLEN GOODS MARKET

Although this chapter is focused on the victims of property crime, it is useful to gain a better understanding of just how stolen goods are disposed of. That information might help to better explain why property crimes have such low clearance rates that were described above.

This topic applies to all the conventional property crimes in this chapter except for vandalism and arson. For all the other property crimes, how the stolen goods are disposed of, including getting them converted into cash, is something most robbers, burglars, motor vehicle thieves, and those who steal smartphones and other electronics have to consider. What used to be referred to as a **fence**, the person who will accept the stolen goods and give the thief cash for it, is now referred to as the "**stolen goods market**" (Schneider, 2005).

Dr. Jacqueline Schneider's research in her article, "Stolen Goods Markets: Methods of Disposal," is based on qualitative in-depth face-to-face interviews with 50 incarcerated male thieves whose thefts were accomplished through burglary and shoplifting. They were 22, on average, and their stealing was in Shropshire, England, a community around 138 miles from London.

In Table 8.1, you will see the first choice of those burglars was to sell it to a handler or fence, followed by selling to friends. The third choice was to use it themselves, and the fourth was to trade it for drugs. Absolutely no one stated that they would sell it to family or give the stolen goods away. (It could be hypothesized that they would not sell the stolen goods to family because their family might be unaware of their criminal activities. This is, of course, only a hypothesis since their families were not interviewed.) (Schneider, 2005: 134)

TABLE 8.1. Preferred Method of Disposal for Shoplifted Goods

Method	First Choice, N (%)
Sell it to handlers/fence	19 (38)
Sell it to friends	12 (24)
Use it myself	8 (16)
Trade it for drugs	4 (8)
Other	1 (2)
Sell it to family	0 (0)
Give it away	0 (0)
Not applicable	6 (12)*

"*These interviewees did not admit to stealing from shops."

Source: Reprinted from Schneider, 2005: 134) (N = number)

Stuart Henry, in his report, "On the Fence," published in the *British Journal of Law and Society* in 1977, cautioned that "recent evidence suggests that the main support of illegal sales from the thief is the legitimate businessman." (Henry, 1977: 132) Henry continues, quoting the District Attorney for Los Angeles: " Too many legitimate businessmen are willing to buy hot merchandise if it assures them of higher profit." (Henry, 1977: 133)

ROBBERY

Just five of the infamous and glamorized robbers throughout U.S. history that are associated with the violent property crime of robbery are Bonnie and Clyde, John Dillinger, Baby Face Nelson, and Jesse James. (Alder, 2019) As you will see from the anecdotes of real-life **robbery** victims that follow, there is nothing glamorous about being robbed:

- Three men in their 20s, along with a female driver, were involved in stealing the property of a family in downtown Los Angeles before taking off in a gray car. The 26-year-old father was pistol-whipped on the head and shot in the arm. A 2-year-old and his 28-year-old mother ran to safety. (ABC7.com, 2021)

- A 41-year-old woman was charged in federal court with the armed robbery of a bank in Liberty, Missouri. The robber allegedly handed the bank teller a note that read, "Hand me all the money or I will shoot." The teller gave the robber, who appeared to have a gun, money from the cash drawer. The robber made off with $971 in cash and was arrested two days later. (Houx, 2021)
- Staff at a petrol station in Dublin, Ireland were held up by three teenagers, aged 18, with a handgun. A regular patrol car with an armed detective just happened to drive by as the robbery was unfolding. The alleged robbers were promptly detained. (*Irish Times*, 2001)

Those are just a few of the hundreds of thousands of real-life robberies that take place every day in the United States and around the world. In 2019, there were a reported 267,988 robberies in the United States. But since we know that many crimes, as many as half, go unreported, the number of actual robberies may be double that number. Of those 267,988 robberies, a reported 509 resulted in the death of the victim. (FBI, Expanded Homicide Data Table 10, *2019 Crime in the United States.*)

You may recall from Chapter 7, "Primary and Secondary Victims of Homicide," the third real-life example at the beginning of that chapter was about a student who was hit over the head with a golf club so the 15-year-old robber could steal her bicycle. She died several days later from her injuries. If you do the math, percentage-wise 509 robbery-homicides out of 267,988 robberies in 2019 may seem like a relatively small number. But tell that to the family, friends, and co-workers of those murdered victims who were killed during the commission of a robbery so the offender could steal a bicycle, money, a smartphone, or a necklace.

Yes, robberies are scary crimes for the victim. According to the FBI's NIBRS definition, robbery involves "The taking, or attempting to take, anything of value under confrontational circumstances from the control, custody, or care of another person by force or threat of force or violence and/or by putting the victim in fear of immediate harm." (NIBRS, 2012)

Robbery involves face to face confrontation with one or more assailants who just might have a weapon or the victim might also get beaten up.

The **clearance rate**—the number of reported offenses that lead to the arrest of a suspect—for robbery is just 30.4 percent of all reported robberies in the United States for 2018. It is a higher clearance rate than for burglary, which was only 13.9 percent. Still, in addition to being a traumatizing experience for robbery victims, it is rare for the property that is stolen by thieves to be recovered.

With 34 percent of the robberies in 2018 in the United States involving the presence of a firearm, and since by definition a robbery involves face to face confrontation with the offender, it is clear why robbery is considered a violent crime whether or not there is injury to the victim. An even higher percentage of robberies are considered a **strong-arm robbery** (also referred to as a **mugging** or a **yoking**) meaning the show of force is using hands, feet, fists, or teeth during the robbery. In 2018, for reported robberies, 88.7 percent involved a firearm, other weapon, a knife or other cutting instrument (an armed robbery), or were a strong-arm robbery. (Federal Bureau of Investigation, 2018 UCR Reports, Table 19.)

Facts About Robbery

As noted above, armed versus unarmed is a key consideration regarding a robbery. Table 8.2 shows the breakdown for 2018 of weapons used in a robber, according to the FBI UCR (Uniform Crime Reporting) Program.

TABLE 8.2. Weapons Used During Robbery, 2018

Weapon	Percentage
Strong-arm tactics (hands, feet, fists)	38.2
Firearms	33.9
Knifes or cutting instruments	7.4
Other dangerous weapons	9.2

Source: FBI, *2018 Crime in the United States*

Losses in 2018 from robberies averaged $2,119 per robbery, according to the FBI Uniform Crime Reporting (UCR) with total estimated robbery losses of $598 million. The losses were highest in residences, totaling an estimated $4,600 per offense.

What are some of the other key considerations for victims and robbery? First is the relationship between the robber and the victim. In 2015, according to the Office of Victims of Crime (OVC), more than 50 percent of robbers were strangers to their victims.

The profile of the typical robbery victim is that he is a male, between the ages of 18 and 24, and unmarried. Robbery victims are more likely to be Black and Hispanic than white. The most common place for robberies to occur is on the street. A trend reported in a government special report by Caroline Wolf Harlow, Ph.D., "Robbery Victims" notes this important fact about robberies: "In the majority of victimizations two or more offenders worked together." (Harlow, 1987:2) Dr. Wolf also points out that robbery is often not a standalone crime, meaning, it occurs in the commission of another crime. She states: "Robbery often occurs in conjunction with other crimes. From 1976 through 1984, for example, between 9.3 percent and 10.8 percent of all homicides were perpetrated with robbery as the circumstance or motive. Three percent of robbery victims between 1973 and 1984 were also raped; 8 percent suffered a burglary; and 4 percent, a motor vehicle theft." (Harlow, 1987:1)

The FBI's 2018 statistics breakdown of the location of those 282,061 robberies are shown in Figure 8.1.

FIGURE 8.1 | **Robberies by Location***

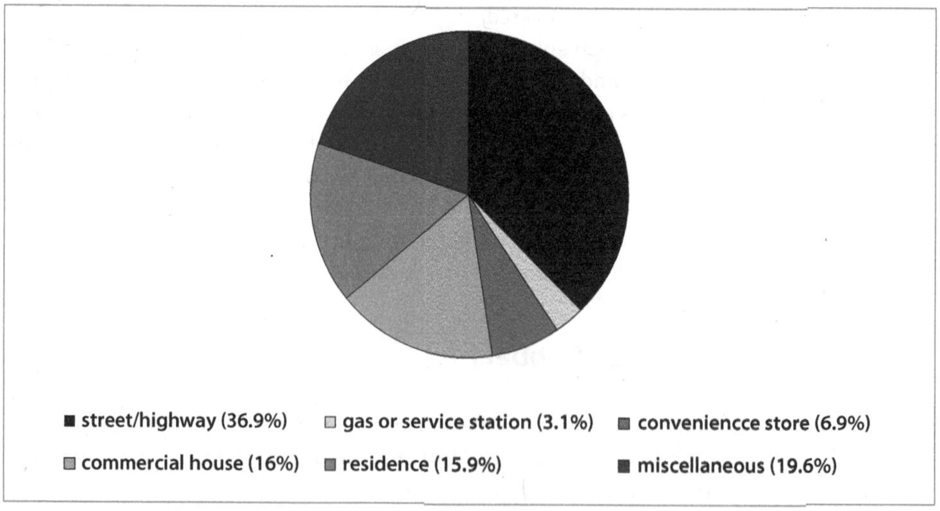

Source: Robberies by location, FBI *2018 Crime in the United States* Table 1.

* Bank (1.6%) is not included in Figure 8.1

Although the year for Dr. Harlow's report might be somewhat dated, the facts that it shares about robbery are still valid, namely

- attacks occur in over half of the robberies
- one-third of the robbery victims were injured
- injuries are more likely to occur in the following situations—the victim was female, the robbery happened at night, there was more than one offender, or there was a weapon
- two-thirds of the victims had property stolen (Harlow, Summary, "Robbery Victims")

Remember that there were a reported 267,988 robberies in the United States in 2019, which is also estimated to be only half or even less than half of the actual number of robberies because of underreporting by 40-50 percent. Consider that 1 in 3 robbery victims get injured, not to mention the 509 who died that year, victims of **robbery-homicide**.

Although statistically, as noted above, the typical robbery victim is a minority single male between the ages of 18 and 24, the story about the following famous robbery victim demonstrates that anyone could be a victim of robbery. The robbery victim in this case was Kim Kardashian, who was robbed in a Paris hotel which journalist Mark Seal describes as more like a home than a hotel in his article about the robbery, "The Inside Story of the Kim Kardashian Paris Hotel Heist." Kardashian, who is known around the world for her reality TV show, financial empire, marriage to Kanye West, and being part of the Kardashian clan, was robbed of her 20-karat diamond ring which, according to Seal, her husband had recently bought for $4 million. (Seal, 2016)

Sadly, what followed after Kardashian's victimization was one of the more well-publicized cases of **victim blame**, whereby the blame for the crime shifts from the perpetrator to the victim. Far too many wondered whether the victim was to blame for the robbery because she had bragged about her ring and had shown it off on social media. Some even fell into the victim defounding trap by wondering whether she had staged the crime to get the insurance money for her ring or whether it was all just a publicity stunt to generate attention. The public response to Kardashian's victimization, including the horrifying experience of being tied up, is highlighted in Alex Abad-Santos' article, "We don't treat Kim Kardashian like a person. Her robbery exposed that" published at Vox.com a few days after the armed robbery. (Abad-Santos, 2016)

After all the false accusations were dispelled, and public opinion reached the consensus that Kardashian was, indeed, a victim of armed robbery, it turned into a teaching moment—that anyone could become the victim of a crime including the violent crime of armed robbery.

Robbery: Special Circumstances

Robbery-homicide. We already answered the key question at the beginning of this chapter about how likely a robbery is to turn into a robbery-homicide. To recap, in the United States in 2018, out of 14,123 murder victims, 548 were killed during the commission of a robbery. That is down by 137 murder victims from the 685 who died during a robbery in 2013 and substantially down from the 2,500 who died during the commission of a robbery in 1980. Still, the unfortunate fact that 548 murder victimizations occurred during the commission of a robbery makes each of those a violent property crime, which helps to explain how much fear robbery invokes. According to Zimring and Zuehl's classic study of robbery-homicide in Chicago, 16 percent of the homicides that year were robbery-homicides at the rate of 3.8 per 100,000 population. They predicted that those numbers were underreported.

In Philip J. Cook's comprehensive study of robbery entitled, "Robbery Violence," published in the *Journal of Criminal Law and Criminology*, some interesting facts about robbery-homicide, also known as **robbery-murder**, are shared:

- Robbery murders, like non-robbery murders, are more likely to be committed with a gun (65%) with weapons present in only 17 percent of all robberies.
- Robbery murder offenders are more likely to be strangers (in 73 percent of robbery murders the perpetrator is a stranger compared to only 12 percent in non-felony murders although that percentage might be higher if there was more information for the "unknown" victim-offender relationships).
- Robbery murder victims are older than victims of either non-felonious murder or robbery (Cook, 1987: 357-376).

As Cook notes, "Armed robbery is far more likely to result in death than is an **un-armed robbery**." (Cook, 1987: 366)

Robbery- homicide may also include what is known as **felony murder**. Those are the situations where an accomplice to robbery, who is not the shooter or the one who wields the knife, but is part of the felony that was being committed when the murder was also committed, even though the murder was by another offender, that offender will also be guilty of felony murder.

To put famous faces on the secondary victims of two robbery-homicides let us remember the deaths of Marie and Terence Duffy, parents to Patrick Duffy, who stared in the hit TV show *Dallas*. They were killed during a robbery at their Montana bar in 1986. A 19-year-old was sentenced in 1987 to 75 years for one murder, 75 years for the second murder, 20 years for robbery, and 10 years for assault, with the sentences to run consecutively. (Conroy, 1987)

Another famous secondary victim of robbery-homicide is basketball legend Michael Jordan. In 1993, as ABC News reports shared in their 2012 article, "Stars Whose Parents Have Been Murdered," Michael Jordan's father James R. Jordan had pulled off the side of the road to take a nap and was shot to death; his luxury car stolen. Weeks later, Jordan's father's body was discovered in a swamp. The perpetrators of that robbery-homicide were caught by tracing the calls they had made using James Jordan's cell phone; they were subsequently sentenced to life in prison. (ABCNews.com, June 25, 2012)

In Chapter 7, "Primary and Secondary Victims of Homicide," you read about Charisse Coleman and her older brother Russell who was the victim of a robbery-homicide in Shreveport, Louisiana. Russell, an artist, was working as a clerk at a liquor store. Three men robbed the store, shooting and killing Russell in the process of that robbery. Refer back to that interview for a detailed account of how just one robbery-homicide impacts the family of the victim.

Bank robberies. There are other robberies besides robbery-homicides that have special circumstances, like bank robberies. The three main types of bank robberies are:

1. robbing someone who is withdrawing money from the ATM
2. robbing a bank where the teller is asked to turn over the cash in his or her drawer
3. bank robberies involving hostage taking

Whereas most robberies of individuals as discussed throughout this chapter are considered crimes against the state with convictions resulting in time in a state penitentiary, since 1934 it has been a federal crime to rob any national bank or state member bank of the Federal Reserve System. Therefore, investigations of bank robberies are handled by the Federal Bureau of Investigation (FBI) and offenders, if convicted, are sentenced to time in a federal prison. The FBI has been associated with bank robberies as far back as the 1930s and the infamous John Dillinger who robbed 24 banks with the help of the "Dillinger Gang."

According to the FBI, in 2018 in the United States, there were 3,033 bank robberies. Most of the cases (2,707) involved commercial banks. The remainder were divided among credit unions (215), armored carrier companies (10), savings and loan associations (23), mutual savings banks (5), and unknown (15). Friday was the most popular day of the week for bank robberies and 3-6 P.M. was the most popular time for a bank to be robbed. Branch offices were by far the most common places for the robberies to occur (2,826) versus main offices (93). Thirty-four were injured in these 3,033 crimes with 9 taken hostage. In 2019, the (FBI, fbi.gov) individuals to die during the commission of a bank robbery were four perpetrators.

The chance of getting caught is much greater for bank robbers: the clearance rate is 60 percent, almost double the overall clearance rate for all robberies (which was 30.4%). Despite the higher clearance rate, unfortunately bank robbery may still happen for the same reason convicted bank robber Willie Sutton (1901-1980) supposedly answered when asked why he robbed banks, "Because that's where the money is."

Ironically, in his 1976 memoir, Willie Sutton claimed he never actually said that infamous line. Here is what he wrote about it: "I never said it. The credit belongs to some enterprising reporter who apparently felt a need to fill out his copy. I can't even remember when I first read it. It just seemed to appear one day, and then it was everywhere. If anybody had asked me, I'd have probably said it. . . . Why did I rob banks? Because I enjoyed it. I loved it. I was more alive when I was inside a bank, robbing it, than at any other time in my life. . . ." (Sutton and Linn, *Where the Money Was*, 1976)

Robbing banks may have been a thrill for infamous Willie Sutton but it was a tragedy for the four who died in the United States in 2018 during bank robberies or the 34 who were injured, including 9 customers and 15 employees (the others who were injured included 2 law officers, 3 guards, 3 perpetrators, and 2 "other"), or the 9 hostages that were taken in bank robberies that same year (8 employees and 1 "other"). (FBI *Bank Crime Statistics*, 2018)

Comply or Resist?

One of the biggest controversies in victim-offender interaction regarding robbery is whether a victim should resist or comply. Will compliance increase the likelihood of surviving the robbery and even reduce the probability of getting injured? A study by Philip J. Cook whereby he analyzed National Crime Survey data (the precursor of the NCVS surveys), led him to the realization that there is no definitive answer. As Cook concludes:

> I am convinced that victims should comply with an armed robber's demands in most cases and that it is a particularly dangerous and foolhardy act to forcefully resist a robber with a gun. This judgment is based on what I like to think of as common sense. The data indicate that most victims act as if they agree with this judgment. I further believe that there are exceptions to the "no forceful resistance" rule, cases in which the robber

> intends to inflict serious injury on the victim. The upshot is that some victims save their lives by resisting and some lose their lives by resisting. Currently available data are not helpful in suggesting how to increase the former or to reduce the latter". (Cook, *Journal of Legal Studies, 1986*:416)

Cook's research and writings were published in the 1980s. More recently, in 2014, Marie Rosenkrantz Lindegaard, Wim Bernasco, and Scott Jacques published their findings, based on a review of 104 robbers who described 143 robbery events in a range of quantitative and qualitative data. In their journal article, "Consequences of Expected and Observed Victim Resistance for Offender Violence during Robbery Events," published in *The Journal of Research in Crime and Delinquency*, they conclude: "At the onset of the robbery, offender violence is related to expected victim resistance; during the progression, it is related to observed victim resistance." (Lindegaard, et al., 2014: 32)

In the article, "If confronted by a robber, don't be a hero, police say," published in *The Charlotte Observer*, Cleve R. Wootson Jr. provides two examples of would-be victims and even bystanders who successfully confronted the failed robbers. But his interviews with the police suggest that is *not* the recommended way to deal with these situations. "Robbery victims shouldn't fight back," Wootson Jr. writes, which is what the police suggest if a robbery is in progress.

Here is the list of eight other suggestions that the police recommend robbery victims heed:

- Try to stay calm. Don't make any sudden movements to upset the robber.
- Tell the robber about anything that might surprise him, such as someone who is expected to arrive soon.
- If you must move or reach, tell the robber what you are going to do and why.
- Try to get a good look at the robber so you can describe him later.
- Don't be a hero. It's better to lose your money than your life.
- Give the robber time to leave.
- Note his direction of travel when he leaves.
- Try to get a description of his vehicle ONLY if you can do so without exposing yourself to harm. (Wootson, Jr., August 12, 2015)

Dealing with the Trauma of Robbery

Like scenes out of a Hollywood movie, the words that robbers say to their victims are words that some of these victims will never forget. A 54-year-old woman shared what happened to her 35 years before, when she was working as a cashier at a restaurant. At approximately 9:15 P.M., a masked gunman entered the store. He then pointed a gun in her face and demanded that she open the register. Here are the words he said, words that the victim finds unforgettable: "He said, 'I have never killed anyone before. Please don't become my first. Do as I say, and you will be OK." (Anonymous interview shared with the author, 2020)

The United States Attorney's Office of the Central District of California provides an information sheet entitled, "Robbery Victims." Its focus is on what robbery victims may expect to experience after being the victim of this violent property crime. Remember, whether or not a weapon is present during a robbery, because it involves face to face confrontation with one or more robbers, it is considered a violent crime because the victim fears for his or her life. Here are reactions to being robbed that the U. S. Attorney's Office of Central District of California notes are normal for anyone who has experienced this trauma:

- Fear—being afraid to leave a bank, or an office, or of being in public out of fear of being victimized again.
- Hyper-alertness—startling easily; being "jumpy"
- Guilt—wondering if there is something that could have been done differently to prevent the robbery
- Anger—furious that their life was disrupted by this event; they no longer feel safe
- Isolation—feeling no one can understand what they have been through so they may pull away from family and friends. (U.S. Attorney's office of Central District of California, 2015)

The U.S. Department of Justice, the United States Attorney's Office, Western District of Tennessee, in its publication, *When Bank Employees Become Victims of a Robbery*, adds these reactions: irritability, which may be directed at family and friends; loss of motivation—feeling blue or depressed; apathy and indifference; and chronic fatigue and flashbacks. (The United States Attorneys Office, Western District of Tennessee, May 26, 2020)

How common are any of the above reactions to all types of robbery? Here is a profile of an actual attempted robbery victim, Nance L. Schick, a lawyer who specializes in dispute resolution. Schick shares how she fought with, and thwarted, an attempted robber, and was injured in the process. Seven years later, she still has back pain related to the robbery attempt. For her, the aftermath has been more physical than emotional, but the physical part is all too real.

Profile of an Attempted Robbery Victim: ▪ Nance L. Schick

Nance Schick, lawyer, mediator, trainer. Contributed photo.

Nance L. Schick is a holistic lawyer and conflict resolution coach who, seven years ago, fought back when a 14-year-old male attempted to rob her as she walked home from a workshop in midtown Manhattan. Nance was unaware of how young her assailant was at the time of the attack since his face was obscured by his hoodie, and he seemed much older. At the time this attempted robbery and assault occurred, Nance had already suffered several victimizations over her lifetime, beginning as a five-year-old child. She had been raped at least twice, once at twelve and once after college. She thinks it might have been her instinct not to be a victim again that motivated her to fight back. Nance shares about her assault and the attempted robbery. Her story brings up such issues as the role of ***bystanders****, the police, her guilt over fighting versus complying, as well as the long-term effects of this robbery, seven years later:*

The assault occurred during an attempted robbery on January 19, 2014, at the corner of 35th Street and Broadway. It was around ten o'clock at night. I was on my way home from a twelve-hour training nearby. What to call the violent assault I survived? Was it a mugging? Was it a robbery? When I was grabbed and thrown to the sidewalk, I wasn't thinking I was being robbed. After he crawled on top of me and tried to restrain me, attempted robbery was not my experience. I was being assaulted and trying to avoid being raped or killed. I believe the defendant was charged with second-degree robbery because of the serious injuries he caused me, although no weapon was found. At the scene, I heard him tell one of the off-duty police officers who detained him that he might have had a "blade" in a pocket, but he did not use that on me.

My initial reaction was shock. I remember thinking throughout the assault that I needed to hold onto my phone so I could tell Peter [my boyfriend] I was okay. That was the first thing I did when the police let me have my phone. I was not okay. But I am a lawyer, and I knew I had to hold myself together to document the evidence.

After that, I just wanted to be silent. Peter did, too, and that was when I knew I was going to need help. I have survived multiple abuses, crimes, and hardships in my lifetime. I was not going to let this be the incident that took the power I had spent a lifetime regaining, and I wasn't going to let this end my perfect partnership.

Did bystanders intervene? It depends what you mean by intervening. For the estimated 12 to 20 minutes he was attacking me, I kept wondering why no one was helping. Several bystanders watched the assault, including a man who operated the food truck I was on the sidewalk in front of. Another young man videotaped some of the occurrences while steadying his cell phone with a foam finger, presumably from the [nearby sports event] Others might have called the police. No one physically put themselves between me and my assailant. I heard no one tell him to get off me.

Eventually, the police were called. I don't know if it was by the off-duty police officers who heard my screams but couldn't see me or someone else. The officers eventually figured out what was going on when they saw my assailant run toward the—train, and they brought him down near [a store's] second display window. That was where I saw him next. He was face down on the ground with my phone between his shoulder blades and my boyfriend's name still on the screen. Our call was still connected.

What I want students reading a textbook on victimology and reading about the attempted robbery to know is that it's not as much about the robbery as you might think. Had I known (which I still don't) that the defendant might have just wanted my phone, I could have given it to him. He could have had my wallet, but that wouldn't have gotten him far. I might have had a $1 bill in it, and a bank card that I would have canceled immediately. Even that wouldn't have yielded him much.

The assault was the more difficult part of the attack. He tossed me around with absolutely no concern for me as a human being. For what? A [smartphone] that was already a couple of editions behind? I still wonder what his life was like that this seemed better.

Yes, I still have chronic back and left hip pain that will only get worse as I age. [Since the attempted robbery] I no longer run long distances and might never again. I learned to swim and was getting chiropractic adjustments one to two times per month before the pandemic [beginning in March 2020]. I've learned to live with the pain, but some days that is not as easy as it seems. On my worst days, I could barely walk around the corner. Those days are thankfully quite rare now. Again, I will not let this [crime] define or destroy my life.

Secondary Victims of Robbery

Secondary victims of robbery include the survivors of homicide when the robbery resulted in the victim's death (robbery-homicide). But we should also note that family and friends of robbery victims who survive the experience may additionally be traumatized by what happened. Nance Schick's boyfriend, for example, was listening on the phone as the attack was taking place since she had not hung up her phone. The mother of a teenager who was robbed, who called the police on her son's behalf, described learning about her son's robbery as such a traumatizing experience that she felt as if she was the one who was robbed. (Anonymous interview shared with the author.)

Changing the Image of the Robber

When you read true crime victim stories like the ones shared in this chapter, it is next to impossible to glorify the robber as literature and the media has done for centuries. There is the age old tale from England of Robin Hood, which led to novels and several movies about this most revered of all robbers, or the Depression-era bank robbers and murderers, Bonnie and Clyde, killed in a hail of bullets in 1934. There is a shift in the portrayal of the robber from the cult figures of the 1967 Arthur Penn movie, *Bonnie and Clyde*, starring Warren Beatty and Faye Dunaway, to the 2019 Netflix film, *The Highwaymen*, which instead focuses on the efforts to capture of the pair. *The Highwaymen* looks at Bonnie and Clyde without the glamorization of the movie. (Newman and Benton, 1967; Fusco, 2019) There are, however, more robbers whose names are well-known, like John Dillinger, Baby Face Nelson, Jesse James, or even infamous robberies, like the 1950 Great Brink's Robbery or the 1963 robbery in Buckinghamshire, United Kingdom, known as The Great Train Robbery.

Baltimore, Maryland high school teacher Adam Schwartz raises a very important question in his August 24, 2019, article in the *Baltimore Sun*, "Does Music Glorifying Armed Robbery Lead Teens to Commit Crimes?" He wonders if music glamorizing robbery or what Schwartz says is also known as **hitting licks**, "slang for robbing people" encourages it. Schwartz shares that he was once personally robbed at gun point. He writes, "I was once a lick that got hit. In 1990, my brother and I were robbed in the Shaw neighborhood of D.C. where he then lived. Although this happened long ago, having a fat-barreled pistol pressed to my cheek created an indelible memory." (Schwartz, 2019)

So, does listening to the music of contemporary singers who glorify robber pose a threat? Schwartz fears that it does; the students disagree. Writes Schwartz, "When I share my concerns with students, they tell me I've got it wrong. 'No song is going to make someone just start robbing people,' Michael said. Maybe. Maybe not. Last November, a student of mine was arrested for armed robbery and carjacking. In January, in an unrelated case, another student was charged with a similar crime. Both remain in Central Booking, awaiting trial. I remain surprised that either might've stuck a gun on somebody; neither seemed the type." (Schwartz, 2019)

Schwartz continues: "A recent headline in The Sun reported "assaults, robberies by juveniles on the rise." Moreover, this month, the home security provider ADT analyzed FBI crime data and determined that Baltimore has the highest rate of robbery among U.S. cities." (Schwartz, 2019)

We owe it to all the real-life robbery victims to avoid glamorizing this violent property crime.

BURGLARY

Burglary, another type of property crime, is defined by the FBI Uniform Crime Reporting (UCR) as "the unlawful entry of a structure to commit a felony or theft." One of the most famous burglaries in modern times took place on June 17, 1972, when five men were arrested breaking into the offices of the Democratic National Committee, which was located in the Watergate complex of buildings in Washington, D.C. It later evolved from what had been termed a "third-rate burglary" into the Watergate scandal. When *Washington Post* investigative reporters Bob Woodward and Carl Bernstein uncovered the efforts of President Richard Nixon, who was running for reelection at the time, to cover-up his re-election campaign's link to the burglary, it became the catalyst that two years later led to Nixon's resignation on August 9, 1974, rather than face impeachment. (Woodward and Bernstein, 1974)

Definition

Few burglaries are as infamous as the one that happened in the Watergate complex. But it is still a major property crime that takes a toll on its victims. The definition of **burglary/ breaking and entering** according to the **National Incident-Based Report System (NIBRS)** of the FBI is: "The unlawful entry into a building or other structure with the intent to commit a felony or a theft." Remember that robbery involves face-to-face confrontation between the criminal and the victim. In almost all cases of burglary, the apartment dweller or homeowner or office manager is absent when the burglary takes place.

Where and When Most Burglaries Are Likely to Occur

According to the fact sheet put together by the Office for Victims of Crime and The National Center for Victims of Crime as a 2018 National Crime Victim's Rights Week Resource Guide, burglaries are more likely to occur in a residential dwellings (72%) compared to an office, store, or another non-residential dwelling (28%).

In Table 8.3, you will find more detailed information about where the 1,117,696 reported burglaries occurred in the United States. That year, the most common targets were dwellings

TABLE 8.3. Burglary by Location, 2019 in the United States

Total Number of Reported Burglaries in 2019: 1,117,696	
Residence (dwelling)	702,449
Residence night	236,635
Residence Day	354,396
Residence Unknown	109,415
Nonresidence (store, office, etc.)	415,247
Nonresidence Night	191,663
Nonresidence Day	152,956
Nonresidence Unknown	70,629

Source: FBI, *2019 Crime in the United States*, Table 7, Offense Analysis

(702,449); the next most common location for a burglary were nonresidences such as stores or offices (415,247), with more nonresidence burglaries taking place at night (191,663) than during the day (152,956). There were 70,629 burglaries in the "nonresidence unknown" category as well.

The statistics do confirm daytime residential burglaries (354,398) being more common than nighttime residential burglaries (236,635). However, these statistics do dispute the common belief that all burglaries happen during the day, when homeowners or apartment dwellers would most likely be out of their residence since 236,635 happened at night.

Victim Reactions to Burglary

Stephen Jones, who is a lawyer and who also teaches criminology and other courses at the University of Bristol Law School, shares in the Preface to his textbook, *Criminology,* about the burglary that he and his wife experienced. He begins his Preface in this way: "Recently, I was the victim of a burglary. Various items have disappeared. Placed with a pile of books, the villain was selective. A couple of Beatrice Potter books were taken, whereas a copy of the last edition of this book was ignored." (Jones, *Criminology*)

Jones shared additional details about the burglary in personal communications:

> The burglary occurred at our little place in La Rochelle, France. My wife arrived from England to find there had been a break-in. It was not immediately obvious, as all the doors and windows were closed and there was no mess. She first noticed that the small television set had gone. A closer inspection revealed that several other objects were missing
>
> She visited the main La Rochelle police station where a number of forms were filled in and a reference provided for insurance purposes. Neither of us is fluent in French, so it was difficult to judge whether the officers were sympathetic. I do not recall that any information to assist victims was given. No one has ever been apprehended and no property has been recovered.
>
> The situation affected my wife far more than me. She immediately wanted to add further security to the place. On subsequent visits she has become very apprehensive at any unusual noise about the place. She has always been worried that the original burglars will return. (Jones, 2021)

The reaction of wanting better security in place after the burglary that Stephen Jones shared seems to be a common reaction among burglary victims. Seven years ago, when 22-year-old Mohammed S. was 15, his house was burglarized. "I was in the front of the house and the burglar came through the back of the house," says Mohammed. The burglars stole several laptop computers, a camera, camera accessories, and watches. What precautions has his family taken to try to prevent another burglary from occurring? "We have better locks, a fully functioning security system, and surveillance cameras around the house," says Mohammed. (Anonymous Interview shared with the author)

Another reaction to burglary, besides reassessing the security system and installing a better or new one, or even getting a guard dog, is the feeling of betrayal that victims report when they realize the burglar was someone known to them. It could even have been a family member or the friend of a friend. When 24-year-old Kelly W. was eight years old and living in Trinidad and Tobago, she was the victim of a burglary. Kelly describes what happened and the aftermath, for her and her family and for the offenders: "This crime not only affected me but my family because still up to this day we are uneasy and do feel unsafe although we are not living in that country anymore. The stolen items were jewelry that has been passed down in my family. None of the items stolen from my family home was recovered. I didn't know [the burglars] personally but one of them was a friend of a family member's brother. When they felt that they were about to be caught, because all the evidence pointed to them, they committed suicide so they wouldn't have to face jail time." (Anonymous interview shared with the author.)

Target Hardening as a Response to Being Burglarized

Anyone who has been burglarized knows that it is not just the possessions that have been taken that make this an upsetting experience. After all, most homeowners have home insurance that includes coverage for theft and some have renter's insurance although that is not as common as homeowner's insurance. Unless family heirlooms are stolen, or a lot of priceless keepsakes, or a computer with original materials or confidential work information that cannot easily be replaced, most stolen electronics including TVs can be bought again. What is not as easy to restore or replace, however, is the feeling of safety in one's own residence. That may take installing new locks, moving, time, and even therapy to restore that safe feeling again.

One approach for potential or even previous burglary victims is to consider what is known as "**target hardening.**" That is when someone proactively makes it harder to select a target, such as a person, or even a residence or an office, as a potential victimization incident. The reason that is something to consider is that the clearance rate for burglary is just 13.5 percent, according to the FBI Uniform Crime Reports (UCR). That means 86.5 percent of all burglaries do not lead to the arrest of a suspect let alone a conviction. With statistics like that, it is clear that even if burglaries go down somewhat, with an estimated 2,639,620 burglaries in 2018 and another 1,724,720 trespassing incidents, these crimes are quite frequent. Taking precautions so your apartment or house is a less likely target for a burglary obviously does not eliminate the problem—and reducing or eliminating burglaries altogether is the goal—but it does make a resident or dwelling a harder target to burglarize. Having an up-to-date security system that cannot be disabled by an intruder, having a guard dog, having lighting at all times, video surveillance and making sure that when you are going to be away on vacation or the residence will be unattended is kept confidential, are some of the target hardening measures that can be taken.

Home Invasions

If the homeowner is not in the apartment or house when the burglary occurs, that is truly a blessing. Since we have seen that most burglaries take place during the day precisely because there is the assumption that the premises will be empty, confrontation with the burglar or burglars is unlikely. But if it does occur, it can be by coincidence, because an apartment dweller or homeowner happened to be home that day, or decided to go to work later. There may be some brazen burglars who either plan or do not mind confronting the homeowners. But most prefer an empty abode to increase the likelihood of a quick and clean getaway and decrease the chances of a confrontation or getting caught.

Whether it is planned or it just happens by flukes, a confrontation between the burglar or burglars and the homeowners or apartment dwellers is known as the ***burglar surprise***. This now changes the property crime of burglary into the crime of ***home invasion*** which actually fits in more with the category of the violent crime of robbery.

Here are some startling statistics about home invasions in the United States between 2003 and 2007, related to the estimated 3.7 million burglaries that occurred in each of those years, according to the U.S. Department of Justice, Bureau of Justice Statistics, September 2010, "National Crime Victimization Survey, Victimization During Household Burglary."

- A household member was present in roughly 1 million burglaries and became victims of violent crimes in 266,560 burglaries.
- Offenders were known to their victims in 65 percent of violent burglaries; offenders were strangers in 28 percent.
- About 12 percent of all households violent burglaries occurred while someone was home and he/she faced an offender armed with a firearm.
- Simple assault (15%) was the most common form of violence when a resident was home and violence occurred.

When this author was researching her book *Victims*, she attended a meeting of Parents of Murdered Children (POMC) on Long Island. It was organized by parents whose son had been murdered during a burglary turned home invasion. The son had been home sick from high school that day and the burglars killed him during the commission of their crime. (Yager, 1978)

LARCENY-THEFT

Larceny-theft is defined by the FBI as "unlawful taking, carrying, leading, or riding away of property from the possession or constructive possession of another." In this section you will learn more about selected types of larceny-theft, the most frequent type of property crime (According to the FBI, there were 5, 217, 055 reported larceny-thefts in the United States in 2018.) These are the larceny-thefts that will be covered: the most frequent kind, theft from motor vehicles (except accessories) (27.3%), shoplifting (21.2%), motor vehicle accessories (6.3%), purse-snatching (.4%), and pocket-picking (.5%).

There are no fewer than eight sub-categories of larceny-thefts according to the National Incident-Based Report System (NIBRS) of the FBI.

Here is a list of the eight types of crime within the broad category of larceny/theft:

1. Pocket-picking
2. Purse-snatching
3. Shoplifting
4. Theft from building
5. Theft from coin-operated machine or device
6. Theft from motor vehicle
7. Theft of motor vehicle parts or accessories
8. All other larceny

According to the fact sheet put together by the Office for Victims of Crime and The National Center for Victims of Crime as a 2018 National Crime Victim's Rights Week Resource

FIGURE 8.2. Larceny-Theft in the United States in 2015 by Type

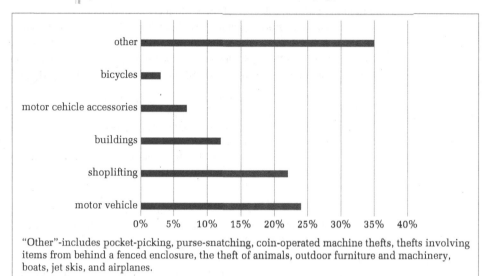

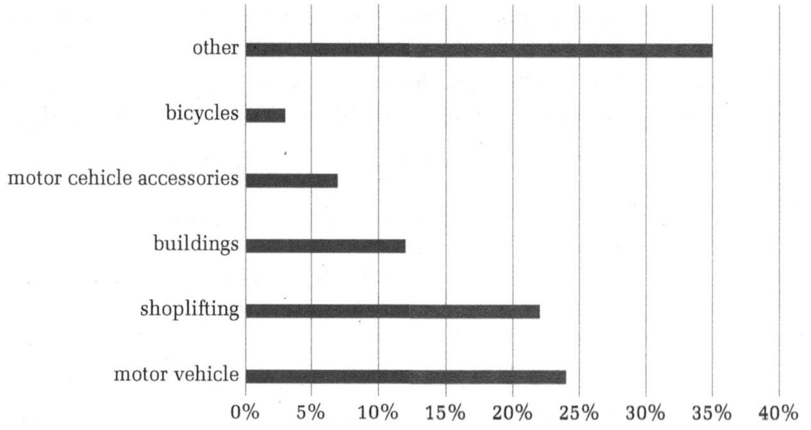

"Other"-includes pocket-picking, purse-snatching, coin-operated machine thefts, thefts involving items from behind a fenced enclosure, the theft of animals, outdoor furniture and machinery, boats, jet skis, and airplanes.

Source: Office for Victims of Crime and The National Center for Victims of Crime as a 2018 National Crime Victim's Rights Week Resource Guide.

Guide, the most common type of larceny-theft in 2015 was motor vehicle theft (24%) followed by shoplifting (22%). Larceny-Theft by Type is indicated further in Figure 8.2.

Purse Snatching and Pickpocketing

Purse-snatching can occur in a variety of locations. If someone is eating out in a restaurant and puts a shoulder bag over the back of her chair, it could be an easy target for a thief who walks by, scoops up the bag in one fell swoop, and is out the door, and in the wind, as they say.

If a woman is in a crowded bus or subway, or even in a congested store, if she has her wallet in her pocketbook, and the purse is not zipped up, someone could reach into that open bag and grab that wallet.

As fewer and fewer people actually carry cash in their wallets, purse-snatchers may be as eager to get credit cards from those wallets as they are to steal money. Because a stolen credit card can quickly be used by the thieves if it has not been reported stolen and either canceled or put on "hold," it is recommended that as soon as a purse is snatched that any credit cards that were in the wallet are immediately reported as stolen.

Unfortunately some people do not keep track of what cards are in their wallet. This can slow down the process of reporting a stolen card. So if you do keep one or more credit cards in your wallet, whether you are a man or a woman, since wallets get stolen out of pants pockets as well, make sure you have ready access to the number of the card and all the details about the card as well as the number to call in case of theft. Have that information in a separate place than your wallet or purse, and even keep a backup copy, so you can readily share that information with the credit card company, the issuing bank, or the police if you are a victim.

Thefts from Motor Vehicles (except theft of motor vehicle parts or accessories)

The NIBRS (National Incident-Based Reporting System) of the FBI defines this crime in this way: "The theft of articles from a motor vehicle, whether locked or unlocked." (NIBRS 2012)

Here are some lessons for potential victims of theft from a car to be a less likely victim:

1. Do not leave valuables, especially a pocketbook, in an unlocked car. Other valuables that should not be left in unlocked cars include cell phones, laptop computers, baby car seat or stroller, bicycle, and other expensive or personal items.
2. If are going to leave something valuable in a *locked* car, make sure that item is not visible.
3. Keep your handbag, backpack, or wallet with you at all times. If this is not feasible because you are working out at a health club or visiting a location that does not allow you to bring in your pocketbook, see if there is a lock box situation that you could use. If you leave these items in your car or trunk, make sure the car is locked and, before you leave home, unless you are traveling internationally, keep as few credit cards and personal documents on your person so there is less to report if your wallet or pocketbook is stolen.
4. Be aware of any extenuating circumstances, such as a family member, friend, or acquaintance's unemployment or drug addictions, in any of the persons that you live with or who might visit you that might make them more likely to steal out of desperation. A study by Johnson et al. published in the *International Review of Victimology* based on 687 parents who had children with drug problems reported that as many as 50.7 percent (half) indicated that they had been the victims of theft or burglary at one point or another by their addicted child. (Johnson, 2018)

In the section below on Motor Vehicle Theft you will read about what is called a **complacency theft** whereby a motor vehicle owner or driver has left the car unlocked or, even worse, the keys in the car, making it that much easier for a car thief to go off with a car. But there are also complacency issues related to this particular kind of larceny-theft, namely making it easier to steal items from cars because the car is unlocked. There are the obvious items stolen out of unlocked cars that will inconvenience the car owner or driver including computers (which may have sensitive business or personal information on it), cell phones, tablets, even wallets or purses. But what if the item taken from the unlocked car is a gun? What if that gun is used to commit a crime? Even if the gun owner is absolved of any wrong doing related to the commission of that crime, the gun owner will have to deal with the guilt associated with that situation.

A reminder about the reported trend of wallets or pocketbooks being stolen out of cars while single drivers, especially women, are pumping gas. It has been recommended that single drivers lock their cars or have their pocketbook with them when they are pumping gas to decrease the likelihood of such thefts.

Shoplifting

Here is the official definition of this well-known property crime: "The theft, by someone other than an employee of the victim, of goods or merchandise exposed for sale." (NIBRS 2012)

The first thing to clear up is the perception that shoplifting is a victimless crime because an individual is not being robbed as is the case in burglary or robbery. But shoplifting most definitely does have victims. The first obvious victim of shoplifting is "the store" or "the business."

Shoplifting causes businesses to have lower profits not just because of the lost goods but the cost of hiring security guards to deal with the issue. These costs usually have to be passed along to the customers in terms of higher prices or in decreased profits which might even cause a business or store to have to go out of business. The second victims of shoplifting are the customers who now have to pay higher prices. The third victim of shoplifting could even be the community who could lose a much-needed business from its mall or downtown shopping area.

There are other consequences to shoplifting that may not be as obvious. That is what happened to Carol V., a 48-year-old widow who let her best friend pressure her into shoplifting a pair of $350 emerald earnings. It led to Carol's arrest and four months in jail. Since her friend and her boyfriend had already left the store when Carol was arrested, they did not suffer any consequences of what turned into a horrific experience, but a life lesson, for Carol. (Anonymous interview shared with the author.)

Here are some facts about shoplifting that you might find interesting based on Rachel Shteir's article, "Five Myths About Shoplifting" from *The Washington Post*, which included key findings from her related book, *The Steal*:

1. Although many assume shoplifting is a crime that women commit more than men, in a 2005 study in Great Britain, there were three times as many men incarcerated for shoplifting as women.
2. Shoplifters cannot easily stop. Shteir interviewed 100 shoplifters. "Many talked about the crime as though it were an illness." She reports writing "Today, kleptomania is considered an impulse-control disorder."
3. Stores are actually having a hard time stopping this crime.
4. Shoplifting dates back at least as far as the time of Shakespeare in 1571.
5. Shoplifters are stealing out of "want" not "need." (Shteir, 2011)

Shoplifting is a crime where perpetrators who are caught may get punished with anything from probation, a fine, or community service to jail time. For some, it may be the first offense that unfortunately starts that offender on a criminal path. For others, like the celebrity convicted shoplifters, it can be a temporary or prolonged derailment of their careers. For all shoplifters, famous or not, there is a stigma associated with the crime as well as a public shaming that hails back to the earliest days of colonial America when shaming was one of the four main ways that offenders were prosecuted (along with branding, fines, whipping, or executions). Examples of the rich and famous who were caught shoplifting, as noted by Maria Ricapito in her 2017 article on celebrity shoplifters, reinforces the belief that shoplifting is an addiction that is not based on need. (Ricapito, 2017) That is in direct contrast to the novel *Les Miserables* by Victor Hugo, originally published in 1862. In that novel, Jean Valjean is sent to prison for stealing a loaf of bread which he stole to feed his starving sister; according to Victor Hugo, his theft was definitely out of need, not want. (Hugo, 1862, 2013)

More typical is the college student from Boston who was caught shoplifting less than $30 of make-up from a major cosmetic store chain in the mall on a visit to her parents on a break from school. The store security guard called the police but the police, upon arrival at the store, and an assessment of the situation, told the security guard and the store to handle the situation internally. The girl's parents were notified, a lawyer was hired, a $1,000 fine was paid, and their daughter was placed on a list that banned her for life from shopping at that particular store or any stores in that chain. The girl's lawyer assured her that the charge would not affect her ability to get her license to become a pharmacist, which was her career goal. The shoplifter certainly had the money for the cosmetics that she stole. Counseling is helping her to figure out why she was driven to shoplift which researchers describe as an addiction. (Anonymous interview shared with the author, 2019)

Facts About Larceny-Theft

In summary, here are some facts about larceny-theft:

- It is the most frequent type of property victimization in the United States.
- It is the top most common kind of victimization of all types in the United States, at 5,086,096.
- According to the FBI, larceny-theft declined 2.8 percent in 2019 when compared with the 2018 estimate.
- There was an even greater decline of 18.0 percent when compared with the 2010 FBI statistics.
- The average value of a larceny-theft in 2019 in the United States was $1,162.
- The loss nationally was estimated at $5.9 billion.
- Over $200 in value included 1,956,531 reported victims; $50 to $200 included 877, 125 reported victims; under $50 included 1,298,910 reported victims. (FBI, 2019, Table 23, "Offense Analysis")
- The percentage of offenses include the following, in order of frequency: all others (29.9%); from cars, except accessories (27.0%); shoplifting (22.2%); from buildings (10%); from motor vehicle accessories (6.5%); bicycle (3.1%); pocket-picking (0.6%); purse-snatching (0.4%); from coin-operated machines (0.2%)
- The terms for larceny-theft crimes, as well as the penalties, vary by state. For example, in Wyoming, instead of referring to it as petit (petty) or grand larceny, it is referred to as **felony theft** (goods or services worth $1,000 or more) or **misdemeanor theft** (stealing goods or services of less than $1,000). In Nevada, less than $1,000 is considered **petit larceny** or **petty larceny**. More than $1,200 it is considered **grand larceny**. In New York, there are degrees of theft—first degree, second degree, third degree, or fourth degree—dependent upon the value of the goods or services stolen. In New York, under $1,000 is petit larceny although there are some exceptions including credit cards, firearms, or religious items valued at just $100 or more. In Virginia, under $200 is petit larceny; more than $200 is grand larceny.
- You will not find information about embezzlement, confidence games, forgery, or check fraud in the FBI Uniform Crime Reporting data on larceny-theft.

> *Sources:* FBI, *2019 Crime in the United States*, "Larceny Theft;" petty and grand larceny data by state compiled by this author from various online attorney sites maintained by attorneys including Nolo's criminaldefenselawyers.com (Wyoming) Rebecca Pirius; johnelledge.com (Virginia); www.shouselaw.com (Nevada); www.criminallawyer-nj.com (Jason A. Volet) (New Jersey); and David Goguen (New York).

Please note that identity theft, definitely a form of theft, will be dealt with in the next chapter, Chapter 9, "Cybercrime, White-Collar Crime, and Economic Crime Victims."

MOTOR VEHICLE THEFT

The National Incident-Based Reporting System (NIBRS) of the FBI quite simply defines motor vehicle theft as "The theft of a motor vehicle." Here are some additional facts about this major property crime in the United States, based on the FBI reports and on information provided by the National Insurance Crime Bureau (NICB). Note that included in the category of motor vehicle thefts are the theft or attempted theft of not just automobiles but also of trucks, busses, motorcycles, scooter, and snowmobiles.

- The financial loss from motor vehicle theft was around $6 billion.
- The average dollar loss per theft was $8,407.
- The rate for motor vehicle theft in 2018 was 228.9 per 100,000 people, which was down from 237.7 in 2017.
- The number of reported vehicles stolen in 2018 was 748,841.
- The top five Metropolitan Statistical areas by motor vehicle theft were Albuquerque, New Mexico, Anchorage, Alaska, Bakersfield, California, Pueblo, Colorado, and Modesto, California.
- The top five states with the most motor vehicle thefts (in descending order, from highest) were California, Texas, Florida, Washington, and Georgia.
- The states with the fewest motor vehicle thefts (in descending order, from lowest) were Vermont, Maine, Wyoming, New Hampshire, and Delaware.
- The five states with the most number of motorcycle thefts were, in descending order, from highest, California, Florida, Texas, New York, and South Carolina.
- New Year's Day is the day when the most motor vehicles are stolen of the 11 major holidays and Christmas Day is the least. (NICB)
- The **clearance rate** in 2019 for motor vehicle thefts was only 13.8 percent meaning that 86.2 percent of all stolen cars are not solved with an arrest. (FBI, *2019 Crime in the United States*)

In Table 8.4, you will see the top ten motor vehicles stolen in the United States in 2018 by type of car and year.

TABLE 8.4. Top 10 Most Stolen Vehicles in the United States in 2018 (In Descending Order of Frequency)

Make of Motor Vehicle	Model Year Most Stolen
Honda Civic	2000
Honda Accord	1997
Ford Pickup (full size)	2006
Chevrolet Pickup (full size)	2004
Toyota Camry	2017
Nissan Altima	2017
Toyota Corolla	2017
GMC Pickup (full size)	2018
Dodge Pickup (full size)	2001
Jeep Cherokee/Grand Cherokee	2000

Source: "NICB's Hot Wheels"

After some property crimes, such as burglary or larceny-theft, especially if there was no contact with the criminal, even some of the victims might say "It's only money," or "I can easily get that replaced." But it is very different with the theft of a motor vehicle. Not only could the motor vehicle be the means of transportation to get someone to work, children to school, or elderly parents to doctor's appointments, the amount of money involved is quite substantial. Even if a motor vehicle owner has car insurance, it might not cover the replacement of the car unless the car owner has gotten what is known as GAP insurance—the difference between the value of the new car and the value given to the used car at the time of the theft. For example, a luxury car that was stolen that cost $36,000 new resulted in the car owner getting a payment from the insurance company of $23,000. That left a gap of $13,000 since that particular car owner had not bought gap insurance. Also, you will not get reimbursed if your car is stolen unless you have a comprehensive coverage policy not just a liability policy.

Here is another hypothetical example. If a 2010 Honda Civic is stolen, if the policy covers theft, after the few days waiting period to see if the car if recovered, when the company does make the reimbursement, it will be based on the current market value. In this case, it would be an average of $8,300. The cost of a 2020 Hondo Civic is approximately $20,000.

In addition to the economic hardship that is caused by having a car stolen, as well as the cost of renting a car, while the claim is being processed, unless the policy covers car rentals during that waiting period, and the inconvenience of the theft, there is the trauma of having something you value, and depend on, and might even have sentimental associations with it taken from the victim. However no motor vehicle lasts forever and that favorite family car that everyone used to go on summer trips, or to visit Grandma on Sundays, would eventually have been sold or donated anyway. But having it stolen is a completely different way of parting with that car. In a worst case scenario, that stolen car would even be used for joyriding, where someone was hurt or killed, or in the commission of a robbery or a worse crime.

We have previously discussed the concept of *target hardening*. It definitely also applies to preventing motor vehicle theft. The best way drivers can decrease the likelihood that they will be a victim of this type of crime is to avoid keeping the key in the car and by locking the car. There developed a problem with some cars because of what is known as a *fob* – a keyless way of starting the car. If someone's car could be easily opened and driven away through technological equipment that criminals can easily purchase, potential victims need to know that they have to contact the car's dealership to circumvent this glitch.

Recently the story of a car theft that led to the victim personally recovering his car was shared with this author. The car that was stolen, the sister of the victim explained, meant a lot to the victim. Beyond the monetary value of the car, he had put a lot of time and effort into customizing that car.

When he discovered it was stolen, he somehow figured out where it might have been driven to. He allegedly asked a police officer to go with him to try to retrieve the car, but he was told that the location he was going to was out of that officer's jurisdiction. So, the victim decided to go there alone.

He arrived and saw three individuals standing near his car. He chased them away and, fortunately, they ran off.

That motor vehicle theft had a happy ending for the victim but if the three car thieves had a weapon, the outcome might have been very different. Refer back to the discussion about complying or resisting that you learned about in the robbery section. Was there another way for the victim to handle the situation that might have put him in less jeopardy?

Complacency Thefts

Potential victims need to know that it is the motor vehicle owners that are too often making it easier for criminals by leaving their keys in the car. These thefts are known as **complacency thefts**. This refers to a situations where motor vehicle owners intentionally or because of forgetfulness leave the key in the car. As Claims Journal points out in their article, "Number of Vehicle Thefts with Keys Left Inside Growing Fast," between 2015 and 2018, according to the NICB, 229,339 or 209 thefts per day were stolen because of keys being left in the car. (Claims Journal, 2019)

Another situation where the key is left in the car that increased the likelihood of a motor vehicle theft is leaving a car to warm up with the key in the car with or without the car locked. Obviously, if the car is unlocked it is almost like having a sign on the car that says "Steal this car." If the car is locked, and the car is warming up, so someone walking past the car can see that the key is in the car, it will be harder to steal it than if the car is unlocked but it is still possible. Usually the person may be inside an apartment or a house while the motor vehicle is warming up so, in theory, confrontation with the motor vehicle thief need not occur. But this scenario does increase the possibility of a face to face confrontation which potential victims want to avoid at all costs so the less the situation is set up where that might happen, the better. That is because criminals might have a weapon and he or she might do something violent out of panic or to avoid detection when the motor vehicle owner arrives.

Complacency thefts rose from just 6.2 percent of all motor vehicle thefts in 2013 to 10 percent of all thefts in 2017. Although it would obviously be an inconvenience for many drivers, if you are alone in your car, and you are pumping gas in a self-serve situation in a questionable neighborhood, you might want to have a second set of car keys so you can lock your car while you are out of the vehicle. Complacency thefts of cars may not, unfortunately, only increase the likelihood that a car can more easily be stolen. If there are occupants in the car when it is stolen, what should have been a non-violent motor vehicle theft has now turned into the dreaded and potentially violent *carjacking*, discussed below.

CARJACKING

Like burglary and arson, motor vehicle theft is usually a non-violent property crime because the victim is not around. But in those rare instances where the victim is still in the car, or near the car, it can turn into a violent **carjacking** with potentially horrific results. Here are just a few examples of a carjacking with tragic outcomes:

- Jon Haworth reported at ABCNews.com about a carjacking that led to one teenager's death. She and her three siblings were left in the family car with the air conditioning running while their mother was picking up food for the family. The 26-year-old suspect allegedly jumped into the vehicle and told the four children to get out. The 18- and 11-year old somehow got out of the van. The suspect drove off and the 8-year old and 13-year old got out of the vehicle. It was unclear if they jumped or were pushed. Both children sustained major injuries and the 13-year-old died at the scene. (Haworth, 2020)

- A 6-year-old Mississippi boy by the name of Kingston, as reported in the *New York Times* by Niraj Chokshi and Daniel Victor, was killed after his mother's car was carjacked. He had been left in the car at 1:15 A.M. as her mother went into a grocery store. Approximately eight hours later, at 9:30 A.M., Kingston was found in the back seat of the car with a gunshot wound to the back of his head. (Chokshi and Victor, 2017)
- A man pleaded guilty to shooting and killing a husband as his wife watched the killing unfold in a carjacking at a mall in New Jersey. There were three defendants involved in the crime.
- A carjacker stole a car that had been left running with three children inside and crashed into a tree. Although everyone was injured, fortunately none of the injuries were fatal.

The National Crime Victimization Survey conducted a special inquiry into carjackings asking their representative sample to share through self-reports about whether they experienced a carjacking between 1993 and 2002. As the Bureau of Justice Statistics statistician Patsy Klaus reports in her July 2004 summary of the findings, there were approximately 38,000 carjacking victimizations during that time period in the United States A weapon was used in 74 percent of those carjackings. Here is the breakdown on those weapons used: firearms (45%); knives (11%); other weapons (18%). (Klaus, 2004)

The self-reports of nonfatal carjackings in the NCVS special study included 130 cases that were identified which consisted of 58 completed carjackings and 72 attempts. Two-thirds of the victims resisted the offender with 24 percent using confrontational techniques such as chasing or trying to catch the offender or threatening or attacking the offender. Injuries of carjacking victims were sustained by 32 percent of completed carjackings and 17 percent of the attempted ones.

According to the NCVS study, 68 percent of the carjackings occurred during the night between 6 P.M. and 6 A.M.. As far as reporting the crime to the police, 98 percent of the completed carjackings and 58 percent of the attempted carjackings were reported.

Some other details from the NCVS special carjacking report note that men were victimized more often than women; Hispanics more than non-Hispanics, and Blacks more than whites although exact statistics were not included in the report. Carjacking victims identified their offenders as white (21%); Black (56%), member of other races including Asian or Native Americans (16%); the carjackers was usually a male (93%) while groups including both males and females committed 3 percent of the carjackings. Women alone committed about 3 percent of the carjackings studied. Finally, in 78 percent of the completed carjacking incidents, there was partial or complete recovery of the property. In 25 percent of the carjackings, there was total recovery of the property. (Klaus, 2004)

Klaus noted that according to the Supplemental Homicide Reports from the FBI's Uniform Crime Reports, there are approximately 15 murders a year that involved car theft. "It is not possible to determine how many of these murders meet the definition of carjacking." (We know that the NCVS does not ask its respondents about murders.)

VANDALISM (EXCEPT ARSON)

The definition of **vandalism,** according to the National Incident-Based Report System (NIBRS) of the FBI is: "To willfully or maliciously destroy, damage, deface, or otherwise injure real or personal property without the consent of the owner or the person having custody or control of it." (NIBRS, 2012) Vandalism is one of those property crimes that is not talked about as often as burglary, robbery, or shoplifting, until someone is either the direct victim of this crime or it is profiled in the media.

A very high profile example of vandalism is what happened on January 6, 2021, when a political protest suddenly turned violent. As protesters stormed the U.S. Capitol building, some of them broke glass, two bronze light fixtures which *New York Times* reporter Sarah Bahr notes were designed in the 19th century by Frederick Law Olmsted, and vandalized with graffiti. (Bahr, January 8, 2021) Excluding the three medical emergencies that were linked to deaths at the riots, there were two fatalities that were initially linked to the vandalism: Brian Sicknick, a 42-year-old Capitol Police force member, and Ashli Babbitt, a 35-year-old Air Force veteran, shot by a Capitol police officer "as she clambered through a broken window leading to the Speaker's Lobby inside the Capitol" according to Jack Healy's *New York Times* report. (Healy, January 11, 2021) Sicknick's death was later ruled as "natural" caused by 'acute brainstem and cerebellar infarcts due to acute basilar artery thrombosis' also known as a stroke." (Viswanatha, 2021)

What is the answer to the question of when does an act, like putting toilet paper all over someone's trees, get categorized as a harmless prank and when does it cross over into the crime of vandalism, like intentionally smashing someone's car windows? Tragically, what happened at the U.S. Capitol on January 6, 2021, when hordes stormed it, causing mayhem and injuries, definitely was not in the "prank" category.

Wirth Law in Tulsa, Oklahoma notes there is a legal difference between a prank and the crime of vandalism. "Although young people often engage in pranks, there can be a legal difference between a prank and acts that are done maliciously," Wirth Law Office writes in their article, "8 Malicious Acts Considered Vandalism in Oklahoma." It continues, "Malice takes a prank and moves it toward vandalism." At their website, Wirth Law lists these malicious acts that are considered vandalism in Oklahoma:

1. Maliciously defacing property
2. Destroying railroad or railroad equipment
3. Vandalizing highways and bridges
4. Damaging fruit and other trees and shrubs
5. Vandalizing landmarks
6. Destroying art, trees, or ornamental improvements
7. Destroying collective literature or art (wirthlawoffice.com, n.d.)

Victims of Vandalism

Victims of vandalism can be schools, apartment houses, homes, commercial properties such as stores, cemeteries, churches, synagogues, mosques, street signs, or government buildings including police stations. On January 6, 2021, the U.S. Capitol in Washington, D.C. was vandalized, as mentioned above, when a siege by a mob and rioters took place. (Judkis and McCarthy, 2021)

Perpetrators may be teens who are doing it as part of a prank. But a prank, if it includes defacing a stop sign so that it becomes illegible and the next two cars that go to that intersection plow into each other because there is no stop sign, that seemingly harmless prank has caused one or more victims of injuries, car damages, or worse.

To some, depending on the type of images that are depicted or even if permission is granted, graffiti might be considered art or even an improvement to a wall but to others, it is vandalism. As Rae Burach writes in her article, "Graffiti Is Art, Not Vandalism," published in *The Temple News*, of Temple University in Philadelphia, she advocates the former. Burach writes, "And even though I regularly see creative graffiti throughout the city, many people fail to recognize it as a viable art form. Instead of being considered a meaningful expression, graffiti is seen as vandalism. This is an unfair label to give to something that requires the same creativity and hard work as other forms of street art." (Burach, 2018)

Example of graffiti.

Could permission of the owner of the building that is the subject of the graffiti be at issue in determining if it is art or vandalism? Glen D. Curry and Scott H. Decker point out that during the 1980s and 1990s, "some cities even introduced mural programs or 'free walls' to provide legal opportunities for urban youths to express their artist creativity." (Curry and Decker, updated 2020 by Adam Zeidan)

If vandalism to a structure is combined with getting back at an individual or a group, it could be a hate crime. If the property owners commit the vandalism themselves as a way of generating income by putting in an insurance claim, that individual would be committing an act of fraud.

The Prevalence of Vandalism

Statistics on the prevalence of vandalism are hard to find but Clairissa D. Breen in her entry on vandalism in the *Encyclopedia of Street Crime in America* refers to a 1990 study by the National Association of School Psychologists. That study estimated the cost to physical property of vandalism in U.S. schools at $600 million (Breen, 2013). Just one business owner, Jim Llg, in just one city, Denver, reported that he estimated $20,000 in vandalism costs related to damages to his building's windows. Those costs were not going to be covered by insurance. (Hindi and Tabachnik, *Denver Post*, 2020)

Here are some additional examples of vandalism "ripped from the headlines":

- Four teens ranging in age from 15 to 17 were arrested in Norman, Oklahoma in April 2016. They allegedly confessed to nearly 80 cases of vandalism, arson, and larceny. (News 9)
- A 35-year-old man was arrested in Sioux Falls, South Dakota for allegedly vandalizing an exhibit of outdoor art sculpture. (Associated Press)
- Graffiti was discovered on the city sidewalk in an area of State Street in Montpelier, Vermont. (WCAX)
- In numerous cities throughout the United States during June and July 2020, in response to the death of George Floyd in police custody, many days and even weeks of vandalism including looting were documented. (Winston and Ormseth, 2020)
- Vandalism may be used as a victim/witness intimidation tactic. (Peter Hermann, "Murder and Vandalism," *Baltimore Sun.*)

Psychologist Philip G. Zimbardo, well-known for his association with the 1972 Stanford Prison Experiment, wrote this about vandalism back in 1972, in an issue of *Bell Telephone Magazine*: "I firmly believe, along with British sociologist Stanley Cohen, one of the few authorities on the subject, that most acts of vandalism make good sense to those who perpetuate them." (Zimbardo, 1972)

Zimbardo concludes with his suggestions about how to prevent it: "we must combat social indifference, apathy, isolation, and the loss of community, neighborhood and family values. We must reaffirm the principle that human rights are more important than property rights and property rights are acknowledged by all only when we all have a share in them."

ARSON

According to the NIBRS (National Incident-Based Reporting System), **arson** is defined as "to unlawfully and intentionally damage, or attempt to damage, any real or personal property by fire or incendiary device."

Here are some statistics about arson victimization in 2018, based on the FBI Uniform Crime Report:

- Law enforcement agencies reported 36,127 arsons.
- More than 43 percent of all arsons involved structures such as residential, storage, or public.
- Arson was done to 7,989 motor vehicles.
- Arsons of industrial/manufacturing structured produced the greatest average dollar losses or $100,578, on average.

The Arson Unit of the Cleveland Police Department offers these interesting additional facts arson and arson victims:

- One fourth of all fires are attributed to arson.
- Half of all arson fires are set by juveniles.
- Over half a million arson fires, including 100,000 building fires, cost the United States more than $2 billion a year, and kill more than 700 people.

Arson-Homicides

Although arson is usually a crime only against property, as is the case with burglaries, when it becomes a burglar surprise with fatal consequences, or a motor vehicle theft, which turns it into a violent carjacking crime, like robbery, and there are hundreds of arson-homicides. In those cases, arson becomes more than a property crime; it becomes another example of violent crime with victim fatalities. Professor Allen D. Sapp, Ph.D. and Timothy G. Huff, a Violent Crime Cast Analyst with the FBI, did a study of Arson-Homicides for the FBI, U.S. Department of Justice. The sample for that study was data for 183 cases of arson-homicide from 36 states and the District of Columbia during the time period 1985 to 1994. The data had been obtained from the FBI's Violent Crime Apprehension Program (VICAP) located at the FBI Academy in Quantico, Virginia. Only 31 of those 183 arson-homicide cases were cleared by an arrest. The co-authors point out that these cases are not all cases of arson-homicide during that time period, but probably also represents unsolved ones. Here is a summary of some of their findings about the arson-homicides that they studied:

- The age range of the arson-homicide victims was from 2 to 91 with the median age of 30.
- The victims were 54.1 percent female and 45.9 percent male.
- Cause of death was available for 177 of the 183 arson-homicide cases studied with fire and fire-related causes accounting for 27.7 percent of the deaths. The next most common case was a tie between gunshot (20.3 percent) and stabbing (20.3), followed by blunt force (14.1), followed by strangulation (11.9).
- Cause of death differed significantly by gender. Gunshot or fire-related deaths were more common for male victims. Females were more often than males to die by asphyxia, blunt force trauma, or stabbing.
- For victims over 60, fire was the most frequent cause of death (32.3 percent).
- Males were twice as likely as females to be alive when the fire injuries occurred.
- The most common locations for arson-homicide were in a residence (41 percent), an open area (19.7 percent), a vehicle (12.6 percent), or a wooded area (10.4 percent).
- When the data was analyzed by the specific location of the victim, it was found that victims were still alive when the fires were set in 62.2 percent of the cases in a residence, 66.7 percent of the trash dumpster victimizations, and 66.7 percent of other buildings.
- In a total of 62 of the cases, another crime took place at the same time as the arson-homicide including burglary (32.3 percent), sexual assault (27.4 percent), and robbery (19.4). Together this accounted for 49 victims out of the sample of 183 cases. Other crimes with a smaller percentage of victims included kidnapping (8.1 percent), auto theft (6.5 percent) and one case each (1.6 percent) of hired killing, prostitution, burglary combined with auto theft, and robbery combined with sexual assault.
- Involvement with drugs was the most common victim lifestyle trait (43.4 percent or 30 victims). The next four most frequent lifestyle characteristics were prostitution (21.7 percent), homosexuality (20.3 percent), and alcoholism (13 percent). (Sapp and Huff, 1995)

As with burglary and motor-vehicle theft, when there is loss of life, and not just property damage, arson becomes a property crime that crosses over into the category of a violent crime.

SUMMARY

Robbery is considered a violent crime, but it is also a property crime. Unlike larceny or theft, robbery involves the threat or use of force which makes the victim fear for his or her life. Rarely is the property that is stolen recovered. Adding to the difficulty of solving a robbery is the reality that so many victims do not report the robbery to the police for the range of reasons discussed in this and previous chapters related to reporting crime patterns including everything from believing the police will not do anything, that the value of the goods stolen was not great enough to make it worth the effort involved in reporting it, to fear of retaliation because at least one of the robbers is known to the victim.

Robbery-homicide is the ultimate consequence of robbery with 548 Americans of the reported 308, 936 robbery victims getting killed in 2018 during a robbery. One out of three robbery victims gets injured. The largest category of robberies (36.9%) take place on the street or highway.

Because robbery is a violent property crime, it can have a traumatic immediate and long-term impact on its victims including the following reactions: fear, hyper-alertness, guilt, anger, and isolation. Even if the victim fails to report the crime, discussing the victimization in a support group for victims may be beneficial in dealing with the resulting trauma. This chapter considers if we are seeing a trend away from the glorification or glamorization of such violent robbers as John Dillinger or Bonnie and Clyde since some contemporary music may be glorifying robbery or what is known by the slang term *hitting licks*. Although the profile of the "typical" robbery victim—a minority single male between the ages of 18 and 24—is shared in this chapter, it is also noted through examples including Kim Kardashian, who was robbed, that anyone could be the victim of robbery.

Although most property crimes, including robberies, are considered crimes against the state, since 1934, bank robberies have been considered federal crimes. Therefore, investigations of bank robberies are handled by the FBI (Federal Bureau of Investigation). According to the FBI, in 2018, there were 3,033 bank robberies in the United States with most of the cases (2,707) involving commercial banks. The remainder were credit unions, armored carrier companies, savings and loan associations, or mutual savings banks.

Robbery can be a very traumatic crime for the victim resulting in the fear of being victimized again leading to being afraid to enter or leave a bank, office, or being out in public. It can lead to hyper-alertness or being "jumpy." Chronic fatigue, apathy, indifference, and irritability are some of the common emotional and physical responses.

In general, residential burglaries are most likely to occur during the day and non-residential dwellings, such as empty office buildings, are more likely to be burglarized at night.

Burglaries upset the victims but as long as they are not present when the burglar or burglars have entered their apartment of home, it is usually experienced as a less traumatic event than a robbery.

Larceny-theft includes pocket-picking, purse-snatching, shoplifting, theft from a building, theft from a coin-operated machine or device, theft from a motor vehicle, theft of motor vehicle parts or accessories, and other larcenies. It is the most frequent of all property crimes in the United States and also the most common type of victimization of all crimes. Depending on the state, and the value of the goods or services that were stolen, the theft may be considered a petit (or petty) larceny or a grand larceny. In 2019, the clearance rate in the United States, according to the FBI official statistics, for larceny-theft, meaning how many reported crimes led to an arrest, was 18.4 percent.

Shoplifting victims are not just the owners of the stores or businesses who might have to lay off employees, or even close, because the losses from shoplifting put the store out of business. It also victimizes the public who will probably have to pay higher prices for goods to cover the cost of the lost revenue from the shoplifting as well as the possibility of having to hire security guards to try to cut down on the shoplifting incidents.

Motor vehicle thefts in the United States have a low clearance rate of just 13.8 percent in 2019. Of the top ten cities where cars are stolen, several are located in California. The average loss from a motor vehicle theft is over $8,000.

The motives behind vandalism range from political unrest and mob riots or violence to teenagers doing it as a prank. It is controversial over whether graffiti is art or a form of vandalism. Having the consent of the building's owner to add art to it can change how the action is considered.

Half of all arsons are committed by juveniles. Arson takes its toll on the victim's property but if there were children or adults in the building or office, and it turns into an arson-homicide, the consequences of this crime are far more serious similar to the tragic outcome when a motor vehicle theft instead turns into a carjacking with a fatality.

KEY TERMS

armed robbery
arson
breaking and entering
burglar surprise
burglary
carjacking
clearance rate
complacency theft
felony murder
felony theft
fence
grand larceny
hitting licks
home invasion
larceny/theft
misdemeanor theft
mugging
National Incident-Based Reporting System (NIBRS)
petit larceny
petty larceny
professional thief
robbery
robbery-homicide
robbery-murder
stolen goods market
strong-arm robbery
target hardening
unarmed robbery
vandalism
victim blame
yoking

REVIEW QUESTIONS

1. What is the definition of a robbery?
2. How many were killed in a robbery-homicide in 2018?
3. What is the most common weapon used during a robbery?
4. What time of day are burglaries most likely to occur?
5. Who are the victims of shoplifting?
6. What is the clearance rate for motor vehicle theft?

7. According to the National Crime Victimization Survey, how many carjackings happened between 1993 and 2002? How often was a weapon used?
8. When is graffiti acceptable and when is it considered vandalism?
9. What are some of the motives behind vandalism?
10. Who are half of the arsonists?

CRITICAL THINKING QUESTIONS

1. Pickpocketing and purse-snatching are included in the crime of larceny/theft rather than robbery. Since those property crimes do involve direct interaction with the victim, do you think that categorization is reasonable or fair? Do you think those crimes should be reclassified as types of robberies? Explain your answer.
2. Why is it important to report a robbery to the police, even if the value of the goods stolen is minimal or there is not enough information about the perpetrator to insure finding him or her?
3. Which of these so-called conventional property crimes discussed in this chapter has the worst impact on its victims? Explain why you chose that particular crime.

ACTIVITIES

1. Divide into teams of two people per team. One of the team will be the First Responder, either the police officer or the EMT (Emergency Medical Technician) first on the scene. The other person will be the robbery victim. Role play for 7 minutes beginning with the first responder's role. What are the very first words you will say to the victim? What might you respond as the victim? After seven minutes, switch places. The victim will now play the role of the first responder and vice versa. After the second seven minutes, come together as a class again and discuss what you said to each other. Were the words comforting? Judgmental? Did anyone fall into a victim blame mindset? When you played the role of the victim, what did you find yourself saying to the first responder?
2. Pick one of the many property crimes you learned about in this chapter. Go to the website for the FBI for the most recent year that statistics are available. Find out what you can about these basic facts about that particular crime in the United States including
   - number of reported victims
   - demographics about the most common victim such as age, race, ethnicity, geographic location (city, suburb, rural), if available
   - presence of weapons
   - location of the crime (at home, on the street, at the office, at a store, etc.)
   - clearance rate for this crime
   - whether or not victims are injured
   - are there more or fewer victims from the previous year? 5 years ago? 10 years ago?

Does this information give you additional insight into that particular crime that helps you to better understand the typical victim? Does it help you develop a plan for how to reduce the number of victims of that particular crime?

3. Pretend you are going on a trip with a friend or with your family. Pick a real or imaginary destination for that trip. You could pick an international destination, like Barcelona, Spain, or Venice, Italy, New Delhi, India, or a domestic one, like New Orleans, Louisiana, or Chicago, Illinois. Do research as to the prevalence of property crimes in that location. Is pick-pocketing or purse-snatching a crime to be concerned about? What could a tourist do to reduce the chance of becoming a property crime victim without falling into the victim blame mindset?

RESOURCES

Directory of Crime Victim Services
Office for Victims of Crime
U.S. Department of Justice
ovc.ojp.gov
Government agency focused on gathering research and disseminating it related to crime victims.

National Center for Victims of Crime
ncvc.org
Educational nonprofit organization offering information on crime victimization.

National Organization for Victim Assistance (NOVA)
trynova.org
National membership organization started in 1976 that offers training and an annual conference for those working with crime victims.

Stolen 911
https://stolen911.com/
Site started by a police detective, now retired who is now a licensed private investigator in California. It helps victims to try to locate their stolen goods and get the goods returned.

Marc Hinch when he was police investigator. Founder of Stolen 911.com. Now retired, Marc is a private investigator specializing in fraud and auto theft. Contributed photo.

CITED WORKS AND ADDITIONAL REFERENCES

Abad-Santos, Alex. October 7, 2016. "We Don't Treat Kim Kardashian Like a Person. Her Robbery Exposed That." Vox.com. Posted at https://www.vox.com/culture/2016/10/7/13186218/kardashian-robbery-conspiracy-backlash

ABC7.com. February 6, 2021. "Caught on Video: Suspects Sought in Armed Robbery of Couple, 2-Year-Old Child in DTLA." Posted at abc7.com

ABC News. June 25, 2012. "Stars Whose Parents Have Been Murdered." Posted online at ABCNews.com

Alder.com. August 21, 2019. "10 Famous Thieves Who Changed History." Posted at alder.com

Bahr, Sarah. January 8, 2021; updated January 11, 2021. "First Inventory of Damage to U.S. Capitol Building Released." *New York Times.* Posted at nytimes.com..

Bartling, Charles. October 28, 2020. "Robber Grabs Cash and Drugs on Chicago Ave." Posted at Evanstonnow.com

Burach, Rae. January 16, 2018. "Graffiti Is Art, Not Vandalism. *Temple News.* Temple University: Philadelphia, PA. Posted at temple-news.com

Belleville, Genevieve, André Marchand, Marie-Hélène St-Hilaire, Melissa Martin, and Cidalia Silva. August 2012. "PTSD and Depression Following Armed Robbery: Patterns of Appearance and Impact on Absenteeism and Use of Health Care Services." *Journal of Traumatic Stress.* 25: 465-468.

Breen, Clairissa D. 2013. "Vandalism." In *The Encyclopedia of Street Crime in America*, edited by Jeffrey Ian Ross. SAGE Publications.

Burach, Rae. January 16, 2018. "Graffiti is Art, Not Vandalism." Commentary, Opinion, *The Temple News* (Temple University publication). Published online at temple-news.com.

Bureau of Justice Statistics. 2018. *National Crime Victimization Survey.* U.S. Department of Justice, 1992-2015.

Chokshi, Niraj and Daniel Victor. May 18, 2017. "Mississippi Boy, 6, Is Killed After Car Is Stolen from His Mother." *New York Times.* Posted at nytimes.com

Claims Journal. March 26, 2019. "Number of Vehicle Thefts with Keys Left Inside Growing Fast" Posted online.

Coleman, Charisse. November 8, 2000. "Life or Death." Indie. Posted online at indyweek.com

Cook, Philip J. Winter 1980. "Reducing Injuries and Death Rates in Robbery." *Policy Analysis.* 6(1): 21-45.

__________. June 1986. "The Relationship between Victim Resistance and Injury in Noncommercial Robbery." *Journal of Legal Studies.* 15(2): 405-416.

__________. Summer 1987. "Robbery Violence." *Journal of Criminal Law and Criminology.* 78: 78-79.

Conroy, Faith. April 16, 1987. "Defendant Sentenced to 180 Years in Duffy Case." Associated Press. Posted at apnews.com

Curry, Glen D. and Scott H. Decker. Revisions in 2006, 2017, and 2020 (by Adam Zeidan). "Graffitti" Published in Britannica.com

Dean, Anabel. July 23, 1991. "Rape: How to Fight Back." *Sydney Morning Herald.* Australia.

Edwards, Rebecca. February 25, 2021. "Eight Surprising Home Burglary Facts and Stats." Posted at safewise.com

JohnElledge.com. August 16, 2018. "What Is the Difference Between Grand and Petit Larceny?" Posted at johnelledge.com

Elklit, Ask. August 2002. "Acute Stress Disorder in Victims of Robbery and Victims of Assault." *Journal of Interpersonal Violence.* 872-887.

Federal Bureau of Investigation. *2019 Crime in the United States.* "Robbery."

__________. *2019 Crime in the United States.* Table 7. Classification by Location.

__________. *2018 UCR Reports.* Table 19. Robbery by Type of Weapon.

__________. "Bank Robberies." Posted at https://www.fbi.gov/investigate/violent-crime/bank-robbery

__________. "Bank Crime Statistics Report, 2018." Posted at https://www.fbi.gov/file-repository/bank-crime-statistics-2018.pdf/view

__________. Fall 2019. "Larceny-Theft." *Crime in the United States. 2018.* Uniform Crime Report. U.S. Department of Justice.

__________., NIBRS (National Incident Basic Reporting System). 2012. "NIBRS Offense Definitions." U.S. Department of Justice. Posted online.

__________. "Willie Sutton." Posted at https://www.fbi.gov/history/famous-cases/willie-sutton

Felson, Marcus and Ronald V. Clarke. 1998. "Opportunity Makes the Thief: Practical Theory for Crime Prevention." Paper 98, Policing and Reducing Crime Unit. London, UK: Police Research Series.

Fisher, Bonnie, Reyns, and Sloan III. 2016. *Introduction to Victimology*. New York: Oxford University Press.

Fusco, John. 2019. *The Highwaymen*. Starring Kevin Costner and Woody Harrelson. Casey Silver Productions. Directed by John Lee Hancock.

Gabor, T., Baril, M., Cusson, M., Elie, D., Leblanc, M., and Normendeau, A. 1987. *Armed Robbery: Cops, Robbers and Victims*. Springfield, IL: Charles C Thomas.

Goguen, David. 2021. "New York Laws on Petit and Grand Larceny." Powered by NOLO. Posted at criminaldefenselawyer.com

Goudie, Chuck. August 6, 2020. "Masked Bank Robbers Take Advantage of COVID-19 Face-Covering Rules." Posted at abc7.com

Gramlich, John. November 20, 2020. "What the Data Says (and Doesn't Say) about Crime in the United States." *News in the Numbers*. Fact Tank. Published by Pew Research. Posted at pewresearch.org

Haidar, Faizan. July 11, 2017. "90% Pickpockets at Delhi Metro Are Women, Be Careful at These 8 Stations: CISF." *Hindustan Times*. New Delhi. Posted online.

Hansen, Maj, Cherie Armour, Mark Shevlin, and Ask Elklit. June 2014. "Investigating the Psychological Impact of Bank Robbery: A Cohort Study." *Journal of Anxiety Disorders*. 28: 454-259.

Harding, Simon, Ross Deuchar, James Densley, and Robert McLean. July 2019. "A Typology of Street Robbery and Gang Organization: Insights from Qualitative Research in Scotland." *British Journal of Criminology*. 59(4): 879-897.

Harlow, Carolyn Wolf. April 1987. "Robbery Victims." Bureau of Justice Statistics. U.S. Department of Justice. Posted at https://bjs.gov/content/pub/pdf/rv.pdf

Haworth, Jon. July 6, 2020. "Girl, 13, Dies After Violent Carjacking of Family Van with 4 Kids Inside." ABCNews.com. Posted online.

Healy, Jack. January 11, 2021 (updated January 16, 2021). "These Are the 5 People Who Died in the Capitol Riot." *New York Times*. Posted at nytimes.com

Henry, Stuart. Summer 1977. "On the Fence." *British Journal of Law and Society*. 4: 124-133.

__________. "The Other Side of the Fence." *Sociological Review*. 793-806.

Hindi, Saja and Sam Tabachnik. May 30, 2020. "Denver Businesses Assess Vandalism, Looting Costs after George Floyd Protests." *Denver Post*. Posted at denverpost.com

Houx, Kellie. February 7, 2021. "Kansas City Woman Charged in Liberty Bank Robbery Case." Published at the mycouriertribune.com site.

Hugo, Victor. 1862, reprinted 2013. *Les Miserables*. Translated by Lee Fahnestock and Norman MacAfee. New York: Signet.

Humphries, Jonathan and Anna MacSwan. Saturday, May 30, 2020. "Hunt for Axe-Wielding Gang Who 'Robbed' Two Teens and Pushed Pregnant Woman into Canal.'" mirror.co.uk.

Irish Times. December 15, 2001. "Three Arrested After Armed Robbery in Dublin." Posted at irishtimes.com

Johnson, Bjorn, Torkey Richert, and Bengt Svensson. 2018. "Parents as Victims of Property Crime Committed by Their Adult Children with Drug Problems: Results from a Self-Report Study." *International Review of Victimology*. 24: 329-346.

Judkis, Maura and Ellen McCarthy. January 8, 2021. "The Capitol Mob Desecrated a Historical Workplace—and Left Behind Some Disturbing Artifacts." *The Washington Post*. Posted at washingtonpost.com

Katz, Jack. 1991. "The Motivation of the Persistent Robber." *Crime and Justice*. 14, 277-306.

Kesslen, Ben. December 27, 2020. "West Virginia Fire That Killed National Guard Member Was Arson, Fire Marshal Says." Posted by nbcnews.com

Klaus, Patsy. July 2004. "National Crime Victimization Survey: Carjacking, 1993-2002." Bureau of Justice Statistics. U.S. Department of Justice.

Lindegaard, Marie Rosenkrantz, Wim Bernasco, and Scott Jacques. February 2015. "Consequences of Expected and Observed Victim Resistance for Offender Violence during Robbery Events." *Journal of Research in Crime and Delinquency*. 52(1): 32-61.

Los Angeles Police Department. "Robbery Prevention." Posted at http://www.lapdonline.org/crime_prevention/content_basic_view/8820

Morgan, Rachel E. and Barbara A. Oudekerk. 2019. *Criminal Victimization, 2018*. Washington, D.C.: Bureau of Justice Statistics.

Mucci Nicola, Giorgi G., Fiz Perez J., Iavicoli I., and Arcangeli G. 2015. "Predictors of Trauma in Bank Employee Robbery Victims." *Neuropsychiatric Disease and* Treatment. 11: 2605-2612.

Narusak, Joe. February 15, 2021. "South Charlotte Homeowners Learn It's Not a 'Kindly Grandma' Stealing Their Mail." Posted at charlotteobserver.com

Nassauer, Anne. February 2018. "How Robberies Succeed or Fail: Analyzing Crime Caught on CCTV." *Journal of Research in Crime & Delinquency.* 55(1): 125-154.

Newman, David and Robert Benton. 1967. *Bonnie and Clyde.* Directed by Arthur Penn. Starring Warren Beatty, Faye Dunaway, and Estelle Parsons. Produced by Warner Bros. Pictures.

Office for Victims of Crime. 2018. "Burglary, Theft, Robbery." Fact Sheet. U.S. Department of Justice. Posted at https://ovc.ncjrs.gov/ncvrw2018/info_flyers/fact_sheets/2018NCVRW_Burglary_508_QC.pdf

__________. 2010. "Robbery: What Is Robbery?" Help Series for Victims of Crime. Posted at https://www.ovc.gov/pubs/helpseries/HelpBrochure_Robbery.html

Olivo, Antonio. "Man Kills Intruder, Is Slain; Violence: Victim, Who Vowed to Fight Back after Previous Robbery, Shouts: 'No One Is Ever Going to Rob Me Again!'" *Los Angeles Times*, June 1, 2000.

Pirius, Rebecca. 2021. "Wyoming Laws on Theft and Shoplifting." Posted at www.criminaldefenselawyer, Published by NOLO.

Prial, Frank J. August 23, 1972. "Two Hold 8 Hostages in a Bank in Brooklyn." *New York Times.* 1.

Ricapito, Maria. August 01, 2017. "Winona ryder and 7 Other Celebrities Who Have Been Sought Stealing." "Real Crime." Posted at www.aetv.com.

Rodriguez, Max. February 16, 2021. "Big Island Suspect Charged with Second-Degree Attempted Murder After Hitting Victim with Her Stolen Car." Posted at khon2.com

Sapp, Allen D. and Timothy G. Huff. Received by NCJRS September 25, 1995. "Arson-Homicides: Findings From a National Study." U.S. Department of Justice, National Institute of Justice. 31 pages.

Seal, Mark. November 22, 2016. "The Inside Story of the Kim Kardashian Paris Hotel Heist." *Vanity Fair.* November 22, 2016. Posted at https://www.vanityfair.com/style/2016/10/solving-kim-kardashian-west-paris-robbery

Schneider, Jacqueline L. January 2005. "Stolen-Goods Markets: Methods of Disposal." *British Journal of Criminology.* 45: 129-140.

Schwartz, Adam. April 24, 2019. "Does Music Glorifying Armed Robbery Lead Teens to Commit Crimes?" *Baltimore Sun.* Posted at https://www.baltimoresun.com/opinion/op-ed/bs-ed-op-0425-drill-artists-20190424-story.html

Shapland, Joanna and Mathew Hall. 2007. "What Do We Know About the Effect of Crime on Victims?" *International Review of Victimology.*14: 175-217.

Shaw, Clifford. 1930. *The Jack Roller.* Chicago, IL: University of Chicago Press.

Shouselaw.com. July 1, 2020. "What's the Difference between Petit and Grand Larceny in Nevada?" Posted at www.shouselaw.com

Shteir, Rachel. 2012. *The Steal: A Cultural History of Shoplifting.* New York: Penguin Books.

__________. August 2, 2011. "Five Myths About Shoplifting." Published in *The Washington Post.*

Sutherland, Edwin H. 1937. *The Professional Thief.* Chicago, IL: University of Chicago Press.

Sutton, Willie and Edwin Linn. 2004. *Where the Money Was.* New York: Broadway Books, Random House (originally published 1976 by Viking Press).

Sylvester, Phil. August 1, 2020. "Is Barcelona the Pickpocket Capital of the World?" Posted at worldnomads.com

Szalavitz, Maia. February 27, 2018. "Why We're Psychologically Hardwired to Blame the Victim." *The Guardian.* Posted at https://www.theguardian.com/us-news/2018/feb/27/victim-blaming-science-behind-psychology-research

Ullman, Sarah E. April 1998. "Does Offender Violence Escalate When Victims Fight Back?" *Journal of Interpersonal Violence.* 2: 179-192.

United States Attorneys Office. Central District of California. June 23, 2015. "Robbery Victims." Posted at https://www.justice.gov/usao-cdca/victimwitness/robbery-victims

United States Attorneys Office. Western District of Missouri. February 8, 2021. "Kansas City Woman Charged With Armed Bank Robbery." Posted at justice.gov

United States Attorneys Office, Western District of Tennessee. May 26, 2020. "When Bank Employees Become Victims of a Robbery."

Viswanatha, Aruna. April 21, 2021. Officer "Brian Sicknick: What We Know About His Death." *Wall Street Journal.* Posted online.

Volet, Jason A. November 23, 2016. "Are Theft Crimes in New Jersey a Misdemeanor or a Felony Offense?" Posted at criminallawyer-nj.com

Weil, Martin. September 18, 2016. "In the District, Several Robbery Victims Fight Back—To Mixed Results." *Washington Post.*

White, R. August 2002. "Understanding Youth Gangs." *Trends and Issues in Crime & Criminal Justice.* Woden: Australian Institute of Criminology.

Williams, Caroline. November 18, 2014. "How Pickpockets Trick Your Mind." Posted at the BBC.com website.

Winton, Richard and Matthew Ormseth. May 28, 2020. "Vandalism During Heated L.A. Protest over George Floyd Death Sparks Concern from Police." *Los Angeles Times.* Posted at latimes.com

Wirth, James M. n.d. "8 Malicious Acts Considered Vandalism in Oklahoma." Posted at wirthlawoffice.com website.

WMTW.com. November 24, 2020. "Maine Man Robbed During Attempted Parking Lot Sale." Posted at WMTW.com.

Woodward, Bob and Carl Bernstein. 1974. *All the President's Men.* New York: Simon & Schuster.

Wootson, Jr., Cleve R. August 12, 2015. "If Confronted by a Robber, Don't be a Hero, Police Say," *The Charlotte Observer.* Posted at https://www.charlotteobserver.com/news/local/crime/article30955707.html

Yager, Jan. 2021. *Help Yourself Now.* New York: Allworth Press, an imprint of Skyhorse.

__________. 2020, 2015, 1978 (originally published by Scribner's). *Victims.* Stamford, CT: Hannacroix Creek. See especially Chapter 5, 'I Want What You've Got' Victims."

Zimbardo, Philip G. July-August 1972. "Vandalism: An Act in Search of a Cause." *Bell Telephone Magazine.*

Zimmerman, Amy. October 11, 2016. "How Kim Kardashian Is Fighting Back After 'Traumatic' Paris Robbery." *Daily Beast.*

Zimring, Franklin E. and James Zuehl. January 1986. "Victim Injury and Death in Urban Robbery: A Chicago Study." *Journal of Legal Studies.* 15: 1-40.

Videos and News Clips

City of Allen, Texas, Police Department. December 8, 2015. "Inside the Mind of a Burglar: Burglar Confessions." Posted at https://www.youtube.com/watch?v=DtwD-c9hn58

Interview with a convicted burglar about how he chooses the homes he burglarizes. 43 minutes.

CBS2 (Chicago). May 29, 2017. ""One Year Later, Family Grieves Robbery Victim." 1:52 minutes. Jeremy Ross reporting. Posted at https://www.youtube.com/watch?v=kPKOL6Riihc

CHAPTER **NINE**

Cybercrime, White-Collar Crime, and Economic Crime Victims

Learning Objectives

After you finish reading this chapter, you should be able to:

1. Define cybercrime and its many forms including hacking, credit card fraud or theft, identity theft, and ransomware.
2. Understand that cybercrime is not always financial; it could include stalking, child pornography, revenge porn, and bullying, among other crimes.
3. Understand the three ways to categorize cybercrime.
4. Know who coined the term *white-collar crime* and when.
5. Define white-collar or economic or financial crime.
6. Define five of the most common types of white-collar crimes—fraud, embezzlement, bribery, forgery, and inside trading—and who are its victims.
7. Explain a Ponzi scheme and know its history beginning with Charles Ponzi (1882-1949) and including Bernie Madoff.
8. Understand what financial crime victims need besides reimbursement.

INTRODUCTION

Why are cybercrimes and white-collar and financial crimes in the same chapter? Some cybercrimes are actually discussed in other chapters, such as cyberstalking in Chapter 13, "Victims of Assault, Domestic Violence, Stalking, and Elder Abuse," in the section on stalking. The cybercrimes that are included in this chapter are those that involve economic fraud, especially credit card fraud. Cybercrimes and white-collar crimes are crimes that hurt its victims in ways that go beyond money. As you will see when you read this chapter, even though financial crimes may sometimes seem a bit complicated to understand or sort out, the harm to the individuals or companies that are impacted need to be recognized and dealt with. The emotional and psychological toll, in addition to the financial devastation, is a concern that needs to be highlighted and better understood. (Ganzini, et al., 1990; Moore and Mills, 1990; U.S. Department of Justice, 2015) Besides the psychological or financial toll of white-collar crime, there are those times when it crosses over into violence. Consider the case of the former assistant who embezzled $90,000 from his boss, Fahim Saleh, a well-known and much-loved tech entrepreneur in New York City. Even though Fahim was said to have worked out a repayment plan for his former employee, the employee allegedly killed and dismembered him. (Parascandola, et al, 2020).

Although there was a study on the psychological toll to white-collar crime victims in 1990 (Ganzini, e. al., 1990), it has taken years for researchers and the public to pay more attention to the emotional and even physical toll of cybercrime and white-collar crime on its victims. In 2020, Randa and Reyns published an article in *Deviant Behavior* that looked at the physical and psychological impact of **identity theft** (stealing key personal information from a victim that enables the thief to open up accounts) on its victims. They relied on data from a sample of 2,299 victims of identity theft from the National Crime Victimization Survey (Randa and Reyns, 2020). Those results are discussed in greater detail below in the section "Emotional and Physical Impact of Cybercrime and White-Collar Crime on Its Victims."

White collar crime includes an array of economic crimes. Some of the better-known crime victimizations include embezzlement, Ponzi schemes, and insider trading. The National Incident-Based Reporting System (NIBRS) lists no fewer than 58 classifications of white-collar offenses. (See Box 9.1 below for that listing.)

Cybercrimes are crimes that occur in cyberspace, which typically means the internet, and its notorious version, the "dark net" or "dark web," a place in cyberspace known primarily to those who operate outside the law. These sites are "dark" because they are like an underground web of mechanisms and gateways that hide activities; they are not indexed or searchable by standard search engines. More on the dark web later in this chapter.

THE EMOTIONAL AND PHYSICAL IMPACT OF CYBERCRIME AND WHITE-COLLAR CRIME ON ITS VICTIMS

Just as there are unique reactions by victims of violent or traditional property crimes, such as rape, robbery, or being the secondary victim of homicide, the same holds true for victims of cybercrimes or white-collar crimes. Although the research is only starting to focus on these reactions, let us examine one of the more recent studies to contribute to our understanding that these crimes impact their victims more than just because of the financial loss.

Researchers Ryan Randa and Bradford W. Reyns, in their study of a sample of 2,299 victims of identity theft from the U.S. National Crime victimization Survey found the economic toll was relatively minor. They discovered the average financial cost to victims was $503 and that just 6 percent of the victims faced such costs. That was because the majority of victims of identity theft had their bank or credit card company reimburse them. Randa and Reyns also point out that the typical victim of theft in 2014 was 25-34 years of age, female, white, with an income of $75,000 or more. (Randa and Reyns, 2020; Harrell, 2015). However, there were definite emotional and physical consequences. Of those who were victims of identity theft in the sample they studied, 37 percent noted feeling either moderately or severely distressed. That distress manifested itself in feelings of anger and/or feeling violated, worried, vulnerable, and "as though they could not trust others." (Randa and Reyns, 2020)

Physical consequences to being the victim of identity theft in their sample included stomach problems, fatigue, back pain, headaches, high blood pressure, and changes in eating and drinking habits. Those who added answers in the "other" response category noted that heart trouble was seen as a consequence. Another finding was that of the 285 in the sample who noted physical consequences related to the identity theft, 21 percent did seek professional help. The most common type of help sought was visiting a doctor or nurse's office, with the next most popular getting medication. Getting therapy or counseling, or visiting the emergency room, were less common ways of getting help. (Randa and Reyns, 2020)

In the earlier 1990 study by Ganzini, McFarland, and Bloom, 77 victims of the Ponzi scheme known as Pac Rim in Oregon, were interviewed by these three mental health professionals. Ganzini and Bloom are MD's and McFarland is an MD, Ph.D. The reported losses for the 450 victims of the Pac Rim Ponzi scheme were much higher than in the Randa and Reyns study of identity theft victims. In fact, 46 percent of those victims lost more than $40,000 and 14 percent of the victims lost more than $100,000. (Ganzini and Bloom, 1990)

Ganzini et al. found that 29 percent of the Pac Rim victims that they interviewed as part of their study experienced a major depressive episode as defined by DSM-III criteria in the first 20 months after their victimization compared to just 2 percent of the control group during the same time frame. They also found that five of the Pac Rim victims developed suicidal ideation following their loss. Another 45 percent of the Pac Rim victims had generalized anxiety disorder compared to only 15 percent in the control group. (Ganzini, et al., 1990) Six months after their loss, 48 percent of those who had suffered a major depressive episode were still having depressive symptoms six months after their victimization compared to just 2 percent in the control group.

Just as Burgess and Holstrom found that a woman's past psychiatric history was a factor in whether symptoms of depression and suicidality were likely to develop after rape (Burgess and Holstrom, 1974), Ganzini et al. found that a fraud victims' psychological profile had to be considered as a predictor of the crime's emotional impact. They conclude: "a previous history of depression, a large financial loss, and a decreased standard of living may increase the risk for major depressive disorder and suicidality and that the depression may be lengthier and more severe than more 'reactive depressions.'" (Ganzini, et al., 1990) The authors conclude: "Similarly the degree of victimization (as measured by increased financial loss and decreased financial resources) and a previous history of major depressive disorder were the most important variables in predicting the development of major depressive disorder in Pac Rim victims after the fraud." (Ganzini, et al., 1990)

UNLIKE OTHER CRIMES, VICTIMS OF ECONOMIC CRIMES MAY BE COMPANIES OR GOVERNMENT AGENCIES AS WELL AS INDIVIDUALS

We have already seen that it is challenging to separate cybercrime from white-collar crime since some cybercrimes are economic and would be considered white-collar crimes, defined as crimes committed by a person of higher standing in the course of carrying out their job. Some cybercrimes, like credit card theft and fraud, tend to be done only in cyberspace but there are also credit card frauds committed in other ways. For example, a **skimmer** is a device placed in gas pumps at gas stations and on ATMs in convenience stores that enables thieves to copy credit card information.

Max Eddy published an article in *PC Magazine* about skimmers.. Eddy notes that "the weird, bulky yellow bit"is the actual skimmer, (Eddy, 2021). (There is more about skimmers below.) Eddy also mentions something called a **shimmer**, which are devices "shimmed into card readers to attack the chips on newer cards." (Eddy, 2021)

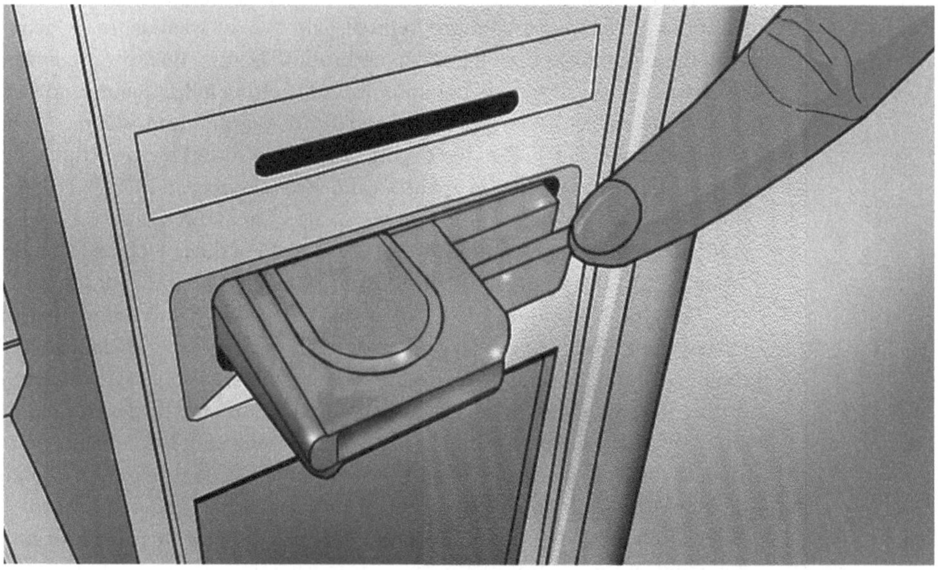

Example of a skimmer used to steal credit card information. Image provided by wikihow.com

Credit card thieves, pickpockets, or mail thieves who gain access to your credit cards or information can do a lot of spending often even before the theft is reported and the cards frozen, and certainly before they are ever caught.

Also important to note is that white-collar criminals also target companies or government agencies. As Cynthia Barnett points out in her U.S. Department of Justice report, "The Measurement of White-Collar Crime Using Uniform Crime Reporting (UCR) Data," "The data show that any effort to measure the impact of white-collar crime that only focuses on individual victims is getting only part of the picture. The impact of these crimes on commercial, financial, governmental, and religious organizations is an integral part of the effect on society as a whole." (Barnett, n.d.)

It needs to be emphasized that in the case of many white-collar crimes, the victims include those who lose their jobs because the crime caused the downfall of their place of employment as well as the family that depended on their income. For example, when an accounting scandal threatened to force WorldCom into bankruptcy back in 2002, 17,000 employees were laid off. (Noguchi, 2002) In the wake of the corporate fraud and accounting irregularities of the 2001 Enron scandal that led to its bankruptcy, thousands lost their jobs and saw their pensions disintegrate as the value of the stock collapsed. The stock price fell from $80 to pennies. It is said that Enron employees lost more than $1 billion in pension holdings. (NPR.com, 2002)

Fisher, et al. point out the two main sources of information on white-collar crime: the first was the Yale White-Collar Crime Project, which lasted from the 1980s through the 1990s; the second is the 2010 National Public Survey on White-Collar Crime, done by the National White-Collar Crime Center. In the Yale White-Collar Crime Project, David Weisburd et al. reported that 95 percent of the victims were organizations for the eight offenses that were included, namely antitrust, securities fraud, mail fraud, false claims, credit fraud, bribery, tax fraud, and bank embezzlement, as compared with the only 28 percent of common crimes with organizations as victims. They also discovered that 16 percent involved a loss of more than $100,000 compared to only 3 percent of conventional crimes with losses that great. Of those studied in the Yale White-Collar Crime Project, 5.7 percent had 100 or more victims compared to 0 percent of the common crimes with that many victims. (Fisher, et al., 2016, based on Weisburd, et al., 1991)

The 2010 National Public Survey on White-Collar Crime, reported on by Rodney Huff, et al., used random-digit dialing to survey 2,503 adults throughout the United States who had experienced white-collar crime during the previous 12 months. They discovered that credit card fraud was the most prevalent crime (39.6%) followed by price misrepresentation (28.1%) followed by unnecessary repairs (22.3%). (Huff, et al., 2010)

Cristina Policastro and Brian K. Payne reported on the results to their telemarketing survey of victims in their article, "Can You Hear Me Now? Telemarketing Fraud Victimization and Lifestyles," published in the *American Journal of Criminal Justice.* The co-authors reanalyzed data that had been collected in the Spring of 2007 as part of a larger study of adult life experiences. (Policastro and Payne, 2015: 625) The sample consisted of 61 adults pursuing services at a medical school and a senior center; 746 adults living in two Southeastern large cities; and 450 undergraduate students enrolled in criminal justice and sociology courses at a Southeast university. The combined total of 1,257 studied had an average age of 40.2 years. The majority were female and White. (Policastro and Payne, 2015: 625-626)

The researchers discovered that males living in disadvantaged areas and those who worked part-time and lived in poor areas had a greater chance of becoming victims of telemarketing fraud. (Policastro and Payne, 2015: 632)

RECOURSES FOR CYBERCRIME AND WHITE-COLLAR CRIME VICTIMS

What further complicates the challenge of understanding cybercrime and white-collar financial crime victimizations, compared to street or conventional crimes, is that civil suits are much more common for white-collar versus conventional crimes. Although there is some development in the popularity of violent and traditional property crime victims bringing lawsuits against their perpetrator or a third party, it is still relatively rare.

In contrast, much white-collar crime is handled outside of the traditional criminal justice system, beginning with the police. Although fraud, bribery, counterfeiting/forgery, and embezzlement are reported as part of the Uniform Crime Reporting (UCR) program and, more recently, the NIBRS annual data collection efforts, there are other ways to deal with these crimes. As Barnett notes in her U.S. Department of Justice report, "much of the investigation and regulation of corporate white-collar crime is left to regulatory agencies and professional association (American Medical Association, American Bar Association, etc.) and not to police or other law enforcement agencies. White-collar offenses, in these cases, probably will be reported to the UCR Program only if criminal charges are filed, which is extremely rare in instances of corporate crime. Corporate crime is usually handled within the regulatory agency (sanctions, cease-and-desist orders, etc.) or corporations are made the subject of civil cases." (A cease-and-desist order is a letter sent to a party requesting that they immediately stop an allegedly illegal practice.) (Barnett, n.d.)

Even if it is not possible to get the money back, victims are encouraged to share what happened to them at the Report Fraud site of the **Federal Trade Commission (FTC)**, which, among other functions, is responsible for promoting consumer protection and for enforcing the U.S. anti-trust laws. They will distribute that report to approximately 3,000 law enforcement personnel. That information could help to build a profile of the fraudsters which might lead to their arrest or at least help to warn others to watch out for those individuals or their con. (Federal Trade Commission, n.d.)

There are programs that are focused on preventing financial exploitation of the elderly, 60 or 65 years of age and up. The Oregon Bankers Association started their Elder Financial Exploitation Prevention Program in 1995; it has become a model nationally. At their website, you can access their training manual as well as their brochure and several videos focusing on specific popular cons, including the ATM fraud, Account Fraud, and Power of Attorney Fraud, among others. (https://www.oregonbankers.com, 2021)

CYBERCRIME AND ITS VICTIMS

Sometimes there is an overlap between white-collar or economic crimes and cybercrimes but, in general, there are distinctions. Let us start by asking a couple of questions: Do you consider someone breaking into someone's home and stealing that family's big screen TV set a criminal and the occupants of the home whose TV was stolen victims of a crime? The answer is obviously *yes*. But what if someone downloads a book that is under copyright protection that had been illegally uploaded to a website? Is the person who illegally uploaded that copyright protected material a criminal? What about the person who downloaded it? Is he/she a criminal? What about the company who produced that product, or the individual author of the material, who will not receive any revenue because of the illegal uploading and downloading? They are just some of the many victims of that type of white-collar or economic crime, that is also known as a cybercrime. In this case, it is also the crime of **intellectual property theft**.

A burglar, if caught, and found guilty, could face any number of punishments, from a slap on the wrist, restitution, or probation, to restitution plus jail or prison time. What about the intellectual property thief? What will his or her punishment be, if caught? What restitution, if any, is available to the victim whose copyrighted material was stolen?

These are not easy questions, and even harder answers. Until recently, these crimes were considered in a different light than the so-called conventional or street property crimes that we studied in the last chapter, Chapter 8, namely robbery, burglary, larceny/heft, motor vehicle theft, graffiti, vandalism, and arson.

Let us look at the economic toll of cybercrime. In the 2018 report, "Economic Impact of Cybercrime," published by the Center for Strategic and International Studies (CSIS) and the software virus protection company, McAfee, it was estimated that global losses due to cybercrime were $600 billion, up from an estimated $445 billion in 2014. (Lewis, 2018) According to the Legal Information Institute of Cornell Law School, referring to the Federal Bureau of Investigation (FBI), it is estimated that in the United States in one year, white-collar crimes cost victims—individuals, the government, and companies—an estimated $300 billion. (Cornell Law School, Legal Information Institutes, n.d.)

More recently, the economic toll of cybercrime, especially **ransomware**, whereby a cybercriminal holds the computer and other data operations of a company hostage until a paid is made, was made clear in just one example: a pipeline that supplied oil to several states was shut down, halting oil delivery. for several days until a $4.4 million ransom was paid. (Suderman and Tucker, 2021). A month later, the Deputy U.S. Attorney General Lisa Monaco announced that the Department of Just ice was able to recovery several million dollars worth of cryptocurrency that had been paid as part of the ransom. (Tucker, 2021) The psychological, economic, and practical impact of the ransomware attack was still being felt as businesses, and individuals, who had not worried about ransomware suddenly knew it was a real crime problem with companies and individuals as victims. (Sanger and Perlroth, 2021) (See further discussions of ransomware below.)

But not all cybercrime is financial. There is also what is known as "**revenge porn**," when a jilted romantic partner posts compromising videos or pictures to get back at their partner, or for money, as well as stalking, harassment, hacking, or piracy, to name a few. See Table 9.1 for a list of cybercrimes along with a definition.

TABLE 9.1. Definitions of Major Types of Cybercrime

Cybercrime	Definition
Hacking	Getting entry to an individual's computer to use it for illegal activities
Credit card fraud or theft	Getting the use of a credit card number or a physical credit card to be used to purchase items and charge them fraudulently to the credit card owner
Identity theft	Stealing key information from an individual such as their Social Security number, or taking the birth date or other identifying details, that allows someone to open up accounts in the stolen identity's name
Espionage	Passing on privileged information that is passed on to governments or rival companies for their illegal use
Piracy	Accepting and illegally using without providing to the creator any renumeration of any kind of intellectual property whether it is text, music, photographs, film, or other visual products that is copyright protected
Fraud	Making claims about a product or a service that are false, such as representing an artwork as authentic when it is a fake and getting monies from those transactions under false pretenses
Phishing	Sending a fake e-mail pretending to be a company or an individual and asking the recipient to click on an attachment or a related file that allows the thief to illegally gain access to the victim's computer or electronic device

(continued)

TABLE 9.1. Definitions of Major Types of Cybercrime (continued)

Cybercrime	Definition
Money laundering	Hiding criminal proceeds or taking money from criminal pursuits and turning it into funds that seem to be from legitimate sources. Known as going from "dirty" to "clean" money
Cyberstalking	Unwelcome actions making the victim feel fearful including gaining access to the victim's social media accounts and reading, and even responding to posts
Cyberbullying	Posting nasty comments, or even fake, vicious reviews for products, or companies, that hurt an individual, a product, or a company's reputation
Cyberterrorism and cyberwar	Using the internet to sabotage systems, infiltrate government agencies and steal information, or to disrupt the infrastructure of a city, state, or countrythrough attacks on water, communication, financial, and air traffic control systems
Romance scams	Using the internet to create one or more false profiles and then manipulating lonely and trusting victims into sending money to these fictitious romantic partners
Ransomware	Using malicious software to get into a system and hold it hostage until the victim, whether it is an individual, a company, or even a government, agrees to pay to allow the data to be accessed
Sexual solicitation	Predators pretending to get trusting minors to believe that they are potential romantic partners, then having them send sexually explicit pictures and subsequently threatening to send the pictures to their parents or their social media network unless they meet them to have sex in person
Child pornography	Offensive and illegal images or films of children under the age of 18, "engaging in sexually explicit conduct" (Marcum, 2019)
Revenge porn	When, out of revenge, a romantic partner, usually an ex-partner, either threatens or actually posts or sends to individuals or groups compromising photographs or videos
Sexual harassment	Using the computer to pester someone by sending unwanted messages that could include inappropriate words or pictures through social media or to their personal or work e-mail
Malware	Putting malicious software into someone's computer such as worms or viruses as a way to hack into someone's private information

Source: Developed from multiple sources including Grabosky, *Cybercrime*, 2016; Marcum, *Cyber Crime*, 2nd edition, 2019; M. Hoppmeyer, prosecutor.

As more and more business and personal banking is done online, cybercrime is certain to keep growing. Potential victims have to do whatever they can to be more alert to fraudulent schemes to avoid falling into their traps, as well as having the best virus protection software possible. A layer of protection is available by Signing up for a monitoring company that will send out alerts about attacks especially if the subscriber's credit card information, e-mail addresses, or personal information such as social security number, date of birth, and other key data is being found on the internet, in any internet breeches, or on what is known as the **dark web**. As we previously mentioned, the dark web is like a network of underground sites that require secret configurations and software to access it. Illegal activity and transactions that happen on the dark web are hard for law enforcement to detect. Because the criminals are operating on the dark web is one good reason why it can take as long as 18 months to 2 years for credit card fraud and other forms of cybercrime to be discovered. In the dark web, information is encrypted and hidden making it challenging and time-consuming for investigators to find the source of the fraud.

The impact of cybercrime on its victims may be more than financial.Take the case of the 67-year-old South African divorced woman who was scammed out of an estimated $90,000 by an alleged romantic con artist who had an estimated 30 aliases that he used to scam countless women. In this case, however, his victim, who had sent additional money to meet him in Nigeria, was found dead. Her death was considered the result of foul play and the alleged scammer was charged. (ABC.net.au, 2014)

CATEGORIZING CYBERCRIME

Cybercrime experts Smith, Grabosky, and Urbas suggest categorizing cybercrime into these three categories: The computer or device targeted in the cybercrime is:

- the *instrument* used to commit the offence;
- the *target* of the offence; or
- *incidental* to the offence Grabosky, 2016: 8)

These categorizations are useful to keep in mind as you read about specific cybercrimes since there can be intersection among these categories. As Grabosky notes, "the distinction between offences where computers are *instruments* and those where computers are *targets* can involve a great deal of overlap." (Grabosky, 2016: 8)

Hacking

Hacking refers to the all-too-common cybercrime whereby someone other than the legitimate computer owner gains access to a victim's computer. Once the unlawful access to the computer is achieved, other crimes can be committed, including, for example, credit card fraud, identity theft, extortion, and even piracy if the computer owner has copyrighted materials on the computer.

Changing passwords frequently can be a help. If potential victims are not willing to take the time to do that, they should at least have passwords that are difficult to guess or they should use different passwords for various accounts. Hopefully the situation has improved since 2017 when it was pointed out by Yael Grauer in his article, "Too Many People are Still Using 'Password' as a Password" just that situation: *password* should not be someone's password. (Grauer, 2017) Potential victims should know that they should avoid using their birthdate or another easily-guessed date, like a wedding anniversary, as a password.

Malware

Another common tool of cybercrime is installing a malicious code or **malware**, sometimes known as a **worm** or a **virus**, on a computer. Another related cybercrime tool is something called a **Trojan horse**, which is a malicious program that seems to be legitimate software but instead allows unauthorized users to gain access to someone's computer. **Phishing schemes** also accomplish something similar. By getting the unsuspecting victims to click on links that seem legitimate, the victims' computer is suddenly infected with one of these cybercrime tools and identity theft, credit card fraud, fraudulent ordering of goods, and even data manipulation may be possible, wreaking havoc on someone's identity, accounts, information, credit cards, and finances.

Identity Theft

David Disraeli is the founder and president of 360NetWorth, Inc. He has been providing financial advice and aging strategies to seniors for 34 years. So, he feels that he should have known better when he got the phone call that led to his identity being stolen and his credit card getting used to rack up hundreds of dollars of purchases. He figures there were two people in on the scam. Fortunately, the major card company was able to cancel the fraudulent charges, but it took hours to sort everything out. Others are not so fortunate. Their fraudulent charges are either accepted because the credit card owners fail to check their statements or the issuing card company is unable or unwilling to cancel out all the charges. (Disraeli, 2021)

Identity theft has become a huge crime problem in America. According to Erika Harrell's U.S. Department of Justice report, "Victims of Identity Theft, 2014," in 2014, an estimated 17.6 million persons, or 7 percent of those ages 16 or older, were victims of identity theft. (Harrell, 2015, revised 2017) According to Randa and Reyns, and their analysis of Harrell's 2014 identity theft report, "the typical victim of identity theft in 2014 was female, white, 25-34 years old, and with an income of $75,000 or more (Harrell, 2015, referred to in Randa and Reyns, 2020)

In 1998, Congress passed the Identity Theft and Assumption Deterrence Act. That makes it a federal crime to use and transfer any name or number without authorized authority. The victim should receive court-mandated restitution from the offender. However, identity theft is often not just undetected but hard to investigate let alone to catch the perpetrator.

Identities may also be stolen through phishing schemes, as mentioned above. This is when a bogus company looks legitimate so the recipient of the e-mail clicks it on and opens a link. Unbeknownst to the victim, that link has now allowed the criminal identity thief to gain access to the victim's computer which may contain confidential information, passwords, and so forth. By clicking on that link, the victim may even have opened up the possibility that a Trojan horse will be installed in his or her computer, permitting the thief to have ongoing access to the victim's transactions.

It is not unreasonable to be suspicious of every single e-mail, especially one that asks you to open an attached file. It is better to be suspicious and cautious than to go through the hassle and cost of straightening out identity theft situations.

We know more about identity theft victims than most other cybercrime victimizations because of the extensive information gathered when the National Crime Victimization Survey (NCVS) added identity theft to the crimes it investigated in 2014. Here is more information about identity theft victims from the report, "Victims of Identity Theft, 2014," put together by Erik Harrell, Ph.D., a Bureau of Justice Statistics statistician. Originally released in September 2015, it was revised and published on November 13, 2017:

- Eighty-six percent (86%) of the victims had an existing credit card or bank account fraudulently used.
- An estimated 1.1 million victims told the interviewer that the fraudulent misuse of their information was used to open a new account such as a loan or a credit card.

- Moderate or severe emotional distress was reported by an estimated 36 percent of the identity theft victims.
- Although half of the identity theft victims were able to resolve the problems in a day or less, about a third (32%) spent a month or more resolving the issues.
- From 2012 to 2014, the number of elderly identity theft victims increased from an estimated 2.1 million to 2.6 million.
- In 2014, almost 79 percent experienced just a single incidence of identity theft but 21% had multiple incidents.
- More females (9,243,300) than males (8,332,900) were the victims of identity theft.
- Identity theft victims tended to be white (13,264,100) compared to African American (1,407,700) or Hispanic (1,789,800).
- The age group most likely to be victimized was 50-64 (5,061,100) followed by 35-49 (5,012,300), followed by those in the 25-34-year age group (3,566,400), followed by those 65 and older (2,596,900) with those in the 18-24 being the lowest in the adult age groups (1,300,800). (Harrell, 2014)

Credit Card Fraud

Credit card fraud occurs in many ways, primarily when someone gains access to a victim's credit card, often through online purchases or in-person transactions, and then uses that card to make as many purchases as possible before the fraud is detected. It is important for potential victims to check their statements often and to make sure to have a good fraud alert system set up with the credit card companies or banks so any suspicious activity can be investigated as quickly as possible.

As noted above, another way that credit cards are fraudulently used is to create a new one using stolen information. One way this is accomplished is by setting up a "skimmer," as discussed earlier in this chapter, on an ATM machine. It takes just seconds to install the skimmer. This is usually done in a convenience store that has a freestanding ATM machine. While the cashier is distracted by the second scammer, the first one puts the skimming device on to the ATM machine. It is undetected throughout the day but every single ATM transaction that takes place feeds that information into the skimmer. The scammers return later in the day, distract the cashier again, and retrieve all the information, creating credit cards and other identity materials that enable them to do all sorts of financial transactions in the identity of the victim whose identity they have stolen.

There are other situations where the victims provide their credit card information to someone they trust, only to learn that trust has been betrayed by the misuse of that card. In some instances, the credit card fraud victim finds out that the person misusing their credit card without permission is a family member whom they gave access to the card. In those instances, since most family members do not want to contact the bank, the credit card company, or the police, the best recourse is usually to retrieve the card from the family member, and work out a repayment plan. If the victim wants the family member to still have access to that card, for emergency use only, it is possible to inform the credit card that there is a cap on spending on the secondary card holder. Victims should pick realistic amounts for the cap. The benefit of this system is that once the secondary card holder hits that limit, the card will not be operational.

If you have even one credit card you should be monitoring your credit to make sure your information has not been compromised. Do you know what your Fair Isaac Corporation

(FICO)® score is? The **FICO score** is a score that ranges from 300 to 850 and is a measure that the three main credit reporting agencies (Experian, Transunion, and Expedia) report to banks, credit card issuers, mortgage companies, even potential employers as a benchmark for how credit worthy an applicant may be. FICO scores are computed based on an individual's credit card debt, the difference between the available credit on a card and how much is owed on the card, how long someone has been employed, and other factors. Regularly reviewing your FICO® score can help you to check that your identity has not been stolen and that your information is accurate. You are eligible for one free credit score report from each of the three credit reporting companies annually. See the Resources section for those website addresses.

Intellectual Property Theft/Piracy

When you watch a movie, at the beginning it will say something about how the movie you are about to watch is copyright protected and then there will be a screen that announces that piracy is not a victimless crime. That is absolutely true. The victims of piracy are the creative individuals who made the product who will not get paid a royalty for any of the pirated copies as well as the companies that paid money to finance the product so it could get made. The actors and actresses who might be entitled to residuals based on how often the movie they appeared in is purchased or downloaded and viewed—legitimately—will not see any of those additional numbers and the related income as well.

Books have been known to be pirated in part or in totality and sold without any compensation to the author or the original publisher. Sometimes the name of the original author is even removed.

Music could be illegally downloaded and played without getting any kind of compensation to the recording artist and his or her music producer or distribution company.

Piracy is a huge white-collar crime today. Unfortunately, it is very hard to track and eliminate even if companies try to follow-up on reports of piracy. Too often the minute one site that is distributing illegal intellectual property is discovered and shut down, another one crops up.

It is key that everyone knows that it is not right to accept and listen to, view, or read pirated material. Respecting copyright is something college students are constantly told to do, especially when they are writing a term paper and they are reminded not to plagiarize.

Reminding everyone that there are real victims to piracy and that it is a crime will hopefully cut down on its prevalence. If no one is willing to pay for a pirated new movie release, the criminals should get the hint that their illegal activities are no longer profitable.

Internet Scammers, Bogus Business Opportunities, and Work-at-Home Schemes

Lillian C. was out several thousand dollars because she fell for a secret shopper internet job scam. (Her story is shared in detail in the Profile section below.) A 90-year-old North Dakota woman lost her life savings of $400,000 dollars in a Jamaican lottery scam. She was paid back only $287 of her stolen funds. The victim was one of more than 100 mostly elderly victims, in 31 states. Thirty-one defendants were prosecuted in the case reported on by the Associated Press in November 2019. Their collective losses amounted to more than $6 million. There are also online romance scams that are bilking victims out of thousands of dollars per person but millions of dollars as a collective group of victims. (AP, 2019)

An example of a bogus business opportunity was the one shared by a 26-year-old woman who told the student who interviewed her that she was scammed out of $3,000. What happened was that she responded to a picture on social media suggesting that she could make money, big time. The businessman claimed he could turn her $200 into $2,000. The fraudster's materials were so convincing that the victim set up a meeting with him the very next day. She even handed him her credit card. You can probably guess the punchline to the story. He vanished, along with her money. When she contacted him again through social media, her messages were not delivered.

Ransomware

As indicated in Table 9.1 above, ransomware is a variety of malicious software that enables scammers to access a system and hold it hostage until the target pays a ransom for its release. Victims of ransomware attacks include everything from an airport in Cleveland, the city governments of Newark, Atlanta, and Sarasota, the Colorado Department of Transportation, and hospitals, to name just a few victims cited in various article and in the CBSNEWS.com report that Scott Pelly did on ransomware. (Pelley, 2019; Blinder and Perlroth, 2018; Freed, 2018; Shear, Perlroth, and Krauss, 2021). Sometimes it was more cost-effective for governments, or businesses, to pay the ransomware fee than risk having all their data corrupted or deleted. Restoring that data could cost millions of dollars so they sometimes think paying a few thousand or even more to the ransomware thieves makes more sense. Unfortunately, by paying those who commit this crime, since detecting who is committing these acts is so challenging, it does make it more enticing for the criminals to keep doing it. As lawyer Jeffrey Allen points out in, "Surviving Ransomware," published in the *American Journal of Family Law*, there are three kinds of ransomware that "break down into three classes of malware":

1. The kind that locks up your screen;
2. The kind that encrypts your files; and
3. A version that makes threats "but do nothing else" (Allen, 2017; 65–66).

As Allen notes, you can advise people to avoid clicking on anything that is sent from someone unfamiliar to them, but you can still have a ransomware attack. His suggestion is to have a fool-proof and failproof backup system so if you do get a ransomware attack, you are able to replicate your data and system rather than being held hostage to the ransomware criminals.

Profile ▪ Lillian C.: a Victim of a Mystery Shopper Scam

The victim was a former executive director of a law firm in Manhattan who had even been a lawyer back in Latin America. But once she came to the United States, she was only able to work at a law firm. The interviewee, who will be called Lillian C. (not her real name) believed that it was because she had lost her job two months before she fell victim to the scam that she fell for it. "I needed money to pay my bills," she says. "This scam looked so real to me that I did not doubt it."

This account was recorded by a student in the author's Victimology class; it is excerpted with permission from both the student and her interviewee.

Here is what the student wrote in her overview to her interviewee's account:

Lillian's story (in her own words):

Two months ago, I lost my job so my husband tried to give me a list of options for me to apply to.

I went to three different interviews, but time was running out, and I needed money to pay my bills.

I received an e-mail from my husband about secret shopper opportunities. After careful consideration, we both decided it was a good idea, and [I had] nothing to lose since I did not have to use my own money, or that's what I thought. I proceeded to apply, and it asked for my address and phone number, but no bank account or any card information so I thought this was safe.

This scam looked so real to me that I did not doubt it. I did think that it was too good to be true, but I got it in a [major delivery service] envelope and had an [major retail store] logo so I believed it, unfortunately.

[I got the letter in the mail on March 8th of this year [2019] and the next day, I went straight to the bank to deposit the check.

A person called "John Smith' [not the real name] sent me an 'official check' for $2,900 by the Members of 1st XYZ Bank [not the real bank name used]. The check looked so real. I mean, I showed it to my husband and he was happy for me because it looked legit. They make you feel like you're doing a deal and getting paid for it. But you're actually not because they're going to take that money right away.

. . . I texted [the number they provided to me] and they kept texting me back constantly to know how I was doing with the mission. I felt kind of intimidated and pressured to do this quickly, but the truth was, no one was forcing me to do it. This is what the letter said, "The funds will be available in a few hours or the next business day. Once funds are available, either withdraw the cash or use your bank card at a [name of store redacted]. There's no [name of store redacted] here in the city so I had to travel all the way to Jersey for this assignment. Continuing on, it said, "Thereafter deduct your commission which is $400 and an extra $100 to cover the cost of gas/transportation as well as the [name of store deleted] and shipping charges for all tasks. The balance of $2,400 will be used to complete your secret assignments. Your first survey will be at a [store name deleted] local/store and [shipping company name deleted] outlet in your locality. We have received several anonymous reports of staff misconduct, turning back customers, unnecessary restrictions, overcharging, and lapses at several of [XXX] and [shipper XXX] outlets in and around you ZIP code. Pertaining to Purchase, Mailing Packages and Deliveries to friends, family, loved ones and business associates. The funds have been provided to visit and patronize the service of a [store] and a shipping outlet to ascertain the situation."

As you can see, this had very detailed instructions on what to do, step by step, and I felt like this was the solution for most of my problems since I could do many of these missions and earn some money.

[So] I withdrew the money the next day and headed to a [store]. Scammers love wire transfers. And they especially love wire transfers done through services like [major wire transfer service] and [another service] where both the sender and receiver can be almost anonymous. Once you send the money through such a service, it's typically gone forever with no way to track it. It's like handing cash to an anonymous stranger.

They wanted me to purchase three [store XXX] money orders in the amount of $800 each. It specified to leave the money order blank and not to write any name on it so I did exactly as it said. After I completed the first task, they texted me saying they had more mystery shopper tasks for me.

The next task was to buy $200 in [retailer] cards, so I did. He then said he would send me the address of the charity that I should mail the cards to, but first I needed to scratch off the silver panels and take pictures of both numbers and send it to him [Mr. Smith].

Student: Didn't you think it was a little sketchy?
Lillian: I did not see the red flags in any of this . . .
Student: Did your bank ever try to contact you or warn you about these sudden expenses?
Lillian: They did, after the damage was done. They gave me the bad news earlier in the morning, the very next day. I received an alert from my bank that my account was overdrawn. The bank had discovered that the check from these other guys was worthless.

Student: What was your reaction when they told you this?

Lillian: I panicked and contacted my bank and asked what they could do to retrieve my money. That's when I learned that I would be responsible for covering the phony check and all overdraft fees.

Student: So even if the check was fake, you were still able to retrieve the money right away?

Lillian: Yes! I did not know that. Apparently, if you are a good customer, your bank assumes that any check you deposit is valid.

Student: How did you try to mitigate your loss?

Lillian: Immediately I took a look at the two wire transfer receipts and noticed that I could check the status of the transfers. One had already gone through, but the other one had not. Luckily I was able to reverse one of the transfers, for $900. Unfortunately, I discovered the current value of the two gift cards. It was zero. Nothing could be done to retrieve that $200. [Or the $2,900 that she had to replenish into her bank account.]

Student: Did you try to contact [the store XXX] and let them know about this too?

Lillian: I checked on their website and there is a page dedicated to Fraud and one of them warns against mystery shoppers . . .

Student: Do you [now] know what's the difference between a real mystery shopper gig and a mystery shopper scam?

Lillian: I just know that a real mystery shopper job will pay little to nothing, but you may get to keep a product or have a free meal. You can actually search for The Mystery Shoppers Professionals Association.[See listing in the Resources.]

Student: How has this experience affected you emotionally or psychologically?

Lillian: Well, it definitely hurt me financially, but also emotionally because it makes me feel ashamed and dumb. I have not told anyone about this. Just my husband and now you, excerpt for a magazine [that I contacted and told my story to]

Student: It's important to know that this can happen to anyone, and now you can help others [to] be aware of this situation.

Lillian: Well, actually, a quick search shows there have been more than 700 reported "Secret Shopper" scams in the U.S. . . . . learned my lesson though. My story is an unfortunate tale that confirms the premise "If it sounds too good to be true, it probably is."

WHITE-COLLAR AND FINANCIAL OR ECONOMIC CRIME VICTIMS

White-collar and economic or financial crime victims is a huge subject that deserves its own textbook. But a textbook on victimology would be incomplete without at least defining white-collar or economic crime, who are its victims, their reactions, compensation programs, and at least discussing some of the top white-collar or financial crime victimizations. As noted previously, there is discussion over whether cybercrime should be treated separately or if it is part of white-collar criminal. As discussed above, cybercrimes include internet scammers, identity theft, credit card fraud, intellectual property theft, piracy, and more. There are also the white-collar crimes that may or may not take place, or rely on, the internet such as corporate fraud, Ponzi schemes, unnecessary repairs or services; embezzlement, and even being the recipient of a bad check because there are insufficient funds to cover it.

Box 9.1. Criminal Behaviors According to the NIBRS (National Incident-Based Reporting System) Classifications of White-Collar Offenses

Academic crime
Adulterated food, drugs, or cosmetics
Anti-trust violation
ATM fraud
Bad checks
Bribery
Check kiting
Combinations in restraint in trade
Computer crime
Confidence game
Contract fraud
Corrupt conduct by juror
Counterfeiting
Defense contract fraud
Ecology law violations
Election law violations
Embezzlement
Employment agency and education-related scams
Environmental law violations
False advertising and misrepresentation of products
False and fraudulent actions on loans, debts, and credits
False pretenses
False report/statement
Forgery
Fraudulent checks
Health and safety laws
Health care providers fraud
Home improvement frauds
Impersonation
Influence peddling
Insider trading
Insufficient funds checks
Insurance fraud
Investment scams
Jury tampering
Kickback
Land sale frauds
Mail fraud
Managerial fraud
Misappropriation
Monopoly in restraint in trade
Ponzi schemes
Procurement fraud
Racketeering Influenced and Corrupt Organizations (RICO)
Religious fraud
Sports bribery
Strategic bankruptcy
Subornation of perjury
Swindle
Tax law violations
Telemarketing or boiler room scams
Telephone fraud
Travel scams
Unauthorized use of a motor vehicle (lawful access but the entrusted vehicle is misappropriated)
Uttering
Uttering bad checks
Welfare fraud
Wire fraud

Source: NIBRS

Defining White-Collar Crime

Sociologist/criminologist Edwin H. Sutherland is credited with coining the term **white-collar criminality.** He used the term initially in a speech presented for the 34th Annual Presidential Address delivered in Philadelphia on December 27, 1939 in the joint meeting with the American Economic Society. Then, a year later, his groundbreaking article, "White-Collar Criminality" was published in the February 1940 issue of the *American Sociological Review.* (Sutherland, 1940)

White collar crime has many names including **economic crime**, **corporate crime**, or **financial crime. White-collar crime** is the term coined by Sutherland to describe crimes that are committed not by the lower classes but by the middle and upper classes and those in corporations usually as part of their job performance.

Considering white-collar crime and its victims has become so commonplace today that it is challenging to think back to a time when crime was only considered the conventional crimes (sometimes referred to as street crimes), violent and nonviolent, that we associate with murder, rape, robbery, aggravated assault, arson, burglary, and larceny-theft. Back in 1939, Sutherland proposed that victims of white-collar crimes were still "real" victims.

As Sutherland wrote: "White-collar criminality in business is expressed most frequently in the form of misrepresentation in financial statements of corporations, manipulation in the stock exchange, commercial bribery, bribery of public officials directly or indirectly in order to secure favorable contracts and legislation, misrepresentation in advertising and salesmanship, embezzlement and misapplication of funds, short weights and measures and mis-grading of commodities, tax frauds, misapplication of funds in receiverships and bankruptcies. These are what Al Capone called 'the legitimate rackets.' These and many others are found in abundance in the business world." (Sutherland, 1940)

Dr. Sutherland continues, describing white-collar crime as "real crime," and criminology and victimology would never be the same! As Sutherland writes: "White-collar crime is real crime. It is not ordinarily called crime and calling it by this name does not make it worse, just as refraining from calling it crime does not make it better than it otherwise would be. It is called crime here in order to bring it within the scope of criminology, which is justified because it is in violation of criminal law. The crucial question in this analysis is the criterion of violation of the criminal law." (Sutherland, 1940: 5)

TYPES OF WHITE-COLLAR OR FINANCIAL CRIMES AND THEIR VICTIMS

Benefits Fraud

This type of fraud involves individuals who misrepresent their eligibility requirements, most commonly by falsifying their income, to receive benefits whether it is food stamps, disability insurance, or unemployment insurance.

Within this category is a unique type of financial fraud that the U.S. Department of Agriculture refers to as **food stamp trafficking**. This is when someone illegally buys or sells food stamp benefits for cash, drugs, weapons, or other items of value. In these cases, the victim is the U.S. government. These schemes may go on undetected for years. If perpetrators are finally caught and serve several years in a federal prison for these crimes, the monies that were stolen, which could be in the millions, may have been spent so reimbursement is unrealistic.

Embezzlement

Embezzlement is a financial crime that takes place when employees steal from their own employer or store. This is a white-collar crime that strikes at the very heart and soul of its victims, because the perpetrator is usually an employee and someone that was trusted and possibly even considered more than an employee but a friend. We mentioned previously the tragic case of the millionaire 33-year-old tech entrepreneur who was willing to work out a payment plan with his ex-personal assistant, who embezzled $90,000 out of his company. In that case, the ex-assistant tragically killed his former boss.

The fines or penalties for embezzlement where, unlike larceny/theft, the person who embezzles has a relationship with the victim, such as a bookkeeper role, or someone entrusted with the care of someone's finances, will vary based on several factors. One consideration is the state where the crime occurred, since state statutes and penalties differ, or whether the crime is under federal jurisdiction. In some states, embezzlement of $1,000 or less is considered a misdemeanor; over that amount, it is considered a felony.

Embezzlement can lead to jail or prison time but it can also lead to unique sentencing agreements. An employee who embezzled an estimated $100,000 from his employer, avoided jail time by agreeing to pay back the money, do community service and probation, and give over to the marina where he worked and embezzled ownership of his prized 26-foot fishing boat.

The elderly, especially those who have given over control of their financial matters, to family members or to paid assistants, can be especially vulnerable to embezzlement if they are no longer capable of double checking the transactions that are being made. Hiring trusted people in the first place, and only relying on family members who are also trustworthy, or even have a second pair of eyes to review all financial matters, are possible ways to cut down on embezzlement.

Ponzi Schemes

The Madoff victims, and the victims of other **Ponzi schemes** (investment scams where returns for early investors are funded by investment funds from later investors, making the success of the fund appear inflated), come from all classes, races, religions, and ethnic groups. They are single and they are married. They are widowed and they are the young. They are sick and they are healthy. They are well-known and famous and they are just the average everyday folk. But what they all had in common is that being a victim of Bernie Madoff's Ponzi scheme was devastating. It has been estimated that as much as $61 billion dollars was lost to his tens of thousands of victims. (Freshman, 2012; Yager, 2010)

What made the Bernie Madoff white-collar crimes so horrific besides the huge number of victims and their enormous financial losses, was the betrayal of trust. Many had known Madoff, and trusted him, as a friend as well as a financial advisor for five or ten years and

Convicted of a multi-billion dollar Ponzi scheme, Bernie Madoff (1938-2021), who died in prison at age 83.

sometimes even for decades. He had held such prestigious positions in the finance world including as a former chairman of the Nasdaq exchange.

Ponzi schemes are named after Charles Ponzi (1882-1949). He arrived from Italy in 1903 and because of his illegal financial activities, his name is now associated with any financial scam that operates with the initial investors getting paid with money from the assets of the new investors.

Bernie Madoff kept his Ponzi scheme going for decades and it actually might have gone on even longer but when the economic downturn of 2008 hit and investors asked for their money back, the scheme fell apart. Madoff got a lengthy prison sentence of 150 years and his two sons died, one from suicide and the other from cancer. Even though it's been a decade since the scandal broke, Madoff's victims are still suffering. As Jim Zarroli writes in his article, "For Madoff Victims, Scars Remain 10 Years Later," Steve Heimoff shared about how he lost his $2 million retirement nest egg. Heimoff told the reporter, "I just stopped going to restaurants, I stopped buying clothing. I stopped going on vacations, I stopped going to movies." Ironically, Heimoff had not even invested directly with Madoff. They had invested with a California fund manager who had put Heimoff's money into Madoff's firm.

Heimoff, who was 62 at the time and forced to refinance his condominium in Oakland, California had even contemplated suicide. "My fear was getting old and decrepit," Heimoff shared. Without any adult children to rely on, he had once been confident he would be able to take care of himself because he had worked so hard to have such a robust retirement account.

Another Madoff victim interviewed for the article was 58 at the time Madoff's Ponzi scheme fell apart. He was going to receive from 60 to 70 percent of the money he invested with Madoff from the court-appointed trustee, but not the returns that he was purportedly growing over the years. So, his retirement income is less than a third of what he had planned it would be.

He shared with Jim Zarroli of NPR the **victim blame** that was widespread back in 2008: "There was a lot of feelings back at that time that people who were invested with Madoff, quote, got what they deserved. That the returns were too good to be true and therefore you took advantage of the system and, you know, ha, we gotcha." (Zarroli, 2018)

Bad Checks (Insufficient Funds)

Writing bad checks is considered a type of financial crime in that it is financial fraud. If the check is written with the knowledge that there are insufficient funds to cover it is viewed differently than if it is done by mistake because of sloppy accounting.

To void unwittingly falling into the category of being a perpetrator of this white-collar crime, if you are still using checks, set up an overdraft situation whereby if you do mistakenly have insufficient funds, while you sort that out, the credit card that you set up as the default for the overdraft will cover the check. You will not, fortunately, be considered by the bank as being someone who is committing fraud, but be aware that when you use a credit card in that manner, the bank usually considers it a cash advance so the funds that are advanced may have a very high default APR rate of as much as 25 percent APR or even higher. So pay off that credit card advance as soon as you can.

Everyone needs to be careful to avoid becoming the victim of receiving a fraudulent check; the first step is to be careful of who you are doing business with. Certainly avoid taking checks from complete strangers. Be aware that if someone accepts a personal check that turns out to be fraudulent, the victim's bank may charge the victims, even if they accepted the fraudulent check through no fault of their own. Also, if a victim believes that check was authentic, other checks could be written against the funds before the insufficient funds situation is made known. There can be a domino effect of bounced checks that victims now cause because of depositing that first fraudulent check.

Although a cashier's check or money orders can be counterfeited, in general, those are safer types of checks to accept over a personal check. If you do use either of those checks, make sure you make a copy of the paperwork. It is still of course possible to get duped.

Counterfeiting/Forgery

The definition of counterfeiting/forgery, according to the NIBRS of the FBI is: "The altering, copying, or imitation of something, without authority or right, with the intent to deceive or defraud by passing the copy or thing altered or imitated as that which is original or genuine; or the selling, buying, or possession of an altered, copies, or imitated thing with the intent to deceive or defraud."

Many stores refuse to accept anything larger than a $20 bill in order to avoid becoming the victim of receiving counterfeit larger bill denominations, such as $50 or $100 bills. Those stores that are still willing to accept larger denominations have ways of testing a bill to check whether it is counterfeit before accepting it.

Bribery

The definition of bribery, according to the NIBRS of the FBI is: "The offering, giving, receiving, or soliciting of anything of value (i.e. a bribe, gratuity, or kickback) to sway the judgment or action of a person in a position of trust or influence." Bribery is an especially complicated white collar crime when it is applied to other countries. It is important to remember that the country you hold your citizenship in is the one that you should be concerned about. It is against the law to bribe a public official in the United States (domestic) or internationally (foreign). The law that prohibits bribing foreign public officials is the Foreign Corrupt Practices Act (FCPA), 15 U.S.C. §§ 78m, 78dd-1, 78dd-2, 78dd-3, and 78ff. It was enacted in 1977. (Yager, 2011)

The law prohibiting bribery of domestic federal officials was enabled in 1962. It is 18 U.S.C. § 201.

Also check out what are the laws in the state you live in regarding bribery.

If you are working in another country, be very careful not to be pulled into that country's approach to bribery. It might be the way business is done, but you could be arrested for violating the Foreign Corrupt Practice Act since you are an American. Also, some countries have such a strict anti-corruption policy that being found guilty of bribery could lead to a lengthy prison sentence or even the death penalty.

Who are the victims of bribery? The citizens of those cities, states, or countries where the bribes are paid, which might lead to more expensive or even inferior products or services.

The hiring of incompetent individuals because of bribery could lead to inferior or even life-threatening services if the requisite skills were bypassed.

Unnecessary Repairs or Services

Victims of unnecessary services or repairs can be fleeced out of hundreds or even thousands of dollars. Car repairs can be requested that are completely unnecessary. Even chimney cleaning, for more than a thousand dollars, can be strongly recommended by some businesses that aggressively seek out customers to the point that homeowners may feel pressured to authorize the service. The elderly are especially vulnerable to being talked into unnecessary repairs or services, especially once they reach an age or stage of life where they may be far too trusting and, although they might not need caregiver help, their mental acuity may not be what it used to be. When and if a scam occurs, even if they do realize what happened, they may be too embarrassed to disclose it to their friends or adult children, often for fear of criticism or of losing their independence.

Tax Fraud

There are certainly many famous names that could be invoked related to tax fraud, beginning with criminal Al Capone who was found guilty of tax evasion after a trial in 1931. (FBI.gov, "Al Capone") He did not get convicted for his more serious violent crime/murder charges, but he was found guilty of tax fraud. He served more than seven years at penitentiaries in Atlanta and Alcatraz. (FBI.gov, "Al Capone")

Tax fraud includes the underreporting of income so the tax liability will be less. A well-regarded and much loved lawyer was found guilty of underreporting his income by $300,000. After the fraud was discovered, he agreed to pay back the taxes that he owed, plus penalties; he was sentenced to three years in a federal prison. He passed away several years later, after his release, at the age of 68.

In addition to the problem of the government not receiving money that is rightfully due, the perpetrator's family is also victimized because of the tax fraud conviction, with its resultant economic hardship to the family on account of the lost job and lost wages and the economic and psychological hardship and shame experienced when a loved one is in jail or prison.

Inventory Shrinkage

In partnership with the University of Florida, the National Retail Federation, in its 2018 report, "2018 National Retail Security Survey," estimated that inventory shrinkage cost retailers, on average, $46.8 million in 2017, or 1.33 percent of sales, on average. (NRF, 2018)

Inventory shrinkage is when the value of a company's inventory is less than it should be because of various actions including employee shrinkage, when employees steal from the company, as well as inventory shrinkage from other sources such as cashier or administrative errors, shoplifting, or vendor fraud. The victims are the public that has to pay higher prices when the cost of the loss is passed along to the customer. Employee shrinkage is when employees steal from their employer through a variety of crimes including shoplifting, cashier or administrative errors, and theft. If the problem is big enough that technology has to be installed to try to minimize or eliminate the problem, those costs may also be passed on to the consumer or it could contribute to the store or company going out of business, or having to lay off employees, to cover the added costs.

Some shoplifters steal for the thrill. They are less concerned with making money from the theft than with getting the goods that they are stealing and getting away with it. Other employee theft perpetrators are interested in reselling the goods that they steal, and making a profit, while even still holding down their job. (Shoplifters are discussed in Chapter 8 as well.)

Insider Trading

Here is how the SEC (Securities Exchange Commission) defines insider trading: ""Insider trading" refers generally to buying or selling a security, in breach of a fiduciary duty or other relationship of trust and confidence, while in possession of material, nonpublic information about the security. Insider trading violations may also include "tipping" such information, securities trading by the person "tipped," and securities trading by those who misappropriate such information." Those who work for a company, as well as financial advisors and brokers, are not allowed to make trades on stocks or commodities if they learn through their position that a dramatic situation is about to unfold that will affect the stock's value up or down. The victims of insider trading are those whose own trades are adversely influenced by the illegal activities of those making sales on illegally obtained information that others were not privy to. As Hansen points out "technically there are legitimate inside traders, like executives at companies, purchasing company stock. But all of that has to be reported on the SEC 10-Ks and 10Qs. They just can't sell or purchase stock based on information that hasn't been made public yet." (Hansen, 2021)

Financial Institution Fraud (FIF)/Mortgage Fraud/ Credit Application Fraud

A lie that affects a bank's determination about whether, for example, to authorize a loan, take on a reduced payoff amount, or agree to repayment terms, is deemed fraud whether it is related to applying for a mortgage or any credit application. Because most banks are federally insured, mortgage fraud is considered a federal crime. Several years ago a guest speaker at the Penology course that this author teaches at John Jay College of Criminal Justice who had previously worked in a state government job shared with the class that he had been found guilty of mortgage fraud and sentenced to three years in a federal prison. He shared that he had inflated his income on his mortgage application. When the lie was discovered, even though he repaid the mortgage that he received, he was sentenced to prison. He warned the students never to lie or inflate any information on any credit or mortgage applications because it could have dire consequences.

Here is the definition of these crimes by the FBI: "Financial institution fraud (FIF) is the class of criminal schemes targeting traditional retail banks, credit unions, and other federally-insured financial institutions. Many FIF schemes involve the compromise of customers' accounts or personal identifying information (PII); when identities are stolen, both the financial institution and customers are considered victims." (FBI, "Financial Institution/Mortgage Fraud," n.d.) In that FBI website document about "What We Investigate," there is also a definition of mortgage fraud. "Mortgage fraud is a sub-category of FIF. It is crime characterized by some type of material misstatement, misrepresentation, or omission in relation to a mortgage loan which is then relied upon by a lender. A lie that influences a bank's decision—about whether for example, to approve a loan, accept a reduced payoff amount, or agree to certain repayment terms—is mortgage fraud."

Health Care Fraud

This type of fraud includes filing claims for procedures that did not take place or were unnecessary; falsifying test results to justify unwarranted procedures; or accepting a **kickback** (a monetary payment) for a patient referral. It also includes **upcoding**, which refers to billing for a more expensive version of a procedure that was performed.

Other types of health care fraud include Medicare fraud, whereby a nurse, physician, or administrative personnel put in for a reimbursement for a service that either was not performed or was performed for a different amount of money, or under a different code than the one that is indicated. Kickbacks, which are usually also considered bribery, can also be part of health care fraud whereby a physician or nurse, or administrative staff, are paid to favor a particular drug or medical equipment over the competition, making recommendations to patients or purchases because of that kickback. Drilling teeth for a fee when there was never a cavity there in the first place or falsifying records or requiring unnecessary procedures for profit are other examples of health care fraud. In addition to the patients who are the victims because they are being exposed to unnecessary risk for medical or dental procedures that are unnecessary, there is also the financial cost to those patients as well as to the insurance companies or other providers who are paying some or all of the medical costs.

Food Stamp Fraud

Food stamp trafficking is a type of fraud whereby the perpetrator illegally buys or sells food stamps for cash, drugs, weapons, or other non-food items. According to the U.S. Department of Agriculture, unlawful possession or use of food stamps benefits amounting to less the $100 is a misdemeanor; more than $100, is considered a felony. Another type of food stamp fraud is if someone underreports their income or providing other false information to make them eligible for the food stamp benefits. This program is only meant for low-income individuals and their families who need the benefits to get food and nutrition.

Securities and Commodities Fraud

Another type of financial crime is known as securities and commodities fraud. This is when an individual intentionally misleads a buyer about the value of a stock or commodity

Phone Scams

Phone scams may start on a phone but then, because so many today have smartphones that are also computers, may move online. When a phone scam is purely a fraudster using a phone to try to extract money from the recipient of the call, it can take many forms. In one especially common tactic targeting seniors, a fraudster calls claiming that a grandchild has been kidnapped and that a ransom is required for their release; one of the rules is not to call the police. In a similar type of call, a fraudster calls claiming to be a grandchild who is stuck in a distant location and needs money to get back home. The fraudster in many cases is so convincing that the recipient of the call withdraws money from their bank account and gets it to the fraudster. Other versions of this type of fraud involve calls from scammers posing as collection agencies, or as IRS agents, and demanding immediate payment of money that is "due" or face dire consequences, such as having assets tapped.

Money Laundering

Money laundering means taking "dirty" money from illegal operations and running it through a legitimate company or service so that the money comes out "clean" without any trace to the original illegal origins. That means that money that was received illegally, perhaps from drug deals or theft, is put through an intricate method of reinvesting it through legitimate businesses, disguising its initial illegal origins.

Misstating a Company's Value at the Point of Sale

If someone is planning to buy a company and the seller hides losses and inflates the value of the company so that the buyer pays far more than the company or its product line is worth, that is a form of fraud because the purchaser will probably pay more for the acquisition based on this false information.

Forgery

Writing someone else's signature on an official document for monetary gain is **forgery**. The juvenile version of this is if a teenager forges their parent's signature on a report card that they don't want their parent to see or imitating the parent's signature on a note about absence as a way of getting a day off from school.

Mail and Wire Fraud

Mail and wire fraud is when someone uses the postal service or sends something electronically to carry out a scheme. If a victim is sent a fake credit card application and, after it is completed and mailed in, the fraudster is able to obtain a credit card or loan in that victim's name, that would be an example of mail fraud. If a letter soliciting money related to a Ponzi scheme is mailed to victims, those letters would be considered mail fraud.

Price Misrepresentation

Price misrepresentation is the financial crime whereby a price has been misrepresented for a commodity that is sold by weight, measure, or count. The victims could be the customer or even the government if the falsification of information about a commodities weight, measure, or count results in reduced taxes.

Fraudulent Business Venture

This type of situation was mentioned related to cybercrime. It also happens outside of the internet and refers to when a company purposefully deceives customers, shareholders, investors, or employees.

Insurance Fraud

There are many types of insurance fraud. One example of insurance fraud would be if someone deliberately causes a fender bender and stages an injury in order to claim compensation from the other driver or the driver's insurance company. If someone has jewelry or certain appraised items insured for their apartment or home and they hide the item, claiming that it was stolen or lost to collect the insurance benefit, that is another example of insurance fraud. Insurance fraud schemes range from falsely claiming the loss of an insured item so that a claim can be filed and reimbursed to inflating the value of items so that if lost or stolen there would be a higher settlement than justified.

Adulterated Foods and Food Fraud

Food fraud crimes are actually crimes against consumers. They also violate the Federal Food, Drug and Cosmetic Act (FFDC). Misrepresenting food that has tested positive for bacteria as being safe is one type crime covered by the FFDC. If victims get sick or die from tainted or adulterated foods, those responsible face prison time as well as huge fines. In 2010, there was an outbreak of Salmonella that was considered responsible for making as many as 56,000 individuals sick. The outbreak was traced to tainted eggs. The father and son who owned the company that sold the eggs pleaded guilty to misdemeanor violations and in a plea deal, were sentenced to three months in prison and a $100,000 fine. Their company had already paid a $6.8 million fine. (Hardee, 2016)

Who Are the Victims of White-Collar or Economic Crime?

Writing in Forbes.com, Roomy Khan notes that the FBI estimates that white collar crime annually costs the United States $500 billion, which is far higher than the estimated $15 billion from "personal property crimes." (Khan, 2018)

So, who are the victims of white-collar crime? According to Laura Pinto Hansen, "The most common victims of financial white-collar crime are the elderly, mentally ill, recent immigrants and the poor, and also employers (in the case of embezzlement or employee theft). The BIG cases make it seem like it really is the wealthy that are victimized (e.g., Madoff's Ponzi scheme)." (Hansen, 2021)

Most of the time we do not learn the names of the victims of white-collar crimes but instead the cases get known by the companies that are associated with the crimes, like the

Enron collapse or the Worldcom account scandals, the conviction of Martha Stewart for lying about why she sold her shares of a biotech company, or the actresses associated with the college admission scandal of 2019, Felicity Huffman and Lori Loughlin. (Noguchi, 2002; Hays and Eaton, 2004; NPR.com, 2002; Taylor, May 2020; Taylor, December 2020)

Unfortunately, the immediate victims of some of the white-collar or economic crimes we will discuss in this section are sometimes made to look as if it was their fault. Consider the small investors whose life savings were depleted by unscrupulous money managers. Yet they are sometimes depicted as someone whose greed or carelessness got them into that predicament.

The victims of white-collar and economic crimes are actually more than just the direct or primary victims. There are secondary victims to white-collar crimes. These are the family and possibly even the business associates of both the perpetrators and the victims. They are secondary victims of the victims because their family members may have lost all of the family's savings. Business associates, including employees or co-owners, may have lost their income or even their business.

Secondary victims of the offenders are those who have to bear the shame and humiliation of having a relative who committed a white-collar or economic crime. In addition to the social stigma, if their family member served time in jail or prison, they may lose financial support during that time. Depending on the situation, they may have to pay some or all of the fines that are part of the sentencing agreement.

In her article, "What Happened to the Students Caught Up in the College Admissions Scandal?" *New York Times* reporter Kate Taylor points out that even if it is their parents who are paying huge fines, doing community service, or even serving time in jail, their children have suffered too. Just some of the consequences she named include getting expelled from school, being "haunted by nightmares and panic attacks, whispered about by classmates, and mocked online." (Taylor, 2020)

Then there are tertiary victims of white-collar crimes, namely the rest of society, who have to pay higher prices for merchandise, increased insurance premiums, and even higher tax rates. Also damaging is the loss of faith in the criminal justice system if those guilty of white-collar crimes costing individuals, companies, and governments thousands, millions, or even more receive little or no sentences. Consider that 17-year-old who confesses to two attempted armed robberies where no one was hurt is sentenced to 40 years in a state prison and a confessed white-collar criminal who embezzles $150,000 from his employer is allowed to make restitution and go on probation.

Dealing with the Criminal Justice System

The devastation that financial crime has on its victims is too often minimized with the phrase, "It's only money." In addition to the psychological and emotional trauma of being deceived and victimized, there is the rare but all too real and horrific situation where the devastation goes way beyond money. As mentioned before, that happened in the July 2020 tragic case of the 33-year-old tech genius, Fahim Saleh, whose ex-personal assistant allegedly embezzled $90,000 from him. The ex-assistant allegedly killed him and then dismembered him with an electric saw. (Slotnik, 2020) This author recalls a former student at The New School sharing that her father had been killed by his business partner.

What made Fahim Salch's murder even more tragic is that Saleh was willing to work things out with his assistant rather than go to the police about the embezzlement. Instead, as Parascandola and other *New York Daily News* reporters wrote in their story about the gruesome killing, "Saleh, rather than going to the NYPD about the missing money, was willing to work out a deal where Haspil could pay back the cash without repercussions, sources said. But the plan fell apart when the assistant responded to his boss' kindness with savage cruelty, the sources said." (Parascandola, 2020)

What should victims of embezzlement, or any other kind of financial crime, do upon realizing they have been victimized? As the U.S. Department of Justice points out in its "Financial Fraud Crime Victims" online publication, fraud crimes can be prosecuted at the state or federal level. There are several factors that need to be considered such as:

- Type of fraud scheme and amount of money stolen
- Laws violated (federal, state, or both)
- Method of operation
- Use of public services (such as the U.S. Postal Service, Telecommunication systems, and Medicare) that fall under federal or state regulation and authority
- Location of the crime (within a state or across state or national borders)

(U. S. Department of Justice, "Financial Fraud Crime Victims")

Compensation Programs

Crime victim state compensation programs are now in place in all 50 states. Those programs are almost universally applied to paying for expenses related to "street crimes": rape, sexual assault, domestic violence, aggravated assault, burglary, or robbery victims. The programs are set up to help eligible families of homicide victims to pay for funerals, cover crime scene clean up expenses, and possible even a one-time payment for loss of earnings. These programs also pay for medical expenses related to victimization injuries. But state crime victim compensation programs are not set up to reimburse those who have lost money because of white collar crimes.

However, if it is a federal crime, the **Mandatory Restitution Act of 1996** made it mandatory for defendants to pay restitution in cases committed after April 24, 1996. Since many defendants lack funds, however, that requirement may be more in principle than in fact. After a conviction, however, a victim may be asked by the U.S. Attorney's Office or by the probation office to prepare a Victim Impact Statement. That statement can include information about the financial harm to the victim in addition to the psychological, medical, or social harm. You will find a blank sample of a Victim Impact Statement for a Financial Crime posted in the Appendices at the publisher's website that accompanies the text, at www.AspenPublishing.com

If someone is the victim of a financial crime, they should call the U.S. Attorney's Office in their area. If there is a Victim-Witness Program, they should contact that program, explain what happened, and see whether their case qualifies as a federal case. If they think it should be handled on the state level, then they can contact the Victim-Witness Program at the local district attorney's office to see what the next steps are.

Regardless of whether it is a state or a federal crime, it is important for the victim to keep all paperwork and/or copies of electronic communications, receipts, bank, investment or medical statements, and any other documentation related to the crime. For example, a scammer attempted to get money out of an elderly man and his wife. What the phone scammer did not know is that his prospective victims were a former head of both the FBI and the CIA, William Webster, and his wife Lydia. In 2014, the Websters got a call from a man who told them that they had won an award. But they were also told to pay a tax up front to claim the money. They decided to get the FBI involved after the phone scammer talked in a very aggressive way, saying threatening things. The FBI was able to identity the scammer who had successfully scammed other victims out of hundreds of thousands of dollars. The outcome was that the scammer was sentenced to nearly six years in prison.

In that case, the Websters did not comply with the scammer's monetary request so they did not lose money and the scammer was actually prosecuted and sentenced to prison. That is an unusual case. Often victims are out their money and the perpetrators are in another country. Even if they are within the United States, figuring out their true identity may be difficult.

UNDERSTANDING THE ECONOMIC AND EMOTIONAL NEEDS OF FINANCIAL CRIME VICTIMS AND OFFERING HELP

In 1997, the Office for Victims of Crime (OVC), which is part of the U.S. Department of Justice, published revised Guidelines for Implementation of the Victims of Crime Act (VOCA), which was originally passed in 1984. In this 1997 revision, these three changes directly applied to victims of financial crimes:

1. An expansion of the definition of *victim* to include financial crime victims.
2. Expanding the definition of *elder abuse* to also include fraud and economic exploitation.
3. Revising the definition of *previously underserved* key areas of concern to also include fraud crime victims.

Because of those changes, VOCA grant funds could now be applied to direct services for victims of fraud. Some of the direct services include: events for public education; mental health assistance and support groups; restitution advocacy; credit counseling; and respite care services for disabled victims.

Victim blame or **victim self-blame** is a common reaction by financial crime victims. Whether it is the victim's family or friends, or the victims themselves, there is that feeling, "How could I have been so gullible?" "Why didn't I know I was being conned?"

In the "Financial Crimes" chapter in the 2000 National Victim Assistance Academy comprehensive overview of victims and their needs, Debbie Deem et al. point to Wells' 1989 article, "White Collar Crime: What About the Victims?" These are the six feelings that Wells noted that financial crime victims suffer, namely:

1. Guilt and shame;
2. Disbelief;
3. Anger;
4. Depression;
5. Sense of betrayal; and

6. Loss of trust (Deem, et al., 2000; Wells, 1989)

Unfortunately, because of their feelings of shame and victim self-blame, too many financial crime victims may be reluctant to seek out professional help. Deem, et al. note these additional concerns that need to be considered for those who work with financial crime victims, namely:

- "Increased susceptibility to physical illness or death.
- The possibility of physical violence within he family of the victim, including elder, child, and/or partner abuse.
- Substance abuse as a reaction to the victimization.
- An increased risk of suicide." (Deem, et al., 2000)

This concept was mentioned previously in *Essentials of Victimology*, and it needs to be referred to again here, namely the phenomenon known as **recurring victimization** or **repeat victimization.** The tendency to be the victim again and again of the same or other financial crimes, particularly for those elders whose families are unaware of the frauds that they have fallen victim to, highlight why getting help the first time it happens is so important.

A web-based survey of 172 Madoff victims (56% female, mean age 60.9 years of age) were examined using the Posttraumatic Stress List Checklist by Audrey Freeman. The result was that 55.7% met the criteria for a diagnosis of PTSD based on the *Diagnostic and Statistical Manual of Mental Disorders*, 4th edition. There were other problems including depression (58%) and health-related problems (34%). A whopping 90 percent stated they had lost confidence in financial institutions. (For a discussion of PTSD, and its symptoms and treatment, refer back to Chapter 6, "Helping the Victim.") (Freeman, 2012: 39) Freeman's 2012 study was important because it highlighted the emotional and health repercussions from the financial loss associated with white-collar crimes like the Madoff Ponzi scheme. Freeman concludes: "The elevated rates of PTSD, coupled with the significant self-reported consequences to health found in this study, suggest that populations affected by sudden and severe financial hardship are in need of social services on a micro and macro level." (Freeman, 2012: 47)

LIMITATIONS ON DATA ABOUT THE VICTIMS OF ECONOMIC CRIMES

As you know by now, the two main sources of data on crime victimization in the United States are the annual NIBRS, provided by the local law enforcement based on each year's reported crimes to the FBI (Federal Bureau of Investigation), and the results of the National Crime Victimization Survey (NCVS), a probability sample based on self-reports of unreported as well as reported crimes, conducted through the Bureau of Justice Statistics and the U.S. Census Bureau. (For more information on the NIBRS and the NCVS see Chapter 4, "Measuring Victimization.")

Although there are sometimes special topics added to the survey, such as identity theft, in 2014, here are the crimes that are tracked on a regular basis in those voluntarily participating

in the survey. (The survey participants must be 12 years old and up and the crime must have occurred within a specific six-month period):
Nonfatal personal crimes

1. Rape or sexual assault
2. Robbery
3. Aggravated and simple assault
4. Personal larceny

Household property crimes

1. Burglary/trespassing
2. Motor vehicle theft
3. Other theft (U.S. Department of Justice)

As you can see from the list of crimes that are focused on, there is a noticeable absence of economic crimes.

The original UCR (Uniform Crime Report) or Summary Reporting System put in place in 1930, for almost 100 years, the only economic crimes that were tracked by the UCR were:

1. Embezzlement
2. Fraud
3. Forgery/counterfeiting
4. All other offenses (Barnett, Criminal Justice Information Services Division)

TABLE 9.2. Arrest Rate per 100,000 Individuals for Reported Property and Economic Crimes According to the UCR

Type of Crime	Total Arrest Rate
All property crimes	635.5
Forgery & counterfeiting	40.7
Fraud	131.5
Embezzlement	6.5

Source: Barnett, U.S. Department of Justice, "The Measurement of White-Collar Crime Using Uniform Crime Reporting (UCR) Data"

Barnett indicates the much lower arrest rate (number of arrests per 100,000 individuals) for the three so-called economic crimes compared to the more traditional property crimes (burglary, larceny/theft, motor vehicle theft), This information is included in Table 9.2.

The good news is that the NIBRS, which became mandatory as of January 1, 2021, has many more categories of crime that local police will be reporting on that would be included in the economic crime category. (Refer back to Box 9.1 above.) We will have more and more data about white-collar crimes as the NIBRS data is collected, analyzed, and disseminated. In NIBRS, for example, fraud is tracked by what type of victim was involved—individual, financial institution, government agency, or company), as well as where the fraud occurred and a description of the property. Another added piece of information within NIBRS is whether or not a computer was used during the commission of the crime, information that should help us to better understand economic crimes being committed through computers and in cyberspace.

SUMMARY

There is some disagreement about whether cybercrime and white-collar or economic crime are the same, different, or if they sometimes overlap. In general, these are crimes that involve finances although, as the chapter points out, sometimes there is a crossover into violence, such as when the employee who embezzled from his boss, even though his boss had forgiven him and worked out a payment plan, killed his boss and dismembered him. Cybercrime can involve stalking, bullying, and terrorism.

In general, these crimes involve fraud and deceit as well as illegal economic gains. The most well-known cybercrime is that of credit card fraud which is also related to another popular version, identity theft. Being careful about clicking on links from those you do not know, changing your password often, and having a good backup system for your data in the event of a ransomware attack, are steps to take to minimize your risk of becoming a victim or even minimizing the possibility of recurring victimization.

White-collar crime is the term coined in 1939 by criminologist/sociologist Edwin H. Sutherland and used to describe crimes that are committed not by the lower classes but by the middle and upper classes and those in corporations. Because of the internet, there are now a whole host of new white-collar crimes under the broad category of cybercrime and including identity theft, bogus business ventures, and internet scams. There are numerous conventional white-collar crimes that involve fraud as well as embezzlement of funds, misrepresentation of the value of a company, inside trading, and the most famous white-collar crime of the last couple of decades, namely the Ponzi scheme of Bernie Madoff that bilked tens of thousands of victims out of billions.

Ganzini, et al., mental health professionals, wrote an article in 1990 discussing how devastating the financial loss was to so many of the 77 victims of the Pac Rim Ponzi scheme that they had treated. They found that 29 percent of the Pac Rim victims had a major depressive episode as defined by DSM-III criteria in the first 20 months after their economic victimization compared to just 2 percent of the control group. The authors concluded: "Similarly the degree of victimization (as measured by increased financial loss and decreased financial resources) and a previous history of major depressive disorder were the most important variables in predicting the development of major depressive disorder in Pac Rim victims after the fraud." (Ganzini, et al., 1990)

More recently, there is a growing awareness that financial victimization takes its emotional and psychological toll, not just a financial one. In reviewing the Bureau of Justice Statistics report by Dr. Harrell related to the 2014 Victims of Identity Theft special research conducted by the NCVS it was found that physical problems followed the identity theft for a month or more, namely: headaches, trouble sleeping, changes in eating or drinking habits, upset stomach, fatigue, high blood pressure, muscle tension or back pain, or some other problem. (Randa and Reyns, 2020)

Understanding the various kinds of cybercrimes and white-collar or economic crimes, as well as who the victims are, will help to offer victims of cybercrime, white-collar, and economic or financial crimes, the understanding, empathy, and psychological help that they need. Getting reimbursed for some, much, or even all of the money that was lost is just one of the needs that individual cybercrime or financial crime victims have. Companies or government agencies, as you have seen in this chapter, may also need help to recover from cybercrime, white-collar, or economic crimes since they will need to restore consumer trust and, in some cases, to deal with the likelihood of going out of business with all the losses to individuals, families, or even communities that it might cause.

KEY TERMS

corporate crime
cybercrime
dark web
economic crime
embezzlement
Federal Trade Commission (FTC)
FICO score
financial crime
food stamp trafficking
forgery
fraud
hacking
identity theft
intellectual property theft
kickback
malware
Mandatory Victims Restitution Act of 1996
phishing schemes
Ponzi scheme
ransomware
recurring (or repeat) victimization
revenge porn
scamming
shimmer
skimmer
Trojan horse
upcoding
victim blame
victim self-blame
virus
white-collar crime
white-collar criminality
worm

REVIEW QUESTIONS

1. Name half a dozen cybercrimes and their definitions.
2. What criminologist/sociologist was white-collar crimes named after and in what year?
3. What are half a dozen white-collar crimes and their definitions?
4. What are some of the physical and psychological aftereffects of being the victim of a white-collar or financial crime?

CRITICAL THINKING QUESTIONS

1. Do you think there is more shame, secrecy, and victim self-blame associated with being the victim of a cybercrime, like identity theft or falling for a phishing scheme, compared to having your pocketbook stolen or your house burglarized? Explain your answer.
2. Should all white-collar crimes be treated as financial crimes requiring only restitution, fines, or community service rather than jail or prison time? Justify your reply.
3. A 19-year-old holds up a couple of convenience stores getting a few hundred dollars for each robbery, is caught, and serves five years in a state prison. A former government employee who had been earning $100,000 gets arrested for fraud, which generated $6 million. She serves 3-1/2 years in a federal prison. Are these sentences fair? Why? Why not? Do we treat white-collar criminals more leniently than those who commit so-called "street" crimes—robbery, burglary, larceny-theft?

ACTIVITIES

1. Make a list of all the confidential information that you need to be keeping a better watch on to avoid being a victim of identity theft or other cybercrimes.
2. Consider piracy and who the victims are. Discuss the topic with your friends and see if they have ever considered whether something they are listening to, watching, or reading online is copyright protected, pirated, or okay to be watching/listening to/ or reading.
3. Pick one of the many cybercrime or white-collar crimes discussed in this chapter. Make a list of ways you and those you know can be less likely victims.
4. Do you have even one credit card? If you do, do you know what your credit score is, known as the FICO® score. Checking this score can help you to make sure that your identity has not been stolen and that your information is accurate. You are entitled to one free credit score report from each of the three credit reporting companies annually. See the resources section for those website addresses.

RESOURCES

Elder Financial Exploitation Prevention Project
Oregon Bankers Association
oregonbankers.com/preventing-elder-financial-exploitation-toolkit.html
A program started in 1995 that has become popular nationally. It focuses on detection, reporting, and prevention/education about the various ways that elderly are especially targeted for financial exploitation. Their training manual is available at their website as well as six short videos "scenarios" on various cybercrimes and white-collar crimes including these frauds: ATM, Power of Attorney, lottery, intimidation, checking, and account.

Federal Bureau of Investigation (FBI)
fbi.gov
FBI field offices have task forces that coordinate with other law enforcement and regulatory agencies including the Securities and Exchange Commission, U.S. Attorney's Offices, Commodity Futures Trading Commission, Financial Industry Regulatory Authority, U.S. Postal Inspection Service, and the IRS (Internal Revenue Service).

Federal Trade Commission (FTC)
ftc.gov
Founded by President Woodrow Wilson in September 1914 to protect consumers and to enforce the U.S. antitrust law.
ReportFraud.ftc.gov
Its Report a Fraud website is a starting point for sharing information about a fraud that has been perpetrated against victims. That information is shared with 3,000 law enforcement personnel with the hope of finding the perpetrators and/or alerting the public to the con man and woman's approach.
consumer.ftc.gov
Federal Trade Commission government site on how to avoid being scams and guidelines on how to report a scam.

MSPA® Americas
https://www.mspa-americas.org/
This is an international trade association started in 1998 by a group of mystery shopping business owners. At the website there is a "Scam Alert" section offering information about how to report a possible scam.

National Insurance Crime Bureau
nicb.org
This is a not-for-profit membership organization that is concerned with the prevention and detection of insurance fraud and vehicle theft.

National White Collar Crime Center (NW3C)
nw3c.org
Founded in 1978 as The Leviticus Project Association. In 1992, it became the National White Collar Crime Center. It now has more than 6,200 member agencies in the United States, its territories, and 15 countries around the world. It provides training and educational materials related to the prevention, probe, and prosecution of economic and "high-tech crime." They now also offer certification in three areas: economic crime forensic examiner; certified cybercrime examiner; and certified cybercrime investigator.

U.S. Securities and Exchange Commission
Investor.gov
The website by the U.S. Securities and Exchange Commission whose purpose is to protect the investor from becoming victims of scams and schemes.

Credit reporting agencies
Each of these agencies will provide a credit report so any fraudulent can be noted and dealt with.
Equifax
equifax.com
Experian
experian.com
TransUnion
transunion.com

CITED WORKS AND ADDITIONAL REFERENCES

ABCsouth.net.au. Posted February 3, 2014. Nigerian police arrest online scammer linked to death of Australian woman Jette Jacobs.

Allen, Jeffrey. (summer 2017?). "Surviving Ransomware." *American Journal of Family Law.* 65-68.

Alonso-Zaldivar, Ricardo. September 27, 2019. "Feds Crack Medicare Gene Test Fraud That Peddled Cheek Swabs." Associated Press. Posted on AOL.com.

Amir, M. 1971. *Patterns of Forcible Rape.* Chicago: University of Chicago Press.

Associated Press. May 21, 2020. "Man Arrested in Fairbanks Charged with Vandalism Spree in Sioux Falls, S.D." Posted at https://www.adn.com/alaska-news/crime-courts/2020/05/21/man-charged-in-fairbanks-with-vandalism-spree-in-downtown-sioux-falls-sd/

Barnett, Cynthia. n.d."The Measurement of White-College Crime Using Uniform Crime Reporting (UCR) Data." NIBRS Publications Series. U.S. Department of Justice, Federal Bureau of Investigation.

Better Business Bureau (BBB). July 28, 2020. Government Impostor Scams Prey on Fear During Pandemic, BBB Study Finds. Posted at bbb.org

Blinder, Alan and Nicole Perlroth. March 27, 2018. "A Cyberattack Hobbles Atlanta, and Security Experts Shudder." *The New York Times.* Posted at nytimes.com

Blum, R.H. 1972. *Deceivers and Deceived.* Springfield, IL: Charles Thomas.

Brenner, Susan W. and Joseph J. Schwerha IV. 2004. "Introduction- Cybercrime: A Note on International Issues." *Information Systems Frontiers.* 6(2): 111-114.

Buchanan, Tom and Monica T. Whitty. 2014. "The Online Dating Romance Scam: Causes and Consequences of Victimhood." *Psychology, Crime & Law.* 20: 261-283.

Bureau of Justice Statistics. n.d. "Data Collection: National Crime Victimization Survey (NCVS)" Office of Justice Programs. Posted online at bjs.gov.

________________. January 2019. "Victims of Identity Theft, 2016." Bureau of Justice Statistics, Office of Justice Programs, U.S. Department of Justice, 1-page summary posted online.

Burgess, Ann Wolbert. 2019. *Victimology: Theories and Applications.* Third edition. Burlington, MA: Jones & Bartlett Learning.

Burgess, Ann Wolbert and L.I. Holmstrom. 1974. "Rape Trauma Syndrome." *American Journal of Psychiatry.* 131: 981-986.

______________. 1978. "Recovery from Rape and Prior Life Stress." *Research in Nursing & Health.* 1: 165-174.

CBS 60 Minutes. May 5, 2019. "How Cybercriminals Hold Data Hostage . . . and Why the Best Solution Is Often Paying a Ransom." Correspondent Scott Pelley.

CBS New York. September 1, 2015. "Bride-To-Be Loses Family Heirlooms As Burglary Spike Plagues Carroll Gardens." CBS Local news. Posted at http://newyork.cbslocl.com

Chouhy, Cecilia. 2018. "Moving Beyond Punitive Interventions: Public Support for Government-Funded Victim Compensation for White-Collar Crime Victims." *Criminology & Public Policy.* 17: 547-551.

Clifford, Stephanie. March 9, 2018. "Martin Shkreli Sentenced to 7 Years in Prison for Fraud." *New York Times.* Posted at https://www.nytimes.com/2018/03/09/business/martin-shkreli-sentenced.html

Clough, Jonathan. December 2011. "Cybercrime." *Commonwealth Law Bulletin.* 37: 671-680.

CNN.com. Updated April 17, 2016. "Enron Fast Facts" CNN Library.

Conrad, Paul. Editorial cartoon. Copyright *Los Angeles Times.*

Copes, Heith, Kent. R. Kerley, Rodney Huff, and John Kane. 2010. "Differentiating Identity Theft: An Exploratory Study of Victims Using a National Victimization Survey." *Journal of Criminal Justice.* 38: 1045-1052.

Cornell Law, Legal Information Institute. N.d. "White-collar crime."

CriminalJustice.com Staff. May 29, 2020. "10 White Collar Crime Casts That Made Headlines." Posted at https://www.criminaljustice.com/10-white-collar-crime-cases-that-made-headlines/

Cross, Cassandra. 2015. "No Laughing Matter: Blaming the Victim of Online Fraud." *International Review of Victimology.* 21: 187-204.

Cullen, Francis T., Richard A. Mathers, Gregory A. Clark, and John B. Cullen. 1983. "Public Support for Punishing White-Collar Crime: Blaming the Victim Registered?" *Journal of Criminal Justice.* 11: 481-493.

Daigle, Leah E. and Lisa R. Muftic. 2016. *Victimology.* Los Angeles, CA: SAGE.

Darby, Edwin. October 18, 1976 "Tracking Corporate Crime." *New York Post.* 36.

Deem, Debbie, Morna Murray, Mario Gaboury, and Christine Edmunds. 2000. "Financial Crimes." Chapter 16 in the NVAA. Archived by the Office for Victims of Crime (OVC). Posted online at ncjrs.gov

Dekmar, Louis M. February 2018. "Solving Crimes in the Lab: Understanding the Role of Forensic Science in Policing." President's Message. *The Police Chief.* 6.

Disraeli, David. Friday, January 19, 2021. Phone interview with the author.

Doroghazi, Robert M. September 2019. "Embezzlement." *The American Journal of Cardiology.* 124: 987.

Downing, Christopher O., Jr., Nicole Capriola and E. Scott Geller. 2018. "Preventing Credit-Card Fraud: A Goal-Setting and Prompting Intervention to Increase Cashers' ID-Checking Behavior." *Journal of Organizational Behavior Management.* 38: 335-344.

Eddy, Max. March 2, 2021. "How to Spot and Avoid Credit Card Skimmers and Shimmers." *PC Magazine.* Posted online at pcmag.com

Federal Trade Commission (FTC). June 2019. What You Need to Know about Romance Scams. Posted at consumer.ftc.gov

FBI (Federal Bureau of Investigation). 2019. *2018 Crime in the United States.* "Arson." Posted at https://ucr.fbi.gov/crime-in-the-u.s/2018/crime-in-the-u.s.-2018/topic-pages/arson

________________. 2019. *2018 Crime in the United States.* "Larceny Theft." Posted at https://ucr.fbi.gov/crime-in-the-u.s/2018/crime-in-the-u.s.-2018/topic-pages/larceny-theft#:~:text=Overview,compared%20with%20the%202017%20estimate.

________________. "Al Capone." Posted at fbi.gov

________________. 2011. "Crime in the United States: 2011." "Property Crime" Posted at https://ucr.fbi.gov/crime-in-the-u.s/2010/crime-in-the-u.s.-2010/property-crime/mvtheftmain

________________. December 03, 2006. "Crime in the Suites: A Look Back at the Enron Case." Posted online at FBI.gov.

________________. July 22, 2005. "Hey, Wanna Buy a Baseball Autographed By . . . Mother Teresa?" Posted online at FBI.gov.

________________. "White-Collar Crime." n.d. Posted at https://www.fbi.gov

Federal Trade Commission (FTC). "Submit a Consumer Complaint to the FTC. n.d. Posted at https://www.ftc.gov/faq/consumer-protection/submit-consumer-complaint-ftc

Fisher, Bonnie S. Fisher, Bradford W. Reyns, and John J. Sloan III. . 2016. *Introduction to Victimology: Contemporary Theory, Research, and Practice* New York: Oxford University Press

Frances, Sari. 2018. Protecting "Protecting Intellectual Property from Digital Piracy." *Information Services & Use.* 38: 37-39.

Frank, E., S.M. Turner, B.P. Stewart, et al. 1981. "Past Psychiatric Symptoms and the Response to Sexual Assault." *Comprehensive Psychiatry.* 22: 479-487.

Frank, E. and B.P. Anderson. 1987. "Psychiatric Disorders in Rape Victims: Past History and the Current Symptomatology." *Comprehensive Psychiatry.* 29: 77-82.

Freed, Benjamin. April 10, 2018. "Colorado Has Spent More than $1million Bailing out from Ransomware Attack." Published online at statescoop.com.

Freeman, Audrey. February 2012. "Financial Disaster as a Risk Factor for Posttraumatic Stress Disorder: Internet Survey of Trauma in Victims of the Madoff Ponzi Scheme." *Health & Social Work.* 37: 39-48.

Galvin, Miranda A., Thomas A. Loughran, Sally S. Simpson, and Mark A. Cohen. 2018. "Victim Compensation Policy and White-Collar Crime: Public Preferences in a National Willingness-to-Pay Survey." *Criminology & Public Policy.* 17: 553.

Ganzini, Linda, Bentson McFarland, and Joseph Bloom. 1990. "Victims of Fraud: Comparing Victims of White Collar and Violent Crime." *Bulletin of the American Academy of Psychiatry Law.* 18: 55-63.

Goosen, Mikael, Ingemar Johansson Seva, and Daniel Larsson. 2016. "Basic Human Values and White-Collar Crime: Findings from Europe. *European Journal of Criminology.* 13: 434-452.

Grabosky, Peter. 2016. *Cybercrime.* New York: Oxford University Press.

Gramlich, John. March 1, 2017. "Most Violent and Property Crimes in the U.S. Go Unsolved." Pew Research. "Facttank: News in Numbers."

Grauer, Yael. December 19, 2017. "Too Many People Are Still Using 'Password' as a Password." Posted at vice.com

Green, Bandn, Stephen Gies, Amanda Bobnis, Nicole Leeper Piquero, Alex R. Piquero, and Eva Velasquez. April 2020. "The Role of Victim Services for Individuals Who Have Experienced Serious Identity-Based Crime." *Victims & Offenders.* 15: 720-743.

Gurliacci, David. September 11, 1999 "Police Say Alleged Forger, Out on Bail, Tried Scam Again." *The Advocate* (Stamford). A3.

Hansen, Laura Pinto. 2021. *White Collar and Corporate Crime: A Case Study Approach.* New York, NY: Wolters Kluwer.

Hardee, Kathy. October 18,, 2016. "Criminal Prosecutions in the Food Industry: Adulteration and Prison Time." *Food and Safety.* Posted at https://www.foodsafetymagazine.com/enewsletter/criminal-prosecutions-in-the-food-industry-adulteration-and-prison-time/

Harrell, Erika. September 2015; Revised November 13, 2017. "Victims of Identity Theft, 2014." Bureau of Justice Statistics (BJS), U.S. Department of Justice, Office of Justice Programs.

Hays, Constance L. and Leslie Eaton. March 6, 2004. "The Martha Stewart Verdict: The Overview; Stewart Found Guilty of Lying in Sales of Stock." *New York Times.* Posted at nytimes.com

Holtfreter, Kristy, Michael D. Reisig, and Travis C. Pratt. 2008. "Low Self-Control, Routine Activities, and Fraud Victimization." *Criminology.* 46: 189-211.

Huamancayo, Neil. May 26, 2021. "Phone Scams and the Elderly." Senior Seminar in Sociology, Sciology 4600, Section 01, Kean University, School of Social Science, Sociology Department, taught by Jan Yager, Ph.D. (Final 31 page paper)

Huff, Rodney, Christian Desilets, and John Kane. December 2010. "National Public Survey on White Collar Crime." Designed by the National White Collar Crime Center.

Infobase. 2015. "American History Online: Crime and Punishment in Colonial America." https://www.wtps.org/cms/lib/NJ01912980/Centricity/Domain/745/crime%20and%20punishment%20in%20colonial%20america.pdf

Jones, Stephen. 2017. *Criminology.* 6th edition. New York: Oxford University Press.

______________. Personal communications, May 17, 2020 and May 23, 2020.

Kempa, Michael. 2010. "Combating White-Collar Crime in Canada: Serving Victim Needs and Market Integrity." *Journal of Financial Crime.* 17: 251-264.

Khan, Roomy. "White-Collar Crimes—Motivations and Triggers." Forbes.com. February 22, 2018. Posted at https://www.forbes.com/sites/roomykhan/2018/02/22/white-collar-crimes-motivations-and-triggers/#7194e3721219

Kshetri, Nir. 2016. "Cybercrime and Cybersecurity in India: Causes, Consequences and Implications for the Future." *Crime, Law and Social Change.* 66: 313-338.

Levenson, Laurie L. November 18, 2016. "White-Collar Crime: Cost to Society." Britannica.com.

Levi, Michael. November 2006. "The Media Construction of Financial White-Collar Crimes." *The British Journal of Criminology.* 16: 1037-1057.

Logan, Matthew W., Mark A. Morgan, Michal L. Benson, and Francis T. Cullen. November 1, 2017. "Coping with Imprisonment: Testing the Special Sensitivity Hypothesis for White-Collar Offenders." *Justice Quarterly.* 36(2): 225-254.

Marcum, Catherine D. 2019. *Cyber Crime.* 2nd edition. Criminal Justice Series. New York: Wolters Kluwer.

McFadden, Robert D. January 13, 1976. "2 Held Here as Confidence Men; Victims' Loss Put at $400,000." *New York Times.* 1, 20.

Moore, Elizabeth and Michael Mills. July 1990. "The Neglected Victims and Unexamined Costs of White-Collar Crime." *Crime & Delinquency.* 36(3): 408-418.

Morgan, Rachel E. and Barbara A. Oudekerk. "Criminal Victimization, 2018." Bureau of Justice Statistics (BJS), U.S. Department of Justice, Office of Justice Programs.

National Health Care Anti-Fraud Association. (NHCAA) "The Challenge of Health Care Fraud." N.d. Posted online at nhcaa.org

New York Times. February 27, 1976. "Four Record Executives Convicted in Payola Case." *New York Times.* 63.

News 9. Posted at https://www.news9.com/story/5e34b3f5527dcf49dad8df2a/Covering%20The%20Capitol%20Unemployment%20Issues

Noguchi, Yuki. June 29, 2002. "WorldCom Lays Off 17,000 Workers." *Washington Post.*

NPR.com. January 22, 2002. "What Enron Employees Have Lost: Tens of Thousands Hit by Job Losses, Plummeting Stock." Posted at legacy.npr.org

Office for Victims of Crime. "Chapter 16—Financial Crimes." The Archives of NCJRS.gov. NVAA 2000 Text. Posted at https://www.ncjrs.gov/ovc_archives/nvaa2000/chapter16.htm

Pak, Eudie. June 24, 2019 (updated May 19, 2020). "Bernie Madoff: Six Famous Victims of His Ponzi Scheme." Biography.com. Posted at https://www.biography.com/news/bernie-madoff-famous-victims

Parascandola, Rocco, Ellen Moynihan, Jordan Rencher, Graham Rayman, and Larry McShane. July 17, 2020. "Ex-assistant Charged with Murder of NYC Tech Entrepeneur Fahim Saleh After Embezzling $90,000 from Victim, Sources Say." *New York Daily News.* Posted at https://www.nydailynews.com/new-york/nyc-crime/ny-former-personal-assistant-arrested-fahim-saleh-murder-20200717-h5dtyqxjbfcprlw6h5ckmhj5p4-story.html

Payne, Brian K. 2018. "White-Collar Cybercrime: White-Collar Crime, Cybercrime, or Both?" *Criminology, Criminal Justice, Law & Society.* 19: 7-33.

Pelley, Scott. May 5, 2019. "How Cybercriminals Hold Data Hostage...And Why the Best Solution Is Often Paying a Random." CBSNews.com. Posted at CBSNews.com

Perri, Frank S. July 25, 2011. "White-Collar Criminals: The 'Kinder, Gentler' Offender?" *Journal of Investigative Psychology and Offender Profiling.* 8: 217-241.

Piquero, Nicole Leeper. 2018. "White-Collar Crime Is Crime: Victims Hurt Just the Same." *Criminology & Public Policy.* 17: 595-600.

Policastro, Christina and Brian K. Payne. 2015. "Can You Hear Me Now? Telemarketing Fraud Victimization and Lifestyles." *American Journal of Criminal Justice.* 40: 620-638.

Pontell, Henry N. and Stephen M. Rosoff. 2009. "White-collar Delinquency." *Crime, Law and Social Change.* 51: 147-162.

Rothe, Dawn L. and David O. Friedrichs. . 2015. *Crimes of Globalization.* New York: Routledge.

Ruggiero, Vincenzo. 2020. "Hypotheses on the Causes of Financial Crime." *Journal of Financial Crime.* 27: 245-257.

Sanger, David E. and Nicole Perlroth. June 3, 2021. "White House Warns Companies to Act Now on Ransomware Defenses." *The New York Times,* posted online at nytimes.com.

Seymour, Anne, Morna Murphy, and Jane Sigmon. Editors. Chapter 16, "Financial Crimes." In 2000 National Victim Assistance Academy. Chapter 16 authors: Debbie Deem, Morna Murray, Mario Gaboury, and Christine Edmunds. Available from the Office for Victims of Crime (OVC), posted at the ncjrs.gov.

Shear, Michael D., Nicole Perlroth, and Clifford Krauss. May 13, 2021, updated June 7, 2021. "Colonial Pipeline Paid roughly $5 Million in Ransom to Hackers." *The New York Times.* Posted at nytimes.com

Siegel, Max H. February 10, 1977. "11 Podiatrists and 2 Crime Figures Indicted in Medicaid Bribery Plot." *New York Times.* L43.

Slotnik, Daniel E. July 17, 2020. "What We Know About the Killing of Tech C.E.O. Fahim Saleh." *The New York Times.* Posted at nytimes.com

Soltes, Eugene. December 14, 2016. "The Psychology of White-Collar Criminals." *The Atlantic.*

Stadler, William A. and Michael L. Benson. 2012. "Revisiting the Guilty Mind: The Neutralization of White-Collar Crime." *Criminal Justice Review.* 37: 494-511.

Steinberg, Jacques. October 21, 1993. "Connecticut Store Owner Sentenced in Tax Fraud." *New York Times.* B: 1..

Suderman, Alan and Eric Tucker. May 8, 2021. "Major U.S. Pipeline Hals Operations After Ransomware Attack." Associated Press (*Los Angeles Times*). Published online at latimes.com.

Sutherland, Edwin H. Annotated and Interpreted by. 1937 (reissued 1972). *The Professional Thief by a Professional Thief.* Chicago, IL: The University of Chicago Press.

______________. 1983. *White Collar Crime: The Uncut Version.* New Haven, CT: Yale University Press.

______________. February 1940. "White-Collar Criminality." *American Sociological Review.* 5(1): 1-12.

Tappan, Paul W. February 1947. "Who Is the Criminal?" *American Sociological Review.* 12(1): 96-102.

Taylor, Kate. February 7, 2020. Updated May 21, 2020. "Former Pimco C.E.P. Gets 9 Months in Prison in College Admissions Case." *New York Times.* Posted at nytimes.com

__________. December 28, 2020. "Lori Loughlin Released From Federal Prison." *New York Times.* Posted at nytimes.com

__________. May 21, 2020. "What Happened to the Students Caught Up in the College Admissions Scandal?" *New York Times.* Posted at https://www.nytimes.com/2020/02/25/us/college-admissions-scandal-students.html

Temple-Raston, Dina. March 12, 2009. "Madoff Pleads Guilty to fraud, Sent to Jail." NPR.org. Posted at https://www.npr.org/templates/story/story.php?storyId=101823851

Thomas, Katie and Reed Abelson. March 14, 2018. "Elizabeth Holes, Theranos C.E.O. and Silicon Valley Star, Accused of Fraud." *New York Times.* Posted at https://www.nytimes.com/2018/03/14/health/theranos-elizabeth-holmes-fraud.html

Tillman, Robert H., Henry N. Pontell, and William K. Black. 2018. *Financial Crime and Crises in the Era of False Profits.* New York: Oxford University Press.

Tomlin, J.W. 1982. "Victims of White Collar Crimes" in H.J. Schneider (ed.). *The Victim in the International Perspective.* New York: Walter de Gruyer.

Tucker, Eric. Updated June 7, 2021. "US Has Recovered Ransom Payment Made After Pipeline Hack." *Chicago Sun Times.* Published online at chcicago.suntimes.com

U.S. Department of Justice. Updated February 10, 2015. "Financial Fraud Crime Victims." Posted at https://www.justice.gov/usao-wdwa/victim-witness/victim-info/financial-fraud

Victims Resource Center (VRC). "Identity Theft and Identity Fraud." Serving Carbon, Luzerne, and Wyoming County in Pennsylvania. Posted at vrcnepa.org

Wells, R.C. 1989. "White Collar Crime: What About the Victim?" *The Investigator Journal* 5: 26-27.

Whitcomb, Dan. February 21, 2019. "Former Enron CEO Jeffrey Skilling Released from Federal Custody." Reuters. Posted at reuters.com

Whitty, Monica T. 2015. "Anatomy of the Online Dating Romance Scam." *Security Journal.* 25: 443-455.

Wisenberg, Solomon L. "White-Collar Crime: The Crash Course." n.d. Posted at https://www.wisenberglaw.com/Articles/White-Collar-Crime-The-Crash-Course.shtml

Yager, Jan. 2016. *125 Ways to Meet the Love of Your Life.* Second edition. Stamford, CT: Hannacroix Creek Books.

______________. 2011. *Grow Global.* Stamford, CT: Hannacroix Creek Books.

______________. 2021. *Help Yourself Now.* New York: Allworth, an imprint of Skyhorse.

______________. July 11, 2010. "How to Avoid Ponzi Schemes." Consumeraffairs.com. Posted at https://www.consumeraffairs.com/boomerific/2010/018_avoiding_ponzi_schemes.html

__________. *Victims.* 2021 (originally published by Scribner's, 1978). With new introduction, updated bibliography and resources. Stamford, CT: Hannacroix Creek.

Yar, Majid. 2005 "The Novelty of 'Cybercrime' An Assessment in Light of Routine Activity Theory." *European Journal of Criminology,* 2: 407-427.

Zarroli, Jim. *See listing below under Videos, Films, Podcasts, and Radio Shows.*

Videos, Films, Podcasts, and Radio Shows

Boiler Room. 2000. Starring Ben Affleck and Vin Diesel. Written and directed by Ben Younger.

FBI. "Former FBI Director William Webster Helps Foil Scam." 3:38 minutes. Posted at https://www.fbi.gov/video-repository/webster-scam-final-021919.mp4/view

Wall Street. 1987. Co-written and directed by Oliver Stone. Starring Michael Douglas and Charlie Sheen. Produced by 20th Century Studios.

Zarroli, Jim. December 23, 2018. "For Madoff Victims, Scars Remain 10 Years Later." R minutes. Posted at: https://www.npr.org/2018/12/23/678238031/for-madoff-victims-scars-remain-10-years-later

CHAPTER **TEN**

Child Victims

Abuse, Neglect, and Other Victimizations

Learning Objectives

After you finish reading this chapter, you should be able to:

1. Estimate the frequency of child abuse and neglect in the United States and worldwide.
2. Highlight the pioneers who brought attention by the medical and academic communities to recognize, treat, research, and prevent child abuse.
3. Identify and explain the five types of child abuse.
4. Identify and explain several of the controversies surrounding the reporting and prosecution of child abuse and neglect allegations.
5. Identify the risk factors for sibling sexual abuse.
6. Describe the ACE study and its importance.

INTRODUCTION

In this chapter, we will examine the neglect and abuse of society's most vulnerable of victims, namely infants, toddlers, and children, those 12 and under. (Teen and College Victims are the subject of Chapter 11.) As noted below, and summarized in Table 10.1, the medical community only started addressing child abuse in the 1960s with the earliest efforts reaching a crescendo of research and publications in the 1970s. The seeds of those efforts, however, go back to the late 1800s. It was then that the first Society for the Prevention of Cruelty to Children (SPCC) was founded in 1875.

We owe a debt of gratitude to the trailblazers listed in Table 10.1, from the fields of medicine, social work, sociology, psychology, criminology, government, law, and organization organizers, for their contributions to the way that victims of child abuse are recognized, treated, and studied, and their perpetrators punished.

REAL-LIFE EXAMPLES OF CHILD ABUSE AND NEGLECT

In 2017, it was estimated that 674,000 were deemed mistreated, based on an investigation by state child protective services (CPS) agencies of 3.5 million. (Administration for Children and Families—ACF, 2019) Who are some of the victims of child abuse and child neglect? Here are just some of them, based on news reports and other sources.

- Police responded to a 911 call from a 10-year-old boy's mother and stepfather. He was found to have severe bruising and puncture wounds and cuts, signs of possible child abuse as the cause of death. (*NY Daily News*, 2021)
- In February 2012, two sons, ages 5 and 7, were visiting with their father. The visit had to be supervised by a social worker because their father was under suspicion because his wife, Susan Powell, had been missing since December 2009. Although a suspect in his wife's disappearance, there was not yet enough evidence to arrest and charge the boys' father. According to the social worker, Powell pulled his sons into the house where the visitation was to take place and locked the door, preventing her from entering. She immediately started to smell something like gas, and as she was calling her supervisor, according to the CNN report, "the house exploded." All inside were killed. (CNN, 2012)
- Five children, ages 6 months, 2, 3, 5, and 7, on June 20th, 2001, were drowned by their mother, Andrea Yates. In July 2006, Yates was found not guilty by reason of insanity after her first conviction in 2002, which sentenced her to life in prison with eligibility for parole in 40 years, was overturned by a January 2005 Texas Court of Appeals. (McLellan, 2006)
- Two-year-old Liam Fee is considered one of Scotland's worst child murder cases. His parents were found guilty of his murder in 2016, two years after his March 2014 death. The abuse that led to his death consisted of more than 30 injuries to his body, the result of being beaten and locked in a cage. (Alderson, 2017)
- Two sons, ages 3 and 14 months, were killed by their mother, Susan Smith, who confessed to their killings on November 3, 1994 after first making up a story about a carjacking. She was sentenced to serve a minimum of 30 years in prison. (Bragg, 1995)

ESTIMATED OCCURRENCE OF CHILD ABUSE AND NEGLECT

Let us start with the most shocking statistic of all: In 2017, it was estimated that 1,720 children in the United States died because of child abuse and neglect, according to the National Child Abuse and Neglect Data System (NCANDS), which is part of the Administration for Children and Families. (Hurley, *New Yorker*, December 12, 2019).

Here are some other statistics on the prevalence of child abuse in America, according to the Administration for Children & Families' 29th Child Maltreatment Report, released on January 15, 2020. Of the estimated 678,000 children determined to be victims of maltreatment in 2018:

- 60.8 percent were neglected.
- 10.7 percent were physically abused.
- 7.0 percent were sexually abused.
- More than 15 percent were victims of two or more maltreatment types. (ACF, 2020)

There is far too much preventable child abuse in America and throughout the world. Child abuse is not just an American problem. In 2016, researchers Hillis, Mercy, Amobi, and Kress published the results of their extensive review of studies from around the world as to its frequency globally. Their conclusion: At least 50 percent of children in Asia, Africa, and North America—1 billion children between the ages of 2 and 17 years of age—experienced violence. (Hillis et al., *Pediatrics*, 2016) That does not, however, minimize the statistical reality, pointed out in this chapter, that the United States has child victimization that are much too high.

Several changes are necessary for the reduction, prevention, and even the elimination of child abuse and neglect to happen. The first is that there needs to be a greater awareness of how frequently child abuse occurs. Second, once detected, it needs to be dealt with more effectively so the abuse stops and the victim gets help as soon as possible. It can no longer be considered a "private" or family matter. Instead, the wellbeing and positive care of every child is the responsibility of the entire family, including siblings, extended family, and the community at large. As you discover later on in this chapter, it was a concerned neighbor, Mrs. Wheeler, back in 1875, who is credited with being the catalyst to the anti-child abuse movement that followed when she sought help for a nine-year-old who could not ask for help herself. As noted in this chapter, 48 of 50 states in the United States now have mandatory reporting of suspected child abuse for certain job categories, from child caregivers to teachers, social workers, crisis counselors and hotline operators, or physicians. That's a start, but more needs to be done to get at the root causes of child abuse as well as other types of victimization of infants and children.

HISTORY AND BACKGROUND

In this chapter, we explore the many forms of child abuse, its victims, and other related issues to victimized children including neglect and missing children and kidnapping. As will also be noted in Chapter 12 "Sexual Violence: Rape, Sexual Abuse, Assault, and Harassment Victims," and Chapter 13, "Victims of Assault, Domestic Violence, Stalking, and Elder Abuse," women used to be considered the property of their husbands. It took centuries for their violations to be considered crimes rather than their husband's right to do with his property as he saw fit.

A similar change in attitude was necessary toward children. Up until the end of the nineteenth century, children were considered the property of their parents, to be disciplined and treated as desired, within the privacy of their own home and the sacred domain of their family.

The first step in a change in that mindset occurred between 1639 and 1680 when the Puritans of colonial Massachusetts passed the first laws "anywhere in the world" according to researcher Elizabeth Pleck against "unnatural severity" to children. (Pleck, 1989:19) In 1639, the colony of New Haven passed the first American law against family violence with a statute that made incest punishable by hanging. However, this law was basically "symbolic" since Pleck found no evidence that anyone was ever prosecuted under that statute. (Pleck, 1989: 22)

A criminal code was written in 1641 and known as the Massachusetts *Body of Laws and Liberties*. These laws included a clause against child abuse. (Pleck, 1989: 22-23) However, Pleck only found evidence of one father of an 11-year-old, Michael Emerson, who was accused of "cruel and excessive beating" for using a flail swing (a large wooden handle attached to a free-swinging stick that was used in the threshing of grain) and with kicking his child. Six months later, the court abated Michael Emerson's fine and released him on a bond of good behavior (Pleck, 1989: 26)

The second era in a reformation of how child victims were considered began in 1875. It was then that Mrs. Wheeler reported that her neighbor, a nine-year-old girl Mary Ellen, was being abused and neglected. But when Mrs. Wheeler discovered there were no laws or policies that could be applied to Mary Ellen's mistreatment, she contacted Henry Bergh who in 1866 in New York City had founded the Society for the Prevention of Cruelty to Animals (SPCA). By intervening on her behalf in court, Bergh was able to get Mary Ellen removed from her abusive caregivers and placed in a children's home. Following that case, that same year, the New York Society for the Prevention of Cruelty to Children was founded.

SPCC accomplished a lot of actions related to the detection and handling of child neglect and abuse cases that were considered controversial at that time. It advocated criminalizing these behaviors that were previously considered the private domain of the family. Private agencies were created that had the power to bring cases of child abuse to the courts which could lead to the removal of the child from the home and the termination of parental rights. From 1875-1890 is considered the "high point of criminalization." (Pleck, 1989: 35, 39)

But the formation of the first Juvenile Justice Court in 1899 in Cook County, Illinois led to a change in the handling of child abuse cases during what has been known as the Progressive Era, between 1900 to 1920. It was during that time that a shift occurred. As Pleck writes, "By the early twentieth century, judges of family courts and heads of SPCCs came to view criminal prosecution and police-like methods as unprofessional and outmoded. They believed that social casework methods were more efficient, humane, and better suited to handling the complicated dynamics of abusing families." (Pleck, 1989: 44-45) As Stephen J. Pfohl points out in his article, "The 'Discovery' of Child Abuse," the 1909 White House Conference on Children "spawned both the 'Mother's Aid' Movement and the American Association for the Study and Prevention of Infant Mortality." The Mothers Aid Movement "drew attention to the benefits of keeping children in the family . . ." (Pfohl, 1977: 314)

According to Pfohl, the development of the medical specialty of pediatric radiology in the 1950s had a lot to do with the "discovery" of child abuse. The ability to take x-rays that would show the presence of multiple breaks and fractures that could no longer be explained away by a parent as the result of just one fall led the medical profession in "the last years of the fifties showed dramatically increased concern for the beaten child." (Pfohl, 1977: 315)

A decade later, in the 1960s, public and medical attention to child abuse became widespread, led by C. Henry Kempe, M.D. Stirred by his writings, child abuse and neglect became a focus of physicians, researchers, and social workers. (Daigle and Muftic, 188) On July 7, 1962, several physicians, including C. Henry Kempe, Frederic N. Silverman, Brandt F. Steele, William Droegemueller, and Henry K. Silver, published their co-authored groundbreaking article, "The Battered-Child Syndrome," in the prestigious *Journal of the American Medical Association* (JAMA). (See Table 10.1 for a timeline of trailblazers in the field of child victimization.)

TABLE 10.1. Pioneers in the Public Awareness, Treatment, and Study of Child Abuse, Its Victims, and Its Prevention

Name	Discipline/Affiliation	Accomplishment	Year
Mrs. Wheeler	concerned neighbor	Takes the maltreatment of 9-year-old Mary Ellen to Henry Bergh	1875
Henry Bergh	founder	Takes case to court, Mary Ellen is removed from abusive situation; New York Society for the Prevention of Cruelty to Children (NYSPCC) is founded	1875
Lucy Flower **Julia Lathrop**	reformers	First Juvenile Justice System, Cook County, Illinois	1899
Hans von Hentig	criminologist	Includes "the young" as general class of likely victims in his groundbreaking book, *The Criminal and His Victim*	1948
Fredric Wertham	psychiatrist	*The Show of Violence* (writes about child murders); Writes about battered children in *Bulletin of the New York Academy of Medicine*, 1972	1949
C. Henry Kempe	pediatrician	Defined child abuse and brought it to the attention of doctors; Co-authored "The Battered Child Syndrome" article in the *Journal of the American Medical Association (JAMA)*; Founded the Kempe Center for the Prevention and Treatment of Child Abuse and Neglect	1962
State of Pennsylvania		First state to require mandatory reporting of child abuse by certain individuals	1963
Children's Bureau		U.S. Department of Health, Education, and Welfare initiates studies on battered child syndrome	1965
David G. Gil	Professor of social policy at Brandeis University	Reports on the Children's Bureau studies; Published *Violence Against Children*; which analyzed key factors in nearly 13,000 child abuse cases between 1967-68	1970
Elizabeth Elmer	social worker, co-founder of Parental Stress Center	*Children in Jeopardy: A Study of Abused Minors and Their Families* (U of Pittsburgh Press)	1967
Dr. Ray E. Helfer	pediatrician & educator	*The Battered Child* (U of Chicago Press)	1968
Vincent Fontana	pediatrician and child abuse expert	Established The Foundling's Child Abuse Rehabilitation Program, New York City; *Somewhere a Child is Crying* (Macmillan) 1973	1972
David Finkelhor	Director of the Crimes Against Children Research Center Ph.D. in Sociology University of New Hampshire	*Sexually Victimized Children* (Free Press)	1979
Richard J. Gelles	Ph.D. in Sociology University of Pennsylvania	*The Violent Home* (SAGE) *Intimate Violence in Families* (SAGE)	1974 1985

(*continued*)

TABLE 10.1. Pioneers in the Public Awareness, Treatment, and Study of Child Abuse, Its Victims, and Its Prevention (continued)

Name	Discipline/Affiliation	Accomplishment	Year
Murray Straus	Sociologist	"Violence in the Family" (paper co-presented at the American Association for the Advancement of Science); Co-authored *Behind Closed Doors: Violence in the American Family* Studied corporal punishment since 1970s	1976 2007
Suzanne K. Steinmetz	Sociologist	Co-author, *Behind Closed Doors*; studied battered husbands	2007

Source: Developed by the author from multiple sources indicated throughout the chapter

INTENTIONAL VS. UNINTENTIONAL CHILD ABUSE

When discussing the neglect and abuse of infants or children, there are two basic categories: intentional and unintentional. In both cases, harm is inflicted but the rationale behind it and the mindset of the offender could be quite different. Here are some examples:

- Overworked and stressed parents who think they dropped their children off at day care but instead left them alone in a hot car all day which lead to their death. In the United States, what is now referred to as **Pediatric Vehicular Heatstroke (PVH)** has resulted in more than 800 deaths of infants and children since 1998. (National Highway Traffic Safety Administration (NHTSA), n.d.)
- In South Africa, in two unrelated cases within one week, a three-year-old and two cousins, ages seven and eight, died in fires when they were left home alone (Bezuidenhout, 2021)
- A parent's or guardian's attention is turned away for a split second at a pool or in a store'—and a child drowns or is kidnapped. "'About 30 to 60 seconds is about all it takes'[to drown]" according to William D. Ramos, American Red Cross Scientific Advisory Council member. (Strybis, 2019)

Facts About Child Abuse in the United States

The 2018 report, Child Maltreatment 2018, the 29th edition of that report, is based on data collected by the Administration on Children, Youth, and Families through the National Child Abuse and Neglect Data System (NCANDS). In 1988, NCANDS was started to put together state child and neglect information. Here are highlights from that report that will provide you with a picture of child abuse and neglect victims today in the United States:

- An estimated 1,700 children died from abuse and neglect at a rate of 2.39 per 100,000 children.
- The majority of perpetrators (77.5%) are the victim's parent.

- There were an estimated 678,000 victims of child abuse and neglect in 2018 in the United States.
- Children under one year are at greatest risk with the highest rate of victimization—26.7 percent per 1,000 children of the same age in the general population.
- The victimization rate for girls is slightly higher than for boys, but not dramatically different: 9.6 versus 8.7 per 1,000 in the population, respectively.
- The overall victimization rate is 9.2 per 1,000 children in the population.
- The highest rate of victimization is for American Indian or Alaska Native children, with a rate of 15.2 per 1,000 children.
- More than 15 percent (15.5) are victims of two or more maltreatment types although 84.5 percent are victims of only one type of abuse. The most common single types of abuse include: neglect only (60.8%); physical abuse only (10.7%); and sexual abuse only (7%).
- African-American children have the second highest victimization rate, 14.0 per 1,000 children. (Administration for Children and Families, 2018)

THE FIVE TYPES OF CHILD ABUSE

What exactly is child abuse? You might immediately think of an infant or toddler being physically hurt, and that is bad enough, but it is more than that. It is generally accepted that there are four distinct types of primary or direct child abuse. A fifth type of abuse has been added because we are now aware that being the secondary or indirect victim to abuse can cause damage as well. All five types of abuse can damage a child's development and even put his or her life in jeopardy, although legal sanctions tend to be focused mostly on the first two. The five types of abuse are:

1. Physical abuse;
2. Child sexual abuse;
3. Neglect;
4. Emotional abuse; and
5. Witnessing child abuse or domestic violence.

Box 10.1. Definitions of Child Abuse and Neglect

Physical child abuse: the intentional or unintentional harm to a child caused by hitting, spanking, shaking, pushing, or using an object resulting in injuries to the child ranging from minor ones to death.

Child sexual abuse: engaging in a sexual act including molestation, oral or anal sex, or intercourse, with a girl or boy who is underage with a perpetrator who may be a relative, trusted authority figure, or a stranger.

Box 10.1. Definitions of Child Abuse and Neglect (continued)

Child neglect: the physical, educational, or medical mistreatment of a child resulting in harm that could even lead to death.

Child emotional neglect: failing to provide the nurturance that an infant, toddler, or child needs to develop the self-esteem and feelings of being loved and cared for necessary for the development of a healthy brain and emotional nature.

Witnessing child abuse or domestic violence: the impact to a child who is the bystander or witness to the abuse of a sibling or the domestic violence to a parent.

Source: Developed by the author from sources noted throughout the chapter.

PHYSICAL CHILD ABUSE

Pediatrician C. Henry Kempe is credited with coining the term "battered child syndrome" back in 1962, used and described in his article of the same name published in the *Journal of American Medical Association*. The battered child syndrome, or what we now refer to as child abuse, was characterized by the injuries that a child suffered because of repeated beatings or neglect. Here is how child abuse expert and Brandeis University professor Dr. David G. Gil defined physical child abuse in his groundbreaking 1970 book, *Violence Against Children*: "Physical abuse of children is the intentional, nonaccidental use of physical force, or intentional nonaccidental acts of omission, on the part of a parent or other caretaker interacting with a child in his care, aimed at hurting, injuring or destroying that child."

Psychiatrist Fredric Wertham described physical child abuse in his 1972 article, "Battered Children and Baffled Adults," detailing the ways that children are physically abused that are as horrific to read about today as it was when he first published these descriptions. As Dr. Wertham writes:

> In a large proportion of cases, methods are used [to batter children] which rarely or never are applied in murdering adults. Children are beaten, kicked, strangled, knocked about, burned, scaled, immersed in ice-cold water, or stomped. They often die after a long martyrdom from internal hemorrhages, brain injuries, ruptured spleen, fat embolism, and other traumatic lesions. In some cases, gasoline is poured over the child and it is set on fire. A most appalling method is slow, deliberate starvation. This usually appears in the records as "malnutrition." . . . (Wertham, 1972: 891)

What Constitutes Physical Abuse?

Few disagree that an infant or child showing up at the emergency room with unexplained broken bones or signs of repeated trauma inflicted by a parent or caregiver is a victim of physical child abuse. But what about spanking? This is a still a very controversial consideration, especially in the United States. Sometimes it takes one case getting national and even international attention to help the public reconsider their previously held notions about a common parenting practice. That happened in 2014 when the media and public paid closer attention to the question of whether spanking is an acceptable way to discipline a child because Vikings running back Adrian Peterson was accused of felony child abuse when he used a switch to spank his four-year-old son. In Dave Campbell's article about Peterson's arrest, his attorney, Rusty Hardin, makes comments that are important to an understanding of physical child abuse since it points out how the treatment or maltreatment of a child can be passed down from generation to generation. "Adrian is a loving father who used his judgment as a parent to discipline his son," said Hardin. "He used the same kind of discipline with his child that he experienced as a child growing up in East Texas." . . . (Parker, 2014)

But is spanking as innocent a way to handle how a child is disciplined as so many might think? Family violence researcher Murray Straus shared the results of a study that he and his colleague Mallie Paschall of the Pacific Institute for Research and Evaluation conducted on 1,510 children—806 children between the ages of two and four and 704 children between the ages of five and nine. According to John Cloud's article about the findings of Straus' study, "Kids Who Get Spanked May Have Lower IQs," published in *Time* magazine on September 26, 2009, approximately three-quarters of those children had had some kind of corporal punishment in the previous two weeks. Dr. Straus, who at that point had spent 40 years studying corporal punishment, suggested that those who were disciplined that way had an IQ that was five points lower than those who were not. The article further notes that the tide of public opinion seems to be leaning away from spanking as an acceptable form of punishment: in 1968, 94 percent agreed with the practice but by 2005, those who said it is "sometimes O.K. to spank a child" dropped to just 72 percent as Cloud adds the caveat "although most researchers believe the actual incidence of corporal punishment is much higher." . . . (Cloud, 2009)

In 2018, the professional association of pediatricians, the American Academy of Pediatrics, updated its previous recommendation against spanking ("corporate punishment") in its 1998 policy statement that "Parents should be encouraged and assisted in developing methods other than spanking in response to undesired behaviors" with a much stronger policy statement. After examining all the relevant research, associating spanking with more aggressive behavior by the age of three, and, in a follow-up study, by age nine concluded: "The AAP recommends that parents do not use spanking, hitting, slapping, threatening, insulting, humiliating, or shaming." (Sege and Siegel, December 2018.)

Determining Whether Physical Abuse Has Occurred

In some cases, it would take an extensive forensic examination done at the right time and under the proper conditions to determine if injuries are, indeed, the result of an accident, or, in the most extreme of cases, a murder. That is the dilemma former babysitter Rosa Jimenez is dealing with 17 years after 21-month-old Bryan Gutierrez choked on a "wad of paper towels the size of a large egg," as Michael Hall described it in his *Texas Monthly* article, "Five Judges Say Rosa Jimenez Was Wrongly Convicted. So Why Is She Dying in Prison?" When young Bryan died three months after he choked on the paper towel that had gotten lodged in his throat, Rosa, who had already been arrested for injury to a child, a first-degree felony, was now indicted for murder. Three years later, her trial ended in her conviction and a 99-year sentence. Rosa's new lawyer asked surgeon and professor Dr. Karen Zur at the Center for Pediatric Airway Disorders at Children's Hospital of Philadelpuhia to look at the evidence and give her expert opinion. As Hall writes in his extensive article: "[Zur] wrote in an affidavit, that 'it is absolutely possible that the child in this case could have stuffed paper towels into his mouth and then accidentally choked on them.' " (Hall, 2020))

Poor Maternal Care during Pregnancy because of Alcohol, Cigarette, or Drug Use

For some infants and children, physical abuse begins even before birth and during the pregnancy. If a mother drinks alcohol during her pregnancy, depending upon how much alcohol she drinks, and for how long during the pregnancy she continues to drink, it can lead to a condition in her newborn known as **fetal alcohol syndrome (FAS)** or the alternative term of FASD (Fetal alcohol spectrum disorders). How severely FAS will impact on the newborn and child is dependent on a range of factors, from the amount of alcohol the mother drank, to the time she stopped in her pregnancy, or if she continued until birth, to the individual differences in infants or children that make it hard to generalize about the severity of the impairment. But the condition can be a devastating one for the child, leading to memory issues, poor social skills, intellectual disability and learning disorders, physical defects including limbs being deformed and having distinctive facial features associated with the condition, heart defects, among other abnormalities related to FAS. (Brierley, 2014)

In February 2016, the Centers for Disease Control and Prevention (CDC) urged women of reproductive age who are pregnant, or are trying to get pregnant, to avoid alcohol. However, there are no federal laws against drinking during pregnancy. According to Alcohol.org. in 2016 there were 16 states that had "legal provisions that may define alcohol use by a pregnant woman as a form of child abuse" namely Alabama, Arizona, Colorado, Florida, Georgia, Illinois, North Dakota, Nevada, Oklahoma, Rhode Island, South Carolina, South Dakota, Texas, Utah, Virginia, and Wisconsin. In their article, "Laws Against Serving Alcohol to Pregnant Women," they also point out that based on their review of data provided by the NIAAA (National Institute on Alcohol Abuse and Alcoholism) and organizations that "actual convictions are rare." That does not mean it is okay to drink while attempting to get pregnant, or while pregnant. The Center for Reproductive Rights is strongly opposed to a punitive approach to encouraging women to do the right thing during their pregnancy, for the baby's sake. In "Punishing Women for Their Behavior During Pregnancy," they point out that fear of being arrested and jailed, or losing parental rights, for drinking alcohol or taking drugs during pregnancy might discourage a woman from seeking treatment for her addiction. (Center for Reproductive Rights, 2000)

So far, the courts have ruled in favor of the non-punitive approach. Nicole Johnson, who is with the American Bar Association Center on Children and the Law, in her article, "Illegal Drug Use While Pregnant is Not Child Abuse," reports on the ruling by the Pennsylvania Supreme Court in this regard. As Johnson writes, "The Pennsylvania Supreme

Court held that a mother's use of opioids while pregnant is not civil child abuse under the Child Protective Services Law (CPSL), which carried with it inclusion in a statewide database of child abuse perpetrators. Using statutory interpretation+, the supreme court reasoned that the definition of 'child, ' under the CPSL, does not include a fetus or unborn child, and a person is not a perpetrator of child abuse unless there is a 'child' at the time of the act." (Johnson, 2019)

Even if such behaviors that have been proven detrimental to the fetus are either not against the law or, if there is a law against it, there is a slim to none chance of the law being enforced, a pregnant woman or someone trying to get pregnant needs to do whatever she is able to do to put the health and well-being of her fetus first.

Smoking cigarettes during pregnancy has also been linked to harming the fetus and then the newborn, including impacting the fetus' normal growth, leading to a low birth weight and the related complications that could cause, and a possible link to these children developing ADHD (Attention Deficit Hyperactivity Disorder), among other conditions including a propensity to smoke themselves.

Finally, using certain illegal drugs, and even some legal prescription drugs, during pregnancy can impact the fetus and newborn. Caffeine needs to be severely limited and possibly even discontinued altogether during the pregnancy. Cocaine, methamphetamine, and marijuana can affect the fetus and the newborn. Taking certain drugs during pregnancy can increase the chance of birth defects, stillborn births, underweight babies, and such health issues in the mother as heart attacks or seizures, which the mother can transmit to her fetus. (WebMD, 2019)

Pediatric Vehicular Heatstroke (PVH)

In 2019, according to the National Highway Safety Transportation Administration (NHSTA), 52 children died because of vehicular heatstroke—being left in a hot car. As previously noted, 850 children in the United States have died from these preventable deaths since 1998. According to noheatstroke.org, here are the statistics that have been determined for the circumstances of these infant and toddler child abuse victims:

54.2%: forgotten by caregiver (460 children)
25.2%: gained access on their own (214 children)
19.1%: knowingly left by caregiver (162)
1.5%: unknown (13)

Of the above statistics, the easiest number to reduce or eliminate will be the 54.2 percent who were forgotten by the caregiver. "Human error" can be corrected with education as well as innovative technological achievements that will alert the driver to a child in the back seat. There are efforts being made by the auto manufacturers to create such a device so there is hope on the horizon to reduce or eliminate this type of child abuse and the excruciating deaths that these infants or children must be enduring as they are literally baked alive in their parents' hot car.

The hardest category to reduce or eliminate are those 19.2 percent of parents or caregivers where it has been proven that the action was not an accident at all but that the parent or caregiver knew the child was in the car but left him or her there anyway. Whether this was due to ignorance of the impact of heat on a child left in a car, or for another more disturbing reason, the adult could be tried for manslaughter or murder.

The third category of causes of these hot car deaths fortunately has a much bigger chance of being eliminated altogether: the 25.2 percent or 214 who "gained access on their own." Solution? Lock the car and do not keep the primary or back up keys in a place where the toddler or child can easily find it and use it to open the car and gain entry only to bake alive. (National Insurance Crime Bureau, 2019)

A source of research, information, and advocacy is Kidsandcars.org. Janette Fennell started Kidsandcars.org to help families whose infant or child are injured or die in vehicle-related incidents. Fennel started the organization after her family was kidnapped, locked in a trunk, and left to die. Janette and her husband did not know if their nine-month-old son, who was still in the back seat of their car, had been kidnapped or hurt. Fortunately the family survived; founding Kidsandcars.org was a result of her family's ordeal. (Fennell, January 21, 2021)

Shaken Baby Syndrome (SBS)

Shaken Baby Syndrome (SBS) is a type of physical child abuse whose typical victim is less than six months of age which can result in an infant's brain damage, cerebral palsy, hearing or vision loss, seizures, extreme irritability, or death. Actions that do not cause Shaken Baby Syndrome include bouncing a baby on your knee, or jogging with a baby, or even tossing a baby in the air. What we're talking about here is the violent shaking of an infant, for just a few seconds, that can cause these severe injuries. Often, vomiting occurs after being violently shaken.

In most of these tragic cases, the perpetrator tearfully explains that he or she shook the baby to try to get the crying to stop. *Shaking a baby should never be done to stop an infant from crying.* These are truly the most tragic of crime victims since the injury and even death caused by the Shaken Baby Syndrome is 100 percent preventable. (Lynoe et. al., 2017)

Munchausen by Proxy Syndrome

Also known as Factitious Disorder Imposed on Another (FDIA), but known more often by the more popular term **Munchausen Syndrome by Proxy (MSBP)**, this is a relatively rare type of child abuse whereby a parent or caregiver fabricates illness and puts the infant, toddler, or child through unnecessary treatments. (Yates and Bass, 2017)

The medical community labels FDIA as a form of mental illness. One estimate is that 2 out of every 100,000 children may have this happen to them. As explained in the *Medical News Today* article by Yvette Brazier, the term Munchausen by Proxy was named after Baron Munchausen who lived in eighteenth-century Germany and he was known for telling exaggerated and even false stories. (Brazier, 2016)

One of the signs to watch for is if a parent or caregiver changes a child's doctors often. This may be her way of avoiding detection that the proposed conditions or illnesses are fabrications. The abusive part of the condition involves the child missing school because of made up ailments but even worse than that is the parent who administers medications to induce conditions that might justify further treatment, such as giving a child a laxative to induce diarrhea. Other symptoms include asthma, allergies, rashes, fainting, fits, seizures, hyperactivity, and vomiting.

Once a doctor confirms that this syndrome is what is really going on and the child is healthy, both the parent and child may need to be treated. The parent for the mental illness that caused her to put her child in harm's way and the child who may have developed health problems caused by being treated for an illness he or she didn't really have. Emotionally, the child may also have to be treated psychologically to deal with the emotional ramifications of being parented by someone who would treat them that way.

Sudden Infant Death Syndrome (SIDS)

Regarding infants, in some cases of **Sudden Infant Death Syndrome (SIDS)**, it may be hard to tell if the infant's death is because of SIDS, a condition whereby an infant does not wake up and there does not seem to be a clear explanation for it, or there was foul play. Marilyn J. Field and Richard E. Behman suggest in *When Children Die* that between 1 and 5 percent of infant deaths attributed to SIDS might result from "intentional suffocation or other abuse. (AAP [American Academy of Pediatrics], 2001)" They note that autopsies are usually performed in 90 percent of SIDS cases "that occur without evident explanation (Iverson, 1999)" (Field and Behman, 2003)

David Finkelhor and Richard Ormrod, in "Homicides of Children and Youth," concur that determining the actual cause of death of an infant can be challenging. Write Finkelhor and Ormrod: "a child who dies from SIDS (sudden infant death syndrome) is difficult to distinguish from one who has been smothered, and a child who has been thrown or intentionally dropped may have injuries similar to those of one who died from an accidental fall." (Finkelhor and Ormrod, 2001:5)

CHILD SEXUAL ABUSE

Child sexual abuse (CAS) is when anyone engages in a sexual act with a girl or boy under the age of consent whether that act is molestation, oral sex, or intercourse. There is basically no such thing as consent when it comes to any kind of sex act with a minor. Even if a minor has agreed to it, a minor who is underage cannot give consent.

There are three basic types of child sexual abuse: incest, unrelated but trusted perpetrators, and stranger perpetrators. **Incest** occurs when the victim and the perpetrator are in the same nuclear family, such as father-daughter, mother-son, brother-sister, or any blood relative that is considered a close tie, such as an uncle or grandfather.

The second type of child sexual abuse is when the perpetrator is unrelated, but a trusted adult or authority figure, like a babysitter, family friend, school teacher, coach, extracurricular instructor, or the spouse of an extended family member, or a stepparent, so there is no blood relation.

The third type, which is the least common, is when the child victim and the perpetrator are strangers. These cases, though rare, will often get the most attention. Yet only 10 percent of the perpetrators of child sexual abuse are strangers; 90 percent are known the victim. (Finkelhor, 2012) That fact should help parents, caregivers, and teachers to revise their "stranger danger" advice to children, broadening their guidance about what to do if a situation makes a child uncomfortable to include anyone, including family members or trusted authority figures.

The complication with reducing, preventing, or treating child abuse and neglect is the frequency with which the perpetrator is the parent. According to the 2021 Child Welfare

Information Gateway summary, "Child Abuse and Neglect Fatalities 2019: Statistics and Interventions," in 2019, the perpetrator in 79.7% of the 1,840 child abuse or neglect fatalities in the United States that year were a parent acting alone or a parent acting along with another parent or individual. (Child Welfare Information Gateway, 2021)

These acts are also considered child sexual abuse: exhibitionism, exposure to pornography, voyeurism, and having phone or internet communications that are in a sexual manner.

Incest

Here is a definition of incest by a psychiatrist, D. James Henderson, M.D., writing in the "Incest" entry in the *Comprehensive Textbook of Psychiatry*: "Incest denotes intimate physical contact accompanied by conscious sexual excitement between individuals within the same socialization unit other than husband and wife or the cultural equivalent, or between individuals who are close blood relatives." (Freedman et al., 1975: 1531).

How widespread is incest? Social psychologist Diana E.H Russell conducted a probability sample of 930 women in San Francisco. Her findings were published in her 1986 book, *The Secret Trauma*. Out of those 930 women, she learned of 187 incest experiences reported by 152 incest victims. For her sample, which Dr. Russell was confident could indicate the prevalence of incest nationally, 16 percent of those 930 women had been sexually abused by a relative by the age of 18 with 4.5 percent abused by their fathers by that age. Twelve percent of the women in her sample reported sexual abuse by a close relative other than a father, such as brother-sister, grandfather-granddaughter, or uncle-niece. (Russell, 1986)

Russell addresses why understanding incest is so vital: "Incestuous abuse is an important social problem because of the intense suffering and sometimes destructive long-term effects that result from it." (Russell, 1986: 11)

Here is a quote from her interview with an adult survivor who was the victim of stepfather-daughter incest at the age of nine: "Sexually I was very messed up for a long time. I feel that I could have ended up in a mental hospital from the experiences. I'm lucky I didn't, but it will affect me forever."

Russell discovered that incestuous abuse by stepfathers was much more prevalent in her survey than biological father incest. There was also a difference in the frequency of the incest with stepfathers versus biological fathers. For stepfathers, 41 percent of the incidents of incest happened more than twenty times; by contrast, only 12 percent of biological father-daughter incest occurred as often. Almost half of the victims of biological father-daughter incest reported that it occurred only once; that was true for only 18 percent of those who were victims of stepfather-daughter incest. (Russell, 1986: 234-235) The age of the victims of both kinds of parent-child sexual abuse was similar with Russell considering the one-year difference not statistically significant: 11.4 years of age for the victims of biological father incest versus 12.1 years for victims of stepfather incest. (Russell, 1986: 240)

Sociologist Russell discovered that of the 29 women who told the researchers that a stepfather was a primary resident during her first 14 years, 17 percent reported being sexually abused by a stepfather. By contrast, only 2.3 percent named a biological father as their abuser. Stated another way, Russell notes that girls are seven times more likely to be sexually abused by a stepfather who raised her than the biological father who reared her.

Here are some other findings from Russell's study that might be of interest in trying to better understand incest:

- Native Americans were overrepresented with the sample having a frequency of 36 percent.
- Having a mother with only a high school education instead of some college or an eighth-grade education or less.
- Being raised by a stepfather.

Whether a mother worked part-time, or full-time outside of the home was *not* considered a high-risk factor.

Profile ▪ FBI Agent Jeffrey Rinek Shares About a 12-Year-Old Female Incest Case That He Handled

For 30 years, Jeffrey Rinek was an FBI agent, handling missing children as well as the tough cases, like the one he shares about in this interview with this author. Retired now, Rinek remembers this case as if it happened yesterday. Rinek, author of In the Name of the Children, *co-authored with Marilee Strong, shares about how it all started when the little girl's aunt came into the FBI field office in Sacramento, where Rinek worked. Her 12-year-old niece told her that she had been traveling across the country with her father, who was a long distance truck driver and she didn't want to get back into the truck. It seemed her father had been sexually assaulting her for an extended period of time. As Rinek explained in the phone interview:*

Her niece said she came to the conclusion that it wasn't fair to her mother to have sex with her father. What the father was doing was not pleasant for her. It was something she had to endure. She used that time in Sacramento visiting with her aunt to reveal [what was going on with her father] because she didn't want to go back into that truck. She was literally driving across the United States with him. She was studying geography at this time, and she would note each state that she was sexually assaulted in by her father. When she got to us, she had 35 states down.

There was a lot of concern by a lot of different agencies in Sacramento of what to do and how to deal with this. Because of my reputation [with the agency for dealing with missing children] I would interview the girl by myself. But the interview would be observed by five or six different people from other agencies.

So we brought the girl into the office. So I interviewed the child for several hours. She explained to me how things started happening with her father and eventually how he started taking her with him. The mother, which is very common, did not complain or object. It's really disheartening when you have assault like this in the home by the parent. It's usually the dad is the assailant and the mom will either defend the dad or act like nothing's happening.

I interviewed her for several hours. I do find there are sexual acts that are in common based on the age of the victim and although I don't want to go into details, she was describing those acts. She was really broken hearted. She was torn between reporting what was done with her. She was concerned about the welfare of her father who was already in custody.

This father was using his 12 year old child like his wife. Their relationship was like a husband and wife. They were traveling across the country almost like a marital relationship.

The father denied everything as is typical with these people when charged. He chose to go to trial, a federal trial. I couldn't go to the trial because I had interviewed her and I could have been a witness. [I heard] the first day of trial, the father stood up announced he was going to plead guilty and take responsibility for what he had done.

At this point, the court was adjoined, and the judge set another hearing where the father would come back to court and be sentenced.

I wanted to hear him so I went to that hearing. I saw the victim come in with her relatives. She left her relatives and came over and sat with me while this was happening.

When her father was called, she just started crying and holding on to me and really really crying when I leaned down to her and said, "Here's what I want you to do. If your father's sentence starts with "I" or "me," you must stop crying. But if he mentions you, you are permitted to cry."

She needless to say, she cried no more because the father's allocution was all about himself.

Once the case was over, she had so much family taking care of her, I didn't have a lot of contact with her. But when I retired, the *Sacramento Bee* did a story about me retiring. She saw that story and asked the reporter to pass on her regards to me, which she did. That meant an awful lot to me.

Risk Factors for Child Sexual Abuse

Researchers Laura K. Murray and Amanda Nguyen, in the Department of Mental Health at Johns Hopkins University School of Public Health, and Judith A. Cohen, M.D., at the Center for Traumatic Stress in Children and Adolescent at Allegheny General Hospital, Drexel University College of Medicine, in Pittsburgh, Pennsylvania, in their article, "Child Sexual Abuse," suggest these risk factors for child sexual abuse:

> Childhood sexual abuse often occurs alongside other forms of abuse or neglect, and in family environments in which there may be low family support and/or high stress, such as high poverty, low parental education, absent or single parenting, parental substance abuse, domestic violence, or low caregiver warmth. [G Perez-Fuentes, et al. and A C Butler] Children who are impulsive, emotionally needy, and who have learning or physical disabilities, mental health problems, or substance use may be at increased risk. [A.C. Butler and E.A. Davies] The risk of CSA also appears to increase in adolescence. [D. Finkelhor, H. Turner, and R. Omrod et al., and E.A. Davies]

Child Sexual Abuse by a Trusted Authority Figure or Non-Familial Caregiver

- An Australian pedophile priest was sentenced to more jail time, according to the Associated Press story. He was convicted in 1994 of abusing 69 children and was sentenced to another two years in May 2020 when four more victims were confirmed. (Associated Press, 2020)
- Jerry Sandusky, who was the assistant coach for the Penn State football team for 15 years, was found guilty on June 22, 2012 of 45 counts of child sexual abuse and sentenced to at least 30 years in prison. (Drape, 2012)
- Larry Nassar, former USA Gymnastics team doctor, was sentenced in July 2017 to 60 years in a federal prison after he plead guilty to possessing **child pornography** and, on January 24, 2018, he was sentenced to 175 years in a state prison for seven counts of sexual assault of minors. (Eggert and Householder, 2018)

- The Tampa Bay Times reported that an ex-nanny was sentenced to 20 years on October 18, 2019 for sexually assaulting an 11-year-old boy. (She subsequently gave birth to their child.) (Sullivan, 2019)

Although in the majority of child sexual abuse cases the perpetrators are family members, being victimized by a trusted authority figure including coaches, priests, teachers, babysitters, or nannies happens often enough that parents and extended family members, as well as friends, physicians, and those who come in contact with infants and children, need to be on the lookout for situations where abuse might occur or, if it is suspected, to stop it sooner than later.

There is a method of getting a child set up for abuse that is known as **grooming** and that is something to be careful about when a parent or even siblings or friends see it occurring with a child. Grooming is when the potential abuser showers the prospective victim with gifts, praise, or even taking the targeted victim on trips where the opportunity for abuse would be more likely. In some cases, the attention on the victim might be innocent and altruistic enough but some of these older teens or adults may have more sinister motives.

As with the family environment that fosters the possibility of sibling abuse (discussed later in the chapter), the family needs to be giving each child enough positive attention that she or he is less likely to be swayed by the pedophile's attention. As the example of the nanny who seduced the 11-year-old in her care demonstrates, it should also never be assumed that potential perpetrators will only be males grooming little girls since it might be older males grooming little boys or older women grooming little boys.

The Academy Award-winning movie *Spotlight*, back in 2015, focused attention on the abuse of boys by priests when it documented the way that the *Boston Globe* unfolded the sexual abuse of priests that had been covered up for decades. (Singer and McCarthy, 2015) More recently, it was revealed that one of the most trusted and revered organizations for boys looking to learn outdoor skills as well as developing relationships with other boys, the Boy Scouts of America, had to declare bankruptcy in the face of allegations of sexual abuse by hundreds of boy scouts.

Child Rape or Molestation by a Stranger

Every type of child sexual abuse has its dynamics that impacted on the victim throughout her or his formative years and into adulthood. For child sexual abuse by a family member or trusted adult authority figure, there are the obvious impacts on the child of trust issues, the failure to develop healthy boundaries between family members, and the issue of keeping the secret and dealing with the guilt that can occur after the secret is shared, especially if there are criminal charges and even incarceration that follow.

Child rape by a stranger has a different dynamic. It is still child sexual abuse, but the consequences of such experience are rarely benign as evidenced by the first-hand account shared by Jennifer Storm. An example of the one in seven girls who is estimated to be raped by the age of 18 in the United States, at the age of 12, Jennifer was raped by a stranger. She openly spoke with this author about what happened to her, including her decline afterwards when she became addicted to alcohol followed by crack cocaine. She finally hit bottom, got into a 28-day recovery program that changed her life, and has been sober ever since. After running a local victim witness assistance program for ten years, she became the victim advocate for the Commonwealth of Pennsylvania. The first edition of her book, *Blackout Girl*, was published in 2008; the second edition in 2020. In an interview with the author, Jennifer, who is now 45 and the parent of a 5-year-old adopted son, shares how that rape at 12 was the beginning of a 10-year decline that included a suicide attempt. But it finally ended in 1997 when she entered a 28-day rehab program. Before the rape, Jennifer was a straight-A student with perfect attendance, and a cheerleader. "I was a happy kid. I had two older brothers. We had a good middle-class home upbringing," Jennifer says.

She explained that her parents decided to let her go out alone that fateful night when she was 12 to a roller-skating rink. On the way to the roller-skating rink, she and her best friend stopped off at a quarry. She got into the car with a 28-year-old who proceeded to rape her.

When she got back to her house after the rape, the police were there because her parents had reported her missing since she had not returned home at the agreed-upon time. When she told her mother what happened, her response was to slap Jennifer across her face. Jennifer explains, "I spent Sunday morning having a rape kit done at the hospital. It completely and totally shifted my life. We didn't have victim advocates. I didn't have anyone with me at the hospital. I had no idea what was going on with my body."

How did her parents deal with Jennifer's rape? Says Jennifer:

> They pretended like it didn't happen. The man was arrested and charged with seven counts. I started a spiral downward. I had significant insomnia. I started skipping school and ended up turning to alcohol because I needed something to numb the pain. I had just turned thirteen, but it wasn't hard to access alcohol.
>
> I attempted to take my own life, but it wasn't really a suicide attempt as much as a cry for help. I wanted someone to see the pain I was in because I couldn't articulate it. I ended up spending that summer in a psych ward which was probably the last place they should have sent me.
>
> My junior and high school years with alcohol gave way to marijuana and cocaine. I became addicted to crack cocaine and was raped again when I was 17 at a friend's house. Raped by my friend's cousin. He was convicted and ended up going to jail. (Reprinted, with permission, from *Victims*, Yager, 2021)

Fortunately, Jennifer was eventually able to heal as she records in *Blackout Girl* and its sequel, *Awakening Blackout Girl: A Survivor's Guide for Healing from Addiction and Sexual Trauma.* (Storm, 2021; Storm, 2008, updated edition, 2021; Yager, 2021)

Although it is not as traumatic as rape, even molestation by a stranger can make a child uncomfortable and traumatized. A young woman interviewee shared in an anonymous student interview about how upset she was when a stranger grabbed her private parts as she was walking up the steps to the subway when she was much younger.

Much more horrific than rape or molestation is when a child is murdered after the rape. It is hard to find statistics for how many rapes were also homicides based on the UCR (Uniform Crime Reports) data since, until the new reporting system in January 2021, the hierarchy rule prevailed. That meant that if a rape resulted in a murder, the worst offense was the way it was tabulated. Hopefully with the new reporting criteria we will have a better understanding of how prevalent this is in the United States. The secondary source of information, the National Crime Victimization Surveys (NCVS), unfortunately cannot shed any better light on child sexual abuse since family members must be 12 and older to participate in the self-report surveys. So, we have no additional information about victimized children from this secondary primary source of crime data for the United States.

Child Pornography

Another behavior that is considered child sexual abuse is child pornography. Sociologist Diana E.H. Russell shares what research has revealed related to child pornography. She writes in *The Secret Trauma:*

> Child pornography may create a predisposition to sexually abuse children in some adults who view it. Because child pornography commonly portrays children as enjoying sexual contact with adults, it seems even more likely that it may undermine some viewers' internal inhibitions against acting out their desires to have sex with children. And when pornography makes it appear that child sexual abuse is something that adults can do without much risk of being caught and punished—a message pornography commonly conveys—it likely undermines viewers' social inhibitions against acting out their desires (Russell 1984) (Quoted in Russell, 1986)

Just one example of how seriously child pornography is viewed by the criminal justice system today is Jared Fogle, the former spokesperson for a major chain of sandwich stores. He pleaded guilty in August 2015 to receiving child pornography and traveling to pay for sex with minors and was sentenced to serving 15 years and 8 months in a federal prison. (Hauser, 2015)

Controversies Involving Allegations of Child Sexual Abuse

Accusing a parent of child sexual abuse during divorce proceedings as a way of ensuring custody will be denied that parent, or using it as a bargaining chip for getting a more generous financial settlement, even has its own name—the **SAID syndrome**. SAID Stands for sexual allegations in divorce. As victimologist Andrew Karmen notes:

> A significant proportion of the allegations handled in family court during a marital breakup are believed to be true, and yet a relatively high number are suspected to be unfounded. Some allegations are deliberate falsehoods, but others could be made by the mother in good faith (she truly believes sexual abuse of her child too place) due to the couple's mutual hostility, distrust, and misunderstandings. Researchers need to identify factors that help to distinguish well-founded accusations from unfounded allegations, so that mental health professionals, lawyers, and judges can make decisions that are in the best interest of the child. (Karmen,2020: 301)

Another controversy related to child sexual abuse is around repressed memories of childhood sexual abuse. Holly Watt details the complicated story of Nicole Kluemper who at 17 recalled having "recovered memories" (or repressed memoires) of her mother abusing her. This was a follow-up to the video the psychiatrist did of her at the age when she initially recalled the abuse. Were the memories true or not? In 1997, the psychiatrist wrote a paper reaffirming the validity of a "recovered memory." Watt describes the debate that the videos that the psychiatrist took of all those years ago unleashed as another expert got involved in the debate over the reliability of Nicole's memories.

Watt shares Nicole's own questioning about her "recovered memory":

> But she is no longer confident about what happened all those years ago. "There are days when I think I was molested by my biological mother and there are days I am fairly convinced it didn't happen. It is a very difficult way to live. More days, I am convinced it is true . . . It feels like someone just took an eraser, sort of, and smudged my life." (Watt, 2017)

Sibling Sexual Abuse

Writing in *Social Work Today*, Margaret Ballantine and Lynne Soine recount how in February 2011, 19-year-old twins Kellie and Kathie shared on the Oprah Winfrey Show that they had been sexually abused by their father but that it had been preceded by 10 years of **sibling abuse** by their two brothers. (Ballantine and Soine, 2012)

Even though abuse by an older sibling is five times more common than parent-child incest, it is hard to know precisely how often it occurs since it is rarely reported to the authorities (Finkelhor, 1980). When parent-child sexual abuse comes to light, it almost automatically becomes a criminal matter. Yet sibling sexual abuse, even if it is by a much older sibling, as long as both siblings are still minors, is not viewed with the same seriousness since it is usually considered aberrant behavior between two consenting children even if that is untrue.

As you will learn in this section on sibling incest, consent is gained through psychological coercion, and threats, although physical threats or the use of weapons are also possible. (Bank and Kahn, *The Sibling Bond*) The consistency to the stories that I heard or read regarding sibling sexual abuse is that the victim was part of a dysfunctional family. I interviewed Claudia (not her real name) when she was fifty-one, married, with two school age children, living in a townhouse in a Manhattan suburb. She is vague about the details of the abuse but she does remember sitting on the lap of her brother, eight years her senior, and he'd say, "I'll pay you fifty cents,' so she figures he must have done something to her but she cannot recall the details. But she doesn't consider what happened to her as incest. "It wasn't like someone came into my bed and raped me. I'm sure in some sense he paid me fifty cents to sit on his lap. There was an agreement. It wasn't an adult doing this. It was none of that stuff that makes for incest. I was twelve. He was eight years older. When I didn't want to, I screamed. So, it wasn't like my brother ever took me by force except that one time in the shower when my brother walked in on me. When I got older, the way he would try to kiss me, always like a French kiss."

You can sense the ambivalence in Claudia's recollections. She wants to minimize what happened to her, on the one hand, and on the other hand, she expressed her disgust and upset when he walked in on her in the shower and kissed her inappropriately.

The prohibition against sexual intimacy between members of the same family has been so widespread throughout history and cross-culturally that some even suggest that it is the only universal taboo. Upon further examination, however, we find it is not that simple: some cultures have sanctioned sexual relations, even marriage, between siblings. Others have punished sexual contact between siblings even more harshly than father-daughter incest.

Evidence from the fourth dynasty of ancient Egypt, around 2700 B.C., suggests that the pharaohs considered a brother-sister marriage to be a privilege for anointed rulers. The Egyptians, who used the same word for married couples as for siblings seemed to extend this royal privilege to all citizens.

Abraham, father of the Hebrews, followed the acceptable customs of his day and married Sarah, his half-sister. Until the time of Moses, such marriages were allowed. From then on, as Deuteronomy states, such unions were forbidden: "Cursed be he that lieth with his sister, the daughter of his father, or the daughter of his mother." (Fifth Book of Moses, 27:22).

But in "Sibling Incest in the Royal Families of Egypt, Peru, and Hawaii," published in the *Journal of Sex Research*, Ray H. Bixler reveals that sibling incest has rarely been sanctioned. One notable exception was the first, second, or third centuries A.D. in Roman Egypt when commoners often entered into brother-sister marriages.

Sociologist S. Kirson Weinberg, in *Incest Behavior*, cross-culturally examined the more typical brother-sister incest taboo. According to Bronislaw Malinowski's study of the Trobriand people of Melanesia, Weinberg writes, "Incest behavior between these participants was a very serious offense. Social pressure upon the offenders, especially the male offender, would have been so furiously intense that it probably would have driven him to suicide."

Freud seems to share Weinberg's viewpoint about the universality of the brother-sister incest taboo in his 1913 essay, "The Horror of Incest." Freud notes that some cultures, such as New Caledonia and Melanesia, beginning at puberty, reduce the likelihood of brother-sister incest by never allowing the siblings to be alone:

> In Melanesia . . . when a boy has reached a certain age he no longer lives at home, but takes up his quarters in the "club house," where he now regularly eats and sleeps. It is true that he may still go to his father's house to ask for food, but if his sister is at home he must go away before eating . . . If by chance a brother and sister meet in the open, she must run away or hide. If a boy knows that certain footprints in the road are his sister's, he will not follow them, nor will she follow his. Indeed, he will not even utter her name, and will avoid the use of a common word if it forms part of her name . . . Similar customs prevail in New Caledonia. If a brother and sister happen to meet on a path, the sister will throw herself into the bushes and he will pass on within turning his head.

Part of the challenge about how to deal with sibling sexual abuse stems from ambivalence about what is normal sexual playfulness between siblings and when sexual curiosity or exploration becomes pathological, harmful, or abusive. Another consideration is that there has been an overemphasis on the parent-child bond, especially between mother and child, as the most important and premiere source of personality formation and socialization. When the sibling bond used to be considered as a factor in a child's development, it was often seen as an extension of the far more paramount parent-child one. Until recently the sibling bond failed to get the attention it deserved with its own distinctively positive and negative childhood and long-term effects on self-esteem and even one's ability to get along with same or opposite sex peers.

But there has been an increased awareness of the importance of sibling relationships in how a child, teen, and adult gets along with others. As psychologist Diane E. Papalia writes in her textbook, *A Child's World*, co-authored with Sally Wendkos Olds:

> *Sibling relationships set the stage for other relationships in children's lives. If children's relationships with brothers and sisters are marked by easy trust and companionship, they may carry this pattern over to their dealings with playmates, classmates, and eventually the friends and lovers of adulthood. If early relationships with siblings have an aggressive cast, this, too, may influence later social relations.* (Papalia and Olds, 1990: 381)

Around the same time there was a new awareness about child abuse, the lack of research on sibling abuse ended with the publication in March 1964 in *Social Issues* by sociologist Donald P. Irish of his article, "Sibling Interaction: A Neglected Aspect of Family Life Research." Beginning in the 1980s, siblings and sibling abuse started to get more attention including the publication of *The Sibling Bond*, by psychologists Stephen Bank and Michael Kahn, and the surveys of sociologist and family abuse expert David Finkelhor. In 1986, Diana E. H. Russell's book, *The Secret Trauma*, devoted an entire chapter to brother-sister incest. Chapter 18 is entitled "Brother-Sister Incest: Breaking the Myth of mutuality." In 1991, Jane Mersky Leder also devoted a chapter to sibling sexual abuse entitled, "Sibling Incest: Dispelling the Myth of Mutuality." (Irish, 1964; Bank and Kahn, 1982; Russell, 1986; Mersky, 1991)

Bank and Kahn share an insight in *The Sibling Bond* that ties into why emotional neglect of a child is so abusive; it sets children up for abuse by others, including sibling. As they write in the last paragraph of their section entitled, "Brother-Sister love," right before the "Sibling Incest" section of the chapter: *"The emotional absence of parents can intensify the mutual dependency and the sexual curiosity of high-access brothers and sisters."* (Italics from the original.)

One of the biggest issues with incest and sibling sexual abuse is why the child and the abuser keep the abuse secret, often for years and even decades. Regarding sibling sexual abuse, psychologists Bank and Kahn explain:

> The secret can always be revealed if one of the children chooses to tell someone; but the emotional payoffs for continuing the relationship tend to outweigh any that could be derived from disclosing it. Children who feel their parents have seriously failed them or hurt them, are likely to agree to continue the incest. Then the secret has enormous potency, for it reminds the children that they have a pact that the parents cannot break. Together the children are more powerful than their parents. (Bank and Kahn, 171)

Victim blame, the tendency of some victims and others to shift some or all of the blame for their victimization from the perpetrator, discussed throughout this textbook with a specific section on it in Chapter 3, "The Discipline of Victimology: Founders, Theories, and Controversies," comes to mind when you read true story is about sibling sexual abuse. Sara was asked, "Do you ever blame yourself?" She replied, "Sometimes I do. I tend to blame myself when I'm down. Some nights I just think about it and wish I could've stopped [him] right then and there but then again, I was so young and did not know what was going on. I know it was not my fault, but I can't help but to blame myself."

Same Sex Sibling Child Sexual Abuse

Although childhood sexual abuse is most often girls being abused by their older brothers, Finkelhor and other researchers found boy victims sexually abused by their brothers as well. In Finkelhor's survey of sexual abuse among several hundred college students, 10 percent of the boys reported having been abused by a sibling, almost always by an older brother. It is probable rare instances of sexual abuse by an older sister of a younger brother are the most underreported of these victimizations since the boy might feel societal pressure to label the experience as a positive one in the interest of gaining sexual prowess.

The male child's reaction to sexual victimization by a sibling is complicated by the ingrained belief that he is supposed to be strong and manly. A boy may be more likely to keep the abuse a secret, especially when it occurs within the family, because of the social pressure to appear powerful. There may also be a reluctance for boys, especially those who identify themselves as heterosexuals, to reveal to an adult what may be mislabeled as a homosexual experience, rather than the sexually abusive one that it really was. Interestingly, Bank and Kahn suggest opposite sex **sibling sexual abuse** may occur because the male sibling uses his sister to prove he is heterosexual.

As with sexually abused young girls, boys are most at risk of becoming victims in their preadolescence, with 11 to 12 the most vulnerable ages. Offenders, as with female child sexual abuse, are three times as likely to be known to the victim than to be a stranger. Finkelhor found that touching and fondling, not intercourse, was the most frequent type of sibling sexual abuse.

Child sexual abuse by a sibling may put the victim in the category of what David Finkelhor refers to as **poly-victim** (also known as **repeat victimization**) whereby an initial victimization sets the victim up for additional ones, beginning during the earliest years with sexual abuse by a sibling. (Finkelhor, 2011:21).

Risk Factors for Sibling Sexual Abuse

What has research and interviews with adult survivors of childhood sibling sexual abuse discovered to be the difference between families where sibling abuse occurs and those where it is lacking? *When parents are emotionally as well as physical absent, siblings, especially brothers and sisters, with unsupervised high access to each other, may try to get from each other the affection and attention they feel they are not getting from their parents.*

Just like adult rape is a crime of power, not sex, the same is true for sibling sexual abuse. Whether it is molestation including oral sex or rape, it is an assault and a crime of power, not a sexual act. Sexual acts are the abuser's tools to be dominant and control his or her weaker victim.

So the first factor in families where sibling sexual abuse occurs is having emotionally distant or abusive parents. The attention from the abuser, even if it is negative, seems like a better alternative than being ignored or neglected by the parents.

The second factor is for the siblings to have unsupervised access to each other.

The third factor is for the siblings to have a power differential—it is almost always the older sibling abusing the younger one whether it is by two, three, five years or more years.

Another dynamic that complicates the situation is the fourth factor—the older sibling (the abuser) is probably being emotionally or even physically victimized by his parents. He, in turn, gains his sense of mastery by abusing his less powerful younger sibling. (What is often known as the "identification with the aggressor" syndrome.)

Finally, the abuser usually uses threats or appeals to the younger sibling ("the victim") to keep the secret that exerts more power over the victim, allowing the abuse to continue.

Here are some other notable factors in the victim's family according to social workers Ballantine and Soine:

> Sibling sexual abuse victims often live in dysfunctional family environments that subtly foster incestuous behavior and are not conducive to disclosing the secret. Sibling incest appears more likely to occur in large families characterized by physical and emotional violence, marital discord, explicit and implicit sexual tensions, and blurred intrafamilial boundaries. Emotionally and/or physically absent parents may empower older siblings to assume parental roles. In short, these families are chaotic and unlikely to recognize the significance of behaviors occurring between siblings. (Ballantine and Soine, 2012)

To stop this cycle and pattern of abuse, the entire family will probably have to be treated including the siblings who were not directly part of the abuse. They may have been witnesses or bystanders, or completely clueless that it was going on. But on some level, they may have known or they may have suffered emotionally because of the stronger alliance between the perpetrator and victim that left them out, even if they did not understand, until the abuse was revealed, the reason for it.

Another distinguishing feature about sibling abuse victims is this: secrecy is pivotal to the continuation of the abuse. In almost all cases, when the sibling sexual abuse is revealed to someone in authority—a parent, another sibling, a teacher, a therapist, a school counselor—an intervention occurs, and the abuse ends. Whether the parents or the person to whom the abuse is confided goes to the police or not is inconsistent, as well as what happens to the abuser in terms of getting arrested, going into therapy, or anything beyond a reprimand. But what seems to be universal is that telling about the abuse puts an end to it.

Other Peer Family Members Committing Child Sexual Abuse: First Cousins

The lines are a bit blurrier when it comes to sexual abuse by a first cousin since in some states, first cousins are even allowed to marry; in others, it is illegal. But whether or not it is legal to marry a first cousin, beyond the mutual sexual exploration between cousins who are the same age, once there is an age or power disparity, especially if it goes beyond innocent and mutually agreeable touching, it enters into the realm of incest. As seen in the previous section, there has been an increase in interest and research into sibling sexual abuse. But studies of sex between first cousins is yet to get the attention of other forms of child sexual abuse.

The author asked 20-year-old Christina R. (not her real name), whose sexual abuse by her older first cousin, eight years her senior, was mentioned at the beginning of Chapter 1, to share about how the #MeToo movement has impacted her since she is a survivor of childhood sexual abuse. Here is what Christina shared about how the #MeToo movement is impacting her reprinted with permission from *Victims*:

> In regard to the #MeToo movement, I think that I put up a guard to protect myself from being triggered when seeing it in the media all the time so I feel very separated from that movement. In not many instances that I saw were stories about family members, so I tended to detach myself from those strong survivors. A couple of times I questioned whether or not to speak out like they did but settled on the fact that I am not one to post or publish my story on Facebook, Instagram, etcetera. I and not sure why, but maybe it was to protect myself.
>
> I have also found myself in many situations where people I was with (acquaintances or friends of friends) were making fun of the movement with jokes or even questioning the honesty of the survivors. I finally got the strength and courage to defend the survivors in a mature and educational way every time anyone made a joke or felt that the stories were made up.
>
> I've always felt that my story is mine, and those I tell is my choice and I know it's safe wherever it goes. In short, the movement hasn't really changed the way I view myself

or what happened to me, but it's made me gain the courage to speak up when people are mishandling the stories that they've seen. (Yager, 2021)

NEGLECT

Neglect includes physical, medical and educational neglect. (Emotional neglect is discussed separately below.) It includes everything from ignoring an infant, toddler, or child, failing to provide adequate nourishment but not to the point of starvation; keeping a child from going to school; prenatal neglect; and inadequate supervision, to name just a few.

Neglect is not to be taken lightly. According to the Child Welfare Information Gateway, part of the U. S. Department of Health and Human Services, Administration for Children and Families, Children's Bureau, in 2019, of the 1,840 children who were estimated to have died due to abuse or neglect that year, 72.9% suffered neglect alone or in combination with another type of abuse such as physical (44.4%), medical neglect (7.8%), sexual abuse (.9%). Psychological abuse (.9%, or other (7.9%). (Child Welfare Information Gateway, 2021). This type of child abuse is probably one of the most challenging child abuse conditions to deal with because if a law has not been broken, there could be nuances in how an infant or child is being raised that the parents or caregivers could consider cultural differences rather than neglect. Since most parents and families consider how they treat their children a private matter, family members or neighbors may be reluctant to report neglect out of fear of reprisals by the parent or caregiver or a reluctance to get involved. Since neglect, unchecked, can lead to worse types of abuse, it may be necessary to report it when such neglect is suspected, even if reported anonymously.

EMOTIONAL NEGLECT

The fourth category of child abuse is emotional neglect. That is when a parent or caregiver can give an infant or child the food he or she needs, a place to sleep, and clothing, but without the emotional interaction and nurturance that makes an infant or child feel loved and cared for, a child can be the victim of emotional neglect with untold damage to an infant or child's self-esteem, attitude toward life, and feelings of self-worth. As noted in the section above in the section on risk factors fostering child sexual abuse, victimization is more likely to occur within the nuclear or extended family, or with a trusted authority figure, if a child is failing to get the attention he or she needs from his or her parents or siblings.

Unfortunately, when that kind of emotional neglect occurs, and is ongoing, a child might give in to a perpetrator because some attention might be better than no attention. This is not, however, to rule out the dubious ways that family members or trusted authority figures, or even strangers, manipulate a child into being the victim of their abuse. Looking at the family dynamics that might set a child up to be a more likely victim absolutely does not imply victim blame. The healthier the child's self-esteem, however, the more likely he or she is to report the abuse to a trusted authority figure and, if the authority figure is the abuser, to find someone else to report to, such as a school advisor, police officer, or even a friend who might report the abuse on her or his friend's behalf.

TREATMENT FOR THE EFFECTS OF CHILDHOOD NEGLECT

In her article, "Childhood Emotional Neglect: How It Can Impact You Now and Later," author Kimberly Holland suggests the following treatments for childhood emotional neglect "whether it's experienced as a child or faced as an adult who was neglected as a child." (Holland, 2019)

1. Therapy with a psychologist or therapist.
2. Family therapy.
3. Parenting classes to teach parents or caregivers the skills "necessary to recognize, listen to, and respond to a child's emotions." (Holland, 2019)

WITNESSING CHILD ABUSE OR DOMESTIC VIOLENCE

The fifth type of child abuse is when a child witnesses child abuse or domestic violence even once or on a continual basis in their home. We talk about the cycle of violence in its relationship to domestic violence—that those who witnessed a parent being abused by a spouse or romantic partner are more likely to abuse their spouses—but it turns out that there is probably a cycle of violence with child abuse as well. Being abused as a child increases the likelihood that a child will grow up to abuse his or her own children. The only way to eliminate passing down from generation to generation of this horrific behavior is to recognize, and stop, the abuse with the current generation of potential victims.

As Pfouts et al. point out in their journal article, "Forgotten Victims of Family Violence," the researchers looked at a population that had been ignored by social workers, case managers, and others who intervene on behalf of the more obvious victims, namely, the bystanders or witnesses to the child abuse of a sibling or even of a parent. As the researchers state, "Family violence scars not only those children or women against whom it is directed, it scars as well those children who must stand by helplessly." They note, in their conclusions about the 24 children in their sample of 141 children who witnessed the abuse of a sibling, "Thirty-seven percent were diagnosed by their caseworkers as depressed and 40 percent as anxious; over 25 percent had undergone therapy at some point." (Pfouts, et. al., 1982)

The 25 percent who had witnessed abuse of their mothers among the 141 children the researchers studied, 40 percent were deemed "anxious" by their caseworkers and 15 percent had been or currently were in therapy. Hypothesizing that their behavior might have "mirrored the adult violence that they observed" they discovered that 16 percent had appeared in juvenile court, 20 percent described as truants, and 58 percent were rated as having a low average or were failing at school. (Pfouts et al.,1982:368)

This fifth category of child abuse is an understudied one that hopefully we will learn more about so we can stop the intergenerational cycle of violence for those who are the primary or direct victims of child abuse but its secondary victims, the bystanders or witnesses to the abuse of their siblings or parent.

CHILD MURDER VICTIMS BY STRANGERS

Previously we looked at the child victims of those crimes where the victim knows the perpetrator, especially by their parents and trusted authority figures. We discussed how an infant, toddler, or child can be the victim of the ultimate crime, being killed, whether it was intentional, like the famous child murders that were described at the beginning of this chapter, or unintentionally, because a drunk parent swerved to avoid another car and crashed his car with the child in the backseat, killing the child instantly, or a young child gains access to a gun in the home that was not properly stored, accidentally shooting himself.

What about child victims of murder by strangers? Fortunately, it is the rarest type of child murder victim, but it still happens all too often. Armand Emamdjomeh and Raoul Ranoa wrote a powerful article, with accompanying photographs, entitled, "L.A. County's Youngest Homicide Victims," published in the *Los Angeles Times*. They profiled infants and toddlers killed by strangers, usually the victim of stray bullets, or caught in the crossfire. As we noted in Chapter 7, "Primary and Secondary Victims of Homicide," overall, most homicide victims are males—more than 85 percent are men or boys—but in the child murders they studied, Emamdjomeh and Ranos found the victims were as likely to be a girl as a boy. males, The Los Angeles Times did a powerful feature a few years ago profiling the faces of its youngest murder victims. Although some of the profiled victims were the victim of abuse or violence in their homes, here you will find thumbnail sketches of some of the younger victims of stranger murder:

- Autumn was just one years old when she died from a gunshot wound, she received when she stood in her crib in her Compton garage.
- Angel was also just one when he was shot and killed by a youth in a dark hoodie who rode up on a bicycle and fired a gun into the crowd; Angel died hours later after emergency surgery could not save him.
- Luis was just 23 days old when he was killed by a stray bullet as he sat in his stroller as his mother was shopping at an outdoor market.
- Suzie was one when she was shot and killed by police when she was caught in the crossfire as police returned fire when they were trying to rescue her and her stepsister when her father, who had held them hostage inside a store, allegedly started shooting at them.

Included in this section is the murder of 20 children by a 20-year-old with mental problems that occurred in December 2012 in Sandy Hook Elementary School in Newtown, Connecticut. There is a discussion of school violence in the next chapter, Chapter 11, "Teen and College Victims," since most of the school violence happens in middle and high school, or college, not in elementary school. The perpetrator of the mass killings at Sandy Hook Elementary School was not another student or teacher. He was an outsider who entered the school and started randomly shooting his victims, who included the 20 children ages six and seven. The killer first shot and killed his mother before going to the school to kill those children, six teachers and faculty, before killing himself. Why that elementary school? Why such little, defenseless, innocent children?

Those questions haunt us.

The impact on the surviving students, teachers, staff, the Newtown, Connecticut community, the nation, and even the world was so great that the Sandy Hook massacre is etched in everyone's consciousness just like the high school massacre at Columbine High School in Littleton, Colorado, 13 years before, discussed in the next chapter on teen victims.

What happened at Sandy Hook is a rarity. As you will see in the discussion of the offenders of child victims that follows, the majority of perpetrators of crime against children between the ages of birth and 12 are their parents or other family members as well as those trusted authority figures who can get close enough to them for the victimization to occur. Any situation where a child is in close contact with an adult, especially if there are no other adults present, such as in extracurricular activities, victimization may occur.

David Finkelhor and Richard Ormrod found distinct patterns that they write about in their important article, "Homicides of Children and Youth," published in October 2001 in the *Juvenile Justice Bulletin*. Here are the highlights:

- The U.S. homicide rate for children is 5 times higher than the rate of 25 developed countries.
- 1,800 juveniles were homicide victims in 1999.
- Homicide is the only major cause of childhood death that increased in the United States during the previous 30 years.
- Minority children are disproportionately impacted by homicide: 52 percent are nonwhite (Black and Hispanic).
- The middle school years are the safest ones for children. The overall homicide rate is 0.6 per 100,000 compared to a rate of 2.6 per 100,000 for children under 6. (Finkelhor and Ormrod, 2001)

CHILD VICTIM OFFENDERS

The perpetrators of crimes against newborns through age 12 are mostly family members or those known to the child. Finkelhor and Ormrod discovered that females are involved in child homicides more than in the homicides of any other age group. (Finkelhore and Ormrod, 2001)

There is consensus about the way the public and even the prison population views those who abuse, neglect, rape, or kill infants or children: they are scorned. Convicted child molesters often must be put into solitary confinement for their own protection when they begin their prison sentences. The inmate population considers sex offenders, especially child molesters, to be the most heinous of offenders because their victims are defenseless children, toddlers, or infants. Many offenders do not go to prison because their victims, especially if it is a family member, fail to report the crime to the police so an arrest might follow or they change their mind and stop cooperating and refuse to be a witness.

Who the offenders are in cases of child victimization varies depends on the type of crime. As we saw in the sections on the four types of child abuse—physical, sexual, neglect, and emotional—the perpetrator is most likely a parent, babysitter or caregiver, or close relative like a sibling, grandparent, or extended family member. For physical abuse, including homicide, the perpetrator may be a mother more than for any other crime of violence. For sexual abuse, the perpetrator is more likely to be a male. As noted throughout this chapter, the perpetrators are overwhelmingly those known to the child victim—a parent, a sibling, a grandparent, an extended family member, a friend, a neighbor, an acquaintance, a caregiver like a babysitter or teacher, or even a member of the clergy.

As most children become more independent and have more freedom to be on their own, there is logically an increase in the possibility that the offender will be a stranger. The challenge that all parents face is how to mesh the need to protect children from that one very bad apple who has murder and mayhem in his heart versus the rite of passage to gain more freedom to bike down the street alone, to walk from the short distance from the school bus to the apartment house, unattended, to play in the front yard without supervision.

Is parental supervision *always* required? If a child gets to the age where more independence is permissible, is a compromise to always have that child accompanied by at least one friend since there is safety in numbers even if it is against one potential perpetrator, or is that impractical and unrealistic? At least it would be two nine-year old pitted against one stranger trying to abduct them, giving the potential victims more of a chance to avoid being taken than if it was just one child.

HOW CHILD ABUSE AND NEGLECT IMPACTS A CHILD

For infants and children, neglect, the most common form of child abuse, can have dramatic impact on these victims with neglect being suspected in sudden infant death syndrome (SIDS). Neglect can also set up a child to become victimized sexually because the emotional deprivation may make him or her more susceptible to attention, even if it is negative attention and even if it is from someone who should not be crossing those boundaries, like a parent, caregiver or babysitter, teacher, cousin, or sibling.

Pediatrician Nadine Burke Harris, M.D., who became the Surgeon General of California in 2019, in her powerful 2015 TEDMed talk, "How childhood trauma affects health across a lifetime," which has been seen by more than 3 million people, documents the medical lifetime consequences to someone who experienced trauma as a child. Not just emotional scars, which we would all expect, but physical ones. Based on the findings of **The Adverse Childhood Experience (ACE) Study,** as Dr. Harris says in her TED talk:

> We now understand better than we ever have before how exposure to early adversity affects the developing brains and bodies of children. It affects areas like the nucleus accumbens, the pleasure and reward center of the brain that is implicated in substance dependence. It inhibits the prefrontal cortex, which is necessary for impulse control and executive function, a critical area for learning. And on MRI scans, we see measurable differences in the amygdala, the brain's fear response center. So, there are real neurologic reasons why folks exposed to high doses of adversity are more likely to engage in high-risk behavior, and that's important to know.
>
> But it turns out that even if you don't engage in any high-risk behavior, you're still more likely to develop heart disease or cancer . . . In the word of Dr. Robert Block, the former President of the American Academy of Pediatrics, "Adverse childhood experiences are the single greatest unaddressed public health threat facing our nation today." (Harris, 2014)

Profile ▪ How Being Physically Abused By His Mother's Boyfriend Impacted a Victim

John T. is now 28 years old. He is African American, growing up in the Midwest. He completed high school and is currently pursuing an Associate's degree. John and the student who interviewed him, who will be referred to as Rebecca S., both granted permission to share John's story.

John's story is very much a "crossover" situation because just after he turned 11, his mother's boyfriend not only poisoned John's mother, John, and his two siblings, but he also poisoned several of the neighbors although it was believed that only John's mother was the intended target. John's brother's dog was poisoned and died after the dog got into the trash and seemed to eat something that had the poison in it. (That autopsy on the dog helped to crack the case of why John's mother and so many others were mysteriously losing their hair and getting sick.)

The way that John's mother's friends and neighbors got poisoned was because she did hair in her spare time, serving her customers tea. His mother was unaware that her boyfriend at the time, who was angry that she wanted to break up with him, had put rat poisoning into the sugar which everyone had been using when they were drinking their tea.

Although John's mother was a victim of attempted murder by her boyfriend, so it was actually a case of domestic violence, the case is mentioned here, in child victims, because of how John's attempted murder by her mother's boyfriend impacted on him. John, as you will see from the excerpted interview that follows, was also the secondary victim of his mother's physical abuse, which landed her in a coma and in a nursing home for two years, of course through no fault of her own.

The crime happened in 2002. His mother's boyfriend, the accused, was in jail starting around a year later, after the crimes were figured out. Several years later, there was a trial and John's mother's ex-boyfriend was found guilty and sentenced to 37 years for seven counts of attempted murder plus other changes. He is eligible for parole in 2025.

John: I got sick at school one day. I couldn't walk. I had tried to get up to go use the bathroom in the middle of class and ended up collapsing in the hallway. [I] had to be rushed to the hospital.

I was in the hospital for about a week. I had to take this medicine to get this stuff out of my system.

These are all the things transpiring over the course of a few weeks. Then my brother's dog, who stayed in the garage in our house, ends up dying.

To make a long story short, they ended up doing an autopsy on the dog and found out he had gotten into the trash and had come into contact with a high dose of thallium which is an element on the periodic tables. It's used in rat poisoning. It's a metal. You can't smell, it. You can't taste it. It's just really harmful in large doses. So they found that the dog had large amounts of that in his system upon his autopsy. They started to test for it in the area because they thought maybe there was thallium since it wasn't used in anything at that time. It hadn't been used since the 80s in rat poison and since it was so harmful they stopped using it in the 80s. So to see it in 2002 in this area in ---- where, affecting [so many]. It was probably seven to eight people across different families. It was alarming to the authorities.

Rebecca: What were the immediate effects of the crime on you?

John: At the time that my mother originally got sick and went into the hospital, for any kid, I guess that's a big deal. Especially considering she was a single parent. My father wasn't really in the picture so all there was was me, her, and my older brother who was in high school at the time. [My mom's boyfriend} didn't live with us. He had his own house, so we lived in our house, he lived in his. So there was really no one there. So once my mother got sick, my oldest brother came back from college. He was the only real adult figure in my life other than, you know, other immediate family. I ended up having trouble in school for a few years after that. But ended up around high school cleaning my act up a little bit.

My mother recovered from the coma and ended up having to get through some rehabilitation in the hospital. Then she ended up getting released after quite some time. This is all within the course of years. [So] from the time I was eleven, until the time I was about fourteen, [my mother] was in the hospital, at nursing homes, and so by the time she finally came home, I was in eighth grade. You can tell there was paranoia. Long term trust issues. I really rarely got to do anything, but understandably so. You know, this woman had been through life altering events.

Rebecca: What challenges has your mother faced since then and how has that affected your relationship with her?

John: She's in a wheelchair. Because of it, she can't walk on her own. She's not paralyzed from the waist down but going into the coma she did get paralyzed from the neck down. It wasn't permanent.

She's in an electronic wheelchair for the most part. She's been in it for almost twenty years now, and you know the anxiety and mental trauma that it's caused for her, the physical limitations that have been put on her are pretty strenuous as well. Like I said, she was in a nursing home for a year or two after getting out of the coma. Then to come back home to a house that was two stories . . . We ended up moving when I was in high school to a different house on one floor. It was a lot more accessible for her.

Other than the typical parent-teenager relationship that's already tough in most regular households, with that added was the fact that I kinda lost my only parent for a few years. When I would think is kind of a critical time for development and parenting. I suffered the burdens of the paranoia that she had so that put a heavy strain on our relationship. So we never really got along that well until after I moved out. I became an adult and obviously was able to see why, and just kinda get away from it.

I got in trouble in school a lot. I ended up getting a "big brother." From a Big Brother/Big Sister program like that. Ended up getting one of those my freshman year in high school after like my fifth time getting suspended in one semester. It was ridiculous. I was just acting up. Doing outlandish stuff but, yeah, my behavior was affected. I acted out for whatever reason. Probably anger, you know, not channeling it the correct way. But, yeah, it took a heavy toll on our relationship indirectly. It's not like I blamed her for any of it, but at the same time, I didn't wanna be the receiver of the trauma from the situation. I mean, we're good now. We talk every week and I know it's a miracle that we even can.

Rebecca: What did you learn, if anything, from being a crime victim that you'd like to share with me?

John: I guess the one thing I learned about this situation is that you gotta be careful who you are involved with. I was too young to really say that I saw many or any warning signs. I didn't pick up on adult business or anything that pertained to adults. I stayed in a child's place for the most part but we [my brothers and me] didn't like him. But that's standard, the children never really like the step parent. But I think there probably were signs other than the dislike or discomfort me and my brothers had for him. There were probably signs, and I think that that's another thing that was probably learned. Be vigilant of those red flags or those bad feelings. Be careful who you associate with, and be careful who you trust. Just be mindful about people intentions because it could be the people closed to you that try to hurt you.

THE FAMILY ENVIRONMENT THAT FOSTERS PHYSICAL ABUSE OR NEGLECT OF CHILDREN

Alcoholism is a factor in physical child abuse. Bob N. shared with a Sociology of Deviance student about the abuse he suffered as a child although, as he explains it:

> I never considered what my parents did to us as child abuse. Man, as far back as I could remember, we were called names, cursed at all the time. We were beaten for the smallest thing we did or didn't do. We became rebellious kids. I remember one time my father beat me so bad he broke my leg and I was taken to the hospital. I told them what he did, but they didn't believe me. My father told them I was mad at him and it happened while I was riding my bike. Other times, we go to school with bruises on our face and body and teachers would look the other way. Both my parents were what you can call "functioning alcoholics."

In "Understanding Child Abuse and Neglect," the National Research Council reinforces the role that dysfunction can play in setting the stage for a child to become a more likely victim:

> Dysfunctions in all aspects of family relations, not just parent-child interactions, are often present in the families of maltreated children, and research is needed to examine whether such dysfunctions contribute to or are consequences of child maltreatment. Anger, conflict, and social isolation are pervasive features of maltreating families. In many cases of maltreatment, there often is not a single maltreated child, but multiple victims. Thus, maltreated children may be exposed to considerable violence involving other family members as well as violence directed toward themselves. A distinctive feature associated with chronically neglecting families is the chaotic and unpredictable character of the family system. The effect on children of repeated acts of violence or constant fluctuations in the makeup of their household, in addition to child neglect, has not been examined in the research literature, although such factors may contribute to unrelatedness and detachment." (National Research Council, 1993:8.)

RESPONSE OF THE CRIMINAL JUSTICE SYSTEM TO CHILD ABUSE AND NEGLECT

Mandatory Reporting

In 1963, Pennsylvania became the first state to have a mandatory reporting of child abuse law for certain individuals in the care, teaching, or treatment of children. Since then, forty-eight states have mandatory reporting laws for those who care for, teach, or treat infants or children. Mandated reporters, depending on the state, include some or all the following professions:

Anyone providing care for a child in a public or private facility	Registered nurses
School employees	Police officers
Social workers	Physicians
	Pharmacists

Members of the clergy
School coaches
Mental health professionals
Medical examiners
Registered nurses
Alcohol and drug counselors
Podiatrists
Employees of the Department of Children and Families
Foster parents
Juvenile or adult parole officers
Juvenile or adult probation officers
Domestic violence counselors
Sexual assault counselors
Child advocates/employee of child advocacy government offices
Dentists and dental hygienists
Any paid youth camp director or assistant director
Licensed physicians, surgeons, or interns
Licensed behavior analysts
Chiropractors

The penalties vary from state to state for failure to report such abuse or neglect. For example, according to "Penalties for Failure to Report and False Reporting of Child Abuse and Neglect" in the Child Welfare Information Gateway, published by the Children's Bureau of the Department of Health and Human Services, failure to report in Colorado is considered a class 3 misdemeanor subject to the punishment provided by law; in California, failure to report abuse or neglect if that abuse or neglect causes death or grave bodily harm, the punishment is up to 1 year in a country jail, a fine of no more than $5,000, or both; in Florida, failure to report suspected child abuse or neglect is considered a third degree felony punishable by a prison term of up to five years and a $5,000 fine, unless there are extenuating circumstances such as the mandated reporter is a victim of domestic violence.

Although there is some variation among the states, in general, mandated reporters have to make an oral report within 12 hours of having reasonable cause to suspect or believe that a child under the age of 18 has been neglected, abused, or has been placed in imminent risk of serious harm. A written report must be submitted within 48 hours of the oral report.

Just as there are harsh penalties for failing to report suspected child abuse or neglect, there are also harsh penalties for making a false report.

Safe Haven Laws

Another pivotal positive step toward protecting the littlest of crime victims was the passage in 1999 in Texas of the first Safe Haven Law. This law was a way of reducing and even eliminating the abandonment of newborns, especially by panicked young mothers, who often were even unaware that they had been pregnant. The Safe Haven Law allows a parent to place a newborn up to the age of 30 days to be given to someone working in one of these approved 24/7 establishments, no questions asked, including police precincts, fire stations, and emergency medical facilities. The place where the infant is left must have 24/7 supervision so that the child infant will be quickly found, and proper care can be provided.

All 50 states now have a Safe Haven Law. The Save Abandoned Babies Foundation estimates that 4,000 babies have been saved since Safe Haven Laws have been implemented.

Megan's Law and the Sex Offender Registry

On July 29, 1994, seven-year-old Megan Kanka in the Hamilton Township, Mercer County, New Jersey was raped and murdered. It was soon determined that the murderer was a sex offender who had two previous convictions for sex crimes against young children. Megan's parents were unaware that this convicted sex offender was living across the street. Richard and Maureen Kanka, Megan's parents, campaigned to make it mandatory that any high-risk sex offenders had to registered in a database that the public could access that could track the residence of a register sex offender. The New Jersey law—Megan's Law—became a model for the federal legislation that was signed by President Bill Clinton on May 17, 1996. It has been a controversial law since a murderer, once he or she has served his or her time in prison, and is no longer under parole supervision, is considered free of the criminal justice system. Sex offenders, however, must remain indefinitely on the sex offender registry.

Megan's Law and the sex registry is a controversial development because of the civil rights of the offender considerations as well as the questions about whether the registry accomplishes what it is intended to achieve, namely, a decrease in sex offenses. In *Criminology*, criminologist Larry J. Siegel highlights the results of the work by Kristen Zgoba and Jill Levenson evaluating the effectiveness of sex offender registration in Florida. As Dr. Siegel writes: "They [Zgoba and Levenson] found that sex offenders were less likely to recidivate than offenders in most other categories of crime, such as robbery or drug sales. Comparing the repeat arrest rates before and after implementation of sex offender registration laws in 1997, Zgoba and Levenson found that there was a statistically significant increase. Obviously, instituting sex offender registration in Florida did not have the desired effect policy makers intended." (Siegel, 2018: 9)

Guardian ad litem (GAL)

Since such a majority of perpetrators of child abuse or neglect are a child's parent or primary caregiver, the court will appoint a **guardian ad litem (GAL)**, who will appear on the child's behalf. The GAL may be an attorney, or it may be a court-appointed special child advocate who has some or extensive training in this area. GALs may also be appointed in child custody cases in divorce proceedings. The appointment of a GAL became mandatory in child abuse and neglect cases following the 1974 passage by the federal government of the child Abuse Prevention and Treatment Act (CAPTA). As lawyer Mary Grams states in her article on guardian ad latems in Law & Inequality, "Mere allegations of abuse are not sufficient to require a judge to appoint a guardian ad litem. For the judge to make an appointment, the party alleging neglect or abuse must substantiate the claim with factual evidence for which the alleged abuser has no reasonable explanation." (Grams, 2004: 111).

Kidnapped and Missing Children: AMBER Alerts

One of the most publicized types of child crime victimizations is that of kidnapped or missing children. These stories grip everyone's emotions because every parent fears that this could happen to them, this could happen to their child. There are some happy endings, even if they are a long time in coming. For example, in China in 2020, a 34-year-old man was reunited through DNA evidence with the parents from whom he had been abducted 32 years before. His father was taking him home from nursery school when he was two years old. He stopped at a hotel to get his son some water and in a split second of distraction, his son was grabbed. All those years later, more than 1,000 miles from the original abduction site, the son was finally found. He had been sold to a family for just $840. (BBC.com, 2020)

Definitely not a happy ending is the tragedy that happened to Adam Walsh and his family. When he was six years old, he was abducted from a store in a shopping mall in Florida. He was found murdered a few weeks later. His father, John Walsh, became a crime victim advocate, hosting the popular TV show, *America's Most Wanted*. Adam's case and his parents' activism led to the passing on the July 27, 2006 by President George W. Bush of the Adam Walsh Child Protection and Safety Act which put sex offenders into three tiers, depending on the severity of their crime. To help locate missing children, John and Reve Walsh co-founded the nonprofit National Center for Missing & Exploited Children. One of their projects is known as Code Adam. It allows stores to sign up to be designated as safe places for a child to run to if she or he is feeling uncomfortable about a potential abduction and needs a safe place to get help. It also trains stores and other establishments in the protocol to follow if a child is reported missing. (codeadam.missingkids.org)

The good news is that of the estimated 800,000 missing children in the United States every year, the majority do return home, safe and sound. Most of the missing children have voluntarily run away from home. Of the 200,000 who have been abducted, most are taken by non-custodial family members. But a disturbingly high number of kidnapped children—58,000—are thought to be taken by non-family members who are known to the child but who have sex or other unsavory plans for the victim. According to Barbara Goldberg, in her Reuters article, "Missing Children in U.S. Nearly Always Make It Home Alive," some do not make it back. Of the 115 children kidnapped annually by strangers, 40 percent (or 46 children) were killed, 57 percent came back alive, and the other cases remain open and unsolved. (Goldberg, 2012)

A way to assist in bringing those children who are abducted home safely is through the AMBER Alert system. It began when nine-year-old Amber Hagerman was abducted on January 15, 1996 as she rode her bicycle in her neighborhood. The abduction by someone in a black pickup truck was seen by bystanders who immediately called 911 to let the police know what had just happened. Unfortunately, the police were not able to find the truck or Amber. Two days later, her body was discovered within five miles of her apartment complex. Amber had been murdered.

There was a collective outrage over the inefficient way that information was disseminated at that time. If only there had been a way to quickly let the public know about Amber's disappearance and the description of the van.

Every state began enacting their own emergency alert plan. Then, in September 2002, the AMBER Alert system, which stands for America's Missing: Broadcast Emergency Response, was started in 26 states. There are certain criteria that must be met for an abduction to be broadcast over the AMBER Alert system, such as the victim being under 17 years of age and in immediate danger. Today all 50 states and 33 other countries participate in the AMBER Alert system.

PREVENTING CHILD ABUSE AND NEGLECT

Some types of child abuse or neglect are relatively easy to prevent; e.g., never leave an infant or a child alone in a car. Following that simple rule will prevent the possibility of a child dying from Pediatric Vehicular Heatstroke (PVH) since it takes just 10 minutes for a car to reach 100 degrees if it is an 80-degree day or 15 minutes for a car to reach 96 degrees on a 70-degree day. According to studies reported by Laura Geggel in Livescience.com, the inside temperature in a car parked in the sun on a 95 degree or hotter day reached 116 degrees within an hour.

Educating those who are trying to get pregnant, as well as pregnant women, and their significant others as well, about the potential danger to the fetus from alcohol, drugs, smoking, and even too much caffeine or certain over the counter medications during pregnancy can go a long way to avoid deliberate or unintentional child abuse in the womb.

Upon delivery, and in those early days, weeks, and months of parenting, especially for the new mother who is inexperienced or the mother with many other small children to care for, having a support network can help reduce the stress and sleeplessness that can lead to child neglect and abuse. If a mother is feeling overwhelmed, seeking out local associations that can offer emotional support and even caregiving suggestions might help as well even requesting a home visit to get some assistance and guidance. Taking it out on the baby is never acceptable since it can have physical, emotional, and legal ramifications. Since 2007, to prevent Shaken Baby Syndrome, the National Center on Shaken Baby Syndrome has had an evidence-based plan known as PURPLE Crying Program available for parents. Their efforts to educate parents in positive ways to deal with the crying that can last as long as five hours that may cause some parents to resort to the life-threatening strategy of shaking the baby are to be applauded and given wide dissemination.

Educating parents about better screening practices when hiring babysitters or any of the teachers or tutors who will have close unsupervised contact with their children may reduce or avoid victimization in the first place. Technology such as "nanny cameras," as long as such surveillance is legal in your area, is a way to monitor unsupervised caregiver behavior especially in the earliest stages of employment when parents are still building trust about those they are relegating their child's care.

SUMMARY

This chapter covered child victims from infancy until age twelve, even discussing how pregnant women have to take care of themselves so they avoid abusing their unborn child.

There are five types of child abuse: physical, sexual, neglect, emotional, and witness to child abuse or family violence. Infant and child victims demand the most attention for study, treatment, and prevention since these victims are usually so defenseless and vulnerable. Those who do survive the abuse or sexual assaults have their entire lives ahead of them, and, for many, that includes dealing with the physical, emotional, and possibly even legal aftermath of the victimization. It is up to the criminal justice system as well as the medical community and society at large to help child victims to heal from these crimes whether it was reported or not.

This chapter also raises some controversies that need to be considered. First, there is evidence that being a child victim of a crime can make it more likely that someone will be victimized again, and even that he or she will become an abuser. (What is known as polyvictimization or repeat victimization.) How can that cycle of violence be avoided?

Second, some accidents to infants, toddlers, or children, may be the result of a parent or caregiver's intentional harm. How can we get better at knowing the difference? What about a case like Rosa Jimenez, the former babysitter to a 21-month-old who choked on a wad of paper towels and died three months later? Was it an accident? Did the toddler ingest the paper towels on his own? The evidence seems to point to that, or was it murder as the jury decided when it gave Rosa a 99-year sentence? (Hall, 2020)

This chapter explored sibling abuse, especially sibling sexual abuse, a type of incest or sexual abuse more common than parent-child sexual abuse but less understood or well-known. Such unique situations related to infants, toddlers, and children were also defined and explored including Munchausen Syndrome by Proxy (MSBP), pediatric vehicular heatstroke (PVH), Shaken Baby Syndrome (SBS), drowning because of parental or caregiver distraction, or the tragedies that occur when children who are not developmentally mature enough to handle sudden emergencies, like a fire, are left home alone.

KEY TERMS

The Adverse Childhood Experience (ACE) Study
battered child syndrome
child abuse
child neglect
child pornography
child sexual abuse
fetal alcohol syndrome (FAS)
guardian ad litem (GAL)
grooming
incest
Munchausen Syndrome by Proxy (MSBP)
neglect
pediatric vehicular heatstroke (PVH)
physical child abuse
poly-victim
SAID syndrome
Shaken Baby Syndrome (SBS)
sibling abuse
sibling sexual abuse
sudden infant death syndrome (SIDS)

REVIEW QUESTIONS

1. What are the five types of child abuse?
2. What are the risk factors that increase the likelihood of child abuse in a family?
3. Why is it so difficult to get accurate data on the actual number of child abuse victims in the United States or globally?
4. What are some of the short- and long-term effects of child abuse on its victims?
5. What does the cycle of violence have to do with child abuse victims?
6. What is a guardian ad litem (GAL) and why may one be necessary in child abuse cases?
7. What percentage of pediatric vehicular heatstroke (PVH) deaths, also known as hot car deaths, are caused intentionally versus unintentionally by absent-minded parents or caregivers?

CRITICAL THINKING QUESTIONS

1. How much latitude should parents be given in how they raise their children? When is it okay for local government to intervene in the care of an infant, toddler, or child? Explain your answer.
2. If a parent is suspected of child abuse, could it ever be a question of poor parenting skills or is it always a criminal matter that requires jail or prison time?

3. Think back to your own formative years. Did you ever get lost in a store even for a few minutes? What did that feel like? Were there any parenting behaviors including how you were disciplined that your parents engaged in that you now view differently after reading this chapter? Which ones? In what way? If you plan on having children, what aspects of the way your parents raised you do you plan to replicate and which ones do you plan to change or avoid all together? Why?

ACTIVITIES

1. Educating children as young as preschoolers about the potential dangers from family members, including siblings, and not just the "stranger danger" approach that is much more common, could help to have more aware children who could be less likely victims. Write a short speech that you would deliver if you could share your suggestions with those children in person in their classroom or in a videoconferencing situation, such as over Zoom, Microsoft Teams, or Skype. What would you say? What examples or statistics would you use to make your point?
2. Consider that you are the prosecutor who has been brought in on a case involving a mother who left her infant in the back seat of her car and went to work. The infant died from the heat. The infant's father, the mother's ex-husband, is pressuring you to charge the mother. The infant's grandmother, is pressuring you to let her daughter go. What would you do? Pursue the case and offer a plea or go to trial? Require probation? Attending parenting classes? Divide into groups of two of four to discuss this.

RESOURCES

American Professional Society on the Abuse of Children
apsac.org
Membership association of professionals who deal with child abuse and neglect.

American Society for the Positive Care of Children (American SPCC)
americanspcc.org
National nonprofit organization including their Positive Parenting For All Facebook group.

Child Molestation Research & Prevention Institute
childmolestationprevention.org
Nonprofit organization conducting research and providing information related to the prevention and treatment of child sexual abuse.

Childhelp
childhelp.org
Nonprofit founded in 1959 by Sara O'Meara and Yvonne Fedderson and dedicated to the prevention of and treatment of child abuse.

Children's Bureau
Office on Child Abuse and Neglect
U.S. Department of Health and Human Services

National Data Archive on Child Abuse and Neglect (NDACAN)
www.ndacan.acf.hhs.gov

Crimes Against Children Research Center
University of New Hampshire
Durham, New Hampshire 03824
unh.edu/ccrc

The Global Partnership to End Violence Against Children
end-violence.org
Started in 2016 by the UN Secretary General, this is a coalition of an estimated 600 organizations from around the world with the goal of ending violence against children.

International Society for Prevention of Child Abuse and Neglect
ispcan.org
Membership organization concerned with child abuse and neglect prevention.

Kempe Foundation for the Prevention and Treatment of Child Abuse and Neglect
Anschutz Medical Campus
Aurora, Colorado 80045
kempe.org

National Center for Missing and Exploited Children (NCMEC)
missingkids.org
Non-profit organization dedicated to finding missing children and ending child sexual and physical abuse and exploitation. Works with families and law enforcement to prevent or recover abducted children. One of its related programs is the CODE ADAM initiative to train and implement a protocol at stores or other establishments if a child goes missing.

National Center on Shaken Baby Syndrome (NCSBS)
dontshake.org
https://www.dontshake.org/
Here is also a site dedicated to their PURPLE Crying baby program: purplecrying.info

ChildAbuseWatch.net
abusewatch.net (covers the United States, South America, and Canada)
abusewatch.au (covers Ireland, UK, and Europe)
abusewatch.info (covers Africa, Australia, and New Zealand)

Kids and Cars
kidsandcars.org
Started by Janette Fennell after she and her family survived being kidnapped, locked in their car trunk, and left to die in 1995 in a California incident. Works with families whose children have been injured or died in a vehicle-related incident.

No Heat Stroke
noheatstroke.org
Developed and maintained by Jan Null, CCM, Department of Meteorology & Climate Science, San Jose State University

Polly Klass® Foundation
pollyklaas.org

Violent Crimes Against Children
FBI Headquarters
Washington, District of Columbia 20535-0001
fbi.gov/investigate/violent-crime/cac

CITED WORKS AND ADDITIONAL REFERENCES

Alcohol.org. Updated on January 29, 2020. Editorial Staff. "Laws Against Serving Alcohol to Pregnant Women." Posted at www.alcohol.org.

Alderson, Reevel. June 20, 2017. "Liam Fee murder: Case Review Highlights 'Missed Opportunities.'" BBC.com

American Psychological Association. August 18, 1997. "Childhood Sibling Abuse Common, But Most Adults Don't Remember It That Way, Study Finds." Press release about study presented by researchers Carol D. Wilson and Marry Ellen Fromuth, Ph.D. at the 105th Annual Convention of the American Psychological Association (APA) in Chicago, IL.

American Society for the Positive Care of Children. May 27, 2019. "the Epidemic of Child Abuse." Website blog. Posted at network127.org.

Armstrong, Louis. 1978. *Kiss Daddy Goodnight.* New York: Hawthorn Press.

Aries, Philippe. 1965. *Centuries of Childhood: A Social History of Family Life.* Translated from the French by Robert Baldick. New York: Vintage.

Associated Press (AP). May 14, 2020. "Australian Pedophile Priest Sentenced to More Jail Time." AP News. Posted at https://apnews.com/0232ceb1e8ed50c719415e86353370be

Ballantine, Margaret and Lynne Soine. November/December 2012. "Sibling Sexual Abuse—Uncovering the Secret." *Social Work Today.*12(6).

Bank, Stephen P. and Michael D. Kahn. 1982. *The Sibling Bond.* New York: Basic Books.

Bass, Ellen and Laura Davis.1994. *The Courage to Heal: A guide for Women Survivors of Child Sexual Abuse.* New York: HarperPerrenial.

BBC.com. May 19, 2020. "China Abductions" Parents Find Son Snatched in Hotel 32 Years Ago." Posted at bbc.con

Berest, Joseph. August 1968. "Medico-Legal Aspects of Incest." *The Journal of Sex Research.*4(3): 195-205.

Best, Joel. 2008. "Missing Children." Entry in *Encyclopedia of Social Problems.* Thousand Oaks, CA: SAGE. 591-593.

Bixler, Ray H. August 1982. "Sibling Incest in the Royal Families of Egypt, Peru, and Hawaii." *The Journal of Sex Research.*18(3): 264-281.

Bok, Sissela. 1984. *Secrets.* New York: Vintage Books.

Bragg, Rick. July 30, 1995. "Susan Smith Verdict Brings Relief to Town." *New York Times.* Posted online at nytimes.com

Brazier, Yvette. June 21, 2016. "Munchausen Syndrome by Proxy." Medically reviewed by Timothy J. Legg, Ph.D., CRNP. *Medical News Today.* Posted online at MedicalNewstoday.com

Butler, A C. 2013. "Child Sexual Assault: Risk Factors for Girls." *Child Abuse & Neglect.* 643-652.

Butler, Sandra. 1978. *Conspiracy of Silence.* San Francisco, CA: New Glide.Campbell, Dave (Associated Press). September 12, 2014. "Vikings' Adrian Peterson Accused of Child Abuse." Posted at https://www.ksl.com/article/31536949/vikings-adrian-peterson-accused-of-child-abuse

Cavanagh, Kate, R. Emerson Dobash, Russell P. Dobash. 2007. "The Murder of Children by Fathers in the Context of Child Abuse." *Child Abuse & Neglect.* 31: 731-746.

Center for Reproductive Rights. September 2, 2000. "Punishing Women for Their Behavior During Pregnancy: An Approach That Undermines Women's Health and Children's Interests." Briefing Paper. Posted at www.reprodutiverights.org. 21 pages.

Child Welfare Information Gateway. 2021 "Child Abuse and Neglect Fatalities 2019: Statistics and Interventions." U.S. Department of Health and Human Services, Administration for Children and Families, Children's Bureau.

____________. 2019. "Penalties for Failure to Report and False Reporting of Child Abuse and Neglect." Washington, DC.: U.S. Department of Health and Human Services, Children's Bureau.

Chon, Don. 2010. "Identification of Child Abuse" entry in *Encyclopedia of Victimology and Crime Prevention*. Bonnie S. Fisher and Steven P. Lab (eds.). Thousand Oaks, CA: SAGE. 73-75.

Cloud, John. September 26, 2009. "Kids Who Get Spanked May Have Lower IQs." *Time,* Saturday. Published online at Time.com.

CNN Wire Staff. February 6, 2012. "Official: Missing Woman's Husband Blows Up House to Kill Himself, 2 Sons." Posted at CNN.com.

Daigle, Leah E. and Lisa R. Muftic. 2016. *Victimology*. Thousand Oaks, CA: SAGE.

Davies, E. A. and A C Jones. 2013. "Risk Factors in Child Sexual Abuse." *Journal of Forensic Psychiatry.* 146-50.

Davis, Carol Anne. 2014. *Children Who Kill: Profiles of Pre-Teen and Teenage Killers.* London, UK: Allison & Busby.

Dockterman, Eliana. June 1, 2019. "These Men Say the Boy Scouts' Sex Abuse Program Is Worse Than Anyone Knew." Posted at Time.com

Doerner, William G. and Steven P. Lab. 2017. *Victimology.* 8th edition. New York: Routledge, Taylor & Francis.

Drape. Joe. June 22, 2012. "Sandusky Guilty of Sexual Abuse of 10 Young Boys." *The New York Times.* Posted at nytimes.com.

Edwards, Jonathan. July 14, 2021. "A Chinese Father Never Stopped Looking for his Son, Who Was Kidnapped at Age 2. They Reunited after 24 Years." *The Washington Post.* Posted online.

Eggert, David and Mike Householder. January 24, 2018. "Gymnastic Doctor Sentenced to 40 to 175 Years in Prison." Associated Press. Posted online at apnews.com.

Felitti, Vincent J., Robert F. Anda, Dale Nordenberg, David F. Williamson, Alison M. Spitz, Valerie Edwards, Mary P. Koss, and James S. Marks. "Relationships of Childhood Abuse and Household Dysfunction to Many of the Leading Causes of Death in Adults: The Adverse Childhood Experiences (ACE) Study." *American Journal of Preventive Medicine.* 14(4): 245-258.

Field M. J., and Behrman R. E., (eds.) 2003. *When Children Die: Improving Palliative and End-of-Life Care for Children and Their Families.* Washington, D.C.:National Academies Press.

Finkelhor, David. 2012. *Characteristics of Crimes Against Juveniles.* Durham, NH: Crimes against Children Research Center.

___________. 2011. "Prevalence of Child Victimization, Abuse, Crime, and Violence Exposure." Chapter 1 in *Violence Against Women and Children: Mapping the Terrain.* J. W. White, M. P. Koss, and A. E. Kazdin (eds.). Washington, D.C.: American Psychological Association. 9-29.

___________. 1980. "Sex Among Siblings: A Survey on Prevalence, Variety, and Effects." *Archives of Sexual Behavior.* 9(1).

___________. 1970. *Violence Against Children: Physical Child Abuse in the United States.* Cambridge, MA: Harvard University Press.

Finkelhor, David and Richard Ormrod. August 2001. "Crimes Against Children by Babysitters." OJJDP Crimes Against Children Series. Rockville, MD: Juvenile Justice Clearinghouse/NCJRS.

___________. October 2001. "Homicides of Children and Youth." Juvenile Justice Bulletin. Office of Justice Programs. Washington, D.C.: Office of Juvenile Justice and Delinquency Prevention.

Finkelhor, David, H. Turner, R. Ormrod, et al. 2009. "Violence, Abuse, and Crime Exposure in a National Sample of children and Youth." *Pediatrics.* 1411-1423.

Finley, Laura L. 2013. "Child Abuse and Domestic Abuse." *Encyclopedia of Domestic Violence and Abuse.* Laura L. Finley (ed.). 1(ABC-CLIO): 76-80.

Fisher, Bonnie S. and Steven P. Lab (eds.). 2010. *Encyclopedia of Victimology and Crime Prevention.* Thousand Oaks, CA: SAGE.

Fontaine, Mia. January 24, 2013. "America Has an Incest Problem." *The Atlantic.*

Freud, Sigmund. 1989 (1913). "The Horror of Incest." Chapter 1 in *Totem and Taboo.* London: Norton.

Fontana, Vincent J. 1973. *Somewhere a Child is Crying: Maltreatment—Causes and Prevention.* New York: Macmillan.

Frohman, Janet. G., Moderator. March 10, 1990. "Sibling Incest: Think Tank Report." In Conjunction with the Sixth National Symposium on Child Sexual Abuse. Huntsville: Alabama.

Gelles, Richard J. February 25, 1977, revised April 1977. "Violence Towards Children in the United States." Presented at the American Association for the Advance of Science, Symposium on "Violence at Home and at School.".

Gil, David G. 1970. *Violence Against Children: Physical Abuse in the United States.* Cambridge, MA: Harvard University Press.

Glasser, M., I. Kolvin, D. Campbell, A. Glasser, Il. Leitch, and S. Farrelly. 2001. "Cycle of Child Sexual Abuse: Links Between Being a Victim and Becoming a Perpetrator." *British Journal of Psychiatry.* 482-494.

Goldberg, Barbara. April 26, 2012. U.S. News (Reuters). "Missing Children in U.S. Nearly Always Make It Home Alive," Posted online at reuters.com.

Grams, Mary. 2004. "Guardian Ad Litem and the Cycle of Domestic Violence: How the Recommendations Turn." *Law & Inequality: A Journal of Theory and Practice.*22(1): 105-139.

Hall, Michael. April 2, 2020. "Five Judges Say Rosa Jimenez Was Wrongly Convicted. So Why Is She Dying in Prison?" *Texas Monthly.* Published online and updated.

Hauser, Christine, November 19, 2015. "Jared Fogle, Former Subway Pitchman, Gets 15-Year Prison Term." *The New York Times.* Posted at nytimes.com

Healthline. "Shaken Baby Syndrome." Posted https://www.healthline.com/health/shaken-baby-syndrome

Henderson, D. James. 1975. "Incest." *Comprehensive Textbook of Psychiatry.* Alfred M. Freedman, Harold I. Kaplan, and Benjamin J. Sadook (eds.). Baltimore, MD: Williams and Wilkins Company. Vol. 2. 2d ed. 1530-1539.

Hillis, Susan, James Mercy, Adaugo Amobi, and Howard Kress. March 2016. "Global Prevalence of Past-Year Violence Against Children: A Systematic Review and Minimum Estimates." *Pediatrics.* 137(3)

Holland, Kimberly. November 25, 2019. Medically revised by Timothy J. Legg, Ph.D., CRNP. "Childhood Emotional Neglect: How It Can Impacting You Now and Later." Posted online at healthline.com

Hurley, Dan. December 12, 2019. "Why Doesn't the U.S. Have an Accurate Count of Child-Abuse Deaths? *New Yorker.* Posted online.

Irish, Donald P. March 1964. "Sibling Interaction: A Neglected Aspect in Family Life Research." *Social Forces.* 42(3): 279-288.

Jansen, Pauline W., Marina Verlinden, Anke Dommisse-van Berkel, Cathelijne Mieloo, Jan van der Ende, Rene Veenstra, Frank C. Verhulst, Wilma Jansen, and Henning Tiemeier. 2012. "Prevalence of Bullying and Victimization Among Children in Early Elementary School: Do Family and School Neighbourhood Socioeconomic Status Matter?" BioMed Central. *Public Health.* 12.

Johnson, Nicole. April 4, 2019. "Illegal Drug Use While Pregnant Is Not Child Abuse." American Bar Association. ABA Center on Children and the Law..

Juntunen, Valerie R. (ed.).2013. *Child Abuse Sourcebook.* 3d Edition. Detroit, MI: Omnigraphics, Inc.

Larcher, Vic and Joe Brierley. May 2014. "Fetal Alcohol Syndrome (FAS) and Fetal Alcohol Spectrum Disorder (FASD) – Diagnoses and Moral Policing : An Ethical Dilemma for Paediatricians. " *Archives of Disease in Childhood.* 99 :969+

Larkby, Cynthia A., Lidush Goldschmidt, Barbara H. Hanusa, and Nancy L. Day. March 1, 2011."Prenatal Alcohol Exposure Is Associated with Conduct Disorder in Adolescence: Findings from a Birth Cohort." *Journal of the American Academy of Child and Adolescent Psychiatry.* 262-271. Available through NIH (National Institutes of Health) Public Access.

Latus, Janine. 2007. *If I Am Missing or Dead.* New York: Simon & Schuster.

Lynoe, Niels, Goran Elinder, Boubou Hailberg, Pia Sundgren, and Andres Eriksson. 2017. "Insufficient Evidence for 'Shaken Baby Syndrome' – A Systematic Review." *Acta Paediatrica.* 106: 1021-1027.

Karmen, Andrew. 2020. *Crime Victims: An Introduction to Victimology.* 10th edition. Boston, MA: Cengage.

Kempe, C. Henry, Frederic N. Silverman, Brandt F. Steele, William W. Droegemueller, and Henry K. Silver. 1962. "The Battered-Child Syndrome." *Journal of the American Medical Association.* 17-24.

KidsMatterInc.org.2016. "Abuse and Neglect." Information sheets. Posted at their website.

Krisel, Brendan. January 15, 2020. "Boyfriend of Killed Harlem 6-Year-Old's Mother Convicted, DA Says." Patch.com.

Mansell, William. September 7, 2019. "2019 Hot Car Deaths Surpass National Average, Automakers Voluntarily Commit to Back Seat Alerts." Posted only at abcnews.com

McLellan, Faith. December 2, 2006. "Mental Health and Justice: The Case of Andrea Yates." *The Lancet.* 368: 1951-1954.

Mersky, Jane. 1991. "Sibling Incest: Dispelling the Myth of Mutuality" (Chapter 10). *Brothers and Sisters: How They Shape Our Lives.* New York: St. Martin's Press.

Meyer, Cheryl L. 2001. *Mothers Who Kill Their Children: Understanding the Acts of Moms from Susan Smith to the "Prom Mom."* New York: NYU Press.

Mones, Paul A. 1991. *When a Child Kills: Abused Children Who Kill Their Parents.* New York: Pocket Books.

Moody, Gwenllian, Rebecca Cannings-John, Kerenza Hood, Alison Kemp and Michael Robling. 2018. "Establishing the International Prevalence of Self-Reported Child Maltreatment: A Systematic Review by Maltreatment Type and Gender l. BMC Public Health. 18:1164.

Murray, Laura K., Amanda Nguyen, and Judith A. Cohen. April 2014. "Child Sexual Abuse." *Child and Adolescent Psychiatric Clinics of North America.* 321-337. Posted by the National Institutes of Health at https://www.ncbi.nlm.nih.gov/pmc/articles/PMC4413451/

Myers, Quinn. May 13, 2019. "How Chicago Women Created the World's First Juvenile Justice System." Posted online at the WBEZ91.5 chicago website.

National Insurance Crime Bureau. March 26, 2019. "Thefts of Vehicles with Keys Left Inside Continue to Rise." Press release. National Research Council. 1993. *Understanding Child Abuse and Neglect.* Washington, D.C.: The National Academies Press. https://doi.org/10.17226/2117.

National Safety Council. "Motor Vehicle Safety Issues." "Hot Car Deaths." Injury Facts. n.d. Posted at https://www.injuryfacts.nsc.org

New York Daily News. March 7, 2021. "'I Really Wish I Heard Something' Neighbors Reeling After Harlem Boy, 10, Dies from Possible Child Abuse." Posted at Newsbreak.com

NIAAA (National Institute on Alcohol Abuse and Alcoholism), NIH (National Institutes of Health). "Civil Commitment." "Pregnancy and Alcohol." Period covered: 1/1/998 through 1/1/2019. Policy topic.

Nietzsche, Friedrich. 1951 (1921). *My Sister and I.* Translated and introduced by Dr. Oscar Levy. New York: Boar's Head.

One Child International. "The Four Types of Child Abuse." 2-page brochure posted at www.childabuse-watch.net. Sources include the National Clearinghouse on Child Abuse and Neglect Information, U.S. Department of Health and Human Services, n.d.

Papalia, Diane E. and Sally Wendkos Olds. 1990. *A Child's World: Infancy Through Adolescence.* 5th edition. New York: McGraw-Hill.

Parker, Ryan. September 12, 2014. "On Twitter, Many Ask Why Adrian Peer's Discipline of Child is at Issue." *Orlando Sentinel.* Posted online at orlandosentinel.com

Perez-Fuentes, G. M. Olfson, and L. Villegas, et al. 2013. "Prevalence and Correlates of Child Sexual Abuse: A National Study." *Comprehesive Psychiatry.* 16-27.

Peters, Joseph J, M.D. July 1976. "Children Who Are Victims of Sexual Assault and the Psychology of Offenders." *American Journal of Psychotherapy.* 30(3): 298-421.

Pfohl, Stephen F. February. 1977. "The 'Discovery' of Child Abuse." *Social Problems.* 24: 310-323.

Pfouts, Jane H. Janice H. Schopler, and H. Carl Henley, Jr. July 1982. "Forgotten Victims of Family Violence." *Social Work.* National Association of Social Workers. 367-368.

Platt, Anthony M. 1969. *The Child Savers: The Invention of Juvenile Delinquency.* Chicago: University of Chicago Press.

Pleck, Elizabeth. 1989. "Criminal Approaches to Family Violence, 1640-1980." *Crime and Justice.* 11:19-57.

Pollack, Daniel and Toby G. Kleinman. June 12, 2018. "Let's Tell It Like It Is: Sexual Abuse by a Cousin Is Incest." *New York Law Journal.*

Quinn, Elizabeth and Sara Brightman. 2015. *Crime Victimization: A Comprehensive Overview.* Durham, NC: Carolina Academic Press.

Quinney, Richard. 1970. *The Social Reality of Crime.* Boston: Little Brown.

Rawson, Kerri. 2019. *A Serial Killer's Daughter.* Nashville, TN: Nelson.

Rush, Florence. 1975. *The Best Kept Secret: Sexual Abuse of Children.* Englewood Cliffs, NJ: Prentice-Hall.

Russell, Diana E. H. 1986. *The Secret Trauma: Incest in the Lives of Girls and Women.* New York: Basic Books.

Sedlak, Andrea J., David Finkelhor, Heather Hammer, and Dana J. Schultz. October 2020. "National Estimates of Missing Children: An Overview." U.S. Department of Justice, Office of Juvenile Justice and Delinquency Prevention, National Incidence Studies of Missing, Abducted, Runaway, and Throwaway Children. (11-page report)

Sege, Robert D. and Benjamin S. Siegel. December 2018. "Effective Discipline to Raise Healthy Children." *Pediatrics.* 142.

Seiler, Naomi K. July-August 2016. "Alcohol and Pregnancy: CDC's Health Advice and the Legal Rights of Pregnant Women." Law and the Public's Health. *Public Health Reports.*, 131: 623+.

Siegel, Larry J. 2018. *Criminology: Theories, Patterns, and Typologies.* 13th edition. Boston, MA: Cengage.

Smith, Selwyn M. and Ruth Hanson. September 1974. "134 Battered Children: A Medical and Psychological Study." *British Medical Journal.* 666-670.

Smith, Selwyn M., Ruth Hanson, and Sheila Noble. December 1974. "Social Aspects of the Battered Baby Syndrome." *The British Journal of Psychiatry.*125: 568-582.

Storm, Jennifer. 2020. *Awakening Blackout Girl.* Century City, MN: Hazelden Publishing.
__________. 2008, updated 2020. *Blackout Girl.* Century City, MN: Hazelden Publishing.
Sullivan, Dan. October 18, 2019. "Ex-Nanny Who Sexually Abused 11-Year-Old, Got Pregnant, Gets 20 Years." *Tampa Bay Times.* Posted at https://www.tampabay.com/news/crime/2019/10/17/ex-nanny-who-sexually-abused-11-year-old-got-pregnant-gets-20-years/
Tampa Bay Times. October 17, 2019. "Ex-Nanny Who Sexually Abused 11-year-old, Got Pregnant, Gets 20 Years." Posted at tampabay.com
Thomson, C.B. 2014. "Our Killing Schools." *Society.* 51: 210-220.
Watt, Holly. September 23, 2017. "Some Days I think I Was Molested, Others I'm Not Sure': Inside a Case of Repressed Memory." *The Guardian.* Also posted online: https://www.theguardian.com/science/2017/sep/23/inside-case-of-repressed-memory-nicole-kluemper
WebMD. August 28, 2019. "Drug Use and Pregnancy." Reviewed by Smitha Bhandari, M.D. Posted at webmd.com
Weinberg, S. Kirson. 1955. *Incest Behavior.* New York: Citadel Press.
Weingarten, Gene. March 8, 2009. "Fatal Distraction: Forgetting a Child in the Backseat of a Car Is a Horrifying Mistake. Is It a Crime?" *Washington Post.*
Wertham, Fredric, M.D. August 1972. "Battered Children and Baffled Adults." *Bulletin of the New York Academy of Medicine,* Second series.48(7): 887-898.
__________________. 1949. *The Show of Violence.* Garden City, New York: Doubleday.
Wiehe, V.R. 1990. *Sibling Abuse: Hidden Physical, Emotional, and Sexual Trauma.* Lexington, MA: Lexington.
Woods, Timothy O. and U.S. Office of Justice Programs, Office for Victims of Crime. Updated April 2008. *First Response to Victims of Crime.* National Sheriffs Association. U.S. Dept of Justice, Office of Justice Programs. 97 pages. Posted at https://www.ovc.gov/publications/infores/pdftxt/FirstResponseGuidebook.pdf
World Health Organization. Report of the consultation on child abuse prevention. 1999. Geneva: WHO. 29–31.
_______________. June 7, 2019. "Violence Against Children." Fact sheets.
Yager, Jan. 2021. *Help Yourself Now.* New York: Allworth, an imprint of Skyhorse.
___________. *Victims.* New introduction, 2021 (originally published 1978 by Scribner's). Stamford, CT: Hannacroix Creek.
Yates, Gregory and Christopher Bass. 2017. "The Perpetrators of Medical Child Abuse (Munchausen Syndrome by Proxy) – A Systematic Review of 796 Cases." *Child Abuse & Neglect.* 72: 45-53.
Young, Leontine R. 1964. *Wednesday's Children: A Study of Child Neglect and Abuse.* New York: McGraw-Hill.
Zalba, Serapro Richard. October 1966. "The Abused Child: I. A Survey of the Problem." *Social Work.* 11(4): 3-16.

Videos and Films

Center on the Developing Child at Harvard University. October 31, 2013. "InBrief: The Science of Neglect." 5:57 minutes. Posted at www.youtube.com/watch?v=bF3j5UVCSCA
"Code Adam." October 5, 2012. Short video demonstrating the 6-step Code Adam program. 5:27 minutes. Posted online at https://www.youtube.com/watch?v=hS48n3p_2mI
Harris, Nadine Burke, M.D. February 17, 2015. "How Childhood Trauma Affects Health Across a Lifetime. 16:02 minutes TED Talk. Posted at https://www.ted.com/talks/nadine_burke_harris_how_childhood_trauma_affects_health_across_a_lifetime?language=en
McCarthy, Tom and Josh Singer. *Spotlight.* 2015. Directed Tom McCarthyStarring Mark Ruffalo and Michael Keaton.

CHAPTER **ELEVEN**

Teen and College Victims

Learning Objectives:

After you finish reading this chapter, you should be able to:

1. Describe the various kinds of victimizations of teens and college students.
2. Identify and explore the prevalence of school violence and its victims.
3. Explain what a status offense is and how it is unique to teenagers.
4. Define *throwaway* and *runaway*.
5. Identify who are the most likely teenage rape victims and their offenders.
6. Define statutory rape and its unique dynamics.
7. Describe dating violence and its victims.
8. Define college hazing and its dangers.
9. Describe the prevalence of substance abuse among teens and its relationship to victimization.
10. Describe and discuss drowsy driving including driving under the influence (DUI) and distracted driving such as texting and some solutions.

WHO ARE THE TEENAGE AND COLLEGE VICTIMS OF CRIME AND SUBSTANCE ABUSE?

- Nicole Giovanni was 14 and lived in suburban Roselle Park, New Jersey when, on February 6, 2005, her mother, who was 46 at the time, entered her daughter's bedroom and bludgeoned her sleeping daughter to death with a hammer and a shovel. Accepting a **plea deal** of **first-degree manslaughter,** Nicole's mother was sentenced to 30 years in prison for the killing of Nicole who was an honor student and freshman in high school. (Qersdyn, 2015)

- In February 2017, 19-year-old Timothy Piazza, a college sophomore, died two days after drinking a large quantity of alcohol related to his hazing at a fraternity house party and a subsequent fall down stairs, leading to traumatic brain injuries. Two years later, in April 2019, three former fraternity members who had pleaded guilty to hazing charges, were sentenced to from 30 days to 9 months in jail, fines of $1,000 to $2,500, and to complete 100 hours of community service. (Holcombe, 2019)
- Sexually assaulted at a school party at age 11 and raped by two men at the age of 14, Noa Pothoven wrote about her struggles on Instagram and in an autobiography. As a 17-year-old, she was said to be suffering from post-traumatic stress disorder (PTSD), depression, and eating disorders. She died from self-starvation. (BBC.com, 2019)
- Johnny Stack was a brilliant 19-year-old living in Colorado, but he had several tough years starting at age 14, when he first tried marijuana. He went to three different universities but had to disenroll from all three because of his continued marijuana use. He was admitted to a mental hospital on two occasions and was on medication, but unfortunately it did not seem to help. He became a dealer as well as a user of high-potency THC marijuana products. In November 2019, Johnny died by suicide. In April 2020, his mother, Laura Stack, a speaker and author, set up a 501(c)3 nonprofit organization, Johnny's Ambassadors, dedicated to educating teens and parents about the dangers of high potency THC marijuana products on adolescent brain development, mental illness, and suicidal ideation. (Stack, 2021, 2020)

OVERVIEW

Although teens and college students from ages 13 to 21 have more maturity and a better chance at self-preservation than infants or children, they still do not have the fully-developed brains of an adult. As the National Institute of Mental Health points out in its fact sheet, "The Teen Brain: 7 Things to Know," "Though the brain may be done growing in size, it does not finish developing and maturing until the mid- to late 20s. The front part of the brain, called the prefrontal cortex, is one of the last brain regions to mature." (NIMH, 2020)

As Carles Feixa put it in "Past and Present of Adolescence in Society: The 'Teen Brain' Debate in Perspective," "The brains of young people are not radically different in structure from those of adults; there is only a difference in the degree of *myelinatin*, which makes brains more reliable and efficient in their reactions and responses but less flexible and less available for new learning. 'The major brain development in the teenage years is the ramping up of the process of myelination which then levels off to some degree in the mid-twenties.'" (Feixa, 2011: 1642)

What does this mean for anyone studying, or working with, teen or college age victims? It means that this is a unique population, distinct from the category of child victims that teens have chronologically moved away from. However, teens, or adolescents, are not yet in the next classification, sequentially, of adults. The courts recognized this fact more than a hundred years ago when the Juvenile Justice System was started in 1899, in Illinois, with the first juvenile court where the focus was on rehabilitation and not on punishment. (Troutman, 2018: 199) Today, however some states consider adults 16, 17, or 18 and up, depending on the crime.)

In this chapter we will discuss some of the major violent and property crimes that teens and college students fall victim to that also befall adults, namely the violent crimes of homicide, rape and sexual assault, robbery, and aggravated assault as well as property crimes including burglary, larceny/theft, and motor vehicle theft. You will also learn about related victimizations that are unique to teens including school violence, dating violence, including bullying, status offenses including runaways, statutory rape, and distracted driving because of texting.

RAPE AND SEXUAL ASSAULT

For teens, as for children, the rapist or the person committing **sexual assault** (contact or sexual activity that a victim has not consented to) is most likely to be someone known to the victim, rather than a stranger. Because of the victim's age, and the decreased likelihood that there will be a babysitter present, the offender in cases where the rape was committed by someone known to the victim, is often a stepparent, an acquaintance, or a trusted authority figure. Stranger rape does occur as well as what has become known as "date rape." In Table 11.1 you will find the statistics for rapes in 2018 by number of offenses and by age for those 13-17 and 17-19, during the teen years.

TABLE 11.1. Rape Victim Statistics Related to Teens and College Students

Younger people are in highest risk group for rape and sexual assault	12-34 are in the highest risk group 15% ages 12-17 54% ages 18-34
Females 16-19	4X more likely to be victims of rape, sexual assault, or attempted rape than general population
Male college students age 18-24	5X more likely to be a victim of rape or sexual assault than non-students
Transgender students are at a higher risk for sexual violence	21% of transgender college students have been sexually assaulted compared to 18% of non-transgender females and 4% of non-transgender males
College-aged female survivors receive help from a victim services agency	1 in 6
Female students age 18-24 reporting to police	Only 20%
Females who are not students ages 18-24 reporting to police	Only 32%
Of sexual abuse juvenile victims who reported to the police	93% knew the perpetrator 59% were acquaintances 34% were family members 7% were strangers

Source: RAINN, "Victims of Sexual Violence: Statistics."

There is more information about the **rape kit** and evidence collection following a rape or other sexual assaults in Chapters 6, "Helping the Victim," and Chapter 12, "Sexual Violence: Victims of Rape, Abuse, Assault, and Harassment." Although this can vary by state, but what will be mentioned here is that teen or college age victims of rape or other kinds of sexual abuse or assault can get a rape kit done even if they do not want to report the crime to the police. In Connecticut, for example, the kit can be put aside for a certain number of years. It will be tested as soon as the victim decides she or he wants to go forward with a case. Most communities also have a sexual assault crime victim advocate who could accompany the victim to the hospital, if requested. Each state is different but in Connecticut, for example, victims are not billed for either the exam at the hospital or collecting of evidence. (The Rowan Center, 2021)

Acquaintance Rape (By Someone Known to the Victim)

Here is a first-person account shared with this author by a college student who was raped by an acquaintance—someone from her high school—when she was 15.

Profile ▪ Acquaintance Rape Survivor Anonymously Shares Her Story

This self-report was shared with the author. Permission was later granted to anonymously reprint her story in this textbook. Further into the self-report, she explains how listening to the hearings related to the confirmation of Judge Brett M. Kavanaugh impacted on her. See The New York Times article by Stolberg and Fandos, "Brett Kavanaugh and Christine Blasey Ford Duel With Tears and Fury," for a recap about what those hearings were like. (Stolberg and Fandos, 2018)

It was New Year's Day of 2015. I was at a friend's house since she was having a huge party. I was fifteen at the time and of course we were all drinking. At the time, we had a big group of friends, and we were also friends with people from every grade in our high school, even a lot of people outside of or high school.

There was this boy from a different high school near ours that I had been crushing on for a couple of weeks. But we hadn't talked or anything too serious. One of my friends had told him that I wanted to "hook up" with him at the New Year's party coming up. To clarify, we referred to "hooking up" as just making out. Nothing more. In all honesty, all I wanted to do was hook up with him. I had no intentions of doing anything more or less with him. I was thinking to myself that once we hook up, that would be it.

It was the night of the party and we had been flirting with each other all night. We definitely had been drinking a lot too. So we were on the first floor of my friend's home by the beer pong table and he was standing next to me and asked me to go upstairs with him. As we were walking upstairs, I was actually excited. I was finally going to hook up with this cute boy that I was crushing on. I would see this as an accomplishment afterwards if anything. So we headed up the stairs and went into an old bedroom that hadn't been used in I don't' know how long. The second we walking into the room, he grabbed me and we started making out.

I just thought "Wow. He's the aggressive type of guy" and didn't think too much of it.

After that, we had been aggressively making out and the "passion" in it escalated very quickly.

Then I noticed that his hands weren't touching my face anymore. His hands were on his pants. He was pulling them down.

At that moment in time, I didn't know what was happening. But then I knew.

He then grabbed my hand and put them down his boxers. That wasn't what I had in mind to do with him and I felt so uncomfortable. Then I knew this was not going to end up well.

From that point, he was pulling his pants down to when he decided to throw me onto the bed. It happened within at least five seconds and we kept making out. He then asked me, "Do you wanna f—?" And I thought I wanted to, so I said, "yes."

He then started to pull my pants off me very aggressively. All of a sudden, I had no pants on and he was taking off his boxers. He then flipped me on to my stomach so my face was in the pillow.

I was scared, mad, and afraid of getting hurt. So as I was face down, I got nervous and I said, "No. I don't want to do this."

He then proceeded to rape me.

I immediately shut down mentally and physical, so I lost all of my senses and feelings.

It was probably the worst thing of my entire life. I had felt so violated. He knew very well that I wasn't enjoying it, but he kept going. I laid there in silence. I looked down and noticed there was a lot of blood all over the bed and myself. He then noticed, put his pants on, made sure he didn't have blood on him, and left.

I immediately started hysterical crying. Once I calmed down, I took everything with blood on it and put it in my friend's laundry room. I wasn't sure of what else to do at that moment in time.

I went straight to my friend's Mom who was there during the party, upstairs in her room. I started hysterical crying in her arms. I didn't tell her that I was raped, but I told her that we had sex and that I got blood everywhere and was very sorry. I never told her what had actually happened.

My best friend told me that he went downstairs and bragged to all of his guy friends that we had just "f—" and so people found out that we did have sex. He only said that and nothing else.

I slept at my friend's house that night and spoke to her the next morning about it, but I didn't actually tell her what happened.

Since that day, I never told anybody what had happened. I suppressed that memory so hard that it had become something that I never wanted to remember because of how horrific it was.

So for the first two weeks, it haunted me and I was nervous that people would find out the real story. At that time, I was fifteen, so I wasn't really too well educated about what rape was and stuff in the relevance and hadn't thought it as a rape.

After a month had gone by, I didn't remember it even happened, it did not affect me in any way whatsoever. I slept fine. I ate normal. I was able to be around my friends like nothing. So essential that memory didn't affect me in any way somehow.

Truthfully, I never shared my story until around two-and-a half years ago. It was when I was sitting in my sociology class and we were watching the live stream of the Doctor Ford versus Kavanagh . . . and she was stating her opening statement when something clicked in my brain. It was at that moment in time where I thought, "That kid at the party I was at forced me to have sex with him even when I said no . . . ."

I got so anxious and shaky and started tearing up in class. That was when that memory came back to me. I was texting my boyfriend during that class and told him I wanted to talk to him about something when I came home. So after school, I went to his house and I sat him down. I told him how the whole Doctor Ford case was getting me and he didn't know why. So, I told him exactly what I [am sharing] just now for the first time since 2015.

I think that a comment I have for people who experienced what I did is to know that you're not alone . . . People shouldn't think they are the only ones. There's always someone that can relate to what happened to you. As well as if you have the courage to report it, then do so.

Acquaintance rape, which some also refer to as **date rape**, described below, is different in that the acquaintance may not have any initial romantic overture to the crime as is the case in a date rape. In acquaintance rape, the perpetrator is not a stranger or a biological family member (incest). Acquaintances could be an older family friend, or a peer.

There is a lot of controversy in many reported acquaintance rape cases because the perpetrator may claim that the victim consented, even though the victim vehemently denies that claim. Although the majority of victims are females, male teens are victims of rape and sexual assault as well. It could be a male in either opposite sex or same sex situations. Because there was usually a preexisting relationship between the perpetrator and the victim in an acquaintance rape, it can be a more challenging rape case for the victim if she or he does press charges than in those cases where the offender was a complete stranger.

Date Rape or Sexual Violence

How prevalent is dating violence? Here are some statistics according to loveisrespect.org:

- Nearly 1.5 million high school students nationwide experience physical abuse from a dating partner in a single year.
- One in three adolescents in the United States is a victim of physical, sexual, emotional or verbal abuse from a dating partner, a figure that far exceeds rates of other types of youth violence.
- One in ten high school students has been purposefully hit, slapped or physically hurt by a boyfriend or girlfriend.

Since teen years technically end at age 20, and the legal age for drinking in the United States is 21, in theory there should not be a need to warn teens to be careful that something is not slipped into their alcoholic drink at a bar or at a party. They should not be in a bar in the first place or drinking alcohol at parties. However, there are teens who use fake IDs to get into a bar, or who frequent bars that unfortunately are known not to check. Even outside of the bar setting, in someone's home, or at a private party, it is important to know about the risk of having a drink "spiked" to make a victim more likely to participate in sex, to pass out, or, if the act occurred, not to remember it.

The government website womenshealth.gov, provides information about date rape drugs, summarized below:

- People who use **date rape drugs** or alcohol to commit sexual assault most often use alcohol alone or in combination with other drugs.
- Someone could use any type of drug, including marijuana, cocaine, or prescription or over-the-counter drugs like antidepressants, tranquilizers, or sleeping aids to overpower a victim or make them not remember an assault.
- Other date rape drugs include *flunitrazepam* (*Rohypnol*), *gamma-hydroxybutyric acid* (GHB), *gamma-butyrolactone* (GBL), and ketamine. These drugs are sometimes called "**club drugs**" because they are often used at dance clubs, concerts, bars, or parties. Most drugs, including club drugs, have nicknames that change over time or are different in

different areas of the country. (*Source:* Adapted from "Date Rape Drugs" posted at womenshealth.gov)

Teen Dating Violence

Dating violence refers to rape and sexual assault and the ultimate, murder, but it also encompasses being mistreated by a date or romantic partner including verbal or physical abuse, or financial exploitation. It can be perpetrated by someone known to the victim, such as a boyfriend or girlfriend who will not take *no* for an answer, or even a date someone has just met. Teens have to be especially careful about agreeing to meet someone for the first time alone that they got to know online or just over the phone. Teens should always meet someone, if they get to the point of feeling enough trust that a face-to-face meeting is permissible, in a public place and probably in a group situation initially. Law enforcement and dating experts agree that teens should never meet someone they have just met especially through social media alone in a secluded, unsupervised situation. "Ripped from the headlines" true tales of first-time meetings that turned deadly abound. Here are some examples:

- Sixteen-year-old Shayna Ritthaler of Wyoming was killed by the 17-year-old boy she met online. He pleaded guilty and accepted a plea bargain deal in her murder. (Ferguson, 2020)
- Seventeen-year-old Bianca Devins of Utica, New York was killed by someone she allegedly met online although some suggested Bianca and her killer had a preexisting relationship. Whether they met online or knew each other, however, Bianca, who had developed a small social media following, met the man, four years her senior, and he killed her in his car, posting a picture of her corpse on the social media site where some of her followers saw it in horror. The site took down the post as soon as they realized what the situation was. (Huffpost, 2019)
- A 14-year-old girl met her date on the internet, talked with him many times, and then met him for the first time at her family's secluded home when all the adults were away for the weekend. When the police arrested the killer, he told them, "'I just snapped.'" (Jacobs, 2002; Yager, 2016, 2004)

Dating violence is an issue that parents, educators, and teens themselves have become more aware of in the last decade or two through the efforts of government and private sector agencies and organizations. There is a big push to help empower teens to stop dating violence. See the listings in the Resource section at the end of this chapter for further details about The National Domestic Violence Hotline, loveisrespect.org, and other sources of information and help.

Drew Crecente was mentioned in previous chapters because his 18-year-old daughter, Jennifer, was shot and killed by her ex-boyfriend. Since that tragedy the day after Valentine's Day in 2006, Drew, who got a law degree to help him in his efforts, has devoted his life to educating teens, their parents, and teachers about the warning signs of dating violence. The nonprofit organization that he started is called Jennifer Ann's Group. At the organization's website, there are various educational materials about dating violence including what the warning signs are. (jenniferann.org)

Together with his mother, a psychologist in Texas, Elizabeth Richeson, Ph.D., Jennifer's grandmother, Drew and Jennifer Ann's Group have helped to pass a law in Texas, H.B. 121. It requires that each Texas school district has to have a policy on intimate partner violence and that the policy includes education and prevention. (Dingfelder, 2010)

According to the CDC (Centers for Disease Control and Prevention), teen dating violence includes the following behaviors:

1. Physical violence
2. Sexual violence
3. Psychological aggression
4. Stalking (CDC, 2021)

Just how widespread is teen dating violence? Here are statistics from the CDC's Youth Risk Behavior Survey and the National Intimate Partner and Sexual Violence Survey:

- In the last year, nearly 1 in 11 female high schools and 1 in 14 males have experienced teen dating violence.
- In the last year, nearly 1 in 8 female and 1 in 26 male high school students reported being subjected to sexual dating violence.
- Twenty-six percent (26%) of the women and 15 percent of the men stated that they had experienced any of these forms of teen dating violence by an intimate partner—physical violence, sexual violence, of stalking—before the age of 18. (CDC, 2021)

In this next anecdote about dating violence, the victim miraculously survived. Daira Hodges was just 14 and a ninth-grade honor student in a middle-class suburb of Memphis, Tennessee when her 14-year-old ex-boyfriend attacked her. As Emily Yellin reports in her *New York Times* article, "Out of Violence, a Survivor and a Scholar," it was just after lunch when her ex-boyfriend dragged Daira into an empty classroom in their junior high school. He attacked and choked her until she lost consciousness. Then he proceeded to stab her 21 times. He left her for dead and went to take a test in algebra. (Yellin, 1998)

Fortunately, somehow, more than an hour after the initial attack, Daira regained consciousness and managed to get herself into the hallway. A classmate fortuitously found her there and she was able to get to the hospital where she spent two weeks in intensive care and another two weeks there before being able to return home.

At the time of the attack, in 1995, the law in Tennessee did not allow her perpetrator to be tried as an adult on attempted murder charges. Therefore, according to state law, he would only stay in state custody until he was 19 years after being found guilty by a jury of attempted second-degree murder. Yelling mentioned that the perpetrator claimed he was set up by a gang member.

In the article about Hodges, who was 17 when the *New York Times* interviewed her about the attack, it was mentioned that after the attack, she had to deal with a punctured liver and having her gallbladder removed. She temporarily could not speak because of all the stab wounds. She still had scars everywhere. "I didn't want to see myself in a mirror for a long time," Daira was quoted as saying. Fortunately she started dating again a year after the attack, not harboring a lifelong fear of boys because of what her ex-boyfriend had done to her.

A testament to her refusal to let the violence that happened to take place at her school define her or derail her, Daira Hodges was going to be graduating from high school the

Wednesday after the *New York Times* article was published. She was not just graduating, she was being honored as the valedictorian of her class. The following Fall, she was going to be starting at a major prestigious university in Nashville, working toward a premedical degree.

Daira said, " 'Before this happened . . . if I cried, it was because something happened to a dog. Maybe I was in a fantasy world. But this opened my eyes. Now I know violence is out there and it always will be.' " (Yellin, 1998)

Stranger Rape

As noted above, according to the Rape Abuse & Incest National Network (RAINN) and other sources, 7 percent of juvenile rape victims who reported to the police said that their assailant was a stranger. (RAIIN; CDC, n.d.) We still need to understand just what it is so here are some examples "ripped from the headlines":

- Paul Walsh, a *Star Tribune* journalist in Minneapolis, reported on a rape by a stranger of a 17-year-old girl who was walking home. Reporter Walsh wrote that she ". . . accepted a ride home along . . . late one night this week from a stranger . . ." and was raped (Walsh, 2012)
- "Stephanie, then 13, was kidnapped from her—neighborhood and raped by a stranger." (Shah, 2006)
- A teenage girl was raped in her home by a stranger who "forced his way into the home, raped her and drove away . . ." (Vezner, 2007)

One of the most famous cases of stranger rape of a teenager was the case of Elizabeth Smart who was abducted at knifepoint out of her bedroom and held captive for nine months when she was repeatedly raped. (Janofsky, 2002) Smart managed to escape. (Heffernan, 2003) She shares parts of her amazing storyin a Tedx talk at the University of Nevada in 2014. (See the link to that talk in the Videos section at the end of this chapter.) She says in her inspirational talk, "Very early on I decided I was not going to let these two captors win." (Smart, 2014).

Sexual Abuse (Not Rape) and Sexual Harassment

Teens may have to deal with sexual molestation that starts during their teen years or as a continuation of what began during childhood, as discussed in the previous chapter, by siblings, parents, stepparents, authority figures, or strangers. Sexual assault may include everything from sexual molestation to sexual harassment at school or at work. Sibling sexual abuse, which is much more common than sexual abuse by other family members, is underreported as siblings fear that the family will be permanently altered if they report it. They may also fear their sibling will retaliate and even that their parents will not believe them. (Ballantine and Soine, 2012)

Refer to Chapter 12, "Sexual Violence: Rape, Sexual Abuse, Assault, and Harassment Victims," for further information about victims of sexual assault or harassment, besides rape, and what to do about it. Also read or review Chapter 10, "Child Victims," for more knowledge about sibling or cousin sexual abuse, which may start in childhood and continue into the teen years.

Sexual harassment is defined by the United States Equal Employment Opportunity Commission (EEOC) in this way:

> It is unlawful to harass a person (an applicant or employee) because of that person's sex. Harassment can include "sexual harassment" or unwelcome sexual advances, requests for sexual favors, and other verbal or physical harassment of a sexual nature.
>
> Harassment does not have to be of a sexual nature, however, and can include offensive remarks about a person's sex. For example, it is illegal to harass a woman by making offensive comments about women in general.
>
> Both victim and the harasser can be either a woman or a man, and the victim and harasser can be the same sex.
>
> Although the law doesn't prohibit simple teasing, offhand comments, or isolated incidents that are not very serious, harassment is illegal when it is so frequent or severe that it creates a hostile or offensive work environment or when it results in an adverse employment decision (such as the victim being fired or demoted).
>
> The harasser can be the victim's supervisor, a supervisor in another area, a co-worker, or someone who is not an employee of the employer, such as a client or customer. (*Source:* www.eeoc.gov website)

Teens need to be educated about what sexual harassment is, and that it is unacceptable at school, in college or university, or at work. Fortunately, there has been a concerted campaign, even before the #metoo movement heightened the discussion about sexual harassment, sexual assault, and rape, with training programs for teachers and faculty provided by the HR departments. Training has become mandatory. Some training is self-paced online and other trainings are in-person workshops. In 2018, for example, New York state made sexual harassment training mandatory for all employers. (NYC Human Rights, n.d.)

Statutory Rape

Statutory rape is a crime that is a unique situation when it comes to rape because it can be a crime even if the underage victim gives consent. That is because if one of the parties in the sexual act is under-age, she or he cannot legally give consent.

At the website Age of Consent (https://www.ageofconsent.net/states) there is a map as well as a list of what the age of consent is for each state. It ranges from a low of 16 in a preponderance of states, like Vermont and Pennsylvania, to 17 in New York and Texas, and the highest is 18 in Wisconsin and Virginia, for example.

Some states also have a "close in age exemption." As the Age of Consent website notes, these laws are also sometimes known as Romeo and Juliet laws. The close in age exemption means that if a state has such an exemption, if a 17-year-old has sex with an 18-year old, and there is a close in age exemption, that sex act would be legal whereas if that 17-year old, where the age of consent was 18, had sex with a 25-year-old it would not be legal and the older person could be accused of statutory rape.

Age of Consent also includes a page that lists the age of consent in selected countries around the world. Those ages range from a low of 11 for Nigeria, 12 for the Philippines, 13 for Niger and Japan, 14 for Brazil, Albania, Australia, and other countries, to as high as 21 for Bahrain. These countries do not have an age of consent because the girl "must be married": to engage in consensual sex: Afghanistan, Iran, Kuwait, Libya, Maldives, Oman, Pakistan, Palestine Gaza Strip, Qatar, UAW, Saudi Arabia, Sudan, UAE, and Yemen.

`Statutory rape could be a charge that a boy or man finds himself facing if the underage girl, who consented to sex, and possibly even lied about her age, has a parent who finds out about the sexual encounter and presses charges. Even if the girl protests that she is in love and that she gave consent, especially if the state does not have a close in age exemption, it might be out of her hands once the situation is brought to the attention of the authorities. Not only might the offender get put on probation, or even sentenced to jail or prison time, but he may get put on the sex offender registry for the rest of his life, unless there are extenuating circumstances that will allow him to be removed after a certain time period.

In her journal article, "From Jailbird to Jailbait: Age of Consent Law and the Constitution of Teenage Sexualities," published in the *William & Mary Journal of Women and the Law,* Kate Sutherland shares this example of the kind of situations statutory rape laws put the offender and their victims in:

> For example, in 1999, 58 percent of defendants prosecuted in California were under the age of 20. In a recent Wisconsin trial, 18-year-old Kevin Gillson was prosecuted after his 15-year-old fiancé became pregnant. Despite a public outcry, he was convicted and his name was entered in a national registry of sex offenders. The terms of the two years of probation to which he was sentenced barred him from contact with his fiancée'. "Thanks to the court system," she said, "I have lost the love of my life and the father of my unborn baby. (Sutherland, 2003)

Physical and Sexual Violence in the Military

Although this chapter is focusing on victimization of teens and college students, it should be mentioned that there are also physical and sexual violence issues in the military. (The minimum age to enlist in the U.S. is seventeen.) The non-profit organization Protect Our Defenders has put together a fact sheet on military sexual violence including sexual harrassment which can be accessed at their website: www.protectourdefenders.com

SCHOOL VIOLENCE

Rape and sexual assault would fit in with the concept of school violence since those are crimes of violence, not sex, but when you hear the phrase, "school violence," most consider the murders or injuries caused to teens because of mass shootings or, occasionally, knife stabbings in high school. Most college and university students, and even law students, or others, who are reading this textbook today, are familiar with the tragic legacy of the April 1999 Columbine High School mass shootings, or the more recent Valentine's Day 2018 incident when a 19-year-old former student shot to death 17 people, mostly teen students, at Marjory Stoneman Douglas High School in Parkland, Florida. According to the Centers for Disease Control and Prevention (CDC), school violence includes much more than gun violence. School violence also includes:

- Weapon use
- Bullying
- Fighting ((e.g., punching, slapping, kicking)
- Cyberbullying
- Gang violence (CDC, "Preventing School Violence")

Just how widespread is school violence? According to the CDC nationwide Youth Risk Behavior Survey (YRBS), during the 12 months before the survey:

- Nearly 9 percent of high school students reported being in a physical fight on school property one or more times.
- About 6 percent of the students had been threatened or injured with some kind of a weapon (gun, knife, or club).
- About 7 percent had not attended school for at least one day during the 30 days before the survey because they felt it would be unsafe on their way to or from school or at school. (CDC, "Preventing School Violence")

Gun Violence (Weapon Use)/High School and College Violence

Let us start with the most horrific of all forms of school violence: weapon use or gun violence especially when it ends in mass casualties and killings. The most notorious of school violence incidents in the United States actually goes back a lot further than that, to August 1, 1966, when a former marine killed 18 students and others, and injured 31 more, from the Tower at the University of Texas at Austin. The night before the murderous rampage, he had stabbed to death his mother and his wife. The next day, of those who were killed or injured, 12 were teenagers, ranging in age from 16 to 19 including two high school students. The rest were already in college or passersby who were older individuals.

It was a tragic and horrific event that received vast media attention even before the days of the internet or YouTube videos. This earliest notorious example of school violence was the subject of songs and TV episodes and even the alleged basis for a number of feature films with the most recent a documentary released in 2016, the 50th anniversary of the rampage, called *The Tower.* Directed by Keith Maitland, it was done in a unique animation style.

A little over a year before Columbine, there was a school shooting at a high school in Springfield, Oregon that rocked the country, judging from the number of newspaper articles that were written about it at that time. (It was not covered in the same live way that would occur in April of the following year during the Columbine mass shootings, described below.) On May 21, 1998, a 15-year-old high school freshman opened fire in the high school cafeteria. He killed two students and his parents, and he injured 22 additional students. The students who were killed were Mikael Nickolauson, age 17, a junior at Thurston High School and Ben Walker, 16, a sophomore, who died at the hospital the night of the shooting. The shooter had previously killed his parents, Bill and Faith Kinkel, ages 59 and 57, respectively. The shooter is serving 111 years in a state penitentiary. The Registrar Guard published an article, "Remembering the Victims of the May 1998 Thurston Shooting," that was published on May 19, 2018, which was the 20th anniversary of the tragedy.

The Springfield, Ohio tragedy seemed to spark a debate and to shine a spotlight on the prevalence of school violence in America. Indeed, CNN.com published an article with the stark and long title, "The US Has Had 57 Times as Many School Shootings as the Other Major Industrialized Nations Combined." In the article, Chip Grabow and Lisa Rose documented that since 2009, the United States had 288 school shootings. During the same time period, there had been 2 in Canada, 2 in France, 1 in Germany, and 0 in Japan, Italy, and the UK. (Grabow and Rose, 2018)

Alas, all that discussion did not stop what would become the most notorious school shooting in the United States the following year, at least until the Virginia Tech massacre in 2007, discussed below. The Columbine High School shooting has certainly had no shortage of films, plays, and other dramatic exposure of the April 20, 1999 example of school violence in the Columbine High School massacre in Littleton, Colorado. On that day, two students murdered 12 students and one teacher and injured 24 before committing suicide. What changed since the University of Texas at Austin tragedy 33 years before was the way that developments in the media enabled the country to watch the drama unfolding almost in real time. Instead of reading about it the next day, or hearing about it on the evening news, there was live reports as the rampage was progressing.

The immediacy of the tragedy, and the extensive coverage given to the bizarre story of two high school students, dressed in black, who planned this mass shooting of their classmates and a teacher, gripped the nation and the world. Psychologists, sociologists, writers, filmmakers, songwriters, and so many others would ponder for decades what could have driven these killers to do what they did and how could it have been prevented.

Most important of all, besides of course the necessity of trying to figure out what caused the horrific mass shooting to try to prevent it from happening again, is to remember the teen victims. Gunned down in the prime of their lives. Never to go to their prom or to get married and have children. Never to graduate and go on to college or join the military or have the careers that they were dreaming about.

It is so important to go beyond the demons that drove two students to kill to remember the joy, laughter, and goals that defined those 14 students who died and the 24 who were injured. Some recovered quickly from their injuries; others had lifelong physical injuries from the bullets, but all experienced psychic, emotional wounds not to mention the entire high school population, staff, and teachers, who were there that day.

Two years after Columbine, on March 5, 2001, at Santana High School in Santee, California, not far from San Diego, the next most infamous example of school violence occurred in the United States when a 15-year-old killed two of his classmates, in the boy's bathroom, randomly chosen, 14-year-old Bryan Zuckor and 17-year-old Randy Gordon. Thirteen other students were injured.

The shooter claimed that he had been bullied and that led to a lot of public debate about the potentially horrific consequences of school bullying, especially since the Columbine killers, two years before, had indicated that they too were bullied. Teachers, however, did not confirm any incidents of the shooter being bullied. In an interview that UTTV did with Williams, the shooter, 12 years after the school violence and murders, written up by Fred Dickey in the *San Diego Union*, other potential causes are explored. The convicted murderer, who pleaded guilty to first-degree murder and received a sentence of 50 years to life, revealed that he "drank alcohol and smoked pot at every opportunity." His parents were divorced and he was being raised by a single working parent, "for many hours of each day, he was unsupervised and unrestrained from running free."

Although teachers might not have agreed that they saw evidence that Williams was bullied, he said in the interview that, as Dickey writes, "small for his age" "he says they punched and kicked him, stole his possessions, even sprayed his pant legs with lighter fluid and set him afire. Beating up on him was fun and easy."

Later in the chapter there is a discussion about teen **bullying** which, as you know, rarely leads to the murder and mayhem but it has been said to be behind such horrific school violence as Columbine and Santana and, more recently, Marjory Stoneman Douglas High School. A year after the horrific Virginia Tech school violence massacre that left 32 college students and faculty dead, as well as the shooter, as everyone searched for an explanation, in an NBC News report, some high school classmates of the shooter, stated that he had been bullied. The article writes that one former classmate shared that the shooter "was bullied by fellow students at school who mocked his shyness and the strange way he talked." The article, "High School Classmates Say Gunman Was Bullied," also noted that as early as November 2005, a full two years before the murderous rampage, school administrators and police were trying to figure out how to handle the student who had been accused of sending unsuitable communications to two female students. He had been referred to a mental health center after police got a provisional detention directive. (NBCNews, April 15, 2008)

The next school violence situation to get the kind of media attention accorded to the tragic events already mentioned in this chapter was Sandy Hook Elementary School, on December 14, 2012, in suburban Newtown, Connecticut. That tragedy, which left 20 children, ages 6 and 7, and 6 staff members, dead was discussed in Chapter 10, "Child Victims," since there were 14 victims who were children. No teens were involved although Adam Lanza, the shooter, at 20, who died at the scene, was just a year beyond his teenage years.

Marjory Stoneman Douglas High School in Parkland, Florida, on February 14, 2018, was the scene of the latest mass shooting with the highest number of teen victims, 14 students between the ages of 14 and 18, and 3 staff members, in their prime, ages 35, 37, and 49. The shooter was a 19-year-old former student at the high school. What made this mass shooting school violence tragedy even more controversial and upsetting was that in 2017, the FBI had allegedly received a tip that someone had posted on social media with the shooter's same name that he was planning to carry out school violence. But the FBI were unable to identity the person before the tragedy occurred. (Burch and Mazzei, 2018) But just how widespread is school violence? How at risk are American teens to be injured or killed at their middle or high schools or colleges?

According to an ABC News report, written by Christina Carrega and published on December 13, 2019, it is more prevalent than you might think. Carrega states that there were 26 school shootings in 2019 based on data and news reports collected by the Gun Violence Archive. September was the most violent month with seven shootings at high schools in Texas, Virginia, South Carolina, and Pennsylvania. Half occurred on Fridays. July was the safest month. In those two dozen incidents, 44 were injured and six were killed. A particularly interesting finding was that 57.6 percent or the majority of the incidents "were at the end of or during sporting events, specifically basketball and football games." (Carrega, 2019)

Another organization, Everytown, a nonprofit that studies gun violence, according to Carrega's article, reported that there were 99 incidents of gunfire on school grounds in 2019 which included 63 injuries and 3 suicides.

Carrega's article profiles every single example of school violence during 2019. One of the profiles, toward the end of the article, is that of the Thursday, November 14, 2019, murder-suicide by a 16-year-old at Saugus High School in Santa Clarita, California. The shooter took the lives of 15-year-old Gracie Anne Muehlberger and 14-year-old Dominic Blackwell, as well as injuring three others, before committing suicide.

Profile ▪ Patrick Korellis, Survivor of a Mass Shooting at Northern Illinois University

On Valentine's Day, 2008, Patrick Korellis went to his class at Northern Illinois University, located in DeKalb, Illinois, two hours outside of Chicago, as he had done so many days before since that semester began. It was his last semester at NIU. Most of the students in the class were freshmen—it was an Intro Geology class—but Patrick needed a few more elective credits to graduate, so he took that class.

This author became aware of Patrick when doing a Google search on school violence. He had recently been interviewed by a local TV station about the 13th anniversary of the mass shooting that killed 5 of his classmates and wounded 21, including Patrick as well as his professor. The 5 victims were Gayle Dubowski, Julianna Gehant, Catalina Garcia, Ryanne Mace, and Dan Parmenter. (Chicago Tribune Staff, 2008) Patrick shared that he had been interning at that TV station when the shooting occurred. (In the Resources section you will find the listing and link to that interview on WGNTV with the related article, "'Feels Like Yesterday': NIU Mass Shooting Survivor Reflects on 13th Anniversary.'")

Patrick has been working at Walgreen's for the last ten years. He was able to put his dual major in meteorology and geography to use in his job as a weather forecaster including mapping out distribution plans for the COVID-19 vaccination effort.

What follows is an edited transcript of the Zoom interview that this author conducted with Patrick in Soc 4700 (Social Deviance) at Kean University on Tuesday, March 2, 2021.

Patrick: It was on Valentine's Day 2008. I was sitting in my geology class. It's a large lecture hall. I usually sit toward the front a little bit so I can see the professor on the stage and pay better attention.

Survivor Patrick Korellis at a memorial for the victims several years after the tragedy.

That day there was about 15 minutes left of class. All of a sudden, the door gets kicked open. He [the shooter] walks in. He had a long trench coat on. He didn't say a word. He had a shotgun and he started shooting at us.

He kept shooting and shooting. At first we thought it might be related to Valentine's Day.

Then everyone in the class started screaming, hiding.

I got under my desk.

Then he stopped shooting and someone yelled, 'He's reloading,"

There were about 300 seats in there but [that day there were] about 150 in the class. Everyone was trying to escape.

He reloaded his shotgun and he shot again. I felt something on my neck. He kept shooting and shooting. I finally made it outside.

I told the students, "Call 911, call 911. There's a shooter."

As soon as I said that, the police started running toward the building.

I had one shoe on. I left my cell phone.

I was holding my head.

As soon as the police found me, [they asked me to] describe the shooter "if you can." Skin color, hair color. He was white. He had a trench coat on. I think he had a tattoo on his neck.

"We're going to try to get you an ambulance." They're backlogged. They were trying to get around thirty ambulances in one spot.

They got me an ambulance.

When I got to the hospital, I had no idea I had also been shot in my arm. The FBI interviewed me again in the hospital room.

That day was so chaotic. When I got to the hospital, there were so many people there. Twenty-one of us were shot. Five of my classmates were killed.

It's a small college hospital in a rural area two hours outside of Chicago. They were trying to organize from most fatal to least, trying to get a hold of the parents.

The college called my Mother and said, "I don't know if you're aware of the situation at NUI but your son's been shot."

My mom said the two-hour drive to campus took her four hours, so I didn't see my parents till four hours later.

I heard crying in the hospital room next to me. One of my classmates didn't make it.

It was one of the worst days in my life.

I found out that as soon as I had left, he shot all the kids who were hiding under the desk.

I'm happy I was able to make it out of there. I still have the shotgun pellets in my head. Because it's near the nerves, the doctors feel it's better to leave the pellets in there. I still have some shotgun pellets in my arm.

It's now been 13 years. The tenth-year memorial they had a large memorial. When we were at that memorial, everyone got alerts on their phone there was a shooting at Parkland, Florida. Little did we know how tragic that would end up being. [The death toll at the mass shooting at Marjory Stoneman Douglas High School was 17 including students, teachers, and even adults shot outside of the school. (Burch and Mazzei, 2018)]

Since that time, I met people from Parkland. I've met people from the concert in Las Vegas. [The worst mass shooting in U.S. history, 58 were killed and more than 600 injured.]

I'm in this private Facebook group of mass shooting survivors. When a new shooting happens, we give advice, we help. [In a previous phone interview with this author, Patrick noted that the private mass shooting survivor group on Facebook has around 1,000 members now.]

Campus was closed for ten days. I was afraid to go back to school but I wanted to go back and finish. It was really hard. I still had bandages on. People were staring at me because they knew I was one of the victims. People were asking how I'm doing. The media presence on campus was difficult.

Question: What helped?

Patrick: Having that support of people that went through it helped. But going back to that class that first day was difficult. But it wasn't the same classroom. That was [still] a crime scene. It was another room. Seeing my classmates again helped, but some didn't want to come back at all. My friend did make it, thankfully. He was sitting next to me. But he didn't end up going back to the campus. But he did make it.

At that time, you're just thinking about yourself. I thought about my life. My life flashed before my eyes. I didn't even think to look for my friend. Something told me to run for the door as fast as I could.

Who knows what would have happened if I stayed under my desk.

Question: What happened to the shooter?

Patrick: As soon as police came in, he killed himself on the stage. [From what I've read or been told] He was mentally ill. He had gone to the university. On that February day, he just decided to drive back up to the campus. He must have known there would be a lot of us in that classroom at that time. He must of peeked in at some point.

We all got interviewed by the FBI asking if we knew him. They asked to see our phones. The police went to the hotel room where he was staying. They took out his hard drive and phone. He had sent his girlfriend a package with a note that read, "I'll always remember you" A stuffed animal and some things they remembered each other by. [But] His girlfriend said he never had any signs. [But} She did get that package from him [with the note], "I'll always remember you."

He went online and purchased a bunch of ammunitions and weapons. He was in a mental institution two years before but it wasn't documented.

Question: Did any of your friends get killed?

Patrick: That was one of the hardest parts. One of the girls, I had exchanged notes with her a couple of times. She was sitting in my row. She was in the middle. I was on the aisle. Her parents came up to me at the one week memorable and they asked me, "Are you Patrick?" They said, "We're Gail's parents. We heard our daughter was in your row. Did you see her?"

I told them, "All I know is that she was sitting toward the middle so it might of made it harder for her to escape."

I had a little **survivor's guilt**, but you're just thinking about your life and yourself. You can't concentrate on what is going on.

Question: How do you feel now compared to right away or even the ten year anniversary three years ago?

Patrick: Yeah, it's a little better now. It was 13 years ago. Each year gets easier. Of course, around Valentine's day it gets difficult. I reconnect with my classmates. We're in a Facebook group. Together we're planning for the 15 year anniversary in 2023.

What do we want? One really nice thing they did for the 10-year memorial. All the parents asked if the survivors could share with them how they're doing 10 years later. Where are they in their careers? Are they married? What have they accomplished?

For the parents [of the 5 who died], we made a little book for them to show how we're doing and what's going on in our lives.

Of the 21 who survived, there are some who don't even want to talk about it. They just don't want to think about that day. Some are doing a lot better. They've moved on. There was one who completely changed her major. She became a police officer. She had 20 pellets in her face. She has scars where they had to remove the pellets because she couldn't breathe. A police officer carried her out. She got help and she wants to help people.

Question: Do you find people are less aware of your tragedy compared to Parkland or Columbine?

Patrick: Yes. Ours, there was "only" 5 deaths and 21 injuries. Also, social media wasn't as big a thing as it was for Parkland. Columbine had more injuries and deaths.

People ask me about a certain kind of gun. All he had was a shotgun and a couple of handguns. I don't know if he had something like the Las Vegas shooter who injured 600 people, maybe more. If that had gone in the back of my head. It's scary to think about.

Question: When you and I had our phone interview last week you mentioned what happens when the weather's cold.

Patrick: Yes, because there's metal in my head, I feel a sharp pain my neck. The metal gets cold first so I have to wear a scarf or a longer hat to cover that area up.

Question: Did you ever think something like this would happen to you?

Patrick: Virginia Tech happened about ten months before ours. [The Virginia Tech University mass shooting by a student led to 33 deaths. (Hauser and O'Connor, 2007).] I was sitting in my dorm room and I said, "Can you imagine if that ever happened here? This is Northern Illinois University. This isn't happening here."

Ten months later, here I was [and it had happened.]

The survivors from Virginia Tech reached out to us. They invited us to their one-year memorial. It was two months after our shooting. I spoke with injured victims. Ours was a year ago. This is what happened to us. I talked to a girl who was in her French class. She was only one of two survivors in her French class. There were 18 in there. The shooter went into their class and killed a lot of their classmates. They pretended that they were dead.

Question: Why do you think you knew to get out of there and not stay under your desk?

Patrick: Some tried to run out. [I thought] Maybe I could follow them out and escape? The adrenalin in my head was nonstop. I'm just going to follow this group of kids trying to get out.

Question: What was it like at graduation that year?

Patrick: The victims received honorary diplomas. The families came up and accepted their honorary diploma. Some of the injured victims were highlighted. I was only one of two that graduated that year.

Question: Do you suffer from PTSD (Post Traumatic Stress Syndrome)?

Patrick: Yes, I do. Any loud noises. It goes over and over again. It took me a while to watch Fourth of July fireworks. If I hear a car backfiring, I get startled. I'll never forget the smell of gunfire from that day.

Bullying Including Cyberbullying

In the all-day training on cybersecurity, James Gierke, who was then a trainer for NOVA (National Organization of Victim Assistance), in coordination with the LifeLock™, co-organizer of the training, which was offered through John Jay College of Criminal Justice, it was stressed that cybercrimes are really just crimes that previously were occurring in person but those crimes have now been moved to cyberspace or the internet. (Gierke, 2016) So when we talk about bullying we need to keep that in mind—that cyberbullying is bullying moved to the internet. Unfortunately, because of the widespread way that vicious rumors, compromising photographs, or nasty comments can be shared through the internet, cyberbullying has an even more immediate, damaging, and even long-term effect on its victims than the kind of taunting and bullying that has notoriously plagued some teens from the beginning of time.

The CDC (Centers for Disease Control and Prevention) lists three types of bullying; cyberbullying, the fourth type, was added to the list:

- Physical bullying (tripping, pushing, hitting, spitting or, if it becomes more extreme, it could move into the "fighting" category of school violence, discussed below; taking someone's possessions; making rude or mean hand gestures; kicking; pinching)
- Verbal bullying (calling someone names, making fun of someone, giving them an unflattering label, inappropriate sexual comments; threatening to cause harm to the victim and/or a family member or friend)
- Social bullying (spreading rumors about someone, sharing secrets that will embarrass someone; purposefully leaving someone out of an activity; telling others to avoid being friends or associating with someone)
- Cyberbullying (when the bullying moves from being experienced at school, on the playground, at parties, or in any other physical spaces into the internet via social media or even through texting)

According to the National Center for Education Statistics, in 2017 approximately 15 percent of students in grades 9 through 12 reported being electronically bullied in the previous 12 months. But that same study of School Crime Supplement to the National Crime Victimization Survey actually saw a decrease in the percentage of students in the age group of 12 to 18 who reported being bullied at school—from 29 to 20 percent between 2005 and 2017. (NCES, Indicator 10)

The U.S. government began a campaign to educate the public, parents, and educators about the dangers of bullying following a national survey on bullying that was published in 2011. The result was their Stop Bullying Now! Campaign. Associated with that campaign is the informative website https://www.stopbullying.gov/

One of the trends in dealing with bullying is trying to help **bystanders** to become what is called an **upstander**, meaning, getting involved and not just passively watching. As the stopbullying.gov website puts it in their page entitled, "Bystanders to Bullying," "An upstander is someone who takes action when they witness bullying. Even one person's support can make a big difference for someone who is being bullied. When youth who are bullied are defended and supported by their peers, they are less anxious and depressed than those who are not."

Fighting

Fighting can include everyone and everything from classmates at school, friends or acquaintances outside of school, to siblings at home. It includes punching, hitting, With all the attention on mass shootings, it is too easy to forget that fighting happens among teens, and someone can get hurt.

Here are some facts about fighting, according to the CDC and its 1991-2017 High School Youth Risk Behavior Survey:

- In 1991, physical fighting had decreased among high school students from 43 percent reporting being in a physical during the previous year, but 24 percent (1 in 4) still reported that was the case.
- On 2017, males are more likely to be in a physical fight (30%) compared to females (17%).
- The pattern of more males than females reporting about physical fights within the last year was consistent across race, ethnicity, and grade levels.
- As the teens age, fighting becomes less frequent beginning with 9th graders (28%), 10th graders (26%), 11th graders (20%), with the lowest at 18% among 12th graders.

The challenge of teen fighting is that, as you know from reading Chapter 7, "Primary and Secondary Victims of Homicide," and you will discover when you read Chapter 13, "Victims of Assault, Domestic Violence, Stalking, and Elder Abuse," if you intentionally (not accidentally) push someone, and the victim is hurt, the perpetrator could be charged with misdemeanor assault, which might lead to probation, a fine, or possibly jail time, but if that intentional push led to the victim falling down and hitting his head and suffering a serious injury, maybe even brain damage, it could be charged as a serious felony, which could result in prison time, and if the victim dies, it could lead to the charge of **involuntary manslaughter**, sometimes also called **criminally negligent homicide.**

Dr. Rashmi Shetgiri, et al., in their journal article, "Why Adolescents Fight: A Qualitative Study of Youth Perspectives on Fighting and Its Prevention," share the results of their qualitative study of 65 participants in 12 focus groups who were between the ages of 13 to 17 years of age. The respondents were all from one urban area. They were motivated to conduct their extensive study because "one in three high-school students is involved in a fight annually."

Perhaps the most unsettling result of this study is that 79 percent of the fighters hurt someone badly enough that the victim needed medical care; 83 percent had been threatened by somebody; over half had threatened someone; and almost one-third had carried a weapon and warned someone with a weapon. (Shetgiri, et al.)

What they discovered by comparing the students who were self-reported fighters versus non-fighters was that the fighters had been exposed to violence in their homes. They were getting mixed messages from their parents about whether fighting was acceptable or not. One fighter shared with the researchers that his uncle had told him, "'You can fight, but don't get into a habit of fighting.'" The researchers state: "Fighters frequently stated that parents and other family members encouraged fighting to maintain respect and modeled fighting behavior."

The reasons they shared for fighting included:

- Self-defense
- To gain/maintain respect
- Due to anger

By contrast, the non-fighters had learned to avoid fighting by:

- Ignoring insults
- Walking away
- Resolving differences by talking
- Avoiding students who fight
- Ignoring rumors and instigators of fighting

A female non-fighter shared that the parents of the fighters never went to school functions or got involved in anything at school. She used that as a possible explanation as to why the fighters fought.

One of the conclusions of the study is that strategies to reduce fighting by high school students may require educating parents as much as teaching fighters to find nonviolent and alternative ways to deal with conflicts.

Gang Violence

According to the FBI (Federal Bureau of Investigation) in their "Gangs" information at their website, there are an estimated 33,000 violent street gangs, motorcycle gangs, and prison gangs that are what they refer to as "criminally active" in the United States today. It is important to address **gang violence** in a chapter on Teen Victims because too many teens are victims of gang violence.

In the information sheets, "Parent's Guide to Gangs," developed by the Office of Juvenile Justice and Delinquency prevention, it is stated that the average age to join a gang is 15 but that youths as young as 12 to 14 are recruited. In 2018, according to the *2018 FBI Crime in the United States* UCR report, there were 308 juvenile gang killings. But that was only the reported ones.

Changes that a parent should look for as signs that their child has joined a gang are detailed in Box 11.1.

Box 11.1. Common Gang Identifiers for Parents (and Teachers)

- Colors—some gangs avoid colors so the police cannot identify them. Others still use a color on bandanas, shirts, belts, shoes, hair bands, and jewelry.
- Symbols and numbers—stars, crowns, pitchforks, three dots in a triangle, and numbers.
- Clothing and apparel.
- Graffiti—used to mark their territory.
- Social media—may be using major social media sites to share about gang activities and post threats and taunts.
- Gang-influenced music and movies—Gangsta/gangster rap—lyrics glorifying street-gang culture.
- Sports items—may be altered to match the gang colors.
- Tattoos—may be found on the hands, neck, face, chest, back, or arms.
- Hand signs—these gestures may be known as "throwing up" or "stacking."
- Withdrawing from family activities and planned events.
- Changed academic performance or declining school attendance.
- Defiant or confrontational behavior.
- Staying out late without reason.
- Unusual desire for secrecy.
- Angry outbursts, excessive aggression.
- Excessive worry about safety, constantly surveying surroundings for danger.
- Sudden negative attitudes about law enforcement or adults in positions of authority (school officials or teachers).
- Change in attitude about school, church, or other normal activities or change in behavior when attending these activities.
- Drastic changes in personal style.
- Withdrawal from longtime friends and forming bonds with an entirely new group-of friends.
- Suspected use of drugs, such as alcohol, inhalants, and narcotics.
- Possession of firearms, ammunitions, or other weapons.
- Nonaccidental physical injuries (such as evidence of being beaten or injuries to hands and knuckles from fighting).
- Unexplained cash or goods, such as clothing, video games, or jewelry.

Source: OJJDP, "Parent's Guide to Gangs," page 3.

STATUS OFFENSES

A **status offense** is an action or behavior that is unlawful or even criminal when committed by a certain group of people, such as minors. An action that is a status offense when committed by a teen would not be a crime if an adult did it. Although status offenses are determined on a state by state basis, here are the typical status offenses that teens have to be aware of:

- Running away
- Truancy

- Defying parents
- Lying
- Violating curfew
- Underage drinking

Why are status offenses so important to understand? Because, unfortunately, being arrested for a status offense may start some teens on the road to delinquency. Although some teens may get a warning, or even probation or community service for being charged with a status offense, some are sent to a reformatory or juvenile prison. Even if their record is wiped clean when they reach 18 or 21, they may have met up with individuals who will have a negative influence on them, they may have missed out on regular school, and they may also begin to see themselves as criminals. Family, friends, and classmates may start to label them as delinquents as well.

Teens runaway for a whole long list of reasons and it might be better to figure out what the teen was running from, and to help him or her resolve those issues. A teen can be arrested for running away but should he or she? Unfortunately, many runaways end up homeless or even becoming victims of human trafficking, as discussed in Chapter 13, "Victims of Assault, Domestic Violence, Stalking, and Elder Abuse" and in Chapter 15, on human trafficking. There are many hotlines for runaways that will help the runaway to make contact with their parents even if they do not want to return home so they can at least have a line of communication and possibly some assistance.

All the other status offenses listed above are, technically, crimes if someone underage is caught committing these offenses. But should these situations be handled by law enforcement or by social workers?

ADDITIONAL TEEN VICTIMS

Murder and Attempted Murder

Out of the 14,123 murder victims in the United States in 2018, 1,126 were under 18 years of age. In Table 11.2 you will see the number of reported homicide victims for teens, ages 13-16 and ages 17-19. In the next Table 11.3, you will see the type of weapons that were used.

TABLE 11.2. Reported Teen Murder Victims in the United States for 2018

Total victims: 14,123	
13-16 years of age	319
17-19 years of age	1,107

Source: 2018 Crime in the United States (FBI), Expanded Homicide Data Table 9.

TABLE 11.3. Reported Teen Murder Victims by Type of Weapon Used

Age	Firearms	Knives	Personal Weapons (hands, fists, feet)	Other Weapon (not stated)
13-16	269	24	7	15
17-19	972	66	6	39

Source: 2018 Crime in the United States (FBI), Expanded Homicide Data Table 9.

For these same age groups, in Table 11.4, you will discover the gender, race, and ethnicity of the murder victims in the United States in 2018. As you will see, there are disproportionately more male murder victims than female, and more Black or African American murder victims than white victims. In 2018, the estimated percentage of Americans who were Black or African American was 12.3 percent. The number of murder victims between the ages of 13 and 19—teen murder victims—was 483 white and 898 Black or African American murder victims. If those numbers were true to the actual percentage of Blacks or African Americans in the United States, there should have been a lot fewer Black or African American murder victims.

TABLE 11.4. 2018 Teen Murder Victims by Gender, Race, and Ethnicity

Age	Gender	Race	Ethnicity
13-16	Male–238 Female–81	White–119 Black–186 Other–11 Unknown–3	Hispanic–64 Non-Hispanic–207 Unknown–32
17-19	Male–948 Female–159	White–364 Black–712 Other–21 Unknown–10	Hispanic–199 Non-Hispanic–709 Unknown–124

Source: FBI, *2018 Crime in the United States*. Expanded Homicide Data, Table 2. Murder Victims by Age, Sex, Race, and Ethnicity, 2018.

Pedro Garcia Jr., at 17, was a murder victim. According to Joe Kovac Jr.'s article about his murder, he had just finished his shift at a fast food restaurant where he worked as a cook. From what the police could piece together about what happened, Pedro had confronted another 17-year-old who was trying to steal someone's bicycle. That teenager shot and killed Pedro, allegedly over the theft of Pedro's gold chain that he was wearing. Pedro died on the night of September 17, 2018. He was the 42d homicide in Bibb County, Georgia that year. Pedro's mother, Brenda, was interviewed two years later. She shared in the interview that Kovac wrote up in his article that when the police knocked on her door, she did not believe them when they told her that her son was dead. Just two years before, she had also lost her brother to murder.

Pedro's mother was quoted as saying, "I can't speak for other parents that have lost their kids, but you never get over it . . . . I miss him . . . . If it wasn't for my other kids, my young daughter, my grandbaby, who knows? They're the ones that motivate me to keep going." (Kovac, 2020)

What makes the murder and attempted murder of teenagers so especially heartbreaking is that they have their whole lives ahead of them. Pedro was working and going to school. He was not in a gang. He was not dealing drugs. He was killed when he was acting as a **Good Samaritan**, trying to stop someone from stealing a bicycle. It was believed that he was killed for the gold necklace he was wearing. (Kovac, 2020)

Robbery

Teens who are ages 13 to 19 are unfortunately targets for robbery because they are starting to have more independence, walking alone from bus stops, to and from school, or even from their cars in parking lots, and having on them the disposable higher-priced electronics, such as cell phones, that are in such demand by thieves. Although newer technology, such as fingerprint and face identification, may be making it more difficult to sell a stolen phone to a **fence** (who will receive the stolen goods) to make the robbery lucrative, teens are still carrying wallets with cash, rather than credit cards, or selling expensive shoes, like the $400 designer running shoes that a teen had stolen during what was supposed to have been a sale in a public parking lot through a buyer "met" through an online social media site.

Without reporting a robbery to the police, there is no chance that they are able to help find the stolen item. There are other reasons teen victims do not want to report to the police such as fear of retaliation, especially if the victim knows who stole their items. If the teen is involved in any criminal activities at the time of the robbery, such as drug dealing, there would be a reluctance to report the robbery.

As you know from reading the robbery chapter, out of the tens of thousands of robberies that occur in the United States each year, the vast majority do not result in a robbery homicide although some statistics report as many as 50 percent resulting in injury. However, in 2018, there were 548 robbery homicide victims in all age groups so robbery is definitely a serious, violent, property crime. (FBI, 2019)

Victims of Other Property Crimes Including Burglary and Larceny-Theft

Teens have to be careful about revealing too much personal information on social media that might set them and their families up for a burglary. If a teen reveals he or she is going on a family vacation and that his/her apartment or home will be unattended, that could make his/her family a more likely target. If teens have a party at their home, they have to be careful about their friends bringing their friends or acquaintances along who could be "casing" the residence for a possible future burglary.

Since most burglaries occur when no one is home, or the office is empty, there are fewer injuries or burglary homicides. The rare instances when that does occur it is because of what is sometimes called the "**burglar surprise.**" That is when a burglar, assuming a location is empty, has one or more family members or employees in the place they were burglarizing. One college student who witnessed a burglar climbing in his bedroom window and stealing his stereo pretended he was asleep as the burglar went out the bedroom door and out of the apartment. In that situation, there was no time to rush away from the assailant. But in the active shooter training that this author participated in, the expert advised against playing dead or (asleep as a related tactic). It was recommended that a better strategy was to get away from the criminal, as fast as possible.

Larceny-theft includes taking property without force such as stealing an unattended bicycle, purse-snatching, shoplifting, pocket-picking; the theft is not done in a violent way nor is it done through fraud. Teenagers need to be careful about leaving their possessions sitting on a table while they stand on a long line to get their lunch in the high school or college cafeteria, for example. Studying the annual FBI statistics for reported crimes emphasizes how frequently larceny theft occurs, and that is only the reported ones. In 2019, there were 5,086,096 larceny-thefts in the United States. (FBI, 2019, Table 2)

Check out Chapter 8, "Property Crime Victims", and Chapter 9, "Cybercrime, White-Collar Crime, and Economic Crime Victims," for information about property crime victimizations.

CRIME ON CAMPUS

We owe a debt of gratitude to those who made what is known as the Clery Act happen. Before this act, how much crime there were on college campuses was much harder to discover. The Clery Act is named after Jeanne Clery, a college student who was raped and murdered in her dormitory room by another student on April 5, 1986. In her memory, her parents became advocates for what became known as the Jeanne Clery Disclosure of Campus Security Policy and Crime Statistics Act, which is known by the shortened name, The Clery Act. This federal law, passed in 1990, requires that colleges report what crimes occur on campus as well as what are their school safety policies. In 2013, the Clery Act was expanded by the Campus Sexual Violence Elimination (SaVE) Act, broadening the Clery requirements to consider all incidents of sexual violence including stalking, dating, violence, domestic violence, or sexual assault.

Rape and Sexual Assault on Campus

Although it may seem like the topic of campus rape is a relatively new concern, as far back as the 1950s, E.J. Kanin and C. Kirkpatrick was studying the phenomenon as reported in "Male Sex Aggression on a College Campus," in 1957. Koss and colleagues drew attention to the problem in the 1980s through studies and publications including "The Scope of Rape: Incidence and Prevalence of Sexual Aggression and Victimization in a National Sample of Higher Education Students." According to Ann Burgess, it was Koss who coined the term *date rape* in 1987. Here are the three situational risk factors for college rape that Koss and her colleagues identified that are still true today:

1. A college culture of excessive drinking;
2. Male peer pressure to "prove one's sexual prowess;" and
3. "Men's own attitudes favoring impersonal sex" (Burgess, 2019; 399, referencing Kamenetz, 2014)

Picture of one of the numerous #MeToo movement signs that became so popular to display in solidarity with victims and survivors.

In 1992, the federal Campus Sexual Assault Victims' Bill of Rights was passed which issued guidelines for colleges and universities about how to deal with rape and sexual assault grievances. Fortunately the #metoo movement has led to increased awareness among all populations, including those in college, that rape is an unacceptable crime and that "No means No." Lisa Fedina, et al. in "How Prevalent Is Campus Sexual Assault in the United States?" point out the difficulty in getting an accurate assessment of just how often rape does occur. Examining 15 years of rape research in this issue, from January 2000 through February 2015, the researchers had these general conclusions:

1. There is a "high prevalence of unwanted sexual contact and sexual coercion."
2. There was a disproportionate number of victims who were LGBTQ (gay, bisexual, transgender, queer/questioning), disabled, and race and ethnicity minorities leading them to suggest there is a "need for responses that are inclusive and culturally specific."
3. Standardized definitions are needed so everyone is addressing the same victimization including "forcible rape," "incapacitated rape," and "drug or alcohol facilitated rape." (Fedina, et al., 2016)

Although it may be challenging to have an exact number of rape victims on campuses because of reporting and other issues, the statistic from the early 2000s based on a sample of 5,446 undergraduate women is something to consider. That Campus Sexual Assault Study, sponsored by the National Institute of Justice, found that "almost 20 percent of undergraduate women had experienced an attempted or a completed sexual assault since entering college" (Burgess, 2019, citing Krebs, et al.) Of course considerations include what is defined as sexual assault, what percentage were attempted versus completed rapes, and since they only surveyed women the percentage of sexual assaults on all students would probably be higher. But clearly having a statistic of 1 out of every 5 college students out of those 5,446 students surveyed as a sexual assault victim is a sobering number that needs to be dramatically reduced.

Sexual violence including rape or assault are key concerns on college campuses. The American College Health Association large-scale college student survey determined that 7.3 percent of females reported experiencing sexual assault in the previous 12 months. (Eisenberg, et al., 2016; American College Health Association, 2012)

According to knowyourix.org, a nonprofit organization founded in 2013, a project of Advocates for Youth, to share information about Title IX and the Clery Act, The Clery Act makes it possible to find out college crime statistics. Crimes that are included are reported victimizations of sexual assaultstalking, intimidation, dating violence, domestic violence, sexual assault, and hate crimes. Although the Clery Act requires that colleges and universities record the date of the report, the date of the crime, and the general location, it does not require the college or university to start an investigation. It also prohibits sharing the identity of the victim. (knowyourix.org, n.d.)

In Chapter 15, you will find a discussion about LGBTQ of all ages, including teens, and the unique challenges those in the LGBTQ community face including their increasing risk of victimization.

Hazing

A uniquely college "tradition" that many consider cruel and unacceptable, and that enters into the category of a crime when someone is injured or dies because of it, is the fraternity or sorority ritual known as **hazing.** Hazing expert Hank Nuwer, a professor at Franklin College in Indiana and the author of four books on the subject, according to the *New York Times* article by Michael Winerip, "When Hazing Goes Very Wrong," estimates that 80 percent of hazing deaths involve alcohol. (Winerip, 2012)

Here is what Arkansas State University advises students about hazing on their website:

> According to Arkansas State Law § 6-5-203, Penalties:
>
> (a) The offense of hazing is a Class B misdemeanor.
>
> (b) Upon conviction of any student of the offense of hazing, he shall, in addition to any punishment imposed by the court, be expelled from the school, college, university, or other educational institution he is attending.

Examples of hazing. Hazing can be subtle, harassing, or violent in nature. It can manifest itself in the form of physical violence, forced physical activities, or psychological and/or emotional harm, which can be violations of law. Although it is impossible to list all possible hazing behaviors because many are context-specific, examples of hazing include everything from requiring fraternity or sorority pledges to perform actions that might be considered silly or harmless pranks to dangerous activities, ending in a fatality. Kasey Varner points out that some of those harmless hazing rituals may include girls not shaving their legs for a week or boys wearing ridiculous costumes to parties. (Varner, 2011; updated 2019)

Unfortunately, there are too many instances when hazing goes horribly wrong, usually involving excessive consumption of alcohol, with fatal consequences. Here are just some of the many examples of hazing deaths:

- George Desdunes, a college sophomore, died in February 2011. (Winerip, 2012)
- Antonio Tomasello, an 18-year-old freshman from Miami, died in October 2019 from a fatal fall after a hazing ritual. Complete details about what happened are still being pursued by Antonio's distraught parents. (Nicolas Bogel-Burroughs, 2021)
- Adam Oakes, a 19-year-old freshman, of Sterling, Virginia, was found dead at an off-campus party which Adam's cousin told the media was a hazing party. (Hauser, 2021)
- Robert Champion, a university drum major, was "beaten to death in November [2012] in a hazing on the band bus." (Winerip, 2012; Montgomery, 2012)

TEENAGERS AND COLLEGE STUDENTS AND DRIVING-RELATED ISSUES

Distracted Driving Including Texting

One of the most preventable victimizations are car accidents caused by distracted driving as well as driving under the influence as well as new driver issues. The National Highway Transportation and Safety Administration (NHTSA) shares these startling statistics:

- 2,841 lives were lost to distracted driving in just 2018.
- 1,730 of those victims were drivers.
- 605 were passengers.
- 400 were pedestrians.
- 77 were bicyclists.

Sending, or receiving, a text while driving is something teens and college students unfortunately are tempted to do and the consequences can be deadly, to the driver, to their passengers, and to those who are hit from the crashes and injured or killed. The NHTSA points out that in a car that is traveling at 55 mph, taking your eyes off the road to read or send a text for 5 seconds, is like "driving the length of an entire football field with your eyes closed." (NHTSA, "Distracted Driving")

Getting the message out that no one should text while driving (TWD) is literally a life and death matter. Of the 36,560 people who died in car accidents in the United States in 2018, distracted driving was the cause of 2,841 of those deaths. (Tamul, et.al., 2021.)

Liberty Mutual insurance company has excellent information at their website about driving measures that help increase safety. (libertymutual.com) So does Edgar Synder & Associates, a law office with offices in Pittsburgh and four other cities in Pennsylvania. In their website blog, "Teen Driver Car Accident Statistics," there is a wealth of information about the challenges that are unique to teenage drivers. (See Cited Works for the link.)

An important idea to get across is that teens should not text—reading or sending a text —even if it is to a parent. Every teen or college student needs a "no texting while driving" policy without any exceptions.

Drowsy Driving

Teens and college students need 8 to 10 hours of sleep a night. More than adults. The combination of a teen driver and exhaustion can be lethal. There is a case from a few years ago that is particularly telling. Several youths had gone out for a fun night and they had a designated driver so they did not have to worry about the driving hazards of drinking and driving or the potential legal complications. When they got pulled over by the police, even though they smelled alcohol in the car from the inebriated passengers, they were fine because the driver had not had a drop to drink. He was, indeed, the designated driver.

Unfortunately, later that night, in the wee hours of the morning, the car crashed. The designated driver was killed and at least one other passenger. The others were injured. What they seemed to think must have happened is that the designated driver fell asleep at the wheel.

There is not enough discussion with teens or public awareness about the dangers of driving without enough sleep. Teens are told not to drink and drive. They need to be reminded that you need to also be completely alert when you drive.

Driving under the Influence—Alcohol or Drugs

In an article published by the Insurance Institute for Highway Safety and the Highway Loss Data Institute, it was revealed that there was a lower awareness of the dangers of driving under the influence of marijuana versus driving under the influence of alcohol. Those statistics were 88 percent of the 2,800 high school students surveyed believed alcohol-impaired driving was wrong compared to only 68 percent of teens who noted that about marijuana. There were similar trends with the 1,000 parents surveyed. Ninety-three percent agreed alcohol-impaired driving was dangerous but only 76 percent of the parents said driving under the influence of marijuana was risky. (IIHS and HLDI, 2017)

Drinking alcohol, smoking marijuana, even taking some prescription drugs can impair driving which can lead to crashes that injure or kill the driver, their passengers, or pedestrians or cyclists or other drivers and passengers in other cars.

If a teen gets arrested for driving under the influence it can have severe consequences to him and to his family who may be paying his car insurance, which will escalate in monthly premiums because of the conviction, as well as paying his or her legal fees. Penalties for driving under the influence, where there was no accident or harm to a second party or car, or even a passenger, can still be quite severe. This will differ depending upon the state the offense occurred in and it depends on how much over the legal limit the teen was at the time he or she was tested and what the rules are in that state. For the same offense, in one state, someone could receive jail time, plus a suspended license, plus fines, plus paying the cost of the court proceedings. Someone else might get a suspended license for six months, a mandatory drug education course, and payment of court fees. But the harm to passengers, other drivers or pedestrians, if there is an accident, is the greatest concern. They are the innocent victims.

Graduated Driving

When a teen gets his or her license, it is a very exciting time. Teens want to give their friends and siblings lifts to anywhere they want to go. Research has shown that this is actually the worst thing that a teen can do. The better thing to do is what has come to be called a **graduated driving** process. Each community or state has its own version of this. For some, it means that for the first 6 months, the new driver can only drive with another related experienced driver over the age of 21. Some allow the new driver to drive a family member, including a sibling, but not someone unrelated to him or her. After 6, 9, or 12 months of driving without a ticket or an accident, the restrictions are lifted and having one or more peers in the car with the teen becomes permissible. A graduating driving program might consider limiting driving at night during the first few months after getting a license. The AAA Foundation for Traffic Safety notes that if a teen driver has other teen passengers in his or her car, the chance of a crash increases by 51 percent. (AAA Foundation for Traffic Safety, 2018)

As the CDC (Center for Disease Control and Prevention) points out, the biggest risk factors for teen drivers are:

- Inexperience (crash risk is highest during the first months after getting the license).
- Driving at night especially for less experienced drivers is linked to a greater likelihood of crashes than during the day (In 2017, 40 percent of car crashes for teen drivers and passengers aged 13-19 occurred between 9 P.M. and 6 A.M.).

- Failing to use a seat belt.
- Any amount of alcohol use.
- Speeding.
- Nighttime driving. (CDC, 2019)

SUBSTANCE ABUSE

At the beginning of this chapter, you learned about Johnny Stack, a 19-year-old who died by suicide; at the time he had developed an addiction to high-potency marijuana. He started using marijuana when he was 14. Middle school and the pre-teen years are a challenging time for almost all youths. So are the high school and college years. Peer pressure can make it hard to resist using drugs, drinking alcohol, even though it is not legal in the United States till 21. Smoking cigarettes, as well as taking prescription medications can have a dramatic impact on a teen's personality, ability to concentrate and even drive a car.

In his textbook, *Social Problems: A Down-to-Earth Approach*, sociologist James M. Henslin shares some intriguing statistics about the prevalence of alcohol consumption in high school Based on several studies including a national survey from 1975-2017 and a University of Michigan study on alcohol consumption, of the 44,000 students who were asked, "Have you drunk alcohol (beer, wine, whiskey, etc.) in the past month? 33 percent of the high school seniors answered *yes* followed by 20 percent of the 10th graders and 8 percent of the 8th graders. Nineteen percent stated in the affirmative that they had been drunk in the past month followed by 9 percent of the 10th graders and 2 percent of the 8th graders. (Henslin, 2020: 93)

Here is what Henslin found out about the smoking of marijuana in the last 30 days for 8th graders, 10th graders, high school seniors, and college students. Based on that same national survey from 1975-2017 and the University of Michigan research, mentioned above, more high school seniors had smoked marijuana in the previous 30 days (22.9%) than college students (22.2%), but not by much. Tenth graders reported 15.7 percent had smoked marijuana in the past 30 days and 5.5% of the 8th graders surveyed answered affirmatively. (Henslin, 2020:95)

In Chapter 15, "Additional Victim situations or Populations," there will be a further discussion of alcohol and drug use.

SUMMARY

Teens and college students are unique populations because they have more independence and maturity but that also opens them up to more potential dangers to become victims. Furthermore, researchers tell us that their brains, including their ability to have impulse control, will not be fully developed until their mid-twenties.

Teens fall victim to all the crimes that adults face including the violent crimes of murder, attempted murder, aggravated assault, and robbery, as well as property crimes including burglary, larceny/theft, and motor vehicle theft. Females are more likely to be raped and sexually abused than males but male teens are also sexual assault victims. Male teens are more likely to be murder victims with Black or African American male teens the group with the highest number of victims in the United States, a number that is disproportionate to their percentage of the population.

Rape and sexual assault are crimes that teens and college students have to be concerned about although it is more likely the perpetrator will be someone known to the victim (90%+) than a stranger (7%). Those situations are referred to as Acquaintance Rape or Date Rape.

Dating violence, especially after a breakup, is a particular concern for teens and college students. For example, Daira Hodges was stabbed by her ex-boyfriend and left for dead when they were in junior high school. Fortunately she survived.

School violence, including the risk of mass shootings as well as bullying, fighting, and gang violence, are other important issues for teens and college students. Mass shootings have occurred far too often in the United States, beginning with the infamous University of Texas at Austin Tower shootings back in 1966 up to the more recent Valentine's Day shooting in 2018 that killed 14 students and three staff at Marjory Stoneman High School in Parkland, Florida.

Violations that are treated like crimes that are unique to teens are the so-called status offenses including being a runaway, violating curfew, truancy, underage drinking, and defying parents. That is because these acts, if committed by an adult, would not be considered crimes.

There is a wide disparity in how status offenses are handled. Some jurisdictions arrest and lock up teens; others have the situations dealt with by social workers.

Another act that is unique to teens is the crime of statutory rape. That is when a male or female below the age of consent in that state has sexual relations. Some states have a "close in age exemption" so that if the underage teen is within four years of the age of the sexual partner, it will be dealt with differently than if it is a 14-year-old having sex with a 30-year-old. Technically statutory rape cannot be consensual even if the underage teen gives consent because she or he is under the legal age of consent.

Such acts as driving under the influence, drowsy driving, distracted driving, especially because of texting while driving (TWD), are other concerns regarding teens and college students. Of the 36,500 people who were killed in car accidents in the United States in 2018, distracted driving was considered the cause in 2,841 of those fatalities. Also, the more teens that a new teen driver has in his or her car, the more dangerous it is, increasing the likelihood of an accident with injuries or fatalities. Graduated driving options seem to help teens get the experience they need at driving in a safer way by systematically removing restrictions as the driver gains experience and confidence.

KEY TERMS

bullying
bystander
club drugs
criminally negligent homicide
date rape
date rape drugs
fence
first degree manslaughter
gang violence
Good Samaritan
graduated driving
hazing
involuntary manslaughter
plea deal
rape kit
second injury
sexual assault
statutory rape
status offense
stranger rape
survivor's guilt
upstander

REVIEW QUESTIONS

1. Why might acquaintance rape or date rape be considered differently by teens, their peers, or the authorities than stranger rape?
2. Who is the most likely perpetrator in the rape of a teen: a stranger or someone known to the victim?
3. What teen age group is most likely to be a victim of murder by the type of weapon used?
4. What are the main types of school violence?
5. Why is physically fighting so dangerous?
6. What gender is the most likely teen homicide victim?
7. What race is the most likely teen homicide victim?
8. What are the items most likely to be stolen from teens during a robbery?
9. What is a status offense?
10. What is drowsy driving so dangerous?
11. What is a good solution to dealing with the likelihood that a less experienced newly-licensed teen driver may have an increased chance of crashes?

CRITICAL THINKING QUESTIONS

1. What are the negative consequences to the teen, his or her family, the school, and the community, of arresting teens for status offenses like truancy and running away? What are alternative ways to handle these situations?

2. If teens at the age of 18 are allowed to join the military and fight for their country, vote for their government officially, and drive a car, should they also be allowed to legally smoke cigarettes if they choose (even though cigarettes are unhealthy), and drink alcohol (if they can do it in a responsible way)?

3. Some schools and colleges are offering Active Shooter trainings. Should it be mandatory? Why? Why not?

4. Should there be agreement as to what a youthful offender is regardless of the crime? If a 15-year-old commits murder, should he be tried "as an adult" even if he is 15?

ACTIVITIES

1. Divide into pairs. One person will be the teen. The other person will be the passenger in the car. The teen is the driver and wants to text while driving. How can the passenger handle the situation? You have 5-7 minutes to discuss this. At the end of the time, switch roles. Then come back together as a class to discuss what you came up with as strategies to deal with this issue.

2. Pick one of the school mass shootings that you have read about in this chapter. Do additional research about the shooting. What did you learn about the victims? What did you

learn about the perpetrator? Is there anything that can be done to prevent situations like this from happening again based on what you have learned about this particular tragedy?

3. Think back to your own earlier teen years, between 13 and 16, 17, or 18. What did you learn about in this chapter that makes you rethink some of the things you did or said during those years? In high school, did you ever witness someone being bullied? If you did, would the concept of going from bystander to upstander have helped you deal with it differently? Did you know anyone who was a crime victim during your middle or high school years?

RESOURCES

Jennifer Ann's Group
Jenniferann.org
Started by Drew Crecente in 2005 soon after his 18-year-old daughter Jennifer was shot and killed by her ex-boyfriend. The nonprofit is dedicated to educating teens, their parents, and teachers about the warning signs of dating violence. Offers related videogames and banners.

National Center for Victims of Crime
ncvc.org

National Crime Prevention Council (NCPC)
ncpc.org
Information clearinghouse

National Dating Abuse Helpline and Love is Respect
1-866-331-9474
Text 77054
loveisrespect.org
Offers information and referrals.

National Domestic Violence Hotline
thehotline.org
Call – 1-800-799-7233
Text – LOVEIS to 1-866-3331-9474

National Institute on Drug Abuse (NIDA), National Institute on Drug Abuse for Teens
teens.drugabuse.gov
Offers information on the effects of drugs on the teen brain.

National Organization for Victim Assistance (NOVA)
trynova.org
Provides victim-related information as well as training for victim advocates.

National Sexual Violence Resource Center (NSVRC)
nsvrc.org

The Trevor Project
thetrevorproject.org
Information related to discrimination or hate crimes against those in the LGBTQ community.

CITED WORKS AND ADDITIONAL REFERENCES

AAA Foundation for Traffic Safety. 2018. "Deadly Combination: Teen Driver and Teen Passenger in Vehicle Increases Risk of Death in a Crash by 51 Percent for Everyone Involved." Press release. Posted at https://newsroom.aaa.com/2018/10/deadly-combination-teen-driver-and-teen-passenger-in-vehicle-increases-risk-of-death-in-a-crash-by-51-percent-for-everyone-involved/#:~:text=New%20research%20from%20the%20AAA,a%20crash%20increased%2051%20percent.

Ageofconsent.com. "Close in Age Exemptions/Romeo and Juliet Laws." Posted at https://www.ageofconsent.net/close-in-age-exemptions

______________. "Legal Age of Consent by Country." Posted at https://www.ageofconsent.net/world

American College Health Association. Spring 2012. "American College Health Association-National College Health Assessment II: Reference Group Data Reporting." Hanover, MD.

Associated Press. April 29, 1999. "Teen Shoots 2, Kills 1 at Canadian School." *The Advocate*. Stamford, CT: A8.

Bacon, John. April 3, 2019. "First Jail Terms Issued in Penn State Fraternity Hazing Death of Timothy Piazza." *USA Today*. Posted at usatoday.com

Ballantine, Margaret and Lynn Soine. November-December 2010. "Sibling Sexual Abuse—Uncovering the Secret." *Social Work Today*. 12(6): 18.

Bank, Stephen P. and Michael D. Kahn. 1982. *The Sibling Bond*. New York: Basic Books.

BBC.com. June 6, 2019. "Why Dutch Teenager Noa's Tragic Death Was Misunderstood." Posted BBC.com.

Becker, Howard S. 1973. *The Outsiders*. New York: Macmillan.

Berest, Joseph. August 1968. "Medico-Legal Aspects of Incest." *Journal of Sex Research*. 4(3): 195-205.

Blos, Peter. 1962. *On Adolescence: A Psychoanalytic Interpretation*. New York: Free Press.

Bogel-Burroughs, Nicholas. March 13, 2021. "A Drunk Hazing, a Fatal Fall and a Cornell Fraternity's Silence." *New York Times*. Posted online at nytimes.com

Bok, Sissela. 1984. *Secrets*. New York: Vintage.

Booher, Dianna Daniels. 1991. *Rape: What Would You Do If . . .?* Revised edition. New York: Julian Messner.

Boynton Health Service. 2012. "2012 College Student Health Survey Report: Health and Health-Related Behaviors." University of Minnesota-Twin Cities Students. Minneapolis, MN: University of Minnesota.

Burch, Audra D.S. and Patricia Mazzei. February 14, 2018. "Death Toll Is at 17 and Could Rise in Florida School Shooting." *New York Times*. Posted at nytimes.com

Burgess, Ann Wolbert. 2019. *Victimology: Theories and Applications*. Third edition. Burlington, MA: Jones & Barlett.

Carrega, Christina. December 13, 2019. "School Shootings Are More Common Than You Think: A Look at the Incidents That Went Under the Radar in 2019." ABCNews.com.

CDC (Centers for Disease Control and Prevention). Last reviewed October 23, 2018. Stopbullying.com "Bystanders to Bullying." Posted at https://www.stopbullying.gov/prevention/bystanders-to-bullying

CDC (Centers for Disease Control and Prevention). Reviewed October 30, 2019. "Teen Drivers: Get the Facts." Posted at https://www.cdc.gov/motorvehiclesafety/teen_drivers/teendrivers_factsheet.html

______________. June 27, 2019. "Preventing School Violence." *Violence Prevention*. 2-page fact sheet. Posted at https://www.cdc.gov/violenceprevention/youthviolence/schoolviolence/fastfact.html

______________. March 5, 2021. "Preventing Teen Dating Violence." Posted at the CDC website.

______________. "Sexual Violence in Youth." National Center for Injury Preventions and Control, Division of Violence Prevention.

Chicago Tribune Staff. February 14, 2009. "These Are the Stories of the Victims of the 2008 Shooting at Northern Illinois University." Posted at chicagotribune.com

Child Trends. 2019. "Teen Homicide, Suicide and Firearm Deaths." Retrieved from https://www.childtrends.org/indicators/teen-homicide-suicide-and-firearm-deaths.

Chiu, Alexis (Associated Press). April 29, 1999. "'Sense of Invincibility' Evaporates at Schools." *The Advocate*. Stamford, CT: A8.

Cloward, Richard and Lloyd Ohlin. 1960. *Delinquency and Opportunity*. New York: Free Press.

Cohen, Albert K. 1955. *Delinquent Boys: The Culture of the Gang*. New York: Free Press.

Claiborne, William. May 22, 1998. "Youth Jailed in Oregon School Rampage." *Washington Post*. A01.

CNN.com. September 27, 2006. "Gunman, Hostage Dead after High School Siege."

Crane-Newman, Molly. September 10, 2019. "Bronx Teen Gets 14 Years in Fatal Classroom Stabbing of Fellow Student." *New York Daily News.*

Dianis, Charles. April 29, 1999. "Student Arrested in Bomb Threat at McMahon High School in Norwalk." *The Advocate.* Stamford, CT: A8.

Dickey, Fred. May 10, 2013. "Column: Killer Recounts Santana High Shooting." *San Diego Tribune.*

Dingfelder, Sadie F. March 2010. "Ending an Epidemic." American Psychological Association, *Monitor.* Posted at apa.org.

Earley, Pete. May 14, 2006. "Slain Detective Helped My Son When the System Wouldn't." *The Advocate.* Stamford, CT: A17.

Eisenberg, Marla E., Katherin A. Lust, Peter J. Hannan, and Carolyn Porta. 2016. "Campus Sexual Violence Resources and Emotional Health of College Women Who Have Experienced Sexual Assault." *Violence and Victims.* 31: 274-284.

Espinola, Maria F. 2013. "Teen Victims of Domestic Abuse." *Encyclopedia of Domestic Violence and Abuse.* Laura L. Finley (ed.). 2(ABC-CLIO): 491-495.

Favero, Marisalva, Sofia Correia Pinto, Amaia Del Campo, Diana Moreira, and Valeria Sousa-Gomes. July 2020. "Power Dress in Black: A Comprehensive Review on Academic Hazing." *Aggression and Violent Behavior.* Published online.

Federal Bureau of Investigation (FBI). *2018 Crime in the United States.* Annual report. Posted at https://ucr.fbi.gov/crime-in-the-u.s/2018/crime-in-the-u.s.-2018

______________. *2018 Crime in the United States.* Expanded homicide data Table 2.

______________. *2018 Crime in the United States.* Murder Circumstances. Table 10.

______________. 2013. *Crime in the United States 2013.* Definition of rape.

______________. "Gangs." Posted at https://www.fbi.gov/investigate/violent-crime/gangs

Fedina, Lisa, Jennifer Lynne Holmes, and Bethany Backes. 2016. "How Prevalent is Campus Sexual Assault in the United States?" *NIJ (National Institute of Justice) Journal.* 277: 26-30.

Feixa, Carles. 2011. "Past and Present of Adolescence in Society: The 'Teen Brain' Debate in Perspective." *Neuroscience and Biobehavioral Reviews.* 35: 1634-1643.

Felitti, Vincent J., Robert F. Anda, Dale Nordenberg, David F. Williamson, Alison M. Spitz, Valerie Edwards, Mary P. Koss, and James S. Marks. "Relationships of Childhood Abuse and Household Dysfunction to Many of the Leading Causes of Death in Adults: The Adverse Childhood Experiences (ACE) Study." *American Journal of Preventive Medicine.* 14(4): 245-258.

Ferguson, Danielle. May 7, 2020. "Sturgis Teen Pleads Guilty to Killing Missing Wyoming Girl." *Sioux Falls Argus Leader.* Posted online at arguleader.com

Fontaine, Mia. January 24, 2013. "America Has an Incest Problem." *The Atlantic.*

Glasser, M., I. Kolvin, D. Campbell, A. Glasser, Il. Leitch, and S. Farrelly. 2001. "Cycle of Child Sexual Abuse: Links Between Being a Victim and Becoming a Perpetrator." *British Journal of Psychiatry.* 482-494.

Gibbs, Nancy and Timothy Roche with reporting by Andrew Goldstein, Maureen Harrington, and Richard Woodbury. December 20, 1999. "Special Report: The Columbine Tapes. In Five Secret Videos They Recorded Before the Massacre, the Killers Reveal Their Hatreds—and Their Lust for Fame." *Time.* 40+ pp.

Giedd, Jay N. 2008. "The Teen Brain: Insights from Neuroimaging." *Journal of Adolescent Health.* 335-343.

GLAAD. "Violence and Bullying." n.d. Posted at https://www.glaad.org/resources/ally/6

Grabow, Chip and Lisa Rose. May 21, 2018. "The US Has Had 57 Times as Many School Shooting as the Other Major Industrialized Nations Combined." CNN.com. Posted at https://www.cnn.com/2018/05/21/us/school-shooting-us-versus-world-trnd/index.html

Gray, Steven. February 16, 2008. "How the NIU Massacre Happened." *Time.* Posted at time.com

Hager, Eli. March 3, 2016. "There Are Still 80 'Youth Prisons' in the U.S. Here Are Five Things to Know About Them." The Marshall Project. Posted at Posted at https://www.themarshallproject.org/2016/03/03/there-are-still-80-youth-prisons-in-the-u-s-here-are-five-things-to-know-about-them

Haskins, James. 1974. *Street Gangs: Yesterday and Today.* New York: Hastings House.

Hauser, Christine. March 1, 2021. "Virginia Fraternity Is Suspended After Death of Student." *New York Times.* Posted at nytimes.

Hauser, Christine and Anahad O'Connor. April 16, 2007. "Virginia Tech Shooting Leaves 33 Dead." *New York Times.* Posted at nytimes.com

Heffernan, Virginia. October 26, 2003. "Abducted Girl Says Her Life is Back to Normal After Ordeal." *The New York Times.* Posted at nytimes.com

Henslin, James M. 2020. *Social Problems: A Down-to-Earth Approach.* New York: Pearson.

Heinzmann, David and Stacy St. Clair. Tribune Reporters. February 15, 2009. *Chicago Tribune.*

Holcombe, Madeline. April 3, 2019. "3 Fraternity Brothers Sentenced to Jail in Penn State Hazing Death." Posted at cnn.com

Insurance Institute for Highway Safety (IIHS) and Highway Loss Data Institute (HLDI). November 21, 2017. "Some Teens, Parents Think Mixing Pot and Driving Is OK." Press release. Posted at https://www.iihs.org/news/detail/some-teens-parents-think-mixing-pot-and-driving-is-ok

Jacobs, Andrew. August 17, 2002. "After Telephone Courtship, A First Date Ends in Death." *New York Times*. Posted at nytimes.com

Janofsky, Michae. June 10, 2002. "Abduction of Utah Girl Inspires Thousands to Join Search." *The New York Times*. Posted at nytimes.com

Jeltsen, Melissa. July 19, 2019, updated July 19, 2019. "A Teen Girl Found Refuge Online—Then Her Murder Went Viral." Huffpost.com.

Kantor, J. and M. Twohey. October 5, 2017. "Harvey Weinstein Paid Off Sexual Harassment Accusers for Decades." *The New York Times*. Posted at nytimes.com

Karmen, Andrew. 2020. *Crime Victims: An Introduction to Victimology*. Tenth edition. Boston: Cengage.

Kattan, Ayelet. March 20, 2001. Column: "A Trend in Suburban Shooting." University Wire.

Kaufman, Michelle R., Debangan Dey, Ciprian Crainiceanu, and Mark Dredze. 2019. "#MeToo and Google Inquiries Into Sexual Violence: A Hashtag Campaign Can Sustain Information Seeking." Journal of Interpersonal Violence. 1-11.

Kearl, H. 2018. "The Facts Behind the #MeToo Movement: A National Study on Sexual Harrassment and Assault." Posted at stopstreetharassment.org

KidsMatterInc.org. 2016. "Abuse and Neglect." Information sheets. Posted at their website.

Korellis, Patrick. February 25, 2071. Phone interview.

_______________. March 2, 2021. Zoom interview with the author. Soc 4700 Social Deviance class at Kean University.

Kovac, Joe, Jr. April 30, 2020, updated May 4, 2020. "Losing Pedro: Murder and Heartbreak in the Words of a Teenage Victim's Mother." *The Telegraph*, published at Macon.com [Georgia].Posted at https://www.macon.com/news/local/crime/article240962771.html

Krisberg, Barry and James Austin (eds.) 1978. *The Children of Ishmael: Critical Perspectives on Juvenile Justice*. Palo Alto, CA: Mayfield

Krishnan, Manisha. November 28, 2018. "How Hazing Escalates to Sexual Assault." Vice.com. Posted at vice.com.

Lewis, Sophie. April 14, 2020. "March 2020 Was the First March Without a School Shooting in the U.S. Since 2002." Posted at CBSNews.com

Liberty Mutual in partnership with HowStuffWorks®. "11 Driving Stats That Might Surprise You." Posted at https://www.libertymutual.com/masterthis/teen-driving-stats

Loveisrespect.org. "Dating Violence Statistics." n.d. posted at https://www.loveisrespect.org/resources/dating-violence-statistics/

Martinez, Ricardo. February 2005. "Teen Crash Victims: Who Are These People and Why Are They Here?" *Annals of Emergency Medicine*. 45(2): 155-156.

Mazzei, Patricia. February 13, 2019. "Parkland: A Year After the School Shooting That Was Supposed to Change Everything." *The New York Times*. Posted at nytimes.com

McCarthy, Terry, with reporting by Polly Forster, Jeffrey Ressner, and Margot Roosevelt. March 19, 2001. "Warning: Andy Williams Here. Unhappy Kid. Tired of Being Picked On. Ready to Blow. Want to Kill Some People. Can Anybody Hear Me? How Did Things Get So Bad?" *Time*. 24+.

McCurley, Carl and Howard N. Snyder. July 2004. "Victims of Violent Juvenile Crime." Office of Justice Programs, Juvenile Justice Bulletin. 8 pp. Posted at https://www.ncjrs.gov/pdffiles1/ojjdp/201628.pdf

Merton, Robert K. October 1938. "Social Structure and Anomie." *American Sociological Review*. 672-282.

Miller, Chanel. 2019. *Know My Name*. New York: Penguin Random House.

Montgomery, Ben. November 10, 2012. "Recounting the Deadly Hazing That Destroyed FAMU Band's Reputation." *Tampa Bay Times*. Posted at tampabay.com

National Center for Education Statistics (NCES). "School Crime." n.d. Posted at https://nces.ed.gov/fastfacts/display.asp?id=49

National Center for Injury Prevention and Control. Division of Violence Prevention. 2016. "Understanding Teen Dating Violence." Fact Sheet. CDC (Center for Diseases Prevention and Control). 2 pp.

National Institute on Drug Abuse (NIDA). April 6, 2020. "The Latest on Vaping-Related Illness and Deaths." NIDA Blog. Posted at https://teens.drugabuse.gov/blog/post/latest-vaping-related-illness-and-deaths

______________. December 2019. "Monitoring the Future Survey: High School and Youth Trends 2019." 8 pages. Posted at https://www.drugabuse.gov/publications/drugfacts/monitoring-future-survey-high-school-youth-trends

National Institute on Drug Abuse for Teens. Revised March 2020. "Drug Overdoses in Youth." Posted at https://teens.drugabuse.gov/drug-facts/drug-overdoses-youth

National Institute of Mental Health. Revised 2020. "The Teen Brain: 7 Things to Know." Posted at https://www.nimh.nih.gov/health/publications/the-teen-brain-7-things-to-know/index.shtml#:~:text=Though%20the%20brain%20may%20be,last%20brain%20regions%20to%20mature.

National Research Council. 1993. *Understanding Child Abuse and Neglect*. Washington, DC: The National Academies Press. https://doi.org/10.17226/2117.

National Safety Council. "Motor Vehicle Safety Issues." "Hot Car Deaths." Injury Facts. n.d. Posted at https://www.injuryfacts.nsc.org

National Sexual Violence Resource Center (NSVRC). "Teen Dating Violence Resource Round-Up for Advocates" n.d. Posted at https://www.nsvrc.org/blogs/teen-dating-violence-resource-round-advocates

National Transportation Safety Board (NTSB). n.d. "Distracted Driving." Posted at https://www.nhtsa.gov/risky-driving/distracted-driving

______________. February 2017. "Drowsy Driving Among Young Drivers." Safety Alert 2-page fact sheet. Posted at https://www.ntsb.gov/safety/safety-alerts/Documents/SA_061.pdf

NBCnews.com April 15, 2008. "High School Classmates Sat Gunman Was Bullied." Posted at nbcnews.com

NCES (National Center for Education Statistics). Last updated: April 2019. "Indicator 10: Bullying at School and Electronic Bullying." Posted at https://nces.ed.gov/programs/crimeindicators/ind_10.asp

New York State Police. July 9, 2020. "Crime Prevention: Teenage Victims of Crime." Fact Sheet.

NPR.org. April 18, 2007. "Remembering Virginia Tech's Shooting Victims." Posted at https://www.npr.org/2007/04/18/9618673/remembering-virginia-techs-shooting-victims

Nutt, Amy Ellis. May 15, 2018. "Among Thousands of LGBTQ Teens, a Survey Finds Anxiety and Fears About Safety." *Washington Post*. Posted at https://www.washingtonpost.com/national/health-science/2018/05/14/083b9ae4-57ab-11e8-b656-a5f8c2a9295d_story.html

NYC Human Rights. N.d. "Sexual Harassment Prevention Training." Posted at 1lnyc.gov

Office of Juvenile Justice and Delinquency Prevention (OJJDP). "Parent's Guide to Gangs." 4 pages. Posted at https://www.nationalgangcenter.gov/Content/Documents/Parents-Guide-to-Gangs.pdf

______________. "Statistical Briefing Book." n.d. 2 pp. Posted at https://www.ojjdp.gov/ojstatbb/victims/faqs.asp

______________. September 2015. "Status Offenders." Literature Review.

Olds, Dorri. January 13, 2012. "Defriending My Rapist." *New York Times*. Townies column.

One Child International. "The Four Types of Child Abuse." 2-page brochure posted at www.childabuse-watch.net. Sources include the National Clearinghouse on Child Abuse and Neglect Information, U.S. Department of Health and Human Services, n.d.

Pfouts, Jane H. Janice H. Schopler, and H. Carl Henley, Jr. July 1982. "Forgotten Victims of Family Violence." *Social Work*. National Association of Social Workers. 367-368.

Qersdyn, Saul. February 6, 2015. "Nicole Giovanni: The Reality Behind Murder in a Small Town." Editorial. *Rosella Park News*. Posted online at roselleparknews.org

Queally, James and Matthew Ormseth. July 16, 2019. "Wielding Machetes and Baseball Bats, MS-13 Carried Out 'Medieval' Killings, Feds Say." *Los Angeles Times*. Posted at https://www.latimes.com/california/story/2019-07-16/ms-13-committed-gruesome-killings

RAINN (Rape Abuse Incest National Network). "Victims of Sexual Violence: Statistics." Posted at https://www.rainn.org/statistics/victims-sexual-violence

Rand, Kristen. May 27, 1998. "School Slayings Couldn't Happen Without Guns." *The Advocate*. Stamford: CT: A19.

The Registrar Guard. May 19, 2018. "Remembering the Victims of the May 1998 Thurston Shooting." *The Registrar Guard*. Posted at https://www.registerguard.com/news/20180519/remembering-victims-of-may-1998-thurston-shooting

Reid, Gerald M., et al. 2019. "Perceived Consequences of Hazing Exposure During the First Year of College: Associations with Childhood Victimization." *Journal of American College Health*. 67: 402-409.

Robinson, Melissa B. April 29, 1999. "Lawmakers Ask for Summit on Violence." *The Advocate.* Stamford: CT: A8.

The Rowan Center. June 2021. "Sexual Assault Crisis Counselor & Advocate Certification Manual." Developed in partnership with the Connecticut Alliance to End Sexual Violence.

Schildkraut, Jaclyn, Evelyn S. Sokolowski, and John Nicoletti. 2020. "The Survivor Network: The Role of Shared Experiences in Mass Shootings Recovery." *Victims & Offenders.* Posted online.

Shah, Allie. April 17, 2006. "Healing After Rape." From the *Star Tribune)* Minneapolis, MN

Shapiro, Emily, Teri Whitcraft, Morgan Winsor, and Zunaira Zaki. February 14, 2020. "Parkland Shooting 2 Years Later: Remembering the 17 Victims of the School Massacre." Posted at https://abcnews.go.com/US/teacher-coach14-year-freshman-florida-high-school-massacre/story?id=53092879

Shetgiri, Rashmi, Simon C. Lee, John Tillitski, Connie Wilson, and Glenn Flores. 2015. "Why Adolescents Fight: A Qualitative Study of Youth Perspectives on Fighting and Its Prevention." *Academic Pediatrics.* 15: 103-110.

Slisco, Aila. July 7, 2020. "Mary Kay Letourneau, Teacher Who Had Affair With Student, Dies of Cancer." Newsweek.com Posted at https://www.newsweek.com/mary-kay-letourneau-teacher-who-had-affair-student-dies-cancer-1516128

Smith, S.G., J. Chen, K. C. Basile, L.K. Gilbert, M.T. Merrick, et.al. 2017. *The National Institute Partner and Sexual Violence Survey (NISVS) 2010-2012 State Report.*

Edgar Snyder & Associates. "Teen Driver Car Accident Statistics." n.d. Website blog. Posted at https://www.edgarsnyder.com/car-accident/who-was-injured/teen/teen-driving-statistics.html

Southall, Ashley. October 24, 2014. "Remains Found in Virginia Identified as Missing Student Hannah Graham." *The New York Times.* Posted at nytimes.com

Stolberg, Sheryl Gay and Nicolas Fandos. September 27, 2018. "Brett Kavanaugh and Christine Blasey Ford Duel With Tears and Furty." *The New York Times.* Posted at nytimes.com

Streisand, Betsy, et al. March 19, 2001. "Betrayed by Their Silence?" *US News & World Report.* 22.

Tamul, Dan, Catherine Einstein, Jessica Hotter, Madison Lanier, Laura Purcell, and Jordan Wolf. 2021. "Narrative Persuasion and Stigma: Using News Accounts to Denormalize Texting While Driving." *Accident Analysis and Prevention* 151. Posted online.

Thorpy, Michael J.; Charles Pollack, and Jan Yager. 2009. *The Encyclopedia of Sleep and Sleep Disorders.* Third edition. New York: Infobase, originally published by Facts on File, Inc.

Thomas, Piri. 1974. *Down These Mean Streets.* New York: Vintage.

Thompson, C. Bradley. 2014. "Our Killing Schools." *Society.* 51: 210-220.

Troutman, Brooke. 2018. "A More Just System of Juvenile Justice Creating a New Standard of Accountability for Juveniles in Illinois." *Journal of Criminal Law and Criminology.* 108: 197-221.

U.S. Department of Health and Human Services. Centers for Disease Control and Prevention. "Child Trends." "Physical fighting by Youth." Posted at https://www.childtrends.org/indicators/physical-fighting-by-youth

______________. 2018. 1991-2017 High School Youth Risk Behavior Survey. Posted at https://nccd.cdc.gov/Youthonline

U.S. Department of Health and Human Services (HHS). Office of Population Affairs. "Opioids and Adolescents. Content reviewed May 13, 2019. Posted at https://www.hhs.gov/ash/oah/adolescent-development/substance-use/drugs/opioids/index.html#prevalence

U.S. Department of Health and Human Services. Office on Women's Health. April 26, 2019. "Date Rape Drugs." Posted at https://www.womenshealth.gov/a-z-topics/date-rape-drugs

Vagianos, A. October 17, 2017. "The 'Me Too' Campaign Was Created by a Black Woman 10 Years Ago." Huffington Post. Posted online at the huffingtonpost.com

Varner, Kasey. July 30, 2011. Updated March 23, 2019. "Despite Stereotypes, Hazing Is Often Harmless." PennLive Editorial.

Vaughan, Kevin and Jeff Kass. With Peggy Lowe, Lynn Bartels, and Carol Kasel. May 18, 2001. "Columbine Had 'Red Flags,' Officials Had Many Chances to Prevent Shooting, Panels Says." *Denver Rocky Mountain News.* 4A.

Vezner, Tad. November 7, 2007. "Teen Raped at Home By Stranger, Police Say." *Pioneer Press.* Posted at twincities.com

Von Hentig, Hans. May-June 1943. "The Pickpocket: Psychology, Tactics, and Technique." *Journal of Criminal Law and Criminology.* 34(1): 11-15.

Walsh, Paul. May 24, 2012. "Police: Teen Accepts Late-night Ride on Lake St., is Raped by Stranger." *Star Tribune.* Posted online at startribune.com

Wang, Judy. February 14, 2021. "'Feels Like Yesterday': NIU Mass Shooting Survivor Reflects on 13th Anniversary." WGNTV.com

Winerip, Michael. April 12, 2012. "When Hazing Goes Very Wrong." *New York Times.* Posted at nytimes.com

Wolfgang, Marvin E. and Franco Ferracuti. 1969. *The Subculture of Violence.* New York: Barnes and Noble reprint.

World Health Organization. 1999. Report of the Consultation on Child Abuse Prevention. Geneva: WHO. 29–31.

Yager, Jan. 2016, 2004. *125 Ways to Meet the Love of Your Life.* Stamford, CT: Hannacroix Creek.

______________. 2021. *Help Yourself Now.* New York: Allworth, an imprint of Skyhorse.

______________. *Victims.* 2021. With a new introduction and updated bibliography and resources. Originally published in 1978 by Scribner. Stamford, CT: Hannacroix Creek.

Yellin, Emily. June 2, 1998. "Out of Violence, a Survivor and a Scholar." *New York Times.* A18.

Zimring, Franklin E. December 2000. "The Common Thread: Diversion in Juvenile Justice." *California Law Review.* 88(6): 2477-2495.

Videos, Films, and TED Talks

Audrie & Daisy. 2016. Documentary directed by Bonni Cohen and Jon Shenk. Actual Films, Production Company. Distributed by Netflix. What happened after the sexual assault of two teenagers" in 2011, to 15-year-old Audrie Pott who lived in California, and in 2012 to Daisy Coleman, who was 14 and lived in a small town in Missouri. 1-1/2 hours.

Smart, Elizabeth. January 31, 2014. "My Story." 11:36 minutes. TEDxUniversity of Nevada. Smart was 14 years old when she was kidnapped at knifepoint out of her bedroom and kept captive and sexually abused for nine months. "Very early on I decided I was not going to let these two captors win." She fortunately managed to escape. Posted at https://www.youtube.com/watch?v=h0C2LPXaEW4

"Tea and Consent." November 16, 2015. 2 minutes 49 Copyright © 2015 Rock Star Dinosaur Pirate Princess and Blue Seat Studios. Posted by Thames Valley Police at www.youtube.com/watch?v=pZwvrxVavnQ

Wang, Judy. February 14, 2021. "'Feels Like Yesterday': NIU Mass Shooting Survivor Reflects on 13th Anniversary.'" WGN-TV Interview. Posted at https://wgntv.com/news/feels-like-yesterday-niu-mass-shooting-survivor-reflects-on-13th-anniversary/

CHAPTER **TWELVE**

Sexual Violence

Rape, Sexual Abuse, Assault, and Harassment Victims*

Learning Objectives

After you finish reading this chapter, you should be able to:

1. Define sexual violence.
2. Know how prevalent is sexual violence in the United States and are the perpetrators more likely to be strangers or someone known to the victim.
3. Consider and define the various types of rape.
4. Understand how often rape is reported to the police and some of the reasons victims are reluctant to come forward.
5. Explain the aftermath of rape.
6. Define sexual harassment.
7. Discuss the secondary victims of rape and sexual assault.

WHAT IS SEXUAL VIOLENCE?

The CDC (Centers for Disease Prevention and Control) defines **sexual violence** as "sexual activity when consent is not obtained or not freely given." (CDC, 2021) That definition is

* *Warning:* In this chapter, you will be reading examples and quotes which at times, by the very nature of rape and other sexual assaults, include descriptions of sexual acts ranging from the general to the specific that some of you might find upsetting or unpleasant. Unfortunately, in order to discuss rape and sexual assaults comprehensively, it is necessary to share the detailed information provided by the victims, law enforcement, medical personnel, lawyers or prosecutors, victim advocates, or rape crisis counselors. Apologies in advance if anyone's sensibilities are inadvertently offended.

obviously a load broader than the crime of **rape**. Sexual violence includes rape but it also includes **sexual abuse**, **sexual assault**, **molestation**, and **sexual harassment**. Sexual violence can occur in-person as well as online or through technology such as sharing or posting compromising sexual photos of someone without his or her consent. (CDC, 2021)

Yes, strangers do jump out of the bushes on occasion, grab someone, and sexually assault or rape him or her—estimates on the percentage of rapes by strangers range from 7% for juveniles to 10% or as high as 19.5% for all adult rapes—but the majority of these crimes are committed by someone known to the victim. In the teen and younger years, the perpetrator might be a family member, trusted authority figure, neighbor, or acquaintance; for adults, it may be the result of what is known as an Acquaintance Rape or a Date Rape, a trusted authority or, less frequently, a family member. (CDC, 2021; RAINN.org, n.d.; Central MN Sexual Assault Center, n.d.)

THE DIVERSE FACES OF SEXUAL VIOLENCE INCLUDING RAPE VICTIMS*

- Chanel Miller is no longer "Emily Doe," the nameless victim of a 2016 sexual assault that happened when she was unconscious behind a dumpster. Yes, her emotional 12-page victim impact statement was read around the world but now she has come forward by her real name including her authorship of the bestselling *Know My Name*. (Finkel, 2020; Miller, 2020)
- Former superstar actor and comedian Bill Cosby who for decades was considered the model of fatherhood through his hit TV program, *The Cosby Show*, was found guilty of drugging and assaulting a former Temple University employee by the name of Andrea Constand. He was sentenced to three to ten years in prison for his crimes. (Bowley and Coscarelli, 2018) (But Cosby was freed in June 2021 when his conviction was overturned.) (Bowley, 2021)
- Once powerful movie producer Harvey Weinstein was found guilty of sexual assaults dating back decades; he received a 23-year prison sentence. One of the many accusers against Weinstein was an aspiring actress who said he raped her in a Manhattan hotel in 2013. (Ransom, 2020)
- A 36-year-old Ph.D. student at a university in the United Kingdom was sentenced to life in prison for 159 sex offenses including 136 rapes of men. The convicted rapist would wait outside bars and nightclubs, taking his victims to his apartment where he would drug them. The assaults took place while his victims were unconscious. They never remembered what had happened but the perpetrator took videos of all the attacks which he stored on his phone. He was finally arrested when one of his victims woke up during the sexual assault and contacted police. (BBC.com, 2020)

The above examples do shatter some of the myths about sexual violence especially rape, such as, that it is a crime that only happens to girls or women. In this chapter, you will learn that rape or sexual assault is more likely to happen between two individuals who know each other as well as between strangers and some of the reasons victims are reluctant to come forward and report the crime.

---

*Please note: This chapter examines adult sexual violence. Child, teen, and college victim sexual violence is explored in Chapter 10, "Child Victims," from pages 383-395, and in Chapter 11, "Teen and College Victims," from pages 417-425.

DEFINITION OF RAPE

According to the FBI Uniform Crime Reporting, prior to 2013, in what is now referred to as the "legacy" definition of rape, the words *forcibly* and *female* were included. That 80-year-old definition of rape was "carnal knowledge of a female forcibly and against her will."

Since 2013, in addition to eliminating the exclusive reference to women as rape victims, the new definition is "penetration, no matter how slight, of the vagina or anus with any body part or object, or oral penetration by a sex organ of another person, without the consent of the victim." (FBI, 2013)

Additional considerations:

- Attempts or assaults to commit rape are also included in the statistics presented here.
- Statutory rape and incest are excluded.

In addition to the official definition of rape, which emphasizes the physical acts that legally constitute rape, it is also important to understand how social scientists, psychologists, criminologists, and victimologists see the crimes of rape and sexual assault. As Gotovac and Towson put it in their article published in *Violence and Victims*, "Rape is not actually about sex; it is a crime of interpersonal violence motivated by aggression, anger, the abuse of power, and the need to exert control over others (Burt, 1980; DeJong, 1999)." (Gotovac and Towson, 2015)

A HISTORY OF RAPE THROUGH THE #METOO MOVEMENT

The last few years have seen a dramatic change in the United States in how rape, sexual assault, sexual harassment, and rape victims are viewed culminating with the conviction and imprisonment of once powerful movie producer Harvey Weinstein for rape with a 23 year prison term. (Ransom, 2020)

In one of the earliest written set of laws, the Code of Hammurabi, the rape of a virgin was considered a property damage against her father. Related to that is the Webster's Dictionary archaic definition of rape as "to seize and take away by force." It was not until the 11th and 12th centuries, according to Kyla Bishop, writing about the history of sexual assault laws in the United States, that "rape began to be considered more as a violent, sexual crime against the victim." Bishop noted that by the end of the next century, another big change would take place when the "Statutes of Westminster allowed the crown to prosecute rapists should the victim's family choose not to do so, signifying a fundamental change in rape being viewed as a crime against the State." (Bishop, 2018.)

Gillian Greensite, in tracing the history of the rape crisis movement, points to the bravery of the African American women who testified before Congress in 1866 as the first step in breaking the silence about rape in America. They were testifying following the Memphis Riot of May 1866 where a number of Black women were gang-raped by a white mob. (Greensite, 2009)

Fast forward to the women's movement of the 1960s and 1970s which was a big impetus in bringing the rights of women, including a woman's right to say "no" to sex, to light. In a landmark article by feminist Susan Griffin, "Rape: The All-American Crime," published in the September 1971 issue of *Ramparts* magazine, the stage was set for the radically new awareness about rape, and the reluctance to sweep it under the rug, or take it in stride any longer. Her influential essay began, "I have never been free of the fear of rape. From a very early age I, like most women, have thought of rape as a part of my natural environment—something to be feared and prayed against like fire or lightning. I never asked why men raped; I simply thought it one of the many mysteries of human nature." (Griffin, 1971)

A year later, in 1972, the first rape crisis centers were started in several cities around the country including Berkley, Boston, Philadelphia, Chicago, and Washington, D.C. Two years after that, in 1974, Michigan passed the first **rape shield law**. This was a breakthrough for rape victims. It stopped the defense from introducing the rape victim's sexual history at trial. That helped to encourage rape victims to come forward since they were not as likely to be put on trial themselves for their past and current sexual relationships if their rape case got to trial.

In the United States, in 1977, in *Coker v. Georgia*, it was ruled that capital punishment could no longer be applied to a convicted rapist. The maximum sentence would be life in prison. This might have actually paved the way for more women coming forward since sending a man to prison for rape is one thing but sending him to death by lethal injection or the electric chair is a whole other level of punishment.

In 1994, the Violence Against Women Act (VAWA), which was co-sponsored by then Senator Joe Biden and Senator Oren Hatch, was signed by President Bill Clinton, passed as part of the Omnibus Crime Bill of 1994. This Act provided $1.6 billion in funding toward research, education, treatment, and criminal justice response at the state level to violence against women including sexual violence. The legislation has been renewed repeatedly including in 2000, 2003, 2005, 2013, and 2019.

Michelle R. Kaufman, et. al. highlight the impact of the #MeToo movement in their article, "#MeToo and Google Inquiries Into Sexual Violence: A Hashtag Campaign Can Sustain Information Seeking." (Note that citations in the excerpt that follow are included in the Cited Works and Additional References section at the end of this chapter.) They write:

> Sexual violence affects approximately 1 in 3 women and nearly 1 in 6 men during their lifetimes in the United States (Smith et al., 2017). Furthermore, an alarming 81% of women and 43% of men have experienced sexual harassment, including both workplace and non-workplace incidents (Kearl, 2018)
>
> The #MeToo Movement has brought new attention to sexual harassment and sexual assault and created an environment where these issues are talked about with regularity in public discourse. While the movement dates back 10 years to activist Tarana Burke (Vagianos, 2017), actor Alyssa Milano used the phrase on Twitter on October 17, 2017 in response to multiple allegations of sexual harassment against Hollywood producer Harvey Weinstein (Kantor & Twohey, 2017). Her tweet read, "If you've been sexually harassed or assaulted write 'me too' as a reply to this tweet." Within 24 hours, 53,000 people, including many other prominent female celebrities, tweeted comments and/or shared stories of their own experiences with sexual violence. Since then, more than 70 additional male public figures were accused of sexual misconduct, resulting in many firings and resignations (Almukhtar, Gold, & Buchanan. 2017).

In the next section, you will find a quick review of the many types of rape, in alphabetical order.

A TYPOLOGY OF RAPE

Acquaintance Rape

This is when the rapist is someone known to the victim but in a nonromantic capacity like a peer or neighbor. In Chapter 11 on teen victims, you read the self-report by a 20-year-old who shared how she was raped when she was 15 by another high school student with whom she only wanted to "hook up." When the kissing was leading to sex, she said "no" but he raped her anyway.

Date Rape

When a woman, or man, is on a date and he or she becomes so intoxicated, or high on drugs, whether voluntarily or by having something slipped into her or his drink, consent cannot be given. Date rape would be the term for such a sexual interaction.

In Chapter 11, "Teen and College Victims," in the section on date rape or sexual violence, there is a discussion of the so-called date rape drugs. Information posted at the womenshealth.gov U.S. government website in the "Date Rape Drugs" section lists the drugs that might be slipped into any kind of a drink, alcoholic or not: gamma-hydroxybutyric acid (GHB), ketamine, and others. It is important to be aware and be careful that this does not happen to someone. Also known as club drugs, it is not just teens or college students who have to be careful to avoid unwittingly being incapacitated by a date rape drug. Also known as "Ruffies," the nickname for the drug Rohypnol, some use the term "ruffies" to describe any kind of club drug. (womenshealth.gov) Side effects of the drugs are memory loss, incapacitation, and altered judgment. (University of Massachusetts at Amherst Police Department, n.d.)

At the beginning of this chapter, the example of the serial rapist who committed an estimated 136 rapes, was shared. (BBC.com, 2020) It was suggested that the rapist was using a date rape drug before he sexually assaulted his victims. Dawn Burnett is the founder of the #SHEROproject Movement. Featured at the website for the project are women who have been abused but who were able to change their lives. Dawn shares about how in her early 20s, right after her first marriage ended, she had an unfortunate experience because of a date rape drug. Dawn writes: "I started going to clubs and meeting what I considered to be fun people until one day I was at a popular tourist location in Central Florida, this was back in 1993; [and someone] slipped a drug in my drink. There were so many thoughts that I was left with and the biggest one was shame. 'How come I wasn't more careful? How could I have trusted a man to bring me a drink?' Most of the moment was a blur; the drug has a way of erasing your memory but it definitely rocked my world and not in a good way." (Burnett, 2019)

Even if alcohol or drugs are not involved, if someone on a date starts off wanting to have sex with his or her partner, but changes his or her mind, but the partner pushes himself or herself on the victim, that is also date rate. The short video listed in the bibliography at the back of this chapter, "Tea Consent" is a useful teaching tool for the concept of consent. Consent has to be freely given and it can be withdrawn at any time at the beginning or in the middle of sexual interactions.

Incest

Incest refers to inappropriate sexual contact including molestation or intercourse between those who are related such as parent-child, siblings, grandparents, even extending to first cousins, aunts and uncles, and to step-parents. Victims of this type of sexual violence tend to be children and, if it continues, teenagers. Rather than dealing with current incest, it is more likely that adults have to deal with the aftermath of the incest they endured as a child or teen, if they have not blanked it out of their memory. (Lawson, 2018) See the section below on the impact of sexual violence on its victims. For a more detailed discussion of incest, please refer to Chapter 10, "Child Victims."

Marital Rape

Since July 5, 1993, **marital rape** has been illegal in all 50 states. It is considered marital rape if a spouse forces his or her partner to have nonconsensual sex. In 1975, Nebraska became the first state to make marital rape a crime. Declaring marital rape a crime was another positive development in women no longer being viewed as the property of their husbands. It should be pointed out that not all countries are as progressive in this matter as the United States. As recently as 2017, for example, in Lebanon a rapist is able to go free if he marries his victim. Although Tunisia, Morocco, and Jordan repealed that law, it was still possible in 2017 in the Philippines, Libya, Cameroon, Angola, Kuwait, and several other countries for rapists to go free if they marry their victim. (NPR, 2017)

Sexual Homicide

Sexual homicide occurs when the rape victim is killed by the rapist. Twenty-four-year-old Imette St. Guillen was a graduate student in criminal justice at John Jay College of Criminal Justice, in New York City, when she went out to a bar with friends, staying behind and leaving the club by herself at 4 A.M. Her mutilated body was found on February 25, 2006. An investigation led to a man who was working as a bouncer at the bar where Imette had gone that night. He was supposed to be on supervised release after serving a 3-1/2 year sentence for a bank robbery that he had committed in 2000 but it was revealed that because of a glitch in the system, no one had been in contact with the killer for several years. It was determined that Imette had been raped and then murdered. They were also able to link her rapist to three previous rapes. (Burgess, 2019; Fahim, 2009).

Imette St. Guillen, a graduate student who was tragically raped and killed in 2006.

It is hard to have accurate statistical data about how widespread sexual homicide is because the hierarchy rule related to the UCR (Uniform Crime Report) might have the crime listed only as a murder rather than a rape and a murder. In 2019, the UCR listed only 8 murders that also included rape: 1 husband, 1 other family, 3 acquaintances, and 2 girlfriends. (FBI, 2019 Table 10). It will be interesting to see if there seems to be an increase in reported sexual homicides in 2021 and going forward now that the NIBRS (National Incident Based Report System) has become mandatory. The NIBRS does not have the hierarchy rule, a crime may now be listed under up to ten offenses.

Highlighting some of the findings from her book, *Sexual Homicide: Patterns and Motives,* Ann Wolbert Burgess notes that in sexual homicide cases, offenders are more likely to be strangers compared to other types of rape (39.2% versus 20.9%). (Burgess, 2019)

Statutory Rape

This unique type of rape occurs when there is consensual sex with a minor who is under the age of consent in that state; there is no threat or use of force. Whether rape is statutory rape or a legal act of consensual sex varies by state. Delaware, along with 34 other states, for example, have 16 as the age of consent. The remaining states have either 17 or 18 as the age of consent. The website Age of Consent reports that Nigeria, at age 11, has the lowest age of consent in the world. Thirteen is the age of consent in Japan. The other extreme is South Korea, where the age of consent is 20. (Ageofconsent.net)

A review of the NIBRS data over a 20-year period from 6,000 police departments revealed that statutory rape is relatively rare—only 5 percent, or 60,362, of the 1.1 million sex crimes that were reported to the NIBRS during that time period included statutory rape. However, the arrest rates were higher: 38 percent of the cases led to an arrest compared to only 26 percent of all other reported sex crimes. It could be tied to the fact that statutory rape usually involves an offender known to the victim whereas other sex crimes may include strangers or unknown assailants. (Bierie and Budd, *Sexual Abuse*, 2018)

Bierie and Budd, in their article, "Romeo, Juliet, and Statutory Rape," note that it is "an important yet understudied topic." Based on their analysis of the NIBRS data, the larger the age difference between the victim and the offender, the more likely there will be an arrest (four years or more). (Bierie and Budd, 2018)

Stranger Rape

Stranger rape occurs when a complete stranger forces himself or herself on a male or female forcing him or her to do any of the sexual acts that are defined as rape. According to the Bureau of Justice Statistics, reporting on violent victimization by strangers between 2005 and 2010, 24.1 percent of rape or sexual assault was committed by strangers. (Harrell, 2012) You will recall in Chapter 11, "Teen and College Victims," that RAINN (Rape, Abuse & Incest National Network) reported there for juvenile victims, 7% were by strangers. At the beginning of this chapter, it was also pointed out that various sources of crime statistics cite stranger rapes between 10% to 19.5% of sexual violence. The majority of crimes are by rapists known to the victim. (CDC, 2021; RAINN.org, n.d.; Central MN Sexual Assault Center, n.d.)

Despite its statistical infrequency, stranger rape is probably the most feared by women of all ages. The reality and horror of stranger rape should not be minimized. Even one victim is one too many.

RAPE VICTIM STATISTICS

In 2018, based on the Uniform Crime Reports of data from local law enforcement reported annually to the FBI, there were a reported 139,380 rapes in the United States. But estimates are that that more than half of all rapes go unreported. The National Sexual Violence Resource Center (NSVRC), a nonprofit organization, suggests in their "Statistics:" "Based on data from the survey, it is estimated that 734,630 people were raped (threatened, attempted, or completed) in the United States in 2018." Obviously that is a very wide range from 139,380 to 734,630 rapes in the United States in 2018 but the message is clear: rape is a violent crime with far too many victims.

As the data in Figure 12.1 indicates, and has been noted previously in this chapter, the most frequent rapist of reported rapes is not a stranger but someone known to the victim.—an acquaintance, current or former spouse, girlfriend, boyfriend, or family member. Stranger rapes accounted for 19.5 percent of all reported rapes in 2018.

FIGURE 12.1 **Percentage of Victim-Offender Relationships**

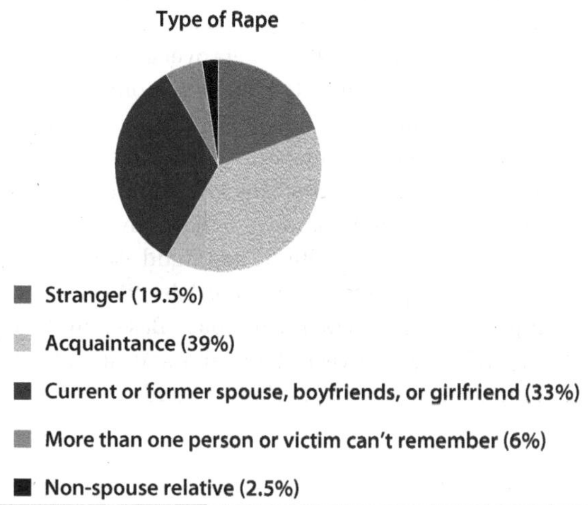

Source: RAINN (Rape, Abuse, & Incent National Network).

The table that follows restates the victim-offender relationship in rapes stated in terms of percentages.

TABLE 12.1. Victim-Offender Relationship in Percentages

Victim-Offender Relationship	Percentage
Acquaintance rapes	39%
Rapes committed by a current or former spouse, boyfriend, or girlfriend	33%
Stranger rapes	19.5%
Rapes committed by more than one person or the victim can't recall	6%
Rape committed by a non-spouse relative	2.5%

Source: RAINN (Rape, Abuse, and Incent National Network).

Age of Victim

According to the Bureau of Justice Statistics, females in the 12 to 34 age group are at the greatest risk for being raped accounting for 69 percent of all reported rapes (15% in the 12-17 age group and 54 percent in the 18 to 34 year old age group). From 35-64, the number of rapes is 28 percent with the lowest incidence for those 65 and over (3%).

Number of Perpetrators

Nine out of ten rape/sexual assault victimization have a single offender based on a study by the Bureau of Justice Statistics, "Sex Offenses and Offenders." (Greenfield, BJS, 1997: 4)

A more recent study by Morgan, Brittain, and Welch, published in the *Journal of Interpersonal Violence*, analyzed the differences between sexual assault with one perpetrator (what they refer to as SPSA—Single Perpetrator Sexual Assault) compared to sexual assault with multiple perpetrators (MPSA). The study consisted of 135 cases of MPSA compared to 139 cases of SP.SA. The study was conducted as a "retrospective review of existing patient notes" (Morgan et al., 2012: 2423). The cases were from a sexual assault referral center in London over a four-year time spa. Here is a summary of their findings:

- Victims of MPSA were "younger, less likely to be white, more likely to report previous self-harm and more likely to sustain injuries than victims of SPSA" (Morgan, et al., 2012: 2415)
- MPSA had more completed rapes and more multiple rapes.
- MPSA, "perpetrators were more likely to meet the victim in an outside location before carrying out the assault in a place of residence that was not the victim's." . . . (Morgan et al., 2012: 2415)
- "Single perpetrator approach and assault is more likely to be inside the victim's or perpetrator's home. . . ." (Morgan et al., 2012: 2420)

MALE RAPE VICTIMS

In 2013, the U.S. government changed the definition of rape so that it included males as well as females. Although we usually associate male victims of rape with situations which are traditionally male only, such as in the military or in prison, sexual assaults between boys and males can occur in a wide range of situations. Although it is rare, women can rape a male as well.

Males are less likely to report rape out of embarrassment. Those who are physically injured are more likely to report it because they need to get medical help. But male rape by males or, in rare instances, by females, does occur. According to the Bureau of Justice Statistics, in the United States one of every ten rape victims is a male (women are victims of attempted or completed rapes at the rate of one out of every six).

Sexual molestation, assault, or rape during the formative years can have an impact on adult relationships for males, as it can for females as well. For example, Cook and Ellis share this example in their article, "The Other #MeToo: Male Sexual Abuse Survivors." "Bill" is 45 years old. Married for 20 years, he and his wife have two children. Bill reports that he and his wife are no longer intimate emotionally, and he finds it difficult to talk with his wife, be affectionate, and often finds himself zoning out when his wife is talking to him. Bill works as a retail supervisor; he noted difficulty holding onto jobs for longer than a year, often due to angry outbursts and irritability that are difficult to control. When directly asked if he has experienced any traumatic events in his life, he reported none. In answering additional intake questions, he noted that some "funny business" had occurred when he was 14 years old when his next-door neighbor touched him inappropriately." (Cook and Ellis, 2020)

Whether the perpetrator is a woman sexually assaulting or raping a man, or a man raping another man, boys and men need to know that they have the same rights as girls and women to be free from sexual assaults or rapes. They are not "weak" if they report what happened to them and seek justice for themselves as well as counseling. They may also need to get medical help including HIV testing for sexually-transmitted diseases, and, even after there are vaccines, which fortunately happened in early 2021, they may have to be tested for COVID-19 if the person sexually assaulting them was not vaccinated.

PRISON SEXUAL VICTIMIZATION

In 2003, Congress passed the Prison Rape Elimination Act (PREA) and signed into law by President George W. Bush. An all-out effort to stop rape in prison followed with wardens and prison superintendents being advised that they would personally be held responsible for any rapes in their facilities. If you visit a jail or prison today, you will usually see big posters or flyers advising the staff and inmates that there is a zero-tolerance policy for rape at that facility.

Be aware that women are sexually assaulted and raped in jails and prisons just like men. Some say that the data shows that women are actually more likely to be raped in prison than men. Research has discovered that transgender women inmates were 13 times more likely to be sexually assaulted in prisons for men. (Jenness and Fenstermaker, 2016)

There is a 28-page report on "Understanding rape in Prison" available at the website for the Maryland Coalition Against Sexual Assault (MCASA). (MCASA, n.d.)

THE AFTERMATH OF RAPE

Decision to Seek Medical Assistance

The first two decisions that a rape victim has to make are whether to call 911 and involve the police and/or whether to seek medical help. These two decisions need not always go hand in hand. (You also may recall from the profile of Karima Holmes, 9-1-1 Operator who also was the Director of the 911 Center in Washington, D.C., in Chapter 6, "Helping the Victim," that rape victims may ask a friend to call for them.)

A victim afraid of retaliation or involving the police and the criminal justice system, if she is over 18, may still seek medical help without the nurse, doctor, or other medical personnel being bound to a mandatory reporting of the sexual assault. Mandatory reporting is true for minors, especially if it is a case of child abuse by someone known to the victim which, as previously stated, it is most likely to be.

However, if a victim goes to the hospital for medical assistance and asks to have a formal rape kit done, in case at a later date she decides to press charges, the police may have to get involved since they may have to be the ones to authorize and store the rape kit.

Getting medical help depends on what injuries, if any, the rape victim experiences. If the rape included successful penetration, getting tested for HIV, sexually-transmitted diseases, and even a pregnancy test are sound procedures even if the victim was not injured. Testing for the coronavirus may also be done. Depending on the victim's religious beliefs, a morning after pill may be requested if the victim wishes to prevent a possible pregnancy.

A similar effort to the **SART** police programs. which stands for **sexual assault response teams**, (described below) have been put in place at hospitals that will be treating the rape victim Those programs are known as **SANE** which stands for sexual assault nurse examiners. **Sexual Assault Nurse Examiner,** which is also know as **SAFE (Sexual Assault Forensic Examiner).** Tennessee had the first SANE program back in the 1970s. Studies indicate that SANE programs help rape victims to deal better with the aftermath of the crime and possibly even aid in improved prosecution rates. (Burgess, pages 123-124) In the state of Connecticut, everyone in the SANE or SAFE program, who will be treating survivors at the hospital, including handling the **rape kit**, is a Registered Nurse (RN), Advanced Practical Registered Nurse (APRN), or a medical doctor (MD). Forty hours of specialized training is required. (Connecticut Alliance to End Sexual Violence and The Rowan Center, 2021)

Please also read or reread the section on rape kits that you will find in Chapter 6, "Helping the Victim."

Decision to Report Being the Victim of Sexual Violence Including Rape to the Police

The reasons a rape victim may decide not to report are complex and very individual. Those reasons may range from fear of retaliation, not wanting to get the rapist in trouble, **victim self-blame**, fear of embarrassment or humiliation if word about the rape gets out, to doubting if police will be able to make an arrest, or if the criminal justice system will pursue the case, or if there will be an adequate punishment, so why bother. The powerful Netflix documentary, *Audrie and Daisy*, cited in Chapter 11, "Teen and College Victims," because the sexual violence victims were ages 15 and 14 respectively are a good example of what can happen to a sexual violence victim when the crime becomes well known. Both situations were complicated but a theme that runs through how their victimization impacted on their lives includes the way that social media and even public sentiment, especially in Daisy's case, called her names for accusing her perpetrators. (The main perpetrator pleaded guilty to child endangerment and served four months in jail.) Audrie committed suicide not long after her ordeal; Daisy seemed to be doing well especially after she met other survivors and they offered each other empathy and support. Tragically, in August 2020, at the age of 23, she also committed suicide. (Stafford, 2020)

For those rape victims who go to the hospital and do a rape examination kit, as well as report the crime to the police, it will be a different experience than what happens when someone keeps the situation to herself or himself, possibly even forgoing any medical treatment. It is important to sexual violence victims to know, if they do go to the hospital to have a rape kit done, they can have it stored anonymously until they are ready to go forward with having the evidence analyzed. It varies by state, but there may be a time limit on that, from three to five years. Check to see if the cost of the rape kit is covered by the state, which it may well be. Victims should not have to pay for the rape kit analysis.

If a rape victim does report the victimization to law enforcement, it is important for police to handle the rape victim in a respectful and compassionate way. Avoid implying directly or indirectly that the victim was "asking for it" or in any way inferring victim blame. It is crucial to get as many details as possible about what happened, including any alcohol or drugs that were consumed right before the rape occurred, but avoid implying that being drunk or high on drugs is an explanation for why the rape victim compiled or it will victimize her a second time. This is what is often called the **second victimization**, or **second injury**, and it is to be avoided. Those are the terms that are associated with the victim, after the offender victimizes him or her, gets victimized again when he/she involves the criminal justice system in what happened in the hope of getting justice. .

Psychologist Paige Leigh Baker-Braxton in her 2018 TED Talk, "LGBT Queering the Narrative of Sexual Violence," makes an excellent case for how the criminal justice system and the medical communities have to treat LGBT rape victims with great sensitivity and in a less judgmental way. (The link to the video in YouTube is at the end of the bibliography.)

In an effort to help rape victims to feel more comfortable during the reporting process, teams known as SART (Sexual Assault Response Team) have been put in place in a majority of local precincts. These teams should coordinate the activities of the various other departments and situations that a rape victim will have to deal with including the medical, forensic, legal, and even victim advocacy issues.

If an Arrest Is Made — The Court Response

If an arrest is made, the rape victim, unless there are multiple victims of the same rapist and the decision is made to have another victim be the main witness in the case, will be involved with the case until its conclusion in either a plea bargain or a trial and, if found guilty, a sentencing. Depending upon the particular district attorney's office, they may honor the important advance in the rights of crime victims by asking the victim what she thinks of the plea they are planning to offer the defendant, If the case does not go to trial, and she testifies, as noted in this chapter, the rape shield laws make it less likely that the victim's current or previous sex life will be up for scrutiny during the trial as a way of discrediting the victim's character or as a way of calling into question her claim that she did not consent to the sex act.

If the defendant is found guilty, once again depending upon the particular court where the case has been tried, the victim may be allowed to give a **victim impact statement** that the judge could consider when deciding on the rapist's punishment. If he or she is ordered to serve time in prison, the victim impact statement may influence the range of years that the rapist is ordered to serve before parole could be considered.

There have been changes made in the previous requirement that a rape allegation have **corroboration** or supporting evidence to substantiate a rape victim's claim that have made it easier and somewhat less traumatizing for rape victims who decide to report their victimization. Previously, corroboration might include such factors as reporting to the police in a timely fashion, the existence of semen as proof of penetration, the rapist using a weapon, and evidence of physical harm to the victim which would indicate that the victim resisted.

Rape victims who are considering whether or not to report their rapes might consider the prevention benefits of sharing the details of what happened to them. Even if they did not see the rapist's face so that an eyewitness description might be impossible if suspects are caught, if the rape victim shares the rapist's *modus operando*, or his signature rapist criminality, it might help to form a better profile of the rapist so that the public could be alerted or law enforcement will have more information to help them to catch the rapist before he strikes again.

The victim who reports the rape to the police will be interviewed by one or two police officers. They will take a statement.

If the woman or man can identify her or his attacker, a warrant may be applied for and, once the warrant is issued, the accused rapist will be arrested. If the accused cannot be located, no arrest will be made. If the attacker is under the age of 16 or another age, depending upon the state the rape occurred in, the case made be sent to Juvenile Court.

An **arraignment** and a setting of **bond** will be held. At the same time the warrant might be applied for, the case might instead be dropped by the rape victim or by the court because there is not enough evidence to pursue it.

Depending upon various factors related to the case, such as whether the victim was a child or not, the case may be sent to a particular court or the case may be dropped for a variety of reasons.

If the case goes forward, it might take up to 18 months for the case to be settled. Initially, after the arraignment, there will be a pre-trial meeting, about two months after the case was transferred to a particular court. At that meeting, it may be decided if the lawyers/prosecutor will plea bargain the case. If they agree to plea bargain, the case goes to sentencing. Or the case might be dropped due to lack of evidence or it might go to trial.

If it goes to trial, the defendant might be found guilty or not guilty. If the defendant is found not guilty, he goes free. If he is found guilty, the case now goes to the pre-sentence investigation phase. After the pre-sentence investigation is complete, the sentencing is decided and the defendant is either placed on **probation** (placed under supervision but in lieu of jail, possibly including doing community service and possibly wearing an ankle monitor to have movements tracked), or sent to jail or prison. He is sent to jail if the sentence is under one year; prison if it is one year or longer. After serving a certain amount of time, the defendant may be eligible for **parole**, or he may elect to complete the entire sentence to avoid having the restrictive conditions placed on him after release while still under parole, which might last as long as one to five or more years.

It is said that anywhere from 20 to 40 percent of rape victims report their crime. Of those who who report their crime, a relatively small percentage of those cases will lead to an arrest. Of those who are arrested, an even smaller percentage will be charged with the rape. Of those who are charged, the majority of those cases will be settled through a **plea bargain**, rather than going to trial. Of those that go to trial, of those that are convicted, out of the original 1000 reported rapes, as few as 25 may go to prison. (RAINN.org, n.d.)

In theory, a rape case could be pursued without the rape victim cooperating. In that case, it makes it harder to win the case.

Although prison is the most common sentence for the few who are convicted of rape, since it is a violent crime, and considered one of the most serious violent crimes, anecdotally there are exceptions to that. The convicted perpetrator in Chanel Miller's rape case, whose perpetrator was a star university athlete, served only three months in jail. (Shapiro, 2019)

If rape victims feel they should get financial restitution and possibly even be part of a **restorative justice** option with or without prison time, that might be an outcome to pursue. If restorative justice is an option, the rape victim, offender, and mediator work out a course of action that is agreeable to all parties. As you know from Chapter 2, "An Anthropological and Historical View of Crime Victims and Victims' Rights," the victim used to be able to work out an agreement with the offender for criminal wrongs but that right was removed in time as the king and then the state took over on the victim's behalf. A **civil suit** against the rapist or a negligent third party might be another option. (See Chapter 6, "Helping the Victim," for more information on civil suits.)

Sex Offender Registration

On July 29, 1994, in New Jersey, Megan Kanka, a 7-year-old girl, was enticed by her neighbor to come over and play with his puppies. Once she entered his house, the rapist sexually assaulted Megan. Then he strangled her with a belt.

The tragedy sparked a public outcry when the killer was caught and it was revealed that he was recently released from prison having served time for two previous sex offense convictions.

That situation led to what became known as **Megan's Law**. That law requires that known sex offenders who fall into three distinct risk categories have lifelong requirements placed on them ranging from the lowest level of risk, which requires the state to notify local law enforcement that a convicted sex offender has been released from custody or prison, to the highest risk category, which requires the community to know that a sex offender is living amongst them. Some states have specific rules about where a convicted sex offender is allowed to live or work if a school, playground, park, or childcare facility is within a certain number of feet.

As criminologist Larry Siegel points out in his textbook, *Criminology*, in the "Do Sex Registration Laws Really Work?" it is debatable if these laws are working. Siegel points to a 2015 study by Zgoba and Levenson in Florida that found that on comparing before and after arrest rates there was actually a statistically significant *increase* in repeat arrest rates after the sex offender registration laws were enacted in 1997. Siegel notes, "Obviously, instituting sex offender registration in Florida did not have the desired effect policy makers intended . . . These results challenge the effectiveness of sex offender registration laws. Rather than deter crime, sex offender laws may merely cause sex offenders to be more cautious while giving parents a false sense of security." (Siegel, 2018:9)

REACTIONS TO RAPE

Five Areas of Concern for All Sexual Assault Victims

Here are the five areas that sexual assault victims need help with:

1. Victim's physical safety;
2. Medical issues;
3. Victim's emotional state;
4. Legal issues; and
5. Victim's support system (*Rape and Sexual Abuse Crisis Center Training Manual*, 1995:10).

The groundbreaking empirical study of psychiatric nurse and rape victim researcher Dr. Ann Wolbert Burgess and sociologist and fellow researcher Dr. Lynda Lytle Holmstrom, back in the 1970s, highlighted the treatment of rape victims by police, hospitals, and courts. The co-authors studied the experiences of 115 victims—113 were female. (Burgess and Holmstrom had co-founded the Victim Counseling Program at Boston City Hospital.) As the Boston College tribute to Dr. Holmstrom pointed out in April 2021, "As reviewers noted, the book [*The Victim of Rape*] made clear that rape does not end after the attacker leaves. The victim's suffering can be heightened or diminished based on the response of the three institutions." (Boston College Trustees, April 2021)

Here is an overview of key issues related to each of those concerns.

- Is the victim in a safe situation?
- Should police be called?
- Does the victim have medical injuries that require an ambulance?
- *Victims need to be told not to bathe or change clothes* and to bring new clothes to the doctor or hospital.
- Remind the victim that going to the hospital does not automatically mean that the rape will be reported to the police.
- Ask the open-ended question to the victim, "How are you are feeling now?"
- "It is important that the victim understand that no matter what happened, no matter what anyone has said to her, the rape was not her fault."
- The rape victim may be going through what is known as the **rape trauma syndrome** (see separate discussion below).
- Suggest that the victim talk with a counselor at a rape crisis or crime victim counseling center about what happened.
- Discuss with the victim her legal options including reporting the crime to the police, sexual assault laws, criminal trials, and even a civil suit as a possibility.
- Another legal option is to let the victim know about state crime victim compensation, what it is, what expenses might be covered by it, eligibility to apply, procedures for applying, and so forth. Every state has a state crime victim compensation plan with its own guidelines and benefits so it is best to find out the specific procedures for each state where the crime occurred.
- Identify who the victim is able to call such as a crime victim advocate and meet her at the hospital, or have a friend or family member come to her apartment or home to stay with her after the assault. (Doerner and Lab, 2017: 219-223; Connecticut Alliance to End Sexual Violence and The Rowan Center, 2021; Rape and Sexual Abuse Crisis Center, Inc., 1995; Osborne-Crowley, 2018)

Rape Trauma Syndrome

Rape trauma syndrome is a term that applies to physical and psychological symptoms experienced by rape victims after the assault. There are two phases in the rape victim or **rape trauma syndrome**. The first is the acute phase which is characterized by disorganization. Feelings such as anger, fear, and anxiety are common in this acute phase. Victims who do not show these feelings, but are withholding their reactions, who are numb, are still in this acute phase.

There are physical reactions to being raped beyond the bruises and injuries the rape victim may have experienced. Sleep and eating patterns may be interrupted and there may be dreams and nightmares. Experts report that there may be symptoms related to the specific focus of the attack. For example, if someone was forced to have oral sex, they may say that their mouth or throat feels irritated. There may be musculoskeletal pain, or gynecological and menstrual issues.

Other emotional reactions in this acute phase include being afraid of dying, getting injured, or being maimed. There may be a fear of sex as well as a lack of a sex drive and even a more generalized aversion to men.

The second phase of the rape trauma syndrome is the reorganization phase, which is for most a prolonged-term evolution. It may take weeks, it may take months, it may even take years. A 62-year-old woman was raped by the *coyote* who helped her migrate from Columbia by way of Mexico 28 years ago. What made her even more upset by the rape is that her best friend had vouched for the man. It took her 18 years from when the rape incident happened to finally tell her husband, to whom she was married for five years at that point, and her children, who were now grown, about what happened to her. Previously she was afraid of being judged or not being believed. She says, "My entire family was so sad that I had kept this secret for such a long time, and suffered alone." Today she wishes she could press charges against the rapist but she does not know his real name or where to find him. The immediate effects of the rape were that it took her a long time to establish a relationship, especially a serious one, with a male. The long-term effects of the attack are that she suffers from anxiety and panic attacks. (Anonymous interview shared with the author, 2018) The third phase of the Rape Trauma Syndrome is the Resolution Phase. Survivors (victims) of rape are more accepting of what happened. (Doerner and Lab, 2017; 219-223; RAINN.org, n.d.; Burgess and Holmstrom, 1974)

POSSIBLE VICTIM REACTIONS DURING AND AFTER SEXUAL VIOLENCE

Sexual violence victims may describe themselves as detaching from reality while they are being assaulted. The term for this is **disassociation.** This defense mechanism for dealing with the trauma can occur during or after the sexual violence. Here is how a survivor described that experience in her TV interview: "A lot of victims and survivors will say they detach and you really do," McGowan, 44, said Tuesday on 'Good Morning America.' "You float up above your body because you're trying to figure out . . . Literally when he grabbed me I was thinking, 'Oh I hope I still have lipstick on for the camera.' " (Kindelan, 2018)

When a sexual violence victim shares that she or he was frozen when the assault was happening, that is actually substantiated by what we have learned about the brain. Experiencing trauma, like the trauma of sexual violence, can impact on the "fight or flight" reaction to danger. If someone cannot do either, it can lead to a response that is known as **tonic immobility** which is when someone "freezes." (Loess, 2020)

Memory impairment is another reaction, which can help explain why many sexual violence victims have trouble recalling the exact details of what happened. In her article, "The Effects of Sexual Assault on the Brain and Body," Priya Loess, Ph.D. explains that memory impairment is ". . . another survival response. In times of distress, the amygdala, which is the part of the brain that responds to stress and fearful emotions, takes over and redirects attention. During an assault, attention may shift as a coping mechanism, making it hard to recount what happened." (Loess, 2020)

By now, most everyone has heard of **PTSD** (post-traumatic stress disorder). This occurs when someone goes through a traumatic event and new experiences can cause a "trigger" or recall of that original event, re-experiencing the original distress. Is a sexual violence victim having PTSD? The National Center for PTSD has this response: "The only way to know for sure if you have PTSD is to talk with a mental health care provider. The provider will ask you about your trauma, your symptoms and any other problems you have." (ptsd.va.gov)

In Chapter 6, "Helping the Victim," there was a discussion of various therapies that are being used, with success, to treat PTSD in survivors, including survivors of rape and sexual assault. Licensed mental health counselor Mary Joye LMHC works with victims of sexual abuse. She shares some insights about the challenges of helping these survivors to deal with their PTSD: "It takes a long time to process the damage. People disassociate particularly rape and sexual assault crime victims. Education to the public needs to work on blaming the perpetrator and how they manipulated the victim instead of blaming the victim." As Joye was quoted as saying in chapter 6, but it bears repeating in this chapter on rape, "They acknowledge its presence, but they learn not to allow it to take over. Rape happened to me, instead of saying, 'I am a rape victim.'" (Joye, January 13, 2021)

The Association of Rape, Sexual Assault and Eating Disorders

The association among rape, sexual assault, and eating disorders may be a familiar idea to you, or you might find it somewhat of a surprise, but it is a potential consequence of sexual violence that needs to be mentioned. There has been more attention by psychiatrists, researchers, and eating disorder experts on the correlation between childhood sexual abuse, especially incest, and eating disorders, notably **anorexia nervosa**, which is characterized by severe starvation, and **bulimia**, which involves vomiting up food to avoid weight gain. (Schwartz and Cohn, editors, 1996) As you know, children and teens are explored in their own chapters, Chapters 10 and 11. That childhood or teenage sexual abuse or rape can impact on adult eating disorders such as anorexia nervosa, bulimia, and also obesity, still bear noting. An example of this was shared with this author when she was conducting research into childhood and teenage sexual abuse as well as eating disorders, by a 31-year-old woman who was currently 244 pounds—100 pounds overweight. She shared: "'I was molested by a neighbor at age eight, by a step-uncle at twelve, and raped by an acquaintance at age fourteen." (Yager, 2015)

This section looks at eating disorders, rape, and sexual assault, regardless of when the sexual abuse occurred. However, even if the sexual abuse or rape occurred during the formative years, it is the eating disorders that are manifested during the adult years that are the concern. Of course if someone always had a normal weight and a healthy association with exercise as well as a positive body image and suddenly, following an adult rape or sexual assault, that all abruptly changes, it should be easier to see a direct correlation between those dramatic changes and the sexual violence.

In "The Connection Between Eating Disorders and Sexual Violence" by Laura Palumbo, published at the website for the National Sexual Violence Resource Center (NSVRC), which was founded by the Pennsylvania Coalition Against Rape, it is noted that "Understanding the connection between sexual trauma and eating disorders is vital for those working with survivors of sexual assault and individuals recovering from an eating disorder." (Palumbo, 2018)

In addition to the three eating disorders already mentioned—anorexia, bulimia, and obesity—there are other conditions including over-exercising, abusing laxatives, negative body image and poor self-esteem,

Developing an eating disorder can happen all of a sudden, after sexual trauma as well as the PTSD (post-traumatic stress disorder) associated with it, or it could be part of an earlier pattern that was successfully dealt with but the new sexual trauma has exacerbated those previous eating disorder-related challenges. This author conducted a study of 26 adult survivors of childhood or teenage sexual abuse including incest. In addition to distributing an extensive written survey, there were selected follow-up phone or in-person interviews. Respondents were asked to check off any of a number of conditions that they might currently be experiencing. Every single respondent who answered that question checked off "low self-esteem" and 16 indicated they had overeating and weight issues including at least 5 who stated that they weighed between 200 and 300 pounds and 4 who reported being 10 to 30 pounds overweight. (Yager, 2015)

A 43-year-old single social service worker from a Western state, who is 5'2" and weighs 206 pounds, shared that she was abused as a child by her brother, a family friend, and then from the age of 13 until 16 by a health care professional. She shared: "My perfectionism/controlling/compulsive/workaholic behavior are all driven by not wanting to ever be caught off guard again . . . And the one thing I've ever been able to trust has been food." (Yager, 2015)

Here are just some of the ways that being the victim of rape or sexual assault can impact on eating, body image, and self-esteem:

- Whether the rape or sexual assault was attempted or completed, the experience means someone tried to take control of the victim, or succeeded in gaining control.
- Food and eating, and even exercising, may be a way to regain that control.

Overeating, or even refusing to eat, may be a way of trying to regain power over one's own body. (Yager, 2015) There are trained professionals available for rape or sexual assault victims who may find they have developed an eating disorder since their attack. All states and most countries offer government-funded crime victim compensation including either direct free counseling services or reimbursement of services that are approved. You have to check with your state or city if you are in another country to see if they require reporting the sexual assault to the police or if there is a time period for either reporting or for how long ago the assault had to have occurred. Some services may even offer free or sliding scale or lower-cost fees regardless of the time that the crime occurred or whether it was reported to the police.

RAPE CONTROVERSIES

Victim Defounding

The issue of **victim defounding,** meaning whether or not a victim's accusations are true, is something law enforcement, police, and the criminal justice system have to deal with for all crimes. Victim defounding, if proven, could lead to the conclusion that a rape claim was actually a **false accusation.** However, a study by Lisak et. al. over a 10 year period of 136 sexual assault cases determined that the prevalence of false allegations was between 2% and 10%. (Lisak, et.al., 2010: 1318)

Questioning the victim's side of things unfortunately reaches a crescendo with rape and sexual assault victims, since so often it can be a "he said, she said" situation, even with forensic evidence. That is because the issue of consent is pivotal and sometimes even subjective. The victim and the accused can be on diametrically opposed sides in that declaration. There are also rape cases where the evidence is so clearly in support of the victim's accusation that the lack of consent is irrefutable, such as if the victim was inebriated or drugged to the point that consent was impossible.

But in many other cases, especially what are known as date rape or acquaintance rape cases, that the "he said, she said" controversy is more likely to manifest itself. Here is a typical scenario: a couple go out on a date; they go back to the girl's apartment and they start to make out. The girl is completely in agreement with the foreplay but as it gets to something more than kissing and fondling, she changes her mind and no longer wants to have sex with her date. She says, "No," but he does not stop. She is 120 pounds and he is 240 pounds. He overpowers her and rapes her. Afterwards, she cries, calls the police, and gets him arrested. He either denies hearing her say "no" or says that he thought "no" was just her way of acting hard to get.

Are some rape victims lying? Why would someone do that? Is it out of fear that the victim's account might be questioned that so many rape victims—an estimated 60 percent—fail to report the crime? Here are the oft-quoted findings of Dr. Eugene Kanin's study reported on in February 1994 about the false accusations of rape in a sample of 109 cases during a nine-year period. Forty-five cases or 41 percent of the total forcible rape cases were found to be false. The motives behind the false accusations Dr. Kanin found are these three:

1. to obtain sympathy and attention;
2. to seek revenge; or
3. to provide an alibi.

Two famous cases of rape allegations that proved to be false are that of 15-year-old Tawana Brawley, back in November 1987 in New York state, and the Duke University allegations, in March 2006. In both high-profile cases, an African American woman accused white men of rape. Brawley's case gained the attention of Al Sharpton, a spokesperson for civil rights, among others. But the following October, a grand jury, after hearing the testimony and examining the evidence, concluded that no rape had occurred. (Winerip, 2013)

The second well-known example of rape allegations that turned out to be false is the case in mid-March 2006 of three Duke University Lacrosse team members. A month after the allegations, the coach resigned, and the remainder of the lacrosse season was suspended. Thirteen months later, the three young men were found innocent. A year later, the alleged victim graduated from Duke with a degree in psychology. In 2008, she published a memoir, sharing that she was previously raped at the age of 14. In November 2013, the victim was found guilty of stabbing her boyfriend who died from his injuries; she claimed she acted in self-defense. She was sentenced to 14 to 18 years in prison for second degree murder. (Calame, 2007; BBC.com, 2013)

According to one of the leading articles in this area, "False allegations of Sexual Assault: An Analysis of Ten Years of Reported Cases," between 2% and 10% of the 136 cases they analyzed over a 10-year period were coded as false allegations. (Lisak, et. al., 2010)

Victim Blame

One of the most hurtful things you can do or say to a rape or sexual assault victim is that she or he is to blame. Victims most often fall into the victim blame syndrome on their own so having those close to them or even the medical community or first responders imply or insinuate that she or he is in any way responsible for what happened just exacerbates the victim blame negative mentality. Victims will say to themselves, "Why didn't I do this?" or "I shouldn't have done that," or "Why did I say that?" so you certainly, as a family, friend, or first responder dealing with a rape victim, should not be saying any of those things as well.

Here is the tricky part. As you will see in the section on how to reduce or eliminate rape or sexual assault later in this chapter, there is a fine line between victim blame and helping potential victims to avoid victimization by engaging in certain behaviors that may avoid or de-escalate a situation from rising to the level of an assault or rape. But fortunately it is possible to help victims or would be victims to take better control of their everyday realities so they are less likely to be a rape victim while still avoiding implying or directly stating that for the completed rape, there is victim blame.

As Susan Storm writes in "10 Things Not to Say to a Sexual Abuse Survivor," there are three basic rules: "Believe them; Support Them, Don't Criticize the Survivor's Actions Leading Up to the Assault." (Susan Storm, 2015)

SEXUAL VICTIMIZATION BESIDES RAPE

Sexual Assault and Unwanted Sexual Contact

According to the NIJ (National Institute of Justice) report on rape and sexual violence, "Sexual assault covers a wide range of unwanted behavior—up to but not including penetration—that are attempted or completed against a victim's will or when a victim cannot consent because of age, disability, or the influence of alcohol or drugs." (NIJ, 2010). It might involve actual or threatened physical force, weapons, or intimidation, and could include touching of intimate body parts, voyeurism, unwanted exposure to pornography, and publicly showing images taken privately or without the victim's knowledge. (NIJ, 2010)

Unwanted sexual contact, under the heading of sexual assault, is another form of sexual victimization. It may include groping or touching without sexual penetration. There are two kinds: (1) **unwanted sexual contact with force** and (2) the non-forceful kind that is referred to as **coerced sexual contact**.

Although few disagree that sexual harassment, stalking, or sexual assault that is forceful and intrusive is a form of sexual victimization, unwanted sexual contact is somewhat more controversial as to what legal action, if any, should be taken against the perpetrator. A homeless man, for example, groped a teenager as she walked up the stairs to her train. She found the nearby police and told them what happened. She wanted the man arrested but the police preferred to issue a warning to the man. The teenager was furious that they did not see the situation as a more serious victimization. (Anonymous interview shared with author)

One does need to consider if someone is not reprimanded, or given counseling or other mental health aid, for unwanted sexual contact if that might be seen as a green light to keep doing it and/or to go on to more heinous sexual victimization. Are there any scientific studies addressing this issue or is this an area of exploration that victimologists or criminologists need to be investigating?

Sexual Harassment

Although this is a crime that freelancers or independent contractors and performing artists can fall victim to, we most often associate sexual harassment with traditional workplace situations. Previously swept under the rug in many instances, including giving the victims large settlements in exchange for their silence, sexual harassment is when someone in power abuses that power and manipulates someone into performing a sex act in exchange for a promotion or some other work-related perk. Sexual harassment also refers to sexual comments, innuendos, unwelcome sexual advances, or physical conduct or contact that is one-sided and not invited by the victim.

This type of behavior has gotten much more attention since the turn of the century. Companies have mandatory training to help their employees to avoid falling into the trap of behaving in a manner that could be considered sexual harassment. It also sensitives victims to actions that they may previously have tolerated but now they realize it is unacceptable conduct.

Sexual harassment clip art.

Eric Knightly is a California-based attorney who specializes in sexual harassment cases especially in the workplace. Occasionally there is a case that has a criminal component to it such as a violent sexual assault. Most of his cases are civil cases. But that does not mean that it should be tolerated. Says Knightly, "The cases I learn about are really severe conduct. I would put them into categories. You could have just words. With words, I would make the distinction between commenting on someone once or all the time. Then you have someone who might ask someone out and the woman declines it. The next level up is, 'Sleep with me or I won't promote you or you'll get fired.' Being rude to somebody and using sexualized terms, a lot of sexual harassment is not illegal, but it could lead to a large money judgment." (Knightly, January 15, 2021)

SECONDARY VICTIMS OF RAPE AND SEXUAL ASSAULT

Secondary victimization applies to sexual violence although unlike the secondary victims of homicide, who are dealing with the loss of their loved one, the rape or sexual assault victim survived. Yes, there are instances of sexual homicide but it is much more likely that family and friends of a sexual violence victim will need to help and support the primary victim during the recovery process.

Depending upon the relationship to the victim, this may or may not be an easy order to fill. If the rape victim was married or in a serious, romantic relationship at the time of the sexual attack, it is going to take work by both parties not to let the victimization make it hard for them to function as a sexual couple. Complicating this situation is that some victims may not even tell their spouse or romantic partner about the rape. Feelings of shame, fear, embarrassment, or even fear of what the spouse will do if he/she finds out what happened, can stop the victim from sharing about the rape or sexual assault, especially if she or he did not report it to the police. If the victim has not reported the crime to the police, or shared about it with a spouse or romantic partner, there may be behavior changes, especially when it comes to sexual intimacy, that cannot easily be explained. There are consequences to telling and not telling the romantic partner.

If the secondary victim of rape and sexual assault is having a hard time dealing with their loved one's victimization, they should look into counseling for themselves. It could be one-on-one or becoming part of a support group for those whose loved ones have been sexually assaulted.

In addition to the most direct secondary victims of rape and sexual assault, the romantic partners, are the victim's children. What should they share with their children? Age will of course be a big factor but it might also be personalities and what is going on in the children, teen, or adult child's life. If they are told what happened to their parent, do they now need to also get counseling or to join a support group? Will the romantic partner or children be advised that they are allowed to share this information with others or is this just something they need to know because they are family but it is not something that the victim wants broadcast beyond the immediate family?

Secondary victims of rape and sexual assault should be versed in the rape trauma syndrome as well as the symptoms for PTSD so they can watch for changes in their loved one's mood, sleep habits, and even the possibility of suicidal ideation that might require immediate intervention to prevent an even greater tragedy than the rape or sexual assault.

Understanding victim blame and being on the lookout for subtle or overt ways of communicating victim blame are important ways that the secondary victims, including friends as well as family, can help the victim in her or his healing, however long it takes. If the victim had to leave a job because of sexual harassment, secondary victims need to steer clear of making statements like, "How are you going to find a job now?" even if an apology, "Sorry, I didn't mean that!" quickly follows. The damage is done. The hurt may stay.

It is also absolutely normal and understandable for the secondary victims to feel many of the same emotions that their loved one is feeling in the aftermath of the sexual assault, from anger and rage to helplessness, fear, and sadness.

This is a dramatic violent crime that has happened to a family member, loved one, or friend and it is something that needs to be acknowledged and dealt with. But you also need to let the victim lead. If she or he wants to talk about it, fine. If avoiding the topic is preferred, respect that as well. That does not mean you do not have the right to talk about it with others if, of course, you have already cleared it with the victim or if you are talking to someone who is sworn to secrecy so it is safe to share, such as a clergyman, rabbi, counselor, rape crisis center advocate, or anonymous support group leader or member. Couples counseling might also be an option the secondary and primary victims of rape might want to consider.

Whenever the victim shares about her or his rape or sexual assault, whether it is right after it happens, or days, weeks, months, or even years later, showing compassion, understanding, and being patient while everything returns to normal is key. The experts say that rape and sexual assaults are not crimes of sex but of power and control, but it can manifest itself in sexual feelings, responses, and associations. Time, and professional help, if necessary, may be required especially for the romantic partner in the victim's life to handle what has happened. Some may take it in stride and deal with it much better than others.

RAPE AND SEXUAL VICTIMIZATION PREVENTION

We are in agreement that only the perpetrators are to blame for sexual violence including rape, not the victims, but there are still actions that potential victims can take to reduce the likelihood of victimization.

1. If you go to a bar, or even someone's private home or apartment, especially if this is someone that you are acquainted with but whose character you cannot completely vouch for, be careful what drink they serve you. It could be spiked.
2. Watch your alcohol or drug intake when you are at parties because this also makes someone more vulnerable to attacks.
3. Stay with one or more friends especially if you are walking to your car later at night, or to the bus or train from your place of work. If possible, request a reliable company employee as an escort.
4. If traveling internationally, individuals should know the laws in that country to avoid the unlikely but still possible scenario of being arrested and sentenced to prison for adultery or fornication outside of marriage, even in the event of rape, since those acts are against the law in certain Muslim countries. Since some Muslim countries are also "dry"—no liquor is allowed—if the rape occurred when the victim was drunk, there could be an additional charge, fine, and time in prison for illegally drinking.
5. Men and women, and boys and girls, should know the age of consent in their particular state to avoid being charged with statutory rape even if the sex was consensual.
6. Know the myths about rape and how those myths could set someone up to be a more likely victim. For example, it is a myth that rapists are most likely strangers. It is also a myth that all rape victims are women. Boys and men can and are raped as well.
7. Bystander intervention can help to stop an attack that might be in progress or at least he/she can call for help.

Finally, remember that victims of rape or sexual assault are entitled to the same rights that all crime victims are entitled to namely:

1. The right to be notified about their case
2. The right to be protected from being fired if they are a witness in a case.
3. The right that any statement a victim makes to a rape crisis center victim advocate or counselor may not be allowed as evidence in court.
4. The right to keep a victims' current or prior sexual behavior not be brought as evidence in any trial.
5. The right to have any property the police had to confiscate related to the case to be returned within six months of the conclusion of any criminal proceedings.
6. The right to make a claim for any injuries suffered because of the crime including medical, psychiatric, or social services necessary for the victim's recovery. (Offices of the United States Attorneys, Crime Victims' Rights Act, updated 2016; "Marsy's Law for Florida . . ." 2018)

Profile ▪ Jasmin D., Survivor of Childhood Incest

This author interviewed Jasmin D. back in 1996, when she was 45. She would be 70 years old now. Jasmin worked hard in individual and group therapy to overcome the long-term effects of her childhood trauma. Her abusers were her brother, two years older, and her father. Jasmin never reported either of her abusers. She kept it all a family secret only sharing with her therapist, therapy group, husband, and her researcher. Jasmin's mother was emotionally abusive and distant but she never felt she knew what was happening in her own home all those years.

When it first started we were very young. I was two and he [my brother] was four. He used to do things. I remember when his friends would be around, he would pull my pants down in front of his friends and poke around and do things. [My mother] pretended not to notice. She probably didn't. It's amazing. People will believe a blue wall is red and they will really believe it because that's what they do to survive.

I remember when I got a little older, I was seven and he was nine, he would have me come up to his room. That was when we moved to the new house. He would have me put my mouth on his [private part] and then he would take pictures of me naked and then that continued. The last I really remember anything was when I was fifteen. We were rolling around on the grass. He had been teaching me how to drive so he was 17 and I was 15. I think we both got very turned on at that point and he came down [to my room] that evening. He undressed me and I pretended to be asleep. He felt all over me. I really believe he was ready to have actual intercourse with me [but] then I stopped it. I sat on the edge of the bed and I said, "We've got to talk about this." He was going to [abroad] the next day and that was basically it. But we were always very very close and people would notice it at that time. He would be going to dances and I would be at the same dance sometimes and when we danced, we almost looked like we were a couple. Even though I didn't have sex with him per se, it was oral and it would have become that if I hadn't stopped it.

He and I have actually talked about it [since that time] a couple of times and he expressed a great deal of guilt. We were actually driving our younger brother to his graduate school graduation and he mentioned feeling guilty because he knew anyone who was a victim of sexual abuse how much it affected them and he couldn't help but feel guilty. He read seventy pages of a novel I had written . . . and he couldn't help but feel guilty because he had sensed [the heroine's] rage.

I believe my brother thought it was okay to abuse women because he saw my father doing it. My first memory is lying on top of my father and pushing away from him. My first memories of two years old of my father and my brother. [My father] was not getting any affection from my mother or perhaps I believe any sex either and she put me in the bathroom with my father. . . .

Just [so] you know I didn't have physical intercourse but it was very inappropriate behavior and it made me feel guilty because it made me feel like he was choosing me over my mother but in reality, he was with her.

I was always so tense with my family but now I'm relaxed because I don't care what they think about me. It was my rage that made me tense. I was afraid of myself. I wanted to fucking kill them and I was afraid of that rage that I had. So that's why I used to be so tense. I'm no longer tense. The rage has dissipated. I've been working on this for seven years and I've turned this over to other people. I started a whole unit of survivors at an institution where I work with women prisoners on this issue. I started another survivor group, for survivors and partners of survivors.

In our groups, they say incest is when someone who has power over you misused that power in any way. It can be verbal. It can be physical. It's basically inappropriate behavior and usually it's been someone who has power over a child and misused that child. It can be a family friend. We won't even talk about the physical abuse, the beating with the belts [of my mother]. I was in a mental institution after a very serious suicide attempt. I took one thousand barbiturates when I was eighteen. The first time that happened was the summer before I went to college. My parents left me outside in my night gown and locked the doors. I had to sleep in the car and I ended up having actual intercourse with a friend of my brother's and my mother was very attracted to him.

Students and instructors can download additional excerpts from transcripts of anonymous interviews with victims (survivors) at the product page that accompanies the text, at www.AspenPublishing.com

SUMMARY

By 1993, marital rape was a crime throughout the U.S. Progress was made when the FBI charged the official definition of rape in 2013 to remove the word "forcible" and "female." Rapists are most likely someone known to the victim a whopping 74 percent known versus 19.5 percent unknown, based on the 2018 UCR report. Whether or not to report a rape is still complicated for its victims. There are many kinds of rapes including acquaintance rape, date rape, incest, marital rape, stranger rape, and sexual homicide, where the rape victim is killed which is relatively rare (23 reported rape or sexual assault-related homicides in 2018 out of over 100,000 reported rapes) but there may be concerns about the statistics.

There are five key ways that rape and sexual assault victims need to be helped after their victimization, namely, ensuring the victim's physical safety; medical issues; the victim's emotional state; legal issues; and the victim's own support system. The direct victim will go through a lot after the rape, a typical reaction known as the rape trauma syndrome. There are immediate effects—the acute phase—as well as a second stage—the outward adjustment phase. The third phase is the Resolution Phase. Victims of rape may also experience PTSD.

A key concept to keep in mind is to avoid victim blame. Everyone has heard comments such as "Why was she wearing that outfit?" or "Why was she out alone at night?"

Researchers have found that sexual violence impacts on the brain causing such reaction as tonic immobility, disassociation, memory impairment, and, down the line, PTSD. In addition to helping the victim deal with her physical, emotional, and legal issues related to the rape, there are secondary victims of rape that also have needs that should be addressed. Their world has been turned upside down as well, especially if the victim is married or has a significant romantic partner. The couple may need individual or couples counseling or becoming part of a survivor support group or secondary victim support group to deal with the aftermath of the rape. Sexual harassment is a victimization that needs to be addressed even if it is not as horrific as the violent crime of rape.

KEY TERMS

acquaintance rape
anorexia nervosa
arraignment
bond
bulimia
coerced sexual contact
corroboration
date rape
disassociation
false accusation
incest
marital rape
Megan's Law
parole
plea bargain
probation
PTSD (post traumatic stress disorder)
rape
rape kit
rape shield law
rape trauma syndrome
restorative justice
SAFE (Sexual Assault Forensic Examiner)
SANE (Sexual Assault Nurse Examiner)
SART (sexual assault response teams)
second injury
second victimization
sexual assault
sexual harassment
sexual homicide
stranger rape
Tonic immobility
unwanted sexual contact
unwanted sexual contact with force
victim blame
victim defounding
victim impact statement

REVIEW QUESTIONS

1. Define sexual violence.
2. What are the major differences between the definition of rape since 2013 and the previous definition now known as the "legacy" definition?
3. Who are the most likely perpetrators of sexual violence of adults?
4. What are some symptoms of the acute phase of rape trauma syndrome?
5. Is rape a crime of sex or power?
6. How common is rape homicide?
7. What act was passed in 2003 to deal with rape in correctional facilities?

CRITICAL THINKING QUESTIONS

1. Why do you think sexual violence victims have the lowest rates of reporting to the police of all violent crimes? Explain your answer.

2. What changes do you think the United States and other countries have to make to see a dramatic decline in sexual violence in all age groups, races, ethnicities, genders, and sezual orientations? List some of those suggestions that individuals, agencies, schools, or law enforcement, the government, the media, and communities could implement to bring a dramatic reduction and even an elimination in sexual violence.

ACTIVITIES

1. You will be divided into teams of three with each team assigned one of the common types of rape: acquaintance, date, stranger, family member (incest), or gang rape. Your team will pick a notetaker for the group. Brainstorm about the rape you were assigned and write down myths and realities about your particular type of rape and its victim. Elect a reporter for your team to share with the entire class about your rape category.
2. Have a discussion of how rape victims are usually treated when they encounter the following individuals after the rape: police officer, SANE (Sexual Assault Nurse Examiner), doctor, TV reporter, family member, friend, or mental health professional. What are the best things to say? How do you avoid falling into the victim blame trap?

RESOURCES

American Bar Association
Commission on Domestic & Sexual Violence
americanbar.org/groups/domestic_violence
From the website: "Our mission is to increase access to justice for victims of domestic violence, sexual assault and stalking by mobilizing the legal profession."

CDC (Centers for Disease Control and Prevention)
https://www.cdc.gov/violenceprevention/sexualviolence/prevention.html
U.S. government agency that is part of U.S. Department of Health & Human Services, that offers information on sexual violence issues including statistics, rape prevention, and education.

National Sexual Assault Hotline
1-800-799-SAFE (7233)
24 hour website offering free help. Operated by RAINN (See separate listing below)

National Sexual Violence Resource Center (NSVRC)
nsvrc.org
Founded in 2000 by the Pennsylvania Commission on Women, this research center nonprofit is concerned with conducting research into sexual violence and educating the public. Sponsors Sexual Assault Awareness Month (SAAM) every April.

RAINN (Rape, Abuse & Incest National Network)
rainn.org
A leading source of advocacy, educational, statistics, and direct help clearinghouse related to rape, sexual abuse, and incest. Started more than 25 years ago.

SHERO Project Movement
sheroprojectmvmt.org
Dawn Burnett founded SHEROs as a place to tell her story and to have other survivors of abuse to share theirs.

CITED WORKS AND ADDITIONAL REFERENCES

Alani, Hannah. January 29, 2020. "Victim of Brutal West Town Rape Must Return to Chicago to Face Attacker After Rufus Carson Rejects Plea Deal, Prosecutors Say." Blockclubchiago.org

Almukhtar, Sarah, Michael Gold, and Larry Buchanan. Updated February 8, 2018. "After Weinstein: 71 Men Accused of Sexual Misconduct and Their Fall From Power." *The New York Times.* Posted at nytimes.com

Amir, Menachem. 1967. "Victim Precipitated Forcible Rape." *Journal of Criminal Law and Criminology.* 58(4): 493-502.

BBC.com. January 6, 2020. "Reynhard Sinaga: 'Evil Sexual Predator' Jailed for Life for 136 Rapes." Posted at BBC.com.

__________. November 22, 2013. "Duke Lacrosse Accuser Crystal Mangum Guilty of Murder." Posted at bbc.com.

Bierie, David M. and Kristen M. Budd. 2018. "Romeo, Juliet, and Statutory Rape." *Sexual Abuse.* 30: 296-321.

Bishop, Kyla. April 15, 2018. "A Flection on the History of Sexual Assault Laws in the United States." *The Arkansas Journal of Social Change and Public Service* (online post)

Bonn, Scott A. December 30, 2019. "Examining Serial Killer Ted Bundy." Posted online psychologday-today.come

Boston College Trustees. April 2021. "In Memoriam: Lynda Lytle Holmstrom." Posted online at bc.edu.

Bowley, Bill. December 10, 2019. "Bill Cosby Loses Appeal of Sexual Assault Conviction." *New York Times,* Posted at https://www.nytimes.com/2019/12/10/arts/television/bill-cosby-appeal-sexual-assault.html

Bowley, Graham. June 30, 2021. "Bill Cosby Is Freed After Serving Three Years of his Sentence for Sexual Assault." *The New York Times.* Posted online at nytimes.com

Bowley, Graham and Joe Coscarelli. September 15, 2018. "Bill Cosby, Once a Model of Fatherhood, Is Sentenced to Prison." *New York Times.* Posted at nytimes.com

Bownes, I.T., E.C. O'Gorman, and A. Sayers. 1991. "Rape—A Comparison of Stranger and Acquaintance Assaults." *Medicine, Science, and the Law.* 102-109.

Bremner, J. Douglas. 2006. "Traumatic Stress: Effects on the Brain." *Dialogues in Clinical Neuroscience.* 8:445-451.

Brownmiller, Susan. 1975. *Against Our Will: Men, Women and Rape.* New York: Simon & Schuster.

Burgess, Ann Wolbert. 2019. *Victimology.* Third edition. Burlington, MA: Jones & Bartlett.

Burgess, Ann Wolbert and L.L. Holmstrom. 1974. "Rape Trauma Syndrome." *American Journal of Psychiatry.* 131: 981-986.

Burstow, Bonnie. 2003. "Toward a Radical Understanding of Trauma and Trauma Work." *Violence Against Women.* 9: 1293-1317.

Burt, M. R. 1980. "Cultural Myths and Supports for Rape." *Journal of Personality and Social Psychology,* 38, 217–230

Calamate, Byron. April 22, 2007. "Revisiting the Times's Coverage of the Duke Rape Case." *The New York Times,* The Public Editor. Posted at nytimes.com

CDC (Centers for Disease Control and Prevention) February 5, 2021 "Preventing Sexual Violence." Posted online.

Central MN Sexual Assault Center. n.d. "Facts About Sexual Assault." Posted online at cmsac.org

Cohen, Shawn, Reuven Fenton, Frank Rosario, and Daniel Prendergast. April 28, 2015. "Shelter Worker Gunned Down by Ex-Resident After Escaping Rape." *New York Post.*

Connecticut Alliance to End Sexual Violence and The Rowan Center. June 7-23, 2021. *Sexual Assault Crisis Counselor & Advocate Certification Manual and Training.* Seven modules.

Connecticut Municipal Police Training Council. March 1995. "Table 1: Patterns of Rape." Included in the Rape and Sexual Abuse Crisis Center, Inc. (Renamed The Rowan Center). *Training Manual.* Stamford, CT.

Cook, Joan M. and Amy E. Ellis. April 8, 2020. "The Other #MeToo: Male Sexual Abuse Survivors." *Psychiatric Times.*

Davis, Randy J. Arthur J. Lurigio, and Susan Herman (eds.). 2013. *Victims of Crime.* Fourth edition. Thousand Oaks, CA: SAGE.

Daigle, Leah E. and Lisa R. Muftic. 2016. *Victimology.* Thousand Oaks, CA: SAGE.

DeJong, W. (1999). "Rape and Physical Attractiveness: Judgments Concerning the Likelihood of Victimization." *Psychological Reports,* 85, 32–34.

Doerner, William G. and Steven P. Lab. 2017 Eighth Edition. *Victimology*. New York: Routledge.

Eyewitness News. November 11, 2019. "NYPD: 13-Year-Old Girl Raped While Walking to Friend's House in Brooklyn."

Fahim, Kareem. May 11, 2009. "In Bouncer's Murder Trial, Victim's Friend Recalls Their Last Night." *New York Times*. Posted at nytimes.com

Fedina, Lisa, Jennifer Lynne Holmes, and Bethany Backes. 2016. "How Prevalent Is Campus Sexual Assault in the United States?" *NIJ Journal*. 277: 26-30. Posted at https://www.ncjrs.gov/pdffiles1/nij/249827.pdf

Finkel, Jori. August 5, 2020. "Chanel Miller's Secret Source of Strength." *New York Times*. Posted at nytimes.com

Fisher, Bonnie S., Bradford W. Reyns, and John J. Sloan III. 2016. *Introduction to Victimology: Contemporary Theory, Research, and Practice*. New York: Oxford University Press.

Funkenstein, Daniel H. May 1955. "The Physiology of Fear and Anger." *Scientific American*.

Gerard, Ralph W. September 1953. "What Is Memory?" *Scientific American*.

Gewirtz-Meydan, Ateret and David Finkelhor. 2020. "Sexual Abuse and Assault in a Large National Sample of Children and Adolescents." *Child Maltreatment*. 25: 203-214

Goleman, Daniel. December 10, 1991. "New Studies Map the Mind of the Rapist." *New York Times*. C1, C10.

______________. April 14, 1992. "Therapies Offer Hope for Sex Offenders." *New York Times*. C1, C11.

Gotovac, Sandra and Shelagh Towson. 2015. "Perceptions of Sexual Assault Victims/Survivors: The Influence of Sexual History and Body Weight." *Violence and Victims*. 30: 66-80.

Gravelin, Claire R., Monica Biernat, and Caroline E. Bucher. January 2019. *Frontiers in Psychology, Review*. 9: 1-22.

Greenfield, Lawrence A. February 1997. "Sex Offenses and Offenders." Bureau of Justice Statistics, U.S. Department of Justice, Office of Justice Program.

Greensite, Gillian. November 1, 2009. "History of the Rape Crisis Movement." CALCASA—California Coalition Against Sexual Assault. Newsletter. Posted at https://www.calcasa.org/2009/11/history-of-the-rape-crisis-movement/

Griffin, Susan. November 3, September 1971. "Rape: The All-American Crime." *Ramparts*. 10.

____________. *Rape: The Politics of Consciousness*. 1986. New York: HarperCollins.

Groth, A. Nicholas with H. Jean Birnbaum. 1979. *Men Who Rape*. New York: Basic Books.

Guelden, Marlene and John Kim. "How to Interview a Rape Victim and Survive." Marin Rape Crisis Center, CA. 4 pages.

Harrell, Erika. December 2012. "Violent Victimization Committed by Strangers, 1993-2010." Bureau of Justice Statistics, Office of Justice Programs, U.S. Department of Justice.

Hodge, Lisa and Lia Bryant. 2019. "Masking the Self: Understanding the Link Between Eating Disorders and Child Sexual Abuse." *Qualitative Social Work*. 18: 247-264.

Hogan, Terry. Sunday, April 9, 1989. "The Real Issue of Victims' Rights Is The Lack of Rights." Connecticut Opinion. *New York Times*.

Holmstrom, Lynda Lytle and Ann Wolbert Burgess. 1978. *The Victim of Rape: Institutional Reactions*. New York: Wiley.

Hughes, Isabel. October 15, 2019. "Pennsylvania Man Charged in Decades-Old Rape Case After DNA Links Him to Attack." USAToday.com

Illinois Criminal Justice Information Authority. Updated 1993. "When the Rapist Is Someone You Know." Published by the Illinois Coalition Against Sexual Assault.

Jenness, Vlerie and Sara Fenstermaker. February 2016. "Forty Years After Brownmiller: Prisons for Men, Transgender Inmates, and the Rape of the Feminine." *Gender & Society*. 30: 14-29.

Kamenetz, Anya. November 30, 2014. "The History of Campus Sexual Assault." NPR (National Public Radio). Posted at https://www.npr.org/sections/ed/2014/11/30/366348383/the-history-of-campus-sexual-assault

Kanin, E.J. September 1957. "Male Aggression in Dating Courtship Relations." *American Journal of Sociology*. 63(2): 197-204.

Kantor, J., & Twohey, M. October 5, 2017. "Harvey Weinstein Paid off Sexual Harrassment Accusers for Decades." *The New York Times*.

Karmen, Andrew. 2020. *Crime Victims: An Introduction to Victimology*. Tenth edition. Boston, MA: Cengage.

Katz, Jennifer, Rena Pazienza, Rachel Olin, and Hillary Rich. 2015. "That's What Friends Are For: Bystander Responses to Friends or Strangers at Risk for Party Rape Victimization." *Journal of Interpersonal Violence* 30: 2775-2792.

Kaufman, Michelle R., Debangan Dey, Ciprian Crainiceanu, and Mark Dredze. August 2019. "#MeToo and Google Inquiries Into Sexual Violence: A Hashtag Campaign Can Sustain Information Seeking" *Journal of Interpersonal Violence.*

Kearl, H. 2018. "The Facts behind the #MeToo movement: A National Study on Sexual Harassment and Assault." Retrieved from stopstreetharassment.org

Keefe, John R., Shannon Wiltsey Stirman, Zachary D. Cohen, Robert J. DeRubeis, Brian N. Smith, and Patricia A. Resick. 2018. "In Rape Trauma PTSD, Patient Characteristics Indicate Which Trauma-Focused Treatment They are Most Likely to Complete." *Depress Anxiety* 35: 330-338.

Kindelan, Katie. February 2, 2018. "Rose McGowan's Account of Detaching From Reality During Alleged Rape is Common: Experts." *Good Morning America.* Posted at goodmorningamerica.com

Kirkpatrick, C. and E.J. Kanin. 1957. "Male Aggression on a College Campus." *American Sociological Review.* 22(1): 52-58.

Koss, M.P., C.A. Gidycz, and N. Wisniewski. 1987. "The Scope of Rape: Incidence and Prevalence of Sexual Aggression and Victimization in a National Sample of Higher Education Students." *Journal of Counseling and Clinical Psychology.* 55(2): 162-170.

Krebs, C.P., C.L. Lindquist, D. Ara, T.D. Warren, B.S. Fisher, and S.L. Martin. 2007. *Campus Sexual Assault (CSA) Study: Final Report.* Washington, D.C. National Institute of Justice.

Lawson, David M. March 6, 2018. "Understanding and Treating Survivors of Incest." *Counseling Today.*

Levenson, Eric, Lauren del Valle, and Sonia Moghe. March 11, 2020. "Harvey Weinstein Sentenced to 23 Years in Prison after Addressing His Accusers in Court." CNN. Posted at https://www.cnn.com/2020/03/11/us/harvey-weinstein-sentence/index.html

Levenson, Jill S. and Kristen M. Zgoba. "Community Protection Policies and Repeat Sexual Offenses in Florida." *International Journal of Offender Therapy and Comparative Criminology.* First published online March 10, 2015. Cited in Larry J. Siegel, *Criminology.* Thirteenth edition. Cengage: 9.

Lisak, David, Lori Gardinier, Sarah C. Nicksa, and Ashley M. Cote. 2010. "False Allegations of Sexual Assault: An Analysis of Ten Years of Reported Cases." *Violence Against Women* 16: 1318-1334.

Loess, Priyadarshani (Priya). July 2020. "The Effects of Sexual Assault on the Brain and Body." Portland Psychotherapy. Posted online.

Logan, T.K. and Jennifer Cole. August 2007. "Differential Characteristics of Intimate Partner, Acquaintance, and Stranger Rape Survivors Examined by a Sexual Assault Nurse Examiner (SANE)." *Journal of Interpersonal Violence.* 22: 1066-1076.

Luo, Tsun-Yin. August 2000. "'Marrying My Rapist?!' The Cultural Trauma among Chinese Rape Survivors." *Gender & Society.* 14(4): 581-597.

MacDonald, J.M. 1971. *Rape Offenders and Their Victims.* Illinois: Charles Thomas.

Mansnerus, Laura. Sunday, February 19, 1989. "The Rape Laws Change Faster Than Perceptions." *New York Times.*

MACSA (Maryland Coalitation Against Sexual Assault). "Understanding Rape in Prison." (Originally by Hallie Martyniuk and published by the Pennsylvania Coalition Against Rape (PCAR), 2013). Retrieved from https://mcasa.org/providers/resources-on-specific-topics/prea/prea-resources-and-webinars/ under

Miller, Chanel. 2020. *Know My Name.* New York: Penguin Books.

Molinari, E., M. Selvini, and F. Lenzini. December 2003. "Sexual Abuse and Eating Disorders: Clinical Cases." *International Journal of Eating and Weight Disorders.* 8: 253-262.

Morgan, Louise, Bernadette Brittain, and Jan Welch. 2012. "Multiple Perpetrator Sexual Assault: How Does it Differ from Assault by a Single Perpetrator?" *Journal of Interpersonal Violence.* 27: 2415-2436

National Institute of Justice (NIJ). October 25, 2010. "Overview of Rape and Sexual Violence." Retrieved from https://nij.ojp.gov/topics/articles/overview-rape-and-sexual-violence

Newman, Sandra. May 11, 2017. "What Kind of Person Makes False Rape Accusations?" *Quartz.* Posted at https://qz.com/980766/the-truth-about-false-rape-accusations/

Nickerson, John. September 21, 2016. "Man Sentenced for 1988 Rape, Kidnapping." *The Advocate.* Stamford, CT: A3.

Olds, Dorri. January 13, 2012. "Defriending My Rapist." *New York Times.* Opinion Pages, Townies.

______________. April 15, 2020. Interview.

______________. November 2018. Interview with SMK.

Osborne-Crowley, Lucia. July 6, 2018. "I Was the 'Perfect' Rape Victim but Still I Didn't Go to Police." Posted at abc.net.

Palumbo, Laura. February 26, 2018. "The Connection Between Eating Disorders and Sexual Violence." Blog posted at nsvrc.org

RAIIN.org, n.d. "The Criminal Justice System: Statistics. Posted online at RAINN.org.

____________. 2008. "Rape Trauma Syndrome." Posted at RAINN.org.

Ransom, Jan. March 6, 2020. "As Weinstein Awaits Prison, Prosecutors Detail 40 Years of Accusations." *New York Times.* Posted at nytimes.com

Rape and Sexual Abuse Crisis Center, Inc. (renamed The Rowan Center). March 1995. *Training Manual.* Stamford: CT.

________________. March 1995. "Helping a Victim of Sexual Harassment." Reprinted in Rape and Sexual Abuse Crisis Center, Inc. (Renamed The Rowan Center). *Training Manual.* Stamford: CT.

________________. March 1995. "Helping the Rape Victim." "Five Areas of Concern for All Sexual Assault Victims." Reprinted in Rape and Sexual Abuse Crisis Center, Inc. (Renamed The Rowan Center). *Training Manual.* Stamford, CT: 6 pages.

________________. February-March 1995, Sessions I, II, III, IV, and IV. "Volunteer Training Agenda." Rape and Sexual Abuse Crisis Center, Inc. (Renamed The Rowan Center).

Raphelson, Samantha. August 9, 2017. "Countries Around the World Move to Repeal 'Marry Your Rapist' Laws." Posted at npr.org

Russell, Diana E.H. 1986. *The Secret Trauma: Incest in the Lives of Girls and Women.* New York: Basic Books.

Ryan, William. 1976, 1971. *Blaming the Victim.* Revised and updated edition. New York: Vintage, a Division of Random House.

Samenov, Stanton E. 2014. *Inside the Criminal Mind.* Revised and updated edition. Broadway Books, Random House.

Santo, Alysia. July 25, 2018. "Prison Rape Allegations Are on the Rise. But the Accusations Are Still Rarely Found to Be True." *The Marshall Project.* Posted at www.themarshallproject.org

Schick, Nance. June 10, 2020. Interview.

Schwartz, Mark F. and Leigh Cohn, editors. 1996. *Sexual Abuse and Eating Disorders.* Bristol, PA: Brunner/Mazel.

Sebold, Alice. February 26, 1989. "Speaking of the Unspeakable." *New York Times Magazine.* 16.

Seelye, Katharine. February 15, 2021. "Kathleen Ham, Who Met Her Rapist Twice in Court, Dies at 73." *New York Times.* Posted at nytimes.com

Shapiro, Emily. October 31, 2020. "How the 'Golden State Killer,' A Serial Rapist, Murderer, Evaded Capture for Decades." Published at abc11.com

______________. September 24, 2019. "'Humiliated': Chanel Miller, Survivor in Brock Turner Sex Assault Case, Shares Her Story of Trauma and Recovery." ABCNews.com Posted online

Sharp, Debra Publosi. August 20, 2014. Interview.

______________. 2004. *Shattered.* New York: Atria, Simon & Schuster.

Shipp, E.R. July 28, 1991. "Bearing Witness to the Unbearable." *New York Times.* Section 4: 1.

Siegel, Larry J. 2018. *Criminology: Theories, Patterns, and Typologies.* Thirteenth edition. Boston, MA: Cengage.

Silverman, Daniel C., M.D. January 1978. "Sharing the Crisis of Rape: Counseling the Mates and Families of Victims." *American Journal of Orthopsychiatry.* 48(1): 166-173.

Storm, Susan. August 8, 2015. "10 Things Not to Say to a Sexual Abuse Survivor." Posted at psychologyjunkie.com

Surrell, April and Ida M. Johnson. 2020. "An Examination of Women's Experiences with Reporting Sexual Victimization Behind Prison Walls." *The Prison Journal.* 1-22.

Susan. (Anonymous) Speech. Friday, November 16, 1979. "The Victims of Crime: Breaking Through Stereotypes." 3 pages.

Stolberg, Sheryl Gay and Nicholas Fandos. September 27, 2018. "Brett Kavanaugh and Christine Blasey Ford Duel with Tears and Fury." *New York Times.* Posted at https://www.nytimes.com/2018/09/27/us/politics/brett-kavanaugh-confirmation-hearings.html

Styles, Ruth. December 15, 2020. "I Still Struggle with It-but I'm okay." Dailymail.com (UK)

Symonds, Martin, M.D. April 10, 1975. "The Psychological Patterns of Response of Victims to Rape." Presented at Seminar on Rape, John Jay College of Criminal Justice and American Academy for Professional Law Enforcement. 18 pages.

_______________. 1975. "Victims of Violence: Psychological Effects and After Effects." *American Journal of Psychoanalysis.* 35(1).

Treuer, Tamas, Magdalena Koperdak, Sandor Rosza, and Janos Furedi. 2005. "The Impact of Physical and Sexual Abuse on Body Image in Eating Disorders." *European Eating Disorders Review.* 13: 106-111.

Ullman, Sarah E. April 1998. "Does Offender Violence Escalate When Rape Victims Fight Back?" *Journal of Interpersonal Violence.* 13.

U.S. Department of Justice. Updated July 22, 2016. "Crime Victims' Rights Act (CVRA)." Posted by the Offices of the United States Attorneys.

University of Massachusetts Police Department (at Amherst). n.d. "Date Rape Drugs."

Vagianos, A. October 17, 2017, October 17. "The "Me Too" Campaign was Created by a Black Woman 10 years ago." Huffington Post.

Walker, Sarah-Jane Lilley, Marianne Hester, Duncan McPhee, and Demi Patsios. July 2019. "Rape, Inequality and the Criminal Justice Response in England: The Importance of Age and Gender." *Criminology & Criminal Justice.*

Waller, Glenn. 1993. "Sexual Abuse and Eating Disorders." *British Journal of Psychiatry.* 162: 771-775.

Williams, J.E. 1984. "Secondary Victimization: Confronting Public Attitudes About Rape." *Victimology.* 9: 66-81.

Winerip, Michael. June 3, 2013. "Revising a rape Scandal That Would Have Been Monstrous if True." *The New York Times*, Retro repost. Posted at nytimes.com.

Woods, Timothy O. and United States Office of Justice Programs. National Sheriffs Association. 2001. *First Response to Victims of Crime: A Handbook for Law Enforcement Officers on How to Approach and Help Elderly Victims, Victims of Sexual Assault, Child Victims, Victims of Domestic Violence, Victims of Alcohol-Related Driving Crashes, Survivors of Homicide Victims.* Updated December 2001. U.S. Department of Justice, Office for Victims of Crime. Reprinted April 2008.

Yager, Jan. 2015. *The Fast Track Guide to Losing Weight and Keeping It Off.* Stamford, CT: Hannacroix Creek.

______________. 2021. *Help Yourself Now.* New York: Allworth, an imprint of Skyhorse.

______________. 2011. *The Pretty One.* Stamford, CT: Hannacroix Creek.

______________. 2021, 2015, 1978, *Victims.* Stamford, CT: Hannacroix Creek (originally published by Scribner's)

Videos, TED Talks, and Documentaries

Centers for Disease Control and Prevention (CDC). February 1, 2018. "What is Sexual Violence?" 1:31 minutes Posted at https://www.youtube.com/watch?v=LWctQH4C0P8&t=91s

Finkelstein, Shari, producer. Published March 8, 2009. "The Fragility of Memory." Eyewitness Testimony Part 2. Lesley Stahl, 60 Minutes. 13:06 minutes. YouTube.com

Paige Leigh Baker-Braxton. July 24, 2018. "LGBT Queering the Narrative of Sexual Violence" TEDxChicago. 14:16 minutes. Posted at https://www.youtube.com/watch?v=xHGmU4ITXdo

"Tea Consent" short video. May 13, 2015. Produced by Blue Seat Studios. Animated video using making tea to explore the concept of consent related to sex. 2:49 minutes Posted at https://www.youtube.com/watch?v=fGoWLWS4-kU

Williams, Reagan. Posted April 3, 2017. "Rape Culture." TEDxArkansas State University. 17:43 minutes.

Audrie and Daisy. 2016. Netflix documentary. Directed and produced by Bonnie Cohen; co-directed by Jon Shenk.

Marsy's Law for Florida Supports National Crime Victims Week for 2018. April 11, 2018. 2:55 minutes. Posted at https://www.youtube.com/watch?v=g6F0cIFiOzY&t=175s

KET Kentucky Educational Television. January 24, 2018. *Closer Look: Marsy's Law | Legislative Update Extras* | 6:26 minutes. Posted at https://www.youtube.com/watch?v=xTUkrz9zCQo

Victims of Assault, Domestic Violence, Stalking, and Elder Abuse

Learning Objectives

After you finish reading this chapter, you should be able to:

1. Define assault, including aggravated assault, simple assault, and intimidation.
2. Know how widespread reported aggravated assault is in the United States.
3. Discuss the most common reasons for aggravated assault.
4. Discuss the change in how domestic violence, also known as intimate partner violence (IPV), is handled by the criminal justice system.
5. Develop an awareness of the range of domestic violence from emotional neglect and sexual abuse to physical abuse.
6. Know who coined the term *battered woman syndrome* in 1979 and what it refers to.
7. Be aware of the main reasons that battered men or women stay with the person hurting them.
8. Describe when and how victims of family violence leave including the availability of shelters.
9. Understand the effect on children and teens of witnessing family violence.
10. Learn about honor killings, one of the most extreme forms of family violence.
11. Understand the definition of stalking and when it became a crime.
12. Have an awareness of the extent of elder abuse and who are its typical victims.

OVERVIEW

This chapter begins with definitions of **assault** including simple assault, **aggravated assault**, and intimidation, defined below, followed by explorations of domestic violence, stalking, and elder abuse. Aggravated assault is, statistically, the most common violent crime in the United States with 821,182 reported aggravated assaults in 2019. (FBI, 2019) Based on the National Crime Victimization Survey, in 2018 **simple assault**, defined below, was estimated at 2,058,470 incidents and was even more widespread. (Morgan and Oudekerk, 2019: Table 16)

As you probably know, **domestic violence** may or may not include physical assault; there may be emotional, verbal, sexual, or even financial abuse. The same is true for elder abuse. According to the American Psychological Association, **elder abuse** may include physical, sexual, and emotional abuse; financial/material exploitation; neglect; abandonment; and self-neglect. (American Psychological Association, 2008).

ASSAULT

The Bureau of Justice Statistics defines *assault* as "an unlawful physical attack or threat of attack." (Bureau of Justice Statistics) The National Incident-Based Reporting System (NIBRS), which is part of the Uniform Crime Reporting System of the FBI and the U.S. Department of Justice, defines assault offenses in this way: "An unlawful attack by one person upon another."

As mentioned in Chapter 1, "Victimology: An Overview," in the section on types of crimes, and in Chapter 4, "Measuring Victimization: Why and How," the NIBRS definition of assault, as well as the three types of assault, described below, are not for the basis for charging someone with a crime. Each state has its own statutes which would be used for the purpose of charging someone with assault. The NIBRS definitions reprinted here are built on common-law definitions located in *Black's Law Dictionary*, the UCR Handbook, and the National Crime Information Center (NCIC) Uniform Offense Classifications.

- Aggravated Assault—An unlawful attack by one person upon another wherein the offender uses a weapon or displays it in a threatening manner, or the victim suffers obvious severe or aggravated bodily injury involving apparent broken bones, loss of teeth, possible internal injury, severe laceration, or loss of consciousness. This also includes assault with disease (as in cases when the offender is aware that he/she is infected with a deadly disease and deliberately attempts to inflict the disease by biting, spitting, etc.).
- Simple Assault—An unlawful physical attack by one person upon another where neither the offender displays a weapon, nor the victim suffers obvious severe or aggravated bodily injury involving apparent broken bones, loss of teeth, possible internal injury, severe laceration, or loss of consciousness.
- Intimidation—To unlawfully place another person in reasonable fear of bodily harm through the use of threatening words and/or other conduct, but without displaying a weapon or subjecting the victim to actual physical attack. (FBI, UCR, NIBRS, 2017)

Simple Assault

Box 13.1 summarizes some important facts about simple assault.

Box 13.1. Facts About Simple Assault

- More than half of the offenders are strangers.
- For male victims, 41 percent of the time they know their offenders.
- Only 23 percent of the offenders are strangers when the victim is a female.
- For females, in 74 percent of the simple assault cases, the offender is someone known to the victim including family members, acquaintances or friends, or intimate partners.
- The highest rate for victimization by age is 15-17, followed by 21-24, then 35-49, with the lowest victimization rate by age in the 65+ age group.
- Whites are assaulted at almost the exact rate as Blacks (a rate of 1,220 or 1,230 per 100,000, respectively).

Sources: Doerner and Lab, 2019 based on the Bureau of Justice Statistics, National Crime Victimization Survey, 2016.

Aggravated Assault

Of the four main violent crimes—murder, robbery, rape, and aggravated assault—aggravated assault is the most common reported violent crime in the United States. As noted above, in 2019, there were 821,182 *reported* aggravated assaults. (FBI, 2019) According to the Bureau of Justice Statistics (BJS) and the National Crime Victimization Survey (NCVS), between 2006 and 2010, 44 percent of aggravated assaults were *not reported* to the police. (You probably recall from Chapter 4 that the NCVS is based on self-reports about reported and unreported.) crimes during the last 6 months with a randomized sample of surveyed Americans (BJS, 2012)

Other terms for aggravated assault are **attempted murder**, assault with intent to kill, assault with intent to do great bodily harm, as well as assault. (Pittman, and Handy, 1964: 463) Alesia Litteral, whose attempted murder a year and a half ago is discussed in greater detail as a Profile in Chapter 15, "Additional Victim Situations and Populations," is a survivor of attempted murder by her husband who shot her 7 times and stabbed her 37 times before killing himself. The doctor did not think Alesia would make it. She explains, "My niece was working in the emergency room. She came and called my half-sister. She said that the doctor told her, 'I will do what I can but I think I'm looking at a corpse.'" at Fortunately, she survived. "This trauma has changed me in such a way that I am not really sure who I am yet," Alesia says. "I'm still strong, but in a very different way." (Litteral, 2021)

Firearms were used to commit aggravated assaults 27.6 percent of the time; bodily weapons such as hands, fists, or feet were used in 25.2 percent of aggravated assaults, 17.5 percent used knives or cutting instruments, and 29.8 percent used "other weapons." (FBI, 2019: Table 19) By contrast, firearms were used in 73.7 percent of the reported murders in 2019. (FBI, 2019: Expanded Homicide Data Table 7) This contrast in the weapons used in both crimes is important to emphasize; you will find these statistics summarized in Figure 13.1.

FIGURE 13.1. **Firearms and Other Weapons in Aggravated Assault Versus Firearms in Murder for 2019 (N=821, 182)**

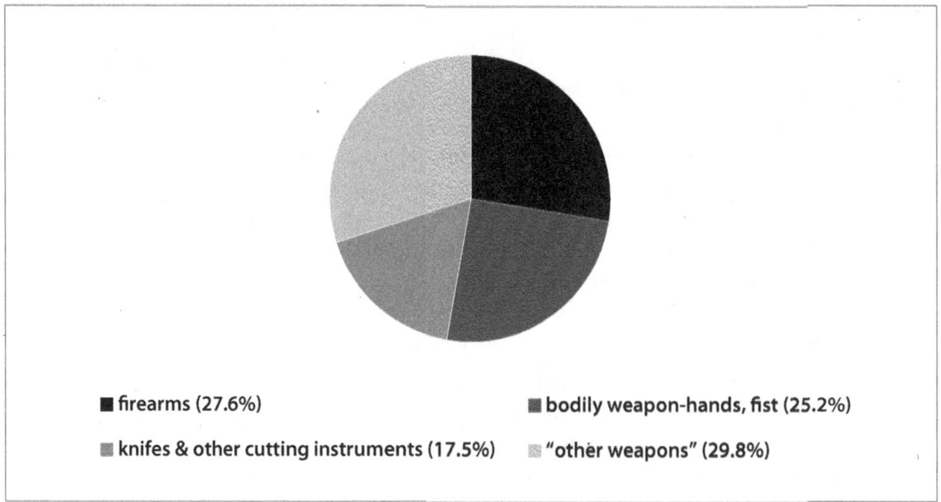

Source: FBI, *2019 Crime in the United States*, "Aggravated Assault"

FIGURE 13.2. **Percentage of Reported Murders in 2019 Where Firearms Were Used (N=16, 445)**

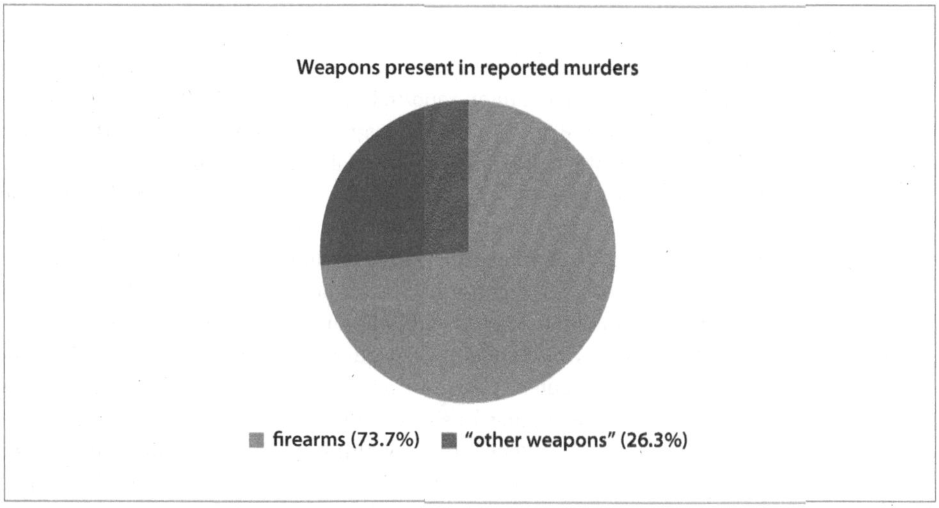

Source: FBI, *2019 Crime in the United States*, "Expanded Homicide Data Table 7"

In Figure 13.2 that follows, the presence of firearms in reported murders is indicated.

Box 13.2 summarizes key details about aggravated assault.

Figure 13.3 summarizes information about the age of aggravated assault victims in 2018. As you can see from Figure 13.3, the two highest age groups for aggravated assault victimization, based on the National Crime Victimization Survey (NCVS), are in the 35-49-year-old (29%) age group followed by the 50+ age group (28%).

Box 13.2. Facts About Aggravated Assault

- In 2015, an estimated 3 in 1,000 persons in the United States was a victim of aggravated assault.
- 60% of aggravated assault (and simple assault) victims reported no injury.
- 60% of the aggravated assault victims who reported an injury received medical treatment.
- Most assaults in 2015 were committed by someone the victim knew.
- On women, 66% of the aggravated assaults- were committed by non-strangers and 34% were committed by strangers.
- On men, 58% of the aggravated assaults on men were committed by non-strangers and 47% were committed by strangers.

Sources: Morgan and Oudekerk, *2018 Crime Victimization* and "Assault," 2018 National Crime Victims' Rights Week Resource Guide

FIGURE 13.3. Age of Aggravated Assault Victims in 2018

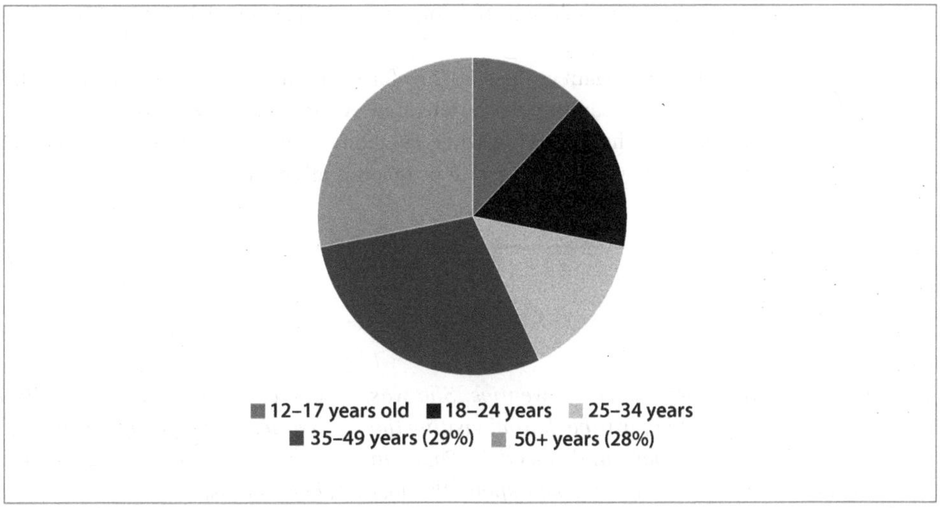

Source: "Assault," 2018 National Crime Victims' Rights Week Resource Guide

Figure 13.4 summarizes information about aggravated assault in the 2018 in the United States by the location and sex of the victim.

Looking over the results in Figure 13.4, it is possible that the difference in the number of female victims at or near the victim's home by gender—56 percent of women compared

FIGURE 13.4. **Aggravated Assault in 2018 in the United States by Location and Sex of the Victim**

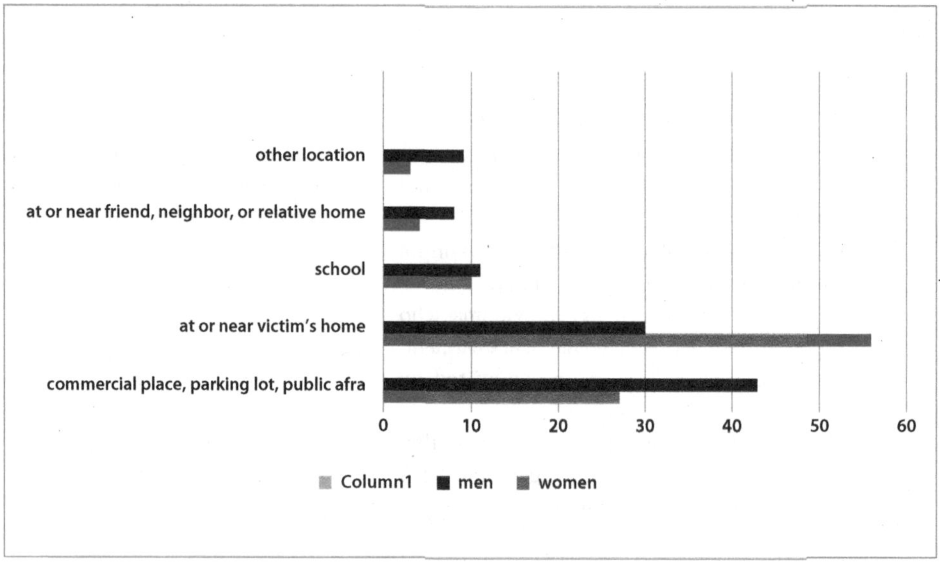

Source: "Assault," 2018 National Crime Victims' Rights Week Resource Guide

to 30 percent of men—fits in with the greater likelihood that many of them were victims of domestic violence or intimate partner violence (IPV), discussed in greater detail below. There are male victims of domestic violence, as will be noted, but it is still a crime with more female than male victims.

Looking again at the statistics for location of the assault in Table 13.4, 43 percent of the males were assaulted in a public area. As noted in Chapter 6, the speed, and competency, of the medical help arriving when someone is injured due to a crime can make the difference between an aggravated assault or the victim's death.

Profile of an Aggravated Assault Victim – Banu P.

Banu is a woman in her early twenties. She was in Egypt in 2020 on her way back from visiting the Pyramids. She was born and raised in Pakistan in a middle-class family but she spent the last five years studying and traveling internationally. Until this incident, Banu shared "never did I ever face any harm." That would all change in an instant. She has returned to Turkey, where she lives now. It was from there that she e-mailed a detailed account of what happened in response to one of this author's HARO (Help-a-Reporter-Out) queries. She gave permission to anonymously excerpt her self-report as well as excerpts from her e-mails.

One evening, after spending a blissful day with the Pyramids, I returned to a city two hours away from the capital Cairo, where I was living and where my project was based. I took a rickshaw around 7 o'clock from a very busy street.

It wasn't new to me. I had taken a rickshaw from the same area a couple of times before . . . The rickshaw driver was a young man. His face didn't give the slightest him [hint] of his evil intensions . . .

He took a turn towards the right direction, but after some while, he again took a turn to another road, while he was supposed to drive just straight. Nevertheless, I didn't say much. I thought he was taking a longer route just to charge more money . . . But the road started getting darker. I felt scared, still completely ignoring any chance of his evil intentions other than charging more money. . . . [I] said that it's too long. Please return to the highway and use that way as I am always using that.

He listened and again took a turn. He asked me where I was from and also said that he had a friend from Pakistan. . . Let me mention here that all this time, he was addressing me as "Abla" meaning sister.

I was then very close to the school. I could see its name that was written in big blue and white lighted letters. Some 500 meters from away, there was a narrow road (on the same side as the school was), he turned then. Now I was frustrated and again directed him towards the school. After taking that turn, he stopped, probably after 100-200 meters. Said "Abla", jumped out, came to the back seat to sit next to me, pulled out a knife, and put it on my throat and said, "Don't scream."

I am still confused about this part, in my memory, he said these two words in English, but I have a slight doubt. If it was in Arabic, I wouldn't have understood it anyway.

But I screamed and jumped out. I was wearing a small backpack, had a jacket, a small pouch (containing money, I intended to pay him) and a plastic bag containing 2 falafel sandwiches I had bought right before taking the rickshaw.

I ran with all that while screaming. I was wearing a long skirt. I still wonder how I didn't trip. I remember my spectacles dropping. Again don't know how. Was it because just of me running, or because while jumping out, his hands with the knife at my throat moved and touched/rubbed against my spectacles and dropped them down? I had a bottle [of water] in the side pockets of my backpack. It dropped too.

. . . I managed to run and stood in the middle of the highway. Plenty of cars were passing. I was screaming and waving to them. Some stopped, some probably nearly missed hitting me. I don't think I had any fear of getting hit by a car at that point.

I saw the rickshaw getting to the highway as well, coming toward me. I thought, will he run over me? Will he pull out his arm and hit me?

He just passed.

Two to four guys came running. They heard me screaming and knew it was related to the rickshaw as I heard them saying *tuk-tuk* [auto rickshaw]. I was crying and walking. They were asking me things. I didn't understand. I think using my hands, I referred to having a knife on my throat. They understood.

. . . Another car stopped. There was a woman in the front seat. Those 2-4 guys said something to her. Maybe the man in the driving seat was her husband. She was a woman, which made me somewhat comfortable to sit in the car. In less than a minute, we reached our school. The woman also got off. She held me, tried to calm me down, told something to the guards at the gate. I remember her saying Sakina—[peace].

I escaped a knife attack from a rickshaw driver [but] more than the incident itself, the reactions of the people around me disappointed me and made it harder for me to handle everything. I decided to leave that place for the sake of my mental health and came to Turkey, where I was living for the last five years.

I am afraid that this incident will haunt me in [the] future and I don't want to leave it untreated . . . I think I am suffering from PTSD. It took away part of my soul, but I empathize with people more now, and I hope that with time I will get stronger. But right now, I have hateful feelings towards so many things.

DOMESTIC VIOLENCE

There are several terms for this type of victimization: **domestic violence** as well as **intimate partner violence (IPV).** *Domestic violence* encompasses the range of crimes that occur within a family including elder abuse, discussed below, and other family violence such as child abuse and neglect, discussed in its own chapter, Chapter 10, "Child Victims" and even teenagers assaulting their parents or parents attacking their adolescents which can lead to teenage runaways, IPV or Intimate Partner Violence, discussed in this section, stalking, only refers to romantic partners who may be married or just cohabitating; they may be a heterosexual couple or a same-sex couple. As you will see in the section on stalking, which follows IPV, most stalking victims are stalked by their current or former intimate partner.

INTIMATE PARTNER VIOLENCE (IPV)

Although there are many types of intimate partner abuse, including emotional, verbal, sexual and even financial abuse, it is the physical violence that usually gets the police and the criminal justice system involved. Depending upon how severe the partner's injuries are, it may also get the emergency medical technicians (EMTs) involved and the hospital. Because IPV is closest to the crime of aggravated assault, it is included in the same chapter.

Intimate Partner Violence, or IPV, refers to any behavior within a romantic opposite-sex or same-sex relationship that causes emotional, physical, financial. or sexual abuse, to the extreme of **intimate partner homicide**. Other terms for IPV that have been previously used are wife battering and domestic violence. In Box 13.3 you will find out some key statistics about IPV in the United States.

Box 13.3. Facts About Intimate Partner Violence

- 1 in 4 women will be IPV victims during their lifetime.
- 1 in 9 men will be an IPV victim during their lifetime.
- According to the Centers for Disease Control and Prevention (CDC), 9 percent of high school students reported being physically hurt by a boyfriend or girlfriend in the 12 months before being surveyed. (See Chapter 11, "Teen and College Victims," for a further discussion of teen dating violence.)
- American Indian and Alaska Native Women experience assault and IPV at higher rates than any other ethnicity with 84 percent experiencing violence during their lifetime.
- IPV is reported in 56 percent of the estimated 1.3 nonfatal domestic violence cases between 2006 and 2015.

Box 13.3. Facts About Intimate Partner Violence (continued)

- There were an estimated 600,000 unreported nonfatal IPVs between 2006 and 2015.
- In 2012 in New York State, courts issued 304,239 **orders of protection** (also sometimes known as **restraining orders**).
- Romantic partners do not leave because of what is known as the "cycle of violence" (described below) previously termed "the battered woman syndrome" by Dr. Lenore Walker in 1979.
- IPVs with serious violence (31%) were more likely to go unreported due to fear of reprisal than simple assault victimizations (13%).
- Female victimizations (24%) were four times more likely as male victimizations (6%) to go unreported because of a fear of reprisal.

Sources: Bureau of Justice Statistics, "Police Response to Domestic Violence, 2006-1015," NCADV (National Coalition Against Domestic Violence), "Statistics," NCADV, "Domestic Violence Against American Indian and Alaska Native Women," CDC, "Understanding Teen Dating Violence" Fact Sheet, 2016

Victims Are Female and Male

The first point about domestic violence or IPV that victimologists know is that it happens to men as well as women, and that certain ethnic groups, like Native Americans and Alaskan Natives, as noted above, experience it in great frequency over their lifetime. Male victims of domestic violence are discussed in a separate section but at this point, let it be noted that they are not just victims of same sex domestic violence as might be assumed. The perpetrator may also be a female partner or spouse attacking the male. But the majority of cases of domestic violence are males attacking females. We also probably know more about female victims because, until recently, studies tended to include only women respondents. For example, the 2005 landmark study by the World Health Organization (WHO), which examined 24,000 *women* in 10 countries, discovered that domestic violence was more common in a woman's life than assault or rape by acquaintances or strangers. (Garcia-Moreno, et. al., 2005) An important finding, but unfortunately it did not look at male victims.

The History of the Criminalization of Domestic Violence

Elizabeth Pleck has provided much of the information we have about the early history of how the legal system dealt with family violence in her seminal article, "Criminal Approaches to

Family Violence, 1640-1980." In Chapter 10, "Child Victims," her findings related to children were highlighted. Here it should be noted that between 1640 and 1680, Pleck points out that the Puritans of colonial Massachusetts enacted the first laws anywhere in the world—not just in the "New World" (the way America was once described)—against wife beating. In 1641, the Massachusetts *Body of Laws and Liberties* included a provision against wife abuse. It stated, "Everie marryed woeman shall be free from bodilie correction or stripes by her husband, unleasse it be in his owne defence upon her assault." Pleck notes that several years later, the law was amended to prohibit husband beating. (Pleak, 1989)

In 1672, Plymouth Colony, Pleck notes, most likely followed Massachusetts Bay Colony in enacting laws against spouse abuse with these penalties: wife beating punished with a whipping or a five-pound fine; husband beating punished with a sentence that the court would determine. (Pleck, 1989: 19, 22)

However, Pleck points out that the laws against wife beating were more ceremonial than practical. She writes, "Criminal laws against family violence were intended mainly to serve symbolic purposes—to define the boundary between saint and sinner, to demonstrate to God and community a vigilance against sin, and to shore up proper authority in the household and in society. While the Puritans passed laws against family violence, these were rarely enforced and when they were, offenders usually received lenient sentences. In keeping with these motives, Puritan laws punished both abuses of authority and acts of disobedience or rebellion against legitimate authority." (Pleck, 1989: 25)

To back up her point, Pleck examined court records from 1633 to 1802. She discovered only 12 out of the 19 family violence cases that were prosecuted involved wife beating. Interestingly, Pleck notes that in wife beating cases, "judges tended to inquire whether a wife provoked her husband into beating her." (Pleck, 1989: 25-26) Shades of victim blame?

Pleck notes that over time or, as she put it, "as Puritans became Yankees," there were fewer complaints of wife assault with only four listed between 1663 and 1682. In the 1700s, in the first half there are no complaints noted and in the second half, only two. (Pleck, 1989: 27)

But times were changing. Although the trend at that time was for family matters to be seen as private ones, to be resolved privately, with the establishment of police departments in cities, beginning with Boston in 1838 followed by New York City in 1845, that was going to change. (Potter, 2013)

The next milestone in family violence occurred in 1850 when Tennessee enacted a law against wife beating. (Pleck, 1989: 29) A study by Friedman and Percival, reported on by Pleck, of the police courts from 1870 to 1920 in Oakland, California, revealed that half of the arrests for wife abuse were tried in the police court as public order violations. About half were convicted or pleaded guilty. The sentence was to go to jail or pay a fine. Most opted for jail since they did not have the money to pay a fine but because wives were dependent on their spouses for support, they would often borrow money from friends or use their savings to pay for their spouse's release. (Pleck, 1989: 30-31)

Pleck addresses the infamous "the rule of the thumb" which was supposedly a way of letting a husband off the hook for beating his wife if the stick that he used was no wider than his thumb. She traces it back to England and a Judge Buller, who, in 1783, was supposedly the first one to assess the rule as characterized by a cartoon as "Judge Thumb." (Pleck, 1989: 32)

However, according to Pleck, "No American judge ever endorsed the 'rule of thumb,' and before the Civil War, two American states passed "statutes against wife beating." (Pleck, 1989: 12) That wife beating "was not against the law" in nineteenth-century America seems to stem from three appellate court rulings that were issued between 1824 and 1868 in Mississippi and North Carolina. As Pleck writes, "According to these court rulings, a husband had the legitimate right to discipline his wife physically, as long as it was done in a moderate manner." (Pleck, 1989: 32-33)

In 1875, there was a movement to address child abuse, highlighted by the establishment of the Society for the Prevention of Cruelty to Children (SPCC) in New York City. Although protection of children from abuse was a growing issue in America, reaching national attention with the 1960s publication in a medical journal of "The Battered Child Syndrome," it was the women's movement of the 1970s that raised awareness about wife battering and, in time, the reality that there was also husband battering.

It makes sense that wife battering as a crime became a bigger focus in conjunction with the women's movement if you look back historically at the wives who bailed out their husbands who were convicted of family violence, rather than have them go to jail, because they needed the spouse's financial support. One of the strongest messages of the women's movement is that women can make it on their own. They can get jobs, contribute to the family household income or, if necessary, be the sole supporter for the family if the husband is undesirable or, worse, abusive. The women's movement helped women in the United States to feel, in general, that they were no longer the property of their husbands, an outmoded centuries-old concept that had been used to excuse rape, sexual assault, and domestic violence for far too long. In 1976, Nebraska was the first state to make it a crime to rape your spouse. They eliminated the marital rape law exception. By 1993, all 50 states had followed suit.

Risk Factors in IPV

The many risk factors for IPV are detailed in Box 13.4.In general, however, the biggest risk factors are a younger woman or girl, with a limited education, who is poor, who has low self-esteem, and, as Pfouts, et al, point out in their article, "Forgotten Victims of Family Violence," the children who witnessed family violence during their formative years. In their sample of 141 children, 17.7 percent or 25 witnessed their mothers being abused. (Pfouts, 1982)

This relates to a male victim of family violence, John W. who tried to explain in his interview shared with this author why he might have allowed himself to be abused by his female romantic partner. He pointed to the battering that his father endured by his mother that John witnessed. John even stated that his parents are still together to this day; his father seemingly accepting the abuse by remaining. As Pfouts et al. state in their journal article, "It is likely, for one thing, that these children (along with their abused siblings) may be abusing husbands and abused wives of the next generation." (Pfouts, et al., 1982: 368)

Anger management and impulse control issues are risk factors in domestic violence. Fortunately, there is help for those who have those concerns including individual counseling, anger management classes, or support groups. The perpetrator has to recognize that he has a problem that he needs to work on before he hurts his beloved.

Author Janine Latus, (on the right) a survivor of domestic violence, and her sister Amy (bride). Contributed photo.

In her compelling memoir, *If I am Missing or Dead: A Sister's Story of Love, Murder, and Liberation*, Janine Latus discusses the domestic violence she endured in her first marriage. She was able to get out before it was too late. She also writes about her sister Amy's abusive romantic relationship that ended tragically with her sister's death at the hands of her boyfriend who served ten years for the crime. At various points in the memoir, Latus talks about her abusive father, the father figure who was their first teacher about relationships. She even includes quotes from her father that show how he was verbally abusive toward his wife, Latus' mother, when he says, "Your mother's a wimp, Dad says." (Latus, 2007:18)

Dysfunctional early family and teenage romantic relationships can set someone up for negative romantic relationships later on. What is needed is positive socialization about loving, non-physical, supportive, and nurturing intimate relationships that are the opposite of domestic violence. Of course conflict may arise in all intimate relationships but witnessing examples of parents or a parent and his/her intimate partner working out their conflicts through negotiation and discussion instead of resorting to any kind of physical violence or emotional abuse may go a long way in reducing or eliminating IPV.

Box 13.4. Risk Factors for Intimate Partner Violence Perpetration

Individual Risk Factors

- Low self-esteem
- Low income
- Low academic achievement/low verbal IQ
- Young age
- Aggressive or delinquent behavior as a youth
- Heavy alcohol and drug use
- Depression and suicide attempts
- Anger and hostility
- Lack of nonviolent social problem-solving skills
- Antisocial personality traits and conduct problems
- Poor behavioral control/impulsiveness
- Borderline personality traits
- Prior history of being physically abusive
- Having few friends and being isolated from other people
- Unemployment
- Emotional dependence and insecurity
- Belief in strict gender roles (e.g., male dominance and aggression in relationships)
- Desire for power and control in relationships
- Hostility towards women
- Attitudes accepting or justifying IPV
- Being a victim of physical or psychological abuse (consistently one of the strongest predictors of perpetration)
- Witnessing IPV between parents as a child
- History of experiencing poor parenting as a child
- History of experiencing physical discipline as a child
- Unplanned pregnancy

Relationship Factors

- Marital conflict-fights, tension, and other struggles
- Jealousy, possessiveness, and negative emotion within an intimate relationship
- Marital instability-divorces or separations
- Dominance and control of the relationship by one partner over the other
- Economic stress
- Unhealthy family relationships and interactions
- Association with antisocial and aggressive peers
- Parents with less than a high-school education
- Social isolation/lack of social support

Community Factors

- Poverty and associated factors (e.g., overcrowding, high unemployment rates)
- Low social capital (lack of institutions, relationships, and norms that shape a community's social interactions)
- Poor neighborhood support and cohesion
- Weak community sanctions against IPV (e.g., unwillingness of neighbors to intervene in situations where they witness violence)
- High alcohol outlet density

Box 13.4. Risk Factors for Intimate Partner Violence Perpetration (continued)

Societal Factors

- Traditional gender norms and gender inequality (e.g., women should stay at home, not enter workforce, and be submissive; men support the family and make the decisions)
- Cultural norms that support aggression toward others
- Societal income inequality
- Weak health, educational, economic, and social policies/laws

Source: Reprinted from the CDC (Centers for Disease Control and Prevention" Violence Prevention program, 2-page flyer, "Risk and Protective Factors for Perpetration"

Signs of Abuse in a Romantic Relationship

In reading the transcripts of more than 30 interviews of real-life cases of those who have suffered intimate partner violence—3 male and 27 female—most point to the *emotional abuse* as the first step in the violence. If the abusive partner does not successfully deal with his or her problems so that emotional abuse stops, it seems to escalate to the next type of abuse, physical, the abuse where it is more likely that the police will get involved, or there will be bodily injuries.. It is at this point that most victims are forced to make the difficult decision if she or he will get a restraining order or order of protection against the abuser, who will probably be forced to leave or get arrested for violating the order of protection or, if the abuse is in an active situation, if the police are called, having the abuser arrested.

The third type of abuse is *sexual abuse*, and this may occur in some instances although it is less common than physical abuse. Financial abuse or exploitation is another form of abuse in domestic violence situations whereby the abusing romantic partner exerts far more control over the couple's finances than what is typical or acceptable.

The words that IPV victims will often use to describe the abusive partner, and the actions outside the normal range of positive romantic partner behavior that they engage in, include:

- Controlling
- Suspicious
- Paranoid
- Discouraging any other relationships besides the one with the abuser including connections with family, friends, and especially opposite sex platonic friendships which brings up their jealous feelings
- Jealousy
- Drinking problem

- Drug problem
- Possessiveness
- Poor anger management
- Poor impulse control
- Low self-esteem

The Cycle of Violence

In 1977, psychologist Lenore Walker wrote a journal article entitled, "Who are the Battered Women?" In that article, she talked about two important phenomena: what came to be known as the *battered woman syndrome*, the title of her book published in 1984, a syndrome which is also referred to by some as the **cycle of violence**, as well as the concept of *learned helplessness*. (Walker, 1977, 1979, 1984).

All these concepts are pivotal in answer to the often-asked questions about family violence: "Why Do They Stay?"

Phase 1: Tension. The first part of the cycle, previously known as the *battered woman syndrome*, is the *tension building*. That is when the romantic partner starts to act in an abusive manner, but it can be more subtle, such as emotional abuse. In this phase, the abuser may intimidate or threaten the partner, which can make the victim more dependent or less likely to leave. It could be anything from telling the victim that it is unlikely she could make it out in the world without him or even saying that he will spread rumors about her to her family or others that she will never live down.

For many victims, they are stunned at the change that occurs in their romantic partner that turns him into a completely different person than the one she thought she knew. For some, it is the strain of living together, a far different emotional commitment than just dating. For others, the strain starts after they have children. The emotional, time, and financial demands of parenting prove overwhelming and the abusive partner takes it out on his or her spouse.

Twenty-six-year-old Olivia T. was in the romantic relationship for a year before the violence caused her to end it. Olivia explains that initially, she was happy with her boyfriend. They would spend a lot of time together but after he moved in with her, everything changed. Perhaps part of the challenge was that he also moved one of his friends in with them.

Olivia explains:

> That's when he started to act differently and jealously. He started to tell me what to wear. Deleting contacts on my phone so I couldn't talk to any guys. I had no guy friends. Even cut off some of my relatives. He had me taking care of him [his friend] as well. I didn't think anything of it because we had so many good memories. Alas, because I thought it was normal in a relationship. There are many couples who get jealous over their spouse. [But] I was young and naïve. I thought I knew what love was and I thought I found it in that person. (Anonymous interview shared with the author.)

The "Power and Control Wheel," developed by the Domestic Abuse Intervention Programs in Duluth, Minnesota, and reprinted below with their permission, is an excellent way of understanding the complexities of domestic violence. (Figure 13.5)

FIGURE 13.5. The Power and Control Wheel

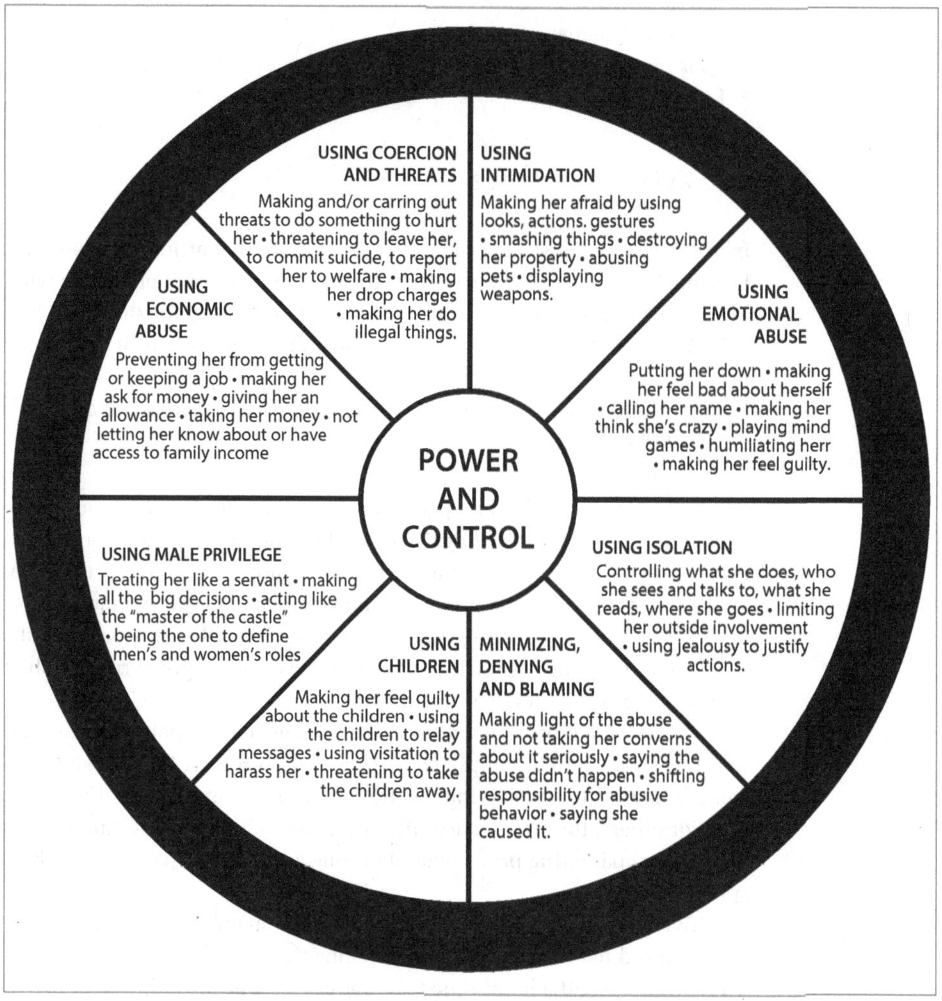

Source: Domestic Abuse Intervention Programs (DAIP), Duluth, Minnesota (www.TheDuluthModel.org)

Emotional Abuse. During the tension building is the emotional abuse part of domestic violence. If domestic violence includes physical abuse, it might be included in the statistics for aggravated assault or even attempted murder. But if the abuse is only emotional, that is a victimization that is a lot harder to criminalize even though emotional scars run deep. Mannette Morgan, author of *Finding Your Voice*, was such a domestic violence victim. She married her high school sweetheart and had two children by the time she was 21. "I was emotionally abused," says Mannette. One day, when she was 23, she was watching the *Phil Donohue* talk show on TV and the person being interviewed talked about depression. The interview resonated with Mannette and she realized that she was in an extremely negative situation for her and her children. "Within six months, I was out of there." She moved in with a friend for two weeks as she figured out what she would do next." (Yager, 2021)

Fortunately, Mannette landed on her feet, started a business and, years later, found love with a second husband who treated her in the way she learned she deserved to be treated. When he died nine years later, she eventually fell in love again and remarried to a man who also treats her well. She never let herself be mistreated the way she had been in her first marriage.

Mannette shared that when she called up her first husband to let him know that she had written a book and that he was in it, although he was not named, "His comment was, 'I never beat you.' "

Her book, and the accompanying workbook, *Finding Your Voice Workbook,* is her way of helping others to gain the courage to create the positive life that they are meant to have. Through her speeches, life coaching, and writing, she tells current victims, and those who have made the break, "I get you. You're worth so much more than the abuse you've experienced." (Yager, 2021)

Financial Abuse. Domestic violence (DV) victims may have their finances controlled by their perpetrators. Working out a way of handling individual and joint money is a challenge for all couples. When there is a DV situation, the abuser may become the victim of all kinds of financial abuses including using credit cards without permission, putting property under someone else's name without the other party's agreement, when one of the partners controls all the money so the other partner has to ask "permission" to buy anything, changing the terms of a partner's will under duress or through emotional manipulation or threats, or fraudulently obtaining power of attorney. Although we most often associate financial abuse with the elderly, it can happen to anyone at any age. (See Chapter 9, "Cybercrime, White-Collar Crime, and Economic Crime Victims," for the discussion of financial abuse as it applies to elder abuse.)

Phase 2: Violence. Mannette left her abusive marriage before it got to the second phase, the *violent phase.* In most cases, there is something that happens to precipitate the violence: something that is said; some incident that triggers it. But it does not have to be a major incident although the abuser finds it to be something that requires a violent response. If he, or she, is under the influence of drinking or drugs, the smallest thing can trigger a violent response. The violence may include anything from hitting, punching, throwing things, slamming car doors, stabbing, slapping, taking a hammer to a refrigerator door, right next to where the victim was standing, to throwing a flammable liquid on to the victim, and lighting it.

For some abused women or men, it just takes one violent incident for them to leave. They do not get into the cycle of violence because they are gone before phase three. But if a girl or woman, boy or man, is in love, especially if it is the first time their romantic partner became violent, particularly if they were inebriated or high, they may try to explain it away. Give him or her another chance. He's fine (she's fine) when he's (she's) sober. It's the drugs, not him (or her). Also, since they have now seen the violence that their loved one is capable of, they may be more frightened by the prospect of leaving than they were when it was just emotional abuse.

Phase 3: The "Honeymoon" Olivia, discussed above, got away after a violent phase was just too violent for her to excuse her ex- boyfriend's behavior anymore. The "Honeymoon" or "Make Up" phase is the way that victims find themselves staying, weeks, months, and even decades in an abusive romantic relationship. This is when the abuser becomes the Hyde in the Dr. Jekyll and Mr. Hyde dual personality, also the title of the novel by Robert Louis Stevenson. (Stevenson, 1886). Her abuser returns to the sweet, loving, caring romantic partner that she fell in love with in the first place. That makes it even harder to leave. Barbara C. has been the victim of domestic violence for seven years. Even though she is only 24, she has been with the abuser since she was 17, dating him "on and off" since she was 13. They have been married the last five years. She describes what the honeymoon phase of her cycle of violence is like:

> After he would hit me, the next day he would apologize and say he'll never do it again, and then give me a gift. Either a necklace, bracelet, or flowers. He said he would change, and then time would go on where we would go back to our normal life as if nothing happened. He'd be the guy I fell in love with again and during those moments, I would believe that he had changed and if I wasn't sure, his mother would reassure me that he had. (Anonymous interview shared with the author)

CALLING 911 (CALLING THE POLICE)

As you learned from the interview in Chapter 6 with 911 operator Karima Holmes, the first call is usually to 911. The 911 operator will determine, based on what she or he learns, as well as the caller's preferences, if an ambulance will be called, the police, the fire department, or all three.

For our discussion about calling the police, let us assume the caller has asked the police to respond. "In the old days" it is said that even when the police were called, they might consider the couple fighting "a private matter" to work out amongst themselves.

The newer way of thinking, however, is that even if you are married, or part of a family, there are basic human rights to being safe and treated with respect and care that are every individual's right. Being a child, or being a spouse, does not give anyone the right to emotional, physical, or sexual abuse. When physical or sexual abuse is occurring and the perpetrator will not stop despite requests to do so, calling 911 is an alternative to someone taking matters into his/her own hands.

A key factor in revising the approach to domestic violence calls by the police was the experiment undertaken by the Minneapolis Police Department and the Police Foundation from early 1981 to mid-1982.Three-hundred-thirty (330) DV cases were studied. In a nutshell, the study discovered that of the three standard police approaches to domestic violence – counseling both parties, sending the abuser away from home for several hours, or arresting the suspect – arrest led to a lower occurrence of repeat violence over the next 6 months (10%) versus 19% for advise situations or 24% when the suspect was just sent away. (Sherman and Berk, 1984a) It should be noted that this study, which has had widespread impact on law enforcement and lawmakers, was based on follow-up interviews with just 205 of the 330 cases, was done at one point in time (1981–1982), was based on just one unique American city (Minneapolis), and was conducted through the police and the Police Foundation. (Sherman and Berk, 1984a; Sherman and Berk, 1984b; Doerner and Lab, 2017: 261–268)

Remember that when the police arrive, it is not up to the victim to tell the police whether she wants the abuser arrested. The police make that decision based on the evidence they are presented with as well as the statutes in their state regarding this situation.

Every so often both parties have to be arrested until it is sorted out who is the abuser and who is the victim since in some instances what the situation is may be unclear.

Sometimes calling police is out of the hands of the victim as was the case with Olivia T., mentioned above. Her bystander called police.

At one extreme are the victims who are reluctant to call the police because they know there is a trend now to mandatory arrest of the perpetrator. They may be reluctant to call police because they fear retaliation by the abuser. They may fear, if the abuser is arrested, that he will lose his job and she will be left without a source of financial support. She may fear the *stigma* of being known as the neighbor, friend, or family member who allowed herself to be in an abusive situation.

However, the police are not marriage counselors. They are representatives of law enforcement and should be considered in that serious light. When should police be called? It is hard to generalize since each situation is unique and usually complicated but a deciding factor would be to consider calling the police if there is imminent danger of injury or death.

GETTING HELP

There is help for those dealing with domestic violence in the form of 24-hour hotlines, organizations, like Safe Horizon, with counselors and support groups to offer help, as well as **shelters** for those who must leave and who fear for their safety. Legal help includes getting a restraining order to keep the abuser physically away or he will be arrested. If a perpetrator has physically harmed the victim, the type of charge, and what degree of that charge, as well as what the sentence might be, if found guilty, will vary greatly based on numerous factors including if it is a first offense, the injuries to the victim, even what state the crime took place in. For example, a domestic violence victim whose spouse threw a flammable liquid on her and set her on fire during the course of an argument was sentenced to 12 years in prison. (Anonymous interview shared with the author 2020)

There is a great variety in charges and punishments in domestic violence cases depending upon the severity of the violence, the statutes in the particular state where it occurs, and many other factors related to the offender and the circumstances. If someone is found guilty of a domestic violence charge that is considered a misdemeanor, the punishment might include probation and participating in a mandatory domestic violence rehabilitation program as well as a $2,000 fine and possibly even up to a year in jail.

If the charge is deemed a more serious felony, the punishment could be two to four years in a state prison and a fine of $6,000 or more. Beyond the time in jail or prison, or the fine, is the conviction on someone's record that can lead to losing a current job and having greater difficulty finding a new one. It also means being labeled a domestic violence abuser, a label that can cancel out many or all other positive achievements.

Counseling

Victims of domestic violence have to focus on the consequences of the criminal behavior to them. If they get too involved in the penalties to the perpetrator, they may not get the restraining order, call the police, press charges, or do what it takes to get justice for themselves. Help for the victims of domestic violence, in addition to assistance getting out of a possibly dangerous situation, may mean getting counseling to figure out why the victim got into the abusive situation in the first place. Even more importantly, if the victim stays in the relationship after the emotional abuse began, and especially after even *one* physical or sexual assault occurred, the question is, what issues need to be addressed to avoid being in an abusive situation again. Too many victims swear off romance because of these tragic violent relationships but that is not the answer. The emotional and even the physical effects of isolation mean that, in a way, the abuser has won if it means giving up having a healthy and happy romantic relationship, even having a family of one's own.

Battered woman syndrome (BWS) expert Dr. Lenore E. Walker points out that BWS "has been identified as a subcategory of posttraumatic stress disorder (PTSD)." (Walker, 2009) She continues, "Although not all battered women meet all the DSM-IV-TR criteria for PTSD, a sufficient number do, thus, a form of trauma treatment is most helpful." (Walker, 2009) Please refer back to Chapter 6, "Helping the Victim," for a discussion of PTSD as well as the trauma therapy that is available to the BWS victim/survivor.

Staying

Much research has focused on why women, or men, leave abusive relationships. There is less attention on why some abused partners stay. Studying why someone stays, however, may help to better understand how to facilitate the path toward leaving and independence. Silke Meyer conducted 29 in-depth interviews with 29 women in Southeast Queensland, Australia. The interviews were carried out between August 2008 and February 2009. The average age of the study participants was 38 with a range of 21 to 62. The majority of the participants (89.7%) were victims of several physical and emotional abuse including pushing, shoving, having something thrown, punching, kicking, cutting or choking the victim, and the use of weapons or other objects that could be considered weapons. (Meyer, 2012: 184)

Another factor that Meyer considered was how long the victims stayed in the abusive intimate partnership relationship. It was a mean of 9.7 years with a range of 6 months to 36 years. A key factor is that at the time of the interview, at least temporarily, the interviewee was no longer with her abusive partner. There was an average of 2.05 years since the woman was with her partner with almost half of the women (48.3%) separated from their abusive partner within the 12 months before the interview.

The results led Meyer to conclude there were two key reasons that the women had previously stayed:

1. Children
2. Financial dependence

Of the interviewees, 62 percent told the researcher that they would return to their abusive partner because of their children. Here's an excerpt from one of the interviews that highlights this reason for saying: "I suppose it's very hard because when you have a house and furniture and it's your children's home, it's very hard to pack up and leave. The home is a secure place. It might be violent but still, that's their bedroom." (Meyer, 2012: 187)

Now to the second main reason the women in that survey stayed: financial dependence. As Meyer explains, the women she interviewed shared with her that they realized if they left the abuser it "often meant walking out with nothing but the few belongings they were able to pack for themselves and their children when the opportunity arose." (Meyer, 2012: 288)

Becoming more financially independent was the road to leaving. For some, it would mean depending on government benefits once they lost their partner's financial support. Others found another way to gain the funds needed to leave. As one victim put it, "I think when we went over to the caravan park I probably should have gotten out then . . . but I didn't have any money . . . So what I used to do was I used to start to sneak some money away. So I did that for five years. I was slowly sneaking money away. . . ." (Meyer, 2012: 188)

Leaving

Every situation is different, but, in general, statistically it is known that it is from the time a woman (or man) makes the decision to leave the abusive relationship until actually leaving that is the most dangerous for her or him. A plan needs to be in place especially if there is a history of violence and there are unresolved anger issues that cause a victim to fear for her or his life and even the lives of her or his children, extended family members, and perhaps even friends. The hundreds of domestic violence centers throughout the United States and internationally can help victims to leave safely. As the Crime Victims Treatment Center in Manhattan, New York states in their booklet, "Domestic, Intimate Partner and Family Violence," have a "go bag" available so you can make a quick exit. Also, victims need to have copies of important paperwork put into one safe place so it will be available to her Social Security after she exits. In her wallet and pocketbook should be such essential documents as social security card, ID/driver's license, passport, phone numbers of relatives and friends, and the hotline number for domestic violence help. (Crime Victims Treatment Center)

Tracie Yamauchi of Tracie Investigations based in Arlington, Texas aids victims, particularly domestic abuse victims, by helping them to get out of abusive situations without a disastrous result.

"On average, it may take seven attempts to get away," says Tracie stating a statistic that many others dealing with domestic violence restate.

When Tracie's firm gets involved, they do something called a *civil standby*; and they arrange with the attorneys, police, and the courts so they can remove a victim "with a one-time shot." "We're able to get a protective order," says Tracie. Tracie continues, "We present that to the abuser as well as we offer the victim protection to get away. We also help them put a plan in place so we can get them somewhere safe. We coordinate with helping them to get away."

Often there is no more than a three-minute time frame for her exit. "Often times they have small children with them," says Tracie. "She needs to have access to those children when we arrive or there is the fear that she might lose those children." (Yager, 2021)

Most help centers for crime victims or domestic violence victims offer victims a range of services from finding a shelter for immediate, safe housing to legal referrals, individual therapy or support groups, or crisis intervention as well as treatment for any physical issues at the ER (emergency room) in a local hospital.

Shelters

In 1971, Erin Pizzey founded the first domestic violence shelter in West London known as Chiswick Women's Aid. Now known as the Refuge, the mission of that first shelter is the same as the mandate for the thousands of shelters that have been established since that time. (Pizzey, 1974) The goal is to offer a free, safe, and temporary place for women suffering from domestic violence where they can leave their spouses, without fear of being found and harmed, as they figure out what the next steps will be in their new lives. Most shelters also house the children of the women who have left their spouses. You will not be able to find the address of the shelters. That information is only given out to the women who will be living there on an "as needed" basis. There are domestic violence centers, however, that offer help to women and men dealing with domestic violence. Through those centers a victim can learn about the available shelters in their area.

Shelters are usually only necessary in extreme cases where the victim fears for her life if she stays or if she leaves. Leaving and moving to a shelter is the preferred option to staying and being the victim of homicide or being put in the position to defend herself and kill the abuser. Even if the criminal justice system deems it a justifiable killing in self-defense, the victim will have to live with the reality that she has killed someone she once loved and who may also be the father of their children.

EXTREME SOLUTIONS: WHEN WOMEN USE FORCE OR VIOLENCE IN ABUSIVE RELATIONSHIPS

According to the National Coalition Against Domestic Violence, here are the reasons that women use force:

- "The desire to defend their self-respect against their partners' verbal and/or emotional attacks;
- To defend their children;
- A refusal to be victimized again;
- Being passive did not work so maybe using violence will; and
- To gain short-term control over a chaotic abusive situation"

This paragraph concludes with a clear view against women using force: "By using force, these women have not successfully controlled their partners' behaviors. Instead, their use of force has put the women at increased risk of physical injury and escalated the violence against them." (NCADV, n.d.)

In *Crime Victims*, criminologist Andrew Karmen highlights five conditions that are necessary for a violent action that led to someone's death to be considered self-defense. Should these same standards be applied to victims of domestic violence or do those complicated situations offer some modification of these rules?

1. The threat by the aggressor must be imminent.
2. If the assailant retreats, removing a victim from imminent danger, force may no longer be used.
3. The target has to have the belief that harm is imminent and that belief must be a reasonable one.
4. The degree of force used to repel the attack must be in proportion to the threat of injury or death posed by the aggressor.
5. Timing of the target's action must be appropriate. It is considered illegal to make the strike either too late or too soon. (Karmen, 2020, 455)

Profile ▪ Mary L. Reflects on the Domestic Violence She Endured When She Was Pregnant and the Fatal End to the Abuse

Mary L. grew up in a small village in a country near Venezuela in South America. She now lives in a southern state in the United States She is a 65-year-old widow who takes care of her grandchildren. A student interviewed Mary for her Victimology class. Mary agreed to be interviewed because "I hope my story can help others." They both also agreed to have Mary's story retold in this textbook. Mary's anonymity is being maintained.

Mary will tell her story in her own words. It also includes sexual abuse at an early age and running away from home at 17. The questions listed below are the verbatim questions asked by the student.

Question: Have you ever been a victim of a crime?

I feel like I was the victim of many crimes starting from when I was born. My mother worked very hard to take care of me and my five siblings. We were very poor and struggled daily for food to eat. My mother would go to work and leave us in the care of a neighbor. At five, I was sexually abused by my neighbor's son. This abuse continued until I was six years old. My mother found out and we moved to a different village. Things were okay for a while. I guess we just survived. No one cared if we went to school or studied. At age 12, my mother met a man and married him. I remember he would beat us quite often when he drank, and my mother would beat us some more for making him mad.

I ran away from home at age 17. I met a man and married him because he had a house and money to take care of me. The physical and sexual abuse started right away. He would also drink heavily. When he drank, he would come home and beat me for no reason, and I had to have sex with him whenever he wanted [it]. I had no say in the relationship and my only responsibility was to take care of the house and George [not his real name], my husband.

Question: Why did you not leave him?

I did not leave him because I had no one to go to. I felt hopeless. I did not have any family I could count on and I did not have any education. I did not graduate from high school. I felt like I was not good at anything. He made me feel worthless.

Question: Did you ever call the police?

The neighbors called the police several times because sometimes he would drag me into the yard and beat me and the neighbors would witness this, and sometimes call the police.

Question: Was George ever arrested?

One night—I remember it like it was yesterday—it was the day before Christmas Day and George had asked me to fry him some fish. I was six months pregnant with our first child. I was pregnant many times before, but George would kill the babies when he beat me, so I lost a lot of babies. Anyway, I was just finished frying the fish, and George came home after a day of drinking. I served him the fish, and after taking a few bites, he got up and started hitting me because I had forgotten to get him something to drink.

I begged him to stop. I kept saying, "Stop George. Stop George. You are going to kill me."

I don't know what came over me. I do not even remember picking up the pan of oil, but I remember hitting him with the pan.

The next thing I knew, the police were at the house, and they were saying that I killed George. I had thrown the pan of hot oil on him, and hit him several times in his head, and that had caused him to die.

Question: I am so sorry this happened. What happened next?

I was put in prison and because my neighbors testified of the abuse, I was only given five years. [But] It was hard time also because the jails [in [my country] are very rough. But I met some nice women who had many stories like mine.

Question: What happened to your baby?

When my son was born, he was sent to live with my sister, who said she would take care of him until I got out of prison.

Question: What happened when you got out of prison?

I went to live with my sister and my son and my sister's children. I was still young and so I went to learn a trade at a trade school. I learned to cook well and I used to sell food. My sister moved to the United States and, seven years later, she sent for me and my son to live in [place].

Question: Do you ever think that George was also a victim in this case because you killed him?

Yes, I do. But at the time, I did not know what else to do. I just snapped, I guess.

Question: How does this crime affect you in your life today?

It still haunts me that I killed George every day. I was never in another relationship. I just live for my son. I attended church and read my Bible and pray every day for forgiveness. I also have meetings at my church to tell women about my experiences and encourage them to leave the situations, because my abuse happened many years ago. But [because] the penalties are stiffer now for murder and domestic violence.

Question: Do you ever receive therapy?

No. Back in my country, you dealt with the abuse and praying that God would help you. When I came here to America, I was busy trying to make a good life for me and my son. I just try to deal with things on my own, and live day by day.

Question: How did George's family feel about you killing him and the abuse?

They supported me because they said that he had a long history of anger problems as a child and would even hit his mother. So they were sad he died I guess. But the entire village knew how bad [it was and that] he would beat me. His mother lived two houses away from us in [my country] but she would never help me really because she was afraid of him. When I came to America, I never heard from them again.

In Box 13.5 you will read a summary of some of the facts related to an aspect of IPV that is the most tragic: when men murder their romantic partners.

Box 13.5. When Men Murder Women in Domestic Violence Relationships

In 2017, there were 1,948 females murdered by males in single victim/single offender incidents that were submitted to the FBI for its Supplementary Homicide Report. A female intimate acquaintance is defined as a wife, common-law wife, ex-wife, or girlfriend. The key findings of this study are highlighted, in the sections that follow.

Box 13.5. When Men Murder Women in Domestic Violence Relationships (continued)

- For homicides in which the victim to offender relationship could be identified, 92 percent of female victims (1,611 out of 1,759) were murdered by a male they knew.
- Nearly 11 times as many females were murdered by a male they knew (1,611 victims) than were killed by male strangers (148 victims).
- For victims who knew their offenders, 62 percent (997) of female homicide victims were wives or intimate acquaintances of their killers.
- Arguments were the reason given for 289 women being shot and killed by their husband or an intimate acquaintance.
- In 82 percent of all incidents where the circumstances could be determined, homicides were unrelated to the commission of another felony, such as rape or robbery.

Source: Violence Policy Center, "When Men Murder Women: An Analysis of 2017 Homicide Data," Posted online, vpc.org, Copyright 2019.

MALE VICTIMS OF DOMESTIC VIOLENCE

The National Intimate Partner and Sexual Violence Survey (NISVS) 2011 survey revealed that nearly 16 million men have endured some type of severe physical violence by an IPV. Drijber et al. in "Male Victims of Domestic Violence" report on the findings of the 372 men who completed their online question about the abuse they experienced. The co-authors concluded: "When men are victims of DV they are physically as well as psychologically abused with the female (ex)partners often being their perpetrator." (Drijber et al., 2012)

Do the men report this abuse by their female significant others?

The co-authors continue: "The most important reason for men not to report the abuse is the belief the police would not take any actions." Within the article, the additional reasons for failing to report the DV to the police was a fear of not being taken seriously (49%), followed by the belief that police cannot do anything (35%), followed by shame (31%). They conclude: "Our findings suggest society should be aware that men are victims of DV and feel the need to talk about it and desire support." (Drijber et al., 2012, 173, 175)

Although the researchers did not focus on same sex relationships, they did find that 6 percent of the victims were said to be abused by a male (ex) partner. Males who were DV victims were predisposed to becoming DV victims by these conditions: alcoholism, depression, physical disability, past history of abusive relationships, the perpetrator having childhood abuse, rigid partner roles, and external stressors including poverty and loss of work. (Drijber et al., 176)

* * *

In conclusion, DV (domestic violence) or IPV (intimate partner violence) is a crime with male and female victims, single and married. It is a crime that impacts on the entire family since research has discovered that children who grow up in homes where they witness domestic violence may become prone to becoming victims themselves or even perpetrators. Even if they are fortunate to avoid being victims or perpetrators of abuse when they grow up, as Dr. Nadine Burke Harris discusses in her memorable TED Talk, "How childhood trauma affects health across a lifetime," there are physical and emotional consequences in adulthood if children grow up amidst family violence. (Harris, 2015)

PREGNANCY IS ONE OF THE RISK FACTORS FOR HOMICIDE IN WOMEN

In 2001, in JAMA (*Journal of the American Medical Association*), Diana Cheng and Isabelle L. Horon pointed out a phenomenon that had been overlooked before, one of the biggest risk factors for death during pregnancy. In addition to the medical and physiological issues related to the pregnancy, that risk factor was the actual announcement of being pregnant that was associated with an unusually high number of murders of the pregnant woman. That is what happened to Jenn, a woman who was in love with her married boss. Upon announcing that she was pregnant, tragically she was killed. Tracy Schott is a social worker who became a filmmaker and director of the documentary *Finding Jenn's Voice* to tell Jenn's story and to draw attention to a problem that was not widely known before. Says Tracy, "It is a documentary film about intimate partner homicide and the increased risks of violence during pregnancy. The film is based on the tragic murder of Jennifer Snyder in 2011 by her married boyfriend after he learned that she was pregnant. I went on to interview dozens of survivors of IPV and homicide attempts and featured eleven of them in my film." (Schott, 2021; Schott, 2014)

In their 2001 study, conducted through Maryland's Department of Health and Mental Health, Horon and Cheng found that there were 247 pregnancy-associated deaths between 1993 and 1998. Here were the causes:

- 20% were due to homicide (N=50)
- 19% were due to cardiovascular (heart) disorders (N=48)

In contrast to non-pregnant women during that time period, homicide was the fifth leading cause of death. (Ramsay, 2001; Horon and Cheng, 2001)

Profile of a Survivor of Attempted Murder by Her Ex-Husband - Monique Faison Ross

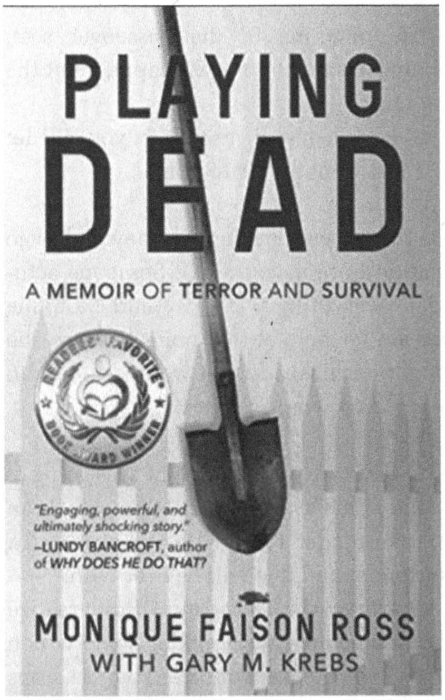

Playing Dead by Monique Faison Ross with Gary M. Krebs.

Author and attempted murder survivor Monique Faison Ross.
Photo credit: TimeFrozen Photography

In her guest presentation this author's my winter intensive Victimology class at John Jay College of Criminal Justice on Monday, January 11, 2021, Monique was asked why she wanted to write her memoir about her attempted murder, Playing Dead, *co-authored with Gary M. Krebs, 20 years after the crime. She explained that now that her children are all grown up and adults, she wanted to share her story so they would learn the details from her about what happened. Monique also wanted to help others who might be in an abusive relationship, including pointing to several resources related to domestic violence that readers should know about.*

The background to Monique's story is that she and her husband had been married for 13 years and had three children together. But after Chris [not his real name] got rough with Monique, they separated, as a road to divorce. (Later on in the interview, Monique shares that Chris tried to strangle her, which is what led to their separation.)

About six months into the separation, Monique and her ex-husband whom she calls Chris—not his real name—talked on the phone. Chris, who was with the military, shared that he had been dating and even had a girlfriend. Since he had shared about his social life, Monique figured it was okay to share that she had gone out with someone at work the night before and that they had a good time. She was wrong that it was okay to communicate that to Chris, dead wrong.

Here is an excerpt from Monique's interview about what followed:

Monique: It was that moment that I shared that information that life spiraled out of control. That simple conversation, that simple mention of a date, he immediately confronted the guy I worked with. I don't know how he figured out who it was but he began stalking me and the guy. It was that moment that I mentioned someone else.

The stalking went on for three months. We had to get injunctions. He was arrested multiple times for the stalking. We didn't grow up in homes dealing with the police. We didn't grow up in homes where people were arrested. This was not familiar territory. His bond kept getting raised till ultimately his parents had to put up their home to make the bond to get him out of jail. That's how high the stakes had gotten.

. . . Chris stalked me roughly every 45 minutes. It's really important to look at the Power and Control Wheel. I didn't think I was the victim of domestic violence. I was averaging ten 911 calls every week for the stalking. I never opened up once about it because I didn't think it [domestic violence] applied to me. I didn't realize where strangulation and stalking can lead and it often leads to a fatal outcome for the victim or for their family member.

The stalking is what I'm sure caused my PTSD more even than the attempted murder because it's hard to explain what it's like to always be looking over your shoulder. I'd see him following me. I went to the grocery store and I'd see him at a distance, watching me.

He rounded my building every 45 minutes. It was a kinda cul de sac design and he'd circle around to see.

At work, he was always there. Chris would show up at work. He [actually] caused me to lose my job. I don't know what he said to my boss, my supervisor . . . I was on a 90-day probationary period. Whatever he said to her, they let me go. They said to me, "When all this is over, we'll take you right back. But we can't risk other employees."

Time goes on. Three months. He's out of jail after one of his arrests and the police catch him circling and stalking and he leads them on a high speed chase.

I gave them his girlfriend's address.

The one thing that Monique does fault the police about: when they went to Chris's girlfriend's house to find him, they never got back to Monique to let her know that he was not there. If they had done that, she might have been better prepared to deal with what happened next. She had assumed that he had been arrested again and in jail. But that is not what happened. Instead, the next morning, Monique was making lunch for her three kids and Chris showed up. Monique was afraid he would do something to the kids so she got the neighbor's teenage daughter to take the two kids who were in the car.

Monique: He puts me in the passenger seat, throws my keys in, and I'm kidnapped, but the kids are safe.

He said, "I just want to talk to you. I'll let you go. I just want to talk to you."

Because the car was leaking oil, they had to go to a gas station to replace the oil. Someone actually asked if everything was okay and Monique did not scream for help at that point because she really thought her husband just wanted to talk to her and everything would be fine.

Monique: I was more worried that he was going to be shot and killed by the police. I thought, "I can get him to surrender. I'll go with him peacefully. He'll surrender and this will be over with."

We get around the corner and I didn't realize there was someone in the model home which was about two blocks from us. The car stops in front of a house that was completed [but empty]. The landscape had just been done. Chris says he's going to go into the house and see if someone could help but now I know that he was looking for something to kill me with.

By this time, it's about six hours later. I try talking to him.

He says, "Okay. I'm ready. You can go with me. We'll wait for the police and I'll turn myself in."

At this point, he hasn't done anything that's so horrendous that it can't be fixed.

He says he'll look at that house. I'm trying to keep him calm.

But now my gut is beginning to say, "Something is off here." But I couldn't go to the unthinkable. I keep my distance from him.

The door's unlocked. He opens the garage and says, "See, you can get out over there."

He removes the shovel from the group.

"Why are you doing that?"

"I was just seeing what they have."

At that moment, I turned to run, but it was too late.

First he dazes me by hitting my head on the cement garage floor. With that first blow to my head, blood splatters everywhere. So he goes on like that. I won't go into the details. In the time he believes he's killed me, he checks my pulse. He opens my eyes and I could hear him clearly when he says, "You're not dead yet" but I didn't answer. I was praying my breathing and my pulse would slow when I was laying there as still as I possibly could.

He drags me into the heavily wooded area and whacks my head multiple times, believing that I would die if I wasn't dead, throws the shovel, and walks off.

When Monique and the detective retraced what probably happened, they figured out she was probably out for 45 minutes. Then she managed to get out of the woods and collapsed in the street. A stranger put her into his car and drove a few blocks to a model home so she could call the police. EMTs and the hospital helicopter soon landed and Monique was on her way to the trauma unit.

She was found around two or three o'clock in the afternoon. Chris was shot around three in the morning the next day by a rookie policeman, but he survived.

In a cruel irony, he was taken to the same ICU unit as his victim, Monique. This happened in Florida and they had both grown up and had family in California so everyone was flying in from the West Coast.

The abuse continued in the ICU when even after the injuries and attempted murder that Monique suffered, Chris put in the police reports that she hit him first. Monique finds that suggestion infuriating.

Says Monique, "First of all, my fingerprints weren't on the shovel. I never even had the chance to hit him first."

Chris survived and eventually took a plea deal for 26 years. Around four years into his incarceration, Monique found out that he had been granted a trial. To avoid that for the sake of her children a new plea agreement was reached with Chris getting 16 years. He was released in 2016. Chris has never admitted to what he did to Monique. She explains she still lives in fear and may always keep looking over her shoulder:

Monique: I never wanted to tell the story publicly but friends encouraged me to tell the story. They said people needed to hear my story and the kids were old enough. I didn't educate myself about what domestic violence is. Black eyes, broken bones, and isolation. But it doesn't always have to look like that. I didn't know things like strangulation and stalking are two of the most lethal acts.

HONOR KILLINGS

The United Nations estimates that as many as 5,000 women are honor killing victims each year. What is an honor killing? It is when a girl or woman is killed in order to "'cleanse family honor' "after an individual has brought perceived shame or dishonor to a family or community by violating social norms." (Selby and Rodriguez, 2019) One honor killing that provoked activism against it was the killing of 26-year-old social media star in Pakistan, Qandeel Baloch, by her brother, on July 16, 2016, because she supposedly embarrassed her family because of "'revealing' clothes and striking pouty poses'" that she posted. (Selby and Rodriguez, 2019) Human Rights Watch lists these countries reporting honor killings: Pakistan, India, Afghanistan, Egypt, Palestine, the United States, Jordan, the United Kingdom, Bangladesh, Brazil, Ecuador, Israel, Italy, Morocco, Sweden, Turkey, and Uganda. (Human Rights Watch reported on by Selby and Rodriguez, 2019)

STALKING

Stalking is defined as "harassing or threatening behavior that an individual engages in repeatedly, such as following a person, appearing at a person's home or place of business, making harassing phone calls, leaving written messages or objects, or vandalizing a person's property. These actions may or may not be accompanied by a credible threat of serious harm, and they may or may not be precursors to an assault or murder." (Tjaden and Thoennes, 1998:1). It eventually became an actual crime in 1990. Prior to that, the first famous stalking victim is the December 8, 1980 death of former Beatles band member John Lennon, who was shot five times in the back and killed by a fan who had stalked him. (Associated Press, 1981)

The next stalking tragedy to get international attention happened just two years later, in 1982. The victim, actress Theresa Saldana, who had stared in the movie *Raging Bull*, was stabbed ten times by a fan who had been stalking her. Fortunately, she survived because a deliveryman who happened to be passing by stopped the man who was trying to kill her, holding him till the arrival of the police. (Grimes, 2016)

But it was the murder seven years later of beloved TV star and actress Rebecca Schaffer on July 18, 1989 by an obsessed fan who stalked her that finally gave stalking its attention as a dangerous action that needed to be criminalized. (Associated Press, 1989) A year later, in 1990, California enacted anti-stalking laws, with all 50 states eventually following suit. (National Institute of Justice, 1996)

THE LINK BETWEEN STALKING AND DOMESTIC VIOLENCE

A U.S. Department of Justice telephone survey of 8,000 men and 8,000 women discovered that 32 percent of the men and 59 percent of the women who had been stalked had once had an intimate relationship with the stalker. (U.S. Department of Justice, cited in Douglas and Dutton, 2001). The link between stalking and homicide was also noted in Chapter 7, "Primary and Secondary Victims of Homicide," and sexual assault, which was in addressed in the previous chapter, Chapter 12, "Sexual Violence: Rape, Sexual Abuse, Assault, and Harassment Victims."

Douglas and Dutton found a clear relationship between stalking and domestic violence in their 27-page journal article, "Assessing the Link Between stalking and Domestic Violence," published in the journal, *Aggression and Violent Behavior*. The co-authors conclude: "It appears that the most typicals talking scenario involves ex-intimate partners. Violence is common in the past relationship, and is common during the stalking episode. Domestic stalkers and certain batterers share a host of common characterological similarities, such as BPOs [borderline personality organization] [disorder], jealousy, anger, abandonment, rage, poorly integrated ego and primitive defenses, dysfunctional attachment styles, substance abuse, and emotional volatility. . . ." (Douglas and Dutton, 2001: 544)

Stalking Statistics

A study by Beth Bjerregaard, "An Empirical Study of Stalking Victimization," found that 25 percent of the women and 11 percent of the men in their study of 788 undergraduate and graduate students had been stalked. The students who participated in the anonymous survey were randomly selected from a list provided by the registrar's office at a large southeastern public university in the Spring semester of 1997. (Bjerregaard, 2000)

What about more recent statistics regarding the prevalence of stalking, especially since cyberstalking—stalking someone through social media on the internet—has become another form of stalking that may or may not lead to in-person stalking? Here are some facts about stalking prepared in 2018 by the Office for Victims of Crime and The National Center for Victims of Crime:

- Although stalking is a crime in all 50 states, most do not consider stalking a felony when it first occurs.
- In 51 percent of the states, two or more different instances of stalking behavior are necessary to deem it a felony.
- As noted in Figure 13.6 and previously, current or former intimate partners are the most common stalkers.
- When the stalking was reported to the police, 32 percent of the victims noted that police talked with the offender or issued a warning; just 8 percent stated that the offender was arrested. Almost 20 percent of the stalking victims indicated that police did not take any action. (Baum et al., 2009)

FIGURE 13.6. Victim Relationship to Stalker by Victim Sex

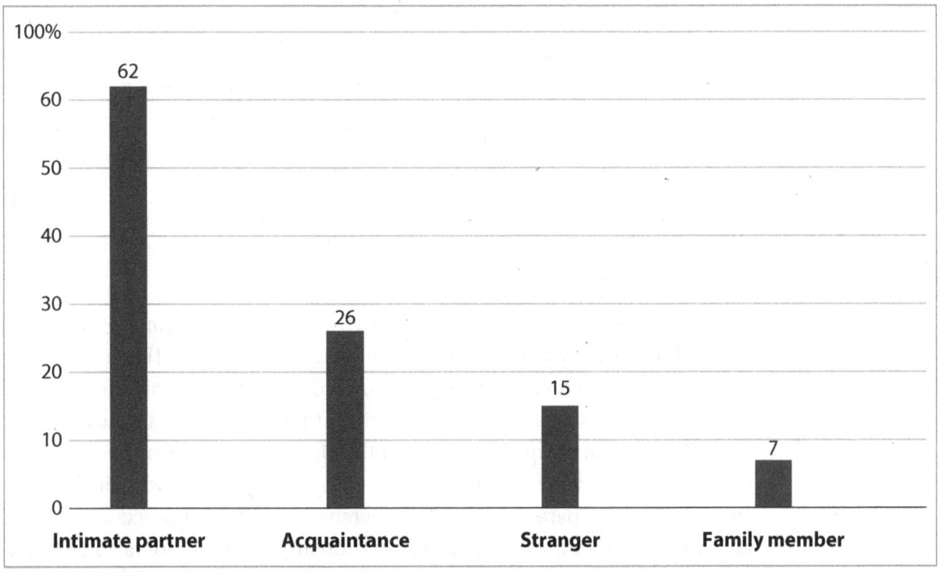

Source: Office for Victims of Crime (OVC) nd The National Center for Victims of Crime, 2018 National Crime Victims' Rights Week Resource Guide

Stalking was also mentioned in Chapter 7, "Primary and Secondary Victims of Homicide," since research has found an astonishingly high connection between stalking and homicide. In the study carried out by J. Monckton Smith, K. Szymanska and S. Haile with the Homicide Research Group at the University of Gloucestershire Centre for Learning and Innovation in Public Protection in the United Kingdom, it was discovered that of the 358 cases of homicide that were studied, stalking behavior was present in 94 percent of the cases. In 94 percent of the cases there was an "obsession" with the victim; in 88 percent, there was a "fixation." In all the cases that were studied in the United Kingdom in 2012, 2013, and 2014, the victims were female and the perpetrators were male. Possibly to avoid that 94 percent statistic causing too much alarm, the researchers point out that stalking occurs a lot more frequently than homicide. They write, "The prevalence of stalking is much higher than the incidence of homicide, so it must be considered that even though stalking can create serious health issues for its victims, and can be menacing, only a very small proportion end in homicide." (Smith, Szymanska, and Haile, 2017) But the connection between stalking and homicide is all too real.

Dr. Lorraine Sheridan, a forensic psychologist and senior lecturer in forensic psychology at the University of Leicester, identified a typology of four distinct stalkers and their victims:

1. Ex-partner harassment—bitterness toward the previous relationship; new relationships make the stalker feel jealous and causes aggressive behavior.
2. Infatuation harassment—Dr. Sheridan notes that the "target is 'beloved' rather than 'victim' and the focus of fantasy; stalker is usually a teenager or in mid-life.
3. Delusional fixation stalking—this stalker has a high risk of violence and sexual assault; police and mental health professionals are probably aware of this stalker; they believe there was a previous relationship with the victim although there never was one.
4. Sadistic stalking—this stalker, according to Dr. Sheridan, could be highly dangerous; he "can target family and friends in an attempt to isolate victim and further enhance control;" there could have been an "initial low level acquaintance;" "progressive escalation of control over all aspects of victim's life.'" (Sheridan, *2006*)

Even though cyberstalking takes place on the internet so technically it should not be as dangerous as being stalked in person, it can cause the victim extreme emotional distress and embarrassment as well as leading to in-person stalking.

ELDER ABUSE

According to Mark S. Lachs, M.D.-M.P.H. and Karl A. Pillemer, Ph.D., it was in the 1970s that elder abuse was first described in the medical literature. (Lachs and Pillemer, 2015: 1947.) Although there is no universally acknowledged definition of elder abuse, the National Center on Elder Abuse suggests this definition put forth by the Elder Justice Roadmap, an initiative of the U.S. Department of Justice and the Department of Health and Human Services: "physical, sexual, or psychological abuse, as well as neglect, abandonments, and financial exploitation of an older person by another person or entity, that occurs in any setting (e.g. home, community, or facility), either in a relationship where there is an expectation of trust and/or when an older person is targeted based on age or disability." (NCEA.acl.gov)

A study by R. Acierno, M.A. Hernandez, A.B. Amstadter, H.S. Resnick, K. Steve, W. Muzzy, and D.G. Kilpatrick, published in the *American Journal of Public Health,* found, as might be predicted, that financial abuse was the most common type of elder abuse. The next most common types of elder abuse, in order of most to least common, were potential neglect, emotional mistreatment, physical mistreatment, and sexual mistreatment. (Acierno et al., 2010)

As noted above, Elder abuse is not just physical abuse. It could include some or all of the following types of abuse:

- Physical abuse
- Physical neglect
- Emotional or psychological abuse including verbal abuse

- Financial abuse and exploitation
- Elder fraud
- Abandonment, loneliness, and isolation
- Sexual abuse
- Health care fraud

Elder abuse may occur in an institutional setting, if a senior has moved to assisted living or a nursing home, or if the elder remains in the home, it could take place in the home. The perpetrator could be a paid or unpaid caregiver such as an adult child or even a grandchild or spouse.

Elder Abuse Statistics

Here are some statistics related to elder abuse in the United States:

- An estimated 1 in 10 Americans who are over the age of 60 have experienced some form of elder abuse.
- Recent studies showed that nearly half of those with dementia suffer abuse or neglect.
- In almost 60 percent of the cases, the abuser is a family member.
- Two-thirds of the abusers are adult children or spouses.
- Abusers are both men and women. (*MEDSURG Nursing*, 2017: 123)

Most vulnerable to becoming victims of elder abuse are those seniors who are in poor health and have mobility problems, such as Parkinson's disease, or have mental deficiencies including dementia and related conditions such as Alzheimer's.

Those elders or seniors who are most likely to become victims of abuse are the ones who actually fall into one of the two categories that we just discussed, namely, physically or mentally disabled. If someone is 90, as long as he or she is in excellent health, has all his or her faculties, and is surrounded by a loving, supportive network of family and friends, abuse should be less likely to happen. The FBI has posted on YouTube a short informative video about how the former FBI Director, William Webster, and his wife helped the agency to catch a lottery scammer who tried to scam them. At the point they helped lead to his arrest, the scammer had bilked seniors out of $300,000 through his scams. The video, also mentioned in Chapter 9, is listed in the Resources section at the end of this chapter, is informative because it shows the tactics that this scammer used, and even the harsh words he used when he threatens the couple who are refusing to cooperate. The scammer was convicted and sentenced to six years in prison.

The two basic situations where elder abuse occurs are through paid or unpaid caregivers who are helping the elder in his or her home or apartment, or caregivers in an institutional setting. Elders could be abused by children, grandchildren, extended family members, spouses, romantic partners, as well as the staff in assisted living and nursing home facilities. Unscrupulous service providers including repair people, lawyers, or financial consultants may also abuse the elderly. Because those who become physically or mentally disabled because of age are especially vulnerable to all the types of abuse and neglect noted above, this is a population that requires a lot of attention.

Sometimes the family is unaware that the older person has been losing his or her sharpness and that abuse happens because of that development. For example, if a senior who is living alone and/or starting to have memory issues watches one of those TV shows or commercials that promotes buying various products, and then purchases something off of the TV or the internet, he or she may be unaware that the item is being purchased on a subscription basis. One month's supply of a product may suddenly become a purchase that is renewed monthly for months or even years unbeknownst to the family members, until they open up a closet and find dozens of items that were assumed by the senior to have been a one-time purchase.

The National Council on Aging (NCA) estimates that 1 in 10 Americans aged 60 and over have experienced some type of elder abuse. Some estimates go as high as 5 million seniors getting abused every year. According to the NCA, in 60 percent of the cases, as mentioned earlier, the perpetrators are family members, with two-thirds of those being adult children or spouses. (NCA, "Elder Abuse Facts.")

The consequences of elder abuse can be severe with the NCA estimating that abused elders have a 300 percent increased risk of death matched to those who have not been mistreated. The estimates for what elder financial fraud or abuse costs Americans ranges from $2.9 billion to $36.5 billion annually.

One-way elders can try to avoid becoming the victims of abuse or neglect is to put documents and plans in place while they are still physically and mentally of sound mind. Choose a trusted family member or, if necessary, a paid trust service provider to have power of attorney if the senior will no longer be able to make medical or financial decisions at a certain point. Ask seniors to write or update their will while they are still in excellent health and put all key documents in a safe place so everything can be found if the senior develops memory issues at some point.

Since social isolation has been associated with elder abuse, the NCA recommends staying active in the community and connected with family and friends. This was especially challenging during 2020 because of the COVID-19 pandemic that afflicted the United States and the world, with seniors in the most vulnerable population. Although vaccines became available by early 2021 and it was becoming possible for seniors to go back to interacting in person two weeks after becoming fully vaccinated, the mental and physical toll that the COVID-19 pandemic took on them will take months or possibly even years to overcome. Videoconferencing and keeping in touch with family members via e-mail and text messaging was a way to try to cut down on the isolation that the pandemic caused. Those seniors who found caregivers were worried about interacting with them because of the risk that they might get the virus. Nursing homes that had adopted strict "no visitors" policies were relieved that there was finally hope for seniors to have visitors again.

Isolated seniors have to be especially careful about allowing their loneliness to put them in compromising positions. Services for seniors with health-related issues, such as readers to those who have developed **macular degeneration**, an age-related condition that makes it hard to see, or paid caregivers, may be asked to sign a written statement that they will not allow the client to rewrite their will giving them money from their estate or changing the beneficiaries on their insurance policy. The needy elder, whose family and friends may have moved away, or who is in an institution and sees the paid staff more often than family members, could be taken advantage of if clear guidelines are not established.

As the population ages, putting into place strategies to recognize and avoid, elder abuse will help untold millions of elders who at some point will be completely dependent and unable to help themselves. An interdisciplinary approach to the elder abuse challenge is necessary. That means doctors, nurses, social workers, and law enforcement have to coordinate their efforts to detect, and deal with, elder abuse.

A Closer Look at the Various Types of Elder Abuse

Risk of violent or property crime victimization. Getting older, in general, puts you in a "protected class." Although seniors may be more vulnerable to some of the abuses and neglects discussed below, those 65 and up are actually less likely to be victims of violent crime or conventional property crimes. According to the Bureau of Justice Statistics, those age 65 and up have the lowest chance of becoming a crime victim of the major violent and property crimes. Considering the Routine Activity Theory of Cohen and Felson, we see that seniors are less likely to be a target because they are, in general, at home more. Even before the pandemic of 2020 required staying home, retired seniors are less likely to be out and about as much as those still working or younger singles going out to bars or other places at night. Lifestyle theory also comes into play here in that the lifestyle of most seniors is to be more protective and cautious. Those who are still living on their own, whether they have a partner or not, especially if they have mobility issues, will usually compensate for those restrictions by avoiding crowds or situations where they might be a more likely target for crime.

Physical abuse. The National Center on Elder Abuse defines physical abuse in this way: "The most commonly documented physical impacts of elder abuse include: welts, wounds, and injuries (bruises, lacerations, dental problems, head injuries, broken bones, pressure sores); persistent physical pain and soreness; nutrition and hydration issues; sleep disturbances; increased susceptibility to new illnesses (including sexually transmitted diseases); exacerbation of pre-existing health conditions; and increased risks for premature death." (National Center on Elder Abuse, 2020)

Physical neglect. Neglect is more subtle than abuse. Abuse is usually something physical that you can see. But neglect could be anything from failing to change the pads that an incontinent senior has to wear so that he or she is sitting in his or her own urine for hours or even days to providing minimal meals on an irregular basis, if the senior is completely dependent on someone for care.

Psychological or emotional abuse or neglect including verbal. A national prevalence study was conducted in Canada beginning in September 2013. It was an interesting study in that it explored what kind of abuse and neglect the 267 older adults, aged 55 and up, had over their lifetime. The results were that psychological, physical, and sexual abuse was most common during childhood, but the most common type of abuse at each life stage was psychological abuse. (McDonald and Thomas, 2013)

Financial abuse and exploitation. This is a different type of economic abuse than the elder fraud that is discussed below. Financial abuse is when someone takes control of the finances of an elder and mishandles that trust. Financial abuse could include everything from talking a senior into investing in a financial scheme that is faulty, like the Ponzi scheme that Bernie Madoff conned so many thousands to participate in, to writing counterfeit checks to make purchases with the senior's funds that were not agreed to.

A study by J. Peterson, et. al., published in the *Journal of General Internal Medicine*, found that the most common perpetrators of financial abuse or exploitation were family members (57.9%), followed by friends and neighbors (16.9%), and lastly by homecare aids (14.9%). (Peterson et al., 2014)

Elder fraud. These are the crimes that seniors are the more likely victims. Fraud can occur by phone or over the internet. Those who are living alone are especially vulnerable to being deceived by fraudsters who call and have such convincing pitches. They know how to get the trust of their senior victims, and they act quickly on the debit or credit card information they have stolen. If it was a credit card fraud, the senior victim might be able to get the charges disallowed by the bank or credit card company that issued the card. A fraud alert would have to be placed on the card along with freezing the card and disputing the charges. But if a debit card was used, if the victim freely shared her or his debit card information, if the bank account is drained, unless it is possible to track down the criminal and seek restitution, the victim is probably out those funds. There has been a push to start compensating victims of white-collar crimes like fraud, but until that happens, most government-funded crime compensation funds cover health care costs related to injuries incurred if someone is the victim of a so-called conventional or violent crime like robbery, rape, or aggravated assault. In the Resource section you will find the phone number for the National Elder Fraud Hotline.

This author recently learned by reading the transcript of an interviewee in a student study of seniors and phone scams of a 69-year-old woman who several years ago fell for a sweepstakes telephone fraud. She voluntarily shared her debit card information so she could supposedly get the dream trip of a lifetime for herself and her husband, who was not in their apartment when the victim was involved in the phone call that led to the fraud. It cost her $4,000 since her entire bank account was drained. (Huamancayo, 2021)

A Canadian senior was scammed out of her $400,000 bank account. (Shypula, 2015) A 67-year-old Australian woman lost more than just her money. She fell for a romantic scam that cost her $90,000 but she was found dead in South Africa where she had gone to meet her alleged romantic partner. A 28-year-old man who was the alleged fraudster was arrested by the Nigerian authorities a year later. (Reuters staff, 2014)

Abandonment, loneliness, and isolation. Adult children may be busy with their own lives and if a parent is widowed or if seniors are single and do not have any adult children to even turn to, they may be alone and abandoned for days or weeks on end. One of the consequences of abandonment is loneliness and we know that loneliness, which is different from spending time alone in a productive, joyful way, can lead to depression. Depression can lead to suicide attempts or suicide. According to the CDC, in 2017, of the 47,000 suicides in the United States, more than 8,500 were aged 65 and over. Males are at a higher risk from age 65 and up but both female and male seniors aged 85 and up are the second most at risk age group for suicide. (Balaban and Stone, 2019)

Sexual abuse. Not as common as financial fraud of seniors, sexual abuse is something to watch out for especially for those who have dementia so they may be unaware of what is happening to them.

Here are the warning signs that sexual abuse has occurred according to RAINN (Rape, Abuse & Incest National Network):

- An elder's report of being sexually assaulted or raped
- Bruises around the breasts or genital area
- Torn, stained, or bloody underclothing

- Unexplained vaginal or anal bleeding
- Unexplained venereal disease or genital infections (RAINN website, www.rainn.org)

Health care fraud. Seniors, especially those who live alone or who have diminished capacity because of memory loss, have to be careful that they are not taken advantage of related to health care costs. Attorney James Ruane lists these ten signs of health care fraud that the elderly may experience in elder care, but most also apply to elders who are living on their own as well who are frequenting medical services:

1. Duplicate billing for the same medical service
2. Evidence of inadequate care
3. Evidence of incorrect medication
4. False use of health care information
5. Inappropriate billing of services
6. Incorrect information on explanation of benefit paperwork
7. Misrepresentation of provider, date, or location or services
8. Problems with the care facility
9. Waiving deductibles ("A medical service or company should never waive deductibles; proceed with caution" Ruane warns.)
10. Waiving co-payments (Ruane, 2020)

As you know from reading Chapter 10, "Child Victims," there are mandatory reporting laws for reporting child abuse. If elder abuse is suspected, check out if your state has a mandatory elder abuse reporting procedure. especially if an elder is in a nursing home or other care facility. You can find that out at the map at the National Center on Elder Abuse. Many cities have also created an adult protective service agency, similar to the child protective agencies that handle issues related to child care. You can check out if such an agency is available in your community if you suspect an elder abuse situation.

The Most Vulnerable Population for Elder Abuse: Physical or Mental Disabilities and Disorders

This is a topic that will be discussed again in Chapter 15, "Additional Victim Situations and Populations," but in this chapter, let us just mention that seniors who are physically or mentally disabled are at the greatest risk for elder abuse. These disabilities include everything from dementia to macular degeneration, mentioned previously, which reduces a senior's ability to see or even read vital documents that they could be asked to sign impacting their financial situation or even their independence. One study found that those with dementia had an abuse rate of 27.5 percent to 55 percent. (Tronetti, 2014)

In addition to the increased risk for elder abuse of all kinds for those with dementia and memory loss are the issues related to mobility including Parkinson's disease and other conditions associated with aging. If an elder is confined to a wheelchair and he or she is totally dependent on others for his or her basic needs, delays in providing those services is a form of neglect and even abuse if it goes on long enough.

SUMMARY

Aggravated assault is the most frequent violent crime. It is defined by the FBI as "an unlawful attack by one person upon another for the purpose of inflicting severe or aggravated bodily injury." Some believe that the presence or absence of a firearm may make the difference between a crime being an aggravated assault or a homicide. Others say that the speed with which a victim receives medical aid can be a major factor as well. Victims of aggravated assault differ by gender and place of the assault. There are more aggravated assaults between those known to the victim than strangers but for males, the assault is more likely to take place in a commercial place outside of the home but for women, within the home is the more common place for their assaults. That may be an indication of domestic violence (DV) or intimate partner violence (IPV) that has become a physical assault, not just an emotional one.

We have come a long way from the centuries-old view of women as the property of men who could control them economically as well as even physically including having sex whenever they wanted once married. According to Elizabeth Pleck, in 1641, the Massachusetts *Body of Laws and Liberties* of colonial American became the first law against wife beating in the world. Marital rape was outlawed in 1976 and the definition of rape was changed so marital rape was not excluded in 2013.

Intimate partner violence is a crime that affects more women than men with one in four women in the United States as victims of DV, but one in nine men may also be DV victims. Those male victims may be in heterosexual relationships, not just same-sex ones. DV is an underreported crime because victims fear the police will be forced to arrest their partner, which they may be required to do, by law, if the evidence points to DV occurring. They may fear retaliation by their partner as well as loss of income if their partner is in jail or serves prison time or even loses his job because of the charges. There is also the fear of being labeled a victim of DV. To avoid the tragic deaths of women by their partner's or women becoming the killers in self-defense, victims need to get out of an abusive situation safely and as soon as the abuse is discovered. The domestic violence shelter movement started in 1971 in London with the founding by Erin Pizzey of the first shelter for abused women who need a safe place to get away from her abuser.

Stalking became a crime following the tragic stalking and murder of Rebecca Schaffer in 1989. The next year, California passed a law making stalking a crime. All 50 states followed. Forensic psychologist Dr. Lorraine Sheridan developed a typology of four distinct types of stalkers: ex-partner harassment; infatuation harassment; delusional fixation stalking; sadistic stalking. The most common type of relationship between the offender and the victim in stalking is that of current or former romantic partner.

Like domestic violence, which covers everything from emotional, sexual, physical, or financial abuse, elder abuse also encompasses many abuses with financial exploitation, neglect, and physical abuse key concerns. Elders who are physically or mentally dependent, including those with dementia, are especially vulnerable. The abuse can occur in the home, with caregivers who are family members or paid attendants, or in nursing home or even assisted living residence. Males ages 65 and up are most at risk for suicide due to loneliness followed by both genders ages 85 and up. Abandonment, loneliness, and isolation are linked to the depression that can lead to suicide attempts or suicide. Elders need to be included wherever they are living.

KEY TERMS

aggravated assault
attempted murder
cycle of violence
domestic violence
elder abuse
honor killing
intimidation
IPV (Intimate Partner Violence)
DV (Domestic violence)
macular degeneration
protective order (PO) (or order of protection)
Power Control Wheel
restraining order
shelters
simple assault
stalking

REVIEW QUESTIONS

1. How do you define aggravated assault?
2. How common is aggravated assault in the United States?
3. When was the first law against wife beating enacted and where?
4. What do IPV and DV stand for?
5. What is the concept that is used to explain why victims stay in the abusive relationship?
6. When is the most dangerous time in an abusive relationship for the victim?
7. What state was the first one to pass a legal statute making stalking a crime?
8. What is the most common relationship between the stalker and the victim?
9. What are the various types of elder abuse?

CRITICAL THINKING QUESTIONS

1. Why do you think growing up in a household where there was child abuse or being the witness to a parent being abused by the other parent predisposes an adult to becoming a victim of domestic violence? Support your answer.

2. Do you think the same conditions that are required for someone claiming they killed someone in self-defense should be applied to domestic violence situations or should there be a different standard applied since some victims fear they will be at greater risk of being killed even if they do leave their abuser? Support your answer with statistics and examples.

3. Explain the dangers of cyberstalking even if the stalker is not technically face to face with his or her victim.

4. Refer back to the Profile/Interview with Mary that you read in this chapter. Consider what happened to her, the various crimes that she was a victim of, and her husband George's fate. What were some of the interventions that could have taken place in her native country in South America that might have changed the outcome? Do you think how Mary handled her husband's behavior was an example of self-defense or justifiable homicide? Why? Why not? Do you agree with the sentence she received for killing her husband? Support your answer.

ACTIVITIES

Do a search on the internet of articles related to sports figures who have been accused of domestic violence and, if found guilty, what their sentences turned out to be. Divide into small groups of three students per group and discuss at least one of those cases. (If this is being done as an online only class, some videoconferencing programs do allow you to divide up into groups.) Do you agree or disagree with the way the criminal justice system handled a particular case? Why? Why not?

RESOURCES

Assault

National Center for Victims of Crime (NCVC)
www.ncvc.org
Offers information and referrals for all types of crime victims.

National Organization for Victim Assistance (NOVA)
www.trynova.org
Membership organization providing information and training for those who offer services to victims and for victims/survivors.

Domestic Violence including IPV

American Bar Association
Commission on Domestic & Sexual Violence
americanbar.org/groups/domestic_violence
From the website: "Our mission is to increase access to justice for victims of domestic violence, sexual assault and stalking by mobilizing the legal profession."

National Coalition Against Domestic Violence (NCADV)
ncadv.org
A membership organization dedicated to advocacy and education to reduce or eliminate domestic violence.

National Domestic Violence Hotline
thehotline.org
Call – 1-800-799-7233
Text – LOVEIS to 1-866-3331-9474

Office on Violence Against Women (U.S. Department of Justice)
usdoj.gov/ovw
From the website: "The Office on Violence Against Women (OVW) provides federal leadership in developing the national capacity to reduce violence against women and administer justice for and strengthen services to victims of domestic violence, dating violence, sexual assault, and stalking."

Safe Horizons
safehorizon.org
New York-based program offering information as well as direct help to victims of domestic violence.

Stalking

Stalking Resource Center
victimsofcrime.org/stalking-resource-center

Developed and run by the National Center for Victims of Crime. Offers educational information and training related to stalking.

Elder Abuse

National Center on Elder Abuse--U.S. Administration on Aging
ncea.acl.gov
This is an information clearinghouse with data on the various types of elder abuse.

National Elder Fraud Hotline
1-833-FRAUD-11 or 1-833-372-8311
The U.S. Department of Justice (DOJ) and the Office for Victims of Crime created this free resource for anyone age 60 and up to be able to report fraud.

CITED WORKS AND ADDITIONAL REFERENCES

Acierno, R., M.A. Hernandez, A.B. Amstadter, H.S Resnick, K. Steve, W. Muzzy, and D.G. Kilpatrick. 2010. "Prevalence and Correlates of Emotional, Physical, Sexual, and Financial Abuse and Potential Neglect in the United States: The National Elder Mistreatment Study." *American Journal of Public Health*. 2: 292-297.

Adams, David. 2009. "Predisposing Childhood Factors for Men Who Kill Their Intimate Partners." *Victims and Offenders*. 215-229.

Allen, Roy B. 1986. "Measuring the Severity of Physical Injury Among Assault and Homicide Victims." *Journal of Quantitative Criminology*. 2(2): 139-156.

American College of Obstetricians and Gynecologists. February 2012. "Intimate Partner Violence." Committee Opinion No. 518. Posted at acog.org

Anetzberger, Georgia J. Fall 2012. "An Update on the Nature and Scope of Elder Abuse." *Generations: Journal of the American Society on Aging*. 36(3): 12-20.

Annese, John. January 11, 2018. "Mom Found Dead in Brooklyn Apartment Building After Cops Ignored Her 911 Call Was Strangled." *Daily News*. Posted online.

Ascione, P. and P. Arkow. 1999. *Child Abuse, Domestic Violence, and Animal Abuse: Linking the Circles for Compassion for Prevention and Intervention*. West Lafayette, IN: Purdue University Press.

Associated Press. July 14, 2014. "The Celebrity Murder That Changed How Stalkers Are Treated." Posted online at pagesix.com

__________. July 20, 1989. "Man Is Being Held in Actress's Death." *The New York Times*. Archived at nytimes.com

__________. May 15, 1981. "Tape By Hinckley is Said to Reveal Obsession With Slaying of Lennon." *The New York Times*. Archived at nytimes.com

Bancroft, L., J. Silverman, and D. Ritchie. 2011. *The Batterer as Parent: Addressing the Impact of Domestic Violence on Family Dynamics*. Thousand Oaks, CA: SAGE.

Baum, K., S. Catalano, M. Rand, & C. Rose. 2009. "Stalking victimization in the United States." Bureau of Justice Statistics Special Report. Washington, DC: U.S. Department of Justice.

Bergman, Paul. "Assault, Battery, and Aggravated Assaulted." *Nolo Legal Encyclopedia*. Posted online at https://www.nolo.com/legal-encyclopedia/assault-battery-aggravated-assault-33775.html

Berk, Richard A., Phyllis J. Newton, and Sarah Fenstermaker Berk. August 1986. "What a Difference a Day Makes: An Empirical Study of the Impact of Shelters for Battered Women." *Journal of Marriage and the Family*. 48: 481-490.

Bjerregaard, Beth. 2000. "An Empirical Study of Stalking Victimization." *Violence and Victims* 15: 389-406.

Boffey, Philip M. April 5, 1983. "Domestic Violence Study Favors Arrest." *New York Times*. C1 ff.

Brown, Maleaha L. April 5, 1983. "When Pros Become Cons: Ending the NFL's History of Domestic Violence Leniency." *Family Law Quarterly*. 50(1): 8,185 words.

Bureau of Justice Statistics. *Criminal Victimization, 2018*. National Crime Victimization Survey.

__________. May 2017. "Police Response to Domestic Violence, 2006-2015." Summary 1-page report. U.S. Department of Justice, Office of Justice Programs.

Burgess, Ann Wolbert. 2019. *Victimology: Theories and Applications.* Third edition. Burlington, MA: Jones & Bartlett.

Center for Disease Control (CDC), National Center for Injury Prevention and Control, Division of Violence Prevention. 2016. "Understanding Teen Dating Violence." Fact Sheet. Posted at file:///C:/Users/hanna/Downloads/cdc_38280_DS1%20(1).pdf

____________. October 8, 2019. "Risk and Protective Factors for Perpetration." *Violence Prevention.* 2-page fact sheet. Posted at https://www.cdc.gov/violenceprevention/intimatepartnerviolence/riskprotectivefactors.html

Chouhy, Cecilia. 2018. "Moving Beyond Punitive Intervention." *Criminology & Public Policy.* 17: 547-551.

Cooper, Andrea. August 2005. "My Dad Went to Prison for Killing My Molester." Cosmogirl.com 124, 126.

Daigle, Leah E. and Lisa R. Muftic. 2016. *Victimology.* Thousand Oaks, CA: SAGE.

D'Alessio, Stewart J. and Lisa Stolzenberg. June 2003. "Race and the Probability of Arrest." *Social Forces.* 81(4): 1381-1397.

Danis, Fran S. April 2003. "The Criminalization of Domestic Violence: What Social Workers Need to Know." *Social Work.* 48(2): 237-246.

Dobash, R. Emerson and Russell Dobash. 1979. *Violence Against Wives: The Case Against Patriarchy.* New York: Free Press.

Doerner, William G. and Steve P. Lab. 2017. *Victimology.* Eighth edition. New York: Routledge.

Domestic Abuse Intervention Programs. "Power and Control Wheel." Duluth, MN.

Douglas, Kevin and Donald G. Dutton. 2001. "Assessing the Link between Stalking and Domestic Violence." *Aggression and Violent Behavior.* 6: 519-546.

Drijber, Babette, Udo J.L. Reijnders, and Manon Ceelen. February 2013. "Male Victims of Domestic Violence." *Journal of Family Violence.* 28(2): 173-178. Published online.

Druzin, Bryan H. and Jessica Li. Spring. 2011. "The Criminalization of Lying: Under What Circumstances, If Any, Should Lies Be Made Criminal?" *Journal of Criminal Law and Criminology.* 101: 529-573.

Estrellado, Alicia F. and Jennifer (MI) Loh. 2019. "To Stay in or Leave an Abusive Relationship: Losses and Gains Experienced by Battered Filipino Women." *Journal of Interpersonal Violence.* 34: 1843-1863.

Eterovic-Soric, Brett, Kim-Kwang Raymond Choo, Helen Ashman, and Sameera Mubarak. 2017. "Stalking the Stalkers-Detecting and Deterring Stalking Behaviours Using Technology: A Review." *Computers & Security.* 70: 278-289.

Federal Bureau of Investigation (FBI). 2020. "Aggravated Assault." *2019 Crime in the United States.* Criminal Justice Information Services Division. Posted online.

______________. 2020. "Expanded Homicide." Table 7. 2019 Crime in the United States. Criminal Justice Information Services Division. Posted online.

Felson, Richard B. 1996. "Big People Hit Little People: Sex Differences in Physical Power and Interpersonal Violence." *Criminology.* 34: 433-452.

___________. and Alison C. Cares. December 2005. "Gender and Seriousness of Assaults on Intimate Partners and Other Victims." *Journal of Marriage and Family.* 67: 1182-1195.

Finkelhor, David. 2011. "Prevalence of Child Victimization, Abuse, Crime, and Violence Exposure." Chapter 1 in *Violence Against Women and Children: Mapping the Terrain.* J.W. White, M.P. Koss, and A.E. Kazdin (eds.). Washington, DC: American Psychological Association. 9-24.

Finley, Laura L. 2013. "Child Abuse and Domestic Abuse." *Encyclopedia of Domestic Violence and Abuse.* Laura L. Finley (ed.). 1(ABC-CLIO): 76-80. Posted online. Published by Gale eBooks.

Fisher, Bonnie S., Bradford W. Reyns, and John J. Sloan III. 2016. "Introduction." *Victimology: Contemporary Theory, Research, and Practice.* New York: Oxford University Press.

Fox, Maragalit. January 23, 2013. "Linda Riss Pugach, Whose Life Was Ripped From Headlines, Dies at 75." *The New York Times.* Posted at nytimes.com

Garcia-Moreno, Claudia, Henrica A.F.M. Jansen, Mary Ellsberg, Lori Heise, and Charlotte Watts. 2005. "WHO (World Health Organization) Multi-country Study on Women's Health and Domestic Violence Against Women." Geneva, Switzerland.

Gelles, Richard J. July 2000. "Estimating the Incidence and Prevalence of Violence Against Women." *Violence Against Women.* 6(7): 784-804.

_____________. October 1979. "The Myth of Battered Husbands—and New Facts About Family Violence." *Ms.* 8: 65-73.

_____________. November 1980. "Violence in the Family: A Review of Research in the Seventies." *Journal of Marriage and the Family.* 873-885.

Gelles, Richard J. and Claire Pedrick-Cornell. 1985. *Intimate Violence in Families.* Beverly Hills, CA: Sage.

Gelles, Richard J. and Murray Straus A. 1988. *Intimate Violence.* New York: Simon & Schuster.

Gondolf, Edward W. June 1995. "Alcohol Abuse, Wife Assault, and Power Needs." *Social Service Review.* 69(2): 275-284.

Goode, William J. November 1971. "Force and Violence in the Family." *Journal of Marriage and the Family.* 33(4): 624-636.

Grams, Mary. 2004. "Guardians Ad Litem and the Cycle of Domestic Violence: How the Recommendations Turn." *Law & Inequality: A Journal of Theory and Practice.* 22(1): 105-139.

Grierson, Jamie. April 24, 2017. "Stalking Behaviour Identified in 94% of Murders, Study." *The Guardian.* Posted online at theguardian.com

Grimes, William. June 8, 2016. "Teresa Saldana, Actress and Attack Survivor, Dies at 61." *New York Times.* Posted online, nytimes.com

Groves, B. 2003. *Children Who See Too Much: Lessons from the Child Witness to Violence Project.* Boston, MA: Beacon.

Hardesty, J. and G. Chung. 2006. "Intimate Partner Violence, Parental Divorce, and Child Custody: Directions for Intervention and Future Research." *Family Relations.* 55: 200-210.

Hardwick, Julie. March 2006. "Early Modern Perspectives on the Long History of Domestic Violence: The Case of Seventeenth Century France." *The Journal of Modern History.* 1-36.

Hayes, Brittany, Coleen E. Mills, Joshua D. Freilich, and Steven M Chermak. 2018. "Are Honor Killings Unique? A Comparison of Honor Killings, Domestic Violence Homicides, and Hate Homicides by Far-Right Extremists." *Homicide Studies* 11: 70-93.

Horon, Isabelle L. and Diana Cheng. March 21, 2001. "Enhanced Surveillance for Pregnancy-Associated Mortality-Maryland, 1993-1998." *Journal of the American Medical Association (JAMA).* 285: 1455-1459.

Huamancayo, Neil. May 26, 2021. "Phone Scams and the Elderly." Senior Seminar in Sociology, Sciology 4600, Section 01, Kean University, School of Social Science, Sociology Department, taught by Jan Yager, Ph.D. (Final 31-page-paper)

Jerin, Robert A. and Laura J. Moriarty. 1998. *Victims of Crime.* Chicago, IL: Nelson-Hall.

Johnson, Dark. "Abused Women Get Leverage in Connecticut." June 15, 1986. *New York Times.* Section 4: 8.

Kardile, Mangal and Carmelle Peisah. 2017. "Elder Abuse by Abandonment in India: A Novel Community Awareness and Intervention Strategy." Letter. *International Psychogeriatrics.* 29: 1035-1036.

Karmen, Andrew.2020. *Crime Victims.* Tenth edition. Boston, MA: Cengage.

Kernic, M.D. Monary-Ernsdorff, and V. Holt. 2005. "Children in the Crossfire: Child Custody Determinations Among Couples with a History of Intimate Partner Violence." *Violence Against Women.* 11: 991-1021.

Kreizman, Maris. May 11, 2019. "Listening to My Neighbors Fight." *The Atlantic.*

Lachs, Mark S. and Karl A. Pillemer. 2015. "Elder Abuse." *The New England Journal of Medicine.* 373: 1747-1756.

Laslett, Barbara. August 1973. "The Family as a Public and Private Institution: An Historical Perspective." *Journal of Marriage and the Family.* 35(3): 480-492.

Latus, Janine. 2007. *If I Am Missing or Dead.* New York: Simon & Schuster.

Litteral, Alesia. Thursday, January 7, 2021. Phone interview with the author.

Lopez, Ray, and Paula Newton. April 25, 2020. "Domestic Assault May Have Triggered Canadian Rampage That Left 22 Dead, Police Say." Posted at MSN.com.

Malsch, Marijke. April 25, 2020. "Stalking: Do Criminalization and Punishment Help? *Punishment & Society.* 9: 201-209.

McDonald, L. and C. Thomas. 2013. "Elder Abuse Through a Life Course Lens." *International Psychogeriatrics.* 25: 1235-1243.

MEDSURG Nursing. March-April 2017. "Elder Abuse Statistics." 26: 124.

Merton, Robert K. October 1938. "Social Structure and Anomie." *American Sociological Review.* 3: 672-682.

Meyer, Silke. 2012. "Why Women Stay: A Theoretical Examination of Rational Choice and Moral Reasoning in the Context of Intimate Partner Violence." *Australian & New Zealand Journal of Criminology.* 45: 179-193.

McColgan, Aileen. Winter 1993. "In Defence of Battered Women Who Kill." *Oxford Journal of Legal Studies.* 13(1): 508-529.

Morgan, Mannette. 2019. *Finding Your Voice.* Made For Success Publishing.

______________. 2020. *Finding Your Voice Workbook.* Made For Success Publishing.

Morgan, Rachel E. and Barbara A. Oudekerk. September 2019. *2018 Crime Victimization*. Bureau of Justice Statistics, U.S. Department of Justice.

National Center for Victims of Crime, Office for Victims of Crime, U.S. Department of Justice. "Assault." 2-page fact sheet for 2018 National Crime Victims' Rights Week Resource Guide: Crime and Victimization Fact Sheets.

National Center on Elder Abuse (NCEA) "Statistics and Data." Posted at ncea.acl.gov

National Coalition Against Domestic Violence (NCADV), n.d. "Why Do Women Use Force or Violence in Intimate Partner Relationships?" (2-page fact sheets, posted online)

National Council on Aging (NCA). "Elder Abuse Facts." n.d. Posted at https://www.ncoa.org/public-policy-action/elder-justice/elder-abuse-facts/

National Institute of Justice (NIJ) April 1996. "Domestic Violence, Stalking, and Antistalking Legislation." An Annual Report to Congress under the Violence Against Women Act. Reported edited by Mary Graham. Office of Justice Programs, U.S. Department of Justice.

Obeid, Nadine, Doris F. Change, and Jeremy Ginges. 2010. "Beliefs About Wife Beating: An Exploratory Study with Lebanese Students." *Violence Against Women*. 691-712.

Office of the Attorney General, State of New York. n.d. "Stalking: Realities and Responses."

Office for the Victims of Crime. "Supporting Male Survivors of Violence Initiative." Vision 21. One page.

The Office for Victims of Crime and The National Center for Victims of Crime. n.d. "Stalking." 2018 National Crime Victims' Rights Week Resource Guide: Crime and Victimization Fact Sheets.

O'Reilly, Jane. September 5, 1983. "Wife Beating: The Silent Crime." *Time*. 23 ff.

Oudekerk, Barbara A. October 2020. "Violent Victimization by Race or Ethnicity, 2005-2019." U.S. Department of Justice, Bureau of Justice Statistics.

Pagelow, Mildred. 1981. *Women Battering: Victims and Their Experiences*. Beverly Hills, CA: SAGE.

Pittman, David J. and William Handy. December 1964. "Patterns in Criminal Aggravated Assault." *Journal of Criminal Law, Criminology, and Police Science*. 55(1): 462-470.

Pizzey, Erin. 1974. *Scream Quietly or the Neighbors Will Hear*. London, UK: Penguin.

Pfouts, Jane H., Janice H. Schopler, and H. Carl Henley, Jr. July 1982. "Forgotten Victims of Family Violence." *Social Work*. 27(4): 367-368.

Pleck, Elizabeth. 1989. "Criminal Approaches to Family Violence, 1640-1980." *Crime and Justice*. 11: 19-57.

Pokorny, Alex D. December 1965. "Human Violence: A Comparison of Homicide, Aggravated Assault, Suicide, and Attempted Suicide." *Journal of Criminal Law, Criminology, and Police Science*. 56(4): 488-497.

Potter, Gary. June 25, 2013. "The History of Policing in the United States, Part 1." Blog published at Police Studies Online.

Ramsay, Sarah. March 31, 2001. "Study Uncovers 'Disturbing' Level of Pregnancy-Associated Homicide." *The Lancet*. 357: 1021.

Reuters staff. February 4, 2014. "Nigeria Arrests Man in $90,000 Romance Scam in Australian Widow." Posted at reuters.com.

Riggs, David S., Dean G. Kilpatrick, and Heidi S. Resnick. December 1992. "Long-Term Psychological Distress Associated with Marital Rape and Aggravated Assault: A Comparison to Other Crime Victims." *Journal of Family Violence*. 7(4): 283-296.

Ross, Monique Faison. January 11, 2021. Guest presentation and interview. John Jay College of Criminal Justice Victimology Course.

__________. with Gary Krebs. 2019. *Playing Dead: A Memoir of Terror and Survival*. CA: WildBlue.

Roth Davis Trial Lawyers LLC. 2020. "How Long Can You Be Jailed for a Domestic Violence Charge?" https://www.copleyroth.com/long-can-jailed-domestic-violence-charge/

Ruane, James. 2020. "Ten Signs of Healthcare Fraud Against the Elderly in Elder Care." Posted at www.nuaneattorneys.com

Selby, Daniele and Leah Rodriguez. April 9, 2019. "How Activists Helped Change Pakistan's Honor-Killing Law." Posted at globalcitizen.org

Seligman, Martin. 1975. *Helplessness: On Depression, Development, and Death*. San Francisco, CA: Freeman.

Sheridan, Lorraine. Spring 2006. "Stalking: Causes and Effect." Originally published in the Spring 2006 edition of *Graduate Review*. Reprinted by the University of Leicester.

Sherman, Lawrence W. and Richard A. Berk. April 1984. "The Minneapolis Domestic Violence Experiment." *Police Foundation Reports*. 13 pages.

____________. 1984. "The Specific Deterrent Effects of Arrest for Domestic Violence." *American Sociological Review*. 49(2): 261-272.

Schott, Tracy. January 22, 2021. Phone interview with the author.

Shuhong, Zhao. 2020. "Characteristics of Intimate Partner Homicide in China: Compared with Previous Studies in Other Countries." *International Journal of Offender Therapy and Comparative Criminology*. 64: 210-231.

Shypula, Brian. April 23, 2015. "Brantford Senior Loses $400,000 in Online Romance Scam." Published online at Toronto.com

Smith, J. Monckton, K. Szymanska, and S. Haile with the Homicide Research Group at the University of Gloucestershire, Centre for Learning and Innovation in Public Protection, in association with Suzy Lamplugh Trust. 2017. "Exploring the Relationship between Stalking and Homicide." Foreword by Rachel Griffin.

Snyder, Rachel Louise. December 20, 2019. "When Can a Woman Who Kills Her Abuser Claim Self-Defense?" *New Yorker*. Posted at newyork.com

State of New York. Revised January 2014. Office for the Prevention of Domestic Violence. *Domestic Violence: Finding Safety & Support*. 79-page booklet.

Steinmetz, Suzanne K. 1978. "The Battered Husband Syndrome." *Victimology*. 2(3-4): 499-509.

Stevenson, Robert Louis. 1886, reprinted 2017. *The Strange Case of Dr. Jekyll and Mr Hyde: and other Stories*. New York: Macmillan.

Stiles, Eric. Ivonne Ortiz and Casey Keene. "Serving Male-Identified Survivors of Intimate Partner Violence." National Resource Center on Domestic Violence. 13 pages.

Stone, Lawrence. 1977. *The Family, Sex and Marriage in England, 1500-1800*. New York: Harper & Row.

Straus, Murray, Richard J. Gelles, and Suzanne K. Steinmetz. 2007. *Behind Closed Doors: Violence in the American Family*. Transaction Publishers.

Strube, Michael J. and Linda S. Barbour. November 1983. "The Decision to Leave an Abusive Relationship: Economic Dependence and Psychological Commitment." *Journal of Marriage and the Family*. 45: 785-793.

The Times and Democrat. April 17, 2020. "Staying at Home Putting Some in New Danger."

Thrasher, John and Toby Handfield. 2018. "Honor and Violence: An Account of Feuds, Duels, and Honor Killings." *Human Nature* 29: 371-389

Time. March 20, 1978. "The Battered Husband." 69.

Tjaden, Patricia and Nancy Thoennes. April 1998. "Stalking in America: Findings From the National Violence Against Women Survey." U.S. Department of Justice, Office of Justice Programs, National Institute of Justice and Centers for Disease Control and Prevention. Research in Brief.

Torpy, Janet M., M.D. (writer), Richard M. Glass (ed.), and Cassio Lynm, illustrator). August 4, 2010. "Intimate Partner Violence." JAMA Patient Page, *Journal of the American Medical Association*. 596.

Tronetti, P. 2014. "Evaluating Abuse in the Patient with Dementia." *Clinics in Geriatric Medicine*. 30: 825-838.

University of Leicester. Spring 2006. "News and Events Archive." Features: Stalking: Cause and Effect. Article first appeared in *Graduates Review*.

U.S. Department of Justice, Department of Health and Human Services. M.T. Connolly, Brandl, and R. Brekman. 2014. *The Elder Justice Roadmap: An Initiative to Respond to an Emerging Health, Justice, Financial, and Social Crisis*.

Vandello, Joseph A. and Dov Cohen. 2003. "Male Honor and Female Fidelity: Implicit Cultural Scripts That Perpetuate Domestic Violence." *Journal of Personality and Social Psychology*. 84: 997-1010.

Violence Policy Center. September 15, 2015. "More than 1,600 Women Murdered by Men in One Year, New Study Finds." Press release.

Walker, Lenore. 1979. *The Battered Woman*. New York: Harper & Row.

____________. 2016, 1984. *The Battered Woman Syndrome*. Fourth edition. New York: Springer.

____________. July 8, 2009. *Psychiatric Times*. 26(7). Online.

____________. 2006. "Battered Woman Syndrome: Empirical Findings. *Annals of the New York Academy of Science*. 1087: 142-157.

____________. 1977-1978. "Battered Women and Learned Helplessness." *Victimology*. 2(3/4): 525-534.

____________. April 1989. "Psychology and Violence Against Women." *American Psychologist*. 44: 695-702.

____________. Spring 1977. "Who Are the Battered Women?" *Frontiers: A Journal of Women Studies*. 2(1): 52-57.

Wallace, Ron. 2015. "Domestic Violence and Intimate Partner Violence: What's the Difference?" Posted at https://inpu blicsafety.com/2015/10/domestic-violence-and-intimate-partner-violence-whats-the-difference/

Yager, Jan. *Victims*. 2021. Originally published by Scribner's in 1978 under the name J.L. Barkas. Published with a new introduction and updated bibliography and resource section. Stamford, CT: Hannacroix Creek.

Zimring, Franklin E. January 1972. "The Medium Is the Message: Firearm Caliber as a Determinant of Death from Assault." *The Journal of Legal Studies*. 1(1): 72-123.

Videos, Films, and Documentaries

The Burning Bed. 1984. Staring Farrah Fawcett. Based on the novel by Faith McNulty, *The Burning Bed*. Written by Rose Leiman Goldemberg. Directed by Robert Greenwald.

FBI. "Former FBI Director William Webster Helps Foil Scam." 3:38 minutes. Posted at https://www.fbi.gov/video-repository/webster-scam-final-021919.mp4/view

Harris, Nadine Burke, M.D. Feb 17, 2015. "How Childhood Trauma Affects Health Across a Lifetime." TED Talk 16 minutes. Posted at https://www.youtube.com/watch?v=95ovIJ3dsNk

Midsommar. 2019. Written and Directed by Ari Aster. Starring Florence Pugh, Jack Reynor, and Vilhelm Blomgren.

Lazarus, Margaret and Renner Wunderlich. 1994. *Defending Our Lives*. Documentary. 42 minutes. An Academy Award® winning video about women who killed their abusers and went to prison because of it.

Lifetime Television in partnership with The National Center for Victims of Crime. January 2, 2008. "Stalking: Real Crime, Real Fear." 17:02 minutes February 2015 This is the story of how the stalking of Peggy Klinke by a former partner ended with her murder. Posted at https://www.youtube.com/watch?v=K3bTc22pq-o

Schott, Tracy. 2014. *Finding Jenn's Voice*. Documentary. (voices4change.net) Edited by R. Bradley Bass.

Survivors of intimate partner homicide attempts share their stories in *Finding Jenn's Voice*.

Steiner, Leslie Morgan. January 25, 2013. "Why domestic violence victims don't leave." TED talk. 15:59 Posted at Why domestic violence victims don't leave | Leslie Morgan Steiner – YouTube Posted at https://www.youtube.com/watch?v=V1yW5IsnSjo.

CHAPTER **FOURTEEN**

Victims of the Criminal Justice System

Prisoners Who Are Victims, Families of the Incarcerated, and the Falsely Accused

Learning Objectives

After you finish reading this chapter, you should be able to:

1. Identify instances of maltreatment of the accused and the incarcerated and what needs to be done to stop such situations.
2. Be aware of the frequency of suicide in American jails and prisons.
3. Define police brutality and excessive force by law enforcement, how prevalent it is, and what can be done about it.
4. Consider how incarceration impacts on the the family of the incarcerated, especially the children.
5. Take into account examples of false accusations and the psychological and financial toll that takes on the accused.

OVERVIEW

The issues addressed in this chapter might seem outside the scope of a textbook on victimology since we are looking at those who have been convicted of a crime. But the examples and concerns in this chapter are regarding what could be called miscarriages of justice as well as abuses of power. Throughout this textbook, we have discussed the concept of primary and secondary victims. In the case of those who are incarcerated for crimes they did commit, so they are not wrongly accused, we need to consider the secondary victims of incarceration, namely, the family of those in jail or prison especially the children as well as the wives and the parents and siblings. With a prison population that is one of the largest in the world, and definitely a leader compared to other Westernized countries—1,435,500 in state and federal prisons according to the Vera Institute although the Prison Policy Initiative puts the figure much higher, at 2.3 million—as well as 3.6 million on probation, in lieu of jail or prison, but under supervision, as well as another 870,000 on parole, whereby the rest of a sentence is served outside of prison but also under supervision. That brings the total to almost 7 million Americans under the supervision of the criminal justice system or as the Prison Police Initiative puts it "1 out of 5 incarcerated people in the world is incarcerated in the U.S." (Kang-Brown et. al., 2019; Sawyer and Wagner, 2020) Consider the number of spouses, children, parents, and siblings, as well as close friends, who have a loved one in jail or prison and you can see how huge a challenge it is that those secondary victims of incarceration are helped through a very trying time in their lives.

Sing Sing Correctional Facility, maximum-security state prison based in Ossining, New York, view from Rockland Lake State Park.

Police brutality and excessive force has always been a concern but it became the major focus, besides COVID-19, during 2020 following the death of George Floyd. His death at the hands of a police officer, whose actions were videotaped by a bystander, and shared online throughout the United States and internationally, sparked protests, riots, and demands for defunding the police and reform in police training. (Burch, et. al., 2021) As the death of this author's distant cousin by the NYPD back in 1999 indicates, excessive force accusations and tragedies are not new. (Newman, 1999) What is new, however, is the even more concerted effort nationally as well as locally to make sweeping changes. See the suggestions below under *police brutality and excessive force* that research has suggested *can* make a positive difference in reducing police brutality (including two ineffective strategies). (Woodward and Mark, 2020)

INCARCERATED INMATES WHO ARE VICTIMS

In this section, through several real-life examples, it is clear that every arrest, every incarceration in a jail or prison, whether for a few hours, days, weeks, months, or decades, has to be specifically considered. Just as behind each victim of crime is an individual, a daughter, a son, a parent, a sibling, a spouse, a friend, and not just a statistic representing a murder victim, someone who was raped, or someone who was robbed. The same is true for those who are incarcerated. They are not just faceless criminals, inmates, convicts, or numbers assigned to them by the state or federal government. They are boys or girls, if they are still juveniles, and men and women, if they are 18 and up, who need to be seen and treated as the individuals that they are.

The Prison Policy Institutive and others make a point that 600,000 who are incarcerated are released each year (which obviously includes those incarcerated for very short times) which means that avoiding being arrested again and especially getting sent back to jail or prison, is a very reason issue. (Sawyer and Wagner, 2020) In this section, however, you will read about those whose incarceration had fatal consequences. Each situation, and the circumstances behind their deaths related to their brush with the criminal justice system, is unique, just as they were all a diverse group. What they all share, however, is that they met untimely deaths disproportionate to the crimes they were accused of or convicted of.

Kalief Browder, arrested at 16 for allegedly stealing a backpack

Probably one of the most famous examples of a victim of the criminal justice system that comes to mind is the case of Kalief Browder. We might not even know about his case if not for the *New Yorker* magazine profile by Jennifer Gonnerman that brought his extreme situation to light. If you are not already familiar with this story, it definitely bears repeating. He was a 16-year-old African American teen, the youngest of seven siblings, who was accused of stealing a backpack, arrested, and locked up in Riker's Island, the infamous New York City jail where thousands are incarcerated while they await a plea deal or a trial, serve out their sentence for a misdemeanor conviction, or are placed awaiting relocation to a state prison after being found guilty of a felony. (Gonnerman, 2014)

What was so shocking about Kalief Browder's situation, once it became known, was that he had been incarcerated for three years awaiting trial after his mother was unable to post his $3,000 bail. Most astonishing of all was that in addition to trying to commit suicide, he spent more than 400 days in solitary confinement. (Eyder Peralta, NPR; Gonnerman, 2014)

In 2013, Kalief's case was dismissed and he was finally released from jail. As Gonnerman wrote in her New Yorker article, "Being around so many people felt strange. Except for a few weeks, he had been in solitary confinement for the previous seventeen months." (Gonnerman, 2014)

Sadly, and tragically, two years later, Kalief committed suicide. He was just 22 years old and, at the time of his suicide, was a student at a community college.

Eyder Peralta's article about Browder's ordeal, published after his unfortunate suicide was announced, quotes Kalief's comments from the *New Yorker* article by Jennifer Gonnerman on how Riker's had damaged him: "'People tell me because I have this case against the city I'm all right . . . But I'm not all right. I'm messed up. I know that I might see some money from

Sandra Bland was a 28-year-old woman who was arrested on July 10, 2015 after being stopped for a minor traffic violation escalated into being charged with assaulting a police officer. She was found dead from suicide three days later in her jail cell.

Soon after Pedro Ruiz, who had been arrested for an alleged shooting, was moved to a new cell, his cellmate allegedly killed him.

this case, but that's not going to help me mentally. I'm mentally scared right now. That's how I feel. Because there are certain things that changed about me and they might not go back."

Was Kalief Browder's suicide after his release preventable? Are there any other situations like Kalief Browder's happening in jails today that have not yet been detected that might have similar immediate or long-term dramatic consequences?

Sandra Bland, the motor vehicle violation and stop that went all wrong

Two other jail-related suicides or homicides come to mind. The first is another famous case: Sandra Bland. She was arrested in July 2015 after she got into an altercation with the arresting officer following her being stopped for a traffic violation. Three days after being imprisoned, while awaiting a solution to her case, she was found hanging in her cell, an apparent suicide. (Montgomery, 2019) Sandra Bland's case received extensive attention in the media including an update in 2019 when *CBS Morning News* showed the very brief footage from Bland's own cell phone taken during the arrest. Neither the $2 million settlement to her family, nor the fact that the arresting officer is no longer working in law enforcement, according to the *CBS This Morning* report, can undo Bland's untimely death following what should have been a routine traffic violation stop.

Pedro Ruiz, allegedly killed in jail by his cellmate

Finally, there is the case of 19-year-old Pedro Ruiz. You probably have not heard about the death of Pedro Ruiz but his death in custody created a lot of attention in Chicago, Illinois, where it occurred. Pedro had been arrested on January 29th 2019 for allegedly being the shooter in an incident that left a man with several gunshot wound injuries. On February 1st, Ruiz was placed in a cell with a 24-year-old who allegedly beat Ruiz to death with a sock filled with bars of soap just half an hour after he had been placed in that cell. In addition to being members of rival gangs, the alleged murderer had been on video attacking another inmate in a brutal beating a few months previously. According to the article by Elvia Malagon, Ruiz's mother shares that "her son worked construction jobs, liked sports, and as a child participated in *Ballet Folklorico*, traditional dances from Mexico. At his funeral, the family heard from an elderly man who said Ruiz had frequently helped him get to and from a store to pick up groceries." (Malagon, 2020) In February 2020, Ruiz' family sued the alleged killer, Cook County, and the Sheriff for **wrongful death** (causing death due to negligence or other actions; bereaved families can sue). (CBS Chicago; Malagon, 2020)

***

Although it happened many decades ago, let us still remember the inmates and staff who were killed during the Attica prison riots of 1971. Herman Badillo, who was a Borough President of the Bronx, and a United States Representative, co-authored a book with Milton Haynes, an Associated Press (AP) reporter, about those riots entitled, *A Bill of No Rights: Attica and the American Prison System.* They tracked down the reason for the incarceration of the 30+ inmates who died in those deadly riots. Just a few were incarcerated for murder. Most were in Attica for lesser offenses including at least one for burglary which probably carried a sentence back then of 5-10 years at the most. For all of those inmates, however, getting caught up in those riots proved to be deadly. (Badillo and Haynes, 1972)

Facts about Suicide and Homicide in Local Jails, State, and Federal Prisons

This section shares statistics about local jails as well as state and federal prisons related to two key issues: suicide and homicide. That does not diminish the issue of aggravated assault in jails or prisons, theft between inmates or even by authority figures, rape and sexual assault, hate crimes related to race or ethnicity, religion, sexual orientation, and even what gang an inmate might belong to. Even extortion happens in jails and prisons. For example,; the mother of a 21-year-old incarcerated for dealing drugs shared with this author that she sent money to her son who passed it on to the inmate who threatened to assault or even kill her son if she did not comply. When her family could no longer pay, she went to the superintendent of the prison, agreeing to tell him what was going on only if her son was immediately transferred to another facility, because they both feared retaliation if he remained in that prison; the transfer was done.

However, we are focusing on the most severe situations that happen in jail or prison, suicide and homicide, because those are outcomes related to incarceration that are lethal and cannot be reversed. Unless an inmate has legally been convicted of a capital crime with a death sentence that has been deemed constitutional in the state where the case was tried, or, if it was a federal crime, an acceptable federal sentence, no jail, state, or federal inmate should be killed in prison or die by their own hand.

Suicide is of course an unfortunate act to the families and friends who have killed themselves, but it is much harder to make statements about the reasons behind those deaths in jail or prisons compared to homicides. Is an inmate's suicide related to the incarceration experience or pre-existing emotional problems? Although the researchers in their summary do not indicate whether this fact is referring to suicides and homicides, but here is a sobering fact about local jail mortalities: "About 40 percent of inmate deaths in 2016 occurred within the first 7 days of admission to jail." That is clearly a statistic that will hopefully lead to better outreach and preventive efforts on the part of the local jails and their staffs. (Carson and Cowhig, 2020)

Here are additional highlights from two Bureau of Justice Statistics department reports on mortality in *local jails* from 2000-2016 (Carson and Cowhig, 2020) and from 2000 to 2013 (Noonan, Rohloff, and Ginder, 2015)

Every year from 2000 to 2013, suicide was the leading cause of death of inmates in local jails. (Carson and Cowhig, 2020; Noonan, Rohloff, and Ginder, 2015. (Note: If a statistic is not attributed to the Noonan, Rohloff, and Ginder report, it is from the Carson and Cowhig report.)

- Suicide accounted for nearly a third of jail deaths in 2016 (31%) followed by heart disease (28%).
- In 2016, whites had a mortality rate in jails that was more than double that of Black inmates (240 deaths per 100,000 white inmates versus 118 deaths per 100,000 Black inmates).
- In 2016, white jail inmates had a mortality rate almost triple the rate for Hispanic inmates (240 deaths per 100,000 white inmates versus 87 deaths per 100,000 Hispanic inmates).
- The number of suicides in local jails for 2001-2013 was 4,134. (Noonan, Rohloff, and Ginder, 2015: 20)
- The number of homicides in local jails for 2001-2013 was 302. (Noonan, Rohloff, and Ginder, 2015: 20)
- In 2016, about 3 percent of jail inmates died from homicide, an increase from about 2 percent in 2000, including deaths due to injuries sustained before admission.
- Almost half of all suicides among jail inmates from 2000 to 2016 happened in general housing (47%).
- From 2000 to 2016, the mortality rate from drug or alcohol intoxication more than doubled, from 6 to 15 deaths per 100,000 inmates (Carson and Cowhig, "Mortality in Local Jails, 2000-2016," 2020: 1-2, 5.)

Here are highlights about suicide and homicide in *state and federal prisons*, 2001-2016:

- Ninety percent (90%) of the deaths among state and federal prisoners from 2001 to 2016, or a total of 59,036 occurred in state prisons (53,051) compared to only ten percent (10%) occurring in federal prisons (5,985).
- From 2001-2016, there were 3,300 suicides in state prisons, which represented 6.2 percent of all deaths, and 260 suicides in federal prisons, representing 4.3 percent of all deaths.
- From 2001-2016, there were 1,024 homicides in state prisons which represented 1.9 percent (2%) of all deaths and 160 homicides of federal prisoners, which represented 2.7 percent (3%) of all deaths.
- Eight states (Texas, California, Florida, Pennsylvania, New York, Michigan, Ohio, and Georgia) accounted for more than half of all deaths in state prisons from 2001 to 2016 with Texas and California accounting for 23 percent of all deaths.
- More than half of all deaths in state prisons in 2016 (55%) were of white prisoners although they made up less than one-third (31%) of state prisoners.
- In 2016, homicide deaths, which include deaths due to injuries that were sustained before incarceration, accounted for 2.5 percent of deaths in state prisons and 3.6 percent of deaths in federal prisons.

- In 2016, just 4 percent of those who died in state prisons were female; 96 percent were male. (Carson and Cowhig, 2020)
- In their report, Noonan, Rohloff, and Ginder point out that from 2000-2013 in state prisons here are the statistics for death by suicide (2,577) and death by homicide (762). (Noonan, Rohloff, and Ginder, 2015)

A New Killer in Jails and Prisons: COVID-19

As addressed above, suicide and homicide are life-threatening concerns for the estimated 2.3 million who are incarcerated in the United States. But the coronavirus pandemic of 2020 brought a new threat to residential institutions, including, obviously, those who are incarcerated in jails and prisons: illness and even death from the virus.

Cary Aspinwall, Keri Blakinger, and Joseph Neff, with additional reporting by Tom Meagher, tell the heartbreaking stories of women who were dying in prison because they contracted COVID-19. The very first story in their article is that of Melissa Ann Horn, 49, a Virginia woman incarcerated in a state prison in Virginia since 2016 who had been convicted of manufacturing meth and violating probation related to a previous larceny charge.

Another woman who succumbed to COVID-19 in federal prison was Andrea Circle Bear, a citizen of the Cheyenne Sioux River tribe. According to The Marshall Project article, Andrea was serving a two year sentence as part of a plea deal for "maintaining a drug-involved" home where methamphetamine was sold. A mother of five, at the time of her incarceration she was also pregnant. Within a few days, Andrea developed symptoms that turned out to be COVID-19. Her conditioned worsened so she had to be put on a ventilator. Her grandmother got a call letting her know the situation and that her new great grandchild had to be delivered by an emergency C-section. Three weeks later, Andrea died, never recovering from the deadly virus.

Andrea Circle Bear, mother of five, who died of COVID-19 while incarcerated for a plea bargained two-year sentence.

The Marshall Project, the journalism site staffed with reporters focused solely on the criminal justice system, in partnership with the Associated Press, has been tracking COVID-19 in prisons since March 2020. They have been keeping track of the numbers who have tested positive for the virus as well as the number of inmates who have died from COVID-19 and the number of prison staff who have also died from the virus. Those numbers are shared in Table 14.1, as of January 22, 2021. (*The New York Times* updated its statistics on April 16, 2021, and reported a total of 2,990 inmates and correctional officers had died from COVID-19. (*The New York Times*, 2021)

TABLE 14.1. COVID-19 Cases and Deaths in U.S. State and Federal Prisons

Total number of cases	386,765
Inmate deaths from COVID-19 in state and federal prisons	2,459
Staff deaths from COVID-19	191

Source: The Marshall Project. Data collected beginning in March 2020 in partnership with the Associated Press, as of March 2, 2021 (Green, 2021)

It is well-known that the confined spaces of jails and prisons, in housing as well as even in other areas where "social distancing" is near to impossible, has led to a higher infection and mortality rate than in the general population. This fact led to the releasing of tens of thousands of inmates in order to reduce the size of the prison populations, as noted by Peter Eisler et al. in their Reuters article on the situation. Some victim groups, such as those behind Marsy's law, which requires victims to be notified if the incarcerated offender is being released, voiced their objections to the hasty releases. (Eisler, et al., "Special Report," Reuters, 2020).

FAMILY AND FRIENDS OF THE INCARCERATED

As noted above, every one of those 2.3 million who are incarcerated in the United States has a family and friends. All of the nearly 7 million in the U.S. who are under the supervision of the criminal justice system also have family and friends who are impacted by the rules that those under supervised release need to adhere to.

Even though this is a textbook on victimology with a focus on primary, secondary, and even tertiary victims, the family and friends of the incarcerated represent another category of victims that is often overlooked but whose sense of loss and suffering is all too real. They too have to deal with a wide range of issues including the loss of contact, lost income if the incarcerated was contributing to the family's economic viability, and the stigma and emotional or psychological toll of having an incarcerated family member.

These family and friends could be seen as falling into two situational categories:

1. those whose family members are guilty of the crime that they were convicted of; or
2. those whose family members were wrongly-accused but convicted anyway.

The separation and loss that family, especially spouses, parents, and children, and friends feel, is the same for both groups, but for those in the second group there is the added sense of outrage about miscarriage of justice. Those whose family members were falsely or wrongly accused or convicted and incarcerated will be discussed in the last section of this chapter. In the section that follows, we will address the issues faced by the family and friends of the incarcerated who are guilty as charged.

Family and Friends of Those Who Are Guilty of the Crime

The unique group within the first situational category above, namely the family and friends of those who *did* commit the crimes that they were accused of and convicted for, face, among other concerns, a lengthy separation of months, years, or possibly even decades. In this section, we will look at the stories of several families that reflect the issues they face and how they cope.

For example, Manuel, (not his real name) who is now 25-years-old, was recently released from a Massachusetts state prison where he served five years for armed robbery. Manuel had held up the same convenience store several times within the one week. He pled guilty to the charges and took a plea-deal sentence of five years that some might consider a gift compared to the sentence that he might have received.

At the time he accepted his five-year plea deal, his child was born. His girlfriend gave up her parental rights to Manuel's mother, who raised his child while he was in prison. His child had minimal contact with Manuel during his incarceration. Upon release, after working at a minimum-wage restaurant job, Manuel took a job in construction. He promised to never again do anything that would get him locked up in prison and away from his child. (Based on transcript of anonymous interview shared with the author, n.d.)

The five years that Manuel spent in prison for three armed robberies contrasts greatly with the 40-year sentence imposed on Blake Smith who, at 17, committed two robberies with a BB gun. Unlike Manuel, who accepted a plea deal, Blake's court-appointed attorney waived a jury trial or plea bargain with the ADA and agreed to a **bench trial** with only a judge. Blake had done well in school, written a play, acted in commercials, and was basically a "good kid" who made two bad decisions: (1) expressing his adolescent rebellion by leaving home in New Orleans to go to Houston where (2) he attempted to commit the two robberies with a BB gun that got him arrested. According to Blake's mother, Tosha Smith Mills, Blake was going through a phase in his adolescence that motivated him to leave New Orleans and connect with family members in Texas.

Blake's mother, Tosha, does not deny that her son deserved to be punished for what he did. Blake did commit two robberies. He did break the law. But both the attorney and Blake's mother, thought that the judge would take Blake's positive prior accomplishments into consideration, his age—just 17—and maybe even give him probation. Blake's mother thought that if he were to do any jail or prison time, hopefully he could get sentenced as a juvenile, go to a juvenile facility, and be out by the time he turned 18, or even 21, or maybe even get probation with community service.

However, the judge threw the proverbial book at Blake. He was sentenced to 40 years in state prison in Texas—two consecutive sentences of 40 years for aggravated assault with a weapon—with no chance of parole until he served a full 20 years.

Now 28, Blake has served almost 11 years of his double 40 year sentences. During the coronavirus situation, the facility that he was in was on lockdown, and he was in his cell 23 hours a day with just 1 hour out of the cell.

In March 2020, the COVID-19 situation was declared a health emergency and a pandemic. Due to COVID-19, no visitors were allowed to any prisons and for months; his mother was unable to visit him—even if she could have spared the time or afforded the expense of traveling from New Orleans to Texas.

Tosha Smith Mills has written a memoir entitled, *Momma I Should Have Listened: A Voice of Pain and Power*, with contributions by her son, B.J. Smith, to shine a light on the deep anguish that family members go through when a loved one is incarcerated. This is especially true when they are incarcerated in remote state prisons or in federal prisons located in other states that can be hundreds or thousands of miles away. Besides the distance, there is the difficulty of visiting face to face and the complicated emotions that go with having a loved one in prison.

Tosha Mills writes in her memoir about what it is like to be a mother with an incarcerated son: "When I found out my son had committed a crime, it felt impossible and surreal. Surely, it was just a nightmare and I would wake up at any second. I felt like I needed to be rescued from a burning building that had collapsed on me ten times over and, after collapsing, I had to be resuscitated when I was certain I was already dead." (Mills, 2017)

She and her son have to deal with Blake's incarceration as well as continuing to see if there is a way to get his excessive sentence reevaluated and hopefully reduced.

Blake's sentence brings up that issue that needs to be addressed: excessive sentencing.

Manuel and Blake's examples highlight the separation and lost time faced by families of those who are guilty of the crime for which they were convicted, as well as a sense of the variability and unpredictability of sentencing.

Emily Widra and Prison Policy highlight in the article, "New Data: People With Incarcerated Loved Ones Have Shorter Life Expectancies and Poorer Health," that life expectancy is cut short by 2.6 years and there are also health consequences to family members. A woman whose partner is incarcerated is more likely to have ". . . excessive depression, hypertension (high blood pressure)" and "children with incarcerated parents are at increased risk for mental health problems and substance use disorders., which have long-term impacts on health." (Sundaresh, et. al., 2021; Widra, 2021; Wakefield, et. al., 2016)

As mentioned in the Preface, Kerri Rawson and her husband and their two children are trying to live as normal a life as possible. To recap for those who do not know her story, on Friday, February 25, 2005, when she was 26 years old, there was a knock on the door of her apartment in Detroit, Michigan where she was attending graduate school and working as a substitute teacher. It was the FBI. The agent was there to inform her that Kerri's father had been arrested suspected of being the BTK serial killer. He also had to collect a DNA sample.

As she shares in her memoir, *A Serial Killer's Daughter,* Kerri, who was unaware of her father's murderous crimes beginning 30 years before, explains that she sees herself as a victim. In our interviews, she also said she sees her husband, brother, and mother as victims of her father as well. As Kerri writes in her memoir:

> I'm now able to say—without shame or fear—I'm a trauma, crime, and abuse victim. I live with anxiety, depression, and PTSD.
>
> What's in my past is what it is; it can't be changed—Dad murdered ten people and devastated countless lives. Yet on the days when I'm not wrestling with hard, terrible truths, I will tell you. I love my dad—the one I mainly knew. I miss him (*Source:* Kerri Rawson, *A Serial Killer's Daughter*, copyright © 2019, reprinted with permission of Thomas Nelson. All rights reserved.).

It is hard to comprehend what Kerri Rawson lives with on a daily basis because of her father's murderous deeds. A grown woman, married, with her own family, she has made the decision not to visit her father in prison.

Children of the Incarcerated

But what about the young children of those who are incarcerated? It is definitely important to address the emotional, financial, and social needs of the children of the incarcerated.

One question that is often asked, and is actually also the title of a classic article dating back to 1978 on this important subject, is: "Should children visit their parents in prison?" (Sack and Seidler, 1978) The researchers interviewed 22 children between the ages of 5 and 15 whose fathers were incarcerated at the Oregon State Penitentiary. Each interview lasted 30 minutes and was conducted in the visitor waiting room. Sack and Seidler emphasize that they only interviewed children who had already developed a steady pattern of family visits, averaging two to four times a month. They did not interview children who had only started to visit a father in prison for the first time or those who only visited on an intermittent basis.

Their findings seemed to confirm the conclusions of a previous study about the children of prisoners, published in 1965 by Friedman and Esselstyn. That study found that "teachers rated such children [with incarcerated parents] below average in social and psychological characteristics more frequently than comparable controls." (Sack and Seidler, 1978)

Sack and Seidler found the children in their study were more isolated in peer relationships when compared to classmates without incarcerated parents. The researchers noted that six children told them that they lacked any friends at all and four children told the researchers that their friends' parents were not going to let them come over for a playdate because their 'Dad's in jail.' Out of the 22 children that they studied, only six seemed to have what the researchers considered "normal peer contacts." (Sack and Seidler, 1978)

An interesting finding in their study were the number of boys (N = 10) who were interviewed who shared that they wanted to become policemen (5) or a lawyer (1) who "'helps the bad guys get a break.'" (Sack and Seidler, 1978)

Formerly incarcerated men and women who have been guest presenters over the years in the Penology course this author has been teaching at John Jay College of Criminal Justice since August 2014 often comment on the toll incarceration took on their relationships with their children. One of their goals upon release, in addition to getting a job and staying out of trouble with the law, was to repair their connections with their children, who usually had grown up by that point. In most cases, visits to their incarcerated parent happened rarely, if at all, especially since for longer sentences, of ten years or more, the significant other or spouse often divorced the incarcerated partner making it even harder for the child or teen to get to prison for a visit.

The Osborne Association, an innovative program headquartered in the Bronx, started by prison reformer and former Sing Sing Correctional Facility warden Thomas Osborne, has a room set up for children to be able to do videoconferencing meetings with their incarcerated parent. This was put in place long before COVID-19 and related restrictions on prison visits made it impossible to visit in person. This author saw the room at the Bronx headquarters of the Osborne Association and it was brightly colored and appealing visually with comfortable seating. It was offered as an option to families who thought the trip to the prison, which might be hours away from their home, was too difficult to get to in person or the experience of going into the prison for the family visit would be more traumatic than conducting it via videoconferencing.

Addressing in part the sadness and confusion experienced by children who have a parent in prison, talk show host John Oliver included a segment with Sesame Street Muppets at the end of a *Last Week Tonight* feature on the prison system. The tone, both serious and hopeful, can be shown in classroom settings or similar situations; children with incarcerated parents may find it gives them greater strength to deal with their situation knowing that there are others whose parents may be incarcerated as well. Also, by bringing the issue into the mainstream on a major TV show, which is also posted and continually available through YouTube, makes it less of a secret or an issue fraught with shame. The clip, entitled "Prison with Sesame Street," is just 2:29 minutes long. The URL is provided in the Resources section at the end of this chapter

The isolation and stigma that Sack and Seidler highlighted in their 1978 study is still an issue today but, as noted, there have been increasing efforts to pay attention to the unique needs of the children of the millions who are incarcerated in jail, temporarily, or in prison, for longer sentences.

In most cases, prison impacts children and spouses of the incarcerated the most. But there are also parents and siblings and extended family members who have to deal with the aftermath of incarceration of a loved one—daughters, sons, mothers, cousins, aunts, uncles—and, to a lesser degree than being related to someone in prison, are the friends of the incarcerated. The prison time might be for a white-collar crime, like tax evasion, or a violent crime, like molesting a daughter's friend when she was there for a sleepover. It will of course be a different psychological burden for the family if the crime their loved one is incarcerated for is even worse, like murder.

These family members and friends are dealing with the criminal justice system usually through no fault of their own. They are often dealing with financial issues because their loved one, who might have been the main provider, is locked up or they are dealing with the emotional angst of separation. What we as a society can at least help them with is not to stigmatize them because they are related to, or a friend to, a convicted offender. They need support from family and friends as well as from the community since the whole family in a way goes to jail or prison when someone's family member or friend is incarcerated.

VICTIMS OF EXCESSIVE SENTENCING

As Tosha Mills Smith has said in our many phone interviews or guest presentations in this author's classes at John Jay College of Criminal Justice, she expected her 17-year-old son to do some prison time because of the two robberies he committed. What she has protested, and continues to object to, is his excessive sentence of two 40-year sentences, to be served consecutively, not concurrently, in a state prison in Texas. Parole cannot even be considered until he has served 20 years.

Was Blake's sentence "fair?" What is a fair sentence? Excessive sentencing is an issue that needs to be addressed at the local, state, and federal level. As you know by now, from reading *Essentials of Victimology*, or from other courses in criminal justice or the law that you have taken, in the United States we basically have 51 systems of justice, 50 separate state systems, and one federal system.

This is a topic that requires its own book! As you may know, there are two basic types of sentencing: indeterminate and determinate. **Indeterminate sentencing** means that there is a range of time that can be applied to a conviction, with a minimum amount that must be served before parole could be considered. **Determinate sentencing** means a fixed time. **Mandatory sentencing** may also be the term that is used. Neither system is ideal since having consistency in sentencing is one of the greatest challenges that the criminal justice system faces. What factors should be considered? Someone's previous criminal record? A victim impact statement? If there are dependent children at home that need one or more parents to be present during their formative years? If there is an admission of guilt? If there is an apology or signs of remorse?

Since excessive sentencing is outside the scope of this victimology textbook, it is still an issue where too many offenders are victimized by the system. (Gardner, 1980). There are organizations that are trying to address this very real imbalance in the American criminal justice system including the National Association of Criminal Defense Lawyers (NACDL) and the NACDL Foundation for Criminal Justice; Equal Justice Initiative (EJI), based in Montgomery, Alabama, and founded by Bryan Stevenson, whose first case was dramatized in the hit movie, *Just Mercy*, based on the book of the same name; Mothers Against Mandatory Minimums (MAMM); and The Sentencing Project, to name a few.

VICTIMS OF FALSE ARREST AND IMPRISONMENT (EXONEREES)

Added to the financial and emotional toll that arrest, conviction, and incarceration has on the offender and his or her family and friends is the stress of knowing that the arrest, conviction, and incarceration were based on false testimony or questionable evidence. The movie *Just Mercy*, starring Jamie Foxx, Michael B. Jordan, and Brie Larson, is the true story of criminal justice activist Bryan Stevenson, an African American Harvard-educated lawyer who takes on the case of Walter McMillian, who was wrongfully-convicted for the murder of an 18-year-old woman and put on death row. Stevenson eventually succeeded in getting McMillian's conviction thrown out after six years on death row. Stevenson, as mentioned above, heads EJI and is also a Professor of Law at New York University Law School. (Stevenson, 2019)

In his book, *Let the Lord Sort Them: The Rise and Fall of the Death Penalty*, Maurice Chammah shares the story of Eddie Ellis, who was convicted of the 1983 murder of Bertie Elizabeth Eakens, an elderly resident of an apartment complex. Ellis had been fired as a maintenance worker at the apartment complex where Eakens lived. As Chammah explains, evidence that pointed to Ellis included his fingerprints on Bertie's door and that "he'd been seen driving a car that resembled her yellow Cadillac." (Chammah, 2021: 79)

A few hours before Ellis' scheduled execution in Texas, new evidence was revealed by the widow of a man who had died a year before, an acquaintance of Elllis'. After some effort, his widow and legal advocate Danalynn Recer found her husband's handwritten note confessing to Bertie's murder. Unfortunately, the legitimacy of the note was called into question, a stay of execution was denied, and 38-year-old Edward Ellis was executed. (Chammah, 2021: 81)

Since its founding in 1992, The Innocence Project has exonerated 367 prisoners. Here are just three of those cases:

- Herman Atkins served 12 years before being exonerated by DNA evidence for the rape and robbery crimes he had been convicted of.
- Jimmy Ray Bromgard served 15 years before he was exonerated by DNA evidence for the rape of an eight-year-old girl. The Innocence Project lists these contributing causes to his wrongful conviction: "eyewitness misidentification, inadequate defense, and unvalidated or improper forensic science."

- Stephan Cowans spent six years in prison for a home invasion and six other charges, including armed assault with intent to murder. He was exonerated by DNA. Contributing causes of his conviction included "eyewitness misidentification, government misconduct, unvalidated or improper forensic science." (Source: The Innocence Project website)

If you go to the website for The Innocence Project, an organization that helps to overturn the wrongful convictions of those who are incarcerated based on DNA evidence, you will find story after story that is both heart wrenching and hopeful of the wrongfully convicted who are now not just out of prison but exonerated. Just one of those many stories and real-life examples is that of Marvin Anderson who, at the age of 18, was wrongfully convicted of rape, forcible sodomy, abduction, and robbery. He served 15 years and was on parole for 5 years. Even though he was already out of prison, he wanted to have his case taken up by The Innocence Project so he could get exonerated. On August 21, 2002, that triumphant event occurred, starting a new page in Anderson's life, which had been completely derailed for two decades beginning with his sentencing to 20 years when he was wrongfully convicted on December 14, 1982. In addition to his regular job, Anderson is now the fire chief for a volunteer fire company in Virginia. (The Innocence Project website n.d.)

VICTIMS OF FALSE ALLEGATIONS

Granting immunity or a reduced sentence to those who implicate others has unfortunately led to untold numbers of falsely-accused teens and men and women getting charged and possibly even found guilty and incarcerated.

Previously in Chapter 10, "Child Victims: Abuse, Neglect, and Other Victimizations," the **SAID Syndrome** (Sexual Allegations In Divorce) was discussed whereby to gain the upper hand in divorce proceedings, a parent will coerce their child into making false allegations against the other parent for financial gain or to tip the scales in their favor regarding custody determinations.

When there are co-defendants in robbery, rape, or murder cases, the defendant accepting partial or full immunity, or a reduced sentence, to testify against the other co-defendant or defendants may eventually not turn out to be the most guilty party. By the time the situation is sorted out, months, years, or even decades can go, as in the case of an African American man in his mid-40s was released after serving 22 years of a 23 years-to-life sentence largely based on the testimony of someone given a reduced sentence whom other eye witnesses claimed was the actual killer.

Adam Bolotin, a Chicago-based criminal defense attorney, shared this case that he defended that was an example of someone being falsely accused. It took almost two years for his client's case to work its way through the justice system before a trial occurred. The criminal charges against his client stemmed from his daughter's ugly divorce. Soon after Bolotin's client's daughter separated from her husband, the client's 12-year-old granddaughter, who was not getting along with her mother, wanted to go live with her father, but the mother refused. To make her case that she needed to leave the maternal home, the granddaughter claimed that her grandfather, who was 70 years old, had been molesting her. Bolotin's client was found innocent. Perjury charges were not pursued against his granddaughter. A man's reputation was tarnished and more than a year of his life put on hold as the case worked its way through the court system, not to mention the private legal fees that had to be met. But in that particular case, his client was found not guilty so he did not have to serve an extended prison sentence or get registered as a sex offender.

When they announced the verdict, Bolotin's client stood up, and profusely thanked the jury with "tears streaming down his face."

Bolotin points out that in this case of false accusation, there are no winners. Even though his client was acquitted, "half of that family is not going to formally accept that our client didn't do what she said." (Bolotin, 2021)

Legal fees and defending one's reputation are consequences of false accusations. **False accusations**, as noted above, are usually made by those with a vested interest in falsely accusing someone—shifting the blame or guilt for a crime from themselves to someone else, who is actually innocent. Or, there could be other motives such as money, revenge, or, in the case of SAID Syndrome false accusations, custody issues. The accusation is made by a person. But, in a new twist, the *New York Times* reported in its June 24, 2020 story by Kashmir Hill, "Wrongfully Accused by an Algorithm," that a suspect had been falsely accused based on a mistaken match in what Hill wrote "may be the first known account of an American being wrongfully arrested based on a flawed match from a facial recognition algorithm . . ."

Hill goes on to note that manufacturers of this crime-fighting technology defend it by stressing that it is intended as an aid in apprehension, not to be the only basis for it. As Hill writes, "This is what technology providers and law enforcement always emphasize when defending facial recognition: It is only supposed to be a clue in the case, not a smoking gun. Before arresting Mr. Williams, investigators might have sought other evidence that he committed the theft, such as eyewitness testimony, location data from his phone or proof that he owned the clothing that the suspect was wearing."

POLICE BRUTALITY AND EXCESSIVE FORCE

Once again, this is a topic that deserves its own chapter or even its own textbook in courses in police science or criminology. But it is too timely and pivotal a topic to be left out of this victimology textbook. As mentioned before, this author personally knew that tragedies occur related to excessive force when, in August 1999, her mother's first cousin, Doris Busch Boskey, discovered on the evening news that night that her youngest son had been shot to death by the NYPD. It turned out to be a case of misunderstanding; the "hammer" that 29-year-old Gidone Busch, a medical school drop out with depression issues related to the diagnosis of a kidney problem in 1991, was allegedly holding was actually a religious object that he used for praying. According to Andy Newman's article in *The New York Times* about Gidone's death, he "was fired upon at least 12 times. . ." (Newman, 1999)

As mentioned in the introduction to this chapter, George Floyd's tragic death related to former Minneapolis police officer Derek Chauvin's kneeling on Mr. Flloyd for nearly 9 minutes, ignited a fire storm of outrage over police brutality and the use of excessive force in making arrests. (Burch, Harmon, Taverine, and Badger, 2021) Floyd's alleged crime was trying to buy a carton of cigarettes with a counterfeit $20 bill. (Eligon, Dewen, Arango, and Bogel-Burroughs, 2021)

Woodward and Mark report in businessinsider.com on research that includes six techniques that are proven to reduce or eliminate police brutality, and two that are ineffective. Here are those suggestions:

> 1. "Eliminate language in police union contracts that limits officer accountability"
> 2. "Track complaints about officers' use of force"
> 3. "Scale up non-police organizations to respond to emergency calls"
> 4. "Encourage federal oversight for police."
> 5. "Demilitarization is essential." (A Pentagon program known as 1033 enables police and sheriff departments to receive surplus military equipment, which the research/researchers/authors suggest exacerbates the excessive force issue.)
> 6. "More restrictive laws governing use of force"
>
> Interestingly, the two ways that Woodward and Mark indicate from the research do not work are: implicit bias trainings and body cameras. (Woodward and Mark, 2020)

***

In this one chapter it is impossible to explore the myriad of issues that should be considered when reviewing the treatment of the nearly 7 million boys and girls, men and women, plus their families, who are either under the supervision of the criminal justice system or impacted by it. This chapter touched upon some key issues but there are others to be considered; some were addressed, even briefly, in previous chapters, such as the fact that eight states ban those previously convicted of any crimes from applying for crime compensation benefits for being a victim of a crime totally unrelated to their prior offense. In other countries, such as Norway, just the fact that someone's liberty is taken away and he or she is incarcerated is the punishment. Prisons are more like upscale college dormitory rooms. The prison in Frankfurt, Germany that this author visited and toured in October 2015 was also a model for its design and appealing individual rooms. A stark comparison to so many of the American prisons, such as one of the maximum security state prisons that incarcerates more than 1,000 male offenders. It was originally built in the early 1800s although that part of the prison was closed down. The newer parts that are in operation today date from the early to mid-1900s although several of the main facilities do not have air conditioning.

This chapter is going to end by suggesting that you consider finding and watching the TED Talk by Ashley Rubin, Ph.D. entitled, "A Brief History of Prisons." She starts her TED Talk by recalling the impact that a child's murder had on her when she was just eight. It was her impetus to begin her lifelong concern about prisons, victims, and offenders. Dr. Rubin concludes the talk by questioning why prisons, a relatively new way of handling criminals, dating back just to the 1800s, is still needed and if it is to persist as a solution for dealing with criminals, who should be incarcerated in prisons and for how long?

SUMMARY

Although it might seem unusual to have a chapter devoted to those who have been convicted of violent or property crimes against victims in a textbook on victimology, it is important to remember that offenders can be victims too, especially if their sentence is excessive for the crime that they committed, or if they are put in solitary confinement for any amount of time or especially for a long time period. The kinds of tragedies like the death of a newly-incarcerated inmate at the hands of his cellmate from a rival gang are situations that should never be allowed to happen.

Those who are falsely accused, like the grandfather mentioned above, are also victims, losing time and being burdened with court costs as well as a tarnished reputation.

The families of those who are incarcerated are victims of their loved one's actions. They have to deal with the loss of income while their family member is incarcerated, the cost of traveling to and from jail or prison for visits, when in-person visits are permissible, and the time away from children, especially during their formative years. There is the stigma of having a spouse, parent or sibling in prison that takes a toll on the peer relations of the children studied by Sacks and Seidler.

This chapter also addressed the offenders who are the ultimate victims of the criminal justice system—those who are killed while incarcerated as well as those who commit suicide in jail or prison. Practically everyone knows the name of Sandra Bland, whose arrest after a traffic violation escalated into a confrontation with the police officer, with her suicide in jail just a few days later. But there were more than 3,500 men and women who committed suicide in a ten year period in the United States in local jails whose names are only known to the family and friends they left behind.

KEY TERMS

determinate sentencing
false accusation
indeterminate sentencing
mandatory sentencing
SAID Syndrome
wrongful death

REVIEW QUESTIONS

1. How many Americans are currently incarcerated in state and federal prisons?
2. What issue did Sandra Bland's case shed a light on in America's jails?
3. What happened to Pedro Ruiz in Cook County jail and how often does it happen in jails and prisons in the United States?
4. Who also suffers when someone is incarcerated?
5. What was the key finding of the research into children who visit their parents in prison that was conducted by Sack and Seidler?
6. What inmate population has The Innocence Project been focusing on and what is the main way they get wrong convictions overturned?
7. What are at least two ways that researchers suggest police brutality and excessive force can be reduced?

CRITICAL THINKING QUESTIONS

1. Do an internet search on the prisons of Norway. You will probably find out about a prison known as Bastoy Prison. Watch videos about this prison and read articles about it. How is that prison different from the typical American prison? Would a prison like that work in the United States? Why? Why not?

2. Consider jail and prison suicides. Who should be held responsible or is it an individual act by the offender that would have happened regardless of their incarceration?
3. Is there a way to achieve fair and consistent sentencing for violent and nonviolent crimes in each state and in the federal sector? What are some of the ways you might be able to achieve that?

ACTIVITIES

1. Create an ideal prison that helps those who have been convicted of crimes they did commit to gain self-awareness and even education or job skills so they will become productive members of society upon their release. What kinds of services will you offer in your prison? Will it even be a prison or an alternative to traditional prisons?
2. Do an internet search on one particular crime. See what you can find about various true-life cases in several states and even internationally. What are the range of sentences and the factors that might account for those disparities? How might you change current practices so that there is more consistency in sentencing?
3. Divide into pairs or groups of four and brainstorm how to help children and teens who have incarcerated parents. Be as creative and innovative in your suggestions as possible. Consider some of the activities that have been implemented by others, such as how children whose parents died in 9-11 have been helped, that could be adapted to the children of the incarcerated. Would you include discussion groups about the possible shame or stigma that children of the incarcerated might be feeling Why? Why not?

RESOURCES

Equal Justice Initiative
eji.org
Set up by Bryan Stevenson to help those falsely accused especially those on Death Row. Also concerned with the issue of excessive versus fair sentencing.

Families Against Mandatory Minimums (FAMM)
ramm.org
Grass roots organization trying to reverse the harsh so-called Rockefeller mandatory drug laws that landed men and women in prison for excessively long sentences for drug offenses.

The Innocence Project
innocenceproject.org/
Founded in 1992, the Innocence Project, through DNA evidence, has helped to get hundreds of inmates freed and even exonerated for wrongful convictions.

The Marshall Project
themarshallproject.org
Research and reporting project dedicated to writing original articles, and organizing into one place, information about the criminal justice system. Anyone studying victimology or planning to work in the criminal justice system should consider subscribing to their free daily newsletter. In addition to original related articles, this is a portal of links to articles from major news and publication outlets so accessing the information in one place is easier.

Stand Together
standtogether.org
Founded in 2003 by business leader Charles Koch to bring together businesses and organizations to tackle big issues like poverty and improving the criminal justice system.

The Sentencing Project
sentencingproject.org
For more than 30 years, this project has been working to end mass incarceration and to seek alternatives to prison.

CITED WORKS AND ADDITIONAL REFERENCES

Amani, Saloumeh. "The Disappearance of Fariba Amani." Posted at the International Crime Victims Association website.

Aspinwall, Cary, Keri Blakinger, Joseph Neff, and Tom Meagher. May 14, 2020. "What Women Dying in Prison from COVID-19 Tell Us About Female Incarceration." The Marshall Project. Posted at https://www.themarshallproject.org/2020/05/14/what-women-dying-in-prison-from-covid-19-tell-us-about-female-incarceration

Aspinwall, Cary, Keri Blakinger, and Joseph Neff. May 14, 2020. "Why Women Dying in Prisons Are Among the Less Visible Victims of Covid-19." *The Guardian.* Posted at https://www.theguardian.com/us-news/2020/may/14/women-prisons-coronavirus-victims

Associated Press. July 13, 2021. "Inmate Killed in Assault at fountain Prison." *U.S. News & World Report.* Posed at usnews.com.

Badillo, Herman and Milton Haynes. 1972. *A Bill of No Rights: Attica and the American Prison System.* New York: Outerbridge and Lazard, distributed by Dutton.

Bogel-Burroughs, Nicholas and Vanessa Swales. April 29, 2020, updated June 16, 2020. "Prisoner with Coronavirus Dies After Giving Birth While on Ventilator." *New York Times.*

Bolotin, Adam. January 8, 2021. Phone interview with author.

Borysenko, Karlyn. February 12, 2020. "The Dark Side of #MeToo: What Happens When Men Are Falsely Accused." Forbes.com. Posted at Forbes.com. https://www.forbes.com/sites/karlynborysenko/2020/02/12/the-dark-side-of-metoo-what-happens-when-men-are-falsely-accused/#62ba7171864d

Brodsky, Doris Busch. December 1, 2000. Phone interview with author.

Burch, Audra D.S., Amy Harmon, Sabrina Tavernise, and Emily Badger. Updated June 4, 2021. "The Death of George Floyd Reignited a Movement. What Happens Now?" *The New York Times.* Posted at nytimes.com

Carson, E. Ann and Mary P. Cowhig. February 2020. "Mortality in Local Jails, 2000-2016-Statistical Tables." U.S. Department of Justice, Office of Justice Programs, Bureau of Justice Statistics. Posted at https://www.bjs.gov/content/pub/pdf/mlj0016st.pdf

________________. February 2020. "Mortality in State and Federal Prisons, 2001-2016 – Statistical Tables." U.S. Department of Justice, Office of Justice Programs, Bureau of Justice Statistics. Posted at https://www.bjs.gov/content/pub/pdf/msfp0116st.pdf

CBS Chicago. February 11, 2020. "Family of Pedro Ruiz, Killed in Cell at Cook County Jail, Sues Sheriff and Cellmate Christian Gonzalez." CBS Chicago. Posted at https://chicago.cbslocal.com/2020/02/11/cook-county-jail-death-lawsuit-murder-pedro-ruiz-christian-gonzalez/#:~:text=linkedin-,Family%20Of%20Pedro%20Ruiz%2C%20Killed%20In%20Cell%20At%20Cook%20County,Sheriff%20And%20Cellmate%20Christian%20Gonzalez.

Chammah, Maurice. *Let the Lord Sort Them: The Rise and Fall of the Death Penalty.* New York: Crown, 2021.

Chandler, Kim. July 13, 2021. "Inmate Killed in Assault at Fountain Prison." Associated Press, posed at apnews.com

Dershowitz, Alan. 2019. *Guilt By Accusation: The Challenge of Proving Innocence in the Age of #metoo.* New York: Hot Books, an imprint of Skyhorse.

Doerner, William G. and Steven P. Lab. 2017. *Victimology.* Eighth edition. New York: Routledge.

Eisler, Peter, Linda So, Ned Parker, and Brad Heath. May 18, 2020. "Special Report: 'Death Sentence'—The Hidden Coronavirus Toll in U.S. Jails and Prisons." Reuters. Posted at https://www.reuters.com/article/us-health-coronavirus-usa-jails-specailr/special-report-death-sentence-the-hidden-coronavirus-toll-in-us-jails-and-prisons-idUSKBN22U1V2

Eligon, John, Shaila Dwan, Tim Arango, and Nicholas Bogel-Burroughs. Updated April 7, 2021. "Clerk Who questioned $20 Bill Watched Floyd Arrest With 'Disbelief and Guilt.'" *The New York Times.* Posted at nytimes.com

Fagan, Abigail A. and Paul Mazerolle. 2011. "Repeat Offending and Repeat Victimization: Assessing Similarities and Differences in Psychosocial Risk Factors." *Crime & Delinquency.* 57: 732-755.

Gardner, M.R. 1980. "Determinate Sentencing Movement and the Eighth Amendment: Excessive Punishment Before and After *Rummel v. Estelle.*" *The Duke Law Journal.* 6: 1103-1140.

Gonnerman, Jennifer. September 29, 2014. "Before the Law." *New Yorker.* Posted at newyorker.com. (Published in the print publication on October 6, 2014)

_____________. June 7, 2015. "Kalief Browder, 1993-2015." *New Yorker.* Posted at https://www.newyorker.com/news/news-desk/kalief-browder-1993-2015

Green. Emily. March 10, 2021. "Why the Marshall Project Is Tracking COVID-19 in America's Prisons." Posted at streetroots.org

Hill, Kashmir. June 24, 2020; updated June 25, 2020. "Wrongly Accused by an Algorithm." *New York Times.* Posted at https://www.nytimes.com/2020/06/24/technology/facial-recognition-arrest.html

Hudson, H.R. D. Anglin, J. Yarborough, K. Hardaway, M. Russell, J. Strote, M. Canter, and B. Blum. December 1998. "Suicide by Cop." *Annals of Emergency Medicine.* Posted at https://pubmed.ncbi.nlm.nih.gov/9832661/

The Innocence Project. n.d. "Marvin Anderson" Posted at https://innocenceproject.org/cases/marvin-anderson/

James, Erwin. February 25, 2013. "The Norwegian Prison Where Inmates Are Treated Like People." Posted online and published at theguardian.com (UK)

Kang-Brown, Jacob, Chase Montagnet, Eital Schattner-Elmaleh, and Oliver Hinds. 2020. "People in Prison in 2019." Published by the Vera Institute of Justice, Brooklyn, New York.

Malagon, Elvia. February 12, 2020. "Family of Chicago Man Beaten to Death in Cook County Jail Cell Files Lawsuit: 'Nothing Is Going to Take Away This Pain.'" *Chicago Tribune.* Posted at chicagotribune .com

The Marshall Project. January 22, 2021. "A State-by-State Look at Coronavirus in Prisons." Posted at themarshallproject.org

Mills, Tosha Smith with contributions by B.J. Smith. 2017. *Momma I Should Have Listened.* Independent Publishing.

_____________. October 22, 2020 and July 11, 2021. Personal communication with author.

Montgomery, David. May 8, 2019. "The Death of Sandra Bland: Is There Anything Left to Investigate?" *New York Times.* Posted at https://www.nytimes.com/2019/05/08/us/sandra-bland-texas-death.html

Motkin, Holly. December 24, 2020."President Trump Pardons Former Cop Who Spent 10 Years in Prison After Her K9 Bit Suspect." *The Police Tribune.*

National Center for PTSD. May 2019. "Understanding PTSD and PTSD Treatment." 16 pages. Posted at https://www.ptsd.va.gov/publications/print/understandingptsd_booklet.pdf

National Institute of Justice. March 7, 2014. "Prison Rape Elimination Act." Posted at https://nij.ojp.gov/topics/articles/prison-rape-elimination-act

The New York Times. Updated April 16, 2021. Originally published in 2020. "Coronavirus in the U.S.: Latest Map nd Case Count." *The New York Times.* Posted at nytimes.com

Newman, Andy. August 31, 1999. "Disturbed Man Wielding a Hammer Is Killed by Police in Brooklyn." *The New York Times.* Posted at nytimes.com

Noonan, Margaret, Harley Rohloff, and Scott Ginder. August 2015. "Mortality in Local Jails and State Prisons, 2000-2013- Statistical Tables." Bureau of Justice Statistics, Office of Justice Programs, U.S. Department of Justice.

Peralta, Eyder. June 8, 2015. "Kalief Browder, Jailed for Years Without Trial, Kills Himself." NPR.org. Posted at https://www.npr.org/sections/thetwo-way/2015/06/08/412842780/kalief-browder-jailed-for-years-at-rikers-island-without-trial-commits-suicide

Perske, Robert. October 2011. "Perske's List: False Confessions from 75 Persons with Intellectual Disability." American Association on Intellectual and Developmental Disabilities. 49(5): 365-373.

Posted at https://www.aaidd.org/docs/default-source/publications/perske-s-list-false-confessions-from-75-persons-with-intellectual-disability.pdf

Sack, William H. and Jack Seidler. 1978. "Should Children Visit Their Parents in Prison? *Law and Human Behavior.* 2: 261-266.

Sawyer, Wendy and Peter Wagner. March 24, 2020. "Mass Incarceration: The Whole Pie 2020." Prison Policy Initiative. Posted at prisonpolicy.org.

Shafer, Stephen. 1968. *The Victim and His Criminal: A Study in Functional Responsibility.* New York: Random House.

Stevenson, Bryan. 2015. *Just Mercy.* One World reprint edition.

Sundaresh, Ram, Yi Youngman, Harvey D. Tyler, Brita Roy, Carley Riley, Hedwig Lee, Christopher Wildeman, and Emily A. Wang. May 28, 2021. "Exposure to Family Member Incarceration and Adult Well-being in the United States." JAMA Network Open. Posted online at jamanetworkopen.

Von Hentig, Hans. 1979. *The Criminal & His Victim: Studies in the Sociobiology of Crime.* With a New Preface by Marvin Wolfgang. New York: Schocken. (Originally published 1948 by Yale University Press.)

Wakefield, Sara, Hedwig Lee, and Christopher Wildeman. May 2016. "Tough on Crime, Tough on Families? Criminal Justice and Family Life in America." ANNALS, AAPSS.

Widra, Emily. July 13, 2021. "New Data: People With Incarcerated Loved Ones Have Shorter Life Expectancies and Poorer Health." Prison Policy Initiative Updates. Posted at aol.com. Sent from prisonpolicy.org.

Woodward, Aylin and Michelle Mark. June 3, 2020. "Research Shows There are at Least 6 Proven Ways to Reduce Police Brutality—and 2 Strategies That Don't Work." Published at the BusinessInsidser.com website.

Yager, Jan. 2021. *Help Yourself Now.* New York: Allworth, an imprint of Skyhorse.

______________. 2021, 2015, 1978. *Victims.* Stamford, CT: Hannacroix Creek.(Originally published by Scribner's)

Videos, and TED Talks

CBS This Morning. May 8, 2019. "Newly Released Video Shows Sandra Bland's Arrest from Her Point of View." 2:39 minutes. Posted at youtube.com/watch?v=iUmhNHURKX8

John Oliver. October 26, 2015. "John Oliver—Prison with Sesame Street." 2:29 minutes. October 26, 2015. Posted on YouTube at http://www.youtube.com/watch?v=dcPPo90p4lk

______________. July 21, 2014. "Prison: Last Week Tonight with John Oliver." 17:42 minutes. Posted at http://www.youtube.com/watch?v=_Pz3syET3DY&t=130s

Just Mercy. 2019. Directed by Destin Daniel Cretton. Staring Michael B. Jordan as the real life story of Harvard law school graduate Bryan Stevenson who moves back to Alabama and takes on a death penalty case. The movie is based on the nonfiction book of the same title.

Michelle Raymond. Apr 8, 2019 "The Invisible Victims of Crime." 8:38 minutes. TEDxRoyalTunbridgeWells "I was victimized and even unaware that I had become a victim," says Raymond whose husband had been arrested for crimes which she does not detail. Posted at https://www.youtube.com/watch?v=HEFezmxePAk

Ashley Rubin. February 8, 2019. "A Brief History of Prisons." TEDxMississauga. 13:43 minutes. Dr Rubin begins by sharing how a murder in California of a young girl when Rubin was just eight got her interested in studying crime and prisons. She ends this well-done and information talk about prisons with questions about why do we need prisons and if we do need them, who should be incarcerated. Posted at https://www.youtube.com/watch?v=KPO3EkA__Xg

Texas Department of Public Safety. July 23, 2015. "Full Sandra Bland Arrest Video." 47:31 minutes. Posted at youtube.com/watch?v=2kI7mzowxus by the *Wall Street Journal.*

CHAPTER **FIFTEEN**

Additional Victim Situations or Populations

Workplace Crime, Terrorism, Hate Crimes, Victimizations Based on Sexual Orientation, Human Trafficking, Persons with Disabilities and Disorders, and More

Learning Objectives

After you finish reading this chapter, you should be able to:

1. Evaluate the type of crimes that are most common in the workplace.
2. Discuss the source of the phrase "going postal" applied to workplace crime.
3. Define terrorism.
4. Name the six types of terrorism attacks.
5. Define the two main types of human trafficking.
6. Discuss the difference between prostitution or sex work and sex trafficking.
7. Identify people with physical, intellectual, and developmental disabilities and if they are at an increased risk of crime victimization.
8. Understand the newer option for the criminal justice system to handle those who are mentally ill who are arrested instead of only being released or incarcerated.
9. Define a hate crime.
10. Outline the scope of the problem of hate crimes in the United States and internationally.
11. Know what laws the federal government has enacted to try to find out the frequency of hate crimes as well as make it a punishable offense.
12. Know the statistics that reflect how members of LGBTQ community are at greater risk of violent crime victimizations.
13. Understand whether animal cruelty and neglect are considered crimes.
14. Describe how those who have been through a natural disaster may be more likely victims.

OVERVIEW

In this chapter you will learn about victimizations that affect certain segments of the population or occur in certain situations. As noted in the subtitle to this chapter, and in the learning objectives, Chapter 15 covers an important and diverse range of additional victims including workplace crime, terrorism, hate crimes, human trafficking, persons with intellectual, developmental, physical, or mental disabilities and disorders, animal cruelty, natural disasters, and cruise ship crimes victims.

WORKPLACE CRIME

When it happens, **workplace crime**, especially when it involves violence, often makes the news. That is because we all expect the place where we work to be a refuge and safe place to spend 8 or 10 hours a day. Doing the work at most jobs is enough of a challenge. Workers do not want to fear their safety, or fear that their wallet, handbag, or briefcase will be stolen even if they lock it up in their desk drawer.

Any kind of property or violent crime—homicide, aggravated assault, larceny-theft, white-collar crime, cybercrime, rape, sexual assault, sexual harassment, robbery, kidnapping, or hostage-taking—that we have discussed so far in this textbook can take place at work. Even the property crimes of arson and vandalism can leave injured or dead workers and must be counted in the list of potential workplace crimes and violent victimizations.

Certain types of crime that we associate with work were already discussed in earlier chapters. For example, cybercrime, including identity theft, embezzlement, and employee theft were addressed in Chapter 9, "Cybercrime, White-Collar Crime, and Economic Crime Victims."

Until the dramatic change in work habits necessitated by the COVID-19 pandemic in the Spring of 2020, which sent millions of office workers home to work remotely for the year, the outside office was generally seen as a positive feature of business employment and a good place to spend part of one's day, regardless of the sometimes lengthy commute from home. Working in an office enables interacting with others and provides access to specialized or high-speed equipment, convenient meeting spaces, and on-site IT specialists. Since the start of the pandemic, many office workers and businesses have made working remotely a functional and successful adaptation. But as millions and, eventually, even billions are vaccinated against the COVID-19 in 2021 and beyond, part of the workforce will most likely return to outside offices. Of course, some will choose to continue working remotely from home, but the social, and even career, benefits of interacting in person will motivate other workers, especially younger, single ones, to get back into the workplace, even if it is only part-time.

With that return to the outside office in greater numbers, the potential for workplace crime and violence will also return. So, just who are the victims of workplace violence? Larceny/theft occurs at work. Wallets are stolen, as well as laptops or smartphones. Individuals may also be robbed in the workplace, face to face. The offices may be burglarized at night when the office tends to be vacant. If any of these crimes occur in the workplace, employees should be encouraged to report the crime to human resources and the local police.

Most state employment laws require that employers carry worker's compensation insurance for their employees, which should cover medical expenses, counseling, and related out-of-pocket expenses as well as two-thirds of the employee's salary until they can return to work. (Gueli, Esq., 2018)

Workplace Violence Victims

In Box 15.1, you will find definitions for the four types of workplace violence, as defined by the National Institute for Occupational Safety and Health, and posted at the CDC (Centers for Disease Control and Prevention) website.

Box 15.1 Four Types of Workplace Violence

Type 1—Criminal Intent

In Type 1 violence, the perpetrator has no legitimate relationship to the business or its employees and is usually committing the act of violence in conjunction with another crime such as robbery, shoplifting, or trespassing.

Type 2—Customer/Client

Also referred to as client-on-worker violence.

Type 3—Worker-on-Worker (Co-Worker or Employer-Employee Violence)

Type 4—Personal Relationship

The violence is because of a relationship outside of the workplace. This would be the situation if someone is in a domestic violence situation and the abuser tracks the worker down and commits violence against her/him in the workplace, possibly injuring or killing others as well.

Source: Adapted from "Types of Workplace Violence," posted at the CDC website, February 7, 2020. Content source: National Institute for Occupational Safety and Health.

Workplace Homicide and Its Victims

On Tuesday, January 26, 2021, 43-year-old pediatrician Dr. Katherine Lindley Dodson, a married mother of three, went to her job at a medical group for children in Austin, Texas. Tragically, after a standoff that lasted several hours, a terminally ill doctor, who had allegedly been turned down for a volunteer position, shot and killed Dr. Dodson before committing suicide.

How common are workplace homicides like this? In 2016, according to the U.S. Bureau of Labor Statistics, there were 500 workplace homicides across the United States. That was an increase of 83 homicides from the 2015 level. It is noted that workplace homicides accounted for 10 percent of fatal occupational injuries in the United States during 2016, after workplace accidents. The majority of victims were males (83% or 409 victims) compared to females (18% or 91 victims). (U.S. Bureau of Labor Statistics, 2018) According to the union AFL-CIO, the number of workplace homicide victims has increased. In its October 2020 report, "Death on the Job: The Toll of Neglect," it reported violent workplace deaths included 828 victims, the second leading cause of death at work after traumatic accident-related injuries. (AFL-CIO, 2020)

In Table 15.1 you will see data for the type of assailant and gender of work-related homicides in 2016 in the United States For women, the highest percentage and number of victims were those killed by a relative or domestic partner (40% or 36 female victims). This is an important statistic to consider. As Tiesman, et al. point out in their journal article, "Workplace Homicides Among U.S. Women: The Role of Intimate Partner Violence," for women, the second most frequent type of perpetrator of workplace homicide (after a robber) is a "personal relation." Tiesman and her co-authors studied 648 women who had been killed on the job between 2003 and 2008. Of the 181 (33%) who were killed by a "personal relation" the majority were "intimate partners" (78% or 142 women). They also note that "over half of workplace homicides perpetrated by intimate partners occurred in parking lots and public buildings (n= 291, 51%)." (Tiesman, et al., 2012)

In contrast to women, in the highest percentage of male workplace murders the perpetrator was a robber (33% or 137 male victims).

TABLE 15.1. Work-Related Homicide in the United States by Type of Assailant and Gender of Victim in 2016

Assailant Type	Women		Men	
	Number	Percent	Number	Percent
Total	91	100%	409	100%
Robber	15	16	137	33
Unspecified	16	18	117	29
Inmate, detainee, suspect	4	4	53	13
Coworker or work associate	13	14	53	13
Student, patient, or customer/client	7	8	42	10
Relative or domestic partner	36	40	7	2

Source: U.S. Bureau of Labor Statistics, January 23, 2018.

Everyone knows what that image and the words, "Crime Scene Do Not Cross" means.

Here are some additional examples of workplace violence fatalities:

- In October of 2017 a carpenter who had been fired from his construction job at a building on the West Side of Manhattan returned to the building and shot and killed the 37-year-old foreman before killing himself. (Mays and Baker, 2017)
- In Newington, Connecticut on March 7, 1998, a disgruntled accountant allegedly upset about not being promoted, and other work-related grievances, stabbed and shot to death four executives, including the State Lottery president, before killing himself. (Rabinovitz, 1998)
- In Wakefield, Massachusetts, on December 26th, 2000, according to the *New York Times* report, "A software tester at an Internet consulting company here came to work as usual today, talked with his coworkers and then, the authorities said, took out a semiautomatic rifle and a shotgun and killed seven of them." (Goldberg, 2000)
- On March 16, 2021, a 21-year-old shot and killed eight people in Atlanta at three different massage parlors in the Atlanta area. Six of the victims of this **spree killing** were Asian; two were Caucasian. (Fausset and Vigdor, 2021)
- On October 12, 2011, a man walked into a hair salon in Orange County, California, and killed his ex-wife, Michelle Fournier, who worked there, along with the salon's owner, and six customers. (Lovett, 2011). Six years later, he was sentenced to life in prison. (Gerber and Queally, 2017)

Probably one of the most famous examples of workplace violence and homicide in the last 40 years happened on August 20, 1986, at a post office in Edmond, Oklahoma. This event is said to be the source of the phrase, "**going postal**" that is associated with workplace violence. At 7 A.M. that morning, a postal worker using three different firearms shot and killed 14 employees, including one of his two supervisors, within fifteen minutes. Six other employees were injured. The rampage ended when the killer committed suicide. (Applebome, 1986)

However, in their report, "Workplace Violence," the FBI claimed that the inference that there is a prevalence of postal worker-related murders is a "myth." As they note in their report: "a Postal Service commission reported in 2000 that postal employees are actually less likely to be homicide victims than other workers." (*Source:* Report of the United States Postal Service Commission on a Safe and Secure Workplace, quoted in U.S. Postal Service Annual Report, 2000.)

Yet besides the infamous 1986 Edmond, Oklahoma post office rampage, 1991 was a year that saw two mass shootings related to ex-postal workers. Four were killed in October 1991 in Ridgewood, New Jersey, and three were killed a month later in Royal Oak, Michigan. Then, in late January 2006, a former postal service worker returned to the sorting plant where she worked and shot and killed five former co-workers before committing suicide. (The Higgins Firm, 2021; Smith, 1991; Levin, 1991)

These type of workplace killings are the ones that the media focuses on and the ones that most employees fear the most. Yet statistically, more than 67 percent of workplace killings result from robberies and not co-worker killing sprees (13%), client or customer outbursts (7%), or visitors who are romantic partners or relatives seeking out a worker (9%). These statistics are based on a study of workplace homicides between the years 1992 and 1998 where the relationship between the offender and victim could be established. (Sygnatur and Toscano, 2000) As noted above, however, when you break those statistics down by gender, for women being killed at work by a personal relation (33%) was only second to robbery (39%) as the leading cause. (Tiesman, et al., 2012)

Ana Charle, first mentioned in Chapter 4, "Measuring Crime Victimization," was one of those 7 percent of victims killed in a workplace crime whose perpetrator was a client or customer. In her case, the 36-year-old mother of two, who directed a men's shelter in the Bronx, fought off her attacker, who was trying to sexually assault her, as she walked to her car. But the perpetrator went after her and shot her several times in the head and chest, killing Ana. (Baker, 2015) (Two years later, the 41-year-old perpetrator was found guilty and sentenced to life in prison without parole.) (NY1, 2017)

Workplace Violence Victims by Occupation

The U.S. Bureau of Labor Statistics noted that cashiers had the largest number of workplace homicides in 2016—54 victims—which was an increase from 35 in 2015. As noted below in the section on Prostitution within the Human Trafficking section, prostitutes had the highest homicide rate in the United States during the 1980s with a crude mortality rate of 204 per 100,000, Compare that to the workplace homicide rates during that same time period for occupations that have a higher workplace violence homicide rate such as the 4 per 100,000 for female liquor store workers or 29 per 100,000 for male taxicab drivers. (Shelley, 2010) However, health care workers, according to the "Workplace Violence in Healthcare, 2018" fact sheet, issued by the U.S. Bureau of Labor Statistics, accounted for 73 percent of all nonfatal workplace injuries and illness due to violence in 2018.

Almost everyone knows that police work is dangerous, but so is health care. (Please refer back to Chapter 7, "Primary and Secondary Victims of Homicide," which includes a discussion of police deaths.) James P. Phillips, M.D., in his article "Workplace Violence Against Health Care Workers in the United States," published in the April 28, 2016, issue of *The New England Journal of Medicine*, provides an in-depth look at this issue. According to Dr. Phillips, between 2011 and 2013, nearly 75 percent of workplace assaults occurred in health care settings. (Phillips, 2016: 1661) The highest rates were reported by emergency department nurses with 100 percent reporting verbal assault and 82.1 percent reporting physical assault during the previous year. (Phillips, 2016: 1663). The effect of these workplace assaults on the health care victims includes increased rates of missed workdays, burnout, job dissatisfaction, as well as decreased productivity and feeling unsafe. Dr. Phillips further points out that those unsafe feelings have led to "some health care workers to protect themselves by carrying weapons, typically knives or firearms." (Phillips, 2016: 1665.)

In his report, "Prosecutors in State Courts, 2005," Steven W. Perry, a statistician at the Bureau of Justice Statistics, wrote that he discovered that 40 percent of staff at state prosecutor's offices had a work-related threat or assault. He reported that chief prosecutors were the victims of battery or assault in 2005 in 3 percent of all offices and 6 percent of assistant prosecutors were victims of similar violent offenses. The more frequent types of work-related victimizations involved threats: 47 percent of chief prosecutors in all offices received a threatening letter, 31 percent a threatening phone call, and 31 percent a face-to-face threat. (Rates were somewhat lower for threats to assistant prosecutors, also known as ADAs: 29 percent for letters, 28 percent for calls, and 31 percent for face-to-face threats.) (Perry, 2006:7)

Types of Workplace Violence

Although you may most often associate workplace violence with murder at the workplace, and those incidents are by far the most dramatic, workplace violence includes more than that. All the other violent crimes that can happen in non-work situations also occur at work including assault, robbery, rape, as well as the nonviolent crime of larceny-theft. Bullying and sexual harassment are also workplace victimizations that may escalate to something more serious and violent. (Employee theft and inventory shrinkage, including shoplifting, were discussed in Chapter 9, "Cybercrime, White-Collar, and Economic Crime Victims.")

Table 15.2 describes the four types of workplace violent victimizations as well as an example.

TABLE 15.2. Four Types of Workplace Violence Victimizations and Examples

Type	Description	Example
1	Perpetrator has no relationship to anyone at work	Armed robbery
2	Perpetrator is customer or patient	Patient, high on drugs, assaults a nurse
3	Perpetrator is current or former employee	Recently fired employee hits, shoots, or kills former supervisor
4	Perpetrator has relationship with employee, not the workplace	Ex-partner assaults his ex-wife at her workplace

Source: Types based on Phillips, *New England Journal of Medicine, 2016.*
Revised examples provided by Yager.

A study of workplace violence conducted by the Bureau of Justice Statistics based on an analysis of the National Crime Victimization Survey data of reported and unreported crimes in the United States during a specific time period discovered these trends. Between 1993 and 1999, the occupations with the highest percentage rate of violent victimizations in the workplace were police officers (260.8 per 1,000 workers), followed by correction officers (155.7 per 1,000), followed by taxicab drivers (128.3 per 1,000). The occupation with the fourth-highest rate was private security guards (86.6 per 1,000), followed by bartenders (81.6), custodial mental health workers (69.0), special education teachers (68.4), gas station workers (68.3), professional mental health workers (68.2), convenience store cashiers (53.9),and junior high school teachers (54.2). According to that study, nurses had a higher violent victimization rate than physicians (21.9 for nurses compared to 16.2 for by physicians.) In the teaching category, college and university professors had the lowest violence victimization rate (1.6) compared to high school teachers (38.1) and elementary school teachers (16.8).

In 2018, according to information compiled by the National Safety Council from government sources, including the Occupational Safety and Health Administration, assaults at work led to 20,790 injuries as well as 453 fatalities. The number of nonfatal and fatal assault-related workplace injuries was highest among 25-to 34-year-olds.

Box 15.2 reprints the warning signs that workplace violence might be imminent issued by the National Safety Council.

Box 15.2. Warning Signs of Employee's Workplace Violence Vulnerability

The National Safety Council (NSC) suggests becoming aware of these warning signs of workplace violence:

- Excessive use of alcohol or drugs;
- Unexplained absenteeism, change in behavior or decline in job performance;
- Depression, withdrawal or suicidal comments;
- Resistance to changes at work or persistent complaining about unfair treatment;
- Violation of company policies;
- Emotional responses to criticism, mood swings; and
- Paranoia.

Source: National Safety Council, "Assaults Fourth Leading Cause of Workplace Deaths."

TERRORISM AND ITS VICTIMS

Terrorism accomplishes what the Latin root of the word, *terrere,* means, namely, to frighten. Whether it is domestic terrorism caused by certain groups who are from within a country, or international terrorism perpetrated by foreigners, the result is the same. It makes citizens fearful to travel, to go about their daily business, and to feel safe and sound.

Criminologist Larry Siegel defines terrorism as "the illegal use of force against innocent people to achieve a political objective." (Siegel, 2018: 405) Siegel describes these contemporary forms of terrorism:

1. Revolutionary terrorists (using terror to replace the current government).
2. Political terrorists (they want to reshape the present government but not replace it).
3. Nationalist terrorism (feeling their minority religious or ethnic group is persecuted under majority rule, wants to create an independent state).
4. Retributive terrorism ("motivated by anger against the existing social and political regime whose policies they find offensive"). (Siegel, 2018: 411)
5. State-sponsored terrorism ("a repressive government regime forces its citizens into obedience, oppresses minorities, and stifles political dissent"). (Siegel, 2018: 413)
6. Lone-actor terrorists (for example, the two Tsarnaev brothers who carried out the 2013 Boston Marathon bombings; they reportedly acted alone). (Winter, 2018)

There are two basic types of terrorism victims: (1) incidental victims who are literally in the wrong place at the wrong time and (2) more targeted particular individuals or members of certain groups.

In the first group, the *location* is the target, and the victims are randomly chosen just because they happen to be at that place. One example that immediately comes to mind is the thousands of workers who just went to their jobs or boarded a flight on the morning of September 11th, 2001, and, sadly, died when four planes taken over by terrorists crashed into the Twin Towers in lower Manhattan, the Pentagon in Washington D.C., and onto a rural field in Pennsylvania after the passengers took control away from the hijackers, forcing them to miss the intended target (still not known with any certainty to this day). (Barron, 2001)

Other random, innocent terrorist victims include the shoppers who were at a December 2016 Berlin Christmas market when a truck driven by a terrorist rammed into them, killing 11 pedestrians. (Eddy and Smale, 2016) Also, in May 2017, a suicide bomber killed 22 and injured hundreds at a concert in Manchester, England where Ariana Grande was performing. (Smith and Chan, 2017) In random situations such as those, the target might be selected because it has meaning to the terrorists, such as five-star hotels that attract foreign tourists in major international cities, or public transportation. But in all those situations, the terrorists are not aiming for a specific individual.

The second type of terrorist victims, as mentioned above, are more targeted as particular individuals as well as persons who represent a group, such as the journalists who were kidnapped, held captive, and then beheaded by terrorists. Just two of those victims who were tragically killed on camera included American journalist James Wright Foley in August 2014 and (Stowe, 2018) American Israeli journalist Steven Sotloff who was killed in September 2014 at the age of 31. Sotloff had been kidnapped the previous August while he was covering the Syrian war and refugee crisis. Sotloff was a freelance journalist, reporting for *Time* magazine and other news outlets. (BBC.com, 2014)

Another example of a specific targeted terrorist victim includes American journalist Daniel Pearl who was working for the *Wall Street Journal* in 2002 when he was kidnapped and later beheaded in Pakistan. (*New York Times*, Editorial, 2002)

What unites those who are murdered or injured because of terrorism is that their murder is considered an act of extremism based on ideology as distinct from victimization associated with the so-called conventional violent or property crimes.

The next distinction when exploring terrorism and its victims is whether or not it is an act of international or transnational terrorism, or an act of domestic terrorism.

After that, a third concern related to victims of terrorism is the issue of dealing with the wounds related to the attack. Whether those injuries are caused by a conventional violent crime or an act of terrorism, there are physical and psychological wounds that have to be treated, such as wounds caused by bullets, shrapnel, burns, or loss of a limb, as well as the short-and long-term psychological aftermath including the possibility of **PTSD (post-traumatic stress disorder)**. For example, singer Ariana Grande, who was performing in Manchester when the terrorist bombing occurred, in 2017 killing at least 22 people, shared that she had "anxiety" and "signs of PTSD" following the attack. (Young, 2019)

Primary and Secondary Victims of Terrorism

Three died and hundreds were injured during the Boston Marathon bombing on April 15, 2013. (Eligan and Cooper, 2013) The FBI defines domestic terrorism as "violent, criminal acts committed by individuals and/or groups to further ideological goals stemming from domestic influences, such as those of a political, religious, social, racial, or environmental nature." (FBI, "What We Investigate: Terrorism," n.d.)

Here are some examples of domestic terrorism in the United States beginning with three of the most well-known occurrences in the last 25 years: (1) the April 19, 1995 bombing of a federal building in Oklahoma City, killing 168 men, women, and children and injuring several hundred others; (Johnston, 1995) (2) the El Paso, Texas shooting in a department store's parking lot and store in August 2019 that claimed 20 lives and has been labeled domestic terrorism (Romero and Bogel-Burroughs, 2019); and (3) The Charlottesville, Virginia car attack in 2017, which killed 32-year-old Heather Heyer and has been labeled domestic terrorism. The driver drove his car into the victim. (He was sentenced to life in federal prison.) (Bergen, 2017; Caron, 2017; Savage, 2017; Smith, 2019)

It is hard to decide if the Boston Marathon terrorist bombings should be considered a domestic or international terrorism attack since one of the two perpetrators, Dzhokhar Tsarnaev, who had moved to the United States in 2002, became a naturalized citizen in 2012. At the time of the bombings, carried out with his brother, he was a student at the state university in Massachusetts. Dr. Anne Speckhard, Director of the International Center for the Study of Violent Extremism, has conducted extensive research into the background of the Boston Marathon bombers, especially the older brother, Tamerlan, considered by many to be the mastermind of the attacks. Many believed he influenced his younger brother to help him to carry out his bombings. Speckhard reports that she interviewed over 400 "extremists and terrorists, their family members and close associates and even their hostages in many countries all over the world." (Speckhard, 2013) She indicates that according to Tamerlan's younger brother and partner in the Boston Marathon bombings, "Tamerlan was upset with the United States and planned to attack Americans due to the wars in Afghanistan and Iraq." (Speckhard, 2013)

Three victims died in the Boston Marathon bombings—Krystle Campbell, 29, a restaurant manager; Martin Richard, an 8-year-old third grade student; and Lu Lingzi, 23, a graduate student from Shenyang, China who was studying at Boston University—and more than 260 were wounded. (Parker and Bidgood, 2015)

Lynn Julian Crisci, mentioned previously in Chapter 1, "Victimology: An Overview," is one of the hundreds who were wounded in the Boston Marathon bombings. She was standing near the finish line at the Boston Marathon on April 15, 2013, when one of the bombs went off causing her to get blast force trauma, hearing problems, and back ailments that she still deals with eight years later.

"I got very lucky that I didn't get hit with shrapnel," says Lynn, who is now 44 years old. She lives near the bomb site, so she has to deal with the PTSD of regularly walking by the place where it happened. For financial reasons, she is unable to move away.

"Part of my injuries are from the panic and stampede," says Lynn. "It's not their fault. It's fear. It's human nature. Some of the people were in the bleachers across the street. Some people were crushed when they were trying to escape, and I went into the bar that was right behind me only because my dog scratched my face and snapped me out of shock first."

Lynn still goes to a support group of fellow survivors but, Lynn explains, "the original survivor support groups, which were divided between external and internal injuries, stopped in 2016, I believe. The current support groups, in which I'm still active on Facebook and Zoom are part of Strength to Strength. I'm also a proud advocate on their Patient Advisory Counsel. Their URL is StoSglobal.org."

"Internal injuries can be the hardest to diagnose, even harder to treat, and healing from them can last a lifetime," Lynn continues. (Crisci, 2020; Crisci, 2021)

Psychiatrist and terrorism expert Carole Lieberman, M.D. notes that there are differences between victims of terrorism and victims of other crimes. "Terrorism victims are different from crime victims in a number of ways," says Dr. Lieberman. "For example, a victim of terrorism has a harder time healing privately because they're usually more than one victim at a time whether from 9/11 where there were thousands or even from a car ramming incident where there might have been less than a dozen."

Dr. Lieberman continues, "There is media interest in the terrorist victim's experience and sometimes that gets in the way of grieving what happened or processing what happened."

Author of *Lions and Tigers and Terrorists Oh My!* among other books on terrorism, Dr. Lieberman explains: "Sometimes terrorism victims are embarrassed to share very personal things. For example, in my first terrorism book that was published in London, I was talking with a family who experienced having lost their daughter in 7/7 (London's 9/11.) The family felt like their daughter was revealing herself to them in signs. They would 'see' her at certain events, and they would agree, 'That must be our daughter!' 'This is our sister!' 'She's coming back to tell us she's okay. She wants us not to worry because she's okay.' They were afraid of being judged for sharing their intimate beliefs. I was mentioning that because if there is all this public interest, it is hard for victims to reveal these things. They might even question if they have to reveal these things. That makes it a little harder."

Finally, Dr. Lieberman notes that terrorism victims have shared with her that people feel responsible for the terrorist act. "Should we have done something differently as a society to have [been] preventing this kind of act," she says. "We are all victims of terrorism whether it is in the United States, London, or France. We're all victims." (Yager, 2021b)

Profile ■ **Christina Stanton, Survivor of 9/11 Attacks**

Christina Stanton. Contributed photo.

Christina Stanton is a survivor of the 9/11 attacks, but she is not the typical victim in that she and her husband lived six blocks away from the Twin Towers but were not working in the buildings that collapsed. Still, almost 20 years later, she and her husband are dealing with physical and psychological aftereffects of being present during the attacks. In addition to PTSD, Christina, who is now 51, has leukemia and Non-Hodgkin's lymphoma. Her husband has skin issues which they know are related to 9/11.

They were in their apartment on the 24th floor of a building six blocks away from the Twin Towers when the first plane crashed into the first tower. "When the second plane came in, the shock waves of that plane going into the second building actually blew us back into our apartment. We had left our terrace doors open."

They grabbed their Boston terrier and ran down the stairs. Christine was still in her pajamas and did not even have her shoes on. "When the two Towers came down," she explains, "it covered us with dust and debris. We were completely yellow."

They walked away from the buildings and got on a boat that took them to New Jersey. They did not get back into their apartment for another five months after the 9/11 terrorist attacks.

The apartment clean up was paid for by the compensation fund and they were given generous donations from their church to pay for the veterinarian bills for their dog who had licked the debris getting glass and other debilitating substances into his system. "Our dog almost died," she says. "It shredded his insides."

"We had PTSD that we had to deal with," explains Christina, who has been working as a walking tour guide in New York City for almost two decades. She also wrote a book entitled, *Out of the Shadows of 9/11*, subtitled *An Inspiring Tale of Escape and Transformation*. (Stanton, 2019)

Christina knows that as bad as the experience was for her, her husband, and their dog, others had it much worse because they did not survive. Her husband lost a fraternity brother named Jim whom he was close to in the 9/11 terrorist attacks. "They never did find any trace of Jim's body," says Christina.

She wants people to know that there was even more destruction caused by the planes than the actual towers. "It surprises people that the destruction was much bigger of a radius than was reported. People are dying because of 9/11. They just passed the amount of people who are dying from the toxins [who died in the attacks]. They're still identifying body parts."

Profile ▪ Mary Siller-Scullin of the Tunnel2Towers Foundation

As noted previously in Chapter 7, Mary Siller-Scullin lost her brother Stephen Siller in the 9/11 attacks. He was the youngest of seven siblings. "He was 34," she says. "He had five children." Because of the Tunnel2Towers Foundation that her family established in her brother's memory, Steven's story is widely known. In case you are not familiar with it, a short overview, from the foundation's website follows:

> . . . On September 11, 2001, Stephen, who was assigned to Brooklyn's Squad 1, had just finished his shift and was on his way to play golf with his brothers when he got word over his scanner of a plane hitting the North Tower of the World Trade Center. Upon hearing the news, Stephen called his wife Sally and asked her to tell his brothers he would catch up with them later. He returned to Squad 1 to get his gear. Stephen drove his truck to the entrance of the Brooklyn Battery Tunnel, but it had already been closed for security purposes. Determined to carry out his duty, he strapped 60 lbs. of gear to his back, and raced on foot through the tunnel to the Twin Towers, where he gave up his life while saving others. . . .

The nonprofit Tunnel2Towers Foundation has raised over $250 million since it was founded in her youngest brother's memory and honor. Among their many activities is paying off the mortgage of a spouse whose partner was killed in the line of duty, including firefighters, police officers, and the military.

In a phone interview, this author asked Mary how long it took her to get back to her old self, to deal with her brother's death during the 9/11 terrorist attacks. "I don't think I am my old self," she said. "I think I am an okay version of myself, but that experience and the experiences that I've had since, working with families who have a lot of tragic loss, have shaped me in a very different way."

How had she changed?

"I think innocence. I think I've lost a certain amount of innocence because I came face to face with the reality of evil, and that's something I never expected to understand so deeply and intimately. I also learning that we must transform and transcend evil and for me and my family, that is by doing good through the Foundation."

The long-term effects of the 9/11 terrorist attacks are still being felt in the United States, and in other countries, the home countries of victims, almost two decades later. Dr. Lieberman says, "There have been studies about how after 9/11, people who watched hours and hours of the Twin Towers falling developed PTSD even though they weren't in New York. If they kept watching the Towers falling again and again for a certain number of hours, they developed PTSD. They could be in Kansas. Statistics also shows that obesity, alcohol, self-cutting, drug abuse, and even suicide went up after 9/11." (Yager, 2021b)

Statistics on Terrorism and Fear of Terrorism

A study conducted by Pew Research in April 2020 found that terrorism was the number two international concern of Americans, after the COVID-19 pandemic. (Poushter and Fagan, 2020)

In 2018, according to the report prepared for the Department of State, Bureau of Counterterrorism and Countering Violent Extremism, by the Development Services Group, Inc., of the Global Terrorism Trends and Analysis Center, there were terrorist incidents in 84 countries and territories. That amounted to 8,093 terrorist incidents. There were 32,836 deaths related to those terrorist attacks. Of those incidents, 901 attacks had more than 10 deaths. (Development Services Group, "Annex of Statistical Information," 2018: 5)

There were 22,651 people injured in 2018 related to those 8,093 terrorist attacks. There were 3,534 kidnapping victims or hostages related to those attacks, (Development Services Group, 6)

January had the highest number of terrorist attacks in 2018 (843) but November had the greatest number of deaths (3,966). (Development Services Group, 7) The hotspots for terrorist attacks in 2018 included Afghanistan, West Africa, the Middle East, and South Asia including Mali, India, Pakistan, Somalia, Kenya, Syria, and Yemen. (Development Services Group, 5, 6)

Terrorist Victim Financial Controversies

The subtitle of the journal article "Victims of Terrorism Policies: Should Victims of Terrorism Be Treated Differently?" by Hans-Jörg Albrecht and Michael Kilchling articulates a victim compensation issue very well. (Albrecht and Kilchling, 2007)

There was a very large fund created for victims after the September 11th Terrorist Attacks. As reporter Lucette Lagnado points out in her article "Terrorism's Forgotten Victims," one of the "largest private charities, the Sept. 11 Fund, has collected more than $450 million and distributed $205 million." (Lagnado, 2002)

Lagnado begins her article with an anecdote about a terrorist victim few may have heard about, Nachum Sasonkin. He, along with another Orthodox Jewish student, were victims of a terrorist attack as the van they were in was crossing the Brooklyn Bridge. His classmate, Ari Halberstam, died but Nachum lived although his injuries were severe. In the article, written eight years after the attack, the reporter shares that Nachum is disabled with a bullet still deep inside his brain. He "sways when he walks, and when he talks, he sometimes slurs his words."

Nachum is quoted as asking, "What is the difference between me and the victims of 9/11? Why can't I get help?"

He is not the only terrorist victim who did not participate in a major compensation fund to ask that question. What about victims of conventional crimes who are injured or restitution to the family members of those who are killed? State compensation funds, if the victim's family qualifies, are usually capped at anywhere from $10,000 to $25,000, to cover a lifetime of lost earnings.

The concern is that victims of some terrorist actions, such as 9/11, have a better chance of collecting compensation because the shocking impact and high visibility of those attacks in which they were victimized generated funding independent of state or federal forces. You can see how controversial the concept of paying out funds based on a determination of the value of each individual was by the title of this related The *New York Times* article, "After Weighing Cost of Lives, 9/11 Fund Completes Its Task." (Chen, 2004) Kenneth R. Feinberg was the administrator of the Sept. 11 Victim Compensation Fund, as it was called. According to the article, 97% of the 2,973 families of those who died and were eligible, had applied to the fund. The payments ranged from $250,000 to $7.1 million with the average of almost $2.1 million per family. (Chen, 2004)

For the sake of comparison, the cap on a payment to an eligible family who lost a loved one—spouse, son, daughter, next of kin—to homicide in the state of New York is $30,000. (New York State Crime Victims Board, n.d. brochure) Reducing the payments to victims of terrorism is certainly not suggested. But should there be an increase in the payment to eligible families of those who are killed because of conventional crimes?

HATE CRIMES

We are so used to hearing the term **hate crime** (or **bias crime**) that it may be hard to imagine that it was only back in 1981 that the state of Wisconsin became the first state to pass a hate crime or bias crime law in the United States. The two approaches to dealing with hate crimes are to add time to the sentencing already being imposed for another kind of crime, such as aggravated assault or vandalism, because that crime was motivated by hate. Another approach is to have new separate offenses that are deemed hate crimes. In 1990, the passage of The Hate Crime Statistics Act (HCSA) required that the Justice Department collect statistics about any crimes directed at individuals because of race, religion, ethnicity, sexual orientation, gender, and gender identity, or disability.

James Byrd Jr., killed because of a hate crime on June 7th, 1998.

In 1998, two horrific hate crimes occurred that dramatically impacted on the public and criminal justice awareness of the need to recognize and punish hate crimes. The first was the killing of James Byrd Jr., a 49-year-old African American, on June 7th, 1998, in Jasper, Texas. He was beaten and then he was chained to a pickup truck and dragged for three miles. The three white supremacists responsible for Byrd's murder were apprehended. (Cropper, 1998) One received life in prison and the other two got the death penalty. (Reuters, 1999) The first of the convicted killers, Lawrence Russell Brewer, was executed by the state of Texas in 2011. The second convicted killer, John William King, was executed in 2019. (Robertson, 2019)

College student and hate crime victim Matthew Shepard, who died on October 7th, 1998.

A few months later, on October 7th, 1998, a 21-year-old college student, Matthew Shepard, who was gay, was tied to a fence, beaten, and left for dead. He was found by a cyclist and brought to the hospital, but he died five days later. (Brooke, 1998)

The Matthew Shepard Foundation was started by Matthew's parents, Judy and Dennis Shepard, to advocate for laws against hate crimes. In 2009, the Matthew Shepard and James Byrd, Jr. Hate Crimes Prevention Act was passed. Another effort of the foundation is providing hate crime training to law enforcement officers as well as assistant district attorneys. According to the foundation's website, since 2017 they have provided hate crime training to more than 1,000 law enforcement officers and 76 prosecutors.

In the Appendices for this book at the publisher's website www.AspenPublishing.com you will find more information on **The Matthew Shepard and James Byrd, Jr. Hate Crimes Prevention Act of 2009.**

The brutal killings of James Byrd Jr. and Matthew Shepard represent two major targeted victims for hate crimes, as indicated in Table 15.1, namely on the basis of race (or ethnicity or ancestry) or gender identity.

TABLE 15.3. Categories of Incidents of Hate Crimes, 2018 (Listed in order of frequency)

Total number of incidents	7,120
Race/ethnicity/ancestry	4,047
Religion	1,419
Sexual orientation	1,196
Gender identity	168
Disability	159
Gender	47

Source: FBI, Incidents, Offenses, Hate Crime Victims and Known Offenders by Bias Motivation, 2018, Table 1.

In Table 15.3 you found the number of hate crime incidents in the United States in 2018, based on the FBI UCR report, as well as what category those hate crimes fall into. As you can see, hate crimes related to race, ethnicity, or ancestry are the most common followed by those associated with religion.

Here is how the FBI defines a hate crime: A hate crime is a traditional offense like murder, arson, or vandalism with an added element of bias. For the purposes of collecting statistics, the FBI has defined a hate crime as a 'criminal offense against a person or property motivated in whole or in part by an offender's bias against a race, religion, disability, sexual orientation, ethnicity, gender, or gender identity.' Hate itself is not a crime—and the FBI is mindful of protecting freedom of speech and other civil liberties." (FBI, "What We Investigate: Hate Crimes.")

If a crime is determined to have elements of hate associated with it, if the perpetrator is found guilty, there can be "enhancements" on the sentencing. So having a crime deemed a hate crime is more than just a distinction.

According to the FBI, in 2018 these were the reasons for reported hate crimes in the United States:

- 59.6 percent of the victims were targeted because of the offenders' bias against race/ethnicity/ancestry.
- 18.7 percent were victimized because of bias against religion.
- 16.7 percent were targeted because of bias against sexual orientation.
- 2.2 percent were victims of gender-identity bias.
- 2.1 percent were targeted because of bias against disability.
- 0.7 percent (61 individuals) were victims of gender bias.

Source: FBI 2018 Hate Crime Statistics, Table 1.

It should be pointed out that hate crimes are an international concern. In March 2019, in New Zealand, 50 people were killed when someone shot up worshippers at two mosques. (Cave, 2020) The Office for Democratic Institutions and Human Rights (ODIHR), Tolerance and Non-2019 Hate Discrimination Department, headquartered in Warsaw, Poland, reported on its 2019 Hate Crime Data. Here are some of its key findings:

- "the vast majority of hate crimes go unreported"
- 6,964 incidents were reported to ODIHR
- The largest number were racism and xenophobia [bias against people from other countries] (3,033 incidents)
- The next biggest number of incidents was anti-Semitism (1,704)
- The third largest number of hate crime incidents were based on sexual orientation or gender identity (1,278)
- Bias against Christians is the next category of hate crime victims (577)
- Muslim hate crimes is next (511)
- The last three groups that are in their reported hate crime review for 2019 are: Roma and Sinti [slang term is "gypsies"] (101), gender (70), and disability (21).

Source: OSCE ODIHR Hate Crime Reporting, 2019 Hate Crime Data Key Findings

Hate Crime Victim Demographics

According to the Bureau of Justice Statistics (BJS), which is part of the Office of Justice Programs, U.S. Department of Justice, males and females had similar rates of hate crime victimization in the United States between 2004 and 2015. Hispanics (1.3 per 1,000 persons) had a higher rate of violent hate crime victimization versus that of non-Hispanic whites (0.7 per 1,000). Households earning less than $24.999 had the highest rate of victimization. (BJS, "Hate Crime Victimization, 2004-2015".)

There is a wide discrepancy in the number of hate crimes reported by the two different major crime data agencies in the in the United States First, hate crimes reported by the Uniform Crime Reporting (UCR) Program which, as you know, is a program whereby local law enforcement sent their data for the reported major crimes that year to the FBI (Federal Bureau of Investigation) for tabulating. As noted in the tables that follow, the UCR, as reported by the FBI, in 2018 shared basic information about a reported 7,120 incidents.

Consider the results of the 2019 Hate Crime Statistics report of the FBI issued through the National Incident-Based Reporting System (NIBRS), the newer system replacing the UCR. With 15,588 law enforcement agencies participating in the Hate Crime Statistics Program, and reporting on incidents and offenses reported for 2019, 8,559 offenses involving 7.314 hate crime incidents. The percentages of those incidents by the type of hate crime being reported are the following (in order of most to least common): 55.8 percent motivated by race/ethnicity/ancestry bias; 21.4 percent religion; 16.8 percent sexual orientation; 2.8 percent gender-identity bias; 2.2 percent disability bias; 1.0 percent by gender bias. (FBI, 2019, Table 1)

The National Criminal Victimization Survey (NCVS) tracks the number of hate crimes in given years, on the basis of interviews with a selected number of households about reported and unreported crimes that happened to anyone in the household above the age of 12 in the previous six months. According to the NCVS, there were approximately 250,000 hate crime victims in the United States every year between 2005 and 2015. (OVC, "Hate Crime) That is based on the June 2017 cumulative report by Madeline Masucci and Lynn Langton, of the Bureau of Justice Statistics, "Hate Crime Victimization, 2004-2015."

Table 15.4 shows the breakdown for the reported incidents that were listed in Table 15.3 by number of incidents by the race or ethnic group that the hate crime was directed against in 2018. The numbers in Table 15.4 indicate that the most common race or ethnicity reported hate crimes in the United States in 2018 were anti-Black followed by anti-white. Anti-Asian had more reported hate crime incidents than Anti-Arabic but keep in mind that these statistics are based on just hate crimes that were reported to the local police. In 2021, a new report found a 169% increase in the first quarter of 2021 in anti-Asian hate crimes, The increase is 223% in New York City. Explanations for this increase usually point to the informal or sporatic government official blame for COVID-19 on a possible leak from a lab in China. Others have blamed the hate crime increase against Asian because of referring to the virus as the "China virus." (Yam, 2021)

TABLE 15.4. Categories of Race Incidents of Hate Crimes in the United States by Race or Ethnicity, 2018

Total incidents: 4,047 (Listed in order of frequency)

Race/Ethnicity	Number of Incidents
Anti-Black	1,943
Anti-white	762
Anti-Hispanic	485
Anti-American Indian	194
Anti-other race/ethnicity/ancestry	276
Anti-Asian	148
Anti-Arabic	82

Source: FBI, Incidents, offenses, Hate Crime Victims and Known Offenders by Bias Motivation, 2018, Table 1.

Table 15.5 shows the number of anti-religion reported hate crimes based on the type of religion. As noted in this table, the vast preponderance of religion hate crime incidents are anti-Jewish with the second group in a much smaller number as anti-Islam or Muslim.

TABLE 15.5. Number of Incidents of Reported Hate Crimes in the United States Against Religion

(Listed in order of decreasing frequency) Total incidents for 2018: 1,419

Religion Targeted for Hate	Number of Reported Incidents in 2018
Anti-Jewish	835
Anti-Islam (Muslim)	188
Anti-Sikh	60
Anti-Catholic	53
Anti-Protestant	34
Anti- Hindu	12
Anti-Buddhist	10
Anti-Mormon	9

Source: FBI, Incidents, offenses, Hate Crime Victims and Known Offenders by Bias Motivation, 2018, Table 1.

Other types of reported hate crimes are hate crimes based on disability and gender identity. There were 159 reported disability hate crimes with 99 of those complaints as anti-mental disability and 60 as anti-physical disability. The disabled as victims is discussed in a separate section below.

The NIBRS has found that these three offenses are most frequently motivated by hate or bias:

1. Destruction/damage/vandalism
2. Intimidation
3. Simple assault

The NIBRS reports hate crime details associated with these 13 offenses:

1. Murder and non-negligent manslaughter
2. Rape
3. Aggravated assault
4. Simple assault
5. Intimidation
6. Human trafficking—commercial sex acts
7. Human trafficking—involuntary servitude
8. Robbery
9. Burglary
10. Larceny-theft
11. More vehicle theft
12. Arson
13. Destruction/damage/vandalism (FBI, "Hate Crimes," n.d.)

VICTIMS OF RACISM BASED ON SKIN COLOR

Hate crimes because of religion or gender identity and sexual orientation will be discussed below under Victims of Anti-Semitism and Other Anti-Religion Bias and **LGBTQ (Lesbian, Gay, Bisexual, Transgender, Queer or Questioning)**.

The type of actions that hate crimes cover range from simple assaults to murder of individuals as well as institutional crimes that include arson or vandalism. A well-known hate crime and massacre based on racism occurred at a church in Charleston, South Carolina on June 17, 2015 when 21-year-old Dylann Roof, posing as a participant in a church study group, opened fire on the church goers. He killed six women and three men, ranging in age from 26 to 87. The FBI was called in to assist local police in their search for the killer whose actions were considered a hate crime. (Horowitz, Corasaniti, and Southall, 2015) He was captured the morning after the massacre, more than 200 miles away from the crime scene in North Carolina. (Dunn, Washburn, and Gordon, 2015) A year and a half later, he was found guilty and sentenced to death. (Hersher, 2017)

Remembering the names of nine victims of this well-known hate crime is not easy to do. Unfortunately, it is much easier to recall the name of the one killer. But it is important to remember those victims of the worst hate crime imaginable: murder. The hometown newspaper, the *Charlestown Observer,* published an article, with photographs, sharing thumbnail sketches about the victims. Tywanza Sanders at 26 was the youngest of the victims. According to the Associated Press, the *Charlestown Observer* article reported his Instagram account described him as a poet, artist, and businessman.

Susie Jackson at 87 was the oldest victim of the Emanuel AME Church hate crime killings. A long-time member of the church, she sang in its choir and, according to her grandson, enjoying playing the slot machines. She was looking forward to a church-sponsored bus trip to Chicago in just a few days. (*Charlotte Observer*, 2015)

Here are the names of the other victims: the Rev. Clementa Pinckney, Cynthia Hurd, the Rev. Sharonda Coleman-Singleton, Ethel Lance, Depayne Middleton Doctor, the Rev. Daniel Simmons, and Myra Thompson. (NPR staff, 2015)

The most severe victimizations based on skin color in the United States (outside slavery, which was outlawed on January 31, 1865) were the lynchings that occurred between 1877 and 1950. The Equal Justice Initiative (EJI), a research, legal, and advocacy program founded by Bryan Stevenson and based in Montgomery, Alabama, provides legal representation for those falsely accused of a crime. EJI has researched lynching extensively. In the third edition of their study, *Lynching in America: Confronting the Legacy of Racial Terror*, posted online, an estimated 4,384 lynchings are discussed. Those 4,384 represent 4,084 in 12 Southern states as well as another 300 lynchings in other states. (EJI, 2017)

Lynching means killing someone for an alleged offense, usually by hanging, often without a trial. The term *lynching* itself is said to be coined after Virginia planter and politician Charles Lynch (1736-1796), who served during the American revolutionary war and was known for the extreme punitive measures he took against British Loyalists or "Tories," including, according to the Merriam-Webster Dictionary, "hanging, shooting and whipping, with little concern for a proper trial," so much so that "in 1782 Virginia governor Thomas Jefferson cautioned Lynch directly" about his methods. Lynch himself used the phrase "Lynch's law" in a 1782 letter. (*Merriam-Webster Dictionary*, "Lynch Law.")

The lynchings that took place between 1877 and 1950 were used primarily against Blacks as a way of spreading fear and to assert control. These violent expressions of racism were based on skin color. In the section that follows, we will discuss hate crimes based on religion..

VICTIMS OF ANTI-SEMITISM AND OTHER ANTI-RELIGION BIAS

There is a long history throughout the world of hate crimes based on religion. The most famous is of course the crucifixion of Jesus which for a majority of the world was used to mark the beginning of the current era, 1 A.D. Another famous example of hate crimes based on religion is the Holocaust which occurred between 1941 and 1945 when approximately 6 million Jews, or an estimated two-thirds of the Jews in Europe at that time, were exterminated. (*Holocaust Encyclopedia*, 2020) It is also estimated that another five million non-Jews were killed during the Holocaust including Jehovah's Witnesses, Catholic priests, and Christian pastors. (Schwartz, n.d.) More recently, in 2018, 11 worshippers at the Tree of Life synagogue in Pittsburgh were murdered and four police officers were wounded. The *New York Times* reported that the killer was "shouting anti-Semitic slurs" as he "opened fire." (Robertson, Mele, and Tavernise, 2018)

In Box 15.2 you will find a reprint of the article this author wrote that was published initially in the *London Jewish Chronicle,* and then reprinted on the Op-Ed page of the *New York Times.* When this author arrived in Germany to begin her three-week research trip, it was only 27 years since World War II had ended. Almost all the Germans this author met during that trip, regardless of their ages, wanted to put that dark period in their history behind them. Most stated that they were unaware of the genocide that was being done to the Jews although some admitted to knowing that there were labor camps and ghettos. But they claimed they were unaware that Jews were being exterminated on a grand scale. When asked what their textbooks revealed about that part of Germany history, this author was told that it simply stated that in 1933, Adolf Hitler came to power and in 1945, World War II ended. There was a huge gap about what happened in-between.

In time, Germany learned to accept its past and not to hide from it. But Jews have not returned to live in Germany to the extent they were residing there in 1933. According to the *Holocaust Encyclopedia*, in 1933, when the population of Germany was estimated at 67 million, there were 505,000 Jews. In 2018, with Germany's population now estimated at 80 million, there were approximately 115,000 Jew living there. (*Holocaust Encyclopedia*, 2021)

Box 15.2. "No Boundaries to Hatred" by Dr. Jan Yager (a/k/a Janet Barkas)

No Boundaries to Hatred

By Janet Barkas
(a/k/a Dr. Jan Yager)
Originally published on Monday, January 14, 1974, in the Op-Ed section of *The New York Times*
(*Reprinted by permission of Dr. Jan Yager with selected updates/explanatory information added by Dr. Jan Yager*)

LONDON—My grandmother was angry that I could bring myself to journey to Germany. To make matters worse, I was flying Lufthansa[1] from New York rather than Pan Am[2]. I was meeting with such former associates of Adolf Hitler as Albert Speer[3], architect and chief of armaments of the Third Reich; Gerda Christian[4], Hitler's secretary from 1933-45; and Winifred Wagner[5], Richard Wagner's daughter-in-law. It was the culmination of a year's research on Hitler.

Heidelberg was my first stop, to see Albert Speer. The students at the bar the first evening of my arrival were not interested in my background. Their hostility was directed at my . . . [self-taught] German and the fact that I was American. I met a young, blond-haired man who claimed agreement with the philosophical basis of [National] Socialism. "If only Hitler had not campaigned against the Jews," he said, "everything else he wanted for Germany was positive."

■

In a student cafeteria at Heidelberg, I met a young married couple. We walked to a nearby restaurant and talked there for hours, sipping draughts of beer. Then they asked the question: "Are you Jewish?"

"Yes."

The young woman drew back, seeming confused by my admission.

"But you don't look Jewish, and your name isn't Jewish."

I explained that it was a Greek name. The conversation petered out.

The next morning, Albert Speer. His attractive, bronzed wife, casually dressed in brown pants and matching knit top, provided freshly squeezed orange juice. Speer discussed my research on Hitler. It was a pleasant chat, though he seemed to be recapitulating sections of his book on the Third Reich.

During the long ride up the Rhine to Dusseldorf, I vowed to put to Mrs. Christian those questions I had not asked Speer.

Her flat was furnished and in the style of her most important period, the thirties.

"Did you dislike the Jews?" I asked.

"You don't know what it was like," she said. "A Jewish girl of sixteen was like a German girl of twenty. My mother was afraid to let me associate with them. They wore lipstick and were 'fast.'"

There was no hesitancy in her voice. She continued eagerly. "It was terrible. All the doctors and lawyers were Jews. The Germans were out of work, too, and couldn't get a job because the Jews had them all."

She did not disagree [stated emphatically] that "Hitler was the best boss" she had ever.

■

Back down the Rhine. Dachau[6]. [Nazi extermination camp] Everything clean and new. The original barracks had been torn down. Only replicas stood there. In front of one of the gas chambers was a young family, the father taking pictures of his son. Is this what Dachau will become? A tourist attraction immortalized in a scrapbook?

■

From Dachau, the long train ride to Bayreuth, the national center for Wagnerian opera and the home of Winifred Wagner, Richard Wagner's daughter-in-law and associate of Adolf Hitler. We talked for over two hours.

"Did you know I provided Hitler with the paper and pencils he used to write Mein Kampf?" [Hitler's 1925 autobiographical Nazi manifesto] she asked, proudly in perfect English since she was born and attended school in England.

I asked, "How do you feel about anti-Semitism?"

"Oh, it's not the same today," she said coldly. "It's hard to tell who is a Jew now. The differences are not as great. But I can always tell a Jew when I see one," she observed, staring directly at me.

Time had not brought Mrs. Wagner to reconsider her attitudes any more than it had mellowed Mrs. Christian.

■

Back in New York, I met a handsome 40-year-old. He had never dated a Jewish girl before and felt compelled to tell me why he hated Jews. "There are only 14 million Jews in the world. Any people which gets into so much trouble over so many years must deserve it. They're an ugly race and the Jews in New York are the worst. They are so obnoxious."

Box 15.2. "No Boundaries to Hatred" by Dr. Jan Yager (Continued)

So, hatred was not just in the heart of the country, any particular country. It was something in the heart of a person.

---

[1]Lufthansa was a state-owned airline until 1994 when it became privatized. (Reuters, "A Privatizing of Lufthansa," The New York Times, March 5, 1994, Section D, Page 5.

[2]Pan Am was a major U.S. airline, founded in 1927, until it was disbanded in 1991. (Agis Salpukas, "Pan Am Loses Aid From Delta," December 4, 1991, The New York Times, Section D, Page 1.

[3]UPI, "Albert Speer Dies at 76; Close Associate of Hitler." The New York Times, September 2, 1981, Section A, Page 18.

[4]The Associated Press (AP), July 17, 1997. "Gerda Christian, 83, Secretary for Hitler." The New York Times, July 17, 1997, Section B, Page 10.

[5]The Editors of Encyclopedia Britannica. Updated June 19, 2021. "Winifred Wagner." Posted online at Britannica.com; "Frau Wagner" by Janet Barkas (a/k/a Dr. Jan Yager), July 1972, Opera News, Vol. 37, pages 20-21.

[6]United States Holocaust Memorial Museum (USHMM), "Dachau." Edited March 24, 2021. (Considered the first concentration camp, established in March 1933. An estimated 200,000+ were incarcerated there and at least 28,000 were killed there.) Posted online at encyclopedia.ushmm.org

---

This article is reprinted from The London Jewish Chronicle.

VICTIMS OF OTHER RELIGIOUS HATE CRIMES

Hate crimes based on religions besides being Jewish occur but sometimes there is an event that gets tied to an upsurge in those kinds of crimes. That is what tragically happened after the terrorist attacks in America on September 11, 2001, when 19 Arab Muslims hijacked four commercial aircraft and flew three of them into the Pentagon and the Twin Towers of the World Trade Center.. The fourth plane was prevented from hitting its intended target when the passengers caused it to crash into a field in Pennsylvania. (Gold and Farley, 2001)

These horrific terrorist attacks, killing an estimated 2,928 passengers including those working in the Twin Towers, led to a dramatic increase in discrimination against Arab-Americans and Muslim-Americans as well as Sikh-Americans and South Asian-Americans. More than just religious discrimination, there were actual murders tied to what came to be known as **Islamophobia**. The first hate crime murder victim after 9/11 was Balbir Singh Sodhi. The killer allegedly told a restaurant employee that he was "going to go out and shoot some towel heads." Sodhi was actually a Sikh from India, but mistaken by the killer as being of the same heritage as the 9/11 murder-suicide killers. (Lewin, 2001; Solis (AP), 2012) And on September 15th and October 4th, just four days and less than a month after 9/11, another killer shot and killed grocery store owner Waquar Hassan, an immigrant from Pakistan, at his store, and then Vasudev Patel, an immigrant who was actually from India. (Williams, 2011)

George Washington University Law School faculty member Cynthia Lee, in her chapter entitled, "Hate Crimes and the War on Terror," points out that the more than 1,000 anti-Muslim or anti-Arab hate crime incidents after 9/11 were because of what she refers to as the "construction of the Arab-as-terrorist stereotype." She notes that the Arab-as-terrorist stereotype actually predated 9/11. Lee refers to the research conducted in 1980 by Dr. Jack Shaheen, Professor Emeritus at Southern Ilinois University. He examined more than 900 feature films released between 1896 and 2011 and he found that in the majority of those films "Arabs were portrayed as bad guys." (Lee, 2008)

Decreasing the number of hate crimes based on religion requires a concerted and successful effort to decrease or eliminate the stereotypes that unfortunately give potential perpetrators their justification for the crimes they commit against individuals who are chosen just because they seem to be a member of the hated group. This was highlighted back in 2015 when three murders, which had originally been characterized as arising out of a parking space dispute at the apartment complex where the shooter and two of his victims lived. Prosecutors presented enough evidence that the shooter was actually guilty of hate crimes, even though North Carolina does not have a hate crime statute, but the federal government does. The shooter pleaded guilty to killing Rzan Mohammade Abu-Salha, 19; her sister, Yusor Mohammade Abu-Salha, 21; and Yusor's new husband, Deah Shaddy Barakat, 23. They were targeted because of their dress and religion. The killer got three consecutive life sentences. (Neff, The Marshall Project, 2019)

After the 9/11 terrorist attacks, multiple hate crime victims were attacked in New York City and in other places throughout the United States. Sikhs were even attacked, often mistaken for a Muslim. As noted above, in the days, weeks, and months right after the September 11th terrorist attacks, there were numerous incidents of attacks and even killings of Muslims, Arabics, and Sikhs. It was assumed that it might have been related to the fact that the 19 terrorists who attacked the World Trade Center, the Pentagon, and were on the plane that crashed in Pennsylvania were all from Middle East countries including Saudi Arabia (15), United Arab Emirates (2), Egypt (1), and Lebanon (1), and were of Muslim or Arabic descent. (CNN, "September 11 Hijackers Fast Facts") You may recall from Table 15.1, above, that it was noted that Sikhs were the third most frequent source of reported religious-based hate crimes in the U.S. in 2018, behind anti-Jewish and anti-Muslim/Arab hate crimes.

VICTIMS OF HATE CRIMES BASED ON SEXUAL ORIENTATION: LGBTQ (LESBIAN, GAY, BISEXUAL, TRANSGENDER, AND QUESTIONING) VICTIMS

Respecting and protecting the rights of those in the LGBTQ community against prejudice and discrimination but especially against crimes of violence is a concern in most societies. In the United States, legal advances for gay rights have been made especially in the last 20 years with gay marriage becoming legal in 2015 and a U.S. Supreme Court decision on June 15, 2020 in *Bostock v. Clayton County, Georgia.* That historic ruling declared that Title VII of the 1964 Civil Rights Act banning employment discrimination on the basis of race, religion, nationality, and sex also included sexual orientation and gender identity, which covers the LGBTQ community.

But there are still those who are **homophobic**, meaning they have a phobia about anyone who is LGBTQ and not heterosexual. Their discriminatory behavior may include anything from a disapproving glance or hurtful comments and slurs, to the types of actions that are deemed hate crimes ranging from assault to murder, as in the horrific death of Matthew Shepard, described above. Researchers have found that those who are LGBTQ are victims of violent crimes at the rate of 71.1 per 1,000 persons in a year, compared to 19.2 per 1,000 in a year in the general population. (Galvan, 2020)

As noted below, those who are **transgender**, including those born male who transition to female or vice versa, are the target of violent crime including murder to a disproportionate degree. But there are signs in the United States at least that progress is being made with a wider acceptance of transgender that might help to reverse that trend. In July 2020, it was announced that 23-year-old Valentina Sampaio, a transgender woman, would be the first transgender woman to be featured in the internationally popular *Sports Illustrated* swimsuit issue. The model was born in a fishing village in northern Brazil which is significant because, as Derrick Bryson Taylor reports in his *New York Times* article, Brazil had the largest number of transgender killings of any country in 2019—130 that year. (Derrick Bryson Taylor, 2020)

The advances in the United States and other countries does not obscure the reality that there is still a need for change in how LGBTQ are treated around the world. Consider that there are 71 countries where homosexuality is still illegal, according to Daniel Avery, writing in *Newsweek*. The article was published because of this event, as Avery writes: "This week, the kingdom of Brunei enacted draconian laws that penalize same-sex relations and adultery with death by stoning." (Avery, 2019) You are not alone if you have never heard of Brunei but it is a country in Southeast Asia with a population of approximately 464,500, according to the CIA World Fact Book. (CIA, 2020)

Avery points out that even if the laws against being gay are "not strictly enforced" in a particular country, "they're routinely used to threaten and discriminate against LGBTQ citizens." (Avery, 2019) Hristina Byrnes, writing for *24/7 Wall Street*, and published in *USA Today*, points out 13 countries where being gay is not just illegal but possibly punishable by death, imprisonment, even flogging, although some of the conditions that apply to make it a capital offense are unclear: Brunei, Iran, Mauritania, Nigeria, Qatar, Saudi Arabia, Afghanistan, Somalia, Sudan, United Arab Emirates, and Pakistan. However, the reporter also points out that public pressure caused Brunei that made homosexual acts a capital crime led to a change as "the sultan of Brunei announced the latter laws would be placed under a moratorium." (Byrnes, 2019) Byrnes points out that in Afghanistan, where "same-sex relationships are not recognized" an **honor killing**, where a relative kills a gay man or woman "to restore the family's honor, are not unheard of." (Byrnes, 2019)

According to the FBI, in 2018, there were 168 reported gender identity hate crimes in the United States. Anti-transgender were 142 of those reports and 26 were anti-gender non-conforming. Since it is well-known that the transgender and gender non-conforming communities are some of the most targeted groups for hate crimes in the United States including violence—44 transgender or gender non-conforming individuals were killed in 2020 according to the Human Rights Campaign, an LGBTQ advocacy group—those hate crime statistics may be underreported. (HRC, n.d.)

In 2018, there were 1,196 reported hate crimes related to sexual orientation. Table 15.6 shows, in order of descending frequency, the group that was targeted for sexual orientation incidents. Anti-gay hate crimes had the largest number of incidents (728).

TABLE 15.6. Sexual Orientation Hate Crimes in the United States in 2018, According to the FBI
Total incidents: 1,196 (Listed in order of descending frequency)

Type of Sexual Orientation Hate Crime	Number of Reported Incidents
Anti-gay	728
Anti-mixed group	303
Anti-lesbian	129
Anti-bisexual	21
Anti-heterosexual	17

Source: FBI, Incidents, offenses, Hate Crime Victims and Known Offenders by Bias Motivation, 2018, Table 1.

An online survey was conducted between April and December 2017 by the Human Rights Campaign Foundation and the University of Connecticut with approximately 12,000 youths between the ages of 13 and 17, who self-identified as LGBTQ. Respondents were solicited through advertisements on social media including Twitter, Instagram, Facebook, and Snapchat, and, as reported by Amy Ellis Nutt in *The Washington Post* in May 2018, three-quarters of the teens indicated they had been verbally threatened because of their sexual identity. Trouble sleeping was reported by 95 percent. Only 26 percent described themselves as feeling safe in their classrooms. Transgender teens seemed to have one of the bigger challenges with about half indicating they were unable to use school restrooms or locker rooms that matched their gender identity.

In Box 15.5, you will find a case highlight provided by the U.S. Justice Department at their website entitled, "Sexual Orientation," with the subtitle, "Assisting Communities Facing Conflict and Tension Based on Sexual Orientation." The case that is highlighted refers to a gay student who was attacked in the bathroom at the university he was attending. As you will see, the unfortunate hate crime incident led to a training initiative for students, faculty, and law enforcement related to the LGBTQ community. In the case highlight, the references to CRS stand for Community Relations Service, which is part of the Department of Justice (DOJ).

Box 15.3. Case Highlight

In March 2018, a University of Montana-Missoula male student was attacked in a campus men's restroom. The assailant urinated on the victim and used an anti-gay slur. The victim did not report the incident until encouraged by university faculty. The victim then submitted a complaint to the Title IX office, which subsequently reported the complaint to campus police.

CRS learned about the incident and contacted the university with information about available services. At the time, university leaders asked CRS to provide training and conflict resolution services for faculty, students and campus law enforcement. On November 30, 2018, CRS facilitated a Hate Crimes Forum for the approximately 60 members of the campus community to strengthen campus safety, define hate crimes and bias incidents, provide information on how to report a hate crime or bias incident, and encourage an atmosphere of inclusion for all students. The three-panel program included community advocates and representatives from law enforcement, the Montana Human Rights bureau, and the Montana Human Rights Network. Staff from university resource centers, including the Student Advocacy Resource Center; the Diversity Advisory Council to the President; and the University Branch Center, a resource center for underrepresented students, spoke about how the campus community could respond to hate crimes and bias incidents on and off campus in their community.

Source: U.S. Justice Department, "Strengthening Hate Crime Awareness on a University Campus Missoula, MT"

VICTIMS OF HUMAN TRAFFICKING

Human trafficking has also been called modern slavery. It is an international crime with victims from around the world. Those victims may end up in American cities because they have been trafficked through promises, deceit, and sometimes even by kidnapping. Human trafficking victims are of all ages, but some groups, such as **throwaway** or **runaway** teens, are more vulnerable to becoming victims. Throwaways are teens whose parents have thrown them out of their apartment or home and runaways are teens who have voluntarily left. Desperate to make money, and despondent over their situation, these teens may end up getting trafficked as prostitutes.

Human Trafficking Search (HTS) is a project of the O.L. Pathy Family Foundation (OLP), a private foundation dedicated to ending human trafficking, among other social issues. It was started in 2006 According to their website, this a huge problem: "While it is difficult to quantify the number of victims of human trafficking because the crime is inherently underground, the **International Labor Organization** estimates that ***40.3 million*** people were victims of modern slavery in 2016. Of those ***40.3 million***, almost **25 *million*** were victims of forced labor and ***15.4 million*** were in forced marriage. There is an average of 5.4 victims of trafficking for every 1,000 people in the world." (HTS.org)

Young people from within the United States and from countries around the world, especially poorer ones, might be told that there is a wonderful job waiting for them in a certain city. They may be promised work in a factory, a job as a nanny, or even work as a model for a photographer. Once they arrive, their designated contact, actually a trafficker, may take away their passports and inform them that they are now under the complete control of the trafficker if they want to eventually get their passport back. Some are willing to put up with the situation, even though they are being trafficked and often also physically abused, because they feel it is better than the conditions in the country that they fled from. According to human trafficking expert Professor Louise Shelley these groups are especially active in trafficking women for sex: "Russian-speaking, Thai, Japanese *yakuza* (a crime syndicate), and Indian" (Shelley, 2010: 5-6)

Some boys and girls who end up being trafficked, especially from the poorest countries, have actually been sold by their parents because they were unable to care for all their children. (Shelley, 2010: 97-98)

Organized crime has become involved in human trafficking because it is very lucrative. As Shelley notes in her book, *Human Trafficking*, "Traffickers choose to trade in humans . . . because there are low start-up costs, minimal risks, high profits, and large demand. For organized crime groups, human beings have one added advantage over drugs: they can be sold repeatedly." (Shelley, 2010: 3)

According to Shelley, trafficking is the second most profitable transnational crime, after drug dealing, but more profitable than selling arms, which is number three. (Shelley, 2015: 7)

Even scarier is Professor Shelley's revelation that profit is not the only reason behind human traffickers. There are even worse motives. She writes, "Some consciously engage in this activity to fund a terrorist group, a guerilla movement, or an insurgency. Others trade in people to provide suicide bombers." (Shelley, 2010: 3)

In 2000, and with reauthorization in 2003, 2005, and 2008, Congress and the Presidents signed into law "The Trafficking Victims Protection Act (TVPA)." The two types of trafficking that are targeted are sex trafficking and labor trafficking. The TVPA defines these types of trafficking acts in this way:

> "Sex trafficking in which a commercial sex act is induced by force, fraud, or coercion, or in which the person induced to perform such an act has not attained 18 years of age."
>
> "The recruitment, harboring, transportation, provision, or obtaining of a person for labor or services through the use of force, fraud, or coercion for the purpose of subjection to involuntary servitude, peonage, debt bondage, or slavery." (Bureau of Justice Assistance, Anti-Human Trafficking Task Force Initiative.)

Here is the story of a 21-year-old sex trafficking victim, reprinted from the website of the Department of Homeland Security. The name is fictitious and some of the details were changed to protect the victim's identity:

> I was 17 around when I met "Robert." It started off with me and my friend meeting him for social purposes. It just went on for about nine months and we were living in different hotels the entire time and I don't even remember how many men there were. I was a runaway and wasn't living anywhere stable, so since I was underage most of the time, I sort of needed him in order to get hotels and move around.
>
> I had already been a prostitute since I was 15 and I think I just didn't even know what was right or wrong and how I should be treated. Towards the end, he held me against my will in a hostage situation and forced me to prostitute and took all the money and just beat me severely.
>
> The last time I saw him, he was just beating me until he was absolutely tired. I was covered in bruises. My face was completely disfigured and it's causing me issues with my back to this day because of the way he was beating me and torturing me. That was probably the worst. There was a client in the room, and he was having an issue with something I couldn't do because I was all beat up. I didn't want to do it anymore. I didn't want to do anything. He wanted the money back. When Robert and him were talking I ran out of the room and somehow was able to run faster than him.
>
> I didn't tell anyone. I kept it to myself until I got a call from the FBI that he'd been arrested for something else and asked would I talk. Having to go face everything and realize how serious everything was. For the longest time I didn't even think it was that serious.
>
> At the trial, it felt empowering to look at him the entire time. I'm sure it drove him crazy. He can never touch me but he had to look at me and listen and it made me feel good.
>
> I had to learn that if I don't at least have some kind of love and value for myself, no one ever will. My advice to other girls would be to let people help you. It's not your fault and that you didn't deserve it. It's OK to be hurt about it because a lot of people will act like it never happened, because that's what I was going to do too. — "Laura" 21
>
> *Source:* U.S. Department of Homeland Security website.

In Box 15.4, you will find guidelines from the National Human Trafficking Resource Center about how to identify human trafficking victims from their behavior.

Box 15.4. Identifying Human Trafficking Victims

Human trafficking may occur in the following situations:

- Prostitution and escort services;
- Pornography, stripping, or exotic dancing;
- Massage parlors;
- Sexual services publicized on the internet or in newspapers;
- Agricultural or ranch work;
- Factory work or sweatshops;
- Businesses like hotels, nail salons or home-cleaning services;
- Domestic labor (cleaning, childcare, elder-care, etc. within a home);
- Restaurants, bars, or cantinas; or
- Begging, street peddling, or door-to-door sales

Victims of human trafficking may exhibit any of the following:

- Evidence of being controlled either physically or psychologically;
- Inability to leave home or place of work;
- Inability to speak for oneself or share one's own information;
- Information is provided by someone accompanying the individual;
- Loss of control of one's own identification documents (ID or passport);
- Have few or no personal possessions;
- Owe a large debt that the individual is unable to pay off; or
- Loss of sense of time or space, not knowing where they are or what city or state they are in.

Source: Reprinted from "Identifying Victims of Human Trafficking" Fact Sheet from the National Human Trafficking Resource Center

Here is an example of two human trafficking victims. The Department of Homeland Security, along with two other government agencies, were able to finally stop the trafficker:

> The trafficker, a former resident of Georgia and a citizen of Nigeria, traveled to her home country in 2001 and enticed a 17-year old girl to come to the United States to work as her nanny. Once here, she abused the girl, beating her for not cleaning well, for not responding fast enough to her crying child, and for talking back to her. A witness to the abuse, a friend of hers, helped the victim escape. The defendant was not deterred and traveled back to Nigeria to lure a second victim, who was subjected to the same treatment and abuse. Eventually, the second victim also escaped. This case was investigated by Homeland Security Investigations (HIS), the FBI and the State Department's Diplomatic Security Services. It was complicated by the fact that the defendant left the country during the investigation. The defendant was found and arrested at a Houston airport as she tried to re-enter the country. The defendant was prosecuted and convicted on eight counts by a federal jury.
>
> *Source:* Homeland Security, "Blue campaign,""Imprisoned In Your Neighborhood"

PROSTITUTION

Prostitution (or "sex work") is legal and regulated in some countries, such as Germany, Austria, Greece, and Switzerland, and in some counties in the state of Nevada, but it is still illegal everywhere else. (Henslin, 2020: 50) Prostitution has also been linked to human trafficking since it is a way to earn money that teens, men, and women especially from countries around the world can be thrown into. (Shelley, 2010: 54-55, 73)

The tie between prostitution and human trafficking occurs when some victims, under the control of the traffickers who take their passport away, are forced to become prostitutes. If they work in a city where prostitution is illegal, they may be reluctant to get their health care needs attended to. That may make them more vulnerable to getting STDs (sexually transmitted diseases) as well as decreasing the likelihood they will report to the police about physical abuse by their customers. The crime associated with prostitution is that of solicitation, or asking someone to engage in sex for money. The customers of a prostitute, who might previously have been known as a *hooker* but is generally now known by the preferred term of *sex worker*, may be referred to as a *john* or a *trick*.

Human trafficking expert and Professor Louise Shelley shares the results of a study by Potterat, et al. that the workplace homicide rate for prostitutes is dramatically higher than for those in occupations known to be extremely dangerous. The workplace homicide rate during the 1980s in the United States for prostitutes is 204 per 100,000 individuals compared to 4 per 100,000 for female liquor store workers, known to be a dangerous occupation, or compared to 29 per 100,000, for male taxicab drivers, another occupation that is known to be a more dangerous one. (Shelley, 2010: 73; Potterat, et. a., 2009). Shelley continues by sharing a Canadian commission that found that the death rate for prostitutes was *forty times* higher when compared to that of the overall population. (Italics added) (Shelley, 2010: 73-74; Farley, 2006)

In her article published in *Gender Issues*, "Prostitution and Human Trafficking for Sexual Exploitation," Svitlana Batsyukova points out an important distinction between prostitution and sex trafficking. She writes, "The difference between those two is that in the case of prostitution, women, girls, and men chose their path voluntarily (depending on the law, this may be legal or not, but this is what they chose to do for a living); in the case of human trafficking they are usually forced into prostitution and other sex services." (Batsyukova, 2007)

PEOPLE WITH DISABILITIES AND VICTIMIZATION

Those who are physically disabled, as well as those who are intellectually or developmentally disabled, or dealing with mental illness or disorders, are especially vulnerable to victimization. In general, those who are in any of these categories tend to be more dependent on others. That makes them open to abuse by unscrupulous caregivers or, depending on the disability, to being unable to get out of situations as quickly as others, such as potential robberies on the street, or to size up situations and realize that they are in jeopardy and get away. Mogens Nygaard Christoffersen addressing this issue in his research article published in *Child Abuse & Neglect*, stated that "statistics on crime against adolescents show that adolescents with disabilities have a higher risk of victimization than other adolescents." (Christoffersen, 2019; Fisher, Hodapp, & Dykens, 2008; Fitzsimons, 2009; Harrell, 2016; Jones, et al., 2012; Leeb, et al., 2012; Marge, 2003; Petersilia, 2001; Spencer, et al., 2005)

There are many groups of individuals within the broad category of people with disabilities who may be more susceptible to victimization. These categories include those with physical disabilities as well as those who have **intellectual disabilities** or **developmental disabilities**. Those who have mental health disorders, disabilities, or illnesses are considered in a separate section below.

Persons with Physical Disabilities

According to Hughes et. al., worldwide, 15 percent of adults have a disability. (Hughes et al., *The Lancet*, 2012) This is a group of potential victims that needs to be addressed since the disabled have a much greater risk of victimization. Hughes et al. pinpoints these reasons behind their increased risk of interpersonal violence:

- Exclusion from education and employment
- The need for personal assistance with daily living
- Reduced physical and emotional defenses
- Communication barriers that hamper the reporting of violence
- Societal stigma
- Discrimination (Hughes, et al., *The Lancet*, 2012: 1621)

Karin Willison has been in a wheelchair all her life due to cerebral palsy at birth. On November 28, 2014, she was attacked in her home in San Diego, California and thrown out of her wheelchair by a masked intruder who turned out to be a former home caregiver and her boyfriend. They were both found guilty of this and other crimes and sent to prison. The crime and subsequent death threats sent by the perpetrators so terrified her, that Karin packed up and moved to the Midwest.

Willison, who is a writer, has a website, https://www.freewheelintravel.org/, where she writes about life and travel with a disability. She says that since people with disabilities are "set up to be victimized," she recommends taking these precautions to decrease the likelihood that what happened to her will happen to another person with a physical disability:

1. Whenever possible, try to hire someone you get through a referral so there is some accountability.
2. Before you hire someone, do an extensive background check.
3. Look up whoever you are considering employing and see who they live with.
4. Check the applicant's social media for any red flags. (Yager, 2021)

Audrey Demmitt, R.N., summarizes the findings of the National Crime Victimization Survey from 2009 to 2014 in her article, "Crime Against Persons with Disabilities: The Facts." published in *Vision Aware*, about the increased potential for being a crime victim of those who have visual impairment. She notes these interesting conclusions from the study:

- Those with disabilities have a three times higher rate of victimization than those without disabilities.
- Visual impairment was the only physical disability category where females were more likely to be the victim than males (31.9 per 1,000 versus 22.8 per 1,000 respectively).
- Visual impairment was the only category of disability where those with the condition were less likely than those without disabilities to report to police that they had been the victim of a crime.

- Age groups with the lowest to the highest rate of victimization were 16- to 19-year-old (highest) followed by 12- to 15-year-old with 65 and over having the lowest victimization rate for those with and without disabilities.
- Those with disabilities have more victimization during the day (59%) compared to those without disabilities (53%). (Demmit, n.d.)

Two of the issues that you need to be aware of regarding physical disabilities and victims are that there may be underreporting of the crimes and there may be caregiver abuse. The National Council on Disability proposed that the leading risk factor for becoming a crime victim is being a victim previously. Unfortunately, those with physical disabilities can be more vulnerable to victimization and once that first victimization occurs, they may be victimized again, what is known as **repeat victimization or poly-victimization**. This recurring victimization pattern is not just associated with those with physical disabilities. Researchers discovered that among the mentally disordered victims of violence that were studied (N=262), "across four waves of data collected during a 1-year longitudinal study." (Teasdale, Daigle, and Ballard, 2014) Sixty-four percent of victims had a recurring victimization "at a later point in time." But there were some distinctions based on the type of mental disorders (substance abuse disorder or major depressions versus those with manic disorder or a schizophrenia spectrum disorder.) (Teasdale, et al., 2014)

In July 2021, a 10-episode mini-series entitled *Dr. Death* premiered on the Peacock network. It told the true story of a Dallas neurosurgeon, Christopher Duntsch, played by Joshua Jackson, who performed surgeries on those with disabilities related to their spines or necks. He was so incompetent that he left his patients worse off after the surgery; one had to use a wheelchair, another was left a quadriplegic and two died. The series also starred Alec Baldwin and Christian Slater as two doctors determined to stop the doctor from operating any more. The drama highlights how vulnerable the disabled are since they have to completely trust that their physician is skilled and competent and that they will be better off after their surgery. (Ellis, 2021; Dorian, et. al., 2019)

Persons with Intellectual and Developmental Disabilities

The American Association on Intellectual and Developmental Disabilities (AAIDD) notes that intellectual disability is a type of disability within the "umbrella" term of developmental disabilities. Intellectual disability "covers the same population of individuals who were diagnosed previously with mental retardation in number, kind, level type, duration of disability, and the need of people with this disability for individualized services and supports." (AAID, "Frequently Asked Questions on Intellectual Disability.")

Like other individuals who are disabled, those with developmental or intellectual disabilities are at greater risk of victimization. The National Council on Disability in its report, "Breaking the Silence on Crime Victims with Disabilities," discovered this fact as reported in their 2007 statement: from 15,000 to 19,000 people with developmental disabilities are raped each year in the United States. Although it is more than a decade since that fact was shared, the increased risk of the intellectually disabled to rape and other crimes of interpersonal violence are trends worth noting.

Fortunately, sectors in the criminal justice system are aware of the increased risk of victimization of those who are intellectually or developmentally disabled and adjusting to minimize or avoid those incidents. For example, at the Federal Prison in Danbury, Connecticut (FCI Danbury) to reduce the greater likelihood of intellectually disabled inmates getting victimized, they have a paid buddy system. An inmate with normal cognitive and mental abilities applies for the job, and is carefully screened, to reside in a special unit in the facility. The two inmates live together in a cell. The mentor job is one of the higher paid jobs at the facility. (Educational tours of FCI Danbury Correctional Facility by this author, 2017, 2019)

The Office for Victims of Crime and the national nonprofit organization, NOVA (National Organization for Victim Assistance), partnered on a project known as "Working with Crime Victims with Disabilities." There is a website devoted to this issue. It is called End Abuse of People with Disabilities, which is a project of the Center on Victimization and Safety at the Vera Institute of Justice. (Tyiskka, 1998)

MENTAL DISORDERS, MENTAL ILLNESS, AND PTSD

The relationship among mental disorders or emotional problems, mental illness, and PTSD and becoming a victim is a huge topic. In this section, let us explore some of the key issues that need to be considered for a rounded view of victimology and victimization. This is an important issue to consider, especially for the severely mentally ill. As Linda A. Teplin et al., in their study "Crime Victimization in Adults with Severe Mental Illness: Comparison With the National Crime Victimization Survey," discovered that, within the past year, those with severe mental illness (SMI) were victims of crime at a rate more than *11 times higher* than the general population. Among the 16 agencies that they studied, more than one quarter of persons with SMI had been victims of a violent crime within the past year. (Teplin, et al., 2005: 911.)

The reason this is such a challenging topic to explore related to victimization is that it involves individuals with a range of mental challenges, from stress and everyday emotional issues to mental disorders that are treated with medication and through therapy, to SMI (severe mental illness) to situational issues, such as PTSD (post-traumatic stress disorder) and even trauma responses to a current or previous victimization.

Mental Disorders, Mental State, and Victimization

How might having emotional or psychological challenges make someone more vulnerable to victimization? This question actually goes all the way back to the earliest victimologists. As you may recall, Hans von Hentig and Beniamin Mendelsohn pointed out through their typologies that there were mental factors that might be tied to victimization. Especially consider von Hentig's eighth type, the depressed, as noted in Schafer's *The Victim and His Criminal.* (Schafer, 1968; Von Hentig, 1948)

But we have fortunately come a long way from the outdated views about those with mental disorders compared to the days of von Hentig in the 1940s and 1950s. Even our terminology has changed.

Mental health issues that impact potential victims, as well as offenders, include everything from anxiety, depression, psychosis including schizophrenia to PTSD (post-traumatic stress disorders), and phobias. You know by now that except in the strictest incidences where that idea is justified, victimologists today try to steer clear of the victim blame mindset that was previously more prevalent. But it is definitely hard not to consider psychological predispositions in the victim's mental state as a factor.

The mental states that make someone more prone to victimization can be obvious and clear or subtle. In the obvious and clear realm, consider someone who has extremely low self-esteem and a history of allowing family members and even friends to take advantage of her.

She is of course set up to be a more likely victim of domestic abuse and even violence. She or he might put herself or himself in situations where a criminal can take advantage of them because they are unable to say "no." For example, consider an out of work employee who is so desperate to make money that she falls for overtures from a scammer about a mystery shopper offer only to find herself scammed out of several thousand dollars. Her stressed state of mind contributed to her susceptibility and led her to accept and act on an offer that she might have scrutinized more carefully had she not been so upset over her financial situation.

Victimization of Those with Mental Illness

An interesting article, "Crime victimization of persons with severe mental illness in Taiwan," published in the *Australian and New Zealand Journal of Psychiatry*, focuses on whether or not those who have severe mental illness (SMI) are more likely to be victims of crime than the general population. Chien-Chi Hsu and colleagues had 155 subjects in their study between the ages of 17 and 66 with the mean age of 37.4. (Chien-Chi Hsu, et al., 2009)

Face-to-face interviews were conducted, and respondents were asked if they had been the victim of a crime in the last 12 months. Out of the total number of respondents, 26 patients, or 16.8 percent, had been the victim of at least one personal crime in the previous 12 months. That is a lot higher than the annual prevalence rate of 11.3 percent. The most common non-violent crime was theft, and the most common violent crime was assault. What is especially notable is the rate of victimization for violent crime for the SMI that they studied compared to the general population: 251.6 incidents per 1,000 persons per year compared to just 68.1 in the general population.

Inpatients were significantly more likely to be victimized (24.6%) compared to day-care (or out) patients (11.7%). Those with a history of alcohol abuse (52.4%), who had a diagnosis of a major affective disorder (30.3%), were more likely to have been victimized than those who had schizophrenia (7.6%). (Chien-Chi Hsu, et al., 2009)

Those with Mental Illness and the Criminal Justice System

Judge Steve Leifman helped to develop an alternative to incarceration program for those with mental illness or disorders in Dade County, Florida. Before this program, a judge had only two choices when presented with an offender who had been arrested for various crimes: send him to prison or set him free. If the offender needed treatment for his mental illness, how could the courts make sure he or she received it?

Judge Steve Leifman says, "The longer I am a judge, the more convinced I am that prison and jail for most people with serious mental illnesses does not work. Prison and jail are not the answer for dealing with people with mental illnesses." (Judge Leifman, 2020)

Fortunately the alternative to incarceration program in Dade County was so successful in dropping the recidivism rate to such low levels that they are building a treatment facility that will offer an in-patient and out-patient option for treatment for these unique individuals.

Gary Nosacek's 25-year-old son had stopped taking his medication for his mental disorders and he thinks that is what led to the violent outburst that caused him to throw his videogame controller at his father when he asked him to turn down the sound. Gary and his wife Cindy, their son's mother, were injured—Gary had two black eyes and a broken nose, and his wife had a cut on her head—and their son was taken away by the police. Fortunately, he was not shot or killed during the arrest because his son had gone up to his room where he did have a collection of knives. (When the police were taking him away, Gary discovered that his son had two weeks' worth of medication in his room. He figured out that his son was putting the medication in his mouth but then spitting it out.)

His son was in jail for several months until a plea deal could be worked out which included pleading guilty to domestic abuse, going to anger management sessions, and meeting with a social worker.

Gary misses his son, but it is the son who used to do charity activities with his father in middle school and high school that he wants back. "That's the guy I remember," he said in our phone interview. "The monster that took him over because he wasn't taking his medication. That guy I have no use for," he continues.

He wants those who will be going into law enforcement or any other part of the criminal justice system to know that when they are dealing with individuals with mental disorders or illness there is "no one size fits all solution," he says. "They have to realize they will be dealing with irrational people and they're confronting a situation that's not rational on the other person's end. You don't know what the other person is going through at the time. You don't know if they're on Mars, if they're hearing voices inside their head telling them to do something. They have to take the cues from what is the situation. Is it totally violent or is the violent part already diffused? You have to stay alert."

Gary says, "People keep saying to me, 'Why do you think that happened? Does he [your son] feel sorry about it?' "

He tries to make it clear to them by answering, "You're trying to rationally explain crazy and you can't. You can't figure out what made sense to him at that time."

In her book, *Insane: America's Criminal Treatment of Mental Illness*, author Alisa Roth points out that between 1950 and 2000, the number of Americans treated in psychiatric institutions shrank from 500,000 to around 50,000. At the same time, the number of men and women who are incarcerated exploded. Roth estimates that roughly half of those incarcerated in the county jails in Michigan have mental illness. In state prisons, she estimates nearly one quarter of the inmates have a mental illness. (Roth, 2018: 2)

A special report by the Bureau of Justice Statistics, "Indicators of Mental Health Problems Reported by Prisoners and Jail Inmates, 2011-12," estimates that 1 in 7 state and federal prisons (14%) and 1 in 4 jail inmates (26%) met the definition within the previous 30 days to the survey for having serious psychological distress (SPD). Here is an even higher statistic to keep in mind: "37% of prisoners and 44% of jail inmates had been told in the past by a mental health professional that they had a mental disorder." (Bureau of Justice Statistics, 2017)

Perhaps the statement made by a veteran female police officer to a student interviewer and allowed to be shared in this textbook, is not that far from the truth: "I have always believed that police officers are social workers with guns." Getting additional training in how to handle those who have mental disorders and illness might be a strong consideration for those going into law enforcement, corrections, and even law, counseling, and rehabilitation. Many police departments, even beginning at the police academy level, are doing just that. It is called Crisis Intervention Training (CIT) or Crisis Intervention Team (CIT) programs. As Rogers et al. point out in their article, "Effectiveness of Police Crisis Intervention Training Programs," of the approximately 1,000 individuals fatally shot by police officers in the United States in 2018, it is estimated that 25 percent of those involved in those shootings were people with mental illness (PMI). (Rogers et al., 2019: 1; Saleh, et al., 2018.)

Certainly, the program started by Judge Steve Leifman, mentioned above, treating those who are arrested who are mentally ill and not career criminals outside of prison is a step in the right direction. It is aiding those with mental illness and disorders so they can get the treatment that they need, it helps to put criminal justice resources into helping those who are criminals, and it helps society by avoiding the confrontations between the mentally ill and law enforcement that too often end with tragic consequences.

There are training models around the world that if adopted here should help reduce the number of tragedies that occur between the mentally ill and the police when called for assistance, or even how the mentally ill are treated if they land in jail or prison. Diversionary programs may be in everyone's best interest—offender, victim, and society. The CIT approach is still being studied for its effectiveness as well as what the standards of training are in the thousands of programs that have been implemented in police precincts throughout the United States and even in Canada, the United Kingdom, and Australia. (Rogers, et al., 2019: 4) The often-cited Memphis model of CIT training includes 40 hours of instruction from community mental health workers, people with mental illness (PMI) and their family members and advocates, as well as police officers who are knowledgeable about CIT. (Rogers, et al., 2019:2). Is that enough training? Here is what Rogers et al. report: "A survey of police officers indicated that CIT-trained officers perceived themselves as less likely to escalate to the use of force in a hypothetical mental health crisis encounter." (Rogers et al., 2019: 4; Steadman and Morrissette, 2016)

As Gary Nosacek's previous excerpted interview indicates, often the victims are family members. That was also the case with Alesia Litteral, whose profile and story follow. Unfortunately, her husband was no longer on much-needed medication for his mental health issues. He had alcoholism problems and on the day described below, he snapped, with double tragic consequences.

Profile Alesia ▪ A Survivor of Attempted Murder by Her Husband Who Had a Drinking Problem and Had Stopped Taking His Medication

No one would deny that 56-year-old Alesia Litteral has had more than her share of tragedies. In 1985, her brother's wife shot him seven times, and he died. Alesia's only child, a son from her first marriage, died at the age of 25 in 2013 from a heroin overdose. Then, in 2019, Alesia was shot seven times and stabbed more than 37 times by her husband, who then committed suicide. "Never in my life did I think that would happen to me," Alesia said in the phone interview with this author. She shared about her husband's ***alcoholism*** *[also known as* ***alcohol use disorder*** *or AUD) and how he was no longer on medication. Then she went into details about what happened that fateful day. She had wanted her husband to leave but since it was Alesia's family home, she did not want to be the one to leave.*

This interview is also an example of what this author mentioned at the beginning of this textbook, namely the idea of situations in victimology that have overlap. Although Alesia's interview is being excerpted in Chapter 15, related to substance abuse and mental illness issues of her husband, it could be included in Chapter 13, "Victims of Assault, Domestic Violence, Stalking, and Elder Abuse," since, in the last year, Alesia reported that they were having domestic violence-related issues.

It [that attack] was the scariest thing I've ever been through. Everybody knew he was an alcoholic. At the clinics, I would stay with him night after night and watch him go through DTs. He was on [medication] for the weeks [before the attack] but they took him off of it because they didn't want him to get addicted.

A few days before this happened, I was trying to get him out of the house.

The day this happened . . . he drank beer and got trashed and then he came home to me. He told me twice, "You're dying tonight bitch. I'm killing you."

I came in the house and called my best friend, but she didn't answer.

My husband walked up to me and he smiled, and he just started shooting and stabbing me. I'm still on voice mail. He's ripping my hair out, trying to get the phone out of my hand, trying to cut my nose off.

There were blood curdling screams. At the very end, all you hear is, "I loved you so much." I mean it's just terrible.

He tortured me. He thought I was dead. I must have blacked out. When I came to, I was at the front door. I didn't know how I got there. I tried to stand up, and I fell down. I [managed] to stand up again. I had four locks.

I managed to throw myself outside. I was screaming for help. My neighbors came out. They heard the shots.

I said, "Call 911." My neighbor's wife came over. She was trying to help me.

[Then] the cops came. None of us knew that he [my husband] was dead. They originally thought somebody came in and tried to kill both of us. They were searching the neighborhood. They were praying over me in the driveway.

My niece was working in the emergency room. She came. She called my half-sister. The doctor told her, "I will do what I can, but I think I'm looking at a corpse."

They didn't think I'd make it, but I did.

They gave me twenty units of blood. I had three surgeries in two days. They put me in a coma for a week. Nobody told me that my husband was dead. As soon as [I was told he was dead] it was a weight lifted off of me. He had been threatening to kill me for a year.

So now I'm in therapy. I'm hoping that I can get through this. I would like to be a speaker. I want to help some people. You just don't know, and people don't listen.

I begged my husband to get help. I was in the hospital [with him] multiple times. "If he doesn't stop drinking, it's going to kill him."

It did kill him, but not in the way he thought it would.

***Question:** What's the number one thing you want people to know from what happened to you?*

Domestic violence is very real. If somebody tells you that they need help, you gotta listen. Here I am. I'm in pain every day. If you're in a situation where you're feeling threatened, get out.

***Question:** Who's been there for you?*

Yes, I do have some good friends. I do have some good friends who are helping me. When I came out of the hospital, when they took the bullets out of me, I had to have my injuries packed and repacked, and I had to be on a wound pack. I had to have that done. People have been bringing me food because of COVID-19, because my immune system is down so far. My protein levels have totally bummed out. People bring me food. People take me to my appointments and stuff like that.

When I first got out of the hospital, I thanked God every day. When this happened, I was on the phone and he was shooting and stabbing. I could see my Mom, my son, my Dad, all my relatives who had passed on and I could see angels around me, protecting me.

***Question:** How long did it take you to get over your injuries?*

I'm still dealing with those. Both my lungs were collapsed. He stabbed me in my kidney. Eighty percent of my liver. He ripped my hair out of my head. He tried to cut the end of my nose off. I still have limited use of my hands. I put my one hand up to block a bullet that was going through my chest area and so the bullet went through my index finger, which broke it. I cannot use that finger. The nerve endings in my hand are extremely raw. I have no strength. He stabbed me in my palm because I was fighting. They took 2 bullets out of my right arm. I still have one in my back. My left hand is completely numb.

I will probably be dealing with this for probably the rest of my life. I have nightmares. I have headaches. I'm in pain all the time.

ALCOHOL, DRUGS, AND SUBSTANCE ABUSE ISSUES

Substance abuse issues could take up an entire chapter or even a textbook of its own. We know, going all the way back to Dr. Marvin Wolfgang's 1957 study of victim-precipitated homicide, that there was a "*significant* association between VP [victim precipitated] homicide and alcohol in the homicide situation." Note that the italicizing of *significant* was in Wolfgang's original article.

Since an entire chapter on substance abuse, crime, and victimization is outside the scope of this textbook, this author will highlight key facts about the issue related to victimization that readers need to know. This information is compiled from various sources, as indicated after each statement. Readers are encouraged to do further reading on this topic if they wish to find out more about substance abuse and victimization.

- According to Ullman et al., women with histories of sexual victimization and other traumas, such as child abuse, may be more inclined to drink as a coping behavior, perhaps in response to PTSD symptoms. (Ulman, Relyea, Peter-Hagene, and Vasquez, 2013.)
- Since 2005, 77 fraternity members have died from hazing-related rituals; alcohol is the cause in 82 percent of fatal hazing incidents. (The Recovery Village, n.d.)
- According to the CDC (Centers for Disease Control and Prevention), "in 2019, 70,630 drug overdose deaths occurred in the United States for an age-adjusted rate of 21.6 per 100,000 standard population." (Hedegaard, et al., 2020)
- How many overdose deaths were due to **fentanyl**, a synthetic opioid that is 50 to 100 times more potent than morphine? It is sometimes mixed with heroin or cocaine, without the user's knowledge, which can have fatal consequences. An estimated 36,000 people died from overdoses in 2019 related to synthetic opioids. (CDC, 2021)
- "Alcohol was present in 74 percent of the VP [victim-precipitated] homicide cases and in 60 percent of the non-VP cases. The proportional difference results in a significant association between alcohol and VP homicide." (Wolfgang, 1957: 8-9)
- "Victims had been drinking immediately prior to their death in more VP cases (69 %) than in non-VP cases (47 %)." (Wolfgang, 1957: 9)
- "Of the 370 [homicide] cases for which there was adequate information, intoxicants were present, according to police records, in 53.5 percent of the homicidal scenes." (Voss and Hepburn, 1968: 5050}
- "The ingestion of alcohol was more common in homicide than in assault, as was a drinking episode between offender and victim prior to the crime." (Pittman and Handy, 1964: 470)
- "A *significant* association was found between VP rapes and the presence of alcohol. Alcohol was present in the rape situation (alcohol present either in the victim alone or in both the offender and the victim), in 53 percent of the VP cases and in 25 percent of the non-VP cases." (Italics in original.) (Amir, 1967: 496)
- **Neonatal abstinence syndrome** is a condition when babies are born addicted to heroin, barbiturates, alcohol, or cocaine, because the mother was abusing drugs during her pregnancy. Those babies need to go through a painful withdrawal after they are born which can include having tremors and being unable to sleep. (Henslin, 2020:103; Hamdan, 2010; Rosen, 2017)
- Those with expensive drug addiction habits can victimize family members to pay for their drugs. For example, a man in the United Kingdom admitted that he was forging his mother's signature on checks to fund his $300 a day drug habit. "Stealing from loved ones is all too common among addicts . . ." (UK Rehab, n.d.)

- Twenty-year-old Stone Foltz died on March 7, 2021 after drinking "'copious amounts of alcohol'" during a fraternity rush event at an Ohio University, according to Joe Harrington's article on hazing. (Harrington, 2021)

ANIMAL CRUELTY AND WILDLIFE VICTIMS

Americans care about how their animals are treated. Prominent New Yorker Henry Bergh founded the ASPCA (American Society for the Prevention of Cruelty to Animals) on April 10, 1866 (ASPCA.org), almost a decade before he helped to found, in 1874, at the behest of Etta Wheeler, the New York Society for the Prevention of Cruelty to Children (NYSPCC). Wheeler was concerned about the way eight-year-old Mary Ellen Wilson was being treated by her foster parents. (Mallon, 2013) The NYSPCC credits the founding with Elbridge Gerry as well as Bergh (nyspcc.org).

A detailed discussion of animal cruelty victims is outside the scope of this victimology textbook. However, it does need to be mentioned as a category of special victims. Animal cruelty is usually a misdemeanor, handled with a fine, but if the cruelty is done maliciously with grave indifference to life it can be elevated to a felony. There is a specialized field known as **veterinary forensics**. In addition to observation of an animal, that field enables veterinarians to obtain evidence of animal abuse through collecting of what is known as *trace evidence* in forensics as well as *DNA samples*.

Enjuris®, an information platform on the internet providing legal information, posted an article entitled, "Can I Sue Someone for Killing or Hurting My Dog?" contributed by an Enjuris Editor. A key point shared in the article is that how animal injuries or death are handled varies from state to state. (This is a different issue than owner liability if a dog or other animal bites or scratches someone. That also varies by state.) The article points out that some states consider dogs and other pets in the "'personal property'" category. "They will award enough for you to go buy another dog, but nothing else." (Enjuris.com) There are exceptions, however, such as a 2006 case of pet owners in Ontario, Canada, successfully suing a kennel where they had boarded their dog when they went on vacation. The dog was able to escape and was never found. The pet owner was so upset when she learned what had happened to her dog that she had insomnia and nightmares, causing her to miss work. The court ruled that the kennel was negligent because they had not taken the proper measures to make sure the fence was secured. The pet owner was awarded $2,527 including $1,417 "in general damages for pain and suffering associated with the loss of the dog.") (Enjuris.com/blog)

Marcus, a "backyard dog," was rescued by PETA's Community Animal Project fieldworkers in September 2019 after suffering from a flea infestation that caused anemia and a chewed off tail. Brought to PETA, Marcus received blood transfusions, was neutered, and there was surgery done on his tail.
Photo credit: Courtesy of People for the Ethical Treatment of Animals (PETA)

In all 50 states, dog fighting is considered a felony. The most infamous dog fighting conviction that led to prison time is that of Atlanta Falcons quarterback Michael Vick who pleaded guilty back in November 2007 to charges related to a dogfighting enterprise on land that Vick owned. According to the report, Vick pleaded guilty to helping to kill six to eight pit bulls among other charges. (Cleveland19.com, 2007) Vick served 19 months at a federal prison in Leavenworth, Kansas. (*New York Times*, 2009)

Animal Abuse and Its Ties to Human Violence and Other Crimes

Similar to the definitions of child or elder abuse, animal abuse is any act of abuse or neglect that is intentional such as physically hitting an animal, failing to provide it with proper food or drink, and even keeping an animal in a hot car where it may expire.

In March 2018 this emaciated companion animal and "backyard dog" was visited by PETA's Community Animal Project.
Photo credit: Courtesy of People for the Ethical Treatment of Animals (PETA)

Seeing a parallel among animal cruelty or abuse to child or elder abuse is appropriate because all three populations, especially in the case of child and animal abuse, are totally dependent on their caregivers for survival. Failing to give animals the attention that they need is not as clearly a case of animal cruelty, although it is to be expected that animal owners will provide such nurturance. But certainly physical abuse can be easily documented, and it is against the law. What is known as **Intentional Animal Torture and Cruelty (IATC)** offenses are not just offenses to the animals. The perpetrators may also use those behaviors to punish their victims, usually family members including children and seniors, by tormenting their pets. (Elkins, 2019)

As Faye Elkins writes in the *Dispatch*, an e-newsletter of the COPS Office (United States Department of Justice), "FBI research indicates that most serial killers, school shooters, and mass murderers tortured animals as children." (Elkins, 2019)

Cynthia Hodges published an extensive article entitled, "The Link: Cruelty to Animals and Violence Towards People," that includes no fewer than 121 references. Hodges research led her to conclude: "Communities must acknowledge that the abuse of any living being is unacceptable and endangers *everyone* . . . . Recognizing that cruelty to animals is a significant form of aggressive and antisocial behavior may help further the understanding and prevention of violence." (Hodges, 2008)

Researchers Arluke, Levin, Luke, and Ascione, however, caution against being too hasty to draw a simplistic cause and effect between animal abuse and violence toward humans. In "The Relationship of Animal Abuse to Violence and Other Forms of Antisocial Behavior," they note that their research suggests there may be a link, but it is not clear cut or consistent. They point out that it is commonly believed that serial killer Jeffrey Dahmer tortured animals. However, their research found otherwise. They write: "There is no evidence that Dahmer abused animals, only that he was fascinated with dead animals and collected road kill (Fox & Levin, 1994)." (Arluke, Levin, et al., 1999: 972.)

There is an association known as The National Link Coalition. It is a membership organization founded on the belief that there is a link between cruelty to animals, and abusive behavior toward children, romantic partners, and the elderly. As they state on the homepage of their website: "Mistreating animals is no longer seen as an isolated incident that can be ignored: it is often an indicator or predictor crime and a 'red flag' warning sign that other family members in the household may not be safe." (Nationallinkcoalition.org)

Check out the work of Professor Piers Beirne at the University of Southern Maine. He has been researching and writing about animal abuse for decades. He has even coined a term for it: **nonspeciesist criminology**. (Beirne, 1999)

Dr. Kimberly Spanjol shares about the emerging field of Green Criminology, which includes animal abuse and cruelty as some of its concerns:

> The victimization of nature and non-human animals began receiving attention from criminologists in the early 1990s, approximately three decades after the environmental and animal rights movements gained traction. Green Criminology examines interconnected harms committed against humans, non-humans and the environment (Beirne and South, 2007). Associated with Eco-Global Criminology, Transnational Environmental Crime, Non-Speciesist Criminology, and Wildlife Criminology (Beirne, 2009; Cazaux, 2017; White, 2011; Nurse and Wyatt, 2020) the sub-field of Green Criminology is often thought of as a branch of "White-Collar Crime"—that is economic, corporate, and state sponsored crime—as perpetrators are frequently corporate entities and government institutions that are often in collusion. However, perpetrators can be individual actors as well (White, 2011). For example, governments, transnational corporations, military, and ordinary people all commit harms and crimes that impact humans, non-human animals, and the environment, and are of interest to Green Criminologists (Beirne and South, 2012). (Spanjol, March 14, 2021)

Wildlife Animal Victims

A subcategory within the field of animal abuse and cruelty is that of cruelty and especially the killing of wildlife, particularly unique endangered species. Many never even heard about wildlife animal victims, or perhaps they did not consider wildlife killings, until the July 2015 killing of Cecil the Lion. A dentist from the United States killed Cecil the Lion outside Zimbabwe's Hwange National Park and that killing caused an international uproar. Cecil was 13 years old. The lion lived in that national park. The lion was said to be "well known to visitors" (Hall, 2016, republished 2018). In the article, "Cecil the Lion Died Amid Controversy—Here's What Happened Since," Jani Hall notes that when the international uproar finally quieted down, the shooter was able to produce documentation showing that he had the right to kill the lion. He explained he "said he didn't know that the animal he'd shot was the beloved Cecil." (Hall, 2016) One of the outcomes of Cecil's killing was that more than 40 airlines banned taking trophies from killing any of these animals on their planes: lions, rhinos, elephants, leopards, and Cape buffalo. (Cummings, 2015)

There are many prominent nonprofit wildlife and conservationist organizations working on behalf of wildlife animals to slow down or eliminate the killing of endangered wildlife. Headquartered in Switzerland, and started in 1963, CITIES (the Convention on International Trade in Endangered Species of Wild Fauna and Flora) is to make sure that international trade does not destroy particular wild fauna (animals) or flora (plants) species especially of a particular region. (https://cites.org/)

Also started in the 1960s is The International Fund for Animal Welfare (IFAW), founded by Brian Davies in 1969. The original goal was to halt the commercial hunting of whitecoat seals on Canada's East Coast. (IFAW website, ifaw.org)

Here is a list of wildlife animals and birds of prey that the organization is concerned with protecting:

- Tigers
- African bush elephants
- Seals
- Koalas
- Whales
- Pangolins
- North Atlantic Right Whales
- Indian rhinos
- Birds of prey (hawks, owls, eagles, vultures, and falcons) (ifaw.org website)

Koala bear in Australia. Photo credit: Jan Yager, Ph.D.

Another nonprofit organization that is working hard to stop illegal wildlife trade is the World Wildlife Fund (WWF), headquartered in Washington, D.C. In this chapter we addressed human trafficking. Wildlife trafficking is also big business. Some of the illegal activities include poaching of elephants for ivory or killing tigers for their bones and skins. WWF in its article, "Illegal Wildlife Trade," points out that rhino (rhinoceros) poaching in South Africa increased from 13 to 1,004 animals between 2007 and 2013. (WWF.org) For those who are interested in learning more about victims of animal cruelty, as well as victims of wildlife crimes, such as poaching of engendered species, organizations are listed in the Resources section in the back of the chapter.

Natural Disaster Victims

Like animal cruelty victims, a detailed discussion of victims of natural disasters is outside the scope of this textbook. Of course we all know that natural disasters happen. Tornadoes. Hurricanes. Earthquakes. Floods. But what needs to be addressed related to victimology is when those who suffer because of a natural disaster are unduly victimized by neglectful behaviors by those who could have prevented the disaster or, if an unavoidable disaster occurs, who are victimized by such a poor or delayed response to disaster victims that it goes to bordering on a criminal offense. The slow response is considered criminal. Finally, there are those who take advantage of the vulnerable position survivors of natural disasters are in. They commit a wide range of property crimes from stealing and looting to overcharging on repairs to telephone or online scams offering government or private sector help that never comes.

An example of victimizations related to a natural disaster is what happened in the aftermath of Hurricane Katrina. It hit the city of New Orleans especially hard as well as surrounding areas. It was a multi-day event lasting from August 23-31, 2005.

There were so many crimes related to Hurricane Katrina that in September 2015, the Department of Justice established the Hurricane Katrina Fraud Task Force. The new Task Force was charged with "deterring, detecting, and prosecuting individuals who try to take advantage of disasters related to Hurricanes Katrina, Rita, Wilma, Gustav, and Ike, as well as other natural disasters." (Govtech.com, News Report, 2008) During its third year of operation, from 2007-2008, it was announced that 907 individuals were going to be charged in 43 federal judicial districts across the country in disaster-related fraud cases. (Govtech.com, News Report 2008)

The crimes can be worse than fraud. It took more than ten years, but in February 2019 a ten-year sentence was finally given to Roland Bourgeois Jr., 56, a white man, related to his shotgun attack on three Black men in the mayhem that ensued after Hurricane Katrina in August 2005. He had originally been indicted in 2010. Bourgeois' guilty plea in October 2019 ruled out a trial. (McGill, AP News, 2019)

FEMA, which is part of the U.S. Department of Homeland Security, is the government agency in charge of responses to natural disasters. Disaster victims deserve as immediate a response as is feasible without unduly risking the lives of those providing immediate help including evacuations, emergency shelter, food, and other essential supplies. Nonprofit and volunteer organizations like the American Red Cross and local, state, and other federal agencies may also provide aid.

Secondary to the actual natural disaster is for the public to be alerted to possible scams that may divert much-needed contributions from real charities to bogus ones that steal the funds. Anyone seeking to donate after a natural disaster has to be extra vigilant in checking out the authenticity of any disaster-related charities. The ones that are scams will take a scam victim's money and also gain contact details and possibly even their credit card information from the victims. The other problem with this type of a scam is that the money does not get to the disaster victims but instead it goes to the fraudsters.

As the tragedy of a collapsed building in Surfside, Florida leaving dozens dead or homeless was unfolding in June 2021, unfortunately so were the scammers and fraudsters. They were trying to get money from generous, caring citizens who just wanted to donate through crowdfunding sites to pay for funerals or to help out survivors who had lost their homes and all their possessions. (Musumed, 2021; Montgomery, 2021)

Three sites that enable potential contributors to check out the legitimacy of a charity include Charity Navigator, Charity Watch, and GuideStar.

Many Americans may be unaware that the National Center for Disaster Fraud (NCDF), which is a partnership between the U.S. Department of Justice and different regulatory and law enforcement agencies, was formed in 2005 after Hurricane Katrina. It handles any claims of fraud related to natural disasters including coronavirus-related (COVID-19) complaints. There is a NCDF Hotline (see the listing in the Resources below) or victim claims can be submitted through the NCDF Web Complaint Form (the link is also included in the Resource section below).

Although the many types of disaster-related victimizations that occurred after Hurricane Katrina may be the most well-known including the deaths that were said to be caused by delays in getting help, businesses (and their owners) were the victims of looting, vandalism, and fraud. In 2016, for example, Pamela Pritt reported on the warning from FEMA about scammers who might pose as inspectors, government representatives, volunteers, or contractors. This was related to the aftermath of the West Virginian flood that was referred to as "a 1,000-year flood event." (Pritt, 2016)

In addition to the violence or property crime victimizations that may occur during or following a natural disaster, just like with non-disaster-related victimizations, there is the potential for PTSD (post-traumatic stress disorder) and other psychological reactions to the natural disaster including depression and anxiety. Rhonda Rees, a publicist, shared in an interview how hard it was on her when she lost everything in one of the biggest fires that ravaged California at the end of 2018. Rhonda said in a phone interview: "I was living in a nice mobile home community. One hundred ten of our homes burned down. After my home was destroyed, I lived in 22 places in a year. I posted about it on Facebook. I didn't really have family and friends come through for me, but I got more love from total and complete strangers. There were disaster relief, community, church and synagogue groups that assigned people to help me. They were wonderful in many ways. The overall snub I received from many individuals who knew me over the years, I took on the chin [but] it bothered me a lot. Here's the biggest disaster of my life, where are they [friends and family]? I had strangers give me thousands of dollars, and clothes, but the people who knew me for forty or fifty years were only asking, 'How's your insurance?' I was shocked.

"To this day, many of them haven't done anything. Why didn't they pick up the phone, or write? Couldn't they have said, 'Are you homeless?' I didn't ask them for any help. It's not like I begged and they were avoiding the call. I never asked them for anything. I never expected it. How many live through a disaster? You never imagine how people will act until you're there. I don't need to explain to people, 'I'm the victim.' If I can't rely on certain individuals that I've known for many years at a time like that, then, when can I? The real heroes in all of this were the strangers in the community. They were brilliant. If it wasn't for them, I wouldn't have made it. The government didn't step in either. You can only take 'so much.'" (Rees, 2020)

In *Help Yourself Now*, this author discusses why everyone needs to have their important documents in a central place where it could be quickly grabbed if a natural disaster strikes. Sometimes there is literally just seconds to get to safety. Emergency physician Stephanie Benjamin, M.D. shares tips related to documents and even prescriptions. In addition to the originals that she suggests storing in a fireproof waterproof safe in your home, she also suggests having digital copies on a password protected flash drive. (Yager, 2021: 208) Store those copies on that flash drive in another location even the safe deposit box at the bank, if you have one.

CRUISE SHIP CRIME VICTIMS

The crime that shocked the cruise ship world was the disappearance of 26-year-old George Smith from a luxury cruise ship. He was on a honeymoon in July 2005 with his wife when he disappeared sometime after 4 A.M. off the coast of Turkey. (Cowan, 2005) Foul play and possibly murder was alleged, but there was never enough to point to any suspects or to confirm that he had just accidentally fallen overboard. (Cowan, 2006)

At the time this happened, little was known about the number of crimes that occur on cruise ships. There was no mandatory reporting of crimes on cruise ships. Since cruise ships sail on the high seas, it was even questionable who had jurisdiction if a crime did occur.

The public pressure to make the cruise ship industry more accountable and visible about crime victimization dangers led to the passage of the Cruise Vessel Security and Safety

Act (CVSSA). It was initially passed in 2010, with amendments in 2014. The federal government agencies behind the act, and its mandates, as stated at the website at the Maritime Administration of the U.S. Transportation Administration are as follows: "Under the Cruise Vessel Security and Safety Act (CVSSA) of 2010 (Public Law 111-207), the Federal Bureau of Investigation (FBI), the U.S. Coast Guard (USCG), and the Maritime Administration (MARAD) cooperatively established model training standards covering crime prevention, detection, evidence preservation, and reporting of criminal activities in the international maritime environment." (U.S. Transportation Administration, Maritime Administration, 2020)

Going missing, like George Smith, and being presumed dead, is probably the biggest crime fear that anyone might have related to cruise ships. Stories of those who have vanished on cruise ships are shared at the website for the International Cruise Victims Association (ICV), an association founded to bring attention to the cruise ship industry and to have a place where victims of cruise ship-related crimes or neglect could share. Fariba Amani, for example, disappeared on February 29, 2012. She was a 47-year-old mother of two from Vancouver, Canada. Her story is shared by her sister at the website for the International Cruise Victims Association. (Amani) There is also a blog posted through thetruecrimefiles.com about Fariba's case. (thetruecrimefiles.com, 2017)

Although disappearances are the most dramatic, serious, and horrific cruise ship victimizations that cause concern, looking over the FBI's statistics for 2019, covering the eight categories listed below, by far the more common crime on cruise ships was sexual assault: 101 on the twelve major cruise ships that report to the FBI. But keep in mind that just one major cruise line in 2018 operating four or more ships had approximately 5.7 million passengers. According to Michael Goldstein, writing in his Forbes.com article, "Is Cruise Ship Crime Continuing to Climb?" that even with a reported rise in incidents between 2017 and 2018, the number of victimizations are low when you consider that 14.2 million North Americans went on a cruise in 2018. After citing the finding of criminologist Dr. James Alan Fox that "there are 25 times fewer allegations of major crime [on a cruise ship] then on land," Goldstein concludes, "On the other hand, violent crime is devastating to its victims and their families. Even one assault at sea is too many." (Goldstein, 2019)

Here are the 8 categories of crime that 12 major cruise ships report to the FBI:

1. Homicide
2. Death (suspicious)
3. Missing (U.S. national)
4. Kidnapping
5. Assault with serious bodily injury
6. Firing or tampering with vessel
7. Theft greater than $10,000
8. Sexual assault

In addition to the 101 sexual assaults during 2019 previously mentioned, here are the cruise ship 2019 crime statistics as compiled and posted by the FBI:

- Homicide—0
- Death (suspicious)—5

- Missing (U.S. national)—2
- Kidnapping—0
- Assault with serious bodily injury—12
- Firing or tampering with vessel—2
- Theft greater than $10,000—15
- Sexual assault—101

Source: FBI, Cruise Vessel Security and Safety Act (CVSSA) Statistical Complication, January 1-December 21, 2019.

Falling overboard, getting sexually assaulted, or having something stolen are definitely crime-related concerns but another issue is getting prompt medical care if there is an emergency. In November 2019, a federal jury awarded millions to the family of a 70-year-old Miami man who died after he suffered a heart attack on a cruise ship in Alaska. The claim was that the cruise ship failed to provide the passenger with adequate medical care leading up to his fatal heart attack. (NBCMiami.com, 2019)

The complication about just who is responsible for what goes on when someone is on a cruise ship was highlighted by the trapping of tens of thousands of cruise ship workers. They were unable to get back to their homelands during the Spring of 2020 when the COVID-19 pandemic led to "crew members who were trapped at sea" as Austin Carr put it in his article, "The Cruise Ship Suicides." Passengers were sent home by chartered flights. Carr writes, "After the guests went home, tens of thousands of workers stayed at sea for months. Some described feeling like prisoners or pieces of cargo with no ETA." (Carr, 2020) Carr profiles several crew members including 28-year-old Jozsef Szaller who died by suicide on May 9, 2020. (Carr, 2020)

As the restrictions on travel lifted in the homelands of the workers, more and more were able to return home. But some had been trapped at sea for six months, as Hannah Sparks reported in her article, "Stranded Cruise Ship Workers Finally Going Home After 6 Months." (Sparks, 2020)

SUMMARY

Workplace crime includes property crimes like theft but the crimes that most people are most fearful of are workplace killings, especially mass shootings. There were 500 killings at work in 2016; homicide has become the second most common cause of death in the workplace after accidents. Although most fear the "going postal" type of workplace violence, whereby a disgruntled co-worker stabs or shoots and injures or kills his or her colleagues or supervisors, the more common form of workplace violence leading to murder is done during robberies (67%). Only 13 percent of workplace murders occur because of co-worker-related violence; 7 percent because of customers or clients; and 9 percent because of romantic partners or family members fatal confrontations at the workplace. (Sygnatur and Toscano, 2000)

Not all occupations have an equal victimization rate. Police officers have the highest workplace violence rate followed by health care workers, taxicab drivers, and bartenders. Jobs that deal with a lot of cash, with solo workers in vulnerable situations, also have higher workplace crime rates.

Victims of international and domestic terrorism may experience injuries as well as emotional trauma, PTSD, and the ultimate crime of murder. Victims may be chosen at random, as symbols of the hatred that the perpetrators feel toward a particular country or group, or the attacks might be targeted, as when journalists are singled out by hostage taking and murder when they are reporting on controversial stories or in war torn areas around the world.

Human trafficking is a global problem as well as a domestic one. Svitlana Batsyukova points out an important distinction between prostitution and sex trafficking. According to Batsyukova, someone chooses to become a prostitute; someone is forced into performing sex because of sex trafficking. (Batsyukova, 2007)

Although prostitution is legal in some countries around the world, it is illegal throughout the United States except in a few counties in Nevada. The workplace homicide rate for prostitutes, or sex workers, is one of the highest rates for any occupation: 204 per 100,000 population. Compare that rate to one of the more dangerous occupations, male taxicab drivers, with a murder rate of 29 per 100,000 (Shelley, 2010:73).

Those with physical and developmental or intellectual disabilities are at a higher risk for victimization. Mental health issues can also increase someone's risk for victimization. Research has found that 25 percent of the approximately 1,000 persons shot in the United States by the police during 2018 were considered PMI (persons with mental illness). There has been a growth of what is called Crisis Intervention Training (CIT) programs for police to try to improve the way they respond to emergency calls where they find a PMI. (Rogers et al., 2019)

The victim interview by this author discussed how his 25-year-old who had stopped taking his medication became irrational and attacked his parents. The chapter also profiled Alesia Litteral, who was nearly killed by her husband who had an extreme drinking problem and who was also no longer on his psychological medication.

Alcohol and drug use are tied to many victim-related situations from the increased likelihood that women who have had a sexual victimization as well as other traumas, such as child abuse, are more likely to drink as a way of coping. (Ullman, et al., 2013). The presence of alcohol was seen as a factor in the homicides that Wolfgang considered victim-precipitated (VP). Alcohol was present in either the victim, the offender, or both in 74 percent of the VP cases compared to only 60 percent in the non-VP cases. (Wolfgang, 1957) Alcohol poisoning or drinking excessive amounts of alcohol is considered a major factor in hazing deaths at fraternities on college campuses. (Harrington, 2021)

Additional victim situations and populations that were addressed in this chapter included animals, who should not be abused or neglected. There was also a brief discussion of the possible link between animal torture during the formative years and serial killers in adulthood. The victims of natural disaster who can become victims of scams as well as even unnecessary victimization due to delays in getting help are also explored. Finally, the unique special population of cruise ship passengers on major commercial ships is discussed related to the prevalence of violent or property crime victimization.

KEY TERMS

alcohol use disorder (AUD)
alcoholism
bias crime (hate crime)
developmental disabilities
fentanyl
going postal
hate crime
hazing
homophobic
homosexuality
honor killing
human trafficking
intellectual disabilities
Intentional Animal Torture and Cruelty (IATC)
Islamophobia
LGBTQ (Lesbian, Gay, Bisexual, Transgender, or Questioning)
lynching
National Crime Victimization Survey (NCVS)
neonatal abstinence syndrome
NIBRS (National Incident-Based Reporting System)
nonspeciesist criminology
post-traumatic stress disorder (PTSD)
prostitution
repeat victimization (polyvictimization)
runaway
spree killing
throwaway
transgender
veterinary forensics
workplace violence

REVIEW QUESTIONS

1. What are the main type of workplace crime?
2. What percentage of workplace violence killings happened because of emotional or violent outbursts compared to robberies?
3. What are the two main types of terrorism that the United States is concerned about deterring?
4. Who are typical human trafficking victims?
5. What is the difference between prostitution and sex trafficking?
6. Are those with severe mental illness (SMI) more likely to become crime victims compared to the general population?
7. Are adolescents with disabilities at a higher risk of victimization than other teens?
8. What was the first state to pass a hate crime statute?
9. What two victims were the motivation behind the stiffer hate crime law of 1998, named after both victims?
10. What are the three most common types of hate crimes, in descending order of frequency?
11. How many Jews are estimated to have been killed during the Holocaust?
12. What event in American history was a catalyst to an increase in hate crimes including murder against Arabs and Muslims?
13. What are two federal laws that advanced the rights of the LGBTQ community?
14. What is the definition of animal cruelty or neglect?
15. Why are natural disaster victims and those who want to help them more susceptible to becoming crime victims or victims of donation scams?

16. Upon examination of the number of actual reported major cruise ship victims versus the number of passengers in a typical (pre-pandemic) year, are there a greater or fewer number of major crime victims at sea versus on the land?

CRITICAL THINKING QUESTIONS

1. You are a specially appointed person whose job it will be to decide how much money each victim of a major international terrorism incident should be awarded. What should be the criteria for deciding how much money a family of the deceased will receive? What are the criteria you will be using? Explain why and how you are using those guidelines.
2. Do you think creating an alternative court system that is based on treatment rather than punishment is the correct way to handle the mentally ill who have been arrested? Is it possible these new approaches could be misused to avoid punishment? How would you safeguard against that?
3. Why is it important to remember those who were murdered during the Holocaust? Why do you think there are some who deny the Holocaust ever happened?
4. If you were sitting on a jury for a case of aggravated assault and you found out the attack was motivated by racism or anti-Semitism, if found guilty, would you be inclined to recommend a harsher sentence? Why or why not?
5. What are some helpful techniques or activities that might assist homophobic men or women in becoming more tolerant of the LGBTQ community?
6. Consider a natural disaster that has occurred in the United States or globally during the last five years. Do independent research on that disaster. How quick and effective was the response to the victims? Was there any crime related to the disaster that could have prevented it or led to handling it differently?

ACTIVITIES

1. Whether this is a traditional in-person class, a hybrid with distance learning and in-person learning, or a completely DL (distance learning) class, divide into groups of four. (In Zoom, you can do this automatically through the Breakout Room function.) Pick a topic from the list of special victim situations or groups in this chapter. Discuss key issues related to that topic such as risk factors, demographics of victims, how to prevent the victimization, and other related topics for further research.
2. Watch one of the following movies and write a short report about how it supports a better understanding of the discrimination or racism and related hate crimes that those who are discriminated against have to deal with: *Loving* (2015); *Selma* (2014); *The Hate U Give* (2019); *Do the Right Thing* (1989).

3. Watch one of the following movies and write an analysis about the anti-gay/hate crime aspects as applied to the LGBTQ community: *Boys Don't Cry* (1989) and *Brokeback Mountain* (2005).

4. Design a campaign about animal welfare where you teach pet owners to be more responsive to their pet's physical and emotional needs. Include definitions and explanations about what constitutes animal cruelty and neglect. Should a brochure reinforcing these guidelines be distributed to those who purchase or adopt a pet if such information is not currently readily provided?

RESOURCES

Workplace Crime

Occupational Safety and Health Administration
osha.gov
A regulatory agency concerned with safety in the workplace including workplace violence and murders.

Terrorism Victims

Strength to Strength
stosglobal.org
Support group for survivors of terrorism including the Boston Marathon Bombing in 2013.

Terrorism Research Initiative (TRI)
terrorism-research.org
Founded in 2007. More than 16 research institutions and more than 120 terrorism academics from more than 30 countries are members. Includes a Teaching About Terrorism initiative as part of its projects.

Department of Homeland Security
dhs.gov
In 2002, Homeland Security was set up, combining 22 different departments of the federal government under one agency. Keeping America safe from international or domestic threats is its mission.

Human Trafficking Victims

End Slavery Now
endslaverynow.org
Started in 2009, this organization partners with other anti-slavery (anti-human trafficking) organizations.

National Human Trafficking Hotline
humantraffickinghotline.org
1-888-373-7888
Started in 2007, this is a private effort through the parent organization, Polaris, with funding provided by the U.S. DepOartment of Health and Human Services and additional donations.

U.S. Department of Justice
Anti-Human Trafficking Task Force Initiative
ovc.ojp.gov/program/human-trafficking/overview

Offers information as well as funding to qualified groups to stop human trafficking.

Intellectual, Physical, and Mental Disabilities and Disorders

American Association on Intellectual and Developmental Disabilities (AAIDD)
aaidd.org
Membership organization providing information on those with intellectual and developmental disabilities including an annual conference. Intellectual disability appears before age 22.

Anxiety and Depression Association of America
adaa.org

Depression and Bipolar Support Alliance
dbsalliance.org

End the Abuse of People with Disabilities
endabusepwd.org
Because violence against those with disabilities happens at two to three times the rate of those in the general population, this organization is dedicated to finding and spreading the word about strategies that can lower this victimization rate.

National Disability Rights Network
ndrn.org

Mental Health America (MHA)
mhanational.org
Clifford W. Beers founded MHA back in 1909. It is a nonprofit organization concerned with the requirements of those who have mental illness.

National Center for PTSD (Post Traumatic Stress Disorder)
ptsd.va.gov

National Institute of Mental Health (NIMH)
nimh.nih.gov
NIMH is the leading federal agency conducting research into mental disorders. It is one of the 27 Institutes and Centers that are part of the National Institutes of Health (NIH).

National Suicide Prevention Lifeline
1-800-272-TALK (8255)
Or test the crisis Text Line (text HELLO to 741741)

Hate Crime

National Center for Victims of Crime
victimconnect.org

U.S. Department of Justice
justice.gov/hatecrimes/get-help-now

Racism

Equal Justice Initiative (EJI)
eji.org
Founded in Montgomery, Alabama by Bryan Stevenson, dedicated to helping those falsely accused of a crime.

NAACP
naacp.org
Founded in 1909 by sociologist William DuBois and others. Educational and advocacy organization dedicated to eliminating discrimination based on race.

Religious Discrimination Including Anti-Semitism

ACLU (American Civil Liberties Union)
aclu.org
Founded in the early 1900s, the ACLU is a membership organization concerned with a range of rights including religious liberty, LGBQ, disability, and women's rights, and many more issues.

Anti-Defamation League
adl.org
From its origins fighting anti-Semitism more than 100 years ago, the ADL is dedicated to raising public awareness about, and eliminating, all kinds of hate crime and protecting religious liberty.

Hindu American Foundation
Hinduamerican.org
Advocacy group on behalf of Hindu Americans founded in 2003.

Muslim Advocates
Muslimadvocates.org
Advocacy organization for Muslims dealing with legal issues including hate crimes.

International Federation of Christians and Jews (IFCJ)
ifcj.org
Non-profit founded in 1983 to foster positive connections between Christians and Jews.

United States Holocaust Memorial Museum
ushmm.org
Opened in 1993, the Museum educates its visitors about the Holocaust.

LGBTQ

The Center (The Lesbian, Gay, Bisexual & Transgender Community Center)
Founded in 1983
gaycenter.org

Human Rights Campaign (HRC)
hrc.org
Founded in 1980, and headquartered in Washington, D.C., HRC is a LGBTQ advocacy group.

The Trevor Project
thetrevorproject.org
From the website: "Founded in 1988 by the creators of the Academy Award®-winning short film TREVOR, The Trevor Project is the leading national organization providing crisis intervention and suicide prevention services to lesbian, gay, bisexual, transgender, queer & questioning (LGBTQ) young people under 25."

Animal Rights Including Anti-Cruelty and Neglect

American Society for the Prevention of Cruelty to Animals (ASPCA)
aspca.org
Founded in 1866, the ASPCA offers direct services to care for animals as well as shelters for lost, strayed, or unwanted animals and educational programs to prevent cruelty to animals.

Defenders of Wildlife
defenders.org
Founded in 1925, this is a membership organization concerned with wildlife conservation including educational programs aimed at eliminating inhumane treatment of wildlife.

American Humane Society
americanhumane.org
Founded in 1877, the American Humane society is devoted to animal welfare including rescuing animals and their famed "No Animals Were Harmed"® Hollywood program to ensure animals are not hurt during the filming of a movie.

Animal Law Web Center
animallaw.info
Animal Law Web Center
Michigan State University College of Law
648 North Shaw Lane
East Lansing, Michigan 48824-1300
Offers information through its website on various animal law-related topics.

The Latham Foundation for the Promotion of Human Education
latham.org
Founded in 1918, it is a foundation dedicated to the advancement of humane education including kindness to animals.

National Link Coalition
nationallinkcoalition.org
Their tag line is: "Working together to stop violence against animals and people."

PETA (People for the Ethical Treatment of Animals)
PETA.org
Founded in 1980, PETA is an international non-profit membership organization that is concerned with protecting the rights of animals and to stopping animal abuse.

World Wildlife Fund, Inc. (WWF)
worldwildlife.org
Founded in 1961 first in Switzerland followed by another organization in the United States the same year.

Natural Disasters

American National Red Cross
redcross.org
Founded in 1881, the American National Red Cross is part of a global organization that provides disaster relief, organized blood donations, and trains and certifies in health and safety first aid.

FEMA Federal Emergency Management Agency)
FEMA.gov
Started in 1979, FEMA is part of the U.S. Department of Homeland Security. Its main mission is to help people prepare for, and deal with, natural disasters including hurricanes, floods, tornadoes, and earthquakes.

National Center for Disaster Fraud (NCDF)
Since 2005, this agency, established after Hurricane Katrina, is the coordinating agency for natural and "man-made" disasters. Here is the link to file a complaint online: https://www.justice.gov/disaster-fraud/webform/ncdf-disaster-complaint-form

Cruise Ship Victims

International Cruise Victims Association (ICV)
internationalcruisevictims.org
Headquartered in Arizona, this is a membership association of victims, family members and friends, crew members, and media reporters who are concerned with crime on cruise ships. In addition to the information provided at their website, ICV is an advocacy group.

U.S. Department of Transportation
transportation.gov/
The Federal Maritime Commission (FMC) and the U.S. Coast Guard are two of the federal agencies concerned with safety at sea. The Cruise Vessel Security and Safety Act of 2010 mandates that any incidents of crime at sea should be reported to the FBI (Federal Bureau of Investigation).

CITED WORKS AND ADDITIONAL REFERENCES

AFL-CIO. October 2020. "Death on the Job: The Toll of Neglect." Twenty-ninth edition. Posted at aflcio.org

Agnew, R. 1998. "The Causes of Animal Abuse: A Social-Psychological Analysis." *Theoretical Criminology.* 22: 177-209.

Alarms.org. January 14, 2020. "Women Are Being Murdered on the Job at an Alarming Rate." Posted at alarms.org

Albrecht, Hans Jorg and Michael Kilchling. 2007. "Victims of Terrorism Policies: Should Victims of Terrorism Be Treated Differently?" *European Journal on Criminal Policy and Research,*13-31.

Alvarez-Lister, M. Soledad, Noemí Peredad, Georgina Guilera, Judit Abad, and Anna Segura. 2017. "Victimization and Poly-Victimization in Adolescent Outpatients from Mental Health Centers: A Case-Control Study. *Journal of Family Violence.* 32: 197-205.

Amani, Saloumeh. "The Disappearance of Fariba Amani." Posted at the International Cruise Victims Association website.

Amir, Menachem. 1967. "Victim Precipitated Forcible Rape." *Journal of Criminal Law, Criminology and Police Science.* 58: 493-502.

Anderson, Valerie R., Teresa C. Kulig, and Christopher J. Sullivan. October 2019. "Estimating the Prevalence of Human Trafficking in Ohio, 2014-2016." *American Journal of Public Health.* 109: 1396-1399.

Argersinger, Jo Ann E. (ed.). 2009. *The Triangle Fire: A Brief History with Documents.* New York: Macmillan.

Arluke, Arnold. 2006. *Just a Dog: Understanding Animal Cruelty and Ourselves.* Philadelphia, PA: Temple University Press.

Arluke, Arnold, Jack Levin, Carter Luke, and Frank Ascione. September 1999. "The Relationship of Animal Abuse to Violence and Other Forms of Antisocial Behavior." *Journal of Interpersonal Violence.* 14: 963-975.

Ascione, Frank R. 2000. "Animal Abuse and Youth Violence." *Juvenile Justice Bulletin.* U.S. Department of Justice.

___________. editor. 2010. *The International Handbook of Animal Abuse and Cruelty: Theory, Research, and Application.* West Lafayette, IN: Purdue University Press.

___________. 2000. *Safe Haven for Pets: Guidelines for Programs Sheltering Pets for Women Who Are Battered.* Logan, UT: Sponsored by the Geraldine R. Dodge Foundation.

Ascione, F.R., Arkow, P. 2002. *Child Abuse, Domestic Violence and Animal Abuse: Linking the Circles of Compassion for Prevention and Intervention.* Purdue University Press.

Avery, Daniel. April 4, 2019. "71 Countries Where Homosexuality Is Illegal." *Newsweek.* Posted at https://www.newsweek.com/73-countries-where-its-illegal-be-gay-1385974

Barkas, Janet. (a/k/a Jan Yager) 1975, 2015. *The Vegetable Passion: A History of the Vegetarian State of Mind.* New York: Scribner's. (Republished in 2015 by Hannacroix Creek Books)

Barkas, Janet (a/k/a Jan Yager) January 14, 1974. "No Boundaries to Hatred." *New York Times,* Op-Ed page. Posted at Article-NoBoundariestoHatred-JanYager-NewYorkTimes-OpEd_piece.pdf (drjanyager.com)

Barron, James. September 11, 2001. "Thousands Feared Dead as World Trade Center Is Toppled." *New York Times.* Posted at nytimes.com

Batsyukova, Svitlana.(2007 "Prostitution and Human Trafficking for Sexual Exploitation." *Gender Issues.* 24: 46-50.

BBC.com. September 3, 2014. "Steven Sotloff: U.S. Journalist Murdered by ISIS."

Beirne, Piers. 2009. *Confronting Animal Abuse: Law, Criminology, and Human-Animal Relationships.* Lanham, MD: Rowman & Littlefield.

___________. 2002. "Criminology and Animal Studies: A Sociological View." *Society & Animals.* 10: 381-386.

___________. 1999. "For a Nonspeciesist Criminology: Animal Abuse as an Object of Study." *Criminology.* 37: 117-148.

__________. 2018. *Murdering Animals.* London: Palgrave Macmillan.

Beirne, Piers and Nigel South. 2012. *Issues in Green Criminology: Confronting Harms Against Environments, Humanity and Other Animals.* London: Routledge.

Bergen, Peter. August 13, 2017. "Charlottesville Killing was an Act of Domestic Terrorism." Posted at CNN.com.

Bertolesi, Lorenzo. November 2017. "Restorative Justice: A New Path for Justice Toward Non-Human Animals." *Victims and Responsibility.* 111-123.

Bissonnette, M., A. Wall, C. Wekerle, C. McKee, S.A. Hinson, and R.E. & D. Tsianis. 1997. "Is a Post-Traumatic Stress Director (PTSD) Mediational Model a Valid Framework for Understanding Undergraduate Drinking Behavior?"' *(Summary) Alcoholism: Clinical and Experimental Research.* 21: 54A/

Blinder, Alan, Amy Harmon, and Richard A. Oppel, Jr. June 3, 2019. "'I Will Not Say His Name': Police Try to End Notoriety of Gunmen in Mass Shootings." *New York Times.* Posted at https://www.nytimes.com/2019/06/03/us/dewayne-craddock-va-beach-shooting.html

Blinder, Alana and Kevin Sack. January 10, 2017. "Dylann Roof Is Sentenced to Death in Charleston Church Massacre." *New York Times.* Posted at nytimes.com

Blume, Harvey. December 19, 2001. "The Other NYPD Murder." *The American Prospect.*

Blumenthal, Ralph. March 2, 1993. "Inquiry Is Pressed on Cause of Blast at Trade Center." *New York Times.* 1: B4.

Bogel-Burroughs, Nicholas and Vanessa Swales. April 29, 2020; updated June 16, 2020. "Prisoner with Coronavirus Dies After Giving Birth While on Ventilator." *New York Times.*

Borysenko, Karlyn. February 12, 2020. "The Dark Side of #MeToo: What Happens When Men Are Falsely Accused." Forbes.com. Posted at Forbes.com. https://www.forbes.com/sites/karlynborysenko/2020/02/12/the-dark-side-of-metoo-what-happens-when-men-are-falsely-accused/#62ba7171864d

Boukli, Avi and Justin Kotze, editors. 2018. *Zemiology: Reconnecting Crime and Social Harm.* London: Palgrave Macmillan.

Brinkley-Rubinstein, Lauren, Josie Sivaraman, David L. Rosen, David H. Cloud, Gary Junker, Scott Proescholdbell, Meghan E. Shanahan, and Shabbar I. Ranapurwala. October 4, 2019. "Association of Restrictive Housing During Incarceration with Mortality After Release." *Journal of the American Medical Association (JAMA) Network Open.* Posted at file:///C:/Users/hanna/Downloads/brinkley-rubinstein_2019_oi_190480.pdf

Bronson, Jennifer and Marcus Berzofsky. June 2017. "Indicators of Mental Health Problems Reported by Prisons and Jail Inmates, 2011-12." Bureau of Justice Statistics, U.S. Department of Justice.

Brooke, James. October 13, 1998. "Gay Man Dies from Attack, Fanning Outrage and Debate." *New York Times.* Posted at nytimes.com

Bureau of Justice Statistics (BJS), Office of Justice Programs, U.S. Department of Justice. BJS, "Drug Use and Crime." Posted at https://www.bjs.gov/index.cfm?ty=tp&tid=352

__________. June 2017. "Hate Crime Statistics." Fact sheet.

__________. December 2001. "Violence in the Workplace, 1993-1999." National Crime Victimization Survey. Special Report. Posted at https://www.bjs.gov/content/pub/pdf/vw99.pdf

Byrnes, Hristina. June 14, 2019, updated June 19, 2019. "13 Countries Where Being Gay Is Legally Punishable by Death." 24/7 Wall Street, published in *USA Today.* Posted at https://www.usatoday.com/story/money/2019/06/14/countries-where-being-gay-is-legally-punishable-by-death/39574685/

Cai, Welyi, Audra D.S. Burch, and Jugai K. Patel. April 3, 2021. "Swelling Anti-Asian Violence: Who Is Being Attacked Where." *The New York Times.* Posted at nytimes.com

Caron, Christina. August 13, 2017. "Heather Heyer, Charlottesville Victim, Is Recalled as 'a Strong Woman.'" *New York Times.* Posted at nytimes.com

Carr, Austin. December 30, 2020. "The Cruise Ship Suicides." Posted at Bloomberg.com

Carson, E. Ann and Mary P. Cowhig. February 2020. "Mortality in Local Jails, 2000-2016—Statistical Tables." U.S. Department of Justice, Office of Justice Programs, Bureau of Justice Statistics. Posted at https://www.bjs.gov/content/pub/pdf/mlj0016st.pdf

__________. February 2020. "Mortality in State and Federal Prisons, 2001-2016—Statistical Tables." U.S. Department of Justice, Office of Justice Programs, Bureau of Justice Statistics. Posted at https://www.bjs.gov/content/pub/pdf/msfp0116st.pdf

Cave, Damien. March 25, 2020. "Man Pleads Guilty in New Zealand Mosque Massacre." *The New York Times.* Posted at nytimes.com

Cazaux, G. 2017. "Beauty and the Beast: Animal Abuse from a Non-speciesist Criminological Perspective." *Green Criminology,* 61-82

CDC (Centers for Disease Control and Prevention) Reviewed March 3, 2021. "Drug Overdose Deaths." Retrieved from https://www.cdc.gov/drugoverdose/deaths/index.html

______________. Reviewed February 7, 2020. "Types of Workplace Violence." The National Institute for Occupational Safety & Health (NIOSH). Posted at cdc.gov

Chappell, Bill. November 20, 2015. "American Among the Dead in Radisson Hotel Attack in Mali." NPR.org.

Charlotte Observer (and wire reports including the Associated Press). June 15, 2015, updated June 16, 2015. "9 Charleston Shooting Victims Remembered." *Charlotte Observer.* Posted at https://www.charlotteobserver.com/news/local/article24903601.html

Chen, David W. June 15, 2004. "After Weighing Cost of Lives, 9/11 Fund Completes Its Task." *The New York Times.* Posted at nytimes.com

Christoffersen, Mogens Nygaard. December 2019. ""Violent Crime against Children with Disabilities: A Nationwide Prospective Birth Cohort-Study." *Child Abuse & Neglect.* 98. Downloaded from ScienceDirect.

CIA (Central Intelligence Agency). April 2020. "Brunei." *World Fact Book.* Posted at https://www.cia.gov/library/publications/the-world-factbook/geos/bx.html

Cleveland19.com. November 19, 2007. "Vick Surrenders, Taken to Jail Before Sentencing on Dogfighting Charge." Posted at cleveland19.com

CNN Editorial Research. "Boston Marathon Terror Attacks Timeline." Updated May 2020. CNN.com. Posted at https://www.cnn.com/2013/06/03/us/boston-marathon-terror-attack-fast-facts/index.html

____________. "September 11 Hijackers Fast Facts." Updated September 8, 2019. Posted at https://www.cnn.com/2013/07/27/us/september-11th-hijackers-fast-facts/index.html

Cole, Jennifer and Ginny Sprang. 2015. "Sex Trafficking of Minors in Metropolitan, Micropolitan, and Rural Communities." *Journal of Child Abuse & Neglect.* 40: 113-123.

Cook, Michael. March 21, 2019. "The Ignored Factor in New Zealand's Mass Shooting." Article republished from MarcatorNet and posted at Intellectual Takeout.

Covert, Bryce. May 13, 2014. "Why Are So Many Women Being Murdered at Work?" Posted to arcive.thinkprogress.org.

Cowan, Alison Leigh. January 5, 2006. "Bride Recounts Disappearance of Husband During Cruise." *New York Times.* Posted at nytimes.com

___________. July 8, 2005. "Greenwich Man Disappears From Ship on His Honeymoon." *New York Times.* Posted at nytimes.com

Crime Victims Board (CVB) (Renamed Office of Victim Services), New York State. Revised 7/5/07. "A Guide to Crime Victims Compensation in New York State." Updated website URL: https//ovs.ny.gov

Cropper, Carol Marie. June 10, 1998. "Black Man Fatally Dragged in a Possible Racial Killing." *New York Times.* Posted at nytimes.com

Cruise Vessel Security and Safety Act (CVSSA). January 1, 2019—March 31, 2019. "Statistical Compilation." Posted online.

Cummings, William. Posted August 3, 2015. Updated August 4, 2015. "Airlines Ban Hunters 'Big-Game' 'Trophies' After Uproar Over Cecil the Lion." *USA Today*, posted online at usatoday.com.

Currie, Cheryl L. 2012. "Corrigendum to 'Animal Cruelty by Children Exposed to Domestic Violence.' *Child Abuse & Neglect.*

Demmitt, Audrey. n.d. "Crimes Against Persons with Disabilities: The Facts." Posted at https://visionaware.org/emotional-support/dealing-with-crime-or-domestic-violence-as-a-person-with-a-disability/crime-against-persons-with-disabilities/

Dennis, Latoya. March 19, 2019. "Number of Hate Crimes and Hate Incidents on Rise Around the World." Published at WUWM.com

Dershowitz, Alan. 2019. *Guilt by Accusation: The Challenge of Proving Innocence in the Age of #MeToo.* New York: Hot Books, an imprint of Skyhorse.

Development Services Group, Inc., Global Terrorism Trends and Analysis Center. Prepared for Department of State, Bureau of Counterterrorism and Countering Violent Extremism. "Annex of Statistical Information: County Reports on Terrorism 2018." October 2019. 47 pages. Posted at https://www.state.gov/wp-content/uploads/2019/10/DSG-Statistical-Annex-2018.pdf

Doerner, William G. and Steven P. Lab. 2017. *Victimology.* Eighth edition. New York: Routledge.

Dolven, Taylor and Jacqueline Charles. June 15, 2020. "42,000 Cruise Ship Workers Still Trapped at Sea." *Tampa Bay Times*. Posted at https://www.tampabay.com/news/business/2020/06/15/42000-cruise-ship-workers-still-trapped-at-sea/

Donaghue, Erin. November 16, 2020. "Hate Crime Murders Surged to Record High in 2019, FBI Data Show." Posted at cbsnews.com

Dorian, David, Ryan Hinds, and Serena Thompson. August 1, 2019. "The Controversy Around Estimating Deaths from Medical Error." Posted at healthydebate.ca.

Doucette, Mitchell, Maria T. Bulzacchelli, Shannon Frattaroli, and Cassandra K. Crifasi. 2019. "Workplace Homicides Committed by Firearm: Recent Trends and Narrative Text Analysis." Distributed through Open Access.

Dunn, Andrew, Mark Washburn, and Michael Gordon. June 19, 2015. "Shelby Police Chief Describes Arrest of Charleston Shooting Suspect." *The Charlotte Observer*.

Durkheim, Emile. 1901, 1982. *The Rules of Sociology Method*. Translated by W. Halls. New York: Free Press.

The Economist. October 13, 2017. "Hazing Deaths on American College Campuses Remain Far Too Common." Posted at economist.com.

Eddy, Melissa and Alison Smale. December 19, 2016. "Berlin Crash Is Suspected to Be a Terror Attack, Police Say." *New York Times*. Posted at nytimes.com

Edwards, D.S., L. McMcMenemy, S.A. Stapley, H.D.L. Patel, and J.C. Clasper. 2016. "40 Years of Terrorist Bombings—A Meta-Analysis of the Casualty and Injury Profile. *International Journal Care Injured*. 646-652.

Eide, Helene Marie K. and Kariane G. Westrheim. 2020. "Norwegian Prison Officers' Perspectives on Professionalism and Professional Development Opportunities in Their Occupation." *Journal of Prison Education & Reentry*. 6: 316-332.

Eligan, John and Michael Cooper. April 15, 2013. "Blasts at Boston Marathon Kill 3 and Injure 100." *New York Times*. Posted at nytimes.com

Elkins, Faye. Senior Technical Writer. April 2019. 12. "Animal Cruelty: A Serious Crime Leading to Horrific Outcomes." COPS (Community Policing Dispatch). E-newsletter. Published by the U.S. Department of Justice. Posted at https://cops.usdoj.gov/html/dispatch/04-2019/animal_cruelty.html#:~:text=Moreover%2C%20FBI%20research%20indicates%20that,the%20harm%20to%20the%20animals.

EncyclopediaBritannica.com. Published February 10, 2020."Terrorism." https://www.britannica.com/topic/terrorism

Fagan, Abigail A. and Paul Mazerolle. 2011. "Repeat Offending and Repeat Victimization: Assessing Similarities and Differences in Psychosocial Risk Factors." *Crime & Delinquency*. 57: 732-755.

Fausset, Richard and Neil Vigdor. March 16, 2021, updated March 19, 2021. "8 People Killed in Atlanta-Area Massage Parlor Shootings." *New York Times*. Posted at nytimes.com

FBI. (Federal Bureau of Investigation). *2019 Hate Crime Statistics*.

__________. *2018 Hate Crime Statistics*. Posted at https://ucr.fbi.gov/hate-crime/2018/topic-pages/victims

__________. n.d. "Hate Crime." Fact sheet. Posted at fbi.gov.

__________. "Scams and Safety: Elder Fraud." Posted at https://www.fbi.gov/scams-and-safety/common-scams-and-crimes/elder-fraud

__________. n.d. "What We Investigate: Hate Crimes." Posted https://www.fbi.gov/investigate/civil-rights/hate-crimes

__________. "What We Investigate: Terrorism," n.d. Posted at fbi.gov

__________. 2002. Critical Incident Response Group. National Center for the Analysis of Violent Crime. "Workplace Violence: Issues in Response." Special Agent Eugene A. Rugala (ed.). 80 pages. Posted at file:///C:/Users/hanna/Downloads/workplace_violence.pdf

Fieldstadt, Elisha. February 8, 2021. "Grandfather of Toddler Who Fell Out of Cruise Ship Window Sentenced to 3 Years' Probation." Posted at NBC News.com.

Felson, Marcus and Lawrence E. Cohen. 1980. "Human Ecology and Crime: A Routine Activity Approach." *Human Ecology*. 8: 389-406.

Fisher, M.H. R.M. Hodapp, and E. M. Dykens (2008) "Child Abuse Among Children with Disabilities: What We Know and What We Need to Know." *International Review of Research in Mental Retardation, 35*, 251-289.

Fitzsimons, N.M. 2009. *Combating Violence and Abuse of People with Disabilities*. Baltimore, MD: Brookes Publishing.

Flynn, C. 2000. "Battered Women and Their Animal Companions: Symbolic Interaction Between Human and Nonhuman Animals." *Society & Animals*. 8: 100-127.

Fox, J. and J. Levin. 1994. *Overkill*. New York: Plenum.

Fralin, Gordon Godfrey. July 1, 1955. "Charles Lynch, Originator of the Term Lynch Law." University of Richmond, Master's Thesis.

Frank, Anna. 1947, 1993. *Anna Frank: The Diary of a Young Girl*. New York: Bantam Books.

Friedrichs, David O. 2002. "Occupational Crime, Occupational Deviance, and Workplace Crime: Sorting Out the Difference." *Criminal Justice*. 2: 243-256.

Fuller-Thomson, Esme and Sarah Brennenstuhl. April 28-May 4, 2012. "People with Disabilities: The Forgotten Victims of Violence." *The Lancet*. 379: 1573-1574.

Galwvan, Astrid. October 2, 2020. Associated Press. "Study Finds LGBTQ People Much Likelier to Be Crime Victims." Published by PBS News Hour and posted to pbs.org/newshour

Gephardt Daily Staff. May 25, 2020. "Police ID Woman They Say was Killed by Utah Man She Met on Tinder App." Posted at https://www.eastidahonews.com/2020/05/police-id-woman-they-say-was-killed-by-utah-man-she-met-on-tinder-app/

Gerber, Marisa and James Queally. September 22, 2017. "Man Who Killed 8 People at California Nail Salon Gets Life in Prison." *Los Angeles Times*. Posted at sun-sentinel.com

Gerstenfeld, Phyllis B. 2018. *Hate Crimes: Causes, Controls, and Controversies*. Fourth edition. Los Angeles, CA: SAGE.

Gold, Matea and Maggie Farely. September 12, 2001. "world Trade Center anad pentagon Attacked on Sept. 11, 2001." *Los Angeles Times*. Posted at latimes.com

Goldstein, Michael. December 4, 2019. "Is Cruise Ship Crime Continuing to Climb?" Forbes.com Posted at https://www.forbes.com/sites/michaelgoldstein/2019/12/04/is-cruise-ship-crime-continuing-to-climb/#10fb3b8b193e

Govtech.com. October 13, 2008. "Hurricane Katrina Fraud Task Force Brings Storm of Justice." Emergency Management. News Report. Posted at https://www.govtech.com/em/disaster/Hurricane-Katrina-Fraud-Task.html

Grant, Heath, Cathryn Lavery, and Kimberly Spanjol. "Critical Understanding about Animal Cruelty for Law Enforcement Practitioners." *Journal of Law Enforcement*. 4. Posted online.

_______________. Summer 2016. "Understanding about Animal Cruelty: Why Animal Abuse Is a Critical Concern for Law Enforcement Practitioners, and Promising Antidote to Youth Violence." *The Latham Letter*.

Green, Anthony and Donna Cooper. April 2012. "Auditing the Cost of the Virginia Tech Massacre." Published at AmericanProgress.Org.

Greenwood, A. September 2014. "Oregon Court Says Animals Can Be Crime Victims, Like People. So What Does That Mean?" *Huffington Post*.

Hall, Jani. June 30, 2016. Posted October 15, 2018. "Cecil the Lion Died Amid Controversy—Here's What Happened Since." www.nationalgeographic.com

Hamdan, Ashraf H. March 3, 2010. "Neonatal Abstinence Syndrome." *Emedicine Pediatrics*. 1-25.

Harlow, Caroline Wolf. November 2005. "Hate Crime Reported by Victims and Police." Bureau of Justice Statistics, Special Report, National Criminal Victimization Survey and Uniform Crime Reporting.

Hellman, D.S. and N. Blackman. 1966. "Enuresis, Fire-Setting and Cruelty to Animals: A Triad Predictive of Adult Crime." *American Journal of Psychiatry*. 22: 1431-1435

Harrell, E. 2016. "Crimes Against Persons with Disabilities, 2009-2014—Statistical Tables." Bureau of Justice of Statistics.

Harrington, Joe. March 8, 2021. "What Is Hazing and Why Does It Exist on College Campuses?" *The Columbus Dispatch*. Posted at dispatch.com

Hedegaard, Holly, Arialdi M. Minino, and Margaret Warner. December 2020. "Drug Overdose Deaths in the United States, 1999-2019." CDC Center for Disease Control and Prevention, U.S. Department of Health & Human Services.

Henslin, James M. 2020. *Social Problems: A Down-to-Earth Approach*. Thirteenth Edition. Hoboken, NJ: Pearson.

Hernandez, Salvador. March 27, 2007. "Testimony Before House Committee on Transportation and Infrastructure." Posted by the FBI at https://archives.fbi.gov/archives/news/testimony/crimes-against-americans-on-cruise-ships#:~:text=Of%20the%20184%20cases%20that,percent%20and%2022%20percent%20respectively.

Hersher, Rebecca. January 10, 2017. "Dylann Roof Sentenced to Death." NPR.org.

Hicks, Jonathan P. March 2, 1993. "A Legal Threshold Is Crossed by Gay Couples in New York." *New York Times*. 1: B3.

Hiday, Virginia Aldige, Marvin S. Swartz, Jeffrey W. Swanson, Randy Borum, and H. Ryan Wagner. January 1, 1999. "Criminal Victimization of Persons with Severe Mental Illness." Published online at https://ps.psychiatryonline.org/doi/full/10.1176/ps.50.1.62

Hines, Morgan. "12,000 Crew Members Still on Cruise Ships in U.S. Waters Months After COVID-19 Pandemic Shut Cruising Down." *USA Today*. Posted at the usatoday.com site.

Hodges, Cynthia. 2008. "The Link: Cruelty to Animals and Violence Towards People." Michigan State University College of Law. Posted at www.animallaw.info.

Horowitz, Jason, Nick Corasaniti, and Ashley Southall. June 17, 2015. "Nine Killed in Shooting at Black Church in Charleston." *New York Times*. Posted at nytimes.com

Hsu, Chien-Chi, Chuen-Jim Sheu, Shen-Ing Liu, Yi-Wen Sun, Shu-I Wu, and Ying Lin. 2009. Crime Victimization of Persons with Severe Mental Illness in Taiwan. *Australian and New Zealand Journal of Psychiatry*. 43: 460-466.

Hudson, H.R., D. Anglin, J. Yarbrough, K. Hardaway, M. Russell, J. Strote, M. Canter, and B. Blum. December 1998. "Suicide by Cop." *Annals of Emergency Medicine*. Posted at https://pubmed.ncbi.nlm.nih.gov/9832661/

Hughes, Karen, Mark A. Bellis, Lisa Jones, Sara Wood, Geoff Bates, Lindsay Eckley, Ellie McCoy, Christopher Mikton, Tom Shakespeare, and Alana Officer. April 28, 2012. "Prevalence and Risk of Violence Against Adults with Disabilities: A Systematic Review and Meta-Analysis of Observational Studies." *The Lancet*. 1621-1629.

Human Rights Campaign (HRC). n.d. "Violence Against the Transgender and Gender Non-Conforming Community in 2020." Posted at https://www.hrc.org/resources/violence-against-the-trans-and-gender-non-conforming-community-in-2020

Jenness, Valerie and Ryken Grattet. 2001. *Making Hate a Crime: From Social Movement to Law Enforcement*. New York: Russell Sage Foundation in Coordination with the American Sociological Association.

Johnston, David. April 25, 1995. "Terror in Oklahoma: The Overview; Oklahoma Bombing Plotted for Months, Officials Say." *New York Times*. Posted at nytimes.com

Jones, L., M.A. Bellis, S. Wood, K. Hughes, E. McCoy, L. Eckley, and A. Officer. 2012. "Prevalence and Risk of Violence against Children with Disabilities: A Systematic Review and Meta-Analysis of Observational Studies. *Lancet*. 380: 899-907.

Karmen, Andrew. 2020. *Crime Victims: An Introduction to Victimology*. Tenth edition. Boston, MA: Cengage.

Kesey, Ken. 1962. *One Flew Over the Cuckoo's Nest*. New York: Signet.

Kimura, Reo. 2007. "Recovery and Reconstruction Calendar." *Journal of Disaster Research* 2: 465-473.

Kirchheimer, Sid. n.d. "7 Ways to Spot Fake Charities After a Disaster." Posted at AARP.org.

Knight-Ridder newspapers. January 20, 1993. *The Baltimore Sun*. "TV Crews Film Florida Man as He Kills His Ex-Wife Man Flees After Shooting at Daughter's Gravesite." Posted at baltimoresun.com

Kolen, Amy. Spring 2001. "Fire." *The Massachusetts Review*. 42: 13-36.

Kristof, Nicholas. September 3, 2014. "When Reporting Is Dangerous." *New York Times*.

Lagnado, Lucette. March 11, 2002. "Terrorism's Forgotten Victims." *Wall Street Journal*. B1, B4.

Lee, Cynthia. 2008. "Hate Crimes and the War on Terror." In *Hate Crimes: Perspectives and Approaches*. Barbara Perry (ed.).

Lee, Trymaine. August 26, 2010. "Rumor to Fact in Tales of Post-Katrina Violence." *New York Times*. Posted at nytimes.com

Leeb, Rebecca T., Rebecca H. Bitsko, Melissa T. Merrick, and Brian S. Armour. 2012. "Does Childhood Disability Increase Risk for Child Abuse and Neglect?" *Journal of Mental Health Research in Intellectual Disabilities*. 5: 4-31.

Leifman, Judge Steven. Thursday, November 12, 2020. Zoom interview with the author as part of the graduate course, "Forensic Health, The Law, and the Criminal Justice System," Iona College.

Lennon, John J. July 9, 2019. "The Murderer, the Writer, the Reckoning." *New York Review of Books*. Posted at nybooks.com

Lentz, Susan A. and B. Grant Stitt. May 1996. "Women as Victims in 'Victimless Crimes': The Case of Prostitution." *Journal of Contemporary Criminal Justice*. 12: 173-186.

Lewin, Barbro. (September 2007) "Who Cares About Disabled Victims of Crime? Barriers and Facilitators for Redress." *Journal of Policy and Practice in Intellectual Disabilities*. 3: 170-176.

Lewin, Tamar. September 17, 2001. "Sikh Owner of Gas Station Is Fatally Shot in Rampage." *The New York Times.* Posted online at nytimes.

Liptak, Adam. June 15, 2020. "Civil Rights Law Protects Gay and Transgender Workers, Supreme Court Rules." *New York Times.* Posted at https://www.nytimes.com/2020/06/15/us/gay-transgender-workers-supreme-court.html

Litteral, Alesia. January 7, 2021. Phone interview with the author.

Lockwood, R. and R. Arkow. 2016. "Animal Abuse and Interpersonal Violence: The Cruelty Connection and Its Implications for Veterinary Pathology." *Veterinary Pathology.* 53: 910-918.

Loeb, R.T., R.H. Bitsko, M.T. Merrick, and RB.S. Armour. 2012. "Does Childhood Disability Increase Risk for Child Abuse and Neglect?" *Journal of Mental Health Research in Intellectual Disabilities.* 5: 4-31.

Lovette, Ian. October 13, 2011. "Custody Battle May Have Fueled Killings at Salon, Victims' Kim Say." *New York Times.* Posted at nytimes.com

Lyon, Ed. February 4, 2019. "Imprisoning America's Mentally Ill." *Prison Legal News.* Posted at prisonlegalnews.org

Makary, Martin A. and Michael Daniel. May 2016. "Medical Error—the Third Leading Cause of Death in the US." *British Medical Journal.* May 2-8, 2016. Vol. 353.

Mallon, Gerald P. 2013. "From the Editor: The Legend of Mary Ellen Wilson and Etta Wheeler: Child Maltreatment and Protection Today." *Child Welfare.* 91: 9-11.

Marge, D. K. 2003. *A Call to Action: Ending Crimes of Violence Against Children and Adults with Disabilities.* New York: SUNY Upstate Medical University. State University of New York.

Masucci, Madeline and Lynn Langton. June 2017. "Hate Crime Victimization, 2004-2015." U.S. Department of Justice, Office of Justice Programs. Posted at https://www.bjs.gov/content/pub/pdf/hcv0415.pdf

Matkin, Holly. December 24, 2020. "President Trump Pardons Former Cop Who Spent 10 Years in Prison After Her K9 Bit Suspect." *USA Today* reporting. Posted at PoliceTribune.com.

Mauro, Tara. September 2007. "The Many Victims of Substance Abuse." *Psychiatry.* 43-51.

McDermott, Brett M. and Vanessa E. Cobham. 2012. "Family Functioning in the Aftermath of a Natural Disaster." BioMedCentral. *BMC Psychiatry.*

McGill, Kevin. February 14, 2019. "10-year Sentence in Race-Based Post-Katrina Shooting." Associated Press News (AP News). Posted at https://apnews.com/c02405b06817450e9d1bcd43a1ae5725

Merck, Melinda D. (ed.). 2007. *Veterinary Forensics: Animal Cruelty Investigations.* Blackwell.

Merriam-Webster Dictionary. "Lynch Law." Posted at merriam-webster.com

Montgomery. Madeline. June 29, 2021. "Scam Warnings Issued Following Surfside Condo Collapse." CBS12.com

Mugan, Mike. February 25, 2021. Presentation on Animal Cruelty. Iona College. Criminal Justice Club.

Musumed, Natalie. June 30, 2021. "Scammers Are Setting Up Fake Online Fundraisers in the Wake of the Florida Condo Collapse Disaster, Official Warns." Posted at www.insider.com

Nandi, Arijit, Melissa Tracy, John R. Beard, David Vlahov, and Sandro Galea. 2009. "Patterns and Predictors of Trajectories of Depression After an Urban Disaster." *Annals of Epidemiology.* 19: 761-770.

National Center for Elder Abuse (NCEA). "Signs of Elder Abuse." Posted at https://ncea.acl.gov/NCEA/media/STEAP-10-31-2019/STEAP_04_SignsEAFactSheet_web.pdf

National Center for PTSD. May 2019. "Understanding PTSD and PTSD Treatment." 16 pages Posted at https://www.ptsd.va.gov/publications/print/understandingptsd_booklet.pdf

National Council on Disabilities. May 27, 2007. "Breaking the Silence on Crime Victims with Disabilities." Posted at https://ncd.gov/publications/2007/May212007

National Disability Council (NDC). "Appropriate Terms to Use." Posted at http://nda.ie/Publications/Attitudes/Appropriate-Terms-to-Use-about-Disability/

National Human Trafficking Resource Center. "Identifying Victims of Human Trafficking Fact Sheet." Posted at https://www.acf.hhs.gov/sites/default/files/orr/fact_sheet_identifying_victims_of_human_trafficking.pdf

National Institute of Mental Health (NIMH). "Coping with Traumatic Events." Revised January 2020. Posted at https://www.nimh.nih.gov/health/topics/coping-with-traumatic-events/index.shtml

_______________. n.d. "Post-Traumatic Stress Disorder." Posted at https://www.nimh.nih.gov/health/publications/post-traumatic-stress-disorder-ptsd/index.shtml

NBCMiami.com. November 21, 2019. "Daughter of Man Who Died on Cruise Ship Speaks After Jury Awards Millions."

NCADV.org. n.d. "Why Do Victims Stay?" Posted at ncadv.org

National Institute on Alcohol Abuse and Alcoholism (NIAAA), National Institute of Health. October 2019. "College Drinking."

National Link Coalition. n.d. "The Link." Homepage of nationallinkcoalition.org

National Safety Council. n.d. "Assaults Fourth Leading Cause of Workplace Deaths." Posted at https://www.nsc.org/work-safety/safety-topics/workplace-violence.

Neal, David J. March 11, 2019. "Heart Attack Lawsuit Verdict Orders Norwegian Cruise Line to Pay Passenger $2 Million." *Miami Herald*. Posted at miamiherald.com

Neff, Joseph, with additional reported by Shalia Dewan. June 12, 2019. "Court Focuses on Motive as Shooter Pleads Guilty to Killing Muslim Students." Posted at TheMarshallProject.org.

Neria, Y., A. Nandi, and S. Galen. 2007. "Post-Traumatic Stress Disorder Following Disasters: A Systematic Review." *Psychological Medicine* 38: 467-480.

Newberry, Michelle. 2017. "Pets in Danger: Exploring the Link Between Domestic Violence and Animal Abuse." *Aggression and Violent Behavior*. 34: 273-281

New York Times. Editorial. February 22, 2002. "The Murder of Daniel Pearl. Posted at nytimes.com

New York Times. May 20, 2009. "Vick is Released from Prison." Posted at nytimes.com.

Nosacek, Gary. December 12, 2019. Phone interview with author. Nurse, A. and T. Wyatt 2020. *Wildlife Criminology*. Bristol, UK: Bristol University Press.

NPR staff. June 18, 2015. "The Victims: 9 Were Slain at Charleston's Emanuel AME Church." Posted at npr.org

Nurse, Angus and Tanya Wyatt. 2020. *Wildlife Criminology*. Bristol, UK (University of Bristol): Policy Press.

O'Connell, A.J. April 15, 2007 "Student Dies of Apparent Overdose." *Stamford Times*. A1, A2.

Office for Victims of Crime (OVC). 2002. "First Response to Victims of Crime with a Disability."

__________. 2018. "Hate Crime Fact Sheet." *2018 National Crime Victims' Rights Week Resource Guide: Crime and Victimization Fact Sheets*. Posted at https://ovc.ojp.gov/sites/g/files/xyckuh226/files/ncvrw2018/info_flyers/fact_sheets/2018NCVRW_HateCrime_508_QC.pdf

__________. n.d. "Working with Victims of Crime with Disabilities." By Cheryl Guidry Tyiska, Director of Victim Services, National Organization for Victim Assistance. Posted at https://www.ncjrs.gov/ovc_archives/factsheets/disable.htm

Ogle, Richard L. and Denise D. Walker. 2006. "Alcohol and Violence." In *Encyclopedia of Interpersonal Violence*. C. Renzetti and J. Edelson (eds.). Thousand Oaks, CA: SAGE. 19-20.

OSCE ODIHR Hate Crime Reporting. 2019. "What Is Hate Crime?" Organization for Security and Co-Operation in Europe (OSCE) / Office for Democratic Institutions and Human Rights (ODIHR). Posted online at hatecrime.osce.org

Parker, Diantha and Jess Bidgood. January 1, 2015. "Boston Marathon Bombing: What We Know." *New York Times*. Posted at nytimes.com

Pascus, Brian. August 10, 2019. "What Is 'Domestic Terrorism' and What Can the Law Do about It? CBSNews.com.

Perske, Robert. October 2011. "Perske's List: False Confessions from 75 Persons with Intellectual Disability." American Association on Intellectual and Developmental Disabilities. 49(5): 365-373. Posted at https://www.aaidd.org/docs/default-source/publications/perske-s-list-false-confessions-from-75-persons-with-intellectual-disability.pdf

Petersilia, Joan R. 2001. "Crime Victims with Developmental Disabilities: A Review Essay." *Criminal Justice and Behavior*. 28: 655-694.

Phillips. James P. April 28, 2016. "Workplace Violence: Violence Against Health Care Workers in the United States." *New England Journal of Medicine*, 1661-1669.

Pittman, David J. and William Handy. December 1964. "Patterns in Criminal Aggravated Assault." *Journal of Criminal Law, Criminology, and Police Science*. 55:462-470

Possley, Maurice. Posted May 30, 2018, updated March 21, 2019. "Gary Bush." *The National Registry of Exonerations*. Posted at https://www.law.umich.edu/special/exoneration/Pages/casedetail.aspx?caseid=5332

Poushter, Jacob and Moira Fagan. April 13, 2020. "Americans See Spread of Disease as Top International Threat, Along with Terrorism, Nuclear Weapons, Cyberattacks." Pewresearch.com. Posted at https://www.pewresearch.org/global/2020/04/13/americans-see-spread-of-disease-as-top-international-threat-along-with-terrorism-nuclear-weapons-cyberattacks/

Pritt, Pamela. June 30, 2016. "FEMA Warns of Disaster-Related Fraud." Posted at govtech.com

Ralph, Sue, Carmel Capewell, and Elizabeth Bonnett. 2016. "Disability Hate Crime: Persecuted for Difference." *British Journal of Special Education*. 43: 215-231.

The Recovery Village. n.d. "Hazing in College: Impact of Hazing on Substance Abuse." Posted at therecoveryvillage.com
Rees, Rhonda. August 14, 2020. Phone interview.
Reuters. November 19, 1999. "Third Defendant Is Convicted in Dragging Death in Texas." *New York Times.* Posted at nytimes.com
Richer, Alanna Durkin. July 31, 2020. "Court Overturns Boston Marathon Bomber's Death Sentence." Posted at APnews.com
Richland Source. August 12, 2019. "Domestic Violence Motive Emerges in Fleming Falls Shooting." Posted at richlandsource.com
Robertson, Campbell. April 24, 2019."Texas Executes White Supremacist for 1998 Dragging Death of James Byrd Jr." *New York Times.* Posted at nytimes.com
Robertson, Campbell, Christopher Mele, and Sabrina Tavernise. October 27, 2019. "11 Killed in Synagogue Massacre; Suspect Charged with 29 Counts." *New York Times.* Posted at nytimes.com.
Rogers, Michael S., Dale E. McNiel, and Renee L. Binder. 2019. "Effectiveness of Police Crisis Intervention Training Programs." *American Academy of Psychiatry and the Law.* 4. Posted online.
Romero, Simon and Nicholas Bogel-Burroughs. August 4, 2019. "El Paso Shooting: Massacre That Killed 20 Being Investigated as Domestic Terrorism." *New York Times.* Posted at nytimes.com
Rosen, Meghan. May 31, 2017. "For Babies Exposed to Opioids in the Womb, Parents May Be the Best Medicine." *Science News.*
Roth, Alisa. 2018, 2020. *Insane: America's Criminal Treatment of Mental Illness.* New York: Basic Books.
Sachs, Susan. September 2, 1999. "Man Shot by City Officers Was on a Troubled Quest." *New York Times.* A: 1.
Salt, Henry. 1892. *Animals' Rights.* Clarkes Summit, PA: Society for Animal Rights.
Sampson, Hannah. December 6, 2019. "Reports of Sexual Assault on Cruises in Late Summer Spiked 67 Percent from Last Year." *Washington Post.* Posted at https://www.washingtonpost.com/travel/2019/12/06/reports-sexual-assault-cruises-late-summer-spiked-percent-last-year/
Sant, Geoffrey. 2012. "Victimless Crime Take on a New Meaning: Did California's Victims' Rights Amendment Eliminate the Right to Be Recognized as a Victim," *Journal of Legislation.* 39: 43-68.
Savage, Charlie. August 13, 2017. A Hate Crime? How the Charlottesville Car Attack May Become a Federal Case." *New York Times.* Posted at nytimes.com
Schwartz, Terese. The Holocaust: Non-Jewish Victims. Posted at Jewishvirtuallibrary.org
Seear, Kate and Suzanne Fraser. 2014. "The Addict as Victim: Producing the 'Problem' of Addiction in Australian Victims of Crime Compensation Laws." *International Journal of Drug Policy.* 25: 826-835.
Sentient Media. December 20, 2018. "Animal Cruelty: What Is It and How Can We Stop It for Good?"
Shafer, Stephen. 1968. *The Victim and His Criminal: A Study in Functional Responsibility.* New York: Random House.
Shandro, Jamie, et al. October 2016. "Human Trafficking: A Guide to Identification and Approach for the Emergency Physician." *Annals of Emergency Medicine.* 68: 501-508.
Shelley, Louse. 2010. *Human Trafficking: A Global Perspective.* New York: Cambridge University Press.
Siegel, Larry J. 2018. *Criminology: Theories, Patterns, and Typologies.* Thirteenth edition. Boston: Cengage.
Siegel, Miriam, Candace Y. Johnson, C. Lawson, M. Ridenour, and Daniel Hartley. March 27, 2020. "Nonfatal Violent Workplace Crime Characteristics and Rates by Occupation—United States, 2007-2015." *Morbidity and Mortality Weekly Report.* 69: 324-328.
Silver, Eric. 2002. "Mental Disorder and Violent Victimization: The Mediating Role of Involvement in Conflicted Social Relationships." *Criminology.* 40: 191-212.
Smith, Mitch. June 28, 2019. "James Fields Sentenced to Life in Prison for Death of Heather Heyer in Charlottesville." *New York Times.* Posted at nytimes.com.
Smith, Rory and Sewel Chan. May 22, 2017. "Ariana Grande Manchester Concert Ends in Explosion, Panic and Death." *New York Times.* Posted at nytimes.com
Snow, Anita (Associated Press). September 15, 2019. "Correction: Sikh Killed–Anniversary Story." ABCNews.com. Posted at https://abcnews.go.com/US/wireStory/arizona-sikh-preaches-love-18-years-post-911-65613832
Solis, Dianne. March 16, 2012. "Widow, Daughters of Man Slain in 9/11 Hate Crime in Dallas Become Americans." *Dallas News* (Associated Press). Posted at dallasnews.com
Spanjol, Kimberly. March 14, 2021. Personal communication.
________________. February 26, 2021. Personal communication.

_______________. February 19, 2021. Zoom interview.

Speckhard, Anne. June 2019. "The Boston Marathon Bombers: The Lethal Cocktail That Turned Troubled Youth to Terrorism." *Perspectives on Terrorism*. 7: 64-78.

Spencer, N., E. Devereux, A. Wallace, R. Sundrum, M. Shenoy, C. Bacchus, et al. 2005. "Disabling Conditions and Registration for Child Abuse and Neglect: A Population-Based Study." *Pediatrics*. 116: 609-613.

Stanton, Christina. Tuesday, January 19, 2021. Guest Presentation at John Jay College of Criminal Justice, Victimology.

____________. 2019. *Out of the Shadows of 9/11: An Inspiring Tale of Escape and Transformation*. New York: Loving All Nations Press.

_____________. Wednesday, January 13, 2021. Phone interview.

Steadman, Henry J. and David Morrissette. October 2016. "Police Responses to Persons With Mental Illness: Going Beyond CIT Training." *Psychiatric Services*. 67: 1054-1056.

Stitt, Grant. 1988. "Victimless Crime: A Definitional Issue." *Journal of Crime and Justice*. 11: 87-102.

Stowe, Stacey. December 21, 2019. "Life After Horrific Death for the Journalist James Foley." *New York Times*. Posted at nytimes.com

Sullivan, S.P. September 23, 2014. "FBI Adds Animal Cruelty as "Crime Against Society." Uniform Crime Report. Retrieved from fivesparrow.org

Swanson, Kim. 2014. *The Emergency Nurse as Crime Victim: Workplace Violence Contributors, Consequences, and Reporting Behavior*. ProQuest Dissertations Publishing.

Sygnatur, Eric F. and Guy A. Toscano. Spring 2000. "Work-Related Homicides: The Facts." *Compensation and Working Conditions*. Office of Safety, Health and Working Conditions. Bureau of Labor Statistics. 3-8+

Taylor, Derrick Bryson. July 11, 2020. "Valentina Sampaio Is the First Transgender Model for Sports Illustrated." *New York Times*. Posted at https://www.nytimes.com/2020/07/11/business/media/valentina-sampaio-transgender-sports-illustrated.html.

Teasdale, Brent, Leah E. Daigle, and Ellen Ballard. 2014. "Trajectories of Recurring Victimization Among People with Major Mental Disorders." *Journal of Interpersonal Violence*. 29: 987-1005.

Teplin, Linda A., Gary M. McClelland, Karen M. Abram, and Dana A. Weiner. "Crime Victimization in Adults with Severe Mental Illness." *Archives of General Psychiatry*. August 2005. Volume 62. Pages 911-921. Posted at https://www.ncbi.nlm.nih.gov/pmc/articles/PMC1389236/

Thetruecrimefiles.com October 16, 2017. "The Disappearance of Fariba Amani." Blog posted at the truecrimefiles site.

Thomas, Tierra. October 14, 2020. "Domestic Abuse Survivor Reflects on Life One Year After Being Shot." Thrive Reporter, RichlandSource.com.

Tiesman, Hope M, Kelly K. Gurka, Srinivas Konda, Jeffrey H. Coben, and Harlan E. Amandus. April 2012. "Workplace Homicides Among U.S. Women: The Role of Intimate Partner Violence." *Annals of Epidemiology*. 12(4): 277-284.

Tyiska, Cheryl Guidry. 1998. "Working with Victims of crime with Disabilities." National Organization of Victim Assistance (NOVA). Findings from the Symposium included in the OVC Bulletin, U.S. Department of Justice, Office for Victims of Crime.

2LivesFoundation.org. "About Steven: Steven Joel Sotloff." Posted at 2livesfoundation.org

UK Rehab. n.d. "How Addiction Often Causes People to Steal from Those They Love."

Ullman, Sarah E., Mark Relyea, Liana Peter-Hagene, and Amanda L. Vasquez. 2013. "Trauma Histories, Substance Use Coping, PTSD, and Problem Substance Use Among Sexual Assault Victims." *Addictive Behaviors*. 38: 2219-2223.

United States Holocaust Memorial Museum. December 8, 2020. "Documented Numbers of Victims of the Holocaust and Nazi Persecution." Washington, DC. Posted at encycloepdia.ushmm.org

U.S. Department of Homeland Security. Blue Campaign. "Human Interest Stories: Imprisoned in Your Neighborhood." Posted at www.dhs.gov/blue-campaign/human-interest-stories

_______________. " Reviewed 11/12/2017. In Their Own Words." https://www.ice.gov/features/human-trafficking-victim-shares-story

U.S. Justice Department. "The Matthew Shepard and James Byrd Jr. Hate Crime Prevention Act of 2009. Posted at justice.gov

_______________. Updated September 28, 2020. "September 11th Victim Compensation Fund." Online information. For more information, go to vcf.gov

______________. "Strengthening Hate Crime Awareness on a University Campus Missoula, MT." The website is entitled, "Sexual Orientation," with information "Assisting Communities Facing Conflict and Tension Based on Sexual Orientation." Posted at https://www.justice.gov/crs/our-focus/sexual-orientation

Von Drehle, David. 2003. *Triangle: The Fire That Changed America.* New York: Atlantic Monthly Press.

Von Hentig, Hans. 1948, 1979. *The Criminal & His Victim: Studies in the Sociobiology of Crime.* With a New Preface by Marvin Wolfgang. New York: Schocken (originally published by Yale University Press).

Voss, Harwin L. and John R. Hepburn. 1968. "Patterns in Criminal Homicide in Chicago." *The Journal of Criminal Law, Criminology, and Police Science.* 50: 499-508.

Walker, Jim. October 8, 2016. "Accurate Cruise Crime Statistics Finally Available." Cruise Law News. October 8, 2016. Posted at https://www.cruiselawnews.com/2016/10/articles/crime/accurate-cruise-crime-statistics-finally-available/

Walters, Glenn D. 2020. "Explaining the Drug-Crime Connection with Peers, Proactive Criminal Thinking, and Victimization: Systemic, Cognitive Social Learning, and Person Proximity Mechanisms." *Psychology of Addictive Behaviors.*

Wareham, Jamie. November 18, 2019. "Murdered, Hanged and Lynched: 331 Trans People Killed This Year." Forbes.com. Posted at https://www.forbes.com/sites/jamiewareham/2019/11/18/murdered-hanged-and-lynched-331-trans-people-killed-this-year/#552b924f2d48

White, Rob. 2011. *Transnational Environmental Crime: Toward an Eco-global Criminology.* New York: Routledge.

Widom, Cathy Spatz, Sally J. Czaja, and Mary Ann Dutton. 2008. "Childhood Victimization and Lifetime Revictimization." *Child Abuse & Neglect.* 32: 785-796.

Williams, Timothy. July 18, 2011."The Hated and the Hater, Both Touched by Crime." *The New York Times,* posted at nytimes.com

Windau, Janice, Eric Sygnatur, and Guy Toscano. June 1999. "Profile of Work Injuries Incurred by Young Workers." Bureau of Labor Statistics. *Monthly Labor Review.* 3-10.

Winter, Tom. October 23, 2018. "Boston Marathon Bomber Told FBI Agents He and His Brother Acted Alone, Court Documents Says." Posted at NBCnews.com

Wolfgang, Marvin E. May-June 1957. "Victim-Precipitated Criminal Homicide." *Journal of Criminal Law and Criminology.* 48(1).

Worsham, Lynn. 1998. "Going Postal: Pedagogic Violence and the Schooling of Emotion." 18(2): 213-245. *JAC: A Journal of Composition Theory.*

Wright, Jeremy and Christopher Hensley. 2003. "From Animal Cruelty to Serial Murder: Applying the Graduation Hypothesis." *International Journal of Offender Therapy and Comparative Criminology.* 47: 71-88.

Yager, Jan. March 15, 1988. "Precaution Best Defense Against Crime in the Office." *Newsday.* 47.

______________. 2021. *Help Yourself Now.* New York: Allworth, an imprint of Skyhorse.

______________. 2021, 2015. 1978. *Victims.* Stamford, CT: Hannacroix Creek. (First edition published by Scribner's).

Yam, Kimmy. April 28, 2021. "New Report Finds 169 Percent Surge in Anti-Asian The Crimes During the First Quarter." Posted at NBCNews.com.

Young, Sarah. Friday, April 12, 2019. "Ariana Grande Shows Impact of PTSD on her Brain After Manchester Terrorist Attack." Posted at the Independent.co.uk.

Videos, TED Talks, Films, Podcasts, and Streaming Series

"An American History of Hate Crimes." September 14, 2018. 3:02 minutes. Newsy.

Christian, Claudia. "How I Overcame Alcoholism." TEDx London. May 31, 2016. 16:32 minutes. Posted at https://www.youtube.com/watch?v=mYsmyIEp0m8

City of Houston. "RUN. HIDE. FIGHT.® Surviving an Active Shooter Event" July 23, 2012. 5:55 minutes https://www.youtube.com/watch?v=5VcSwejU2D0

Dr. Death. July 15, 2021. Peacock TV series inspired by the 2018 podcast, "Dr. Death." Written by Patrick Macmanus, starring Joshua Jackson, Alec Baldwin, and Christian Slater.

"Dr. Death." 2018, 2020. Podcast, reported and hosted by Laura Beil and produced by Wondery, dealing with medical malpractice. Season 1 dealt with Dr. Duntsch whose conviction and imprisonment for life became a TV series. Season 2 focused on an oncologist who erroneously prescribed chemotherapy.

Foster, Landon. "Coming Out about the Barrier I Did Not Break Because of the Courage I Did Not Have." TEDxUSF talk. May 31, 2018. 13.43 minutes. Posted at https://www.youtube.com/watch?v=KqwF6iog4Lg

A Gentleman's Agreement. 1947. Starring Gregory Peck and John Garfield. Directed by Elia Kazan. 2 hours. Based on the novel by Laura B. Hobson. Screenplay by Moss Hart. Revised screenplay by Elia Kazan.

Boys Don't Cry. 1999. Staring Hillary Swank. Directed by Kimberly Peirce. Real-life dramatization of what happened to Brandon Teena, a transgender male who meets up with hatred and discrimination in Nebraska. Distributed by Fox Searchlight Pictures. Co-written by Peirce and Andy Bieren. 118 minutes.

Schindler's List. 1993. Directed by Steven Spielberg. Polish factory owner Oskar Schindler. This is the true story of how he saved more than 1,200 Jews from the Nazis.

Stevenson, Ed. October 3, 2016. "Seeing Drug and Alcohol Addiction in a New Light." TEDxCoeurdalene. 15:18 minutes. Posted at https://www.youtube.com/watch?v=KYrJ1VV6CWI

Trevor. Produced by Peggy Rajski and Randy Stone. Written by James Lecesne. 16 minutes. Danny Troob, musical score. This is the 1994 Academy Award® winning short film that was the inspiration for founding of The Trevor Project. (See description above in Resources.) Posted at https://www.youtube.com/watch?v=CO5uKgTETSI

CHAPTER **SIXTEEN**

Summing Up and Conclusion

Careers Related to Victimology, the Media, the Discipline's Future, and More

Learning Objectives

After you finish reading this chapter, you should be able to:

1. Identify and discuss at least five careers for victimologists or that studying victimology can help you to pursue.
2. Identify the way that victims are depicted in the media and if change is necessary.
3. Understand the difference between crime prevention and victimization reduction.
4. Discuss several of the issues that the discipline is facing and its potential future.

OVERVIEW

In this final chapter in *Essentials of Victimology*, you will find an annotated listing of the more than 60 diverse careers that should benefit from studying Victimology, occupations you might even consider, the media and victims, the debatable idea of crime victimization reduction, the future of the discipline of victimology, concluding thoughts and, finally, some of the additional materials you will find posted at the publisher's page for this book at their website, www.AspenPublishing.com.

We have covered a lot of diverse topics in this textbook that impact on anyone who wants to understand the victim part of crime as well as other situations where there are victims such as natural disasters and even the so-called victimless crimes of alcoholism and drug addiction. Hopefully you have learned a lot by reading *Essentials of Victimology*. Whether you are taking victimology because it is a required course for your major, or as an elective because you just thought the course sounded interesting, or you are in a graduate program, in this section of this final chapter we will address victimology as a career as well as jobs and careers that studying victimology will be useful for.

CAREERS AND VICTIMOLOGY

As you will see from the descriptions of the 60+ jobs or careers that studying victimology will help you with, there is more to victimology than just becoming a professor of this unique field, teaching at a college or university, or being a victim advocate, helping rape, domestic violence, and other victims to deal with their victimization.

There are eight broad categories of jobs or careers that studying victimology will help you with, including:

1. Research and Teaching
2. Advocacy, Counseling, and Mediating
3. Law Enforcement
4. Criminology
5. Law and the Courts
6. Corrections
7. Medicine
8. Applied Careers

Two sources of information about salary ranges for any of the jobs identified below is the job search portal https://www.Indeed.com or the old standby government publication, *Occupational Outlook Handbook* (https://www.bls.gov/ooh/) published by the U.S. Bureau of Labor Statistics. At Indeed.com, you may set up a free alert for any of the jobs you are interested in by putting in the keyword as well as the location and how many miles beyond that location you want to receive job listings.

The social media site https://www.Linkedin.com, has also become a leading job search option. Monster.com and Careerbuilder.com are other options as are the sites for government jobs including https://www.usajobs.gov for jobs in the federal government. Remember to also search local and state job sites for additional job listings. You may use the 60 listings below for possible keywords to put into any of these sites, based on the areas you are interested in. But remember that these job titles are general guidelines. The same job may have a different title in various sites so remember to read the job description, as well as the requirements, to see if this is what you are looking for.

RESEARCH AND TEACHING

Victimologist

The person who scientifically studies victims is what we have been labeling a victimologist. We have broadened the type of victims the victimologist studies, or teaches about, from the more narrow view of just crime victims to the broader view of anyone who is a victim ranging from natural disasters to the supposedly "victimless" crimes of alcoholism and drug addiction.

Victimologists may work in a variety of government or private company settings, researching crime and other victims, or they may teach at colleges, universities, or graduate schools. They may not call themselves forensic victimologists, but if they have taken courses, and developed an expertise by working in the field, in examining crime scenes, this could be one of their jobs as a victimologist.

A victimologist may combine various job functions under the umbrella of "victimologist" including teaching, crime victim advocacy, research, and even forensic examinations. The American Society of Criminology (ASC) has a Division of Victimology with members and a periodic newsletter. The division also presents panels and roundtables at the annual ASC meeting. For more information, go to: https://ascdov.org/

Expert Witness

Victimologists and especially those who specialize in forensic victimology may be called to be an expert witness in a trial. They might be called because of the forensic findings by studying the crime scene, results that are requested to be presented as evidence at the trial. The expert witness will be asked to state his or her name as well as what his or her credentials are that make him an expert witness. Credentials are very important in validating the authority of the expert witness but having experience in the field is possibly even more important.

An expert witness may be called in either a criminal or a civil case. As noted in Chapter 6, "Helping the Victim," to win a criminal trial, the offender must be guilty beyond a reasonable doubt. To win a civil case, the offender must be found guilty by a lower standard of guilt, namely by the "preponderance of evidence." The types of cases that an expert witness with a forensic victimology background might be called in for cover a wide range from distinguishing between a murder and a suicide to determining if a worker was pushed or fell at a construction site. As Bonnie S. Fisher and Steven P. Lab write in their encyclopedia entry on the expert witness, "An expert witness is an advocate for the truth who works for neither the prosecution nor the defense." (Fisher and Lab, 364)

Crime Data/Statistics Researcher

Compiling research data is a highly-specialized and well-paid application of studying victimology. You could work for the local, city, state, federal, or international governments. In addition to studying victimology and taking courses in research methods, especially quantitative research, someone who pursues this career has to have a personality and mental mindset that has a keen attention to details, is patient, and very careful in checking and rechecking data. Being an excellent researcher, in general, and writer are additional skills since presenting the research findings in an accessible way, for other experts, those in the field, students, or the public, may be part of the job.

Some researchers are able to have their names associated with the data that they research and that they analyze and present. Others may not be accorded that level of recognition, as when the company or agency that employs them is credited as the data's author. So it helps not to be too focused on prominence and realize ahead of time that if you pursue this field you might not get the recognition that you might get if you conduct research and publish it under your own name in other capacities.

Behavioral Analyst

This is a highly trained position requiring at least a master's degree in applied behavior analysis or forensic science, and preferably a Ph.D. in forensic psychology, sociology, or criminology, that requires visiting crime scenes and interviewing victims, witnesses, and bystanders to figure out what happened in each situation.

Victim Organization Administrator

There are national organizations dedicated to helping crime victims. These organizations need someone to run them. Two of the long-standing victim organizations are NOVA (National Organization of Victim Assistance), based in Alexandria, Virginia, and the National Center for Victims of Crime, based in Washington, D.C. Check out the website for each organization, listed in the Resources section. There are job openings often listed as well as volunteer or internship opportunities.

These organizations cover all types of crime victims. There are also centers that specialize in a particular type of victim, discussed below, such as rape crisis center, domestic violence centers, and others.

Teacher

Those who study victimology are in the position of sharing that knowledge with others as they seek to answer the question, "Who are the victims?" Those who teach about victims, even if it is not referred to as victimology, could share it with a range of students from elementary, middle, and high school students to college and university students, those in graduate school, law school, police academies, and continuing education. Those knowledgeable about victimology and crime victims could be called upon to teach about victims in training sessions at various victim crisis centers or victim-witness assistance programs, noted throughout the textbook and in these job and career descriptions.

Sociologist

As you probably know, sociologists are those who scientifically study group behavior. Sociologists may have majored in sociology, or many other majors, followed by a master's degree although most go on to obtain their Ph.D. Sociologists specialize in such areas as family, health, criminal justice issues including studying criminals and victims, race and ethnic studies, or media and marketing. One of many educational paths might be to obtain a master's in victim studies, criminology, cybersecurity, or sociology, followed by a Ph.D. in sociology.

Forensic Victimology

As Dr. Turvey writes in his textbook, *Forensic Victimology*, in defining forensic victimology, "It gives readers the means and rationale for examining victims with a scientific mindset, as opposed to the mindset of a police officer, victim's advocate, or treatment professional." (Turvey, 2014 page xi)

In addition to all the information that someone studying basic victimology would study, here are additional concerns that someone would study in forensic victimology: false allegations of crime; false confessions; forensic science; crime scene analysis; expert testimony; and wrongful convictions. In addition, here are other issues that forensic victimology looks at, similar to in victimology, namely constructing a victim profile, how victims are handled in the criminal justice system, 911 emergency response to a crime, and the dynamics of a range of crimes including domestic violence, sexual assault, homicide, school or workplace shootings, sex trafficking, child abuse, among other offenses.

ADVOCACY, COUNSELING, AND MEDIATING

911 Operator

Handling emergency calls is such an important part of the whole process in victimization that it brings enough drama to be the source of two hit TV shows on Fox: *9-1-1*, created by Ryan Murphy, and premiering in January 2018 and *9-1-1 Lone Star*," set in Texas, which premiered in January 2020.

The 911 operators are the first part of the "system" that the victim will encounter since that is who is called to get to the police, emergency medical help, and/or fire personnel. Education requirements usually include a high school diploma or a GED. Most jobs also have on-the-job training. Some communities may require CPR training as well (since 911 operators may be required to tell someone over phone how to administer CPR until help arrives).

For a further discussion of what it is like to be a 911 Operator, including a recollection of one of her most memorable 911 calls, refer back to Karima Holmes' profile in Chapter 6, "Helping the Victim.")

Crime Victim Compensation Board Administrator

Every state has a crime victim compensation board which administers a fund that reimburses eligible victims for a range of expenses related to funerals, crime scene clean up, injuries, or, especially in the case of homicide, loss of wages. You can find your state board by doing an internet search or going to the National Association of Crime Victim Compensation Boards (http://www.nacvcb.org/) and linking to your state and its website. Working for your state board may include everything from considering applications to writing or revising information for the website or related brochures, working with local law enforcement and hospitals to make sure their personnel are aware of what the compensation boards may offer eligible crime victims, or dealing with the media.

Crime Victim Advocate

Some crime victim advocates are also counselors so you may want to read through both of these thumbnail sketches. In a broader way, however, the crime victim advocate will be attached to a local crime victim center, or hotline, which may be based at the local police precinct (see listing below), at the local district attorney's office (see listing below), or at an independent crime victim center. That local center may service all crime victims or it may be specialized by type of crime, such as a crisis center for victims of rape or another center specializing in offering help for domestic violence victims.

When a crime has been reported, a crime victim advocate may be assigned to that victim through the local police, the hospital, or the victim witness assistance program at the district attorneys' office.

The crime victim advocate may be with the assigned victim through any and all of the procedures that the victim has to go through, depending on the particular case. For example, if a victim has been raped, and she is at the hospital getting a rape kit done, the nurse might ask if it's okay to call in a crime victim advocate to help her through the procedures. If the victim agrees, the crime victim advocate should arrive within 20 to 45 minutes of the call.

One of the major functions of a crime victim advocate initially at the hospital, in addition to being a source of information and emotional support for the victim, is to let the victim know that it is her (or his) choice if the police will be called. In a rape case, calling the police is not automatic.

One of the primary goals of the crime victim advocate is to help the victim feel a restored sense of control in her or his life. That means presenting options and allowing the victim to choose what to do. Restoring that sense of control is an important first step in helping victims cope because a victim of a rape or robbery may have been confronted by an attacker who says "Do what I say or I'll kill you."

There is a lot of confusion about what kind of salary a crime victim advocate might receive because there are paid crime victim advocates who are trained but there are also unpaid volunteers. Although those who are volunteers do not receive financial compensation; however, they receive valuable training for functioning as a volunteer in the first place, as well as on-the-job training by doing the work of an advocate. Some volunteers are using the experience as a stepping stone to a paid position. Others are using it to learn more about crime victims and victimology and to help in getting into graduate school or even fulfilling an on-the-job requirement that might be part of a course or a degree.

Paid crime victim advocates can make a decent salary, depending upon who is offering the position and how much experience the advocate may bring to the position. Obviously salaries are higher for advocates with experience than those at the entry level.

Crime Victim Counselor

Some crime victim advocates are also volunteers or paid counselors. This is not to be confused with the psychologist, psychiatrist, mental health counselor, or social worker described below. Crime victim counselors, even volunteer counselors, all have to go through at least 40 hours of training about how to counsel victims. The pay level for crime victim counselors may be higher if becoming a crime victim counselor is one of your functions but your overall training, and job title, is one of the more specialized categories below, namely, forensic psychologist, psychologist specializing in crime victims, psychiatrist specializing in crime victims, mental health counselor, or social worker.

Depending on the state, you may need to be certified to be able to get reimbursed by a health insurance company which is why if you become a crime victim counselor as part of your training for one of those other counselor jobs, you may earn more money.

Crime victim counselors, regardless of training, will be focused on helping a crime victim to deal with what happened and to go forward in their lives. As noted below, there are also specialized crime victim counselors and/or advocates, by type of crime such as a counselor for victims of rape, domestic violence, child abuse, or elder abuse. One of the advantages of picking the type of victim you will specialize in is that not only will you get to know the typical victim reactions, and needs, but you will also get familiar with the resources that are available for that type of victim. The downside is that it could get repetitious to only deal with one type of crime victim. As with advocacy positions, these positions range from volunteer to paid. Some volunteers begin in that capacity but once they log in a certain number of hours, or finish their undergraduate or graduate degrees, they get promoted to a paid counseling position at the current or another agency or organization.

Rape Victim Counselor/Advocate

This is a victimology-related position that could be volunteer or paid and it covers the same skills and activities as the general crime victim advocate or counselor, described above, but it is focused on victims of rape, sexual assault, and sexual harassment. In addition to helping specific victims, and their families, to deal with the crime and its aftermath, there may be opportunities to visit elementary, middle, and high schools to offer educational talks about rape prevention. Sexual harassment training has become mandatory in many states and there may be opportunities to offer it although advanced training, and even certification, to teach such a course, online or in person, may be required.

Domestic Violence Counselor/Advocate

Someone helping victims of domestic violence as an advocate or a counselor will do much the same activities as someone working with rape victims except for a very big difference: the IPV (intimate partner violence) victim may need help getting out, moving to a shelter or another safe place, before she or her children her harmed. Working in the domestic violence field, you may work directly with victims at the office or on a hotline or you might be stationed at the shelter where the IPV victims and their children retreat to once they decide to leave.

Homicide Survivors Counselor/Advocate

This unique group of secondary victims may need immediate as well as long-term help. The advocacy part, like for the other specialized victim advocate positions, includes helping the victim to navigate the criminal justice system. The counseling part may mean listening and providing feedback one-on-one with the homicide victim survivor or being a facilitator in a support group for several survivors. (Homicide survivors are the spouse, romantic partner, children, siblings, cousins, parents, friends, and even co-workers of the homicide victim.)

Administrator for a Crime Victim Center

Every crime victim center that provides advocacy and counseling needs an administrator. The administrator may also perform those other functions or will just be an administrator as well as a fund raiser. They may also supervise or direct the training of volunteers as well as paid staff and even deal with the media. (Crime victim centers may be government or privately-funded and run agencies.)

Elder Abuse Specialist

Those who are dealing with victims of elder abuse may be working with the families of the elderly who are in nursing home situations where abuse is suspected. If the family member is the suspected abuser, they will have procedures that they have to follow to get the alleged abuse verified including reporting the situation to the police or another government agency. Some, not all, have mandatory reporting by physicians, caregivers, medical workers, nursing home staff, paramedic, and others, such as the Adult Protective Services Act of Florida. Alaska has mandatory reporting of suspected elder abuse within 24 hours of first detecting signs of it. To find out what is required in any particulate state, RAINN (Rape, Abuse & Incest

National Network) has information archived at their site that is easily searchable: https://apps.rainn.org/policy/compare/elderly.cfm

Child Abuse Specialist

All 50 states require mandatory reporting by individuals in certain jobs of any suspected child abuse, including doctors nurses, social workers, therapists, and others. Child abuse specialists are usually social workers so refer to that listing below for more information.

Social Worker

These trained counselors study the signs of child abuse as part of their preparation. Since so many of the child abuse cases will be referred to the child services division of a community or city, the social worker will get assigned the case and will be asked to investigate. Understanding the dynamics behind child abuse and its victims as well as having a knowledge of teen victims will help anyone going into a social work career. Check with the state or county where you want to practice social work for specific requirements. Some may require completing a Masters of Social Work degree, passing an exam given by the Association of Social Work Boards (ASWB), and extensive field work under the supervision of a Licensed Clinical Social Worker. The NASW (National Association of Social Workers) (socialworkers.org), a professional membership association, provides career-related information.

Forensic Psychologist

This has become a very popular major, graduate degree, and career for those who might have majored in criminology or criminal justice previously. Although the focus for a **forensic psychologist** is why a criminal commits a crime, understanding the other half of that equation, the victim, can only help someone pursuing this field. Although some positions may only require a master's degree, most require a doctorate in forensic psychology as well as getting licensed, which varies by state. Forensic psychologists usually specialize in criminal, family, or civil cases; they may be asked to testify in court as an expert witness. Forensic psychologists work in a range of settings including prisons, police departments, hospitals, or as consultants. A related professional membership association is The International Association for Correctional and Forensic Psychology (https://www.myiacfp.org)

Psychologist Specializing in Crime Victims

Counseling crime victims will of course benefit by studying the victim. A leading expert in this field of the last 50 years was Morton Bard, who was a police officer before becoming a psychologist and professor at City University of New York, as well as an expert on crime victims. He co-authored the popular book, *A Crime Victim's Book*, back in the mid-1970s. He combined his practical experience in the field as a police officer who interviewed victims as part of his job with his later academic training.

Psychiatrist Specializing in Crime Victims

Dr. Martin Symonds had a similar background to Morton Bard, Ph.D. in that he went from a police officer to a psychiatrist specializing in the treatment of crime victims. Instead of becoming a police officer, studying victimology is a way to at least have a strong background in victims besides the medical and graduate training in psychiatry.

Mental Health Counselor

If someone becomes a mental health counselor, even if he or she has a practice with a wide range of patients, victimology training will help to understand what victims go through. The term **mental health counselor** applies to a range of jobs or careers, some requiring a master's in counseling (for example, Master of Arts in Counseling; Master of Arts in Rehabilitation Studies), some requiring a Ph.D., or some just requiring on-the-job supervised experience.

Grief Counselor

This is a job for someone who is an expert with those going through grief. The grief could be related to loss of a spouse because of illness or an accident, but it could also be due to homicide.

Trauma Counselor

There are counselors who specialize in getting over trauma. The trauma could be more than victimization and it could be recent or long-standing traumas. Someone specializing in this type of counseling might be affiliated with a hospital, crime victim center, or private practice.

Human Trafficking Investigator

There are a range of jobs available in this field that may be located in government or through non-profit efforts to stop human trafficking, or to help the victims. Someone who specializes in becoming a human trafficking investigator may work for a local, state, or federal agency or private non-profit organization that is focused on direct help to victims or educating businesses and the public about the issue.

Restorative Justice Program Administrator

There is a growing trend toward restorative justice as an alternative to prisons whereby the criminal, the victim, the mediator, and a representative of the community all agree on a program that the offender must follow to avoid prison. Administrators are needed in this field.

There are restorative justice jobs in schools (elementary, middle and high school), colleges and universities, the courts, corrections, and as an independent consultant. The National Association of Community and Restorative Justice (NACRJ) is a related nonprofit membership association (https://nacrj.org)

Dispute Resolution Mediator

In addition to needing an administrator to run the restorative justice program, there is a need for mediators who work out the agreement among all parties. Most dispute resolution or mediator jobs in the private, government, or independent consultant sectors require a bachelor's degree. Majors and minors are from a wide range of disciplines including law, criminology, victimology, sociology, communications, psychology, and dispute resolution, among others. Even taking courses in this area, or obtaining a certificate in dispute resolution, should prove useful. A law degree or a Ph.D. is another valued credential. The professional membership association for those in the field of meditation and dispute resolution is the Association for Conflict Resolution® (https://acrnet.org)

LAW ENFORCEMENT

Police Officer

Officers working in law enforcement may work at a local police precinct or for a sheriff's department. Jobs are available at the local, state, federal, and international level.

One of the most controversial and challenging jobs in the criminal justice system in the United States today is that of police officer. Requirements vary from local precinct to local precinct, from state to state, and even to federal, as does salary and benefits. Some require a four-year degree, others only a high school diploma. A mandatory six months of training is usually required. Studying victimology certainly should be useful to anyone planning to become a police officer.

The police officer arriving on the scene needs to quickly assess the situation and assess the level of threat in the situation. Sadly, two police officers who answered a domestic violence call did not even get a chance to do that. When they arrived at the door of the residence of the location of the domestic disturbance, the 23-year-old assailant shot and killed them. When two additional officers arrived, the assailant reportedly shot himself. (Osborne and Mendez, 2020)

In more typical cases, after responding police officers make the assessment that a scene is safe and secure for the victims, they will secure the evidence in the crime scene. If medical help has not already been requested, they will do that. Once evidence has been obtained and secured, they may take testimonies from the victims and any additional witnesses.

Forensic Scientist/CSI Investigator

This is a photo released by the FBI showing an FBI Evidence Response Team.

Although off the air now and only available in reruns on cable television, the hit TV show, *CSI,* for a decade educated Americans and viewers around the world about the day-to-day activities of the forensic scientist or crime scene investigator (CSI). Going to a crime scene, running tests, and comparing the evidence to the preconceived notion about "who done it" is what this job is all about. Although *CSI* focused on murder scenes, there is a need for forensic evidence in more than just murder scene including rape, robbery, and other crimes.

Getting as complete a picture of who the victim was is a key part of the crime scene analysis process. If an offender is already suspected, and even arrested, that is one type of scenario. But if the offender has left the scene of the crime, finding out as much information as possible about the victim, his or her relationships, the details of his or her most recent activities, and other crucial details may help to figure out who the offender was. Obviously the procedure will be different if it is the crime scene of a homicide victim or another type of crime where the victim is available for questioning.

Detective

Detectives are specialized police officers who are trained to investigate crime scenes. At least a high school diploma is required for this job although many require a college degree with a specialization in criminology or criminal justice. Several years on the job as a police officer are also usually required. A detective will gather the evidence and interview potential suspects, among other duties related to dealing with a criminal case.

Homicide Investigator

This is a police officer who specializes in homicide. Some departments also have a robbery-homicide unit as well. Some of the tasks include interviewing witnesses, analyzing evidence including fingerprints, arresting suspects, and testifying in court if there is a trial.

CRIMINOLOGY

Criminologist

Having a Ph.D. in criminology, sociology, or criminal justice is usually the criteria for being called a criminologist. Criminologists are scientifically studying crime and criminal behavior. In addition to teaching at the undergraduate college or graduate school level, there may be opportunities for criminologists to be consultants to government or private companies, such as security firms, who may benefit from their expertise.

Cybercrime/Cyber Security

A combination of training in computer science and in criminology would be an ideal education for someone pursuing cybercrime or cyber security. The skills that cyber security requires are in demand today by all businesses especially big ones and by governments as well. Cyber security experts can be those who investigate cybercrimes or they can be those who are working on ways to prevent the breaches in the first place. Understanding the way that victims behave, as a way to better grasp programs and plans that might make someone less susceptible to becoming victims of these cybercrimes, might be helpful for the cyber security experts to know. This has become one of the most in-demand jobs in victimology and criminology. Having the combination of computer skills and criminology knowledge is a winning combination that is challenging to find. Depending on what city or state you will work in, and whether or not you have an MS or MA degree beyond a BA, salaries may start close to or at the $100K range and go up from there.

Criminal or Victim Profiler

Victim profiling, and criminal profiling, might be described as two sides of the same coin. You are profiling (analyzing psychological and behavioral characteristics) the possible or actual victim because you want to figure out who the offender might be. Conversely, you might be profiling the criminal to determine who was or will be his or her next victim.

Crime Analyst

Those who have this job may be law enforcement or civilians. This is a job for someone who likes conducting research, collecting data, analyzing it, and writing about it. Having a degree in criminal justice, victimology or criminology will be helpful; research methods courses are especially useful. The data that the crime analyst compiles may be useful to detectives or investigators who are trying to solve a crime or even see a pattern in a series of similar crimes. Crime analysts look for tendencies in where crimes are occurring as well as what is known about the victims.

Polygraph Examiner

Also known as the lie detector test, the person who administers the **polygraph** exam is trained to do this job so they administer the test is as professional a way as possible. They also learn how to read the reports and convey that information to the interested parties. John Larson, a police officer with a Ph.D. in physiology, invented the polygraph test in 1921. (Carlsen, 2010) Although the test is often inadmissible in many cases, and it is no longer used in all but highly selective pre-employment situations, the information from the test may still be useful in a variety of government and private segment situations. The American Polygraph Association certifies examiners, a distinction that is useful to anyone who wants to go to the top of this field.

Criminal Justice Reformer

There are a wide range of paid and unpaid jobs that are dedicated to reforming the criminal justice field in the United States and internationally. Each of those programs or organizations has administrative jobs as well as jobs dependent on the specialized knowledge of a victimologist. Some of the top organizations that would fit under the category of criminal justice reformer are the New York-based Vera Institute of Justice and the Washington, D.C.-based The Sentencing Project. There is also the well-known The Innocence Project which since its founding in 1992 has led to the release of hundreds of wrongly-convicted offenders, freed through **DNA evidence**. You could even consider The Fortune Society, started by former Broadway producer David Rothenberg a form of criminal justice reform. It has helped untold thousands of ex-offenders to avoid going back to a life of crime after their release in the 50 years since it was founded. They have a need for administrators and counselors.

LAW AND THE COURTS

Defense Attorney/Lawyer

Defense attorneys will be defending those who are accused but it still will be helpful to know about victimology especially since so many criminal defense attorneys start off in the district attorney's office, on behalf of the victim/witness.

Lawyer Specializing in Civil Suits for Victims

Some lawyers specialize in bringing civil suits on behalf of victims against the offender, whether he or she has been found guilty in a criminal case or not, as well as against third parties who are deemed negligent.

Assistant District Attorney (ADA)

Since the assistant district attorney (also known as prosecutors) is usually pursuing a case because a victim has come forward with a complaint, knowing as much as possible about victims can only help ADAs at their job. As you know from reading this textbook so far, only around 5 percent of all criminal cases actually go to trial. The rest are plea bargained. That does not even include all the cases that are dismissed and do not even get that far. But whether or not a case goes to trial, and whether or not the defendant is found guilty and, if found guilty, whether or not probation, a fine, and jail or prison time is imposed, there are usually one or many victims behind each of those cases.

Victim Witness Assistance Specialist

There are victim-witness assistance specialists in the federal as well as the state criminal justice systems. At the federal level, the Victim-Witness Assistance Program and those who run it are there to ensure that crime victims get the rights that they were accorded by the Crime Victims' Rights Act of 2004.

Victim witness assistance programs were put into state district attorney offices beginning in the 1970s. In New York City, for example, the Manhattan District Attorney's office calls their program the Witness Aid Services Unit. Counseling and various social services are offered through the program. In Illinois, in Chicago, the program is called the Cook's County State's Attorney's Office Victim Witness Assistance Unit, founded in 1981. One of their mandates is to offer victims and witnesses information and referrals to services that they might need. Keeping the victim informed about the status of their case is one of its many services to the victim/witness in a criminal case.

Paralegal

For some, working as a **paralegal** is a steppingstone to eventually becoming a lawyer. For others, it is a lifelong career. Paralegals assist attorneys, handling detailed work related to the briefs that attorneys are preparing, conducting research, and fact checking. A high school diploma or an Associate's degree from a two year college is required but a degree from a four year college or university will help to garner a higher starting salary. Getting a certificate in paralegal training as well as taking courses related to this specialized administrative and managerial job will also be helpful. Paralegals need to have an attention to detail, computer skills, plus excellent time management skills that enables the paralegal to meet deadlines consistently. The professional membership association for paralegals is NALA, The Paralegal Association (https://nala.org). They list paralegal job postings at the Career Center portion of their site.

CORRECTIONS

Corrections Officer

Some institutions require a college degree; others only require a high school diploma or a 2 year degree. There is a mandatory training period. Corrections officers do not carry weapons inside the prison so there is a need to learn other techniques to keep the inmates in line that is humane and reliable. Good communication skills will help the corrections officer.

Corrections Counselor

Correctional counselors meet with inmates individually and helps them work out programs to make the best use of their time inside the prison as well as working on plans about how to productively turn their lives around when they get out.

Parole officer

Parole officers work with the formerly incarcerated who are able to complete the rest of their sentence under strict supervision. In this role, you help the formerly incarcerated to rejoin the community, focusing on employment and avoiding rearrest. Requires a bachelor's degree.

Penologist

A penologist scientifically studies punishment including prisons and alternatives. Penologists are researchers who conduct scientific qualitative and quantitative studies about punishment, including prisons. They may be professors with a Ph. D. teaching courses in penology as well as consultants on prisons.

Probation officer

Those who have been offered an alternative to incarceration, such as completing community service or taking a drug and alcohol educational program, are supervised by a probation officer. A BA in criminology, sociology, criminal justice, psychology, or a related field is required.

Warden or Superintendent

This is the one person in charge of the jail or prison. Minimum requirements are a high school diploma or GED, but an Associate's or bachelor's degree in criminal justice, corrections, criminology, police studies, or law enforcement, and even a related master's degree, is helpful. Other prerequisites are one or more years of experience working in correctional administration.

MEDICINE AND RELATED CAREERS

Paramedic (EMT-Emergency Medicine Technician) or Ambulance Worker

These individuals may be first on the scene, even before the police. Training usually takes six months because 120 to 150 hours are required. Paramedics need to pass a state certification test. Educational requirements usually include taking courses in biology, anatomy, basic life support, and similar courses.

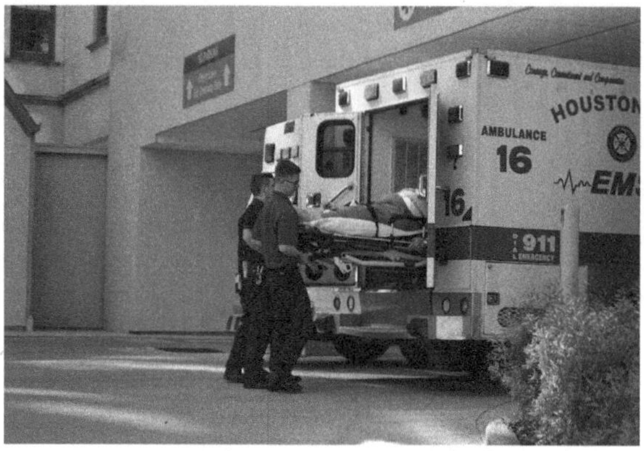

EMT workers loading someone into an ambulance.

Doctor

Victims need to see general practitioners and specialists because of what has happened to them. This includes everyone from a surgeon, if there were extensive injuries requiring surgery, to specialists, such as an orthopedic surgeon, if there were broken bones due to an assault.

Nurse

All kinds of nurses will be dealing with victims from the ER (Emergency Room) nurse to the **Sexual Assault Nurse Examiner** (SANE) if there is a rape or sexual assault victim who needs to be examined and a rape kit prepared. Those who are part of a hospital's SANE staff are usually required to have specialized training related to rape kit and handling the examination of someone who has been the victim of sexual violence.

Sexual Assault Forensic Examiner (SAFE)

Newer term for medical staff trained to examine sexual violence victims and to handle a rape kit. That is because those in the program may be Registered Nurses as well as medical doctors and Advanced Practical Registered Nurse (APRN). They will all have gone through the necessary specializing training as mandated by their state and the participating hospital.

Forensic Nursing

Nursing specialty combining the training of a registered nurse (RNs) with criminology and victimology knowledge. Forensic nurses treat victims of domestic abuse, child abuse, human trafficking, assault, and sexual violence, collect evidence, and may testify in court. Forensic nurse Dr. Ann Wolbert Burgess, who has a doctorate and is Connell School of Nursing Professor at Boston College, has testified in numerous cases including the trial of the Menendez brothers, convicted of killing their parents in 1989. (Giacobbe, 2019) Forensic nurses may work in hospitals, psychiatric institutions, medical examiner's offices, and correction facilities. (Dr Burgess' work on sexual homicide and her rape victim research and advocacy work in the 1970s, along with sociologist Dr. Lynda Lytle Holmstrom, was discussed in Chapter 12, "Sexual Violence.")

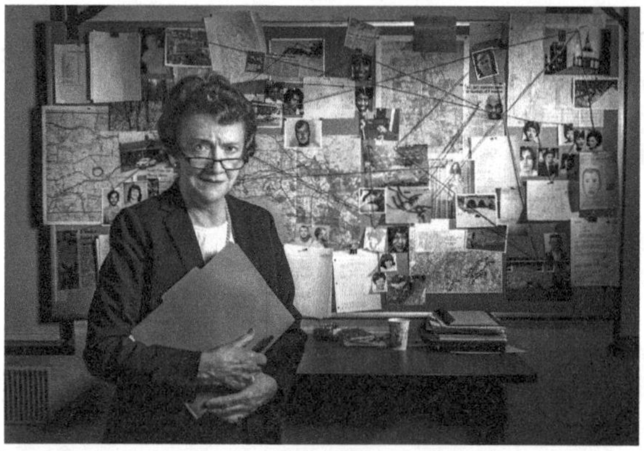

Dr. Ann Wolbert Burgess, said to be the real-life inspiration for the Dr. Wendy Carr character in the Netflix series, *Mindhunter*, based on how Dr. Burgess helped transform the FBI's way of investigating serial killers. (Giacobbe, 2019)
Photo credit: Gary Wayne Gilbert
(Permission granted from Boston College magazine.)

Medical Examiner (ME)

A medical examiner has to get a college degree plus a medical degree and then to specialize in becoming a medical examiner. Any suspicious death should be given an autopsy although sometimes families will deny that request if it is seen as an optional situation whether for religious, personal, or other reasons. Since so many of the bodies that will be autopsied will be those of crime victims, having taken courses in victimology, or at least understanding victims, could be an excellent course of study for a future ME.

Morgue Worker

This is the person who handles the bodies that the ME (medical examiner) will examine, if the morgue worker works in a morgue. Other locations for this job include a funeral home or a hospital. A high school diploma is a requirement for this position however some employers do require an Associate's Degree in Mortuary Science.

Coroner

This is the secondary, alternative system to investigate suspicious deaths in a community. Some states even have a state ME as well as a coroner system. Coroners are either appointed or elected. Being a doctor is not a requirement. Some coroners are funeral directors or sheriffs.

Funeral Director

After the autopsy, in the case of a suspicious death or known murder or homicide, the body may be sent to a funeral home to prepare for burial or cremation. If the funeral director and his or her staff are trained to understand victim reactions, especially those of the secondary victims of homicide, it will certainly be beneficial as they deal with one of the worst tragedies any family can endure.

APPLIED CAREERS

Consultant to Security Company

Since security companies will be selling to victims or potential victims, having a knowledge of victimology will be useful. Having the statistics for various kinds of crimes in general, such as burglary, and even in a particular community in particular, could help a consultant to.a security company to help the potential customers to feel more confident in the product they are buying.

Fraud Examiner (also referred to as forensic accountants)

These accountants have special training in fraud examination and forensic accounting. The association for fraud accountants is the Association of Certified Fraud Examiners (ACFE). A bachelor's degree and/or a master's degree in accounting is a requirement for this position which could be found in the private or public sector. Some of the situations that might be dealt with include everything from money laundering, insurance claims, or securities fraud to embezzlement, credit card fraud, or bankruptcy fraud.

Government Jobs Including Working for FEMA (Federal Emergency Management Agency)

Victims of natural disaster will benefit from knowledgeable workers such as those who work in the head offices, or go out in the field, where there are natural disasters with tens of thousands of victims.

There are a wide range of government jobs at the local, city, state, national, and even international level available to those who have an understanding of crime victims. Check out the government websites and put in any of the terms on this listing of 40+ possible jobs or careers to see what they are looking for.

Crime Reporter

Having a background in victimology will be useful to crime reporters who will be interviewing primary victims as well as secondary victims and criminal justice administrators. In rare instances, they may even be interviewing the perpetrators. Learning the best way to talk to a victim or a victim's family, to avoid what Dr. Martin Symonds and others referred to as the "second injury," will be useful background to have. (Symonds, 1980, 2010)

Crime Writer — Fiction or Nonfiction

Since all crimes have one or more victims, as well as perpetrators, understanding what the victim typically experiences should help the crime writer of non-fiction or novels to have a well-rounded view of what Mendelsohn referred to as the "penal couple." Readers will expect the writer to have a level of knowledge about crime, the criminal justice system, and victimization that will make their writings believable.

Podcaster

There is a 2020 podcast called "Victimology." It is hosted by Melissa Lee, who is the podcaster, sponsored by The ORACL3 Network Productions. "Victimology" is through Spreaker, a podcast service; it is also available through Audible.com. One of the podcast episodes is an interview with Steven David Lampley about a 51-year-old case, the unsolved murder of 12-year-old Kathy Jones in Nashville, Tennessee. There are many true crime podcasts but those may be focused on the perpetrator. Here are a few additional crime victim podcasts: *These Are Their Stories: The Law & Order Podcast* and *Broken: Seeking Justice.*

Training to become a podcaster may include studying voice, public speaking, and broadcasting, in college or in a specialized professional school, or working with a mentor or coach to learn the necessary interview skills. There are podcast services, such as Patreon and Spreaker, that offer packages for hosting and archiving your podcast. Knowledge of victimology, criminology, and criminal justice topics, including major or minoring in those fields, or in a graduate program, should help a podcaster to have an excellent background for the interviews that usually make up each podcast.

Crime Prevention/Victimization Reduction Trainer

Going into schools, or even giving talks at community centers, are activities that the **crime prevention** or **victimization reduction** trainer would do. There used to be government grants available for such educational programs. Private corporations have funds available to similar efforts but usually the group applying has to be a registered non-profit organization.

Life Coach

A life coach could be a useful person to a crime victim who is recovering from trauma. A behavioral analyst quoted in a previous chapter shared that she often refers some of the victims she interviews to a coach because she finds their "where do we go from here" approach better suited for a particular victim. Others she feels need to go back and reconsider the victimization. Those victims might be referred to a therapist instead.

Photographer

Another interesting applied career that would benefit from studying Victimology is that of photographer. Government or civilian photography jobs for those who are skilled in this area are available at the local, state, or federal level, including for the FBI.

VICTIMS IN THE MEDIA

Fortunately we have come a long way from the romanticized portrait of bank robbers and murderers such as Bonnie and Clyde, in the 1967 movie, *Bonnie and Clyde*, and the bestselling 1975 novel *Looking for Mr. Goodbar*, made into a 1977 movie of the same name, whose alleged real-life inspiration was just a school teacher stopping by at a bar and going home with someone whom she met. It led to a murder but that is what so many singles have been known to do, without tragic consequences or putting the blame on the victim.

The media seems to be going out of its way these days to profile the victims of crime and downplay the criminals. Still, we know the name of the mass shooter at Marjory Stoneman Douglas High School, on February 14, 2018, in Parkland, Florida, but it may be hard for many to recall the name of even one of the 17 victims. Maybe the name of Meadow Pollack is better known because her father did more media interviews, or Jaime Guttenberg, because her father Fred Guttenberg also did media interviews and became outspoken for gun safety. He also authored a book, *Find the Helpers*. But few can name many of the victims. Ditto for the victims of the Columbine High School or Sandy Hook Elementary School massacres, or the injured who survived. But many can name the killers. (Rodriguez, 2018; Guttenberg 2021; Guttenberg, 2020)

Wikipedia is to be commended for sharing (https://www.miamiherald.com/news/local/community/broward/xpjh0p/picture200809794/alternates/LANDSCAPE_1140/meadow pollack) the names of the victims of mass shootings, including back to the first infamous one, the University of Texas at Austin Tower shooting in 1966. The name of every victim, and his or her age, for the Parkland, Florida mass shooting is included in the Wikipedia listing for "Stoneman Douglas High School Shooting." (Wikipedia, 2021)

Still there is, for better or worse, a fascination with why the offender did what he did. Law abiding citizens have a need to separate the offenders and the victims into the "us" versus "we" categories as much as to maintain the just world hypothesis that if you do the right thing you will not become a victim as they do that if you avoid the wrong thing you will not become an accused or convicted offender. We saw in Chapter 14, "Victims of the Criminal Justice System" where we explored exonerated offenders, who served many and even decades in prison for crimes they did not do, that there are those who do the right thing but for a variety of reasons find themselves on the wrong side of the law.

Yes, there are those who are fascinated by the perpetrator, rather than the victim. Jason Moss became so fascinated with serial killers that he wrote to many of them and met many of them especially the Killer Clown, John Wayne Gacy.

Moss' book, co-authored with Jeffrey Kottler, Ph.D., is prophetically entitled *The Last Victim*. Published in 1999, and an instant bestseller, it is disturbing to learn that on June 6, 2006, lawyer and author Jason Moss shot and killed himself. In that way, he tragically made himself the last victim.

The media might benefit from taking even one course in victimology if they will be interviewing primary and secondary crime victims for the TV, radio, podcast, or social media reports. Maercker and Mehr surveyed 63 victims of armed robbery and domestic violence to see if the media reports of their crimes triggered PTSD responses. They did not find a direct correlation between those two events but they did find that there was an overall negative feeling toward the media's treatment of them. Only 5 percent of the respondents felt "pleased" by the media coverage of their victimization and only 11 percent "felt supported." Instead, two thirds reported that reading, listening to, or watching reports about their crime victimization made them feel "sad" and 50 percent said it made them feel frightened. Even though the study did not find PTSD was triggered by the media coverage, the researchers did find that "persons with higher psychological well-being seem to have somewhat less negative responses to reports on their cases." The researchers suggest that the media try harder to keep that in mind when they are selecting what victims to interview and what crimes to cover. (Maercker and Mehr, 2006)

Victims and mental health counselors interviewed by this author concurred. Mary Joye, a mental health counselor who does trauma therapy with crime victims, agrees that the media has to be more mindful of how it talks to, and depicts, crime victims. She says, "The media treats certain victims of crime better than others. For example, the human trafficking crisis is globally reprehensible, and no one seems to talk about it because they believe the victim has something to do with it by not telling or not trying to escape. But they have nowhere to go. They have no finances and truly, as counterintuitive as this may sound, the common denominator of almost every victim is a lack of finances to escape, get away, or exit a toxic or criminal situation. Other victims of crime sometimes live in places where there's a high likelihood of being a victim." Those crime victims deserve to be covered as well. Not just the ones who are famous or whose cases seem to be the ones that the listeners, viewers, or readers are more likely to identify with.

VICTIMIZATION REDUCTION VERSUS CRIME PREVENTION

One of the founding fathers of sociology, Emile Durkheim, back in the late 1890s made the controversial statement that crime is inevitable. (Durkheim, 1895) It is as controversial now as it was more than a hundred years ago, because idealists want to suggest that crime can be eliminated. Especially now that we are all well versed in the psychological financial, legal, medical, and societal impact of crime on an individual, his or her family and friends, and even on schools, workplaces, and society as a whole, it is reassuring to think of a time when crime does not exist.

That is the idea behind crime prevention. Get rid of crime. No more burglaries. No more robberies. Turn the cybercriminals into computer scientists who are gainfully employed by the leading technology companies, not hackers who are committing cybercrime. No more murderers. Everyone is talking out their problems. There is no need for gun control because no one even wants to own, let alone use, a gun. No, playing videogames that simulate gun fire or shooting arrows at camp during archery lessons are the closest to weaponry that anyone gets to.

Sound unrealistic? Unfortunately, it is.

Crime will always be with us to a greater or lesser degree because, unfortunately, there will always be criminals even if it is just one criminal out for revenge, or unwilling to work to make money but instead committed to stealing it, or one rapist who needs a therapist but unfortunately instead commits multiple rapes before he gets the help he so badly needs.

The reality of crime does not negate the importance of taking steps to reduce crime. We do, fortunately, now have measures that have been proven to reduce crime. That is, unfortunately, a whole other book and one that would probably fall under the category of criminology, not victimology. Just to mention a few of those techniques: we know that identifying the ring leaders in a community who are committing most of the crime, the strategy employed by National Network for Safe Communities (https://www.nnscommunities.org/), founded a decade ago by David Kennedy, and run out of John Jay College of Criminal Justice, is a strategy that is working. Cullen and Jonson, sociologists/criminologist in their textbook *Correctional Theory*, make a strong case for prisons rarely working; rehabilitation has better results. By addressing the criminogenic problems that landed an offender in prison in the first place, there is a greater likelihood that he or she will not commit crimes upon release, and create more victims. (Cullen and Jonson, 2017)

But this is a victimology textbook, so we are going to focus on what victims can do and this is going to be a controversial concept because it walks the fine line between victimization prevention and victim blame. However, it is possible to help victims to become more savvy about how they can decrease the likelihood that they will be targeted for crime while still avoiding the trap of victim blame.

It is a subtle but imperative distinction: Someone has the right to walk down the street at 11 o'clock at night, alone, and not be mugged, stabbed, or killed by a gang but that same person also needs to learn that he made a choice to walk down that street alone in that neighborhood and that choice had consequences.

So this section of *Essentials of Victimology* is dedicated to all past, current, and future victims so that you can make choices based on what we have learned from criminals that might help you to be a less likely target or victim. Because we cannot control crime, in general, but you can take charge of your own behavior. Which of course does not mean that if some deranged individual with a high-powered rifle chooses to randomly shoot at concert goers, as the Las Vegas killer did in October 2017, being wounded or killed is preventable. (Belson, et. al., 2017) But there are still some situations and behaviors that, when carefully considered or reconsidered, may reduce at least some of your risk of victimization.

Take Stock Over Your Abode and Yourself

Security equipment has increased exponentially in the last few years with the introduction of affordable surveillance apparatus, especially the Ring alarm system. That installation enables you to see who is ringing your doorbell whether or not you are home. The reason this is just one of many measures someone could take to make their home less desirable to a burglar is that in that video created by a police department in Texas and posted to YouTube (See the listing in the Videos section at the end of the chapter), which lasts almost an hour, the convicted burglar shares exactly what he looks for in a house that makes it a more desirable choice for him.

In criminology we refer to the process that the burglar of that Texas educational video is sharing with video viewers as Rational Choice Theory. Yes, he is confirming that he is making clear and rational choices about what homes he is going to burglarize. It is not some impulsive or random act as some might have thought it would be.

So here are some tips to minimize the likelihood of being a victim of a property crime at an apartment or a home, or even if walking in the street:

In an apartment situation:

- Do not allow packages to be placed outside your door if you are not home. Have an alternative way to get those packages even if you have to use an off-site lockbox situation that many delivery companies or services, including Amazon, are utilizing, especially around the holidays.
- Avoid publicizing through social media or even in casual conversation vacation plans that might announce that your apartment will be vacant.
- Ask a neighbor you trust to keep an eye out for any strangers to your apartment especially if you will be away.
- Have a lock on an interior bathroom so that if you are in your apartment and someone breaks in and you are unable to get out a window or the only front exit, you will be able to lock out the intruder as you call 911.
- If you live so high up that you might break a leg or worse if you jumped out of a window if there is an intruder, invest in a rope ladder that you keep in a convenient location. Do a test run with the ladder to make sure you will be ready, willing, and able to use it in a split-second emergency.
- Always have a second person with you when repairs or deliveries are being made. If you live alone, ask a relative or friend to stop by.
- Do not keep jewelry or valuables in an obvious place. Hide it well.
- Keep the door locked and do *not* put an extra key under the welcome mat!

In a home:

- Invest in a security system, preferably one that is electronic so wires cannot be cut by the burglar or possible intruder and one that can be monitored off site as well.
- Keep bushes trimmed around the house so the entrances and exits are visible at all times.
- Avoid having a ladder near the house especially if it is a two story home.
- Do not keep jewelry or valuables in an obvious place. Hide those well.
- Always have a second person with you when repairs or deliveries are being made. If you live alone, ask a relative or friend to stop by.

- Keep all doors locked.
- Have a door for protection or a sign announcing that you have a dog.
- Have a system for lights going on and off outside so the house is never dark even if you are away. Rather than motion detection lights, which will only go on if there is motion to detect, consider getting lights that absorb the sun during the day and automatically go on at night without having to be turned on.
- If you get newspapers delivered, if you are going on a trip, make sure the deliveries stop or have a trusted neighbor pick up the deliveries. Newspapers scattered on a lawn is a telltale sign that no one is home.
- If you are going away, or even in general, make sure your mailbox is collected regularly. Ideally, install a locked mailbox. It is more expensive than a traditional mailbox but it at least avoids having someone just drive by and collect your mail, finding out names and other information about the homeowners or stealing credit card offers and more.

If you are walking, driving, or biking:

- Be aware. Avoid putting ear buds in your ear and being oblivious to what is going on around you including reading your phone as you are walking in the street.
- Use your judgment but in general, do not fall for the, "Can I use your phone?" trap that is a technique that some robbers use as the would-be caller runs off with the phone.
- Consider avoid wearing expensive jewelry especially in crowded, public situations including thick, gold chains that unfortunately can get snatched from your neck.
- If you have to walk alone at night, arrange for an escort.
- If you call for a car, check out the license plate number or associated number to your order before getting into the car.
- If possible, especially late at night or in questionable neighborhoods, have one or more friends, co-workers, or family members walking with you.
- On your bicycle, stay alert.
- If you are driving a car and stop for gas, women need to know that grabbing the woman's pocketbook out of the car, along with her wallet, has become a new crime to watch out for since women are pumping gas themselves. If you are going to pump gas, lock your car and take the key with you so no one can gain unlawful entry. (This also avoids a potential carjacking situation.)
- When you go to withdraw cash from an ATM, be aware of your surroundings and avoid doing it during late night or early morning hours when there are fewer people around to help you or to discourage robbers.
- Only frequent ATMs in places that are open and without obstructions as well as, if possible, in banks with security guards in that area or nearby.

Violent crime reduced victimization suggestions:

- In family, friend, or acquaintance disputes, walk away before it escalates to violence.
- If you have one, keep firearms locked up and especially make sure children or teens cannot get into the lockbox.
- In abusive situations, get out before it escalates to physical violence. Refer to the suggestions in Chapter 13, "Victims of Assault, Domestic Violence, Stalking, and Elder Abuse."

- Avoid accepting a drink from anyone you do not know well at a party or in a bar situation since it might be spiked with a "date rape" drug.
- Being paranoid is not recommended but trusting your instincts if you feel someone is "not right" and might harm you, and staying away, may serve you well.
- If you meet someone through social media, if you get to the point that you feel confident enough to meet in person, always meet in a public place. It might sound excessively cautious but it might be prudent to consider doing a background check first if it is someone who is a total stranger to you.
- Teach children and teens that in addition to be suspicious of strangers, especially those who are being overly friendly, since the majority of victimizations are by family members, acquaintances, or friends—someone known to the victim—learning when someone is making you uncomfortable, and extricating yourself from the situation, and asking someone for help, is better than a blanket rule to "beware of strangers."
- If a child or teen or even an adult is asked to do something that is uncomfortable and then asked to "not tell" that is when they need the confidence to know that they should tell.

All the above suggestions could be seen as extensions of some of the leading contemporary theories of victimization, including the Routine Activity Theory, which would suggest that being more informed about a situation can reduce the likelihood that it will put someone in jeopardy or create a victimization, as well as Lifestyle Exposure Theory, which suggests by avoiding certain activities, such as going out to bars late at night, where arguments may occur, or coming home alone in the wee hours of the morning, when someone is more vulnerable to crime, victimization is less likely. The same applies for Deviant Place Theory, which suggests that being in places or situations where crime is more likely, such as working as a journalist in a war-torn country, or living in a particularly crime-ridden city neighborhood, can increase someone's likelihood of becoming a victim.

REDUCING THE POTENTIAL FOR VICTIMIZATION AMONG HIGH RISK POPULATIONS

What is being proposed is that there needs to be a stronger alliance and cooperation among psychiatrists, psychologists, sociologists, forensic psychologists, criminologists, and victimologists to understand the behaviors that might make someone a more likely victim or even a more likely perpetrator. In the case of Andrea Yates, she may have been suffering from postpartum depression when she drowned her five young children. In that case, their mother's depression made the children more likely victims. That was a murder not a murder-suicide but the underlying causes to that mother's horrific act may be the same.

Let us mention again the concept of **repeat victimization** which was originally discussed in Chapter 3 in the section on controversies in the field of victimology. This is the proven finding that being exposed to victimization during childhood, or previously, such as the primary victim of child abuse or the witness to domestic violence between parents, are more likely to become victimized themselves, and repeatedly.

For some victims, the awareness that being a victim once as a child or teen has set them up for additional victimizations is a particularly important first step in stopping the pattern also known as polyvictimization. By substituting for the question, "Why me?" the statement,

"Not me!" without any hint of victim blame it could empower victims (survivors) to become more cautious, suspicious, and better practiced at self-preservation.

THE FUTURE OF THE DISCIPLINE OF VICTIMOLOGY

In Chapter 3, "The Discipline of Victimology," we explored the early roots of the discipline, tracing them back to lawyer Beniamin Mendelsohn, who is credited with coining the term *victimology* in 1947, and criminologist Hans von Hentig, who wrote a journal article about victim-offender relationships in 1940. They are considered the co-founders of the discipline. It has been asserted that Mendelsohn always wanted victimology to be a separate discipline, parallel to criminology but not a branch of criminology. Mendelsohn thought criminology was too narrow because it only addressed crime. He envisioned victimology to be a much broader field, studying victims of crime as well as victims of any event where someone is put in the position of being a victim including victims of natural disasters. (Mendelsohn, 1978; Von Hentig, 1940; Von Hentig, 1948)

As mentioned previously, there is a Division of Victimology within the American Society of Criminology. That membership organization, founded in 1941, boasts 3,700 members from 60 countries with the Victimology section having 200 members from throughout the United States and internationally. The Academy of Criminal Justice Sciences (ACJS) also has a Section on Victimology.

There are several journals specifically for victimology: *The International Review of Victimology* and the *Journal of Victimology and Victim Justice*. Both journals are published by the academic publisher, SAGE, out of California with offices around the world. The peer- reviewed journal *Victims & Offenders* is published by Taylor & Francis. Its first volume was released in 2006. In 2021, the journal became established as the official journal of the DOV (Division of Victimology) of the ASC. Additional victimology journals include the *Journal of Interpersonal Violence* and *Homicide Studies*, sponsored by the Homicide Research Working Group. Both journals are published by SAGE.

At the beginning of this chapter, we explored the 60+ careers that studying victimology will help you with. The field of victimology has broad implications to untold undergraduate and graduate students in fields as diverse as law and sociology, criminology and psychology, criminal justice and computer science, research methods and statistics, and even journalism. But what about the future of the discipline? Sadly, if you visit the site for the American Society of Victimology (http://american-society-victimology.org/) you receive a notice that says Archive Site. Not currently Active.

Hopefully the American Society of Victimology will be reactivated and become the force in the field that it could be since its name is a nice parallel to the American Society of Criminology. Fortunately, the World Society of Victimology (worldsocietyofvictimology.org), founded in 1979, is still active. An international meeting is held every few years at a different location around the world. From June 5-8, 2022, The International Symposium on Victimology is convening in San Sebastian, Basque Country, Spain. The theme of that conference is "Victimization in a Digital World: Responding To and Connecting with Victims." This membership organization has a student rate.

Here is its mission statement from their website:

> The purpose of the WSV is to advance victimological research and practices around the world; to encourage interdisciplinary and comparative work and research in this field and to advance cooperation between international, national, regional and local agencies and other groups who are concerned with the problems of victims.

Beniamin Mendelsohn would be pleased. Instead of referring specifically to crime victims, the mission statement instead ends further in line with his original vision, to a more general "victims."

But to kick the discipline up a notch, Masters and Ph.D. programs in victimology must be as valued and as popular as MA or MS or Ph.D. programs in criminology or forensic psychology. More research needs to be done into victimology, and victims, including international research and research resulting in new theories of victimization. The discipline is in need of a theory that will create as much of a stir to criminologists, victimologists, sociologists, and even psychologists as Marvin E. Wolfgang's "Victim Precipitated Criminal Homicide" research, journal article, and subsequent book did in the late 1950s. (Wolfgang, 1957; Wolfgang, 1958)

IN CONCLUSION

We are fortunately finally seeing a shift from a *criminal* justice system to a *justice system* that is concerned with the rights of victims *and* criminals. We of course will never completely return to the victim justice system whereby the victim, not the state, could directly deal with the offender. But a justice system that takes into account the rights of both the accused *and* the victimized is a big step. Consider how in Washington, D.C., victims are able to get an attorney to represent their interest in a criminal case, and it will be provided to them for free. (See the short video created in 2020 by the Network for Victim Recovery of DC, listed in the Resources section below.) Some countries, such as Germany, are innovative by making their criminal justice system more "victim friendly." (Walther, 2006)

***

Victims can become survivors and even thrivers. We know that becoming a victim once may set some victims up for repeat victimization. So, if that first victimization cannot be avoided, perhaps because it was during childhood or some random act that was inescapable, at least through education and counseling, and even self-introspection, additional victimizations may be prevented.

Even the family and friends of those whose loved one was killed can become survivors of homicide. The horrific tragedy they have experienced, the loss they have endured that is greater than anyone can imagine, does not have to define the life of the victim who was taken from them or even their own lives. We remember those who have died because of victimization, and we offer understanding and help to those who have been directly injured physically, psychologically traumatized, and financially compromised.

Victimology is an evidence-based social science providing a better understanding of direct and indirect victims, as well as those who respond to, and help victims, so they are less likely to fall victim to the "second injury." (Symonds, 1980) A victimization happened and cannot be undone, but victimology offers tools to helping primary victims and their families, the secondary victims, to heal.

The consensus is that victimization creates a before and after mindset, especially when it is a more violent crime, or the financial loss is more catastrophic, as it was for the thousands of victims of white-collar criminal Bernie Madoff. Becoming a victim impacts victims but it need not become someone's new label or self-identity. Being a survivor and thriver are reasonable goals that victimology can help those who have experienced victimization to achieve.

But for too many, crime victims continue to be in a group that no one wants to be associated with. But for two many, Yet no one has disproven Durkheim's belief stated in 1895 that crime is a part of every society. (Durkheim, 1895) For some, victimization may occur as long as there is crime.

If change is to occur in the United States, or in any country that deals with victimization, whether it is violent or "only" money and property, we need everyone to be open to thinking about crime, its victims, its consequences, and how we can reduce how much crime occurs, and to destigmatize those who are victims through no fault of their own. Victim blame in any form is counterproductive.

The powerful documentary *Audrie & Daisy*, mentioned previously, is a reminder that we have a lot of work to do to help survivors of violence to heal. Audrie and Daisy were sexually assaulted at the ages of 15 and 14, respectively. In the original 2016 documentary, distributed by Netflix, we learn that soon after her sexual assault, Audrie took her own life because of the shame and despair she felt when the victimization was shared on social media.

The situation with Daisy, however, ends on a note of hope. Originally devastated not just by the sexual assault or by getting drunk almost to the point of alcohol poisoning and being left outside in the bitter cold overnight after the assault, it was the social media name calling that made it harder to heal. Other sexual violence victims reached out to Daisy, however, and the documentary ends on a positive note; we all feel that Daisy is going to overcome this tragic event in her life. After all, look at Elizabeth Smart, the Utah teen who was abducted from her bedroom, held captive for nine months, and repeatedly raped. She recorded a TED Talk in 2014, sharing in detail about her initial abduction on June 5, 2002. Like Daisy, Elizabeth was 14.

Elizabeth Smart was 26 when she recorded her upbeat and inspirational TED Talk entitled, "My Story." You definitely feel that she has dealt with her horrific ordeal and has gone on with her life despite an experience that could have broken so many others. (Smart, 2014)

Sadly, Daisy Coleman would not get to celebrate her 26th birthday. On August 4, 2020, at the age of 23, nine years after being the victim of sexual violence at the age of 14 she took her own life. It was said that she could not deal with the depression that consumed her. (Stafford, 2020)

Daisy Coleman's suicide in 2020, and Audrie's suicide back in 2011, soon after her victimization, highlights how much more work we all have to do to help survivors of violent crime, whether they report it or not, immediately after the assault and in the long term.

I want to reiterate in a slightly different version the powerful title of survivor of sexual assault Chanel Miller's memoir, *Know My Name*, and say "Say Their Names." (Miller, 2020) Yes, say the names of the 8 massage parlor workers, owner, or others who were gunned down in Atlanta,—Delaina Ashley Yaun Gonzalez, Paul Andre Michaels, Xiaojie Tan, Daoyou Feng, Hyun Jung Grant, Suncha Kim, Soon Chung Park, Yong Ae Yue, Elcias Hernandez-Ortiz—(Rosa-Aquino, 2021)—or the 26 children, staff, and teachers who died in the Sandy Hook Elementary School massacre, Jessica Rekos, Olivia Engel, Avielle Richman, Jesse Lewis, Grace Audrey McDonnell, Noah Pozner, Ana Marquez-Greene, Emilie Parker, Charlotte Bacon, Catherine Hubbard, Josephine Gay, Daniel Barden, James Mattioli, Caroline Previdi, Allison Wyatt, Victoria Soto, Lauren Rousseau, Dawn Hochsprung, Mary Sherlach, Rachel Davino, Anne Marie Murphy, Nancy Lanza, Chase Kowalski, Madeline Hsu, Dylan Hockley, Jack Pinto, and Benjamin Wheeler (Kranz and Harrington, 2018)—or the 77 teens and adults who died in the Norway mass murders that included 8 adults killed in an Oslo bombing followed by 69 teens, young adults, and adults killed in the Utoeya island shooting —BBC.com, in 2016, 5 years after the July 2011 attacks, listed every single victim by name in their article, "Norway Attacks: The Victims" (BBC.com, 2016)—or the hundreds of thousands or more of unnamed victims whose victimizations never get covered in the media so we do not know their names, of robbery, fraud, burglary, carjacking, vandalism, arson, domestic violence, elder abuse, child abuse, healthcare crimes, or any other physical, material, or psychological harm that was done to them, by someone they knew or by a complete stranger. Say their names. Offer understanding and help. Let them tell their stories.

Melvin Lerner and his colleagues came up with the powerful concept that people want to believe in the "just world" hypothesis. (Lerner, 1971; Lerner, 1997) So in order to avoid revictimizing those who have been victims and their loved ones, we need to deal with victimization head-on, facing reality and making it better. As comforting as it might be to believe in a "just world," that fantasy is too often linked to falling into the victim blame or victim self-blame trap when someone does become a victim.

There is much work to be done to help those who have already been victimized and to reducing crime and minimizing the chances of victimization. We have covered many of those issues throughout this textbook. Just some of those notable changes that could make a big difference in the challenges that current, past, or potential victims face include better training for law enforcement in how they handle 911 calls especially if an individual has mental disorders or is off his/her medication; improved gun safety that could lead to a reduction in gun violence and related injuries or deaths; a concerted effort to encourage more reporting of crime which is estimated at under 50% for actual victimizations and even lower for certain crimes, like sexual violence; improved clearance rates, meaning there is an arrest for a reported crime—as you know, those rates in the U.S. are quite low, just 45.5 percent of violent crimes and 17.2 percent of property crimes in 2019—and, finally, since as many as 80-90% of violent crimes, especially rapes at college, are committed by someone known to the victim, getting away from just teaching "stranger danger" but instead educating children, teens, and adults about the warning signs that someone might be a perpetrator, and what to do about it, will go far in helping to reduce sexual violence. (Brooks III, 2018; King, 2021; Morgan and Truman, 2020; FBI *2019 Crime in the United States*, "Clearances;" Office of the Attorney General (Texas), n.d.: 36; National Institute of Justice, 2008)

Let us end this victimology textbook on an upbeat note. The lives of the majority of victims of crime may not, in most cases, be the stuff of true crime bestsellers, and the work of a victimologist may not even be as popular as that of the criminologist, who traditionally explores the motivations of the criminal. But it is important work and victims, we have seen, can be just about anyone, and they are. The more we learn about victims, and understand why they become victims, what their experiences are like, and what society can do to make them whole again, the more we will serve those well who have been victimized. If Durkheim's belief that crime is normal and inevitable, which means that there will always be crime victims, is true then we need to help those who are victimized. If crime cannot be eliminated completely, hopefully it is possible to at least have less of it.

Those are the last words of the main part of this textbook. Pat yourself on the back for finishing all 16 chapters, plus the Preface. There are several Appendices posted at the page for this book at the publisher's website www.AspenPublishing.com that you might find useful. You will find specific laws that were mentioned in this textbook, including VOCA (Victims of Crime Act) of 1984 as well as a sample Victim Impact Statement for financial crimes, and other related materials. Other materials in those Appendices include an original Power Point that this author created entitled, "International Aspects of Victimology," that is based on the chapter of the same title from Harvey Wallace and Cliff Roberson's textbook, *Victimology*. (Wallace and Roberson, 2015) Also in the Appendices is the complete self-report by Bill, whose excerpted comments about his sexual assault by an uncle at age 9 were profiled briefly at the end of Chapter 1. Additional anonymous or named, with permission, interviews will be found in that Appendices section.

After this chapter, there is a Glossary which contains definitions of all the key terms that you found at the end of each chapter.

There is an Acknowledgements page where this author thanks the many individuals who helped her to make this textbook possible. If a victim or service provider wished to remain anonymous of course his/her name will not be included. But my gratitude to everyone who shared with this author recently, or over the years, is just as strong whether someone is named or anonymous.

Following the Acknowledgements section is a list of Photo Credits.

Finally, after the Index, there is an About the Author if you wish to learn more about this author.

Thank you for continuing on this journey through victimology as you completed this entire textbook! It is an honor to be your guide! Your feedback is welcome and appreciated!

SUMMARY

This chapter begins by annotating more than 60 jobs and careers that are directly or indirectly related to victimology. Those careers were divided into eight key areas, namely, research, teaching, victim advocacy, law, corrections, law enforcement, counseling, and applied fields.

After the career development part of this chapter, there is a brief discussion of whether victims find it cathartic to talk with the media or if they feel as if they are being used for a story.

The updated end to the story of Daisy Coleman, who was sexually assaulted at 14, attacked on social media for coming forward about her victimization, is that Coleman took her own life in August 2020. She seemed to have been dealing with what happened to her when the Netflix documentary ends in 2016. Alas, at 23, it was said her depression seemed to be behind her suicide. This tragic outcome is a strong reminder that, for some, being a crime victim has both short and long term powerful consequences.

The chapter concludes on an upbeat note, emphasizing how primary victims can become survivors, triumphing despite what they have gone through, directly or even if they are secondary victims, because of the victimization and even the murder or homicide of a loved one.

The future of victimology is discussed. Will it become as strong a discipline, parallel to criminology, or will it be considered a branch of criminology, within the master discipline of criminology, as some have suggested it should be?

Hopefully *Essentials of Victimology* will help readers who are going into fields related to victimology and to helping victims in some way, such as law enforcement, law, forensic psychology, FBI, crime victim advocacy counseling, rehabilitation, social work, corrections, or even research and teaching, to remove the stigma associated with crime victimization. In that way, primary, secondary, tertiary, and quaternary victims may get the understanding, help, empathy, restitution, information, and compassion that they have earned and that they deserve.

KEY TERMS

crime prevention
DNA evidence
expert witness
forensic psychologist
medical examiner
mental health counselor
ME (medical examiner)
paralegal
polygraph
repeat victimization
SANE (sexual assault nurse examiner)
victim blame
victimization reduction

REVIEW QUESTIONS

1. What are at least two jobs or careers that someone who wants to help victims would be qualified for?
2. Why is learning about victimology helpful to law enforcement?
3. What does a forensic psychologist do and how does studying victimology help in that field?
4. What do social workers do that relies on information that victimologists uncover?
5. What are at least two tips that potential victims should consider that might make them less likely to become violent personal or property crime victims?
6. How can the media be sensitive to the needs of primary and secondary victims?
7. Why is it important to try to avoid repeat victimization?

CRITICAL THINKING QUESTIONS

1. Do you think it is better for victimology to be part of criminology or for it to be a separate discipline? Why? Support your answer.

2. Where do you see the discipline of victimology in another 50 years?

4. You are at the end of this textbook with the assumption that you read all sixteen chapters and the preface. Out of everything you read, what is the #1 most meaningful concept you have learned that will help you understand victimology and contribute to a better understanding of the criminal justice field in general? Why did you pick that concept?

5. Out of all the longer profiles or shorter anonymous anecdotes or examples "ripped from the headlines," what primary or secondary victim report that you read about did you find most memorable? Why?

6. If you could have unlimited funds to design and carry out a study within the field of victimology, what would it be? Who or what would you study and why?

ACTIVITIES

1. Make a list of the five journal articles or additional books you want to read related to victimology. Make a timeline for accomplishing your goal of reading those materials. You can find citations for those journal articles in this chapter or any of the previous chapters. You should be able to locate a free copy of those articles through your college library.

2. If you are interested in the field of victimology, consider joining one of the associations that deal with victimology including the ACJS, ASC, and WSV (listed below). Most have student memberships. Take the time to visit the website for those associations, listed below in the resource section, and see if there is a benefit to joining. Remember that you may learn as much from the colleagues you meet, and the information you share with each other, as you do from readings and of course your own experiences.

3. Make a list of the top ten ideas or facts that you learned from this textbook that you did not know before.

RESOURCES

Associations

Academy of Criminal Justice Sciences (ACJS)
Section on Victimology
acjs.org/page/VictimologySection
Membership association of those in the criminal justice field. This is the section on victimology for those teaching, researching, and working in the victimology field.

American Society of Criminology (ASC)
Division of Victimology
ascdov.org
The specialized division of those teaching, researching, and working in the field of victimology.

American Sociology Association (ASA)
asanet.org
Founded in 1905, a professional membership organization of sociologists which includes a student membership option. There are various sections that you may also join including several related to crime, deviance, corrections, and criminology.

World Society of Victimology (WSV)
worldsocietyofvictimology.org
Founded in 1973 on the heels of the First International Symposium on Victimology that was organized by Israel Drapkin and held in Israel.

Job search sites

Indeed
indeed.com
Create an "alert" for the jobs that you are looking for and you will be sent listings openings for that meet that category. Can also indicate the geographic area you prefer.

Linkedin.com
linkedin.com
Professional networking free social media site for connecting with millions throughout the United States and internationally. You may also post status updates about what you are researching. There is a job search function as well.

U.S. Government Jobsite
usajobs.gov
The main job search portal for the U.S. government.

Certificate, undergraduate, or graduate degree programs in Victimology or Victim Studies*

Please note this is not a comprehensive list. For more listings, contact the Victimology divisions of the ASC (American Society of Criminology) or the ACJS (Academy of Criminal Justice Sciences), listed above.

Sam Houston State University (SHSU)
Department of Victim Studies
Huntsvile, Texas 77341

Offers an undergraduate BS or BA degree with a concentration in Victim Studies. Here is the URL for the program's website:
https://www.shsu.edu/programs/bachelor-degree-in-victim-studies/

There is also a Master of Science in Victim Services Management (MSVSM). The graduate program is fully online. Courses are National Advocate Credentialing Program-approved. Here is the link to the website for the program:
https://online.shsu.edu/degrees/graduate/victim-services-management/

John Jay College of Criminal Justice
City University of New York
New York, New York 10019

For graduates, Advanced Certificate, Victimology Studies, is offered through the Forensic Psychology Department. The 12 credit certificate program includes four 3-credit courses. For more information, here is the URL:
https://jjay.smartcatalogig.com/en/2020/Graduate-Bulletin/Certificates-Offered/Victimology-Studies-Advance-Certificate

Alliant International University
Six campuses throughout California
Certificate program is online
https://www.alliant.edu/forensics-certiifcates/forensic-victimology

Offers a three course Certificate in Forensic Victimology program. The credits in the certificate program can be applied toward the MS Degree in Forensic Behavioural Science or the MS in Forensic Leadership Administration.

Algonquin College
Ottawa Campus, Canada

This is a 1-year graduate certificate program that can be completed online. It leads to an Ontario College Graduate Certificate in Victimology. Includes 140 hours of fieldwork related work in such settings as police services, women's shelters, victim advocacy centers. Here is the link for more information: https://www.algonquincollege.com/ppsi/program/victimology/

Stockton University
Galloway, New Jersey

A public university, Stockton's School of Social and Behavioral Sciences offers a minor in Victimology and Victim Services. The program requires the completion of 20 credits (five courses) related to victims and victim-related issues. For more information, go to: https://stockton.edu/social-behavioral-sciences/victimology.html

CITED WORKS AND ADDITIONAL REFERENCES

Barkas, Seth Alan. 2005. *In the Great Together: One Act Plays.* Stamford, CT: Hannacroix Creek.
BBC.com March 15, 2016. "Norwalk Attacks: The Victims." Oslo Bombing. Utoeya Island Shooting. Posted at bbc.com
Belson, Ken, Jennifer Medina, and Richard Perez-Pena. October 2, 2017. "A Burst of Gunfire, a Pause, Then Carnage in Las Vegas That Would Not Stop." *The New York Times.* Posted at nytimes.com.
Blinder, Alan, Amy Harmon and Richard A. Oppel, Jr. June 3, 2019. "'I Will Not Say His Name': Police Try to End Notoriety of Gunmen in Mass Shootings." *New York Times.* Posted at https://www.nytimes.com/2019/06/03/us/dewayne-craddock-va-beach-shooting.html
Brooks III, William G. February 22, 2018. "Police Need More Mental Health Training." Published online at thehill.com

Burgess, Ann Wolbert. August 10, 2021. Personal communication.

Burgess, Ann Wolbert and Lynda Lytle Holmstrom. 1974. "Rape Trauma Syndrome." *American Journal of Psychiatry*. 131: 981-986.

____________. October 1973. "The Rape Victim in the Emergency Ward." *American Journal of Nursing*. 73: 1741-45.

Burgess, Anthony. May 18, 1976. Personal communication.

Carlsen, Ezra. Spring 2010. "Truth in the Machine: Three Berkeley men Converged to Create the Lie Detector." *California Magazine* (Berkeley.edu).

Clevenger, Shelly (ASC DOV Chair). July 12, 2021. E-mail. Message announcing *Victims and Offenders* journal to become official journal of the DOV (Division of Victimology) of the ASC.

Dunn, Jennifer L. February 2005. " 'Victims' and 'Survivors' Emerging Vocabularies of Motive for 'Battered Women Who Stay'." *Sociological Inquiry*. 75(1): 1-30.

Durkheim, Emile. 1893, 1933. *The Division of Labor in Society*. Translated by George Simpson. New York: Free Press.

____________. 1895, 2014. *The Rules of Sociological Method*. New York: Free Press.

____________. 1897. 1952. Translated by John A. Spaulding and George Simpson. *Suicide*. London: Routledge & Kegan Paul.

FBI (Federal Bureau of Investigation). Released 2020. 2019 *Crime in the United States*. "Clearances. Posted at the fbi.gov website.

Fisher, Bonnie S. and Steven P. Lab. 2010. *Encyclopedia of Victimology and Crime Prevention*. Thousand Oaks, CA: SAGE.

Fosburgh, Lacey. October 17, 1975. "Finding Mr. Goodbar." *New Times* magazine. 5(8): 54-56, 57, 58-59, 60, 62-69.

Gest, Ted, with Pamela Ellis-Simon, Scott Minerbrook, and Anne Moncreiff Arrarte. July 31, 1989."Victims of Crime." *U.S. News & World Report*. 16-19.

Giacobbe, Alyssa. July 7, 2019. "Mastermind." *Boston College Magazine*. Posted online at bc.edu.

Grayson, Betty and Morris I. Stein. March 1981. "Attracting Assault: Victims' Nonverbal Cues. *Journal of Communication*. 31: 68-75.

Guttenberg, Fred. 2020. *Find the Helpers*. Coral Gables, FL: Mango.

____________. April 15, 2021. Guest Zoom interview, "Victiomology," Iona College, New Rochelle, NY, Dr. Jan Yager.

Hustmyre, Chuck and Jay Dixit. January 1, 2009. "Marked for Mayhem." *Psychology Today*. Posted at psychologytoday.com. (Article reviewed October 29, 2020)

Johnston, Tracy. February 1978. "Who Else Is Looking for Mr. Goodbar?" *Ms*. 24, 26.

Jones, Kay. July 11, 2020. "Two Texas Police Officers Fatally Shot While Responding to a Domestic Disturbance." CNN.com. Posted at https://www.cnn.com/2020/07/11/us/texas-police-officers-fatally-shot/index.html

King, Taylor. April 14, 2021. "Address Gun Violence by going After the Root Causes." Brennan Center for Justice. Posted online at brennancenter.org

Kranz, Michal and Rebecca Harrington. December 14, 2018. "It's Been 6 Years Since the Sandy Hook Shooting. Here are the Name sand Pictures of the 27 Victims, including 20 Children, Who Were Murdered That Day." Posted at the Business Insider.com

Lerner, Melvin J. 1971. "Observer's Evaluations of a Victim: Justice, Guilt, and Veridical Perception." *Journal of Personality and Social Psychology*. 20: 17-35.

____________. 1997. "What Does the Belief in a Just World Protect Us From: The Dread of Death or the Fear of Undeserved Suffering?" *Psychology Inquiry*. 8:29-32.

Lerner, Melvin J. and Dale T. Miller. 1978. "Just World Research and the Attribution Process: Looking Back and Ahead." Psychological Bulletin. 85. 1030-1051.

Maercker, Andreas and Astrid Mehr. 2006. "What If Victims Read a Newspaper Report about Their Victimization? A Study on the Relationship to PTSD Symptoms in Crime Victims." *European Psychologist*. 11(2): 137-142.

Meier, Robert F. and Terance D. Miethe. 1993. "Understanding Theories of Criminal Victimization." *Crime and Justice*. 17: 459-499.

Mendelsohn, B. May-June 1963. "The Origin of the Doctrine of Victimology." *Excerpta Criminologica*. 3(3). Reprinted in Israel Drapkin and Emilio Viano (eds.). 1974. *Victimology*. Lexington, MA: Lexington Books. Chapter 1, 3-11.

Mendelsohn, Beniamin. August-October 1937. "Methods to Be Used by Counsel for the Defense in the Researches Made into the Personality of the Criminal." *Revue de Droit Penal et de Criminologie*. France.

______________. "The Origin of the Doctrine of Victimology."

______________. November 24, 1978. Personal correspondence.

______________. January 19, 1978. Personal correspondence.

Mendelson, B. September 1973. "Victimology and the Needs of Contemporary Society." *The Israeli Journal of Psychiatry and Related Disciplines*. 11(3): 1-9. https://www.crimeandjustice.org.uk/sites/crimeandjustice.org.uk/files/09627250108552963.pdf

Moore, Thomas. July 31, 1989. "Death of a Bard." *U.S. News & World Report*. 20-21, 23, 24-25.

Morgan, Rachel E. and Jennifer L. Truman. September 2020. "Criminal Victimization, 2019." U.S. Department of Justice, Office of Justice Programs, Bureau of Justice Statistics.

Mulley, Kate. Spring 2001. "Victimized by the Media." *Criminal Justice Matters*. 43(1): 30-31.

National Institute of Justice (NIJ). September 30, 2008. "Most Victims Know their Attacker." Posted at the ojp.gov website.

Osborne, Mark and Michelle Mendez. July 11, 2020. "2 Police Officers Shot and Killed in McAllen, Texas." Posted online at ABCNews.go.com

Quinney, Richard. June 24, 2020. Personal communication.

______________. 1970. *The Social Reality of Crime*. Boston: Little, Brown.

______________. November 1972. "Who Is the Victim?" *Criminology*. 314-323.

Rasmi, Adam. "July 11, 2017. "Dubai's Camel Races Embrace Robot Jockeys." Posted at the Daily Beast. Thedailybeast.com

Rosa-Aquino, Paola. March 21, 2021. "These Are the Victims of the Atlanta Spa Shootings." *New York Magazine*. Published at nymag.com

Rosoff, Stephen, Henry Pontell, and Robert Tillman. 2019. *Profit Without Honor*. Seventh edition. New York: Pearson.

Samenow, Stanton E. 2014, 2004, 1984. *Inside the Criminal Mind*. Revised and updated edition. New York: Broadway Books, Random House.

Schafer, Stephen. 1968. *The Victim and His Criminal: A Study in Functional Responsibility*. New York: Random House.

Schur, Edwin M. 1965. *Crimes Without Victims: Deviant Behavior and Public Policy: Abortion, Homosexuality, Drug Addiction*. Englewood Cliffs, NJ: Prentice-Hall.

Shaw, Clifford.1969. *Juvenile Delinquency in Urban Areas*. Chicago, IL: University of Chicago Press.

Shimon, Marilyn. 2016. *First One In, Last One Out: Auschwitz Survivor 31321*.

Siegel, Larry. 2018. *Criminology*. Thirteenth edition. Boston, MA: Cengage.

Stafford, Margaret. August 6, 2020. "Daisy Colmean, Advocate for Sexual assault Victims Who was Featured in Netflix Documentary, Dies at 23." *The Washington Post*. Posted online.

Stark, Rodney. November 1987. "Deviant Places: A Theory of the Ecology of Crime." *Criminology*. 893-910.

Sutherland, Edwin H. 1924. *Criminology*. Philadelphia, PA: J.B. Lippincott.

Sykes, Graham M. and David Matza. December 1957. "Techniques of Neutralization." *American Sociological Review*. 22: 664-670.

Symonds Martin. 1980, reprinted 2010. "The "Second Injury" to Victims of Violent Acts." *American Journal of Psychoanalysis*. 70:34-41.

Thrasher, Frederic. 2013 (1927). *The Gang*. Chicago, IL: University of Chicago Press.

Trevino, A. Javier, and Richard Quinney. 2019. *Clinard and Quinney's Criminal Behavior Systems*. Fourth edition. New York: Routledge.

Turvey, Brent E., et al. 2014, 2009. *Forensic Victimology: Examining Violent Crime Victims in Investigative and Legal Contexts*. Boston, MA: Academic Press, an imprint of Elsevier.

Tyler, Kimberly A. and Morgan R. Beal. 2010. "The High-Risk Environment of Homeless Young Adults: Consequences for Physical and Sexual Victimization." *Violence and Victims*. 25: 101-115.

U.S. News & World Report. July 1, 1989. "Victims of Crime." Cover story and issue.

Von Hentig, Hans. 1948. *The Criminal and His Victim: Studies in the Sociobiology of Crime*. New Haven, CT: Yale University Press. Reprint edition, 1979, with a Preface by Marvin E. Wolfgang. Schocken.

______________. September-October 1940. "Remarks on the Interaction of Perpetrator and Victim." *Journal of Criminal Law and Criminology*. 31(3): 303-309.

Wallace, Harvey and Cliff Roberson. 2015. *Victimology*. Fourth edition. New York: Pearson.

Walther, Susan. December 2006. "Victims' Rights in the German Court System." *Federal Sentencing Reporter*. 19: 113-118.

Wertham, Frederic. 1949. *The Show of Violence*. New York: Doubleday.

Wikipedia. July 22, 2021. "Mass Shootings in the United States." Retrieved from https://en.wikipedia.org/wiki/Mass_shootings_in_the_United_States

Williams, Christopher. Winter 1996. "An Environmental Victimology." *Social Justice*. 23(4): 16-40.

Wolfgang, Marvin. 1958. *Patterns of Criminal Homicide*. Philadelphia, PA: University of Pennsylvania Press.

______________. May-June 1957. "Victim-Precipitated Homicide." *Journal of Criminal Law, Criminology, and Police Science*. 48(1): 1-11.

Yager, Jan. 2021. *Help Yourself Now*. New York: Allworth, an imprint of Skyhorse.

___________. *Victims*. 2021. Original book published by Scribner's in 1978. With a new introduction, updated bibliography and resources. Stamford, CT: Hannacroix Creek.

___________. (a/k/a J.L. Barkas). May 1977. "Victims of Crime and Social Change." Goddard Graduate Program, Masters in Criminal Justice. Dr. Arthur Niederhoffer, Thesis Advisor.

Zaykowski, Heather and Lena Campagna. 2014. "Teaching Theories of Victimology." *Journal of Criminal Justice Education*. 25:4: 452-467.

Videos, Documentaries, Podcasts, Series, and TED Talks

Audrie & Daisy. 2016. Documentary directed by Bonni Cohen and Jon Shenk. Actual Films, Production Company. Distributed by Netflix. What happened after the sexual assault of two teenager in 2011, to 15-year-old Audrie Pott who lived in California, and in 2012 to Daisy Coleman, who was 14 and lived in a small town in Missouri. 1-1/2 hours.

"Inside the City: Victim Advocate." City of Vancouver, Washington. 1:31 minutes Posted at youtube.com

"Crime Victims' Rights: Working with Victims of Crime" June 8, 2020. 3:17 minutes Produced by Network for Victim Recovery of DC. Posted at https://www.youtube.com/watch?v=j_kcmKVQOIw

Lost Girls: An Unsolved American Mystery. 2020. Netflix release. Based on a true story.

City of Allen Police Department. December 8, 2015. "Inside the Mind of a Thief: Burglar Confessions." 43 minutes. Interview done in jail with a professional burglar about what makes him choose to burglarize one home over another. https://www.youtube.com/watch?v=DtwD-c9hn58

"The Minds Behind Mindhunter." September 24, 2018. Interviews with Dr. Ann Wolbert Burgess and John E. Douglas. Boston College. 1:23 hours. Posted at https://www.youtube.com/watch?v=gh1nrN97fPg

Mindhunter. 2017. Netflix series. Season 1. Based on the 1995 true-crime book, Mindhunter, by John E. Douglas and Matt Olshaker. Directed by David Fincher. Traces the beginnings of the Behavioral Science Unit at the FBI in the late 1970s.

Mindhunter. 2019. Netflix series. Season 2. Continues the development of the Behavioral Science Unit at the FBI, in the early 1980s.

Smart, Elizabeth. January 31, 2014. "My Story." TedxUniversityofNevada. Elizabeth Smart, who was abducted, kidnapped, and raped for nine months when she was 14 years old. She shares the details of what happened the night she was abducted, how she survived "the nine-month long nightmare" as well as how she has dealt with it since then. 11:46 minutes. Posted at https://www.youtube.com/watch?v=h0C2LPXaEW4

Lee, Melissa. "Victimology" Posted at https://www.listennotes.com/podcasts/victimology-oracl3-network-93i80S4rEZh/

GLOSSARY

A

Acquaintance rape Rape by someone known to the victim. Also known as date rape. For a definition of rape, see *Rape*.

Admissible Evidence that can be presented in court.

Adverse Childhood Experience (ACE) Study Study of approximately 13,500 participants between 1995 and 1997 that analyzed the impact of early child abuse and neglect on adult health and mortality. Put simply, the higher someone's ACE score, the greater the chance of having physical and psychological problems including heart disease and cancer and even suicidal ideation. (Felitti, et. al. 1998)

Aggravated assault "An unlawful attack by one person upon another wherein the offender uses a weapon or displays it in a threatening manner, or the victim suffers obvious severe or aggravated bodily injury involving apparent broken bones, loss of teeth, possible internal injury, severe laceration, or loss of consciousness . . . ." (NIBRS, 2018)

Alcohol use disorder (AUD) Also known as alcoholism, AUD is the inability to stop drinking because of emotional or physical dependency on it.

Alcoholism Physical and emotional dependency on drinking that prevents someone from stopping despite negative consequences.

Animal cruelty "Intentionally, knowingly, or recklessly taking an action that mistreats or kills any animal without just cause, such as torturing, tormenting, mutilation, maiming, poisoning, or abandonment." (NIBRS, 2018)

Anorexia nervosa Complex eating disorder that impacts eating habits and body image leading to a weight loss that can become life-threatening.

Armed robbery Type of robbery that includes a weapon.

Arraignment Court proceeding where the accused is formally charged with the commission of a crime. A plea of guilty or not guilty is expected to be entered.

Arrest warrant A judge or magistrate issues an arrest warrant, also known as a *warrant*, on behalf of the state, allowing someone's detention.

Arson "To unlawfully and intentionally damage or attempt to damage any real or personal property by fire or incendiary device." (NIBRS, 2018)

Assault offenses "An unlawful attack by one person upon another." (NIBRS, 2018)

Attempted murder The unsuccessful act of killing someone. May also be called *attempted homicide*.

B

B.C.E. (Before Common Era) The term B.C.E. (Before Common Era) refers to events before the C.E. (Common Era). Used in connection with the Gregorian calendar, which considers the beginning of the Common Era as the year 1. The term B.C.E. replaced the term B.C. (Before Christ).

Bail The temporary release of an accused individual with the promise to return to court. Where cash bail is allowed, a monetary amount is posted to encourage the return of the defendant for subsequent court hearings.

Bail bond When someone accused of a crime is asked to pay a certain amount of money to prompt that he/she will return to court for his/her next appearance.

Battered child syndrome Now referred to as child abuse; characterized by the injuries that a child suffered because of repeated beatings or neglect. Pediatrician C. Henry Kempe M.D., in 1962, along with his colleagues, identified the repeated mistreatment of a child in their groundbreaking article, "The Battered Child Syndrome." (Kempe, et. al., 1962)

Bench warrant A judge issues this if a defendant fails to return to court at the predetermined time/date.

Bias crime See *Hate crime*.

Blood feud Bitter disagreement between two families because of a crime, usually a murder, committed against a family member.

Blood money The money that the offender or the offender's family pays to the victim or the victim's family to avoid a *blood feud*.

Body of Liberties The first legal code in New England, established in Massachusetts in 1641.

Bond This is what is posted by someone, usually a bail bond company, to get someone out of jail with the agreement that he/she will return at a predetermined time/date.

Bot In Saxon England, compensation for injury that was given to the victim.

Breaking and entering "The unlawful entry into a building or other structure with the intent to commit a felony or a theft." (NIBRS, 2021)

Briana's Law Requires that all New York police officers including state police receive CPR training preceding employment. as well as every two to four years on the job; proficiency in the technique is required.

Bribery "(Except Sports Bribery) The offering, giving, receiving, or soliciting of anything of value (i.e., a bribe, gratuity, or kickback) to sway the judgment or action of a person in a position of trust or influence." (NIBRS, 2018)

Bulimia An eating disorder that includes bingeing followed by purging (vomiting) that may, in some cases, be related to early childhood or teenage sexual abuse.

Bullying The actions of a bully. "Bullying is unwanted, aggressive behavior among school-aged children that involves a real or perceived power imbalance." (stopbullying.gov) Teens and adults may also be bullied at school or work.

Burglar surprise See *Home invasion*.

Burglary/Breaking and Entering "The unlawful entry into a building or some other structure to commit a felony or a theft." (NIBRS, 2021)

Busse The payment or compensation to the victim when a crime was committed or to the victim's family or kin in the case of homicide. Also known as the *wergild.*

Bystander Someone who is nearby when a crime is committed.

Bystander effect The phenomenon who the more people that are bystanders, the less likely someone is to get involved.

C

Capital punishment The right of the state or the federal government to legally cause the death of someone convicted of a capital crime.

Carjacking When someone steals someone's car, and the person is either still in it or is nearby.

Caste A strict station in a society based on birth that in ancient India was associated with the different way an offender, or victim, was held accountable, or treated, because of a crime.

Child abuse Mistreatment of a child that could be physical, sexual, or emotional.

Child neglect Failing to provide an infant or child with physical comfort, such as food, shelter, clothing, or with attention and affection.

Child pornography Obscene or sexually explicit images of children. Such images are illegal to photograph, film, or distribute.

Child sexual abuse Sexual abuse of a child including fondling, touching, oral sex, or penetration.

Civil court Some victims may choose to seek justice through the civil court system. Defendants who are found liable are accountable to their victims in the form of financial compensation, not for crimes against the state.

Civil suit In a civil suit, a victim can sue and seek financial redress from the offender or a responsible third party. See *Civil court.*

Clearance rate Refers to the number of arrests for a particular offense in a given year.

Club drugs Slang term for drugs that are misused to get someone passed out or unable to fight back if he/she is attacked or raped. Also known as date rape drugs.

Code of Draco Code of ancient Athens.

Code of Hammurabi Babylonian code (from the eighteenth century B.C.E. or earlier) associated with the phrase "an eye for an eye and a tooth for a tooth" representing its form of justice. Very detailed rules were set forth as to how a victim was to be compensated and an offender to be punished or fined, based on the crime that was committed and the status of the offender or victim, freeman, slave, or noble.

Code of Ur-Nammu Written by King Ur-Nammu who ruled from 2047-2030 B.C.E. as the founder of the Third Dynasty of Ur in Sumer. Here is an example: *If a man committed a kidnapping, he is to be imprisoned and pay fifteen shekels of silver.*

CODIS (Combined DNA Index System) The FBI's extensive database of millions of DNA profiles.

Coerced sexual contact Unwanted or nonconsensual sexual activity. That is never okay. Sex has to be consensual at all times.

Cognitive interview A technique that helps victims or witnesses to have better recall of what happened in the events that they are trying to remember.

Collective responsibility In primitive societies, the entire clan is wronged if a member of their kinship group is victimized and, conversely, the clan collectively bears the shame of their kin's criminal act.

Compassion fatigue A form of burnout experienced by first responders, such as 911 operators, the police, emergency medical technicians (EMTs), crime victim advocates or counselors, and others helping those who deal with crime victims.

Compensatory damages In a civil suit related to a victimization, a judge and a jury are able to award compensatory damages to the victim, if the plaintiff wins, for losses that the injured party suffered.

Complacency theft Actions by the victim that make it easier for a theft to occur. An example is when a car owner or driver leaves their car unlocked or leaves, even worse, the keys in the unlocked car, making it that much easier for a car thief to steal the car.

Complainant The complainant is the person signing the complaint, an important step in the arrest process. This is the official court document that has to be signed. In that complaint, either a victim or a witness will accuse someone of committing a crime. In some states, in the case of domestic violence, the state or police could be the complainant.

Complaint In civil court, a *complaint* is the document filed by the plaintiff and served on the defendant, setting out the plaintiff's factual allegations that show the defendant is responsible for the plaintiff's injuries. In criminal law, it is referred to as a *criminal complaint*, a statement about the alleged crime that is filed in court and that starts the criminal justice process.

Complaint and answer In a civil case, filing a *complaint,* the initial step in a potential lawsuit, is followed by the *answer,* the opening formal reply by the defense to the complaint.

Conditional release May be used synonymously for *parole*. When inmates have served a certain amount of their overall sentence, they may go before a parole board and, if approved, be granted conditional release. Paroled individuals have to adhere to specific conditions as they serve the remainder of their sentence in the community rather than in prison.

Continuance If the ADA (Assistant District Attorney), also known as the prosecutor, or the defendant's lawyer needs more time, they may ask for a continuance, which is an extension of time.

Conventional crimes A term applied to violent personal or property crimes such as murder, rape, robbery, burglary, aggravated assault, or motor vehicle theft; also known as street crimes. In contrast to white-collar crimes.

Corporate crime Another term for white-collar crime, a term coined by criminologist/sociologist Edwin Sutherland to describe crimes that are committed by the middle and upper classes and those in corporations usually as part of their job performance.

Corpus Juris Civilis A century after the Twelve Tables, to update Roman laws, the *Corpus Juris Civilis,* also known as The Justinian Code, because it was created by Emperor Justinian I, were set down in 528-529 C.E.

Corroboration A secondary source of evidence to confirm an accusation.

Co-victims of homicide Family or close friends of the homicide victim.

Co-victims People close to the victim, such as their family, friends, and co-workers, who are also affected by the crime.

Counterfeiting/Forgery "The altering, copying, or imitation of something, without authority or right, with the intent to deceive or defraud by passing the copy or thing altered or imitated as that which is original or genuine; or, the selling, buying, or possession of an altered, copied, or imitated thing with the intent to deceive or defraud." (NIBRS, 2018)

CPR Cardiopulmonary resuscitation is an emergency procedure to help someone breathe and get blood circulating to their brain especially in instances of cardiac arrest.

CPTED (Crime Prevention Through Environmental Design) Dealing with structural issues that might be contributing to crime as a way of reducing the likelihood of victimization.

Crime An action or behavior that breaches a criminal law and is open to punishment.

Crime Index Reports the rate and number of violent and property crimes by crime type, including murder, rape, robbery, burglary, larceny/theft, motor vehicle theft, arson, and aggravated assault. Also known as the UCR Crime Index.

Crime mapping Using crime statistics to determine where crime is more frequent.

Crime prevention An approach to victimization that tries to reduce crime by helping potential victims to be more proactive in their attitudes and behaviors. It might also address environmental or systemic issues such as unemployment, gang violence, and family dysfunction that might be contributing to crime..

Crime victim advocate A trained individual, paid or volunteer, who provides a range of services for crime victims from staffing the victim hotline to accompanying a victim to the hospital or to court.

Crime victim compensation program A state or federal government-sponsored program, usually based on funds received from court-ordered restitution or the sale of seized properties. Physical injuries, funeral costs, and reimbursement for psychological counseling are some of the benefits for those meeting the eligibility requirements, which vary by state.

Criminal homicide The unlawful killing of a person without justification.

Criminal justice system In the United States, the system that includes the police, courts, and corrections (jails and prisons).

Criminal law Law that relates to crime.

Criminally negligent homicide Occurs when someone has been killed by someone in a dangerous, negligent, or reckless manner.

Criminology The scientific study of criminal behavior and criminals including what causes them to commit crime.

Crowdfunding A way to raise funds through online platforms such as GoFundMe, Kickstarter, and Indiegogo, among numerous others, to pay for expenses related to victimization.

Cybercrime Crimes such as identity theft, credit card fraud, or cyberstalking that are committed online.

Cycle of violence Behavior pattern common in domestic violence situations, whereby the perpetrator, is alternatively loving and thoughtful with episodes of rage that increase in frequency until there is an outburst that could include physical or sexual violence, or emotional abuse, followed by apologies and promises to change, but the cycle repeats.

D

Dark web A network that is not visible through typical search engines and is often associated with illegal activities including identity theft, drug dealing, prostitution, and other illicit actions.

Date rape See *Acquaintance rape.*

Date rape drugs See *Club drugs.*

Death notification The process of informing the next of kin, usually by the police, when someone is killed, has committed suicide, or died under suspicious circumstances. If possible, making the notification in person is the preferred approach.

Death penalty Synonymous with capital punishment. When the state or federal government issues the sentence of death for a crime, usually especially heinous murders, or for federal offenses including espionage, terrorism, or treason. In the United States, 23 states no longer allow the death penalty.

Defounding When a police officer arrives at a crime scene, or when a victim reports a crime, if law enforcement considers the evidence and listens to the testimonies and determines that a crime happened, but the circumstances are different from how the victim's version, it is called *defounding.*

Determinate sentencing When a conviction has a set number of years in prison associated with the punishment.

Deterrence Actions that discourage the commission of a crime. *Specific deterrence* is when punishment deters the offender from committing another crime. *General deterrence* is when knowing about someone else's punishment will deter others.

Developmental disabilities Impairments in a range of conditions including language, learning, and behavior including autism, ADHD, intellectual ability, cerebral palsy, Down syndrome, and fetal alcohol syndrome.

Deviance Going against a norm or what is expected in society. Acting in a deviant way is not necessarily a crime. Someone has to break a criminal law for their actions to be deemed criminal.

Deviant Place Theory The idea that people are more likely to become crime victims if they live in, work at, or visit places that have a greater amount of crime.

Direct victims Those who personally experience the crime.

Disassociation Phenomenon reported by sexual violence victims of becoming detached from what is happening during their victimization.

DNA evidence Forensic technique that is used in criminal investigations, relying on the unique DNA (Deoxyribonucleic acid) genetic information about each individual.

Domestic violence (DV) Violence that occurs between romantic couples or spouses, whether they are opposite sex or same sex couples. The term could also be applied to child or teen abuse or elder abuse.

Driving Under the Influence "Driving or operating a motor vehicle or common carrier while mentally or physically impaired as the result of consuming an alcoholic beverage or using a drug or narcotic." (NIBRS, 2018)

Drug/Narcotics Offenses (Except Driving Under the Influence) "The violation of laws prohibiting the production, distribution, and/or use of certain controlled substances and the equipment or devices utilized in their preparation and/or use." (NIBRS, 2018)

E

Early intervention The evidence-based penology theory that suggests helping pregnant women, new parents, as well as infants, children, and teens to deal with issues that might lead to criminal behavior later on is a way to reduce later teen or adult criminality.

Economic crime See *Financial crime.*

Elder abuse Mistreatment of someone over the age of 65, including physical, sexual, or financial abuse or emotional neglect or abuse.

Eldercide Killing of a senior age 60 and older.

Embezzlement "The unlawful misappropriation by an offender to his/her own use or purpose of money, property, or some other thing of value entrusted to his/her care, custody, or control." (NIBRS, 2018)

EMS (Emergency Medical Services) Network providing emergency medical services.

Environmental victimology The study of crimes related to the environment. Some see it as a subcategory of "green criminology."

Ethnography The study of cultures by witnessing the society firsthand either as an observer or a participant observer.

Evaluation research Determining the effectiveness of programs such as crime victim crisis centers or restorative justice.

Evidence Proof that can be used to confirm someone's guilt or innocence such as DNA evidence, testimonies, fingerprints, blood samples, or the presence of a murder weapon. Evidence may be direct or circumstantial.

Excusable homicide See *Justifiable homicide.*

Expert witness In a jury trial, this refers to someone with specialized knowledge who is called by the defense or the prosecution. Examples include forensic, medical, and mental health experts.

F

False accusation When a child, teen, or adult falsely accuses someone of a crime.

Federal Trade Commission (FTC) Founded by President Woodrow Wilson in September 1914 to protect consumers and to enforce the U.S. antitrust laws. ReportFraud.ftc.gov is a starting point to share information about a fraud.

Felony A serious crime punishable by time in prison of one year or longer.

Felony murder A criminal offense in the American criminal justice system whereby if someone is participating in a criminal act and during the course of that crime someone dies, that individual is as guilty as if he wielded the knife or shot the victim.

Felony theft The theft of an item or service valued above a certain dollar amount that makes it a more serious theft rather than a misdemeanor theft. Felony thefts can result in jail or prison time.

Fence An individual or business receiving stolen goods and then reselling those goods to others. The recipients of the stolen goods may or may not be aware that they are buying ill-gotten products.

Fentanyl Powerful synthetic opioid which resembles morphine but is 50 to 100 times more potent.

Fetal Alcohol Syndrome (FAS) A condition that can occur in a newborn if during her pregnancy a mother drinks alcohol, depending upon how much was consumed and how often. Also known as FASD (Fetal alcohol spectrum disorders).

FICO® score Your credit score is known as the *FICO® (Fair Isaac Corporation)* score. It ranges from 300 to 850 and it advises those who review the score, such as companies or even potential employers, about how credit worthy someone is considered. Regular checking for any suspicious activity is a reassurance that identity theft has not occurred.

Filicide If a parent or caregiver kills a child.

Financial crime In contrast to the so-called conventional or street crimes of murder, robbery, and rape, financial or economic crimes involve money. Some financial crimes may also be considered white-collar crimes in that the crimes were related to carrying out a job-related company function such as the crimes of embezzlement, tax evasion, bribery, or fraud.

First degree manslaughter When someone dies because an individual, intending to cause serious physical injury to another, caused his/her death.

First degree murder Intentional killing with premeditation

Food stamp trafficking This is when someone illegally buys or sells food stamp benefits for cash, drugs, weapons, or other items of value. In these cases, the victim is the U.S. government and its citizens since their tax dollars make this government program possible.

Forcible rape See *Rape.*

Forensic evidence Includes evidence that is obtained through scientific means including DNA testing, ballistics, and blood samples. Also known as *criminalistics.*

Forensic nursing Specialized branch of nursing where nurses are trained to work with crime victims to gather medical evidence and provide expert testimony that can be used in court.

Forensic psychologist A subspecialty of psychology that includes the application of psychological expertise to the criminal justice system.

Forensic victimology The subtitle of the textbook *Forensic Victimology, Examining Violent Crimes in Investigative and Legal Contexts,* helps to further define this field.

Forgery See C*ounterfeiting/Forgery*

Formal defendant Term for the person who was arrested.

Forward telescoping Reporting a crime victimization as taking place more recently than it really happened.

Fraud "Fraud Offenses – (Except Counterfeiting/Forgery and Bad Checks) The intentional perversion of the truth for the purpose of inducing another person or other entity, in reliance upon it to part with something of value or to surrender a legal right." (NIBRS, 2018)

Friedensgeld The portion that the victim or king received when someone had a crime committed against them in Saxon England.

G

Gang violence When a group of individuals band together, and part of their collective actions includes committing violent crimes.

Gewedde See *Friedensgeld.*

Go-between A mediator, negotiator, or intermediary in disputes.

Going postal A type of workplace violence whereby a disgruntled co-worker stabs or shoots and injures or kills his or her colleagues or supervisors. The term is said to have originated in 1986 when a postal worker in Oklahoma shot and killed 14 and injured 6 others.

Graduated driving A way to try to reduce the number of accidents or fatalities among new drivers by having a graduated driving program whereby what hours of the day driving is permitted is regulated as well as who may be in the car with the new driver.

Grand jury Whether or not a charge should be made against someone can be determined by those citizens who make up a grand jury.

Grand larceny This varies by state, but it puts larceny/theft into a category with stiffer penalties based on the value of the item or service that was stolen.

Grooming When an authority figure sets up a child or teen for sexual abuse by gaining their trust and loyalty through activities they do together as well as by bestowing gifts and attention.

Guardian ad litem (GAL) A guardian that a court appoints to watch after someone during a case. If a child lacks an adequate caregiver, one will be appointed to watch out for the child's interest during a court case.

H

Hacking/Computer Invasion "Wrongfully gaining access to another person's or institution's computer software, hardware, or networks without authorized permissions or security clearances." (NIBRS, 2020)

Hate crime An attack against individuals or groups because of their race, religion, gender, ethnicity, or sexual orientation. At the state and federal level, tougher penalties may be imposed if a crime is determined to be a hate crime in addition to another crime such as robbery, aggravated assault, or rape.

Hazing When a college fraternity or sorority requires pledges to do actions, such as drinking an excessive amount of alcohol, that may be harmful, leading to injury or death.

Hierarchy rule No longer practiced under the newer NIBRS reporting system, the UCR system required that law enforcement only report to the FBI the more serious offense even if one incident included multiple offenses.

Hitting licks Slang expression for robbing people.

Home invasion When a burglar enters an apartment or a home thinking it was empty, but he/she confronts the residents. May also be referred to as a burglar surprise.

Homicide "The killing of one human being by another." (NIBRS, 2021)

Homicide survivors Family members of those who were killed. Other terms are *secondary victims of homicide* or *co-victims of homicide*.

Homophobic Descriptive term for those who have a phobia about or antipathy for anyone who practices homosexuality.

Homosexuality When two people of the same sex are romantically attracted to each other or engaged in a romantic relationship. Today many consider the term *gay* has become more acceptable than *homosexuality*.

Honor killings Illegal and rare but still informally practiced in certain countries around the world, these killings, usually against females, are carried out by family members if they feel the family's honor has been blemished. Examples in those cultures practicing honor killings include adultery or if a girl has a romantic relationship with someone other than a chosen suitor.

Hot spots Places in a community that have more crime than other areas.

Human trafficking "Human Trafficking Offenses - The inducement of a person to perform a commercial sex act, or labor, or services, through force, fraud, or coercion." (NIBRS, 2018)

I

Identity theft "Wrongfully obtaining and using another person's personal data (e.g., name, date of birth, Social Security number, driver's license number)." (NIBRS, 2018)

Identification with the aggressor Psychological defense mechanism of relating to the victimizer that could be considered another version of the Stockholm Syndrome.

Incapacitation One of the theories of punishment that says that putting someone in jail or prison is an appropriate and/or recommended way to deal with the offender.

Incest "Nonforcible sexual intercourse between persons who are related to each other within the degrees wherein marriage is prohibited by law." (NIBRS, 2018) The term may also be applied to any kind of inappropriate sexual contact between close relatives including an adult and a minor or siblings such as sexual molestation and fondling.

Incidence rate A statistical measure of the frequency that an event occurs over a specific period of time such as how many murders occur in a certain year.

Incident report Formal recording of the facts related to a crime.

In-depth interviewing A technique used to find out all the details of what happened during the crime in describing it to police or prosecutors as well as after the crime, as a way of helping the victim to deal with it.

Indeterminate sentencing When a sentence includes a range of years, such as 15 to 25, which could lead to release at the lower end of the range based on good behavior in prison and other considerations.

Indictable offense A serious crime for which a grand jury determines there is enough evidence to bring charges. The court signs a warrant complaint when a crime that is an indictable or serious offense has been committed, or there was an attempt to commit it, such as murder, robbery, and sexual assault. (Replaced the term *felony offense.*)

Indirect victims Family members or close friends of the primary victim who are indirectly impacted by a crime. Also known as *secondary* or *co-victims.*

Infanticide The killing of an infant.

In-person lineup When a crime is reported and an alleged offender is arrested, the victim or witness may be asked to look at several individuals in an in-person lineup at the police station.

Intellectual disabilities Also referred to as ID, a term used to describe those ages 18 and younger who have intelligence and life skills that are below average.

Intellectual property theft Also known as piracy, the creator or creators of the product is a victim because he/she is cut out of any profits for the product that is illegally being pirated.

Intentional animal torture and cruelty (IATC) The physical or sexual abuse or torture of animals.

International Association of Chiefs of Police (IACP) Founded in 1893, this association of chiefs of police was the initiator of the UCR (Uniform Crime Report) dating back to 1920s. The IACP holds an annual conference.

INTERPOL (International Criminal Police Organization) A global organization that encourages cooperation among police departments especially sharing information with each other about those who are most wanted for criminal activity.

Intimate partner violence (IPV) The term that some use to describe domestic violence that includes physical or sexual abuse and violence.

Intimidation "To unlawfully place another person in reasonable fear of bodily harm through the use of threatening words and/or other conduct but without displaying a weapon or subjecting the victim to actual physical attack." (NIBRS, 2018) Considered one of the Assault Offenses; the other two are Aggravated Assault and Simple Assault.

Invalidicide Killing an invalid.

Involuntary manslaughter The unintentional killing of another.

Islamophobia Discrimination and prejudice against Arab Americans and Muslim-Americans.

J

Judgment proof When an offender does not have any income or savings so that he or she would be able to actually comply with any restitution ordered by the court to the victim.

Just deserts An approach to corrections that sees punishment as the goal. It is not concerned with helping the offender to reform. Another term for a correctional theory known as *retribution.*

Just world hypothesis Psychologist Melvin Lerner's research finding that there is a belief in a just world to enable people to go about their daily lives without fear. Could be considered a possible explanation for why so many fall into the *victim blame* mentality. (Lerner, 1971)

Justifiable homicide "The killing of a perpetrator of a serious criminal offense by a peace officer in the line of duty, or the killing, during the commission of a serious criminal offense, of the perpetrator by a private individual. (This is not a crime in the UCR Program.)" (NIBRS, 2018)

K

Kickback A form of bribery which is used to influence the actions or judgment of someone in power.

Kidnapping/Abduction "The unlawful seizure, transportation, and/or detention of a person against his/her will, or of a minor without the consent of his/her custodial parent (s) or legal guardian." (NIBRS, 2018)

Kin Relatives or family members.

L

Larceny/theft "Larceny/Theft Offenses - The unlawful taking, carrying, leading, or riding away of property from the possession or constructive possession of another person." (NIBRS, 2018)

Law Enforcement Officers Killed and Assaulted Information (LEOKAI) Data collected by the FBI (Federal Bureau of Investigation) about the assaults or deaths in the line-of-duty (on the job) including information about the race, ethnicity, and sex of the victim officer.

Laws of Manu One of the first written law codes. Based on the Hindu culture. Estimated to have been written between 200 B.C.E. to 200 C.E.

Leges Henrici A legal treatise written down by an unknown Norman under the reign of King Henry I of England between 1114 and 1118. It contains Anglo-Saxon and Norman laws formalizing offenses that were now crimes against the king or government.

Levirate A practice in certain cultures of when a man marries his brother's widow.

LGBTQ (lesbian, gay, bisexual, transgender, or questioning) Acronym for lesbian, gay, bisexual, transgender and queer or questioning. These terms are used to describe a person's sexual orientation or gender identity.

Lifestyle Exposure Theory Theory based on the premise that differences in victimization rates can be explained by the differences in the exposure to crime based on such demographics as age, gender, even occupation.

Lifestyle Theory See *Lifestyle Exposure Theory*.

Lynching A form of vigilantism whereby a mob, without legal authority, takes the law into their own hands, often in the form of hanging, instead of following due process.

M

Macular degeneration An age-related condition that makes it hard to see. As a precaution against elder abuse fraud, services for seniors with this and other health conditions, such as readers, or paid caregivers, may be asked to sign a written statement that they will not allow the client to rewrite their will giving them money from their estate or changing the beneficiaries on their insurance policy.

MADD (Mothers Against Drunk Driving) Non-profit organization started in 1980 by Candace Lightner after the death of her 13-year-old daughter who was killed by a drunk driver who was a repeat offender.

Magna Carta Influential document signed by King John of England on June 15, 1215, to assure political civil liberties. Established the principle that everyone is subject to the law, even the king, and guarantees the rights of individuals, the right to justice and the right to a fair trial.

Malum in se Refers to something being wrong or evil. Examples of actions that most would consider *malum in se* are murder, rape, and robbery.

Malum prohibita Refers to something being wrong because it is prohibited by a statute or a law. Some examples of acts that might be considered *malum prohibita*, but not *malum in se*, are jaywalking, drug use, and parking violations.

Malware Malicious software such as worms or viruses introduced into someone's computer to hack into someone's private data.

Mandatory sentencing A fixed number of years that a convicted offender must serve before release. Compare to indeterminate sentencing where there is a range of years from a minimum to a maximum.

Mandatory Victims Restitution Act of 1996 On April 24, 1996, became a federal law by Congress that restitution had to be made by defendants in many federal crimes.

Manslaughter Killing someone without malice or aforethought.

Maori Indigenous people of New Zealand whose community problem solving became the basis of the *restorative justice* concept that has become popular in the United States and globally as an alternative to jail or prison.

Marital rape When a legal spouse rapes a partner. Also known as *spousal rape.*

Marsy's Law Law ensuring that victims of crime have equal, constitutional rights to those accused and convicted of crimes. Named after college student Marsalee (Marsy) Nicholas who was stalked and killed by her ex-boyfriend in 1983.

Mass murder The murder of four or more people at once. (FBI definition)

Materials-based methods Also known as nonreactive research measures which means using preexisting data collected by others to do a secondary data analysis of the results applied to different considerations or measures.

Matricide When a mother is killed by her child.

Mediator A neutral party who is trained to help two or more individuals to reach an agreement.

Medical examiner (ME) Professional (usually a trained pathologist) who is trained to investigate suspicious deaths and determine the cause of death. The alternative approach is the coroner who may be a public official, lawyer, or citizen.

Megan's Law Mandatory requirement that any high-risk sex offenders had to be registered in a database that the public could access and track the residence of a registered sex offender. The New Jersey law—Megan's Law—became a model for the federal legislation that was signed by President Bill Clinton on May 17, 1996.

Memory decay A tendency to forget, change, or embellish memories related to a crime that was experienced or witnessed. This can impact the charges against someone or even whether a crime, such as rape or molestation during early childhood, occurred.

Mens rea Refers to criminal intent with its literal meaning "guilty mind."

Mental health counselor Someone with training in psychological issues who could help victims deal with the emotional aftermath of victimization.

#MeToo movement Founded in 2006, it became widespread in 2017. It is a social movement that led to increased awareness about sexual harassment, abuse, and rape and that "no means no."

Miranda rights The 1966 *Miranda v. Arizona* U.S. Supreme Court law guarantees that anyone who is in police custody and accused of a crime has to be told that they have the right to remain silent and to avoid self-incrimination.

Misdemeanor Criminal offense that could result in incarceration in jail for up to one year (but no longer) and/or payment of a fine, community service, or restorative justice.

Misdemeanor theft Similar to petit larceny, when the theft of an object or service is below the dollar amount set by law classifying it as a misdemeanor (versus a felony).

Modus operandi The way a criminal commits a crime. Determining the *modus operandi* can help to solve the cases.

Money laundering Process of concealing the origins of illegally obtained money, typically by means funneling funds through foreign banks or legitimate businesses.

Mosaic Code Ancient law of the Hebrews. Includes the Ten Commandments, including the code "Thou Shalt Not Kill," and the first five books of the Bible.

Motor vehicle theft "The theft of a motor vehicle." (NIBRS, 2018)

Mug shot The photograph that is taken upon arrest when a defendant is booked and his/her key information is also taken.

Mugging Another term for a robbery. Popular in the 1960s-1980s. Not used as much anymore.

Munchausen by Proxy Syndrome Relatively rare type of child abuse whereby a parent or caregiver fabricates illness and puts the infant, toddler, or child through unnecessary treatments. Also known as *Factitious Disorder Imposed on Another (FDIA).*

Murder "Murder and Nonnegligent Manslaughter - The willful (nonnegligent) killing of one human being by another." (NIBRS, 2018)

Murder-suicide A murder whereby the killer commits suicide after first killing one or more people.

N

Narrative victimology Using a victim's story to explore how a crime has impacted a victim.

National Crime Victimization Survey (NCVS) One of the two major sources of crime data in the United States. Interviews are done in a self-report manner, conducted in-person or administered by phone by members of the U.S. Census Bureau on behalf of the Bureau of Justice Statistics under the U.S. Department of Justice. It involves intensively interviewing randomly selected Americans about their crime victimizations during the previous six months to collect information about reported and unreported crimes.

Neglect Occurs when a person who is responsible fails to meet a dependent's basic needs. Not as serious as abuse but considered a crime especially as it relates to such dependent individuals as children (child abuse and neglect), the elderly (elder abuse and neglect), and animals (animal abuse and neglect).

Negligent manslaughter "The killing of another person through negligence." (NIBRS, 2018)

Neonatal abstinence syndrome A condition when babies are born addicted to heroin, barbiturates, alcohol, or cocaine because the mother was abusing drugs or alcohol during her pregnancy considered harmful to the developing fetus.

New age for the victim The decades from the 1960s through the end of the twentieth century during which concern for the rights of crime victims became more of a primary issue after centuries of being secondary to the criminal.

NIBRS (National Incident-Based Reporting System) The official way that local law enforcement information is collected and sent to the FBI for annual analysis and publication, as of January 1, 2021.

The NIBRS is more detailed than the previous UCR, which had been used as a paper reporting system beginning in 1930.

No-knock warrant A warrant that has been issued by a judge that allows law enforcement to enter the premises without ringing the doorbell or giving advance notice of their intention to enter.

Non-negligent homicide The willful killing of one human being by another.

Nonreactive research Research, such as document analysis, so-called content analysis, or secondary analysis of previous research, where the person or place under study is unaware of the study. Unobtrusively studying individuals without their knowledge or permission may be nonreactive but whether it is ethical or not is questionable since permission for the study/research has not been obtained.

Nonspeciesist criminology Criminologist Piers Beirne uses this term to refer to animal abuse as an important concern for criminology.

NVDRS (National Violent Death Reporting System) A state-based reporting system that takes information from more than 600 sources of data related to homicide and suicide and compiles it into one database. Administered through the CDC (Centers for Disease Control and Prevention).

O

Observer Someone who monitors an agency or situation for proper handling. There are also those known as court watchers who monitor that the court system is working fairly.

P

Paralegal Someone trained to assist a lawyer, government agency, or law office with certain tasks related to the legal profession.

Parole Allowing a prisoner to leave jail or prison early because they have been approved by the parole board. It is said to have started in the mid-1800s in a penal colony at Norfolk Island in Australia by Alexander Maconochie when inmates were allowed to earn "marks" for good behavior, allowing them to get released early.

Parricide When someone kills his/her parents.

Participant observer Someone who actively engages in and observes a culture or an agency or situation as a social scientist or member of the criminal justice system, taking notes on how people are interacting.

Pediatric Vehicular Heatstroke (PVH) Occurs due to intense heat when an infant, toddler, or child is left unattended in a car, with no ability to leave the vehicle on their own. Often results in death.

Penal couple Refers to the fact that every crime has two parties: the offender and the victim. Term attributed to Beniamin Mendelsohn.

Petit larceny See *petty larceny.*

Petty larceny Theft of property or services below a certain dollar amount, which varies by state and may range from as low as $200 to as high as $2,500. Usually considered a misdemeanor. If the theft exceeds that dollar amount, it may be reclassified as a felony along with more severe penalties.

Phishing schemes A form of cybercrime when someone intentionally sends an e-mail with false information requesting that the recipient click on a link that enables the hacker to gain control of the victim's computer and/or their stored data.

Photo array See *Photo lineup.*

Photo display See *Photo lineup.*

Photo lineup A procedure that law enforcement uses to confirm the identity of an accused suspect. The photo lineup has to be put together in a way that does not unintentionally highlight one particular person which might lead the victim or witness to choose that individual.

Physical child abuse Physical violence done to an infant, toddler, or child including shaking, pushing, dropping, hitting, or burning.

Plea bargain Arrangement where the accused, through his or her attorney, is offered a specific punishment by the prosecutor instead of going to trial. Also known as "to cop a plea."

Plea deal See *Plea bargain.*

Plea disposition conference A conference during which the defense attorney can discuss with a judge whether there is a plea that might be offered in exchange for a guilty plea, and thereby avoid a trial.

Pocket-picking "The theft of articles from another person's physical possession by stealth where the victim is not immediately aware a theft occurred." (NIBRS, 2020)

Police lineup See *Photo lineup.*

Polygraph Machine used to detect if someone is telling the truth. In general, polygraph tests are not considered admissible in court. Also known as a lie detector test.

Poly-victim Victims, especially children, who are submitted to multiple victimizations such as sexual abuse, exposure to domestic violence, bullying, and being physically abused or neglected. (Also known as poly-victimization).

Ponzi scheme A fraudulent economic investment whereby returns for early investors are paid out of funds from the latest investors. Since there are no actual investments or profits, if any investors, especially the original ones, ask to take out all their funds from the investment, the whole scheme falls apart leaving most investors destitute.

Post-traumatic stress disorder (PTSD) See *PTSD.*

Power Control Wheel A descriptive wheel depicting domestic violence patterns created by the Domestic Abuse Intervention Programs (DAIP) as part of The Duluth (Minnesota) Model.

Pre-trial conference There are two basic types. One is where the prosecutor and defense attorney use this conference to try to reach a plea bargain agreement. The other is where the judge uses the pre-trial conference to consider the evidence and clarify any concerns or logistics related to the case and the upcoming trial.

Prevalence rate The number of individuals experiencing a specific situation per 1,000, 10,000 or 100,000 such as the number of murder victims per 1,000. Also known as *prevalence.*

Primary victims Those who directly or actually experience the crime rather than those around the victims, known as secondary victims.

Private law The laws between individuals or institutions rather than with individuals and the government. Examples include contracts and torts.

Probable cause The standard that gives police the right to make an arrest, carry out a search, or seize property; also refers to the same criterion for the court to issue a warrant for the same procedures.

Probation In lieu of jail or prison, someone can be ordered to be on probation, including doing community service, which requires them to report to a probation officer and follow a strict set of rules. If they do not comply, their original sentence, which included jail or prison time, can be instituted.

Professional thief Someone who makes his/her living by stealing on a regular rather than an occasional basis.

Prolonged grief disorder (PGD) A condition that occurs when someone has not successfully dealt with the death of their loved one even if enough time has passed that most others have gone through the grieving process and moved on.

Prostitution "Prostitution Offenses - To unlawfully engage in or promote sexual activities for anything of value." (NIBRS, 2018)

Protective order (PO) Issued by the court, stipulates how far away physically someone has to be from someone who has been granted the order. It is most common in cases of domestic violence. Also known as a restraining order or order of protection.

PTSD (post-traumatic stress disorder) Mental health condition triggered by a traumatic event, such as being raped or physically abused. Symptoms may include flashbacks, nightmares and severe anxiety, as well as uncontrollable thoughts about the event, both immediately afterwards as well as on an ongoing basis.

Public law Laws between individuals and the government. Examples include criminal law and tax law.

Punitive damages Also known as exemplary damages, it is the money awarded to the plaintiff in a civil lawsuit because the defendant was found guilty of negligence that caused the crime or harm.

Q

Qualitative methods Research techniques that include interviews, observations, and surveys.

Quantitative data Research that is dependent on collecting and analyzing larger numbers of data especially through the use of surveys.

Quaternary victims Includes the family and friends of the tertiary victims, those who are helping victims who may share examples and anecdotes with others. They may also withhold for a variety of reasons, including confidentiality issues, which can also impact their relationships.

R

Radical victimology The perspective that government and corporations should play a bigger role in preventing crime in the first place.

Ransomware Malicious software that enables hackers to break into an individual, company, or government agency's computer system and hold the data hostage until a ransom is paid.

Rape "(Except Statutory Rape) - The carnal knowledge of a person, without the consent of the victim, including instances where the victim is incapable of giving consent because of his/her age or because of his/her temporary or permanent mental or physical incapacity." (NIBRS, 2018)

Rape kit After a rape, a forensic examination of the rape victim is put into a kit that could be used in potentially charging a suspect. It is usually performed at a hospital by a *Sexual Assault Nurse Examiner (SANE)* or *Sexual Assault Forensic Examiner (SAFE).*

Rape shield law Law that stops the defense from introducing the rape victim's sexual history at trial. In 1974, Michigan passed the first rape shield law.

Rape trauma syndrome Abbreviated RTS, this refers to the psychological and physical symptoms that a rape victim may experience immediately following the crime or in weeks, months, or even years later.

Rape-homicide When someone is raped and also killed by the rapist.

Raw number Refers to the actual data or numbers that are being studied.

Recidivism When those who have been released from jail or prison are rearrested or, in some cases, imprisoned again.

Recurring victimization See *Repeat victimization.*

Reentry An approach in correctional theory that addresses how ex-offenders adjust once they are released from jail or prison with the goal of not recidivating.

Rehabilitation A correctional theory that prioritizes the transformation of the inmate in prison to get at the criminogenic factors that contributed to his or her incarceration. The goal of rehabilitation is for the inmate to change and lead a law-abiding life upon release.

Reparations Granting of money to a victim. Also known as compensation or restitution.

Repeat victimization Becoming a victim more than once. The victimizations could be the same crime, or it could be other crimes. Also known as poly-victimization.

Respondent Someone who participates in a study whether by being interviewed or completing a questionnaire.

Response time How long it takes emergency professionals to get to the scene of a crime or accident including the police, EMS (Emergency Medical Services) workers, or the fire department.

Restitution The funds that are awarded to a victim paid out by the offender or, if it is a government compensation program, by the government, although offenders may pay into the government's funding program.

Restorative justice An alternative to jail or prison time whereby the offender meets with the victim, a member of the community, a representative of the restorative justice program, and/or a facilitator or meditator, and possibly even a lawyer or judge, to work out a plan that is agreeable to everyone. Admission of guilt by the offender, and an apology to the victim, makes it challenging to implement in every situation. Also known as RJ.

Restraining order See *Protective order.*

Retribution Obtaining justice through punishment; when a criminal is punished for the harm that he/she has caused without concern about whether or not he/she is being rehabilitated or whether he/she will commit another crime upon release. Usually refers to incarceration.

Revenge porn When someone puts on the internet compromising and revealing pictures, usually nude, of someone that they know usually in retaliation for an unwanted breakup. Whether it is considered a crime varies by state. Civil remedies may be possible

Robbery "The taking or attempting to take anything of value under confrontational circumstances from the control, custody, or care of another person by force or threat of force or violence and/or by putting the victim in fear of immediate harm." (NIBRS, 2020)

Robbery-homicide A robbery or mugging that also includes the homicide of the victim. (Not to be confused with the Robbery Homicide Division (RHD), established in 1969, as part of the Los Angeles Police Department (LAPD). It combined two divisions that were previously separate.)

Robbery-murder When a mugging or robbery also includes killing the victim.

Routine Activity Theory (RAT) A theory advanced in 1979 by criminologists Marcus Felson and Lawrence E. Cohen that the three conditions that are necessary for a crime to occur are a motivated offender, a suitable target, and lack of adequate guardianship. (Cohen and Felson, 1979)

Runaways Since they are underage and under the supervision of their parents or guardians, being a *runaway* (running away from family, home, or institution) is considered a status offense.

S

SAFE (Sexual Assault Forensic Exam) A process whereby a skilled and trained health care professional collects DNA evidence from a rape or sexual assault victim's body or clothing.

SAFE (Sexual Assault Forensic Examiner) A medical professional including a registered nurse or medical doctor who is trained to administer a rape kit.

SAID syndrome (Sexual Allegations In Divorce) False allegations of sexual misconduct by a child or teenager against one of their parents. The child is coaxed to make those accusations against a parent or another caregiver to try to gain a custody or monetary advantage in a custody battle or divorce proceeding.

SANE (Sexual Assault Nurse Examiner) A nursing professional trained with specialized education and clinical preparation in medical forensic care, including preparation of the rape kit.

SART (Sexual Assault Response Team) Teams that have been put in place in a majority of local precincts to coordinate the activities of the various other departments and situations that a rape victim will have to deal with including the medical, forensic, legal, and even victim advocacy issues. SART is an effort to help sexual violence victims to feel more comfortable during the reporting process.

Scamming When someone deceives someone by phone or online. Scammers gain the victim's trust and then proceed to obtain credit card information or access to bank accounts that they drain. Some of the scams include lottery, dating or romance, mystery shopper, and misrepresentation as agents of major companies seeking verification of key account information.

SCPT (Situational Crime Prevention theory) Efforts to reduce crime victimization through target hardening and other crime prevention techniques. Related to situational victimization.

Second degree murder Unplanned but intentional killing of another such as an argument that escalates into murder; also includes death that happened because of a thoughtless indifference for life.

Second injury What Dr. Martin Symonds, a police officer who became a leading psychiatrist specializing in treating crime victims, referred to as the way victims may be retraumatized by the criminal justice system. (Symonds, 1980, 2010)

Secondary victimization When those who are supposed to help victims actually revictimize them because of victim blaming attitudes or statements. (This is different from repeat victimization whereby a victim suffers from more than one or multiple crimes.)

Secondary victims Those close to the victim, such as family members or friends, who are also impacted when their loved one is a primary or direct victim of a crime.

Secondary victims of homicide Family members or close friends of the homicide or murder victim who are impacted by their loved one's homicide or murder. Also known as survivors of homicide, or homicide survivors,

Self-report When someone independently shares their recollection of events.

Senilicide Killing of old people.

Serial killer Someone who kills three or more people.

Sex worker Someone who makes money by selling sex. Another term for prostitute.

Sexual assault Unwanted touching, attempted rape, or molestation.

Sexual harassment Unwelcome and unwarranted comments referencing sexual activity or pushing for sexual favors or interaction in a quid pro quo situation, such as you do this for me, and I will advance your career. May occur at work or in school or extracurricular sports activity settings.

Sexual homicide When the victim is intentionally killed, and the perpetrator has also been involved in sexual behavior with the victim. Also known as sexual killing.

Sexual molestation See *Sexual abuse.*

Sexual violence An umbrella terms that refers to any kind of violation that is sexual from sexual harassment to abuse, assault, molestation, and rape.

Shaken Baby Syndrome (SBS) A form of child abuse whereby an infant can experience severe brain damage or even death if shaken for as little as five seconds.

Shelter A place of refuge for battered partners who are seeking a place to be safe from their perpetrators. Also refers to the free places for those who are homeless who prefer to have a roof over their heads than to be living on the street.

Skimmer A device between the credit card's chip and the ATM chip reader that enables the cybercriminal to steal the consumer's information.

SHR (Supplementary Homicide Reports) Database about each homicide maintained by the FBI (Federal Bureau of Investigation).

Sibling abuse Refers to the various ways that siblings can abuse each other including physical, sexual, emotional, and financial.

Sibling sexual abuse When a sibling takes advantage of a sister or brother by sexually abusing her/him through molestation, oral sex, penetration, or rape.

Simple assault "An unlawful physical attack by one person upon another where neither the offender displays a weapon, nor the victim suffers obvious severe or aggravated bodily injury involving apparent broken bones, loss of teeth, possible internal injury, severe laceration, or loss of consciousness." (NIBRS, 2018)

Situational victimization Reducing crime victimization by making it harder through efforts such as target hardening. Also known as SCPT.

Skimmer The way that cybercriminals illegally gather the credit card information of unsuspecting consumers. May be attached to an otherwise legitimate ATM machine.

Social sciences The scientific study behind such academic disciplines as anthropology, psychology, political science, media studies, archaeology, economics, linguistics, and history.

Sociology Scientific study of the behavior of groups defined as two or more individuals.

Spree killing Killing of two or more individuals within a brief time period.

SRS (Summary Reporting System) The traditional UCR SRS which collected data regularly from local police precincts and sheriffs, sharing it with the FBI.

Stalking Unwelcome attention by someone, either in-person or online, including watching, sending e-mails, making phone calls, sending letters, or showing up uninvited at someone's door.

State and federal constitutions The laws that govern a particular state or the entire United States.

Statement Can refer to a suspect making a declaration of his/her knowledge of the events under question. In a criminal trial, an opening statement will be made by the prosecutor who has the burden of proof.

Status offense Crimes that, if committed by an adult, would not be considered a crime, such as when a child or teen is a runaway, stays out after curfew, or stays away from school under the age of 16.

Statute A written law passed by the legislature at the federal or state level.

Statute of limitations (SOL) In a criminal case, the number of years a victim has to bring charges. It varies by crime and by state although some crimes, such as murder, have no statute of limitations. Other crimes, like rape, may have a statute of limitations from 3 to 30 years.

Statutory rape "Nonforcible sexual intercourse with a person who is under the statutory age of consent." (NIBRS, 2018)

Stockholm Syndrome Based on a real-life hostage taking situation during a bank robbery whereby the hostages seemed to form a bond with their captors. Afterwards it was expanded to refer to any situation where the victim seems to have a positive connection to their assailant.

Stolen goods market Also known as *fences*, this is how goods that are stolen find their buyers including in stores such as pawn shops or jewelry stores, through online sites, or even selling on the street.

Stop the Bleed® A training program run by the American College of Surgeons pursuant to a licensing arrangement granted to by the Department of Defense. It helps civilians learn how to stop someone who has a major injury from bleeding out. (stopthebleed.org)

Stranger rape Rape where the rapist is a complete stranger to the victim, without any prior connection.

Street crimes Term previously applied to such conventional crimes as murder, rape, and robbery, in contrast to economic crimes committed in the course of doing business. Term is no longer widely used since it gives the false impression that major crimes are likely to occur in the street instead of at home or in the office.

Strong-arm robbery Threat of or the actual theft from a victim, where no weapon was present.

Sudden infant death syndrome (SIDS) When a baby under a year of age dies unexpectedly in their sleep. Because the causes of SIDS are unknown, and it is such a mysterious tragic occurrence, it is important to distinguish it from homicide.

Survey A research technique to find out information. Surveys can be administered by mail, through the internet, over the phone, or in person. It usually involves a pre-set number of questions.

Survivor For many, this is the preferred term to *victim* when referring to the victim of a crime and/or a victim's self-definition. This use of the term *survivor* is not to be confused with those who are the survivors of homicide (family or friends of the deceased).

Survivor guilt May be experienced by those whose loved ones are killed who may feel guilty they were spared.

T

Target hardening An approach to crime prevention through environmental design such as by making buildings more secure by putting obstacles in front to stop vehicles from slamming into people or buildings, or making computer systems less vulnerable to cybercrime.

Tertiary victims Those who deal with crime victims on a continual basis such as first responders including police officers, EMTs, crime victim advocates, and even therapists, who may suffer from compassion fatigue or burnout.

Theftbote Beginning with Edward III, the King of England, (1312-1377), it became a misdemeanor crime for a victim to accept return of stolen goods or make a deal with the criminal in exchange for an agreement not to prosecute because it was seen to deny the King the compensation he should get from the criminal.

Third party civil suit When a crime victim or a victim's family sues a third party seeking to prove that their actions or negligence were responsible for the occurrence of the crime.

Third party victim rights litigation When a crime is committed, in addition to an individual who might be responsible for the crime, there may be third party that could be held responsible in a civil suit, if the third party was deemed to be negligent. Successful civil suits can result in the awarding of financial damages but not confinement, like in a criminal suit.

Thomas Theorem Proposed in 1928 by sociologist William Thomas and his wife Dorothy that if you define a situation as real, it is real in its consequences.

Throwaway Children or teenagers literally thrown out by a parent or caregiver and left to fend for themselves.

Tonic immobility Refers to the way that sexual violence victims may become physically or mentally frozen and unable to move or even speak or scream during or after their victimization.

Tort A civil wrong that may cause the claimant to experience harm or a loss that could be the focus of a civil suit to claim financial compensation for the damages.

Trace evidence Includes human or animal hair, clothing fibers, or gunshot residue, and can be transferred by heat or contact, becoming a consideration in the investigation of a crime.

Transgender Someone becomes another gender than the one assigned at birth. Transgender individuals may or may not undergo drug or surgical treatments to change to their preferred gender.

Treaty of Verdun Treaty signed in August 843 that divided the Carolingian Empire into three territories among the three sons of Charlemagne's grandson, Louis the Pious.

Trojan horse Malware that enables the hacker to gain access to the victim's computer system.

Twelve Tables In ancient Rome, a set of laws about the rights and obligations of citizens inscribed on twelve bronze tables.

Typology Creating a classification system that organizes data into a system based on any number of factors. In victimology, early co-founders Hans von Hentig and Beniamin Mendelsohn created victim typologies.

U

UCR (Uniform Crime Report) System of reporting crimes initially proposed by the International Association of Chiefs of Police (IACP) which led to local police reporting crime annually to the FBI beginning in 1930. On January 1, 2021, the NIBRS (National Incident-Based Reporting System) replaced it.

Unarmed robbery Theft by force but without a weapon.

Unfounding When law enforcement determines, based on further investigation, that a crime has not been committed.

Uniform Crime Reporting (UCR) Program Collecting crime data from local law enforcement since 1930.

United Nations Office on Drugs and Crime (UNODC) Founded in 1997, this United Nations office focuses its efforts on reducing or eliminating organized crime, illegal drug activity, human trafficking, and terrorism.

Unwanted sexual contact A type of sexual abuse or assault.

Unwanted sexual contact with force Considered a type of sexual assault.

Upcoding When medical personnel enter the code for a more expensive procedure than the one that was preformed to get a higher reimbursement.

Upstander Someone who speaks up if he/she observes bullying or any unacceptable behavior. The term is used by schools to encourage students to actively intervene.

V

Vandalism "Destruction/Damage/Vandalism of Property – (Except Arson) - To willfully or maliciously destroy, damage, deface, or otherwise injure real or personal property without the consent of the owner or the person having custody or control of it." (NIBRS, 2018)

Vehicular homicide When someone is killed besides the driver because of the driver's negligent or murderous actions.

Vehicular manslaughter When someone dies because of the reckless driving of another, including driving under the influence (drunk driving).

Veterinary forensics Applying to animals the forensic techniques to help investigate animal cruelty and abuse.

Vicarious traumatic stress See *Compassion fatigue.*

Victim Someone who has been physically, financially, sexually, legally, or psychologically harmed by the criminal actions of another.

Victim blame When blame for a crime is shifted from the criminal to the victim. It may be practiced by the media, family members, friends, co-workers or even the victim himself/herself. However, in *Essentials of Victimology*, the term *victim self-blame* is proposed for victims who blame themselves.

Victim defounding See *Defounding.*

Victim facilitation When a victim's actions, such as leaving the door of a car unlocked, might contribute to becoming the victim of a crime.

Victim impact statement (VIS) A statement about how the crime has impacted a victim or, in the case of homicide, the family of the victim (secondary victims of homicide) that victims may be allowed to share at various points in the criminal proceedings including presentencing or prior to a parole hearing.

Victim justice system A phrase used in *Essentials of Victimology* to juxtapose the common term of the *criminal* justice system.

Victim precipitation The controversial concept that a victim might actually precipitate a criminal act by his/her behavior.

Victim self-blame A version of victim blame whereby victims shift some or all of the blame for their victimization from the perpetrator to their own behavior whether it was something they said, did, wore, or failed to do. See also *Victim blame.*

Victimization rate The number of victims per 1,000 in stating rates for such crimes as burglary or murder or per 100,000 in stating the rates for cities or countries.

Victimization reduction Refers to lowering the rate of crime, overall or related to specific crimes, which would lead to a reduction in victimization.

Victimless crimes Because they are between consenting adults, certain crimes such as recreational illegal drug use or prostitution some may consider to be victimless crimes..

Victim-offender relationship Association between the victim and offender, such as being members of the same family, friends, acquaintances, employer-employee, caregiver, or strangers.

Victimology The scientific study of those who have suffered physical, sexual, financial, legal, or psychological harm as the result of being the victim of a crime as well as their treatment by the criminal justice system, the media, and society.

Victim-precipitated homicide The controversial theory that a victim is responsible for getting killed especially if he/she was the first to show or use a weapon or physical violence. First proposed by Dr. Marvin Wolfgang in his article, "Victim-Precipitated Homicide," published in 1957. (Wolfgang, 1957)

Victim-precipitated rape Menachem Amir tried to do for rape what Wolfgang did for homicide, but the concept of victim-precipitated rape, and the criteria that Amir used, have led to wide criticism of his findings. (Amir, 1967)

Victims of Crimes Act (VOCA) In 1984, Congress created VOCA to distribute funds to state and federal agencies and organizations assisting crime victims.

Vigilante committees These bands of men took the law into their own hands to deal with the stealing and murder, and other situations if they lacked access to regular courts, such as in the frontiers, or if they preferred to bypass them.

Vigilantism When individuals without legal authority take the law into their own hands and without following due process.

virus A malevolent code that can infect a computer, changing how it operates, compromising its data.

Voir dire Procedure followed to interview prospective jurors as to their suitability until the number of jurors plus any alternatives are selected.

W

warrant See *Arrest warrant.*

Wer In Saxon England, the payment to the victim's family for the homicide of a family member.

Wergild* or *wergeld In the Middle Ages, the term for the payment or compensation to the victim when a crime was committed or to the victim's family or kin in the case of homicide. Other terms for it are *blood money, busse, emenda,* and *lendis.*

Werther Effect Also known as *copycat suicide phenomenon.* A term coined in 1974 to describe imitative suicide. Traced back to Goethe's novel, published in 1774 when he was 25, *The Sorrows of Young Werther,* where there were copycat suicides like the novel's protagonist. (Seeman, 2017)

White-collar crimes Crimes committed by those carrying out their job, or by those in professions, such as the bookkeeper who embezzles or the company executive who inflates the company's value to a prospective buyer.

White-collar criminality Term coined by Edwin Sutherland in 1939 for economic crimes committed by middle and upper classes usually during the course of their jobs. In contrast to the so-called conventional or street crimes (murder, rape, robbery, larceny/theft, etc.). (Sutherland, 1940)

Wite The payment to the king or head of state by the offender or the offender's family.

Witness Someone who observes a crime taking place. A victim may also be a witness.

Workplace violence Physical abuse, aggression, or a threat that occurs at work.

Worm Malware that can infect and spread to other computers as a way of gaining control of someone's stored data.

Wrongful death Claim in a civil suit usually brought by the family of the deceased.

Y

Yoking A mugging without a weapon.

CITED WORKS

Amir, Menachem. 1967. "Victim Precipitated Forcible Rape." *Journal of Criminal Law, Criminology & Police Science* 58: 493-502.

Cohen, Lawrence E. and Marcus Felson. August 1979. "Social Change and Crime Rate Trends: A Routine Activity Approach." *American Sociological Review.* 44: 588-608.

Felitti, Vincent J., Robert F. Anda, Dale Nordenberg, David F. Williamson, Alison M. Spitz, Valerie Edwards, Mary P. Koss, and James S. Marks. 1998. "Relationship of Childhood Abuse and Household Dysfunction to Many of the Leading Causes of Death in Adults: The Adverse Childhood Experiences (ACE) Study." *American Journal of Preventive Medicine.* 14: 245-258.

Kempe, C. Henry, Frederic N. Silverman, and Brandt F. Steele. July 7, 1962. "The Battered-Child Syndrome." *JAMA (Journal of American Medical Association).* 181: 17-24.

Lerner, Melvin J. 1971 "Observers Evaluation of a Victim: Justice, Guilt, and Veridical Perception." *Journal of Personality and Social Psychology* 20: 127–135.

National Incident-Based Reporting System (NIBRS). Released Fall 2018. U.S. Department of Justice, Federal Bureau of Investigation (FBI) "NIBRS Offense Definitions" Posted at https://ucr.fbi.gov/nibrs/2017/resource-pages/nibrs_offense_definitions-2017.pdf

________________. Released 04/15/2021. "2021 National Incident-Based Reporting System User Manual." Prepared by the Criminal Justice Information Services Division, Crime Statistics Management Unit, U.S. Department of Justice, FBI.

Seeman, Mary V. 2017. "The Marilyn Monroe Group and the Werther Effect." *Case Reports Journal.* 1.

Sutherland, Edwin H. February 1940. "White-Collar Criminality." *American Sociological Review.* 5: 1-12.

Symonds, Martin. 1980, 2010. "The 'Second Injury' to Victims of Violent Acts." *The American Journal of Psychoanalysis.* 70: 34-41.

Wolfgang, Marvin. May-June 1957. "Victim-Precipitated Criminal Homicide." *The Journal of Criminal Law, Criminology, and Police Science.* 48: 1-11.

CITED WORKS AND ADDITIONAL REFERENCES

(also **Resources and Audiovisual Materials- Videos, Films, Podcasts, TED Talks, etc.**)

Please note: Just a reminder that you will find Cited Works and Additional References, as well as Resources and Audiovisual Materials—Videos, Films, Podcasts, TED Talks, etc.—related to each of the sixteen chapters of *Essentials of Victimology*, at the end of each chapter.

Additional references, resources, or audiovisual materials, post-publication, related to each of the chapters, will be added when deemed necessary by this author at the product page for this book which you will find at the publisher's website: www.AspenPublishing.com

Professors, students, and service providers are welcome to e-mail this author with suggestions about any further articles, books, films, videos, podcasts, TED Talks, and even Resources, related to Victimology and the topics covered in *Essentials of Victimology* for consideration to be reviewed and/or possibly added to that supplementary list: drjanyager123@gmail.com

ACKNOWLEDGMENTS

This author would like to start by thanking the hard-working team at Aspen Publishing, this textbook's publisher, who have put time and effort into the many drafts, revisions, and related tasks for this book in an exemplary way. Thanks, especially to managing and acquisitions editor Stacie Goosman for believing in me and in this new book, and for always answering my questions in a thorough and timely fashion.

Thanks also to development editor Elizabeth (Betsy) Kenny, production editor Paul Sobel, former photo and permissions editor Michelle Humphrey, permissions editor Corinne Pulicay, and publisher Joe Terry. Thanks also to Jordan Jepsen, my first managing editor.

There are many more to thank including the production staff for the e-book version of the textbook as well as the textbook's copyeditor Peggy Rehberger, and the sales team. Even if you are not named individually, please know how grateful I am to all of you for making *Essentials of Victimology* happen.

Next, this author would like to thank the conscientious peer reviewers who generously shared their feedback, suggestions, and comments. I know how busy we academics are, so I am especially grateful that all these peer reviewers made reading, and responding, to the drafts of this new textbook a priority.

Thanks to everyone who was gracious enough with your time and insights to either do an interview with this author, one-on-one, or to participate in an in-person, or Zoom videoconferencing interview for an undergraduate or graduate course this author was teaching. Thanks as well as the victims/survivors and/or service providers including lawyers, police officers, and crime victim advocates, among others, who were interviewed in-person, over the phone, or via Zoom or filled out the confidential survey related to this new book.

This author would like to acknowledge and thank all the guest speakers at her Victimology and other related courses including Social Deviance, Forensic Health, the Law, and the Criminal Justice System, Penology, and Criminology. Thank you for the time you took to share either your own crime victimizations, the loss of a loved one and your secondary victimization of homicide, as well as those who shared their expertise as lawyers, prosecutors, judges, crime victim counselors, social workers, correction officers, superintendent of a maximum security state prison, and others. I want to especially thank Nicole Hockley, Kaitin Roig-DeBellis (*Choosing Hope*), Martin Tantleff, Kevin Gres, Judge Steve Leifman, Patrick Korellis, Charisse Coleman, Fred Guttenberg (*Find the Helpers*), Nance Schick, Jeffrey Rinek, Tosha Smith Mills, Julio Briones, Val Reyes-Jimenez, Kerri Rawson, Bernard Kerik (*From Jailer to Jailed*), Janine Latus (*If I Am Missing or Dead*), Jennifer Storm (*Blackout Girl*). Dorri Olds, Drew Crecente, Superintendent Michael Capra, Barry Campbell, David Rothenberg, founder of the Fortune Society, David Friedrichs (*Crimes of Globalization*), Jimmy Santiago, Baca, Richard Hoffman, Maurice Chammah (*Let the Lord Sort Them*), Monique Faison Ross (*Playing Dead*), Robert Katzberg (*The Vanishing Trial*), Tereson D., Laura Stack, Jonathan Hay, Valorie First, Randy Kearse (*Changin' Your Game Plan*), Liz Pryor (*Look at You Now*), Karima Holmes, Christina Stanton, Ken Nichols, John Dussich, Vincent N. Parrillo, Joseph

Imperatrice, Anthony Papa (*This Side of Freedom*), Gina Carr, April Feeney, Jennifer Bradley, and others.

Thanks to criminologist and author, Richard Quinney, whom this author has considered a mentor since he read her book, *Victims*, back in 1978, and we struck up a correspondence, as well as to David Friederichs, criminologist and author, who also was a friend of the author's late brother, Seth Alan Barkas, at NYU, plus so many other colleagues and/or department chairs for their support and friendship over the years including Robert Garot, Jayne Mooney, Jacob Felson, Virginia Cannon, Marcus Aldredge, Greg Snyder, Shelly Clevenger, Kimberly Spanjol, Henry Pontell, Andrew Karmen, Susan Ostrow, Maria Volpe, Eileen B. Hoffman, Esther Kreider-Verhalle, David Green, Amy Adamczyk, Jana Arsovska, Eileen Clancy, Baz Dreisinger, Carla Barrett, Gail Garfield, Crystal Jackson, Joyce Nova, Richard Ocejo, Sheetal Ranjan, Robyn Goldstein, Julia Navarro, David Brotherton, Rosemary Barbaret, James Ganvas, Louis Kontos, Patricia Johnson, Antonio Pastrana Jr., Tarun Banerjee, Andrea Siegal, Janet L. Mullings, Callie Marie Rennison, Jillian Turanovic, Rachael Powers, Mike Brown, and the late Barry Spunt. I appreciate so much the support and administrative staff at the colleges and universities where I am privileged and honored to teach including Alisa Thomas, Theresa Rockett, Ruth Tekle, Keisha Griffin, Frankie Cruz, and Melissa Hicks.

Over the years, I have been able to interview, in person or by phone, or correspond with, others in the field of victimology and related fields including Erin Pizzey, Charlotte Hullinger, and Bob Hullinger, co-founders of POMC (Parents of Murdered Children).

The following pioneers in the field may be gone but they are not forgotten; I want to acknowledge the opportunity that I had to interview them by phone or in person including Frederic Wertham, Marvin Wolfgang, Beniamin Mendelsohn, Frank Carrington, Arthur Niederhoffer, Martin Symonds, Morton Bard, and Edith Surgan.

Others that I contacted that helped me currently or previously as I researched this and related articles or books include Lisbet Chiriboga, Deborah Brenner-Liss, Jaime Hobbs, Barbara Gordon, Melissa Hoppmeyer, Kathryn Marsh, Adam Bolotin, Mary Joye, Gary Nosacek, Dawn Burnett, Sarah Fogel, Karen Gross, Carrie Mead, Rhonda Rees, Mary Siller-Scullin, Nicole Anderson, Darcy Maulsby, Denise Brown, Judge Joseph G. Gubbay, Blake Smith, Alba Reyes, Michelle Rodriguez, Darcie Rowan, Molly Blair, Melissa Lee, Doris Busch, Karin Willison, Lynn Julian Crisci, Carmen Mead, Kurt Varricchio, David Disraeli, Alesia Litteral, Louie Free, Carole Lieberman, Cindy Collins, C J Scarlet, John Wolfson, Alyssa Giacobbe, Lee Pellegrini, Ann Wolbert Burgess, Lenore E. A. Walker, and so many others. If anyone was left out, apologies in advance. Your help is still appreciated.

Dr. Neiderhoffer was my mentor for my masters in criminal justice and the thesis advisor for my thesis, "Victims of Crime and Social Change" (Goddard College Graduate Program, 1977). I had the privilege of taking a graduate course with Dr. Martin Symonds, "Psychology of the Victim," one of that unusual group of police officers turned Ph.D.s or M.D.s (which also included Dr. Niederhoffer and Dr. Bard) at John Jay College of Criminal Justice back in Spring 1976. This author also wants to thank the late David Caplovitz, her professor at The City University of New York Graduate Center, who was a brilliant scholar as well as a dedicated and thoughtful professor. Ditto for Cynthia Epstein, and the late Ed Sagarin, Sam Bloom, Patricia Kendall, and so many others at CUNY Graduate Center whose research, writings, and teachings helped to shape my doctoral education.

Thanks to Sidney Offit whose recommendation all those many years ago led to this author's first college level teaching job, at The New School for Social Research. That course, "The Roots of Violence," was the beginning of my lifelong commitment to teaching undergraduate or graduate students, and even adult learners, to better understand the criminal justice system and everyone associated with it including offenders and victims. Thank you to the guest speakers in that course including federal Judge Jack Weinstein (who passed away at the age of 99 on June 15, 2021), the late bestselling author Peter Maas (*Serpico*), Tom Wicker (*Attica*), Lt David Durk, and others. For that course, the students and this author visited New York City's morgue and the morgue museum. She was fortunate to be allowed to do several very educational "ride alongs" with the NYPD.

Thank you to the late Charles Scribner Jr. and the editors and staff at Scribner's, including Patricia Cristol and Susan Richman, who were involved in the publication of my first three nonfiction books including my book on crime victims, *Victims*, initially published in 1978. Your faith in this author and in that book that a well-respected colleague and leader in the field of victimology recently referred to as a "seminal work" is something she will never take for granted.

Thanks to this author's undergraduate and graduate students who, over the years, have conducted literally hundreds of confidential, anonymous interviews with primary and secondary crime victims as well as police officers, forensic psychologists, police, probation, parole, and correction officers, lawyers, prosecutors, judges, and others. Even though you are not thanked or acknowledged by name or individually, please know that each and every one of you are appreciated. Your professor is proud of all of you and how you are applying what you learned in the Victimology or other course or courses that you studied with her.

Thanks to the Stamford, Connecticut-based The Rowan Center, in conjunction with the Connecticut Alliance to End Sexual Violence, for the 40-hour intensive certification program that this author participated in from June 7 through June 23, 2021. This was the second time this author completed this training. The first time was back in 1995 when the center and training was called the Sexual Assault Crisis Counselor & Advocate program. This recertification training was intensive and handled with such professionalism and expertise by the main trainer, Jessica Feighan, as well as the supplementary trainers, Rowan Center staff members Marsha P., who is head of volunteer services and an adult advocate, and Kelly I., a case manager and bilingual educator. Thank you as well to the fourteen men and women who participated in that June 2021 training.

Gratitude to the various college and university libraries that were so pivotal in researching and writing this textbook especially the Lloyd George Sealy Library John Jay College of Criminal Justice, The Cheng Library at William Paterson University, and The Ryan Library at Iona College. During the height of the pandemic, being able to especially access materials online, 24/7, made it possible to keep pushing forward on researching and writing this textbook even if in-person visits were often curtailed.

Thank you to this author's husband, children, grandchildren, extended family, and friends who have supported me emotionally through the research and writing of this textbook and even over the previous decades that this author has dedicated to teaching, researching, writing, and advocacy about and on behalf of crime victims and their loved ones.

Finally, this author wants to take a moment to remember the life of her 23-year-old older brother, Seth Alan Barkas, who died from the injuries he sustained during a violent robbery by a teenage gang. His murder, when she was 20 years old and a senior in college, inspired this author's life-long journey to understand everything there is to know about crime, the justice system, and most of all, about its victims and Victimology.

PHOTO CREDITS*

(In alphabetical order)

Prepared by The Froebe Group on behalf of Aspen Publishing**

#MeToo. Image provided by Mihai Surdu / unsplash.com.

A "backyard dog" named Chico, visited by PETA's Community Animal Project in March 2018. Image courtesy of People for the Ethical Treatment of Animals.

A "backyard dog" named Marcus who was rescued by PETA's Community Animal Project in September 2019. Image courtesy of People for the Ethical Treatment of Animals.

Ambulance. Image provided by Jose de Azpiazu / unsplash.com.

Amy Latus (left) and Janine Latus (right). Contributed photo, courtesy of Janine Latus.

ATM with skimmer. Image provided by wikihow.com / CC BY NC SA 3.0.

Seth Alan Barkas (1945-1969) Contributed photo courtesy of Jan Yager, Ph.D.

Ann Wolbert Burgess. Non-exclusive permission granted from *Boston College* magazine where this photo was first published on July 7, 2019, entitled, "Mastermind," by Alyssa Giacobbe. Photo credit: Gary Wayne Gilbert

Beniamin Mendelsohn. Image provided by Jeff G / CC 3.0.

Charisse Coleman and her brother Russell in 1987 on her wedding day; Russell as Best Man. Contributed photo, courtesy of Charisse Coleman.

Code of Hammurabi. Image provided by Mbzt / CC BY 3.0.

Crime Tape. Image provided by Gerd Altmann / pixabay.com.

The Definition of Insanity PBS still.

Diana Rodriguez-Martin. Contributed photo, courtesy of Alba Reyes and Michele Rodriguez.

Dorri Olds as a teenager. Contributed photo, courtesy of Dorri Olds.

End the Backlog. Picture of the press conference with actress Mariska Hargitay and others. Fair use.

FBI evidence response team. Public domain photo release by the FBI.

* *Selected photo credits including Dr Burgess, Tracy Schott, and Dr. Walker provided by Dr. Jan Yager*

** *Note that CC stands for Creative Commons License*

Fred Guttenberg and his daughter, Jaime Guttenberg. Contributed photo, courtesy of Fred Guttenberg.

Graffiti. Image provided by Olha Kostenko / Alamy Stock Vector.

Harassment clip art. Public domain.

Hospital. Image provided by Gorodenkoff / Shutterstock.

Inuit, 1999. Image provided by Ansgar Walk / CC BY 2.5, photo.

Jennifer and Drew Crecente. Contributed photo, courtesy of Drew Crecente.

Jennifer Crecente, by Dr. Elizabeth L. Richeson, Jennifer's grandmother. Contributed photo, courtesy of Drew Crecente.

Karima Holmes. Image courtesy of Karima Holmes.

Koala bear. Photographed in Australia. Image courtesy of Jan Yager, Ph.D.

Man in prison, by fongbeerredhot / Shutterstock.

Marc Hinch. Contributed photo, courtesy of Marc Hinch.

Monique Faison Ross. Image provided by Monique. Photo credit: TimeFrozen Photography.

Nance Schick. Image courtesy of Nance Schick.

Paramedic, by F. Muhammad / pixabay.com

Patrick Korellis on 4/14/2012, on the 14-year memorial of the Northern Illinois University shooting. Contributed photo, courtesy of Patrick Korellis.

The Refuge, Copyright (c) Julian Nieman. Reproduced with permission by The Refuge.

Police at Crime Scene. Image provided by LightField Studios / Shutterstock

Police Officer. Image provided by BodyWorn by Utility / pixabay.com

Police talking to a victim. Image provided by Robert Kneschke / Shutterstock.

Power and Control Wheel. Reprinted with permission by the Domestic Abuse Intervention Program (DAIP), Duluth, MN.

Psychologist having session with her patient in office. Image provided by wavebreakmedia / Shutterstock.

Sing Sing Correctional Facility. Image provided by Brett Weinstein (NRbelex) at en.wikipedia / CC BY-SA 2.5.

Survivors of intimate partner homicide attempts share their stories.

© Finding Jenn's Voice, 2015. Contributed by Tracy Schott, Producer/Director.

Imette St Guillen. Graduate student who was killed. Fair use.

Stephen Siller. Images courtesy of Tunnel to Towers Foundation.

Target hardening, the Houses of Parliament in London, UK. Image provided by Maxy Naylor at English Wikipedia.

Teacher in Classroom. Image provided by Stefan Meller / pixabay.com.

Tereson and her son Eden. Image courtesy of Tereson.

Tereson's ex-husband Terry. Image courtesy of his daughter.

Dr. Lenore E. Walker. Contributed photo.

World Trade Center Attack on 9/11/2001. Image provided by Robert on Flickr / CC 2.0.

INDEX

H

ABOUT THE AUTHOR

Jan Yager, Ph.D., the former J.L. (Janet Lee) Barkas, has a Ph.D. in Sociology from The City University of New York Graduate Center, where she had a predoctoral fellowship from the National Science Foundation. She also has an M.A. in Criminal Justice from Goddard College Graduate Program. Her master's thesis was entitled, "Victims of Crime and Social Change." Her thesis advisor was Dr. Arthur J. Niederhoffer, a police officer who became a Sociology Professor at John Jay College of Criminal Justice.

Dr. Yager did a year of graduate work in art therapy at Hahnemann Medical College in Philadelphia. Part of her art therapy training was to do an internship in the in-patient psychiatric ward at a city hospital in Philadelphia. Her second semester internship was at a residence for children who had been removed from their abusive family situations.

The author has been teaching at the college level since her mid-twenties beginning at The New School followed by Temple University, St. John's University, Penn State, New York Institute of Technology (fulltime 1983-1985), and the University of Connecticut (1999-2006). Since 2014, Dr. Yager has been teaching criminology and sociology courses in the Department of Sociology at John Jay College of Criminal Justice, one of the senior colleges of The City University of New York (CUNY). Since August 2015, Dr. Yager, an Adjunct Associate Professor, has been teaching Victimology every semester, and often during Winter and Summer breaks, at John Jay College of Criminal Justice and beginning in Spring 2021, also at Iona College.

Dr. Yager has received the John Jay Sociology Department's Adjunct Teaching Excellence Award in 2021 and 2017 and its Adjunct Mentoring Excellence Award in 2021, 2020, 2019, and 2016. Other colleges and universities where Dr. Yager has taught undergraduate and graduate courses include Kean University, New York Film Academy, William Paterson University, and Sam Houston State University.

A prolific author, Dr. Yager has published more than 50 books which have been translated into 34 languages. Her award-winning nonfiction titles include *Victims*, originally published by Scribner's in 1978 under her maiden name of J.L. Barkas, *When Friendship Hurts*, published by Simon & Schuster and translated into 29 languages, *Help Yourself Now; Time Management and Other Essential Skills for College Students; How to Finish Everything You Start; Friendgevity; Effective Business and Nonfiction Writing*; *Friendshifts; Business Protocol; 125 Ways to Meet the Love of Your Life;* crime novels including *Untimely Death* and *Just Your Everyday People,* co-authored with her husband Fred Yager; *On the Run*, as well as the novel, *The Pretty One*, a study of a best-selling therapist who is a survivor of childhood sexual abuse.

Dr. Yager's practical experience in the criminal justice system includes working on a crime victim hotline, developing and running a crime prevention resource center through Marymount Manhattan College, participating in a volunteer program to help women incarcerated at Bedford Hills Correctional Facility with their reentry upon release, being a participant observer for 1-1/2 years in a support group for adult survivors of childhood and teenage sexual abuse, certifying (1995) and then recertifying (June 2021) as a crisis counselor/advocate in the state of Connecticut. Dr. Yager's extensive original research into victimization and crime has also included conducting in-depth in-person and phone interviews, distributing and analyzing surveys, as well as visits to shelters, prisons, police departments, and crime victim programs throughout the United States and in Canada, England, France, the Netherlands, and Germany.

It was the murder of her 23-year-old older brother, Seth Alan Barkas, by a teenage gang that started Dr. Yager on her decades-long journey to study, teach, and advocate for crime victims as well as for those who help them, and for the secondary victims --their family and friends.

For more information on Dr. Yager, to read her blogs, or to sign up for her free newsletter or her mailing list, visit her main website: https://www.drjanyager.com. To contact Dr. Yager: drjanyager123@gmail.com.